Grace Callahan

THE MODERN LIBRARY
of the World's Best Books

>>>

THE ORIGIN OF SPECIES
AND
THE DESCENT OF MAN

>>

The publishers will be pleased to send, upon request, an illustrated folder setting forth the purpose and scope of THE MODERN LIBRARY, *and listing each volume in the series. Every reader of books will find titles he has been looking for, handsomely printed, in unabridged editions, and at an unusually low price.*

>>>

THE ORIGIN OF SPECIES

BY MEANS OF NATURAL SELECTION

OR THE PRESERVATION OF FAVORED
RACES IN THE STRUGGLE FOR LIFE

AND

THE DESCENT OF MAN

AND SELECTION IN RELATION TO SEX

BY

CHARLES DARWIN

BENNETT A. CERF · DONALD S. KLOPFER

THE MODERN LIBRARY

NEW YORK

THE MODERN LIBRARY

IS PUBLISHED BY

RANDOM HOUSE, INC.

BENNETT A. CERF • DONALD S. KLOPFER • ROBERT K. HAAS

Manufactured in the United States of America
Printed by Parkway Printing Company   *Bound by H. Wolff*

CHARLES DARWIN
(1809-1882)

A NOTE ON THIS EDITION OF "THE ORIGIN OF SPECIES" AND "THE DESCENT OF MAN"

IN bringing together for the first time in one volume the two principal works of Charles Darwin, the editors of the Modern Library are in a sense fulfilling a part of the author's intention. *The Descent of Man* is, in truth, a sequel and an amplification of *The Origin of Species* and belongs with it as corroborative scientific evidence of the theories of evolution set forth in the earlier work. Darwin's statement in *The Origin of Species* that "light would be thrown on the origin of man and his history" is justified by the wealth of data contained in *The Descent of Man*. To these facts are added in the section *Selection in Relation to Sex* a mass of observations in support of the hypothesis that sexual selection exercises a major influence in the evolution of species. Of the history of these books and their epoch-making consequences upon the scientific and religious thought of our time it would be superfluous to comment. They remain in the 20th century, in spite of a few minor scientific revisions, one of the greatest achievements in humanity's quest for enlightenment.

BIBLIOGRAPHY

Journal of a Naturalist (1836).

Narrative of the Surveying Voyages of H.M.S. Adventure and Beagle (1840-1843).

The Origin of Species by Means of Natural Selection (1859).

A Naturalist's Voyage (1860).

On the Various Contrivances by Which Orchids Are Fertilized by Insects (1862).

The Movements and Habits of Climbing Plants (1865).

The Variation of Animals and Plants Under Domestication (1868).

The Descent of Man and Selection in Relation to Sex (1871).

The Expression of the Emotions in Man and Animals (1872).

Insectivorous Plants (1875).

The Effects of Cross and Self-Fertilization in the Vegetable Kingdom (1876).

Volcanic Islands (1876).

Different Forms of Flowers (1877).

The Power of Movement in Plants (1880).

CONTENTS

THE ORIGIN OF SPECIES

CHAPTER I

VARIATION UNDER DOMESTICATION

CHAPTER II

VARIATION UNDER NATURE

CHAPTER III

STRUGGLE FOR EXISTENCE

CHAPTER VIII

INSTINCT

CHAPTER IX

HYBRIDISM

CHAPTER X

ON THE IMPERFECTION OF THE GEOLOGICAL RECORD

CHAPTER XI

ON THE GEOLOGICAL SUCCESSION OF ORGANIC BEINGS

CHAPTER XII

GEOGRAPHICAL DISTRIBUTION

CHAPTER XIII

GEOGRAPHICAL DISTRIBUTION—*continued*

CHAPTER XIV

MUTUAL AFFINITIES OF ORGANIC BEINGS: MORPHOLOGY: EMBRYOLOGY: RUDIMENTARY ORGANS

CHAPTER XV

RECAPITULATION AND CONCLUSION

THE DESCENT OF MAN

PART I

THE DESCENT OR ORIGIN OF MAN

CHAPTER I

THE EVIDENCE OF THE DESCENT OF MAN FROM SOME LOWER FORM

CHAPTER II

ON THE MANNER OF DEVELOPMENT OF MAN FROM SOME LOWER FORM

CHAPTER III

COMPARISON OF THE MENTAL POWERS OF MAN AND THE LOWER ANIMALS

PART II

SEXUAL SELECTION

CHAPTER VIII

PRINCIPLES OF SEXUAL SELECTION

CHAPTER IX

SECONDARY SEXUAL CHARACTERS IN THE LOWER CLASSES OF THE ANIMAL KINGDOM

CHAPTER X

SECONDARY SEXUAL CHARACTERS OF INSECTS

CHAPTER XI

INSECTS, continued.—ORDER LEPIDOPTERA
(BUTTERFLIES AND MOTHS)

CHAPTER XVI

BIRDS—*concluded*

CHAPTER XVII

SECONDARY SEXUAL CHARACTERS OF MAMMALS

CHAPTER XVIII

SECONDARY SEXUAL CHARACTERS OF MAMMALS—*continued*

PART III

SEXUAL SELECTION IN RELATION TO MAN

AND CONCLUSION

CHAPTER XIX

SECONDARY SEXUAL CHARACTERS OF MAN

CHAPTER XX

SECONDARY SEXUAL CHARACTERS OF MAN—*continued*

CHAPTER XXI

GENERAL SUMMARY AND CONCLUSION

THE ORIGIN OF SPECIES

"But with regard to the material world, we can at least go so far as this—
we can perceive that events are brought about not by insulated interpositions
of Divine power, exerted in each particular case, but by the establishment of
general laws."

WHEWELL: *Bridgewater Treatise.*

"The only distinct meaning of the word 'natural' is *stated, fixed,* or *settled;*
since what is natural as much requires and presupposes an intelligent agent
to render it so, *i. e.,* to effect it continually or at stated times, as what is super-
natural or miraculous does to effect it for once."

BUTLER: *Analogy of Revealed Religion.*

"To conclude, therefore, let no man out of a weak conceit of sobriety, or an
ill-applied moderation, think or maintain, that a man can search too far or be
too well studied in the book of God's word, or in the book of God's works;
divinity or philosophy; but rather let men endeavour an endless progress or
proficience in both."

BACON: *Advancement of Learning.*

Down, Beckenham, Kent,
  First Edition, November 24th, 1859.
  Sixth Edition, Jan. 1872.

AN HISTORICAL SKETCH

OF THE PROGRESS OF OPINION ON THE ORIGIN OF SPECIES,

PREVIOUSLY TO THE PUBLICATION OF THE FIRST EDITION OF THIS WORK

I WILL here give a brief sketch of the progress of opinion on the Origin of Species. Until recently the great majority of naturalists believed that species were immutable productions, and had been separately created. This view has been ably maintained by many authors. Some few naturalists, on the other hand, have believed that species undergo modification, and that the existing forms of life are the descendants by true generation of pre-existing forms. Passing over allusions to the subject in the classical writers,* the first author who in modern times has treated it in a scientific spirit was Buffon. But as his opinions fluctuated greatly at different periods, and as he does not enter on the causes or means of the transformation of species, I need not here enter on details.

Lamarck was the first man whose conclusions on the subject excited much attention. This justly celebrated naturalist first published his views in 1801; he much enlarged them in 1809 in his 'Philosophie Zoologique,' and subsequently, in 1815, in the Introduction to his 'Hist. Nat. des Animaux sans Vertébres.' In these works he upholds the doctrine that all species, including man, are descended from other species. He first did the eminent service of arousing attention to the probability of all change in the organic, as well as in the inorganic world, being the result of law, and

---

* Aristotle, in his 'Physicæ Auscultationes' (lib. 2, cap. 8, s. 2), after remarking that rain does not fall in order to make the corn grow, any more than it falls to spoil the farmer's corn when threshed out of doors, applies the same argument to organisation; and adds (as translated by Mr. Clair Grece, who first pointed out the passage to me), "So what hinders the different parts [of the body] from having this merely accidental relation in nature? as the teeth, for example, grow by necessity, the front ones sharp, adapted for dividing, and the grinders flat, and serviceable for masticating the food; since they were not made for the sake of this, but it was the result of accident. And in like manner as to the other parts in which there appears to exist an adaptation to an end. Wheresoever, therefore, all things together (that is all the parts of one whole) happened like as if they were made for the sake of something, these were preserved, having been appropriately constituted by an internal spontaneity; and whatsoever things were not thus constituted, perished, and still perish." We here see the principle of natural selection shadowed forth, but how little Aristotle fully comprehended the principle, is shown by his remarks on the formation of the teeth.

not of miraculous interposition. Lamarck seems to have been chiefly led to his conclusion on the gradual change of species, by the difficulty of distinguishing species and varieties, by the almost perfect gradation of forms in certain groups, and by the analogy of domestic productions. With respect to the means of modification, he attributed something to the direct action of the physical conditions of life, something to the crossing of already existing forms, and much to use and disuse, that is, to the effects of habit. To this latter agency he seems to attribute all the beautiful adaptations in nature;—such as the long neck of the giraffe for browsing on the branches of trees. But he likewise believed in a law of progressive development; and as all the forms of life thus tend to progress, in order to account for the existence at the present day of simple productions, he maintains that such forms are now spontaneously generated.*

Geoffroy Saint-Hilaire, as is stated in his 'Life,' written by his son, suspected, as early as 1795, that what we call species are various degenerations of the same type. It was not until 1828 that he published his conviction that the same forms have not been perpetuated since the origin of all things. Geoffroy seems to have relied chiefly on the conditions of life, or the '*monde ambiant*' as the cause of change. He was cautious in drawing conclusions, and did not believe that existing species are now undergoing modification; and, as his son adds, "C'est donc un problème à réserver entièrement à l'avenir, supposé même que l'avenir doive avoir prise sur lui."

In 1813, Dr. W. C. Wells read before the Royal Society 'An Account of a White female, part of whose skin resembles that of a Negro'; but his paper was not published until his famous 'Two Essays upon Dew and Single Vision' appeared in 1818. In this paper he distinctly recognises the principle of natural selection, and this is the first recognition which has been indicated; but he applies it only to the races of man, and to certain characters alone. After remarking that Negroes and mulattoes enjoy an immunity from certain tropical diseases, he observes, firstly, that all animals tend to vary in some degree, and, secondly, that agriculturists improve their domesticated animals by selection; and then, he adds, but

---

* I have taken the date of the first publication of Lamarck from Isid. Geoffroy Saint-Hilaire's ('Hist. Nat. Générale,' tom. ii. p. 405, 1859) excellent history of opinion on this subject. In this work a full account is given of Buffon's conclusions on the same subject. It is curious how largely my grandfather, Dr. Erasmus Darwin, anticipated the views and erroneous grounds of opinion of Lamarck in his 'Zoonomia' (vol. i. pp. 500-510), published in 1794. According to Isid. Geoffroy there is no doubt that Goethe was an extreme partisan of similar views, as shown in the Introduction to a work written in 1794 and 1795, but not published till long afterwards: he has pointedly remarked ('Goethe als Naturforscher,' von Dr. Karl Meding, s. 34) that the future question for naturalists will be how, for instance, cattle got their horns, and not for what they are used. It is rather a singular instance of the manner in which similar views arise at about the same time, that Goethe in Germany, Dr. Darwin in England, and Geoffroy Saint-Hilaire (as we shall immediately see) in France, came to the same conclusion on the origin of species, in the years 1794-5.

what is done in this latter case "by art, seems to be done with equal effi-
cacy, though more slowly, by nature, in the formation of varieties of mankind, fitted for the country which they inhabit. Of the accidental varieties
of man, which would occur among the first few and scattered inhabitants
of the middle regions of Africa, some one would be better fitted than the
others to bear the diseases of the country. This race would consequently
multiply, while the others would decrease; not only from their inability
to sustain the attacks of disease, but from their incapacity of contending
with their more vigorous neighbours. The colour of this vigorous race I
take for granted, from what has been already said, would be dark. But
the same disposition to form varieties still existing, a darker and a darker
race would in the course of time occur: and as the darkest would be the
best fitted for the climate, this would at length become the most prevalent, if not the only race, in the particular country in which it had originated." He then extends these same views to the white inhabitants of
colder climates. I am indebted to Mr. Rowley, of the United States, for
having called my attention, through Mr. Brace, to the above passage in
Dr. Wells' work.

The Hon. and Rev. W. Herbert, afterwards Dean of Manchester, in the
fourth volume of the 'Horticultural Transactions,' 1822, and in his work
on the 'Amaryllidaceæ' (1837, pp. 19, 339), declares that "horticultural
experiments have established, beyond the possibility of refutation, that
botanical species are only a higher and more permanent class of varieties." He extends the same view to animals. The Dean believes that single species of each genus were created in an originally highly plastic
condition, and that these have produced, chiefly by intercrossing, but
likewise by variation, all our existing species.

In 1826 Professor Grant, in the concluding paragraph in his well-
known paper ('Edinburgh Philosophical Journal,' vol. xiv. p. 283) on the
Spongilla, clearly declares his belief that species are descended from other
species, and that they become improved in the course of modification.
This same view was given in his 55th Lecture, published in the 'Lancet'
in 1834.

In 1831 Mr. Patrick Matthew published his work on 'Naval Timber
and Arboriculture,' in which he gives precisely the same view on the origin of species as that (presently to be alluded to) propounded by Mr.
Wallace and myself in the 'Linnean Journal,' and as that enlarged in the
present volume. Unfortunately the view was given by Mr. Matthew very
briefly in scattered passages in an Appendix to a work on a different subject, so that it remained unnoticed until Mr. Matthew himself drew attention to it in the 'Gardener's Chronicle,' on April 7th, 1860. The differences of Mr. Matthew's view from mine are not of much importance: he
seems to consider that the world was nearly depopulated at successive
periods, and then re-stocked; and he gives as an alternative, that new
forms may be generated "without the presence of any mould or germ of
former aggregates." I am not sure that I understand some passages; but
it seems that he attributes much influence to the direct action of the con-

ditions of life. He clearly saw, however, the full force of the principle of natural selection.

The celebrated geologist and naturalist, Von Buch, in his excellent 'Description Physique des Isles Canaries' (1836, p. 147), clearly expresses his belief that varieties slowly become changed into permanent species, which are no longer capable of intercrossing.

Rafinesque, in his 'New Flora of North America,' published in 1836, wrote (p. 6) as follows:—"All species might have been varieties once, and many varieties are gradually becoming species by assuming constant and peculiar characters;" but farther on (p. 18) he adds, "except the original types or ancestors of the genus."

In 1843-44 Professor Haldeman ('Boston Journal of Nat. Hist. U. States,' vol. iv. p. 468) has ably given the arguments for and against the hypothesis of the development and modification of species: he seems to lean towards the side of change.

The 'Vestiges of Creation' appeared in 1844. In the tenth and much improved edition (1853) the anonymous author says (p. 155):—"The proposition determined on after much consideration is, that the several series of animated beings, from the simplest and oldest up to the highest and most recent, are, under the providence of God, the results, *first*, of an impulse which has been imparted to the forms of life, advancing them, in definite times, by generation, through grades of organisation terminating in the highest dicotyledons and vertebrata, these grades being few in number, and generally marked by intervals of organic character, which we find to be a practical difficulty in ascertaining affinities; *second*, of another impulse connected with the vital forces, tending, in the course of generations, to modify organic structures in accordance with external circumstances, as food, the nature of the habitat, and the meteoric agencies, these being the 'adaptations' of the natural theologian." The author apparently believes that organisation progresses by sudden leaps, but that the effects produced by the conditions of life are gradual. He argues with much force on general grounds that species are not immutable productions. But I cannot see how the two supposed "impulses" account in a scientific sense for the numerous and beautiful coadaptations which we see throughout nature; I cannot see that we thus gain any insight how, for instance, a woodpecker has become adapted to its peculiar habits of life. The work, from its powerful and brilliant style, though displaying in the earlier editions little accurate knowledge and a great want of scientific caution, immediately had a very wide circulation. In my opinion it has done excellent service in this country in calling attention to the subject, in removing prejudice, and in thus preparing the ground for the reception of analogous views.

In 1846 the veteran geologist M. J. d'Omalius d'Halloy published in an excellent though short paper ('Bulletins de l'Acad. Roy. Bruxelles,' tom. xiii. p. 581) his opinion that it is more probable that new species have been produced by descent with modification than that they have been separately created: the author first promulgated this opinion in 1831.

Professor Owen, in 1849 ('Nature of Limbs,' p. 86), wrote as follows:—"The archetypal idea was manifested in the flesh under diverse such modifications, upon this planet, long prior to the existence of those animal species that actually exemplify it. To what natural laws or secondary causes the orderly succession and progression of such organic phenomena may have been committed, we, as yet, are ignorant." In his Address to the British Association, in 1858, he speaks (p. li.) of "the axiom of the continuous operation of creative power, or of the ordained becoming of living things." Farther on (p. xc.), after referring to geographical distribution, he adds, "These phenomena shake our confidence in the conclusion that the Apteryx of New Zealand and the Red Grouse of England were distinct creations in and for those islands respectively. Always, also, it may be well to bear in mind that by the word 'creation' the zoologist means 'a process he knows not what.'" He amplifies this idea by adding that when such cases as that of the Red Grouse are "enumerated by the zoologist as evidence of distinct creation of the bird in and for such islands, he chiefly expresses that he knows not how the Red Grouse came to be there, and there exclusively; signifying also, by this mode of expressing such ignorance, his belief that both the bird and the islands owed their origin to a great first Creative Cause." If we interpret these sentences given in the same Address, one by the other, it appears that this eminent philosopher felt in 1858 his confidence shaken that the Apteryx and the Red Grouse first appeared in their respective homes, "he knew not how," or by some process "he knew not what."

This Address was delivered after the papers by Mr. Wallace and myself on the Origin of Species, presently to be referred to, had been read before the Linnean Society. When the first edition of this work was published, I was so completely deceived, as were many others, by such expressions as "the continuous operation of creative power," that I included Professor Owen with other palæontologists as being firmly convinced of the immutability of species; but it appears ('Anat. of Vertebrates,' vol. iii. p. 796) that this was on my part a preposterous error. In the last edition of this work I inferred, and the inference still seems to me perfectly just, from a passage beginning with the words "no doubt the type-form," &c. (Ibid. vol. i. p. xxxv.), that Professor Owen admitted that natural selection may have done something in the formation of a new species; but this it appears (Ibid. vol. iii. p. 798) is inaccurate and without evidence. I also gave some extracts from a correspondence between Professor Owen and the Editor of the 'London Review,' from which it appeared manifest to the Editor as well as to myself, that Professor Owen claimed to have promulgated the theory of natural selection before I had done so; and I expressed my surprise and satisfaction at this announcement; but as far as it is possible to understand certain recently published passages (Ibid. vol. iii. p. 798) I have either partially or wholly again fallen into error. It is consolatory to me that others find Professor Owen's controversial writings as difficult to understand and to reconcile with each other, as I do. As far as the mere enunciation of the principle of natural selection is concerned, it is quite immaterial whether or not Professor Owen preceded me, for both of us, as shown in this historical sketch, were long ago preceded by Dr. Wells and Mr. Matthew.

M. Isidore Geoffroy Saint-Hilaire, in his lectures delivered in 1850 (of which a Résumé appeared in the 'Revue et Mag. de Zoolog.,' Jan. 1851), briefly gives his reason for believing that specific characters "sont fixés, pour chaque espèce, tant qu'elle se perpétue au milieu des mêmes circonstances: ils se modifient, si les circonstances ambiantes viennent à changer." "En-résumé, *l'observation* des animaux sauvages démontre déjà la variabilité *limitée* des espèces. Les *expériences* sur les animaux sauvages, devenus domestiques, et sur les animaux domestiques redevenus sauvages, la démontrent plus clairement encore. Ces mêmes expériences prouvent, de plus, que les différences produites peuvent être de *valeur générique.*" In his 'Hist. Nat. Générale' (tom. ii. p. 430, 1859) he amplifies analogous conclusions.

From a circular lately issued it appears that Dr. Freke, in 1851 ('Dublin Medical Press,' p. 322), propounded the doctrine that all organic beings have descended from one primordial form. His grounds of belief and treatment of the subject are wholly different from mine; but as Dr. Freke has now (1861) published his Essay on the 'Origin of Species by means of Organic Affinity,' the difficult attempt to give any idea of his views would be superfluous on my part.

Mr. Herbert Spencer, in an Essay (originally published in the 'Leader,' March, 1852, and republished in his 'Essays,' in 1858), has contrasted the theories of the Creation and the Development of organic beings with remarkable skill and force. He argues from the analogy of domestic productions, from the changes which the embryos of many species undergo, from the difficulty of distinguishing species and varieties, and from the principle of general gradation, that species have been modified; and he attributes the modification to the change of circumstances. The author (1855) has also treated Psychology on the principle of the necessary acquirement of each mental power and capacity by gradation.

In 1852 M. Naudin, a distinguished botanist, expressly stated, in an admirable paper on the Origin of Species ('Revue Horticole,' p. 102; since partly republished in the 'Nouvelles Archives du Muséum,' tom. i. p. 171), his belief that species are formed in an analogous manner as varieties are under cultivation; and the latter process he attributes to man's power of selection. But he does not show how selection acts under nature. He believes, like Dean Herbert, that species, when nascent, were more plastic than at present. He lays weight on what he calls the principle of finality, "puissance mystérieuse, indéterminée; fatalité pour les uns; pour les autres, volonté providentielle, dont l'action incessante sur les êtres vivants détermine, à toutes les époques de l'existence du monde, la forme, le volume, et la durée de chacun d'eux, en raison de sa destinée dans l'ordre de choses dont il fait partie. C'est cette puissance qui harmonise chaque membre à l'ensemble, en l'appropriant à la fonction qu'il doit remplir dans l'organisme général de la nature, fonction qui est pour lui sa raison d'être." *

In 1853 a celebrated geologist, Count Keyserling ('Bulletin de la Soc. Géolog.,' 2nd Ser., tom. x. p. 357), suggested that as new diseases, supposed to have been caused by some miasma, have arisen and spread over the world, so at certain periods the germs of existing species may have been chemically affected by circumambient molecules of a particular nature, and thus have given rise to new forms.

In this same year, 1853, Dr. Schaaffhausen published an excellent pamphlet ('Verhand. des Naturhist. Vereins der Preuss. Rheinlands,' &c.), in which he maintains the development of organic forms on the earth. He infers that many species have kept true for long periods, whereas a few have become modified. The distinction of species he explains by the destruction of intermediate graduated forms. "Thus living plants and animals are not separated from the extinct by new creations, but are to be regarded as their descendants through continued reproduction."

A well-known French botanist, M. Lecoq, writes in 1854 ('Etudes sur Géograph. Bot.,' tom. i. p. 250), "On voit que nos recherches sur la fixité ou la variation de l'espèce, nous conduisent directement aux idées émises, par deux hommes justement célèbres, Geoffroy Saint-Hilaire et Goethe." Some other passages scattered through M. Lecoq's large work, make it a little doubtful how far he extends his views on the modification of species.

The 'Philosophy of Creation' has been treated in a masterly manner by the Rev. Baden Powell, in his 'Essays on the Unity of Worlds,' 1855. Nothing can be more striking than the manner in which he shows that the introduction of new species is "a regular, not a casual phenomenon," or, as Sir John Herschel expresses it, "a natural in contradistinction to a miraculous process."

The third volume of the 'Journal of the Linnean Society' contains papers, read July 1st, 1858, by Mr. Wallace and myself, in which, as stated in the introductory remarks to this volume, the theory of Natural Selection is promulgated by Mr. Wallace with admirable force and clearness.

Von Baer, towards whom all zoologists feel so profound a respect, expressed about the year 1859 (see Prof. Rudolph Wagner, 'Zoologisch-Anthropologische Untersuchungen,' 1861, s. 51) his conviction, chiefly

---

* From references in Bronn's 'Untersuchungen über die Entwickelungs-Gesetze,' it appears that the celebrated botanist and palæontologist Unger published, in 1852, his belief that species undergo development and modification. Dalton, likewise, in Pander and Dalton's work on Fossil Sloths, expressed, in 1821, a similar belief. Similar views have, as is well known, been maintained by Oken in his mystical 'Natur-Philosophie.' From other references in Godron's work 'Sur l'Espèce,' it seems that Bory St. Vincent, Burdach, Poiret, and Fries, have all admitted that new species are continually being produced.

I may add, that of the thirty-four authors named in this Historical Sketch, who believe in the modification of species, or at least disbelieve in separate acts of creation, twenty-seven have written on special branches of natural history or geology.

grounded on the laws of geographical distribution, that forms now perfectly distinct have descended from a single parent-form.

In June, 1859, Professor Huxley gave a lecture before the Royal Institution on the 'Persistent Types of Animal Life.' Referring to such cases, he remarks, "It is difficult to comprehend the meaning of such facts as these, if we suppose that each species of animal and plant, or each great type of organisation, was formed and placed upon the surface of the globe at long intervals by a distinct act of creative power; and it is well to recollect that such an assumption is as unsupported by tradition or revelation as it is opposed to the general analogy of nature. If, on the other hand, we view 'Persistent Types' in relation to that hypothesis which supposes the species living at any time to be the result of the gradual modification of pre-existing species a hypothesis which, though unproven, and sadly damaged by some of its supporters, is yet the only one to which physiology lends any countenance; their existence would seem to show that the amount of modification which living beings have undergone during geological time is but very small in relation to the whole series of changes which they have suffered."

In December, 1859, Dr. Hooker published his 'Introduction to the Australian Flora.' In the first part of this great work he admits the truth of the descent and modification of species, and supports this doctrine by many original observations.

The first edition of this work was published on November 24th, 1859, and the second edition on January 7th, 1860.

INTRODUCTION

WHEN on board H.M.S. 'Beagle,' as naturalist, I was much struck with certain facts in the distribution of the organic beings inhabiting South America, and in the geological relations of the present to the past inhabitants of that continent. These facts, as will be seen in the latter chapters of this volume, seemed to throw some light on the origin of species—that mystery of mysteries, as it has been called by one of our greatest philosophers. On my return home, it occurred to me, in 1837, that something might perhaps be made out on this question by patiently accumulating and reflecting on all sorts of facts which could possibly have any bearing on it. After five years' work I allowed myself to speculate on the subject, and drew up some short notes; these I enlarged in 1844 into a sketch of the conclusions, which then seemed to me probable: from that period to the present day I have steadily pursued the same object. I hope that I may be excused for entering on these personal details, as I give them to show that I have not been hasty in coming to a decision.

My work is now (1859) nearly finished; but as it will take me many more years to complete it, and as my health is far from strong, I have been urged to publish this Abstract. I have more especially been induced to do this, as Mr. Wallace, who is now studying the natural history of the Malay archipelago, has arrived at almost exactly the same general conclusions that I have on the origin of species. In 1858 he sent me a memoir on this subject, with a request that I would forward it to Sir Charles Lyell, who sent it to the Linnean Society, and it is published in the third volume of the Journal of that society. Sir C. Lyell and Dr. Hooker, who both knew of my work—the latter having read my sketch of 1844—honoured me by thinking it advisable to publish, with Mr. Wallace's excellent memoir, some brief extracts from my manuscripts.

This Abstract, which I now publish, must necessarily be imperfect. I cannot here give references and authorities for my several statements; and I must trust to the reader reposing some confidence in my accuracy. No doubt errors will have crept in, though I hope I have always been cautious in trusting to good authorities alone. I can here give only the general conclusions at which I have arrived, with a few facts in illustration, but which, I hope, in most cases will suffice. No one can feel more sensible than I do of the necessity of hereafter publishing in detail all the facts, with references, on which my conclusions have been grounded; and I hope in a future work to do this. For I am well aware that scarcely a single point is discussed in this volume on which facts cannot be adduced, often apparently leading to conclusions directly opposite to those at which I have arrived. A fair result can be obtained only by fully stating and balancing the facts and arguments on both sides of each question; and this is here impossible.

I much regret that want of space prevents my having the satisfaction of acknowledging the generous assistance which I have received from very many naturalists, some of them personally unknown to me. I cannot, however, let this opportunity pass without expressing my deep obligations to Dr. Hooker, who, for the last fifteen years, has aided me in every possible way by his large stores of knowledge and his excellent judgment.

In considering the Origin of Species, it is quite conceivable that a naturalist, reflecting on the mutual affinities of organic beings, on their embryological relations, their geographical distribution, geological succession, and other such facts, might come to the conclusion that species had not been independently created, but had descended, like varieties, from other species. Nevertheless, such a conclusion, even if well founded, would be unsatisfactory, until it could be shown how the innumerable species inhabiting this world have been modified, so as to acquire that perfection of structure and coadaptation which justly excites our admiration. Naturalists continually refer to external conditions, such as climate, food, &c., as the only possible cause of variation. In one limited sense, as we shall hereafter see, this may be true; but it is preposterous to attribute to mere external conditions, the structure, for instance, of the woodpecker, with its feet, tail, beak, and tongue, so admirably adapted to catch insects under the bark of trees. In the case of the mistletoe, which draws its nourishment from certain trees, which has seeds that must be transported by certain birds, and which has flowers with separate sexes absolutely requiring the agency of certain insects to bring pollen from one flower to the other, it is equally preposterous to account for the structure of this parasite, with its relations to several distinct organic beings, by the effects of external conditions, or of habit, or of the volition of the plant itself.

It is, therefore, of the highest importance to gain a clear insight into the means of modification and coadaptation. At the commencement of my observations it seemed to me probable that a careful study of domesticated animals and of cultivated plants would offer the best chance of making out this obscure problem. Nor have I been disappointed; in this and in all other perplexing cases I have invariably found that our knowledge, imperfect though it be, of variation under domestication, afforded the best and safest clue. I may venture to express my conviction of the high value of such studies, although they have been very commonly neglected by naturalists.

From these considerations, I shall devote the first chapter of this Abstract to Variation under Domestication. We shall thus see that a large amount of hereditary modification is at least possible; and, what is equally or more important, we shall see how great is the power of man in accumulating by his Selection successive slight variations. I will then pass on to the variability of species in a state of nature; but I shall, unfortunately, be compelled to treat this subject far too briefly, as it can be treated properly only by giving long catalogues of facts. We shall, however, be enabled to discuss what circumstances are most favourable to variation. In the next chapter the Struggle for Existence amongst all organic beings throughout the world, which inevitably follows from the high geometrical ratio of their increase, will be considered. This is the doctrine of Malthus, applied to the whole animal and vegetable kingdoms. As many more individuals of each species are born than can possibly survive; and as, consequently, there is a frequently recurring struggle for existence, it follows that any being, if it vary however slightly in any manner profitable to itself, under the complex and sometimes varying conditions of life, will have a better chance of surviving, and thus be *naturally selected*. From the strong principle of inheritance, any selected variety will tend to propagate its new and modified form.

This fundamental subject of Natural Selection will be treated at some length in the fourth chapter; and we shall then see how Natural Selection almost inevitably causes much Extinction of the less improved forms of life, and leads to what I have called Divergence of Character. In the next chapter I shall discuss the complex and little known laws of variation. In the five succeeding chapters, the most apparent and gravest difficulties in accepting the theory will be given: namely, first, the difficulties of transitions, or how a simple being or a simple organ can be changed and perfected into a highly developed being or into an elaborately constructed organ; secondly, the subject of Instinct, or the mental powers of animals; thirdly, Hybridism, or the infertility of species and the fertility of varieties when intercrossed; and fourthly, the imperfection of the Geological Record. In the next chapter I shall consider the geological succession of organic beings throughout time; in the twelfth and thirteenth, their geographical distribution throughout space; in the fourteenth, their classification or mutual affinities, both when mature and in an embryonic condition. In the last chapter I shall give a brief recapitulation of the whole work, and a few concluding remarks.

No one ought to feel surprise at much remaining as yet unexplained in regard to the origin of species and varieties, if he make due allowance for our profound ignorance in regard to the mutual relations of the many beings which live around us. Who can explain why one species ranges widely and is very numerous, and why another allied species has a narrow range and is rare? Yet these relations are of the highest importance, for they determine the present welfare and, as I believe, the future success and modification of every inhabitant of this world. Still less do we know of the mutual relations of the innumerable inhabitants of the world during the many past geological epochs in its history. Although much remains obscure, and will long remain obscure, I can entertain no doubt, after the most deliberate study and dispassionate judgment of which I am capable, that the view which most naturalists until recently entertained, and which I formerly entertained—namely, that each species has been independently created—is erroneous. I am fully convinced that species are not immutable; but that those belonging to what are called the same genera are lineal descendants of some other and generally extinct species, in the same manner as the acknowledged varieties of any one species are the descendants of that species. Furthermore, I am convinced that Natural Selection has been the most important, but not the exclusive, means of modification.

CHAPTER I

VARIATION UNDER DOMESTICATION

Causes of Variability—Effects of Habit and the use or disuse of Parts—Correlated Variation—Inheritance—Character of Domestic Varieties—Difficulty of distinguishing between Varieties and Species—Origin of Domestic Varieties from one or more Species—Domestic Pigeons, their Differences and Origin— Principles of Selection, anciently followed, their Effects—Methodical and Unconscious Selection—Unknown Origin of our Domestic Productions—Circumstances favourable to Man's power of Selection.

Causes of Variability

WHEN we compare the individuals of the same variety or sub-variety of our older cultivated plants and animals, one of the first points which strikes us is, that they generally differ more from each other than do the individuals of any one species or variety in a state of nature. And if we reflect on the vast diversity of the plants and animals which have been cultivated, and which have varied during all ages under the most different climates and treatment, we are driven to conclude that this great variability is due to our domestic productions having been raised under conditions of life not so uniform as, and somewhat different from, those to which the parent species had been exposed under nature. There is, also, some probability in the view propounded by Andrew Knight, that this variability may be partly connected with excess of food. It seems clear that organic beings must be exposed during several generations to new conditions to cause any great amount of variation; and that, when the organisation has once begun to vary, it generally continues varying for many generations. No case is on record of a variable organism ceasing to vary under cultivation. Our oldest cultivated plants, such as wheat, still yield new varieties: our oldest domesticated animals are still capable of rapid improvement or modification.

As far as I am able to judge, after long attending to the subject, the conditions of life appear to act in two ways,—directly on the whole organisation or on certain parts alone, and indirectly by affecting the reproductive system. With respect to the direct action, we must bear in mind that in every case, as Professor Weismann has lately insisted, and as I have incidentally shown in my work on 'Variation under Domestication,' there are two factors: namely, the nature of the organism, and the nature of the conditions. The former seems to be much the more important; for nearly similar variations sometimes arise under, as far as we can judge, dissimilar conditions; and, on the other hand, dissimilar variations arise under conditions which appear to be nearly uniform. The effects on the offspring are either definite or indefinite. They may be considered as definite when all or nearly all the offspring of individuals exposed to certain conditions during several generations are modified in the same manner. It is extremely difficult to come to any conclusion in regard to the extent of the changes which have been thus definitely induced. There can, however, be little doubt about many slight changes,—such as size from the amount of food, colour from the nature of the food, thickness of the skin and hair from climate, &c. Each of the endless variations which we see in the plumage of our fowls must have had some efficient cause; and if the same cause were to act uniformly during a long series of generations on many individuals, all probably would be modified in the same manner. Such facts as the complex and extraordinary out-growths which variably follow from the insertion of a minute drop of poison by a gall-producing insect, show us what singular modifications might result in the case of plants from a chemical change in the nature of the sap.

Indefinite variability is a much more common result of changed conditions than definite variability, and has probably played a more important part in the formation of our domestic races. We see indefinite variability in the endless slight peculiarities which distinguish the individuals of the same species, and which cannot be accounted for by inheritance from either parent or from some more remote ancestor. Even strongly marked differences occasionally appear in the young of the same litter, and in seedlings from the same seed-capsule. At long intervals of time, out of millions of individuals reared in the same country and fed on nearly the same food, deviations of structure so strongly pronounced as to deserve to be called monstrosities arise; but monstrosities cannot be separated by any distinct line from slighter variations. All such changes of structure, whether extremely slight or strongly marked, which appear amongst many individuals living together, may be considered as the indefinite effects of the conditions of life on each individual organism, in nearly the same manner as the chill affects different men in an indefinite manner, according to their state of body or constitution, causing coughs or colds, rheumatism, or inflammation of various organs.

With respect to what I have called the indirect action of changed conditions, namely, through the reproductive system of being affected, we may infer that variability is thus induced, partly from the fact of this system being extremely sensitive to any change in the conditions, and partly from the similarity, as Kölreuter and others have remarked, between the variability which follows from the crossing of distinct species, and that which may be observed with plants and animals when reared under new or unnatural conditions. Many facts clearly show how eminently susceptible the reproductive system is to very slight changes in the surrounding conditions. Nothing is more easy than to tame an animal, and few things more difficult than to get it to breed freely under confinement, even when the male and female unite. How many animals there are which will not breed, though kept in an almost free state in their native country! This is generally, but erroneously, attributed to vitiated instincts. Many culti-vated plants display the utmost vigour, and yet rarely or never seed! In some few cases it has been discovered that a very trifling change, such as a little more or less water at some particular period of growth, will deter-mine whether or not a plant will produce seeds. I cannot here give the de-tails which I have collected and elsewhere published on this curious subject; but to show how singular the laws are which determine the re-production of animals under confinement, I may mention that carnivor-ous animals, even from the tropics, breed in this country pretty freely under confinement, with the exception of the plantigrades or bear family, which seldom produce young; whereas carnivorous birds, with the rarest exceptions, hardly ever lay fertile eggs. Many exotic plants have pollen utterly worthless, in the same condition as in the most sterile hybrids. When, on the one hand, we see domesticated animals and plants, though often weak and sickly, breeding freely under confinement; and when, on the other hand, we see individuals, though taken young from a state of nature perfectly tamed, long-lived and healthy (of which I could give numerous instances), yet having their reproductive system so seriously affected by unperceived causes as to fail to act, we need not be surprised at this system, when it does act under confinement, acting irregularly, and producing offspring somewhat unlike their parents. I may add, that as some organisms breed freely under the most unnatural conditions (for instance, rabbits and ferrets kept in hutches), showing that their repro-ductive organs are not easily affected; so will some animals and plants withstand domestication or cultivation, and vary very slightly—perhaps hardly more than in a state of nature.

Some naturalists have maintained that all variations are connected with the act of sexual reproduction; but this is certainly an error; for I have given in another work a long list of "sporting plants," as they are called by gardeners;—that is, of plants which have suddenly produced a single bud with a new and sometimes widely different character from that of the other buds on the same plant. These bud variations, as they may be named, can be propagated by grafts, offsets, &c., and sometimes by seed. They occur rarely under nature, but are far from rare under culture. As a single bud out of the many thousands, produced year after year on the same tree under uniform conditions, has been known suddenly to assume a new character; and as buds on distinct trees, growing under different conditions, have sometimes yielded nearly the same variety—for in-stance, buds on peach-trees producing nectarines, and buds on common roses producing moss-roses—we clearly see that the nature of the condi-tions is of subordinate importance in comparison with the nature of the organism in determining each particular form of variation;—perhaps of not more importance than the nature of the spark, by which a mass of combustible matter is ignited, has in determining the nature of the flames.

Effects of Habit and of the Use or Disuse of Parts; Correlated Variation; Inheritance

Changed habits produce an inherited effect, as in the period of the flowering of plants when transported from one climate to another. With animals the increased use or disuse of parts has had a more marked influence; thus I find in the domestic duck that the bones of the wing weigh less and the bones of the leg more, in proportion to the whole skeleton, than do the same bones in the wild-duck; and this change may be safely attributed to the domestic duck flying much less, and walking more, than its wild parents. The great and inherited development of the udders in cows and goats in countries where they are habitually milked, in comparison with these organs in other countries, is probably another instance of the effects of use. Not one of our domestic animals can be named which has not in some country drooping ears; and the view which has been suggested that the drooping is due to disuse of the muscles of the ear, from the animals being seldom much alarmed, seems probable.

Many laws regulate variation, some few of which can be dimly seen, and will hereafter be briefly discussed. I will here only allude to what may be called correlated variation. Important changes in the embryo or larva will probably entail changes in the mature animal. In monstrosities, the correlations between quite distinct parts are very curious; and many instances are given in Isidore Geoffroy St. Hilaire's great work on this subject. Breeders believe that long limbs are almost always accompanied by an elongated head. Some instances of correlation are quite whimsical: thus cats which are entirely white and have blue eyes are generally deaf; but it has been lately stated by Mr. Tait that this is confined to the males. Colour and constitutional peculiarities go together, of which many remarkable cases could be given amongst animals and plants. From facts collected by Heusinger, it appears that white sheep and pigs are injured by certain plants, whilst dark-coloured individuals escape: Professor Wyman has recently communicated to me a good illustration of this fact; on asking some farmers in Virginia how it was that all their pigs were black, they informed him that the pigs ate the paint-root (Lachnanthes), which coloured their bones pink, and which caused the hoofs of all but the black varieties to drop off; and one of the "crackers" (*i.e.* Virginia squatters) added, "we select the black members of a litter for raising, as they alone have a good chance of living." Hairless dogs have imperfect teeth; long-haired and coarse-haired animals are apt to have, as is asserted, long or many horns; pigeons with feathered feet have skin between their outer toes; pigeons with short beaks have small feet, and those with long beaks large feet. Hence if man goes on selecting, and thus augmenting, any peculiarity, he will almost certainly modify unintentionally other parts of the structure, owing to the mysterious laws of correlation.

The results of the various, unknown, or but dimly understood laws of variation are infinitely complex and diversified. It is well worth while carefully to study the several treatises on some of our old cultivated

plants, as on the hyacinth, potato, even the dahlia, &c.; and it is really
surprising to note the endless points of structure and constitution in
which the varieties and sub-varieties differ slightly from each other. The
whole organisation seems to have become plastic, and departs in a slight
degree from that of the parental type.

Any variation which is not inherited is unimportant for us. But the
number and diversity of inheritable deviations of structure, both those of
slight and those of considerable physiological importance, are endless. Dr.
Prosper Lucas's treatise, in two large volumes, is the fullest and the best
on this subject. No breeder doubts how strong is the tendency to inheritance; that like produces like is his fundamental belief: doubts have been
thrown on this principle only by theoretical writers. When any deviation
of structure often appears, and we see it in the father and child, we cannot tell whether it may not be due to the same cause having acted on
both; but when amongst individuals, apparently exposed to the same conditions, any very rare deviation, due to some extraordinary combination
of circumstances, appears in the parent—say, once amongst several million individuals—and it reappears in the child, the mere doctrine of
chances almost compels us to attribute its reappearance to inheritance.
Every one must have heard of cases of albinism, prickly skin, hairy
bodies, &c., appearing in several members of the same family. If strange
and rare deviations of structure are really inherited, less strange and
commoner deviations may be freely admitted to be inheritable. Perhaps
the correct way of viewing the whole subject would be, to look at the inheritance of every character whatever as the rule, and non-inheritance as
the anomaly.

The laws governing inheritance are for the most part unknown. No one
can say why the same peculiarity in different individuals of the same species, or in different species, is sometimes inherited and sometimes not so;
why the child often reverts in certain characters to its grandfather or
grandmother or more remote ancestor; why a peculiarity is often transmitted from one sex to both sexes, or to one sex alone, more commonly
but not exclusively to the like sex. It is a fact of some importance to us,
that peculiarities appearing in the males of our domestic breeds are often
transmitted, either exclusively or in a much greater degree, to the males
alone. A much more important rule, which I think may be trusted, is that,
at whatever period of life a peculiarity first appears, it tends to reappear
in the offspring at a corresponding age, though sometimes earlier. In
many cases this could not be otherwise; thus the inherited peculiarities in
the horns of cattle could appear only in the offspring when nearly mature; peculiarities in the silkworm are known to appear at the corresponding caterpillar or cocoon stage. But hereditary diseases and some
other facts make me believe that the rule has a wider extension, and that,
when there is no apparent reason why a peculiarity should appear at any
particular age, yet that it does tend to appear in the offspring at the same
period at which it first appeared in the parent. I believe this rule to be of
the highest importance in explaining the laws of embryology. These re-

marks are of course confined to the first *appearance* of the peculiarity, and not to the primary cause which may have acted on the ovules or on the male element; in nearly the same manner as the increased length of the horns in the offspring from a short-horned cow by a long-horned bull, though appearing late in life, is clearly due to the male element.

Having alluded to the subject of reversion, I may here refer to a statement often made by naturalists—namely, that our domestic varieties, when run wild, gradually but invariably revert in character to their aboriginal stocks. Hence it has been argued that no deductions can be drawn from domestic races to species in a state of nature. I have in vain endeavoured to discover on what decisive facts the above statement has so often and so boldly been made. There would be great difficulty in proving its truth: we may safely conclude that very many of the most strongly marked domestic varieties could not possibly live in a wild state. In many cases, we do not know what the aboriginal stock was, and so could not tell whether or not nearly perfect reversion had ensued. It would be necessary, in order to prevent the effects of intercrossing, that only a single variety should have been turned loose in its new home. Nevertheless, as our varieties certainly do occasionally revert in some of their characters to ancestral forms, it seems to me not improbable that if we could succeed in naturalising, or were to cultivate, during many generations, the several races, for instance, of the cabbage, in very poor soil (in which case, however, some effect would have to be attributed to the *definite* action of the poor soil), that they would, to a large extent, or even wholly, revert to the wild aboriginal stock. Whether or not the experiment would succeed, is not of great importance for our line of argument; for by the experiment itself the conditions of life are changed. If it could be shown that our domestic varieties manifested a strong tendency to reversion,—that is, to lose their acquired characters, whilst kept under the same conditions, and whilst kept in a considerable body, so that free intercrossing might check, by blending together, any slight deviations in their structure, in such case, I grant that we could deduce nothing from domestic varieties in regard to species. But there is not a shadow of evidence in favour of this view: to assert that we could not breed our cart and race-horses, long and short-horned cattle, and poultry of various breeds, and esculent vegetables, for an unlimited number of generations, would be opposed to all experience.

Character of Domestic Varieties; difficulty of distinguishing between Varieties and Species; origin of Domestic Varieties from one or more Species

When we look to the hereditary varieties or races of our domestic animals and plants, and compare them with closely allied species, we generally perceive in each domestic race, as already remarked, less uniformity of character than in true species. Domestic races often have a somewhat monstrous character; by which I mean, that, although differing from each other, and from other species of the same genus, in several trifling respects, they often differ in an extreme degree in some one part, both when compared one with another, and more especially when compared with the species under nature to which they are nearest allied. With these exceptions (and with that of the perfect fertility of varieties when crossed,—a subject hereafter to be discussed), domestic races of the same species differ from each other in the same manner as do the closely-allied species of the same genus in a state of nature, but the differences in most cases are less in degree. This must be admitted as true, for the domestic races of many animals and plants have been ranked by some competent judges as the descendants of aboriginally distinct species, and by other competent judges as mere varieties. If any well marked distinction existed between a domestic race and a species, this source of doubt would not so perpetually recur. It has often been stated that domestic races do not differ from each other in character of generic value. It can be shown that this statement is not correct; but naturalists differ much in determining what characters are of generic value; all such valuations being at present empirical. When it is explained how genera originate under nature, it will be seen that we have no right to expect often to find a generic amount of difference in our domesticated races.

In attempting to estimate the amount of structural difference between allied domestic races, we are soon involved in doubt, from not knowing whether they are descended from one or several parent species. This point, if it could be cleared up, would be interesting; if, for instance, it could be shown that the greyhound, bloodhound, terrier, spaniel, and bull-dog, which we all know propagate their kind truly, were the offspring of any single species, then such facts would have great weight in making us doubt about the immutability of the many closely allied natural species—for instance, of the many foxes—inhabiting different quarters of the world. I do not believe, as we shall presently see, that the whole amount of difference between the several breeds of the dog has been produced under domestication; I believe that a small part of the difference is due to their being descended from distinct species. In the case of strongly marked races of some other domesticated species, there is presumptive or even strong evidence, that all are descended from a single wild stock.

It has often been assumed that man has chosen for domestication animals and plants having an extraordinary inherent tendency to vary, and likewise to withstand diverse climates. I do not dispute that these capacities have added largely to the value of most of our domesticated productions: but how could a savage possibly know, when he first tamed an animal, whether it would vary in succeeding generations, and whether it would endure other climates? Has the little variability of the ass and goose, or the small power of endurance of warmth by the reindeer, or of cold by the common camel, prevented their domestication? I cannot doubt that if other animals and plants, equal in number to our domesticated productions, and belonging to equally diverse classes and countries, were taken from a state of nature, and could be made to breed for an equal number of generations under domestication, they would on an average vary as largely as the parent species of our existing domesticated productions have varied.

In the case of most of our anciently domesticated animals and plants, it is not possible to come to any definite conclusion, whether they are descended from one or several wild species. The argument mainly relied on by those who believe in the multiple origin of our domestic animals is, that we find in the most ancient times, on the monuments of Egypt, and in the lake-habitations of Switzerland, much diversity in the breeds; and that some of these ancient breeds closely resemble, or are even identical with, those still existing. But this only throws far backwards the history of civilisation, and shows that animals were domesticated at a much earlier period than has hitherto been supposed. The lake-inhabitants of Switzerland cultivated several kinds of wheat and barley, the pea, the poppy for oil, and flax; and they possessed several domesticated animals. They also carried on commerce with other nations. All this clearly shows, as Heer has remarked, that they had at this early age progressed considerably in civilisation; and this again implies a long continued previous period of less advanced civilisation, during which the domesticated animals, kept by different tribes in different districts, might have varied and given rise to distinct races. Since the discovery of flint tools in the superficial formations of many parts of the world, all geologists believe that barbarian man existed at an enormously remote period; and we know that at the present day there is hardly a tribe so barbarous, as not to have domesticated at least the dog.

The origin of most of our domestic animals will probably for ever remain vague. But I may here state, that, looking to the domestic dogs of the whole world, I have, after a laborious collection of all known facts, come to the conclusion that several wild species of Canidæ have been tamed, and that their blood, in some cases mingled together, flows in the veins of our domestic breeds. In regard to sheep and goats I can form no decided opinion. From facts communicated to me by Mr. Blyth, on the habits, voice, constitution, and structure of the humped Indian cattle, it is almost certain that they are descended from a different aboriginal stock from our European cattle; and some competent judges believe that these latter have had two or three wild progenitors,—whether or not these deserve to be called species. This conclusion, as well as that of the specific distinction between the humped and common cattle, may, indeed, be looked upon as established by the admirable researches of Professor Rütimeyer. With respect to horses, from reasons which I cannot here give, I am doubtfully inclined to believe, in opposition to several authors, that all the races belong to the same species. Having kept nearly all the English breeds of the fowl alive, having bred and crossed them, and examined their skeletons, it appears to me almost certain that all are the descendants of the wild Indian fowl, Gallus bankiva; and this is the conclusion of

Mr. Blyth, and of others who have studied this bird in India. In regard to ducks and rabbits, some breeds of which differ much from each other, the evidence is clear that they are all descended from the common wild duck and rabbit.

The doctrine of the origin of our several domestic races from several aboriginal stocks, has been carried to an absurd extreme by some authors. They believe that every race which breeds true, let the distinctive characters be ever so slight, has had its wild prototype. At this rate there must have existed at least a score of species of wild cattle, as many sheep, and several goats, in Europe alone, and several even within Great Britain. One author believes that there formerly existed eleven wild species of sheep peculiar to Great Britain! When we bear in mind that Britain has now not one peculiar mammal, and France but few distinct from those of Germany, and so with Hungary, Spain, &c., but that each of these kingdoms possesses several peculiar breeds of cattle, sheep, &c., we must admit that many domestic breeds must have originated in Europe; for whence otherwise could they have been derived? So it is in India. Even in the case of the breeds of the domestic dog throughout the world, which I admit are descended from several wild species, it cannot be doubted that there has been an immense amount of inherited variation; for who will believe that animals closely resembling the Italian greyhound, the bloodhound, the bull-dog, pug-dog, or Blenheim spaniel, &c.—so unlike all wild Canidæ—ever existed in a state of nature? It has often been loosely said that all our races of dogs have been produced by the crossing of a few aboriginal species; but by crossing we can only get forms in some degree intermediate between their parents; and if we account for our several domestic races by this process, we must admit the former existence of the most extreme forms, as the Italian greyhound, bloodhound, bull-dog, &c., in the wild state. Moreover, the possibility of making distinct races by crossing has been greatly exaggerated. Many cases are on record, showing that a race may be modified by occasional crosses, if aided by the careful selection of the individuals which present the desired character; but to obtain a race intermediate between two quite distinct races, would be very difficult. Sir J. Sebright expressly experimented with this object and failed. The offspring from the first cross between two pure breeds is tolerably and sometimes (as I have found with pigeons) quite uniform in character, and everything seems simple enough; but when these mongrels are crossed one with another for several generations, hardly two of them are alike, and then the difficulty of the task becomes manifest.

Breeds of the Domestic Pigeon, their Differences and Origin

Believing that it is always best to study some special group, I have, after deliberation, taken up domestic pigeons. I have kept every breed which I could purchase or obtain, and have been most kindly favoured with skins from several quarters of the world, more especially by the Hon. W. Elliot from India, and by the Hon. C. Murray from Persia.

Many treatises in different languages have been published on pigeons, and some of them are very important, as being of considerable antiquity. I have associated with several eminent fanciers, and have been permitted to join two of the London Pigeon Clubs. The diversity of the breeds is something astonishing. Compare the English carrier and the short-faced tumbler, and see the wonderful difference in their beaks, entailing corresponding differences in their skulls. The carrier, more especially the male bird, is also remarkable from the wonderful development of the carunculated skin about the head; and this is accompanied by greatly elongated eyelids, very large external orifices to the nostrils, and a wide gape of mouth. The short-faced tumbler has a beak in outline almost like that of a finch; and the common tumbler has the singular inherited habit of flying at a great height in a compact flock, and tumbling in the air head over heels. The runt is a bird of great size, with long massive beak and large feet; some of the sub-breeds of runts have very long necks, others very long wings and tails, others singularly short tails. The barb is allied to the carrier, but, instead of a long beak has a very short and broad one. The pouter has a much elongated body, wings, and legs; and its enormously developed crop, which it glories in inflating, may well excite astonishment and even laughter. The turbit has a short and conical beak, with a line of reversed feathers down the breast; and it has the habit of continually expanding slightly, the upper part of the œsophagus. The Jacobin has the feathers so much reversed along the back of the neck that they form a hood; and it has, proportionally to its size, elongated wing and tail feathers. The trumpeter and laugher, as their names express, utter a very different coo from the other breeds. The fantail has thirty or even forty tail-feathers, instead of twelve or fourteen—the normal number in all the members of the great pigeon family: these feathers are kept expanded, and are carried so erect, that in good birds the head and tail touch: the oil-gland is quite aborted. Several other less distinct breeds might be specified.

In the skeletons of the several breeds, the development of the bones of the face in length and breadth and curvature differs enormously. The shape, as well as the breadth and length of the ramus of the lower jaw, varies in a highly remarkable manner. The caudal and sacral vertebræ vary in number; as does the number of the ribs, together with their relative breadth and the presence of processes. The size and shape of the apertures in the sternum are highly variable; so is the degree of divergence and relative size of the two arms of the furcula. The proportional width of the gape of mouth, the proportional length of the eyelids, of the orifice of the nostrils, of the tongue (not always in strict correlation with the length of beak), the size of the crop and of the upper part of the œsophagus; the development and abortion of the oil-gland; the number of the primary wing and caudal feathers; the relative length of the wing and tail to each other and to the body; the relative length of the leg and foot; the number of scutellæ on the toes, the development of skin between the toes, are all points of structure which are variable. The period at which the perfect plumage is acquired varies, as does the state of the down with which the nestling birds are clothed when hatched. The shape and size of the eggs vary. The manner of flight, and in some breeds the voice and disposition, differ remarkably. Lastly, in certain breeds, the males and females have come to differ in a slight degree from each other.

Altogether at least a score of pigeons might be chosen, which, if shown to an ornithologist, and he were told that they were wild birds, would certainly be ranked by him as well-defined species. Moreover, I do not believe that any ornithologist would in this case place the English carrier, the short-faced tumbler, the runt, the barb, pouter, and fantail in the same genus; more especially as in each of these breeds several truly-inherited sub-breeds, or species, as he would call them, could be shown him.

Great as are the differences between the breeds of the pigeon, I am fully convinced that the common opinion of naturalists is correct, namely, that all are descended from the rock-pigeon (Columba livia), including under this term several geographical races or sub-species, which differ from each other in the most trifling respects. As several of the reasons which have led me to this belief are in some degree applicable in other cases, I will here briefly give them. If the several breeds are not varieties, and have not proceeded from the rock-pigeon, they must have descended from at least seven or eight aboriginal stocks; for it is impossible to make the present domestic breeds by the crossing of any lesser number: how, for instance, could a pouter be produced by crossing two breeds unless one of the parent-stocks possessed the characteristic enormous crop? The supposed aboriginal stocks must all have been rock-pigeons, that is, they did not breed or willingly perch on trees. But besides C. livia, with its geographical sub-species, only two or three other species of rock-pigeons are known; and these have not any of the characters of the domestic breeds. Hence the supposed aboriginal stocks must either still exist in the countries where they were originally domesticated, and yet be unknown to ornithologists; and this, considering their size, habits, and remarkable characters, seems improbable; or they must have become extinct in the wild state. But birds breeding on precipices, and good fliers, are unlikely to be exterminated; and the common rock-pigeon, which has the same habits with the domestic breeds, has not been exterminated even on several of the smaller British islets, or on the shores of the Mediterranean. Hence the supposed extermination of so many species having similar habits with the rock-pigeon seems a very rash assumption. Moreover, the several above-named domesticated breeds have been transported to all parts of the world, and, therefore, some of them must have been carried back again into their native country; but not one has become wild or feral, though the dovecot-pigeon, which is the rock-pigeon in a very slightly altered state, has become feral in several places. Again, all recent experience shows that it is difficult to get wild animals to breed freely under domestication; yet on the hypothesis of the multiple origin of our pigeons, it must be assumed that at least seven or eight species were so thoroughly domesticated in ancient times by half-civilised man, as to be quite prolific under confinement.

An argument of great weight, and applicable in several other cases, is, that the above-specified breeds, though agreeing generally with the wild rock-pigeon in constitution, habits, voice, colouring, and in most parts of their structure, yet are certainly highly abnormal in other parts; we may look in vain through the whole great family of Columbidæ for a beak like that of the English carrier, or that of the short-faced tumbler, or barb; for reversed feathers like those of the Jacobin; for a crop like that of the pouter; for tail-feathers like those of the fantail. Hence it must be assumed not only that half-civilised man succeeded in thoroughly domesticating several species, but that he intentionally or by chance picked out extraordinarily abnormal species; and further, that these very species have since all become extinct or unknown. So many strange contingencies are improbable in the highest degree.

Some facts in regard to the colouring of pigeons well deserve consideration. The rock-pigeon is of a slaty-blue, with white loins; but the Indian sub-species, C. intermedia of Strickland, has this part bluish. The tail has a terminal dark bar, with the outer feathers externally edged at the base with white. The wings have two black bars. Some semi-domestic breeds, and some truly wild breeds, have, besides the two black bars, the wings chequered with black. These several marks do not occur together in any other species of the whole family. Now, in every one of the domestic breeds, taking thoroughly well-bred birds, all the above marks, even to the white edging of the outer tail-feathers, sometimes concur perfectly developed. Moreover, when birds belonging to two or more distinct breeds are crossed, none of which are blue or have any of the above-specified marks, the mongrel offspring are very apt suddenly to acquire these characters. To give one instance out of several which I have observed:—I crossed some white fantails, which breed very true, with some black barbs—and it so happens that blue varieties of barbs are so rare that I never heard of an instance in England; and the mongrels were black, brown, and mottled. I also crossed a barb with a spot, which is a white bird with a red tail and red spot on the forehead, and which notoriously breeds very true; the mongrels were dusky and mottled. I then crossed one of the mongrel barb-fantails with a mongrel barb-spot, and they produced a bird of as beautiful a blue colour, with the white loins, double black wing-bar, and barred and white-edged tail-feathers, as any wild-rock pigeon! We can understand these facts, on the well-known principle of reversion to ancestral characters, if all the domestic breeds are descended from the rock-pigeon. But if we deny this, we must make one of the two following highly improbable suppositions. Either, first, that all the several imagined aboriginal stocks were coloured and marked like the rock-pigeon, although no other existing species is thus coloured and marked, so that in each separate breed there might be a tendency to revert to the very same colours and markings. Or, secondly, that each breed, even the purest, has within a dozen, or at most within a score, of generations, been crossed by the rock-pigeon: I say within a dozen or twenty generations, for no instance is known of crossed descendants reverting to an ancestor of foreign blood, removed by a greater number of generations. In a breed which has been crossed only once, the tendency to revert to any character derived from such a cross will naturally become less and less, as in each succeeding generation there will be less of the foreign blood; but when there has been no cross, and there is a tendency in the breed to revert to a character which was lost during some former generation, this tendency, for all that we can see to the contrary, may be transmitted undiminished for an indefinite number of generations. These two distinct cases of reversion are often confounded together by those who have written on inheritance.

Lastly, the hybrids or mongrels from between all the breeds of the pigeon are perfectly fertile, as I can state from my own observations, purposely made, on the most distinct breeds. Now, hardly any cases have been ascertained with certainty of hybrids from two quite distinct species of animals being perfectly fertile. Some authors believe that long-continued domestication eliminates this strong tendency to sterility in species. From the history of the dog, and of some other domestic animals, this conclusion is probably quite correct, if applied to species closely related to each other. But to extend it so far as to suppose that species, aboriginally as distinct as carriers, tumblers, pouters, and fantails now are, should yield offspring perfectly fertile *inter se,* would be rash in the extreme.

From these several reasons, namely,—the improbability of man having formerly made seven or eight supposed species of pigeons to breed freely under domestication;—these supposed species being quite unknown in a wild state, and their not having become anywhere feral;—these species presenting certain very abnormal characters, as compared with all other Columbidæ, though so like the rock-pigeon in most respects;—the occasional re-appearance of the blue colour and various black marks in all the breeds, both when kept pure and when crossed;—and lastly, the mongrel offspring being perfectly fertile;—from these several reasons taken together, we may safely conclude that all our domestic breeds are descended from the rock-pigeon or Columba livia with its geographical sub-species.

In favour of this view, I may add, firstly, that the wild C. livia has been found capable of domestication in Europe and in India; and that it agrees in habits and in a great number of points of structure with all the domestic breeds. Secondly, that, although an English carrier or a short-faced tumbler differs immensely in certain characters from the rock-pigeon, yet that, by comparing the several sub-breeds of these two races, more especially those brought from distant countries, we can make, between them and the rock-pigeon, an almost perfect series; so we can in some other cases, but not with all the breeds. Thirdly, those characters which are mainly distinctive of each breed are in each eminently variable, for instance the wattle and length of beak of the carrier, the shortness of that of the tumbler, and the number of tail-feathers in the fantail; and the explanation of this fact will be obvious when we treat of Selection. Fourthly, pigeons have been watched and tended with the utmost care, and loved by many people. They have been domesticated for thousands of years in several quarters of the world; the earliest known record of pigeons is in the fifth Ægyptian dynasty, about 3000 B. C., as was pointed out to me by Professor Lepsius; but Mr. Birch informs me that pigeons are given in a bill of fare in the previous dynasty. In the time of the Romans, as we hear from Pliny, immense prices were given for pigeons; "nay, they are come to this pass, that they can reckon up their pedigree and race." Pigeons were much valued by Akber Khan in India, about the year 1600; never less than 20,000 pigeons were taken with the court. "The monarchs of Iran and Turan sent him some very rare birds;" and continues the courtly historian, "His Majesty by crossing the breeds, which method was never practised before, has improved them astonishingly." About this same period the Dutch were as eager about pigeons as were the old Romans. The paramount importance of these considerations in explaining the immense amount of variation which pigeons have undergone, will likewise be obvious when we treat of Selection. We shall then, also, see how it is that the several breeds so often have a somewhat monstrous character. It is also a most favourable circumstance for the production of distinct breeds, that male and female pigeons can be easily mated for life; and thus different breeds can be kept together in the same aviary.

I have discussed the probable origin of domestic pigeons at some, yet quite insufficient, length; because when I first kept pigeons and watched the several kinds, well knowing how truly they breed, I felt fully as much difficulty in believing that since they had been domesticated they had all proceeded from a common parent, as any naturalist could in coming to a similar conclusion in regard to the many species of finches, or other groups of birds, in nature. One circumstance has struck me much; namely, that nearly all the breeders of the various domestic animals and the cultivators of plants, with whom I have conversed, or whose treatises I have read, are firmly convinced that the several breeds to which each has attended, are descended from so many aboriginally distinct species. Ask, as I have asked, a celebrated raiser of Hereford cattle, whether his cattle might not have descended from Long-horns, or both from a common parent-stock, and he will laugh you to scorn. I have never met a pigeon, or poultry, or duck, or rabbit fancier, who was not fully convinced that each main breed was descended from a distinct species. Van Mons, in his treatise on pears and apples, shows how utterly he disbelieves that the several sorts, for instance a Ribston-pippin or Codlin-apple, could ever have proceeded from the seeds of the same tree. Innumerable other examples could be given. The explanation, I think, is simple: from long-continued study they are strongly impressed with the differences between the several races; and though they well know that each race varies slightly, for they win their prizes by selecting such slight differences, yet they ignore all general arguments, and refuse to sum up in their minds slight differences accumulated during many successive generations. May not those naturalists who, knowing far less of the laws of inheritance than does the breeder, and knowing no more than he does of the intermediate links in the long lines of descent, yet admit that many of our domestic races are descended from the same parents—may they not learn a lesson of caution, when they deride the idea of species in a state of nature being lineal descendants of other species?

Principles of Selection anciently followed, and their Effects

Let us now briefly consider the steps by which domestic races have been produced, either from one or from several allied species. Some effect may be attributed to the direct and definite action of the external conditions of life, and some to habit; but he would be a bold man who would account by such agencies for the differences between a dray- and race-horse, a greyhound and bloodhound, a carrier and tumbler pigeon. One of the most remarkable features in our domesticated races is that we see in them adaptation, not indeed to the animal's or plant's own good, but to man's use or fancy. Some variations useful to him have probably arisen suddenly, or by one step; many botanists, for instance, believe that the fuller's teasel, with its hooks, which cannot be rivalled by any mechanical contrivance, is only a variety of the wild Dipsacus; and this amount of change may have suddenly arisen in a seedling. So it has probably been with the turnspit dog; and this is known to have been the case with the ancon sheep. But when we compare the dray-horse and race-horse, the dromedary and camel, the various breeds of sheep fitted either for cultivated land or mountain pasture, with the wool of one breed good for one purpose, and that of another breed for another purpose; when we compare the many breeds of dogs, each good for man in different ways; when we compare the game-cock, so pertinacious in battle, with other breeds so little quarrelsome, with "everlasting layers" which never desire to sit, and with the bantam so small and elegant; when we compare the host of agricultural, culinary, orchard, and flower-garden races of plants, most useful to man at different seasons and for different purposes, or so beautiful in his eyes, we must, I think, look further than to mere variability. We cannot suppose that all the breeds were suddenly produced as perfect and as useful as we now see them; indeed, in many cases, we know that this has not been their history. The key is man's power of accumulative selection: nature gives successive variations; man adds them up in certain directions useful to him. In this sense he may be said to have made for himself useful breeds.

The great power of this principle of selection is not hypothetical. It is certain that several of our eminent breeders have, even within a single lifetime, modified to a large extent their breeds of cattle and sheep. In order fully to realise what they have done, it is almost necessary to read several of the many treatises devoted to this subject, and to inspect the animals. Breeders habitually speak of an animal's organisation as something plastic, which they can model almost as they please. If I had space I could quote numerous passages to this effect from highly competent authorities. Youatt, who was probably better acquainted with the works of agriculturists than almost any other individual, and who was himself a very good judge of animals, speaks of the principle of selection as "that which enables the agriculturist, not only to modify the character of his flock, but to change it altogether. It is the magician's wand, by means of which he may summon into life whatever form and mould he pleases." Lord Somerville, speaking of what breeders have done for sheep, says:— "It would seem as if they had chalked out upon a wall a form perfect in itself, and then had given it existence." In Saxony the importance of the principle of selection in regard to merino sheep is so fully recognised, that men follow it as a trade: the sheep are placed on a table and are studied, like a picture by a connoisseur; this is done three times at intervals of months, and the sheep are each time marked and classed, so that the very best may ultimately be selected for breeding.

What English breeders have actually effected is proved by the enormous prices given for animals with a good pedigree; and these have been exported to almost every quarter of the world. The improvement is by no means generally due to crossing different breeds; all the best breeders are strongly opposed to this practice, except sometimes amongst closely allied sub-breeds. And when a cross has been made, the closest selection is far more indispensable even than in ordinary cases. If selection consisted merely in separating some very distinct variety, and breeding from it, the principle would be so obvious as hardly to be worth notice; but its importance consists in the great effect produced by the accumulation in one direction, during successive generations, of differences absolutely inappreciable by an uneducated eye—differences which I for one have vainly attempted to appreciate. Not one man in a thousand has accuracy of eye and judgment sufficient to become an eminent breeder. If gifted with these qualities, and he studies his subject for years, and devotes his lifetime to it with indomitable perseverance, he will succeed, and may make great improvements; if he wants any of these qualities, he will assuredly fail. Few would readily believe in the natural capacity and years of practice requisite to become even a skilful pigeon-fancier.

The same principles are followed by horticulturists; but the variations are here often more abrupt. No one supposes that our choicest productions have been produced by a single variation from the aboriginal stock. We have proofs that this has not been so in several cases in which exact records have been kept; thus, to give a very trifling instance, the steadily-increasing size of the common gooseberry may be quoted. We see an astonishing improvement in many florists' flowers, when the flowers of the present day are compared with drawings made only twenty or thirty years ago. When a race of plants is once pretty well established, the seed-raisers do not pick out the best plants, but merely go over their seed-beds, and pull up the "rogues," as they call the plants that deviate from the proper standard. With animals this kind of selection is, in fact, likewise followed; for hardly any one is so careless as to breed from his worst animals.

In regard to plants, there is another means of observing the accumulated effects of selection—namely, by comparing the diversity of flowers in the different varieties of the same species in the flower-garden; the diversity of leaves, pods, or tubers, or whatever part is valued, in the kitchen garden, in comparison with the flowers of the same varieties; and the diversity of fruit of the same species in the orchard, in comparison with the leaves and flowers of the same set of varieties. See how different the leaves of the cabbage are, and how extremely alike the flowers; how unlike the flowers of the heartsease are, and how alike the leaves; how much the fruit of the different kinds of gooseberries differ in size, colour, shape, and hairiness, and yet the flowers present very slight differences. It is not that the varieties which differ largely in some one point do not differ at all in other points; this is hardly ever,—I speak after careful observation,—perhaps never, the case. The law of correlated variation, the importance of which should never be overlooked, will ensure some differences; but, as a general rule, it cannot be doubted that the continued selection of slight variations, either in the leaves, the flowers, or the fruit, will produce races differing from each other chiefly in these characters.

It may be objected that the principle of selection has been reduced to methodical practice for scarcely more than three-quarters of a century; it has certainly been more attended to of late years, and many treatises have been published on the subject; and the result has been, in a corresponding degree, rapid and important. But it is very far from true that the principle is a modern discovery. I could give several references to works of high antiquity, in which the full importance of the principle is acknowledged. In rude and barbarous periods of English history choice animals were often imported, and laws were passed to prevent their exportation: the destruction of horses under a certain size was ordered, and this may be compared to the "roguing" of plants by nurserymen. The principle of selection I find distinctly given in an ancient Chinese encyclopædia. Explicit rules are laid down by some of the Roman classical writers. From passages in Genesis, it is clear that the colour of domestic animals was at that early period attended to. Savages now sometimes cross their dogs with wild canine animals, to improve the breed, and they formerly did so, as is attested by passages in Pliny. The savages in South Africa match their draught cattle by colour, as do some of the Esquimaux their teams of dogs. Livingstone states that good domestic breeds are highly valued by the Negroes in the interior of Africa who have not associated with Europeans. Some of these facts do not show actual selection, but they show that the breeding of domestic animals was carefully attended to in ancient times, and is now attended to by the lowest savages. It would, indeed, have been a strange fact, had attention not been paid to breeding, for the inheritance of good and bad qualities is so obvious.

Unconscious Selection

At the present time, eminent breeders try by methodical selection, with a distinct object in view, to make a new strain or sub-breed, superior to anything of the kind in the country. But, for our purpose, a form of Selection, which may be called Unconscious, and which results from every one trying to possess and breed from the best individual animals, is more important. Thus, a man who intends keeping pointers naturally tries to get as good dogs as he can, and afterwards breeds from his own best dogs, but he has no wish or expectation of permanently altering the breed. Nevertheless we may infer that this process, continued during centuries, would improve and modify any breed, in the same way as Bakewell, Collins, &c., by this very same process, only carried on more methodically, did greatly modify, even during their lifetimes, the forms and qualities of their cattle. Slow and insensible changes of this kind can never be recognised unless actual measurements or careful drawings of the breeds in question have been made long ago, which may serve for comparison. In some cases, however, unchanged, or but little changed individuals of the same breed exist in less civilised districts, where the breed has been less improved. There is reason to believe that King Charles's spaniel has been unconsciously modified to a large extent since the time of that monarch. Some highly competent authorities are convinced that the setter is directly derived from the spaniel, and has probably been slowly altered from it. It is known that the English pointer has been greatly changed within the last century, and in this case the change has, it is believed, been chiefly effected by crosses with the foxhound; but what concerns us is, that the change has been effected unconsciously and gradually, and yet so effectually, that, though the old Spanish pointer certainly came from Spain, Mr. Borrow has not seen, as I am informed by him, any native dog in Spain like our pointer.

By a similar process of selection, and by careful training, English race-horses have come to surpass in fleetness and size the parent Arabs, so that the latter, by the regulations for the Goodwood Races, are favoured in the weights which they carry. Lord Spencer and others have shown how the cattle of England have increased in weight and in early maturity, compared with the stock formerly kept in this country. By comparing the accounts given in various old treatises of the former and present state of carrier and tumbler pigeons in Britain, India, and Persia, we can trace the stages through which they have insensibly passed, and come to differ so greatly from the rock-pigeon.

Youatt gives an excellent illustration of the effects of a course of selection, which may be considered as unconscious, in so far that the breeders could never have expected, or even wished, to produce the result which ensued—namely, the production of two distinct strains. The two flocks of Leicester sheep kept by Mr. Buckley and Mr. Burgess, as Mr. Youatt remarks, "have been purely bred from the original stock of Mr. Bakewell for upwards of fifty years. There is not a suspicion existing in the mind of any one at all acquainted with the subject, that the owner of either of them has deviated in any one instance from the pure blood of Mr. Bakewell's flock, and yet the difference between the sheep possessed by these two gentlemen is so great that they have the appearance of being quite different varieties."

If there exist savages so barbarous as never to think of the inherited character of the offspring of their domestic animals, yet any one animal particularly useful to them, for any special purpose, would be carefully preserved during famines and other accidents, to which savages are so liable, and such choice animals would thus generally leave more offspring than the inferior ones; so that in this case there would be a kind of unconscious selection going on. We see the value set on animals even by the barbarians of Tierra del Fuego, by their killing and devouring their old women, in times of dearth, as of less value than their dogs.

In plants the same gradual process of improvement, through the occasional preservation of the best individuals, whether or not sufficiently distinct to be ranked at their first appearance, as distinct varieties, and whether or not two or more species or races have become blended together by crossing, may plainly be recognised in the increased size and beauty which we now see in the varieties of the heartsease, rose, pelargonium, dahlia, and other plants, when compared with the older varieties or with their parent-stocks. No one would ever expect to get a first-rate heartsease or dahlia from the seed of a wild plant. No one would expect to raise a first-rate melting pear from the seed of the wild pear, though he might succeed from a poor seedling growing wild, if it had come from a garden-stock. The pear though cultivated in classical times, appears, from Pliny's description, to have been a fruit of very inferior quality. I have seen great surprise expressed in horticultural works at the wonderful skill of gardeners, in having produced such splendid results from such poor materials; but the art has been simple, and, as far as the final result is concerned, has been followed almost unconsciously. It has consisted in always cultivating the best-known variety, sowing its seeds, and, when a slightly better variety chanced to appear, selecting it, and so onwards. But the gardeners of the classical period, who cultivated the best pears which they could procure, never thought what splendid fruit we should eat; though we owe our excellent fruit in some small degree, to their having naturally chosen and preserved the best varieties they could anywhere find.

A large amount of change, thus slowly and unconsciously accumulated, explains, as I believe, the well-known fact, that in a number of cases we cannot recognise, and therefore do not know, the wild parent-stocks of the plants which have been longest cultivated in our flower and kitchen gardens. If it has taken centuries or thousands of years to improve or modify most of our plants up to their present standard of usefulness to man, we can understand how it is that neither Australia, the Cape of Good Hope, nor any other region inhabited by quite uncivilised man, has afforded us a single plant worth culture. It is not that these countries, so rich in species, do not by a strange chance possess the aboriginal stocks of any useful plants, but that the native plants have not been improved by continued selection up to a standard of perfection comparable with that acquired by the plants in countries anciently civilised.

In regard to the domestic animals kept by uncivilised man, it should not be overlooked that they almost always have to struggle for their own food, at least during certain seasons. And in two countries very differently circumstanced, individuals of the same species, having slightly different constitutions or structure would often succeed better in the one country than in the other; and thus by a process of "natural selection," as will hereafter be more fully explained, two sub-breeds might be formed. This, perhaps, partly explains why the varieties kept by savages, as has been remarked by some authors, have more of the character of true species than the varieties kept in civilised countries.

On the view here given of the important part which selection by man has played, it becomes at once obvious, how it is that our domestic races show adaptation in their structure or in their habits to man's wants or fancies. We can, I think, further understand the frequently abnormal characters of our domestic races, and likewise their differences being so great in external characters, and relatively so slight in internal parts or organs. Man can hardly select, or only with much difficulty, any deviation of structure excepting such as is externally visible; and indeed he rarely cares for what is internal. He can never act by selection, excepting on variations which are first given to him in some slight degree by nature. No man would ever try to make a fantail till he saw a pigeon with a tail developed in some slight degree in an unusual manner, or a pouter till he saw a pigeon with a crop of somewhat unusual size; and the more abnormal or unusual any character was when it first appeared, the more likely it would be to catch his attention. But to use such an expression as trying to make a fantail, is, I have no doubt, in most cases, utterly incorrect. The man who first selected a pigeon with a slightly larger tail, never dreamed what the descendants of that pigeon would become through long-continued, partly unconscious and partly methodical, selection. Perhaps the parent-bird of all fantails had only fourteen tail-feathers somewhat expanded, like the present Java fantail, or like individuals of other and distinct breeds, in which as many as seventeen tail-feathers have been counted. Perhaps the first pouter-pigeon did not inflate its crop much more than the turbit now does the upper part of its œsophagus,—a habit which is disregarded by all fanciers, as it is not one of the points of the breed.

Nor let it be thought that some great deviation of structure would be necessary to catch the fancier's eye: he perceives extremely small differences, and it is in human nature to value any novelty, however slight, in one's own possession. Nor must the value which would formerly have been set on any slight differences in the individuals of the same species, be judged of by the value which is now set on them, after several breeds have fairly been established. It is known that with pigeons many slight variations now occasionally appear, but these are rejected as faults or deviations from the standard of perfection in each breed. The common goose has not given rise to any marked varieties; hence the Toulouse and the common breed, which differ only in colour, that most fleeting of characters, have lately been exhibited as distinct at our poultry-shows.

These views appear to explain what has sometimes been noticed—namely, that we know hardly anything about the origin or history of any of our domestic breeds. But, in fact, a breed, like a dialect of a language, can hardly be said to have a distinct origin. A man preserves and breeds from an individual with some slight deviation of structure, or takes more care than usual in matching his best animals, and thus improves them, and the improved animals slowly spread in the immediate neighbourhood. But they will as yet hardly have a distinct name, and from being only slightly valued, their history will have been disregarded. When further improved by the same slow and gradual process, they will spread more widely, and will be recognised as something distinct and valuable, and will then probably first receive a provincial name. In semi-civilised countries, with little free communication, the spreading of a new sub-breed would be a slow process. As soon as the points of value are once acknowledged, the principle, as I have called it, of unconscious selection will always tend,—perhaps more at one period than at another, as the breed rises or falls in fashion,—perhaps more in one district than in another, according to the state of civilisation of the inhabitants,—slowly to add to the characteristic features of the breed, whatever they may be. But the chance will be infinitely small of any record having been preserved of such slow, varying, and insensible changes.

Circumstances favourable to Man's Power of Selection

I will now say a few words on the circumstances, favourable, or the reverse, to man's power of selection. A high degree of variability is obviously favourable, as freely giving the materials for selection to work on; not that mere individual differences are not amply sufficient, with extreme care, to allow of the accumulation of a large amount of modification in almost any desired direction. But as variations manifestly useful or pleasing to man appear only occasionally, the chance of their appearance will be much increased by a large number of individuals being kept. Hence, number is of the highest importance for success. On this principle Marshall formerly remarked, with respect to the sheep of parts of Yorkshire, "as they generally belong to poor people, and are mostly *in small lots,* they never can be improved." On the other hand, nurserymen, from keeping large stocks of the same plant, are generally far more successful than amateurs in raising new and valuable varieties. A large number of individuals of an animal or plant can be reared only where the conditions for its propagation are favourable. When the individuals are scanty, all will be allowed to breed, whatever their quality may be, and this will effectually prevent selection. But probably the most important element is that the animal or plant should be so highly valued by man, that the closest attention is paid to even the slightest deviations in its qualities or structure. Unless such attention be paid nothing can be effected. I have seen it gravely remarked, that it was most fortunate that the strawberry began to vary just when gardeners began to attend to this plant. No doubt the strawberry had always varied since it was cultivated, but the slightest varieties had been neglected. As soon, however, as gardeners picked out individual plants with slightly larger, earlier, or better fruit, and raised seedlings from them, and again picked out the best seedlings and bred from them, then (with some aid by crossing distinct species) those many admirable varieties of the strawberry were raised which have appeared during the last half-century.

With animals, facility in preventing crosses is an important element in the formation of new races,—at least, in a country which is already stocked with other races. In this respect enclosure of the land plays a part. Wandering savages or the inhabitants of open plains rarely possess more than one breed of the same species. Pigeons can be mated for life, and this is a great convenience to the fancier, for thus many races may be improved and kept true, though mingled in the same aviary; and this circumstance must have largely favoured the formation of new breeds. Pigeons, I may add, can be propagated in great numbers and at a very quick rate, and inferior birds may be freely rejected, as when killed they serve for food. On the other hand, cats, from their nocturnal rambling habits cannot be easily matched, and, although so much valued by women and children, we rarely see a distinct breed long kept up; such breeds as we do sometimes see are almost always imported from some other country. Although I do not doubt that some domestic animals vary less than others, yet the rarity or absence of distinct breeds of the cat, the donkey, peacock, goose, &c., may be attributed in main part to selection not having been brought into play: in cats, from the difficulty in pairing them; in donkeys, from only a few being kept by poor people, and little attention paid to their breeding; for recently in certain parts of Spain and of the United States this animal has been surprisingly modified and improved by careful selection: in peacocks, from not being very easily reared and a large stock not kept: in geese, from being valuable only for two purposes, food and feathers, and more especially from no pleasure having been felt in the display of distinct breeds; but the goose, under the conditions to which it is exposed when domesticated, seems to have a singularly inflexible organisation, though it has varied to a slight extent, as I have elsewhere described.

Some authors have maintained that the amount of variation in our domestic productions is soon reached, and can never afterwards be exceeded. It would be somewhat rash to assert that the limit has been attained in any one case; for almost all our animals and plants have been greatly improved in many ways within a recent period; and this implies variation. It would be equally rash to assert that characters now increased to their utmost limit, could not, after remaining fixed for many centuries, again vary under new conditions of life. No doubt, as Mr. Wallace has remarked with much truth, a limit will be at last reached. For instance, there must be a limit to the fleetness of any terrestrial animal, as this will be determined by the friction to be overcome, the weight of body to be carried, and the power of contraction in the muscular fibres. But what concerns us is that the domestic varieties of the same species differ from each other in almost every character, which man has attended to and selected, more than do the distinct species of the same genera. Isidore Geoffroy St. Hilaire has proved this in regard to size, and so it is with colour and probably with the length of hair. With respect to fleetness, which depends on many bodily characters, Eclipse was far fleeter, and a dray-horse is incomparably stronger than any two natural species belonging to the same genus. So with plants, the seeds of the different varieties of the bean or maize probably differ more in size, than do the seeds of the distinct species in any one genus in the same two families. The same remark holds good in regard to the fruit of the several varieties of the plum, and still more strongly with the melon, as well as in many other analogous cases.

To sum up on the origin of our domestic races of animals and plants. Changed conditions of life are of the highest importance in causing variability, both by acting directly on the organisation, and indirectly by affecting the reproductive system. It is not probable that variability is an inherent and necessary contingent, under all circumstances. The greater or less force of inheritance and reversion, determine whether variations shall endure. Variability is governed by many unknown laws, of which correlated growth is probably the most important. Something, but how much we do not know, may be attributed to the definite action of the conditions of life. Some, perhaps a great, effect may be attributed to the increased use or disuse of parts. The final result is thus rendered infinitely complex. In some cases the intercrossing of aboriginally distinct species appears to have played an important part in the origin of our breeds. When several breeds have once been formed in any country, their occasional intercrossing, with the aid of selection, has, no doubt, largely aided in the formation of new sub-breeds; but the importance of crossing has been much exaggerated, both in regard to animals and to those plants which are propagated by seed. With plants which are temporarily propagated by cuttings, buds, &c., the importance of crossing is immense; for the cultivator may here disregard the extreme variability both of hybrids and of mongrels, and the sterility of hybrids; but plants not propagated by seed are of little importance to us, for their endurance is only temporary. Over all these causes of Change, the accumulative action of Selection, whether applied methodically and quickly, or unconsciously and slowly but more efficiently seems to have been the predominant Power.

CHAPTER II

VARIATION UNDER NATURE

Variability—Individual differences—Doubtful species—Wide ranging, much diffused, and common species, vary most—Species of the larger genera in each country vary more frequently than the species of the smaller genera—Many of the species of the larger genera resemble varieties in being very closely, but unequally, related to each other, and in having restricted ranges.

BEFORE applying the principles arrived at in the last chapter to organic beings in a state of nature, we must briefly discuss whether these latter are subject to any variation. To treat this subject properly, a long catalogue of dry facts ought to be given; but these I shall reserve for a future work. Nor shall I here discuss the various definitions which have been given of the term species. No one definition has satisfied all naturalists; yet every naturalist knows vaguely what he means when he speaks of a species. Generally the term includes the unknown element of a distant act of creation. The term "variety" is almost equally difficult to define; but here community of descent is almost universally implied, though it can rarely be proved. We have also what are called monstrosities; but they graduate into varieties. By a monstrosity I presume is meant some considerable deviation of structure, generally injurious, or not useful to the species. Some authors use the term "variation" in a technical sense, as implying a modification directly due to the physical conditions of life; and "variations" in this sense are supposed not to be inherited; but who can say that the dwarfed condition of shells in the brackish waters of the Baltic, or dwarfed plants on Alpine summits, or the thicker fur of an animal from far northwards, would not in some cases be inherited for at least a few generations? And in this case I presume that the form would be called a variety.

It may be doubted whether sudden and considerable deviations of structure such as we occasionally see in our domestic productions, more especially with plants, are ever permanently propagated in a state of nature. Almost every part of every organic being is so beautifully related to its complex conditions of life that it seems as improbable that any part should have been suddenly produced perfect, as that a complex machine should have been invented by man in a perfect state. Under domestication monstrosities sometimes occur which resemble normal structures in widely different animals. Thus pigs have occasionally been born with a

38

sort of proboscis, and if any wild species of the same genus had naturally possessed a proboscis, it might have been argued that this had appeared as a monstrosity; but I have as yet failed to find, after diligent search, cases of monstrosities resembling normal structures in nearly allied forms, and these alone bear on the question. If monstrous forms of this kind ever do appear in a state of nature and are capable of reproduction (which is not always the case), as they occur rarely and singularly, their preservation would depend on unusually favourable circumstances. They would, also, during the first and succeeding generations cross with the ordinary form, and thus their abnormal character would almost inevitably be lost. But I shall have to return in a future chapter to the preservation and perpetuation of single or occasional variations.

Individual Differences

The many slight differences which appear in the offspring from the same parents, or which it may be presumed have thus arisen, from being observed in the individuals of the same species inhabiting the same confined locality, may be called individual differences. No one supposes that all the individuals of the same species are cast in the same actual mould. These individual differences are of the highest importance for us, for they are often inherited, as must be familiar to every one; and they thus afford materials for natural selection to act on and accumulate, in the same manner as man accumulates in any given direction individual differences in his domesticated productions. These individual differences generally affect what naturalists consider unimportant parts; but I could show by a long catalogue of facts, that parts which must be called important, whether viewed under a physiological or classificatory point of view, sometimes vary in the individuals of the same species. I am convinced that the most experienced naturalist would be surprised at the number of the cases of variability, even in important parts of structure, which he could collect on good authority, as I have collected, during a course of years. It should be remembered that systematists are far from being pleased at finding variability in important characters, and that there are not many men who will laboriously examine internal and important organs, and compare them in many specimens of the same species. It would never have been expected that the branching of the main nerves close to the great central ganglion of an insect would have been variable in the same species; it might have been thought that changes of this nature could have been effected only by slow degrees; yet Sir J. Lubbock has shown a degree of variability in these main nerves in Coccus, which may almost be compared to the irregular branching of a stem of a tree. This philosophical naturalist, I may add, has also shown that the muscles in the larvæ of certain insects are far from uniform. Authors sometimes argue in a circle when they state that important organs never vary; for these same authors practically rank those parts as important (as some few naturalists have honestly confessed) which do not vary; and, under this point of view, no instance will ever be found of an important part varying; but under any other point of view many instances assuredly can be given.

There is one point connected with individual differences, which is extremely perplexing: I refer to those genera which have been called "protean" or "polymorphic," in which the species present an inordinate amount of variation. With respect to many of these forms, hardly two naturalists agree whether to rank them as species or as varieties. We may instance Rubus, Rosa, and Hieracium amongst plants, several genera of insects and of Brachiopod shells. In most polymorphic genera some of the species have fixed and definite characters. Genera which are polymorphic in one country seem to be, with a few exceptions, polymorphic in other countries, and likewise, judging from Brachiopod shells, at former periods of time. These facts are very perplexing, for they seem to show that this kind of variability is independent of the conditions of life. I am inclined to suspect that we see, at least in some of these polymorphic genera, variations which are of no service or disservice to the species, and which consequently have not been seized on and rendered definite by natural selection, as hereafter to be explained.

Individuals of the same species often present, as is known to every one, great differences of structure, independently of variation, as in the two sexes of various animals, in the two or three castes of sterile females or workers amongst insects, and in the immature and larval states of many of the lower animals. There are, also, cases of dimorphism and trimorphism, both with animals and plants. Thus, Mr. Wallace, who has lately called attention to the subject, has shown that the females of certain species of butterflies, in the Malayan archipelago, regularly appear under two or even three conspicuously distinct forms, not connected by intermediate varieties. Fritz Müller has described analogous but more extraordinary cases with the males of certain Brazilian Crustaceans: thus, the male of the Tanais regularly occurs under two distinct forms; one of these has strong and differently shaped pincers, and the other has antennæ much more abundantly furnished with smelling-hairs. Although in most of these cases, the two or three forms, both with animals and plants are not now connected by intermediate gradations, it is probable that they were once thus connected. Mr. Wallace, for instance, describes a certain butterfly which presents in the same island a great range of varieties connected by intermediate links, and the extreme links of the chain closely resemble the two forms of an allied dimorphic species inhabiting another part of the Malay archipelago. Thus also with ants, the several worker-castes are generally quite distinct; but in some cases, as we shall hereafter see, the castes are connected together by finely graduated varieties. So it is, as I myself observed, with some dimorphic plants. It certainly at first appears a highly remarkable fact that the same female butterfly should have the power of producing at the same time three distinct female forms and a male; and that an hermaphrodite plant should produce from the same seed-capsule three distinct hermaphrodite forms, bearing three different kinds of females and three or even six different kinds of males. Nevertheless these cases are only exaggerations of the common fact that the female produces offspring of two sexes which sometimes differ from each other in a wonderful manner.

Doubtful Species

The forms which possess in some considerable degree the character of species, but which are so closely similar to other forms, or are so closely linked to them by intermediate gradations, that naturalists do not like to rank them as distinct species, are in several respects the most important for us. We have every reason to believe that many of these doubtful and closely allied forms have permanently retained their characters for a long time; for as long, as far as we know, as have good and true species. Practically, when a naturalist can unite by means of intermediate links any two forms, he treats the one as a variety of the other; ranking the most common, but sometimes the one first described, as the species, and the other as the variety. But cases of great difficulty, which I will not here enumerate, sometimes arise in deciding whether or not to rank one form as a variety of another, even when they are closely connected by intermediate links; nor will the commonly-assumed hybrid nature of the intermediate forms always remove the difficulty. In very many cases, however, one form is ranked as a variety of another, not because the intermediate links have actually been found, but because analogy leads the observer to suppose either that they do now somewhere exist, or may formerly have existed; and here a wide door for the entry of doubt and conjecture is opened.

Hence, in determining whether a form should be ranked as a species or a variety, the opinion of naturalists having sound judgment and wide experience seems the only guide to follow. We must, however, in many cases, decide by a majority of naturalists, for few well-marked and well-known varieties can be named which have not been ranked as species by at least some competent judges.

That varieties of this doubtful nature are far from uncommon cannot be disputed. Compare the several floras of Great Britain, of France, or of the United States, drawn up by different botanists, and see what a surprising number of forms have been ranked by one botanist as good species, and by another as mere varieties. Mr. H. C. Watson, to whom I lie under deep obligation for assistance of all kinds, has marked for me 182 British plants, which are generally considered as varieties, but which have all been ranked by botanists as species; and in making this list he has omitted many trifling varieties, but which nevertheless have been ranked by some botanists as species, and he has entirely omitted several highly polymorphic genera. Under genera, including the most polymorphic forms, Mr. Babington gives 251 species, whereas Mr. Bentham gives only 112,—a difference of 139 doubtful forms! Amongst animals which unite for each birth, and which are highly locomotive, doubtful forms, ranked by one zoologist as a species and by another as a variety, can rarely be found within the same country, but are common in separated areas. How many of the birds and insects in North America and Europe, which differ very slightly from each other, have been ranked by one eminent naturalist as undoubted species, and by another as varieties, or, as they are often called, geographical races! Mr. Wallace, in several valuable papers on the various animals, especially on the Lepidoptera, inhabiting the islands of the great Malayan archipelago, shows that they may be classed under four heads, namely, as variable forms, as local forms, as geographical races or sub-species, and as true representative species. The first or variable forms vary much within the limits of the same island. The local forms are moderately constant and distinct in each separate island; but when all from the several islands are compared together, the differences are seen to be so slight and graduated, that it is impossible to define or describe them, though at the same time the extreme forms are sufficiently distinct. The geographical races or sub-species are local forms completely fixed and isolated; but as they do not differ from each other by strongly marked and important characters, "there is no possible test but individual opinion to determine which of them shall be considered as species and which as varieties." Lastly, representatives species fill the same place in the natural economy of each island as do the local forms and sub-species; but as they are distinguished from each other by a greater amount of difference than that between the local forms and sub-species, they are almost universally ranked by naturalists as true species. Nevertheless, no certain criterion can possibly be given by which variable forms, local forms, sub-species, and representative species can be recognised.

Many years ago, when comparing, and seeing others compare, the birds from the closely neighbouring islands of the Galapagos archipelago, one with another, and with those from the American mainland, I was much struck how entirely vague and arbitrary is the distinction between species and varieties. On the islets of the little Madeira group there are many insects which are characterised as varieties in Mr. Wollaston's admirable work, but which would certainly be ranked as distinct species by many entomologists. Even Ireland has a few animals, now generally regarded as varieties, but which have been ranked as species by some zoologists. Several experienced ornithologists consider our British red grouse as only a strongly-marked race of a Norwegian species, whereas the greater number rank it as an undoubted species peculiar to Great Britain. A wide distance between the homes of two doubtful forms leads many naturalists to rank them as distinct species; but what distance, it has been well asked, will suffice; if that between America and Europe is ample, will that between Europe and the Azores, or Madeira, or the Canaries, or between the several islets of these small archipelagos, be sufficient?

Mr. B. D. Walsh, a distinguished entomologist of the United States, has described what he calls Phytophagic varieties and Phytophagic species. Most vegetable-feeding insects live on one kind of plant or on one group of plants; some feed indiscriminately on many kinds, but do not in consequence vary. In several cases, however, insects found living on different plants, have been observed by Mr. Walsh to present in their larval or mature state, or in both states, slight, though constant differences in colour, size, or in the nature of their secretions. In some instances the males alone, in other instances both males and females, have been observed thus to differ in a slight degree. When the differences are rather more strongly marked, and when both sexes and all ages are affected, the forms are ranked by all entomologists as good species. But no observer can determine for another, even if he can do so for himself, which of these Phytophagic forms ought to be called species and which varieties. Mr. Walsh ranks the forms which it may be supposed would freely intercross, as varieties; and those which appear to have lost this power, as species. As the differences depend on the insects having long fed on distinct plants, it cannot be expected that intermediate links connecting the several forms should now be found. The naturalist thus loses his best guide in determining whether to rank doubtful forms as varieties or species. This likewise necessarily occurs with closely allied organisms, which inhabit distinct continents or islands. When, on the other hand, an animal or plant ranges over the same continent, or inhabits many islands in the same archipelago, and presents different forms in the different areas, there is always a good chance that intermediate forms will be discovered which will link together the extreme states, and these are then degraded to the rank of varieties.

Some few naturalists maintain that animals never present varieties; but then these same naturalists rank the slightest difference as of specific value; and when the same identical form is met with in two distant countries, or in two geological formations, they believe that two distinct species are hidden under the same dress. The term species thus comes to be a mere useless abstraction, implying and assuming a separate act of creation. It is certain that many forms, considered by highly-competent judges to be varieties, resemble species so completely in character, that they have been thus ranked by other highly-competent judges. But to discuss whether they ought to be called species or varieties, before any definition of these terms has been generally accepted, is vainly to beat the air.

Many of the cases of strongly-marked varieties or doubtful species well deserve consideration; for several interesting lines of argument, from geographical distribution, analogical variation, hybridism, &c., have been brought to bear in the attempt to determine their rank; but space does not here permit me to discuss them. Close investigation, in many cases, will no doubt bring naturalists to agree how to rank doubtful forms. Yet it must be confessed that it is in the best-known countries that we find the greatest number of them. I have been struck with the fact, that if any animal or plant in a state of nature be highly useful to man, or from any cause closely attracts his attention, varieties of it will almost universally be found recorded. These varieties, moreover, will often be ranked by some authors as species. Look at the common oak, how closely it has been studied; yet a German author makes more than a dozen species out of forms, which are almost universally considered by other botanists to be varieties; and in this country the highest botanical authorities and practical men can be quoted to show that the sessile and pedunculated oaks are either good and distinct species or mere varieties.

I may here allude to a remarkable memoir lately published by A. de Candolle, on the oaks of the whole world. No one ever had more ample materials for the discrimination of the species, or could have worked on them with more zeal and sagacity. He first gives in detail all the many points of structure which vary in the several species, and estimates numerically the relative frequency of the variations. He specifies above a dozen characters which may be found varying even on the same branch, sometimes according to age or development, sometimes without any assignable reason. Such characters are not of course of specific value, but they are, as Asa Gray has remarked in commenting on this memoir, such as generally enter into specific definitions. De Candolle then goes on to say that he gives the rank of species to the forms that differ by characters never varying on the same tree, and never found connected by intermediate states. After this discussion, the result of so much labour, he emphatically remarks: "They are mistaken, who repeat that the greater part of our species are clearly limited, and that the doubtful species are in a feeble minority. This seemed to be true, so long as a genus was imperfectly known, and its species were founded upon a few specimens, that is to say, were provisional. Just as we come to know them better, intermediate forms flow in, and doubts as to specific limits augment." He also adds that it is the best-known species which present the greatest number of spontaneous varieties and sub-varieties. Thus Quercus robur has twenty-eight varieties, all of which, excepting six, are clustered round three sub-species, namely, Q. pedunculata, sessiliflora, and pubescens. The forms which connect these three sub-species are comparatively rare; and, as Asa Gray again remarks, if these connecting forms which are now rare, were to become wholly extinct, the three sub-species would hold exactly the same relation to each other, as do the four or five provisionally admitted species which closely surround the typical Quercus robur. Finally, De Candolle admits that out of the 300 species, which will be enumerated in his Prodromus as belonging to the oak family, at least two-thirds are provisional species, that is, are not known strictly to fulfil the definition above given of a true species. It should be added that De Candolle no longer believes that species are immutable creations, but concludes that the derivative theory is the most natural one, "and the most accordant with the known facts in palæontology, geographical botany and zoology, of anatomical structure and classification."

When a young naturalist commences the study of a group of organisms quite unknown to him, he is at first much perplexed in determining what differences to consider as specific, and what as varietal; for he knows nothing of the amount and kind of variation to which the group is subject; and this shows, at least, how very generally there is some variation. But if he confine his attention to one class within one country, he will soon make up his mind how to rank most of the doubtful forms. His general tendency will be to make many species, for he will become impressed, just like the pigeon or poultry fancier before alluded to, with the amount of difference in the forms which he is continually studying; and he has little general knowledge of analogical variation in other groups and in other countries, by which to correct his first impressions. As he extends the range of his observations, he will meet with more cases of difficulty; for he will encounter a greater number of closely-allied forms. But if his observations be widely extended, he will in the end generally be able to make up his own mind: but he will succeed in this at the expense of admitting much variation,—and the truth of this admission will often be disputed by other naturalists. When he comes to study allied forms brought from countries not now continuous, in which case he cannot hope to find intermediate links, he will be compelled to trust almost entirely to analogy, and his difficulties will rise to a climax.

Certainly no clear line of demarcation has as yet been drawn between species and sub-species—that is, the forms which in the opinion of some naturalists come very near to, but do not quite arrive at, the rank of species: or, again, between sub-species and well-marked varieties, or between lesser varieties and individual differences. These differences blend into each other by an insensible series; and a series impresses the mind with the idea of an actual passage.

Hence I look at individual differences, though of small interest to the systematist, as of the highest importance for us, as being the first steps towards such slight varieties as are barely thought worth recording in works on natural history. And I look at varieties which are in any degree more distinct and permanent, as steps towards more strongly-marked and permanent varieties; and at the latter, as leading to sub-species, and then to species. The passage from one stage of difference to another may, in many cases, be the simple result of the nature of the organism and of the different physical conditions to which it has long been exposed; but with respect to the more important and adaptive characters, the passage from one stage of difference to another, may be safely attributed to the cumulative action of natural selection, hereafter to be explained, and to the effects of the increased use or disuse of parts. A well-marked variety may therefore be called an incipient species; but whether this belief is justifiable must be judged by the weight of the various facts and considerations to be given throughout this work.

It need not be supposed that all varieties or incipient species attain the rank of species. They may become extinct, or they may endure as varieties for very long periods, as has been shown to be the case by Mr. Wollaston with the varieties of certain fossil land-shells in Madeira, and with plants by Gaston de Saporta. If a variety were to flourish so as to exceed in numbers the parent species, it would then rank as the species, and the species as the variety; or it might come to supplant and exterminate the parent species; or both might co-exist, and both rank as independent species. But we shall hereafter return to this subject.

From these remarks it will be seen that I look at the term species as one arbitrarily given, for the sake of convenience, to a set of individuals closely resembling each other, and that it does not essentially differ from the term variety, which is given to less distinct and more fluctuating forms. The term variety, again, in comparison with mere individual differences, is also applied arbitrarily, for convenience' sake.

Wide-ranging, much diffused, and common Species vary most

Guided by theoretical consideration, I thought that some interesting results might be obtained in regard to the nature and relations of the species which vary most, by tabulating all the varieties in several well-worked floras. At first this seemed a simple task; but Mr. H. C. Watson, to whom I am much indebted for valuable advice and assistance on this subject, soon convinced me that there were many difficulties, as did subsequently Dr. Hooker, even in stronger terms. I shall reserve for a future work the discussion of these difficulties, and the tables of the proportional numbers of the varying species. Dr. Hooker permits me to add that after having carefully read my manuscript, and examined the tables, he thinks that the following statements are fairly well established. The whole subject, however, treated as it necessarily here is with much brevity, is rather perplexing, and allusions cannot be avoided to the "struggle for existence," "divergence of character," and other questions, hereafter to be discussed.

Alphonse de Candolle and others have shown that plants which have very wide ranges generally present varieties; and this might have been expected, as they are exposed to diverse physical conditions, and as they come into competition (which, as we shall hereafter see, is an equally or more important circumstance) with different sets of organic beings. But my tables further show that, in any limited country, the species which are the most common, that is abound most in individuals, and the species which are most widely diffused within their own country (and this is a different consideration from wide range, and to a certain extent from commonness), oftenest give rise to varieties sufficiently well marked to have been recorded in botanical works. Hence it is the most flourishing, or, as they may be called, the dominant species,—those which range widely, are the most diffused in their own country, and are the most numerous in individuals,—which oftenest produce well-marked varieties, or, as I consider them, incipient species. And this, perhaps, might have been anticipated; for, as varieties, in order to become in any degree permanent, necessarily have to struggle with the other inhabitants of the country, the species which are already dominant will be the most likely to yield offspring, which, though in some slight degree modified, still inherit those advantages that enabled their parents to become dominant over their compatriots. In these remarks on predominance, it should be understood that reference is made only to the forms which come into competition with each other, and more especially to the members of the same genus or class having nearly similar habits of life. With respect to the number of individuals or commonness of species, the comparison of course relates only to the members of the same group. One of the higher plants may be said to be dominant if it be more numerous in individuals and more widely diffused than the other plants of the same country, which live under nearly the same conditions. A plant of this kind is not the less dominant because some conferva inhabiting the water or some parasitic fungus is infinitely more numerous in individuals and more widely diffused. But if the conferva or parasitic fungus exceeds its allies in the above respects, it will then be dominant within its own class.

Species of the Larger Genera in each Country vary more frequently than the Species of the Smaller Genera

If the plants inhabiting a country, as described in any Flora, be divided into two equal masses, all those in the larger genera (*i. e.*, those including many species) being placed on one side, and all those in the smaller genera on the other side, the former will be found to include a somewhat larger number of the very common and much diffused or dominant species. This might have been anticipated; for the mere fact of many species of the same genus inhabiting any country, shows that there is something in the organic or inorganic conditions of that country favourable to the genus; and, consequently, we might have expected to have found in the larger genera or those including many species, a larger proportional number of dominant species. But so many causes tend to obscure this result, that I am surprised that my tables show even a small majority on the side of the larger genera. I will here allude to only two causes of obscurity. Fresh-water and salt-loving plants generally have very wide ranges and are much diffused, but this seems to be connected with the nature of the stations inhabited by them, and has little or no relation to the size of the genera to which the species belong. Again, plants low in the scale of organisation are generally much more widely diffused than plants higher in the scale; and here again there is no close relation to the size of the genera. The cause of lowly-organised plants ranging widely will be discussed in our chapter on Geographical Distribution.

From looking at species as only strongly-marked and well-defined varieties, I was led to anticipate that the species of the larger genera in each country would oftener present varieties, than the species of the smaller genera; for wherever many closely related species (*i. e.*, species of the same genus) have been formed, many varieties or incipient species ought, as a general rule, to be now forming. Where many large trees grow, we expect to find saplings. Where many species of a genus have been formed through variation, circumstances have been favourable for variation; and hence we might expect that the circumstances would generally be still favourable to variation. On the other hand, if we look at each species as a special act of creation, there is no apparent reason why more varieties should occur in a group having many species, than in one having few.

To test the truth of this anticipation I have arranged the plants of twelve countries, and the coleopterous insects of two districts, into two nearly equal masses, the species of the larger genera on one side, and those of the smaller genera on the other side, and it has invariably proved to be the case that a larger proportion of the species on the side of the larger genera presented varieties, than on the side of the smaller genera. Moreover, the species of the large genera which present any varieties, invariably present a larger average number of varieties than do the species of the small genera. Both these results follow when another division is made, and when all the least genera, with from only one to four species, are altogether excluded from the tables. These facts are of plain signification on the view that species are only strongly-marked and permanent varieties; for wherever many species of the same genus have been formed, or where, if we may use the expression, the manufactory of species has been active, we ought generally to find the manufactory still in action, more especially as we have every reason to believe the process of manufacturing new species to be a slow one. And this certainly holds true, if varieties be looked at as incipient species; for my tables clearly show as a general rule that, wherever many species of a genus have been formed, the species of that genus present a number of varieties, that is of incipient species, beyond the average. It is not that all large genera are now varying much, and are thus increasing in the number of their species, or that no small genera are now varying and increasing; for if this had been so, it would have been fatal to my theory; inasmuch as geology plainly tells us that small genera have in the lapse of time often increased greatly in size; and that large genera have often come to their maxima, decline, and disappeared. All that we want to show is, that, when many species of a genus have been formed, on an average many are still forming; and this certainly holds good.

Many of the Species included within the Larger Genera resemble Varieties in being very closely, but unequally, related to each other, and in having restricted ranges.

There are other relations between the species of large genera and their recorded varieties which deserve notice. We have seen that there is no infallible criterion by which to distinguish species and well-marked varieties; and when intermediate links have not been found between doubtful forms, naturalists are compelled to come to a determination by the amount of difference between them, judging by analogy whether or not the amount suffices to raise one or both to the rank of species. Hence the amount of difference is one very important criterion in settling whether two forms should be ranked as species or varieties. Now Fries has remarked in regard to plants, and Westwood in regard to insects, that in large genera the amount of difference between the species is often exceedingly small. I have endeavoured to test this numerically by averages, and, as far as my imperfect results go, they confirm the view. I have also consulted some sagacious and experienced observers, and, after deliberation, they concur in this view. In this respect, therefore, the species of the larger genera resemble varieties, more than do the species of the smaller genera. Or the case may be put in another way, and it may be said, that in the larger genera, in which a number of varieties or incipient species greater than the average are now manufacturing, many of the species already manufactured still to a certain extent resemble varieties, for they differ from each other by less than the usual amount of difference.

Moreover, the species of the larger genera are related to each other, in the same manner as the varieties of any one species are related to each other. No naturalist pretends that all the species of a genus are equally distinct from each other; they may generally be divided into sub-genera, or sections, or lesser groups. As Fries has well remarked, little groups of species are generally clustered like satellites around other species. And what are varieties but groups of forms, unequally related to each other, and clustered round certain forms—that is, round their parent-species. Undoubtedly there is one most important point of difference between varieties and species; namely, that the amount of difference between varieties, when compared with each other or with their parent-species, is much less than that between the species of the same genus. But when we come to discuss the principle, as I call it, of Divergence of Character, we shall see how this may be explained, and how the lesser differences between varieties tend to increase into the greater differences between species.

There is one other point which is worth notice. Varieties generally have much restricted ranges: this statement is indeed scarcely more than a truism, for, if a variety were found to have a wider range than that of its supposed parent-species, their denominations would be reversed. But there is reason to believe that the species which are very closely allied to other species, and in so far resemble varieties, often have much restricted ranges. For instance, Mr. H. C. Watson has marked for me in the well-sifted London Catalogue of plants (4th edition) 63 plants which are therein ranked as species, but which he considers as so closely allied to other species as to be of doubtful value: these 63 reputed species range on an average over 6.9 of the provinces into which Mr. Watson has divided Great Britain. Now, in this same Catalogue, 53 acknowledged varieties are recorded, and these range over 7.7 provinces; whereas, the species to which these varieties belong range over 14.3 provinces. So that the acknowledged varieties have nearly the same restricted average range, as have the closely allied forms, marked for me by Mr. Watson as doubtful species, but which are almost universally ranked by British botanists as good and true species.

Summary

Finally, varieties cannot be distinguished from species,—except, first, by the discovery of intermediate linking forms; and, secondly, by a certain indefinite amount of difference between them; for two forms, if differing very little, are generally ranked as varieties, notwithstanding that they cannot be closely connected; but the amount of difference considered necessary to give to any two forms the rank of species cannot be defined. In genera having more than the average number of species in any country, the species of these genera have more than the average number of varieties. In large genera the species are apt to be closely, but unequally, allied together, forming little clusters round other species. Species very closely allied to other species apparently have restricted ranges. In all these respects the species of large genera present a strong analogy with varieties. And we can clearly understand these analogies, if species once existed as varieties, and thus originated; whereas, these analogies are utterly inexplicable if species are independent creations.

We have, also, seen that it is the most flourishing or dominant species of the larger genera within each class which on an average yield the greatest number of varieties; and varieties, as we shall hereafter see, tend to become converted into new and distinct species. Thus the larger genera tend to become larger; and throughout nature the forms of life which are now dominant tend to become still more dominant by leaving many modified and dominant descendants. But by steps hereafter to be explained, the larger genera also tend to break up into smaller genera. And thus, the forms of life throughout the universe become divided into groups subordinate to groups.

CHAPTER III

Its bearing on natural selection—The term used in a wide sense—Geometrical ratio of increase—Rapid increase of naturalised animals and plants—Nature of the checks to increase—Competition universal—Effects of Climate—Protection from the number of individuals—Complex relations of all animals and plants throughout nature—Struggle for life most severe between individuals and varieties of the same species: often severe between species of the same genus—The relation of organism to organism the most important of all relations.

BEFORE entering on the subject of this chapter, I must make a few preliminary remarks, to show how the struggle for existence bears on Natural Selection. It has been seen in the last chapter that amongst organic beings in a state of nature there is some individual variability: indeed I am not aware that this has ever been disputed. It is immaterial for us whether a multitude of doubtful forms be called species or sub-species or varieties; what rank, for instance, the two or three hundred doubtful forms of British plants are entitled to hold, if the existence of any well-marked varieties be admitted. But the mere existence of individual variability and of some few well-marked varieties, though necessary as the foundation for the work, helps us but little in understanding how species arise in nature. How have all those exquisite adaptations of one part of the organisation to another part, and to the conditions of life, and of one organic being to another being, been perfected? We see these beautiful co-adaptations most plainly in the woodpecker and the mistletoe; and only a little less plainly in the humblest parasite which clings to the hairs of a quadruped or feathers of a bird; in the structure of the beetle which dives through the water; in the plumed seed which is wafted by the gentlest breeze; in short, we see beautiful adaptations everywhere and in every part of the organic world.

Again, it may be asked, how is it that varieties, which I have called incipient species, become ultimately converted into good and distinct species which in most cases obviously differ from each other far more than do the varieties of the same species? How do those groups of species, which constitute what are called distinct genera, and which differ from each other more than do the species of the same genus, arise? All these results, as we shall more fully see in the next chapter, follow from the struggle for life. Owing to this struggle, variations, however slight and from whatever cause proceeding, if they be in any degree profitable to the individuals of a species, in their infinitely complex relations to other organic beings and to their physical conditions of life, will tend to the preservation of such individuals, and will generally be inherited by the offspring. The offspring, also, will thus have a better chance of surviving, for, of the many individuals of any species which are periodically born, but a small number can survive. I have called this principle, by which each slight variation, if useful, is preserved, by the term Natural Selection, in order to mark its relation to man's power of selection. But the expression often used by Mr. Herbert Spencer of the Survival of the Fittest is more accurate, and is sometimes equally convenient. We have seen that man by selection can certainly produce great results, and can adapt organic beings to his own uses, through the accumulation of slight but useful variations, given to him by the hand of Nature. But Natural Selection, as we shall hereafter see, is a power incessantly ready for action, and is as immeasurably superior to man's feeble efforts, as the works of Nature are to those of Art.

We will now discuss in a little more detail the struggle for existence. In my future work this subject will be treated, as it well deserves, at greater length. The elder De Candolle and Lyell have largely and philosophically shown that all organic beings are exposed to severe competition. In regard to plants, no one has treated this subject with more spirit and ability than W. Herbert, Dean of Manchester, evidently the result of his great horticultural knowledge. Nothing is easier than to admit in words the truth of the universal struggle for life, or more difficult—at least I have found it so—than constantly to bear this conclusion in mind. Yet unless it be thoroughly engrained in the mind, the whole economy of nature, with every fact on distribution, rarity, abundance, extinction, and variation, will be dimly seen or quite misunderstood. We behold the face of nature bright with gladness, we often see superabundance of food; we do not see or we forget, that the birds which are idly singing round us mostly live on insects or seeds, and are thus constantly destroying life; or we forget how largely these songsters, or their eggs, or their nestlings, are destroyed by birds and beasts of prey; we do not always bear in mind, that, though food may be now superabundant, it is not so at all seasons of each recurring year.

The Term, Struggle for Existence, used in a large sense

I should premise that I use this term in a large and metaphorical sense including dependence of one being on another, and including (which is more important) not only the life of the individual, but success in leaving progeny. Two canine animals, in a time of dearth, may be truly said to struggle with each other which shall get food and live. But a plant on the edge of a desert is said to struggle for life against the drought, though more properly it should be said to be dependent on the moisture. A plant which annually produces a thousand seeds, of which only one of an average comes to maturity, may be more truly said to struggle with the plants of the same and other kinds which already clothe the ground. The mistletoe is dependent on the apple and a few other trees, but can only in a farfetched sense be said to struggle with these trees, for, if too many of these parasites grow on the same tree, it languishes and dies. But several seedling mistletoes, growing close together on the same branch, may more truly be said to struggle with each other. As the mistletoe is disseminated by birds, its existence depends on them; and it may methodically be said to struggle with other fruit-bearing plants, in tempting the birds to devour and thus disseminate its seeds. In these several senses, which pass into each other, I use for convenience' sake the general term of Struggle for Existence.

Geometrical Ratio of Increase

A struggle for existence inevitably follows from the high rate at which all organic beings tend to increase. Every being, which during its natural lifetime produces several eggs or seeds, must suffer destruction during some period of its life, and during some season or occasional year, otherwise, on the principle of geometrical increase, its numbers would quickly become so inordinately great that no country could support the product. Hence, as more individuals are produced than can possibly survive, there must in every case be a struggle for existence, either one individual with another of the same species, or with the individuals of distinct species, or with the physical conditions of life. It is the doctrine of Malthus applied with manifold force to the whole animal and vegetable kingdoms; for in this case there can be no artificial increase of food, and no prudential restraint from marriage. Although some species may be now increasing, more or less rapidly, in numbers, all cannot do so, for the world would not hold them.

There is no exception to the rule that every organic being naturally increases at so high a rate, that, if not destroyed, the earth would soon be covered by the progeny of a single pair. Even slow-breeding man has doubled in twenty-five years, and at this rate, in less than a thousand years, there would literally not be standing-room for his progeny. Linnæus has calculated that if an annual plant produced only two seeds—and there is no plant so unproductive as this—and their seedlings next year produced two, and so on, then in twenty years there should be a million plants. The elephant is reckoned the slowest breeder of all known animals, and I have taken some pains to estimate its probable minimum rate of natural increase; it will be safest to assume that it begins breeding when thirty years old, and goes on breeding till ninety years old, bringing forth six young in the interval, and surviving till one hundred years old; if this be so, after a period of from 740 to 750 years there would be nearly nineteen million elephants alive, descended from the first pair.

But we have better evidence on this subject than mere theoretical calculations, namely, the numerous recorded cases of the astonishingly rapid increase of various animals in a state of nature, when circumstances have been favourable to them during two or three following seasons. Still more striking is the evidence from our domestic animals of many kinds which have run wild in several parts of the world; if the statements of the rate of increase of slow-breeding cattle and horses in South America, and latterly in Australia, had not been well authenticated, they would have been incredible. So it is with plants; cases could be given of introduced plants which have become common throughout whole islands in a period of less than ten years. Several of the plants, such as the cardoon and a tall thistle, which are now the commonest over the whole plains of La Plata, clothing square leagues of surface almost to the exclusion of every other plant, have been introduced from Europe; and there are plants which now range in India, as I hear from Dr. Falconer, from Cape Comorin to the Himalaya, which have been imported from America since its discovery. In such cases, and endless others could be given, no one supposes, that the fertility of the animals or plants has been suddenly and temporarily increased in any sensible degree. The obvious explanation is that the conditions of life have been highly favourable, and that there has consequently been less destruction of the old and young, and that nearly all the young have been enabled to breed. Their geometrical ratio of increase, the result of which never fails to be surprising, simply explains their extraordinarily rapid increase and wide diffusion in their new homes.

In a state of nature almost every full-grown plant annually produces seed, and amongst animals there are very few which do not annually pair. Hence we may confidently assert, that all plants and animals are tending to increase at a geometrical ratio,—that all would rapidly stock every station in which they could anyhow exist,—and that this geometrical tendency to increase must be checked by destruction at some period of life. Our familiarity with the larger domestic animals tends, I think, to mislead us: we see no great destruction falling on them, but we do not keep in mind that thousands are annually slaughtered for food, and that in a state of nature an equal number would have somehow to be disposed of.

The only difference between organisms which annually produce eggs or seeds by the thousand, and those which produce extremely few, is, that the slow-breeders would require a few more years to people, under favourable conditions, a whole district, let it be ever so large. The condor lays a couple of eggs and the ostrich a score, and yet in the same country the condor may be the more numerous of the two; the Fulmar petrel lays but one egg, yet it is believed to be the most numerous bird in the world. One fly deposits hundreds of eggs, and another, like the hippobosca, a single one; but this difference does not determine how many individuals of the two species can be supported in a district. A large number of eggs is of some importance to those species which depend on a fluctuating amount of food, for it allows them rapidly to increase in number. But the real importance of a large number of eggs or seeds is to make up for much destruction at some period of life; and this period in the great majority of cases is an early one. If an animal can in any way protect its own eggs or young, a small number may be produced, and yet the average stock be fully kept up; but if many eggs or young are destroyed, many must be produced, or the species will become extinct. It would suffice to keep up the full number of a tree, which lived on an average for a thousand years, if a single seed were produced once in a thousand years, supposing that this seed were never destroyed, and could be ensured to germinate in a fitting place. So that, in all cases, the average number of any animal or plant depends only indirectly on the number of its eggs or seeds.

In looking at Nature, it is most necessary to keep the foregoing considerations always in mind—never to forget that every single organic being may be said to be striving to the utmost to increase in numbers; that each lives by a struggle at some period of its life; that heavy destruction inevitably falls either on the young or old, during each generation or at recurrent intervals. Lighten any check, mitigate the destruction ever so little, and the number of the species will almost instantaneously increase to any amount.

Nature of the Checks to Increase

The causes which check the natural tendency of each species to increase are most obscure. Look at the most vigorous species; by as much as it swarms in numbers, by so much will it tend to increase still further. We know not exactly what the checks are even in a single instance. Nor will this surprise any one who reflects how ignorant we are on this head, even in regard to mankind, although so incomparably better known than any other animal. This subject of the checks to increase has been ably treated by several authors, and I hope in a future work to discuss it at considerable length, more especially in regard to the feral animals of South America. Here I will make only a few remarks, just to recall to the reader's mind some of the chief points. Eggs or very young animals seem generally to suffer most, but this is not invariably the case. With plants there is a vast destruction of seeds, but, from some observations which I have made it appears that the seedlings suffer most from germinating in ground already thickly stocked with other plants. Seedlings, also, are destroyed in vast numbers by various enemies; for instance, on a piece of ground three feet long and two wide, dug and cleared, and where there could be no choking from other plants, I marked all the seedlings of our native weeds as they came up, and out of 357 no less than 295 were destroyed, chiefly by slugs and insects. If turf which has long been mown, and the case would be the same with turf closely browsed by quadrupeds, be let to grow, the more vigorous plants gradually kill the less vigorous, though fully grown plants; thus out of twenty species growing on a little plot of mown turf (three feet by four) nine species perished, from the other species being allowed to grow up freely.

The amount of food for each species of course gives the extreme limit to which each can increase; but very frequently it is not the obtaining food, but the serving as prey to other animals, which determines the average numbers of a species. Thus, there seems to be little doubt that the stock of partridges, grouse, and hares on any large estate depends chiefly on the destruction of vermin. If not one head of game were shot during the next twenty years in England, and, at the same time, if no vermin were destroyed, there would, in all probability, be less game than at present, although hundreds of thousands of game animals are now annually shot. On the other hand, in some cases, as with the elephant, none are destroyed by beasts of prey; for even the tiger in India most rarely dares to attack a young elephant protected by its dam.

Climate plays an important part in determining the average number of a species, and periodical seasons of extreme cold or drought seem to be the most effective of all checks. I estimated (chiefly from the greatly reduced numbers of nests in the spring) that the winter of 1854-5 destroyed four-fifths of the birds in my own grounds; and this is a tremendous destruction, when we remember that ten per cent. is an extraordinarily severe mortality from epidemics with man. The action of climate seems at first sight to be quite independent of the struggle for existence; but in so far as climate chiefly acts in reducing food, it brings on the most severe struggle between the individuals, whether of the same or of distinct species, which subsist on the same kind of food. Even when climate, for instance, extreme cold, acts directly, it will be the least vigorous individuals, or those which have got least food through the advancing winter, which will suffer most. When we travel from south to north, or from a damp region to a dry, we invariably see some species gradually getting rarer and rarer, and finally disappearing; and the change of climate being conspicuous, we are tempted to attribute the whole effect to its direct action. But this is a false view; we forget that each species, even where it most abounds, is constantly suffering enormous destruction at some period of its life, from enemies or from competitors for the same place and food; and if these enemies or competitors be in the least degree favoured by any slight change of climate, they will increase in numbers; and as each area is already fully stocked with inhabitants, the other species must decrease. When we travel southward and see a species decreasing in numbers, we may feel sure that the cause lies quite as much in other species being favoured, as in this one being hurt. So it is when we travel northward, but in a somewhat lesser degree, for the number of species of all kinds, and therefore of competitors, decreases northwards; hence in going northwards, or in ascending a mountain, we far oftener meet with stunted forms, due to the *directly* injurious action of climate, than we do in proceeding southwards or in descending a mountain. When we reach the Arctic regions, or snow-capped summits, or absolute deserts, the struggle for life is almost exclusively with the elements.

That climate acts in main part indirectly by favouring other species, we clearly see in the prodigious number of plants which in our gardens can perfectly well endure our climate, but which never become naturalised, for they cannot compete with our native plants nor resist destruction by our native animals.

When a species, owing to highly favourable circumstances, increases inordinately in numbers in a small tract, epidemics—at least, this seems generally to occur with our game animals—often ensue; and here we have a limiting check independent of the struggle for life. But even some of these so-called epidemics appear to be due to parasitic worms, which have from some cause, possibly in part through facility of diffusion amongst the crowded animals, been disproportionally favoured: and here comes in a sort of struggle between the parasite and its prey.

On the other hand, in many cases, a large stock of individuals of the same species, relatively to the numbers of its enemies, is absolutely necessary for its preservation. Thus we can easily raise plenty of corn and rape-seed, &c., in our fields, because the seeds are in great excess compared with the number of birds which feed on them; nor can the birds, though having a super-abundance of food at this one season, increase in number proportionally to the supply of seed, as their numbers are checked during the winter; but any one who has tried, knows how troublesome it is to get seed from a few wheat or other such plants in a garden: I have in this case lost every single seed. This view of the necessity of a large stock of the same species for its preservation, explains, I believe, some singular facts in nature such as that of very rare plants being sometimes extremely abundant, in the few spots where they do exist; and that of some social plants being social, that is abounding in individuals, even on the extreme verge of their range. For in such cases, we may believe, that a plant could exist only where the conditions of its life were so favourable that many could exist together, and thus save the species from utter destruction. I should add that the good effects of intercrossing, and the ill effects of close interbreeding, no doubt come into play in many of these cases; but I will not here enlarge on this subject.

Complex Relations of all Animals and Plants to each other in the Struggle for Existence

Many cases are on record showing how complex and unexpected are the checks and relations between organic beings, which have to struggle together in the same country. I will give only a single instance, which, though a simple one, interested me. In Staffordshire, on the estate of a relation, where I had ample means of investigation, there was a large and extremely barren heath, which had never been touched by the hand of man; but several hundred acres of exactly the same nature had been enclosed twenty-five years previously and planted with Scotch fir. The change in the native vegetation of the planted part of the heath was most remarkable, more than is generally seen in passing from one quite different soil to another: not only the proportional numbers of the heath-plants were wholly changed, but twelve species of plants (not counting grasses and carices) flourished in the plantations, which could not be found on the heath. The effect on the insects must have been still greater, for six insectivorous birds were very common in the plantations, which were not to be seen on the heath; and the heath was frequented by two or three distinct insectivorous birds. Here we see how potent has been the effect of the introduction of a single tree, nothing whatever else having been done, with the exception of the land having been enclosed, so that cattle could not enter. But how important an element enclosure is, I plainly saw near Farnham, in Surrey. Here there are extensive heaths, with a few clumps of old Scotch firs on the distant hilltops: within the last ten years large spaces have been enclosed, and self-sown firs are now springing up in multitudes, so close together that all cannot live. When I ascertained that these young trees had not been sown or planted, I was so much surprised at their numbers that I went to several points of view, whence I could examine hundreds of acres of the unenclosed heath, and literally I could not see a single Scotch fir, except the old planted clumps. But on looking closely between the stems of the heath, I found a multitude of seedlings and little trees which had been perpetually browsed down by the cattle. In one square yard, at a point some hundred yards distant from one of the old clumps, I counted thirty-two little trees; and one of them, with twenty-six rings of growth, had, during many years tried to raise its head above the stems of the heath, and had failed. No wonder that, as soon as the land was enclosed, it became thickly clothed with vigorously growing young firs. Yet the heath was so extremely barren and so extensive that no one would ever have imagined that cattle would have so closely and effectually searched it for food.

Here we see that cattle absolutely determine the existence of the Scotch fir; but in several parts of the world insects determine the existence of cattle. Perhaps Paraguay offers the most curious instance of this; for here neither cattle nor horses nor dogs have ever run wild, though they swarm southward and northward in a feral state; and Azara and Rengger have shown that this is caused by the greater number in Paraguay of a certain fly, which lays its eggs in the navels of these animals when first born. The increase of these flies, numerous as they are, must be habitually checked by some means, probably by other parasitic insects. Hence, if certain insectivorous birds were to decrease in Paraguay, the parasitic insects would probably increase; and this would lessen the number of the navel-frequenting flies—then cattle and horses would become feral, and this would certainly greatly alter (as indeed I have observed in parts of South America) the vegetation: this again would largely affect the insects; and this, as we have just seen in Staffordshire, the insectivorous birds, and so onwards in ever-increasing circles of complexity. Not that under nature the relations will ever be as simple as this. Battle within battle must be continually recurring with varying success; and yet in the long-run the forces are so nicely balanced, that the face of nature remains for long periods of time uniform, though assuredly the merest trifle would give the victory to one organic being over another. Nevertheless, so profound is our ignorance, and so high our presumption, that we marvel when we hear of the extinction of an organic being; and as we do not see the cause, we invoke cataclysms to desolate the world, or invent laws on the duration of the forms of life!

I am tempted to give one more instance showing how plants and animals remote in the scale of nature, are bound together by a web of complex relations. I shall hereafter have occasion to show that the exotic
Lobelia fulgens is never visited in my garden by insects, and consequently, from its peculiar structure, never sets a seed. Nearly all our orchidaceous plants absolutely require the visits of insects to remove their pollen-masses and thus to fertilise them. I find from experiments that humble-bees are almost indispensable to the fertilisation of the heartsease
(Viola tricolor), for other bees do not visit this flower. I have also found
that the visits of bees are necessary for the fertilisation of some kinds of
clover; for instance, 20 heads of Dutch clover (Trifolium repens) yielded
2,290 seeds, but 20 other heads protected from bees produced not one.
Again, 100 heads of red clover (T. pratense) produced 2,700 seeds, but
the same number of protected heads produced not a single seed. Humble-
bees alone visit red clover, as other bees cannot reach the nectar. It has
been suggested that moths may fertilise the clovers; but I doubt whether
they could do so in the case of the red clover, from their weight not being sufficient to depress the wing petals. Hence we may infer as highly
probable that, if the whole genus of humble-bees became extinct or very
rare in England, the heartsease and red clover would become very rare,
or wholly disappear. The number of humble-bees in any district depends
in a great measure upon the number of field-mice, which destroy their
combs and nests; and Col. Newman, who has long attended to the habits
of humble-bees, believes that "more than two-thirds of them are thus destroyed all over England." Now the number of mice is largely dependent,
as every one knows, on the number of cats; and Col. Newman says, "Near
villages and small towns I have found the nests of humble-bees more
numerous than elsewhere, which I attribute to the number of cats that
destroy the mice." Hence it is quite credible that the presence of a feline
animal in large numbers in a district might determine, through the intervention first of mice and then of bees, the frequency of certain flowers in
that district!

In the case of every species, many different checks, acting at different
periods of life, and during different seasons or years, probably come into
play; some one check or some few being generally the most potent; but
all will concur in determining the average number or even the existence
of the species. In some cases it can be shown that widely-different checks
act on the same species in different districts. When we look at the plants
and bushes clothing an entangled bank, we are tempted to attribute their
proportional numbers and kinds to what we call chance. But how false a
view is this! Every one has heard that when an American forest is cut
down a very different vegetation springs up; but it has been observed
that ancient Indian ruins in the Southern United States, which must
formerly have been cleared of trees, now display the same beautiful diversity and proportion of kinds as in the surrounding virgin forest. What
a struggle must have gone on during long centuries between the several
kinds of trees each annually scattering its seeds by the thousand; what

war between insect and insect—between insects, snails, and other animals with birds and beasts of prey—all striving to increase, all feeding on each other, or on the trees, their seeds and seedlings, or on the other plants which first clothed the ground and thus checked the growth of the trees! Throw up a handful of feathers, and all fall to the ground according to definite laws; but how simple is the problem where each shall fall compared to that of the action and reaction of the innumerable plants and animals which have determined, in the course of centuries, the proportional numbers and kinds of trees now growing on the old Indian ruins!

The dependency of one organic being on another, as of a parasite on its prey, lies generally between beings remote in the scale of nature. This is likewise sometimes the case with those which may be strictly said to struggle with each other for existence, as in the case of locusts and grass-feeding quadrupeds. But the struggle will almost invariably be most severe between the individuals of the same species, for they frequent the same districts, require the same food, and are exposed to the same dangers. In the case of varieties of the same species, the struggle will generally be almost equally severe, and we sometimes see the contest soon decided: for instance, if several varieties of wheat be sown together, and the mixed seed be resown, some of the varieties which best suit the soil or climate, or are naturally the most fertile, will beat the others and so yield more seed, and will consequently in a few years supplant the other varieties. To keep up a mixed stock of even such extremely close varieties as the variously-coloured sweet peas, they must be each year harvested separately, and the seed then mixed in due proportion, otherwise the weaker kinds will steadily decrease in number and disappear. So again with the varieties of sheep; it has been asserted that certain mountain-varieties will starve out other mountain-varieties, so that they cannot be kept together. The same result has followed from keeping together different varieties of the medicinal leech. It may even be doubted whether the varieties of any of our domestic plants or animals have so exactly the same strength, habits, and constitution, that the original proportions of a mixed stock (crossing being prevented) could be kept up for half-a-dozen generations, if they were allowed to struggle together, in the same manner as beings in a state of nature, and if the seed or young were not annually preserved in due proportion.

Struggle for Life most severe between Individuals and Varieties of the same Species

As the species of the same genus usually have, though by no means invariably, much similarity in habits and constitution, and always in structure, the struggle will generally be more severe between them, if they come into competition with each other, than between the species of distinct genera. We see this in the recent extension over parts of the United States of one species of swallow having caused the decrease of another species. The recent increase of the missel-thrush in parts of Scotland has caused the decrease of the song-thrush. How frequently we hear of one species of rat taking the place of another species under the most different climates! In Russia the small Asiatic cockroach has everywhere driven before it its great congener. In Australia the imported hive-bee is rapidly exterminating the small, stingless native bee. One species of charlock has been known to supplant another species; and so in other cases. We can dimly see why the competition should be most severe between allied forms, which fill nearly the same place in the economy of nature; but probably in no one case could we precisely say why one species has been victorious over another in the great battle of life.

A corollary of the highest importance may be deduced from the foregoing remarks, namely, that the structure of every organic being is related, in the most essential yet often hidden manner, to that of all the other organic beings, with which it comes into competition for food or residence, or from which it has to escape, or on which it preys. This is obvious in the structure of the teeth and talons of the tiger; and in that of the legs and claws of the parasite which clings to the hair on the tiger's body. But in the beautifully plumed seed of the dandelion, and in the flattened and fringed legs of the water-beetle, the relation seems at first confined to the elements of air and water. Yet the advantage of plumed seeds no doubt stands in the closest relation to the land being already thickly clothed with other plants; so that the seeds may be widely distributed and fall on unoccupied ground. In the water-beetle, the structure of its legs, so well adapted for diving, allows it to compete with other aquatic insects, to hunt for its own prey, and to escape serving as prey to other animals.

The store of nutriment laid up within the seeds of many plants seems at first to have no sort of relation to other plants. But from the strong growth of young plants produced from such seeds, as peas and beans, when sown in the midst of long grass, it may be suspected that the chief use of the nutriment in the seed is to favour the growth of the seedlings, whilst struggling with other plants growing vigorously all around.

Look at a plant in the midst of its range, why does it not double or quadruple its numbers? We know that it can perfectly well withstand a little more heat or cold, dampness or dryness, for elsewhere it ranges into slightly hotter or colder, damper or drier districts. In this case we can clearly see that if we wish in imagination to give the plant the power of increasing in number, we should have to give it some advantage over its competitors, or over the animals which prey on it. On the confines of its geographical range, a change of constitution with respect to climate would clearly be an advantage to our plant; but we have reason to believe that only a few plants or animals range so far, that they are destroyed exclusively by the rigour of the climate. Not until we reach the extreme confines of life, in the Arctic regions or on the borders of an utter desert, will competition cease. The land may be extremely cold or dry, yet there will be competition between some few species, or between the individuals of the same species, for the warmest or dampest spots.

Hence we can see that when a plant or animal is placed in a new country amongst new competitors, the conditions of its life will generally be changed in an essential manner, although the climate may be exactly the same as in its former home. If its average numbers are to increase in its new home, we should have to modify it in a different way to what we should have had to do in its native country; for we should have to give it some advantage over a different set of competitors or enemies.

It is good thus to try in imagination to give to any one species an advantage over another. Probably in no single instance should we know what to do. This ought to convince us of our ignorance on the mutual relations of all organic beings; a conviction as necessary, as it is difficult to acquire. All that we can do, is to keep steadily in mind that each organic being is striving to increase in a geometrical ratio; that each at some period of its life, during some season of the year, during each generation or at intervals, has to struggle for life and to suffer great destruction. When we reflect on this struggle, we may console ourselves with the full belief, that the war of nature is not incessant, that no fear is felt, that death is generally prompt, and that the vigorous, the healthy, and the happy survive and multiply.

CHAPTER IV

NATURAL SELECTION; OR THE SURVIVAL OF THE FITTEST

*Natural Selection—its power compared with man's selection—its power on char-
acters of trifling importance—its power at all ages and on both sexes—Sexual
Selection—On the generality of intercrosses between individuals of the same
species—Circumstances favourable and unfavourable to the results of Natural
Selection, namely, intercrossing, isolation, number of individuals—Slow action—
Extinction caused by Natural Selection—Divergence of Character, related to
the diversity of inhabitants of any small area, and to naturalisation—Action
of Natural Selection, through Divergence of Character, and Extinction, on the
descendants from a common parent—Explains the grouping of all organic
beings—Advance in organisation—Low forms preserved—Convergence of character—Indefinite multiplication of species—Summary.*

How will the struggle for existence, briefly discussed in the last chapter,
act in regard to variation? Can the principle of selection, which we have
seen is so potent in the hands of man, apply under nature? I think we
shall see that it can act most efficiently. Let the endless number of slight
variations and individual differences occurring in our domestic productions, and, in a lesser degree, in those under nature, be borne in mind; as
well as the strength of the hereditary tendency. Under domestication, it
may be truly said that the whole organisation becomes in some degree
plastic. But the variability, which we almost universally meet with in our
domestic productions, is not directly produced, as Hooker and Asa Gray
have well remarked, by man; he can neither originate varieties, nor prevent their occurrence; he can preserve and accumulate such as do occur.
Unintentionally he exposes organic beings to new and changing conditions of life, and variability ensues; but similar changes of conditions
might and do occur under nature. Let it also be borne in mind how infinitely complex and close-fitting are the mutual relations of all organic
beings to each other and to their physical conditions of life; and consequently what infinitely varied diversities of structure might be of use to
each being under changing conditions of life. Can it, then, be thought improbable, seeing that variations useful to man have undoubtedly occurred, that other variations useful in some way to each being in the great
and complex battle of life, should occur in the course of many successive
generations. If such do occur, can we doubt (remembering that many
more individuals are born than can possibly survive) that individuals
having any advantage, however slight, over others, would have the best
chance of surviving and of procreating their kind? On the other hand, we

may feel sure that any variation in the least degree injurious would be rigidly destroyed. This preservation of favourable individual differences and variations, and the destruction of those which are injurious, I have called Natural Selection, or the Survival of the Fittest. Variations neither useful nor injurious would not be affected by natural selection, and would be left either a fluctuating element, as perhaps we see in certain polymorphic species, or would ultimately become fixed, owing to the nature of the organism and the nature of the conditions.

Several writers have misapprehended or objected to the term Natural Selection. Some have even imagined that natural selection induces variability, whereas it implies only the preservation of such variations as arise and are beneficial to the being under its conditions of life. No one objects to agriculturists speaking of the potent effects of man's selection; and in this case the individual differences given by nature, which man for some object selects, must of necessity first occur. Others have objected that the term selection implies conscious choice in the animals which become modified; and it has even been urged that, as plants have no volition, natural selection is not applicable to them! In the literal sense of the word, no doubt, natural selection is a false term; but who ever objected to chemists speaking of the elective affinities of the various elements?—and yet an acid cannot strictly be said to elect the base with which it in preference combines. It has been said that I speak of natural selection as an active power or Deity; but who objects to an author speaking of the attraction of gravity as ruling the movements of the planets? Every one knows what is meant and is implied by such metaphorical expressions; and they are almost necessary for brevity. So again it is difficult to avoid personifying the word Nature; but I mean by Nature, only the aggregate action and product of many natural laws, and by laws the sequence of events as ascertained by us. With a little familiarity such superficial objections will be forgotten.

We shall best understand the probable course of natural selection by taking the case of a country undergoing some slight physical change, for instance, of climate. The proportional numbers of its inhabitants will almost immediately undergo a change, and some species will probably become extinct. We may conclude, from what we have seen of the intimate and complex manner in which the inhabitants of each country are bound together, that any change in the numerical proportions of the inhabitants, independently of the change of climate itself, would seriously affect the others. If the country were open on its borders, new forms would certainly immigrate, and this would likewise seriously disturb the relations of some of the former inhabitants. Let it be remembered how powerful the influence of a single introduced tree or mammal has been shown to be. But in the case of an island, or of a country partly surrounded by barriers, into which new and better adapted forms could not freely enter, we should then have places in the economy of nature which would assuredly be better filled up, if some of the original inhabitants were in some manner modified; for, had the area been open to immigration, these same places would have been seized on by intruders. In such cases, slight modifications, which in any way favoured the individuals of any species, by better adapting them to their altered conditions, would tend to be preserved; and natural selection would have free scope for the work of improvement.

We have good reason to believe, as shown in the first chapter, that changes in the conditions of life give a tendency to increased variability; and in the foregoing cases the conditions have changed, and this would manifestly be favourable to natural selection, by affording a better chance of the occurrence of profitable variations. Unless such occur, natural selection can do nothing. Under the term of "variations," it must never be forgotten that mere individual differences are included. As man can produce a great result with his domestic animals and plants by adding up in any given direction individual differences, so could natural selection, but far more easily from having incomparably longer time for action. Nor do I believe that any great physical change, as of climate, or any unusual degree of isolation to check immigration, is necessary in order that new and unoccupied places should be left, for natural selection to fill up by improving some of the varying inhabitants. For as all the inhabitants of each country are struggling together with nicely balanced forces, extremely slight modifications in the structure or habits of one species would often give it an advantage over others; and still further modifications of the same kind would often still further increase the advantage, as long as the species continued under the same conditions of life and profited by similar means of subsistence and defence. No country can be named in which all the native inhabitants are now so perfectly adapted to each other and to the physical conditions under which they live, that none of them could be still better adapted or improved; for in all countries, the natives have been so far conquered by naturalised productions, that they have allowed some foreigners to take firm possession of the land. And as foreigners have thus in every country beaten some of the natives, we may safely conclude that the natives might have been modified with advantage, so as to have better resisted the intruders.

As man can produce, and certainly has produced, a great result by his methodical and unconscious means of selection, what may not natural selection effect? Man can act only on external and visible characters: Nature, if I may be allowed to personify the natural preservation or survival of the fittest, cares nothing for appearances, except in so far as they are useful to any being. She can act on every internal organ, on every shade of constitutional difference, on the whole machinery of life. Man selects only for his own good: Nature only for that of the being which she tends. Every selected character is fully exercised by her, as is implied by the fact of their selection. Man keeps the natives of many climates in the same country; he seldom exercises each selected character in some peculiar and fitting manner; he feeds a long and a short beaked pigeon on the same food; he does not exercise a long-backed or long-legged quadruped in any peculiar manner; he exposes sheep with long and short wool to the same climate. He does not allow the most vigorous males to struggle for the females. He does not rigidly destroy all inferior animals, but protects during each varying season, as far as lies in his power, all his productions. He often begins his selection by some half-monstrous form; or at least by some modification prominent enough to catch the eye or to be plainly useful to him. Under nature, the slightest differences of structure or constitution may well turn the nicely balanced scale in the struggle for life, and so be preserved. How fleeting are the wishes and efforts of man! how short his time! and consequently how poor will be his results, compared with those accumulated by Nature during whole geological periods! Can we wonder, then, that Nature's productions should be far "truer" in character than man's productions; that they should be infinitely better adapted to the most complex conditions of life, and should plainly bear the stamp of far higher workmanship?

It may metaphorically be said that natural selection is daily and hourly scrutinising, throughout the world, the slightest variations; rejecting those that are bad, preserving and adding up all that are good; silently and insensibly working, *whenever and wherever opportunity offers*, at the improvement of each organic being in relation to its organic and inorganic conditions of life. We see nothing of these slow changes in progress, until the hand of time has marked the lapse of ages, and then so imperfect is our view into long-past geological ages, that we see only that the forms of life are now different from what they formerly were.

In order that any great amount of modification should be effected in a species, a variety when once formed must again, perhaps after a long interval of time, vary or present individual differences of the same favourable nature as before; and these must be again preserved, and so onwards step by step. Seeing that individual differences of the same kind perpetually recur, this can hardly be considered as an unwarrantable assumption. But whether it is true, we can judge only by seeing how far the hypothesis accords with and explains the general phenomena of nature. On the other hand, the ordinary belief that the amount of possible variation is a strictly limited quantity is likewise a simple assumption.

Although natural selection can act only through and for the good of each being, yet characters and structures, which we are apt to consider as of very trifling importance, may thus be acted on. When we see leaf-eating insects green, and bark-feeders mottled-grey; the alpine ptarmigan white in winter, the red-grouse the colour of heather, we must believe that these tints are of service to these birds and insects in preserving them from danger. Grouse, if not destroyed at some period of their lives would increase ·in countless numbers; they are known to suffer largely from birds of prey; and hawks are guided by eyesight to their prey—so much so, that on parts of the Continent persons are warned not to keep white pigeons, as being the most liable to destruction. Hence natural selection might be effective in giving the proper colour to each kind of grouse, and in keeping that colour, when once acquired, true and constant. Nor ought we to think that the occasional destruction of an animal of any particular colour would produce little effect: we should remember how essential it is in a flock of white sheep to destroy a lamb with the faintest trace of black. We have seen how the colour of the hogs, which feed on the "paint-root" in Virginia, determines whether they shall live or die. In plants, the down on the fruit and the colour of the flesh are considered by botanists as characters of the most trifling importance: yet we hear from an excellent horticulturist, Downing, that in the United States, smooth-skinned fruits suffer far more from a beetle, a Curculio, than those with down; that purple plums suffer far more from a certain disease than yellow plums; whereas another disease attacks yellow-fleshed peaches far more than those with other coloured flesh. If, with all the aids of art, these slight differences make a great difference in cultivating the several varieties, assuredly, in a state of nature, where the trees would have to struggle with other trees, and with a host of enemies, such differences would effectually settle which variety, whether a smooth or downy, a yellow or purple fleshed fruit, should succeed.

In looking at many small points of difference between species, which, as far as our ignorance permits us to judge, seem quite unimportant, we must not forget that climate, food, &c., have no doubt produced some direct effect. It is also necessary to bear in mind that, owing to the law of correlation, when one part varies, and the variations are accumulated through natural selection, other modifications, often of the most unexpected nature, will ensue.

As we see that those variations which, under domestication, appear at any particular period of life, tend to reappear in the offspring at the same period;—for instance, in the shape, size, and flavour of the seeds of the many varieties of our culinary and agricultural plants; in the caterpillar and cocoon stages of the varieties of the silk-worm; in the eggs of poultry, and in the colour of the down of their chickens; in the horns of our sheep and cattle when nearly adult;—so in a state of nature natural selection will be enabled to act on and modify organic beings at any age, by the accumulation of variations profitable at that age, and by their inheritance at a corresponding age. If it profit a plant to have its seeds more and more widely disseminated by the wind, I can see no greater difficulty in this being effected through natural selection, than in the cotton-planter increasing and improving by selection the down in the pods on his cotton-trees. Natural selection may modify and adapt the larva of an insect to a score of contingencies, wholly different from those which concern the mature insect; and these modifications may effect, through correlation, the structure of the adult. So, conversely, modifications in the adult may affect the structure of the larva; but in all cases natural selection will ensure that they shall not be injurious: for if they were so, the species would become extinct.

Natural selection will modify the structure of the young in relation to the parent, and of the parent in relation to the young. In social animals it will adapt the structure of each individual for the benefit of the whole community; if the community profits by the selected change. What natural selection cannot do, is to modify the structure of one species, without giving it any advantage, for the good of another species; and though statements to this effect may be found in works of natural history, I cannot find one case which will bear investigation. A structure used only once in an animal's life, if of high importance to it, might be modified to any extent by natural selection; for instance, the great jaws possessed by certain insects, used exclusively for opening the cocoon—or the hard tip to the beak of unhatched birds, used for breaking the egg. It has been asserted, that of the best short-beaked tumbler-pigeons a greater number perish in the egg than are able to get out of it; so that fanciers assist in the act of hatching. Now if nature had to make the beak of a full-grown pigeon very short for the bird's own advantage, the process of modification would be very slow, and there would be simultaneously the most rigorous selection of all the young birds within the egg, which had the most powerful and hardest beaks, for all with weak beaks would inevitably perish; or, more delicate and more easily broken shells might be selected, the thickness of the shell being known to vary like every other structure.

It may be well here to remark that with all beings there must be much fortuitous destruction, which can have little or no influence on the course of natural selection. For instance a vast number of eggs or seeds are annually devoured, and these could be modified through natural selection only if they varied in some manner which protected them from their enemies. Yet many of these eggs or seeds would perhaps, if not destroyed, have yielded individuals better adapted to their conditions of life than any of those which happened to survive. So again a vast number of mature animals and plants, whether or not they be the best adapted to their conditions, must be annually destroyed by accidental causes, which would not be in the least degree mitigated by certain changes of structure or constitution which would in other ways be beneficial to the species. But let the destruction of the adults be ever so heavy, if the number which can exist in any district be not wholly kept down by such causes,—or again let the destruction of eggs or seeds be so great that only a hundredth or a thousandth part are developed,—yet of those which do survive, the best adapted individuals, supposing that there is any variability in a favourable direction, will tend to propagate their kind in larger numbers than the less well adapted. If the numbers be wholly kept down by the causes just indicated, as will often have been the case, natural selection will be powerless in certain beneficial directions; but this is no valid objection to its efficiency at other times and in other ways; for we are far from having any reason to suppose that many species ever undergo modification and improvement at the same time in the same area.

Sexual Selection

Inasmuch as peculiarities often appear under domestication in one sex and become hereditarily attached to that sex, so no doubt it will be under nature. Thus it is rendered possible for the two sexes to be modified

through natural selection in relation to different habits of life, as is sometimes the case; or for one sex to be modified in relation to the other sex, as
commonly occurs. This leads me to say a few words on what I have called
Sexual Selection. This form of selection depends, not on a struggle for existence in relation to other organic beings or to external conditions, but on
a struggle between the individuals of one sex, generally the males, for the
possession of the other sex. The result is not death to the unsuccessful
competitor, but few or no offspring. Sexual selection is, therefore, less rigorous than natural selection. Generally, the most vigorous males, those
which are best fitted for their places in nature, will leave most progeny.
But in many cases, victory depends not so much on general vigor, as on
having special weapons, confined to the male sex. A hornless stag or spur-
less cock would have a poor chance of leaving numerous offspring. Sexual
selection, by always allowing the victor to breed, might surely give indomitable courage, length to the spur, and strength to the wing to strike
in the spurred leg, in nearly the same manner as does the brutal cock-
fighter by the careful selection of his best cocks. How low in the scale of
nature the law of battle descends, I know not; male alligators have been
described as fighting, bellowing, and whirling round, like Indians in a
war-dance, for the possession of the females; male salmons have been observed fighting all day long; male stag-beetles sometimes bear wounds
from the huge mandibles of other males; the males of certain hymenopterous insects have been frequently seen by that inimitable observer M.
Fabre, fighting for a particular female who sits by, an apparently unconcerned beholder of the struggle, and then retires with the conqueror. The
war is, perhaps, severest between the males of polygamous animals, and
these seem oftenest provided with special weapons. The males of carnivorous animals are already well armed; though to them and to others,
special means of defence may be given through means of sexual selection,
as the mane of the lion, and the hooked jaw to the male salmon; for the
shield may be as important for victory, as the sword or spear.

Amongst birds, the contest is often of a more peaceful character. All
those who have attended to the subject, believe that there is the severest
rivalry between the males of many species to attract, by singing, the females. The rock-thrush of Guiana, birds of paradise, and some others,
congregate; and successive males display with the most elaborate care,
and show off in the best manner, their gorgeous plumage; they likewise
perform strange antics before the females, which, standing by as specta-
tors, at last choose the most attractive partner. Those who have closely
attended to birds in confinement well know that they often take individual preferences and dislikes: thus Sir R. Heron has described how a pied
peacock was eminently attractive to all his hen birds. I cannot here enter
on the necessary details; but if man can in a short time give beauty and
an elegant carriage to his bantams, according to his standard of beauty, I
can see no good reason to doubt that female birds, by selecting, during
thousands of generations, the most melodious or beautiful males, according to their standard of beauty, might produce a marked effect. Some

well-known laws, with respect to the plumage of male and female birds, in comparison with the plumage of the young, can partly be explained through the action of sexual selection on variations occurring at different ages, and transmitted to the males alone or to both sexes at corresponding ages; but I have not space here to enter on this subject.

Thus it is, as I believe, that when the males and females of any animal have the same general habits of life, but differ in structure, colour, or ornament, such differences have been mainly caused by sexual selection: that is, by individual males having had, in successive generations, some slight advantage over other males, in their weapons, means of defence, or charms, which they have transmitted to their male offspring alone. Yet, I would not wish to attribute all sexual differences to this agency: for we see in our domestic animals peculiarities arising and becoming attached to the male sex, which apparently have not been augmented through selection by man. The tuft of hair on the breast of the wild turkey-cock cannot be of any use, and it is doubtful whether it can be ornamental in the eyes of the female bird;—indeed, had the tuft appeared under domestication, it would have been called a monstrosity.

Illustrations of the Action of Natural Selection, or the Survival of the Fittest

In order to make it clear how, as I believe, natural selection acts, I must beg permission to give one or two imaginary illustrations. Let us take the case of a wolf, which preys on various animals, securing some by craft, some by strength, and some by fleetness; and let us suppose that the fleetest prey, a deer for instance, had from any change in the country increased in numbers, or that other prey had decreased in numbers, during that season of the year when the wolf was hardest pressed for food. Under such circumstances the swiftest and slimmest wolves would have the best chance of surviving and so be preserved or selected,—provided always that they retained strength to master their prey at this or some other period of the year, when they were compelled to prey on other animals. I can see no more reason to doubt that this would be the result, than that man should be able to improve the fleetness of his greyhounds by careful and methodical selection, or by that kind of unconscious selection which follows from each man trying to keep the best dogs without any thought of modifying the breed. I may add, that, according to Mr. Pierce, there are two varieties of the wolf inhabiting the Catskill Mountains, in the United States, one with a light greyhound-like form, which pursues deer, and the other more bulky, with shorter legs, which more frequently attacks the shepherd's flocks.

It should be observed that, in the above illustration, I speak of the slimmest individual wolves, and not of any single strongly-marked variation having been preserved. In former editions of this work I sometimes spoke as if this latter alternative had frequently occurred. I saw the great importance of individual differences, and this led me fully to discuss the results of unconscious selection by man, which depends on the preservation of all the more or less valuable individuals, and on the destruction of the worst. I saw, also, that the preservation in a state of nature of any occasional deviation of structure, such as a monstrosity, would be a rare event; and that, if at first preserved, it would generally be lost by subsequent intercrossing with ordinary individuals. Nevertheless, until reading an able and valuable article in the 'North British Review' (1867), I did not appreciate how rarely single variations, whether slight or strongly-marked, could be perpetuated. The author takes the case of a pair of animals, producing during their lifetime two hundred offspring, of which, from various causes of destruction, only two on an average survive to procreate their kind. This is rather an extreme estimate for most of the higher animals, but by no means so for many of the lower organisms. He then shows that if a single individual were born, which varied in some manner, giving it twice as good a chance of life as that of the other individuals, yet the chances would be strongly against its survival. Supposing it to survive and to breed, and that half its young inherited the favourable variation; still, as the Reviewer goes on to show, the young would have only a slightly better chance of surviving and breeding; and this chance would go on decreasing in the succeeding generations. The justice of these remarks cannot, I think, be disputed. If, for instance, a bird of some kind could procure its food more easily by having its beak curved, and if one were born with its beak strongly curved, and which consequently flourished, nevertheless there would be a very poor chance of this one individual perpetuating its kind to the exclusion of the common form; but there can hardly be a doubt, judging by what we see taking place under domestication, that this result would follow from the preservation during many generations of a large number of individuals with more or less strongly curved beaks, and from the destruction of a still larger number with the straightest beaks.

It should not, however, be overlooked that certain rather strongly marked variations, which no one would rank as mere individual differences, frequently recur owing to a similar organisation being similarly acted on—of which fact numerous instances could be given with our domestic productions. In such cases, if the varying individual did not actually transmit to its offspring its newly-acquired character, it would undoubtedly transmit to them, as long as the existing conditions remained the same, a still stronger tendency to vary in the same manner. There can also be little doubt that the tendency to vary in the same manner has often been so strong that all the individuals of the same species have been similarly modified without the aid of any form of selection. Or only a third, fifth, or tenth part of the individuals may have been thus affected, of which fact several instances could be given. Thus Graba estimates that about one-fifth of the guillemots in the Faroe Islands consist of a variety so well marked, that it was formerly ranked as a distinct species under the name of Uria lacrymans. In cases of this kind, if the variation were of a beneficial nature, the original form would soon be supplanted by the modified form, through the survival of the fittest.

To the effects of intercrossing in eliminating variations of all kinds, I shall have to recur; but it may be here remarked that most animals and plants keep to their proper homes, and do not needlessly wander about; we see this even with migratory birds, which almost always return to the same spot. Consequently each newly-formed variety would generally be at first local, as seems to be the common rule with varieties in a state of nature; so that similarly modified individuals would soon exist in a small body together, and would often breed together. If the new variety were successful in its battle for life, it would slowly spread from a central district, competing with and conquering the unchanged individuals on the margins of an ever-increasing circle.

It may be worth while to give another and more complex illustration of the action of natural selection. Certain plants excrete sweet juice, apparently for the sake of eliminating something injurious from the sap: this is effected, for instance, by glands at the base of the stipules in some Leguminosæ, and at the backs of the leaves of the common laurel. This juice, though small in quantity, is greedily sought by insects; but their visits do not in any way benefit the plant. Now, let us suppose that the juice or nectar was excreted from the inside of the flowers of a certain number of plants of any species. Insects in seeking the nectar would get dusted with pollen, and would often transport it from one flower to another. The flowers of two distinct individuals of the same species would thus get crossed; and the act of crossing, as can be fully proved, gives rise to vigorous seedlings which consequently would have the best chance of flourishing and surviving. The plants which produced flowers with the largest glands or nectaries, excreting most nectar, would oftenest be visited by insects, and would oftenest be crossed; and so in the long-run would gain the upper hand and form a local variety. The flowers, also, which had their stamens and pistils placed, in relation to the size and habits of the particular insects which visited them, so as to favour in any degree the transportal of the pollen, would likewise be favoured. We might have taken the case of insects visiting flowers for the sake of collecting pollen instead of nectar; and as pollen is formed for the sole purpose of fertilisation, its destruction appears to be a simple loss to the plant; yet if a little pollen were carried, at first occasionally and then habitually, by the pollen-devouring insects from flower to flower, and a cross thus effected, although nine-tenths of the pollen were destroyed it might still be a great gain to the plant to be thus robbed; and the individuals which produced more and more pollen, and had larger anthers, would be selected.

When our plant, by the above process long continued, had been rendered highly attractive to insects, they would, unintentionally on their part, regularly carry pollen from flower to flower; and that they do this effectually, I could easily show by many striking facts. I will give only one, as likewise illustrating one step in the separation of the sexes of plants. Some holly-trees bear only male flowers, which have four stamens producing a rather small quantity of pollen, and a rudimentary pistil; other holly-trees bear only female flowers; these have a full-sized pistil, and four stamens with shrivelled anthers, in which not a grain of pollen can be detected. Having found a female tree exactly sixty yards from a male tree, I put the stigmas of twenty flowers, taken from different branches, under the microscope, and on all, without exception, there were a few pollen-grains, and on some a profusion. As the wind had set for several days from the female to the male tree, the pollen could not thus have been carried. The weather had been cold and boisterous, and therefore not favourable to bees, nevertheless every female flower which I examined had been effectually fertilised by the bees, which had flown from tree to tree in search of nectar. But to return to our imaginary case: as soon as the plant had been rendered so highly attractive to insects that pollen was regularly carried from flower to flower, another process might commence. No naturalist doubts the advantage of what has been called the "physiological division of labour;" hence we may believe that it would be advantageous to a plant to produce stamens alone in one flower or on one whole plant, and pistils alone in another flower or on another plant. In plants under culture and placed under new conditions of life, sometimes the male organs and sometimes the female organs become more or less impotent; now if we suppose this to occur in ever so slight a degree under nature, then, as pollen is already carried regularly from flower to flower, and as a more complete separation of the sexes of our plant would be advantageous on the principle of the division of labour, individuals with this tendency more and more increased, would be continually favoured or selected, until at last a complete separation of the sexes might be effected. It would take up too much space to show the various steps, through dimorphism and other means, by which the separation of the sexes in plants of various kinds is apparently now in progress; but I may add that some of the species of holly in North America, are, according to Asa Gray, in an exactly intermediate condition, or, as he expresses it, are more or less diœciously polygamous.

Let us now turn to the nectar-feeding insects; we may suppose the plant, of which we have been slowly increasing the nectar by continued selection, to be a common plant; and that certain insects depended in main part on its nectar for food. I could give many facts showing how anxious bees are to save time: for instance, their habit of cutting holes and sucking the nectar at the bases of certain flowers, which, with a very little more trouble, they can enter by the mouth. Bearing such facts in mind, it may be believed that under certain circumstances individual differences in the curvature or length of the proboscis, &c., too slight to be appreciated by us, might profit a bee or other insect, so that certain individuals would be able to obtain their food more quickly than others; and thus the communities to which they belonged would flourish and throw off many swarms inheriting the same peculiarities. The tubes of the corolla of the common red and incarnate clovers (Trifolium pratense and incarnatum) do not on a hasty glance appear to differ in length; yet the hive-bee can easily suck the nectar out of the incarnate clover, but not out of the common red clover, which is visited by humble-bees alone; so that whole fields of red clover offer in vain an abundant supply of precious nectar to the hive-bee. That this nectar is much liked by the hive-bee is certain; for I have repeatedly seen, but only in the autumn, many hive-bees sucking the flowers through holes bitten in the base of the tube by humble-bees. The difference in the length of the corolla in the two kinds of clover, which determines the visits of the hive-bee, must be very trifling; for I have been assured that when red clover has been mown, the flowers of the second crop are somewhat smaller, and that these are visited by many hive-bees. I do not know whether this statement is accurate; nor whether another published statement can be trusted, namely, that the Ligurian bee which is generally considered a mere variety of the common hive-bee, and which freely crosses with it, is able to reach and suck the nectar of the red clover. Thus, in a country where this kind of clover abounded, it might be a great advantage to the hive-bee to have a slightly longer or differently constructed proboscis. On the other hand, as the fertility of this clover absolutely depends on bees visiting the flowers, if humble-bees were to become rare in any country, it might be a great advantage to the plant to have a shorter or more deeply divided corolla, so that the hive-bees should be enabled to suck its flowers. Thus I can understand how a flower and a bee might slowly become, either simultaneously or one after the other, modified and adapted to each other in the most perfect manner, by the continued preservation of all the individuals which presented slight deviations of structure mutually favourable to each other.

I am well aware that this doctrine of natural selection, exemplified in the above imaginary instances, is open to the same objections which were first urged against Sir Charles Lyell's noble views on "the modern changes of the earth, as illustrative of geology;" but we now seldom hear the agencies which we see still at work, spoken of as trifling or insignificant, when used in explaining the excavation of the deepest valleys or the formation of long lines of inland cliffs. Natural selection acts only by the preservation and accumulation of small inherited modifications, each profitable to the preserved being; and as modern geology has almost banished such views as the excavation of a great valley by a single diluvial wave, so will natural selection banish the belief of the continued creation of new organic beings, or of any great and sudden modification in their structure.

On the Intercrossing of Individuals

I must here introduce a short digression. In the case of animals and plants with separated sexes, it is of course obvious that two individuals must always (with the exception of the curious and not well-understood cases of parthenogenesis) unite for each birth; but in the case of hermaphrodites this is far from obvious. Nevertheless there is reason to believe that with all hermaphrodites two individuals, either occasionally or habitually, concur for the reproduction of their kind. This view was long ago doubtfully suggested by Sprengel, Knight and Kölreuter. We shall presently see its importance; but I must here treat the subject with extreme brevity, though I have the materials prepared for an ample discussion. All vertebrate animals, all insects, and some other large groups of animals, pair for each birth. Modern research has much diminished the number of supposed hermaphrodites, and of real hermaphrodites a large number pair; that is, two individuals regularly unite for reproduction, which is all that concerns us. But still there are many hermaphrodite animals which certainly do not habitually pair, and a vast majority of plants are hermaphrodites. What reason, it may be asked, is there for supposing in these cases that two individuals ever concur in reproduction? As it is impossible here to enter on details, I must trust to some general considerations alone.

In the first place, I have collected so large a body of facts, and made so many experiments, showing, in accordance with the almost universal belief of breeders, that with animals and plants a cross between different varieties, or between individuals of the same variety but of another strain, gives vigour and fertility to the offspring; and on the other hand, that *close* interbreeding diminishes vigour and fertility; that these facts alone incline me to believe that it is a general law of nature that no organic being fertilises itself for a perpetuity of generations; but that a cross with another individual is occasionally—perhaps at long intervals of time—indispensable.

On the belief that this is a law of nature, we can, I think, understand several large classes of facts, such as the following, which on any other view are inexplicable. Every hybridizer knows how unfavourable exposure to wet is to the fertilisation of a flower, yet what a multitude of flowers have their anthers and stigmas fully exposed to the weather! If an occasional cross be indispensable, notwithstanding that the plant's own anthers and pistil stand so near each other as almost to insure self-fertilisation, the fullest freedom for the entrance of pollen from another individual will explain the above state of exposure of the organs. Many flowers, on the other hand, have their organs of fructification closely enclosed, as in the great papilionaceous or pea-family; but these almost invariably present beautiful and curious adaptations in relation to the visits of insects. So necessary are the visits of bees to many papilionaceous flowers, that their fertility is greatly diminished if these visits be prevented. Now, it is scarcely possible for insects to fly from flower and flower, and not to carry pollen from one to the other, to the great good of the plant. Insects act like a camel-hair pencil, and it is sufficient, to ensure fertilisation, just to touch with the same brush the anthers of one flower and then the stigma of another; but it must not be supposed that bees would thus produce a multitude of hybrids between distinct species; for if a plant's own pollen and that from another species are placed on the same stigma, the former is so prepotent that it invariably and completely destroys, as has been shown by Gärtner, the influence of the foreign pollen.

When the stamens of a flower suddenly spring towards the pistil, or slowly move one after the other towards it, the contrivance seems adapted solely to ensure self-fertilisation; and no doubt it is useful for this end: but the agency of insects is often required to cause the stamens to spring forward, as Kölreuter has shown to be the case with the barberry; and in this very genus, which seems to have a special contrivance for self-fertilisation, it is well known that, if closely allied forms or varieties are planted near each other, it is hardly possible to raise pure seedlings, so largely do they naturally cross. In numerous other cases, far from self-fertilisation being favoured, there are special contrivances which effectually prevent the stigma receiving pollen from its own flower, as I could show from the works of Sprengel and others, as well as from my own observations: for instance, in Lobelia fulgens, there is a real beautiful and elaborate contrivance by which all the infinitely numerous pollen-granules are swept out of the conjoined anthers of each flower, before the stigma of that individual flower is ready to receive them; and as this flower is never visited, at least in my garden, by insects, it never sets a seed, though by placing pollen from one flower on the stigma of another, I raise plenty of seedlings. Another species of Lobelia which is visited by bees, seeds freely in my garden. In very many other cases, though there is no special mechanical contrivance to prevent the stigma receiving pollen from the same flower, yet, as Sprengel, and more recently Hildebrand, and others, have shown, and as I can confirm, either the anthers burst before the stigma is ready for fertilisation, or the stigma is ready before the pollen of that flower is ready, so that these so-named dichogamous plants have in fact separated sexes, and must habitually be crossed. So it is with the reciprocally dimorphic and trimorphic plants previously alluded to. How strange are these facts! How strange that the pollen and stigmatic surface of the same flower, though placed so close together, as if for the very purpose of self-fertilisation, should be in so many cases mutually useless to each other! How simply are these facts explained on the view of an occasional cross with a distinct individual being advantageous or indispensable!

If several varieties of the cabbage, radish, onion, and of some other plants, be allowed to seed near each other, a large majority of the seedlings thus raised turn out, as I have found, mongrels: for instance, I raised 233 seedling cabbages from some plants of different varieties growing near each other, and of these only 78 were true to their kind, and some even of these were not perfectly true. Yet the pistil of each cabbage-flower is surrounded not only by its own six stamens but by those of the many other flowers on the same plant; and the pollen of each flower readily gets on its own stigma without insect agency; for I have found that plants carefully protected from insects produce the full number of pods. How, then, comes it that such a vast number of the seedlings are mongrelized? It must arise from the pollen of a distinct *variety* having a prepotent effect over the flower's own pollen; and that this is part of the general law of good being derived from the intercrossing of distinct individuals of the same species. When distinct *species* are crossed the case is reversed, for a plant's own pollen is almost always prepotent over foreign pollen; but to this subject we shall return in a future chapter.

In the case of a large tree covered with innumerable flowers, it may be objected that pollen could seldom be carried from tree to tree, and at most only from flower to flower on the same tree; and flowers on the same tree can be considered as distinct individuals only in a limited sense. I believe this objection to be valid, but that nature has largely provided against it by giving to trees a strong tendency to bear flowers with separated sexes. When the sexes are separated, although the male and female flowers may be produced on the same tree, pollen must be regularly carried from flower to flower; and this will give a better chance of pollen being occasionally carried from tree to tree. That trees belonging to all Orders have their sexes more often separated than other plants, I find to be the case in this country; and at my request Dr. Hooker tabulated the trees of New Zealand, and Dr. Asa Gray those of the United States, and the result was as I anticipated. On the other hand, Dr. Hooker informs me that the rule does not hold good in Australia: but if most of the Australian trees are dichogamous, the same result would follow as if they bore flowers with separated sexes. I have made these few remarks on trees simply to call attention to the subject.

Turning for a brief space to animals: various terrestrial species are hermaphrodites, such as the land-mollusca and earth-worms; but these all pair. As yet I have not found a single terrestrial animal which can fertilise itself. This remarkable fact, which offers so strong a contrast with terrestrial plants, is intelligible on the view of an occasional cross being indispensable; for owing to the nature of the fertilising element there are no means, analogous to the action of insects and of the wind with plants, by which an occasional cross could be effected with terrestrial animals without the concurrence of two individuals. Of aquatic animals, there are many self-fertilising hermaphrodites; but here the currents of water offer an obvious means for an occasional cross. As in the case of flowers, I have as yet failed, after consultation with one of the highest authorities, namely, Professor Huxley, to discover a single hermaphrodite animal with the organs of reproduction so perfectly enclosed that access from without, and the occasional influence of a distinct individual, can be shown to be physically impossible. Cirripedes long appeared to me to present, under this point of view, a case of great difficulty; but I have been enabled, by a fortunate chance, to prove that two individuals, though both are self-fertilising hermaphrodites, do sometimes cross.

It must have struck most naturalists as a strange anomaly that, both with animals and plants, some species of the same family and even of the same genus, though agreeing closely with each other in their whole organisation, are hermaphrodites, and some unisexual. But if, in fact, all hermaphrodites do occasionally intercross, the difference between them and unisexual species is, as far as function is concerned, very small.

From these several considerations and from the many special facts which I have collected, but which I am unable here to give, it appears that with animals and plants an occasional intercross between distinct individuals is a very general, if not universal, law of nature.

Circumstances favourable for the production of new forms through Natural Selection

This is an extremely intricate subject. A great amount of variability, under which term individual differences are always included, will evidently be favourable. A large number of individuals, by giving a better chance within any given period for the appearance of profitable variations, will compensate for a lesser amount of variability in each individual, and is, I believe, a highly important element of success. Though Nature grants long periods of time for the work of natural selection, she does not grant an indefinite period; for as all organic beings are striving to seize on each place in the economy of nature, if any one species does not become modified and improved in a corresponding degree with its competitors, it will be exterminated. Unless favourable variations be inherited by some at least of the offspring, nothing can be effected by natural selection. The tendency to reversion may often check or prevent the work; but as this tendency has not prevented man from forming by selection numerous domestic races, why should it prevail against natural selection?

In the case of methodical selection, a breeder selects for some definite object, and if the individuals be allowed freely to intercross, his work will completely fail. But when many men, without intending to alter the breed, have a nearly common standard of perfection, and all try to procure and breed from the best animals, improvement surely but slowly follows from this unconscious process of selection, notwithstanding that there is no separation of selected individuals. Thus it will be under nature; for within a confined area, with some place in the natural polity not perfectly occupied, all the individuals varying in the right direction, though in different degrees, will tend to be preserved. But if the area be large, its several districts will almost certainly present different conditions of life; and then, if the same species undergoes modification in different districts, the newly-formed varieties will intercross on the confines of each. But we shall see in the sixth chapter that intermediate varieties, inhabiting intermediate districts, will in the long run generally be supplanted by one of the adjoining varieties. Intercrossing will chiefly affect those animals which unite for each birth and wander much, and which do not breed at a very quick rate. Hence with animals of this nature, for instance, birds, varieties will generally be confined to separated countries; and this I find to be the case. With hermaphrodite organisms which cross only occasionally, and likewise with animals which unite for each birth, but which wander little and can increase at a rapid rate, a new and improved variety might be quickly formed on any one spot, and might there maintain itself in a body and afterwards spread, so that the individuals of the new variety would chiefly cross together. On this principle, nurserymen always prefer saving seed from a large body of plants, as the chance of intercrossing is thus lessened.

Even with animals which unite for each birth, and which do not propagate rapidly, we must not assume that free intercrossing would always eliminate the effects of natural selection; for I can bring forward a considerable body of facts showing that within the same area, two varieties of the same animal may long remain distinct, from haunting different stations, from breeding at slightly different seasons, or from the individuals of each variety preferring to pair together.

Intercrossing plays a very important part in nature by keeping the individuals of the same species, or of the same variety, true and uniform in character. It will obviously thus act far more efficiently with those animals which unite for each birth; but, as already stated, we have reason to believe that occasional intercrosses take place with all animals and plants. Even if these take place only at long intervals of time, the young thus produced will gain so much in vigour and fertility over the offspring from long-continued self-fertilisation, that they will have a better chance of surviving and propagating their kind; and thus in the long run the influence of crosses, even at rare intervals, will be great. With respect to organic beings extremely low in the scale, which do not propagate sexually, nor conjugate, and which cannot possibly intercross, uniformity of character can be retained by them under the same conditions of life, only through the principle of inheritance, and through natural selection which will destroy any individuals departing from the proper type. If the conditions of life change and the form undergoes modification, uniformity of character can be given to the modified offspring, solely by natural selection preserving similar favourable variations.

Isolation, also, is an important element in the modification of species through natural selection. In a confined or isolated area, if not very large, the organic and inorganic conditions of life will generally be almost uniform; so that natural selection will tend to modify all the varying individuals of the same species in the same manner. Intercrossing with the inhabitants of the surrounding districts will, also, be thus prevented. Moritz Wagner has lately published an interesting essay on this subject, and has shown that the service rendered by isolation in preventing crosses between newly-formed varieties is probably greater even than I supposed. But from reasons already assigned I can by no means agree with this naturalist, that migration and isolation are necessary elements for the formation of new species. The importance of isolation is likewise great in preventing, after any physical change in the conditions, such as of climate, elevation of the land, &c., the immigration of better adapted organisms; and thus new places in the natural economy of the district will be left open to be filled up by the modification of the old inhabitants. Lastly, isolation will give time for a new variety to be improved at a slow rate; and this may sometimes be of much importance. If, however, an isolated area be very small, either from being surrounded by barriers, or from having very peculiar physical conditions, the total number of the inhabitants will be small; and this will retard the production of new species, through natural selection by decreasing the chances of favourable variations arising.

The mere lapse of time by itself does nothing, either for or against natural selection. I state this because it has been erroneously asserted that the element of time has been assumed by me to play an all-important part in modifying species, as if all the forms of life were necessarily undergoing change through some innate law. Lapse of time is only so far important, and its importance in this respect is great, that it gives a better chance of beneficial variations arising and of their being selected, accumulated, and fixed. It likewise tends to increase the direct action of the physical conditions of life, in relation to the constitution of each organism.

If we turn to nature to test the truth of these remarks, and look at any small isolated area, such as an oceanic island, although the number of species inhabiting it is small, as we shall see in our chapter on Geographical Distribution; yet of these species a very large proportion are endemic, —that is, have been produced there and nowhere else in the world. Hence an oceanic island at first sight seems to have been highly favourable for the production of new species. But we may thus deceive ourselves, for to ascertain whether a small isolated area, or a large open area like a continent, has been most favourable for the production of new organic forms, we ought to make the comparison within equal times; and this we are incapable of doing.

Although isolation is of great importance in the production of new species, on the whole I am inclined to believe that largeness of area is still more important, especially for the production of species which shall prove capable of enduring for a long period, and of spreading widely. Throughout a great and open area, not only will there be a better chance of favourable variations, arising from the large number of individuals of the same species there supported, but the conditions of life are much more complex from the large number of already existing species; and if some of these many species become modified and improved, others will have to be improved in a corresponding degree, or they will be exterminated. Each new form, also, as soon as it has been much improved, will be able to spread over the open and continuous area, and will thus come into competition with many other forms. Moreover, great areas, though now continuous, will often, owing to former oscillations of level, have existed in a broken condition; so that the good effects of isolation will generally, to a certain extent, have concurred. Finally, I conclude that, although small isolated areas have been in some respects highly favourable for the production of new species, yet that the course of modification will generally have been more rapid on large areas; and what is more important, that the new forms produced on large areas, which already have been victorious over many competitors, will be those that will spread most widely, and will give rise to the greatest number of new varieties and species. They will thus play a more important part in the changing history of the organic world.

In accordance with this view, we can, perhaps, understand some facts which will be again alluded to in our chapter on Geographical Distribution; for instance, the fact of the productions of the smaller continent of Australia now yielding before those of the larger Europæo-Asiatic area. Thus, also, it is that continental productions have everywhere become so largely naturalised on islands. On a small island, the race for life will have been less severe, and there will have been less modification and less extermination. Hence, we can understand how it is that the flora of Madeira, according to Oswald Heer, resembles to a certain extent the extinct tertiary flora of Europe. All fresh-water basins, taken together, make a small area compared with that of the sea or of the land. Consequently, the competition between fresh-water productions will have been less severe than elsewhere; new forms will have been then more slowly produced, and old forms more slowly exterminated. And it is in fresh-water basins that we find seven genera of Ganoid fishes, remnants of a once preponderant order: and in fresh water we find some of the most anomalous forms now known in the world as the Ornithorhynchus and Lepidosiren which, like fossils, connect to a certain extent orders at present widely sundered in the natural scale. These anomalous forms may be called living fossils; they have endured to the present day, from having inhabited a confined area, and from having been exposed to less varied, and therefore less severe, competition.

To sum up, as far as the extreme intricacy of the subject permits, the circumstances favourable and unfavourable for the production of new species through natural selection. I conclude that for terrestrial productions a large continental area, which has undergone many oscillations of level, will have been the most favourable for the production of many new forms of life, fitted to endure for a long time and to spread widely. Whilst the area existed as a continent, the inhabitants will have been numerous in individuals and kinds, and will have been subjected to severe competition. When converted by subsidence into large separate islands, there will still have existed many individuals of the same species on each island: intercrossing on the confines of the range of each new species will have been checked: after physical changes of any kind, immigration will have been prevented, so that new places in the polity of each island will have had to be filled up by the modification of the old inhabitants; and time will have been allowed for the varieties in each to become well modified and perfected. When, by renewed elevation, the islands were reconverted into a continental area, there will again have been very severe competition: the most favoured or improved varieties will have been enabled to spread: there will have been much extinction of the less improved forms, and the relative proportional numbers of the various inhabitants of the reunited continent will again have been changed; and again there will have been a fair field for natural selection to improve still further the inhabitants, and thus to produce new species.

That natural selection generally acts with extreme slowness I fully admit. It can act only when there are places in the natural polity of a district which can be better occupied by the modification of some of its existing inhabitants. The occurrence of such places will often depend on physical changes, which generally take place very slowly, and on the immigration of better adapted forms being prevented. As some few of the old inhabitants become modified, the mutual relations of others will often be disturbed; and this will create new places, ready to be filled up by better adapted forms, but all this will take place very slowly. Although all the individuals of the same species differ in some slight degree from each other, it would often be long before differences of the right nature in various parts of the organisation might occur. The result would often be greatly retarded by free intercrossing. Many will exclaim that these several causes are amply sufficient to neutralise the power of natural selection. I do not believe so. But I do believe that natural selection will generally act very slowly, only at long intervals of time, and only on a few of the inhabitants of the same region. I further believe that these slow, intermittent results accord well with what geology tells us of the rate and manner at which the inhabitants of the world have changed.

Slow though the process of selection may be, if feeble man can do much by artificial selection, I can see no limit to the amount of change, to the beauty and complexity of the coadaptations between all organic beings, one with another and with their physical conditions of life, which may have been effected in the long course of time through nature's power of selection, that is by the survival of the fittest.

Extinction caused by Natural Selection

This subject will be more fully discussed in our chapter on Geology; but it must here be alluded to from being intimately connected with natural selection. Natural selection acts solely through the preservation of variations in some way advantageous, which consequently endure. Owing to the high geometrical rate of increase of all organic beings, each area is already fully stocked with inhabitants; and it follows from this, that as the favoured forms increase in number, so, generally, will the less favoured decrease and become rare. Rarity, as geology tells us, is the precursor to extinction. We can see that any form which is represented by few individuals will run a good chance of utter extinction, during great fluctuations in the nature of the seasons, or from a temporary increase in the number of its enemies. But we may go further than this; for, as new forms are produced, unless we admit that specific forms can go on indefinitely increasing in number, many old forms must become extinct. That the number of specific forms has not indefinitely increased, geology plainly tells us; and we shall presently attempt to show why it is that the number of species throughout the world has not become immeasurably great.

We have seen that the species which are most numerous in individuals have the best chance of producing favourable variations within any given period. We have evidence of this, in the facts stated in the second chapter showing that it is the common and diffused or dominant species which offer the greatest number of recorded varieties. Hence, rare species will be less quickly modified or improved within any given period; they will consequently be beaten in the race for life by the modified and improved descendants of the commoner species.

From these several considerations I think it inevitably follows, that as new species in the course of time are formed through natural selection, others will become rarer and rarer, and finally extinct. The forms which stand in closest competition with those undergoing modification and improvement will naturally suffer most. And we have seen in the chapter on the Struggle for Existence that it is the most closely-allied forms,—varieties of the same species, and species of the same genus or of related genera,—which, from having nearly the same structure, constitution, and habits, generally come into the severest competition with each other; consequently, each new variety or species, during the progress of its formation, will generally press hardest on its nearest kindred, and tend to exterminate them. We see the same process of extermination amongst our domesticated productions, through the selection of improved forms by man. Many curious instances could be given showing how quickly new breeds of cattle, sheep, and other animals, and varieties of flowers, take the place of older and inferior kinds. In Yorkshire, it is historically known that the ancient black cattle were displaced by the long-horns, and that these "were swept away by the short-horns" (I quote the words of an agricultural writer) "as if by some murderous pestilence."

Divergence of Character

The principle, which I have designated by this term, is of high importance, and explains, as I believe, several important facts. In the first place, varieties, even strongly-marked ones, though having somewhat of the character of species—as is shown by the hopeless doubts in many cases how to rank them—yet certainly differ far less from each other than do good and distinct species. Nevertheless, according to my view, varieties are species in the process of formation, or are, as I have called them, incipient species. How, then, does the lesser difference between varieties become augmented into the greater difference between species? That this does habitually happen, we must infer from most of the innumerable species throughout nature presenting well-marked differences; whereas varieties, the supposed prototypes and parents of future well-marked species, present slight and ill-defined differences. Mere chance, as we may call it, might cause one variety to differ in some character from its parents, and the offspring of this variety again to differ from its parent in the very same character and in a greater degree; but this alone would never account for so habitual and large a degree of difference as that between the species of the same genus.

As has always been my practice, I have sought light on this head from our domestic productions. We shall here find something analogous. It will be admitted that the production of races so different as short-horn and Hereford cattle, race and cart horses, the several breeds of pigeons, &c., could never have been effected by the mere chance accumulation of similar variations during many successive generations. In practice, a fancier is, for instance, struck by a pigeon having a slightly shorter beak; another fancier is struck by a pigeon having a rather longer beak; and on the acknowledged principle that "fanciers do not and will not admire a medium standard, but like extremes," they both go on (as has actually occurred with the sub-breeds of the tumbler-pigeon) choosing and breeding from birds with longer and longer beaks, or with shorter and shorter beaks. Again, we may suppose that at an early period of history, the men of one nation or district required swifter horses, whilst those of another required stronger and bulkier horses. The early differences would be very slight; but, in the course of time, from the continued selection of swifter horses in the one case, and of stronger ones in the other, the differences would become greater, and would be noted as forming two sub-breeds. Ultimately, after the lapse of centuries, these sub-breeds would become converted into two well-established and distinct breeds. As the differences became greater, the inferior animals with intermediate characters, being neither swift nor very strong, would not have been used for breeding, and will thus have tended to disappear. Here, then, we see in man's productions the action of what may be called the principle of divergence, causing differences, at first barely appreciable, steadily to increase, and the breeds to diverge in character, both from each other and from their common parent.

But how, it may be asked, can any analogous principle apply in nature? I believe it can and does apply most efficiently (though it was a long time before I saw how), from the simple circumstance that the more diversified the descendants from any one species become in structure, constitution, and habits, by so much will they be better enabled to seize on many and widely diversified places in the polity of nature, and so be enabled to increase in numbers.

We can clearly discern this in the case of animals with simple habits. Take the case of a carnivorous quadruped, of which the number that can be supported in any country has long ago arrived at its full average. If its natural power of increase be allowed to act, it can succeed in increasing (the country not undergoing any change in conditions) only by its varying descendants seizing on places at present occupied by other animals: some of them, for instance, being enabled to feed on new kinds of prey, either dead or alive; some inhabiting new stations, climbing trees, frequenting water, and some perhaps becoming less carnivorous. The more diversified in habits and structure the descendants of our carnivorous ani-

mals become, the more places they will be enabled to occupy. What applies to one animal will apply throughout all time to all animals—that is,
if they vary—for otherwise natural selection can effect nothing. So it will
be with plants. It has been experimentally proved, that if a plot of ground
be sown with one species of grass, and a similar plot be sown with several
distinct genera of grasses, a greater number of plants and a greater weight
of dry herbage can be raised in the latter than in the former case. The
same has been found to hold good when one variety and several mixed varieties of wheat have been sown on equal spaces of ground. Hence, if any
one species of grass were to go on varying, and the varieties were continually selected which differed from each other in the same manner, though
in a very slight degree, as do the distinct species and genera of grasses, a
greater number of individual plants of this species, including its modified
descendants, would succeed in living on the same piece of ground. And
we know that each species and each variety of grass is annually sowing
almost countless seeds; and is thus striving, as it may be said, to the utmost to increase in number. Consequently, in the course of many thousand generations, the most distinct varieties of any one species of grass
would have the best chance of succeeding and of increasing in numbers,
and thus of supplanting the less distinct varieties; and varieties, when
rendered very distinct from each other, take the rank of species.

The truth of the principle that the greatest amount of life can be supported by great diversification of structure, is seen under many natural
circumstances. In an extremely small area, especially if freely open to immigration, and where the contest between individual and individual must
be very severe, we always find great diversity in its inhabitants. For instance, I found that a piece of turf, three feet by four in size which had
been exposed for many years to exactly the same conditions, supported
twenty species of plants, and these belonged to eighteen genera and to
eight orders, which shows how much these plants differed from each other. So it is with the plants and insects on small and uniform islets: also in
small ponds of fresh water. Farmers find that they can raise most food by
a rotation of plants belonging to the most different orders: nature follows
what may be called a simultaneous rotation. Most of the animals and
plants which live close round any small piece of ground, could live on it
(supposing its nature not to be in any way peculiar), and may be said to
be striving to the utmost to live there; but, it is seen, that where they
come into the closest competition, the advantages of diversification of
structure, with the accompanying differences of habit and constitution,
determine that the inhabitants, which thus jostle each other most closely,
shall, as a general rule, belong to what we call different genera and orders.

The same principle is seen in the naturalisation of plants through
man's agency in foreign lands. It might have been expected that the
plants which would succeed in becoming naturalised in any land would
generally have been closely allied to the indigenes; for these are commonly looked at as specially created and adapted for their own country. It
might also, perhaps, have been expected that naturalised plants would

have belonged to a few groups more especially adapted to certain stations in their new homes. But the case is very different; and Alph. de Candolle has well remarked, in his great and admirable work, that floras gain by naturalisation, proportionally with the number of the native genera and species far more in new genera than in new species. To give a single instance: in the last edition of Dr. Asa Gray's 'Manual of the Flora of the Northern United States,' 260 naturalised plants are enumerated, and these belong to 162 genera. We thus see that these naturalised plants are of a highly diversified nature. They differ, moreover, to a large extent, from the indigenes, for out of the 162 naturalised genera, no less than 100 genera are not there indigenous, and thus a large proportional addition is made to the genera now living in the United States.

By considering the nature of the plants or animals which have in any country struggled successfully with the indigenes and have there become naturalised, we may gain some crude idea in what manner some of the natives would have to be modified, in order to gain an advantage over their compatriots; and we may at least infer that diversification of structure, amounting to new generic differences, would be profitable to them.

The advantage of diversification of structure in the inhabitants of the same region is, in fact, the same as that of the physiological division of labour in the organs of the same individual body—a subject so well elucidated by Milne Edwards. No physiologist doubts that a stomach adapted to digest vegetable matter alone, or flesh alone, draws most nutriment from these substances. So in the general economy of any land, the more widely and perfectly the animals and plants are diversified for different habits of life, so will a greater number of individuals be capable of there supporting themselves. A set of animals, with their organisation but little diversified, could hardly compete with a set more perfectly diversified in structure. It may be doubted, for instance, whether the Australian marsupials, which are divided into groups differing but little from each other, and feebly representing, as Mr. Waterhouse and others have remarked, our carnivorous, ruminant, and rodent mammals, could successfully compete with these well-developed orders. In the Australian mammals, we see the process of diversification in an early and incomplete stage of development.

The Probable Effects of the Action of Natural Selection through Divergence of Character and Extinction, on the Descendants of a Common Ancestor.

After the foregoing discussion, which has been much compressed, we may assume that the modified descendants of any one species will succeed so much the better as they become more diversified in structure, and are thus enabled to encroach on places occupied by other beings. Now let us see how this principle of benefit being derived from divergence of character, combined with the principles of natural selection and of extinction, tends to act.

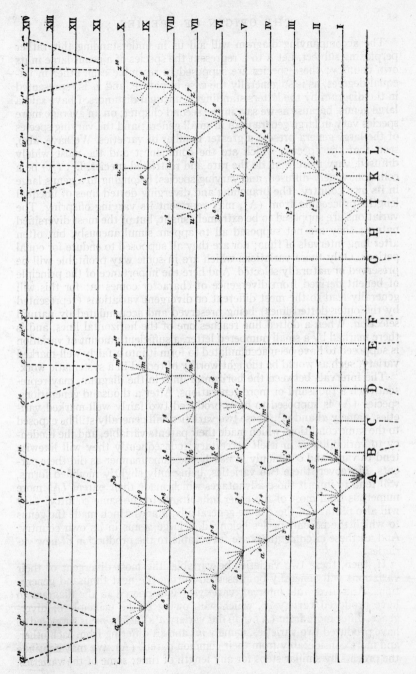

The accompanying diagram will aid us in understanding this rather perplexing subject. Let A to L represent the species of a genus large in its own country; these species are supposed to resemble each other in unequal degrees, as is so generally the case in nature, and as is represented in the diagram by the letters standing at unequal distances. I have said a large genus, because as we saw in the second chapter, on an average more species vary in large genera than in small genera; and the varying species of the large genera present a greater number of varieties. We have, also, seen that the species, which are the commonest and the most widely diffused, vary more than do the rare and restricted species. Let (A) be a common, widely-diffused, and varying species, belonging to a genus large in its own country. The branching and diverging dotted lines of unequal lengths proceeding from (A), may represent its varying offspring. The variations are supposed to be extremely slight, but of the most diversified nature; they are not supposed all to appear simultaneously, but often after long intervals of time; nor are they all supposed to endure for equal periods. Only those variations which are in some way profitable will be preserved or naturally selected. And here the importance of the principle of benefit derived from divergence of character comes in; for this will generally lead to the most different or divergent variations (represented by the outer dotted lines) being preserved and accumulated by natural selection. When a dotted line reaches one of the horizontal lines, and is there marked by a small numbered letter, a sufficient amount of variation is supposed to have been accumulated to form it into a fairly well-marked variety, such as would be thought worthy of record in a systematic work.

The intervals between the horizontal lines in the diagram, may represent each a thousand or more generations. After a thousand generations, species (A) is supposed to have produced two fairly well-marked varieties, namely a^1 and m^1. These two varieties will generally still be exposed to the same conditions which made their parents variable, and the tendency to variability is in itself hereditary; consequently they will likewise tend to vary, and commonly in nearly the same manner as did their parents. Moreover, these two varieties, being only slightly modified forms, will tend to inherit those advantages which made their parent (A) more numerous than most of the other inhabitants of the same country; they will also partake of those more general advantages which made the genus to which the parent-species belonged, a large genus in its own country. And all these circumstances are favourable to the production of new varieties.

If, then, these two varieties be variable, the most divergent of their variations will generally be preserved during the next thousand generations. And after this interval, variety a^1 is supposed in the diagram to have produced variety a^2, which will, owing to the principle of divergence, differ more from (A) than did variety a^1. Variety m^1 is supposed to have produced two varieties, namely m^2 and s^2, differing from each other, and more considerably from their common parent (A). We may continue the process by similar steps for any length of time; some of the varieties, after each thousand generations, producing only a single variety, but in a more and more modified condition, some producing two or three varieties, and some failing to produce any. Thus the varieties or modified descendants of the common parent (A), will generally go on increasing in number and diverging in character. In the diagram the process is represented up to the ten-thousandth generation, and under a condensed and simplified form up to the fourteen-thousandth generation.

But I must here remark that I do not suppose that the process ever goes on so regularly as is represented in the diagram, though in itself made somewhat irregular, nor that it goes on continuously; it is far more probable that each form remains for long periods unaltered, and then again undergoes modification. Nor do I suppose that the most divergent varieties are invariably preserved: a medium form may often long endure, and may or may not produce more than one modified descendant; for natural selection will always act according to the nature of the places which are either unoccupied or not perfectly occupied by other beings; and this will depend on infinitely complex relations. But as a general rule, the more diversified in structure the descendants from any one species can be rendered, the more places they will be enabled to seize on, and the more their modified progeny will increase. In our diagram the line of succession is broken at regular intervals by small numbered letters marking the successive forms which have become sufficiently distinct to be recorded as varieties. But these breaks are imaginary, and might have been inserted anywhere, after intervals long enough to allow the accumulation of a considerable amount of divergent variation.

As all the modified descendants from a common and widely-diffused species, belonging to a large genus, will tend to partake of the same advantages which made their parent successful in life, they will generally go on multiplying in number as well as diverging in character: this is represented in the diagram by the several divergent branches proceeding from (A). The modified offspring from the later and more highly improved branches in the lines of descent, will, it is probable, often take the place of, and so destroy, the earlier and less improved branches: this is represented in the diagram by some of the lower branches not reaching to the upper horizontal lines. In some cases no doubt the process of modification will be confined to a single line of descent and the number of modified descendants will not be increased; although the amount of divergent modification may have been augmented. This case would be represented in the diagram, if all the lines proceeding from (A) were removed, excepting that from a^1 to a^{10}. In the same way the English race-horse and English pointer have apparently both gone on slowly diverging in character from their original stocks, without either having given off any fresh branches or races.

After ten thousand generations, species (A) is supposed to have produced three forms, a^{10}, f^{10}, and m^{10}, which, from having diverged in character during the successive generations, will have come to differ largely, but perhaps unequally, from each other and from their common parent. If we suppose the amount of change between each horizontal line in our diagram to be excessively small, these three forms may still be only well-marked varieties; but we have only to suppose the steps in the process of modification to be more numerous or greater in amount, to convert these three forms into doubtful or at least into well-defined species. Thus the diagram illustrates the steps by which the small differences distinguishing varieties are increased into the larger differences distinguishing species. By continuing the same process for a greater number of generations (as shown in the diagram in a condensed and simplified manner), we get eight species, marked by the letters between a^{14} and m^{14}, all descended from (A). Thus, as I believe, species are multiplied and genera are formed.

In a large genus it is probable that more than one species would vary. In the diagram I have assumed that a second species (I) has produced, by analogous steps, after ten thousand generations, either two well-marked varieties (w^{10} and z^{10}) or two species, according to the amount of change supposed to be represented between the horizontal lines. After fourteen thousand generations, six new species, marked by the letters n^{14} to z^{14}, are supposed to have been produced. In any genus, the species which are already very different in character from each other, will generally tend to produce the greatest number of modified descendants; for these will have the best chance of seizing on new and widely different places in the polity of nature: hence in the diagram I have chosen the extreme species (A), and the nearly extreme species (I), as those which have largely varied, and have given rise to new varieties and species. The other nine species (marked by capital letters) of our original genus, may for long but unequal periods continue to transmit unaltered descendants; and this is shown in the diagram by the dotted lines unequally prolonged upwards.

But during the process of modification, represented in the diagram, another of our principles, namely that of extinction, will have played an important part. As in each fully stocked country natural selection necessarily acts by the selected form having some advantage in the struggle for life over other forms, there will be a constant tendency in the improved descendants of any one species to supplant and exterminate in each stage of descent their predecessors and their original progenitor. For it should be remembered that the competition will generally be most severe between those forms which are most nearly related to each other in habits, constitution, and structure. Hence all the intermediate forms between the earlier and later states, that is between the less and more improved states of the same species, as well as the original parent-species itself, will generally tend to become extinct. So it probably will be with many whole collateral lines of descent, which will be conquered by later and improved lines. If, however, the modified offspring of a species get into some distinct country, or become quickly adapted to some quite new station, in which offspring and progenitor do not come into competition, both may continue to exist.

If, then, our diagram be assumed to represent a considerable amount of modification, species (A) and all the earlier varieties will have become extinct, being replaced by eight new species (a^{14} to m^{14}); and species (I) will be replaced by six (n^{14} to z^{14}) new species.

But we may go further than this. The original species of our genus were supposed to resemble each other in unequal degrees, as is so generally the case in nature; species (A) being more nearly related to B, C, and D, than to the other species; and species (I) more to G, H, K, L, than to the others. These two species (A) and (I) were also supposed to be very common and widely diffused species, so that they must originally have had some advantage over most of the other species of the genus. Their modified descendants, fourteen in number at the fourteen-thousandth generation, will probably have inherited some of the same advantages: they have also been modified and improved in a diversified manner at each stage of descent, so as to have become adapted to many related places in the natural economy of their country. It seems, therefore, extremely probable that they will have taken the places of, and thus exterminated not only their parents (A) and (I), but likewise some of the original species which were most nearly related to their parents. Hence very few of the original species will have transmitted offspring to the fourteen-thousandth generation. We may suppose that only one, (F), of the two species (E and F) which were least closely related to the other nine original species, has transmitted descendants to this late stage of descent.

The new species in our diagram descended from the original eleven species, will now be fifteen in number. Owing to the divergent tendency of natural selection, the extreme amount of difference in character between species a^{14} and z^{14} will be much greater than that between the most distinct of the original eleven species. The new species, moreover, will be allied to each other in a widely different manner. Of the eight descendants from (A) the three marked a^{14}, q^{14}, p^{14}, will be nearly related from having recently branched off from a^{10}; b^{14}, and f^{14}, from having diverged at an earlier period from a^5, will be in some degree distinct from the three first-named species; and lastly, o^{14}, e^{14}, and m^{14}, will be nearly related one to the other, but, from having diverged at the first commencement of the process of modification, will be widely different from the other five species, and may constitute a sub-genus or a distinct genus.

The six descendants from (I) will form two sub-genera or genera. But as the original species (I) differed largely from (A), standing nearly at the extreme end of the original genus, the six descendants from (I) will, owing to inheritance alone, differ considerably from the eight descendants from (A); the two groups, moreover, are supposed to have gone on diverging in different directions. The intermediate species, also (and this is a very important consideration), which connected the original species (A) and (I), have all become, excepting (F), extinct, and have left no descendants. Hence the six new species descended from (I), and the eight descendants from (A), will have to be ranked as very distinct genera, or even as distinct sub-families.

Thus it is, as I believe, that two or more genera are produced by descent with modification, from two or more species of the same genus. And the two or more parent-species are supposed to be descended from some one species of an earlier genus. In our diagram, this is indicated by the broken lines, beneath the capital letters, converging in sub-branches downwards towards a single point; this point represents a species, the supposed progenitor of our several new sub-genera and genera.

It is worth while to reflect for a moment on the character of the new species F^{14}, which is supposed not to have diverged much in character, but to have retained the form of (F), either unaltered or altered only in a slight degree. In this case, its affinities to the other fourteen new species will be of a curious and circuitous nature. Being descended from a form which stood between the parent-species (A) and (I), now supposed to be extinct and unknown, it will be in some degree intermediate in character between the two groups descended from these two species. But as these two groups have gone on diverging in character from the type of their parents, the new species (F^{14}) will not be directly intermediate between them, but rather between types of the two groups; and every naturalist will be able to call such cases before his mind.

In the diagram, each horizontal line has hitherto been supposed to represent a thousand generations, but each may represent a million or more generations; it may also represent a section of the successive strata of the earth's crust including extinct remains. We shall, when we come to our chapter on Geology, have to refer again to this subject, and I think we shall then see that the diagram throws light on the affinities of extinct beings, which, though generally belonging to the same orders, families, or genera, with those now living, yet are often, in some degree, intermediate in character between existing groups; and we can understand this fact, for the extinct species lived at various remote epochs when the branching lines of descent had diverged less.

I see no reason to limit the process of modification, as now explained, to the formation of genera alone. If, in the diagram, we suppose the amount of change, represented by each successive group of diverging dotted lines to be great, the forms marked a^{14} to p^{14}, those marked b^{14} and f^{14}, and those marked o^{14} to m^{14}, will form three very distinct genera. We shall also have two very distinct genera descended from (I), differing widely from the descendants of (A). These two groups of genera will thus form two distinct families, or orders, according to the amount of divergent modification supposed to be represented in the diagram. And the two new families, or orders, are descended from two species of the original genus, and these are supposed to be descended from some still more ancient and unknown form.

We have seen that in each country it is the species belonging to the larger genera which oftenest present varieties or incipient species. This, indeed, might have been expected; for, as natural selection acts through one form having some advantage over other forms in the struggle for existence, it will chiefly act on those which already have some advantage;

and the largeness of any group shows that its species have inherited from a common ancestor some advantage in common. Hence, the struggle for the production of new and modified descendants will mainly lie between the larger groups which are all trying to increase in number. One large group will slowly conquer another large group, reduce its numbers, and thus lessen its chance of further variation and improvement. Within the same large group, the later and more highly perfected sub-groups, from branching out and seizing on many new places in the polity of Nature, will constantly tend to supplant and destroy the earlier and less improved sub-groups. Small and broken groups and sub-groups will finally disappear. Looking to the future, we can predict that the groups of organic beings which are now large and triumphant, and which are least broken up, that is, which have as yet suffered least extinction, will, for a long period, continue to increase. But which groups will ultimately prevail, no man can predict; for we know that many groups formerly most extensively developed, have now become extinct. Looking still more remotely to the future, we may predict that, owing to the continued and steady increase of the larger groups, a multitude of smaller groups will become utterly extinct, and leave no modified descendants; and consequently that, of the species living at any one period, extremely few will transmit descendants to a remote futurity. I shall have to return to this subject in the chapter on Classification, but I may add that as, according to this view, extremely few of the more ancient species have transmitted descendants to the present day, and, as all the descendants of the same species form a class, we can understand how it is that there exist so few classes in each main division of the animal and vegetable kingdoms. Although few of the most ancient species have left modified descendants, yet, at remote geological periods, the earth may have been almost as well peopled with species of many genera, families, orders, and classes, as at the present time.

On the Degree to which Organization tends to advance

Natural Selection acts exclusively by the preservation and accumulation of variations, which are beneficial under the organic and inorganic conditions to which each creature is exposed at all periods of life. The ultimate result is that each creature tends to become more and more improved in relation to its conditions. This improvement inevitably leads to the gradual advancement of the organisation of the greater number of living beings throughout the world. But here we enter on a very intricate subject, for naturalists have not defined to each other's satisfaction what is meant by an advance in organisation. Amongst the vertebrata the degree of intellect and an approach in structure to man clearly come into play. It might be thought that the amount of change which the various parts and organs pass through in their development from the embryo to maturity would suffice as a standard of comparison; but there are cases, as with certain parasitic crustaceans, in which several parts of the structure become less perfect, so that the mature animal cannot be called higher than its larva. Von Baer's standard seems the most widely applicable and the best, namely, the amount of differentiation of the parts of the same organic being, in the adult state as I should be inclined to add, and their specialisation for different functions; or, as Milne Edwards would express it, the completeness of the division of physiological labour. But we shall see how obscure this subject is if we look, for instance, to fishes, amongst which some naturalists rank those as highest which, like the sharks, approach nearest to amphibians; whilst other naturalists rank the common bony or teleostean fishes as the highest, inasmuch as they are most strictly fish-like and differ most from the other vertebrate classes. We see still more plainly the obscurity of the subject by turning to plants, amongst which the standard of intellect is of course quite excluded; and here some botanists rank those plants as highest which have every organ, as sepals, petals, stamens, and pistils, fully developed in each flower; whereas other botanists, probably with more truth, look at the plants which have their several organs much modified and reduced in number as the highest.

If we take as the standard of high organisation, the amount of differentiation and specialisation of the several organs in each being when adult (and this will include the advancement of the brain for intellectual purposes), natural selection clearly leads towards this standard: for all physiologists admit that the specialisation of organs, inasmuch as in this state they perform their functions better, is an advantage to each being; and hence the accumulation of variations tending towards specialisation is within the scope of natural selection. On the other hand, we can see, bearing in mind that all organic beings are striving to increase at a high ratio and to seize on every unoccupied or less well occupied place in the economy of nature, that it is quite possible for natural selection gradually to fit a being to a situation in which several organs would be superfluous or useless: in such cases there would be retrogression in the scale of organisation. Whether organisation on the whole has actually advanced from the remotest geological periods to the present day will be more conveniently discussed in our chapter on Geological Succession.

But it may be objected that if all organic beings thus tend to rise in the scale, how is it that throughout the world a multitude of the lowest forms still exist; and how is it that in each great class some forms are far more highly developed than others? Why have not the more highly developed forms everywhere supplanted and exterminated the lower? Lamarck, who believed in an innate and inevitable tendency towards perfection in all organic beings, seems to have felt this difficulty so strongly, that he was led to suppose that new and simple forms are continually being produced by spontaneous generation. Science has not as yet proved the truth of this belief, whatever the future may reveal. On our theory the continued existence of lowly organisms offers no difficulty; for natural selection, or the survival of the fittest, does not necessarily include progressive development—it only takes advantage of such variations as arise and are beneficial to each creature under its complex relations of life. And it may be asked what advantage, as far as we can see, would it be to an infusoriar animalcule—to an intestinal worm—or even to an earthworm, to be high· ly organised. If it were no advantage, these forms would be left, by nat· ural selection, unimproved or but little improved, and might remain foi indefinite ages in their present lowly condition. And geology tells us that some of the lowest forms, as the infusoria and rhizopods, have remained for an enormous period in nearly their present state. But to suppose that most of the many now existing low forms have not in the least advanced since the first dawn of life would be extremely rash; for every naturalist who has dissected some of the beings now ranked as very low in the scale, must have been struck with their really wondrous and beautiful organisa- tion.

Nearly the same remarks are applicable if we look to the different grades of organisation within the same great group; for instance, in the vertebrata, to the co-existence of mammals and fish—amongst mam- malia, to the co-existence of man and the ornithorhynchus—amongst fishes, to the co-existence of the shark and the lancelot (Amphioxus), which latter fish in the extreme simplicity of its structure approaches the invertebrate classes. But mammals and fish hardly come into competition with each other; the advancement of the whole class of mammals, or of certain members in this class, to the highest grade would not lead to their taking the place of fishes. Physiologists believe that the brain must be bathed by warm blood to be highly active, and this requires aërial res- piration; so that warm-blooded mammals when inhabiting the water lie under a disadvantage in having to come continually to the surface to breathe. With fishes, members of the shark family would not tend to sup- plant the lancelet; for the lancelet, as I hear from Fritz Müller, has as sole companion and competitor on the barren sandy shore of South Bra- zil, an anomalous annelid. The three lowest orders of mammals, namely, marsupials, edentata, and rodents, co-exist in South America in the same region with numerous monkeys, and probably interfere little with each other. Although organisation, on the whole, may have advanced and be still advancing throughout the world, yet the scale will always present many degrees of perfection; for the high advancement of certain whole classes, or of certain members of each class, does not at all necessarily lead to the extinction of those groups with which they do not enter into close competition. In some cases, as we shall hereafter see, lowly organ- ised forms appear to have been preserved to the present day, from in- habiting confined or peculiar stations, where they have been subjected to less severe competition, and where their scanty numbers have retarded the chance of favourable variations arising.

Finally, I believe that many lowly organised forms now exist through- out the world, from various causes. In some cases variations or individual differences of a favourable nature may never have arisen for natural se- lection to act on and accumulate. In no case, probably, has time sufficed for the utmost possible amount of development. In some few cases there has been what we must call retrogression of organisation. But the main

cause lies in the fact that under very simple conditions of life a high organisation would be of no service,—possibly would be of actual disservice, as being of a more delicate nature, and more liable to be put out of
order and injured.

Looking to the first dawn of life, when all organic beings, as we may
believe, presented the simplest structure, how, it has been asked, could
the first steps in the advancement or differentiation of parts have arisen?
Mr. Herbert Spencer would probably answer that, as soon as simple unicellular organism came by growth or division to be compounded of several cells, or became attached to any supporting surface, his law "that
homologous units of any order become differentiated in proportion as
their relations to incident forces become different" would come into action. But as we have no facts to guide us, speculation on the subject is almost useless. It is, however, an error to suppose that there would be no
struggle for existence, and, consequently, no natural selection, until many
forms had been produced: variations in a single species inhabiting an isolated station might be beneficial, and thus the whole mass of individuals
might be modified, or two distinct forms might arise. But, as I remarked
towards the close of the Introduction, no one ought to feel surprise at
much remaining as yet unexplained on the origin of species, if we make
due allowance for our profound ignorance on the mutual relations of the
inhabitants of the world at the present time, and still more so during past
ages.

Convergence of Character

Mr. H. C. Watson thinks that I have overrated the importance of divergence of character (in which, however, he apparently believes), and
that convergence, as it may be called, has likewise played a part. If two
species, belonging to two distinct though allied genera, had both produced a large number of new and divergent forms, it is conceivable that these
might approach each other so closely that they would have all to be classed under the same genus; and thus the descendants of two distinct genera
would converge into one. But it would in most cases be extremely rash to
attribute to convergence a close and general similarity of structure in the
modified descendants of widely distinct forms. The shape of a crystal is
determined solely by the molecular forces, and it is not surprising that
dissimilar substances should sometimes assume the same form; but with
organic beings we should bear in mind that the form of each depends on
an infinitude of complex relations, namely on the variations which have
arisen, these being due to causes far too intricate to be followed out,—on
the nature of the variations which have been preserved or selected, and
this depends on the surrounding physical conditions, and in a still higher
degree on the surrounding organisms with which each being has come into
competition,—and lastly, on inheritance (in itself a fluctuating element)
from innumerable progenitors, all of which have had their forms determined through equally complex relations. It is incredible that the de-

scendants of two organisms, which had originally differed in a marked manner, should ever afterwards converge so closely as to lead to a near approach to identity throughout their whole organisation. If this had occurred, we should meet with the same form, independently of genetic connection, recurring in widely separated geological formations; and the balance of evidence is opposed to any such an admission.

Mr. Watson has also objected that the continued action of natural selection, together with divergence of character, would tend to make an indefinite number of specific forms. As far as mere inorganic conditions are concerned, it seems probable that a sufficient number of species would soon become adapted to all considerable diversities of heat, moisture, &c.; but I fully admit that the mutual relations of organic beings are more important; and as the number of species in any country goes on increasing, the organic conditions of life must become more and more complex. Consequently there seems at first sight no limit to the amount of profitable diversification of structure, and therefore no limit to the number of species which might be produced. We do not know that even the most prolific area is fully stocked with specific forms: at the Cape of Good Hope and in Australia, which support such an astonishing number of species, many European plants have become naturalised. But geology shows us, that from an early part of the tertiary period the number of species of shells, and that from the middle part of this same period the number of mammals, has not greatly or at all increased. What then checks an indefinite increase in the number of species? The amount of life (I do not mean the number of specific forms) supported on an area must have a limit, depending so largely as it does on physical conditions; therefore, if an area be inhabited by very many species, each or nearly each species will be represented by few individuals; and such species will be liable to extermination from accidental fluctuations in the nature of the seasons or in the number of their enemies. The process of extermination in such cases would be rapid, whereas the production of new species must always be slow. Imagine the extreme case of as many species as individuals in England, and the first severe winter or very dry summer would exterminate thousands on thousands of species. Rare species, and each species will become rare if the number of species in any country becomes indefinitely increased, will, on the principle often explained, present within a given period few favourable variations; consequently, the process of giving birth to new specific forms would thus be retarded. When any species becomes very rare, close interbreeding will help to exterminate it; authors have thought that this comes into play in accounting for the deterioration of the Aurochs in Lithuania, of Red Deer in Scotland, and of Bears in Norway, &c. Lastly, and this I am inclined to think is the most important element, a dominant species, which has already beaten many competitors in its own home, will tend to spread and supplant many others. Alph. de Candolle has shown that those species which spread widely, tend generally to spread *very* widely; consequently, they will tend to supplant and exterminate several species in several areas, and thus check the inordinate increase of specific forms throughout the world. Dr. Hooker has recently shown that in the S.E. corner of Australia, where, apparently, there are many invaders from different quarters of the globe, the endemic Australian species have been greatly reduced in number. How much weight to attribute to these several considerations I will not pretend to say; but conjointly they must limit in each country the tendency to an indefinite augmentation of specific forms.

Summary of Chapter

If under changing conditions of life organic beings present individual differences in almost every part of their structure, and this cannot be disputed; if there be, owing to their geometrical rate of increase, a severe struggle for life at some age, season, or year, and this certainly cannot be disputed; then, considering the infinite complexity of the relations of all organic beings to each other and to their conditions of life, causing an infinite diversity in structure, constitution, and habits, to be advantageous to them, it would be a most extraordinary fact if no variations had ever occurred useful to each being's own welfare, in the same manner as so many variations have occurred useful to man. But if variations useful to any organic being ever do occur, assuredly individuals thus characterised will have the best chance of being preserved in the struggle for life; and from the strong principle of inheritance, these will tend to produce offspring similarly characterised. This principle of preservation, or the survival of the fittest, I have called Natural Selection. It leads to the improvement of each creature in relation to its organic and inorganic conditions of life; and consequently, in most cases, to what must be regarded as an advance in organisation. Nevertheless, low and simple forms will long endure if well fitted for their simple conditions of life.

Natural selection, on the principle of qualities being inherited at corresponding ages, can modify the egg, seed, or young, as easily as the adult. Amongst many animals, sexual selection will have given its aid to ordinary selection, by assuring to the most vigorous and best adapted males the greatest number of offspring. Sexual selection will also give characters useful to the males alone, in their struggles or rivalry with other males; and these characters will be transmitted to one sex or to both sexes, according to the form of inheritance which prevails.

Whether natural selection has really thus acted in adapting the various forms of life to their several conditions and stations, must be judged by the general tenor and balance of evidence given in the following chapters. But we have already seen how it entails extinction; and how largely extinction has acted in the world's history, geology plainly declares. Natural selection, also leads to divergence of character; for the more organic beings diverge in structure, habits, and constitution, by so much the more can a large number be supported on the area,—of which we see proof by looking to the inhabitants of any small spot, and to the productions naturalised in foreign lands. Therefore, during the modification of the descendants of any one species, and during the incessant struggle of all species to increase in numbers, the more diversified the descendants become, the better will be their chance of success in the battle for life. Thus the small differences distinguishing varieties of the same species, steadily tend to increase, till they equal the greater differences between species of the same genus, or even of distinct genera.

We have seen that it is the common, the widely-diffused and widely-ranging species, belonging to the larger genera within each class, which vary most; and these tend to transmit to their modified offspring that superiority which now makes them dominant in their own countries. Natural selection, as has just been remarked, leads to divergence of character and to much extinction of the less improved and intermediate forms of life. On these principles, the nature of the affinities, and the generally well-defined distinctions between the innumerable organic beings in each class throughout the world, may be explained. It is a truly wonderful fact —the wonder of which we are apt to overlook from familiarity—that all animals and all plants throughout all time and space should be related to each other in groups, subordinate to groups, in the manner which we everywhere behold—namely, varieties of the same species most closely related, species of the same genus less closely and unequally related, forming sections and sub-genera, species of distinct genera much less closely related, and genera related in different degrees, forming sub-families, families, orders, sub-classes and classes. The several subordinate groups in any class cannot be ranked in a single file, but seem clustered round points, and these round other points, and so on in almost endless cycles. If species had been independently created, no explanation would have been possible of this kind of classification; but it is explained through inheritance and the complex action of natural selection, entailing extinction and divergence of character, as we have seen illustrated in the diagram.

The affinities of all the beings of the same class have sometimes been represented by a great tree. I believe this simile largely speaks the truth. The green and budding twigs may represent existing species; and those produced during former years may represent the long succession of extinct species. At each period of growth all the growing twigs have tried to branch out on all sides, and to overtop and kill the surrounding twigs and branches, in the same manner as species and groups of species have at all times overmastered other species in the great battle for life. The limbs divided into great branches, and these into lesser and lesser branches, were themselves once, when the tree was young, budding twigs, and this connection of the former and present buds by ramifying branches may well represent the classification of all extinct and living species in groups subordinate to groups. Of the many twigs which flourished when the tree was a mere bush, only two or three, now grown into great branches, yet survive and bear the other branches; so with the species which lived during long-past geological periods, very few have left living and modified descendants. From the first growth of the tree, many a limb and branch has decayed and dropped off; and these fallen branches of various sizes may represent those whole orders, families, and genera which have now no living representatives, and which are known to us only in a fossil state. As we here and there see a thin straggling branch springing from a fork low down in a tree, and which by some chance has been favoured and is still alive on its summit, so we occasionally see an animal like the Ornithorhynchus or Lepidosiren, which in some small degree connects by its affinities two large branches of life, and which has apparently been saved from fatal competition by having inhabited a protected station. As buds give rise by growth to fresh buds, and these, if vigorous, branch out and overtop on all sides many a feebler branch, so by generation I believe it has been with the great Tree of Life, which fills with its dead and broken branches the crust of the earth, and covers the surface with its ever-branching and beautiful ramifications.

CHAPTER V

LAWS OF VARIATION

Effects of changed conditions—Use and disuse, combined with natural selection; organs of flight and of vision—Acclimatisation—Correlated variation—Compensation and economy of growth—False correlations—Multiple, rudimentary, and lowly organised structures variable—Parts developed in an unusual manner are highly variable; specific characters more variable than generic: secondary sexual characters variable—Species of the same genus vary in an analogous manner—Reversions to long-lost characters—Summary.

I HAVE hitherto sometimes spoken as if the variations—so common and multiform with organic beings under domestication, and in a lesser degree with those under nature—were due to chance. This, of course, is a wholly incorrect expression, but it serves to acknowledge plainly our ignorance of the cause of each particular variation. Some authors believe it to be as much the function of the reproductive system to produce individual differences, or slight deviations of structure, as to make the child like its parents. But the fact of variations and monstrosities occurring much more frequently under domestication than under nature, and the greater variability of species having wider ranges than of those with restricted ranges, lead to the conclusion that variability is generally related to the conditions of life to which each species has been exposed during several successive generations. In the first chapter I attempted to show that changed conditions act in two ways, directly on the whole organisation or on certain parts alone, and indirectly through the reproductive system. In all cases there are two factors, the nature of the organism, which is much the most important of the two, and the nature of the conditions. The direct action of changed conditions leads to definite or indefinite results. In the latter case the organisation seems to become plastic, and we have much fluctuating variability. In the former case the nature of the organism is such that it yields readily, when subjected to certain conditions, and all, or nearly all the individuals become modified in the same way.

It is very difficult to decide how far changed conditions, such as of climate, food, &c., have acted in a definite manner. There is reason to believe that in the course of time the effects have been greater than can be proved by clear evidence. But we may safely conclude that the innumerable complex co-adaptations of structure, which we see throughout nature between various organic beings, cannot be attributed simply to such action. In the following cases the conditions seem to have produced some slight definite effect: E. Forbes asserts that shells at their southern limit, and when living in shallow water, are more brightly coloured than those of the same species from further north or from a greater depth; but this certainly does not always hold good. Mr. Gould believes that birds of the same species are more brightly coloured under a clear atmosphere, than when living near the coast or on islands, and Wollaston is convinced that residence near the sea affects the colours of insects. Moquin-Tandon gives a list of plants which, when growing near the sea-shore, have their leaves in some degree fleshy, though not elsewhere fleshy. These slightly varying organisms are interesting in as far as they present characters analogous to those possessed by the species which are confined to similar conditions.

When a variation is of the slightest use to any being, we cannot tell how much to attribute to the accumulative action of natural selection, and how much to the definite action of the conditions of life. Thus, it is well known to furriers that animals of the same species have thicker and better fur the further north they live; but who can tell how much of this difference may be due to the warmest-clad individuals having been favoured and preserved during many generations, and how much to the action of the severe climate? for it would appear that climate has some direct action on the hair of our domestic quadrupeds.

Instances could be given of similar varieties being produced from the same species under external conditions of life as different as can well be conceived; and, on the other hand, of dissimilar varieties being produced under apparently the same external conditions. Again, innumerable instances are known to every naturalist, of species keeping true, or not varying at all, although living under the most opposite climates. Such considerations as these incline me to lay less weight on the direct action of the surrounding conditions, than on a tendency to vary, due to causes of which we are quite ignorant.

In one sense the conditions of life may be said, not only to cause variability, either directly or indirectly, but likewise to include natural selection, for the conditions determine whether this or that variety shall survive. But when man is the selecting agent, we clearly see that the two elements of change are distinct; variability is in some manner excited, but it is the will of man which accumulates the variations in certain directions; and it is this latter agency which answers to the survival of the fittest under nature.

Effects of the increased Use and Disuse of Parts, as controlled by Natural Selection

From the facts alluded to in the first chapter, I think there can be no doubt that use in our domestic animals has strengthened and enlarged certain parts, and disuse diminished them; and that such modifications are inherited. Under free nature, we have no standard of comparison, by which to judge of the effects of long-continued use or disuse, for we know not the parent-forms; but many animals possess structures which can be best explained by the effects of disuse. As Professor Owen has remarked, there is no greater anomaly in nature than a bird that cannot fly; yet there are several in this state. The logger-headed duck of South America can only flap along the surface of the water, and has its wings in nearly the same condition as the domestic Aylesbury duck: it is a remarkable fact that the young birds, according to Mr. Cunningham, can fly, while the adults have lost this power. As the larger ground-feeding birds seldom take flight except to escape danger, it is probable that the nearly wingless condition of several birds, now inhabiting or which lately inhabited several oceanic islands, tenanted by no beast of prey, has been caused by disuse. The ostrich indeed inhabits continents, and is exposed to danger from which it cannot escape by flight, but it can defend itself by kicking its enemies, as efficiently as many quadrupeds. We may believe that the progenitor of the ostrich genus had habits like those of the bustard, and that, as the size and weight of its body were increased during successive generations, its legs were used more, and its wings less, until they became incapable of flight.

Kirby has remarked (and I have observed the same fact) that the anterior tarsi, or feet, of many male dung-feeding beetles are often broken off; he examined seventeen specimens in his own collection, and not one had even a relic left. In the Onites apelles the tarsi are so habitually lost, that the insect has been described as not having them. In some other genera they are present, but in a rudimentary condition. In the Ateuchus or sacred beetle of the Egyptians, they are totally deficient. The evidence that accidental mutilations can be inherited is at present not decisive; but the remarkable cases observed by Brown-Séquard in guinea-pigs, of the inherited effects of operations, should make us cautious in denying this tendency. Hence it will perhaps be safest to look at the entire absence of the anterior tarsi in Ateuchus, and their rudimentary condition in some other genera, not as cases of inherited mutilations, but as due to the effects of long-continued disuse; for as many dung-feeding beetles are generally found with their tarsi lost, this must happen early in life; therefore the tarsi cannot be of much importance or be much used by these insects.

In some cases we might easily put down to disuse modifications of structure which are wholly, or mainly, due to natural selection. Mr. Wollaston has discovered the remarkable fact that 200 beetles, out of the 550 species (but more are now known) inhabiting Madeira, are so far deficient in wings that they cannot fly; and that, of the twenty-nine endemic genera, no less than twenty-three have all their species in this condition! Several facts,—namely, that beetles in many parts of the world are frequently blown to sea and perish; that the beetles in Madeira, as observed by Mr. Wollaston, lie much concealed, until the wind lulls and the sun shines; that the proportion of wingless beetles is larger on the exposed Desertas than in Madeira itself; and especially the extraordinary fact, so strongly insisted on by Mr. Wollastan, that certain large groups of beetles, elsewhere excessively numerous, which absolutely require the use of their wings, are here almost entirely absent;—these several considerations make me believe that the wingless condition of so many Madeira beetles is mainly due to the action of natural selection, combined probably with disuse. For during many successive generations each individual beetle which flew least, either from its wings having been ever so little less perfectly developed or from indolent habit, will have had the best chance of surviving from not being blown out to sea; and, on the other hand, those beetles which most readily took to flight would oftenest have been blown to sea, and thus destroyed.

The insects in Madeira which are not ground-feeders, and which, as certain flower-feeding coleoptera and lepidoptera, must habitually use their wings to gain their subsistence, have, as Mr. Wollaston suspects, their wings not at all reduced, but even enlarged. This is quite compatible with the action of natural selection. For when a new insect first arrived on the island, the tendency of natural selection to enlarge or to reduce the wings, would depend on whether a greater number of individuals were saved by successfully battling with the winds, or by giving up the attempt and rarely or never flying. As with mariners shipwrecked near a coast, it would have been better for the good swimmers if they had been able to swim still further, whereas it would have been better for the bad swimmers if they had not been able to swim at all and had stuck to the wreck.

The eyes of moles and of some burrowing rodents are rudimentary in size, and in some cases are quite covered by skin and fur. This state of the eyes is probably due to gradual reduction from disuse, but aided perhaps by natural selection. In South America, a burrowing rodent, the tuco-tuco, or Ctenomys, is even more subterranean in its habits than the mole; and I was assured by a Spaniard, who had often caught them, that they were frequently blind. One which I kept alive was certainly in this condition, the cause, as appeared on dissection, having been inflammation of the nictitating membrane. As frequent inflammation of the eyes must be injurious to any animal, and as eyes are certainly not necessary to animals having subterranean habits, a reduction in their size, with the adhesion of the eyelids and growth of fur over them, might in such case be an advantage; and if so, natural selection would aid the effects of disuse.

It is well known that several animals, belonging to the most different classes, which inhabit the caves of Carniola and of Kentucky, are blind. In some of the crabs the foot-stalk for the eye remains, though the eye is gone;—the stand for the telescope is there, though the telescope with its glasses has been lost. As it is difficult to imagine that eyes, though useless, could be in any way injurious to animals living in darkness, their loss may be attributed to disuse. In one of the blind animals, namely, the cave-rat (Noetoma), two of which were captured by Professor Silliman at above half a mile distance from the mouth of the cave, and therefore not in the profoundest depths, the eyes were lustrous and of large size; and these animals, as I am informed by Professor Silliman, after having been exposed for about a month to a graduated light, acquired a dim perception of objects.

It is difficult to imagine conditions of life more similar than deep limestone caverns under a nearly similar climate; so that, in accordance with the old view of the blind animals having been separately created for the American and European caverns, very close similarity in their organisation and affinities might have been expected. This is certainly not the case if we look at the two whole faunas; and with respect to the insects alone, Schiödte has remarked, "We are accordingly prevented from considering the entire phenomenon in any other light than something purely local, and the similarity which is exhibited in a few forms between the Mammoth cave (in Kentucky) and the caves in Carniola, otherwise than as a very plain expression of that analogy which subsists generally between the fauna of Europe and of North America." On my view we must suppose that American animals, having in most cases ordinary powers of vision, slowly migrated by successive generations from the outer world into the deeper and deeper recesses of the Kentucky caves, as did European animals into the caves of Europe. We have some evidence of this gradation of habit; for, as Schiödte remarks, "We accordingly look upon the subterranean faunas as small ramifications which have penetrated into the earth from the geographically limited faunas of the adjacent tracts, and which, as they extended themselves into darkness, have been accommodated to surrounding circumstances. Animals not far remote from ordinary forms, prepare the transition from light to darkness. Next follow those that are constructed for twilight; and, last of all, those destined for total darkness, and whose formation is quite peculiar." These remarks of Schiödte's it should be understood, apply not to the same, but to distinct species. By the time that an animal had reached, after numberless generations, the deepest recesses, disuse will on this view have more or less perfectly obliterated its eyes, and natural selection will often have effected other changes, such as an increase in the length of the antennæ or palpi, as a compensation for blindness. Notwithstanding such modifications, we might expect still to see in the cave-animals of America, affinities to the other inhabitants of that continent, and in those of Europe to the inhabitants of the European continent. And this is the case with some of the American cave-animals, as I hear from Professor Dana; and some of the European cave-insects are very closely allied to those of the surrounding country. It would be difficult to give any rational explanation of the affinities of the blind cave-animals to the other inhabitants of the two continents on the ordinary view of their independent creation. That several of the inhabitants of the caves of the Old and New Worlds should be closely related, we might expect from the well-known relationship of most of their other productions. As a blind species of Bathyscia is found in abundance on shady rocks far from caves, the loss of vision in the cave-species of this one genus has probably had no relation to its dark habitation; for it is natural that an insect already deprived of vision should readily become adapted to dark caverns. Another blind genus (Anophthalmus) offers this remarkable peculiarity, that the species, as Mr. Murray observes, have not as yet been found anywhere except in caves; yet those which inhabit the several caves of Europe and America are distinct; but it is possible that the progenitors of these several species, whilst they were furnished with eyes, may formerly have ranged over both continents, and then have become extinct, excepting in their present secluded abodes. Far from feeling surprise that some of the cave-animals should be very anomalous, as Agassiz has remarked in regard to the blind fish, the Amblyopsis, and as is the case with blind Proteus with reference to the reptiles of Europe, I am only surprised that more wrecks of ancient life have not been preserved, owing to the less severe competition to which the scanty inhabitants of these dark abodes will have been exposed.

Acclimatisation

Habit is hereditary with plants, as in the period of flowering, in the time of sleep, in the amount of rain requisite for seeds to germinate, &c., and this leads me to say a few words on acclimatisation. As it is extremely common for distinct species belonging to the same genus to inhabit hot and cold countries, if it be true that all the species of the same genus are descended from a single parent-form, acclimatisation must be readily effected during a long course of descent. It is notorious that each species is adapted to the climate of its own home: species from an arctic or even from a temperate region cannot endure a tropical climate, or conversely. So again, many succulent plants cannot endure a damp climate. But the degree of adaptation of species to the climates under which they live is often overrated. We may infer this from our frequent inability to predict whether or not an imported plant will endure our climate, and from the number of plants and animals brought from different countries which are here perfectly healthy. We have reason to believe that species in a state of nature are closely limited in their ranges by the competition of other organic beings quite as much as, or more than, by adaptation to particular climates. But whether or not this adaptation is in most cases very close, we have evidence with some few plants, of their becoming, to a certain extent, naturally habituated to different temperatures; that is, they become acclimatised: thus the pines and rhododendrons, raised from seed collected by Dr. Hooker from the same species growing at different heights on the Himalaya, were found to possess in this country different constitutional powers of resisting cold. Mr. Thwaites informs me that he has observed similar facts in Ceylon; analogous observations have been made by Mr. H. C. Watson on European species of plants brought from the Azores to England; and I could give other cases. In regard to animals, several authentic instances could be adduced of species having largely extended, within historical times, their range from warmer to cooler latitudes, and conversely; but we do not positively know that these animals were strictly adapted to their native climate, though in all ordinary cases we assume such to be the case; nor do we know that they have subsequently become specially acclimatised to their new homes, so as to be better fitted for them than they were at first.

As we may infer that our domestic animals were originally chosen by uncivilised man because they were useful and because they bred readily under confinement, and not because they were subsequently found capable of far-extended transportation, the common and extraordinary capacity in our domestic animals of not only withstanding the most different climates, but of being perfectly fertile (a far severer test) under them, may be used as an argument that a large proportion of other animals now in a state of nature could easily be brought to bear widely different climates. We must not, however, push the foregoing argument too far, on account of the probable origin of some of our domestic animals from several wild stocks; the blood, for instance, of a tropical and arctic wolf may perhaps be mingled in our domestic breeds. The rat and mouse cannot be considered as domestic animals, but they have been transported by man to many parts of the world, and now have a far wider range than any other rodent; for they live under the cold climate of Faroe in the north and of the Falklands in the south, and on many an island in the torrid zones. Hence adaptation to any special climate may be looked at as a quality readily grafted on an innate wide flexibility of constitution, common to most animals. On this view, the capacity of enduring the most different climates by man himself and by his domestic animals, and the fact of the extinct elephant and rhinoceros having formerly endured a glacial climate, whereas the living species are now all tropical or sub-tropical in their habits, ought not to be looked at as anomalies, but as examples of a very common flexibility of constitution, brought, under peculiar circumstances, into action.

How much of the acclimatisation of species to any peculiar climate is due to mere habit, and how much to the natural selection of varieties having different innate constitutions, and how much to both means combined, is an obscure question. That habit or custom has some influence, I must believe, both from analogy and from the incessant advice given in agricultural works, even in the ancient Encyclopædias of China, to be very cautious in transporting animals from one district to another. And as it is not likely that man should have succeeded in selecting so many breeds and sub-breeds with constitutions specially fitted for their own districts, the result must, I think, be due to habit. On the other hand, natural selection would inevitably tend to preserve those individuals which were born with constitutions best adapted to any country which they inhabited. In treatises on many kinds of cultivated plants, certain varieties are said to withstand certain climates better than others; this is strikingly shown in works on fruit-trees published in the United States, in which certain varieties are habitually recommended for the northern and others for the southern States; and as most of these varieties are of recent origin, they cannot owe their constitutional differences to habit. The case of the Jerusalem artichoke, which is never propagated in England by seed, and of which consequently new varieties have not been produced, has even been advanced, as proving that acclimatisation cannot be effected, for it is now as tender as ever it was! The case, also, of the kidney-bean has been often cited for a similar purpose, and with much greater weight; but until someone will sow, during a score of generations, his kidney-beans so early that a very large proportion are destroyed by frost, and then collect seed from the few survivors, with care to prevent accidental crosses, and then again get seed from these seedlings, with the same precautions, the experiment cannot be said to have been tried. Nor let it be supposed that differences in the constitution of seedling kidney-beans never appear, for an account has been published how much more hardy some seedlings are than others; and of this fact I have myself observed striking instances.

On the whole, we may conclude that habit, or use and disuse, have, in some cases, played a considerable part in the modification of the constitution and structure; but that the effects have often been largely combined with, and sometimes overmastered by, the natural selection of innate variations.

Correlated Variation

I mean by this expression that the whole organisation is so tied together during its growth and development, that when slight variations in any one part occur, and are accumulated through natural selection, other parts become modified. This is a very important subject, most imperfectly understood, and no doubt wholly different classes of facts may be here easily confounded together. We shall presently see that simple inheritance often gives the false appearance of correlation. One of the most obvious real cases is, that variations of structure arising in the young or larvæ naturally tend to affect the structure of the mature animal. The several parts of the body which are homologous, and which, at an early embryonic period, are identical in structure, and which are necessarily exposed to similar conditions, seem eminently liable to vary in a like manner: we see this in the right and left sides of the body varying in the same manner; in the front and hind legs, and even in the jaws and limbs, varying together, for the lower jaw is believed by some anatomists to be homologous with the limbs. These tendencies, I do not doubt, may be mastered more or less completely by natural selection; thus a family of stags once existed with an antler only on one side; and if this had been of any great use to the breed, it might probably have been rendered permanent by selection.

Homologous parts, as has been remarked by some authors, tend to cohere, this is often seen in monstrous plants: and nothing is more common than the union of homologous parts in normal structures, as in the union of the petals into a tube. Hard parts seem to affect the form of adjoining soft parts; it is believed by some authors that with birds the diversity in the shape of the pelvis causes the remarkable diversity in the shape of their kidneys. Others believe that the shape of the pelvis in the human mother influences by pressure the shape of the head of the child. In snakes, according to Schlegel, the form of the body and the manner of swallowing determine the position and form of several of the most important viscera.

The nature of the bond is frequently quite obscure. M. Is. Geoffroy St. Hilaire has forcibly remarked, that certain malconformations frequently, and that others rarely, co-exist, without our being able to assign any reason. What can be more singular than the relation in cats between complete whiteness and blue eyes with deafness, or between the tortoise-shell colour and the female sex; or in pigeons between their feathered feet and skin betwixt the outer toes, or between the presence of more or less down on the young pigeon when first hatched, with the future colour of its plumage; or, again, the relation between the hair and teeth in the naked Turkish dog, though here no doubt homology comes into play? With respect to this latter case of correlation, I think it can hardly be accidental, that the two orders of mammals which are most abnormal in their dermal covering, viz., Cetacea (whales) and Edentata (armadilloes, scaly ant-eaters, &c.,) are likewise on the whole the most abnormal in their teeth; but there are so many exceptions to this rule, as Mr. Mivart has remarked, that it has little value.

I know of no case better adapted to show the importance of the laws of correlation and variation, independently of utility and therefore of natural selection, than that of the difference between the outer and inner flowers in some Compositous and Umbelliferous plants. Every one is familiar with the difference between the ray and central florets of, for instance, the daisy, and this difference is often accompanied with the partial or complete abortion of the reproductive organs. But in some of these plants, the seeds also differ in shape and sculpture. These differences have sometimes been attributed to the pressure of the involucra on the florets, or to their mutual pressure, and the shape of the seeds in the ray-florets of some Compositæ countenances this idea; but with the Umbelliferæ, it is by no means, as Dr. Hooker informs me, the species with the densest heads which most frequently differ in their inner and outer flowers. It might have been thought that the development of the ray-petals by drawing nourishment from the reproductive organs causes their abortion; but this can hardly be the sole cause, for in some Compositæ the seeds of the outer and inner florets differ, without any difference in the corolla. Possibly these several differences may be connected with the different flow of nutriment towards the central and external flowers: we know, at least, that with irregular flowers, those nearest to the axis are most subject to peloria, that is to become abnormally symmetrical. I may add, as an instance of this fact, and as a striking case of correlation, that in many pelargoniums, the two upper petals in the central flower of the truss often lose their patches of darker colour; and when this occurs, the adherent

nectary is quite aborted; the central flower thus becoming peloric or regular. When the colour is absent from only one of the two upper petals,
the nectary is not quite aborted but is much shortened.

With respect to the development of the corolla, Sprengel's idea that
the ray-florets serve to attract insects, whose agency is highly advantageous or necessary for the fertilisation of these plants, is highly probable; and if so, natural selection may have come into play. But with respect to the seeds, it seem impossible that their differences in shape, which
are not always correlated with any difference in the corolla, can be in any
way beneficial: yet in the Umbelliferæ these differences are of such apparent importance—the seeds being sometimes orthospermous in the exterior flowers and cœlospermous in the central flowers,—that the elder De
Candolle founded his main divisions in the order on such characters.
Hence modifications of structure, viewed by systematists as of high value,
may be wholly due to the laws of variation and correlation, without being,
as far as we can judge, of the slightest service to the species.

We may often falsely attribute to correlated variation structures which
are common to whole groups of species, and which in truth are simply
due to inheritance; for an ancient progenitor may have acquired through
natural selection some one modification in structure, and, after thousands
of generations, some other and independent modification; and these two
modifications, having been transmitted to a whole group of descendants
with diverse habits, would naturally be thought to be in some necessary
manner correlated. Some other correlations are apparently due to the
manner in which natural selection can alone act. For instance, Alph. de
Candolle has remarked that winged seeds are never found in fruits which
do not open; I should explain this rule by the impossibility of seeds
gradually becoming winged through natural selection, unless the capsules
were open; for in this case alone could the seeds, which were a little better adapted to be wafted by the wind, gain an advantage over others less
well fitted for wide dispersal.

Compensation and Economy of Growth

The elder Geoffroy and Goethe propounded, at about the same time,
their law of compensation or balancement of growth; or, as Goethe expressed it, "in order to spend on one side, nature is forced to economise on
the other side." I think this holds true to a certain extent with our domestic productions: if nourishment flows to one part or organ in excess, it
rarely flows, at least in excess, to another part; thus it is difficult to get a
cow to give much milk and to fatten readily. The same varieties of the
cabbage do not yield abundant and nutritious foliage and a copious supply of oil-bearing seeds. When the seeds in our fruits become atrophied,
the fruit itself gains largely in size and quality. In our poultry, a large
tuft of feathers on the head is generally accompanied by a diminished
comb, and a large beard by diminished wattles. With species in a state of
nature it can hardly be maintained that the law is of universal applica-

tion; but many good observers, more especially botanists, believe in its truth. I will not, however, here give any instances, for I see hardly any way of distinguishing between the effects, on the one hand, of a part being largely developed through natural selection and another and adjoining part being reduced by this same process or by disuse, and, on the other hand, the actual withdrawal of nutriment from one part owing to the excess of growth in another and adjoining part.

I suspect, also, that some of the cases of compensation which have been advanced, and likewise some other facts, may be merged under a more general principle, namely, that natural selection is continually trying to economise every part of the organization. If under changed conditions of life a structure, before useful, becomes less useful, its diminution will be favoured, for it will profit the individual not to have its nutriment wasted in building up an useless structure. I can thus only understand a fact with which I was much struck when examining cirripedes, and of which many analogous instances could be given: namely, that when a cirripede is parasitic within another cirripede and is thus protected, it loses more or less completely its own shell or carapace. This is the case with the male Ibla, and in a truly extraordinary manner with the Proteolepas: for the carapace in all other cirripedes consists of the three highly-important anterior segments of the head enormously developed, and furnished with great nerves and muscles; but in the parasitic and protected Proteolepas, the whole anterior part of the head is reduced to the merest rudiment attached to the bases of the prehensile antennæ. Now the saving of a large and complex structure, when rendered superfluous, would be a decided advantage to each successive individual of the species; for in the struggle for life to which every animal is exposed, each would have a better chance of supporting itself, by less nutriment being wasted.

Thus, as I believe, natural selection will tend in the long run to reduce any part of the organisation, as soon as it becomes, through changed habits, superfluous, without by any means causing some other part to be largely developed in a corresponding degree. And, conversely, that natural selection may perfectly well succeed in largely developing an organ without requiring as a necessary compensation the reduction of some adjoining part.

Multiple, Rudimentary, and Lowly-organised Structures are Variable

It seems to be a rule, as remarked by Is. Geoffroy St. Hilaire, both with varieties and species, that when any part or organ is repeated many times in the same individual (as the vertebræ in snakes, and the stamens in polyandrous flowers) the number is variable; whereas the same part or organ, when it occurs in lesser numbers, is constant. The same author as well as some botanists have further remarked that multiple parts are extremely liable to vary in structure. As "vegetable repetition," to use Prof. Owen's expression, is a sign of low organisation, the foregoing statements accord with the common opinion of naturalists, that beings which stand low in the scale of nature are more variable than those which are higher. I presume that lowness here means that the several parts of the organisation have been but little specialised for particular functions; and as long as the same part has to perform diversified work, we can perhaps see why it should remain variable, that is, why natural selection should not have preserved or rejected each little deviation of form as carefully as when the part has to serve for some one special purpose. In the same way that a knife which has to cut all sorts of things may be of almost any shape; whilst a tool for some particular purpose must be of some particular shape. Natural selection, it should never be forgotten, can act solely through and for the advantage of each being.

Rudimentary parts, as it is generally admitted, are apt to be highly variable. We shall have to recur to this subject; and I will here only add that their variability seems to result from their uselessness, and consequently from natural selection having had no power to check deviations in their structure.

A Part developed in any Species in an extraordinary degree or manner, in comparison with the same Part in allied Species, tends to be highly variable

Several years ago I was much struck by a remark, to the above effect, made by Mr. Waterhouse. Professor Owen, also, seems to have come to a nearly similar conclusion. It is hopeless to attempt to convince any one of the truth of the above proposition without giving the long array of facts which I have collected, and which cannot possibly be here introduced. I can only state my conviction that it is a rule of high generality. I am aware of several causes of error, but I hope that I have made due allowance for them. It should be understood that the rule by no means applies to any part, however unusually developed, unless it be unusually developed in one species or in a few species in comparison with the same part in many closely allied species. Thus, the wing of a bat is a most abnormal structure in the class of mammals, but the rule would not apply here, because the whole group of bats possesses wings; it would apply only if some one species had wings developed in a remarkable manner in comparison with the other species of the same genus. The rule applies very strongly in the case of secondary sexual characters, when displayed in any unusual manner. The term, secondary sexual characters, used by Hunter, relates to characters which are attached to one sex, but are not directly connected with the act of reproduction. The rule applies to males and females; but more rarely to the females, as they seldom offer remarkable secondary sexual characters. The rule being so plainly applicable in the case of secondary sexual characters, may be due to the great variability of these characters, whether or not displayed in any unusual manner —of which fact I think there can be little doubt. But that our rule is not confined to secondary sexual characters is clearly shown in the case of hermaphrodite cirripedes; I particularly attended to Mr. Waterhouse's remark, whilst investigating this Order, and I am fully convinced that the rule almost always holds good. I shall, in a future work, give a list of all the more remarkable cases; I will here give only one, as it illustrates the rule in its largest application. The opercular valves of sessile cirripedes (rock barnacles) are, in every sense of the word, very important structures, and they differ extremely little even in distinct genera; but in the several species of one genus, Pyrgoma, these valves present a marvellous amount of diversification; the homologous valves in the different species being sometimes wholly unlike in shape; and the amount of variation in the individuals of the same species is so great, that it is no exaggeration to state that the varieties of the same species differ more from each other in the characters derived from these important organs, than do the species belonging to other distinct genera.

As with birds the individuals of the same species, inhabiting the same country, vary extremely little, I have particularly attended to them; and the rule certainly seems to hold good in this class. I cannot make out that it applies to plants, and this would have seriously shaken my belief in its truth, had not the great variability in plants made it particularly difficult to compare their relative degrees of variability.

When we see any part or organ developed in a remarkable degree or manner in a species, the fair presumption is that it is of high importance to that species: nevertheless it is in this case eminently liable to variation. Why should this be so? On the view that each species has been independently created, with all its parts as we now see them, I can see no explanation. But on the view that groups of species are descended from some other species, and have been modified through natural selection, I think we can obtain some light. First let me make some preliminary remarks. If, in our domestic animals, any part or the whole animal be neglected, and no selection be applied, that part (for instance, the comb in the Dorking fowl) or the whole breed will cease to have a uniform character: and the breed may be said to be degenerating. In rudimentary organs, and in those which have been but little specialised for any particular purpose, and perhaps in polymorphic groups, we see a nearly parallel case; for in such cases natural selection either has not or cannot have come into full play, and thus the organisation is left in a fluctuating condition. But what here more particularly concerns us is, that those points in our domestic animals, which at the present time are undergoing rapid change by continued selection, are also eminently liable to variation. Look at the individuals of the same breed of the pigeon, and see what a prodigious amount of difference there is in the beaks of tumblers, in the beaks and wattle of carriers, in the carriage and tail of fantails, &c., these being the points now mainly attended to by English fanciers. Even in the same sub-breed, as in that of the short-faced tumbler, it is notoriously difficult to breed nearly perfect birds, many departing widely from the standard. There may truly be said to be a constant struggle going on between, on the one hand, the tendency to reversion to a less perfect state, as well as an innate tendency to new variations, and, on the other hand, the power of steady selection to keep the breed true. In the long run selection gains the day, and we do not expect to fail so completely as to breed a bird as coarse as a common tumbler pigeon from a good short-faced strain. But as long as selection is rapidly going on, much variability in the parts undergoing modification may always be expected.

Now let us turn to nature. When a part has been developed in an extraordinary manner in any one species, compared with the other species of the same genus, we may conclude that this part has undergone an extraordinary amount of modification since the period when the several species branched off from the common progenitor of the genus. This period will seldom be remote in any extreme degree, as species rarely endure for more than one geological period. An extraordinary amount of modification implies an unusually large and long-continued amount of variability, which has continually been accumulated by natural selection for the benefit of the species. But as the variability of the extraordinarily developed part or organ has been so great and long-continued within a period not excessively remote, we might, as a general rule, still expect to find more variability in such parts than in other parts of the organisation which have remained for a much longer period nearly constant. And this, I am convinced, is the case. That the struggle between natural selection on the one hand, and the tendency to reversion and variability on the other hand, will in the course of time cease; and that the most abnormally developed organs may be made constant, I see no reason to doubt. Hence, when an organ, however abnormal it may be, has been transmitted in approximately the same condition to many modified descendants, as in the case of the wing of the bat, it must have existed, according to our theory, for an immense period in nearly the same state; and thus it has come not to be more variable than any other structure. It is only in those cases in which the modification has been comparatively recent and extraordinarily great that we ought to find the *generative variability,* as it may be called, still present in a high degree. For in this case the variability will seldom as yet have been fixed by the continued selection of the individuals varying in the required manner and degree, and by the continued rejection of those tending to revert to a former and less-modified condition.

Specific Characters more Variable than Generic Characters

The principle discussed under the last heading may be applied to our present subject. It is notorious that specific characters are more variable than generic. To explain by a simple example what is meant: if in a large genus of plants some species had blue flowers and some had red, the colour would be only a specific character, and no one would be surprised at one of the blue species varying into red, or conversely; but if all the species had blue flowers, the colour would become a generic character, and its variation would be a more unusual circumstance. I have chosen this example because the explanation which most naturalists would advance is not here applicable, namely, that specific characters are more variable than generic, because they are taken from parts of less physiological importance than those commonly used for classing genera. I believe this explanation is partly, yet only indirectly, true; I shall, however, have to return to this point in the chapter on Classification. It would be almost superfluous to adduce evidence in support of the statement, that ordinary specific characters are more variable than generic; but with respect to important characters I have repeatedly noticed in works on natural history, that when an author remarks with surprise that some important organ or part, which is generally very constant throughout a large group of species, *differs* considerably in closely-allied species, it is often *variable* in the individuals of the same species. And this fact shows that a character, which is generally of generic value, when it sinks in value and becomes only of specific value, often becomes variable, though its physiological importance may remain the same. Something of the same kind applies to monstrosities: at least Is. Geoffroy St. Hilaire apparently entertains no doubt, that the more an organ normally differs in the different species of the same group, the more subject it is to anomalies in the individuals.

On the ordinary view of each species having been independently created, why should that part of the structure, which differs from the same part in other independently-created species of the same genus, be more variable than those parts which are closely alike in the several species? I do not see that any explanation can be given. But on the view that species are only strongly marked and fixed varieties, we might expect often to find them still continuing to vary in those parts of their structure which have varied within a moderately recent period, and which have thus come to differ. Or to state the case in another manner:—the points in which all the species of a genus resemble each other, and in which they differ from allied genera, are called generic characters; and these characters may be attributed to inheritance from a common progenitor, for it can rarely have happened that natural selection will have modified several distinct species, fitted to more or less widely-different habits, in exactly the same manner: and as these so-called generic characters have been inherited from before the period when the several species first branched off from their common progenitor, and subsequently have not varied or come to differ in any degree, or only in a slight degree, it is not probable that they should vary at the present day. On the other hand, the points in which species differ from other species of the same genus are called specific characters; and as these specific characters have varied and come to differ since the period when the species branched off from a common progenitor, it is probable that they should still often be in some degree variable,—at least more variable than those parts of the organisation which have for a very long period remained constant.

Secondary Sexual Characters Variable.—I think it will be admitted by naturalists, without my entering on details, that secondary sexual characters are highly variable. It will also be admitted that species of the same group differ from each other more widely in their secondary sexual characters, than in other parts of their organisation: compare, for instance, the amount of difference between the males of gallinaceous birds, in which secondary sexual characters are strongly displayed, with the amount of difference between the females. The cause of the original variability of these characters is not manifest; but we can see why they should not have been rendered as constant and uniform as others, for they are accumulated by sexual selection, which is less rigid in its action than ordinary selection, as it does not entail death, but only gives fewer offspring to the less favoured males. Whatever the cause may be of the variability of secondary sexual characters, as they are highly variable, sexual selection will have had a wide scope for action, and may thus have succeeded in giving to the species of the same group a greater amount of difference in these than in other respects.

It is a remarkable fact, that the secondary differences between the two sexes of the same species are generally displayed in the very same parts of the organisation in which the species of the same genus differ from each other. Of this fact I will give in illustration the two first instances which happen to stand on my list; and as the differences in these cases are of a very unusual nature, the relation can hardly be accidental. The same number of joints in the tarsi is a character common to very large groups of beetles, but in the Engidæ, as Westwood has remarked, the number varies greatly; and the number likewise differs in the two sexes of the same species. Again in the fossorial hymenoptera, the neuration of the wings is a character of the highest importance, because common to large groups; but in certain genera the neuration differs in the different species, and likewise in the two sexes of the same species. Sir J. Lubbock has recently remarked, that several minute crustaceans offer excellent illustrations of this law. "In Pontella, for instance, the sexual characters are afforded mainly by the anterior antennæ and by the fifth pair of legs: the specific differences also are principally given by these organs." This relation has a clear meaning on my view: I look at all the species of the same genus as having as certainly descended from a common progenitor, as have the two sexes of any one species. Consequently, whatever part of the structure of the common progenitor, or of its early descendants, became variable, variations of this part would, it is highly probable, be taken advantage of by natural and sexual selection, in order to fit the several species to their several places in the economy of nature, and likewise to fit the two sexes of the same species to each other, or to fit the males to struggle with other males for the possession of the females.

Finally, then, I conclude that the greater variability of specific characters, or those which distinguish species from species, than of generic characters, or those which are possessed by all the species;—that the frequent extreme variability of any part which is developed in a species in an extraordinary manner in comparison with the same part in its congeners; and the slight degree of variability in a part, however extraordinarily it may be developed, if it be common to a whole group of species;—that the great variability of secondary sexual characters, and their great difference in closely allied species;—that secondary sexual and ordinary specific differences are generally displayed in the same parts of the organisation, —are all principles closely connected together. All being mainly due to the species of the same group being the descendants of a common progenitor, from whom they have inherited much in common,—to parts which have recently and largely varied being more likely still to go on varying than parts which have long been inherited and have not varied—to natural selection having more or less completely, according to the lapse of time, overmastered the tendency to reversion and to further variability, —to sexual selection being less rigid than ordinary selection,—and to variations in the same parts having been accumulated by natural and sexual selection, and having been thus adapted for secondary sexual, and for ordinary purposes.

Distinct Species present analogous Variations, so that a Variety of one Species often assumes a Character proper to an allied Species, or reverts to some of the Characters of an early Progenitor.—These propositions will be most readily understood by looking to our domestic races. The most distinct breeds of the pigeon, in countries widely apart, present subvarieties with reversed feathers on the head, and with feathers on the feet, —characters not possessed by the aboriginal rock-pigeon; these then are analogous variations in two or more distinct races. The frequent presence of fourteen or even sixteen tail-feathers in the pouter may be considered as a variation representing the normal structure of another race, the fantail. I presume that no one will doubt that all such analogous variations are due to the several races of the pigeon having inherited from a common parent the same constitution and tendency to variation, when acted on by similar unknown influences. In the vegetable kingdom we have a case of analogous variation, in the enlarged stems, or as commonly called roots, of the Swedish turnip and Ruta baga, plants which several botanists rank as varieties produced by cultivation from a common parent: if this be not so, the case will then be one of analogous variation in two so-called distinct species; and to these a third may be added, namely, the common turnip. According to the ordinary view of each species having been independently created, we should have to attribute this similarity in the enlarged stems of these three plants, not to the *vera causa* of community of descent, and a consequent tendency to vary in a like manner, but to three separate yet closely related acts of creation. Many similar cases of analogous variation have been observed by Naudin in the great gourd-family, and by various authors in our cereals. Similar cases occurring with insects under natural conditions have lately been discussed with much ability by Mr. Walsh, who has grouped them under his law of Equable Variability.

With pigeons, however, we have another case, namely, the occasional appearance in all the breeds, of slaty-blue birds with two black bars on the wings, white loins, a bar at the end of the tail, with the outer feathers externally edged near their basis with white. As all these marks are characteristic of the parent rock-pigeon, I presume that no one will doubt that this is a case of reversion, and not of a new yet analogous variation appearing in the several breeds. We may, I think, confidently come to this conclusion, because, as we have seen, these coloured marks are eminently liable to appear in the crossed offspring of two distinct and differently coloured breeds; and in this case there is nothing in the external conditions of life to cause the reappearance of the slaty-blue, with the several marks, beyond the influence of the mere act of crossing on the laws of inheritance.

No doubt it is a very surprising fact that characters should reappear after having been lost for many, probably for hundreds of generations. But when a breed has been crossed only once by some other breed, the offspring occasionally show for many generations a tendency to revert in character to the foreign breed—some say, for a dozen or even a score of generations. After twelve generations, the proportion of blood, to use a common expression, from one ancestor, is only 1 in 2048; and yet, as we see, it is generally believed that a tendency to reversion is retained by this remnant of foreign blood. In a breed which has not been crossed, but in which *both* parents have lost some character which their progenitor possessed, the tendency, whether strong or weak, to reproduce the lost character might, as was formerly remarked, for all that we can see to the contrary, be transmitted for almost any number of generations. When a character which has been lost in a breed, reappears after a great number of generations, the most probable hypothesis is, not that one individual suddenly takes after an ancestor removed by some hundred generations, but that in each successive generation the character in question has been lying latent, and at last, under unknown favourable conditions, is developed. With the barb-pigeon, for instance, which very rarely produces a blue bird, it is probable that there is a latent tendency in each generation to produce blue plumage. The abstract improbability of such a tendency being transmitted through a vast number of generations, is not greater than that of quite useless or rudimentary organs being similarly transmitted. A mere tendency to produce a rudiment is indeed sometimes thus inherited.

As all the species of the same genus are supposed to be descended from a common progenitor, it might be expected that they would occasionally vary in an analogous manner; so that the varieties of two or more species would resemble each other, or that a variety of one species would resemble in certain characters another and distinct species,—this other species being, according to our view, only a well-marked and permanent variety. But characters exclusively due to analogous variation would probably be of an unimportant nature, for the preservation of all functionally important characters will have been determined through natural selection, in accordance with the different habits of the species. It might further be expected that the species of the same genus would occasionally exhibit reversions to long lost characters. As, however, we do not know the com-

mon ancestors of any natural group, we cannot distinguish between reversionary and analogous characters. If, for instance, we did not know that
the parent rock-pigeon was not feather-footed or turn-crowned, we could
not have told, whether such characters in our domestic breeds were reversions or only analogous variations; but we might have inferred that
the blue colour was a case of reversion from the number of the markings,
which are correlated with this tint, and which would not probably have
all appeared together from simple variation. More especially we might
have inferred this, from the blue colour and the several marks so often
appearing when differently coloured breeds are crossed. Hence, although
under nature it must generally be left doubtful, what cases are reversions
to formerly existing characters, and what are new but analogous variations, yet we ought, on our theory, sometimes to find the varying offspring of a species assuming characters which are already present in other
members of the same group. And this undoubtedly is the case.

The difficulty in distinguishing variable species is largely due to the
varieties mocking, as it were, other species of the same genus. A considerable catalogue, also, could be given of forms intermediate between two
other forms, which themselves can only doubtfully be ranked as species;
and this shows, unless all these closely allied forms be considered as independently created species, that they have in varying assumed some of
the characters of the others. But the best evidence of analogous variations is afforded by parts or organs which are generally constant in character, but which occasionally vary so as to resemble, in some degree, the
same part or organ in an allied species. I have collected a long list of such
cases; but here, as before, I lie under the great disadvantage of not being
able to give them. I can only repeat that such cases certainly occur, and
seem to me very remarkable.

I will, however, give one curious and complex case, not indeed as affecting any important character, but from occurring in several species of
the same genus, partly under domestication and partly under nature. It is
a case almost certainly of reversion. The ass sometimes has very distinct
transverse bars on its legs, like those on the legs of the zebra: it has been
asserted that these are plainest in the foal, and, from inquiries which I
have made, I believe this to be true. The stripe on the shoulder is sometimes double, and is very variable in length and outline. A white ass, but
not an albino, has been described without either spinal or shoulder stripe:
and these stripes are sometimes very obscure, or actually quite lost, in
dark-coloured asses. The koulan of Pallas is said to have been seen with a
double shoulder-stripe. Mr. Blyth has seen a specimen of the hemionus
with a distinct shoulder-stripe, though it properly has none; and I have
been informed by Colonel Poole that the foals of this species are generally striped on the legs, and faintly on the shoulder. The quagga, though
so plainly barred like a zebra over the body, is without bars on the legs;
but Dr. Gray has figured one specimen with very distinct zebra-like bars
on the hocks.

With respect to the horse, I have collected cases in England of the spinal stripe in horses of the most distinct breeds, and of *all* colours: transverse bars on the legs are not rare in duns, mouse-duns, and in one instance in a chestnut: a faint shoulder-stripe may sometimes be seen in duns, and I have seen a trace in a bay horse. My son made a careful examination and sketch for me of a dun Belgian cart-horse with a double stripe on each shoulder and with leg-stripes; I have myself seen a dun Devonshire pony, and a small dun Welsh pony has been carefully described to me, both with *three* parallel stripes on each shoulder.

In the north-west part of India the Kattywar breed of horses is so generally striped, that, as I hear from Colonel Poole, who examined this breed for the Indian Government, a horse without stripes is not considered as purely-bred. The spine is always striped; the legs are generally barred; and the shoulder-stripe, which is sometimes double and sometimes treble, is common; the side of the face, moreover, is sometimes striped. The stripes are often plainest in the foal; and sometimes quite disappear in old horses. Colonel Poole has seen both gray and bay Kattywar horses striped when first foaled. I have also reason to suspect, from information given me by Mr. W. W. Edwards, that with the English racehorse the spinal stripe is much commoner in the foal than in the full-grown animal. I have myself recently bred a foal from a bay mare (offspring of a Turkoman horse and a Flemish mare) by a bay English racehorse; this foal when a week old was marked on its hinder quarters and on its forehead with numerous, very narrow, dark, zebra-like bars, and its legs were feebly striped: all the stripes soon disappeared completely. Without here entering on further details, I may state that I have collected cases of leg and shoulder stripes in horses of very different breeds in various countries from Britain to Eastern China; and from Norway in the north to the Malay Archipelago in the south. In all parts of the world these stripes occur far oftenest in duns and mouse-duns; by the term dun a large range of colour is included, from one between brown and black to a close approach to cream-colour.

I am aware that Colonel Hamilton Smith, who has written on this subject, believes that the several breeds of the horse are descended from several aboriginal species—one of which, the dun, was striped; and that the above-described appearances are all due to ancient crosses with the dun stock. But this view may be safely rejected; for it is highly improbable that the heavy Belgian cart-horse, Welsh ponies, Norwegian cobs, the lanky Kattywar race, &c., inhabiting the most distant parts of the world, should all have been crossed with one supposed aboriginal stock.

Now let us turn to the effects of crossing the several species of the horse-genus. Rollin asserts, that the common mule from the ass and horse is particularly apt to have bars on its legs; according to Mr. Gosse, in certain parts of the United States about nine out of ten mules have striped legs. I once saw a mule with its legs so much striped that any one might have thought that it was a hybrid-zebra; and Mr. W. C. Martin, in his excellent treatise on the horse, has given a figure of a similar mule. In four coloured drawings, which I have seen, of hybrids between the ass and zebra, the legs were much more plainly barred than the rest of the body; and in one of them there was a double shoulder-stripe. In Lord Morton's famous hybrid, from a chestnut mare and male quagga, the hybrid, and even the pure offspring subsequently produced from the same mare by a black Arabian sire, were much more plainly barred across the legs than is even the pure quagga. Lastly, and this is another most remarkable case, a hybrid has been figured by Dr. Gray (and he informs me that he knows of a second case) from the ass and the hemionus; and this hybrid, though the ass only occasionally has stripes on its legs and the hemionus has none and has not even a shoulder-stripe, nevertheless had all four legs barred, and had three short shoulder-stripes, like those on the dun Devonshire and Welsh ponies, and even had some zebra-like stripes on the sides of its face. With respect to this last fact, I was so convinced that not even a stripe of colour appears from what is commonly called chance, that I was led solely from the occurrence of the face-stripes on this hybrid from the ass and hemionus to ask Colonel Poole whether such face-stripes ever occurred in the eminently striped Kattywar breed of horses, and was, as we have seen, answered in the affirmative.

What now are we to say to these several facts? We see several distinct species of the horse-genus becoming, by simple variation, striped on the legs like a zebra, or striped on the shoulders like an ass. In the horse we see this tendency strong whenever a dun tint appears—a tint which approaches to that of the general colouring of the other species of the genus. The appearance of the stripes is not accompanied by any change of form or by any other new character. We see this tendency to become striped most strongly displayed in hybrids from between several of the most distinct species. Now observe the case of the several breeds of pigeons: they are descended from a pigeon (including two or three sub-species or geographical races) of a bluish colour, with certain bars and other marks; and when any breed assumes by simple variation a bluish tint, these bars and other marks invariably reappear; but without any other change of form or character. When the oldest and truest breeds of various colours are crossed, we see a strong tendency for the blue tint and bars and marks to reappear in the mongrels. I have stated that the most probable hypothesis to account for the reappearance of very ancient characters, is— that there is a *tendency* in the young of each successive generation to produce the long-lost character, and that this tendency, from unknown causes, sometimes prevails. And we have just seen that in several species of the horse-genus the stripes are either plainer or appear more commonly in the young than in the old. Call the breeds of pigeons, some of which have bred true for centuries, species; and how exactly parallel is the case with that of the species of the horse-genus! For myself, I venture confidently to look back thousands on thousands of generations, and I see an animal striped like a zebra, but perhaps otherwise very differently constructed, the common parent of our domestic horse (whether or not it be descended from one or more wild stocks) of the ass, the hemionus, quagga, and zebra.

He who believes that each equine species was independently created, will, I presume, assert that each species has been created with a tendency to vary, both under nature and under domestication, in this particular manner, so as often to become striped like the other species of the genus; and that each has been created with a strong tendency, when crossed with species inhabiting distant quarters of the world, to produce hybrids resembling in their stripes, not their own parents, but other species of the genus. To admit this view is, as it seems to me, to reject a real for an unreal, or at least for an unknown, cause. It makes the works of God a mere mockery and deception; I would almost as soon believe that the old and ignorant cosmogonists, that fossil shells had never lived, but had been created in stone so as to mock the shells living on the sea-shore.

Summary.—Our ignorance of the laws of variation is profound. Not in one case out of a hundred can we pretend to assign any reason why this or that part has varied. But whenever we have the means of instituting a comparison, the same laws appear to have acted in producing the lesser differences between varieties of the same species, and the greater differences between species of the same genus. Changed conditions generally induce mere fluctuating variability, but sometimes they cause direct and definite effects; and these may become strongly marked in the course of time, though we have not sufficient evidence on this head. Habit in producing constitutional peculiarities and use in strengthening and disuse in weakening and diminishing organs, appear in many cases to have been potent in their effects. Homologous parts tend to vary in the same manner, and homologous parts tend to cohere. Modifications in hard parts and in external parts sometimes affect softer and internal parts. When one part is largely developed, perhaps it tends to draw nourishment from the adjoining parts; and every part of the structure which can be saved without detriment will be saved. Changes of structure at an early age may affect parts subsequently developed; and many cases of correlated variation, the nature of which we are unable to understand, undoubtedly occur. Multiple parts are variable in number and in structure, perhaps arising from such parts not having been closely specialised for any particular function, so that their modifications have not been closely checked by natural selection. It follows probably from this same cause, that organic beings low in the scale are more variable than those standing higher in the scale, and which have their whole organisation more specialised. Rudimentary organs, from being useless, are not regulated by natural selection, and hence are variable. Specific characters—that is, the characters which have come to differ since the several species of the same genus branched off from a common parent—are more variable than generic characters, or those which have long been inherited, and have not differed from this same period. In these remarks we have referred to special parts or organs being still variable, because they have recently varied and thus come to differ; but we have also seen in the second chapter that the same principle applies to the whole individual; for in a district where many species of a genus are found—that is, where there has been much former variation and differentiation, or where the manufactory of new specific forms has been actively at work—in that district and amongst these species, we now find, on an average, most varieties. Secondary sexual characters are highly variable, and such characters differ much in the species of the same group. Variability in the same parts of the organisation has generally been taken advantage of in giving secondary sexual differences to the two sexes of the same species, and specific differences to the several species of the same genus. Any part or organ developed to an extraordinary size or in an extraordinary manner, in comparison with the same part or organ in the allied species, must have gone through an extraordinary amount of modification since the genus arose; and thus we can understand why it should often still be variable in a much higher degree than other parts; for variation is a long-continued and slow process, and natural selection will in such cases not as yet have had time to overcome the tendency to further variability and to reversion to a less modified state. But when a species with any extraordinarily-developed organ has become the parent of many modified descendants—which on our view must be a very slow process, requiring a long lapse of time—in this case, natural selection has succeeded in giving a fixed character to the organ, in however extraordinary a manner it may have been developed. Species inheriting nearly the same constitution from a common parent, and exposed to similar influences, naturally tend to present analogous variations, or these same species may occasionally revert to some of the characters of their ancient progenitors. Although new and important modifications may not arise from reversion and analogous variation, such modifications will add to the beautiful and harmonious diversity of nature.

Whatever the cause may be of each slight difference between the offspring and their parents—and a cause for each must exist—we have reason to believe that it is the steady accumulation of beneficial differences which has given rise to all the more important modifications of structure in relation to the habits of each species.

CHAPTER VI

DIFFICULTIES OF THE THEORY

Difficulties of the theory of descent with modification—Absence or rarity of transitional varieties—Transitions in habits of life—Diversified habits in the same species—Species with habits widely different from those of their allies—Organs of extreme perfection—Modes of transition—Cases of difficulty—Natura non facit saltum—Organs of small importance—Organs not in all cases absolutely perfect—The law of Unity of Type and of the Conditions of Existence embraced by the theory of Natural Selection.

LONG before the reader has arrived at this part of my work, a crowd of difficulties will have occurred to him. Some of them are so serious that to this day I can hardly reflect on them without being in some degree staggered; but, to the best of my judgment, the greater number are only apparent, and those that are real are not, I think, fatal to the theory.

These difficulties and objections may be classed under the following heads:—First, why, if species have descended from other species by fine gradations, do we not everywhere see innumerable transitional forms? Why is not all nature in confusion, instead of the species being, as we see them, well defined?

Secondly, is it possible that an animal having, for instance, the structure and habits of a bat, could have been formed by the modification of some other animal with widely different habits and structure? Can we believe that natural selection could produce, on the one hand, an organ of trifling importance, such as the tail of a giraffe, which serves as a fly-flapper, and, on the other hand, an organ so wonderful as the eye?

Thirdly, can instincts be acquired and modified through natural selection? What shall we say to the instinct which leads the bee to make cells, and which has practically anticipated the discoveries of profound mathematicians?

Fourthly, how can we account for species, when crossed, being sterile and producing sterile offspring, whereas, when varieties are crossed, their fertility is unimpaired?

The two first heads will here be discussed; some miscellaneous objections in the following chapter; Instinct and Hybridism in the two succeeding chapters.

On the Absence or Rarity of Transitional Varieties.—As natural selection acts solely by the preservation of profitable modifications, each new form will tend in a fully-stocked country to take the place of, and finally to exterminate, its own less improved parent-form and other less favoured forms with which it comes into competition. Thus extinction and natural selection go hand in hand. Hence, if we look at each species as descended from some unknown form, both the parent and all the transitional varieties will generally have been exterminated by the very process of the formation and perfection of the new form.

But, as by this theory innumerable transitional forms must have existed, why do we not find them embedded in countless numbers in the crust of the earth? It will be more convenient to discuss this question in the chapter on the Imperfection of the Geological Record; and I will here only state that I believe the answer mainly lies in the record being incomparably less perfect than is generally supposed. The crust of the earth is a vast museum; but the natural collections have been imperfectly made, and only at long intervals of time.

But it may be urged that when several closely-allied species inhabit the same territory, we surely ought to find at the present time many transitional forms. Let us take a simple case: in travelling from north to south over a continent, we generally meet at successive intervals with closely allied or representative species, evidently filling nearly the same place in the natural economy of the land. These representative species often meet and interlock; and as the one becomes rarer and rarer, the other becomes more and more frequent, till the one replaces the other. But if we compare these species where they intermingle, they are generally as absolutely distinct from each other in every detail of structure as are specimens taken from the metropolis inhabited by each. By my theory these allied species are descended from a common parent; and during the process of modification, each has become adapted to the conditions of life of its own region, and has supplanted and exterminated its original parent-form and all the transitional varieties between its past and present states. Hence we ought not to expect at the present time to meet with numerous transitional varieties in each region, though they must have existed there, and may be embedded there in a fossil condition. But in the intermediate region, having intermediate conditions of life, why do we not now find closely-linking intermediate varieties? This difficulty for a long time quite confounded me. But I think it can be in large part explained.

In the first place we should be extremely cautious in inferring, because an area is now continuous, that it has been continuous during a long period. Geology would lead us to believe that most continents have been broken up into islands even during the later tertiary periods; and in such islands distinct species might have been separately formed without the possibility of intermediate varieties existing in the intermediate zones. By changes in the form of the land and of climate, marine areas now continuous must often have existed within recent times in a far less continuous and uniform condition than at present. But I will pass over this way of escaping from the difficulty; for I believe that many perfectly defined species have been formed on strictly continuous areas; though I do not, doubt that the formerly broken condition of areas now continuous, has played an important part in the formation of new species, more especially with freely-crossing and wandering animals.

In looking at species as they are now distributed over a wide area, we generally find them tolerably numerous over a large territory, then becoming somewhat abruptly rarer and rarer on the confines, and finally disappearing. Hence the neutral territory, between two representative species is generally narrow in comparison with the territory proper to each. We see the same fact in ascending mountains, and sometimes it is quite remarkable how abruptly, as Alph. de Candolle has observed, a common alpine species disappears. The same fact has been noticed by E. Forbes in sounding the depths of the sea with the dredge. To those who look at climate and the physical conditions of life as the all-important elements of distribution, these facts ought to cause surprise, as climate and height or depth graduate away insensibly. But when we bear in mind that almost every species, even in its metropolis, would increase immensely in numbers, were it not for other competing species; that nearly all either prey on or serve as prey for others; in short, that each organic being is either directly or indirectly related in the most important manner to other organic beings,—we see that the range of the inhabitants of any country by no means exclusively depends on insensibly changing physical conditions, but in a large part on the presence of other species, on which it lives, or by which it is destroyed, or with which it comes into competition; and as these species are already defined objects, not blending one into another by insensible gradations, the range of any one species, depending as it does on the range of others, will tend to be sharply defined. Moreover, each species on the confines of its range, where it exists in lessened numbers, will, during fluctuations in the number of its enemies or of its prey, or in the nature of the seasons, be extremely liable to utter extermination; and thus its geographical range will come to be still more sharply defined.

As allied or representative species, when inhabiting a continuous area, are generally distributed in such a manner that each has a wide range, with a comparatively narrow neutral territory between them, in which they become rather suddenly rarer and rarer; then, as varieties do not essentially differ from species, the same rule will probably apply to both; and if we take a varying species inhabiting a very large area, we shall have to adapt two varieties to two large areas, and a third variety to a narrow intermediate zone. The intermediate variety, consequently, will exist in lesser numbers from inhabiting a narrow and lesser area; and practically, as far as I can make out, this rule holds good with varieties in a state of nature. I have met with striking instances of the rule in the case of varieties intermediate between well-marked varieties in the genus Balanus. And it would appear from information given me by Mr. Watson, Dr. Asa Gray, and Mr. Wollaston, that generally, when varieties intermediate between two other forms occur, they are much rarer numerically than the forms which they connect. Now, if we may trust these facts and inferences, and conclude that varieties linking two other varieties together generally have existed in lesser numbers than the forms which they connect, then we can understand why intermediate varieties should not endure for very long periods:—why, as a general rule, they should be exterminated and disappear, sooner than the forms which they originally linked together.

For any form existing in lesser numbers would, as already remarked, run a greater chance of being exterminated than one existing in large numbers; and in this particular case the intermediate form would be eminently liable to the inroads of closely-allied forms existing on both sides of it. But it is a far more important consideration, that during the process of further modification, by which two varieties are supposed to be converted and perfected into two distinct species, the two which exist in larger numbers, from inhabiting larger areas, will have a great advantage over the intermediate variety, which exists in smaller numbers in a narrow and intermediate zone. For forms existing in larger numbers will have a better chance, within any given period, of presenting further favourable variations for natural selection to seize on, than will the rarer forms which exist in lesser numbers. Hence, the more common forms, in the race for life, will tend to beat and supplant the less common forms, for these will be more slowly modified and improved. It is the same principle which, as I believe, accounts for the common species in each country, as shown in the second chapter, presenting on an average a greater number of well-marked varieties than do the rarer species. I may illustrate what I mean by supposing three varieties of sheep to be kept, one adapted to an extensive mountainous region; a second to a comparatively narrow, hilly tract; and a third to the wide plains at the base; and that the inhabitants are all trying with equal steadiness and skill to improve their stocks by selection; the chances in this case will be strongly in favour of the great holders on the mountains or on the plains, improving their breeds more quickly than the small holders on the intermediate narrow, hilly tract; and consequently the improved mountain or plain breed will soon take the place of the less improved hill breed; and thus the two breeds, which originally existed in greater numbers, will come into close contact with each other, without the interposition of the supplanted, intermediate hill variety.

To sum up, I believe that species come to be tolerably well-defined objects, and do not at any one period present an inextricable chaos of varying and intermediate links; first, because new varieties are very slowly formed, for variation is a slow process, and natural selection can do nothing until favourable individual differences or variations occur, and until a place in the natural polity of the country can be better filled by some modification of some one or more of its inhabitants. And such new places will depend on slow changes of climate, or on the occasional immigration of new inhabitants, and, probably, in a still more important degree, on some of the old inhabitants becoming slowly modified, with the new forms thus produced, and the old ones acting and reacting on each other. So that, in any one region and at any one time, we ought to see only a few species presenting slight modifications of structure in some degree permanent; and this assuredly we do see.

Secondly, areas now continuous must often have existed within the recent period as isolated portions, in which many forms, more especially amongst the classes which unite for each birth and wander much, may have separately been rendered sufficiently distinct to rank as representative species. In this case, intermediate varieties between the several representative species and their common parent, must formerly have existed within each isolated portion of the land, but these links during the process of natural selection will have been supplanted and exterminated, so that they will no longer be found in a living state.

Thirdly, when two or more varieties have been formed in different portions of a strictly continuous area, intermediate varieties will, it is probable, at first have been formed in the intermediate zones, but they will generally have had a short duration. For these intermediate varieties will, from reasons already assigned (namely from what we know of the actual distribution of closely allied or representative species, and likewise of acknowledged varieties), exist in the intermediate zones in lesser numbers than the varieties which they tend to connect. From this cause alone the intermediate varieties will be liable to accidental extermination; and during the process of further modification through natural selection, they will almost certainly be beaten and supplanted by the forms which they connect; for these from existing in greater numbers will, in the aggregate, present more varieties, and thus be further improved through natural selection and gain further advantages.

Lastly, looking not to any one time, but to all time, if my theory be true, numberless intermediate varieties, linking closely together all the species of the same group, must assuredly have existed; but the very process of natural selection constantly tends, as has been so often remarked, to exterminate the parent-forms and the intermediate links. Consequently evidence of their former existence could be found only amongst fossil remains, which are preserved, as we shall attempt to show in a future chapter, in an extremely imperfect and intermittent record.

On the Origin and Transitions of Organic Beings with peculiar Habits and Structure.—It has been asked by the opponents of such views as I hold, how, for instance, could a land carnivorous animal have been converted into one with aquatic habits; for how could the animal in its transitional state have subsisted? It would be easy to show that there now exist carnivorous animals presenting close intermediate grades from strictly terrestrial to aquatic habits; and as each exists by a struggle for life, it is clear that each must be well adapted to its place in nature. Look at the Mustela vison of North America, which has webbed feet, and which resembles an otter in its fur, short legs, and form of tail. During the summer this animal dives for and preys on fish, but during the long winter it leaves the frozen waters, and preys, like other pole-cats, on mice and land animals. If a different case had been taken, and it had been asked how an insectivorous quadruped could possibly have been converted into a flying bat, the question would have been far more difficult to answer. Yet I think such difficulties have little weight.

Here, as on other occasions, I lie under a heavy disadvantage, for, out of the many striking cases which I have collected, I can only give one or two instances of transitional habits and structures in allied species; and of diversified habits, either constant or occasional, in the same species. And it seems to me that nothing less than a long list of such cases is sufficient to lessen the difficulty in any particular case like that of the bat.

Look at the family of squirrels; here we have the finest gradation from animals with their tails only slightly flattened, and from others, as Sir J. Richardson has remarked, with the posterior part of their bodies rather wide and with the skin on their flanks rather full, to the so-called flying squirrels; and flying squirrels have their limbs and even the base of the tail united by a broad expanse of skin, which serves as a parachute and allows them to glide through the air to an astonishing distance from tree to tree. We cannot doubt that each structure is of use to each kind of squirrel in its own country, by enabling it to escape birds or beasts of prey, to collect food more quickly, or, as there is reason to believe, to lessen the danger from occasional falls. But it does not follow from this fact that the structure of each squirrel is the best that it is possible to conceive under all possible conditions. Let the climate and vegetation change, let other competing rodents or new beasts of prey immigrate, or old ones become modified, and all analogy would lead us to believe that some at least of the squirrels would decrease in numbers or become exterminated, unless they also become modified and improved in structure in a corresponding manner. Therefore, I can see no difficulty, more especially under changing conditions of life, in the continued preservation of individuals with fuller and fuller flank-membranes, each modification being useful, each being propagated, until, by the accumulated effects of this process of natural selection, a perfect so-called flying squirrel was produced.

Now look at the Galeopithecus or so-called flying lemur, which formerly was ranked amongst bats, but is now believed to belong to the Insectivora. An extremely wide flank-membrane stretches from the corners of the jaw to the tail, and includes the limbs with the elongated fingers. This flank-membrane is furnished with an extensor muscle. Although no graduated links of structure, fitted for gliding through the air, now connect the Galeopithecus with the other Insectivora, yet there is no difficulty in supposing that such links formerly existed, and that each was developed in the same manner as with the less perfectly gliding squirrels; each grade of structure having been useful to its possessor. Nor can I see any insuperable difficulty in further believing that the membrane connected fingers and fore-arm of the Galeopithecus might have been greatly lengthened by natural selection; and this, as far as the organs of flight are concerned, would have converted the animal into a bat. In certain bats in which the wing-membrane extends from the top of the shoulder to the tail and includes the hind-legs, we perhaps see traces of an apparatus originally fitted for gliding through the air rather than for flight.

If about a dozen genera of birds were to become extinct, who would have ventured to surmise that birds might have existed which used their wings solely as flappers, like the logger-headed duck (Micropterus of Eyton); as fins in the water and as front-legs on the land, like the penguin; as sails, like the ostrich; and functionally for no purpose, like the Apteryx? Yet the structure of each of these birds is good for it, under the conditions of life to which it is exposed, for each has to live by a struggle; but it is not necessarily the best possible under all possible conditions. It must not be inferred from these remarks that any of the grades of wing-structure here alluded to, which perhaps may all be the result of disuse, indicate the steps by which birds actually acquired their perfect power of flight; but they serve to show what diversified means of transition are at least possible.

Seeing that a few members of such water-breathing classes as the Crustacea and Mollusca are adapted to live on the land; and seeing that we have flying birds and mammals, flying insects of the most diversified types, and formerly had flying reptiles, it is conceivable that flying-fish, which now glide far through the air, slightly rising and turning by the aid of their fluttering fins, might have been modified into perfectly winged animals. If this had been effected, who would have ever imagined that in an early transitional state they had been the inhabitants of the open ocean, and had used their incipient organs of flight exclusively, as far as we know, to escape being devoured by other fish?

When we see any structure highly perfected for any particular habit, as the wings of a bird for flight, we should bear in mind that animals displaying early transitional grades of the structure will seldom have survived to the present day, for they will have been supplanted by their successors, which were gradually rendered more perfect through natural selection. Furthermore, we may conclude that transitional states between structures fitted for very different habits of life will rarely have been developed at an early period in great numbers and under many subordinate forms. Thus, to return to our imaginary illustration of the flying-fish, it does not seem probable that fishes capable of true flight would have been developed under many subordinate forms, for taking prey of many kinds in many ways, on the land and in the water, until their organs of flight had come to a high stage of perfection, so as to have given them a decided advantage over other animals in the battle for life. Hence the chance of discovering species with transitional grades of structure in a fossil condition will always be less, from their having existed in lesser numbers, than in the case of species with fully developed structures.

I will now give two or three instances both of diversified and of changed habits in the individuals of the same species. In either case it would be easy for natural selection to adapt the structure of the animal to its changed habits, or exclusively to one of its several habits. It is, however, difficult to decide, and immaterial for us, whether habits generally change first and structure afterwards; or whether slight modifications of structure lead to changed habits; both probably often occurring almost simultaneously. Of cases of changed habits it will suffice merely to allude to that of the many British insects which now feed on exotic plants, or exclusively on artificial substances. Of diversified habits innumerable instances could be given: I have often watched a tyrant flycatcher (Saurophagus sulphuratus) in South America, hovering over one spot and then proceeding to another, like a kestrel, and at other times standing stationary on the margin of water, and then dashing into it like a kingfisher at a fish. In our own country the larger titmouse (Parus major) may be seen climbing branches, almost like a creeper; it sometimes, like a shrike, kills small birds by blows on the head; and I have many times seen and heard it hammering the seeds of the yew on a branch, and thus breaking them like a nuthatch. In North America the black bear was seen by Hearne swimming for hours with widely open mouth, thus catching, almost like a whale, insects in the water.

As we sometimes see individuals following habits different from those proper to their species and to the other species of the same genus, we might expect that such individuals would occasionally give rise to new species, having anomalous habits, and with their structure either slightly or considerably modified from that of their type. And such instances occur in nature. Can a more striking instance of adaptation be given than that of a woodpecker for climbing trees and seizing insects in the chinks of the bark? Yet in North America there are woodpeckers which feed largely on fruit, and others with elongated wings which chase insects on the wing. On the plains of La Plata, where hardly a tree grows, there is a woodpecker (Colaptes campestris) which has two toes before and two behind, a long pointed tongue, pointed tail-feathers, sufficiently stiff to support the bird in a vertical position on a post, but not so stiff as in the typical woodpeckers, and a straight strong beak. The beak, however, is not so straight or so strong as in the typical woodpeckers, but it is strong enough to bore into wood. Hence this Colaptes in all the essential parts of its structure is a woodpecker. Even in such trifling characters as the colouring, the harsh tone of the voice, and undulatory flight, its close blood-relationship to our common woodpecker is plainly declared; yet, as I can assert, not only from my own observation, but from those of the accurate Azara, in certain large districts it does not climb trees, and it makes its nest in holes in banks! In certain other districts, however, this same woodpecker, as Mr. Hudson states, frequents trees, and bores holes in the trunk for its nest. I may mention as another illustration of the varied habits of this genus, that a Mexican Colaptes has been described by De Saussure as boring holes into hard wood in order to lay up a store of acorns.

Petrels are the most aërial and oceanic of birds, but in the quiet sounds of Tierra del Fuego, the Puffinuria berardi, in its general habits, in its astonishing power of diving, in its manner of swimming and of flying when made to take flight, would be mistaken by any one for an auk or a grebe; nevertheless it is essentially a petrel, but with many parts of its organisation profoundly modified in relation to its new habits of life; whereas the woodpecker of La Plata has had its structure only slightly modified. In the case of the water-ouzel, the acutest observer by examining its dead body would never have suspected its sub-aquatic habits; yet this bird, which is allied to the thrush family, subsists by diving—using its wings under water, and grasping stones with its feet. All the members of the great order of Hymenopterous insects are terrestrial, excepting the genus Proctotrupes, which Sir John Lubbock has discovered to be aquatic in its habits; it often enters the water and dives about by the use not of its legs but of its wings, and remains as long as four hours beneath the surface; yet it exhibits no modification in structure in accordance with its abnormal habits.

He who believes that each being has been created as we now see it, must occasionally have felt surprise when he has met with an animal having habits and structure not in agreement. What can be plainer than that the webbed feet of ducks and geese are formed for swimming? Yet there are upland geese with webbed feet which rarely go near the water; and no one except Audubon has seen the frigate-bird, which has all its four toes webbed, alight on the surface of the ocean. On the other hand, grebes and coots are eminently aquatic, although their toes are only bordered by membrane. What seems plainer than that the long toes, not furnished with membrane of the Grallatores are formed for walking over swamps and floating plants?—the water-hen and landrail are members of this order, yet the first is nearly as aquatic as the coot, and the second nearly as terrestrial as the quail or partridge. In such cases, and many others could be given, habits have changed without a corresponding change of structure. The webbed feet of the upland goose may be said to have become almost rudimentary in function, though not in structure. In the frigate-bird, the deeply scooped membrane between the toes shows that structure has begun to change.

He who believes in separate and innumerable acts of creation may say, that in these cases it has pleased the Creator to cause a being of one type to take the place of one belonging to another type; but this seems to me only re-stating the fact in dignified language. He who believes in the struggle for existence and in the principle of natural selection, will acknowledge that every organic being is constantly endeavouring to increase in numbers; and that if any one being varies ever so little, either in habits or structure, and thus gains an advantage over some other inhabitant of the same country, it will seize on the place of that inhabitant, however different that may be from its own place. Hence it will cause him no surprise that there should be geese and frigate-birds with webbed feet, living on the dry land and rarely alighting on the water, that there should be long-toed corncrakes, living in meadows instead of in swamps; that there should be woodpeckers where hardly a tree grows; that there should be diving thrushes and diving Hymenoptera, and petrels with the habits of auks.

Organs of extreme Perfection and Complication

To suppose that the eye with all its inimitable contrivances for adjusting the focus to different distances, for admitting different amounts of light, and for the correction of spherical and chromatic aberration, could have been formed by natural selection, seems, I freely confess, absurd in the highest degree. When it was first said that the sun stood still and the world turned round, the common sense of mankind declared the doctrine false; but the old saying of *Vox populi, vox Dei,* as every philosopher knows, cannot be trusted in science. Reason tells me, that if numerous gradations from a simple and imperfect eye to one complex and perfect can be shown to exist, each grade being useful to its possessor, as is certainly the case; if further, the eye ever varies and the variations be inherited, as is likewise certainly the case; and if such variations should be useful to any animal under changing conditions of life, then the difficulty of believing that a perfect and complex eye could be formed by natural selection, though insuperable by our imagination, should not be considered as subversive of the theory. How a nerve comes to be sensitive to light, hardly concerns us more than how life itself originated; but I may remark that, as some of the lowest organisms, in which nerves cannot be detected, are capable of perceiving light, it does not seem impossible that certain sensitive elements in their sarcode should become aggregated and developed into nerves, endowed with this special sensibility.

In searching for the gradations through which an organ in any species has been perfected, we ought to look exclusively to its lineal progenitors; but this is scarcely ever possible, and we are forced to look to other species and genera of the same group, that is to the collateral descendants from the same parent-form, in order to see what gradations are possible, and for the chance of some gradations having been transmitted in an unaltered or little altered condition. But the state of the same organ in distinct classes may incidentally throw light on the steps by which it has been perfected.

The simplest organ which can be called an eye consists of an optic nerve, surrounded by pigment-cells and covered by translucent skin, but without any lens or other refractive body. We may, however, according to M. Jourdain, descend even a step lower and find aggregates of pigment-cells, apparently serving as organs of vision, without any nerves, and resting merely on sarcodic tissue. Eyes of the above simple nature are not capable of distinct vision, and serve only to distinguish light from darkness. In certain star-fishes, small depressions in the layer of pigment which surrounds the nerve are filled, as described by the author just quoted, with transparent gelatinous matter, projecting with a convex surface, like the cornea in the higher animals. He suggests that this serves not to form an image, but only to concentrate the luminous rays and render their perception more easy. In this concentration of the rays we gain the first and by far the most important step towards the formation of a true, picture-forming eye; for we have only to place the naked extremity of the optic nerve, which in some of the lower animals lies deeply buried in the body, and in some near the surface, at the right distance from the concentrating apparatus, and an image will be formed on it.

In the great class of the Articulata, we may start from an optic nerve simply coated with pigment, the latter sometimes forming a sort of pupil, but destitute of a lens or other optical contrivance. With insects it is now known that the numerous facets on the cornea of their great compound eyes form true lenses, and that the cones include curiously modified nervous filaments. But these organs in the Articulata are so much diversified that Müller formerly made three main classes with seven subdivisions, besides a fourth main class of aggregated simple eyes.

When we reflect on these facts, here given much too briefly, with respect to the wide, diversified, and graduated range of structure in the eyes of the lower animals; and when we bear in mind how small the number of all living forms must be in comparison with those which have become extinct, the difficulty ceases to be very great in believing that natural selection may have converted the simple apparatus of an optic nerve, coated with pigment and invested by transparent membrane, into an optical instrument as perfect as is possessed by any member of the Articulate Class.

He who will go thus far, ought not to hesitate to go one step further, if he finds on finishing this volume that large bodies of facts, otherwise inexplicable, can be explained by the theory of modification through natural selection; he ought to admit that with a structure even as perfect as an eagle's eye might thus be formed, although in this case he does not know the transitional states. It has been objected that in order to modify the eye and still preserve it as a perfect instrument, many changes would have to be effected simultaneously, which, it is assumed, could not be done through natural selection; but as I have attempted to show in my work on the variation of domestic animals, it is not necessary to suppose that the modifications were all simultaneous, if they were extremely slight and gradual. Different kinds of modification would, also, serve for the same general purpose: as Mr. Wallace has remarked, "if a lens has too short or too long a focus, it may be amended either by an alteration of curvature, or an alteration of density; if the curvature be irregular, and the rays do not converge to a point, then any increased regularity of curvature will be an improvement. So the contraction of the iris and the muscular movements of the eye are neither of them essential to vision, but only improvements which might have been added and perfected at any stage of the construction of the instrument." Within the highest division of the animal kingdom, namely, the Vertebrata, we can start from an eye so simple, that it consists, as in the lancelet, of a little sack of transparent skin, furnished with a nerve and lined with pigment, but destitute of any other apparatus. In fishes and reptiles, as Owen has remarked, "the range of gradations of dioptric structures is very great." It is a significant fact that even in man, according to the high authority of Virchow, the beautiful crystalline lens is formed in the embryo by an accumulation of epidermic cells, lying in a sack-like fold of the skin; and the vitreous body is formed from embryonic sub-cutaneous tissue. To arrive, however, at a just conclusion regarding the formation of the eye, with all its marvellous yet not absolutely perfect characters, it is indispensable that the reason should conquer the imagination; but I have felt the difficulty far too keenly to be surprised at others hesitating to extend the principle of natural selection to so startling a length.

It is scarcely possible to avoid comparing the eye with a telescope. We know that this instrument has been perfected by the long-continued efforts of the highest human intellects; and we naturally infer that the eye has been formed by a somewhat analogous process. But may not this inference be presumptuous? Have we any right to assume that the Creator works by intellectual powers like those of man? If we must compare the eye to an optical instrument, we ought in imagination to take a thick layer of transparent tissue, with spaces filled with fluid, and with a nerve sensitive to light beneath, and then suppose every part of this layer to be continually changing slowly in density, so as to separate into layers of different densities and thicknesses, placed at different distances from each other, and with the surfaces of each layer slowly changing in form. Further we must suppose that there is a power, represented by natural selection or the survival of the fittest, always intently watching each slight alteration in the transparent layers; and carefully preserving each which, under varied circumstances, in any way or in any degree, tends to produce a distincter image. We must suppose each new state of the instrument to be multiplied by the million; each to be preserved until a better one is produced, and then the old ones to be all destroyed. In living bodies, variation will cause the slight alterations, generation will multiply them almost infinitely, and natural selection will pick out with unerring skill each improvement. Let this process go on for millions of years; and during each year on millions of individuals of many kinds; and may we not believe that a living optical instrument might thus be formed as superior to one of glass, as the works of the Creator are to those of man?

Modes of Transition

If it could be demonstrated that any complex organ existed, which could not possibly have been formed by numerous, successive, slight modifications, my theory would absolutely break down. But I can find out no such case. No doubt many organs exist of which we do not know the transitional grades, more especially if we look to much-isolated species, round which, according to the theory, there has been much extinction. Or again, if we take an organ common to all the members of a class, for in this latter case the organ must have been originally formed at a remote period, since which all the many members of the class have been developed; and in order to discover the early transitional grades through which the organ has passed, we should have to look to very ancient ancestral forms, long since become extinct.

We should be extremely cautious in concluding that an organ could not have been formed by transitional gradations of some kind. Numerous cases could be given amongst the lower aminals of the same organ performing at the same time wholly distinct functions; thus in the larva of the dragon-fly and in the fish Cobites the alimentary canal respires, digests, and excretes. In the Hydra, the animal may be turned inside out, and the exterior surface will then digest and the stomach respire. In such cases natural selection might specialise, if any advantage were thus gained, the whole or part of an organ, which had previously performed two functions, for one function alone, and thus by insensible steps greatly change its nature. Many plants are known which regularly produce at the same time differently constructed flowers; and if such plants were to produce one kind alone, a great change would be effected with comparative suddenness in the character of the species. It is, however, probable that the two sorts of flowers borne by the same plant were originally differentiated by finely graduated steps, which may still be followed in some few cases.

Again, two distinct organs, or the same organ under two very different forms, may simultaneously perform in the same individual the same function, and this is an extremely important means of transition: to give one instance,—there are fish with gills or branchiæ that breathe the air dissolved in the water, at the same time that they breathe free air in their swimbladders, this latter organ being divided by highly vascular partitions and having a ductus pneumaticus for the supply of air. To give another instance from the vegetable kingdom: plants climb by three distinct means, by spirally twining, by clasping a support with their sensitive tendrils, and by the emission of aërial rootlets; these three means are usually found in distinct groups, but some few species exhibit two of the means, or even all three, combined in the same individual. In all such cases one of the two organs might readily be modified and perfected so as to perform all the work, being aided during the progress of modification by the other organ; and then this other organ might be modified for some other and quite distinct purpose, or be wholly obliterated.

The illustration of the swimbladder in fishes is a good one, because it shows us clearly the highly important fact that an organ originally constructed for one purpose, namely, flotation, may be converted into one for a widely different purpose, namely, respiration. The swimbladder has, also, been worked in as an accessory to the auditory organs of certain fishes. All physiologists admit that the swimbladder is homologous, or "ideally similar" in position and structure with the lungs of the higher vertebrate animals: hence there is no reason to doubt that the swimbladder has actually been converted into lungs, or an organ used exclusively for respiration.

According to this view it may be inferred that all vertebrate animals with true lungs are descended by ordinary generation from an ancient and unknown prototype, which was furnished with a floating apparatus or swimbladder. We can thus, as I infer from Owen's interesting description of these parts, understand the strange fact that every particle of food and drink which we swallow has to pass over the orifice of the trachea, with some risk of falling into the lungs, notwithstanding the beautiful contrivance by which the glottis is closed. In the higher Vertebrate the branchiæ have wholly disappeared—but in the embryo the slits on the sides of the neck and the loop-like course of the arteries still mark their former position. But it is conceivable that the now utterly lost branchiæ might have been gradually worked in by natural selection for some distinct purpose: for instance, Landois has shown that the wings of insects are developed from the tracheæ; it is therefore highly probable that in this great class organs which once served for respiration have been actually converted into organs for flight.

In considering transitions of organs, it is so important to bear in mind the probability of conversion from one function to another, that I will give another instance. Pedunculated cirripedes have two minute folds of skin, called by me the ovigerous frena, which serve, through the means of a sticky secretion, to retain the eggs until they are hatched within the sack. These cirripedes have no branchiæ, the whole surface of the body and of the sack, together with the small frena, serving for respiration. The Balanidæ or sessile cirripedes, on the other hand, have no ovigerous frena, the eggs lying loose at the bottom of the sack, within the well-enclosed shell; but they have, in the same relative position with the frena, large, much-folded membranes, which freely communicate with the circulatory lacunæ of the sack and body, and which have been considered by all naturalists to act as branchiæ. Now I think no one will dispute that the ovigerous frena in the one family are strictly homologous with the branchiæ of the other family; indeed, they graduate into each other. Therefore it need not be doubted that the two little folds of skin, which originally served as ovigerous frena, but which, likewise, very slightly aided in the act of respiration, have been gradually converted by natural selection into branchiæ, simply through an increase in their size and the obliteration of their adhesive glands. If all pedunculated cirripedes had become extinct, and they have suffered far more extinction than have sessile cirripedes, who would ever have imagined that the branchiæ in this latter family had originally existed as organs for preventing the ova from being washed out of the sack?

There is another possible mode of transition, namely, through the acceleration or retardation of the period of reproduction. This has lately been insisted on by Prof. Cope and others in the United States. It is now known that some animals are capable of reproduction at a very early age, before they have acquired their perfect characters; and if this power became thoroughly well developed in a species, it seems probable that the adult stage of development would sooner or later be lost; and in this case, especially if the larva differed much from the mature form, the character of the species would be greatly changed and degraded. Again, not a few animals, after arriving at maturity, go on changing in character during nearly their whole lives. With mammals, for instance, the form of the skull is often much altered with age, of which Dr. Murie has given some striking instances with seals; every one knows how the horns of stags become more and more branched, and the plumes of some birds become more finely developed, as they grow older. Prof. Cope states that the teeth of certain lizards change much in shape with advancing years; with crustaceans not only many trivial, but some important parts assume a new character, as recorded by Fritz Müller, after maturity. In all such cases, —and many could be given,—if the age for reproduction were retarded, the character of the species, at least in its adult state, would be modified; nor is it improbable that the previous and earlier stages of development would in some cases be hurried through and finally lost. Whether species have often or ever been modified through this comparatively sudden mode of transition, I can form no opinion; but if this has occurred, it is probable that the differences between the young and the mature, and between the mature and the old, were primordially acquired by graduated steps.

Special Difficulties of the Theory of Natural Selection

Although we must be extremely cautious in concluding that any organ could not have been produced by successive, small, transitional gradations, yet undoubtedly serious cases of difficulty occur.

One of the most serious is that of neuter insects, which are often differently constructed from either the males or fertile females; but this case will be treated of in the next chapter. The electric organs of fishes offer another case of special difficulty; for it is impossible to conceive by what steps these wondrous organs have been produced. But this is not surprising, for we do not even know of what use they are. In the Gymnotus and Torpedo they no doubt serve as powerful means of defence, and perhaps for securing prey; yet in the Ray, as observed by Matteucci, an analogous organ in the tail manifests but little electricity, even when the animal is greatly irritated; so little, that it can hardly be of any use for the above purposes. Moreover, in the Ray, besides the organ just referred to, there is, as Dr. R. M'Donnell has shown, another organ near the head, not known to be electrical, but which appears to be the real homologue of the electric battery in the Torpedo. It is generally admitted that there exists between these organs and ordinary muscle a close analogy, in intimate structure, in the distribution of the nerves, and in the manner in which they are acted on by various reagents. It should, also, be especially observed that muscular contraction is accompanied by an electrical discharge; and, as Dr. Radcliffe insists, "in the electrical apparatus of the torpedo during rest, there would seem to be a charge in every respect like that which is met with in muscle and nerve during rest, and the discharge of the torpedo, instead of being peculiar, may be only another form of the discharge which depends upon the action of muscle and motor nerve." Beyond this we cannot at present go in the way of explanation; but as we know so little about the uses of these organs, and as we know nothing about the habits and structure of the progenitors of the existing electric fishes, it would be extremely bold to maintain that no serviceable transitions are possible by which these organs might have been gradually developed.

These organs appear at first to offer another and far more serious difficulty; for they occur in about a dozen kinds of fish, of which several are widely remote in their affinities. When the same organ is found in several members of the same class, especially if in members having very different habits of life, we may generally attribute its presence to inheritance from a common ancestor; and its absence in some of the members to loss through disuse or natural selection. So that, if the electric organs had been inherited from some one ancient progenitor, we might have expected that all electric fishes would have been specially related to each other; but this is far from the case. Nor does geology at all lead to the belief that most fishes formerly possessed electric organs, which their modified descendants have now lost. But when we look at the subject more closely, we find in the several fishes provided with electric organs, that these are situated in different parts of the body,—that they differ in construction, as in the arrangement of the plates, and, according to Pacini, in the process or means by which the electricity is excited—and lastly, in being supplied with nerves proceeding from different sources, and this is perhaps the most important of all the differences. Hence in the several fishes furnished with electric organs, these cannot be considered as homologous, but only as analogous in function. Consequently there is no reason to suppose that they have been inherited from a common progenitor; for had this been the case they would have closely resembled each other in all respects. Thus the difficulty of an organ, apparently the same, arising in several remotely allied species, disappears, leaving only the lesser yet still great difficulty; namely, by what graduated steps these organs have been developed in each separate group of fishes.

The luminous organs which occur in a few insects, belonging to widely different families, and which are situated in different parts of the body, offer, under our present state of ignorance, a difficulty almost exactly parallel with that of the electric organs. Other similar cases could be given; for instance in plants, the very curious contrivance of a mass of pollen-grains, borne on a foot-stalk with an adhesive gland, is apparently the same in Orchis and Asclepias,—genera almost as remote as is possible amongst flowering plants; but here again the parts are not homologous. In all cases of beings, far removed from each other in the scale of organisation, which are furnished with similar and peculiar organs, it will be found that although the general appearance and function of the organs may be the same, yet fundamental differences between them can always be detected. For instance, the eyes of cephalopods or cuttle-fish and of vertebrate animals appear wonderfully alike; and in such widely sundered groups no part of this resemblance can be due to inheritance from a common progenitor. Mr. Mivart has advanced this case as one of special difficulty, but I am unable to see the force of his argument. An organ for vision must be formed of transparent tissue, and must include some sort of lens for throwing an image at the back of a darkened chamber. Beyond this superficial resemblance, there is hardly any real similarity between the eyes of cuttle-fish and vertebrates, as may be seen by consulting Hensen's admirable memoir on these organs in the Cephalopoda. It is impossible for me here to enter on details, but I may specify a few of the points of difference. The crystalline lens in the higher cuttle-fish consists of two parts, placed one behind the other like two lenses, both having a very different structure and disposition to what occurs in the vertebrata. The retina is wholly different, with an actual inversion of the elemental parts, and with a large nervous ganglion included within the membranes of the eye. The relations of the muscles are as different as it is possible to conceive, and so in other points. Hence it is not a little difficult to decide how far even the same terms ought to be employed in describing the eyes of the Cephalopoda and Vertebrata. It is, of course, open to any one to deny that the eye in either case could have been developed through the natural selection of successive slight variations; but if this be admitted in the one case, it is clearly possible in the other; and fundamental differences of structure in the visual organs of two groups might have been anticipated, in accordance with this view of their manner of formation. As two men have sometimes independently hit on the same invention, so in the several foregoing cases it appears that natural selection, working for the good of each being, and taking advantage of all favourable variations, has produced similar organs, as far as function is concerned, in distinct organic beings, which owe none of their structure in common to inheritance from a common progenitor.

Fritz Müller, in order to test the conclusions arrived at in this volume, has followed out with much care a nearly similar line of argument. Several families of crustaceans include a few species, possessing an air-breathing apparatus and fitted to live out of the water. In two of these families, which were more especially examined by Müller, and which are nearly related to each other, the species agree most closely in all important characters; namely, in their sense organs, circulating system, in the position of the tufts of hair within their complex stomachs, and lastly in the whole structure of the water-breathing branchiæ, even to the microscopical hooks by which they are cleansed. Hence it might have been expected that in the few species belonging to both families which live on the land, the equally important air-breathing apparatus would have been the same; for why should this one apparatus, given for the same purpose, have been made to differ, whilst all the other important organs were closely similar or rather identical.

Fritz Müller argues that this close similarity in so many points of structure must, in accordance with the views advanced by me, be accounted for by inheritance from a common progenitor. But as the vast majority of the species in the above two families, as well as most other crustaceans, are aquatic in their habits, it is improbable in the highest degree, that their common progenitor should have been adapted for breathing air. Müller was thus led carefully to examine the apparatus in the air-breathing species; and he found it to differ in each in several important points, as in the position of the orifices, in the manner in which they are opened and closed, and in some accessory details. Now such differences are intelligible, and might even have been expected, on the supposition that species belonging to distinct families had slowly become adapted to live more and more out of water, and to breathe the air. For these species, from belonging to distinct families, would have differed to a certain extent, and in accordance with the principle that the nature of each variation depends on two factors, viz., the nature of the organism and that of the surrounding conditions, their variability assuredly would not have been exactly the same. Consequently natural selection would have had different materials or variations to work on, in order to arrive at the same functional result; and the structures thus acquired would almost necessarily have differed. On the hypothesis of separate acts of creation the whole case remains unintelligible. This line of argument seems to have had great weight in leading Fritz Müller to accept the views maintained by me in this volume.

Another distinguished zoologist, the late Professor Claparède, has argued in the same manner, and has arrived at the same result. He shows that there are parasitic mites (Acaridæ), belonging to distinct sub-families and families, which are furnished with hair-claspers. These organs must have been independently developed, as they could not have been inherited from a common progenitor; and in the several groups they are formed by the modification of the fore-legs,—of the hind-legs,—of the maxillæ or lips,—and of appendages on the under side of the hind part of the body.

In the foregoing cases, we see the same end gained and the same function performed, in beings not at all or only remotely allied, by organs in appearance, though not in development, closely similar. On the other hand, it is a common rule throughout nature that the same end should be gained, even sometimes in the case of closely-related beings, by the most diversified means. How differently constructed is the feathered wing of a bird and the membrane-covered wing of a bat; and still more so the four wings of a butterfly, the two wings of a fly, and the two wings with the elytra of a beetle. Bivalve shells are made to open and shut, but on what a number of patterns is the hinge constructed,—from the long row of neatly interlocking teeth in a Nucula to the simple ligament of a Mussel! Seeds are disseminated by their minuteness,—by their capsule being converted into a light balloon-like envelope,—by being embedded in pulp or flesh, formed of the most diverse parts, and rendered nutritious, as well as conspicuously coloured, so as to attract and be devoured by birds,—

by having hooks and grapnels of many kinds and serrated awns, so as to adhere to the fur of quadrupeds,—and by being furnished with wings and plumes, as different in shape as they are elegant in structure, so as to be wafted by every breeze. I will give one other instance; for this subject of the same end being gained by the most diversified means well deserves attention. Some authors maintain that organic beings have been formed in many ways for the sake of mere variety, almost like toys in a shop, but such a view of nature is incredible. With plants having separated sexes, and with those in which, though hermaphrodites, the pollen does not spontaneously fall on the stigma, some aid is necessary for their fertilisation. With several kinds this is effected by the pollen-grains, which are light and incoherent, being blown by the wind through mere chance on to the stigma; and this is the simplest plan which can well be conceived. An almost equally simple, though very different, plan occurs in many plants in which a symmetrical flower secretes a few drops of nectar, and is consequently visited by insects; and these carry the pollen from the anthers to the stigma.

From this simple stage we may pass through an inexhaustible number of contrivances, all for the same purpose and effected in essentially the same manner, but entailing changes in every part of the flower. The nectar may be stored in variously shaped receptacles, with the stamens and pistils modified in many ways, sometimes forming trap-like contrivances, and sometimes capable of neatly adapted movements through irritability or elasticity. From such structures we may advance till we come to such a case of extraordinary adaptation as that lately described by Dr. Crüger in the Coryanthes. This orchid has part of its labellum or lower lip hollowed out into a great bucket, into which drops of almost pure water continually fall from two secreting horns which stand above it; and when the bucket is half full, the water overflows by a spout on one side. The basal part of the labellum stands over the bucket, and is itself hollowed out into a sort of chamber with two lateral entrances; within this chamber there are curious fleshy ridges. The most ingenious man, if he had not witnessed what takes place, could never have imagined what purpose all these parts serve. But Dr. Crüger saw crowds of large humble-bees visiting the gigantic flowers of this orchid, not in order to suck nectar, but to gnaw off the ridges within the chamber above the bucket; in doing this they frequently pushed each other into the bucket, and their wings being thus wetted they could not fly away, but were compelled to crawl out through the passage formed by the spout or overflow. Dr. Crüger saw a "continual procession" of bees thus crawling out of their involuntary bath. The passage is narrow, and is roofed over by the column, so that a bee, in forcing its way out, first rubs its back against the viscid stigma and then against the viscid glands of the pollen-masses. The pollen-masses are thus glued to the back of the bee which first happens to crawl out through the passage of a lately expanded flower, and are thus carried away. Dr. Crüger sent me a flower in spirits of wine, with a bee which he had killed before it had quite crawled out with a pollen-mass still fastened to its back. When the bee, thus provided, flies to another flower, or to the same flower a second time, and is pushed by its comrades into the bucket and then crawls out by the passagé, the pollen-mass necessarily comes first into contact with the viscid stigma, and adheres to it, and the flower is fertilised. Now at last we see the full use of every part of the flower, of the water-secreting horns, of the bucket half full of water, which prevents the bees from flying away, and forces them to crawl out through the spout, and rub against the properly placed viscid pollen-masses and the viscid stigma.

The construction of the flower in another closely allied orchid, namely the Catasetum, is widely different, though serving the same end; and is equally curious. Bees visit these flowers, like those of the Coryanthes, in order to gnaw the labellum; in doing this they inevitably touch a long, tapering, sensitive projection; or, as I have called it, the antenna. This antenna, when touched, transmits a sensation or vibration to a certain membrane which is instantly ruptured; this sets free a spring by which the pollen-mass is shot forth, like an arrow, in the right direction, and adheres by its viscid extremity to the back of the bee. The pollen-mass of the male plant (for the sexes are separate in this orchid) is thus carried to the flower of the female plant where it is brought into contact with the stigma, which is viscid enough to break certain elastic threads, and retaining the pollen, fertilisation is effected.

How, it may be asked, in the foregoing and in innumerable other instances, can we understand the graduated scale of complexity and the multifarious means for gaining the same end. The answer no doubt is, as already remarked, that when two forms vary, which already differ from each other in some slight degree, the variability will not be of the same exact nature, and consequently the results obtained through natural selection for the same general purpose will not be the same. We should also bear in mind that every highly developed organism has passed through many changes; and that each modified structure tends to be inherited, so that each modification will not readily be quite lost, but may be again and again further altered. Hence the structure of each part of each species, for whatever purpose it may serve, is the sum of many inherited changes, through which the species has passed during its successive adaptations to changed habits and conditions of life.

Finally then, although in many cases it is most difficult even to conjecture by what transitions organs have arrived at their present state; yet, considering how small the proportion of living and known forms is to the extinct and unknown, I have been astonished how rarely an organ can be named, towards which no transitional grade is known to lead. It certainly is true, that new organs appearing as if created for some special purpose, rarely or never appear in any being;—as indeed is shown by that old, but somewhat exaggerated, canon in natural history of "Natura non facit saltum." We meet with this admission in the writings of almost every experienced naturalist; or as Milne Edwards has well expressed it, Nature is prodigal in variety, but niggard in innovation. Why, on the theory of

Creation, should there be so much variety and so little real novelty? Why should all the parts and organs of many independent beings, each supposed to have been separately created for its proper place in nature, be so commonly linked together by graduated steps? Why should not Nature take a sudden leap from structure to structure? On the theory of natural selection, we can clearly understand why she should not; for natural selection acts only by taking advantage of slight successive variations; she can never take a great and sudden leap, but must advance by short and sure, though slow steps.

Organs of little apparent Importance, as affected by Natural Selection

As natural selection acts by life and death,—by the survival of the fittest, and by the destruction of the less well-fitted individuals,—I have sometimes felt great difficulty in understanding the origin or formation of parts of little importance; almost as great, though of a very different kind, as in the case of the most perfect and complex organs.

In the first place, we are much too ignorant in regard to the whole economy of any one organic being, to say what slight modifications would be of importance or not. In a former chapter I have given instances of very trifling characters, such as the down on fruit and the colour of its flesh, the colour of the skin and hair of quadrupeds, which, from being correlated with constitutional differences or from determining the attacks of insects, might assuredly be acted on by natural selection. The tail of the giraffe looks like an artificially constructed fly-flapper; and it seems at first incredible that this could have been adapted for its present purpose by successive slight modifications, each better and better fitted, for so trifling an object as to drive away flies; yet we should pause before being too positive even in this case, for we know that the distribution and existence of cattle and other animals in South America absolutely depend on their power of resisting the attacks of insects: so that individuals which could by any means defend themselves from these small enemies, would be able to range into new pastures and thus gain a great advantage. It is not that the larger quadrupeds are actually destroyed (except in some rare cases) by flies, but they are incessantly harassed and their strength reduced, so that they are more subject to disease, or not so well enabled in a coming dearth to search for food, or to escape from beasts of prey.

Organs now of trifling importance have probably in some cases been of high importance to an early progenitor, and, after having been slowly perfected at a former period, have been transmitted to existing species in nearly the same state, although now of very slight use; but any actually injurious deviations in their structure would of course have been checked by natural selection. Seeing how important an organ of locomotion the tail is in most aquatic animals, its general presence and use for many purposes in so many land animals, which in their lungs or modified swim-bladders betray their aquatic origin, may perhaps be thus accounted for. A well-developed tail having been formed in an aquatic animal, it might subsequently come to be worked in for all sorts of purposes,—as a fly-flapper, an organ of prehension, or as an aid in turning, as in the case of the dog, though the aid in this latter respect must be slight, for the hare, with hardly any tail, can double still more quickly.

In the second place, we may easily err in attributing importance to characters, and in believing that they have been developed through natural selection. We must by no means overlook the effects of the definite action of changed conditions of life,—of so-called spontaneous variations, which seem to depend in a quite subordinate degree on the nature of the conditions,—of the tendency to reversion to long-lost characters,—of the complex laws of growth, such as of correlation, compensation, of the pressure of one part on another, &c.,—and finally of sexual selection, by which characters of use to one sex are often gained and then transmitted more or less perfectly to the other sex, though of no use to this sex. But structures thus indirectly gained, although at first of no advantage to a species, may subsequently have been taken advantage of by its modified descendants, under new conditions of life and newly acquired habits.

If green woodpeckers alone had existed, and we did not know that there were many black and pied kinds, I dare say that we should have thought that the green colour was a beautiful adaptation to conceal this tree-frequenting bird from its enemies; and consequently that it was a character of importance, and had been acquired through natural selection; as it is, the colour is probably in chief part due to sexual selection. A trailing palm in the Malay Archipelago climbs the loftiest trees by the aid of exquisitely constructed hooks clustered around the ends of the branches, and this contrivance, no doubt, is of the highest service to the plant; but as we see nearly similar hooks on many trees which are not climbers, and which, as there is reason to believe from the distribution of the thorn-bearing species in Africa and South America, serve as a defence against browsing quadrupeds, so the spikes on the palm may at first have been developed for this object, and subsequently have been improved and taken advantage of by the plant, as it underwent further modification and became a climber. The naked skin on the head of a vulture is generally considered as a direct adaptation for wallowing in putridity; and so it may be, or it may possibly be due to the direct action of putrid matter; but we should be very cautious in drawing any such inference, when we see that the skin on the head of the clean-feeding male Turkey is likewise naked. The sutures in the skulls of young mammals have been advanced as a beautiful adaptation for aiding parturition, and no doubt they facilitate, or may be indispensable for this act; but as sutures occur in the skulls of young birds and reptiles, which have only to escape from a broken egg, we may infer that this structure has arisen from the laws of growth, and has been taken advantage of in the parturition of the higher animals.

We are profoundly ignorant of the cause of each slight variation or individual difference; and we are immediately made conscious of this by reflecting on the differences between the breeds of our domesticated animals in different countries,—more especially in the less civilised countries where there has been but little methodical selection. Animals kept by savages in different countries often have to struggle for their own subsistence, and are exposed to a certain extent to natural selection, and individuals with slightly different constitutions would succeed best under different climates. With cattle susceptibility to the attacks of flies is correlated with colour, as is the liability to be poisoned by certain plants; so that even colour would be thus subjected to the action of natural selection. Some observers are convinced that a damp climate affects the growth of the hair, and that with the hair the horns are correlated. Mountain breeds always differ from lowland breeds; and a mountainous country would probably affect the hind limbs from exercising them more, and possibly even the form of the pelvis; and then by the law of homologous variation, the front limbs and the head would probably be affected. The shape, also, of the pelvis might affect by pressure the shape of certain parts of the young in the womb. The laborious breathing necessary in high regions tends, as we have good reason to believe, to increase the size of the chest; and again correlation would come into play. The effects of lessened exercise together with abundant food on the whole organisation is probably still more important; and this, as H. von Nathusius has lately shown in his excellent Treatise, is apparently one chief cause of the great modification which the breeds of swine have undergone. But we are far too ignorant to speculate on the relative importance of the several known and unknown causes of variation; and I have made these remarks only to show that, if we are unable to account for the characteristic differences of our several domestic breeds, which nevertheless are generally admitted to have arisen through ordinary generation from one or a few parent-stocks, we ought not to lay too much stress on our ignorance of the precise cause of the slight analogous differences between true species.

Utilitarian Doctrine, how far true: Beauty, how acquired

The foregoing remarks lead me to say a few words on the protest lately made by some naturalists, against the utilitarian doctrine that every detail of structure has been produced for the good of its possessor. They believe that many structures have been created for the sake of beauty, to delight man or the Creator (but this latter point is beyond the scope of scientific discussion), or for the sake of mere variety, a view already discussed. Such doctrines, if true, would be absolutely fatal to my theory. I fully admit that many structures are now of no direct use to their possessors, and may never have been of any use to their progenitors; but this does not prove that they were formed solely for beauty or variety. No doubt the definite action of changed conditions, and the various causes of modifications, lately specified, have all produced an effect, probably a great effect, independently of any advantage thus gained. But a still more important consideration is that the chief part of the organisation of every living creature is due to inheritance; and consequently, though each being assuredly is well fitted for its place in nature, many structures have now no very close and direct relation to present habits of life. Thus, we can hardly believe that the webbed feet of the upland goose or of the frigate-bird are of special use to these birds; we cannot believe that the similar bones in the arm of the monkey, in the fore-leg of the horse, in the wing of the bat, and in the flipper of the seal, are of special use to these animals. We may safely attribute these structures to inheritance. But webbed feet no doubt were as useful to the progenitor of the upland goose and of the frigate-bird, as they now are to the most aquatic of living birds. So we may believe that the progenitor of the seal did not possess a flipper, but a foot with five toes fitted for walking or grasping; but we may further venture to believe that the several bones in the limbs of the monkey, horse, and bat, were originally developed, on the principle of utility, probably through the reduction of more numerous bones in the fin of some ancient fish-like progenitor of the whole class. It is scarcely possible to decide how much allowance ought to be made for such causes of change, as the definite action of external conditions, so-called spontaneous variations, and the complex laws of growth; but with these important exceptions, we may conclude that the structure of every living creature either now is, or was formerly, of some direct or indirect use to its possessor.

With respect to the belief that organic beings have been created beautiful for the delight of man,—a belief which it has been pronounced is subversive of my whole theory,—I may first remark that the sense of beauty obviously depends on the nature of the mind, irrespective of any real quality in the admired object; and that the idea of what is beautiful, is not innate or unalterable. We see this, for instance, in the men of different races admiring an entirely different standard of beauty in their women. If beautiful objects had been created solely for man's gratification, it ought to be shown that before man appeared, there was less beauty on the face of the earth than since he came on the stage. Were the beautiful volute and cone shells of the Eocene epoch, and the gracefully sculptured ammonites of the Secondary period, created that man might ages afterwards admire them in his cabinet? Few objects are more beautiful than the minute siliceous cases of the diatomaceæ: were these created that they might be examined and admired under the higher powers of the microscope? The beauty in this latter case, and in many others, is apparently wholly due to symmetry of growth. Flowers rank amongst the most beautiful productions of nature; but they have been rendered conspicuous in contrast with the green leaves, and in consequence at the same time beautiful, so that they may be easily observed by insects. I have come to this conclusion from finding it an invariable rule that when a flower is fertilised by the wind it never has a gaily-coloured corolla. Several plants habitually produce two kinds of flowers; one kind open and coloured so as to attract insects; the other closed, not coloured, destitute of nectar, and never visited by insects. Hence we may conclude that, if insects had not been developed on the face of the earth, our plants would not have been decked with beautiful flowers, but would have produced only such poor flowers as we see on our fir, oak, nut and ash trees, on grasses, spinach, docks, and nettles, which are all fertilised through the agency of the wind. A similar line of argument holds good with fruits; that a ripe strawberry or cherry is as pleasing to the eye as to the palate,—that the gaily-coloured fruit of the spindle-wood tree and the scarlet berries of the holly are beautiful objects,—will be admitted by every one. But this beauty serves merely as a guide to birds and beasts, in order that the fruit may be devoured and the matured seeds disseminated: I infer that this is the case from having as yet found no exception to the rule that seeds are always thus disseminated when embedded within a fruit of any kind (that is within a fleshy or pulpy envelope), if it be coloured of any brilliant tint, or rendered conspicuous by being white or black.

On the other hand, I willingly admit that a great number of male animals, as all our most gorgeous birds, some fishes, reptiles, and mammals, and a host of magnificently coloured butterflies, have been rendered beautiful for beauty's sake; but this has been effected through sexual selection, that is, by the more beautiful males having been continually preferred by the females, and not for the delight of man. So it is with the music of birds. We may infer from all this that a nearly similar taste for beautiful colours and for musical sounds runs through a large part of the animal kingdom. When the female is as beautifully coloured as the male, which is not rarely the case with birds and butterflies, the cause apparently lies in the colours acquired through sexual selection having been transmitted to both sexes, instead of to the males alone. How the sense of beauty in its simplest form—that is, the reception of a peculiar kind of pleasure from certain colours, forms, and sounds—was first developed in the mind of man and of the lower animals, is a very obscure subject. The same sort of difficulty is presented, if we enquire how it is that certain flavours and odours give pleasure, and others displeasure. Habit in all these cases appears to have come to a certain extent into play; but there must be some fundamental cause in the constitution of the nervous system in each species.

Natural selection cannot possibly produce any modification in a species exclusively for the good of another species; though throughout nature one species incessantly takes advantage of, and profits by, the structures of others. But natural selection can and does often produce structures for the direct injury of other animals, as we see in the fang of the adder, and in the ovipositor of the ichneumon, by which its eggs are deposited in the living bodies of other insects. If it could be proved that any part of the structure of any one species had been formed for the exclusive good of another species, it would annihilate my theory, for such could not have been produced through natural selection. Although many statements may be found in works on natural history to this effect, I cannot find even one which seems to me of any weight. It is admitted that the rattlesnake has a poison-fang for its own defence, and for the destruction of its prey; but some authors suppose that at the same time it is furnished with a rattle for its own injury, namely, to warn its prey. I would almost as soon believe that the cat curls the end of its tail when preparing to spring, in order to warn the doomed mouse. It is a much more probable view that the rattlesnake uses its rattle, the cobra expands its frill, and the puff-adder swells whilst hissing so loudly and harshly, in order to alarm the many birds and beasts which are known to attack even the most venomous species. Snakes act on the same principle which makes the hen ruffle her feathers and expand her wings when a dog approaches her chickens; but I have not space here to enlarge on the many ways by which animals endeavour to frighten away their enemies.

Natural selection will never produce in a being any structure more injurious than beneficial to that being, for natural selection acts solely by and for the good of each. No organ will be formed, as Paley has remarked, for the purpose of causing pain or for doing an injury to its possessor. If a fair balance be struck between the good and evil caused by each part, each will be found on the whole advantageous. After the lapse of time, under changing conditions of life, if any part comes to be injurious, it will be modified; or if it be not so, the being will become extinct as myriads have become extinct.

Natural selection tends only to make each organic being as perfect as, or slightly more perfect than, the other inhabitants of the same country with which it comes into competition. And we see that this is the standard of perfection attained under nature. The endemic productions of New Zealand, for instance, are perfect one compared with another; but they are now rapidly yielding before the advancing legions of plants and animals introduced from Europe. Natural selection will not produce absolute perfection, nor do we always meet, as far as we can judge, with this high standard under nature. The correction for the aberration of light is said by Müller not to be perfect even in that most perfect organ, the human eye. Helmholtz, whose judgment no one will dispute, after describing in the strongest terms the wonderful powers of the human eye, adds these remarkable words: "That which we have discovered in the way of inexactness and imperfection in the optical machine and in the image on the retina, is as nothing in comparison with the incongruities which we have just come across in the domain of the sensations. One might say that nature has taken delight in accumulating contradictions in order to remove all foundation from the theory of a pre-existing harmony between the external and internal worlds." If our reason leads us to admire with enthusiasm a multitude of inimitable contrivances in nature, this same reason tells us, though we may easily err on both sides, that some other contrivances are less perfect. Can we consider the sting of the bee as perfect, which, when used against many kinds of enemies, cannot be withdrawn, owing to the backward serratures, and thus inevitably causes the death of the insect by tearing out its viscera?

If we look at the sting of the bee, as having existed in a remote progenitor, as a boring and serrated instrument, like that in so many members of the same great order, and that it has since been modified but not perfected for its present purpose, with the poison originally adapted for some other object, such as to produce galls, since intensified, we can perhaps understand how it is that the use of the sting should so often cause the insect's own death: for if on the whole the power of stinging be useful to the social community, it will fulfil all the requirements of natural selection, though it may cause the death of some few members. If we admire the truly wonderful power of scent by which the males of many insects find their females, can we admire the production for this single purpose of thousands of drones, which are utterly useless to the community for any other purpose, and which are ultimately slaughtered by their industrious and sterile sisters? It may be difficult, but we ought to admire the savage instinctive hatred of the queen-bee, which urges her to destroy the young queens, her daughters, as soon as they are born, or to perish herself in the combat; for undoubtedly this is for the good of the community; and maternal love or maternal hatred, though the latter fortunately is most rare, is all the same to the inexorable principle of natural selection. If we admire the several ingenious contrivances, by which orchids and many other plants are fertilised through insect agency, can we consider as equally perfect the elaboration of dense clouds of pollen by our fir-trees, so that a few granules may be wafted by chance on to the ovules?

Summary: the Law of Unity of Type and of the Conditions of Existence embraced by the Theory of Natural Selection

We have in this chapter discussed some of the difficulties and objections which may be urged against the theory. Many of them are serious; but I think that in the discussion light has been thrown on several facts, which on the belief of independent acts of creation are utterly obscure. We have seen that species at any one period are not indefinitely variable, and are not linked together by a multitude of intermediate gradations, partly because the process of natural selection is always very slow, and at any one time acts only on a few forms; and partly because the very process of natural selection implies the continual supplanting and extinction of preceding and intermediate gradations. Closely allied species, now living on a continuous area, must often have been formed when the area was not continuous, and when the conditions of life did not insensibly graduate away from one part to another. When two varieties are formed in two districts of a continuous area, an intermediate variety will often be formed, fitted for an intermediate zone; but from reasons assigned, the intermediate variety will usually exist in lesser numbers than the two forms which it connects; consequently the two latter, during the course of further modification, from existing in greater numbers, will have a great advantage over the less numerous intermediate variety, and will thus generally succeed in supplanting and exterminating it.

We have seen in this chapter how cautious we should be in concluding that the most different habits of life could not graduate into each other;

that a bat, for instance, could not have been formed by natural selection from an animal which at first only glided through the air.

We have seen that a species under new conditions of life may change its habits; or it may have diversified habits, with some very unlike those of its nearest congeners. Hence we can understand, bearing in mind that each organic being is trying to live wherever it can live, how it has arisen that there are upland geese with webbed feet, ground woodpeckers, diving thrushes, and petrels with the habits of auks.

Although the belief that an organ so perfect as the eye could have been formed by natural selection, is enough to stagger any one; yet in the case of any organ, if we know of a long series of gradations in complexity, each good for its possessor, then, under changing conditions of life, there is no logical impossibility in the acquirement of any conceivable degree of perfection through natural selection. In the cases in which we know of no intermediate or transitional states, we should be extremely cautious in concluding that none can have existed, for the metamorphoses of many organs show what wonderful changes in function are at least possible. For instance, a swimbladder has apparently been converted into an airbreathing lung. The same organ having performed simultaneously very different functions, and then having been in part or in whole specialised for one function; and two distinct organs having performed at the same time the same function, the one having been perfected whilst aided by the other, must often have largely facilitated transitions.

We have seen that in two beings widely remote from each other in the natural scale, organs serving for the same purpose and in external appearance closely similar may have been separately and independently formed; but when such organs are closely examined, essential differences in their structure can almost always be detected; and this naturally follows from the principle of natural selection. On the other hand, the common rule throughout nature is infinite diversity of structure for gaining the same end; and this again naturally follows from the same great principle.

In many cases we are far too ignorant to be enabled to assert that a part or organ is so unimportant for the welfare of a species, that modifications in its structure could not have been slowly accumulated by means of natural selection. In many other cases, modifications are probably the direct result of the laws of variation or of growth, independently of any good having been thus gained. But even such structures have often, as we may feel assured, been subsequently taken advantage of, and still further modified, for the good of species under new conditions of life. We may, also, believe that a part formerly of high importance has frequently been retained (as the tail of an aquatic animal by its terrestrial descendants), though it has become of such small importance that it could not, in its present state, have been acquired by means of natural selection.

Natural selection can produce nothing in one species for the exclusive good or injury of another; though it may well produce parts, organs, and excretions highly useful or even indispensable, or again highly injurious to another species, but in all cases at the same time useful to the possessor. In each well-stocked country natural selection acts through the competition of the inhabitants, and consequently leads to success in the battle for life, only in accordance with the standard of that particular country. Hence the inhabitants of one country, generally the smaller one, often yield to the inhabitants of another and generally the larger country. For in the larger country there will have existed more individuals and more diversified forms, and the competition will have been severer, and thus the standard of perfection will have been rendered higher. Natural selection will not necessarily lead to absolute perfection; nor, as far as we can judge by our limited faculties, can absolute perfection be everywhere predicated.

On the theory of natural selection we can clearly understand the full meaning of that old canon in natural history, "Natura non facit saltum." This canon, if we look to the present inhabitants alone of the world, is not strictly correct; but if we include all those of past times, whether known or unknown, it must on this theory be strictly true.

It is generally acknowledged that all organic beings have been formed on two great laws—Unity of Type, and the Conditions of Existence. By unity of type is meant that fundamental agreement in structure which we see in organic beings of the same class, and which is quite independent of their habits of life. On my theory, unity of type is explained by unity of descent. The expression of conditions of existence, so often insisted on by the illustrious Cuvier, is fully embraced by the principle of natural selection. For natural selection acts by either now adapting the varying parts of each being to its organic and inorganic conditions of life; or by having adapted them during past periods of time: the adaptations being aided in many cases by the increased use or disuse of parts, being affected by the direct action of the external conditions of life, and subjected in all cases to the several laws of growth and variation. Hence, in fact, the law of the Conditions of Existence is the higher law; as it includes, through the inheritance of former variations and adaptations, that of Unity of Type.

CHAPTER VII

MISCELLANEOUS OBJECTIONS TO THE THEORY OF NATURAL SELECTION

Longevity—Modifications not necessarily simultaneous—Modifications apparently of no direct service—Progressive development—Characters of small functional importance, the most constant—Supposed incompetence of natural selection to account for the incipient stages of useful structures—Causes which interfere with the acquisition through natural selection of useful structures—Gradations of structure with changed functions—Widely different organs in members of the same class, developed from one and the same source—Reasons for disbelieving in great and abrupt modifications.

I WILL devote this chapter to the consideration of various miscellaneous objections which have been advanced against my views, as some of the previous discussions may thus be made clearer; but it would be useless to discuss all of them, as many have been made by writers who have not taken the trouble to understand the subject. Thus a distinguished German naturalist has asserted that the weakest part of my theory is, that I consider all organic beings as imperfect: what I have really said is, that all are not as perfect as they might have been in relation to their conditions; and this is shown to be the case by so many native forms in many quarters of the world having yielded their places to intruding foreigners. Nor can organic beings, even if they were at any one time perfectly adapted to their conditions of life, have remained so, when their conditions changed, unless they themselves likewise changed; and no one will dispute that the physical conditions of each country, as well as the numbers and kinds of its inhabitants, have undergone many mutations.

A critic has lately insisted, with some parade of mathematical accuracy, that longevity is a great advantage to all species, so that he who believes in natural selection "must arrange his genealogical tree" in such a manner that all the descendants have longer lives than their progenitors! Cannot our critic conceive that a biennial plant or one of the lower animals might range into a cold climate and perish there every winter; and yet, owing to advantages gained through natural selection, survive from year to year by means of its seeds or ova? Mr. E. Ray Lankester has recently discussed this subject, and he concludes, as far as its extreme complexity allows him to form a judgment, that longevity is generally related to the standard of each species in the scale of organisation, as well as to the amount of expenditure in reproduction and in general activity. And these conditions have, it is probable, been largely determined through natural selection.

It has been argued that, as none of the animals and plants of Egypt, of which we know anything, have changed during the last three or four thousand years, so probably have none in any part of the world. But, as Mr. G. H. Lewes has remarked, this line of argument proves too much, for the ancient domestic races figured on the Egyptian monuments, or embalmed, are closely similar or even identical with those now living; yet all naturalists admit that such races have been produced through the modification of their original types. The many animals which have remained unchanged since the commencement of the glacial period, would have been an incomparably stronger case, for these have been exposed to great changes of climate and have migrated over great distances; whereas, in Egypt, during the last several thousand years, the conditions of life, as far as we know, have remained absolutely uniform. The fact of little or no modification having been effected since the glacial period would have been of some avail against those who believe in an innate and necessary law of development, but is powerless against the doctrine of natural selection or the survival of the fittest, which implies that when variations or individual differences of a beneficial nature happen to arise, these will be preserved; but this will be effected only under certain favourable circumstances.

The celebrated palæontologist, Bronn, at the close of his German translation of this work, asks, how, on the principle of natural selection, can a variety live side by side with the parent species? If both have become fitted for slightly different habits of life or conditions, they might live together; and if we lay on one side polymorphic species, in which the variability seems to be of a peculiar nature, and all mere temporary variations, such as size, albinism, &c., the more permanent varieties are generally found, as far as I can discover, inhabiting distinct stations,—such as high land or low land, dry or moist districts. Moreover, in the case of animals which wander much about and cross freely, their varieties seem to be generally confined to distinct regions.

Bronn also insists that distinct species never differ from each other in single characters, but in many parts; and he asks, how it always comes that many parts of the organisation should have been modified at the same time through variation and natural selection? But there is no necessity for supposing that all the parts of any being have been simultaneously modified. The most striking modifications, excellently adapted for some purpose, might, as was formerly remarked, be acquired by successive variations, if slight, first in one part and then in another; and as they would be transmitted all together, they would appear to us as if they had been simultaneously developed. The best answer, however, to the above objection is afforded by those domestic races which have been modified, chiefly through man's power of selection, for some special purpose. Look at the race and dray horse, or at the greyhound and mastiff. Their whole frames and even their mental characteristics have been modified; but if we could trace each step in the history of their transformation,—and the latter steps can be traced,—we should not see great and simultaneous changes, but first one part and then another slightly modified and improved. Even when selection has been applied by man to some one character alone,—of which our cultivated plants offer the best instances,—it will invariably be found that although this one part, whether it be the flower, fruit, or leaves, has been greatly changed, almost all the other parts have been slightly modified. This may be attributed partly to the principle of correlated growth, and partly to so-called spontaneous variation.

A much more serious objection has been urged by Bronn, and recently by Broca, namely, that many characters appear to be of no service whatever to their possessors, and therefore cannot have been influenced through natural selection. Bronn adduces the length of the ears and tails in the different species of hares and mice,—the complex folds of enamel in the teeth of many animals, and a multitude of analogous cases. With respect to plants, this subject has been discussed by Nägeli in an admirable essay. He admits that natural selection has effected much, but he insists that the families of plants differ chiefly from each other in morphological characters, which appear to be quite unimportant for the welfare of the species. He consequently believes in an innate tendency towards progressive and more perfect development. He specifies the arrangement of the cells in the tissues, and of the leaves on the axis, as cases in which natural selection could not have acted. To these may be added the numerical divisions in the parts of the flower, the position of the ovules, the shape of the seed, when not of any use for dissemination, &c.

There is much force in the above objection. Nevertheless, we ought, in the first place, to be extremely cautious in pretending to decide what structures now are, or have formerly been, of use to each species. In the second place, it should always be borne in mind that when one part is modified, so will be other parts, through certain dimly seen causes, such as an increased or diminished flow of nutriment to a part, mutual pressure, an early developed part affecting one subsequently developed, and so forth,—as well as through other causes which lead to the many mysterious cases of correlation, which we do not in the least understand. These agencies may be all grouped together, for the sake of brevity, under the expression of the laws of growth. In the third place, we have to allow for the direct and definite action of changed conditions of life, and for so-called spontaneous variations, in which the nature of the conditions apparently plays a quite subordinate part. Bud-variations, such as the appearance of a moss-rose on a common rose, or of a nectarine on a peach-tree offer good instances of spontaneous variations; but even in these cases, if we bear in mind the power of a minute drop of poison in producing complex galls, we ought not to feel too sure that the above variations are not the effect of some local change in the nature of the sap, due to some change in the conditions. There must be some efficient cause for each slight individual difference, as well as for more strongly marked variations which occasionally arise; and if the unknown cause were to act persistently, it is almost certain that all the individuals of the species would be similarly modified.

In the earlier editions of this work I under-rated, as it now seems probable, the frequency and importance of modifications due to spontaneous variability. But it is impossible to attribute to this cause the innumerable structures which are so well adapted to the habits of life of each species. I can no more believe in this than that the well-adapted form of a race-horse or greyhound, which before the principle of selection by man was well understood, excited so much surprise in the minds of the older naturalists, can thus be explained.

It may be worth while to illustrate some of the foregoing remarks. With respect to the assumed inutility of various parts and organs, it is hardly necessary to observe that even in the higher and best-known animals many structures exist, which are so highly developed that no one doubts that they are of importance, yet their use has not been, or has only recently been, ascertained. As Bronn gives the length of the ears and tail in the several species of mice as instances, though trifling ones, of differences in structure which can be of no special use, I may mention that, according to Dr. Schöbl, the external ears of the common mouse are supplied in an extraordinary manner with nerves, so that they no doubt serve as tactile organs; hence the length of the ears can hardly be quite unimportant. We shall, also, presently see that the tail is a highly useful prehensile organ to some of the species; and its use would be much influenced by its length.

With respect to plants, to which on account of Nägeli's essay I shall confine myself in the following remarks, it will be admitted that the flowers of orchids present a multitude of curious structures, which a few years ago would have been considered as mere morphological differences without any special function; but they are now known to be of the highest importance for the fertilisation of the species through the aid of insects, and have probably been gained through natural selection. No one until lately would have imagined that in dimorphic and trimorphic plants the different lengths of the stamens and pistils, and their arrangement, could have been of any service, but now we know this to be the case.

In certain whole groups of plants the ovules stand erect, and in others they are suspended; and within the same ovarium of some few plants, one ovule holds the former and a second ovule the latter position. These positions seem at first purely morphological, or of no physiological signification; but Dr. Hooker informs me that within the same ovarium, the upper ovules alone in some cases, and in other cases the lower ones alone are fertilised; and he suggests that this probably depends on the direction in which the pollen-tubes enter the ovarium. If so, the position of the ovules, even when one is erect and the other suspended within the same ovarium, would follow from the selection of any slight deviations in position which favoured their fertilisation, and the production of seed.

Several plants belonging to distinct orders habitually produce flowers of two kinds,—the one open of the ordinary structure, the other closed and imperfect. These two kinds of flowers sometimes differ wonderfully in structure, yet may be seen to graduate into each other on the same plant. The ordinary and open flowers can be intercrossed; and the benefits which certainly are derived from this process are thus secured. The closed and imperfect flowers are, however, manifestly of high importance, as they yield with the utmost safety a large stock of seed, with the expenditure of wonderfully little pollen. The two kinds of flowers often differ much, as just stated, in structure. The petals in the imperfect flowers almost always consist of mere rudiments, and the pollen-grains are reduced in diameter. In Ononis columnæ five of the alternate stamens are rudimentary; and in some species of Viola three stamens are in this state, two retaining their proper function, but being of very small size. In six out of thirty of the closed flowers in an Indian violet (name unknown, for the plants have never produced with me perfect flowers), the sepals are reduced from the normal number of five to three. In one section of the Malpighiaceæ the closed flowers, according to A. de Jussieu, are still further modified, for the five stamens which stand opposite to the sepals are all aborted, a sixth stamen standing opposite to a petal being alone developed; and this stamen is not present in the ordinary flowers of these species; the style is aborted; and the ovaria are reduced from three to two. Now although natural selection may well have had the power to prevent some of the flowers from expanding, and to reduce the amount of pollen, when rendered by the closure of the flowers superfluous, yet hardly any of the above special modifications can have been thus determined, but must have followed from the laws of growth, including the functional inactivity of parts, during the progress of the reduction of the pollen and the closure of the flowers.

It is so necessary to appreciate the important effects of the laws of growth, that I will give some additional cases of another kind, namely of differences in the same part or organ, due to differences in relative position on the same plant. In the Spanish chestnut, and in certain fir-trees, the angles of divergence of the leaves differ, according to Schacht, in the nearly horizontal and in the upright branches. In the common rue and some other plants, one flower, usually the central or terminal one, opens first, and has five sepals and petals, and five divisions to the ovarium; whilst all the other flowers on the plant are tetramerous. In the British Adoxa the uppermost flower generally has two calyx-lobes with the other organs tetramerous, whilst the surrounding flowers generally have three calyx-lobes with the other organs pentamerous. In many Compositæ and Umbelliferæ (and in some other plants) the circumferential flowers have their corollas much more developed than those of the centre; and this seems often connected with the abortion of the reproductive organs. It is a more curious fact, previously referred to, that the achenes or seeds of the circumference and centre sometimes differ greatly in form, colour, and other characters. In Carthamus and some other Compositæ the central achenes alone are furnished with a pappus; and in Hyoseris the same head yields achenes of three different forms. In certain Umbelliferæ the exterior seeds, according to Tausch, are orthospermous, and the central one cœlospermous, and this is a character which was considered by De Candolle to be in other species of the highest systematic importance. Prof. Braun mentions a Fumariaceous genus, in which the flowers in the lower part of the spike bear oval, ribbed, one-seeded nutlets; and in the upper part of the spike, lanceolate, two-valved, and two-seeded siliques. In these several cases, with the exception of that of the well developed ray-florets, which are of service in making the flowers conspicuous to insects, natural selection cannot, as far as we can judge, have come into play, or only in a quite subordinate manner. All these modifications follow from the relative position and inter-action of the parts; and it can hardly be doubted that if all the flowers and leaves on the same plant had been subjected to the same external and internal condition, as are the flowers and leaves in certain positions, all would have been modified in the same manner.

In numerous other cases we find modifications of structure, which are considered by botanists to be generally of a highly important nature, affecting only some of the flowers on the same plant, or occurring on distinct plants, which grow close together under the same conditions. As these variations seem of no special use to the plants, they cannot have been influenced by natural selection. Of their cause we are quite ignorant; we cannot even attribute them, as in the last class of cases, to any proximate agency, such as relative position. I will give only a few instances. It is so common to observe on the same plant, flowers indifferently tetramerous, pentamerous, &c., that I need not give examples; but as numerical variations are comparatively rare when the parts are few, I may mention that, according to De Candolle, the flowers of Papaver bracteatum offer either two sepals with four petals (which is the common type with poppies), or three sepals with six petals. The manner in which the petals are folded in the bud is in most groups a very constant morphological character; but Professor Asa Gray states that with some species of Mimulus, the æstivation is almost as frequently that of the Rhinanthideæ as of the Antirrhinideæ, to which latter tribe the genus belongs. Aug. St. Hilaire gives the following cases: the genus Zanthoxylon belongs to a division of the Rutaceæ with a single ovary, but in some species flowers may be found on the same plant, and even in the same panicle, with either one or two ovaries. In Helianthemum the capsule has been described as unilocular or 3-locular; and in H. mutabile, "Une lame, *plus ou moins large*, s'étend entre le pericarpe et le placenta." In the flowers of Saponaria officinalis, Dr. Masters has observed instances of both marginal and free central placentation. Lastly, St. Hilaire found towards the southern extreme of the range of Gomphia oleæformis two forms which he did not at first doubt were distinct species, but he subsequently saw them growing on the same bush; and he then adds, "Voilà donc dans un même individu des loges et un style qui se rattachent tantôt à un axe verticale et tantôt à un gynobase."

We thus see that with plants many morphological changes may be attributed to the laws of growth and the inter-action of parts, independently of natural selection. But with respect to Nägeli's doctrine of an innate tendency towards perfection or progressive development, can it be said in the case of these strongly pronounced variations, that the plants have been caught in the act of progressing towards a higher state of development? On the contrary, I should infer from the mere fact of the parts in question differing or varying greatly on the same plant, that such modifications were of extremely small importance to the plants themselves, of whatever importance they may generally be to us for our classifications. The acquisition of a useless part can hardly be said to raise an organism in the natural scale; and in the case of the imperfect, closed flowers above described, if any new principle has to be invoked, it must be one of retrogression rather than of progression; and so it must be with many parasitic and degraded animals. We are ignorant of the exciting cause of the above specified modifications; but if the unknown cause were to act almost uniformly for a length of time, we may infer that the result would be almost uniform; and in this case all the individuals of the species would be modified in the same manner.

From the fact of the above characters being unimportant for the welfare of the species, any slight variations which occurred in them would not have been accumulated and augmented through natural selection. A structure which has been developed through long-continued selection, when it ceases to be of service to a species, generally becomes variable, as we see with rudimentary organs; for it will no longer be regulated by this same power of selection. But when, from the nature of the organism and of the conditions, modifications have been induced which are unimportant for the welfare of the species, they may be, and apparently often have been, transmitted in nearly the same state to numerous, otherwise modified, descendants. It cannot have been of much importance to the greater number of mammals, birds, or reptiles, whether they were clothed with hair, feathers, or scales; yet hair has been transmitted to almost all mammals, feathers to all birds, and scales to all true reptiles. A structure, whatever it may be, which is common to many allied forms, is ranked by us as of high systematic importance, and consequently is often assumed to be of high vital importance to the species. Thus, as I am inclined to believe, morphological differences, which we consider as important—such as the arrangement of the leaves, the divisions of the flower or of the ovarium, the position of the ovules, &c.—first appeared in many cases as fluctuating variations, which sooner or later became constant through the nature of the organism and of the surrounding conditions, as well as through the intercrossing of distinct individuals, but not through natural selection; for as these morphological characters do not affect the welfare of the species, any slight deviations in them could not have been governed or accumulated through this latter agency. It is a strange result which we thus arrive at, namely that characters of slight vital importance to the species, are the most important to the systematist; but, as we shall hereafter see when we treat of the genetic principle of classification, this is by no means so paradoxical as it may at first appear.

Although we have no good evidence of the existence in organic beings of an innate tendency towards progressive development, yet this necessarily follows, as I have attempted to show in the fourth chapter, through the continued action of natural selection. For the best definition which has ever been given of a high standard of organisation, is the degree to which the parts have been specialised or differentiated; and natural selection tends towards this end, inasmuch as the parts are thus enabled to perform their functions more efficiently.

A distinguished zoologist, Mr. St. George Mivart, has recently collected all the objections which have ever been advanced by myself and others against the theory of natural selection, as propounded by Mr. Wallace and myself, and has illustrated them with admirable art and force. When thus marshalled, they make a formidable array; and as it forms no part of Mr. Mivart's plan to give the various facts and considerations opposed to his conclusions, no slight effort of reason and memory is left to the reader, who may wish to weigh the evidence on both sides. When discussing special cases, Mr. Mivart passes over the effects of the increased use and disuse of parts, which I have always maintained to be highly important, and have treated in my 'Variation under Domestication' at greater length than, as I believe, any other writer. He likewise often assumes that I attribute nothing to variation, independently of natural selection, whereas in the work just referred to I have collected a greater number of well-established cases than can be found in any other work known to me. My judgment may not be trustworthy, but after reading with care Mr. Mivart's book, and comparing each section with what I have said on the same head, I never before felt so strongly convinced of the general truth of the conclusions here arrived at, subject, of course, in so intricate a subject, to much partial error.

All Mr. Mivart's objections will be, or have been, considered in the present volume. The one new point which appears to have struck many readers is, "that natural selection is incompetent to account for the incipient stages of useful structures." This subject is intimately connected with that of the gradation of characters, often accompanied by a change of function,—for instance, the conversion of a swim-bladder into lungs,—points which were discussed in the last chapter under two headings. Nevertheless, I will here consider in some detail several of the cases advanced by Mr. Mivart, selecting those which are the most illustrative, as want of space prevents me from considering all.

The giraffe, by its lofty stature, much elongated neck, fore-legs, head and tongue, has its whole frame beautifully adapted for browsing on the higher branches of trees. It can thus obtain food beyond the reach of the other Ungulata or hoofed animals inhabiting the same country; and this must be a great advantage to it during dearths. The Niata cattle in S

America show us how small a difference in structure may make, during such periods, a great difference in preserving an animal's life. These cattle can browse as well as others on grass, but from the projection of the lower jaw they cannot, during the often recurrent droughts, browse on the twigs of trees, reeds, &c., to which food the common cattle and horses are then driven; so that at these times the Niatas perish, if not fed by their owners. Before coming to Mr. Mivart's objections, it may be well to explain once again how natural selection will act in all ordinary cases. Man has modified some of his animals, without necessarily having attended to special points of structure, by simply preserving and breeding from the fleetest individuals, as with the race-horse and greyhound, or as with the game-cock, by breeding from the victorious birds. So under nature with the nascent giraffe the individuals which were the highest browsers, and were able during dearths to reach even an inch or two above the others, will often have been preserved; for they will have roamed over the whole country in search of food. That the individuals of the same species often differ slightly in the relative lengths of all their parts may be seen in many works of natural history, in which careful measurements are given. These slight proportional differences, due to the laws of growth and variation, are not of the slightest use or importance to most species. But it will have been otherwise with the nascent giraffe, considering its probable habits of life; for those individuals which had some one part or several parts of their bodies rather more elongated than usual, would generally have survived. These will have intercrossed and left offspring, either inheriting the same bodily peculiarities, or with a tendency to vary again in the same manner; whilst the individuals, less favoured in the same respects, will have been the most liable to perish.

We here see that there is no need to separate single pairs, as man does, when he methodically improves a breed: natural selection will preserve and thus separate all the superior individuals, allowing them freely to intercross, and will destroy all the inferior individuals. By this process long-continued, which exactly corresponds with what I have called unconscious selection by man, combined no doubt in a most important manner with the inherited effects of the increased use of parts, it seems to me almost certain that an ordinary hoofed quadruped might be converted into a giraffe.

To this conclusion Mr. Mivart brings forward two objections. One is that the increased size of the body would obviously require an increased supply of food, and he considers it as "very problematical whether the disadvantages thence arising would not, in times of scarcity, more than counterbalance the advantages." But as the giraffe does actually exist in large numbers in S. Africa, and as some of the largest antelopes in the world, taller than an ox, abound there, why should we doubt that, as far as size is concerned, intermediate gradations could formerly have existed there, subjected as now to severe dearths. Assuredly the being able to reach, at each stage of increased size, to a supply of food, left untouched by the other hoofed quadrupeds of the country, would have been of some advantage to the nascent giraffe. Nor must we overlook the fact, that increased bulk would act as a protection against almost all beasts of prey excepting the lion; and against this animal, its tall neck,—and the taller the better,—would, as Mr. Chauncey Wright has remarked, serve as a watch-tower. It is from this cause, as Sir S. Baker remarks, that no animal is more difficult to stalk than the giraffe. This animal also uses its long neck as a means of offence or defence, by violently swinging his head armed with stump-like horns. The preservation of each species can rarely be determined by any one advantage, but by the union of all, great and small.

Mr. Mivart then asks (and this is his second objection), if natural selection be so potent, and if high browsing be so great an advantage, why has not any other hoofed quadruped acquired a long neck and lofty stature, besides the giraffe, and, in a lesser degree, the camel, guanaco, and macrauchenia? Or, again, why has not any member of the group acquired a long proboscis? With respect to S. Africa, which was formerly inhabited by numerous herds of the giraffe, the answer is not difficult, and can best be given by an illustration. In every meadow in England in which trees grow, we see the lower branches trimmed or planed to an exact level by the browsing of the horses or cattle; and what advantage would it be, for instance, to sheep, if kept there, to acquire slightly longer necks? In every district some one kind of animal will almost certainly be able to browse higher than the others; and it is almost equally certain that this one kind alone could have its neck elongated for this purpose, through natural selection and the effects of increased use. In S. Africa the competition for browsing on the higher branches of the acacias and other trees must be between giraffe and giraffe, and not with the other ungulate animals.

Why, in other quarters of the world, various animals belonging to this same order have not acquired either an elongated neck or a proboscis, cannot be distinctly answered; but it is as unreasonable to expect a distinct answer to such a question, as why some event in the history of mankind did not occur in one country, whilst it did in another. We are ignorant with respect to the conditions which determine the numbers and range of each species; and we cannot even conjecture what changes of structure would be favourable to its increase in some new country. We can, however, see in a general manner that various causes might have interfered with the development of a long neck or proboscis. To reach the foliage at a considerable height (without climbing, for which hoofed animals are singularly ill-constructed) implies greatly increased bulk of body; and we know that some areas support singularly few large quadrupeds, for instance S. America, though it is so luxuriant; whilst S. Africa abounds with them to an unparalleled degree. Why this should be so, we do not know; nor why the later tertiary periods should have been so much more favourable for their existence than the present time. Whatever the causes may have been, we can see that certain districts and times would have been much more favourable than others for the development of so large a quadruped as the giraffe.

In order that an animal should acquire some structure specially and largely developed, it is almost indispensable that several other parts should be modified and co-adapted. Although every part of the body varies slightly, it does not follow that the necessary parts should always vary in the right direction and to the right degree. With the different species of our domesticated animals we know that the parts vary in a different manner and degree; and that some species are much more variable than others. Even if the fitting variations did arise, it does not follow that natural selection would be able to act on them, and produce a structure which apparently would be beneficial to the species. For instance, if the number of individuals existing in a country is determined chiefly through destruction by beasts of prey,—by external or internal parasites, &c.,—as seems often to be the case, then natural selection will be able to do little, or will be greatly retarded, in modifying any particular structure for obtaining food. Lastly, natural selection is a slow process, and the same favourable conditions must long endure in order that any marked effect should thus be produced. Except by assigning such general and vague reasons, we cannot explain why, in many quarters of the world, hoofed quadrupeds have not acquired much elongated necks or other means for browsing on the higher branches of trees.

Objections of the same nature as the foregoing have been advanced by many writers. In each case various causes, besides the general ones just indicated, have probably interfered with the acquisition through natural selection of structures, which it is thought would be beneficial to certain species. One writer asks, why has not the ostrich acquired the power of flight? But a moment's reflection will show what an enormous supply of food would be necessary to give to this bird of the desert force to move its huge body through the air. Oceanic islands are inhabited by bats and seals, but by no terrestrial mammals; yet as some of these bats are peculiar species, they must have long inhabited their present homes. Therefore Sir C. Lyell asks, and assigns certain reasons in answer, why have not seals and bats given birth on such islands to forms fitted to live on the land? But seals would necessarily be first converted into terrestrial carnivorous animals of considerable size, and bats into terrestrial insectivorous animals; for the former there would be no prey; for the bats ground-insects would serve as food, but these would already be largely preyed on by the reptiles or birds, which first colonise and abound on most oceanic islands. Gradations of structure, with each stage beneficial to a changing species, will be favoured only under certain peculiar conditions. A strictly terrestrial animal, by occasionally hunting for food in shallow water, then in streams or lakes, might at last be converted into an animal so thoroughly aquatic as to brave the open ocean. But seals would not find on oceanic islands the conditions favourable to their gradual reconversion into a terrestrial form. Bats, as formerly shown, probably acquired their wings by at first gliding through the air from tree to tree, like the so-called flying squirrels, for the sake of escaping from their enemies, or for avoiding falls; but when the power of true flight had once been acquired, it would never be reconverted back, at least for the above purposes, into the less efficient power of gliding through the air. Bats might, indeed, like many birds, have had their wings greatly reduced in size, or completely lost, through disuse; but in this case it would be necessary that they should first have acquired the power of running quickly on the ground, by the aid of their hind legs alone, so as to compete with birds or other ground animals; and for such a change a bat seems singularly ill-fitted. These conjectural remarks have been made merely to show that a transition of structure, with each step beneficial, is a highly complex affair; and that there is nothing strange in a transition not having occurred in any particular case.

Lastly, more than one writer has asked, why have some animals had their mental powers more highly developed than others, as such development would be advantageous to all? Why have not apes acquired the intellectual powers of man? Various causes could be assigned; but as they are conjectural, and their relative probability cannot be weighed, it would be useless to give them. A definite answer to the latter question ought not to be expected, seeing that no one can solve the simpler problem why, of two races of savages, one has risen higher in the scale of civilisation than the other; and this apparently implies increased brain-power.

We will return to Mr. Mivart's other objections. Insects often resemble for the sake of protection various objects, such as green or decayed leaves, dead twigs, bits of lichen, flowers, spines, excrement of birds, and living insects; but to this latter point I shall hereafter recur. The resemblance is often wonderfully close, and is not confined to colour, but extends to form, and even to the manner in which the insects hold themselves. The caterpillars which project motionless like dead twigs from the bushes on which they feed, offer an excellent instance of a resemblance of this kind. The cases of the imitation of such objects as the excrement of birds, are rare and exceptional. On this head, Mr. Mivart remarks, "As, according to Mr. Darwin's theory, there is a constant tendency to indefinite variation, and as the minute incipient variations will be in *all directions*, they must tend to neutralise each other, and at first to form such unstable modifications that it is difficult, if not impossible, to see how such indefinite oscillations of infinitesimal beginnings can ever build up a sufficiently appreciable resemblance to a leaf, bamboo, or other object, for Natural Selection to seize upon and perpetuate."

But in all the foregoing cases the insects in their original state no doubt presented some rude and accidental resemblance to an object commonly found in the stations frequented by them. Nor is this at all improbable, considering the almost infinite number of surrounding objects and the diversity in form and colour of the hosts of insects which exist. As some rude resemblance is necessary for the first start, we can understand how it is that the larger and higher animals do not (with the exception, as far as I know, of one fish) resemble for the sake of protection special objects, but only the surface which commonly surrounds them, and this chiefly in colour. Assuming that an insect originally happened to resemble in some degree a dead twig or a decayed leaf, and that it varied slightly in many ways, then all the variations which rendered the insect at all more like any such object, and thus favoured its escape, would be preserved, whilst other variations would be neglected and ultimately lost; or, if they rendered the insect at all less like the imitated object, they would be eliminated. There would indeed be force in Mr. Mivart's objection, if we were to attempt to account for the above resemblances, independently of natural selection, through mere fluctuating variability; but as the case stands there is none.

Nor can I see any force in Mr. Mivart's difficulty with respect to "the last touches of perfection in the mimicry;" as in the case given by Mr. Wallace, of a walking-stick insect (Ceroxylus laceratus), which resembles "a stick grown over by a creeping moss or jungermannia." So close was this resemblance, that a native Dyak maintained that the foliaceous excrescences were really moss. Insects are preyed on by birds and other enemies, whose sight is probably sharper than ours, and every grade in resemblance which aided an insect to escape notice or detection, would tend towards its preservation; and the more perfect the resemblance so much the better for the insect. Considering the nature of the differences between the species in the group which includes the above Ceroxylus, there is nothing improbable in this insect having varied in the irregularities on its surface, and in these having become more or less green-coloured; for in every group the characters which differ in the several species are the most apt to vary, whilst the generic characters, or those common to all the species, are the most constant.

The Greenland whale is one of the most wonderful animals in the world, and the baleen, or whale-bone, one of its greatest peculiarities. The baleen consists of a row, on each side, of the upper jaw, of about 300 plates or laminæ, which stand close together transversely to the longer axis of the mouth. Within the main row there are some subsidiary rows. The extremities and inner margins of all the plates are frayed into stiff bristles, which clothe the whole gigantic palate, and serve to strain or sift the water, and thus to secure the minute prey on which these great animals subsist. The middle and longest lamina in the Greenland whale is ten, twelve, or even fifteen feet in length; but in the different species of Cetaceans there are gradations in length; the middle lamina being in one species, according to Scoresby, four feet, in another three, in another eighteen inches, and in the Balænoptera rostrata only about nine inches in length. The quality of the whale-bone also differs in the different species.

With respect to the baleen, Mr. Mivart remarks that if it "had once attained such a size and development as to be at all useful, then its preservation and augmentation within serviceable limits would be promoted by natural selection alone. But how to obtain the beginning of such useful development?" In answer, it may be asked, why should not the early progenitors of the whales with baleen have possessed a mouth constructed something like the lamellated beak of a duck? Ducks, like whales, subsist by sifting the mud and water; and the family has sometimes been called *Criblatores,* or sifters. I hope that I may not be misconstrued into saying that the progenitors of whales did actually possess mouths lamellated like the beak of a duck. I wish only to show that this is not incredible, and that the immense plates of baleen in the Greenland whale might have been developed from such lamellæ by finely graduated steps, each of service to its possessor.

The beak of a shoveller-duck (Spatula clypeata) is a more beautiful and complex structure than the mouth of a whale. The upper mandible is furnished on each side (in the specimen examined by me) with a row or comb formed of 188 thin, elastic lamellæ, obliquely bevelled so as to be pointed, and placed transversely to the longer axis of the mouth. They arise from the palate, and are attached by flexible membrane to the sides of the mandible. Those standing towards the middle are the longest, being about one-third of an inch in length, and they project .14 of an inch beneath the edge. At their bases there is a short subsidiary row of obliquely transverse lamellæ. In these several respects they resemble the plates of baleen in the mouth of a whale. But towards the extremity of the beak they differ much, as they project inwards, instead of straight downwards. The entire head of the shoveller, though incomparably less bulky, is about one-eighteenth of the length of the head of a moderately large Balænoptera rostrata, in which species the baleen is only nine inches long; so that if we were to make the head of the shoveller as long as that of the Balænoptera, the lamellæ would be six inches in length,—that is, two-thirds of the length of the baleen in this species of whale. The lower mandible of the shoveller-duck is furnished with lamellæ of equal length with those above, but finer; and in being thus furnished it differs conspicuously from the lower jaw of a whale, which is destitute of baleen. On the other hand the extremities of these lower lamellæ are frayed into fine bristly points, so that they thus curiously resemble the plates of baleen. In the genus Prion, a member of the distinct family of the Petrels, the upper mandible alone is furnished with lamellæ, which are well developed and project beneath the margin; so that the beak of this bird resembles in this respect the mouth of a whale.

From the highly developed structure of the shoveller's beak we may proceed (as I have learnt from information and specimens sent to me by Mr. Salvin), without any great break, as far as fitness for sifting is concerned, through the beak of the Merganetta armata, and in some respects through that of the Aix sponsa, to the beak of the common duck. In this latter species, the lamellæ are much coarser than in the shoveller, and are firmly attached to the sides of the mandible; they are only about 50 in number on each side, and do not project at all beneath the margin. They are square-topped, and are edged with translucent hardish tissue, as if for crushing food. The edges of the lower mandible are crossed by numerous fine ridges, which project very little. Although the beak is thus very inferior as a sifter to that of the shoveller, yet this bird, as every one knows, constantly uses it for this purpose. There are other species, as I hear from Mr. Salvin, in which the lamellæ are considerably less developed than in the common duck; but I do not know whether they use their beaks for sifting the water.

Turning to another group of the same family. In the Egyptian goose (Chenalopex) the beak closely resembles that of the common ducks; but the lamellæ are not so numerous, nor so distinct from each other, nor do they project so much inwards; yet this goose, as I am informed by Mr. E. Bartlett, "uses its bill like a duck by throwing the water out at the corners." Its chief food, however, is grass, which it crops like the common goose. In this latter bird, the lamellæ of the upper mandible are much coarser than in the common duck, almost confluent, about 27 in number on each side, and terminating upwards in teeth-like knobs. The palate is also covered with hard rounded knobs. The edges of the lower mandible are serrated with teeth much more prominent, coarser, and sharper than in the duck. The common goose does not sift the water, but uses its beak exclusively for tearing or cutting herbage, for which purpose it is so well fitted, that it can crop grass closer than almost any other animal. There are other species of geese, as I hear from Mr. Bartlett, in which the lamellæ are less developed than in the common goose.

We thus see that a member of the duck family, with a beak constructed like that of the common goose and adapted solely for grazing, or even a member with a beak having less well-developed lamellæ, might be converted by small changes into a species like the Egpytian goose,—this into one like the common duck,—and, lastly into one like the shoveller, provided with a beak almost exclusively adapted for sifting the water; for this bird could hardly use any part of its beak, except the hooked tip, for seizing or tearing solid food. The beak of a goose, as I may add, might also be converted by small changes into one provided with prominent, recurved teeth, like those of the Merganser (a member of the same family), serving for the widely different purpose of securing live fish.

Returning to the whales. The Hyperoodon bidens is destitute of true teeth in an efficient condition, but its palate is roughened, according to Lacepède, with small, unequal, hard points of horn. There is, therefore, nothing improbable in supposing that some early Cetacean form was provided with similar points of horn on the palate, but rather more regularly placed, and which, like the knobs on the beak of the goose, aided it in seizing or tearing its food. If so, it will hardly be denied that the points might have been converted through variation and natural selection into lamellæ as well developed as those of the Egyptian goose, in which case they would have been used both for seizing objects and for sifting the water; then into lamellæ like those of the domestic duck; and so onwards, until they became as well constructed as those of the shoveller, in which case they would have served exclusively as a sifting apparatus. From this stage, in which the lamellæ would be two-thirds of the length of the plates of baleen in the Balænoptera rostrata, gradations, which may be observed in still-existing Cetaceans, lead us onwards to the enormous plates of baleen in the Greenland whale. Nor is there the least reason to doubt that each step in this scale might have been as serviceable to certain ancient Cetaceans, with the functions of the parts slowly changing during the progress of development, as are the gradations in the beaks of the different existing members of the duck-family. We should bear in mind that each species of duck is subjected to a severe struggle for existence, and that the structure of every part of its frame must be well adapted to its conditions of life.

The Pleuronectidæ, or Flat-fish, are remarkable for their asymmetrical bodies. They rest on one side,—in the greater number of species on the left, but in some on the right side; and occasionally reversed adult specimens occur. The lower, or resting-surface, resembles at first sight the ventral surface of an ordinary fish: it is of a white colour, less developed in many ways than the upper side, with the lateral fins often of smaller size. But the eyes offer the most remarkable peculiarity; for they are both placed on the upper side of the head. During early youth, however, they stand opposite to each other, and the whole body is then symmetrical, with both sides equally coloured. Soon the eye proper to the lower side begins to glide slowly round the head to the upper side; but does not pass right through the skull, as was formerly thought to be the case. It is obvious that unless the lower eye did thus travel round, it could not be used by the fish whilst lying in its habitual position on one side. The lower eye would, also, have been liable to be abraded by the sandy bottom. That the Pleuronectidæ are admirably adapted by their flattened and asymmetrical structure for their habits of life, is manifest from several species, such as soles, flounders, &c., being extremely common. The chief advantages thus gained seem to be protection from their enemies, and facility for feeding on the ground. The different members, however, of the family present, as Schiödte remarks, "a long series of forms exhibiting a gradual transition from Hippoglossus pinguis, which does not in any considerable degree alter the shape in which it leaves the ovum, to the soles, which are entirely thrown to one side."

Mr. Mivart has taken up this case, and remarks that a sudden spontaneous transformation in the position of the eyes is hardly conceivable, in which I quite agree with him. He then adds: "if the transit was gradual, then how such transit of one eye a minute fraction of the journey towards the other side of the head could benefit the individual is, indeed, far from clear. It seems, even, that such an incipient transformation must rather have been injurious." But he might have found an answer to this objection in the excellent observations published in 1867 by Malm. The Pleuronectidæ, whilst very young and still symmetrical, with their eyes standing on opposite sides of the head, cannot long retain a vertical position, owing to the excessive depth of their bodies, the small size of their lateral fins, and to their being destitute of a swimbladder. Hence soon growing tired, they fall to the bottom on one side. Whilst thus at rest they often twist, as Malm observed, the lower eye upwards, to see above them; and they do this so vigorously that the eye is pressed hard against the upper part of the orbit. The forehead between the eyes consequently becomes, as could be plainly seen, temporarily contracted in breadth. On one occasion Malm saw a young fish raise and depress the lower eye through an angular distance of about seventy degrees.

We should remember that the skull at this early age is cartilaginous and flexible, so that it readily yields to muscular action. It is also known with the higher animals, even after early youth, that the skull yields and is altered in shape, if the skin or muscles be permanently contracted through disease or some accident. With long-eared rabbits, if one ear lops forwards and downwards, its weight drags forward all the bones of the skull on the same side, of which I have given a figure. Malm states that the newly-hatched young of perches, salmon, and several other symmetrical fishes, have the habit of occasionally resting on one side at the bottom; and he has observed that they often then strain their lower eyes so as to look upwards; and their skulls are thus rendered rather crooked. These fishes, however, are soon able to hold themselves in a vertical position, and no permanent effect is thus produced. With the Pleuronectidæ, on the other hand, the older they grow the more habitually they rest on one side, owing to the increasing flatness of their bodies, and a permanent effect is thus produced on the form of the head, and on the position of the eyes. Judging from analogy, the tendency to distortion would no doubt be increased through the principle of inheritance. Schiödte believes, in opposition to some other naturalists, that the Pleuronectidæ are not quite symmetrical even in the embryo; and if this be so, we could understand how it is that certain species, whilst young, habitually fall over and rest on the left side, and other species on the right side. Malm adds, in confirmation of the above view, that the adult Trachypterus arcticus, which is not a member of the Pleuronectidæ, rests on its left side at the bottom, and swims diagonally through the water; and in this fish, the two sides of the head are said to be somewhat dissimilar. Our great authority on Fishes, Dr. Günther, concludes his abstract of Malm's paper, by remarking that "the author gives a very simple explanation of the abnormal condition of the Pleuronectoids."

We thus see that the first stages of the transit of the eye from one side of the head to the other, which Mr. Mivart considers would be injurious, may be attributed to the habit, no doubt beneficial to the individual and to the species, of endeavouring to look upwards with both eyes, whilst resting on one side at the bottom. We may also attribute to the inherited effects of use the fact of the mouth in several kinds of flat-fish being bent towards the lower surface, with the jaw bones stronger and more effective on this, the eyeless side of the head, than on the other, for the sake, as Dr. Traquair supposes, of feeding with ease on the ground. Disuse, on the other hand, will account for the less developed condition of the whole inferior half of the body, including the lateral fins; though Yarrell thinks that the reduced size of these fins is advantageous to the fish, as "there is so much less room for their action, than with the larger fins above." Perhaps the lesser number of teeth in the proportion of four to seven in the upper halves of the two jaws of the plaice, to twenty-five to thirty in the lower halves, may likewise be accounted for by disuse. From the colourless state of the ventral surface of most fishes and of many other animals, we may reasonably suppose that the absence of colour in flat-fish on the side, whether it be the right or left, which is undermost, is due to the exclusion of light. But it cannot be supposed that the peculiar speckled appearance of the upper side of the sole, so like the sandy bed of the sea, or the power in some species, as recently shown by Pouchet, of changing their colour in accordance with the surrounding surface, or the presence of bony tubercles on the upper side of the turbot, are due to the action of the light. Here natural selection has probably come into play, as well as in adapting the general shape of the body of these fishes, and many other peculiarities, to their habits of life. We should keep in mind, as I have before insisted, that the inherited effects of the increased use of parts, and perhaps of their disuse, will be strengthened by natural selection. For all spontaneous variations in the right direction will thus be preserved; as will those individuals which inherit in the highest degree the effects of the increased and beneficial use of any part. How much to attribute in each particular case to the effects of use, and how much to natural selection, it seems impossible to decide.

I may give another instance of a structure which apparently owes its origin exclusively to use or habit. The extremity of the tail in some American monkeys has been converted into a wonderfully perfect prehensile organ, and serves as a fifth hand. A reviewer who agrees with Mr. Mivart in every detail, remarks on this structure: "It is impossible to believe that in any number of ages the first slight incipient tendency to grasp could preserve the lives of the individuals possessing it, or favour their chance of having and of rearing offspring." But there is no necessity for any such belief. Habit, and this almost implies that some benefit great or small is thus derived, would in all probability suffice for the work. Brehm saw the young of an African monkey (Cercopithecus) clinging to the under surface of their mother by their hands, and at the same time they hooked their little tails round that of their mother. Professor Henslow kept in confinement some harvest mice (Mus messorius) which do not possess a structurally prehensile tail; but he frequently observed that they curled their tails round the branches of a bush placed in the cage, and thus aided themselves in climbing. I have received an analogous account from Dr. Günther, who has seen a mouse thus suspend itself. If the harvest mouse had been more strictly arboreal, it would perhaps have had its tail rendered structurally prehensile, as is the case with some members of the same order. Why Cercopithecus, considering its habits whilst young, has not become thus provided, it would be difficult to say. It is, however, possible that the long tail of this monkey may be of more service to it as a balancing organ in making its prodigious leaps, than as a prehensile organ.

The mammary glands are common to the whole class of mammals, and are indispensable for their existence; they must, therefore, have been developed at an extremely remote period, and we can know nothing posi- tively about their manner of development. Mr. Mivart asks: "Is it con- ceivable that the young of any animal was ever saved from destruction by accidentally sucking a drop of scarcely nutritious fluid from an acci- dentally hypertrophied cutaneous gland of its mother? And even if one was so, what chance was there of the perpetuation of such a variation?" But the case is not here put fairly. It is admitted by most evolutionists that mammals are descended from a marsupial form; and if so, the mam- mary glands will have been at first developed within the marsupial sack. In the case of the fish (Hippocampus) the eggs are hatched, and the young are reared for a time, within a sack of this nature; and an Ameri- can naturalist, Mr. Lockwood, believes from what he has seen of the de- velopment of the young, that they are nourished by a secretion from the cutaneous glands of the sack. Now with the early progenitors of mam- mals, almost before they deserved to be thus designated, is it not at least possible that the young might have been similarly nourished? And in this case, the individuals which secreted a fluid, in some degree or manner the most nutritious, so as to partake of the nature of milk, would in the long run have reared a larger number of well-nourished offspring, than would the individuals which secreted a poorer fluid; and thus the cutaneous glands, which are the homologues of the mammary glands, would have been improved or rendered more effective. It accords with the widely ex- tended principle of specialisation, that the glands over a certain space of the sack should have become more highly developed than the remainder; and they would then have formed a breast, but at first without a nipple, as we see in the Ornithorhyncus, at the base of the mammalian series. Through what agency the glands over a certain space became more highly specialised than the others, I will not pretend to decide, whether in part through compensation of growth, the effects of use, or of natural selec- tion.

The development of the mammary glands would have been of no ser- vice, and could not have been effected through natural selection, unless the young at the same time were able to partake of the secretion. There is no greater difficulty in understanding how young mammals have instinc- tively learnt to suck the breast, than in understanding how unhatched chickens have learnt to break the egg-shell by tapping against it with their specially adapted beaks; or how a few hours after leaving the shell they have learnt to pick up grains of food. In such cases the most prob- able solution seems to be, that the habit was at first acquired by practice at a more advanced age, and afterwards transmitted to the offspring at an earlier age. But the young kangaroo is said not to suck, only to cling to the nipple of its mother, who has the power of injecting milk into the mouth of her helpless, half-formed offspring. On this head, Mr. Mivart remarks: "Did no special provision exist, the young one must infallibly be choked by the intrusion of the milk into the windpipe. But there *is* a special provision. The larynx is so elongated that it rises up into the pos- terior end of the nasal passage, and is thus enabled to give free entrance to the air for the lungs, while the milk passes harmlessly on each side of this elongated larynx, and so safely attains the gullet behind it." Mr. Mivart then asks how did natural selection remove in the adult kangaroo (and in most other mammals, on the assumption that they are descended from a marsupial form), "this at least perfectly innocent and harmless structure?" It may be suggested in answer that the voice, which is certainly of high importance to many animals, could hardly have been used with full force as long as the larynx entered the nasal passage; and Professor Flower has suggested to me that this structure would have greatly interfered with an animal swallowing solid food.

We will now turn for a short space to the lower divisions of the animal kingdom. The Echinodermata (star-fishes, sea-urchins, &c.) are furnished with remarkable organs, called pedicellariæ, which consist, when well developed, of a tridacytle forceps—that is, of one formed of three serrated arms, neatly fitting together and placed on the summit of a flexible stem, moved by muscles. These forceps can firmly seize hold of any object; and Alexander Agassiz has seen an Echinus or sea-urchin rapidly passing particles of excrement from forceps to forceps down certain lines of its body, in order that its shell should not be fouled. But there is no doubt that besides removing dirt of all kinds, they subserve other functions; and one of these apparently is defence.

With respect to these organs, Mr. Mivart, as on so many previous occasions, asks: "What would be the utility of the *first rudimentary beginnings* of such structures, and how could such incipient buddings have ever preserved the life of a single Echinus?" He adds, "not even the *sudden* development of the snapping action could have been beneficial without the freely moveable stalk, nor could the latter have been efficient without the snapping jaws, yet no minute merely indefinite variations could simultaneously evolve these complex co-ordinations of structure; to deny this seems to do no less than to affirm a startling paradox. Paradoxical as this may appear to Mr. Mivart, tridactyle forcepses, immovably fixed at the base, but capable of a snapping action, certainly exist on some star-fishes; and this is intelligible if they serve, at least in part, as a means of defence. Mr. Agassiz, to whose great kindness I am indebted for much information on the subject, informs me that there are other star-fishes, in which one of the three arms of the forceps is reduced to a support for the other two; and again, other genera in which the third arm is completely lost. In Echinoneus, the shell is described by M. Perrier as bearing two kinds of pedicellariæ, one resembling those of Echinus, and the other those of Spatangus; and such cases are always interesting as affording the means of apparently sudden transitions, through the abortion of one of the two states of an organ.

With respect to the steps by which these curious organs have been evolved, Mr. Agassiz infers from his own researches and those of Müller, that both in star-fishes and sea-urchins the pedicellariæ must undoubtedly be looked at as modified spines. This may be inferred from their manner of development in the individual, as well as from a long and perfect series of gradations in different species and genera, from simple granules to ordinary spines, to perfect tridactyle pedicellariæ. The gradations extend even to the manner in which ordinary spines and pedicellariæ with their supporting calcareous rods are articulated to the shell. In certain genera of star-fishes, "the very combinations needed to show that the pedicellariæ are only modified branching spines" may be found. Thus we have fixed spines, with three equi-distant, serrated, moveable branches, articulated to near their bases; and higher up, on the same spine, three other moveable branches. Now when the latter arise from the summit of a spine they form in fact a rude tridactyle pedicellaria, and such may be seen on the same spine together with the three lower branches. In this case the identity in nature between the arms of the pedicellariæ and the moveable branches of a spine, is unmistakable. It is generally admitted that the ordinary spines serve as a protection; and if so, there can be no reason to doubt that those furnished with serrated and moveable branches likewise serve for the same purpose; and they would thus serve still more effectively as soon as by meeting together they acted as a prehensile or snapping apparatus. Thus every gradation, from an ordinary fixed spine to a fixed pedicellaria, would be of service.

In certain genera of star-fishes these organs, instead of being fixed or borne on an immoveable support, are placed on the summit of a flexible and muscular, though short, stem; and in this case they probably subserve some additional function besides defence. In the sea-urchins the steps can be followed by which a fixed spine becomes articulated to the shell, and is thus rendered moveable. I wish I had space here to give a fuller abstract of Mr. Agassiz's interesting observations on the development of the pedicellariæ. All possible gradations, as he adds, may likewise be found between the pedicellariæ of the star-fishes and the hooks of the Ophiurians, another group of Echinodermata; and again between the pedicellariæ of sea-urchins and the anchors of the Holothuriæ, also belonging to the same great class.

Certain compound animals, or zoophytes as they have been termed, namely the Polyzoa, are provided with curious organs called avicularia. These differ much in structure in the different species. In their most perfect condition, they curiously resemble the head and beak of a vulture in miniature, seated on a neck and capable of movement, as is likewise the lower jaw or mandible. In one species observed by me all the avicularia on the same branch often moved simultaneously backwards and forwards, with the lower jaw widely open, through an angle of about 90°, in the course of five seconds; and their movement caused the whole polyzoary to tremble. When the jaws are touched with a needle they seize it so firmly that the branch can thus be shaken.

Mr. Mivart adduces this case, chiefly on account of the supposed difficulty of organs, namely the avicularia of the Polyzoa and the pedicellariæ of the Echinodermata, which he considers as "essentially similar," having been developed through natural selection in widely distinct divisions of the animal kingdom. But, as far as structure is concerned, I can see no similarity between tridactyle pedicellariæ and avicularia. The latter resemble somewhat more closely the chelæ or pincers of Crustaceans; and Mr. Mivart might have adduced with equal appropriateness this resemblance as a special difficulty; or even their resemblance to the head and beak of a bird. The avicularia are believed by Mr. Busk, Dr. Smitt, and Dr. Nitsche—naturalists who have carefully studied this group—to be homologous with the zooids and their cells which compose the zoophyte; the moveable lip or lid of the cell corresponding with the lower and moveable mandible of the avicularium. Mr. Busk, however, does not know of any gradations now existing between a zooid and an avicularium. It is therefore impossible to conjecture by what serviceable gradations the one could have been converted into the other: but it by no means follows from this that such gradations have not existed.

As the chelæ of Crustaceans resemble in some degree the avicularia of Polyzoa, both serving as pincers, it may be worth while to show that with the former a long series of serviceable gradations still exists. In the first and simplest stage, the terminal segment of a limb shuts down either on the square summit of the broad penultimate segment, or against one whole side; and is thus enabled to catch hold of an object; but the limb still serves as an organ of locomotion. We next find one corner of the broad penultimate segment slightly prominent, sometimes furnished with irregular teeth; and against these the terminal segments shuts down. By an increase in the size of this projection, with its shape, as well as that of the terminal segment, slightly modified and improved, the pincers are rendered more and more perfect, until we have at last an instrument as efficient as the chelæ of a lobster; and all these gradations can be actually traced.

Besides the avicularia, the Polyzoa possess curious organs called vibracula. These generally consist of long bristles, capable of movement and easily excited. In one species examined by me the vibracula were slightly curved and serrated along the outer margin; and all of them on the same polyzoary often moved simultaneously; so that, acting like long oars, they swept a branch rapidly across the object-glass of my microscope. When a branch was placed on its face, the vibracula became entangled, and they made violent efforts to free themselves. They are supposed to serve as a defence, and may be seen, as Mr. Busk remarks, "to sweep slowly and carefully over the surface of the polyzoary, removing what might be noxious to the delicate inhabitants of the cells when their tentacula are protruded." The avicularia, like the vibracula, probably serve for defence, but they also catch and kill small living animals, which it is believed are afterwards swept by the currents within reach of the tentacula of the zooids. Some species are provided with avicularia and vibracula; some with avicularia alone, and a few with vibracula alone.

It is not easy to imagine two objects more widely different in appearance than a bristle or vibraculum, and an avicularium like the head of a bird; yet they are almost certainly homologous and have been developed from the same common source, namely a zooid with its cell. Hence we can understand how it is that these organs graduate in some cases, as I am informed by Mr. Busk, into each other. Thus with the avicularia of several species of Lepralia, the moveable mandible is so much produced and is so like a bristle, that the presence of the upper or fixed beak alone serves to determine even its avicularian nature. The vibracula may have been directly developed from the lips of the cells, without having passed through the avicularian stage; but it seems more probable that they have passed through this stage, as during the early stages of the transformation, the other parts of the cell with the included zooid could hardly have disappeared at once. In many cases the vibracula have a grooved support at the base, which seems to represent the fixed beak; though this support in some species is quite absent. This view of the development of the vibracula, if trustworthy, is interesting; for supposing that all the species provided with avicularia had become extinct, no one with the most vivid imagination would ever have thought that the vibracula had originally existed as part of an organ, resembling a bird's head or an irregular box or hood. It is interesting to see two such widely different organs developed from a common origin; and as the moveable lip of the cell serves as a protection to the zooid, there is no difficulty in believing that all the gradations, by which the lip became converted first into the lower mandible of an avicularium and then into an elongated bristle, likewise served as a protection in different ways and under different circumstances.

In the vegetable kingdom Mr. Mivart only alludes to two cases, namely the structure of the flowers of orchids, and the movements of climbing plants. With respect to the former, he says, "the explanation of their *origin* is deemed thoroughly unsatisfactory—utterly insufficient to explain the incipient, infinitesimal beginnings of structures which are of utility only when they are considerably developed." As I have fully treated this subject in another work, I will here give only a few details on one alone of the most striking peculiarities of the flowers of orchids, namely their pollinia. A pollinium when highly developed consists of a mass of pollen-grains, affixed to an elastic foot-stalk or caudicle, and this to a little mass of extremely viscid matter. The pollinia are by this means transported by insects from one flower to the stigma of another. In some orchids there is no caudicle to the pollen-masses, and the grains are merely tied together by fine threads; but as these are not confined to orchids, they need not here be considered; yet I may mention that at the base of the orchidaceous series, in Cypripedium, we can see how the threads were probably first developed. In other orchids the threads cohere at one end of the pollen-masses; and this forms the first or nascent trace of a caudicle. That this is the origin of the caudicle, even when of considerable length and highly developed, we have good evidence in the aborted pollen-grains which can sometimes be detected embedded within the central and solid parts.

With respect to the second chief peculiarity, namely the little mass of

viscid matter attached to the end of the caudicle, a long series of gradations can be specified, each of plain service to the plant. In most flowers
belonging to other orders the stigma secretes a little viscid matter. Now in
certain orchids similar viscid matter is secreted, but in much larger quantities by one alone of the three stigmas; and this stigma, perhaps in consequence of the copious secretion, is rendered sterile. When an insect
visits a flower of this kind, it rubs off some of the viscid matter and thus
at the same time drags away some of the pollen-grains. From this simple
condition, which differs but little from that of a multitude of common
flowers, there are endless gradations,—to species in which the pollen-
mass terminates in a very short, free caudicle,—to others in which the
caudicle becomes firmly attached to the viscid matter, with the sterile
stigma itself much modified. In this latter case we have a pollinium in its
most highly developed and perfect condition. He who will carefully examine the flowers of orchids for himself will not deny the existence of the
above series of gradations—from a mass of pollen-grains merely tied together by threads, with the stigma differing but little from that of an ordinary flower, to a highly complex pollinium, admirably adapted for
transportal by insects; nor will he deny that all the gradations in the several species are admirably adapted in relation to the general structure of
each flower for its fertilisation by different insects. In this, and in almost
every other case, the enquiry may be pushed further backwards; and it
may be asked how did the stigma of an ordinary flower become viscid,
but as we do not know the full history of any one group of beings, it is as
useless to ask, as it is hopeless to attempt answering, such questions.

We will now turn to climbing plants. These can be arranged in a long
series, from those which simply twine round a support, to those which I
have called leaf-climbers, and to those provided with tendrils. In these
two latter classes the stems have generally, but not always, lost the power
of twining, though they retain the power of revolving, which the tendrils
likewise possess. The gradations from leaf-climbers to tendril-bearers are
wonderfully close, and certain plants may be indifferently placed in either
class. But in ascending the series from simple twiners to leaf-climbers, an
important quality is added, namely sensitiveness to a touch, by which
means the foot-stalks of the leaves or flowers, or these modified and converted into tendrils, are excited to bend round and clasp the touching object. He who will read my memoir on these plants will, I think, admit that
all the many gradations in function and structure between simple twiners
and tendril-bearers are in each case beneficial in a high degree to the species. For instance, it is clearly a great advantage to a twining plant to become a leaf-climber; and it is probable that every twiner which possessed
leaves with long foot-stalks would have been developed into a leaf-climber if the foot-stalks had possessed in any slight degree the requisite sensitiveness to a touch.

As twining is the simplest means of ascending a support, and forms the
basis of our series, it may naturally be asked how did plants acquire this

power in an incipient degree, afterwards to be improved and increased through natural selection. The power of twining depends, firstly, on the stems whilst young being extremely flexible (but this is a character common to many plants which are not climbers) ; and, secondly, on their continually bending to all points of the compass, one after the other in succession, in the same order. By this movement the stems are inclined to all sides, and are made to move round and round. As soon as the lower part of a stem strikes against any object and is stopped, the upper part still goes on bending and revolving, and thus necessarily twines round and up the support. The revolving movement ceases after the early growth of each shoot. As in many widely separated families of plants, single species and single genera possess the power of revolving, and have thus become twiners, they must have independently acquired it, and cannot have inherited it from a common progenitor. Hence I was led to predict that some slight tendency to a movement of this kind would be found to be far from uncommon with plants which did not climb; and that this had afforded the basis for natural selection to work on and improve. When I made this prediction, I knew of only one imperfect case, namely, of the young flower-peduncles of a Maurandia which revolved slightly and irregularly, like the stems of twining plants, but without making any use of this habit. Soon afterwards Fritz Müller discovered that the young stems of an Alisma and of a Linum,—plants which do not climb and are widely separated in the natural system,—revolved plainly, though irregularly; and he states that he has reason to suspect that this occurs with some other plants. These slight movements appear to be of no service to the plants in question; anyhow, they are not of the least use in the way of climbing, which is the point that concerns us. Nevertheless we can see that if the stems of these plants had been flexible, and if under the conditions to which they are exposed it had profited them to ascend to a height, then the habit of slightly and irregularly revolving might have been increased and utilised through natural selection, until they had become converted into well-developed twining species.

With respect to the sensitiveness of the foot-stalks of the leaves and flowers, and of tendrils, nearly the same remarks are applicable as in the case of the revolving movements of twining plants. As a vast number of species, belonging to widely distinct groups, are endowed with this kind of sensitiveness, it ought to be found in a nascent condition in many plants which have not become climbers. This is the case: I observed that the young flower-peduncles of the above Maurandia curved themselves a little towards the side which was touched. Morren found in several species of Oxalis that the leaves and their foot-stalks moved, especially after exposure to a hot sun, when they were gently and repeatedly touched, or when the plant was shaken. I repeated these observations on some other species of Oxalis with the same result; in some of them the movement was distinct, but was best seen in the young leaves; in others it was extremely slight. It is a more important fact that according to the high authority of

Hofmeister, the young shoots and leaves of all plants move after being shaken; and with climbing plants it is, as we know, only during the early stages of growth that the foot-stalks and tendrils are sensitive.

It is scarcely possible that the above slight movements, due to a touch or shake, in the young and growing organs of plants, can be of any functional importance to them. But plants possess, in obedience to various stimuli, powers of movement, which are of manifest importance to them; for instance, towards and more rarely from the light,—in opposition to, and more rarely in the direction of, the attraction of gravity. When the nerves and muscles of an animal are excited by galvanism or by the absorption of strychnine, the consequent movements may be called an incidental result, for the nerves and muscles have not been rendered specially sensitive to these stimuli. So with plants it appears that, from having the power of movement in obedience to certain stimuli, they are excited in an incidental manner by a touch, or by being shaken. Hence there is no great difficulty in admitting that in the case of leaf-climbers and tendril-bearers, it is this tendency which has been taken advantage of and increased through natural selection. It is, however, probable, from reasons which I have assigned in my memoir, that this will have occurred only with plants which had already acquired the power of revolving, and had thus become twiners.

I have already endeavoured to explain how plants became twiners, namely, by the increase of a tendency to slight and irregular revolving movements, which were at first of no use to them; this movement, as well as that due to a touch or shake, being the incidental result of the power of moving, gained for other and beneficial purposes. Whether, during the gradual development of climbing plants, natural selection has been aided by the inherited effects of use, I will not pretend to decide; but we know that certain periodical movements, for instance the so-called sleep of plants, are governed by habit.

I have now considered enough, perhaps more than enough, of the cases, selected with care by a skilful naturalist, to prove that natural selection is incompetent to account for the incipient stages of useful structures; and I have shown, as I hope, that there is no great difficulty on this head. A good opportunity has thus been afforded for enlarging a little on gradations of structure, often associated with changed functions,—an important subject, which was not treated at sufficient length in the former editions of this work. I will now briefly recapitulate the foregoing cases.

With the giraffe, the continued preservation of the individuals of some extinct high-reaching ruminant, which had the longest necks, legs, &c., and could browse a little above the average height, and the continued destruction of those which could not browse so high, would have sufficed for the production of this remarkable quadruped; but the prolonged use of all the parts together with inheritance will have aided in an important manner in their co-ordination. With the many insects which imitate various objects, there is no improbability in the belief that an accidental resemblance to some common object was in each case the foundation for the work of natural selection, since perfected through the occasional preservation of slight variations which made the resemblance at all closer; and this will have been carried on as long as the insect continued to vary, and as long as a more and more perfect resemblance led to its escape from sharp-sighted enemies. In certain species of whales there is a tendency to the formation of irregular little points of horn on the palate; and it seems to be quite within the scope of natural selection to preserve all favourable variations, until the points were converted first into lamellated knobs or teeth, like those on the beak of a goose,—then into short lamellæ, like those of the domestic ducks,—and then into lamellæ, as perfect as those of the shoveller-duck,—and finally into the gigantic plates of baleen, as in the mouth of the Greenland whale. In the family of the ducks, the lamellæ are first used as teeth, then partly as teeth, and partly as a sifting apparatus, and at last almost exclusively for this latter purpose.

With such structures as the above lamellæ of horn or whalebone, habit or use can have done little or nothing, as far as we can judge, towards their development. On the other hand, the transportal of the lower eye of a flat-fish to the upper side of the head, and the formation of a prehensile tail, may be attributed almost wholly to continued use, together with inheritance. With respect to the mammæ of the higher animals, the most probable conjecture is that primordially the cutaneous glands over the whole surface of a marsupial sack secreted a nutritious fluid; and that these glands were improved in function through natural selection, and concentrated into a confined area, in which case they would have formed a mamma. There is no more difficulty in understanding how the branched spines of some ancient Echinoderm, which served as a defence, became developed through natural selection into tridactyle pedicellariæ, than in understanding the development of the pincers of crustaceans, through slight, serviceable modifications in the ultimate and penultimate segments of a limb, which was at first used solely for locomotion. In the avicularia and vibracula of the Polyzoa we have organs widely different in appearance developed from the same source; and with the vibracula we can understand how the successive gradations might have been of service. With the pollinia of orchids, the threads which originally served to tie together the pollen-grains, can be traced cohering into caudicles; and the steps can likewise be followed by which viscid matter, such as that secreted by the stigmas of ordinary flowers, and still subserving nearly but not quite the same purpose, became attached to the free ends of the caudicles;—all these gradations being of manifest benefit to the plants in question. With respect to climbing plants, I need not repeat what has been so lately said.

It has often been asked, if natural selection be so potent, why has not this or that structure been gained by certain species, to which it would apparently have been advantageous? But it is unreasonable to expect a precise answer to such questions, considering our ignorance of the past history of each species, and of the conditions which at the present day determine its numbers and range. In most cases only general reasons, but in some few cases special reasons, can be assigned. Thus to adapt a species to new habits of life, many co-ordinated modifications are almost indispensable, and it may often have happened that the requisite parts did not vary in the right manner or to the right degree. Many species must have been prevented from increasing in numbers through destructive agencies, which stood in no relation to certain structures, which we imagine would have been gained through natural selection from appearing to us advantageous to the species. In this case, as the struggle for life did not depend on such structures, they could not have been acquired through natural selection. In many cases complex and long-enduring conditions, often of a peculiar nature, are necessary for the development of a structure; and the requisite conditions may seldom have concurred. The belief that any given structure, which we think, often erroneously, would have been beneficial to a species, would have been gained under all circumstances through natural selection, is opposed to what we can understand of its manner of action. Mr. Mivart does not deny that natural selection has effected something; but he considers it as "demonstrably insufficient" to account for the phenomena which I explain by its agency. His chief arguments have now been considered, and the others will hereafter be considered. They seem to me to partake little of the character of demonstration, and to have little weight in comparison with those in favour of the power of natural selection, aided by the other agencies often specified. I am bound to add, that some of the facts and arguments here used by me, have been advanced for the same purpose in an able article lately published in the 'Medico-Chirurgical Review.'

At the present day almost all naturalists admit evolution under some form. Mr. Mivart believes that species change through "an internal force or tendency," about which it is not pretended that anything is known. That species have a capacity for change will be admitted by all evolutionists; but there is no need, as it seems to me, to invoke any internal force beyond the tendency to ordinary variability, which through the aid of selection by man has given rise to many well-adapted domestic races, and which through the aid of natural selection would equally well give rise by graduated steps to natural races or species. The final result will generally have been, as already explained, an advance, but in some few cases a retrogression, in organisation.

Mr. Mivart is further inclined to believe, and some naturalists agree with him, that new species manifest themselves "with suddenness and by modifications appearing at once." For instance, he supposes that the differences between the extinct three-toed Hipparion and the horse arose suddenly. He thinks it difficult to believe that the wing of a bird "was developed in any other way than by a comparatively sudden modification of a marked and important kind;" and apparently he would extend the same view to the wings of bats and pterodactyles. This conclusion, which implies great breaks or discontinuity in the series, appears to me improbable in the highest degree.

Every one who believes in slow and gradual evolution, will of course admit that specific changes may have been as abrupt and as great as any single variation which we meet with under nature, or even under domestication. But as species are more variable when domesticated or cultivated than under their natural conditions, it is not probable that such great and abrupt variations have often occurred under nature, as are known occasionally to arise under domestication. Of these latter variations several may be attributed to reversion; and the characters which thus reappear were, it is probable, in many cases at first gained in a gradual manner. A still greater number must be called monstrosities, such as six-fingered men, porcupine men, Ancon sheep, Niata cattle, &c.; and as they are widely different in character from natural species, they throw very little light on our subject. Excluding such cases of abrupt variations, the few which remain would at best constitute, if found in a state of nature, doubtful species, closely related to their parental types.

My reasons for doubting whether natural species have changed as abruptly as have occasionally domestic races, and for entirely disbelieving that they have changed in the wonderful manner indicated by Mr. Mivart, are as follows. According to our experience, abrupt and strongly marked variations occur in our domesticated productions, singly and at rather long intervals of time. If such occurred under nature, they would be liable, as formerly explained, to be lost by accidental causes of destruction and by subsequent inter-crossing; and so it is known to be under domestication, unless abrupt variations of this kind are specially preserved and separated by the care of man. Hence in order that a new species should suddenly appear in the manner supposed by Mr. Mivart, it is almost necessary to believe, in opposition to all analogy, that several wonderfully changed individuals appeared simultaneously within the same district. This difficulty, as in the case of unconscious selection by man, is avoided on the theory of gradual evolution, through the preservation of a large number of individuals, which varied more or less in any favourable direction, and of the destruction of a large number which varied in an opposite manner.

That many species have been evolved in an extremely gradual manner, there can hardly be a doubt. The species and even the genera of many large natural families are so closely allied together, that it is difficult to distinguish not a few of them. On every continent in proceeding from north to south, from lowland to upland, &c., we meet with a host of closely related or representative species; as we likewise do on certain distinct continents, which we have reason to believe were formerly connected. But in making these and the following remarks, I am compelled to allude to subjects hereafter to be discussed. Look at the many outlying islands round a continent, and see how many of their inhabitants can be raised only to the rank of doubtful species. So it is if we look to past times, and compare the species which have just passed away with those still living within the same areas; or if we compare the fossil species embedded in the sub-stages of the same geological formation. It is indeed manifest that multitudes of species are related in the closest manner to other species that still exist, or have lately existed; and it will hardly be maintained that such species have been developed in an abrupt or sudden manner. Nor should it be forgotten, when we look to the special parts of allied species, instead of to distinct species, that numerous and wonderfully fine gradations can be traced, connecting together widely different structures.

Many large groups of facts are intelligible only on the principle that species have been evolved by very small steps. For instance, the fact that the species included in the larger genera are more closely related to each other, and present a greater number of varieties than do the species in the smaller genera. The former are also grouped in little clusters, like varieties round species, and they present other analogies with varieties, as was shown in our second chapter. On this same principle we can understand how it is that specific characters are more variable than generic characters; and how the parts which are developed in an extraordinary degree or manner are more variable than other parts of the same species. Many analogous facts, all pointing in the same direction, could be added.

Although very many species have almost certainly been produced by steps not greater than those separating fine varieties; yet it may be maintained that some have been developed in a different and abrupt manner. Such an admission, however, ought not to be made without strong evidence being assigned. The vague and in some respects false analogies, as they have been shown to be by Mr. Chauncey Wright, which have been advanced in favour of this view, such as the sudden crystallisation of inorganic substances, or the falling of a facetted spheroid from one facet to another, hardly deserve consideration. One class of facts, however, namely, the sudden appearance of new and distinct forms of life in our geological formations supports at first sight the belief in abrupt development. But the value of this evidence depends entirely on the perfection of the geological record, in relation to periods remote in the history of the world. If the record is as fragmentary as many geologists strenuously assert, there is nothing strange in new forms appearing as if suddenly developed.

Unless we admit transformations as prodigious as those advocated by Mr. Mivart, such as the sudden development of the wings of birds or bats, or the sudden conversion of a Hipparion into a horse, hardly any light is thrown by the belief in abrupt modifications on the deficiency of connecting links in our geological formations. But against the belief in such abrupt changes, embryology enters a strong protest. It is notorious that the wings of birds and bats, and the legs of horses or other quadrupeds, are undistinguishable at an early embryonic period, and that they become differentiated by insensibly fine steps. Embryological resemblances of all kinds can be accounted for, as we shall hereafter see, by the progenitors of our existing species having varied after early youth, and having transmitted their newly acquired characters to their offspring, at a corresponding age. The embryo is thus left almost unaffected, and serves as a record of the past condition of the species. Hence it is that existing species during the early stages of their development so often resemble ancient and extinct forms belonging to the same class. On this view of the meaning of embryological resemblances, and indeed on any view, it is incredible that an animal should have undergone such momentous and abrupt transformations, as those above indicated; and yet should not bear even a trace in its embryonic condition of any sudden modification; every detail in its structure being developed by insensibly fine steps.

He who believes that some ancient form was transformed suddenly through an internal force or tendency into, for instance, one furnished with wings, will be almost compelled to assume, in opposition to all analogy, that many individuals varied simultaneously. It cannot be denied that such abrupt and great changes of structure are widely different from those which most species apparently have undergone. He will further be compelled to believe that many structures beautifully adapted to all the other parts of the same creature and to the surrounding conditions, have been suddenly produced; and of such complex and wonderful co-adaptations, he will not be able to assign a shadow of an explanation. He will be forced to admit that these great and sudden transformations have left no trace of their action on the embryo. To admit all this is, as it seems to me, to enter into the realms of miracle, and to leave those of Science.

CHAPTER VIII

INSTINCT

Instincts comparable with habits, but different in their origin—Instincts graduated —Aphides and ants—Instincts variable—Domestic instincts, their origin— Natural instincts of the cuckoo, molothrus, ostrich, and parasitic bees—Slave-making ants—Hive-bee, its cell-making instinct—Changes of instinct and structure not necessarily simultaneous—Difficulties of the theory of the Natural Selection of instincts—Neuter or sterile insects—Summary.

MANY instincts are so wonderful that their development will probably appear to the reader a difficulty sufficient to overthrow my whole theory. I may here premise that I have nothing to do with the origin of the mental powers, any more than I have with that of life itself. We are concerned only with the diversities of instinct and of the other mental faculties in animals of the same class.

I will not attempt any definition of instinct. It would be easy to show that several distinct mental actions are commonly embraced by this term; but every one understands what is meant, when it is said that instinct impels the cuckoo to migrate and to lay her eggs in other birds' nests. An action, which we ourselves require experience to enable us to perform, when performed by an animal, more especially by a very young one, without experience, and when performed by many individuals in the same way, without their knowing for what purpose it is performed, is usually said to be instinctive. But I could show that none of these characters are universal. A little dose of judgment or reason, as Pierre Huber expresses it, often comes into play, even with animals low in the scale of nature.

Frederick Cuvier and several of the older metaphysicians have compared instinct with habit. This comparison gives, I think, an accurate notion of the frame of mind under which an instinctive action is performed, but not necessarily of its origin. How unconsciously many habitual actions are performed, indeed not rarely in direct opposition to our conscious will! yet they may be modified by the will or reason. Habits easily become associated with other habits, with certain periods of time, and states of the body. When once acquired, they often remain constant throughout life. Several other points of resemblance between instincts and habits could be pointed out. As in repeating a well-known song, so in instincts, one action follows another by a sort of rhythm; if a person be interrupted in a song, or in repeating anything by rote, he is generally forced to go back to recover the habitual train of thought; so P. Huber found it was with a caterpillar, which makes a very complicated hammock; for if he took a caterpillar which had completed its hammock up to, say, the sixth stage of construction, and put it into a hammock completed up only to the third stage, the caterpillar simply re-performed the fourth, fifth, and sixth stages of construction. If, however, a caterpillar were taken out of a hammock made up, for instance, to the third stage, and were put into one finished up to the sixth stage, so that much of its work was already done for it, far from deriving any benefit from this, it was much embarrassed, and in order to complete its hammock, seemed forced to start from the third stage, where it had left off, and thus tried to complete the already finished work.

If we suppose any habitual action to become inherited—and it can be shown that this does sometimes happen—then the resemblance between what originally was a habit and an instinct becomes so close as not to be distinguished. If Mozart, instead of playing the pianoforte at three years old with wonderfully little practice, had played a tune with no practice at all, he might truly be said to have done so instinctively. But it would be a serious error to suppose that the greater number of instincts have been acquired by habit in one generation, and then transmitted by inheritance to succeeding generations. It can be clearly shown that the most wonderful instincts with which we are acquainted, namely, those of the hive-bee and of many ants, could not possibly have been acquired by habit.

It will be universally admitted that instincts are as important as corporeal structures for the welfare of each species, under its present conditions of life. Under changed conditions of life, it is at least possible that slight modifications of instinct might be profitable to a species; and if it can be shown that instincts do vary ever so little, then I can see no difficulty in natural selection preserving and continually accumulating variations of instinct to any extent that was profitable. It is thus, as I believe, that all the most complex and wonderful instincts have originated. As modifications of corporeal structure arise from, and are increased by, use or habit, and are diminished or lost by disuse, so I do not doubt it has been with instincts. But I believe that the effects of habit are in many cases of subordinate importance to the effects of the natural selection of what may be called spontaneous variations of instincts;—that is of variations produced by the same unknown causes which produce slight deviations of bodily structure.

No complex instinct can possibly be produced through natural selection, except by the slow and gradual accumulation of numerous slight, yet profitable, variations. Hence, as in the case of corporeal structures, we ought to find in nature, not the actual transitional gradations by which each complex instinct has been acquired—for these could be found only in the lineal ancestors of each species—but we ought to find in the collateral lines of descent some evidence of such gradations; or we ought at least to be able to show that gradations of some kind are possible; and this we certainly can do. I have been surprised to find, making allowance for the instincts of animals having been but little observed except in Eu-

rope and North America, and for no instinct being known amongst extinct species, how very generally gradations, leading to the most complex
instincts, can be discovered. Changes of instinct may sometimes be facilitated by the same species having different instincts at different periods of
life, or at different seasons of the year, or when placed under different circumstances, &c.; in which case either the one or the other instinct might
be preserved by natural selection. And such instances of diversity of instinct in the same species can be shown to occur in nature.

Again, as in the case of corporeal structure, and conformably to my
theory, the instinct of each species is good for itself, but has never, as far
as we can judge, been produced for the exclusive good of others. One of
the strongest instances of an animal apparently performing an action for
the sole good of another, with which I am acquainted, is that of aphides
voluntarily yielding, as was first observed by Huber, their sweet excretion
to ants: that they do so voluntarily, the following facts show. I removed
all the ants from a group of about a dozen aphides on a dock-plant, and
prevented their attendance during several hours. After this interval, I felt
sure that the aphides would want to excrete. I watched them for some
time through a lens, but not one excreted; I then tickled and stroked
them with a hair in the same manner, as well as I could, as the ants do
with their antennæ; but not one excreted. Afterwards I allowed an ant to
visit them, and it immediately seemed, by its eager way of running about,
to be well aware what a rich flock it had discovered; it then began to play
with its antennæ on the abdomen first of one aphis and then of another;
and each, as soon as it felt the antennæ, immediately lifted up its abdomen and excereted a limpid drop of sweet juice, which was eagerly devoured by the ant. Even the quite young aphides behaved in this manner,
showing that the action was instinctive, and not the result of experience.
It is certain, from the observations of Huber, that the aphides show no
dislike to the ants: if the latter be not present they are at last compelled
to eject their excretion. But as the excretion is extremely viscid, it is no
doubt a convenience to the aphides to have it removed; therefore probably they do not excrete solely for the good of the ants. Although there is no
evidence that any animal performs an action for the exclusive good of another species, yet each tries to take advantage of the instincts of others,
as each takes advantage of the weaker bodily structure of other species.
So again certain instincts cannot be considered as absolutely perfect; but
as details on this and other such points are not indispensable, they may
be here passed over.

As some degree of variation in instincts under a state of nature, and the
inheritance of such variations, are indispensable for the action of natural
selection, as many instances as possible ought to be given; but want of
space prevents me. I can only assert that instincts certainly do vary —for
instance, the migratory instinct, both in extent and direction, and in its
total loss. So it is with the nests of birds, which vary partly in dependence
on the situations chosen, and on the nature and temperature of the country inhabited, but often from causes wholly unknown to us: Audubon has

given several remarkable cases of differences in the nests of the same species in the northern and southern United States. Why, it has been asked,
if instinct be variable, has it not granted to the bee "the ability to use
some other material when wax was deficient"? But what other natural
material could bees use? They will work, as I have seen, with wax hardened with vermilion or softened with lard. Andrew Knight observed that
his bees, instead of laboriously collecting propolis, used a cement of wax
and turpentine, with which he had covered decorticated trees. It has lately been shown that bees, instead of searching for pollen, will gladly use a
very different substance, namely oatmeal. Fear of any particular enemy
is certainly an instinctive quality, as may be seen in nestling birds,
though it is strengthened by experience, and by the sight of fear of the
same enemy in other animals. The fear of man is slowly acquired, as I
have elsewhere shown, by the various animals which inhabit desert islands; and we see an instance of this even in England, in the greater wildness of all our large birds in comparison with our small birds; for the
large birds have been most persecuted by man. We may safely attribute
the greater wildness of our large birds to this cause; for in uninhabited islands large birds are not more fearful than small; and the magpie, so
wary in England, is tame in Norway, as is the hooded crow in Egypt.

That the mental qualities of animals of the same kind, born in a state
of nature, vary much, could be shown by many facts. Several cases could
also be adduced of occasional and strange habits in wild animals, which,
if advantageous to the species, might have given rise, through natural selection, to new instincts. But I am well aware that these general statements, without the facts in detail, will produce but a feeble effect on the
reader's mind. I can only repeat my assurance, that I do not speak with
out good evidence.

Inherited Changes of Habit or Instinct in Domesticated Animals

The possibility, or even probability, of inherited variations of instinct
in a state of nature will be strengthened by briefly considering a few cases
under domestication. We shall thus be enabled to see the part which habit
and the selection of so-called spontaneous variations have played in modifying the mental qualities of our domestic animals. It is notorious how
much domestic animals vary in their mental qualities. With cats, for instance, one naturally takes to catching rats, and another mice, and these
tendencies are known to be inherited. One cat, according to Mr. St. John,
always brought home game-birds, another hares or rabbits, and another
hunted on marshy ground and almost nightly caught woodcocks or
snipes. A number of curious and authentic instances could be given of various shades of disposition and of taste, and likewise of the oddest tricks,
associated with certain frames of mind or periods of time, being inherited.
But let us look to the familiar case of the breeds of the dogs: it cannot be
doubted that young pointers (I have myself seen a striking instance) will
sometimes point and even back other dogs the very first time that they

are taken out; retrieving is certainly in some degree inherited by retrievers; and a tendency to run round, instead of at, a flock of sheep, by shepherd dogs. I cannot see that these actions, performed without experience
by the young, and in nearly the same manner by each individual, performed with eager delight by each breed, and without the end being
known—for the young pointer can no more know that he points to aid his
master, than the white butterfly knows why she lays her eggs on the leaf
of the cabbage—I cannot see that these actions differ essentially from
true instincts. If we were to behold one kind of wolf, when young and
without any training, as soon as it scented its prey, stand motionless like
a statue, and then slowly crawl forward with a peculiar gait; and another
kind of wolf rushing round, instead of at, a herd of deer, and driving them
to a distant point, we should assuredly call these actions instinctive. Domestic instincts, as they may be called, are certainly far less fixed than
natural instincts; but they have been acted on by far less rigorous selection, and have been transmitted for an incomparably shorter period,
under less fixed conditions of life.

How strongly these domestic instincts, habits, and dispositions are inherited, and how curiously they become mingled, is well shown when different breeds of dogs are crossed. Thus it is known that a cross with a
bull-dog has affected for many generations the courage and obstinacy of
greyhounds; and a cross with a greyhound has given to a whole family of
shepherd-dogs a tendency to hunt hares. These domestic instincts, when
thus tested by crossing, resemble natural instincts, which in a like manner
become curiously blended together, and for a long period exhibit traces of
the instincts of either parent: for example, Le Roy describes a dog, whose
great-grandfather was a wolf, and this dog showed a trace of its wild parentage only in one way, by not coming in a straight line to his master,
when called.

Domestic instincts are sometimes spoken of as actions which have become inherited solely from long-continued and compulsory habit; but
this is not true. No one would ever have thought of teaching, or probably
could have taught, the tumbler-pigeon to tumble,—an action which, as I
have witnessed, is performed by young birds, that have never seen a pigeon tumble. We may believe that some one pigeon showed a slight tendency to this strange habit, and that the long-continued selection of the
best individuals in successive generations made tumblers what they now
are; and near Glasgow there are house-tumblers, as I hear from Mr.
Brent, which cannot fly eighteen inches high without going head over
heels. It may be doubted whether any one would have thought of training
a dog to point, had not some one dog naturally shown a tendency in this
line; and this is known occasionally to happen, as I once saw, in a pure
terrier: the act of pointing is probably, as many have thought, only the
exaggerated pause of an animal preparing to spring on its prey. When the
first tendency to point was once displayed, methodical selection and the
inherited effects of compulsory training in each successive generation

would soon complete the work; and unconscious selection is still in progress, as each man tries to procure, without intending to improve the breed, dogs which stand and hunt best. On the other hand, habit alone in some cases has sufficed; hardly any animal is more difficult to tame than the young of the wild rabbit; scarcely any animal is tamer than the young of the tame rabbit; but I can hardly suppose that domestic rabbits have often been selected for tameness alone; so that we must attribute at least the greater part of the inherited change from extreme wildness to extreme tameness, to habit and long-continued close confinement.

Natural instincts are lost under domestication: a remarkable instance of this is seen in those breeds of fowls which very rarely or never become "broody," that is, never wish to sit on their eggs. Familiarity alone prevents our seeing how largely and how permanently the minds of our domestic animals have been modified. It is scarcely possible to doubt that the love of man has become instinctive in the dog. All wolves, foxes, jackals, and species of the cat genus, when kept tame, are most eager to attack poultry, sheep, and pigs; and this tendency has been found incurable in dogs which have been brought home as puppies from countries such as Tierra del Fuego and Australia, where the savages do not keep these domestic animals. How rarely, on the other hand, do our civilised dogs, even when quite young, require to be taught not to attack poultry, sheep, and pigs! No doubt they occasionally do make an attack, and are then beaten; and if not cured, they are destroyed; so that habit and some degree of selection have probably concurred in civilising by inheritance our dogs. On the other hand, young chickens have lost, wholly by habit, that fear of the dog and cat which no doubt was originally instinctive in them; for I am informed by Captain Hutton that the young chickens of the parent-stock, the Gallus bankiva, when reared in India under a hen, are at first excessively wild. So it is with young pheasants reared in England under a hen. It is not that chickens have lost all fear, but fear only of dogs and cats, for if the hen gives the danger-chuckle, they will run (more especially young turkeys) from under her, and conceal themselves in the surrounding grass or thickets; and this is evidently done for the instinctive purpose of allowing as we see in wild ground-birds, their mother to fly away. But this instinct retained by our chickens has become useless under domestication, for the mother-hen has almost lost by disuse the power of flight.

Hence, we may conclude, that under domestication instincts have been acquired, and natural instincts have been lost, partly by habit, and partly by man selecting and accumulating, during successive generations, peculiar mental habits and actions, which at first appeared from what we must in our ignorance call an accident. In some cases compulsory habit alone has sufficed to produce inherited mental changes; in other cases, compulsory habit has done nothing, and all has been the result of selection, pursued both methodically and unconsciously: but in most cases habit and selection have probably concurred.

Special Instincts

We shall, perhaps, best understand how instincts in a state of nature have become modified by selection by considering a few cases. I will select only three,—namely, the instinct which leads the cuckoo to lay her eggs in other birds' nests; the slave-making instinct of certain ants; and the cell-making power of the hive-bee. These two latter instincts have generally and justly been ranked by naturalists as the most wonderful of all known instincts.

Instincts of the Cuckoo.—It is supposed by some naturalists that the more immediate cause of the instinct of the cuckoo is, that she lays her eggs, not daily, but at intervals of two or three days; so that, if she were to make her own nest and sit on her own eggs, those first laid would have to be left for some time unincubated, or there would be eggs and young birds of different ages in the same nest. If this were the case, the process of laying and hatching might be inconveniently long, more especially as she migrates at a very early period; and the first hatched young would probably have to be fed by the male alone. But the American cuckoo is in this predicament; for she makes her own nest, and has eggs and young successively hatched, all at the same time. It has been both asserted and denied that the American cuckoo occasionally lays her eggs in other birds' nests; but I have lately heard from Dr. Merrell, of Iowa, that he once found in Illinois a young cuckoo together with a young jay in the nest of a Blue jay (Garrulus cristatus); and as both were nearly full feathered, there could be no mistake in their identification. I could also give several instances of various birds which have been known occasionally to lay their eggs in other birds' nests. Now let us suppose that the ancient progenitor of our European cuckoo had the habits of the American cuckoo, and that she occasionally laid an egg in another birds' nest. If the old bird profited by this occasional habit through being enabled to migrate earlier or through any other cause; or if the young were made more vigorous by advantage being taken of the mistaken instinct of another species than when reared by their own mother, encumbered as she could hardly fail to be by having eggs and young of different ages at the same time; then the old birds or the fostered young would gain an advantage. And analogy would lead us to believe, that the young thus reared would be apt to follow by inheritance the occasional and aberrant habit of their mother, and in their turn would be apt to lay their eggs in other birds' nests, and thus be more successful in rearing their young. By a continued process of this nature, I believe that the strange instinct of our cuckoo has been generated. It has, also, recently been ascertained on sufficient evidence, by Adolf Müller, that the cuckoo occasionally lays her eggs on the bare ground, sits on them, and feeds her young. This rare event is probably a case of reversion to the long-lost, aboriginal instinct of nidification.

It has been objected that I have not noticed other related instincts and adaptations of structure in the cuckoo, which are spoken of as necessarily co-ordinated. But in all cases, speculation on an instinct known to us only in a single species, is useless, for we have hitherto had no facts to guide us. Until recently the instincts of the European and of the non-parasitic American cuckoo alone were known; now, owing to Mr. Ramsay's observations, we have learnt something about three Australian species, which lay their eggs in other birds' nests. The chief points to be referred to are three: first, that the common cuckoo, with rare exceptions, lays only one egg in a nest, so that the large and voracious young bird receives ample food. Secondly, that the eggs are remarkably small, not exceeding those of the skylark,—a bird about one-fourth as large as the cuckoo. That the small size of the egg is a real cause of adaptation we may infer from the fact of the non-parasitic American cuckoo laying full-sized eggs. Thirdly, that the young cuckoo, soon after birth, has the instinct, the strength, and a properly shaped back for ejecting its foster-brothers, which then perish from cold and hunger. This has been boldly called a beneficent arrangement, in order that the young cuckoo may get sufficient food, and that its foster-brothers may perish before they had acquired much feeling!

Turning now to the Australian species; though these birds generally lay only one egg in a nest, it is not rare to find two and even three eggs in the same nest. In the Bronze cuckoo the eggs vary greatly in size, from eight to ten times in length. Now if it had been of an advantage to this species to have laid eggs even smaller than those now laid, so as to have deceived certain foster-parents, or, as is more probable, to have been hatched within a shorter period (for it is asserted that there is a relation between the size of eggs and the period of their incubation), then there is no difficulty in believing that a race or species might have been formed which would have laid smaller and smaller eggs; for these would have been more safely hatched and reared. Mr. Ramsay remarks that two of the Australian cuckoos, when they lay their eggs in an open nest, manifest a decided preference for nests containing eggs similar in colour to their own. The European species apparently manifests some tendency towards a similar instinct, but not rarely departs from it, as is shown by her laying her dull and pale-coloured eggs in the nest of the Hedge-warbler with bright greenish-blue eggs. Had our cuckoo invariably displayed the above instinct, it would assuredly have been added to those which it is assumed must all have been acquired together. The eggs of the Australian Bronze cuckoo vary, according to Mr. Ramsay, to an extraordinary degree in colour; so that in this respect, as well as in size, natural selection might have secured and fixed any advantageous variation.

In the case of the European cuckoo, the offspring of the foster-parents are commonly ejected from the nest within three days after the cuckoo is hatched; and as the latter at this age is in a most helpless condition, Mr. Gould was formerly inclined to believe that the act of ejection was performed by the foster-parents themselves. But he has now received a trustworthy account of a young cuckoo which was actually seen, whilst still blind and not able even to hold up its own head, in the act of ejecting its foster-brothers. One of these was replaced in the nest by the observer, and was again thrown out. With respect to the means by which this strange and odious instinct was acquired, if it were of great importance for the young cuckoo, as is probably the case, to receive as much food as possible soon after birth, I can see no special difficulty in its having gradually acquired, during successive generations, the blind desire, the strength, and structure necessary for the work of ejection; for those young cuckoos which had such habits and structure best developed would be the most securely reared. The first step towards the acquisition of the proper instinct might have been more unintentional restlessness on the part of the young bird, when somewhat advanced in age and strength; the habit having been afterwards improved, and transmitted to an earlier age. I can see no more difficulty in this, than in the unhatched young of other birds acquiring the instinct to break through their own shells;—or than in young snakes acquiring in their upper jaws, as Owen has remarked, a transitory sharp tooth for cutting through the tough egg-shell. For if each part is liable to individual variations at all ages, and the variations tend to be inherited at a corresponding or earlier age,—propositions which cannot be disputed,—then the instincts and structure of the young could be slowly modified as surely as those of the adult; and both cases must stand or fall together with the whole theory of natural selection.

Some species of Molothrus, a widely distinct genus of American birds, allied to our starlings, have parasitic habits like those of the cuckoo; and the species present an interesting gradation in the perfection of their instincts. The sexes of Molothrus badius are stated by an excellent observer, Mr. Hudson, sometimes to live promiscuously together in flocks, and sometimes to pair. They either build a nest of their own, or seize on one belonging to some other bird, occasionally throwing out the nestlings of the stranger. They either lay their eggs in the nest thus appropriated, or oddly enough build one for themselves on the top of it. They usually sit on their own eggs and rear their own young; but Mr. Hudson says it is probable that they are occasionally parasitic, for he has seen the young of this species following old birds of a distinct kind and clamouring to be fed by them. The parasitic habits of another species of Molothrus, the M. bonariensis, are much more highly developed than those of the last, but are still far from perfect. This bird, as far as it is known, invariably lays its eggs in the nests of strangers; but it is remarkable that several together sometimes commence to build an irregular untidy nest of their own, placed in singularly ill-adapted situations, as on the leaves of a large thistle. They never, however, as far as Mr. Hudson has ascertained, complete a nest for themselves. They often lay so many eggs—from fifteen to twenty—in the same foster-nest, that few or none can possibly be hatched. They have, moreover, the extraordinary habit of pecking holes in the eggs, whether of their own species or of their foster-parents, which they find in the appropriated nests. They drop also many eggs on the bare ground, which are thus wasted. A third species, the M. pecoris of North America, has acquired instincts as perfect as those of the cuckoo, for it never lays more than one egg in a foster-nest, so that the young bird is securely reared. Mr. Hudson is a strong disbeliever in evolution, but he appears to have been so much struck by the imperfect instincts of the Molothrus bonariensis that he quotes my words, and asks, "Must we consider these habits, not as especially endowed or created instincts, but as small consequences of one general law, namely, transition?"

Various birds, as has already been remarked, occasionally lay their eggs in the nests of other birds. This habit is not very uncommon with the Gallinaceæ, and throws some light on the singular instinct of the ostrich. In this family several hen-birds unite and lay first a few eggs in one nest and then in another; and these are hatched by the males. This instinct may probably be accounted for by the fact of the hens laying a large number of eggs, but, as with the cuckoo, at intervals of two or three days. The instinct, however, of the American ostrich, as in the case of the Molothrus bonariensis, has not as yet been perfected; for a surprising number of eggs lie strewed over the plains, so that in one day's hunting I picked up no less than twenty lost and wasted eggs.

Many bees are parasitic, and regularly lay their eggs in the nests of other kinds of bees. This case is more remarkable than that of the cuckoo; for these bees have not only had their instincts but their structure modified in accordance with their parasitic habits; for they do not possess the pollen-collecting apparatus which would have been indispensable if they had stored up food for their own young. Some species of Sphegidæ (wasp-like insects) are likewise parasitic; and M. Fabre has lately shown good reason for believing that, although the Tachytes nigra generally makes its own burrow and stores it with paralysed prey for its own larvæ, yet that, when this insect finds a burrow already made and stored by another sphex, it takes advantage of the prize and becomes for the occasion parasitic. In this case, as with that of the Molothrus or cuckoo, I can see no difficulty in natural selection making an occasional habit permanent, if of advantage to the species, and if the insect whose nest and stored food are feloniously appropriated, be not thus exterminated.

Slave-making instinct.—This remarkable instinct was first discovered in the Formica (Polyerges) rufescens by Pierre Huber, a better observer even than his celebrated father. This ant is absolutely dependent on its slaves; without their aid, the species would certainly become extinct in a single year. The males and fertile female do no work of any kind, and the workers or sterile females, though most energetic and courageous in capturing slaves, do no other work. They are incapable of making their own nests, or of feeding their own larvæ. When the old nest is found inconvenient, and they have to migrate, it is the slaves which determine the migration, and actually carry their masters in their jaws. So utterly helpless are the masters, that when Huber shut up thirty of them without a slave, but with plenty of the food which they like best, and with their own larvæ and pupæ to stimulate them to work, they did nothing; they could not even feed themselves, and many perished of hunger. Huber then introduced a single slave (F. fusca), and she instantly set to work, fed and saved the survivors; made some cells and tended the larvæ, and put all to rights. What can be more extraordinary than these well-ascertained facts? If we had not known of any other slave-making ant, it would have been hopeless to speculate how so wonderful an instinct could have been perfected.

Another species, Formica sanguinea, was likewise first discovered by P. Huber to be a slave-making ant. This species is found in the southern parts of England, and its habits have been attended to by Mr. F. Smith, of the British Museum, to whom I am much indebted for information on this and other subjects. Although fully trusting to the statements of Huber and Mr. Smith, I tried to approach the subject in a sceptical frame of mind, as any one may well be excused for doubting the existence of so extraordinary an instinct as that of making slaves. Hence, I will give the observations which I made in some little detail. I opened fourteen nests of F. sanguinea, and found a few slaves in all. Males and fertile females of the slave species (F. fusca) are found only in their own proper communities, and have never been observed in the nests of F. sanguinea. The slaves are black and not above half the size of their red masters, so that the contrast in their appearance is great. When the nest is slightly disturbed, the slaves occasionally come out, and like their masters are much agitated and defend the nest: when the nest is much disturbed, and the larvæ and pupæ are exposed, the slaves work energetically together with their masters in carrying them away to a place of safety. Hence, it is clear, that the slaves feel quite at home. During the months of June and July, on three successive years, I watched for many hours several nests in Surrey and Sussex, and never saw a slave either leave or enter a nest. As, during these months, the slaves are very few in number, I thought that they might behave differently when more numerous; but Mr. Smith informs me that he has watched the nests at various hours during May, June, and August, both in Surrey and Hampshire, and has never seen the slaves, though present in large numbers in August, either leave or enter the nest. Hence he considers them as strictly household slaves. The masters, on the other hand, may be constantly seen bringing in materials for the nest, and food of all kinds. During the year 1860, however, in the month of July, I came across a community with an unusually large stock of slaves, and I observed a few slaves mingled with their masters leaving the nest, and marching along the same road to a tall Scotch-fir-tree, twenty-five yards distant, which they ascended together, probably in search of aphides or cocci. According to Huber, who had ample opportunities for observation, the slaves in Switzerland habitually work with their masters in making the nest, and they alone open and close the doors in the morning and evening; and, as Huber expressly states, their principal office is to search for aphides. This difference in the usual habits of the masters and slaves in the two countries, probably depends merely on the slaves being captured in greater numbers in Switzerland than in England.

One day I fortunately witnessed a migration of F. sanguinea from one nest to another, and it was a most interesting spectacle to behold the masters carefully carrying their slaves in their jaws instead of being carried by them, as in the case of F. rufescens. Another day my attention was struck by about a score of the slave-makers haunting the same spot, and evidently not in search of food; they approached and were vigorously repulsed by an independent community of the slave-species (F. fusca); sometimes as many as three of these ants clinging to the legs of the slave-making F. sanguinea. The latter ruthlessly killed their small opponents. and carried their dead bodies as food to their nest, twenty-nine yards distant; but they were prevented from getting any pupæ to rear as slaves. I then dug up a small parcel of the pupæ of F. fusca from another nest, and put them down on a bare spot near the place of combat; they were eagerly seized and carried off by the tyrants, who perhaps fancied that, after all, they had been victorious in their late combat.

At the same time I laid on the same place a small parcel of the pupæ of another species, F. flava, with a few of these little yellow ants still clinging to the fragments of their nest. This species is sometimes, though rarely, made into slaves, as has been described by Mr. Smith. Although so small a species, it is very courageous, and I have seen it ferociously attack other ants. In one instance I found to my surprise an independent community of F. flava under a stone beneath a nest of the slave-making F. sanguinea; and when I had accidentally disturbed both nests, the little ants attacked their big neighbours with surprising courage. Now I was curious to ascertain whether F. sanguinea could distinguish the pupæ of F. fusca, which they habitually make into slaves, from those of the little and furious F. flava, which they rarely capture, and it was evident that they did at once distinguish them; for we have seen that they eagerly and instantly seized the pupæ of F. fusca, whereas they were much terrified when they came across the pupæ, or even the earth from the nest, of F. flava, and quickly ran away; but in about a quarter of an hour, shortly after all the little yellow ants had crawled away, they took heart and carried off the pupæ.

One evening I visited another community of F. sanguinea, and found a number of these ants returning home and entering their nests, carrying the dead bodies of F. fusca (showing that it was not a migration) and numerous pupæ. I traced a long file of ants burthened with booty, for about forty yards back, to a very thick clump of heath, whence I saw the last individual of F. sanguinea emerge, carrying a pupa; but I was not able to find the desolated nest in the thick heath. The nest, however, must have been close at hand, for two or three individuals of F. fusca were rushing about in the greatest agitation, and one was perched motionless with its own pupa in its mouth on the top of a spray of heath, an image of despair over its ravaged home.

Such are the facts, though they did not need confirmation by me, in regard to the wonderful instinct of making slaves. Let it be observed what a contrast the instinctive habits of F. sanguinea present with those of the continental F. rufescens. The latter does not build its own nest, does not determine its own migrations, does not collect food for itself or its young, and cannot even feed itself: it is absolutely dependent on its numerous slaves. Formica sanguinea, on the other hand, possesses much fewer slaves, and in the early part of the summer extremely few: the masters determine when and where a new nest shall be formed, and when they migrate, the masters carry the slaves. Both in Switzerland and England the slaves seem to have the exclusive care of the larvæ, and the masters alone go on slave-making expeditions. In Switzerland the slaves and masters work together, making and bringing materials for the nest; both, but chiefly the slaves, tend, and milk, as it may be called their aphides; and thus both collect food for the community. In England the masters alone usually leave the nest to collect building materials and food for themselves, their slaves and larvæ. So that the masters in this country receive much less service from their slaves than they do in Switzerland.

By what steps the instinct of F. sanguinea originated I will not pretend to conjecture. But as ants which are not slave-makers will, as I have seen, carry off the pupæ of other species, if scattered near their nests, it is possible that such pupæ originally stored as food might become developed; and the foreign ants thus unintentionally reared would then follow their proper instincts, and do what work they could. If their presence proved useful to the species which had seized them—if it were more advantageous to this species to capture workers than to procreate them—the habit of collecting pupæ, originally for food, might by natural selection be strengthened and rendered permanent for the very different purpose of raising slaves. When the instinct was once acquired, if carried out to a much less extent even than in our British F. sanguinea, which, as we have seen, is less aided by its slaves than the same species in Switzerland, natural selection might increase and modify the instinct—always supposing each modification to be of use to the species—until an ant was formed as abjectly dependent on its slaves as is the Formica rufescens.

Cell-making instinct of the Hive-Bee.—I will not here enter on minute details on this subject, but will merely give an outline of the conclusions at which I have arrived. He must be a dull man who can examine the exquisite structure of a comb, so beautifully adapted to its end, without enthusiastic admiration. We hear from mathematicians that bees have practically solved a recondite problem, and have made their cells of the proper shape to hold the greatest possible amount of honey, with the least possible consumption of precious wax in their construction. It has been remarked that a skilful workman with fitting tools and measures, would find it very difficult to make cells of wax of the true form, though this is effected by a crowd of bees working in a dark hive. Granting whatever instincts you please, it seems at first quite inconceivable how they can make all the necessary angles and planes, or even perceive when they are correctly made. But the difficulty is not nearly so great as it at first appears: all this beautiful work can be shown, I think, to follow from a few simple instincts.

I was led to investigate this subject by Mr. Waterhouse, who has shown that the form of the cell stands in close relation to the presence of adjoining cells; and the following view may, perhaps, be considered only as a modification of this theory. Let us look to the great principle of gradation, and see whether Nature does not reveal to us her method of work. At one end of a short series we have humble-bees, which use their old cocoons to hold honey, sometimes adding to them short tubes of wax, and likewise making separate and very irregular rounded cells of wax. At the other end of the series we have the cells of the hive-bee, placed in a double layer: each cell, as is well known, is an hexagonal prism, with the basal edges of its six sides bevelled so as to join an inverted pyramid, of three rhombs. These rhombs have certain angles, and the three which form the pyramidal base of a single cell on one side of the comb enter into the composition of the bases of three adjoining cells on the opposite side. In the series between the extreme perfection of the cells of the hive-bee and the simplicity of those of the humble-bee we have the cells of the Mexican Melipona domestica, carefully described and figured by Pierre Huber. The Melipona itself is intermediate in structure between the hive and humble bee, but more nearly related to the latter; it forms a nearly regular waxen comb of cylindrical cells, in which the young are hatched, and, in addition, some large cells of wax for holding honey. These latter cells are nearly spherical and of nearly equal sizes, and are aggregated into an irregular mass. But the important point to notice is, that these cells are always made at that degree of nearness to each other that they would have intersected or broken into each other if the spheres had been completed; but this is never permitted, the bees building perfectly flat walls of wax between the spheres which thus tend to intersect. Hence, each cell consists of an outer spherical portion, and of two, three, or more flat surfaces, according as the cell adjoins two, three, or more other cells. When one cell rests on three other cells, which, from the spheres being nearly of the same size, is very frequently and necessarily the case, the three flat surfaces are united into a pyramid; and this pyramid, as Huber has remarked, is manifestly a gross imitation of the three-sided pyramidal base of the cell of the hive-bee. As in the cells of the hive-bee, so here, the three plane surfaces in any one cell necessarily enter into the construction of three adjoining cells. It is obvious that the Melipona saves wax, and what is more important, labour, by this manner of building; for the flat walls between the adjoining cells are not double, but are of the same thickness as the outer spherical portions, and yet each flat portion forms a part of two cells.

Reflecting on this case, it occurred to me that if the Melipona had made its spheres at some given distance from each other, and had made them of equal sizes and had arranged them symmetrically in a double layer, the resulting structure would have been as perfect as the comb of the hive-bee. Accordingly I wrote to Professor Miller of Cambridge, and this geometer has kindly read over the following statement, drawn up from his information, and tells me that it is strictly correct:—

If a number of equal squares be described with their centres placed in two parallel layers; with the centre of each sphere at the distance of radius $\times \sqrt{2}$, or radius $\times 1.41421$ (or at some lesser distance), from the centres of the six surrounding spheres in the same layer; and at the same distance from the centres of the adjoining spheres in the other and parellel layer; then, if planes of intersection between the several spheres in both layers be formed, there will result a double layer of hexagonal prisms united together by pyramidal bases formed of three rhombs; and the rhombs and the sides of the hexagonal prisms will have every angle identically the same with the best measurements which have been made of the cells of the hive-bee. But I hear from Prof. Wyman, who has made numerous careful measurements, that the accuracy of the workmanship of the bee has been greatly exaggerated; so much so, that whatever the typical form of the cell may be, it is rarely, if ever, realised.

Hence we may safely conclude that, if we could slightly modify the instincts already possessed by the Melipona, and in themselves not very wonderful, this bee would make a structure as wonderfully perfect as that of the hive-bee. We must suppose that Melipona to have the power of forming her cells truly spherical, and of equal sizes; and this would not be very surprising, seeing that she already does so to a certain extent, and seeing what perfectly cylindrical burrows many insects make in wood, apparently by turning round on a fixed point. We must suppose the Melipona to arrange her cells in level layers, as she already does her cylindrical cells; and we must further suppose, and this is the greatest difficulty, that she can somehow judge accurately at what distance to stand from her fellow-labourers when several are making their spheres; but she is already so far enabled to judge of distance, that she always describes her spheres so as to intersect to a certain extent; and then she unites the points of intersection by perfectly flat surfaces. By such modifications of instincts which in themselves are not very wonderful,—hardly more wonderful than those which guide a bird to make its nest,—I believe that the hive-bee has acquired, through natural selection, her inimitable architectural powers.

But this theory can be tested by experiment. Following the example of Mr. Tegetmeier, I separated two combs, and put between them a long, thick, rectangular strip of wax: the bees instantly began to excavate minute circular pits in it; and as they deepened these little pits, they made them wider and wider until they were converted into shallow basins, appearing to the eye perfectly true or parts of a sphere, and of about the diameter of a cell. It was most interesting to observe that, wherever several bees had begun to excavate these basins near together, they had begun their work at such a distance from each other, that by the time the basins had acquired the above-stated width (*i. e.* about the width of an ordinary cell), and were in depth about one-sixth of the diameter of the sphere of which they formed a part, the rims of the basins intersected or broke into each other. As soon as this occurred, the bees ceased to excavate, and began to build up flat walls of wax on the lines of intersection between the basins, so that each hexagonal prism was built upon the scalloped edge of a smooth basin, instead of on the straight edges of a three-sided pyramid as in the case of ordinary cells.

I then put into the hive, instead of a thick, rectangular piece of wax, a thin and narrow, knife-edged ridge, coloured with vermilion. The bees instantly began on both sides to excavate little basins near to each other, in the same way as before; but the ridge of wax was so thin, that the bottoms of the basins, if they had been excavated to the same depth as in the former experiment, would have broken into each other from the opposite sides. The bees, however, did not suffer this to happen, and they stopped their excavations in due time; so that the basins, as soon as they had been a little deepened, came to have flat bases; and these flat bases, formed by thin little plates of the vermilion wax left ungnawed, were situated, as far as the eye could judge, exactly along the planes of imaginary intersection between the basins on the opposite sides of the ridge of wax. In some parts, only small portions, in other parts, large portions of a rhombic plate were thus left between the opposed basins, but the work, from the unnatural state of things, had not been neatly performed. The bees must have worked at very nearly the same rate in circularly gnawing away and deepening the basins on both sides of the ridge of vermilion wax, in order to have thus succeeded in leaving flat plates between the basins, by stopping work at the planes of intersection.

Considering how flexible thin wax is, I do not see that there is any difficulty in the bees, whilst at work on the two sides of a strip of wax, perceiving when they have gnawed the wax away to the proper thinness, and then stopping their work. In ordinary combs it has appeared to me that the bees do not always succeed in working at exactly the same rate from the opposite sides; for I have noticed half-completed rhombs at the base of a just commenced cell, which were slightly concave on one side, where I suppose that the bees had excavated too quickly, and convex on the opposed side where the bees had worked less quickly. In one well-marked instance, I put the comb back into the hive, and allowed the bees to go on working for a short time, and again examined the cell, and I found that the rhombic plate had been completed, and had become *perfectly flat:* it was absolutely impossible, from the extreme thinness of the little plate, that they could have effected this by gnawing away the convex side; and I suspect that the bees in such cases stand on opposite sides and push and bend the ductile and warm wax (which as I have tried is easily done) into its proper intermediate plane, and thus flatten it.

From the experiment of the ridge of vermillion wax we can see that, if the bees were to build for themselves a thin wall of wax, they could make their cells of the proper shape, by standing at the proper distance from each other, by excavating at the same rate, and by endeavouring to make equal spherical hollows, but never allowing the spheres to break into each other. Now bees, as may be clearly seen by examining the edge of a growing comb, do make a rough, circumferential wall or rim all round the comb; and they gnaw this away from the opposite sides, always working circularly as they deepen each cell. They do not make the whole three-sided pyramidal base of any one cell at the same time, but only that one rhombic plate which stands on the extreme growing margin, or the two plates, as the case may be; and they never complete the upper edges of the rhombic plates, until the hexagonal walls are commenced. Some of these statements differ from those made by the justly celebrated elder Huber, but I am convinced of their accuracy; and if I had space, I would show that they are conformable with my theory.

Huber's statement that the very first cell is excavated out of a little parallel-sided wall of wax, is not, as far as I have seen, strictly correct; the first commencement having always been a little hood of wax; but I will not here enter on details. We see how important a part excavation plays in the construction of the cells; but it would be a great error to suppose that the bees cannot build up a rough wall of wax in the proper position—that is, along the plane of intersection between two adjoining spheres. I have several specimens showing clearly that they can do this. Even in the rude circumferential rim or wall of wax round a growing comb, flexures may sometimes be observed, corresponding in position to the planes of the rhombic basal plates of future cells. But the rough wall of wax has in every case to be finished off, by being largely gnawed away on both sides. The manner in which the bees build is curious; they always make the first rough wall from ten to twenty times thicker than the excessively thin finished wall of the cell, which will ultimately be left. We shall understand how they work, by supposing masons first to pile up a broad ridge of cement, and then to begin cutting it away equally on both sides near the ground, till a smooth, very thin wall is left in the middle; the masons always piling up the cut-away cement, and adding fresh cement on the summit of the ridge. We shall thus have a thin wall steadily growing upward but always crowned by a gigantic coping. From all the cells, both those just commenced and those completed, being thus crowned by a strong coping of wax, the bees can cluster and crawl over the comb without injuring the delicate hexagonal walls. These walls, as Professor Miller has kindly ascertained for me, vary greatly in thickness; being, on an average of twelve measurements made near the border of the comb, $\frac{1}{352}$ of an inch in thickness; whereas the basal rhomboidal plates are thicker, nearly in the proportion of three to two, having a mean thickness, from twenty-one measurements, of $\frac{1}{229}$ of an inch. By the above singular manner of building, strength is continually given to the comb, with the utmost ultimate economy of wax.

It seems at first to add to the difficulty of understanding how the cells are made, that a multitude of bees all work together; one bee after working a short time at one cell going to another, so that, as Huber has stated a score of individuals work even at the commencement of the first cell. I was able practically to show this fact, by covering the edges of the hexagonal walls of a single cell, or the extreme margin of the circumferential rim of a growing comb, with an extremely thin layer of melted vermilion wax; and I invariably found that the colour was most delicately diffused by the bees—as delicately as a painter could have done it with his brush —by atoms of the coloured wax having been taken from the spot on which it had been placed, and worked into the growing edges of the cells all round. The work of construction seems to be a sort of balance struck between many bees, all instinctively standing at the same relative distance from each other, all trying to sweep equal spheres, and then building up, or leaving ungnawed, the planes of intersection between these spheres. It was really curious to note in cases of difficulty, as when two pieces of comb met at an angle, how often the bees would pull down and rebuild in different ways the same cell, sometimes recurring to a shape which they had at first rejected.

When bees have a place on which they can stand in their proper positions for working,—for instance, on a slip of wood, placed directly under the middle of a comb growing downwards, so that the comb has to be built over one face of the slip—in this case the bees can lay the foundations of one wall of a new hexagon, in its strictly proper place, projecting beyond the other completed cells. It suffices that the bees should be enabled to stand at their proper relative distances from each other and from the walls of the last completed cells, and then, by striking imaginary spheres, they can build up a wall intermediate between two adjoining spheres; but, as far as I have seen, they never gnaw away and finish off the angles of a cell till a large part both of that cell and of the adjoining cells has been built. This capacity in bees of laying down under certain circumstances a rough wall in its proper place between two just-commenced cells, is important, as it bears on a fact, which seems at first subversive of the foregoing theory; namely, that the cells on the extreme margin of wasp-combs are sometimes strictly hexagonal; but I have not space here to enter on this subject. Nor does there seem to me any great difficulty in a single insect (as in the case of a queen-wasp) making hexagonal cells, if she were to work alternately on the inside and outside of two or three cells commenced at the same time, always standing at the proper relative distance from the parts of the cells just begun, sweeping spheres or cylinders, and building up intermediate planes.

As natural selection acts only by the accumulation of slight modifications of structure or instinct, each profitable to the individual under its conditions of life, it may reasonably be asked, how a long and graduated succession of modified architectural instincts, all tending towards the present perfect plan of construction, could have profited the progenitors of the hive-bee? I think the answer is not difficult: cells constructed like those of the bee or the wasp gain in strength, and save much in labour and space, and in the materials of which they are constructed. With respect to the formation of wax, it is known that bees are often hard pressed to get sufficient nectar, and I am informed by Mr. Tegetmeier that it has been experimentally proved that from twelve to fifteen pounds of dry sugar are consumed by a hive of bees for the secretion of a pound of wax; so that a prodigious quantity of fluid nectar must be collected and consumed by the bees in a hive for the secretion of the wax necessary for the construction of their combs. Moreover, many bees have to remain idle for many days during the process of secretion. A large store of honey is indispensable to support a large stock of bees during the winter; and the security of the hive is known mainly to depend on a large number of bees being support-ed. Hence the saving of wax by largely saving honey and the time con-sumed in collecting the honey must be an important element of success to any family of bees. Of course the success of the species may be dependent on the number of its enemies, or parasites, or on quite distinct causes, and so be altogether independent of the quantity of honey which the bees can collect. But let us suppose that this latter circumstance determined, as it probably often has determined, whether a bee allied to our humble-bees could exist in large numbers in any country; and let us further suppose that the community lived through the winter, and consequently required a store of honey: there can in this case be no doubt that it would be an ad-vantage to our imaginary humble-bee if a slight modification in her in-stincts led her to make her waxen cells near together, so as to intersect a little; for a wall in common even to two adjoining cells would save some little labour and wax. Hence it would continually be more and more ad-vantageous to our humble-bees, if they were to make their cells more and more regular, nearer together, and aggregated into a mass, like the cells of the Melipona; for in this case a large part of the bounding surface of each cell would serve to bound the adjoining cells, and much labour and wax would be saved. Again, from the same cause, it would be advantageous to the Melipona, if she were to make her cells closer together, and more reg-ular in every way than at present; for then, as we have seen, the spherical surfaces would wholly disappear and be replaced by plane surfaces; and the Melipona would make a comb as perfect as that of the hive-bee. Be-yond this stage of perfection in architecture, natural selection could not lead; for the comb of the hive-bee, as far as we can see, is absolutely per-fect in economising labour and wax.

Thus, as I believe, the most wonderful of all known instincts, that of the hive-bee, can be explained by natural selection having taken advant-age of numerous, successive, slight modifications of simpler instincts; nat-ural selection having, by slow degrees, more and more perfectly led the bees to sweep equal spheres at a given distance from each other in a double layer, and to build up and excavate the wax along the planes of in-tersection; the bees, of course, no more knowing that they swept their spheres at one particular distance from each other, than they know what are the several angles of the hexagonal prisms and of the basal rhombic plates; the motive power of the process of natural selection having been the construction of cells of due strength and of the proper size and shape for the larvæ, this being effected with the greatest possible economy of labour and wax; that individual swarm which thus made the best cells with least labour, and least waste of honey in the secretion of wax, having succeeded best, and having transmitted their newly-acquired economical instincts to new swarms, which in their turn will have had the best chance of succeeding in the struggle for existence.

Objections to the Theory of Natural Selection as applied to Instincts:
Neuter and Sterile Insects

It has been objected to the foregoing view of the origin of instincts that "the variations of structure and of instinct must have been simultaneous and accurately adjusted to each other, as a modification in the one with-out an immediate corresponding change in the other would have been fatal." The force of this objection rests entirely on the assumption that the changes in the instincts and structure are abrupt. To take as an illus-tration the case of the larger titmouse (Parus major) alluded to in a pre-vious chapter; this bird often holds the seeds of the yew between its feet on a branch, and hammers with its beak till it gets at the kernel. Now what special difficulty would there be in natural selection preserving all the slight individual variations in the shape of the beak, which were bet-ter and better adapted to break open the seeds, until a beak was formed, as well constructed for this purpose as that of the nuthatch, at the same time that habit, or compulsion, or spontaneous variations of taste, led the bird to become more and more of a seed-eater? In this case the beak is supposed to be slowly modified by natural selection, subsequently to, but in accordance with, slowly changing habits or taste; but let the feet of the titmouse vary and grow larger from correlation with the beak, or from any other unknown cause, and it is not improbable that such larger feet would lead the bird to climb more and more until it acquired the remarkable climbing instinct and power of the nuthatch. In this case a gradual change of structure is supposed to lead to changed instinctive habits. To take one more case: few instincts are more remarkable than that which leads the swift of the Eastern Islands to make its nest wholly of inspissated saliva. Some birds build their nests of mud, believed to be moistened with saliva; and one of the swifts of North America makes its nest (as I have seen) of sticks agglutinated with saliva, and even with flakes of this sub-stance. Is it then very improbable that the natural selection of individual swifts, which secreted more and more saliva, should at last produce a spe-cies with instincts leading it to neglect other materials, and to make its nest exclusively of inspissated saliva? And so in other cases. It must, how-ever, be admitted that in many instances we cannot conjecture whether it was instinct or structure which first varied.

No doubt many instincts of very difficult explanation could be opposed to the theory of natural selection—cases, in which we cannot see how an instinct could have originated; cases, in which no intermediate gradations are known to exist; cases of instincts of such trifling importance, that they could hardly have been acted on by natural selection; cases of instincts almost identically the same in animals so remote in the scale of nature, that we cannot account for their similarity by inheritance from a common progenitor, and consequently must believe that they were independently acquired through natural selection. I will not here enter on these several cases, but will confine myself to one special difficulty, which at first ap-peared to me insuperable, and actually fatal to the whole theory. I allude to the neuters or sterile females in insect-communities; for these neuters often differ widely in instinct and in structure from both the males and fertile females, and yet, from being sterile, they cannot propagate their kind.

The subject well deserves to be discussed at great length, but I will here take only a single case, that of working or sterile ants. How the workers have been rendered sterile is a difficulty; but not much greater than that of any other striking modification of structure; for it can be shown that some insects and other articulate animals in a state of nature occasionally become sterile; and if such insects had been social, and it had been profitable to the community that a number should have been annually born capable of work, but incapable of procreation, I can see no especial difficulty in this having been effected through natural selection. But I must pass over this preliminary difficulty. The great difficulty lies in the working ants differing widely from both the males and the fertile females in structure, as in the shape of the thorax, and in being destitute of wings and sometimes of eyes, and in instinct. As far as instinct alone is concerned, the wonderful difference in this respect between the workers and the perfect females, would have been better exemplified by the hive-bee. If a working ant or other neuter insect had been an ordinary animal, I should have unhesitatingly assumed that all its characters had been slowly acquired through natural selection; namely, by individuals having been born with slight profitable modifications, which were inherited by the offspring; and that these again varied and again were selected, and so onwards. But with the working ant we have an insect differing greatly from its parents, yet absolutely sterile; so that it could never have transmitted successively acquired modifications of structure or instinct to its progeny. It may well be asked how is it possible to reconcile this case with the theory of natural selection?

First, let it be remembered that we have innumerable instances, both in our domestic productions and in those in a state of nature, of all sorts of differences of inherited structure which are correlated with certain ages, and with either sex. We have differences correlated not only with one sex, but with that short period when the reproductive system is active, as in the nuptial plumage of many birds, and in the hooked jaws of the male salmon. We have even slight differences in the horns of different breeds of cattle in relation to an artificially imperfect state of the male sex; for oxen of certain breeds have longer horns than the oxen of other breeds, relatively to the length of the horns in both the bulls and cows of these same breeds. Hence I can see no great difficulty in any character becoming correlated with the sterile condition of certain members of insect-communities: the difficulty lies in understanding how such correlated modifications of structure could have been slowly accumulated by natural selection.

This difficulty, though appearing insuperable, is lessened, or, as I believe, disappears, when it is remembered that selection may be applied to the family, as well as to the individual, and may thus gain the desired end.

Breeders of cattle wish the flesh and fat to be well marbled together: an animal thus characterised has been slaughtered, but the breeder has gone with confidence to the same stock and has succeeded. Such faith may be placed in the power of selection, that a breed of cattle, always yielding oxen with extraordinarily long horns, could, it is probable, be formed by carefully watching which individual bulls and cows, when matched, produced oxen with the longest horns; and yet no ox would ever have propagated its kind. Here is a better and real illustration: according to M. Verlot, some varieties of the double annual Stock from having been long and carefully selected to the right degree, always produce a large proportion of seedlings bearing double and quite sterile flowers; but they likewise yield some single and fertile plants. These latter, by which alone the variety can be propagated, may be compared with the fertile male and female ants, and the double sterile plants with the neuters of the same community. As with the varieties of the stock, so with social insects, selection has been applied to the family, and not to the individual, for the sake of gaining a serviceable end. Hence we may conclude that slight modifications of structure or of instinct, correlated with the sterile condition of certain members of the community, have proved advantageous: consequently the fertile males and females have flourished, and transmitted to their fertile offspring a tendency to produce sterile members with the same modifications. This process must have been repeated many times, until that prodigious amount of difference between the fertile and sterile females of the same species has been produced, which we see in many social insects.

But we have not as yet touched on the acme of the difficulty; namely, the fact that the neuters of several ants differ, not only from the fertile females and males, but from each other, sometimes to an almost incredible degree, and are thus divided into two or even three castes. The castes, moreover, do not commonly graduate into each other, but are perfectly well defined; being as distinct from each other as are any two species of the same genus, or rather as any two genera of the same family. Thus in Eciton, there are working and soldier neuters, with jaws and instincts extraordinarily different: in Cryptocerus, the workers of one caste alone carry a wonderful sort of shield on their heads, the use of which is quite unknown: in the Mexican Myrmecocystus, the workers of one caste never leave the nest; they are fed by the workers of another caste, and they have an enormously developed abdomen which secretes a sort of honey, supplying the place of that excreted by the aphides, or the domestic cattle as they may be called, which our European ants guard and imprison.

It will indeed be thought that I have an overweening confidence in the principle of natural selection, when I do not admit that such wonderful and well-established facts at once annihilate the theory. In the simpler case of neuter insects all of one caste, which, as I believe, have been rendered different from the fertile males and females through natural selection, we may conclude from the analogy of ordinary variations, that the successive, slight, profitable modifications did not first arise in all the neuters in the same nest, but in some few alone; and that by the survival of the communities with females which produced most neuters having the advantageous modifications, all the neuters ultimately came to be thus characterised. According to this view we ought occasionally to find in the same nest neuter insects, presenting gradations of structure; and this we do find, even not rarely, considering how few neuter insects out of Europe have been carefully examined. Mr. F. Smith has shown that the neuters of several British ants differ surprisingly from each other in size and sometimes in colour; and that the extreme forms can be linked together by individuals taken out of the same nest: I have myself compared perfect gradations of this kind. It sometimes happens that the larger or the smaller sized workers are the most numerous; or that both large and small are numerous, whilst those of an intermediate size are scanty in numbers. Formica flava has larger and smaller workers, with some few of intermediate size; and, in this species, as Mr. F. Smith has observed, the larger workers have simple eyes (ocelli), which though small can be plainly distinguished, whereas the smaller workers have their ocelli rudimentary. Having carefully dissected several specimens of these workers, I can affirm that the eyes are far more rudimentary in the smaller workers than can be accounted for merely by their proportionally lesser size; and I fully believe, though I dare not assert so positively, that the workers of intermediate size have their ocelli in an exactly intermediate condition. So that here we have two bodies of sterile workers in the same nest, differing not only in size, but in their organs of vision, yet connected by some few members in an intermediate condition. I may digress by adding, that if the smaller workers had been the most useful to the community, and those males and females had been continually selected, which produced more and more of the smaller workers, until all the workers were in this condition; we should then have had a species of ant with neuters in nearly the same condition as those of Myrmica. For the workers of Myrmica have not even rudiments of ocelli, though the male and female ants of this genus have well-developed ocelli.

I may give one other case: so confidently did I expect occasionally to find gradations of important structures between the different castes of neuters in the same species, that I gladly availed myself of Mr. F. Smith's offer of numerous specimens from the same nest of the driver ant (Anomma) of West Africa. The reader will perhaps best appreciate the amount of difference in these workers, by my giving not the actual measurements, but a strictly accurate illustration: the difference was the same as if we were to see a set of workmen building a house, of whom many were five feet four inches high, and many sixteen feet high; but we must in addition suppose that the larger workmen had heads four instead of three times as big as those of the smaller men, and jaws nearly five times as big. The jaws, moreover, of the working ants of the several sizes differed wonderfully in shape, and in the form and number of the teeth. But the important fact for us is, that, though the workers can be grouped into castes of different size, yet they graduate insensibly into each other, as does the widely-different structure of their jaws. I speak confidently on this latter point, as Sir J. Lubbock made drawings for me, with the camera lucida, of the jaws which I dissected from the workers of the several sizes. Mr. Bates, in his interesting 'Naturalist on the Amazons,' has described analogous cases.

With these facts before me, I believe that natural selection, by acting on the fertile ants or parents, could form a species which should regularly produce neuters, all of large size with one form of jaw, or all of small size with widely different jaws; or lastly, and this is the greatest difficulty, one set of workers of one size and structure, and simultaneously another set of workers of a different size and structure;—a graduated series having first been formed, as in the case of the driver ant, and then the extreme forms having been produced in greater and greater numbers, through the survival of the parents which generated them, until none with an intermediate structure were produced.

An analogous explanation has been given by Mr. Wallace, of the equally complex case, of certain Malayan Butterflies regularly appearing under two or even three distinct female forms; and by Fritz Müller, of certain Brazilian crustaceans likewise appearing under two widely distinct male forms. But this subject need not here be discussed.

I have now explained how, as I believe, the wonderful fact of two distinctly defined castes of sterile workers existing in the same nest, both widely different from each other and from their parents, has originated. We can see how useful their production may have been to a social community of ants, on the same principle that the division of labour is useful to civilised man. Ants, however, work by inherited instincts and by inherited organs or tools, whilst man works by acquired knowledge and manufactured instruments. But I must confess, that, with all my faith in natural selection, I should never have anticipated that this principle could have been efficient in so high a degree, had not the case of these neuter insects led me to this conclusion. I have, therefore, discussed this case, at some little but wholly insufficient length, in order to show the power of natural selection, and likewise because this is by far the most serious special difficulty which my theory has encountered. The case, also, is very interesting, as it proves that with animals, as with plants, any amount of modification may be effected by the accumulation of numerous, slight, spontaneous variations, which are in any way profitable, without exercise or habit having been brought into play. For peculiar habits confined to the workers or sterile females, however long they might be followed, could not possibly affect the males and fertile females, which alone leave descendants. I am surprised that no one has hitherto advanced this demonstrative case of neuter insects, against the well-known doctrine of inherited habit, as advanced by Lamarck.

Summary

I have endeavoured in this chapter briefly to show that the mental qualities of our domestic animals vary, and that the variations are inherited. Still more briefly I have attempted to show that instincts vary slightly in a state of nature. No one will dispute that instincts are of the highest importance to each animal. Therefore there is no real difficulty, under changing conditions of life, in natural selection accumulating to any extent slight modifications of instinct which are in any way useful. In many cases habit or use and disuse have probably come into play. I do not pretend that the facts given in this chapter strengthen in any great degree my theory; but none of the cases of difficulty, to the best of my judgment, annihilate it. On the other hand, the fact that instincts are not always absolutely perfect and are liable to mistakes:—that no instinct can be shown to have been produced for the good of other animals, though animals take advantage of the instincts of others;—that the canon in natural history, of "Natura non facit saltum," is applicable to instincts as well as to corporeal structure, and is plainly explicable on the foregoing views, but is otherwise inexplicable,—all tend to corroborate the theory of natural selection.

This theory is also strengthened by some few other facts in regard to instincts; as by that common case of closely allied, but distinct species, when inhabiting distant parts of the world and living under considerably different conditions of life, yet often retaining nearly the same instincts. For instance, we can understand, on the principle of inheritance, how it is that the thrush of tropical South America lines its nest with mud, in the same peculiar manner as does our British thrush; how it is that the Hornbills of Africa and India have the same extraordinary instinct of plastering up and imprisoning the females in a hole in a tree, with only a small hole left in the plaster through which the males feed them and their young when hatched; how it is that the male wrens (Troglodytes) of North America build "cock-nests," to roost in, like the males of our Kitty-wrens,—a habit wholly unlike that of any other known bird. Finally, it may not be a logical deduction, but to my imagination it is far more satisfactory to look at such instincts as the young cuckoo ejecting its foster-brothers,—ants making slaves,—the larvæ of ichneumonidæ feeding within the live bodies of caterpillars,—not as specially endowed or created instincts, but as small consequences of one general law leading to the advancement of all organic beings,—namely, multiply, vary, let the strongest live and the weakest die.

CHAPTER IX

HYBRIDISM

Distinction between the sterility of first crosses and of hybrids—Sterility various in degree, not universal, affected by close interbreeding, removed by domestication—Laws governing the sterility of hybrids—Sterility not a special endowment, but incidental on other differences, not accumulated by natural selection—Causes of the sterility of first crosses and of hybrids—Parallelism between the effects of changed conditions of life and of crossing—Dimorphism and trimorphism—Fertility of varieties when crossed and of their mongrel offspring not universal—Hybrids and mongrels compared independently of their fertility—Summary.

THE view commonly entertained by naturalists is that species, when inter-crossed, have been specially endowed with sterility, in order to prevent their confusion. This view certainly seems at first highly probable, for species living together could hardly have been kept distinct had they been capable of freely crossing. The subject is in many ways important for us, more especially as the sterility of species when first crossed, and that of their hybrid offspring, cannot have been acquired, as I shall show, by the preservation of successive profitable degrees of sterility. It is an incidental result of differences in the reproductive systems of the parent-species.

In treating this subject, two classes of facts, to a large extent fundamentally different, have generally been confounded; namely, the sterility of species when first crossed, and the sterility of the hybrids produced from them.

Pure species have of course their organs of reproduction in a perfect condition, yet when intercrossed they produce either few or no offspring. Hybrids, on the other hand, have their reproductive organs functionally impotent, as may be clearly seen in the state of the male element in both plants and animals; though the formative organs themselves are perfect in structure, as far as the microscope reveals. In the first case the two sexual elements which go to form the embryo are perfect; in the second case they are either not at all developed, or are imperfectly developed. This distinction is important, when the cause of the sterility, which is common to the two cases, has to be considered. The distinction probably has been slurred over, owing to the sterility in both cases being looked on as a special endowment, beyond the province of our reasoning powers.

The fertility of varieties, that is of the forms known or believed to be descended from common parents, when crossed, and likewise the fertility of their mongrel offspring, is, with reference to my theory, of equal importance with the sterility of species; for it seems to make a broad and clear distinction between varieties and species.

Degrees of Sterility.—First, for the sterility of species when crossed and of their hybrid offspring. It is impossible to study the several memoirs and works of those two conscientious and admirable observers, Kölreuter and Gärtner, who almost devoted their lives to this subject, without being deeply impressed with the high generality of some degree of sterility. Kölreuter makes the rule universal; but then he cuts the knot, for in ten cases in which he found two forms, considered by most authors as distinct species, quite fertile together, he unhesitatingly ranks them as varieties. Gärtner, also, makes the rule equally universal; and he disputes the entire fertility of Kölreuter's ten cases. But in these and in many other cases, Gärtner is obliged carefully to count the seeds, in order to show that there is any degree of sterility. He always compares the maximum number of seeds produced by two species when first crossed, and the maximum produced by their hybrid offspring, with the average number produced by both pure parent-species in a state of nature. But causes of serious error here intervene: a plant, to be hybridised, must be castrated, and, what is often more important, must be secluded in order to prevent pollen being brought to it by insects from other plants. Nearly all the plants experimented on by Gärtner were potted, and were kept in a chamber in his house. That these processes are often injurious to the fertility of a plant cannot be doubted; for Gärtner gives in his table about a score of cases of plants which he castrated, and artificially fertilised with their own pollen, and (excluding all cases such as the Leguminosæ, in which there is an acknowledged difficulty in the manipulation) half of these twenty plants had their fertility in some degree impaired. Moreover, as Gärtner repeatedly crossed some forms, such as the common red and blue pimpernels (Anagallis arvensis and cœrulea), which the best botanists rank as varieties, and found them absolutely sterile, we may doubt whether many species are really so sterile, when intercrossed, as he believed.

It is certain, on the one hand, that the sterility of various species when crossed is so different in degree and graduates away so insensibly, and, on the other hand, that the fertility of pure species is so easily affected by various circumstances, that for all practical purposes it is most difficult to say where perfect fertility ends and sterility begins. I think no better evidence of this can be required than that the two most experienced observers who have ever lived, namely Kölreuter and Gärtner, arrived at diametrically opposite conclusions in regard to some of the very same forms. It is also most instructive to compare—but I have not space here to enter on details—the evidence advanced by our best botanists on the question whether certain doubtful forms should be ranked as species or varieties, with the evidence from fertility adduced by different hybridisers, or by the same observer from experiments made during different years. It can thus be shown that neither sterility nor fertility affords any certain distinction between species and varieties. The evidence from this source graduates away, and is doubtful in the same degree as is the evidence derived from other constitutional and structural differences.

In regard to the sterility of hybrids in successive generations; though Gärtner was enabled to rear some hybrids, carefully guarding them from a cross with either pure parent, for six or seven, and in one case for ten generations, yet he asserts positively that their fertility never increases, but generally decreases greatly and suddenly. With respect to this decrease, it may first be noticed that when any deviation in structure or constitution is common to both parents, this is often transmitted in an augmented degree to the offspring; and both sexual elements in hybrid plants are already affected in some degree. But I believe that their fertility has been diminished in nearly all these cases by an independent cause, namely, by too close interbreeding. I have made so many experiments and collected so many facts, showing on the one hand that an occasional cross with a distinct individual or variety increases the vigour and fertility of the offspring, and on the other hand that very close interbreeding lessens their vigour and fertility, that I cannot doubt the correctness of this conclusion. Hybrids are seldom raised by experimentalists in great numbers; and as the parent-species, or other allied hybrids, generally grow in the same garden, the visits of insects must be carefully prevented during the flowering season: hence hybrids, if left to themselves, will generally be fertilised during each generation by pollen from the same flower; and this would probably be injurious to their fertility, already lessened by their hybrid origin. I am strengthened in this conviction by a remarkable statement repeatedly made by Gärtner, namely, that if even the less fertile hybrids be artificially fertilised with hybrid pollen of the same kind, their fertility, notwithstanding the frequent ill effects from manipulation, sometimes decidedly increases, and goes on increasing. Now, in the process of artificial fertilisation, pollen is as often taken by chance (as I know from my own experience) from the anthers of another flower, as from the anthers of the flower itself which is to be fertilised; so that a cross between two flowers, though probably often on the same plant, would be thus effected. Moreover, whenever complicated experiments are in progress, so careful an observer as Gärtner would have castrated his hybrids, and this would have ensured in each generation a cross with pollen from a distinct flower, either from the same plant or from another plant of the same hybrid nature. And thus, the strange fact of an increase of fertility in the successive generations of *artificially fertilised* hybrids, in contrast with those spontaneously self-fertilised, may, as I believe, be accounted for by too close interbreeding having been avoided.

Now let us turn to the results arrived at by a third most experienced hybridiser, namely, the Hon. and Rev. W. Herbert. He is as emphatic in his conclusion that some hybrids are perfectly fertile—as fertile as the pure parent-species—as are Kölreuter and Gärtner that some degree of sterility between distinct species is a universal law of nature. He experimented on some of the very same species as did Gärtner. The difference in their results may, I think, be in part accounted for by Herbert's great horticultural skill, and by his having hot-houses at his command. Of his many important statements I will here give only a single one as an example, namely, that "every ovule in a pod of Crinum capense fertilised by C. revolutum produced a plant, which I never saw to occur in a case of its natural fecundation." So that here we have perfect or even more than commonly perfect fertility, in a first cross between two distinct species.

This case of the Crinum leads me to refer to a singular fact, namely, that individual plants of certain species of Lobelia, Verbascum and Passiflora, can easily be fertilised by pollen from a distinct species, but not by pollen from the same plant, though this pollen can be proved to be perfectly sound by fertilising other plants or species. In the genus Hippeastrum, in Corydalis as shown by Professor Hildebrand, in various orchids as shown by Mr. Scott and Fritz Müller, all the individuals are in this peculiar condition. So that with some species, certain abnormal individuals, and in other species all the individuals, can actually be hybridised much more readily than they can be fertilised by pollen from the same individual plant! To give one instance, a bulb of Hippeastrum aulicum produced four flowers; three were fertilised by Herbert with their own pollen, and the fourth was subsequently fertilised by the pollen of a compound hybrid descended from three distinct species: the result was that "the ovaries of the three first flowers soon ceased to grow, and after a few days perished entirely, whereas the pod impregnated by the pollen of the hybrid made vigorous growth and rapid progress to maturity, and bore good seed, which vegetated freely." Mr. Herbert tried similar experiments during many years, and always with the same result. These cases serve to show on what slight and mysterious causes the lesser or greater fertility of a species sometimes depends.

The practical experiments of horticulturists, though not made with scientific precision, deserve some notice. It is notorious in how complicated a manner the species of Pelargonium, Fuchsia, Calceolaria, Petunia, Rhododendron, &c., have been crossed, yet many of these hybrids seed freely. For instance, Herbert asserts that a hybrid from Calceolaria integrifolia and plantaginea, species most widely dissimilar in general habit, "reproduces itself as perfectly as if it had been a natural species from the mountains of Chili." I have taken some pains to ascertain the degree of fertility of some of the complex crosses of Rhododendrons, and I am assured that many of them are perfectly fertile. Mr. C. Noble, for instance, informs me that he raises stocks for grafting from a hybrid between Rhod. ponticum and catawbiense, and that this hybrid "seeds as freely as it is possible to imagine." Had hybrids when fairly treated, always gone on decreasing in fertility in each successive generation, as Gärtner believed to be the case, the fact would have been notorious to nurserymen. Horticulturists raise large beds of the same hybrid, and such alone are fairly treated, for by insect agency the several individuals are allowed to cross freely with each other, and the injurious influence of close interbreeding is thus prevented. Any one may readily convince himself of the efficiency of insect-agency by examining the flowers of the more sterile kinds of hybrid Rhododendrons, which produce no pollen, for he will find on their stigmas plenty of pollen brought from other flowers.

In regard to animals, much fewer experiments have been carefully tried than with plants. If our systematic arrangements can be trusted, that is, if the genera of animals are as distinct from each other as are the genera of plants, then we may infer that animals more widely distinct in the scale of nature can be crossed more easily than in the case of plants; but the hybrids themselves are, I think, more sterile. It should, however, be borne in mind that, owing to few animals breeding freely under confinement, few experiments have been fairly tried: for instance, the canary-bird has been crossed with nine distinct species of finches, but, as not one of these breeds freely in confinement, we have no right to expect that the first crosses between them and the canary, or that their hybrids, should be perfectly fertile. Again, with respect to the fertility in successive generations of the more fertile hybrid animals, I hardly know of an instance in which two families of the same hybrid have been raised at the same time from different parents, so as to avoid the ill effects of close interbreeding. On the contrary, brothers and sisters have usually been crossed in each successive generation, in opposition to the constantly repeated admonition of every breeder. And in this case, it is not at all surprising that the inherent sterility in the hybrids should have gone on increasing.

Although I know of hardly any thoroughly well-authenticated cases of perfectly fertile hybrid animals, I have reason to believe that the hybrids from Cervulus vaginalis and Reevesii, and from Phasianus colchicus with P. torquatus, are perfectly fertile. M. Quatrefages states that the hybrids from two moths (Bombyx cynthia and arrindia) were proved in Paris to be fertile *inter se* for eight generations. It has lately been asserted that two such distinct species as the hare and rabbit, when they can be got to breed together, produce offspring, which are highly fertile when crossed with one of the parent-species. The hybrids from the common and Chinese geese (A. cygnoides), species which are so different that they are generally ranked in distinct genera, have often bred in this country with either pure parent, and in one single instance they have bred *inter se*. This was effected by Mr. Eyton, who raised two hybrids from the same parents, but from different hatches; and from these two birds he raised no less than eight hybrids (grandchildren of the pure geese) from one nest. In India, however, these cross-bred geese must be far more fertile; for I am assured by two eminently capable judges, namely Mr. Blyth and Capt. Hutton, that whole flocks of these crossed geese are kept in various parts of the country; and as they are kept for profit, where neither pure parent-species, exists, they must certainly be highly or perfectly fertile.

With our domesticated animals, the various races when crossed together are quite fertile; yet in many cases they are descended from two or more wild species. From this fact we must conclude either that the aboriginal parent-species at first produced perfectly fertile hybrids, or that the hybrids subsequently reared under domestication became quite fertile. This latter alternative, which was first propounded by Pallas, seems by far the most probable, and can, indeed, hardly be doubted. It is, for instance, almost certain that our dogs are descended from several wild stocks; yet, with perhaps the exception of certain indigenous domestic dogs of South America, all are quite fertile together; but analogy makes me greatly doubt, whether the several aboriginal species would at first have freely bred together and have produced quite fertile hybrids. So again I have lately acquired decisive evidence that the crossed offspring from the Indian humped and common cattle are *inter se* perfectly fertile; and from the observations by Rütimeyer on their important osteological differences, as well as from those by Mr. Blyth on their differences in habits, voice, constitution, &c., these two forms must be regarded as good and distinct species. The same remarks may be extended to the two chief races of the pig. We must, therefore, either give up the belief of the universal sterility of species when crossed; or we must look at this sterility in animals, not as an indelible characteristic, but as one capable of being removed by domestication.

Finally, considering all the ascertained facts on the intercrossing of plants and animals, it may be concluded that some degree of sterility, both in first crosses and in hybrids, is an extremely general result; but that it cannot, under our present state of knowledge, be considererd as absolutely universal.

Laws governing the Sterility of first Crosses and of Hybrids

We will now consider a little more in detail the laws governing the sterility of first crosses and of hybrids. Our chief object will be to see whether or not these laws indicate that species have been specially endowed with this quality, in order to prevent their crossing and blending together in utter confusion. The following conclusions are drawn up chiefly from Gärtner's admirable work on the hybridisation of plants. I have taken much pains to ascertain how far they apply to animals, and, considering how scanty our knowledge is in regard to hybrid animals, I have been surprised to find how generally the same rules apply to both kingdoms.

It has been already remarked, that the degree of fertility, both of first crosses and of hybrids, graduates from zero to perfect fertility. It is surprising in how many curious ways this gradation can be shown; but only the barest outline of the facts can here be given. When pollen from a plant of one family is placed on the stigma of a plant of a distinct family, it exerts no more influence than so much inorganic dust. From this absolute zero of fertility, the pollen of different species applied to the stigma of some one species of the same genus, yields a perfect gradation in the number of seeds produced, up to nearly complete or even quite complete fertility; and, as we have seen, in certain abnormal cases, even to an excess of fertility, beyond that which the plant's own pollen produces. So in hybrids themselves, there are some which never have produced, and probably never would produce, even with the pollen of the pure parents, a single fertile seed: but in some of these cases a first trace of fertility may be detected, by the pollen of one of the pure parent-species causing the flower of the hybrid to wither earlier than it otherwise would have done; and the early withering of the flower is well known to be a sign of incipient fertilisation. From this extreme degree of sterility we have self-sterilised hybrids producing a greater and greater number of seeds up to perfect fertility.

The hybrids raised from two species which are very difficult to cross, and which rarely produce any offspring, are generally very sterile; but the parallelism between the difficulty of making a first cross, and the sterility of the hybrids thus produced—two classes of facts which are generally confounded together—is by no means strict. There are many cases, in which two pure species, as in the genus Verbascum, can be united with unusual facility, and produce numerous hybrid offspring, yet these hybrids are remarkably sterile. On the other hand, there are species which can be crossed very rarely, or with extreme difficulty, but the hybrids, when at last produced, are very fertile. Even within the limits of the same genus, for instance in Dianthus, these two opposite cases occur.

The fertility, both of first crosses and of hybrids, is more easily affected by unfavourable conditions, than is that of pure species. But the fertility of first crosses is likewise innately variable; for it is not always the same in degree when the same two species are crossed under the same circumstances; it depends in part upon the constitution of the individuals which happen to have been chosen for the experiment. So it is with hybrids, for their degree of fertility is often found to differ greatly in the several individuals raised from seed out of the same capsule and exposed to the same conditions.

By the term systematic affinity is meant, the general resemblance between species in structure and constitution. Now the fertility of first crosses, and of the hybrids produced from them, is largely governed by their systematic affinity. This is clearly shown by hybrids never having been raised between species ranked by systematists in distinct families; and on the other hand, by very closely allied species generally uniting with facility. But the correspondence between systematic affinity and the facility of crossing is by no means strict. A multitude of cases could be given of very closely allied species which will not unite, or only with extreme difficulty; and on the other hand of very distinct species which unite with the utmost facility. In the same family there may be a genus, as Dianthus, in which very many species can most readily be crossed; and another genus, as Silene, in which the most persevering efforts have failed to produce between extremely close species a single hybrid. Even within the limits of the same genus, we meet with this same difference; for instance, the many species of Nicotiana have been more largely crossed than the species of almost any other genus; but Gärtner found that N. acuminata, which is not a particularly distinct species, obstinately failed to fertilise, or to be fertilised by no less than eight other species of Nicotiana. Many analogous facts could be given.

No one has been able to point out what kind or what amount of difference, in any recognisable character, is sufficient to prevent two species crossing. It can be shown that plants most widely different in habit and general appearance, and having strongly marked differences in every part of the flower, even in the pollen, in the fruit, and in the cotyledons, can be crossed. Annual and perennial plants, deciduous and evergreen trees, plants inhabiting different stations and fitted for extremely different climates, can often be crossed with ease.

By a reciprocal cross between two species, I mean the case, for instance, of a female-ass being first crossed by a stallion, and then a mare by a male-ass; these two species may then be said to have been reciprocally crossed. There is often the widest possible difference in the facility of making reciprocal crosses. Such cases are highly important, for they prove that the capacity in any two species to cross is often completely independent of their systematic affinity, that is of any difference in their structure or constitution, excepting in their reproductive systems. The diversity of the result in reciprocal crosses between the same two species was long ago observed by Kölreuter. To give an instance: Mirabilis jalapa can easily be fertilised by the pollen of M. longiflora, and the hybrids thus produced are sufficiently fertile; but Kölreuter tried more than two hundred times, during eight following years, to fertilise reciprocally M. longiflora with the pollen of M. jalapa, and utterly failed. Several other equally striking cases could be given. Thuret has observed the same fact with certain sea-weeds or Fuci. Gärtner, moreover, found that this difference of facility in making reciprocal crosses is extremely common in a lesser degree. He has observed it even between closely related forms (as Matthiola annua and gilabra) which many botanists rank only as varieties. It is also a remarkable fact, that hybrids raised from reciprocal crosses, though of course compounded of the very same two species, the one species having first been used as the father and then as the mother, though they rarely differ in external characters, yet generally differ in fertility in a small, and occasionally in a high degree.

Several other singular rules could be given from Gärtner: for instance, some species have a remarkable power of crossing with other species; other species of the same genus have a remarkable power of impressing their likeness on their hybrid offspring; but these two powers do not at all necessarily go together. There are certain hybrids which, instead of having, as is usual, an intermediate character between their two parents, always closely resemble one of them; and such hybrids, though externally so like one of their pure parent-species, are with rare exceptions extremely sterile. So again amongst hybrids which are usually intermediate in structure between their parents, exceptional and abnormal individuals sometimes are born, which closely resemble one of their pure parents; and these hybrids are almost always utterly sterile, even when the other hybrids raised from seed from the same capsule have a considerable degree of fertility. These facts show how completely the fertility of a hybrid may be independent of its external resemblance to either pure parent.

Considering the several rules now given, which govern the fertility of first causes and of hybrids, we see that when forms, which must be considered as good and distinct species, are united, their fertility graduates from zero to perfect fertility, or even to fertility under certain conditions in excess; that their fertility, besides being eminently susceptible to favourable and unfavourable conditions, is innately variable; that it is by no means always the same in degree in the first cross and in the hybrids produced from this cross; that the fertility of hybrids is not related to the degree in which they resemble in external appearance either parent; and lastly, that the facility of making a first cross between any two species is not always governed by their systematic affinity or degree of resemblance to each other. This latter statement is clearly proved by the difference in the result of reciprocal crosses between the same two species, for, according as the one species or the other is used as the father or the mother, there is generally some difference, and occasionally the widest possible difference, in the facility of effecting an union. The hybrids, moreover, produced from reciprocal crosses often differ in fertility.

Now do these complex and singular rules indicate that species have been endowed with sterility simply to prevent their becoming confounded in nature? I think not. For why should the sterility be so extremely different in degree, when various species are crossed, all of which we must suppose it would be equally important to keep from blending together? Why should the degree of sterility be innately variable in the individuals of the same species? Why should some species cross with facility, and yet produce very sterile hybrids; and other species cross with extreme difficulty, and yet produce fairly fertile hybrids? Why should there often be so great a difference in the result of a reciprocal cross between the same two species? Why, it may even be asked, has the production of hybrids been permitted? To grant to species the special power of producing hybrids, and then to stop their further propagation by different degrees of sterility, not strictly related to the facility of the first union between their parents, seems a strange arrangement.

The foregoing rules and facts, on the other hand, appear to me clearly to indicate that the sterility both of first crosses and of hybrids is simply incidental or dependent on unknown differences in their reproductive systems; the differences being of so peculiar and limited a nature, that, in reciprocal crosses between the same two species, the male sexual element of the one will often freely act on the female sexual element of the other, but not in a reversed direction. It will be advisable to explain a little more fully by an example what I mean by sterility being incidental on other differences, and not a specially endowed quality. As the capacity of one plant to be grafted or budded on another is unimportant for their welfare in a state of nature, I presume that no one will suppose that this capacity is a *specially* endowed quality, but will admit that it is incidental on differences in the laws of growth of the two plants. We can sometimes see the reason why one tree will not take on another, from differences in their rate of growth, in the hardness of their wood, in the period of the flow or nature of their sap, &c.; but in a multitude of cases we can assign no reason whatever. Great diversity in the size of two plants, one being woody and the other herbaceous, one being evergreen and the other deciduous, and adaptation to widely different climates, do not always prevent the two grafting together. As in hybridisation, so with grafting, the capacity is limited by systematic affinity, for no one has been able to graft together trees belonging to quite distinct families; and, on the other hand, closely allied species, and varieties of the same species, can usually, but not invariably, be grafted with ease. But this capacity, as in hybridisation, is by no means absolutely governed by systematic affinity. Although many distinct genera within the same family have been grafted together, in other cases species of the same genus will not take on each other. The pear can be grafted far more readily on the quince, which is ranked as a distinct genus, than on the apple, which is a member of the same genus. Even different varieties of the pear take with different degrees of facility on the quince; so do different varieties of the apricot and peach on certain varieties of the plum.

As Gärtner found that there was sometimes an innate difference in different *individuals* of the same two species in crossing; so Sageret believes this to be the case with different individuals of the same two species in being grafted together. As in reciprocal crosses, the facility of effecting an union is often very far from equal, so it sometimes is in grafting; the common gooseberry, for instance, cannot be grafted on the currant, whereas the currant will take, though with difficulty, on the gooseberry.

We have seen that the sterility of hybrids, which have their reproductive organs in an imperfect condition, is a different case from the difficulty of uniting two pure species, which have their reproductive organs perfect; yet these two distinct classes of cases run to a large extent parallel. Something analogous occurs in grafting; for Thouin found that three species of Robinia, which seeded freely on their own roots, and which could be grafted with no great difficulty on a fourth species, when thus grafted were rendered barren. On the other hand, certain species of Sorbus, when grafted on other species yielded twice as much fruit as when on their own roots. We are reminded by this latter fact of the extraordinary cases of Hippeastrum, Passiflora, &c., which seed much more freely when fertilised with the pollen of a distinct species, than when fertilised with pollen from the same plant.

We thus see, that, although there is a clear and great difference between the mere adhesion of grafted stocks, and the union of the male and female elements in the act of reproduction, yet that there is a rude degree of parallelism in the results of grafting and of crossing distinct species. And as we must look at the curious and complex laws governing the facility with which trees can be grafted on each other as incidental on unknown differences in their vegetative systems, so I believe that the still more complex laws governing the facility of first crosses are incidental on unknown differences in their reproductive systems. These differences in both cases, follow to a certain extent, as might have been expected, systematic affinity, by which term every kind of resemblance and dissimilarity between organic beings is attempted to be expressed. The facts by no means seem to indicate that the greater or lesser difficulty of either grafting or crossing various species has been a special endowment; although in the case of crossing, the difficulty is as important for the endurance and stability of specific forms, as in the case of grafting it is unimportant for their welfare.

Origin and Causes of the Sterility of first Crosses and of Hybrids

At one time it appeared to me probable, as it has to others, that the sterility of first crosses and of hybrids might have been slowly acquired through the natural selection of slightly lessened degrees of fertility, which, like any other variation, spontaneously appeared in certain individuals of one variety when crossed with those of another variety. For it would clearly be advantageous to two varieties or incipient species, if they could be kept from blending, on the same principle that, when man is selecting at the same time two varieties, it is necessary that he should keep them separate. In the first place, it may be remarked that species inhabiting distinct regions are often sterile when crossed; now it could clearly have been of no advantage to such separated species to have been rendered mutually sterile, and consequently this could not have been effected through natural selection; but it may perhaps be argued, that, if a species was rendered sterile with some one compatriot, sterility with other species would follow as a necessary contingency. In the second place, it is almost as much opposed to the theory of natural selection as to that of special creation, that in reciprocal crosses the male element of one form should have been rendered utterly impotent on a second form, whilst at the same time the male element of this second form is enabled freely to fertilise the first form; for this peculiar state of the reproductive system could hardly have been advantageous to either species.

In considering the probability of natural selection having come into action, in rendering species mutually sterile, the greatest difficulty will be found to lie in the existence of many graduated steps from slightly lessened fertility to absolute sterility. It may be admitted that it would profit an incipient species, if it were rendered in some slight degree sterile when crossed with its parent form or with some other variety; for thus fewer bastardised and deteriorated offspring would be produced to commingle their blood with the new species in process of formation. But he who will take the trouble to reflect on the steps by which this first degree of sterility could be increased through natural selection to that high degree which is common with so many species, and which is universal with species which have been differentiated to a generic or family rank, will find the subject extraordinarily complex. After mature reflection it seems to me that this could not have been effected through natural selection. Take the case of any two species which, when crossed, produced few and sterile offspring; now, what is there which could favour the survival of those individuals which happened to be endowed in a slightly higher degree with mutual infertility, and which thus approached by one small step towards absolute sterility? Yet an advance of this kind, if the theory of natural selection be brought to bear, must have incessantly occurred with many species, for a multitude are mutually quite barren. With sterile neuter insects we have reason to believe that modifications in their structure and fertility have been slowly accumulated by natural selection, from an advantage having been thus indirectly given to the community to which they belonged over other communities of the same species; but an individual animal not belonging to a social community, if rendered slightly sterile when crossed with some other variety, would not thus itself gain any advantage or indirectly give any advantage to the other individuals of the same variety, thus leading to their preservation.

But it would be superfluous to discuss this question in detail; for with plants we have conclusive evidence that the sterility of crossed species must be due to some principle, quite independent of natural selection. Both Gärtner and Kölreuter have proved that in genera including numerous species, a series can be formed from species which when crossed yield fewer and fewer seeds, to species which never produce a single seed, but yet are affected by the pollen of certain other species, for the germen swells. It is here manifestly impossible to select the more sterile individuals, which have already ceased to yield seeds; so that this acme of sterility, when the germen alone is affected, cannot have been gained through selection; and from the laws governing the various grades of sterility being so uniform throughout the animal and vegetable kingdoms, we may infer that the cause, whatever it may be, is the same or nearly the same in all cases.

We will now look a little closer at the probable nature of the differences between species which induce sterility in first crosses and in hybrids. In the case of first crosses, the greater or less difficulty in effecting an union and in obtaining offspring apparently depends on several distinct causes. There must sometimes be a physical impossibility in the male element reaching the ovule, as would be the case with a plant having a pistil too long for the pollen-tubes to reach the ovarium. It has also been observed that when the pollen of one species is placed on the stigma of a distantly allied species, though the pollen-tubes protrude, they do not penetrate the stigmatic surface. Again, the male element may reach the female element but be incapable of causing an embryo to be developed, as seems to have been the case with some of Thuret's experiments on Fuci. No explanation can be given of these facts, any more than why certain trees cannot be grafted on others. Lastly, an embryo may be developed, and then perish at an early period. This latter alternative has not been sufficiently attended to; but I believe, from observations communicated to me by Mr. Hewitt, who has had great experience in hybridising pheasants and fowls, that the early death of the embryo is a very frequent cause of sterility in first crosses. Mr. Salter has recently given the results of an examination of about 500 eggs produced from various crosses between three species of

Gallus and their hybrids; the majority of these eggs had been fertilised; and in the majority of the fertilised eggs, the embryos had either been partially developed and had then perished, or had become nearly mature, but the young chickens had been unable to break through the shell. Of the chickens which were born, more than four-fifths died within the first few days, or at latest weeks, "without any obvious cause, apparently from mere inability to live;" so that from the 500 eggs only twelve chickens were reared. With plants, hybridised embryos probably often perish in a like manner; at least it is known that hybrids raised from very distinct species are sometimes weak and dwarfed, and perish at an early age; of which fact Max Wichura has recently given some striking cases with hybrid willows. It may be here worth noticing that in some cases of parthenogenesis, the embryos within the eggs of silk moths which had not been fertilised, pass through their early stages of development and then perish like the embryos produced by a cross between distinct species. Until becoming acquainted with these facts, I was unwilling to believe in the frequent early death of hybrid embryos; for hybrids, when once born, are generally healthy and long-lived, as we see in the case of the common mule. Hybrids, however, are differently circumstanced before and after birth: when born and living in a country where their two parents live, they are generally placed under suitable conditions of life. But a hybrid partakes of only half of the nature and constitution of its mother; it may therefore before birth, as long as it is nourished within its mother's womb, or within the egg or seed produced by the mother, be exposed to conditions in some degree unsuitable, and consequently be liable to perish at an early period; more especially as all very young beings are eminently sensitive to injurious or unnatural conditions of life. But after all, the cause more probably lies in some imperfection in the original act of impregnation, causing the embryo to be imperfectly developed, rather than in the conditions to which it is subsequently exposed.

In regard to the sterility of hybrids, in which the sexual elements are imperfectly developed, the case is somewhat different. I have more than once alluded to a large body of facts showing that, when animals and plants are removed from their natural conditions, they are extremely liable to have their reproductive systems seriously affected. This, in fact, is the great bar to the domestication of animals. Between the sterility thus superinduced and that of hybrids, there are many points of similarity. In both cases the sterility is independent of general health, and is often accompanied by excess of size or great luxuriance. In both cases the sterility occurs in various degrees; in both, the male element is the most liable to be affected; but sometimes the female more than the male. In both, the tendency goes to a certain extent with systematic affinity, for whole groups of animals and plants are rendered impotent by the same unnatural conditions; and whole groups of species tend to produce sterile hybrids. On the other hand, one species in a group will sometimes resist great changes of conditions with unimpaired fertility; and certain species in a group will produce unusually fertile hybrids. No one can tell, till he tries, whether any particular animal will breed under confinement, or any exotic plant seed freely under culture; nor can he tell till he tries, whether any two species of a genus will produce more or less sterile hybrids. Lastly, when organic beings are placed during several generations under conditions not natural to them, they are extremely liable to vary, which seems to be partly due to their reproductive systems having been specially affected, though in a lesser degree than when sterility ensues. So it is with hybrids, for their offspring in successive generations are eminently liable to vary, as every experimentalist has observed.

Thus we see that when organic beings are placed under new and unnatural conditions, and when hybrids are produced by the unnatural crossing of two species, the reproductive system, independently of the general state of health, is affected in a very similar manner. In the one case, the conditions of life have been disturbed, though often in so slight a degree as to be inappreciable by us; in the other case, or that of hybrids, the external conditions have remained the same, but the organisation has been disturbed by two distinct structures and constitutions, including of course the reproductive systems, having been blended into one. For it is scarcely possible that two organisations should be compounded into one, without some disturbance occurring in the development, or periodical action, or mutual relations of the different parts and organs one to another or to the conditions of life. When hybrids are able to breed *inter se*, they transmit to their offspring from generation to generation the same compounded organisation, and hence we need not be surprised that their sterility, though in some degree variable, does not diminish; it is even apt to increase, this being generally the result, as before explained, of too close interbreeding. The above view of the sterility of hybrids being caused by two constitutions being compounded into one has been strongly maintained by Max Wichura.

It must, however, be owned that we cannot understand, on the above or any other view, several facts with respect to the sterility of hybrids; for instance, the unequal fertility of hybrids produced from reciprocal crosses; or the increased sterility in those hybrids which occasionally and exceptionally resemble closely either pure parent. Nor do I pretend that the foregoing remarks go to the root of the matter; no explanation is offered why an organism, when placed under unnatural conditions, is rendered sterile. All that I have attempted to show is, that in two cases, in some respects allied, sterility is the common result,—in the one case from the conditions of life having been disturbed, in the other case from the organisation having been disturbed by two organisations being compounded into one.

A similar parallelism holds good with an allied yet very different class of facts. It is an old and almost universal belief founded on a considerable body of evidence, which I have elsewhere given, that slight changes in the conditions of life are beneficial to all living things. We see this acted on by farmers and gardeners in their frequent exchanges of seed, tubers, &c., from one soil or climate to another, and back again. During the convalescence of animals, great benefit is derived from almost any change in their habits of life. Again, both with plants and animals, there is the clearest evidence that a cross between individuals of the same species, which differ to a certain extent, gives vigour and fertility to the offspring; and that close interbreeding continued during several generations between the nearest relations, if these be kept under the same conditions of life, almost always leads to decreased size, weakness, or sterility.

Hence it seems that, on the one hand, slight changes in the conditions of life benefit all organic beings, and on the other hand, that slight crosses, that is crosses between the males and females of the same species, which have been subjected to slightly different conditions, or which have slightly varied, give vigour and fertility to the offspring. But, as we have seen, organic beings long habituated to certain uniform conditions under a state of nature, when subjected, as under confinement, to a considerable change in their conditions, very frequently are rendered more or less sterile; and we know that a cross between two forms, that have become widely or specifically different, produce hybrids which are almost always in some degree sterile. I am fully persuaded that this double parallelism is by no means an accident or an illusion. He who is able to explain why the elephant and a multitude of other animals are incapable of breeding when kept under only partial confinement in their native country, will be able to explain the primary cause of hybrids being so generally sterile. He will at the same time be able to explain how it is that the races of some of our domesticated animals, which have often been subjected to new and not uniform conditions, are quite fertile together, although they are descended from distinct species, which would probably have been sterile if aboriginally crossed. The above two parellel series of facts seem to be connected together by some common but unknown bond, which is essentially related to the principle of life; this principle, according to Mr. Herbert Spencer, being that life depends on, or consists in, the incessant action and reaction of various forces, which, as throughout nature, are always tending towards an equilibrium; and when this tendency is slightly disturbed by any change, the vital forces gain in power.

Reciprocal Dimorphism and Trimorphism

This subject may be here briefly discussed, and will be found to throw some light on hybridism. Several plants belonging to distinct orders present two forms, which exist in about equal numbers and which differ in no respect except in their reproductive organs; one form having a long pistil with short stamens, the other a short pistil with long stamens; the two having differently sized pollen-grains. With trimorphic plants there are three forms likewise differing in the lengths of the pistils and stamens, in the size and colour of the pollen-grains, and in some other respects; and as in each of the three forms there are two sets of stamens, the three forms possess altogether six sets of stamens and three kinds of pistils. These organs are so proportioned in length to each other, that half the stamens in two of the forms stand on a level with the stigma of the third form. Now I have shown, and the result has been confirmed by other observers, that, in order to obtain full fertility with these plants, it is necessary that the stigma of the one form should be fertilised by pollen taken from the stamens of corresponding height in another form. So that with dimorphic species two unions, which may be called legitimate, are fully fertile; and two, which may be called illegitimate, are more or less infertile. With trimorphic species six unions are legitimate, or fully fertile,— and twelve are illegitimate, or more or less infertile.

The infertility which may be observed in various dimorphic and trimorphic plants, when they are illegitimately fertilised, that is by pollen taken from stamens not corresponding in height with the pistil, differs much in degree, up to absolute and utter sterility; just in the same manner as occurs in crossing distinct species. As the degree of sterility in the latter case depends in an eminent degree on the conditions of life being more or less favourable, so I have found it with illegitimate unions. It is well known that if pollen of a distinct species be placed on the stigma of a flower, and its own pollen be afterwards, even after a considerable interval of time, placed on the same stigma, its action is so strongly prepotent that it generally annihilates the effect of the foreign pollen; so it is with the pollen of the several forms of the same species, for legitimate pollen is strongly prepotent over illegitimate pollen, when both are placed on the same stigma. I ascertained this by fertilising several flowers, first illegitimately, and twenty-four hours afterwards legitimately with the pollen taken from a peculiarly coloured variety, and all the seedlings were similarly coloured; this shows that the legitimate pollen, though applied twenty-four hours subsequently, had wholly destroyed or prevented the action of the previously applied illegitimate pollen. Again, as in making reciprocal crosses between the same two species, there is occasionally a great difference in the result, so the same thing occurs with trimorphic plants; for instance, the mid-styled form of Lythrum salicaria was illegitimately fertilised with the greatest ease by pollen from the longer stamens of the short-styled form, and yielded many seeds; but the latter form did not yield a single seed when fertilised by the longer stamens of the mid-styled form.

In all these respects, and in others which might be added, the forms of the same undoubted species when illegitimately united behave in exactly the same manner as do two distinct species when crossed. This led me carefully to observe during four years many seedlings, raised from several illegitimate unions. The chief result is that these illegitimate plants, as they may be called, are not fully fertile. It is possible to raise from dimorphic species, both long-styled and short-styled illegitimate plants, and from trimorphic plants all three illegitimate forms. These can then be properly united in a legitimate manner. When this is done, there is no apparent reason why they should not yield as many seeds as did their parents when legitimately fertilised. But such is not the case. They are all infertile, in various degrees; some being so utterly and incurably sterile that they did not yield during four seasons a single seed or even seed-capsule. The sterility of these illegitimate plants, when united with each other in a legitimate manner, may be strictly compared with that of hybrids when crossed *inter se*. If, on the other hand, a hybrid is crossed with either pure parent-species, the sterility is usually much lessened: and so it is when an illegitimate plant is fertilised by a legitimate plant. In the same manner as the sterility of hybrids does not always run parellel with the difficulty of making the first cross between the two parent-species, so the sterility of certain illegitimate plants was unusually great, whilst the sterility of the union from which they were derived was by no means great. With hybrids raised from the same seed-capsule the degree of sterility is innately variable, so it is in a marked manner with illegitimate plants. Lastly, many hybrids are profuse and persistent flowerers, whilst other and more sterile hybrids produce few flowers, and are weak, miserable dwarfs; exactly similar cases occur with the illegitimate offspring of various dimorphic and trimorphic plants.

Altogether there is the closest identity in character and behaviour between illegitimate plants and hybrids. It is hardly an exaggeration to maintain that illegitimate plants are hybrids, produced within the limits of the same species by the improper union of certain forms, whilst ordinary hybrids are produced from an improper union between so-called distinct species. We have also already seen that there is the closest similarity in all respects between first illegitimate unions and first crosses between distinct species. This will perhaps be made more fully apparent by an illustration; we may suppose that a botanist found two well-marked varieties (and such occur) of the long-styled form of the trimorphic Lythrum salicaria, and that he determined to try by crossing whether they were specifically distinct. He would find that they yielded only about one-fifth of the proper number of seeds, and that they behaved in all the other above-specified respects as if they had been two distinct species. But to make the case sure, he would raise plants from his supposed hybridised seed, and he would find that the seedlings were miserably dwarfed and utterly sterile, and that they behaved in all other respects like ordinary hybrids. He might then maintain that he had actually proved, in accordance with the common view, that his two varieties were as good and as distinct species as any in the world; but he would be completely mistaken.

The facts now given on dimorphic and trimorphic plants are important, because they show us, first, that the physiological test of lessened fertility, both in first crosses and in hybrids, is no safe criterion of specific distinction; secondly, because we may conclude that there is some unknown bond which connects the infertility of illegitimate unions with that of their illegitimate offspring, and we are led to extend the same view to first crosses and hybrids; thirdly, because we find, and this seems to me of especial importance, that two or three forms of the same species may exist and may differ in no respect whatever, either in structure or in constitution, relatively to external conditions, and yet be sterile when united in certain ways. For we must remember that it is the union of the sexual elements of individuals of the same form, for instance, of two long-styled forms, which results in sterility; whilst it is the union of the sexual elements proper to two distinct forms which is fertile. Hence the case appears at first sight exactly the reverse of what occurs, in the ordinary unions of the individuals of the same species and with crosses between distinct species. It is, however, doubtful whether this is really so; but I will not enlarge on this obscure subject.

We may, however, infer as probable from the consideration of dimorphic and trimorphic plants, that the sterility of distinct species when crossed and of their hybrid progeny, depends exclusively on the nature of their sexual elements, and not on any difference in their structure or general constitution. We are also led to this same conclusion by considering reciprocal crosses, in which the male of one species cannot be united, or can be united with great difficulty, with the female of a second species, whilst the converse cross can be effected with perfect facility. That excellent observer, Gärtner, likewise concluded that species when crossed are sterile owing to differences confined to their reproductive systems.

Fertility of Varieties when Crossed, and of their Mongrel Offspring, not universal

It may be urged, as an overwhelming argument, that there must be some essential distinction between species and varieties, inasmuch as the latter, however much they may differ from each other in external appearance, cross with perfect facility, and yield perfectly fertile offspring. With some exceptions, presently to be given, I fully admit that this is the rule. But the subject is surrounded by difficulties, for, looking to varieties produced under nature, if two forms hitherto reputed to be varieties be found in any degree sterile together, they are at once ranked by most naturalists as species. For instance, the blue and red pimpernel, which are considered by most botanists as varieties, are said by Gärtner to be quite sterile when crossed, and he subsequently ranks them as undoubted species. If we thus argue in a circle, the fertility of all varieties produced under nature will assuredly have to be granted.

If we turn to varieties, produced, or supposed to have been produced, under domestication, we are still involved in some doubt. For when it is stated, for instance, that certain South American indigenous domestic dogs do not readily unite with European dogs, the explanation which will occur to every one, and probably the true one, is that they are descended from aboriginally distinct species. Nevertheless the perfect fertility of so many domestic races, differing widely from each other in appearance, for instance those of the pigeon, or of the cabbage, is a remarkable fact; more especially when we reflect how many species there are, which, though resembling each other most closely, are utterly sterile when intercrossed. Several considerations, however, render the fertility of domestic varieties less remarkable. In the first place, it may be observed that the amount of external difference between two species is no sure guide to their degree of mutual sterility, so that similar differences in the case of varieties would be no sure guide. It is certain that with species the cause lies exclusively in differences in their sexual constitution. Now the varying conditions to which domesticated animals and cultivated plants have been subjected, have had so little tendency towards modifying the reproductive system in a manner leading to mutual sterility, that we have good grounds for admitting the directly opposite doctrine of Pallas, namely, that such conditions generally eliminate this tendency; so that the domesticated descendants of species, which in their natural state probably would have been in some degree sterile when crossed, become perfectly fertile together. With plants, so far is cultivation from giving a tendency towards sterility between distinct species, that in several well-authenticated cases already alluded to, certain plants have been affected in an opposite manner, for they have become self-impotent whilst still retaining the capacity of fertilising, and being fertilised by, other species. If the Pallasian doctrine of the elimination of sterility through long-continued domestication be admitted, and it can hardly be rejected, it becomes in the highest degree improbable that similar conditions long-continued should likewise induce this tendency; though in certain cases, with species having a peculiar constitution, sterility might occasionally be thus caused. Thus, as I believe, we can understand why with domesticated animals varieties have not been produced which are mutually sterile; and why with plants only a few such cases, immediately to be given, have been observed.

The real difficulty in our present subject is not, as it appears to me, why domestic varieties have not become mutually infertile when crossed, but why this has so generally occurred with natural varieties, as soon as they have been permanently modified in a sufficient degree to take rank as species. We are far from precisely knowing the cause; nor is this surprising, seeing how profoundly ignorant we are in regard to the normal and abnormal action of the reproductive system. But we can see that species, owing to their struggle for existence with numerous competitors, will have been exposed during long periods of time to more uniform conditions, than have domestic varieties; and this may well make a wide difference in the result. For we know how commonly wild animals and plants, when taken from their natural conditions and subjected to captivity, are rendered sterile; and the reproductive functions of organic beings which have always lived under natural conditions would probably in like manner be eminently sensitive to the influence of an unnatural cross. Domesticated productions, on the other hand, which, as shown by the mere fact of their domestication, were not originally highly sensitive to changes in their conditions of life, and which can now generally resist with undiminished fertility repeated changes of conditions, might be expected to produce varieties, which would be little liable to have their reproductive powers injuriously affected by the act of crossing with other varieties which had originated in a like manner.

I have not as yet spoken as if the varieties of the same species were invariably fertile when intercrossed. But it is impossible to resist the evid ence of the existence of a certain amount of sterility in the few following cases, which I will briefly abstract. The evidence is at least as good as that from which we believe in the sterility of a multitude of species. The evidence is, also, derived from hostile witnesses, who in all other cases consider fertility and sterility as safe criterions of specific distinction. Gärtner kept during several years a dwarf kind of maize with yellow seeds, and a tall variety with red seeds growing near each other in his garden; and although these plants have separated sexes, they never naturally crossed. He then fertilised thirteen flowers of the one kind with pollen of the other; but only a single head produced any seed, and this one head produced only five grains. Manipulation in this case could not have been injurious, as the plants have separated sexes. No one, I believe, has suspected that these varieties of maize are distinct species; and it is important to notice that the hybrid plants thus raised were themselves *perfectly* fertile; so that even Gärtner did not venture to consider the two varieties as specifically distinct.

Girou de Buzareingues crossed three varieties of gourd, which like ╷he maize has separated sexes, and he asserts that their mutual fertilization is by so much the less easy as their differences are greater. How far these experiments may be trusted, I know not; but the forms experimented on are ranked by Sageret, who mainly founds his classification by the test of infertility, as varieties, and Naudin has come to the same conclusion.

The following case is far more remarkable, and seems at first incredible; but it is the result of an astonishing number of experiments made during many years on nine species of Verbascum, by so good an observer and so hostile a witness as Gärtner: namely, that the yellow and white varieties when crossed produce less seed than the similarly coloured varieties of the same species. Moreover, he asserts that, when yellow and white varieties of one species are crossed with yellow and white varieties of a *distinct* species, more seed is produced by the crosses between the similarly coloured flowers, than between those which are differently coloured. Mr. Scott also has experimented on the species and varieties of Verbascum; and although unable to confirm Gärtner's results on the crossing of the distinct species, he finds that the dissimilarly coloured varieties of the same species yield fewer seeds, in the proportion of 86 to 100, than the similarly coloured varieties. Yet these varieties differ in no respect except in the colour of their flowers; and one variety can sometimes be raised from the seed of another.

Kölreuter, whose accuracy has been confirmed by every subsequent observer, has proved the remarkable fact, that one particular variety of the common tobacco was more fertile than the other varieties, when crossed with a widely distinct species. He experimented on five forms which are commonly reputed to be varieties, and which he tested by the severest trial, namely, by reciprocal crosses, and he found their mongrel offspring perfectly fertile. But one of these five varieties, when used either as the father or mother, and crossed with the Nicotiana glutinosa, always yielded hybrids not so sterile as those which were produced from the four other varieties when crossed with N. glutinosa. Hence the reproductive system of this one variety must have been in some manner and in some degree modified.

From these facts it can no longer be maintained that varieties when crossed are invariably quite fertile. From the great difficulty of ascertaining the infertility of varieties in a state of nature, for a supposed variety, if proved to be infertile in any degree, would almost universally be ranked as a species;—from man attending only to external characters in his domestic varieties, and from such varieties not having been exposed for very long periods to uniform conditions of life;—from these several considerations we may conclude that fertility does not constitute a fundamental distinction between varieties and species when crossed. The general sterility of crossed species may safely be looked at, not as a special acquirement or endowment, but as incidental on changes of an unknown nature in their sexual elements.

Hybrids and Mongrels compared, independently of their fertility

Independently of the question of fertility, the offspring of species and of varieties when crossed may be compared in several other respects. Gärtner, whose strong wish it was to draw a distinct line between species and varieties, could find very few, and, as it seems to me, quite unimportant differences between the so-called hybrid offspring of species, and the so-called mongrel offspring of varieties. And, on the other hand, they agree most closely in many important respects.

I shall here discuss this subject with extreme brevity. The most important distinction is, that in the first generation mongrels are more variable than hybrids; but Gärtner admits that hybrids from species which have long been cultivated are often variable in the first generation; and I have myself seen striking instances of this fact. Gärtner further admits that hybrids between very closely allied species are more variable than those from very distinct species; and this shows that the difference in the degree of variability graduates away. When mongrels and the more fertile hybrids are propagated for several generations, an extreme amount of variability in the offspring in both cases is notorious; but some few instances of both hybrids and mongrels long retaining a uniform character could be given. The variability, however, in the successive generations of mongrels is, perhaps, greater than in hybrids.

This greater variability in mongrels than in hybrids does not seem at all surprising. For the parents of mongrels are varieties, and mostly domestic varieties (very few experiments having been tried on natural varieties), and this implies that there has been recent variability, which would often continue and would augment that arising from the act of crossing. The slight variability of hybrids in the first generation, in contrast with that in the succeeding generations, is a curious fact and deserves attention. For it bears on the view which I have taken of one of the causes of ordinary variability; namely, that the reproductive system from being eminently sensitive to changed conditions of life, fails under these circumstances to perform its proper function of producing offspring closely similar in all respects to the parent-form. Now hybrids in the first generation are descended from species (excluding those long-cultivated) which have not had their reproductive systems in any way affected, and they are not variable; but hybrids themselves have their reproductive systems seriously affected, and their descendants are highly variable.

But to return to our comparison of mongrels and hybrids: Gärtner states that mongrels are more liable than hybrids to revert to either parent-form; but this, if it be true, is certainly only a difference in degree. Moreover, Gärtner expressly states that hybrids from long cultivated plants are more subject to reversion than hybrids from species in their natural state; and this probably explains the singular difference in the results arrived at by different observers: thus Max Wichura doubts whether hybrids ever revert to their parent-forms, and he experimented on uncultivated species of willows; whilst Naudin, on the other hand, insists in the strongest terms on the almost universal tendency to reversion in hybrids, and he experimented chiefly on cultivated plants. Gärtner further states that when any two species, although most closely allied to each other, are crossed with a third species, the hybrids are widely different from each other; whereas if two very distinct varieties of one species are crossed with another species, the hybrids do not differ much. But this conclusion, as far as I can make out, is founded on a single experiment; and seems directly opposed to the results of several experiments made by Kölreuter.

Such alone are the unimportant differences which Gärtner is able to point out between hybrid and mongrel plants. On the other hand, the degrees and kinds of resemblance in mongrels and in hybrids to their respective parents, more especially in hybrids produced from nearly related species, follow according to Gärtner the same laws. When two species are crossed, one has sometimes a prepotent power of impressing its likeness on the hybrid. So I believe it to be with varieties of plants; and with animals one variety certainly often has this prepotent power over another variety. Hybrid plants produced from a reciprocal cross, generally resemble each other closely; and so it is with mongrel plants from a reciprocal cross. Both hybrids and mongrels can be reduced to either pure parent-form, by repeated crosses in successive generations with either parent.

These several remarks are apparently applicable to animals; but the subject is here much complicated, partly owing to the existence of secondary sexual characters; but more especially owing to prepotency in transmitting likeness running more strongly in one sex than in the other, both when one species is crossed with another, and when one variety is crossed with another variety. For instance, I think those authors are right who maintain that the ass has a prepotent power over the horse, so that both the mule and the hinny resemble more closely the ass than the horse; but that the prepotency runs more strongly in the male than in the female ass, so that the mule, which is the offspring of the male ass and mare, is more like an ass, than is the hinny, which is the offspring of the female ass and stallion.

Much stress has been laid by some authors on the supposed fact, that it is only with mongrels that the offspring are not intermediate in character, but closely resemble one of their parents; but this does sometimes occur with hybrids, yet I grant much less frequently than with mongrels. Looking to the cases which I have collected of cross-bred animals closely resembling one parent, the resemblances seem chiefly confined to characters almost monstrous in their nature, and which have suddenly appeared —such as albinism, melanism, deficiency of tail or horns, or additional fingers and toes; and do not relate to characters which have been slowly acquired through selection. A tendency to sudden reversions to the perfect character of either parent would, also, be much more likely to occur with mongrels, which are descended from varieties often suddenly produced and semi-monstrous in character, than with hybrids, which are descended from species slowly and naturally produced. On the whole, I entirely agree with Dr. Prosper Lucas, who, after arranging an enormous body of facts with respect to animals, comes to the conclusion that the laws of resemblance of the child to its parents are the same, whether the two parents differ little or much from each other, namely, in the union of individuals of the same variety, or of different varieties, or of distinct species.

Independently of the question of fertility and sterility, in all other respects there seems to be a general and close similarity in the offspring of crossed species, and of crossed varieties. If we look at species as having been specially created, and at varieties as having been produced by secondary laws, this similarity would be an astonishing fact. But it harmonises perfectly with the view that there is no essential distinction between species and varieties.

Summary of Chapter

First crosses between forms, sufficiently distinct to be ranked as species, and their hybrids, are very generally, but not universally, sterile. The sterility is of all degrees, and is often so slight that the most careful experimentalists have arrived at diametrically opposite conclusions in ranking forms by this test. The sterility is innately variable in individuals of the same species, and is eminently susceptible to the action of favourable and unfavourable conditions. The degree of sterility does not strictly follow systematic affinity, but is governed by several curious and complex laws. It is generally different, and sometimes widely different in reciprocal crosses between the same two species. It is not always equal in degree in a first cross and in the hybrids produced from this cross.

In the same manner as in grafting trees, the capacity in one species or variety to take on another, is incidental on differences, generally of an unknown nature, in their vegetative systems, so in crossing, the greater or less facility of one species to unite with another is incidental on unknown differences in their reproductive systems. There is no more reason to think that species have been specially endowed with various degrees of sterility to prevent their crossing and blending in nature, than to think that trees have been specially endowed with various and somewhat analogous degrees of difficulty in being grafted together in order to prevent their inarching in our forests.

The sterility of first crosses and of their hybrid progeny has not been acquired through natural selection. In the case of first crosses it seems to depend on several circumstances; in some instances in chief part on the early death of the embryo. In the case of hybrids, it apparently depends on their whole organisation having been disturbed by being compounded from two distinct forms; the sterility being closely allied to that which so frequently affects pure species, when exposed to new and unnatural conditions of life. He who will explain these latter cases will be able to explain the sterility of hybrids. This view is strongly supported by a parallelism of another kind: namely, that, firstly, slight changes in the conditions of life add to the vigour and fertility of all organic beings; and secondly, that the crossing of forms, which have been exposed to slightly different conditions of life or which have varied, favours the size, vigour, and fertility of their offspring. The facts given on the sterility of the illegitimate unions of dimorphic and trimorphic plants and of their illegitimate progeny, perhaps render it probable that some unknown bond in all cases connects the degree of fertility of first unions with that of their offspring. The consideration of these facts on dimorphism, as well as of the results of reciprocal crosses, clearly leads to the conclusion that the primary cause of the sterility of crossed species is confined to differences in their sexual elements. But why, in the case of distinct species, the sexual elements should so generally have become more or less modified, leading to their mutual infertility, we do not know; but it seems to stand in some close relation to species having been exposed for long periods of time to nearly uniform conditions of life.

It is not surprising that the difficulty in crossing any two species, and the sterility of their hybrid offspring, should in most cases correspond, even if due to distinct causes: for both depend on the amount of difference between the species which are crossed. Nor is it surprising that the facility of effecting a first cross, and the fertility of the hybrids thus produced, and the capacity of being grafted together—though this latter capacity evidently depends on widely different circumstances—should all run, to a certain extent, parellel with the systematic affinity of the forms subjected to experiment; for systematic affinity includes resemblances of all kinds.

First crosses between forms known to be varieties, or sufficiently alike to be considered as varieties, and their mongrel offspring, are very generally, but not, as is so often stated, invariably fertile. Nor is this almost universal and perfect fertility surprising, when it is remembered how liable we are to argue in a circle with respect to varieties in a state of nature; and when we remember that the greater number of varieties have been produced under domestication by the selection of mere external differences, and that they have not been long exposed to uniform conditions of life. It should also be especially kept in mind, that long-continued domestication tends to eliminate sterility, and is therefore little likely to induce this same quality. Independently of the question of fertility, in all other respects there is the closest general resemblance between hybrids and mongrels,—in their variability, in their power of absorbing each other by repeated crosses, and in their inheritance of characters from both parent-forms. Finally, then, although we are as ignorant of the precise cause of the sterility of first crosses and of hybrids as we are why animals and plants removed from their natural conditions become sterile, yet the facts given in this chapter do not seem to me opposed to the belief that species aboriginally existed as varieties.

CHAPTER X

ON THE IMPERFECTION OF THE GEOLOGICAL RECORD

On the absence of intermediate varieties at the present day—On the nature of extinct intermediate varieties; on their number—On the lapse of time, as inferred from the rate of denudation and of deposition—On the lapse of time as estimated by years —On the poorness of our palæontological collections—On the intermittence of geological formations—On the denudation of granitic areas—On the absence of intermediate varieties in any one formation—On the sudden appearance of groups of species—On their sudden appearance in the lowest known fossiliferous strata— Antiquity of the habitable earth.

IN the sixth chapter I enumerated the chief objections which might be justly urged against the views maintained in this volume. Most of them have now been discussed. One, namely the distinctness of specific forms, and their not being blended together by innumerable transitional links, is a very obvious difficulty. I assigned reasons why such links do not commonly occur at the present day under the circumstances apparently most favourable for their presence, namely, on an extensive and continuous area with graduated physical conditions. I endeavoured to show, that the life of each species depends in a more important manner on the presence of other already defined organic forms, than on climate, and, therefore, that the really governing conditions of life do not graduate away quite insensibly like heat or moisture. I endeavoured, also, to show that intermediate varieties, from existing in lesser numbers than the forms which they connect, will generally be beaten out and exterminated during the course of further modification and improvement. The main cause, however, of innumerable intermediate links not now occurring everywhere throughout nature, depends on the very process of natural selection, through which new varieties continually take the places of and supplant their parent-forms. But just in proportion as this process of extermination has acted on an enormous scale, so must the number of intermediate varieties, which have formerly existed, be truly enormous. Why then is not every geological formation and every stratum full of such intermediate links? Geology assuredly does not reveal any such finely-graduated organic chain; and this, perhaps, is the most obvious and serious objection which can be urged against the theory. The explanation lies, as I believe, in the extreme imperfection of the geological record.

In the first place, it should always be borne in mind what sort of intermediate forms must, on the theory, have formerly existed. I have found it difficult, when looking at any two species, to avoid picturing to myself forms *directly* intermediate between them. But this is a wholly false view; we should always look for forms intermediate between each species and a common but unknown progenitor; and the progenitor will generally have differed in some respects from all its modified descendants. To give a simple illustration: the fantail and pouter pigeons are both descended from the rock-pigeon; if we possessed all the intermediate varieties which have ever existed, we should have an extremely close series between both and the rock-pigeon; but we should have no varieties directly intermediate between the fantail and pouter; none, for instance, combining a tail somewhat expanded with a crop somewhat enlarged, the characteristic features of these two breeds. These two breeds, moreover, have become so much modified, that, if we had no historical or indirect evidence regarding their origin, it would not have been possible to have determined, from a mere comparison of their structure with that of the rock-pigeon, C. livia, whether they had descended from this species or from some allied form, such as C. œnas.

So, with natural species, if we look to forms very distinct, for instance to the horse and tapir, we have no reason to suppose that links directly intermediate between them ever existed, but between each and an unknown common parent. The common parent will have had in its whole organisation much general resemblance to the tapir and to the horse; but in some points of structure may have differed considerably from both, even perhaps more than they differ from each other. Hence, in all such cases, we should be unable to recognise the parent-form of any two or more species, even if we closely compared the structure of the parent with that of its modified descendants, unless at the same time we had a nearly perfect chain of the intermediate links.

It is just possible by the theory, that one of two living forms might have descended from the other; for instance, a horse from a tapir; and in this case *direct* intermediate links will have existed between them. But such a case would imply that one form had remained for a very long period unaltered, whilst its descendants had undergone a vast amount of change; and the principle of competition between organism and organism, between child and parent, will render this a very rare event; for in all cases the new and improved forms of life tend to supplant the old and unimproved forms.

By the theory of natural selection all living species have been connected with the parent-species of each genus, by differences not greater than we see between the natural and domestic varieties of the same species at the present day; and these parent-species, now generally extinct, have in their turn been similarly connected with more ancient forms; and so on backwards, always converging to the common ancestor of each great class. So that the number of intermediate and transitional links, between all living and extinct species, must have been inconceivably great. But assuredly, if this theory be true, such have lived upon the earth.

On the Lapse of Time, as inferred from the rate of Deposition and extent of Denudation

Independently of our not finding fossil remains of such infinitely numerous connecting links, it may be objected that time cannot have sufficed for so great an amount of organic change, all changes having been effected slowly. It is hardly possible for me to recall to the reader who is not a practical geologist, the facts leading the mind feebly to comprehend the lapse of time. He who can read Sir Charles Lyell's grand work on the Principles of Geology, which the future historian will recognise as having produced a revolution in natural science, and yet does not admit how vast have been the past periods of time, may at once close this volume. Not that it suffices to study the Principles of Geology, or to read special treatises by different observers on separate formations, and to mark how each author attempts to give an inadequate idea of the duration of each formation, or even of each stratum. We can best gain some idea of past time by knowing the agencies at work, and learning how deeply the surface of the land has been denuded, and how much sediment has been deposited. As Lyell has well remarked, the extent and thickness of our sedimentary formations are the result and the measure of the denudation which the earth's crust has elsewhere undergone. Therefore a man should examine for himself the great piles of superimposed strata, and watch the rivulets bringing down mud, and the waves wearing away the sea-cliffs, in order to comprehend something about the duration of past time, the monuments of which we see all around us.

It is good to wander along the coast, when formed of moderately hard rocks, and mark the process of degradation. The tides in most cases reach the cliffs only for a short time twice a day, and the waves eat into them only when they are charged with sand or pebbles; for there is good evidence that pure water effects nothing in wearing away rock. At last the base of the cliff is undermined, huge fragments fall down, and these, remaining fixed, have to be worn away atom by atom, until after being reduced in size they can be rolled about by the waves, and then they are more quickly ground into pebbles, sand, or mud. But how often do we see along the bases of retreating cliffs rounded boulders, all thickly clothed by marine productions, showing how little they are abraded and how seldom they are rolled about! Moreover, if we follow for a few miles any line of rocky cliff, which is undergoing degradation, we find that it is only here and there, along a short length or round a promontory, that the cliffs are at the present time suffering. The appearance of the surface and the vegetation show that elsewhere years have elapsed since the waters washed their base.

We have, however, recently learnt from the observations of Ramsay, in the van of many excellent observers—of Jukes, Geikie, Croll, and others, that subaerial degradation is a much more important agency than coast-action, or the power of the waves. The whole surface of the land is exposed to the chemical action of the air and of the rain-water with its dissolved carbonic acid, and in colder countries to frost; the disintegrated matter is carried down even gentle slopes during heavy rain, and to a greater extent than might be supposed, especially in arid districts, by the wind; it is then transported by the streams and rivers, which when rapid deepen their channels, and triturate the fragments. On a rainy day, even in a gently undulating country, we see the effects of subaerial degradation in the muddy rills which flow down every slope. Messrs. Ramsay and Whitaker have shown, and the observation is a most striking one, that the great lines of escarpment in the Wealden district and those ranging across England, which formerly were looked at as ancient sea-coasts, cannot have been thus formed, for each line is composed of one and the same formation, whilst our sea-cliffs are everywhere formed by the intersection of various formations. This being the case, we are compelled to admit that the escarpments owe their origin in chief part to the rocks of which they are composed having resisted subaerial denudation better than the surrounding surface; this surface consequently has been gradually lowered, with the lines of harder rock left projecting. Nothing impresses the mind with the vast duration of time, according to our ideas of time, more forcibly than the conviction thus gained that subaerial agencies which apparently have so little power, and which seem to work so slowly, have produced great results.

When thus impressed with the slow rate at which the land is worn away through subaerial and littoral action, it is good, in order to appreciate the past duration of time, to consider, on the one hand, the masses of rock which have been removed over many extensive areas, and on the other hand the thickness of our sedimentary formations. I remember having been much struck when viewing volcanic islands, which have been worn by the waves and pared all round into perpendicular cliffs of one or two thousand feet in height; for the gentle slope of the lava-streams, due to their formerly liquid state, showed at a glance how far the hard, rocky beds had once extended into the open ocean. The same story is told still more plainly by faults,—those great cracks along which the strata have been upheaved on one side, or thrown down on the other, to the height or depth of thousands of feet; for since the crust cracked, and it makes no great difference whether the upheaval was sudden, or, as most geologists now believe, was slow and effected by many starts, the surface of the land has been so completely planed down that no trace of these vast dislocations is externally visible. The Craven fault, for instance, extends for upwards of 30 miles, and along this line the vertical displacement of the strata varies from 600 to 3000 feet. Professor Ramsay has published an account of a downthrow in Anglesea of 2300 feet; and he informs me that he fully believes that there is one in Merionethshire of 12,000 feet; yet in these cases there is nothing on the surface of the land to show such prodigious movements; the pile of rocks on either side of the crack having been smoothly swept away.

On the other hand, in all parts of the world the piles of sedimentary

strata are of wonderful thickness. In the Cordillera I estimated one mass
of conglomerate at ten thousand feet; and although conglomerates have
probably been accumulated at a quicker rate than finer sediments, yet
from being formed of worn and rounded pebbles, each of which bears the
stamp of time, they are good to show how slowly the mass must have been
heaped together. Professor Ramsay has given me the maximum thickness,
from actual measurement in most cases, of the successive formations in
different parts of Great Britain; and this is the result:—

	Feet.
Palæozoic strata (not including igneous beds)	57,154
Secondary strata	13,190
Tertiary strata	2,240

—making altogether 72,584 feet; that is, very nearly thirteen and three-
quarters British miles. Some of the formations, which are represented in
England by thin beds, are thousands of feet in thickness on the Continent.
Moreover, between each successive formation, we have, in the opinion of
most geologists, blank periods of enormous length. So that the lofty pile
of sedimentary rocks in Britain gives but an inadequate idea of the time
which has elapsed during their accumulation. The consideration of these
various facts impresses the mind almost in the same manner as does the
vain endeavour to grapple with the idea of eternity.

Nevertheless this impression is partly false. Mr. Croll, in an interesting
paper, remarks that we do not err "in forming too great a conception of
the length of geological periods," but in estimating them by years. When
geologists look at large and complicated phenomena, and then at the figures representing several million years, the two produce a totally different
effect on the mind, and the figures are at once pronounced too small.
In regard to subaerial denudation, Mr. Croll shows, by calculating the
known amount of sediment annually brought down by certain rivers, relatively to their areas of drainage, that 1000 feet of solid rock, as it became
gradually disintegrated, would thus be removed from the mean level of
the whole area in the course of six million years. This seems an astonishing result, and some considerations lead to the suspicion that it may be too
large, but even if halved or quartered it is still very surprising. Few of us,
however, know what a million really means: Mr. Croll gives the following
illustration: take a narrow strip of paper, 83 feet 4 inches in length, and
stretch it along the wall of a large hall; then mark off at one end the tenth
of an inch. This tenth of an inch will represent one hundred years, and
the entire strip a million years. But let it be borne in mind, in relation to
the subject of this work, what a hundred years implies, represented as it is
by a measure utterly insignificant in a hall of the above dimensions. Several eminent breeders, during a single lifetime, have so largely modified
some of the higher animals which propagate their kind much more slowly
than most of the lower animals, that they have formed what well deserves
to be called a new sub-breed. Few men have attended with due care to

any one strain for more than half a century, so that a hundred years represents the work of two breeders in succession. It is not to be supposed that species in a state of nature ever change so quickly as domestic animals under the guidance of methodical selection. The comparison would be in every way fairer with the effects which follow from unconscious selection, that is the preservation of the most useful or beautiful animals, with no intention of modifying the breed; but by this process of unconscious selection, various breeds have been sensibly changed in the course of two or three centuries.

Species, however, probably change much more slowly, and within the same country only a few change at the same time. This slowness follows from all the inhabitants of the same country being already so well adapted to each other, that new places in the polity of nature do not occur until after long intervals, due to the occurrence of physical changes of some kind, or through the immigration of new forms. Moreover variations or individual differences of the right nature, by which some of the inhabitants might be better fitted to their new places under the altered circumstances, would not always occur at once. Unfortunately we have no means of determining, according to the standards of years, how long a period it takes to modify a species; but to the subject of time we must return.

On the Poorness of Palæontological Collections

Now let us turn to our richest geological museums, and what a paltry display we behold! That our collections are imperfect is admitted by every one. The remark of that admirable palæontologist, Edward Forbes, should never be forgotten, namely, that very many fossil species are known and named from single and often broken specimens, or from a few specimens collected on some one spot. Only a small portion of the surface of the earth has been geologically explored, and no part with sufficient care, as the important discoveries made every year in Europe prove. No organism wholly soft can be preserved. Shells and bones decay and disappear when left on the bottom of the sea, where sediment is not accumulating. We probably take a quite erroneous view, when we assume that sediment is being deposited over nearly the whole bed of the sea, at a rate sufficiently quick to embed and preserve fossil remains. Throughout an enormously large proportion of the ocean, the bright blue tint of the water bespeaks its purity. The many cases on record of a formation conformably covered, after an immense interval of time, by another and later formation, without the underlying bed having suffered in the interval any wear and tear, seem explicable only on the view of the bottom of the sea not rarely lying for ages in an unaltered condition. The remains which do become embedded, if in sand or gravel, will, when the beds are upraised, generally be dissolved by the percolation of rain-water charged with carbonic acid. Some of the many kinds of animals which live on the beach between high and low water mark seem to be rarely preserved. For instance, the several species of the Chthamalinæ (a sub-family of sessile cirripedes) coat the rocks all over the world in infinite numbers: they are all strictly littoral, with the exception of a single Mediterranean species, which inhabits deep water, and this has been found fossil in Sicily, whereas not one other species has hitherto been found in any tertiary formation: yet it is known that the genus Chthamalus existed during the Chalk period. Lastly, many great deposits requiring a vast length of time for their accumulation, are entirely destitute of organic remains, without our being able to assign any reason: one of the most striking instances is that of the Flysch formation, which consists of shale and sandstone, several thousand, occasionally even six thousand feet in thickness, and extending for at least 300 miles from Vienna to Switzerland; and although this great mass has been most carefully searched, no fossils, except a few vegetable remains, have been found.

With respect to the terrestrial productions which lived during the Secondary and Palæozoic periods, it is superfluous to state that our evidence is fragmentary in an extreme degree. For instance, until recently not a land-shell was known belonging to either of these vast periods, with the exception of one species discovered by Sir C. Lyell and Dr. Dawson in the carboniferous strata of North America; but now land-shells have been found in the lias. In regard to mammiferous remains, a glance at the historical table published in Lyell's Manual will bring home the truth, how accidental and rare is their preservation, far better than pages of detail. Nor is their rarity surprising, when we remember how large a proportion of the bones of tertiary mammals have been discovered either in caves or in lacustrine deposits; and that not a cave or true lacustrine bed is known belonging to the age of our secondary or palæozoic formations.

But the imperfection in the geological record largely results from another and more important cause than any of the foregoing; namely, from the several formations being separated from each other by wide intervals of time. This doctrine has been emphatically admitted by many geologists and palæontologists, who, like E. Forbes, entirely disbelieve in the change of species. When we see the formations tabulated in written works, or when we follow them in nature, it is difficult to avoid believing that they are closely consecutive. But we know, for instance, from Sir R. Murchison's great work on Russia, what wide gaps there are in that country between the superimposed formations; so it is in North America, and in many other parts of the world. The most skilful geologist if his attention had been confined exclusively to these large territories, would never have suspected that, during the periods which were blank and barren in his own country, great piles of sediment, charged with new and peculiar forms of life, had elsewhere been accumulated. And if, in each separate territory, hardly any idea can be formed of the length of time which has elapsed between the consecutive formations, we may infer that this could nowhere be ascertained. The frequent and great changes in the mineralogical composition of consecutive formations, generally implying great changes in the geography of the surrounding lands, whence the sediment was derived, accord with the belief of vast intervals of time having elapsed between each formation.

We can, I think, see why the geological formations of each region are almost invariably intermittent; that is, have not followed each other in close sequence. Scarcely any fact struck me more when examining many hundred miles of the South American coasts, which have been upraised several hundred feet within the recent period, than the absence of any recent deposits sufficiently extensive to last for even a short geological period. Along the whole west coast, which is inhabited by a peculiar marine fauna, tertiary beds are so poorly developed, that no record of several successive and peculiar marine faunas will probably be preserved to a distant age. A little reflection will explain why, along the rising coast of the western side of South America, no extensive formations with recent or tertiary remains can anywhere be found, though the supply of sediment must for ages have been great, from the enormous degradation of the coast-rocks and from muddy streams entering the sea. The explanation, no doubt, is, that the littoral and sub-littoral deposits are continually worn away, as soon as they are brought up by the slow and gradual rising of the land within the grinding action of the coast-waves.

We may, I think, conclude that sediment must be accumulated in extremely thick, solid, or extensive masses, in order to withstand the incessant action of the waves, when first upraised and during successive oscillations of level as well as the subsequent subaerial degradation. Such thick and extensive accumulations of sediment may be formed in two ways; either in profound depths of the sea, in which case the bottom will not be inhabited by so many and such varied forms of life, as the more shallow seas; and the mass when upraised will give an imperfect record of the organisms which existed in the neighbourhood during the period of its accumulation. Or, sediment may be deposited to any thickness and extent over a shallow bottom, if it continue slowly to subside. In this latter case, as long as the rate of subsidence and the supply of sediment nearly balance each other, the sea will remain shallow and favourable for many and varied forms, and thus a rich fossiliferous formation, thick enough, when upraised, to resist a large amount of denudation, may be formed.

I am convinced that nearly all our ancient formations, which are throughout the greater part of their thickness *rich in fossils*, have thus been formed during subsidence. Since publishing my views on this subject in 1845, I have watched the progress of Geology, and have been surprised to note how author after author, in treating of this or that great formation, has come to the conclusion that it was accumulated during subsidence. I may add, that the only ancient tertiary formation on the west coast of South America, which has been bulky enough to resist such degradation as it has as yet suffered, but which will hardly last to a distant geological age, was deposited during a downward oscillation of level, and thus gained considerable thickness.

All geological facts tell us plainly that each area has undergone slow os cillations of level, and apparently these oscillations have affected wide spaces. Consequently, formations rich in fossils and sufficiently thick and extensive to resist subsequent degradation, will have been formed over wide spaces during periods of subsidence, but only where the supply of sediment was sufficient to keep the sea shallow and to embed and preserve the remains before they had time to decay. On the other hand, as long as the bed of the sea remains stationary, *thick* deposits cannot have been accumulated in the shallow parts, which are the most favourable to life. Still less can this have happened during the alternate periods of elevation; or, to speak more accurately, the beds which were then accumulated will generally have been destroyed by being upraised and brought within the limits of the coast-action.

These remarks apply chiefly to littoral and sub-littoral deposits. In the case of an extensive and shallow sea, such as that within a large part of the Malay Archipelago, where the depth varies from 30 or 40 to 60 fathoms, a widely extended formation might be formed during a period of elevation, and yet not suffer excessively from denudation during its slow upheaval; but the thickness of the formation could not be great, for owing to the elevatory movement it would be less than the depth in which it was formed; nor would the deposit be much consolidated, nor be capped by overlying formations, so that it would run a good chance of being worn away by atmospheric degradation and by the action of the sea during subsequent oscillations of level. It has, however, been suggested by Mr. Hopkins, that if one part of the area, after rising and before being denuded, subsided, the deposit formed during the rising movement, though not thick, might afterwards become protected by fresh accumulations, and thus be preserved for a long period.

Mr. Hopkins also expresses his belief that sedimentary beds of considerable horizontal extent have rarely been completely destroyed. But all geologists, excepting the few who believe that our present metamorphic schists and plutonic rocks once formed the primordial nucleus of the globe, will admit that these latter rocks have been stript of their coverings to an enormous extent. For it is scarcely possible that such rocks could have been solidified and crystallized whilst uncovered; but if the metamorphic action occurred at profound depths of the ocean, the former protecting mantle of rock may not have been very thick. Admitting then that gneiss, mica-schist, granite, diorite, &c., were once necessarily covered up, how can we account for the naked and extensive areas of such rocks in many parts of the world, except on the belief that they have subsequently been completely denuded of all overlying strata? That such extensive areas do exist cannot be doubted: the granitic region of Parime is described by Humboldt as being at least nineteen times as large as Switzerland. South of the Amazon, Boué colours an area composed of rocks of this nature as equal to that of Spain, France, Italy, part of Germany, and the British Islands, all conjoined. This region has not been carefully explored, but from the concurrent testimony of travellers, the granitic area is very large: thus, Von Eschwege gives a detailed section of these rocks.

stretching from Rio de Janeiro for 260 geographical miles inland in a straight line; and I travelled for 150 miles in another direction, and saw nothing but granitic rocks. Numerous specimens, collected along the whole coast from near Rio Janeiro to the mouth of the Plata, a distance of 1100 geographical miles, were examined by me, and they all belonged to this class. Inland, along the whole northern bank of the Plata I saw, besides modern tertiary beds, only one small patch of slightly metamorphosed rock, which alone could have formed a part of the original capping of the granitic series. Turning to a well-known region, namely, to the United States and Canada, as shown in Professor H. D. Rogers's beautiful map, I have estimated the areas by cutting out and weighing the paper, and I find that the metamorphic (excluding "the semi-metamorphic") and granitic rocks exceed, in the proportion of 19 to 12.5, the whole of the newer Palæozoic formations. In many regions the metamorphic and granitic rocks would be found much more widely extended than they appear to be, if all the sedimentary beds were removed which rest unconformably on them, and which could not have formed part of the original mantle under which they were crystallized. Hence it is probable that in some parts of the world whole formations have been completely denuded, with not a wreck left behind.

One remark is here worth a passing notice. During periods of elevation the area of the land and of the adjoining shoal parts of the sea will be increased, and new stations will often be formed:—all circumstances favourable, as previously explained, for the formation of new varieties and species; but during such periods there will generally be a blank in the geological record. On the other hand, during subsidence, the inhabited area and number of inhabitants will decrease (excepting on the shores of a continent when first broken up into an archipelago), and consequently during subsidence, though there will be much extinction, few new varieties or species will be formed; and it is during these very periods of subsidence, that the deposits which are richest in fossils have been accumulated.

On the Absence of Numerous Intermediate Varieties in any Single Formation

From these several considerations, it cannot be doubted that the geological record, viewed as a whole, is extremely imperfect; but if we confine our attention to any one formation, it becomes much more difficult to understand why we do not therein find closely graduated varieties between the allied species which lived at its commencement and at its close. Several cases are on record of the same species presenting varieties in the upper and lower parts of the same formation; thus, Trautschold gives a number of instances with Ammonites; and Hilgendorf has described a most curious case of ten graduated forms of Planorbis multiformis in the successive beds of a fresh-water formation in Switzerland. Although each formation has indisputably required a vast number of years for its deposi-

tion, several reasons can be given why each should not commonly include
a graduated series of links between the species which lived at its commencement and close; but I cannot assign due proportional weight to the
following considerations.

Although each formation may mark a very long lapse of years, each
probably is short compared with the period requisite to change one species
into another. I am aware that two palæontologists, whose opinions are
worthy of much deference, namely Bronn and Woodward, have concluded
that the average duration of each formation is twice or thrice as long as
the average duration of specific forms. But insuperable difficulties, as it
seems to me, prevent us from coming to any just conclusion on this head.
When we see a species first appearing in the middle of any formation, it
would be rash in the extreme to infer that it had not elsewhere previously
existed. So again when we find a species disappearing before the last
layers have been deposited, it would be equally rash to suppose that it
then became extinct. We forget how small the area of Europe is compared
with the rest of the world; nor have the several stages of the same formation throughout Europe been correlated with perfect accuracy.

We may safely infer that with marine animals of all kinds there has
been a large amount of migration due to climatal and other changes; and
when we see a species first appearing in any formation, the probability is
that it only then first immigrated into that area. It is well-known, for instance, that several species appear somewhat earlier in the palæozoic beds
of North America than in those of Europe; time having apparently been
required for their migration from the American to the European seas. In
examining the latest deposits in various quarters of the world, it has
everywhere been noted, that some few still existing species are common in
the deposit, but have become extinct in the immediately surrounding sea;
or, conversely, that some are now abundant in the neighbouring sea, but
are rare or absent in this particular deposit. It is an excellent lesson to reflect on the ascertained amount of migration of the inhabitants of Europe
during the glacial epoch, which forms only a part of one whole geological
period; and likewise to reflect on the changes of level, on the extreme
change of climate, and on the great lapse of time, all included within this
same glacial period. Yet it may be doubted whether, in any quarter of the
world, sedimentary deposits, *including fossil remains*, have gone on accumulating within the same area during the whole of this period. It is not,
for instance, probable that sediment was deposited during the whole of the
glacial period near the mouth of the Mississippi, within that limit of
depth at which marine animals can best flourish: for we know that great
geographical changes occurred in other parts of America during this space
of time. When such beds as were deposited in shallow water near the
mouth of the Mississippi during some part of the glacial period shall have
been upraised, organic remains will probably first appear and disappear
at different levels, owing to the migrations of species and to geographical
changes. And in the distant future, a geologist, examining these beds,
would be tempted to conclude that the average duration of life of the em-

bedded fossils had been less than that of the glacial period, instead of having been really far greater, that is, extending from before the glacial epoch
to the present day.

In order to get a perfect gradation between two forms in the upper and
lower parts of the same formation, the deposit must have gone on continuously accumulating during a long period, sufficient for the slow process of
modification; hence the deposit must be a very thick one; and the species
undergoing change must have lived in the same district throughout the
whole time. But we have seen that a thick formation, fossiliferous
throughout its entire thickness, can accumulate only during a period of
subsidence; and to keep the depth approximately the same, which is necessary that the same marine species may live on the same space, the supply of sediment must nearly counterbalance the amount of subsidence.
But this same movement of subsidence will tend to submerge the area
whence the sediment is derived, and thus diminish the supply, whilst the
downward movement continues. In fact, this nearly exact balancing between the supply of sediment and the amount of subsidence is probably a
rare contingency; for it has been observed by more than one palæontologist, that very thick deposits are usually barren of organic remains, except
near their upper or lower limits.

It would seem that each separate formation, like the whole pile of formations in any country, has generally been intermittent in its accumulation.
When we see, as is so often the case, a formation composed of beds of
widely different mineralogical composition, we may reasonably suspect
that the process of deposition has been more or less interrupted. Nor will
the closest inspection of a formation give us any idea of the length of time
which its deposition may have consumed. Many instances could be given
of beds only a few feet in thickness, representing formations, which are
elsewhere thousands of feet in thickness, and which must have required
an enormous period for their accumulation; yet no one ignorant of this
fact would have even suspected the vast lapse of time represented by the
thinner formation. Many cases could be given of the lower beds of a formation having been upraised, denuded, submerged, and then re-covered by
the upper beds of the same formation,—facts, showing what wide, yet
easily overlooked, intervals have occurred in its accumulation. In other
cases we have the plainest evidence in great fossilised trees, still standing
upright as they grew, of many long intervals of time and changes of level
during the process of deposition, which would not have been suspected,
had not the trees been preserved: thus Sir C. Lyell and Dr. Dawson found
carboniferous beds 1400 feet thick in Nova Scotia, with ancient root-bear-
ing strata, one above the other at no less than sixty-eight different levels.
Hence, when the same species occurs at the bottom, middle, and top of a
formation, the probability is that it has not lived on the same spot during
the whole period of deposition, but has disappeared and reappeared, perhaps many times, during the same geological period. Consequently if it
were to undergo a considerable amount of modification during the deposition of any one geological formation, a section would not include all the

fine intermediate gradations which must on our theory have existed, but abrupt, though perhaps slight, changes of form.

It is all-important to remember that naturalists have no golden rule by which to distinguish species and varieties; they grant some little varia-bility to each species, but when they meet with a somewhat greater amount of difference between any two forms, they rank both as species, unless they are enabled to connect them together by the closest intermedi-ate gradations; and this, from the reasons just assigned, we can seldom hope to effect in any one geological section. Supposing B and C to be two species, and a third, A, to be found in an older and underlying bed; even if A were strictly intermediate between B and C, it would simply be ranked as a third and distinct species, unless at the same time it could be closely connected by intermediate varieties with either one or both forms. Nor should it be forgotten, as before explained, that A might be the actual progenitor of B and C, and yet would not necessarily be strictly interme-diate between them in all respects. So that we might obtain the parent-species, and its several modified descendants from the lower and upper beds of the same formation, and unless we obtained numerous transitional gradations, we should not recognise their blood-relationship, and should consequently rank them as distinct species.

It is notorious on what excessively slight differences many palæontolo-gists have founded their species; and they do this the more readily if the specimens come from different sub-stages of the same formation. Some experienced conchologists are now sinking many of the very fine species of D'Orbigny and others into the rank of varieties; and on this view we do find the kind of evidence of change which on the theory we ought to find. Look again at the later tertiary deposits, which include many shells be-lieved by the majority of naturalists to be identical with existing species; but some excellent naturalists as Agassiz and Pictet, maintain that all these tertiary species are specifically distinct, though the distinction is ad-mitted to be very slight; so that here, unless we believe that these eminent naturalists have been misled by their imaginations, and that these late ter-tiary species really present no difference whatever from their living repre-sentatives, or unless we admit, in opposition to the judgment of most nat-uralists, that these tertiary species are all truly distinct from the recent, we have evidence of the frequent occurrence of slight modifications of the kind required. If we look to rather wider intervals of time, namely, to dis-tinct but consecutive stages of the same great formation, we find that the embedded fossils, though universally ranked as specifically different, yet are far more closely related to each other than are the species found in more widely separated formations; so that here again we have undoubted evidence of change in the direction required by the theory; but to this latter subject I shall return in the following chapter.

With animals and plants that propagate rapidly and do not wander much, there is reason to suspect, as we have formerly seen, that their varieties are generally at first local; and that such local varieties do not spread widely and supplant their parent-forms until they have been modified and perfected in some considerable degree. According to this view, the chance of discovering in a formation in any one country all the early stages of transition between any two forms, is small, for the successive changes are supposed to have been local or confined to some one spot. Most marine animals have a wide range; and we have seen that with plants it is those which have the widest range, that oftenest present varieties; so that, with shells and other marine animals, it is probable that those which had the widest range, far exceeding the limits of the known geological formations in Europe, have oftenest given rise, first to local varieties and ultimately to new species; and this again would greatly lessen the chance of our being able to trace the stages of transition in any one geological formation.

It is a more important consideration, leading to the same result, as lately insisted on by Dr. Falconer, namely, that the period during which each species underwent modification, though long as measured by years, was probably short in comparison with that during which it remained without undergoing any change.

It should not be forgotten, that at the present day, with perfect specimens for examination, two forms can seldom be connected by intermediate varieties, and thus proved to be the same species, until many specimens are collected from many places; and with fossil species this can rarely be done. We shall, perhaps, best perceive the improbability of our being enabled to connect species by numerous, fine, intermediate, fossil links, by asking ourselves whether, for instance, geologists at some future period will be able to prove that our different breeds of cattle, sheep, horses, and dogs are descended from a single stock or from several aboriginal stocks; or, again, whether certain sea-shells inhabiting the shores of North America, which are ranked by some conchologists as distinct species from their European representatives, and by other conchologists as only varieties, are really varieties, or are, as it is called, specifically distinct. This could be effected by the future geologist only by his discovering in a fossil state numerous intermediate gradations; and such success is improbable in the highest degree.

It has been asserted over and over again, by writers who believe in the immutability of species, that geology yields no linking forms. This assertion, as we shall see in the next chapter, is certainly erroneous. As Sir J. Lubbock has remarked, "Every species is a link between other allied forms." If we take a genus having a score of species, recent and extinct, and destroy four-fifths of them, no one doubts that the remainder will stand much more distinct from each other. If the extreme forms in the genus happen to have been thus destroyed, the genus itself will stand more distinct from other allied genera. What geological research has not revealed, is the former existence of infinitely numerous gradations, as fine as existing varieties, connecting together nearly all existing and extinct species. But this ought not to be expected; yet this has been repeatedly advanced as a most serious objection against my views.

It may be worth while to sum up the foregoing remarks on the causes of the imperfection of the geological record under an imaginary illustration. The Malay Archipelago is about the size of Europe from the North Cape to the Mediterranean, and from Britain to Russia; and therefore equals all the geological formations which have been examined with any accuracy, excepting those of the United States of America. I fully agree with Mr. Godwin-Austen, that the present condition of the Malay Archipelago, with its numerous large islands separated by wide and shallow seas, probably represents the former state of Europe, whilst most of our formations were accumulating. The Malay Archipelago is one of the richest regions in organic beings; yet if all the species were to be collected which have ever lived there, how imperfectly would they represent the natural history of the world!

But we have every reason to believe that the terrestrial productions of the archipelago would be preserved in an extremely imperfect manner in the formations which we suppose to be there accumulating. Not many of the strictly littoral animals, or of those which lived on naked submarine rocks, would be embedded; and those embedded in gravel or sand would not endure to a distant epoch. Wherever sediment did not accumulate on the bed of the sea, or where it did not accumulate at a sufficient rate to protect organic bodies from decay, no remains could be preserved.

Formations rich in fossils of many kinds, and of thickness sufficient to last to an age as distant in futurity as the secondary formations lie in the past, would generally be formed in the archipelago only during periods of subsidence. These periods of subsidence would be separated from each other by immense intervals of time, during which the area would be either stationary or rising; whilst rising, the fossiliferous formations on the steeper shores would be destroyed, almost as soon as accumulated, by the incessant coast-action, as we now see on the shores of South America. Even throughout the extensive and shallow seas within the archipelago, sedimentary beds could hardly be accumulated of great thickness during the periods of elevation, or become capped and protected by subsequent deposits, so as to have a good chance of enduring to a very distant future. During the periods of subsidence, there would probably be much extinction of life; during the periods of elevation, there would be much variation, but the geological record would then be less perfect.

It may be doubted whether the duration of any one great period of subsidence over the whole or part of the archipelago, together with a contemporaneous accumulation of sediment, would *exceed* the average duration of the same specific forms; and these contingencies are indispensable for the preservation of all the transitional gradations between any two or more species. If such gradations were not all fully preserved, transitional varieties would merely appear as so many new, though closely allied species. It is also probable that each great period of subsidence would be interrupted by oscillations of level, and that slight climatal changes would intervene during such lengthy periods; and in these cases the inhabitants of the archipelago would migrate, and no closely consecutive record of their modifications could be preserved in any one formation.

Very many of the marine inhabitants of the archipelago now range thousands of miles beyond its confines; and analogy plainly leads to the belief that it would be chiefly these far-ranging species, though only some of them, which would oftenest produce new varieties; and the varieties would at first be local or confined to one place, but if possessed of any decided advantage, or when further modified and improved, they would slowly spread and supplant their parent-forms. When such varieties returned to their ancient homes, as they would differ from their former state in a nearly uniform, though perhaps extremely slight degree, and as they would be found embedded in slightly different sub-stages of the same formation, they would, according to the principles followed by many palæontologists, be ranked as new and distinct species.

If then there be some degree of truth in these remarks, we have no right to expect to find, in our geological formations, an infinite number of those fine transitional forms which, on our theory, have connected all the past and present species of the same group into one long and branching chain of life. We ought only to look for a few links, and such assuredly we do find—some more distantly, some more closely, related to each other; and these links, let them be ever so close, if found in different stages of the same formation, would, by many palæontologists, be ranked as distinct species. But I do not pretend that I should ever have suspected how poor was the record in the best preserved geological sections, had not the absence of innumerable transitional links between the species which lived at the commencement and close of each formation, pressed so hardly on my theory.

On the sudden Appearance of whole Groups of allied Species

The abrupt manner in which whole groups of species suddenly appear in certain formations, has been urged by several palæontologists—for instance, by Agassiz, Pictet, and Sedgwick—as a fatal objection to the belief in the transmutation of species. If numerous species, belonging to the same genera or families, have really started into life at once, the fact would be fatal to the theory of evolution through natural selection. For the development by this means of a group of forms, all of which are descended from some one progenitor, must have been an extremely slow process; and the progenitors must have lived long before their modified descendants. But we continually overrate the perfection of the geological record, and falsely infer, because certain genera or families have not been found beneath a certain stage, that they did not exist before that stage. In all cases positive palæontological evidence may be implicitly trusted; negative evidence is worthless, as experience has so often shown. We continually forget how large the world is, compared with the area over which our geological formations have been carefully examined; we forget that groups of species may elsewhere have long existed, and have slowly multiplied, before they invaded the ancient archipelagoes of Europe and the United States. We do not make due allowance for the intervals of time which have elapsed between our consecutive formations,—longer perhaps in many cases than the time required for the accumulation of each formation. These intervals will have given time for the multiplication of species from some one parent-form: and in the succeeding formation, such groups or species will appear as if suddenly created.

I may here recall a remark formerly made, namely, that it might require a long succession of ages to adapt an organism to some new and peculiar line of life, for instance, to fly through the air; and consequently that the transitional forms would often long remain confined to some one region; but that, when this adaptation had once been effected, and a few species had thus acquired a great advantage over other organisms, a comparatively short time would be necessary to produce many divergent forms, which would spread rapidly and widely, throughout the world. Professor Pictet, in his excellent Review of this work, in commenting on early transitional forms, and taking birds as an illustration, cannot see how the successive modifications of the anterior limbs of a supposed prototype could possibly have been of any advantage. But look at the penguins of the Southern Ocean; have not these birds their front limbs in this precise intermediate state of "neither true arms nor true wings"? Yet these birds hold their place victoriously in the battle for life; for they exist in infinite numbers and of many kinds. I do not suppose that we here see the real transitional grades through which the wings of birds have passed; but what special difficulty is there in believing that it might profit the modified descendants of the penguin, first to become enabled to flap along the surface of the sea like the logger-headed duck, and ultimately to rise from its surface and glide through the air?

I will now give a few examples to illustrate the foregoing remarks, and to show how liable we are to error in supposing that whole groups of species have suddenly been produced. Even in so short an interval as that between the first and second editions of Pictet's great work on Palæontology, published in 1844–46 and in 1853–57, the conclusions on the first appearance and disappearance of several groups of animals have been considerably modified; and a third edition would require still further changes. I may recall the well-known fact that in geological treatises, published not many years ago, mammals were always spoken of as having abruptly come in at the commencement of the tertiary series. And now one of the richest known accumulations of fossil mammals belongs to the middle of the secondary series; and true mammals have been discovered in the new red sandstone at nearly the commencement of this great series. Cuvier used to urge that no monkey occurred in any tertiary stratum; but now extinct species have been discovered in India, South America and in Europe, as far back as the miocene stage. Had it not been for the rare accident of the preservation of the footsteps in the new red sandstone of the United States, who would have ventured to suppose that no less than at least thirty different bird-like animals, some of gigantic size, existed during that period? Not a fragment of bone has been discovered in these beds. Not long ago, palæontologists maintained that the whole class of birds came suddenly into existence during the eocene period; but now we know, on the authority of Professor Owen, that a bird certainly lived during the deposition of the upper greensand; and still more recently, that strange bird, the Archeopteryx, with a long lizard-like tail, bearing a pair of feathers on each joint, and with its wings furnished with two free claws, has been discovered in the oolitic slates of Solenhofen. Hardly any recent discovery shows more forcibly than this, how little we as yet know of the former inhabitants of the world.

I may give another instance, which, from having passed under my own eyes, has much struck me. In a memoir on Fossil Sessile Cirripedes, I stated that, from the large number of existing and extinct tertiary species; from the extraordinary abundance of the individuals of many species all over the world, from the Arctic regions to the equator, inhabiting various zones of depths from the upper tidal limits to 50 fathoms; from the perfect manner in which specimens are preserved in the oldest tertiary beds; from the ease with which even a fragment of a valve can be recognised; from all these circumstances, I inferred that, had sessile cirripedes existed during the secondary periods, they would certainly have been preserved and discovered; and as not one species had then been discovered in beds of this age, I concluded that this great group had been suddenly developed at the commencement of the tertiary series. This was a sore trouble to me, adding as I then thought one more instance of the abrupt appearance of a great group of species. But my work had hardly been published, when a skilful palæontologist, M. Bosquet, sent me a drawing of a perfect specimen of an unmistakable sessile cirripede, which he had himself extracted from the chalk of Belgium. And, as if to make the case as striking as possible, this cirripede was a Chthamalus, a very common, large, and ubiquitous genus, of which not one species has as yet been found even in any tertiary stratum. Still more recently, a Pyrgoma, a member of a distinct sub-family of sessile cirripedes, has been discovered by Mr. Woodward in the upper chalk; so that we now have abundant evidence of the existence of this group of animals during the secondary period.

The case most frequently insisted on by palæontologists of the apparently sudden appearance of a whole group of species, is that of the teleostean fishes, low down, according to Agassiz, in the Chalk period. This group includes the large majority of existing species. But certain Jurassic and Triassic forms are now commonly admitted to be teleostean; and even some palæozoic forms have thus been classed by one high authority. If the teleosteans had really appeared suddenly in the northern hemisphere at the commencement of the chalk formation the fact would have been highly remarkable; but it would not have formed an insuperable difficulty, unless it could likewise have been shown that at the same period the species were suddenly and simultaneously developed in other quarters of the world. It is almost superfluous to remark that hardly any fossil-fish are known from south of the equator; and by running through Pictet's Palæontology it will be seen that very few species are known from several formations in Europe. Some few families of fish now have a confined range; the teleostean fishes might formerly have had a similarly confined range, and after having been largely developed in some one sea, have spread widely. Nor have we any right to suppose that the seas of the world have always been so freely open from south to north as they are at present. Even at this day, if the Malay Archipelago were converted into land, the tropical parts of the Indian Ocean would form a large and perfectly enclosed basin, in which any great group of marine animals might be multiplied: and here they would remain confined, until some of the species became adapted to a cooler climate, and were enabled to double the Southern capes of Africa or Australia, and thus reach other and distant seas.

From these considerations, from our ignorance of the geology of other countries beyond the confines of Europe and the United States, and from the revolution in our palæontological knowledge effected by the discoveries of the last dozen years, it seems to me to be about as rash to dogmatize on the succession of organic forms throughout the world, as it would be for a naturalist to land for five minutes on a barren point in Australia, and then to discuss the number and range of its productions.

On the sudden Appearance of Groups of allied Species in the lowest known Fossiliferous Strata

There is another and allied difficulty, which is much more serious. I allude to the manner in which species belonging to several of the main divisions of the animal kingdom suddenly appear in the lowest known fossiliferous rocks. Most of the arguments which have convinced me that all the existing species of the same group are descended from a single progenitor, apply with equal force to the earliest known species. For instance, it cannot be doubted that all the Cambrian and Silurian trilobites are descended from some one crustacean, which must have lived long before the Cambrian age, and which probably differed greatly from any known animal. Some of the most ancient animals, as the Nautilus, Lingula, &c., do not differ much from living species; and it cannot on our theory be supposed, that these old species were the progenitors of all the species belonging to the same groups which have subsequently appeared, for they are not in any degree intermediate in character.

Consequently, if the theory be true, it is indisputable that before the lowest Cambrian stratum was deposited long periods elapsed, as long as, or probably far longer than, the whole interval from the Cambrian age to the present day; and that during these vast periods the world swarmed with living creatures. Here we encounter a formidable objection; for it seems doubtful whether the earth, in a fit state for the habitation of living creatures, has lasted long enough. Sir W. Thompson concludes that the consolidation of the crust can hardly have occurred less than 20 or more than 400 million years ago, but probably not less than 98 or more than 200 million years. These very wide limits show how doubtful the data are; and other elements may have hereafter to be introduced into the problem. Mr. Croll estimates that about 60 million years have elapsed since the Cambrian period, but this, judging from the small amount of organic change since the commencement of the Glacial epoch, appears a very short time for the many and great mutations of life, which have certainly occurred since the Cambrian formation; and the previous 140 million years can hardly be considered as sufficient for the development of the varied forms of life which already existed during the Cambrian period. It is, however, probable, as Sir William Thompson insists, that the world at a very early period was subjected to more rapid and violent changes in its physical conditions than those now occurring; and such changes would have tended to induce changes at a corresponding rate in the organisms which then existed.

To the question why we do not find rich fossiliferous deposits belonging to these assumed earliest periods prior to the Cambrian system, I can give no satisfactory answer. Several eminent geologists, with Sir R. Murchison at their head, were until recently convinced that we beheld in the organic remains of the lowest Silurian stratum the first dawn of life. Other highly competent judges, as Lyell and E. Forbes, have disputed this conclusion. We should not forget that only a small portion of the world is known with accuracy. Not very long ago M. Barrande added another and lower stage, abounding with new and peculiar species, beneath the then known Silurian system; and now, still lower down in the Lower Cambrian formation, Mr. Hicks has found in South Wales beds rich in trilobites, and containing various molluscs and annelids. The presence of phosphatic nodules and bituminous matter, even in some of the lowest azoic rocks, probably indicates life at these periods; and the existence of the Eozoon in the Laurentian formation of Canada is generally admitted. There are three great series of strata beneath the Silurian system in Canada, in the lowest of which the Eozoon is found. Sir W. Logan states that their "united thickness may possibly far surpass that of all the succeeding rocks, from the base of the palæozoic series to the present time. We are thus carried back to a period so remote, that the appearance of the so-called Primordial fauna (of Barrande) may by some be considered as a comparatively modern event." The Eozoon belongs to the most lowly organised of all classes of animals, but is highly organised for its class; it existed in countless numbers, and, as Dr. Dawson has remarked, certainly preyed on other minute organic beings, which must have lived in great numbers. Thus the words, which I wrote in 1859, about the existence of living beings long before the Cambrian period, and which are almost the same with those since used by Sir W. Logan, have proved true. Nevertheless, the difficulty of assigning any good reason for the absence of vast piles of strata rich in fossils beneath the Cambrian system is very great. It does not seem probable that the most ancient beds have been quite worn away by denudation, or that their fossils have been wholly obliterated by metamorphic action, for if this had been the case we should have found only small remnants of the formations next succeeding them in age, and these would always have existed in partially metamorphosed condition. But the descriptions which we possess of the Silurian deposits over immense territories in Russia and in North America, do not support the view, that the older a formation is, the more invariably it has suffered extreme denudation and metamorphism.

The case at present must remain inexplicable; and may be truly urged as a valid argument against the views here entertained. To show that it may hereafter receive some explanation, I will give the following hypothesis. From the nature of the organic remains which do not appear to have inhabited profound depths, in the several formations of Europe and of the United States; and from the amount of sediment, miles in thickness, of which the formations are composed, we may infer that from first to last large islands or tracts of land, whence the sediment was derived, occurred in the neighbourhood of the now existing continents of Europe and North America. This same view has since been maintained by Agassiz and others. But we do not know what was the state of things in the intervals between the several successive formations; whether Europe and the United States during these intervals existed as dry land, or as a submarine surface near land, on which sediment was not deposited, or as the bed of an open and unfathomable sea.

Looking to the existing oceans, which are thrice as extensive as the land, we see them studded with many islands; but hardly one truly oceanic island (with the exception of New Zealand, if this can be called a truly oceanic island) is as yet known to afford even a remnant of any palæozoic or secondary formation. Hence we may perhaps infer, that during the palæozoic and secondary periods, neither continents nor continental islands existed where our oceans now extend; for had they existed, palæozoic and secondary formations would in all probability have been accumulated from sediment derived from their wear and tear; and these would have been at least partially upheaved by the oscillations of level, which must have intervened during these enormously long periods. If then we may infer anything from these facts, we may infer that, where our oceans now extend, oceans have extended from the remotest period of which we have any record; and on the other hand, that where continents now exist, large tracts of land have existed, subjected no doubt to great oscillations of level, since the Cambrian period. The coloured map appended to my volume on Coral Reefs, led me to conclude that the great oceans are still mainly areas of subsidence, the great archipelagoes still areas of oscillations of level, and the continents areas of elevation. But we have no reason to assume that things have thus remained from the beginning of the world. Our continents seem to have been formed by a preponderance, during many oscillations of level, of the force of elevation; but may not the areas of preponderant movement have changed in the lapse of ages? At a period long antecedent to the Cambrian epoch, continents may have existed where oceans are now spread out; and clear and open oceans may have existed where our continents now stand. Nor should we be justified in assuming that if, for instance, the bed of the Pacific Ocean were now converted into a continent we should there find sedimentary formations in a recognisable condition older than the Cambrian strata, supposing such to have been formerly deposited; for it might well happen that strata which had subsided some miles nearer to the centre of the earth, and which had been pressed on by an enormous weight of superincumbent water, might have undergone far more metamorphic action than strata which have always remained nearer to the surface. The immense areas in some parts of the world, for instance in South America, of naked metamorphic rocks, which must have been heated under great pressure, have always seemed to me to require some special explanation; and we may perhaps believe that we see in these large areas, the many formations long anterior to the Cambrian epoch in a completely metamorphosed and denuded condition.

The several difficulties here discussed, namely—that, though we find in our geological formations many links between the species which now exist and which formerly existed, we do not find infinitely numerous fine transitional forms closely joining them all together;—the sudden manner in which several groups of species first appear in our European formations;—the almost entire absence, as at present known, of formations rich in fossils beneath the Cambrian strata,—are all undoubtedly of the most serious nature. We see this in the fact that the most eminent palæontologists, namely, Cuvier, Agassiz, Barrande, Pictet, Falconer, E. Forbes, &c., and all our greatest geologists, as Lyell, Murchison, Sedgwick, &c., have unanimously, often vehemently, maintained the immutability of species. But Sir Charles Lyell now gives the support of his high authority to the opposite side; and most geologists and palæontologists are much shaken in their former belief. Those who believe that the geological record is in any degree perfect, will undoubtedly at once reject the theory. For my part, following out Lyell's metaphor, I look at the geological record as a history of the world imperfectly kept, and written in a changing dialect; of this history we possess the last volume alone, relating only to two or three countries. Of this volume, only here and there a short chapter has been preserved; and of each page, only here and there a few lines. Each word of the slowly-changing language, more or less different in the successive chapters, may represent the forms of life, which are entombed in our consecutive formations, and which falsely appear to have been abruptly introduced. On this view, the difficulties above discussed are greatly diminished, or even disappear.

CHAPTER XI

ON THE GEOLOGICAL SUCCESSION OF ORGANIC BEINGS

On the slow and successive appearance of new species—On their different rates of change—Species once lost do not reappear—Groups of species follow the same general rules in their appearance and disappearance as do single species—On extinction—On simultaneous changes in the forms of life throughout the world—On the affinities of extinct species to each other and to living species—On the state of development of ancient forms—On the succession of the same types within the same areas—Summary of preceding and present chapter.

LET us now see whether the several facts and laws relating to the geological succession of organic beings accord best with the common view of the immutability of species, or with that of their slow and gradual modification, through variation and natural selection.

New species have appeared very slowly, one after another, both on the land and in the waters. Lyell has shown that it is hardly possible to resist the evidence on this head in the case of the several tertiary stages; and every year tends to fill up the blanks between the stages, and to make the proportion between the lost and existing forms more gradual. In some of the most recent beds, though undoubtedly of high antiquity if measured by years, only one or two species are extinct, and only one or two are new, having appeared there for the first time, either locally, or, as far as we know, on the face of the earth. The secondary formations are more broken; but, as Bronn has remarked, neither the appearance nor disappearance of the many species embedded in each formation has been simultaneous.

Species belonging to different genera and classes have not changed at the same rate, or in the same degree. In the older tertiary beds a few living shells may still be found in the midst of a multitude of extinct forms. Falconer has given a striking instance of a similar fact, for an existing crocodile is associated with many lost mammals and reptiles in the sub-Himalayan deposits. The Silurian Lingula differs but little from the living species of this genus; whereas most of the other Silurian Molluscs and all the Crustaceans have changed greatly. The productions of the land seem to have changed at a quicker rate than those of the sea, of which a striking instance has been observed in Switzerland. There is some reason to believe that organisms high in the scale, change more quickly than those that are low: though there are exceptions to this rule. The amount of organic change, as Pictet has remarked, is not the same in each successive so-called formation. Yet if we compare any but the most closely related formations, all the species will be found to have undergone some change. When a species has once disappeared from the face of the earth, we have no reason to believe that the same identical form ever reappears. The strongest apparent exception to this latter rule is that of the so-called "colonies" of M. Barrande, which intrude for a period in the midst of an older formation, and then allow the pre-existing fauna to reappear; but Lyell's explanation, namely, that it is a case of temporary migration from a distinct geographical province, seems satisfactory.

These several facts accord well with our theory, which includes no fixed law of development, causing all the inhabitants of an area to change abruptly, or simultaneously, or to an equal degree. The process of modification must be slow, and will generally effect only a few species at the same time; for the variability of each species is independent of that of all others. Whether such variations or individual differences as may arise will be accumulated through natural selection in a greater or less degree, thus causing a greater or less amount of permanent modification, will depend on many complex contingencies—on the variations being of a beneficial nature, on the freedom of intercrossing, on the slowly changing physical conditions of the country, on the immigration of new colonists, and on the nature of the other inhabitants with which the varying species come into competition. Hence it is by no means surprising that one species should retain the same identical form much longer than others; or, if changing, should change in a less degree. We find similar relations between the existing inhabitants of distinct countries; for instance, the land-shells and coleopterous insects of Madeira have come to differ considerably from their nearest allies on the continent of Europe, whereas the marine shells and birds have remained unaltered. We can perhaps understand the apparently quicker rate of change in terrestrial and in more highly organised productions compared with marine and lower productions, by the more complex relations of the higher beings to their organic and inorganic conditions of life, as explained in a former chapter. When many of the inhabitants of any area have become modified and improved, we can understand, on the principle of competition, and from the all-important relations of organism to organism in the struggle for life, that any form which did not become in some degree modified and improved, would be liable to extermination. Hence we see why all the species in the same region do at last, if we look to long enough intervals of time, become modified, for otherwise they would become extinct.

In members of the same class the average amount of change, during long and equal periods of time, may, perhaps, be nearly the same; but as the accumulation of enduring formations, rich in fossils, depends on great masses of sediment being deposited on subsiding areas, our formations have been almost necessarily accumulated at wide and irregularly intermittent intervals of time; consequently the amount of organic change exhibited by the fossils embedded in consecutive formations is not equal. Each formation, on this view, does not mark a new and complete act of creation, but only an occasional scene, taken almost at hazard, in an ever slowly changing drama.

We can clearly understand why a species when once lost should never reappear, even if the very same conditions of life, organic and inorganic, should recur. For though the offspring of one species might be adapted (and no doubt this has occurred in innumerable instances) to fill the place of another species in the economy of nature, and thus supplant it; yet the two forms—the old and the new—would not be identically the same; for both would almost certainly inherit different characters from their distinct progenitors; and organisms already differing would vary in a different manner. For instance, it is possible, if all our fantail pigeons were destroyed, that fanciers might make a new breed hardly distinguishable from the present breed; but if the parent rock-pigeon were likewise destroyed, and under nature we have every reason to believe that parent forms are generally supplanted and exterminated by their improved offspring, it is incredible that a fantail, identical with the existing breed, could be raised from any other species of pigeon, or even from any other well-established race of the domestic pigeon, for the successive variations would almost certainly be in some degree different, and the newly-formed variety would probably inherit from its progenitor some characteristic differences.

Groups of species, that is, genera and families, follow the same general rules in their appearance and disappearance as do single species, changing more or less quickly, and in a greater or lesser degree. A group, when it has once disappeared, never reappears; that is, its existence, as long as it lasts, is continuous. I am aware that there are some apparent exceptions to this rule, but the exceptions are surprisingly few, so few that E. Forbes, Pictet, and Woodward (though all strongly opposed to such views as I maintain) admit its truth; and the rule strictly accords with the theory. For all the species of the same group, however long it may have lasted, are the modified descendants one from the other, and all from a common progenitor. In the genus Lingula, for instance, the species which have successively appeared at all ages must have been connected by an unbroken series of generations, from the lowest Silurian stratum to the present day.

We have seen in the last chapter that whole groups of species sometimes falsely appear to have been abruptly developed; and I have attempted to give an explanation of this fact, which if true would be fatal to my views. But such cases are certainly exceptional; the general rule being a gradual increase in number, until the group reaches its maximum, and then, sooner or later, a gradual decrease. If the number of the species included within a genus, or the number of the genera within a family, be represented by a vertical line of varying thickness, ascending through the successive geological formations, in which the species are found, the line will sometimes falsely appear to begin at its lower end, not in a sharp point, but abruptly; it then gradually thickens upwards, often keeping of equal thickness for a space, and ultimately thins out in the upper beds, marking the decrease and final extinction of the species. This gradual increase in number of the species of a group is strictly conformable with the theory, for the species of the same genus, and the genera of the same family, can increase only slowly and progressively; the process of modification and the production of a number of allied forms necessarily being a slow and gradual process,—one species first giving rise to two or three varieties, these being slowly converted into species, which in their turn produce by equally slow steps other varieties and species, and so on, like the branching of a great tree from a single stem, till the group becomes large.

On Extinction

We have as yet only spoken incidentally of the disappearance of species and of groups of species. On the theory of natural selection, the extinction of old forms and the production of new and improved forms are intimately connected together. The old notion of all the inhabitants of the earth having been swept away by catastrophes at successive periods is very generally given up, even by those geologists, as Elie de Beaumont, Murchison, Barrande, &c., whose general views would naturally lead them to this conclusion. On the contrary, we have every reason to believe, from the study of the tertiary formations, that species and groups of species gradually disappear, one after another, first from one spot, then from another, and finally from the world. In some few cases however, as by the breaking of an isthmus and the consequent irruption of a multitude of new inhabitants into an adjoining sea, or by the final subsidence of an island, the process of extinction may have been rapid. Both single species and whole groups of species last for very unequal periods; some groups, as we have seen, have endured from the earliest known dawn of life to the present day; some have disappeared before the close of the palæozoic period. No fixed law seems to determine the length of time during which any single species or any single genus endures. There is reason to believe that the extinction of a whole group of species is generally a slower process than their production: if their appearance and disappearance be represented, as before, by a vertical line of varying thickness the line is found to taper more gradually at its upper end, which marks the progress of extermination, than at its lower end, which marks the first appearance and the early increase in number of the species. In some cases, however, the extermination of whole groups, as of ammonites, towards the close of the secondary period, has been wonderfully sudden.

The extinction of species has been involved in the most gratuitous mystery. Some authors have even supposed that, as the individual has a definite length of life, so have species a definite duration. No one can have marvelled more than I have done at the extinction of species. When I found in La Plata the tooth of a horse embedded with the remains of Mastodon, Megatherium, Toxodon, and other extinct monsters, which all co-existed with still living shells at a very late geological period, I was filled with astonishment; for, seeing that the horse, since its introduction by the Spaniards into South America, has run wild over the whole coun-

try and has increased in numbers at an unparalleled rate, I asked myself
what could so recently have exterminated the former horse under conditions of life apparently so favourable. But my astonishment was ground-
less. Professor Owen soon perceived that the tooth, though so like that of
the existing horse, belonged to an extinct species. Had this horse been still
living, but in some degree rare, no naturalist would have felt the least surprise at its rarity; for rarity is the attribute of a vast number of species
of all classes, in all countries. If we ask ourselves why this or that species
is rare, we answer that something is unfavourable in its conditions of life;
but what that something is we can hardly ever tell. On the supposition of
the fossil horse still existing as a rare species, we might have felt certain,
from the analogy of all other mammals, even of the slow-breeding elephant, and from the history of the naturalisation of the domestic horse in
South America, that under more favourable conditions it would in a very
few years have stocked the whole continent. But we could not have told
what the unfavourable conditions were which checked its increase,
whether some one or several contingencies, and at what period of the
horse's life, and in what degree they severally acted. If the conditions had
gone on, however slowly, becoming less and less favourable, we assuredly
should not have perceived the fact, yet the fossil horse would certainly
have become rarer and rarer, and finally extinct;—its place being seized
on by some more successful competitor.

It is most difficult always to remember that the increase of every creature is constantly being checked by unperceived hostile agencies; and
that these same unperceived agencies are amply sufficient to cause rarity,
and finally extinction. So little is this subject understood, that I have
heard surprise repeatedly expressed at such great monsters as the Mastodon and the more ancient Dinosaurians having become extinct; as if mere
bodily strength gave victory in the battle of life. Mere size, on the contrary, would in some cases determine, as has been remarked by Owen,
quicker extermination from the greater amount of requisite food. Before
man inhabited India or Africa, some cause must have checked the continued increase of the existing elephant. A highly capable judge, Dr. Falconer, believes that it is chiefly insects which, from incessantly harassing and
weakening the elephant in India, check its increase; and this was Bruce's
conclusion with respect to the African elephant in Abyssinia. It is certain
that insects and blood-sucking bats determine the existence of the larger
naturalized quadrupeds in several parts of S. America.

We see in many cases in the more recent tertiary formations, that rarity precedes extinction; and we know that this has been the progress of
events with those animals which have been exterminated, either locally or
wholly, through man's agency. I may repeat what I published in 1845,
namely, that to admit that species generally become rare before they become extinct—to feel no surprise at the rarity of a species, and yet to
marvel greatly when the species ceases to exist, is much the same as to
admit that sickness in the individual is the forerunner of death—to feel

no surprise at sickness, but, when the sick man dies, to wonder and to suspect that he died by some deed of violence.

The theory of natural selection is grounded on the belief that each new
variety and ultimately each new species, is produced and maintained by
having some advantage over those with which it comes into competition;
and the consequent extinction of the less-favoured forms almost inevitably follows. It is the same with our domestic productions; when a new
and slightly improved variety has been raised, it at first supplants the less
improved varieties in the same neighbourhood; when much improved it is
transported far and near, like our short-horn cattle, and takes the place of
other breeds in other countries. Thus the appearance of new forms and
the disappearance of old forms, both those naturally and those artificially
produced, are bound together. In flourishing groups, the number of new
specific forms which have been produced within a given time has at some
periods probably been greater than the number of the old specific forms
which have been exterminated; but we know that species have not gone
on indefinitely increasing, at least during the later geological epochs, so
that, looking to later times, we may believe that the production of new
forms has caused the extinction of about the same number of old forms.

The competition will generally be most severe, as formerly explained
and illustrated by examples, between the forms which are most like each
other in all respects. Hence the improved and modified descendants of a
species will generally cause the extermination of the parent-species; and
if many new forms have been developed from any one species, the nearest
allies of that species, *i.e.* the species of the same genus, will be the most liable to extermination. Thus, as I believe, a number of new species descended from one species, that is a new genus, comes to supplant an old
genus, belonging to the same family. But it must often have happened
that a new species belonging to some one group has seized on the place occupied by a species belonging to a distinct group, and thus have caused its
extermination. If many allied forms be developed from the successful intruder, many will have to yield their places; and it will generally be the
allied forms, which will suffer from some inherited inferiority in common.
But whether it be species belonging to the same or to a distinct class,
which have yielded their places to other modified and improved species, a
few of the sufferers may often be preserved for a long time, from being fitted to some peculiar line of life, or from inhabiting some distant and isolated station, where they will have escaped severe competition. For instance, some species of Trigonia, a great genus of shells in the secondary
formations, survive in the Australian seas; and a few members of the
great and almost extinct group of Ganoid fishes still inhabit our fresh waters. Therefore the utter extinction of a group is generally, as we have
seen, a slower process than its production.

With respect to the apparently sudden extermination of whole families
or orders, as of Trilobites at the close of the palæozoic period and of Ammonites at the close of the secondary period, we must remember what has

been already said on the probable wide intervals of time between our consecutive formations; and in these intervals there may have been much
slow extermination. Moreover, when, by sudden immigration or by unusually rapid development, many species of a new group have taken possession of an area, many of the older species will have been exterminated
in a correspondingly rapid manner; and the forms which thus yield their
places will commonly be allied, for they will partake of the same inferiority in common.

Thus, as it seems to me, the manner in which single species and whole
groups of species become extinct accords well with the theory of natural
selection. We need not marvel at extinction; if we must marvel, let it be
at our own presumption in imagining for a moment that we understand
the many complex contingencies on which the existence of each species
depends. If we forget for an instant that each species tends to increase inordinately, and that some check is always in action, yet seldom perceived
by us, the whole economy of nature will be utterly obscured. Whenever
we can precisely say why this species is more abundant in individuals
than that; why this species and not another can be naturalised in a given
country; then, and not until then, we may justly feel surprise why we
cannot account for the extinction of any particular species or group of
species.

On the Forms of Life changing almost simultaneously throughout the World

Scarcely any palæontological discovery is more striking than the fact
that the forms of life change almost simultaneously throughout the world.
Thus our European Chalk formation can be recognised in many distant
regions, under the most different climates, where not a fragment of the
mineral chalk itself can be found; namely in North America, in equatorial South America, in Tierra del Fuego, at the Cape of Good Hope, and
in the peninsula of India. For at these distant points, the organic remains
in certain beds present an unmistakable resemblance to those of the
Chalk. It is not that the same species are met with; for in some cases not
one species is identically the same, but they belong to the same families,
genera, and sections of genera, and sometimes are similarly characterised
in such trifling points as mere superficial sculpture. Moreover, other
forms, which are not found in the Chalk of Europe, but which occur in
the formations either above or below, occur in the same order at these distant points of the world. In the several successive palæozoic formations of
Russia, Western Europe, and North America, a similar parallelism in the
forms of life has been observed by several authors; so it is, according to
Lyell, with the European and North American tertiary deposits. Even if
the few fossil species which are common to the Old and New Worlds were
kept wholly out of view, the general parallelism in the successive forms of
life, in the palæozoic and tertiary stages, would still be manifest, and the
several formations could be easily correlated.

These observations, however, relate to the marine inhabitants of the world: we have not sufficient data to judge whether the productions of the land and of fresh water at distant points change in the same parallel manner. We may doubt whether they have thus changed: if the Megatherium, Mylodon, Macrauchenia, and Toxodon had been brought to Europe from La Plata, without any information in regard to their geological position, no one would have suspected that they had co-existed with sea-shells all still living; but as these anomalous monsters co-existed with the Mastodon and Horse, it might at least have been inferred that they had lived during one of the later tertiary stages.

When the marine forms of life are spoken of as having changed simultaneously throughout the world, it must not be supposed that this expression relates to the same year, or to the same century, or even that it has a very strict geological sense; for if all the marine animals now living in Europe, and all those that lived in Europe during the pleistocene period (a very remote period as measured by years, including the whole glacial epoch) were compared with those now existing in South America or in Australia, the most skilful naturalist would hardly be able to say whether the present or the pleistocene inhabitants of Europe resembled most closely those of the southern hemisphere. So, again, several highly competent observers maintain that the existing productions of the United States are more closely related to those which lived in Europe during certain late tertiary stages, than to the present inhabitants of Europe; and if this be so, it is evident that fossiliferous beds now deposited on the shores of North America would hereafter be liable to be classed with somewhat older European beds. Nevertheless, looking to a remotely future epoch, there can be little doubt that all the more modern *marine* formations, namely, the upper pliocene, the pleistocene and strictly modern beds of Europe, North and South America, and Australia, from containing fossil remains in some degree allied, and from not including those forms which are found only in the older underlying deposits, would be correctly ranked as simultaneous in a geological sense.

The fact of the forms of life changing simultaneously, in the above large sense, at distant parts of the world, has greatly struck these admirable observers, MM. de Verneuil and d'Archiac. After referring to the parallelism of the palæozoic forms of life in various parts of Europe, they add, "If, struck by this strange sequence, we turn our attention to North America, and there discover a series of analogous phenomena, it will appear certain that all these modifications of species, their extinction, and the introduction of new ones, cannot be owing to mere changes in marine currents or other causes more or less local and temporary, but depend on general laws which govern the whole animal kingdom." M. Barrande has made forcible remarks to precisely the same effect. It is, indeed, quite futile to look to changes of currents, climate, or other physical conditions, as the cause of these great mutations in the forms of life throughout the world, under the most different climates. We must, as Barrande has remarked, look to some special law. We shall see this more clearly when we treat of the present distribution of organic beings, and find how slight is the relation between the physical conditions of various countries and the nature of their inhabitants.

This great fact of the parallel succession of the forms of life throughout the world, is explicable on the theory of natural selection. New species are formed by having some advantage over older forms; and the forms, which are already dominant, or have some advantage over the other forms in their own country, give birth to the greatest number of new varieties or incipient species. We have distinct evidence on this head, in the plants which are dominant, that is, which are commonest and most widely diffused, producing the greatest number of new varieties. It is also natural that the dominant, varying, and far-spreading species, which have already invaded to a certain extent the territories of other species, should be those which would have the best chance of spreading still further, and of giving rise in new countries to other new varieties and species. The process of diffusion would often be very slow, depending on climatal and geographical changes, on strange accidents, and on the gradual acclimatisation of new species to the various climates through which they might have to pass, but in the course of time the dominant forms would generally succeed in spreading and would ultimately prevail. The diffusion would, it is probable, be slower with the terrestrial inhabitants of distinct continents than with the marine inhabitants of the continuous sea. We might therefore expect to find, as we do find, a less strict degree of parallelism in the succession of the productions of the land than with those of the sea.

Thus, as it seems to me, the parallel, and, taken in a large sense, simultaneous, succession of the same forms of life throughout the world, accords well with the principle of new species having been formed by dominant species spreading widely and varying; the new species thus produced being themselves dominant, owing to their having had some advantage over their already dominant parents, as well as over other species, and again spreading, varying, and producing new forms. The old forms which are beaten and which yield their places to the new and victorious forms, will generally be allied in groups, from inheriting some inferiority in common; and therefore, as new and improved groups spread throughout the world, old groups disappear from the world; and the succession of forms everywhere tends to correspond both in their first appearance and final disappearance.

There is one other remark connected with this subject worth making. I have given my reasons for believing that most of our great formations, rich in fossils, were deposited during periods of subsidence; and that blank intervals of vast duration, as far as fossils are concerned, occurred during the periods when the bed of the sea was either stationary or rising, and likewise when sediment was not thrown down quickly enough to embed and preserve organic remains. During these long and blank intervals I suppose that the inhabitants of each region underwent a considerable amount of modification and extinction, and that there was much migration from other parts of the world. As we have reason to believe that large

areas are affected by the same movement, it is probable that strictly contemporaneous formations have often been accumulated over very wide
spaces in the same quarter of the world; but we are very far from having
any right to conclude that this has invariably been the case, and that large
areas have invariably been affected by the same movements. When two
formations have been deposited in two regions during nearly, but not exactly, the same period, we should find in both, from the causes explained
in the foregoing paragraphs, the same general succession in the forms of
life; but the species would not exactly correspond; for there will have
been a little more time in the one region than in the other for modification, extinction, and immigration.

I suspect that cases of this nature occur in Europe. Mr. Prestwich, in
his admirable Memoirs on the eocene deposits of England and France, is
able to draw a close general parallelism between the successive stages in
the two countries; but when he compares certain stages in England with
those in France, although he finds in both a curious accordance in the
numbers of the species belonging to the same genera, yet the species themselves differ in a manner very difficult to account for, considering the
proximity of the two areas,—unless, indeed, it be assumed that an isthmus separated two seas inhabited by distinct, but contemporaneous, faunas. Lyell has made similar observations on some of the later tertiary formations. Barrande, also, shows that there is a striking general parallelism
in the successive Silurian deposits of Bohemia and Scandinavia; nevertheless he finds a surprising amount of difference in the species. If the several formations in these regions have not been deposited during the same
exact periods,—a formation in one region often corresponding with a
blank interval in the other,—and if in both regions the species have gone
on slowly changing during the accumulation of the several formations and
during the long intervals of time between them; in this case the several
formations in the two regions could be arranged in the same order, in accordance with the general succession of the forms of life, and the order
would falsely appear to be strictly parallel; nevertheless the species
would not be all the same in the apparently corresponding stages in the
two regions.

On the Affinities of Extinct Species to each other, and to Living Forms

Let us now look to the mutual affinities of extinct and living species.
All fall into a few grand classes; and this fact is at once explained on the
principle of descent. The more ancient any form is, the more, as a general
rule, it differs from living forms. But, as Buckland long ago remarked, extinct species can all be classed either in still existing groups, or between
them. That the extinct forms of life help to fill up the intervals between
existing genera, families, and orders, is certainly true; but as this statement has often been ignored or even denied, it may be well to make some
remarks on this subject, and to give some instances. If we confine our attention either to the living or to the extinct species of the same class, the

series is far less perfect than if we combine both into one general system. In the writings of Professor Owen we continually meet with the expression of generalised forms, as applied to extinct animals; and in the writings of Agassiz, of prophetic or synthetic types; and these terms imply that such forms are in fact intermediate or connecting links. Another distinguished palæontologist, M. Gaudry, has shown in the most striking manner that many of the fossil mammals discovered by him in Attica serve to break down the intervals between existing genera. Cuvier ranked the Ruminants and Pachyderms as two of the most distinct orders of mammals: but so many fossil links have been disentombed that Owen has had to alter the whole classification, and has placed certain pachyderms in the same sub-order with ruminants; for example, he dissolves by gradations the apparently wide interval between the pig and the camel. The Ungulata or hoofed quadrupeds are now divided into the even-toed or odd-toed divisions; but the Macrauchenia of S. America connects to a certain extent these two grand divisions. No one will deny that the Hipparion is intermediate between the existing horse and certain older ungulate forms. What a wonderful connecting link in the chain of mammals is the Typotherium from S. America, as the name given to it by Professor Gervais expresses, and which cannot be placed in any existing order. The Sirenia form a very distinct group of mammals, and one of the most remarkable peculiarities in the existing dugong and lamentin is the entire absence of hind limbs without even a rudiment being left; but the extinct Halitherium had, according to Professor Flower, an ossified thigh-bone "articulated to a well-defined acetabulum in the pelvis," and it thus makes some approach to ordinary hoofed quadrupeds, to which the Sirenia are in other respects allied. The cetaceans or whales are widely different from all other mammals, but the tertiary Zeuglodon and Squalodon, which have been placed by some naturalists in an order by themselves, are considered by Professor Huxley to be undoubtedly cetaceans, "and to constitute connecting links with the aquatic carnivora."

Even the wide interval between birds and reptiles has been shown by the naturalist just quoted to be partially bridged over in the most unexpected manner, on the one hand, by the ostrich and extinct Archeopteryx, and on the other hand, by the Compsognathus, one of the Dinosaurians— that group which includes the most gigantic of all terrestrial reptiles. Turning to the Invertebrata, Barrande asserts, a higher authority could not be named, that he is every day taught that, although palæozoic animals can certainly be classed under existing groups, yet that at this ancient period the groups were not so distinctly separated from each other as they now are.

Some writers have objected to any extinct species, or group of species, being considered as intermediate between any two living species, or groups of species. If by this term it is meant that an extinct form is directly intermediate in all its characters between two living forms or groups, the objection is probably valid. But in a natural classification many fossil

species certainly stand between living species, and some extinct genera between living genera, even between genera belonging to distinct families.
The most common case, especially with respect to very distinct groups,
such as fish and reptiles, seems to be, that, supposing them to be distinguished at the present day by a score of characters, the ancient members
are separated by a somewhat lesser number of characters; so that the two
groups formerly made a somewhat nearer approach to each other than
they now do.

It is a common belief that the more ancient a form is, by so much the
more it tends to connect by some of its characters groups now widely separated from each other. This remark no doubt must be restricted to those
groups which have undergone much change in the course of geological
ages; and it would be difficult to prove the truth of the proposition, for
every now and then even a living animal, as the Lepidosiren, is discovered
having affinities directed towards very distinct groups. Yet if we compare
the older Reptiles and Betrachians, the older Fish, the older Cephalopods, and the eocene Mammals, with the more recent members of the same
classes, we must admit that there is truth in the remark.

Let us see how far these several facts and inferences accord with the
theory of descent with modification. As the subject is somewhat complex,
I must request the reader to turn to the diagram in the fourth chapter.
We may suppose that the numbered letters in italics represent genera,
and the dotted lines diverging from them the species in each genus. The
diagram is much too simple, too few genera and too few species being giv-
en, but this is unimportant for us. The horizontal lines may represent successive geological formations, and all the forms beneath the uppermost
line may be considered as extinct. The three existing genera a^{14}, q^{14}, p^{14},
will form a small family; b^{14} and f^{14} a closely allied family or sub-family;
and o^{14}, e^{14}, m^{14}, a third family. These three families, together with the
many extinct genera on the several lines of descent diverging from the
parent-form (A) will form an order, for all will have inherited something
in common from their ancient progenitor. On the principle of the continued tendency to divergence of character, which was formerly illustrated
by this diagram, the more recent any form is, the more it will generally
differ from its ancient progenitor. Hence we can understand the rule that
the most ancient fossils differ most from existing forms. We must not,
however, assume that divergence of character is a necessary contingency;
it depends solely on the descendants from a species being thus enabled to
seize on many and different places in the economy of nature. Therefore it
is quite possible, as we have seen in the case of some Silurian forms, that
a species might go on being slightly modified in relation to its slightly altered conditions of life, and yet retain throughout a vast period the same
general characteristics. This is represented in the diagram by the letter
F^{14}.

All the many forms, extinct and recent, descended from (A), make, as
before remarked, one order; and this order, from the continued effects of

extinction and divergence of character, has become divided into several sub-families and families, some of which are supposed to have perished at different periods, and some to have endured to the present day.

By looking at the diagram we can see that if many of the extinct forms supposed to be imbedded in the successive formations, were discovered at several points low down in the series, the three existing families on the uppermost line would be rendered less distinct from each other. If, for instance, the genera a^1, a^5, a^{10}, f^8, m^3, m^6, m^9, were disinterred, these three families would be so closely linked together that they probably would have to be united into one great family, in nearly the same manner as has occurred with ruminants and certain pachyderms. Yet he who objected to consider as intermediate the extinct genera, which thus link together the living genera of three families, would be partly justified, for they are intermediate, not directly, but only by a long and circuitous course through many widely different forms. If many extinct forms were to be discovered above one of the middle horizontal lines or geological formations—for instance, above No. VI.—but none from beneath this line, then only two of the families (those on the left hand, a^{14}, &c., and b^{14}, &c.) would have to be united into one; and there would remain two families, which would be less distinct from each other than they were before the discovery of the fossils. So again if the three families formed of eight genera (a^{14} to m^{14}), on the uppermost line, be supposed to differ from each other by half-a-dozen important characters, then the families which existed at the period marked VI. would certainly have differed from each other by a less number of characters; for they would at this early stage of descent have diverged in a less degree from their common progenitor. Thus it comes that ancient and extinct genera are often in a greater or less degree intermediate in character between their modified descendants, or between their collateral relations.

Under nature the process will be far more complicated than is represented in the diagram; for the groups will have been more numerous; they will have endured for extremely unequal lengths of time, and will have been modified in various degrees. As we possess only the last volume of the geological record, and that in a very broken condition, we have no right to expect, except in rare cases, to fill up the wide intervals in the natural system, and thus to unite distinct families or orders. All that we have a right to expect is, that those groups which have, within known geological periods, undergone much modification, should in the older formations make some slight approach to each other; so that the older members should differ less from each other in some of their characters than do the existing members of the same groups; and this by the concurrent evidence of our best palæontologists is frequently the case.

Thus, on the theory of descent with modification, the main facts with respect to the mutual affinities of the extinct forms of life to each other and to living forms, are explained in a satisfactory manner. And they are wholly inexplicable on any other view.

On this same theory, it is evident that the fauna during any one great period in the earth's history will be intermediate in general character between that which preceded and that which succeeded it. Thus the species which lived at the sixth great stage of descent in the diagram are the modified offspring of those which lived at the fifth stage, and are the parents of those which became still more modified at the seventh stage; hence they could hardly fail to be nearly intermediate in character between the forms of life above and below. We must, however, allow for the entire extinction of some preceding forms, and in any one region for the immigration of new forms from other regions, and for a large amount of modification during the long and blank intervals between the successive formations. Subject to these allowances, the fauna of each geological period undoubtedly is intermediate in character, between the preceding and succeeding faunas. I need give only one instance, namely, the manner in which the fossils of the Devonian system, when this system was first discovered, were at once recognized by palæontologists as intermediate in character between those of the overlying carboniferous, and underlying Silurian systems. But each fauna is not necessarily exactly intermediate, as unequal intervals of time have elapsed between consecutive formations.

It is no real objection to the truth of the statement that the fauna of each period as a whole is nearly intermediate in character between the preceding and succeeding faunas, that certain genera offer exceptions to the rule. For instance, the species of mastodons and elephants, when arranged by Dr. Falconer in two series,—in the first place according to their mutual affinities, and in the second place according to their periods of existence,—do not accord in arrangement. The species extreme in character are not the oldest or the most recent; nor are those which are intermediate in character, intermediate in age. But supposing for an instant, in this and other such cases, that the record of the first appearance and disappearance of the species was complete, which is far from the case, we have no reason to believe that forms successively produced necessarily endure for corresponding lengths of time. A very ancient form may occasionally have lasted much longer than a form elsewhere subsequently produced, especially in the case of terrestrial productions inhabiting separated districts. To compare small things with great; if the principal living and extinct races of the domestic pigeon were arranged in serial affinity, this arrangement would not closely accord with the order in time of their production, and even less with the order of their disappearance; for the parent rock-pigeon still lives; and many varieties between the rock-pigeon and the carrier have become extinct; and carriers which are extreme in the important character of length of beak originated earlier than short-beaked tumblers, which are at the opposite end of the series in this respect.

Closely connected with the statement, that the organic remains from an intermediate formation are in some degree intermediate in character, is the fact, insisted on by all palæontologists, that fossils from two consecutive formations are far more closely related to each other, than are the fossils from two remote formations. Pictet gives as a well-known instance, the general resemblance of the organic remains from the several stages of the Chalk formation, though the species are distinct in each stage. This fact alone, from its generality, seems to have shaken Professor Pictet in his belief in the immutability of species. He who is acquainted with the distribution of existing species over the globe, will not attempt to account for the close resemblance of distinct species in closely consecutive formations, by the physical conditions of the ancient areas having remained nearly the same. Let it be remembered that the forms of life, at least those inhabiting the sea, have changed almost simultaneously throughout the world, and therefore under the most different climates and conditions. Consider the prodigious vicissitudes of climate during the pleistocene period, which includes the whole glacial epoch, and note how little the specific forms of the inhabitants of the sea have been affected.

On the theory of descent, the full meaning of the fossil remains from closely consecutive formations being closely related, though ranked as distinct species, is obvious. As the accumulation of each formation has often been interrupted, and as long blank intervals have intervened between successive formations, we ought not to expect to find, as I attempted to show in the last chapter, in any one or in any two formations, all the intermediate varieties between the species which appeared at the commencement and close of these periods: but we ought to find after intervals, very long as measured by years, but only moderately long as measured geologically, closely allied forms, or, as they have been called by some authors, representative species; and these assuredly we do find. We find, in short, such evidence of the slow and scarcely sensible mutations of specific forms, as we have the right to expect.

On the State of Development of Ancient compared with Living Forms

We have seen in the fourth chapter that the degree of differentiation and specialisation of the parts in organic beings, when arrived at maturity, is the best standard, as yet suggested, of their degree of perfection or highness. We have also seen that, as the specialisation of parts is an advantage to each being, so natural selection will tend to render the organisation of each being more specialised and perfect, and in this sense higher; not but that it may leave many creatures with simple and unimproved structures fitted for simple conditions of life, and in some cases will even degrade or simplify the organisation, yet leaving such degraded beings better fitted for their new walks of life. In another and more general manner, new species become superior to their predecessors; for they have to beat in the struggle for life all the older forms, with which they come into close competition. We may therefore conclude that if under a nearly similar climate the eocene inhabitants of the world could be put into competition with the existing inhabitants, the former would be beaten and exterminated by the latter, as would the secondary by the eocene, and the palæozoic by the secondary forms. So that by this fundamental test of victory in the battle for life, as well as by the standard of the specialisation of organs, modern forms ought, on the theory of natural selection, to stand higher than ancient forms. Is this the case? A large majority of palæontologists would answer in the affirmative; and it seems that this answer must be admitted as true, though difficult of proof.

It is no valid objection to this conclusion, that certain Brachiopods have been but slightly modified from an extremely remote geological epoch; and that certain land and fresh-water shells have remained nearly the same, from the time when, as far as is known, they first appeared. It is not an insuperable difficulty that Foraminifera have not, as insisted on by Dr. Carpenter, progressed in organisation since even the Laurentian epoch; for some organisms would have to remain fitted for simple conditions of life, and what could be better fitted for this end than these lowly organised Protozoa? Such objections as the above would be fatal to my view, if it included advance in organisation as a necessary contingent. They would likewise be fatal, if the above Foraminifera, for instance, could be proved to have first come into existence during the Laurentian epoch, or the above Brachiopods during the Cambrian formation; for in this case, there would not have been time sufficient for the development of these organisms up to the standard which they had then reached. When advanced up to any given point, there is no necessity, on the theory of natural selection, for their further continued progress; though they will, during each successive age, have to be slightly modified, so as to hold their places in relation to slight changes in their conditions. The foregoing objections hinge on the question whether we really know how old the world is, and at what period the various forms of life first appeared; and this may well be disputed.

The problem whether organisation on the whole has advanced is in many ways excessively intricate. The geological record, at all times imperfect, does not extend far enough back to show with unmistakable clearness that within the known history of the world organisation has largely advanced. Even at the present day, looking to members of the same class, naturalists are not unanimous which forms ought to be ranked as highest: thus, some look at the selaceans or sharks, from their approach in some important points of structure to reptiles, as the highest fish; others look at the teleosteans as the highest. The ganoids stand intermediate between the selaceans and teleosteans; the latter at the present day are largely preponderant in number; but formerly selaceans and ganoids alone existed; and in this case, according to the standard of highness chosen, so will it be said that fishes have advanced or retrograded in organisation. To attempt to compare members of distinct types in the scale of highness seem hopeless; who will decide whether a cuttle-fish be higher than a bee—that insect which the great Von Baer believed to be "in fact more highly organised than a fish, although upon another type"? In the complex struggle for life it is quite credible that crustaceans, not very high in their own class, might beat cephalopods, the highest molluscs; and such crustaceans, though not highly developed, would stand

very high in the scale of invertebrate animals, if judged by the most decisive of all trials—the law of battle. Besides these inherent difficulties in
deciding which forms are the most advanced in organisation, we ought
not solely to compare the highest members of a class at any two periods—
though undoubtedly this is one and perhaps the most important element
in striking a balance—but we ought to compare all the members, high and
low, at the two periods. At an ancient epoch the highest and lowest mol-
luscoidal animals, namely, cephalopods and brachiopods, swarmed in
numbers; at the present time both groups are greatly reduced, whilst
others, intermediate in organisation, have largely increased; consequently some naturalists maintain that molluscs were formerly more highly developed than at present; but a stronger case can be made out on the opposite side, by considering the vast reduction of brachiopods, and the fact
that our existing cephalopods, though few in number, are more highly organised than their ancient representatives. We ought also to compare the
relative proportional numbers at any two periods of the high and low
classes throughout the world: if, for instance, at the present day fifty
thousand kinds of vertebrate animals exist, and if we knew that at some
former period only ten thousand kinds existed, we ought to look at this
increase in number in the highest class, which implies a great displacement of lower forms, as a decided advance in the organisation of the
world. We thus see how hopelessly difficult it is to compare with perfect
fairness under such extremely complex relations, the standards of organisation of the imperfectly-known faunas of successive periods.

We shall appreciate this difficulty more clearly, by looking to certain
existing faunas and floras. From the extraordinary manner in which European productions have recently spread over New Zealand, and have
seized on places which must have been previously occupied by the indigenes, we must believe, that if all the animals and plants of Great Britain
were set free in New Zealand, a multitude of British forms would in the
course of time become thoroughly naturalised there, and would exterminate many of the natives. On the other hand, from the fact that hardly a
single inhabitant of the southern hemisphere has become wild in any part
of Europe, we may well doubt whether, if all the productions of New Zealand were set free in Great Britain, any considerable number would be
enabled to seize on places now occupied by our native plants and animals.
Under this point of view, the productions of Great Britain stand much
higher in the scale than those of New Zealand. Yet the most skilful naturalist, from an examination of the species of the two countries, could
not have foreseen this result.

Agassiz and several other highly competent judges insist that ancient
animals resemble to a certain extent the embryos of recent animals belonging to the same classes; and that the geological succession of extinct
forms is nearly parallel with the embryological development of existing
forms. This view accords admirably well with our theory. In a future
chapter I shall attempt to show that the adult differs from its embryo,

owing to variations having supervened at a not early age, and having been inherited at a corresponding age. This process, whilst it leaves the embryo almost unaltered, continually adds, in the course of successive generations, more and more difference to the adult. Thus the embryo comes to be left as a sort of picture, preserved by nature, of the former and less modified condition of the species. This view may be true, and yet may never be capable of proof. Seeing, for instance, that the oldest known mammals, reptiles, and fishes strictly belong to their proper classes, though some of these old forms are in a slight degree less distinct from each other than are the typical members of the same groups at the present day, it would be vain to look for animals having the common embryological character of the Vertebrata, until beds rich in fossils are discovered far beneath the lowest Cambrian strata—a discovery of which the chance is small.

On the Succession of the same Types within the same Areas, during the later Tertiary periods

Mr. Clift many years ago showed that the fossil mammals from the Australian caves were closely allied to the living marsupials of that continent. In South America a similar relationship is manifest, even to an uneducated eye, in the gigantic pieces of armour, like those of the armadillo, found in several parts of La Plata; and Professor Owen has shown in the most striking manner that most of the fossil mammals, buried there in such numbers, are related to South American types. This relationship is even more clearly seen in the wonderful collection of fossil bones made by MM. Lund and Clausen in the caves of Brazil. I was so much impressed with these facts that I strongly insisted, in 1839 and 1845, on this "law of the succession of types,"—on "this wonderful relationship in the same continent between the dead and the living." Professor Owen has subsequently extended the same generalisation to the mammals of the Old World. We see the same law in this author's restorations of the extinct and gigantic birds of New Zealand. We see it also in the birds of the caves of Brazil. Mr. Woodward has shown that the same law holds good with sea-shells, but, from the wide distribution of most molluscs, it is not well displayed by them. Other cases could be added, as the relation between the extinct and living land-shells of Madeira; and between the extinct and living brackish water-shells of the Aralo-Caspian Sea.

Now what does this remarkable law of the succession of the same types within the same areas mean? He would be a bold man who, after comparing the present climate of Australia and of parts of South America, under the same latitude, would attempt to account, on the one hand through dissimilar physical conditions, for the dissimilarity of the inhabitants of these two continents; and, on the other hand through similarity of conditions, for the uniformity of the same types in each continent during the later tertiary periods. Nor can it be pretended that it is an immutable law that marsupials should have been chiefly or solely produced in Australia; or that Edentata and other American types should have been solely produced in South America. For we know that Europe in ancient times was peopled by numerous marsupials; and I have shown in the publications above alluded to, that in America the law of distribution of terrestrial mammals was formerly different from what it now is. North America formerly partook strongly of the present character of the southern half of the continent; and the southern half was formerly more closely allied, than it is at present, to the northern half. In a similar manner we know, from Falconer and Cautley's discoveries, that Northern India was formerly more closely related in its mammals to Africa than it is at the present time. Analogous facts could be given in relation to the distribution of marine animals.

On the theory of descent with modification, the great law of the long enduring, but not immutable, succession of the same types within the same areas, is at once explained; for the inhabitants of each quarter of the world will obviously tend to leave in that quarter, during the next succeeding period of time, closely allied though in some degree modified descendants. If the inhabitants of one continent formerly differed greatly from those of another continent, so will their modified descendants still differ in nearly the same manner and degree. But after very long intervals of time, and after great geographical changes, permitting much intermigration, the feebler will yield to the more dominant forms, and there will be nothing immutable in the distribution of organic beings.

It may be asked in ridicule, whether I suppose that the megatherium and other allied huge monsters, which formerly lived in South America, have left behind them the sloth, armadillo, and anteater, as their degenerate descendants. This cannot for an instant be admitted. These huge animals have become wholly extinct, and have left no progeny. But in the caves of Brazil, there are many extinct species which are closely allied in size and in all other characters to the species still living in South America; and some of these fossils may have been the actual progenitors of the living species. It must not be forgotten that, on our theory, all the species of the same genus are the descendants of some one species; so that, if six genera, each having eight species, be found in one geological formation, and in a succeeding formation there be six other allied or representative genera each with the same number of species, then we may conclude that generally only one species of each of the older genera has left modified descendants, which constitute the new genera containing the several species; the other seven species of each old genus having died out and left no progeny. Or, and this will be a far commoner case, two or three species in two or three alone of the six older genera will be the parents of the new genera: the other species and the other old genera having become utterly extinct. In failing orders, with the genera and species decreasing in numbers as is the case with the Edentata of South America, still fewer genera and species will leave modified blood-descendants.

Summary of the preceding and present Chapters

I have attempted to show that the geological record is extremely imperfect; that only a small portion of the globe has been geologically explored with care; that only certain classes of organic beings have been largely preserved in a fossil state; that the number both of specimens and of species, preserved in our museums, is absolutely as nothing compared with the number of generations which must have passed away even during a single formation; that, owing to subsidence being almost necessary for the accumulation of deposits rich in fossil species of many kinds, and thick enough to outlast future degradation, great intervals of time must have elapsed between most of our successive formations; that there has probably been more extinction during the periods of subsidence, and more variation during the periods of elevation, and during the latter the record will have been less perfectly kept; that each single formation has not been continuously deposited; that the duration of each formation is probably short compared with the average duration of specific forms; that migration has played an important part in the first appearance of new forms in any one area and formation; that widely ranging species are those which have varied most frequently, and have oftenest given rise to new species; that varieties have at first been local; and lastly, although each species must have passed through numerous transitional stages, it is probable that the periods, during which each underwent modification, though many and long as measured by years, have been short in comparison with the periods during which each remained in an unchanged condition. These causes, taken conjointly, will to a large extent explain why —though we do find many links—we do not find interminable varieties, connecting together all extinct and existing forms by the finest graduated steps. It should also be constantly borne in mind that any linking variety between two forms, which might be found, would be ranked, unless the whole chain could be perfectly restored, as a new and distinct species; for it is not pretended that we have any sure criterion by which species and varieties can be discriminated.

He who rejects this view of the imperfection of the geological record, will rightly reject the whole theory. For he may ask in vain where are the numberless transitional links which must formerly have connected the closely allied or representative species, found in the successive stages of the same great formation? He may disbelieve in the immense intervals of time which must have elapsed between our consecutive formations; he may overlook how important a part migration has played, when the formations of any one great region, as those of Europe, are considered; he may urge the apparent, but often falsely apparent, sudden coming in of whole groups of species. He may ask where are the remains of those infinitely numerous organisms which must have existed long before the Cambrian system was deposited? We now know that at least one animal did then exist; but I can answer this last question only by supposing that where our oceans now extend they have extended for an enormous period, and where our oscillating continents now stand they have stood since the commencement of the Cambrian system; but that, long before that epoch, the world presented a widely different aspect; and that the older continents formed of formations older than any known to us, exist now only as remnants in a metamorphosed condition, or lie still buried under the ocean.

Passing from these difficulties, the other great leading facts in palæontology agree admirably with the theory of descent with modification through variation and natural selection. We can thus understand how it is that new species come in slowly and successively; how species of different classes do not necessarily change together, or at the same rate, or in the same degree; yet in the long run that all undergo modification to some extent. The extinction of old forms is the almost inevitable consequence of the productions of new forms. We can understand why, when a species has once disappeared, it never reappears. Groups of species increase in numbers slowly, and endure for unequal periods of time; for the process of modification is necessarily slow, and depends on many complex contingencies. The dominant species belonging to large and dominant groups tend to leave many modified descendants, which form new sub-groups and groups. As these are formed, the species of the less vigorous groups, from their inferiority inherited from a common progenitor, tend to become extinct together, and to leave no modified offspring on the face of the earth. But the utter extinction of a whole group of species has sometimes been a slow process, from the survival of a few descendants, lingering in protected and isolated situations. When a group has once wholly disappeared, it does not reappear; for the link of generation has been broken.

We can understand how it is that dominant forms which spread widely and yield the greatest number of varieties tend to people the world with allied, but modified, descendants; and these will generally succeed in displacing the groups which are their inferiors in the struggle for existence. Hence, after long intervals of time, the productions of the world appear to have changed simultaneously.

We can understand how it is that all the forms of life, ancient and recent, make together a few grand classes. We can understand, from the continued tendency to divergence of character, why the more ancient a form is, the more it generally differs from those now living; why ancient and extinct forms often tend to fill up gaps between existing forms, sometimes blending two groups, previously classed as distinct, into one; but more commonly bringing them only a little closer together. The more ancient a form is, the more often it stands in some degree intermediate between groups now distinct; for the more ancient a form is, the more nearly it will be related to, and consequently resemble, the common progenitor of groups, since become widely divergent. Extinct forms are seldom directly intermediate between existing forms; but are intermediate only by a long and circuitous course through other extinct and different forms. We can clearly see why the organic remains of closely consecutive formations are closely allied; for they are closely linked together by generation. We can clearly see why the remains of an intermediate formation are intermediate in character.

The inhabitants of the world at each successive period in its history have beaten their predecessors in the race for life, and are, in so far, higher in the scale, and their structure has generally become more specialised; and this may account for the common belief held by so many palæontologists, that organisation on the whole has progressed. Extinct and ancient animals resemble to a certain extent the embryos of the more recent animals belonging to the same classes, and this wonderful fact receives a simple explanation according to our views. The succession of the same types of structure within the same areas during the later geological periods ceases to be mysterious, and is intelligible on the principle of inheritance.

If then the geological record be as imperfect as many believe, and it may at least be asserted that the record cannot be proved to be much more perfect, the main objections to the theory of natural selection are greatly diminished or disappear. On the other hand, all the chief laws of palæontology plainly proclaim, as it seems to me, that species have been produced by ordinary generation: old forms having been supplanted by new and improved forms of life, the products of Variation and the Survival of the Fittest.

CHAPTER XII

GEOGRAPHICAL DISTRIBUTION

Present distribution cannot be accounted for by differences in physical conditions—Importance of barriers—Affinity of the productions of the same continent—Centres of creation—Means of dispersal by changes of climate and of the level of the land, and by occasional means—Dispersal during the Glacial period—Alternate Glacial periods in the North and South.

IN considering the distribution of organic beings over the face of the globe, the first great fact which strikes us is, that neither the similarity nor the dissimilarity of the inhabitants of various regions can be wholly accounted for by climatal and other physical conditions. Of late, almost every author who has studied the subject has come to this conclusion. The case of America alone would almost suffice to prove its truth; for if we exclude the arctic and northern temperate parts, all authors agree that one of the most fundamental divisions in geographical distribution is that between the New and Old Worlds; yet if we travel over the vast American continent, from the central parts of the United States to its extreme southern point, we meet with the most diversified conditions; humid districts, arid deserts, lofty mountains, grassy plains, forests, marshes, lakes, and great rivers, under almost every temperature. There is hardly a climate or condition in the Old World which cannot be paralleled in the New—at least as closely as the same species generally require. No doubt small areas can be pointed out in the Old World hotter than any in the New World; but these are not inhabited by a fauna different from that of the surrounding districts; for it is rare to find a group of organisms confined to a small area, of which the conditions are peculiar in only a slight degree. Notwithstanding this general parallelism in the conditions of the Old and New Worlds, how widely different are their living productions!

In the southern hemisphere, if we compare large tracts of land in Australia, South Africa, and western South America, between latitudes 25° and 35°, we shall find parts extremely similar in all their conditions, yet it would not be possible to point out three faunas and floras more utterly dissimilar. Or, again, we may compare the productions of South America south of lat. 35° with those north of 25°, which consequently are separated by a space of ten degrees of latitude, and are exposed to considerably different conditions; yet they are incomparably more closely related to each other than they are to the productions of Australia or Africa under nearly the same climate. Analogous facts could be given with respect to the inhabitants of the sea.

A second great fact which strikes us in our general review is, that barriers of any kind, or obstacles to free migration, are related in a close and important manner to the differences between the productions of various regions. We see this in the great difference in nearly all the terrestrial productions of the New and Old Worlds, excepting in the northern parts, where the land almost joins, and where, under a slightly different climate, there might have been free migration for the northern temperate forms, as there now is for the strictly arctic productions. We see the same fact in the great difference between the inhabitants of Australia, Africa, and South America under the same latitude; for these countries are almost as much isolated from each other as is possible. On each continent, also, we see the same fact; for on the opposite sides of lofty and continuous mountain-ranges, of great deserts and even of large rivers, we find different productions; though as mountain-chains, deserts, &c., are not as impassable, or likely to have endured so long, as the oceans separating continents, the differences are very inferior in degree to those characteristic of distinct continents.

Turning to the sea, we find the same law. The marine inhabitants of the eastern and western shores of South America are very distinct, with extremely few shells, crustacea, or echinodermata in common; but Dr. Günther has recently shown that about thirty per cent. of the fishes are the same on the opposite sides of the isthmus of Panama; and this fact has led naturalists to believe that the isthmus was formerly open. Westward of the shores of America, a wide space of open ocean extends, with not an island as a halting-place for emigrants; here we have a barrier of another kind, and as soon as this is passed we meet in the eastern islands of the Pacific with another and totally distinct fauna. So that three marine faunas range far northward and southward in parallel lines not far from each other, under corresponding climates; but from being separated from each other by impassable barriers, either of land or open sea, they are almost wholly distinct. On the other hand, proceeding still farther westward from the eastern islands of the tropical parts of the Pacific, we encounter no impassable barriers, and we have innumerable islands as halting-places, or continuous coasts, until, after travelling over a hemisphere, we come to the shores of Africa; and over this vast space we meet with no well-defined and distinct marine faunas. Although so few marine animals are common to the above-named three approximate faunas of Eastern and Western America and the Eastern Pacific islands, yet many fishes range from the Pacific into the Indian Ocean, and many shells are common to the eastern islands of the Pacific and the eastern shores of Africa on almost exactly opposite meridians of longitude.

A third great fact, partly included in the foregoing statement, is the affinity of the productions of the same continent or of the same sea, though the species themselves are distinct at different points and stations. It is a law of the widest generality, and every continent offers innumerable instances. Nevertheless the naturalist, in travelling, for instance, from north to south, never fails to be struck by the manner in which successive groups of beings, specifically distinct, though nearly related, replace each other. He hears from closely allied, yet distinct kinds of birds, notes nearly similar, and sees their nests similarly constructed, but not quite alike, with eggs coloured in nearly the same manner. The plains near the Straits of Magellan are inhabited by one species of Rhea (American ostrich) and northward the plains of La Plata by another species of the same genus; and not by a true ostrich or emu, like those inhabiting Africa and Australia under the same latitude. On these same plains of La Plata we see the agouti and bizcacha, animals having nearly the same habits as our hares and rabbits, and belonging to the same order of Rodents, but they plainly display an American type of structure. We ascend the lofty peaks of the Cordillera, and we find an alpine species of bizcacha; we look to the waters, and we do not find the beaver or musk-rat, but the coypu and capybara, rodents of the S. American type. Innumerable other instances could be given. If we look to the islands off the American shore, however much they may differ in geological structure, the inhabitants are essentially American, though they may be all peculiar species. We may look back to past ages, as shown in the last chapter, and we find American types then prevailing on the American continent and in the American seas. We see in these facts some deep organic bond, throughout space and time, over the same areas of land and water, independently of physical conditions. The naturalist must be dull who is not led to enquire what this bond is.

The bond is simply inheritance, that cause which alone, as far as we positively know, produces organisms quite like each other, or, as we see in the case of varieties, nearly alike. The dissimilarity of the inhabitants of different regions may be attributed to modification through variation and natural selection, and probably in a subordinate degree to the definite influence of different physical conditions. The degrees of dissimilarity will depend on the migration of the more dominant forms of life from one region into another having been more or less effectually prevented, at periods more or less remote;—on the nature and number of the former immigrants;—and on the action of the inhabitants on each other in leading to the preservation of different modifications; the relation of organism to organism in the struggle for life being, as I have already often remarked, the most important of all relations. Thus the high importance of barriers comes into play by checking migration; as does time for the slow process of modification through natural selection. Widely-ranging species, abounding in individuals, which have already triumphed over many competitors in their own widely-extended homes, will have the best chance of seizing on new places, when they spread into new countries. In their new homes they will be exposed to new conditions, and will frequently undergo further modification and improvement; and thus they will become still further victorious, and will produce groups of modified descendants. On this principle of inheritance with modification we can understand how it is that sections of genera, whole genera, and even families, are confined to the same areas, as is so commonly and notoriously the case.

There is no evidence, as was remarked in the last chapter, of the existence of any law of necessary development. As the variability of each species is an independent property, and will be taken advantage of by natural selection, only so far as it profits each individual in its complex struggle for life, so the amount of modification in different species will be no uniform quantity. If a number of species, after having long competed with each other in their old home, were to migrate in a body into a new and afterwards isolated country, they would be little liable to modification; for neither migration nor isolation in themselves effect anything. These principles come into play only by bringing organisms into new relations with each other and in a lesser degree with the surrounding physical conditions. As we have seen in the last chapter that some forms have retained nearly the same character from an enormously remote geological period, so certain species have migrated over vast spaces, and have not become greatly or at all modified.

According to these views, it is obvious that the several species of the same genus, though inhabiting the most distant quarters of the world, must originally have proceeded from the same source, as they are descended from the same progenitor. In the case of those species which have undergone during the whole geological periods little modification, there is not much difficulty in believing that they have migrated from the same region; for during the vast geographical and climatal changes which have supervened since ancient times, almost any amount of migration is possible. But in many other cases, in which we have reason to believe that the species of a genus have been produced within comparatively recent times, there is great difficulty on this head. It is also obvious that the individuals of the same species, though now inhabiting distant and isolated regions, must have proceeded from one spot, where their parents were first produced: for, as has been explained, it is incredible that individuals identically the same should have been produced from parents specifically distinct.

Single Centres of supposed Creation.—We are thus brought to the question which has been largely discussed by naturalists, namely, whether species have been created at one or more points of the earth's surface. Undoubtedly there are many cases of extreme difficulty in understanding how the same species could possibly have migrated from some one point to the several distant and isolated points, where now found. Nevertheless the simplicity of the view that each species was first produced within a single region captivates the mind. He who rejects it, rejects the *vera causa* of ordinary generation with subsequent migration, and calls in the agency of a miracle. It is universally admitted, that in most cases the area inhabited by a species is continuous; and that when a plant or animal inhabits two points so distant from each other, or with an interval of such a nature, that the space could not have been easily passed over by migration, the fact is given as something remarkable and exceptional. The incapacity of migrating across a wide sea is more clear in the case of terrestrial mammals than perhaps with any other organic beings; and, accordingly, we find no inexplicable instances of the same mammals inhabiting distant points of the world. No geologist feels any difficulty in Great Britain possessing the same quadrupeds with the rest of Europe, for they were no doubt once united. But if the same species can be produced at two separate points, why do we not find a single mammal common to Europe and Australia or South America? The conditions of life are nearly the same, so that a multitude of European animals and plants have become naturalised in America and Australia; and some of the aboriginal plants are identically the same at these distant points of the northern and southern hemispheres? The answer, as I believe, is, that mammals have not been able to migrate, whereas some plants, from their varied means of dispersal, have migrated across the wide and broken interspaces. The great and striking influence of barriers of all kinds, is intelligible only on the view that the great majority of species have been produced on one side, and have not been able to migrate to the opposite side. Some few families, many sub-families, very many genera, and a still greater number of sections of genera, are confined to a single region; and it has been observed by several naturalists that the most natural genera, or those genera in which the species are most closely related to each other, are generally confined to the same country, or if they have a wide range that their range is continuous. What a strange anomaly it would be, if a directly opposite rule were to prevail, when we go down one step lower in the series, namely, to the individuals of the same species, and these had not been, at least at first, confined to some one region!

Hence it seems to me, as it has to many other naturalists, that the view of each species having been produced in one area alone, and having subsequently migrated from that area as far as its powers of migration and subsistence under past and present conditions permitted, is the most probable. Undoubtedly many cases occur, in which we cannot explain how the same species could have passed from one point to the other. But the geographical and climatal changes which have certainly occurred within recent geological times, must have rendered discontinuous the formerly continuous range of many species. So that we are reduced to consider whether the exceptions to continuity of range are so numerous and of so grave a nature, that we ought to give up the belief, rendered probable by general considerations, that each species has been produced within one area, and has migrated thence as far as it could. It would be hopelessly tedious to discuss all the exceptional cases of the same species, now living at distant and separated points, nor do I for a moment pretend that any explanation could be offered of many instances. But, after some preliminary remarks, I will discuss a few of the most striking classes of facts; namely, the existence of the same species on the summits of distant mountain ranges, and at distant points in the arctic and antarctic regions; and secondly (in the following chapter), the wide distribution of freshwater productions; and thirdly, the occurrence of the same terrestrial species on islands and on the nearest mainland, though separated by hundreds of miles of open sea. If the existence of the same species at distant and isolated points of the earth's surface, can in many instances be explained on the view of each species having migrated from a single birthplace; then, considering our ignorance with respect to former climatal and geographical changes and to the various occasional means of transport, the belief that a single birthplace is the law, seems to me incomparably the safest.

In discussing this subject, we shall be enabled at the same time to consider a point equally important for us, namely, whether the several species of a genus which must on our theory all be descended from a common progenitor, can have migrated, undergoing modification during their migration, from some one area. If, when most of the species inhabiting one region are different from those of another region, though closely allied to them, it can be shown that migration from the one region to the other has probably occurred at some former period, our general view will be much strengthened; for the explanation is obvious on the principle of descent with modification. A volcanic island, for instance, upheaved and formed at the distance of a few hundreds of miles from a continent, would probably receive from it in the course of time a few colonists, and their descendants, though modified, would still be related by inheritance to the inhabitants of that continent. Cases of this nature are common, and are, as we shall hereafter see, inexplicable on the theory of independent creation. This view of the relation of the species of one region to those of another, does not differ much from that advanced by Mr. Wallace, who concludes that "every species has come into existence coincident both in space and time with a pre-existing closely allied species." And it is now well known that he attributes this coincidence to descent with modification.

The question of single or multiple centres of creation differs from another though allied question,—namely, whether all the individuals of the same species are descended from a single pair, or single hermaphrodite, or whether, as some authors suppose, from many individuals simultaneously created. With organic beings which never intercross, if such exist, each species must be descended from a succession of modified varieties, that have supplanted each other, but have never blended with other individuals or varieties of the same species; so that, at each successive stage of modification, all the individuals of the same form will be descended from a single parent. But in the great majority of cases, namely, with all organisms which habitually unite for each birth, or which occasionally intercross, the individuals of the same species inhabiting the same area will be kept nearly uniform by intercrossing; so that many individuals will go on simultaneously changing, and the whole amount of modification at each stage will not be due to descent from a single parent. To illustrate what I mean: our English race-horses differ from the horses of every other breed; but they do not owe their difference and superiority to descent from any single pair, but to continued care in the selecting and training of many individuals during each generation.

Before discussing the three classes of facts, which I have selected as presenting the greatest amount of difficulty on the theory of "single centres of creation," I must say a few words on the means of dispersal.

Means of Dispersal

Sir C. Lyell and other authors have ably treated this subject. I can give here only the briefest abstract of the more important facts. Change of climate must have had a powerful influence on migration. A region now impassable to certain organisms from the nature of its climate, might have been a high road for migration, when the climate was different. I shall, however, presently have to discuss this branch of the subject in some detail. Changes of level in the land must also have been highly influential: a narrow isthmus now separates two marine faunas; submerge it, or let it formerly have been submerged, and the two faunas will now blend together, or may formerly have blended. Where the sea now extends, land may at a former period have connected islands or possibly even continents together, and thus have allowed terrestrial productions to pass from one to the other. No geologist disputes that great mutations of level have occurred within the period of existing organisms. Edward Forbes insisted that all the islands in the Atlantic must have been recently connected with Europe or Africa, and Europe likewise with America. Other authors have thus hypothetically bridged over every ocean, and united almost every island with some mainland. If indeed the arguments used by Forbes are to be trusted, it must be admitted that scarcely a single island exists which has not recently been united to some continent. This view cuts the Gordian knot of the dispersal of the same species to the more distant points, and removes many a difficulty; but to the best of my judgment we are not authorised in admitting such enormous geographical changes within the period of existing species. It seems to me that we have abundant evidence of great oscillations in the level of the land or sea; but not of such vast change in the position and extension of our continents, as to have united them within the recent period to each other and to the several intervening oceanic islands. I freely admit the former existence of many islands, now buried beneath the sea, which may have served as halting-places for plants and for many animals during their migration. In the coral-producing oceans such sunken islands are now marked by rings of coral or atolls standing over them. Whenever it is fully admitted, as it will some day be, that each species has proceeded from a single birthplace, and when in the course of time we know something definite about the means of distribution, we shall be enabled to speculate with security on the former extension of the land. But I do not believe that it will ever be proved that within the recent period most of our continents which now stand quite separate have been continuously, or almost continuously united with each other, and with the many existing oceanic islands. Several facts in distribution,—such as the great difference in the marine faunas on the opposite sides of almost every continent,—the close relation of the tertiary inhabitants of several lands and even seas to their present inhabitants,—the degree of affinity between the mammals inhabiting islands with those of the nearest continent, being in part determined (as we shall hereafter see) by the depth of the intervening ocean,—these and other such facts are opposed to the admission of such prodigious geographical revolutions within the recent period, as are necessary on the view advanced by Forbes and admitted by his followers. The nature and relative proportions of the inhabitants of oceanic islands are likewise opposed to the belief of their former continuity with continents. Nor does the almost universally volcanic composition of such islands favour the admission that they are the wrecks of sunken continents;—if they had originally existed as continental mountain ranges, some at least of the islands would have been formed, like other mountain summits, of granite, metamorphic schists, old fossiliferous and other rocks, instead of consisting of mere piles of volcanic matter.

I must now say a few words on what are called accidental means, but which more properly should be called occasional means of distribution. I shall here confine myself to plants. In botanical works, this or that plant is often stated to be ill adapted for wide dissemination; but the greater or less facilities for transport across the sea may be said to be almost wholly unknown. Until I tried, with Mr. Berkeley's aid, a few experiments, it was not even known how far seeds could resist the injurious action of sea-water. To my surprise I found that out of 87 kinds, 64 germinated after an immersion of 28 days, and a few survived an immersion of 137 days. It deserves notice that certain orders were far more injured than others: nine Leguminosæ were tried, and, with one exception, they resisted the salt-water badly; seven species of the allied orders, Hydrophyllaceæ and Polemoniaceæ, were all killed by a month's immersion. For convenience' sake I chiefly tried small seeds without the capsule or fruit; and as all of these sank in a few days they could not have been floated across wide spaces of the sea, whether or not they were injured by the salt-water. Afterwards I tried some larger fruits, capsules, &c., and some of these floated for a long time. It is well known what a difference there is in the buoyancy of green and seasoned timber; and it occurred to me that floods would often wash into the sea dried plants or branches with seed-capsules or fruit attached to them. Hence I was led to dry the stems and branches of 94 plants with ripe fruit, and to place them on sea-water. The majority sank rapidly, but some which, whilst green, floated for a short time, when dried floated much longer; for instance, ripe hazel-nuts sank immediately, but when dried they floated for 90 days, and afterwards when planted germinated; an asparagus-plant with ripe berries floated for 23 days, when dried it floated for 85 days, and the seeds afterwards germinated; the ripe seeds of Helosciadium sank in two days, when dried they floated for above 90 days, and afterwards germinated. Altogether, out of the 94 dried plants, 18 floated for above 28 days; and some of the 18 floated for a very much longer period. So that as $\frac{64}{87}$ kinds of seeds germinated after an immersion of 28 days; and as $\frac{18}{94}$ distinct species with ripe fruit (but not all the same species as in the foregoing experiment) floated, after being dried, for above 28 days, we may conclude, as far as anything can be inferred from these scanty facts, that the seeds of $\frac{14}{100}$ kinds of plants of any country might be floated by sea-currents during 28 days, and would retain their power of germination. In Johnston's Physical Atlas, the average rate of the several Atlantic currents is 33 miles per diem (some currents running at the rate of 60 miles per diem); on this average, the seeds of $\frac{14}{100}$ plants belonging to one country might be floated across 924 miles of sea to another country, and when stranded, if blown by an inland gale to a favourable spot, would germinate.

Subsequently to my experiments, M. Martens tried similar ones, but in a much better manner, for he placed the seeds in a box in the actual sea, so that they were alternately wet and exposed to the air like really floating plants. He tried 98 seeds, mostly different from mine; but he chose many large fruits and likewise seeds from plants which live near the sea; and this would have favoured both the average length of their flotation and their resistance to the injurious action of the salt-water. On the other hand, he did not previously dry the plants or branches with the fruit; and this, as we have seen, would have caused some of them to have floated much longer. The result was that $\frac{18}{98}$ of his seeds of different kinds floated for 42 days, and were then capable of germination. But I do not doubt that plants exposed to the waves would float for a less time than those protected from violent movement as in our experiments. Therefore it would perhaps be safer to assume that the seeds of about $\frac{10}{100}$ plants of a flora, after having been dried, could be floated across a space of sea 900 miles in width, and would then germinate. The fact of the larger fruits often floating longer than the small, is interesting; as plants with large seeds or fruit which, as Alph. de Candolle has shown, generally have restricted ranges, could hardly be transported by any other means.

Seeds may be occasionally transported in another manner. Drift timber is thrown up on most islands, even on those in the midst of the widest oceans; and the natives of the coral-islands in the Pacific procure stones for their tools, solely from the roots of drifted trees, these stones being a valuable royal tax. I find that when irregularly shaped stones are embedded in the roots of trees, small parcels of earth are frequently enclosed in their interstices and behind them,—so perfectly that not a particle could be washed away during the longest transport: out of one small portion of earth thus *completely* enclosed by the roots of an oak about 50 years old, three dicotyledonous plants germinated: I am certain of the accuracy of this observation. Again, I can show that the carcases of birds, when floating on the sea, sometimes escape being immediately devoured: and many kinds of seeds in the crops of floating birds long retain their vitality: peas and vetches, for instance, are killed by even a few days' immersion in seawater; but some taken out of the crop of a pigeon, which had floated on artificial sea-water for 30 days, to my surprise nearly all germinated.

Living birds can hardly fail to be highly effective agents in the transportation of seeds. I could give many facts showing how frequently birds of many kinds are blown by gales to vast distances across the ocean. We may safely assume that under such circumstances their rate of flight would often be 35 miles an hour; and some authors have given a far higher estimate. I have never seen an instance of nutritious seeds passing through the intestines of a bird; but hard seeds of fruit pass uninjured through even the digestive organs of a turkey. In the course of two months, I picked up in my garden 12 kinds of seeds, out of the excrement of small birds, and these seemed perfect, and some of them, which were tried, germinated. But the following fact is more important: the crops of birds do not secrete gastric juice, and do not, as I know by trial, injure in the least the germination of seeds; now, after a bird has found and devoured a large supply of food, it is positively asserted that all the grains do not pass into the gizzard for twelve or even eighteen hours. A bird in this interval might easily be blown to the distance of 500 miles, and hawks are known to look out for tired birds, and the contents of their torn crops might thus readily get scattered. Some hawks and owls bolt their prey whole, and, after an interval of from twelve to twenty hours, disgorge pellets, which, as I know from experiments made in the Zoological Gardens, include seeds capable of germination. Some seeds of the oat, wheat, millet, canary, hemp, clover, and beet germinated after having been from twelve to twenty-one hours in the stomachs of different birds of prey; and two seeds of beet grew after having been thus retained for two days and fourteen hours. Fresh-water fish, I find, eat seeds of many land and water plants; fish are frequently devoured by birds, and thus the seeds might be transported from place to place. I forced many kinds of seeds into the stomachs of dead fish, and then gave their bodies to fishing-eagles, storks, and pelicans; these birds, after an interval of many hours, either rejected the seeds in pellets or passed them in their excrement; and several of these seeds retained the power of germination. Certain seeds, however, were always killed by this process.

Locusts are sometimes blown to great distances from the land; I myself caught one 370 miles from the coast of Africa, and have heard of others caught at greater distances. The Rev. R. T. Lowe informed Sir C. Lyell that in November, 1844, swarms of locusts visited the island of Madeira. They were in countless numbers, as thick as the flakes of snow in the heaviest snowstorm, and extended upwards as far as could be seen with a telescope. During two or three days they slowly careered round and round in an immense ellipse, at least five or six miles in diameter, and at night alighted on the taller trees, which were completely coated with them. They then disappeared over the sea, as suddenly as they had appeared, and have not since visited the island. Now, in parts of Natal it is believed by some farmers, though on insufficient evidence, that injurious seeds are introduced into their grass-land in the dung left by the great flights of locusts which often visit that country. In consequence of this belief Mr. Weale sent me in a letter a small packet of the dried pellets, out of which I extracted under the microscope several seeds, and raised from them seven grass plants, belonging to two species, of two genera. Hence a swarm of locusts, such as that which visited Madeira, might readily be the means of introducing several kinds of plants into an island lying far from the mainland.

Although the beaks and feet of birds are generally clean, earth sometimes adheres to them: in one case I removed sixty-one grains, and in another case twenty-two grains of dry argillaceous earth from the foot of a partridge, and in the earth there was a pebble as large as the seed of a vetch. Here is a better case: the leg of a woodcock was sent to me by a friend, with a little cake of dry earth attached to the shank, weighing only nine grains; and this contained a seed of the toad-rush (Juncus bufonius) which germinated and flowered. Mr. Swaysland, of Brighton, who during the last forty years has paid close attention to our migratory birds, informs me that he has often shot wagtails (Motacillæ), wheat-ears, and whinchats (Saxicolæ), on their first arrival on our shores, before they had alighted; and he has several times noticed little cakes of earth attached to their feet. Many facts could be given showing how generally soil is charged with seeds. For instance, Prof. Newton sent me the leg of a red-legged partridge (Caccabis rufa) which had been wounded and could not fly, with a ball of hard earth adhering to it, and weighing six and a half ounces. The earth had been kept for three years, but when broken, watered and placed under a bell glass, no less than 82 plants sprung from it: these consisted of 12 monocotyledons, including the common oat, and at least one kind of grass, and of 70 dicotyledons, which consisted, judging from the young leaves, of at least three distinct species. With such facts before us, can we doubt that the many birds which are annually blown by gales across great spaces of ocean, and which annually migrate—for instance, the millions of quails across the Mediterranean—must occasionally transport a few seeds embedded in dirt adhering to their feet or beaks? But I shall have to recur to this subject.

As icebergs are known to be sometimes loaded with earth and stones, and have even carried brushwood, bones, and the nest of a land-bird, it can hardly be doubted that they must occasionally, as suggested by Lyell, have transported seeds from one part to another of the arctic and antarctic regions; and during the Glacial period from one part of the now temperate regions to another. In the Azores, from the large number of plants common to Europe, in comparison with the species on the other islands of the Atlantic, which stand nearer to the mainland, and (as remarked by Mr. H. C. Watson) from their somewhat northern character in comparison with the latitude, I suspected that these islands had been partly stocked by ice-borne seeds, during the Glacial epoch. At my request Sir C. Lyell wrote to M. Hartung to inquire whether he had observed erratic boulders on these islands, and he answered that he had found large fragments of granite and other rocks, which do not occur in the archipelago. Hence we may safely infer that icebergs formerly landed their rocky burthens on the shores of these mid-ocean islands, and it is at least possible that they may have brought thither some few seeds of northern plants.

Considering that these several means of transport, and that other means, which without doubt remain to be discovered, have been in action year after year for tens of thousands of years, it would, I think, be a marvellous fact if many plants had not thus become widely transported. These means of transport are sometimes called accidental, but this is not strictly correct: the currents of the sea are not accidental, nor is the direction of prevalent gales of wind. It should be observed that scarcely any means of transport would carry seeds for very great distances: for seeds do not retain their vitality when exposed for a great length of time to the action of sea-water; nor could they be long carried in the crops or intestines of birds. These means, however, would suffice for occasional transport across tracts of sea some hundred miles in breadth, or from island to island, or from a continent to a neighbouring island, but not from one distant continent to another. The floras of distant continents would not by such means become mingled; but would remain as distinct as they now are. The currents, from their course, would never bring seeds from North America to Britain, though they might and do bring seeds from the West Indies to our western shores, where, if not killed by their very long immersion in salt water, they could not endure our climate. Almost every year, one or two land-birds are blown across the whole Atlantic Ocean, from North America to the western shores of Ireland and England; but seeds could be transported by these rare wanderers only by one means, namely, by dirt adhering to their feet or beaks, which is in itself a rare accident. Even in this case, how small would be the chance of a seed falling on favourable soil, and coming to maturity! But it would be a great error to argue that because a well-stocked island, like Great Britain, has not, as far as is known (and it would be very difficult to prove this), received within the last few centuries, through occasional means of transport, immigrants from Europe or any other continent, that a poorly-stocked island, though standing more remote from the mainland, would not receive colonists by similar means. Out of a hundred kinds of seeds or animals transported to an island, even if far less well-stocked than Britain, perhaps not more than one would be so well fitted to its new home, as to become naturalised. But this is no valid argument against what would be effected by occasional means of transport, during the long lapse of geological time, whilst the island was being upheaved, and before it had become fully stocked with inhabitants. On almost bare land, with few or no destructive insects or birds living there, nearly every seed which chanced to arrive, if fitted for the climate, would germinate and survive.

Dispersal during the Glacial Period

The identity of many plants and animals, on mountain-summits, separated from each other by hundreds of miles of lowlands, where Alpine species could not possibly exist, is one of the most striking cases known of the same species living at distant points without the apparent possibility of their having migrated from one point to the other. It is indeed a remarkable fact to see so many plants of the same species living on the snowy regions of the Alps or Pyrenees, and in the extreme northern parts of Europe; but it is far more remarkable, that the plants on the White Mountains, in the United States of America, are all the same with those of Labrador, and nearly all the same, as we hear from Asa Gray, with those on the loftiest mountains of Europe. Even as long ago as 1747, such facts led Gmelin to conclude that the same species must have been independently created at many distinct points; and we might have remained in this same belief, had not Agassiz and others called vivid attention to the Glacial period, which, as we shall immediately see, affords a simple explanation of these facts. We have evidence of almost every conceivable kind, organic and inorganic, that, within a very recent geological period, central Europe and North America suffered under an arctic climate. The ruins of a house burnt by fire do not tell their tale more plainly than do the mountains of Scotland and Wales, with their scored flanks, polished surfaces, and perched boulders, of the icy streams with which their valleys were lately filled. So greatly has the climate of Europe changed, that in Northern Italy, gigantic moraines, left by old glaciers, are now clothed by the vine and maize. Throughout a large part of the United States, erratic boulders and scored rocks plainly reveal a former cold period.

The former influence of the glacial climate on the distribution of the inhabitants of Europe, as explained by Edward Forbes, is substantially as follows. But we shall follow the changes more readily, by supposing a new glacial period slowly to come on, and then pass away, as formerly occurred. As the cold came on, and as each more southern zone became fitted for the inhabitants of the north, these would take the places of the former inhabitants of the temperate regions. The latter, at the same time, would travel further and further southward, unless they were stopped by barriers, in which case they would perish. The mountains would become covered with snow and ice, and their former Alpine inhabitants would descend to the plains. By the time that the cold had reached its maximum, we should have an arctic fauna and flora, covering the central parts of Europe, as far south as the Alps and Pyrenees, and even stretching into Spain. The now temperate regions of the United States would likewise be covered by arctic plants and animals and these would be nearly the same with those of Europe; for the present circumpolar inhabitants, which we suppose to have everywhere travelled southward, are remarkably uniform round the world.

As the warmth returned, the arctic forms would retreat northward, closely followed up in their retreat by the productions of the more temperate regions. And as the snow melted from the bases of the mountains, the arctic forms would seize on the cleared and thawed ground, always ascending, as the warmth increased and the snow still further disappeared, higher and higher, whilst their brethren were pursuing their northern journey. Hence, when the warmth had fully returned, the same species, which had lately lived together on the European and North American lowlands, would again be found in the arctic regions of the Old and New Worlds, and on many isolated mountain-summits far distant from each other.

Thus we can understand the identity of many plants at points so immensely remote as the mountains of the United States and those of Europe. We can thus also understand the fact that the Alpine plants of each mountain-range are more especially related to the arctic forms living due north or nearly due north of them: for the first migration when the cold came on, and the re-migration on the returning warmth, would generally have been due south and north. The Alpine plants, for example, of Scotland, as remarked by Mr. H. C. Watson, and those of the pyrenees, as remarked by Ramond, are more especially allied to the plants of northern Scandinavia; those of the United States to Labrador; those of the mountains of Siberia to the arctic regions of that country. These views, grounded as they are on the perfectly well-ascertained occurrence of a former Glacial period, seem to me to explain in so satisfactory a manner the present distribution of the Alpine and Arctic productions of Europe and America, that when in other regions we find the same species on distant mountain-summits, we may almost conclude, without other evidence, that a colder climate formerly permitted their migration across the intervening lowlands, now become too warm for their existence.

As the arctic forms moved first southward and afterwards backwards to the north, in unison with the changing climate, they will not have been exposed during their long migration to any great diversity of temperature; and as they all migrated in a body together, their mutual relations will not have been much disturbed. Hence, in accordance with the principles inculcated in this volume, these forms will not have been liable to much modification. But with the Alpine productions, left isolated from the moment of the returning warmth, first at the bases and ultimately on the summits of the mountains, the case will have been somewhat different; for it is not likely that all the same arctic species will have been left on mountain ranges far distant from each other, and have survived there ever since; they will also in all probability, have become mingled with ancient Alpine species, which must have existed on the mountains before the commencement of the Glacial epoch, and which during the coldest period will have been temporarily driven down to the plains; they will, also, have been subsequently exposed to somewhat different climatal influences. Their mutual relations will thus have been in some degree disturbed; consequently they will have been liable to modification; and they have been modified; for if we compare the present Alpine plants and animals of the several great European mountain-ranges one with another, though many of the species remain identically the same, some exist as varieties, some as doubtful forms or sub-species, and some as distinct yet closely allied species representing each other on the several ranges.

In the foregoing illustration I have assumed that at the commencement of our imaginary Glacial period, the arctic productions were as uniform round the polar regions as they are at the present day. But it is also necessary to assume that many sub-arctic and some few temperate forms were the same round the world, for some of the species which now exist on the lower mountain-slopes and on the plains of North America and Europe are the same; and it may be asked how I account for this degree of uniformity in the sub-arctic and temperate forms round the world, at the commencement of the real Glacial period. At the present day, the sub-arctic and northern temperate productions of the Old and New Worlds are separated from each other by the whole Atlantic Ocean and by the northern part of the Pacific. During the Glacial period, when the inhabitants of the Old and New Worlds lived farther southward than they do at present, they must have been still more completely separated from each other by wider spaces of ocean; so that it may well be asked how the same species could then or previously have entered the two continents. The explanation, I believe, lies in the nature of the climate before the commencement of the Glacial period. At this, the newer Pliocene period, the majority of the inhabitants of the world were specifically the same as now, and we have good reason to believe that the climate was warmer than at the present day. Hence we may suppose that the organisms which now live under latitude 60°, lived during the Pliocene period farther north under the Polar Circle, in latitude 66°-67°; and that the present arctic productions then lived on the broken land still nearer to the pole. Now, if we looked at a terrestrial globe, we see under the Polar Circle that there is almost continuous land from western Europe, through Siberia, to eastern America. And this continuity of the circumpolar land, with the consequent freedom under a more favourable climate for intermigration, will account for the supposed uniformity of the sub-arctic and temperate productions of the Old and New Worlds, at a period anterior to the Glacial epoch.

Believing, from reasons before alluded to, that our continents have long remained in nearly the same relative position, though subjected to great oscillations of level, I am strongly inclined to extend the above view, and to infer that during some still earlier and still warmer period, such as the older Pliocene period, a large number of the same plants and animals inhabited the almost continuous circumpolar land; and that these plants and animals, both in the Old and New Worlds, began slowly to migrate southwards as the climate became less warm, long before the commencement of the Glacial period. We now see, as I believe, their descendants, mostly in a modified condition, in the central parts of Europe and the United States. On this view we can understand the relationship with very little identity, between the productions of North America and Europe,—a relationship which is highly remarkable, considering the distance of the two areas, and their separation by the whole Atlantic Ocean. We can further understand the singular fact remarked on by several observers that the productions of Europe and America during the later tertiary stages were more closely related to each other than they are at the present time; for during these warmer periods the northern parts of the Old and New Worlds will have been almost continuously united by land, serving as a bridge, since rendered impassable by cold, for the intermigration of their inhabitants.

During the slowly decreasing warmth of the Pliocene period, as soon as the species in common, which inhabited the New and Old Worlds, migrated south of the Polar Circle, they will have been completely cut off from each other. This separation, as far as the more temperate productions are concerned, must have taken place long ages ago. As the plants and animals migrated southwards, they will have become mingled in the one great region with the native American productions, and would have had to compete with them; and in the other great region, with those of the Old World. Consequently we have here everything favourable for much modification,—for far more modification than with the Alpine productions, left isolated, within a much more recent period, on the several mountain-ranges and on the arctic lands of Europe and N. America. Hence it has come, that when we compare the now living productions of the New and Old Worlds, we find very few identical species (though Asa Gray has lately shown that more plants are identical than was formerly supposed), but we find in every great class many forms, which some naturalists rank as geographical races, and others as distinct species; and a host of closely allied or representative forms which are ranked by all naturalists as specifically distinct.

As on the land, so in the waters of the sea, a slow southern migration of a marine fauna, which, during the Pliocene or even a somewhat earlier period, was nearly uniform along the continuous shores of the Polar Circle, will account, on the theory of modification, for many closely allied forms now living in marine areas completely sundered. Thus, I think, we can understand the presence of some closely allied, still existing and extinct tertiary forms, on the eastern and western shores of temperate North America; and the still more striking fact of many closely allied crustaceans (as described in Dana's admirable work), some fish and other marine animals, inhabiting the Mediterranean and the seas of Japan,—these two areas being now completely separated by the breadth of a whole continent and by wide spaces of ocean.

These cases of close relationship in species either now or formerly inhabiting the seas on the eastern and western shores of North America, the Mediterranean and Japan, and the temperate lands of North America and Europe, are inexplicable on the theory of creation. We cannot maintain that such species have been created alike, in correspondence with the nearly similar physical conditions of the areas; for if we compare, for instance, certain parts of South America with parts of South Africa or Australia, we see countries closely similar in all their physical conditions, with their inhabitants utterly dissimilar.

Alternate Glacial Periods in the North and South

But we must return to our more immediate subject. I am convinced that Forbes's view may be largely extended. In Europe we meet with the plainest evidence of the Glacial period, from the western shores of Britain to the Oural range, and southward to the Pyrenees. We may infer from the frozen mammals and nature of the mountain vegetation, that

Siberia was similarly affected. In the Lebanon, according to Dr. Hooker, perpetual snow formerly covered the central axis, and fed glaciers which rolled 400 feet down the valleys. The same observer has recently found great moraines at a low level on the Atlas range in N. Africa. Along the Himalaya, at points 900 miles apart, glaciers have left the marks of their former low descent; and in Sikkim, Dr. Hooker saw maize growing on ancient and gigantic moraines. Southward of the Asiatic continent, on the opposite side of the equator, we know, from the excellent researches of Dr. J. Haast and Dr. Hector, that in New Zealand immense glaciers formerly descended to a low level; and the same plants found by Dr. Hooker on widely separated mountains in this island tell the same story of a former cold period. From facts communicated to me by the Rev. W. B. Clarke, it appears also that there are traces of former glacial action on the mountains of the south-eastern corner of Australia.

Looking to America; in the northern half, ice-borne fragments of rock have been observed on the eastern side of the continent, as far south as lat. 36°-37°, and on the shores of the Pacific, where the climate is now so different, as far south as lat. 46°. Erratic boulders have, also, been noticed on the Rocky Mountains. In the Cordillera of South America, nearly under the equator, glaciers once extended far below their present level. In Central Chile I examined a vast mound of detritus with great boulders, crossing the Portillo valley, which there can hardly be a doubt once formed a huge moraine; and Mr. D. Forbes informs me that he found in various parts of the Cordillera, from lat. 13° to 30°S., at about the height of 12,000 feet, deeply furrowed rocks, resembling those with which he was familiar in Norway, and likewise great masses of detritus, including grooved pebbles. Along this whole space of the Cordillera true glaciers do not exist even at much more considerable heights. Farther south on both sides of the continent, from lat. 41° to the southernmost extremity, we have the clearest evidence of former glacial action, in numerous immense boulders transported far from their parent source.

From these several facts, namely from the glacial action having extended all round the northern and southern hemispheres—from the period having been in a geological sense recent in both hemispheres—from its having lasted in both during a great length of time, as may be inferred from the amount of work effected—and lastly from glaciers having recently descended to a low level along the whole line of the Cordillera, it at one time appeared to me that we could not avoid the conclusion that the temperature of the whole world had been simultaneously lowered during the Glacial period. But now Mr. Croll, in a series of admirable memoirs, has attempted to show that a glacial condition of climate is the result of various physical causes, brought into operation by an increase in the eccentricity of the earth's orbit. All these causes tend towards the same end; but the most powerful appears to be the indirect influence of the eccentricity of the orbit upon oceanic currents. According to Mr. Croll, cold periods regularly occur every ten or fifteen thousand years; and these at long intervals are extremely severe, owing to certain contingencies, of

which the most important, as Sir C. Lyell has shown, is the relative position of the land and water. Mr. Croll believes that the last great Glacial
period occurred about 240,000 years ago, and endured with slight alterations of climate for about 160,000 years. With respect to more ancient
Glacial periods, several geologists are convinced from direct evidence that
such occurred during the Miocene and Eocene formations, not to mention still more ancient formations. But the most important result for us,
arrived at by Mr. Croll, is that whenever the northern hemisphere passes
through a cold period the temperature of the southern hemisphere is actually raised, with the winters rendered much milder, chiefly through
changes in the direction of the ocean currents. So conversely it will be
with the northern hemisphere, whilst the southern passes through a Glacial period. This conclusion throws so much light on geographical distribution that I am strongly inclined to trust in it; but I will first give the
facts, which demand an explanation.

In South America, Dr. Hooker has shown that besides many closely al-
lied species, between forty and fifty of the flowering plants of Tierra del
Fuego, forming no inconsiderable part of its scanty flora, are common to
North America and Europe, enormously remote as these areas in opposite
hemispheres are from each other. On the lofty mountains of equatorial
America a host of peculiar species belonging to European genera occur.
On the Organ mountains of Brazil, some few temperate European, some
Antarctic, and some Andean genera were found by Gardner, which do not
exist in the low intervening hot countries. On the Silla of Caraccas, the
illustrious Humboldt long ago found species belonging to genera characteristic of the Cordillera.

In Africa, several forms characteristic of Europe and some few representatives of the flora of the Cape of Good Hope occur on the mountains
of Abyssinia. At the Cape of Good Hope a very few European species, believed not to have been introduced by man, and on the mountains several
representative European forms are found, which have not been discovered in the intertropical parts of Africa. Dr. Hooker has also lately shown
that several of the plants living on the upper parts of the lofty island of
Fernando Po and on the neighbouring Cameroon mountains, in the Gulf
of Guinea, are closely related to those on the mountains of Abyssinia, and
likewise to those of temperate Europe. It now also appears, as I hear from
Dr. Hooker, that some of these same temperate plants have been discovered by the Rev. R. T. Lowe on the mountains of the Cape Verde islands.
This extension of the same temperate forms, almost under the equator,
across the whole continent of Africa and to the mountains of the Cape
Verde archipelago, is one of the most astonishing facts ever recorded in
the distribution of plants.

On the Himalaya, and on the isolated mountain-ranges of the peninsula of India, on the heights of Ceylon, and on the volcanic cones of Java,
many plants occur, either identically the same or representing each other,
and at the same time representing plants of Europe, not found in the intervening hot lowlands. A list of the genera of plants collected on the lof-

tier peaks of Java, raises a picture of a collection made on a hillock in Europe! Still more striking is the fact that peculiar Australian forms are represented by certain plants growing on the summits of the mountains of Borneo. Some of these Australian forms, as I hear from Dr. Hooker, extend along the heights of the peninsula of Malacca, and are thinly scattered on the one hand over India, and on the other hand as far north as Japan.

On the southern mountains of Australia, Dr. F. Müller has discovered several European species; other species, not introduced by man, occur on the lowlands; and a long list can be given, as I am informed by Dr. Hooker, of European genera, found in Australia, but not in the intermediate torrid regions. In the admirable 'Introduction to the Flora of New Zealand,' by Dr. Hooker, analogous and striking facts are given in regard to the plants of that large island. Hence we see that certain plants growing on the more lofty mountains of the tropics in all parts of the world, and on the temperate plains of the north and south, are either the same species or varieties of the same species. It should, however, be observed that these plants are not strictly arctic forms; for, as Mr. H. C. Watson has remarked, "in receding from polar towards equatorial latitudes, the Alpine or mountain floras really become less and less Arctic." Besides these identical and closely allied forms, many species inhabiting the same widely sundered areas, belong to genera not now found in the intermediate tropical lowlands.

These brief remarks apply to plants alone; but some few analogous facts could be given in regard to terrestrial animals. In marine productions, similar cases likewise occur; as an example, I may quote a statement by the highest authority, Prof. Dana, that "it is certainly a wonderful fact that New Zealand should have a closer resemblance in its crustacea to Great Britain, its antipode, than to any other part of the world." Sir J. Richardson, also, speaks of the reappearance on the shores of New Zealand, Tasmania, &c., of northern forms of fish. Dr. Hooker informs me that twenty-five species of Algæ are common to New Zealand and to Europe, but have not been found in the intermediate tropical seas.

From the foregoing facts, namely, the presence of temperate forms on the highlands across the whole of equatorial Africa, and along the Peninsula of India, to Ceylon and the Malay Archipelago, and in a less well-marked manner across the wide expanse of tropical South America, it appears almost certain that at some former period, no doubt during the most severe part of a Glacial period, the lowlands of these great continents were everywhere tenanted under the equator by a considerable number of temperate forms. At this period the equatorial climate at the level of the sea was probably about the same with that now experienced at the height of from five to six thousand feet under the same latitude, or perhaps even rather cooler. During this, the coldest period, the lowlands under the equator must have been clothed with a mingled tropical and temperate vegetation, like that described by Hooker as growing luxuriantly at the height of from four to five thousand feet on the lower slopes of the Himalaya, but with perhaps a still greater preponderance of temperate forms. So again in the mountainous island of Fernando Po, in the Gulf of Guinea, Mr. Mann found temperate European forms beginning to appear at the height of about five thousand feet. On the mountains of Panama, at the height of only two thousand feet, Dr. Seemann found the vegetation like that of Mexico, "with forms of the torrid zone harmoniously blended with those of the temperate."

Now let us see whether Mr. Croll's conclusion that when the northern hemisphere suffered from the extreme cold of the great Glacial period, the southern hemisphere was actually warmer, throws any clear light on the present apparently inexplicable distribution of various organisms in the temperate parts of both hemispheres, and on the mountains of the tropics. The Glacial period, as measured by years, must have been very long; and when we remember over what vast spaces some naturalised plants and animals have spread within a few centuries, this period will have been ample for any amount of migration. As the cold became more and more intense, we know that Arctic forms invaded the temperate regions; and, from the facts just given, there can hardly be a doubt that some of the more vigorous, dominant, and widest-spreading temperate forms invaded the equatorial lowlands. The inhabitants of these hot lowlands would at the same time have migrated to the tropical and subtropical regions of the south, for the southern hemisphere was at this period warmer. On the decline of the Glacial period, as both hemispheres gradually recovered their former temperatures, the northern temperate forms living on the lowlands under the equator, would have been driven to their former homes or have been destroyed, being replaced by the equatorial forms returning from the south. Some, however, of the northern temperate forms would almost certainly have ascended any adjoining high land, where, if sufficiently lofty, they would have long survived like the Arctic forms on the mountains of Europe. They might have survived, even if the climate was not perfectly fitted for them, for the change of temperature must have been very slow, and plants undoubtedly possess a certain capacity for acclimatisation, as shown by their transmitting to their offspring different constitutional powers of resisting heat and cold.

In the regular course of events the southern hemisphere would in its turn be subjected to a severe Glacial period, with the northern hemisphere rendered warmer; and then the southern temperate forms would invade the equatorial lowlands. The northern forms which had before been left on the mountains would now descend and mingle with the southern forms. These latter, when the warmth returned, would return to their former homes, leaving some few species on the mountains, and carrying southward with them some of the northern temperate forms which had descended from their mountain fastnesses. Thus, we should have some few species identically the same in the northern and southern temperate zones and on the mountains of the intermediate tropical regions. But the species left during a long time on these mountains, or in opposite hemispheres, would have to compete with many new forms and would be exposed to somewhat different physical conditions; hence they would be eminently liable to modification, and would generally now exist as varieties or as representative species; and this is the case. We must, also, bear in mind the occurrence in both hemispheres of former Glacial periods; for these will account, in accordance with the same principles, for the many quite distinct species inhabiting the same widely separated areas, and belonging to genera not now found in the intermediate torrid zones.

It is a remarkable fact strongly insisted on by Hooker in regard to America, and by Alph. de Candolle in regard to Australia, that many more identical or slightly modified species have migrated from the north to the south, than in a reversed direction. We see, however, a few southern forms on the mountains of Borneo and Abyssinia. I suspect that this preponderant migration from the north to the south is due to the greater extent of land in the north, and to the northern forms having existed in their own homes in greater numbers, and having consequently been advanced through natural selection and competition to a higher stage of perfection, or dominating power, than the southern forms. And thus, when the two sets became commingled in the equatorial regions, during the alternations to the Glacial periods, the northern forms were the more powerful and were able to hold their places on the mountains, and afterwards to migrate southward with the southern forms; but not so the southern in regard to the northern forms. In the same manner at the present day, we see that very many European productions cover the ground in La Plata, New Zealand, and to a lesser degree in Australia, and have beaten the natives; whereas extremely few southern forms have become naturalised in any part of the northern hemisphere, though hides, wool, and other objects likely to carry seeds have been largely imported into Europe during the last two or three centuries from La Plata and during the last forty or fifty years from Australia. The Neilgherrie mountains in India, however, offer a partial exception; for here, as I hear from Dr. Hooker, Australian forms are rapidly sowing themselves and becoming naturalised. Before the last great Glacial period, no doubt the intertropical mountains were stocked with endemic Alpine forms; but these have almost everywhere yielded to the more dominant forms generated in the larger areas and more efficient workshops of the north. In many islands the native productions are nearly equalled, or even outnumbered, by those which have become naturalised; and this is the first stage towards their extinction. Mountains are islands on the land, and their inhabitants have yielded to those produced within the larger areas of the north, just in the same way as the inhabitants of real islands have everywhere yielded and are still yielding to continental forms naturalised through man's agency.

The same principles apply to the distribution of terrestrial animals and of marine productions, in the northern and southern temperate zones, and on the intertropical mountains. When, during the height of the Glacial period, the ocean-currents were widely different to what they now are, some of the inhabitants of the temperate seas might have reached the equator; of these a few would perhaps at once be able to migrate southward, by keeping to the cooler currents, whilst others might remain and survive in the colder depths until the southern hemisphere was in its turn subjected to a glacial climate and permitted their further progress; in nearly the same manner as, according to Forbes, isolated spaces inhabited by Arctic productions exist to the present day in the deeper parts of the northern temperate seas.

I am far from supposing that all the difficulties in regard to the distribution and affinities of the identical and allied species, which now live so widely separated in the north and south, and sometimes on the intermediate mountain-ranges, are removed on the views above given. The exact lines of migration cannot be indicated. We cannot say why certain species and not others have migrated; why certain species have been modified and have given rise to new forms, whilst others have remained unaltered. We cannot hope to explain such facts, until we can say why one species and not another becomes naturalised by man's agency in a foreign land; why one species ranges twice or thrice as far, and is twice or thrice as common, as another species within their own homes.

Various special difficulties also remain to be solved; for instance, the occurrence, as shown by Dr. Hooker, of the same plants at points so enormously remote as Kerguelen Land, New Zealand, and Fuegia; but icebergs, as suggested by Lyell, may have been concerned in their dispersal. The existence at these and other distant points of the southern hemisphere, of species, which, though distinct, belong to genera exclusively confined to the south, is a more remarkable case. Some of these species are so distinct, that we cannot suppose that there has been time since the commencement of the last Glacial period for their migration and subsequent modification to the necessary degree. The facts seem to indicate that distinct species belonging to the same genera have migrated in radiating lines from a common centre; and I am inclined to look in the southern, as in the northern hemisphere, to a former and warmer period, before the commencement of the last Glacial period, when the Antarctic lands now covered with ice, supported a highly peculiar and isolated flora. It may be suspected that before this flora was exterminated during the last Glacial epoch, a few forms had been already widely dispersed to various points of the southern hemisphere by occasional means of transport, and by the aid as halting-places, of now sunken islands. Thus the southern shores of America, Australia, and New Zealand may have become slightly tinted by the same peculiar forms of life.

Sir C. Lyell in a striking passage has speculated, in language almost identical with mine, on the effects of great alterations of climate throughout the world on geographical distribution. And we have now seen that Mr. Croll's conclusion that successive Glacial periods in the one hemisphere coincide with warmer periods in the opposite hemisphere, together with the admission of the slow modification of species, explains a multitude of facts in the distribution of the same and of the allied forms of life in all parts of the globe. The living waters have flowed during one period from the north and during another from the south, and in both cases have reached the equator; but the stream of life has flowed with greater force from the north than in the opposite direction, and has consequently more freely inundated the south. As the tide leaves its drift in horizontal lines, rising higher on the shores where the tide rises highest, so have the living waters left their living drift on our mountain summits, in a line gently rising from the Arctic lowlands to a great altitude under the equator. The various beings thus left stranded may be compared with savage races of man, driven up and surviving in the mountain fastnesses of almost every land, which serves as a record, full of interest to us, of the former inhabitants of the surrounding lowlands.

CHAPTER XIII

GEOGRAPHICAL DISTRIBUTION—*continued*

Distribution of fresh-water productions—On the inhabitants of oceanic islands—Absence of Batrachians and of terrestrial Mammals—On the relation of the inhabitants of islands to those of the nearest mainland—On colonisation from the nearest source with subsequent modification—Summary of the last and present chapter.

Fresh-water Productions

As lakes and river-systems are separated from each other by barriers of land, it might have been thought that fresh-water productions would not have ranged widely within the same country, and as the sea is apparently a still more formidable barrier, that they would never have extended to distant countries. But the case is exactly the reverse. Not only have many fresh-water species, belonging to different classes, an enormous range, but allied species prevail in a remarkable manner throughout the world. When first collecting in the fresh waters of Brazil, I well remember feeling much surprise at the similarity of the fresh-water insects, shells &c., and at the dissimilarity of the surrounding terrestrial beings, compared with those of Britain.

But the wide ranging power of fresh-water productions can, I think, in most cases be explained by their having become fitted, in a manner highly useful to them, for short and frequent migrations from pond to pond, or from stream to stream, within their own countries; and liability to wide dispersal would follow from this capacity as an almost necessary consequence. We can here consider only a few cases; of these, some of the most difficult to explain are presented by fish. It was formerly believed that the same fresh-water species never existed on two continents distant from each other. But Dr. Günther has lately shown that the Galaxias attenuatus inhabits Tasmania, New Zealand, the Falkland Islands, and the mainland of South America. This is a wonderful case, and probably indicates dispersal from an Antarctic centre during a former warm period. This case, however, is rendered in some degree less surprising by the species of this genus having the power of crossing by some unknown means considerable spaces of open ocean: thus there is one species common to New Zealand and to the Auckland Islands, though separated by a distance of about 230 miles. On the same continent fresh-water fish often range widely, and as if capriciously; for in two adjoining river-systems some of the species may be the same, and some wholly different.

It is probable that they are occasionally transported by what may be called accidental means. Thus fishes still alive are not very rarely dropped at distant points by whirlwinds; and it is known that the ova retain their vitality for a considerable time after removal from the water. Their dispersal may, however, be mainly attributed to changes in the level of the land within the recent period, causing rivers to flow into each other. Instances, also, could be given of this having occurred during floods, without any change of level. The wide difference of the fish on the opposite sides of most mountain-ranges, which are continuous, and which consequently must from an early period have completely prevented the inosculation of the river-systems on the two sides, leads to the same conclusion. Some fresh-water fish belong to very ancient forms, and in such cases there will have been ample time for great geographical changes, and consequently time and means for much migration. Moreover, Dr. Günther has recently been led by several considerations to infer that with fishes the same forms have a long endurance. Salt-water fish can with care be slowly accustomed to live in fresh water; and, according to Valenciennes, there is hardly a single group of which all the members are confined to fresh water, so that a marine species belonging to a fresh-water group might travel far along the shores of the sea, and could, it is probable, become adapted without much difficulty to the fresh waters of a distant land.

Some species of fresh-water shells have very wide ranges, and allied species which, on our theory, are descended from a common parent, and must have proceeded from a single source, prevail throughout the world. Their distribution at first perplexed me much, as their ova are not likely to be transported by birds; and the ova, as well as the adults, are immediately killed by sea-water. I could not even understand how some naturalised species have spread rapidly throughout the same country. But two facts, which I have observed—and many others no doubt will be discovered—throw some light on this subject. When ducks suddenly emerge from a pond covered with duck-weed, I have twice seen these little plants adhering to their backs; and it has happened to me, in removing a little duck-weed from one aquarium to another, that I have unintentionally stocked the one with fresh-water shells from the other. But another agency is perhaps more effectual: I suspended the feet of a duck in an aquarium, where many ova of fresh-water shells were hatching; and I found that numbers of the extremely minute and just-hatched shells crawled on the feet, and clung to them so firmly that when taken out of the water they could not be jarred off, though at a somewhat more advanced age they would voluntarily drop off. These just-hatched molluscs, though aquatic in their nature, survived on the duck's feet, in damp air, from twelve to twenty-hours; and in this length of time a duck or heron might fly at least six or seven hundred miles, and if blown across the sea to an oceanic island, or to any other distant point, would be sure to alight on a pool or rivulet. Sir Charles Lyell informs me that a Dytiscus has been caught with an Ancylus (a fresh-water shell like a limpet) firmly adhering to it; and a water-beetle of the same family, a Colymbetes, once flew on board the 'Beagle,' when forty-five miles distant from the nearest land: how much farther it might have been blown by a favouring gale no one can tell.

With respect to plants, it has long been known what enormous ranges many fresh-water, and even marsh species, have, both over continents and to the most remote oceanic islands. This is strikingly illustrated, according to Alph. de Candolle, in those large groups of terrestrial plants, which have very few aquatic members; for the latter seem immediately to acquire, as if in consequence, a wide range. I think favourable means of dispersal explain this fact. I have before mentioned that earth occasionally adheres in some quantity to the feet and beaks of birds. Wading birds, which frequent the muddy edges of ponds, if suddenly flushed, would be the most likely to have muddy feet. Birds of this order wander more than those of any other; and they are occasionally found on the most remote and barren islands of the open ocean; they would not be likely to alight on the surface of the sea, so that any dirt on their feet would not be washed off; and when gaining the land, they would be sure to fly to their natural fresh-water haunts. I do not believe that botanists are aware how charged the mud of ponds is with seeds; I have tried several little experiments, but will here give only the most striking case: I took in February three tablespoonfuls of mud from three different points, beneath water, on the edge of a little pond: this mud when dried weighed only 6¾ ounces; I kept it covered up in my study for six months, pulling up and counting each plant as it grew; the plants were of many kinds, and were altogether 537 in number; and yet the viscid mud was all contained in a breakfast cup! Considering these facts, I think it would be an inexplicable circumstance if water-birds did not transport the seeds of fresh-water plants to unstocked ponds and streams, situated at very distant points. The same agency may have come into play with the eggs of some of the smaller fresh-water animals.

Other and unknown agencies probably have also played a part. I have stated that fresh-water fish eat some kinds of seeds, though they reject many other kinds after having swallowed them; even small fish swallow seeds of moderate size, as of the yellow water-lily and Potamogeton. Herons and other birds, century after century, have gone on daily devouring fish; they then take flight and go to other waters, or are blown across the sea; and we have seen that seeds retain their power of germination, when rejected many hours afterwards in pellets or in the excrement. When I saw the great size of the seeds of that fine water-lily, the Nelumbium, and remembered Alph. de Candolle's remarks on the distribution of this plant, I thought that the means of its dispersal must remain inexplicable; but Audubon states that he found the seeds of the great southern water-lily (probably, according to Dr. Hooker, the Nelumbium luteum) in a heron's stomach. Now this bird must often have flown with its stomach thus

well stocked to distant ponds, and then getting a hearty meal of fish, analogy makes me believe that it would have rejected the seeds in a pellet in
a fit state for germination.

In considering these several means of distribution, it should be remembered that when a pond or stream is first formed, for instance, on a rising
islet, it will be unoccupied; and a single seed or egg will have a good
chance of succeeding. Although there will always be a struggle for life between the inhabitants of the same pond, however few in kind, yet as the
number even in a well-stocked pond is small in comparison with the number of species inhabiting an equal area of land, the competition between
them will probably be less severe than between terrestrial species; consequently an intruder from the waters of a foreign country would have a
better chance of seizing on a new place, than in the case of terrestrial colonists. We should also remember that many fresh-water productions are
low in the scale of nature, and we have reason to believe that such beings
become modified more slowly than the high; and this will give time for
the migration of aquatic species. We should not forget the probability of
many fresh-water forms having formerly ranged continuously over immense areas, and then having become extinct at intermediate points. But
the wide distribution of fresh-water plants and of the lower animals,
whether retaining the same identical form or in some degree modified, apparently depends in main part on the wide dispersal of their seeds and
eggs by animals, more especially by fresh-water birds, which have great
powers of flight, and naturally travel from one piece of water to another.

On the Inhabitants of Oceanic Islands

We now come to the last of the three classes of facts, which I have selected as presenting the greatest amount of difficulty with respect to distribution, on the view that not only all the individuals of the same species
have migrated from some one area, but that allied species, although now
inhabiting the most distant points, have proceeded from a single area,—
the birthplace of their early progenitors. I have already given my reasons
for disbelieving in continental extensions within the period of existing
species, on so enormous a scale that all the many islands of the several
oceans were thus stocked with their present terrestrial inhabitants. This
view removes many difficulties, but it does not accord with all the facts in
regard to the productions of islands. In the following remarks I shall not
confine myself to the mere question of dispersal, but shall consider some
other cases bearing on the truth of the two theories of independent creation and of descent with modification.

The species of all kinds which inhabit oceanic islands are few in number compared with those on equal continental areas: Alph. de Candolle
admits this for plants, and Wollaston for insects. New Zealand, for instance, with its lofty mountains and diversified stations, extending ovei
780 miles of latitude, together with the outlying islands of Auckland,
Campbell and Chatham, contain altogether only 960 kinds of flowering

plants; if we compare this moderate number with the species which swarm over equal areas in South-Western Australia or at the Cape of Good Hope, we must admit that some cause, independently of different physical conditions, has given rise to so great a difference in number. Even the uniform county of Cambridge has 847 plants, and the little island of Anglesea 764, but a few ferns and a few introduced plants are included in these numbers, and the comparison in some other respects is not quite fair. We have evidence that the barren island of Ascension aboriginally possssed less than half-a-dozen flowering plants; yet many species have now become naturalised on it, as they have in New Zealand and on every other oceanic island which can be named. In St. Helena there is reason to believe that the naturalised plants and animals have nearly or quite exterminated many native productions. He who admits the doctrine of the creation of each separate species, will have to admit that a sufficient number of the best adapted plants and animals were not created for oceanic islands; for man has unintentionally stocked them far more fully and prefectly than did nature.

Although in oceanic islands the species are few in number, the proportion of endemic kinds (*i. e.*, those found nowhere else in the world) is often extremely large. If we compare, for instance, the number of endemic land-shells in Madeira, or of endemic birds in the Galapagos Archipelago, with the number found on any continent, and then compare the area of the island with that of the continent, we shall see that this is true. This fact might have been theoretically expected, for, as already explained, species occasionally arriving after long intervals of time in the new and isolated district, and having to compete with new associates, would be eminently liable to modification, and would often produce groups of modified descendants. But it by no means follows that, because in an island nearly all the species of one class are peculiar, those of another class, or of another section of the same class, are peculiar; and this difference seems to depend partly on the species which are not modified having immigrated in a body, so that their mutual relations have not been much disturbed; and partly on the frequent arrival of unmodified immigrants from the mother-country, with which the insular forms have intercrossed. It should be borne in mind that the offspring of such crosses would certainly gain in vigour; so that even an occasional cross would produce more effect than might have been anticipated. I will give a few illustrations of the foregoing remarks: in the Galapagos Islands there are 26 land-birds; of these 21 (or perhaps 23) are peculiar, whereas of the 11 marine birds only 2 are peculiar; and it is obvious that marine birds could arrive at these islands much more easily and frequently than land-birds. Bermuda, on the other hand, which lies at about the same distance from North America as the Galapagos Islands do from South America, and which has a very peculiar soil, does not possess a single endemic land bird, and we know from Mr. J. M. Jones's admirable account of Bermuda, that very many North American birds occasionally or even frequently visit this island. Almost every year, as I am informed by Mr. E.

V. Harcourt, many European and African birds are blown to Madeira; this island is inhabited by 99 kinds of which one alone is peculiar, though very closely related to a European form; and three or four other species are confined to this island and to the Canaries. So that the islands of Bermuda and Madeira have been stocked from the neighbouring continents with birds, which for long ages have there struggled together, and have become mutually co-adapted. Hence when settled in their new homes, each kind will have been kept by the others to its proper place and habits, and will consequently have been but little liable to modification. Any tendency to modification will also have been checked by intercrossing with the unmodified immigrants, often arriving from the mother-country. Madeira again is inhabited by a wonderful number of peculiar land-shells, whereas not one species of sea-shell is peculiar to its shores: now, though we do not know how sea-shells are dispersed, yet we can see that their eggs or larvæ, perhaps attached to seaweed or floating timber, or to the feet of wading-birds, might be transported across three or four hundred miles of open sea far more easily than land-shells. The different orders of insects inhabiting Madeira present nearly parallel cases.

Oceanic islands are sometimes deficient in animals of certain whole classes, and their places are occupied by other classes; thus in the Galapagos Islands reptiles, and in New Zealand gigantic wingless birds, take, or recently took, the place of mammals. Although New Zealand is here spoken of as an oceanic island, it is in some degree doubtful whether it should be so ranked; it is of large size, and is not separated from Australia by a profoundly deep sea; from its geological character and the direction of its mountain-ranges, the Rev. W. B. Clarke has lately maintained that this island, as well as New Caledonia, should be considered as appurtenances of Australia. Turning to plants, Dr. Hooker has shown that in the Galapagos Islands the proportional numbers of the different orders are very different from what they are elsewhere. All such differences in number, and the absence of certain whole groups of animals and plants, are generally accounted for by supposed differences in the physical conditions of the islands; but this explanation is not a little doubtful. Facility of immigration seems to have been fully as important as the nature of the conditions.

Many remarkable little facts could be given with respect to the inhabitants of oceanic islands. For instance, in certain islands not tenanted by a single mammal, some of the endemic plants have beautifully hooked seeds; yet few relations are more manifest than that hooks serve for the transportal of seeds in the wool or fur of quadrupeds. But a hooked seed might be carried to an island by other means; and the plant then becoming modified would form an endemic species, still retaining its hooks, which would form a useless appendage like the shrivelled wings under the soldered wing-covers of many insular beetles. Again, islands often possess trees or bushes belonging to orders which elsewhere include only herbaceous species; now trees, as Alph. de Candolle has shown, generally have, whatever the cause may be, confined ranges. Hence trees would be little likely to reach distant oceanic islands; and an herbaceous plant, which had no chance of successfully competing with the many fully developed trees growing on a continent, might, when established on an island, gain an advantage over other herbaceous plants by growing taller and taller and overtopping them. In this case, natural selection would tend to add to the stature of the plant, to whatever order it belonged, and thus first convert it into a bush and then into a tree.

Absence of Batrachians and Terrestrial Mammals on Oceanic Islands

With respect to the absence of whole orders of animals on oceanic islands, Bory St. Vincent long ago remarked that Batrachians (frogs, toads, newts) are never found on any of the many islands with which the great oceans are studded. I have taken pains to verify this asssertion, and have found it true, with the exception of New Zealand, New Caledonia, the Andaman Islands, and perhaps the Solomon Islands and the Seychelles. But I have already remarked that it is doubtful whether New Zealand and New Caledonia ought to be classed as oceanic islands; and this is still more doubtful with respect to the Andaman and Solomon groups and the Seychelles. This general absence of frogs, toads, and newts on so many true oceanic islands cannot be accounted for by their physical conditions: indeed it seems that islands are peculiarly fitted for these animals; for frogs have been introduced into Madeira, the Azores, and Mauritius, and have multiplied so as to become a nuisance. But as these animals and their spawn are immediately killed (with the exception, as far as known, of one Indian species) by sea-water, there would be great difficulty in their transportal across the sea, and therefore we can see why they do not exist on strictly oceanic islands. But why, on the theory of creation, they should not have been created there, it would be very difficult to explain.

Mammals offer another and similar case. I have carefully searched the oldest voyages, and have not found a single instance, free from doubt, of a terrestrial mammal (excluding domesticated animals kept by the natives) inhabiting an island situated above 300 miles from a continent or great contir.ental island; and many islands situated at a much less distance are equally barren. The Falkland Islands, which are inhabited by a wolf-like fox, come nearest to an exception; but this group cannot be considered as oceanic, as it lies on a bank in connection with the mainland at the distance of about 280 miles; moreover, icebergs formerly brought boulders to its western shores, and they may have formerly transported foxes, as now frequently happens in the arctic regions. Yet it cannot be said that small islands will not support at least small mammals, for they occur in many parts of the world on very small islands, when lying close to a continent; and hardly an island can be named on which our smaller quadrupeds have not become naturalised and greatly multiplied. It cannot be said, on the ordinary view of creation, that there has not been time for the creation of mammals; many volcanic islands are sufficiently ancient, as shown by the stupendous degradation which they have suffered, and by their tertiary strata: there has also been time for the production of endemic species belonging to other classes; and on continents it is known that new species of mammals appear and disappear at a quicker rate than other and lower animals. Although terrestrial mammals do not occur on oceanic islands, aerial mammals do occur on almost every island. New Zealand possesses two bats found nowhere else in the world: Norfolk Island, the Viti Archipelago, the Bonin Islands, the Caroline and Marianne Archipelagoes, and Mauritius, all possess their peculiar bats. Why, it may be asked, has the supposed creative force produced bats and no other mammals on remote islands? On my view this question can easily be answered; for no terrestrial mammal can be transported across a wide space of sea, but bats can fly across. Bats have been seen wandering by day far over the Atlantic Ocean; and two North American species either regularly or occasionally visit Bermuda, at the distance of 600 miles from the mainland. I hear from Mr. Tomes, who has specially studied this family, that many species have enormous ranges, and are found on continents and on far distant islands. Hence we have only to suppose that such wandering species have been modified in their new homes in relation to their new position, and we can understand the presence of endemic bats on oceanic islands, with the absence of all other terrestrial mammals.

Another interesting relation exists, namely, between the depth of the sea separating islands from each other or from the nearest continent, and the degreee of affinity of their mammalian inhabitants. Mr. Windsor Earl has made some striking observations on this head, since greatly extended by Mr. Wallace's admirable researches, in regard to the great Malay Archipelago, which is traversed near Celebes by a space of deep ocean, and this separates two widely distinct mammalian faunas. On either side the islands stand on a moderately shallow submarine bank, and these islands are inhabited by the same or by closely allied quadrupeds. I have not as yet had time to follow up this subject in all quarters of the world; but as far as I have gone, the relation holds good. For instance, Britain is separated by a shallow channel from Europe, and the mammals are the same on both sides; and so it is with all the islands near the shores of Australia. The West Indian Islands, on the other hand, stand on a deeply submerged bank, nearly 1000 fathoms in depth, and here we find American forms, but the species and even the genera are quite distinct. As the amount of modification which animals of all kinds undergo partly depends on the lapse of time, and as the islands which are separated from each other or from the mainland by shallow channels, are more likely to have been continuously united within a recent period than the islands separated by deeper channels, we can understand how it is that a relation exists between the depth of the sea separating two mammalian faunas, and the degree of their affinity,—a relation which is quite inexplicable on the theory of independent acts of creation.

The foregoing statements in regard to the inhabitants of oceanic islands,—namely, the fewness of the species, with a large proportion consisting of endemic forms—the members of certain groups, but not those of other groups in the same class, having been modified—the absence of certain whole orders, as of batrachians and of terrestrial mammals, notwithstanding the presence of aerial bats,—the singular proportions of certain orders of plants,—herbaceous forms having been developed into trees, &c.,—seem to me to accord better with the belief in the efficiency of occasional means of transport, carried on during a long course of time, than with the belief in the former connection of all oceanic islands with the nearest continent; for on this latter view it is probable that the various classes would have immigrated more uniformly, and from the species having entered in a body their mutual relations would not have been much disturbed, and consequently they would either have not been modified, or all the species in a more equable manner.

I do not deny that there are many and serious difficulties in understanding how many of the inhabitants of the more remote islands, whether still retaining the same specific form or subsequently modified, have reached their present homes. But the probability of other islands having once existed as halting-places, of which not a wreck now remains, must not be overlooked. I will specify one difficult case. Almost all oceanic islands, even the most isolated and smallest, are inhabited by land-shells, generally by endemic species, but sometimes by species found elsewhere, —striking instances of which have been given by Dr. A. A. Gould in relation to the Pacific. Now it is notorious that land-shells are easily killed by sea-water; their eggs, at least such as I have tried, sink in it and are killed. Yet there must be some unknown, but occasionally efficient means for their transportal. Would the just-hatched young sometimes adhere to the feet of birds roosting on the ground, and thus get transported? It occurred to me that land-shells, when hybernating and having a membranous diaphragm over the mouth of the shell, might be floated in chinks of drifted timber across moderately wide arms of the sea. And I find that several species in this state withstand uninjured an immersion in sea-water during seven days: one shell, the Helix pomatia, after having been thus treated and again hybernating was put into sea-water for twenty days, and perfectly recovered. During this length of time the shell might have been carried by a marine current of average swiftness, to a distance of 660 geographical miles. As this Helix has a thick calcareous operculum, I removed it, and when it had formed a new membranous one, I again immersed it for fourteen days in sea-water, and again it recovered and crawled away. Baron Aucapitaine has since tried similar experiments: he placed 100 land-shells, belonging to ten species, in a box pierced with holes, and immersed it for a fortnight in the sea. Out of the hundred shells, twenty-seven recovered. The presence of an operculum seems to have been of importance, as out of twelve specimens of Cyclostoma elegans, which is thus furnished, eleven revived. It is remarkable, seeing how well the Helix pomatia resisted with me the salt-water, that not one of fifty-four specimens belonging to four other species of Helix tried by Aucapitaine, recovered. It is, however, not at all probable that land-shells have often been thus transported; the feet of birds offer a more probable method.

On the Relations of the Inhabitants of Islands to those of the nearest Mainland

The most striking and important fact for us is the affinity of the species which inhabit islands to those of the nearest mainland, without being actually the same. Numerous instances could be given. The Galapagos Archipelago, situated under the equator, lies at the distance of between 500 and 600 miles from the shores of South America. Here almost every product of the land and of the water bears the unmistakable stamp of the American continent. There are twenty-six land-birds; of these, twenty-one, or perhaps twenty-three are ranked as distinct species, and would commonly be assumed to have been here created; yet the close affinity of most of these birds to American species is manifest in every character, in their habits, gestures, and tones of voice. So it is with the other animals, and with a large proportion of the plants, as shown by Dr. Hooker in his admirable Flora of this archipelago. The naturalist, looking at the inhabitants of these volcanic islands in the Pacific, distant several hundred miles from the continent, feels that he is standing on American land. Why should this be so? why should the species which are supposed to have been created in the Galapagos Archipelago, and nowhere else, bear so plainly the stamp of affinity to those created in America? There is nothing in the conditions of life, in the geological nature of the islands, in their height or climate, or in the proportions in which the several classes are associated together, which closely resembles the conditions of the South American coast: in fact, there is a considerable dissimilarity in all these respects. On the other hand, there is a considerable degree of resemblance in the volcanic nature of the soil, in the climate, height, and size of the islands, between the Galapagos and Cape Verde Archipelagoes: but what an entire and absolute difference in their inhabitants! The inhabitants of the Cape Verde Islands are related to those of Africa, like those of the Galapagos to America. Facts such as these admit of no sort of explanation on the ordinary view of independent creation; whereas on the view here maintained, it is obvious that the Galapagos Islands would be likely to receive colonists from America, whether by occasional means of transport or (though I do not believe in this doctrine) by formerly continuous land, and the Cape Verde Islands from Africa; such colonists would be liable to modification,—the principle of inheritance still betraying their original birthplace.

Many analogous facts could be given: indeed it is an almost universal rule that the endemic productions of islands are related to those of the nearest continent, or of the nearest large island. The exceptions are few, and most of them can be explained. Thus although Kerguelen Land stands nearer to Africa than to America, the plants are related, and that very closely, as we know from Dr. Hooker's account, to those of America: but on the view that this island has been mainly stocked by seeds brought with earth and stones on icebergs, drifted by the prevailing currents, this anomaly disappears. New Zealand in its endemic planes is much more closely related to Australia, the nearest mainland, than to any other region: and this is what might have been expected; but it is also plainly related to South America, which, although the next nearest continent, is so enormously remote, that the fact becomes an anomaly. But this difficulty partially disappears on the view that New Zealand, South America, and the other southern lands have been stocked in part from a nearly intermediate though distant point, namely from the antarctic islands, when they were clothed with vegetation, during a warmer tertiary period, before the commencement of the last Glacial period. The affinity, which though feeble, I am assured by Dr. Hooker is real, between the flora of the south-western corner of Australia and of the Cape of Good Hope, is a far more remarkable case; but this affinity is confined to the plants, and will, no doubt, some day be explained.

The same law which has determined the relationship between the inhabitants of islands and the nearest mainland, is sometimes displayed on a small scale, but in a most interesting manner, within the limits of the same archipelago. Thus each separate island of the Galapagos Archipelago is tenanted, and the fact is a marvellous one, by many different species; but these species are related to each other in a very much closer manner than to the inhabitants of the American continent, or of any other quarter of the world. This is what might have been expected, for islands situated so near to each other would almost necessarily receive immigrants from the same original source, and from each other. But how is it that many of the immigrants have been differently modified, though only in a small degree, in islands situated within sight of each other, having the same geological nature, the same height, climate, &c.? This long appeared to me a great difficulty: but it arises in chief part from the deeply-seated error of considering the physical conditions of a country as the most important; whereas it cannot be disputed that the nature of the other species with which each has to compete, is at least as important, and generally a far more important element of success. Now if we look to the species which inhabit the Galapagos Archipelago, and are likewise found in other parts of the world, we find that they differ considerably in the several islands. This difference might indeed have been expected if the islands had been stocked by occasional means of transport—a seed, for instance, of one plant having been brought to one island, and that of another plant to another island, though all proceeding from the same general source. Hence, when in former times an immigrant first settled on one of the islands, or when it subsequently spread from one to another, it would undoubtedly be exposed to different conditions in the different islands, for it would have to compete with a different set of organisms; a plant, for instance, would find the ground best fitted for it occupied by somewhat different species in the different islands, and would be exposed to the attacks of somewhat different enemies. If then it varied, natural selection would probably favour different varieties in the different islands. Some species, however, might spread and yet retain the same character throughout the group, just as we see some species spreading widely throughout a continent and remaining the same.

The really surprising fact in this case of the Galapagos Archipelago, and in a lesser degree in some analogous cases, is that each new species after being formed in any one island, did not spread quickly to the other islands. But the islands, though in sight of each other, are separated by deep arms of the sea, in most cases wider than the British Channel, and there is no reason to suppose that they have at any former period been continuously united. The currents of the sea are rapid and sweep between the islands, and gales of wind are extraordinarily rare; so that the islands are far more effectually separated from each other than they appear on a map. Nevertheless some of the species, both of those found in other parts of the world and of those confined to the archipelago, are common to the several islands; and we may infer from their present manner of distribution, that they have spread from one island to the others. But we often take, I think, an erroneous view of the probability of closely-allied species invading each other's territory, when put into free intercommunication. Undoubtedly, if one species has any advantage over another, it will in a very brief time wholly or in part supplant it; but if both are equally well fitted for their own places, both will probably hold their separate places for almost any length of time. Being familiar with the fact that many species, naturalised through man's agency, have spread with astonishing rapidity over wide areas, we are apt to infer that most species would thus spread; but we should remember that the species which become naturalised in new countries are not generally closely allied to the aboriginal inhabitants, but are very distinct forms, belonging in a large proportion of cases, as shown by Alph. de Candolle, to distinct genera. In the Galapagos Archipelago, many even of the birds, though so well adapted for flying from island to island, differ on the different islands; thus there are three closely-allied species of mocking-thrush, each confined to its own island. Now let us suppose the mocking-thrush of Chatham Island to be blown to Charles Island, which has its own mocking-thrush, why should it succeed in establishing itself there? We may safely infer that Charles Island is well stocked with its own species, for annually more eggs are laid and young birds hatched, than can possibly be reared; and we may infer that the mocking-thrush peculiar to Charles's Island is at least as well fitted for its home as is the species peculiar to Chatham Island. Sir C. Lyell and Mr. Wollaston have communicated to me a remarkable fact bearing on this subject; namely, that Madeira and the adjoining islet of Porto Santo possess many distinct but representative species of land-shells, some of which live in crevices of stone; and although large quantities of stone are annually transported from Porto Santo to Madeira, yet this latter island has not become colonised by the Porto Santo species; nevertheless both islands have been colonised by European land-shells, which no doubt had some advantage over the indigenous species. From these considerations I think we need not greatly marvel at the endemic species which inhabit the several islands of the Galapagos Archipelago, not having all spread from island to island. On the same continent, also, preoccupation has probably played an important part in checking the commingling of the species which inhabit different districts with nearly the same physical conditions. Thus, the south-east and south-west corners of Australia have nearly the same physical conditions, and are united by continuous land, yet they are inhabited by a vast number of distinct mammals, birds, and plants; so it is, according to Mr. Bates, with the butterflies and other animals inhabiting the great, open, and continuous valley of the Amazons.

The same principle which governs the general character of the inhabitants of oceanic islands, namely, the relation to the source whence colonists could have been most easily derived, together with their subsequent modification, is of the widest application throughout nature. We see this on every mountain-summit, in every lake and marsh. For Alpine species, excepting in as far as the same species have become widely spread during the Glacial epoch, are related to those of the surrounding lowlands; thus we have in South America, Alpine humming-birds, Alpine rodents, Alpine plants, &c., all strictly belonging to American forms; and it is obvious that a mountain, as it became slowly unheaved, would be colonised from the surrounding lowlands. So it is with the inhabitants of lakes and marshes, excepting in so far as great facility of transport has allowed the same forms to prevail throughout large portions of the world. We see this same principle in the character of most of the blind animals inhabiting the caves of America and of Europe. Other analogous facts could be given. It will, I believe, be found universally true, that wherever in two regions, let them be ever so distant, many closely allied or representative species occur, there will likewise be found some identical species; and wherever many closely-allied species occur, there will be found many forms which some naturalists rank as distinct species, and others as mere varieties; these doubtful forms showing us the steps in the progress of modification.

The relation between the power and extent of migration in certain species, either at the present or at some former period, and the existence at remote points of the world of closely-allied species, is shown in another and more general way. Mr. Gould remarked to me long ago, that in those genera of birds which range over the world, many of the species have very wide ranges. I can hardly doubt that this rule is generally true, though difficult of proof. Amongst mammals, we see it strikingly displayed in Bats, and in a lesser degree in the Felidæ and Canidæ. We see the same rule in the distribution of butterflies and beetles. So it is with most of the inhabitants of fresh water, for many of the genera in the most distinct classes range over the world, and many of the species have enormous ranges. It is not meant that all, but that some of the species have very wide ranges in the genera which range very widely. Nor is it meant that the species in such genera have on an average a very wide range; for this will largely depend on how far the process of modification has gone; for instance, two varieties of the same species inhabit America and Europe, and thus the species has an immense range; but, if variation were to be carried a little further, the two varieties would be ranked as distinct species, and their range would be greatly reduced. Still less is it meant, that species which have the capacity of crossing barriers and ranging widely, as in the case of certain powerfully-winged birds, will necessarily range widely; for we should never forget that to range widely implies not only the power of crossing barriers, but the more important power of being victorious in distant lands in the struggle for life with foreign associates. But according to the view that all the species of a genus, though distributed to the most remote points of the world, are descended from a single progenitor, we ought to find, and I believe as a general rule we do find, that some at least of the species range very widely.

We should bear in mind that many genera in all classes are of ancient origin, and the species in this case will have had ample time for dispersal and subsequent modification. There is also reason to believe from geological evidence, that within each great class the lower organisms change at a slower rate than the higher; consequently they will have had a better chance of ranging widely and of still retaining the same specific character. This fact, together with that of the seeds and eggs of most lowly organised forms being very minute and better fitted for distant transportal, probably accounts for a law which has long been observed, and which has lately been discussed by Alph. de Candolle in regard to plants, namely, that the lower any group of organisms stands the more widely it ranges.

The relations just discussed,—namely, lower organisms ranging more widely than the higher,—some of the species of widely-ranging genera themselves ranging widely,—such facts, as alpine, lacustrine, and marsh productions being generally related to those which live on the surrounding low lands and dry lands,—the striking relationship between the inhabitants of islands and those of the nearest mainland—the still closer relationship of the distinct inhabitants of the islands in the same archipelago—are inexplicable on the ordinary view of the independent creation of each species, but are explicable if we admit colonisation from the nearest or readiest source, together with the subsequent adaptation of the colonists to their new homes.

Summary of the last and present Chapters

In these chapters I have endeavoured to show, that if we make due allowance for our ignorance of the full effects of changes of climate and of the level of the land, which have certainly occurred within the recent period, and of other changes which have probably occurred,—if we remember how ignorant we are with respect to the many curious means of occasional transport,—if we bear in mind, and this is a very important consideration, how often a species may have ranged continuously over a wide area, and then have become extinct in the intermediate tracts,—tne difficulty is not insuperable in believing that all the individuals of the same species, wherever found, are descended from common parents. And we are led to this conclusion, which has been arrived at by many naturalists under the designation of single centres of creation, by various general considerations, more especially from the importance of barriers of all kinds, and from the analogical distribution of sub-genera, genera, and families.

With respect to distinct species belonging to the same genus, which on our theory have spread from one parent-source; if we make the same allowances as before for our ignorance, and remember that some forms of life have changed very slowly, enormous periods of time having been thus granted for their migration, the difficulties are far from insuperable; though in this case, as in that of the individuals of the same species, they are often great.

As exemplifying the effects of climatal changes on distribution, I have attempted to show how important a part the last Glacial period has played, which affected even the equatorial regions, and which, during the alternations of the cold in the north and south, allowed the productions of opposite hemispheres to mingle, and left some of them stranded on the mountain-summits in all parts of the world. As showing how diversified are the means of occasional transport, I have discussed at some little length the means of dispersal of fresh-water productions.

If the difficulties be not insuperable in admitting that in the long course of time all the individuals of the same species, and likewise of the several species belonging to the same genus, have proceeded from some one source; then all the grand leading facts of geographical distribution are explicable on the theory of migration, together with subsequent modification and the multiplication of new forms. We can thus understand the high importance of barriers, whether of land or water, in not only separating, but in apparently forming the several zoological and botanical provinces. We can thus understand the concentration of related species within the same areas; and how it is that under different latitudes, for instance in South America, the inhabitants of the plains and mountains, of the forests, marshes, and deserts, are linked together in so mysterious a manner, and are likewise linked to the extinct beings which formerly inhabited the same continent. Bearing in mind that the mutual relation of organism to organism is of the highest importance, we can see why two areas having nearly the same physical conditions should often be inhabited by very different forms of life; for according to the length of time which has elapsed since the colonists entered one of the regions, or both; according to the nature of the communication which allowed certain forms and not others to enter, either in greater or lesser numbers; according or not, as those which entered happened to come into more or less direct competition with each other and with the aborigines; and according as the immigrants were capable of varying more or less rapidly, there would ensue in the two or more regions, independently of their physical conditions, infinitely diversified conditions of life,—there would be an al-most endless amount of organic action and reaction,—and we should find some groups of beings greatly, and some only slightly modified,—some developed in great force, some existing in scanty numbers—and this we do find in the several great geographical provinces of the world.

On these same principles we can understand, as I have endeavoured to show, why oceanic islands should have few inhabitants, but that of these, a large proportion should be endemic or peculiar; and why, in relation to the means of migration, one group of beings should have all its species pe-culiar, and another group, even within the same class, should have all its species the same with those in an adjoining quarter of the world. We can see why whole groups of organisms, as batrachians and terrestrial mam-mals, should be absent from oceanic islands, whilst the most isolated is-lands should possess their own peculiar species of aerial mammals or bats. We can see why, in islands, there should be some relation between the presence of mammals, in a more or less modified condition, and the depth of the sea between such islands and the mainland. We can clearly see why all the inhabitants of an archipelago, though specifically distinct on the several islets, should be closely related to each other; and should likewise be related, but less closely, to those of the nearest continent, or other source whence immigrants might have been derived. We can see why, if there exists very closely allied or representative species in two areas, how-ever distant from each other, some identical species will almost always there be found.

As the late Edward Forbes often insisted, there is a striking parallelism in the laws of life throughout time and space; the laws governing the suc-cession of forms in past times being nearly the same with those governing at the present time the differences in different areas. We see this in many facts. The endurance of each species and group of species is continuous in time; for the apparent exceptions to the rule are so few, that they may fairly be attributed to our not having as yet discovered in an intermediate deposit certain forms which are absent in it, but which occur both above and below: so in space, it certainly is the general rule that the area inhab-ited by a single species, or by a group of species, is continuous, and the ex-ceptions, which are not rare, may, as I have attempted to show, be ac-counted for by former migrations under different circumstances, or through occasional means of transport, or by the species having become extinct in the intermediate tracts. Both in time and space species and groups of species have their points of maximum development. Groups of species, living during the same period of time, or living within the same area, are often characterised by trifling features in common, as of sculp-ture or colour. In looking to the long succession of past ages, as in looking to distant provinces throughout the world, we find that species in certain classes differ little from each other, whilst those in another class, or only in a different section of the same order, differ greatly from each other. In both time and space the lowly organised members of each class generally change less than the highly organised; but there are in both cases marked exceptions to the rule. According to our theory, these several relations throughout time and space are intelligible; for whether we look to the allied forms of life which have changed during successive ages, or to those which have changed after having migrated into distant quarters, in both cases they are connected by the same bond of ordinary generation; in both cases the laws of variation have been the same, and modifications have been accumulated by the same means of natural selection.

CHAPTER XIV

MUTUAL AFFINITIES OF ORGANIC BEINGS: MORPHOLOGY: EMBRYOLOGY: RUDIMENTARY ORGANS

Classification, groups subordinate to groups—Natural system—Rules and difficulties in classification, explained on the theory of descent with modification—Classification of varieties—Descent always used in classification—Analogical or adaptive characters—Affinities, general, complex, and radiating—Extinction separates and defines groups—Morphology, between members of the same class, between parts of the same individual—Embryology, laws of, explained by variations not supervening at an early age, and being inherited at a corresponding age—Rudimentary organs; their origin explained—Summary.

Classification

FROM the most remote period in the history of the world organic beings have been found to resemble each other in descending degrees, so that they can be classed in groups under groups. This classification is not arbitrary like the grouping of the stars in constellations. The existence of groups would have been of simpler significance, if one group had been exclusively fitted to inhabit the land and another the water; one to feed on flesh, another on vegetable matter, and so on; but the case is widely different, for it is notorious how commonly members of even the same subgroup have different habits. In the second and fourth chapters, on Variation and on Natural Selection, I have attempted to show that within each country it is the widely ranging, the much diffused and common, that is the dominant species, belonging to the larger genera in each class, which vary most. The varieties, or incipient species, thus produced, ultimately become converted into new and distinct species; and these, on the principle of inheritance, tend to produce other new and dominant species. Consequently the groups which are now large, and which generally include many dominant species, tend to go on increasing in size. I further attempted to show that from the varying descendants of each species trying to occupy as many and as different places as possible in the economy of nature, they constantly tend to diverge in character. This latter conclusion is supported by observing the great diversity of forms which, in any small area, come into the closest competition, and by certain facts in naturalisation.

I attempted also to show that there is a steady tendency in the forms which are increasing in number and diverging in character, to supplant and exterminate the preceding, less divergent and less improved forms. I request the reader to turn to the diagram illustrating the action, as formerly explained, of these several principles; and he will see that the inevitable result is, that the modified descendants proceeding from one progenitor become broken up into groups subordinate to groups. In the diagram each letter on the uppermost line may represent a genus including several species, and the whole of the genera along this upper line form together one class, for all are descended from one ancient parent, and, consequently, have inherited something in common. But the three genera on the left hand have, on this same principle, much in common, and form a sub-family, distinct from that containing the next two genera on the right hand, which diverged from a common parent at the fifth stage of descent. These five genera have also much in common, though less than when grouped in sub-families; and they form a family distinct from that containing the three genera still farther to the right hand, which diverged at an earlier period. And all these genera, descended from (A), form an order distinct from the genera descended from (I). So that we here have many species descended from a single progenitor grouped into genera; and the genera into sub-families, families, and orders, all under one great class. The grand fact of the natural subordination of organic beings in groups under groups, which, from its familiarity, does not always sufficiently strike us, is in my judgment thus explained. No doubt organic beings, like all other objects, can be classed in many ways, either artificially by single characters, or more naturally by a number of characters. We know, for instance, that minerals and the elemental substances can be thus arranged. In this case there is of course no relation to genealogical succession, and no cause can at present be assigned for their falling into groups. But with organic beings the case is different, and the view above given accords with their natural arrangment in group under group; and no other explanation has ever been attempted.

Naturalists, as we have seen, try to arrange the species, genera, and families in each class, on what is called the Natural System. But what is meant by this system? Some authors look at it merely as a scheme for arranging together those living objects which are most alike, and for separating those which are most unlike; or as an artificial method of enunciating, as briefly as possible, general propositions,—that is, by one sentence to give the characters common, for instance, to all mammals, by another those common to all carnivora, by another those common to the dog-genus, and then, by adding a single sentence, a full description is given of each kind of dog. The ingenuity and utility of this system are indisputable. But many naturalists think that something more is meant by the Natural System; they believe that it reveals the plan of the Creator; but unless it be specified whether order in time or space, or both, or what else is meant by the plan of the Creator, it seems to me that nothing is thus added to our knowledge. Expressions such as that famous one by Linnæus, which we often meet with in a more or less concealed form, namely, that the characters do not make the genus, but that the genus gives the characters, seem to imply that some deeper bond is included in our classifications than mere resemblance. I believe that this is the case, and that community of descent—the one known cause of close similarity in organic beings—is the bond, which though observed by various degrees of modification, is partially revealed to us by our classifications.

Let us now consider the rules followed in classification, and the difficulties which are encountered on the view that classification either gives some unknown plan of creation, or is simply a scheme for enunciating general propositions and of placing together the forms most like each other. It might have been thought (and was in ancient times thought) that those parts of the structure which determined the habits of life, and the general place of each being in the economy of nature, would be of very high importance in classification. Nothing can be more false. No one regards the external similarity of a mouse to a shrew, of a dugong to a whale, of a whale to a fish, as of any importance. These resemblances, though so intimately connected with the whole life of the being, are ranked as merely "adaptive or analogical characters;" but to the consideration of these resemblances we shall recur. It may even be given as a general rule, that the less any part of the organisation is concerned with special habits, the more important it becomes for classification. As an instance: Owen, in speaking of the dugong, says, "The generative organs, being those which are most remotely related to the habits and food of an animal, I have always regarded as affording very clear indications of its true affinities. We are least likely in the modifications of these organs to mistake a merely adaptive for an essential character." With plants how remarkable it is that the organs of vegetation, on which their nutrition and life depend, are of little significance; whereas the organs of reproduction, with their product the seed and embryo, are of paramount importance! So again in formerly discussing certain morphological characters which are not functionally important, we have seen that they are often of the highest service in classification. This depends on their constancy throughout many allied groups; and their constancy chiefly depends on any slight deviations not having been preserved and accumulated by natural selection, which acts only on serviceable characters.

That the mere physiological importance of an organ does not determine its classificatory value, is almost proved by the fact that in allied groups, in which the same organ, as we have every reason to suppose, has nearly the same physiological value, its classificatory value is widely different. No naturalist can have worked long at any group without being struck with this fact; and it has been fully acknowledged in the writings of almost every author. It will suffice to quote the highest authority, Robert Brown, who, in speaking of certain organs in the Proteaceæ, says their generic importance, "like that of all their parts, not only in this, but, as I apprehend, in every natural family, is very unequal, and in some cases seems to be entirely lost." Again, in another work he says, the genera of the Connaraceæ "differ in having one or more ovaria, in the existence or absence of albumen, in the imbricate or valvular æstivation. Any one of these characters singly is frequently of more than generic importance, though here even when all taken together they appear insufficient to separate Cnestis from Connarus." To give an example amongst insects: in one great division of the Hymenoptera, the antennæ, as Westwood has remarked, are most constant in structure; in another division they differ much, and the differences are of quite subordinate value in classification; yet no one will say that the antennæ in these two divisions of the same order are of unequal physiological importance. Any number of instances could be given of the varying importance for classification of the same important organ within the same group of beings.

Again, no one will say that rudimentary or atrophied organs are of high physiological or vital importance; yet, undoubtedly, organs in this condition are often of much value in classification. No one will dispute that the rudimentary teeth in the upper jaws of young ruminants, and certain rudimentary bones of the leg, are highly serviceable in exhibiting the close affinity between ruminants and pachyderms. Robert Brown has strongly insisted on the fact that the position of the rudimentary florets is of the highest importance in the classification of the grasses.

Numerous instances could be given of characters derived from parts which must be considered of very trifling physiological importance, but which are universally admitted as highly serviceable in the definition of whole groups. For instance, whether or not there is an open passage from the nostrils to the mouth, the only character, according to Owen, which absolutely distinguishes fishes and reptiles—the inflection of the angle of the lower jaw in Marsupials—the manner in which the wings of insects are folded—mere colour in certain Algæ—mere pubescence on parts of the flower in grasses—the nature of the dermal covering, as hair or feathers, in the Vertebrata. If the Ornithorhynchus had been covered with feathers instead of hair, this external and trifling character would have been considered by naturalists as an important aid in determining the degree of affinity of this strange creature to birds.

The importance, for classification, of trifling characters, mainly depend on their being correlated with many other characters of more or less importance. The value indeed of an aggregate of characters is very evident in natural history. Hence, as has often been remarked, a species may depart from its allies in several characters, both of high physiological importance, and of almost universal prevalence, and yet leave us in no doubt where it should be ranked. Hence, also, it has been found that a classification founded on any single character, however important that may be, has always failed; for no part of the organisation is invariably constant. The importance of an aggregate of characters, even when none are important, alone explains the aphorism enunciated by Linnæus, namely, that the characters do not give the genus, but the genus gives the characters; for this seems founded on the appreciation of many trifling points of resemblance, too slight to be defined. Certain plants, belonging to the Malpighiaceæ, bear perfect and degraded flowers; in the latter, as A. de Jussieu has remarked, "the greater number of the characters proper to the species, to the genus, to the family, to the class, disappear, and thus laugh at our classification." When Aspicarpa produced in France, during several years, only these degraded flowers, departing so wonderfully in a number of the most important points of structure from the proper type of the order, yet M. Richard sagaciously saw, as Jussieu observes, that this genus should still be retained amongst the Malpighiaceæ. This case well illustrates the spirit of our classifications.

Practically, when naturalists are at work, they do not trouble themselves about the physiological value of the characters which they use in defining a group or in allocating any particular species. If they find a character nearly uniform, and common to a great number of forms, and not common to others, they use it as one of high value; if common to some lesser number, they use it as of subordinate value. This principle has been broadly confessed by some naturalists to be the true one; and by none more clearly than by that excellent botanist, Aug. St. Hilaire. If several trifling characters are always found in combination, though no apparent bond of connection can be discovered between them, especial value is set on them. As in most groups of animals, important organs, such as those for propelling the blood, or for ærating it, or those for propagating the race, are found nearly uniform, they are considered as highly serviceable in classification; but in some organs all these, the most important vital organs, are found to offer characters of quite subordinate value. Thus, as Fritz Müller has lately remarked, in the same group of crustaceans, Cypridina is furnished with a heart, whilst in two closely allied genera, namely Cypris and Cytherea, there is no such organ; one species of Cypridina has well-developed branchiæ, whilst another species is destitute of them.

We can see why characters derived from the embryo should be of equal importance with those derived from the adult, for a natural classification of course includes all ages. But it is by no means obvious, on the ordinary view, why the structure of the embryo should be more important for this purpose than that of the adult, which alone plays its full part in the economy of nature. Yet it has been strongly urged by those great naturalists, Milne Edwards and Agassiz, that embryological characters are the most important of all; and this doctrine has very generally been admitted as true. Nevertheless, their importance has sometimes been exaggerated, owing to the adaptive characters of larvæ not having been excluded; in order to show this, Fritz Müller arranged by the aid of such characters alone the great class of crustaceans, and the arrangement did not prove a natural one. But there can be no doubt that embryonic, excluding larval characters, are of the highest value for classification, not only with animals but with plants. Thus the main divisions of flowering plants are founded on differences in the embryo,—on the number and position of the cotyledons, and on the mode of development of the plumule and radicle. We shall immediately see why these characters possess so high a value in classification, namely, from the natural system being genealogical in its arrangement.

Our classifications are often plainly influenced by chains of affinities. Nothing can be easier than to define a number of characters common to all birds; but with crustaceans, any such definition has hitherto been found impossible. There are crustaceans at the opposite ends of the series, which have hardly a character in common; yet the species at both ends, from being plainly allied to others, and these to others, and so onwards, can be recognised as unequivocally belonging to this, and to no other class of the Articulata.

Geographical distribution has often been used, though perhaps not quite logically, in classification, more especially in very large groups of closely allied forms. Temminck insists on the utility or even necessity of this practice in certain groups of birds; and it has been followed by several entomologists and botanists.

Finally, with respect to the comparative value of the various groups of species, such as orders, sub-orders, families, sub-families, and genera, they seem to be, at least at present, almost arbitrary. Several of the best botanists, such as Mr. Bentham and others, have strongly insisted on their arbitrary value. Instances could be given amongst plants and insects, of a group first ranked by practised naturalists as only a genus, and then raised to the rank of a sub-family or family; and this has been done, not because further research has detected important structural differences, at first overlooked, but because numerous allied species with slightly different grades of difference, have been subsequently discovered.

All the foregoing rules and aids and difficulties in classification may be explained, if I do not greatly deceive myself, on the view that the Natural System is founded on descent with modification;—that the characters which naturalists consider as showing true affinity between any two or more species, are those which have been inherited from a common parent, all true classification being genealogical;—that community of descent is the hidden bond which naturalists have been unconsciously seeking, and not some unknown plan of creation, or the enunciation of general propositions, and the mere putting together and separating objects more or less alike.

But I must explain my meaning more fully. I believe that the *arrangement* of the groups within each class, in due subordination and relation to each other, must be strictly genealogical in order to be natural; but that the *amount* of difference in the several branches or groups, though allied in the same degree in blood to their common progenitor, may differ greatly, being due to the different degrees of modification which they have undergone; and this is expressed by the forms being ranked under different genera, families, sections, or orders. The reader will best understand what is meant, if he will take the trouble to refer to the diagram in the fourth chapter. We will suppose the letters A to L to represent allied genera existing during the Silurian epoch, and descended from some still earlier form. In three of these genera (A, F, and I), a species has transmitted modified descendants to the present day, represented by the fifteen genera (a^{14} to z^{14}) on the uppermost horizontal line. Now all these modified descendants from a single species, are related in blood or descent in the same degree; they may metaphorically be called cousins to the same millionth degree; yet they differ widely and in different degrees from each other. The forms descended from A, now broken up into two or three families, constitute a distinct order from those descended from I, also broken up into two families. Nor can the existing species, descended from A, be ranked in the same genus with the parent A; or those from I, with the parent I. But the existing genus F^{14} may be supposed to have been but slightly modified; and it will then rank with the parent-genus F; just as some few still living organisms belong to Silurian genera. So that the comparative value of the differences between these organic beings, which are all related to each other in the same degree in blood, has come to be widely different. Nevertheless their genealogical *arrangement* remains strictly true, not only at the present time, but at each successive period of descent. All the modified descendants from A will have inherited something in common from their common parent, as will all the descendants from I; so will it be with each subordinate branch of descendants, at each successive stage. If, however, we suppose any descendant of A, or of I, to have become so much modified as to have lost all traces of its parentage, in this case, its place in the natural system will be lost, as seems to have occurred with some few existing organisms. All the descendants of the genus F, along its whole line of descent, are supposed to have been but little modified, and they form a single genus. But this genus, though much isolated, will still occupy its proper intermediate position. The representation of the groups, as here given in the diagram on a flat surface, is much too simple. The branches ought to have diverged in all directions. If the names of the groups had been simply written down in a linear series, the representation would have been still less natural; and it is notoriously not possible to represent in a series, on a flat surface, the affinities which we discover in nature amongst the beings of the same group. Thus, the natural system is genealogical in its arrangement, like a pedigree: but the amount of modification which the different groups have undergone has to be expressed by ranking them under different so-called genera, sub-families, families, sections, orders, and classes.

It may be worth while to illustrate this view of classification, by taking the case of languages. If we possessed a perfect pedigree of mankind, a genealogical arrangement of the races of man would afford the best classification of the various languages now spoken throughout the world; and if all extinct languages, and all intermediate and slowly changing dialects, were to be included, such an arrangement would be the only possible one. Yet it might be that some ancient languages had altered very little and had given rise to few new languages, whilst others had altered much owing to the spreading, isolation, and state of civilisation of the several co-descended races, and had thus given rise to many new dialects and languages. The various degrees of difference between the languages of the same stock, would have to be expressed by groups subordinate to groups; but the proper or even the only possible arrangement would still be genealogical; and this would be strictly natural, as it would connect together all languages, extinct and recent, by the closest affinities, and would give the filiation and origin of each tongue.

In confirmation of this view, let us glance at the classification of varieties, which are known or believed to be descended from a single species. These are grouped under the species, with the sub-varieties under the varieties; and in some cases, as with the domestic pigeon, with several other grades of difference. Nearly the same rules are followed as in classifying species. Authors have insisted on the necessity of arranging varieties on a natural instead of an artificial system; we are cautioned, for instance, not to class two varieties of the pine-apple together, merely because their fruit, though the most important part, happens to be nearly identical; no one puts the Swedish and common turnip together, though the esculent and thickened stems are so similar. Whatever part is found to be most constant, is used in classing varieties: thus the great agriculturist Marshall says the horns are very useful for this purpose with cattle, because they are less variable than the shape or colour of the body, &c.; whereas with sheep the horns are much less serviceable, because less constant. In classing varieties, I apprehend that if we had a real pedigree, a genealogical classification would be universally preferred; and it has been attempted in some cases. For we might feel sure, whether there had been more or less modification, that the principle of inheritance would keep the forms together which were allied in the greatest number of points. In tumbler pigeons, though some of the sub-varieties differ in the important character of the length of the beak, yet all are kept together from having the common habit of tumbling; but the short-faced breed has nearly or quite lost this habit; nevertheless, without any thought on the subject, these tumblers are kept in the same group, because allied in blood and alike in some other respects.

With species in a state of nature, every naturalist has in fact brought descent into his classification; for he includes in his lowest grade, that of species, the two sexes; and how enormously these sometimes differ in the most important characters, is known to every naturalist: scarcely a single fact can be predicated in common of the adult males and hermaphrodites of certain cirripedes, and yet no one dreams of separating them. As soon as the three Orchidean forms, Monachanthus, Myanthus, and Catasetum, which had previously been ranked as three distinct genera, were known to be sometimes produced on the same plant, they were immediately considered as varieties; and now I have been able to show that they are the male, female, and hermaphrodite forms of the same species. The naturalist includes as one species the various larval stages of the same individual, however much they may differ from each other and from the adult, as well as the so-called alternate generations of Steenstrup, which can only in a technical sense be considered as the same individual. He includes monsters and varieties, not from their partial resemblance to the parent-form, but because they are descended from it.

As descent has universally been used in classing together the individuals of the same species, though the males and females and larvæ are some-times extremely different; and as it has been used in classing varieties which have undergone a certain, and sometimes a considerable amount of modification, may not this same element of descent have been unconcious-ly used in grouping species under genera, and genera under higher groups, all under the so-called natural system? I believe it has been unconsciously used; and thus only can I understand the several rules and guides which have been followed by our best systematists. As we have no written pedi-grees, we are forced to trace community of descent by resemblances of any kind. Therefore we chose those characters which are the least likely to have been modified, in relation to the conditions of life to which each species has been recently exposed. Rudimentary structures on this view are as good as, or even better than, other parts of the organisation. We care not how trifling a character may be—let it be the mere inflection of the angle of the jaw, the manner in which an insect's wing is folded, whe-ther the skin be covered by hair or feathers—if it prevail throughout many and different species, especially those having very different habits of life, it assumes high value; for we can account for its presence in so many forms with such different habits, only by inheritance from a com-mon parent. We may err in this respect in regard to single points of struc-ture, but when several characters, let them be ever so trifling, concur throughout a large group of beings having different habits, we may feel al-most sure, on the theory of descent, that these characters have been inher-ited from a common ancestor; and we know that such aggregated charac-ters have especial value in classification.

We can understand why a species or a group of species may depart from its allies, in several of its most important characteristics, and yet be safely classed with them. This may be safely done, and is often done, as long as a sufficient number of characters, let them be ever so unimportant, be-trays the hidden bond of community of descent. Let two forms have not a single character in common, yet, if these extreme forms are connected to-gether by a chain of intermediate groups, we may at once infer their com-munity of descent, and we put them all into the same class. As we find or-gans of high physiological importance—those which serve to preserve life under the most diverse conditions of existence—are generally the most constant, we attach especial value to them; but if these same organs, in another group or section of a group, are found to differ much, we at once value them less in our classification. We shall presently see why embryo-logical characters are of such high classificatory importance. Geographi-cal distribution may sometimes be brought usefully into play in classing large genera, because all the species of the same genus, inhabiting any distinct and isolated region, are in all probability descended from the same parents.

Analogical Resemblances.—We can understand, on the above views, the very important distinction between real affinities and analogical or adaptive resemblances. Lamarck first called attention to this subject, and he has been ably followed by Macleay and others. The resemblance in the shape of the body and in the fin-like anterior limbs between dugongs and whales, and between these two orders of mammals and fishes, are analogical. So is the resemblance between a mouse and a shrew-mouse (Sorex), which belong to different orders; and the still closer resemblance, insisted on by Mr. Mivart, between the mouse and a small marsupial animal (Antechinus) of Australia. These latter resemblances may be accounted for, as it seems to me, by adaptation for similarly active movements through thickets and herbage, together with concealment from enemies.

Amongst insects there are innumerable similar instances; thus Linnæus, misled by external appearances, actually classed an homopterous insect as a moth. We see something of the same kind even with our domestic varieties, as in the strikingly similar shape of the body in the improved breeds of the Chinese and common pig, which are descended from distinct species; and in the similarly thickened stems of the common and specifically distinct Swedish turnip. The resemblance between the greyhound and the racehorse is hardly more fanciful than the analogies which have been drawn by some authors between widely different animals.

On the view of characters being of real importance for classification, only in so far as they reveal descent, we can clearly understand why analogical or adaptive characters, although of the utmost importance to the welfare of the being, are almost valueless to the systematist. For animals, belonging to two most distinct lines of descent, may have become adapted to similar conditions, and thus have assumed a close external resemblance; but such resemblances will not reveal—will rather tend to conceal their blood-relationship. We can thus also understand the apparent paradox, that the very same characters are analogical when one group is compared with another, but give true affinities when the members of the same group are compared together: thus, the shape of the body and fin-like limbs are only analogical when whales are compared with fishes, being adaptations in both classes for swimming through the water; but between the several members of the whale family, the shape of the body and the fin-like limbs offer characters exhibiting true affinity; for as these parts are so nearly similar throughout the whole family, we cannot doubt that they have been inherited from a common ancestor. So it is with fishes.

Numerous cases could be given of striking resemblances in quite distinct beings between single parts or organs, which have been adapted for the same functions. A good instance is afforded by the close resemblance of the jaws of the dog and Tasmanian wolf or Thylacinus,—animals which are widely sundered in the natural system. But this resemblance is confined to general appearance, as in the prominence of the canines, and in the cutting shape of the molar teeth. For the teeth really differ much: thus the dog has on each side of the upper jaw four pre-molars and only two molars; whilst the Thylacinus has three pre-molars and four molars. The molars also differ much in the two animals in relative size and structure. The adult dentition is preceded by a widely different milk dentition. Any one may of course deny that the teeth in either case have been adap-

ted for tearing flesh, through the natural selection of successive variations; but if this be admitted in the one case, it is unintelligible to me
that it should be denied in the other. I am glad to find that so high an
authority as Professor Flower has come to this same conclusion.

The extraordinary cases given in a former chapter, of widely different
fishes possessing electric organs,—of widely different insects possessing
luminous organs,—and of orchids and asclepiads having pollen-masses
with viscid discs, come under this same head of analogical resemblances.
But these cases are so wonderful that they were introduced as difficulties
or objections to our theory. In all such cases some fundamental difference
in the growth or development of the parts, and generally in their matured
structure, can be detected. The end gained is the same, but the means,
though appearing superficially to be the same, are essentially different.
The principle formerly alluded to under the term of *analogical variation*
has probably in these cases often come into play; that is, the members of
the same class, although only distantly allied, have inherited so much in
common in their constitution, that they are apt to vary under similar exciting causes in a similar manner; and this would obviously aid in the acquirement through natural selection of parts or organs, strikingly like
each other, independently of their direct inheritance from a common progenitor.

As species belonging to distinct classes have often been adapted by successive slight modifications to live under nearly similar circumstances,—
to inhabit, for instance, the three elements of land, air, and water,—we
can perhaps understand how it is that a numerical parallelism has sometimes been observed between the sub-groups of distinct classes. A naturalist, struck with a parallelism of this nature, by arbitrarily raising or
sinking the value of the groups in several classes (and all our experience
shows that their valuation is as yet arbitrary), could easily extend the
parallelism over a wide range; and thus the septenary, quinary, quartern-
ary and ternary classifications have probably arisen.

There is another and curious class of cases in which close external resemblance does not depend on adaptation to similar habits of life, but has
been gained for the sake of protection. I allude to the wonderful manner in which certain butterflies imitate, as first described by Mr. Bates,
other and quite distinct species. This excellent observer has shown that in
some districts of S. America, where, for instance, an Ithomia abounds in
gaudy swarms, another butterfly, namely, a Leptalis, is often found
mingled in the same flock; and the latter so closely resembles the Ithomia
in every shade and stripe of colour and even in the shape of its wings, that
Mr. Bates, with his eyes sharpened by collecting during eleven years,
was, though always on his guard, continually deceived. When the mockers
and the mocked are caught and compared, they are found to be very diff-
rent in essential structure, and to belong not only to distinct genera, but
often to distinct families. Had this mimicry occurred in only one or two
instances, it might have been passed over as a strange coincidence. But,
if we proceed from a district where one Leptalis imitates an Ithomia, an-

other mocking and mocked species belonging to the same two genera, equally close in their resemblance, may be found. Altogether no less than ten genera are enumerated, which include species that imitate other butterflies. The mockers and mocked always inhabit the same region; we never find an imitator living remote from the form which it imitates. The mockers are almost invariably rare insects; the mocked in almost every case abound in swarms. In the same district in which a species of Leptalis closely imitates an Ithomia, there are sometimes other Lepidoptera mimicking the same Ithomia: so that in the same place, species of three genera of butterflies and even a moth are found all closely resembling a butterfly belonging to a fourth genus. It deserves especial notice that many of the mimicking forms of the Leptalis, as well as of the mimicked forms, can be shown by a graduated series to be merely varieties of the same species; whilst others are undoubtedly distinct species. But why, it may be asked, are certain forms treated as the mimicked and others as the mimickers? Mr. Bates satisfactorily answers this question, by showing that the form which is imitated keeps the usual dress of the group to which it belongs, whilst the counterfeiters have changed their dress and do not resemble their nearest allies.

We are next led to inquire what reason can be assigned for certain butterflies and moths so often assuming the dress of another and quite distinct form; why, to the perplexity of naturalists, has nature condescended to the tricks of the stage? Mr. Bates has, no doubt, hit on the true explanation. The mocked forms, which always abound in numbers, must habitually escape destruction to a large extent, otherwise they could not exist in such swarms; and a large amount of evidence has now been collected, showing that they are distasteful to birds and other insect-devouring animals. The mocking forms, on the other hand, that inhabit the same district, are comparatively rare, and belong to rare groups; hence they must suffer habitually from some danger, for otherwise, from the number of eggs laid by all butterflies, they would in three or four generations swarm over the whole country. Now if a member of one of these persecuted and rare groups were to assume a dress so like that of a well-protected species that it continually deceived the practised eye of an entomologist, it would often deceive predaceous birds and insects, and thus often escape destruction. Mr. Bates may almost be said to have actually witnessed the process by which the mimickers have come so closely to resemble the mimicked; for he found that some of the forms of Leptalis which mimic so many others butterflies, varied in an extreme degree. In one district several varieties occurred, and of these one alone resembled to a certain extent, the common Ithomia of the same district. In another district there were two or three varieties, one of which was much commoner than the others, and this closely mocked another form of Ithomia. From facts of this nature, Mr. Bates concludes that the Leptalis first varies; and when a variety happens to resemble in some degree any common butterfly inhabiting the same district, this variety, from its resemblance to a flourishing and little-persecuted kind, has a better chance of escaping destruction from predaceous birds and insects, and is consequently oftener preserved;—"the less perfect degrees of resemblance being generation after generation eliminated, and only the others left to propagate their kind." So that here we have an excellent illustration of natural selection.

Messrs. Wallace and Trimen have likewise described several equally striking cases of imitation in the Lepidoptera of the Malay Archipelago and Africa, and with some other insects. Mr. Wallace has also detected one such case with birds, but we have none with the larger quadrupeds. The much greater frequency of imitation with insects than with other animals, is probably the consequence of their small size; insects cannot defend themselves, excepting indeed the kinds furnished with a string, and I have never heard of an instance of such kinds mocking other insects, though they are mocked; insects cannot easily escape by flight from the larger animals which prey on them; therefore, speaking metaphorically, they are reduced, like most weak creatures, to trickery and dissimulation.

It should be observed that the process of imitation probably never commenced between forms widely dissimilar in colour. But starting with species already somewhat like each other, the closest resemblance, if beneficial, could readily be gained by the above means; and if the imitated form was subsequently and gradually modified through any agency, the imitating form would be led along the same track, and thus be altered to almost any extent, so that it might ultimately assume an appearance or colouring wholly unlike that of the other members of the family to which it belonged. There is, however, some difficulty on this head, for it is necessary to suppose in some cases that ancient members belonging to several distinct groups, before they had diverged to their present extent, accidentally resembled a member of another and protected group in a sufficient degree to afford some slight protection; this having given the basis for the subsequent acquisition of the most perfect resemblance.

On the Nature of the Affinities connecting Organic Beings.—As the modified descendants of dominant species, belonging to the larger genera, tend to inherit the advantages which made the groups to which they belong large and their parents dominant, they are almost sure to spread widely, and to seize on more and more places in the economy of nature. The larger and more dominant groups within each class thus tend to go on increasing in size; and they consequently supplant many smaller and feebler groups. Thus we can account for the fact that all organisms, recent and extinct, are included under a few great orders, and under still fewer classes. As showing how few the higher groups are in number, and how widely they are spread throughout the world, the fact is striking that the discovery of Australia has not added an insect belonging to a new class; and that in the vegetable kingdom, as I learn from Dr. Hooker, it has added only two or three families of small size.

In the chapter on Geological Succession I attempted to show, on the principle of each group having generally diverged much in character during the long-continued process of modification, how it is that the more ancient forms of life often present characters in some degree intermediate between existing groups. As some few of the old and intermediate forms have transmitted to the present day descendants but little modified, these constitute our so-called osculant or aberrant species. The more aberrant any form is, the greater must be the number of connecting forms which have been exterminated and utterly lost. And we have some evidence of abberant groups having suffered severely from extinction, for they are almost always represented by extremely few species; and such species as do occur are generally very distinct from each other, which again implies extinction. The genera Ornithorhynchus and Lepidosiren, for example, would not have been less abberant had each been represented by a dozen species, instead of as at present by a single one, or by two or three. We can, I think, account for this fact only by looking at aberrant groups as forms which have been conquered by more successful competitors, with a few members still preserved under unusually favourable conditions.

Mr. Waterhouse has remarked that, when a member belonging to one group of animals exhibits an affinity to a quite distinct group, this affinity in most cases is general and not special; thus, according to Mr. Waterhouse, of all Rodents, the bizcacha is most nearly related to Marsupials; but in the points in which it approaches this order, its relations are general, that is, not to any one marsupial species more than to another. As these points of affinity are believed to be real and not merely adaptive, they must be due in accordance with our view to inheritance from a common progenitor. Therefore we must suppose either that all Rodents, including the bizcacha, branched off from some ancient Marsupial, which will naturally have been more or less intermediate in character with respect to all existing Marsupials; or that both Rodents and Marsupials branched off from a common progenitor, and that both groups have since undergone much modification in divergent directions. On either view we must suppose that the bizcacha has retained, by inheritance, more of the characters of its ancient progenitor than have other Rodents; and therefore it will not be specially related to any one existing Marsupial, but indirectly to all or nearly all Marsupials, from having partially retained the character of their common progenitor, or of some early member of the group. On the other hand, of all Marsupials, as Mr. Waterhouse has remarked, the Phascolomys resembles most nearly, not any one species, but the general order of Rodents. In this case, however, it may be strongly suspected that the resemblance is only analogical, owing to the Phascolomys having become adapted to habits like those of a Rodent. The elder De Candolle has made nearly similar observations on the general nature of the affinities of distinct families of plants.

On the principle of the multiplication and gradual divergence in character of the species descended from a common progenitor, together with their retention by inheritance of some characters in common, we can understand the excessively complex and radiating affinities by which all the members of the same family or higher group are connected together. For the common progenitor of a whole family, now broken up by extinction into distinct groups and sub-groups, will have transmitted some of its characters, modified in various ways and degrees, to all the species; and they will consequently be related to each other by circuitous lines of affinity of various lengths (as may be seen in the diagrams so often referred to), mounting up through many predecessors. As it is difficult to show the blood-relationship between the numerous kindred of any ancient and noble family even by the aid of a genealogical tree, and almost impossible to do so without this aid, we can understand the extraordinary difficulty which naturalists have experienced in describing, without the aid of a diagram, the various affinities which they perceive between the many living and extinct members of the same great natural class.

Extinction, as we have seen in the fourth chapter, has played an important part in defining and widening the intervals between the several groups in each class. We may thus account for the distinctness of whole classes from each other—for instance, of birds from all other vertebrate animals—by the belief that many ancient forms of life have been utterly lost, through which the early progenitors of birds were formerly connected with the early progenitors of the other and at that time less differentiated vertebrate classes. There has been much less extinction of the forms of life which once connected fishes with batrachians. There has been still less within some whole classes, for instance the Crustacea, for here the most wonderfully diverse forms are still linked together by a long and only partially broken chain of affinities. Extinction has only defined the groups: it has by no means made them; for if every form which has ever lived on this earth were suddenly to reappear, though it would be quite impossible to give definitions by which each group could be distinguished, still a natural classification, or at least a natural arrangement, would be possible. We shall see this by turning to the diagram; the letters, A to L, may represent eleven Silurian genera, some of which have produced large groups of modified descendants, with every link in each branch and sub-branch still alive; and the links not greater than those between existing varieties. In this case it would be quite impossible to give definitions by which the several members of the several groups could be distinguished from their more immediate parents and descendants. Yet the arrangement in the diagram would still hold good and would be natural; for, on the principle of inheritance, all the forms descended, for instance, from A, would have something in common. In a tree we can distinguish this or that branch, though at the actual fork the two unite and blend together. We could not, as I have said, define the several groups; but we could pick out types, or forms, representing most of the characters of each group, whether large or small, and thus give a general idea of the value of the differences between them. This is what we should be driven to, if we were ever to succeed in collecting all the forms in any one class which have lived throughout all time and space. Assuredly we shall never succeed in making so perfect a collection: nevertheless, in certain classes, we are tending towards this end; and Milne Edwards has lately insisted, in an able paper, on the high importance of looking to types, whether or not we can separate and define the groups to which such types belong.

Finally we have seen that natural selection, which follows from the struggle for existence, and which almost inevitably leads to extinction and divergence of character in the descendants from any one parent species, explains that great and universal feature in the affinities of all organic beings, namely, their subordination in group under group. We use the element of descent in classing the individuals of both sexes and of all ages under one species, although they may have but few characters in common; we use descent in classing acknowledged varieties, however different they may be from their parents; and I believe that this element of descent is the hidden bond of connection which naturalists have sought under the term of the Natural System. On this idea of the natural system being, in so far as it has been perfected, genealogical in its arrangement, with the grades of difference expressed by the terms genera, families, orders, &c., we can understand the rules which we are compelled to follow in our classification. We can understand why we value certain resemblances far more than others; why we use rudimentary and useless organs, or others of trifling physiological importance; why, in finding the relations between one group and another, we summarily reject analogical or adaptive characters, and yet use these same characters within the limits of the same group. We can clearly see how it is that all living and extinct forms can be grouped together within a few great classes; and how the several members of each class are connected together by the most complex and radiating lines of affinities. We shall never, probably, disentangle the inextricable web of the affinities between the members of any one class; but when we have a distinct object in view, and do not look to some unknown plan of creation, we may hope to make sure but slow progress.

Professor Häckel in his 'Generelle Morphologie' and in other works, has recently brought his great knowledge and abilities to bear on what he calls phylogeny, or the lines of descent of all organic beings. In drawing up the several series he trusts chiefly to embryological characters, but receives aid from homologous and rudimentary organs, as well as from the successive periods at which the various forms of life are believed to have first appeared in our geological formations. He has thus boldly made a great beginning, and shows us how classification will in the future be treated.

Morphology

We have seen that the members of the same class, independently of their habits of life, resemble each other in the general plan of their organisation. This resemblance is often expressed by the term "unity of type;" or by saying that the several parts and organs in the different species of the class are homologous. The whole subject is included under the general term of Morphology. This is one of the most interesting departments of natural history, and may almost be said to be its very soul. What can be more curious than that the hand of a man, formed for grasping, that of a mole for digging, the leg of the horse, the paddle of the porpoise, and the wing of the bat, should all be constructed on the same pattern, and should include similar bones, in the same relative positions? How curious it is, to give a subordinate though striking instance, that the hind-feet of the kangaroo, which are so well fitted for bounding over the open plains,—those of the climbing, leaf eating koala, equally well fitted for grasping the branches of trees,—those of the ground-dwelling, insect or root-eating, bandicoots,—and those of some other Australian marsupials,—should all be constructed on the same extraordinary type, namely with the bones of the second and third digits extremely slender and enveloped within the same skin, so that they appear like a single toe furnished with two claws. Notwithstanding this similarity of pattern, it is obvious that the hind feet of these several animals are used for as widely different purposes as it is possible to conceive. The case is rendered all the more striking by the American opossums, which follow nearly the same habits of life as some of their Australian relatives, having feet constructed on the ordinary plan. Professor Flower, from whom these statements are taken, remarks in conclusion: "We may call this conformity to type, without getting much nearer to an explanation of the phenomenon;" and he then adds "but is it not powerfully suggestive of true relationship, of inheritance from a common ancestor?"

Geoffroy St. Hilaire has strongly insisted on the high importance of relative position or connexion in homologous parts; they may differ to almost any extent in form and size, and yet remain connected together in the same invariable order. We never find, for instance, the bones of the arm and fore-arm, or of the thigh and leg, transposed. Hence the same names can be given to the homologous bones in widely different animals. We see the same great law in the construction of the mouths of insects: what can be more different than the immensely long spiral proboscis of a sphinx-moth, the curious folded one of a bee or bug, and the great jaws of a beetle?—yet all these organs, serving for such widely different purposes, are formed by infinitely numerous modifications of an upper lip, mandibles, and two pairs of maxillæ. The same law governs the construction of the mouths and limbs of crustaceans. So it is with the flowers of plants.

Nothing can be more hopeless than to attempt to explain this similarity of pattern in members of the same class, by utility or by the doctrine of final causes. The hopelessness of the attempt has been expressly admitted by Owen in his most interesting work on the 'Nature of Limbs.' On the ordinary view of the independent creation of each being, we can only say that so it is;—that it has pleased the Creator to construct all the animals and plants in each great class on a uniform plan; but this is not a scientific explanation.

The explanation is to a large extent simple on the theory of the selection of successive slight modifications,—each modification being profitable in some way to the modified form, but often affecting by correlation other parts of the organisation. In changes of this nature, there will be little or no tendency to alter the original pattern, or to transpose the parts. The bones of a limb might be shortened and flattened to any extent, becoming at the same time enveloped in thick membrane, so as to serve as a fin; or a webbed hand might have all its bones, or certain bones, lengthened to any extent, with the membrane connecting them increased, so as to serve as a wing; yet all these modifications would not tend to alter the framework of the bones or the relative connection of the parts. If we suppose that an early progenitor—the archetype as it may be called—of all mammals, birds, and reptiles, had its limbs constructed on the existing general pattern, for whatever purpose they served, we can at once perceive the plain signification of the homologous construction of the limbs throughout the class. So with the mouths of insects, we have only to suppose that their common progenitor had an upper lip, mandibles, and two pairs of maxillæ, these parts being perhaps very simple in form; and then natural selection will account for the infinite diversity in the structure and functions of the mouths of insects. Nevertheless, it is conceivable that the general pattern of an organ might become so much obscured as to be finally lost, by the reduction and ultimately by the complete abortion of certain parts, by the fusion of other parts, and by the doubling or multiplication of others,—variations which we know to be within the limits of possibility. In the paddles of the gigantic extinct sea-lizards, and in the mouths of certain suctorial crustaceans, the general pattern seems thus to have become partially obscured.

There is another and equally curious branch of our subject; namely, serial homologies, or the comparison of the different parts or organs in the same individual, and not of the same parts or organs in different members of the same class. Most physiologists believe that the bones of the skull are homologous—that is, correspond in number and in relative connexion—with the elemental parts of a certain number of vertebræ. The anterior and posterior limbs in all the higher vertebrate classes are plainly homologous. So it is with the wonderfully complex jaws and legs of crustaceans. It is familiar to almost every one, that in a flower the relative position of the sepals, petals, stamens, and pistils, as well as their intimate structure, are intelligible on the view that they consist of metamorphosed leaves, arranged in a spire. In monstrous plants, we often get direct evidence of the possibility of one organ being transformed into another; and we can actually see, during the early or embryonic stages of development in flowers, as well as in crustaceans and many other animals, that organs, which when mature become extremely different are at first exactly alike.

How inexplicable are the cases of serial homologies on the ordinary view of creation! Why should the brain be enclosed in a box composed of such numerous and such extraordinarily shaped pieces of bone, apparently representing vertebræ? As Owen has remarked, the benefit derived from the yielding of the separate pieces in the act of parturition by mammals, will by no means explain the same construction in the skulls of birds and reptiles. Why should similar bones have been created to form the wing and the leg of a bat, used as they are for such totally different purposes, namely flying and walking? Why should one crustacean, which has an extremely complex mouth formed of many parts, consequently always have fewer legs; or conversely, those with many legs have simpler mouths? Why should the sepals, petals, stamens, and pistils, in each flower, though fitted for such distinct purposes, be all constructed on the same pattern?

On the theory of natural selection, we can, to a certain extent, answer these questions. We need not here consider how the bodies of some animals first became divided into a series of segments, or how they became divided into right and left sides, with corresponding organs, for such questions are almost beyond investigation. It is, however, probable that some serial structures are the result of cells multiplying by division, entailing the multiplication of the parts developed from such cells. It must suffice for our purpose to bear in mind that an indefinite repetition of the same part or organ is the common characteristic, as Owen has remarked, of all low or little specialised forms; therefore the unknown progenitor of the Vertebrata probably possessed many vertebræ; the unknown progenitor of the Articulata, many segments; and the unknown progenitor of flowering plants, many leaves arranged in one or more spires. We have also formerly seen that parts many times repeated are eminently liable to vary, not only in number, but in form. Consequently such parts, being already present in considerable numbers, and being highly variable, would naturally afford the materials for adaptation to the most different purposes; yet they would generally retain, through the force of inheritance, plain traces of their original or fundamental resemblance. They would retain this resemblance all the more, as the variations, which afforded the basis for their subsequent modification through natural selection, would tend from the first to be similar; the parts being at an early stage of growth alike, and being subjected to nearly the same conditions. Such parts, whether more or less modified, unless their common origin became wholly obscured, would be serially homologous.

In the great class of molluscs, though the parts in distinct species can be shown to be homologous, only a few serial homologies, such as the valves of Chitons, can be indicated; that is, we are seldom enabled to say that one part is homologous with another part in the same individual. And we can understand this fact; for in molluscs, even in the lowest members of the class, we do not find nearly so much indefinite repetition of any one part as we find in the other great classes of the animal and vegetable kingdoms.

But morphology is a much more complex subject than it at first appears, as has lately been well shown in a remarkable paper by Mr. E. Ray Lankester, who has drawn an important distinction between certain classes of cases which have all been equally ranked by naturalists as homologous. He proposes to call the structures which resemble each other in distinct animals, owing to their descent from a common progenitor with subsequent modification, *homogenous;* and the resemblances which cannot thus be accounted for, he proposes to call *homoplastic.* For instance, he believes that the hearts of birds and mammals are as a whole homogenous,—that is, have been derived from a common progenitor; but that the four cavities of the heart in the two classes are homoplastic,— that is, have been independently developed. Mr. Lankester also adduces the close resemblance of the parts on the right and left sides of the body, and in the successive segments of the same individual animal; and here we have parts commonly called homologous, which bear no relation to the descent of distinct species from a common progenitor. Homoplastic structures are the same with those which I have classed, though in a very imperfect manner, as analogous modifications or resemblances. Their formation may be attributed in part to distinct organisms, or to distinct parts of the same organism, having varied in an analogous manner; and in part to similar modifications, having been preserved for the same general purpose or function,—of which many instances have been given.

Naturalists frequently speak of the skull as formed of metamorphosed vertebræ; the jaws of crabs as metamorphosed legs; the stamens and pistils in flowers as metamorphosed leaves; but it would in most cases be more correct, as Professor Huxley has remarked, to speak of both skull and vertebræ, jaws and legs, &c., as having been metamorphosed, not one from the other, as they now exist, but from some common and simpler element. Most naturalists, however, use such language only in a metaphorical sense; they are far from meaning that during a long course of descent, primordial organs of any kind—vertebræ in the one case and legs in the other—have actually been converted into skulls or jaws. Yet so strong is the appearance of this having occurred, that naturalists can hardly avoid employing language having this plain signification. According to the views here maintained, such language may be used literally; and the wonderful fact of the jaws, for instance, of a crab retaining numerous characters which they probably would have retained through inheritance, if they had really been metamorphosed from true though extremely simple legs, is in part explained.

Development and Embryology

This is one of the most important subjects in the whole round of history. The metamorphoses of insects, with which every one is familiar, are generally effected abruptly by a few stages; but the transformations are in reality numerous and gradual, though concealed. A certain ephemerous insect (Chlöeon) during its development, moults, as shown by Sir J. Lubbock, above twenty times, and each time undergoes a certain amount of change; and in this case we see the act of metamorphosis performed in a primary and gradual manner. Many insects, and especially certain crustaceans, show us what wonderful changes of structure can be effected during development. Such changes, however, reach their acme in the so-called alternate generations of some of the lower animals. It is, for instance, an astonishing fact that a delicate branching coralline, studded with polypi and attached to a submarine rock, should produce, first by budding and then by transverse division, a host of huge floating jellyfishes; and that these should produce eggs, from which are hatched swimming animalcules, which attach themselves to rocks and become developed into branching corallines; and so on in an endless cycle. The belief in the essential identity of the process of alternate generation and of ordiary metamorphosis has been greatly strengthened by Wagner's discovery of the larva or maggot of a fly, namely the Cecidomyia, producing asexually other larvæ, and these others, which finally are developed into mature males and females, propagating their kind in the ordinary manner by eggs.

It may be worth notice that when Wagner's remarkable discovery was first announced, I was asked how was it possible to account for the larvæ of this fly having acquired the power of asexual reproduction. As long as the case remained unique no answer could be given. But already Grimm has shown that another fly, a Chironomus, reproduces itself in nearly the same manner, and he believes that this occurs frequently in the Order. It is the pupa, and not the larva, of the Chironomus which has this power; and Grimm further shows that this case, to a certain extent, "unites that of the Cecidomyia with the parthenogenesis of the Coccidæ;"—the term parthenogenesis implying that the mature females of the Coccidæ are capable of producing fertile eggs without the concourse of the males. Certain animals belonging to several classes are now known to have the power of ordinary reproduction at an unusually early age; and we have only to accelerate parthenogenetic production by gradual steps to an earlier and earlier age,—Chironomus showing us an almost exactly intermediate stage viz., that of the pupa—and we can perhaps account for the marvellous case of the Cecidomyia.

It has already been stated that various parts in the same individual which are exactly alike during an early embryonic period, become widely different and serve for widely different purposes in the adult state. So again it has been shown that generally the embryos of the most distinct species belonging to the same class are closely similar, but become, when fully developed, widely dissimilar. A better proof of this latter fact cannot be given than the statement by Von Baer that "the embryos of mammalia, of birds, lizards, and snakes, probably also of chelonia are in their earliest states exceedingly like one another, both as a whole and in the mode of development of their parts; so much so, in fact, that we can often distinguish the embryos only by their size. In my possession are two little embryos in spirit, whose names I have omitted to attach, and at present I am quite unable to say to what class they belong. They may be lizards or small birds, or very young mammalia, so complete is the similarity in the mode of formation of the head and trunk in these animals. The extremities, however, are still absent in these embryos. But even if they had existed in the earliest stage of their development we should learn nothing, for the feet of lizards and mammals, the wings and feet of birds, no less than the hands and feet of man, all arise from the same fundamental form." The larvæ of most crustaceans, at corresponding stages of development, closely resemble each other, however different the adult may become; and so it is with very many other animals. A trace of the law of embryonic resemblance occasionally lasts till a rather late age: thus birds of the same genus, and of allied genera, often resemble each other in their immature plumage; as we see in the spotted feathers in the young of the thrush group. In the cat tribe, most of the species when adult are striped or spotted in lines; and stripes or spots can be plainly distinguished in the whelp of the lion and the puma. We occasionally though rarely see something of the same kind in plants; thus the first leaves of the ulex or furze, and the first leaves of the phyllodineous acacias, are pinnate or divided like the ordinary leaves of the leguminosæ.

The points of structure, in which the embryos of widely different animals within the same class resemble each other, often have no direct relation to their conditions of existence. We cannot, for instance, suppose that in the embryos of the vertebrata the peculiar loop-like courses of the arteries near the branchial slits are related to similar conditions,—in the young mammal which is nourished in the womb of its mother, in the egg of the bird which is hatched in a nest, and in the spawn of a frog under water. We have no more reason to believe in such a relation, than we have to believe that the similar bones in the hand of a man, wing of a bat, and fin of a porpoise, are related to similar conditions of life. No one supposes that the stripes on the whelp of a lion, or the spots on the young blackbird, are of any use to these animals.

The case, however, is different when an animal during any part of its embryonic career is active, and has to provide for itself. The period of activity may come on earlier or later in life; but whenever it comes on, the adaptation of the larva to its conditions of life is just as perfect and as beautiful as in the adult animal. In how important a manner this has acted, has recently been well shown by Sir J. Lubbock in his remarks on the close similarity of the larvæ of some insects belonging to very different orders, and on the dissimilarity of the larvæ of other insects within the same order, according to their habits of life. Owing to such adaptations, the similarity of the larvæ of allied animals is sometimes greatly obscured; especially when there is a division of labour during the different stages of development, as when the same larva has during one stage to search for food, and during another stage has to search for a place of attachment. Cases can even be given of the larvæ of allied species, or groups of species, differing more from each other than do the adults. In most cases, however, the larvæ, though active, still obey, more or less closely, the law of common embryonic resemblance. Cirripedes afford a good instance of this; even the illustrious Cuvier did not perceive that a barnacle was a crustacean: but a glance at the larva shows this in an un-

mistakable manner. So again the two main divisions of cirripedes, the pedunculated and sessile, though differing widely in external appearance,
have larvæ in all their stages barely distinguishable.

The embryo in the course of development generally rises in organisation; I use this expression, though I am aware that it is hardly possible
to define clearly what is meant by the organisation being higher or lower.
But no one probably will dispute that the butterfly is higher than the caterpillar. In some cases, however, the mature animal must be considered as
lower in the scale than the larva, as with certain parasitic crustaceans.
To refer once again to cirripedes: the larvæ in the first stage have three
pairs of locomotive organs, a simple single eye, and a prosociformed
mouth, with which they feed largely, for they increase much in size. In
the second stage, answering to the chrysalis stage of butterflies, they have
six pairs of beautifully constructed natatory legs, a pair of magnificent
compound eyes, and extremely complex antennæ; but they have a closed
and imperfect mouth, and cannot feed: their function at this stage is, to
search out by their well-developed organs of sense, and to reach by their
active powers of swimming, a proper place on which to become attached
and to undergo their final metamorphosis. When this is completed they
are fixed for life: their legs are now converted into prehensile organs;
they again obtain a well-constructed mouth; but they have no antennæ,
and their two eyes are now reconverted into a minute, single, simple eye-
spot. In this last and complete state, cirripedes may be considered as
either more highly or more lowly organised than they were in the larval
condition. But in some genera the larvæ become developed into hermaphrodites having the ordinary structure, and into what I have called complemental males; and in the latter the development has assuredly been
retrograde, for the male is a mere sack, which lives for a short time and
is destitute of mouth, stomach, and every other organ of importance, excepting those for reproduction.

We are so much accustomed to see a difference in structure between the
embryo and the adult, that we are tempted to look at this difference as in
some necessary manner contingent on growth. But there is no reason why,
for instance, the wing of a bat, or the fin of a porpoise, should not have
been sketched out with all their parts in proper proportion, as soon as any
part became visible. In some whole groups of animals and in certain members of other groups this is the case, and the embryo does not at any period differ widely from the adult: thus Owen has remarked in regard to
cuttle-fish, "there is no metamorphosis; the cephalopodic character is
manifested long before the parts of the embryo are completed." Land-
shells and fresh-water crustaceans are born having their proper forms,
whilst the marine members of the same two great classes pass through
considerable and often great changes during their development. Spiders,
again, barely undergo any metamorphosis. The larvæ of most insects pass
through a worm-like stage, whether they are active and adapted to diversified habits, or are inactive from being placed in the midst of proper
nutriment or from being fed by their parents; but in some few cases, as in

that of Aphis, if we look to the admirable drawings of the development of this insect, by Professor Huxley, we see hardly any trace of the vermiform stage.

Sometimes it is only the earlier developmental stages which fail. Thus Fritz Müller has made the remarkable discovery that certain shrimp-like crustaceans (allied to Penœus) first appear under the simple nauplius-form, and after passing through two or more zoea-stages, and then through the mysis-stage, finally acquire their mature structure: now in the whole great malacostracan order, to which these crustaceans belong, no other member is as yet known to be first developed under the nauplius-form, though many appear as zoeas; nevertheless Müller assigns reasons for his belief, that if there had been no suppression of development, all these crustaceans would have appeared as nauplii.

How, then, can we explain these several facts in embryology,—namely, the very general, though not universal, difference in structure between the embryo and the adult;—the various parts in the same individual embryo, which ultimately become very unlike and serve for diverse purposes, being at an early period of growth alike;—the common, but not invariable, resemblance between the embryos or larvæ of the most distinct species in the same class;—the embryo often retaining, whilst within the egg or womb, structures which are of no service to it, either at that or at a later period of life; on the other hand, larvæ, which have to provide for their own wants, being perfectly adapted to the surrounding conditions;—and lastly the fact of certain larvæ standing higher in the scale of organisation than the mature animal into which they are developed? I believe that all these facts can be explained, as follows.

It is commonly assumed, perhaps from monstrosities affecting the embryo at a very early period, that slight variations or individual differences necessarily appear at an equally early period. We have little evidence on this head, but what we have certainly points the other way; for it is notorious that breeders of cattle, horses, and various fancy animals, cannot positively tell, until some time after birth, what will be the merits or demerits of their young animals. We see this plainly in our own children; we cannot tell whether a child will be tall or short, or what its precise features will be. The question is not, at what period of life each variation may have been caused, but at what period the effects are displayed. The cause may have acted, and I believe often has acted, on one or both parents before the act of generation. It deserves notice that it is of no importance to a very young animal, as long as it remains in its mother's womb or in the egg, or as long as it is nourished and protected by its parent, whether most of its characters are acquired a little earlier or later in life. It would not signify, for instance, to a bird which obtained its food by having a much-curved beak whether or not whilst young it possessed a beak of this shape, as long as it was fed by its parents.

I have stated in the first chapter, that at whatever age a variation first appears in the parent, it tends to re-appear at a corresponding age in the offspring. Certain variations can only appear at corresponding ages; for instance, peculiarities in the caterpillar, cocoon, or imago states of the silk-moth; or, again, in the full-grown horns of cattle. But variations, which, for all that we can see might have first appeared either earlier or later in life, likewise tend to reappear at a corresponding age in the off-spring and parent. I am far from meaning that this is invariably the case, and I could give several exceptional cases of variations (taking the word in the largest sense) which have supervened at an earlier age in the child than in the parent.

These two principles, namely, that slight variations generally appear at a not very early period of life, and are inherited at a corresponding not early period, explain, as I believe, all the above-specified leading facts in embryology. But first let us look to a few analogous cases in our domestic varieties. Some authors who have written on Dogs, maintain that the greyhound and bulldog, though so different, are really closely allied varieties, descended from the same wild stock; hence I was curious to see how far their puppies differed from each other: I was told by breeders that they differed just as much as their parents, and this, judging by the eye, seemed almost to be the case; but on actually measuring the old dogs and their six-days-old puppies, I found that the puppies had not acquired nearly their full amount of proportional difference. So, again, I was told that the foals of cart and race-horses—breeds which have been almost wholly formed by selection under domestication—differed as much as the full-grown animals; but having had careful measurements made of the dams and of three-days-old colts of race and heavy cart-horses, I find that this is by no means the case.

As we have conclusive evidence that the breeds of the Pigeon are descended from a single wild species, I compared the young within twelve hours after being hatched; I carefully measured the proportions (but will not here give the details) of the beak, width of mouth, length of nostril and of eyelid, size of feet and length of leg, in the wild parent-species, in pouters, fantails, runts, barbs, dragons, carriers, and tumblers. Now some of these birds, when mature, differ in so extraordinary a manner in the length and form of beak, and in other characters, that they would certainly have been ranked as distinct genera if found in a state of nature. But when the nestling birds of these several breeds were placed in a row, though most of them could just be distinguished, the proportional differences in the above specified points were incomparably less than in the full-grown birds. Some characteristic points of difference—for instance, that of the width of mouth—could hardly be detected in the young. But there was one remarkable exception to this rule, for the young of the short-faced tumbler differed from the young of the wild rock-pigeon and of the other breeds, in almost exactly the same proportions as in the adult state.

These facts are explained by the above two principles. Fanciers select their dogs, horses, pigeons, &c., for breeding, when nearly grown up: they are indifferent whether the desired qualities are acquired earlier or later in life, if the full-grown animal possesses them. And the cases just given, more especially that of the pigeons, show that the characteristic differences which have been accumulated by man's selection, and which give value to his breeds, do not generally appear at a very early period of life, and are inherited at a corresponding not early period. But the case of the short-faced tumbler, which when twelve hours old possessed its proper characters, proves that this is not the universal rule; for here the characteristic differences must either have appeared at an earlier period than usual, or, if not so, the differences must have been inherited, not at a corresponding, but at an earlier age.

Now let us apply these two principles to species in a state of nature. Let us take a group of birds, descended from some ancient form and modified through natural selection for different habits. Then, from the many slight successive variations having supervened in the several species at a not early age, and having been inherited at a corresponding age, the young will have been but little modified, and they will still resemble each other much more closely than do the adults,—just as we have seen with the breeds of the pigeon. We may extend this view to widely distinct structures and to whole classes. The fore-limbs, for instance, which once served as legs to a remote progenitor, may have become, through a long course of modification, adapted in one descendant to act as hands, in another as paddles, in another as wings; but on the above two principles the fore-limbs will not have been much modified in the embryos of these several forms; although in each form the fore-limb will differ greatly in the adult state. Whatever influence long-continued use or disuse may have had in modifying the limbs or other parts of any species, this will chiefly or solely have affected it when nearly mature, when it was compelled to use its full powers to gain its own living; and the effects thus produced will have been transmitted to the offspring at a corresponding nearly mature age. Thus the young will not be modified, or will be modified only in a slight degree, through the effects of the increased use or disuse of parts

With some animals the successive variations may have supervened at a very early period of life, or the steps may have been inherited at an earlier age than that at which they first occurred. In either of these cases, the young or embryo will closely resemble the mature parent-form, as we have seen with the short-faced tumbler. And this is the rule of development in certain whole groups, or in certain sub-groups alone, as with cuttle-fish, land-shells, fresh-water crustaceans, spiders, and some members of the great class of insects. With respect to the final cause of the young in such groups not passing through any metamorphosis, we can see that this would follow from the following contingencies; namely, from the young having to provide at a very early age for their own wants, and from their following the same habits of life with their parents; for in this case, it would be indispensable for their existence that they should be modified in the same manner as their parents. Again, with respect to the singular fact that many terrestrial and fresh-water animals do not undergo any metamorphosis, whilst marine members of the same groups pass through various transformations, Fritz Müller has suggested that the process of slowly modifying and adapting an animal to live on the land or in fresh water, instead of in the sea, would be greatly simplified by its not passing through any larval stage; for it is not probable that places well adapted for both the larval and mature stages, under such new and greatly changed habits of life, would commonly be found unoccupied or ill-occupied by other organisms. In this case the gradual acquirement at an earlier and earlier age of the adult structure would be favoured by natural selection; and all traces of former metamorphoses would finally be lost.

If, on the other hand, it profited the young of an animal to follow habits of life slightly different from those of the parent-form, and consequently to be constructed on a slightly different plan, or if it profited a larva already different from its parent to change still further, then, on the principle of inheritance at corresponding ages, the young or the larvæ might be rendered by natural selection more and more different from their parents to any conceivable extent. Differences in the larva might, also, become correlated with successive stages of its development; so that the larva, in the first stage might come to differ greatly from the larva in the second stage, as is the case with many animals. The adult might also become fitted for sites or habits, in which organs of locomotion or of the senses, &c., would be useless; and in this case the metamorphosis would be retrograde.

From the remarks just made we can see how by changes of structure in the young, in conformity with changed habits of life, together with inheritance at corresponding ages, animals might come to pass through stages of development, perfectly distinct from the primordial condition of their adult progenitors. Most of our best authorities are now convinced that the various larval and pupal stages of insects have thus been acquired through adaptation, and not through inheritance from some ancient form. The curious case of Sitaris—a beetle which passes through certain unusual stages of development—will illustrate how this might occur. The first larval form is described by M. Fabre, as an active, minute insect, furnished with six legs, two long antennæ, and four eyes. These larvæ are hatched in the nests of bees; and when the male-bees emerge from their burrows, in the spring, which they do before the females, the larvæ spring on them, and afterwards crawl on to the females whilst paired with the males. As soon as the female bee deposits her eggs on the surface of the honey stored in the cells, the larvæ of the Sitaris leap on the eggs and devour them. Afterwards they undergo a complete change; their eyes disappear; their legs and antennæ become rudimentary, and they feed on honey; so that they now more closely resemble the ordinary larvæ of insects; ultimately they undergo a further transformation, and finally emerge as the perfect beetle. Now, if an insect, undergoing transformations like those of the Sitaris, were to become the progenitor of a whole new class of insects, the course of development of the new class would be widely different from that of our existing insects; and the first larval stage certainly would not represent the former condition of any adult and ancient form.

On the other hand it is highly probable that with many animals the embryonic or larval stages show us, more or less completely, the condition of the progenitor of the whole group in its adult state. In the great class of the Crustacea, forms wonderfully distinct from each other, namely, suctorial parasites, cirripedes, entomostraca, and even the malacostraca, appear at first as larvæ under the nauplius-form; and as these larvæ live and feed in the open sea, and are not adapted for any peculiar habits of life, and from other reasons assigned by Fritz Müller, it is probable that at some very remote period an independent adult animal, resembling the Nauplius, existed, and subsequently produced, along several divergent lines of descent, the above-named great Crustacean groups. So again it is probable, from what we know of the embryos of mammals, birds, fishes, and reptiles, that these animals are the modified descendants of some ancient progenitor, which was furnished in its adult state with branchiæ, a swim-bladder, four fin-like limbs, and a long tail, all fitted for an aquatic life.

As all the organic beings, extinct and recent, which have ever lived, can be arranged within a few great classes; and as all within each class have, according to our theory, been connected together by fine gradations, the best, and, if our collections were nearly perfect, the only possible arrangement, would be genealogical; descent being the hidden bond of connexion which naturalists have been seeking under the term of the Natural System. On this view we can understand how it is that, in the eyes of most naturalists, the structure of the embryo is even more important for classification than that of the adult. In two or more groups of animals, however much they may differ from each other in structure and habits in their adult condition, if they pass through closely similar embryonic stages, we may feel assured that they all are descended from one parent-form, and are therefore closely related. Thus, community in embryonic structure reveals community of descent; but dissimilarity in embryonic development does not prove discommunity of descent, for in one of two groups the developmental stages may have been suppressed, or may have been so greatly modified through adaptation to new habits of life, as to be no longer recognisable. Even in groups, in which the adults have been modified to an extreme degree, community of origin is often revealed by the structure of the larvæ; we have seen, for instance, that cirripedes, though externally so like shell-fish, are at once known by their larvæ to belong to the great class of crustaceans. As the embryo often shows us more or less plainly the structure of the less modified and ancient progenitor of the group, we can see why ancient and extinct forms so often resemble in their adult state the embryos of existing species of the same class. Agassiz believes this to be a universal law of nature; and we may hope hereafter to see the law proved true. It can, however, be proved true only in those cases in which the ancient state of the progenitor of the group has not been wholly obliterated, either by successive variations having supervened at a very early period of growth, or by such variations having been inherited at an earlier age than that at which they first appeared. It should also be borne in mind, that the law may be true, but yet, owing to the geological record not extending far enough back in time, may remain for a long period, or for ever, incapable of demonstration. The law will not strictly hold good in those cases in which an ancient form became adapted in its larvæ state to some special line of life, and transmitted the same larval state to a whole group of descendants; for such larval will not resemble any still more ancient form in its adult state.

Thus, as it seems to me, the leading facts in embryology, which are second to none in importance, are explained on the principle of variations in the many descendants from some one ancient progenitor, having appeared at a not very early period of life, and having been inherited at a corresponding period. Embryology rises greatly in interest, when we look at the embryo as a picture, more or less obscured, of the progenitor, either in its adult or larval state, of all the members of the same great class.

Rudimentary, Atrophied, and Aborted Organs

Organs or parts in this strange condition, bearing the plain stamp of inutility, are extremely common, or even general, throughout nature. It would be impossible to name one of the higher animals in which some part or other is not in a rudimentary condition. In the mammalia, for instance, the males possess rudimentary mammæ; in snakes one lobe of the lungs is rudimentary; in birds the "bastard-wing" may safely be considered as a rudimentary digit, and in some species the whole wing is so far rudimentary that it cannot be used for flight. What can be more curious than the presence of teeth in fœtal whales, which when grown up have not a tooth in their heads; or the teeth, which never cut through the gums, in the upper jaws of unborn calves?

Rudimentary organs plainly declare their origin and meaning in various ways. There are beetles belonging to closely allied species, or even to the same identical species, which have either full-sized and perfect wings, or mere rudiments of membrane, which not rarely lie under wing-covers firmly soldered together; and in these cases it is impossible to doubt, that the rudiments represent wings. Rudimentary organs sometimes retain their potentiality: this occasionally occurs with the mammæ of male mammals, which have been known to become well developed and to secrete milk. So again in the udders in the genus Bos, there are normally four developed and two rudimentary teats; but the latter in our domestic cows sometimes become well developed and yield milk. In regard to plants the petals are sometimes rudimentary, and sometimes well-developed in the individuals of the same species. In certain plants having separated sexes Kölreuter found that by crossing a species, in which the male flowers included a rudiment of a pistil, with an hermaphrodite species, having of course a well-developed pistil, the rudiment in the hybrid offspring was much increased in size; and this clearly shows that the rudimentary and perfect pistils are essentially alike in nature. An animal may possess various parts in a perfect state, and yet they may in one sense be rudimentary, for they are useless: thus the tadpole of the common Sala-mander or Water-newt, as Mr. G. H. Lewes remarks, "has gills, and passes its existence in the water; but the Salamandra atra, which lives high up among the mountains, brings forth its young full-formed. This animal never lives in the water. Yet if we open a gravid female, we find tadpoles inside her with exquisitely feathered gills; and when placed in water they swim about like the tadpoles of the water-newt. Obviously this aquatic organisation has no reference to the future life of the ani-mal, nor has it any adaptation to its embryonic condition; it has solely reference to ancestral adaptations, it repeats a phase in the development of its progenitors."

An organ, serving for two purposes, may become rudimentary or utter-ly aborted for one, even the more important purpose, and remain perfect-ly efficient for the other. Thus in plants, the office of the pistil is to allow the pollen-tubes to reach the ovules within the ovarium. The pistil consists of a stigma supported on a style; but in some Compositæ, the male florets, which of course cannot be fecundated, have a rudimentary pistil, for it is not crowned with a stigma; but the style remains well de-veloped and is clothed in the usual manner with hairs, which serve to brush the pollen out of the surrounding and conjoined anthers. Again, an organ may become rudimentary for its proper purpose, and be used for a distinct one: in certain fishes the swim-bladder seems to be rudimentary for its proper function of giving buoyancy, but has become converted into a nascent breathing organ or lung. Many similar instances could be given.

Useful organs, however little they may be developed, unless we have reason to suppose that they were formerly more highly developed, ought not to be considered as rudimentary. They may be in a nascent condition, and in progress towards further development. Rudimentary organs, on the other hand, are either quite useless, such as teeth which never cut through the gums, or almost useless, such as the wings of an ostrich, which serve merely as sails. As organs in this condition would formerly, when still less developed, have been of even less use than at present, they cannot formerly have been produced through variation and natural selec-tion, which acts solely by the preservation of useful modifications. They have been partially retained by the power of inheritance, and relate to a former state of things. It is, however, often difficult to distinguish beween rudimentary and nascent organs; for we can judge only by analogy whether a part is capable of further development, in which case alone it deserves to be called nascent. Organs in this condition will always be somewhat rare; for beings thus provided will commonly have been sup-planted by their successors with the same organ in a more perfect state, and consequently will have become long ago extinct. The wing of the pen-guin is of high service, acting as a fin; it may, therefore, represent the nascent state of the wing: not that I believe this to be the case; it is more probably a reduced organ, modified for a new function: the wing of the Apteryx, on the other hand, is quite useless, and is truly rudimentary. Owen considers the simple filamentary limbs of the Lepidosiren as the "beginnings of organs which attain full functional development in higher vertebrates;" but, according to the view lately advocated by Dr. Günther, they are probably remnants, consisting of the persistent axis of a fin, with the lateral rays or branches aborted. The mammary glands of the Ornithorhynchus may be considered, in comparison with the udders of a cow, as in a nascent condition. The ovigerous frena of certain cirripedes, which have ceased to give attachment to the ova and are feebly developed, are nascent branchiæ.

Rudimentary organs in the individuals of the same species are very liable to vary in the degree of their development and in other respects. In closely allied species, also, the extent to which the same organ has been reduced occasionally differs much. This latter fact is well exemplified in the state of the wings of female moths belonging to the same family. Rudimentary organs may be utterly aborted; and this imples, that in certain animals or plants, parts are entirely absent which analogy would lead us to expect to find in them, and which are occasionally found in monstrous individuals. Thus in most of the Scrophulariaceæ the fifth stamen is utterly aborted; yet we may conclude that a fifth stamen once existed, for a rudiment of it is found in many species of the family, and this rudiment occasionally becomes perfectly developed, as may sometimes be seen in the common snap-dragon. In tracing the homologies of any part in different members of the same class, nothing is more common, or, in order fully to understand the relations of the parts, more useful than the discovery of rudiments. This is well shown in the drawings given by Owen of the leg-bones of the horse, ox, and rhinoceros.

It is an important fact that rudimentary organs, such as teeth in the upper jaws of whales and ruminants, can often be detected in the embryo, but afterwards wholly disappear. It is also, I believe, a universal rule, that a rudimentary part is of greater size in the embryo relatively to the adjoining parts, than in the adult; so that the organ at this early age is less rudimentary, or even cannot be said to be in any degree rudimentary. Hence rudimentary organs in the adult are often said to have retained their embryonic condition.

I have now given the leading facts with respect to rudimentary organs. In reflecting on them, every one must be struck with astonishment; for the same reasoning power which tells us that most parts and organs are exquisitely adapted for certain purposes, tells us with equal plainness that these rudimentary or atrophied organs are imperfect and useless. In works on natural history, rudimentary organs are generally said to have been created "for the sake of symmetry," or in order "to complete the scheme of nature." But this is not an explanation, merely a re-statement of the fact. Nor is it consistent with itself; thus the boa-constrictor has rudiments of hind-limbs and of a pelvis, and if it be said that these bones have been retained "to complete the scheme of nature," why, as Professor Weismann asks, have they not been retained by other snakes, which do not possess even a vestige of these same bones? What would be the thought of an astronomer who maintained that the satellites revolve in elliptic courses round their planets "for the sake of symmetry," because the planets thus revolve round the sun? An eminent physiologist accounts for the presence of rudimentary organs, by supposing that they serve to excrete matter in excess, or matter injurious to the system; but can we suppose that the minute papilla, which often represents the pistil in male flowers, and which is formed of mere cellular tissue, can thus act? Can we suppose that rudimentary teeth, which are subsequently absorbed, are beneficial to the rapidly growing embryonic calf by removing matter so precious as phosphate of lime? When a man's fingers have been amputated, imperfect nails have been known to appear on the stumps, and I could as soon believe that these vestiges of nails are developed in order to excrete horny matter, as that the rudimentary nails on the fin of the manatee have been developed for this same purpose.

On the view of descent with modification, the origin of rudimentary organs is comparatively simple; and we can understand to a large extent the laws governing their imperfect development. We have plenty of cases of rudimentary organs in our domestic productions,—as the stump of a tail in tailless breeds,—the vestige of an ear in earless breeds of sheep,—the reappearance of minute dangling horns in hornless breeds of cattle, more especially, according to Youatt, in young animals,—and the state of the whole flower in the cauliflower. We often see rudiments of various parts in monsters; but I doubt whether any of these cases throw light on the origin of rudimentary organs in a state of nature, further than by showing that rudiments can be produced; for the balance of evidence clearly indicates that species under nature do not undergo great and abrupt changes. But we learn from the study of our domestic productions that the disuse of parts leads to their reduced size; and that the result is inherited.

It appears probable that disuse has been the main agent in rendering organs rudimentary. It would at first lead by slow steps to the more and more complete reduction of a part, until at last it became rudimentary,—as in the case of the eyes of animals inhabiting dark caverns, and of the wings of birds inhabiting oceanic islands, which have seldom been forced by beasts of prey to take flight, and have ultimately lost the power of flying. Again, an organ, useful under certain conditions, might become injurious under others, as with the wings of beetles living on small and exposed islands; and in this case natural selection will have aided in reducing the organ, until it was rendered harmless and rudimentary.

Any change in structure and function, which can be effected by small stages, is within the power of natural selection; so that an organ rendered, through changed habits of life, useless or injurious for one purpose, might be modified and used for another purpose. An organ might, also, be retained for one alone of its former functions. Organs, originally formed by the aid of natural selection, when rendered useless may well be variable, for their variations can no longer be checked by natural selection. All this agrees well with what we see under nature. Moreover, at whatever period of life either disuse or selection reduces an organ, and this will generally be when the being has come to maturity and has to exert its full powers of action, the principle of inheritance at corresponding ages will tend to reproduce the organ in its reduced state at the same mature age, but will seldom effect it in the embryo. Thus we can understand the greater size of rudimentary organs in the embryo relatively to the adjoining parts, and their lesser relative size in the adult. If, for instance, the digit of an adult animal was used less and less during many generations, owing to some change of habits, or if an organ or gland was less and less functionally exercised, we may infer that it would become reduced in size in the adult descendants of this animal, but would retain nearly its original standard of development in the embryo.

There remains, however, this difficulty. After an organ has ceased being used, and has become in consequence much reduced, how can it be still further reduced in size until the merest vestige is left; and how can it be finally quite obliterated? It is scarcely possible that disuse can go on producing any further effect after the organ has once been rendered functionless. Some additional explanation is here requisite which I cannot give. If, for instance, it could be proved that every part of the organisation tends to vary in a greater degree towards diminution than towards augmentation of size, then we should be able to understand how an organ which has become useless would be rendered, independently of the effects of disuse, rudimentary and would at last be wholly suppressed; for the variations towards diminished size would no longer be checked by natural selection. The principle of the economy of growth, explained in a former chapter, by which the materials forming any part, if not useful to the possessor, are saved as far as possible, will perhaps come into play in rendering a useless part rudimentary. But this principle will almost necessarily be confined to the earlier stages of the process of reduction; for we cannot suppose that a minute papilla, for instance, representing in a male flower the pistil of the female flower, and formed merely of cellular tissue, could be further reduced or absorbed for the sake of economising nutriment.

Finally, as rudimentary organs, by whatever steps they may have been degraded into their present useless condition, are the record of a former state of things, and have been retained solely through the power of inheritance,—we can understand, on the genealogical view of classification, how it is that systematists, in placing organisms in their proper places in the natural system, have often found rudimentary parts as useful as, or even sometimes more useful than, parts of high physiological importance. Rudimentary organs may be compared with the letters in a word, still retained in the spelling, but become useless in the pronunciation, but which serve as a clue for its derivation. On the view of descent with modification, we may conclude that the existence of organs in a rudimentary, imperfect, and useless condition, or quite aborted, far from presenting a strange difficulty, as they assuredly do on the old doctrine of creation, might even have been anticipated in accordance with the views here explained.

Summary

In this chapter I have attempted to show, that the arrangement of all organic beings throughout all time in groups under groups—that the nature of the relationships by which all living and extinct organisms are united by complex, radiating, and circuitous lines of affinities into a few grand classes,—the rules followed and the difficulties encountered by naturalists in their classifications,—the value set upon characters, if constant and prevalent, whether of high or of the most trifling importance, or, as with rudimentary organs, of no importance,—the wide opposition in value between analogical or adaptive characters, and characters of true affinity; and other such rules;—all naturally follow if we admit the common parentage of allied forms, together with their modification through variation and natural selection, with the contingencies of extinction and divergence of character. In considering this view of classification, it should be borne in mind that the element of descent has been universally used in ranking together the sexes, ages, dimorphic forms, and acknowledged varieties of the same species, however much they may differ from each other in structure. If we extend the use of this element of descent,—the one certainly known cause of similarity in organic beings,—we shall understand what is meant by the Natural System: it is genealogical in its attempted arrangement, with the grades of acquired difference marked by the terms, varieties, species, genera, families, orders, and classes.

On this same view of descent with modification, most of the great facts in Morphology become intelligible,—whether we look to the same pattern displayed by the different species of the same class in their homologous organs, to whatever purpose applied; or to the serial and lateral homologies in each individual animal and plant.

On the principle of successive slight variations, not necessarily or generally supervening at a very early period of life, and being inherited at a corresponding period, we can understand the leading facts in Embryology; namely, the close resemblance in the individual embryo of the parts which are homologous, and which when matured become widely different in structure and function; and the resemblance of the homologous parts or organs in allied though distinct species, though fitted in the adult state for habits as different as is possible. Larvæ are active embryos, which have been specially modified in a greater or less degree in relation to their habits of life, with their modifications inherited at a corresponding early age. On these same principles,—and bearing in mind that when organs are reduced in size, either from disuse or through natural selection, it will generally be at that period of life when the being has to provide for its own wants, and bearing in mind how strong is the force of inheritance—the occurrence of rudimentary organs might even have been anticipated. The importance of embryological characters and of rudimentary organs in classification is intelligible, on the view that a natural arrangement must be genealogical.

Finally, the several classes of facts which have been considered in this chapter, seem to me to proclaim so plainly, that the innumerable species, genera and families, with which this world is peopled, are all descended, each within its own class or group, from common parents, and have all been modified in the course of descent, that I should without hesitation adopt this view, even if it were unsupported by other facts or arguments.

CHAPTER XV

Recapitulation of the objections to the theory of Natural Selection—Recapitulation of the general and special circumstances in its favour—Causes of the general belief in the immutability of species—How far the theory of Natural Selection may be extended—Effects of its adoption on the study of Natural History—Concluding Remarks.

As this whole volume is one long argument, it may be convenient to the reader to have the leading facts and inferences briefly recapitulated.

That many and serious objections may be advanced against the theory of descent with modification through variation and natural selection, I do not deny. I have endeavoured to give to them their full force. Nothing at first can appear more difficult to believe than that the more complex organs and instincts have been perfected, not by means superior to, though analogous with, human reason, but by the accumulation of innumerable slight variations, each good for the individual possessor. Nevertheless, this difficulty, though appearing to our imagination insuperably great, cannot be considered real if we admit the following propositions, namely, that all parts of the organisation and instincts offer, at least, individual differences—that there is a struggle for existence leading to the preservation of profitable deviations of structure or instinct—and, lastly, that gradations in the state of perfection of each organ may have existed, each good of its kind. The truth of these propositions cannot, I think, be disputed.

It is, no doubt, extremely difficult even to conjecture by what gradations many structures have been perfected, more especially amongst broken and failing groups of organic beings, which have suffered much extinction, but we see so many strange gradations in nature, that we ought to be extremely cautious in saying that any organ or instinct, or any whole structure, could not have arrived at its present state by many graduated steps. There are, it must be admitted, cases of special difficulty opposed to the theory of natural selection; and one of the most curious of these is the existence in the same community of two or three defined castes of workers or sterile female ants; but I have attempted to show how these difficulties can be mastered.

With respect to the almost universal sterility of species when first crossed, which forms so remarkable a contrast with the almost universal fertility of varieties when crossed, I must refer the reader to the recapitulation of the facts given at the end of the ninth chapter, which seem to me conclusively to show that this sterility is no more a special endowment than is the incapacity of two distinct kinds of trees to be grafted together; but that it is incidental on differences confined to the reproductive systems of the intercrossed species. We see the truth of this conclusion in the vast difference in the results of crossing the same two species reciprocally,— that is, when one species is first used as the father and then as the mother. Analogy from the consideration of dimorphic and trimorphic plants clearly leads to the same conclusion, for when the forms are illegitimately united, they yield few or no seed, and their offspring are more or less sterile; and these forms belong to the same undoubted species, and differ from each other in no respect except in their reproductive organs and functions.

Although the fertility of varieties when intercrossed and of their mongrel offspring has been asserted by so many authors to be universal, this cannot be considered as quite correct after the facts given on the high authority of Gärtner and Kölreuter. Most of the varieties which have been experimented on have been produced under domestication; and as domestication (I do not mean mere confinement) almost certainly tends to eliminate that sterility which, judging from analogy, would have affected the parent-species if intercrossed, we ought not to expect that domestication would likewise induce sterility in their modified descendants when crossed. This elimination of sterility apparently follows from the same cause which allows our domestic animals to breed freely under diversified circumstances; and this again apparently follows from their having been gradually accustomed to frequent changes in their conditions of life.

A double and parallel series of facts seems to throw much light on the sterility of species, when first crossed, and of their hybrid offspring. On the one side, there is good reason to believe that slight changes in the conditions of life give vigour and fertility to all organic beings. We know also that a cross between the distinct individuals of the same variety, and between distinct varieties, increases the number of their offspring, and certainly gives to them increased size and vigour. This is chiefly owing to the forms which are crossed having been exposed to somewhat different conditions of life; for I have ascertained by a laborious series of experiments that if all the individuals of the same variety be subjected during several generations to the same conditions, the good derived from crossing is often much diminished or wholly disappears. This is one side of the case. On the other side, we know that species which have long been exposed to nearly uniform conditions, when they are subjected under confinement to new and greatly changed conditions, either perish, or if they survive, are rendered sterile, though retaining perfect health. This does not occur, or only in a very slight degree, with our domesticated productions, which have long been exposed to fluctuating conditions. Hence when we find that hybrids produced by a cross between two distinct species are few in number, owing to their perishing soon after conception or at a very early age, or if surviving that they are rendered more or less sterile, it seems highly probable that this result is due to their having been in fact subjected to a great change in their conditions of life, from being compounded of two distinct organisations. He who will explain in a definite manner why, for instance, an elephant or a fox will not breed under confinement in its native country, whilst the domestic pig or dog will breed freely under the most diversified conditions, will at the same time be able to give a definite answer to the question why two distinct species, when crossed, as well as their hybrid offspring, are generally rendered more or less sterile, whilst two domesticated varieties when crossed and their mongrel offspring are perfectly fertile.

Turning to geographical distribution, the difficulties encountered on the theory of descent with modification are serious enough. All the individuals of the same species, and all the species of the same genus, or even higher group, are descended from common parents; and therefore, in however distant and isolated parts of the world they may now be found, they must in the course of successive generations have travelled from some one point to all the others. We are often wholly unable even to conjecture how this could have been effected. Yet, as we have reason to believe that some species have retained the same specific form for very long periods of time, immensely long as measured by years, too much stress ought not to be laid on the occasional wide diffusion of the same species; for during very long periods there will always have been a good chance for wide migration by many means. A broken or interrupted range may often be accounted for by the extinction of the species in the intermediate regions. It cannot be denied that we are as yet very ignorant as to the full extent of the various climatal and geographical changes which have affected the earth during modern periods; and such changes will often have facilitated migration. As an example, I have attempted to show how potent has been the influence of the Glacial period on the distribution of the same and of allied species throughout the world. We are as yet profoundly ignorant of the many occasional means of transport. With respect to distinct species of the same genus inhabiting distant and isolated regions, as the process of modification has necessarily been slow, all the means of migration will have been possible during a very long period; and consequently the difficulty of the wide diffusion of the species of the same genus is in some degree lessened.

As according to the theory of natural selection an interminable number of intermediate forms must have existed, linking together all the species in each group by gradations as fine as are our existing varieties, it may be asked: Why do we not see these linking forms all around us? Why are not all organic beings blended together in an inextricable chaos? With respect to existing forms, we should remember that we have no right to expect (excepting in rare cases) to discover *directly* connecting links between them, but only between each and some extinct and supplanted form. Even on a wide area, which has during a long period remained continuous, and of which the climatic and other conditions of life change insensibly in proceeding from a district occupied by one species into another district occupied by a closely allied species, we have no just right to expect often to find intermediate varieties in the intermediate zones. For we have reason to believe that only a few species of a genus ever undergo change; the other species becoming utterly extinct and leaving no modified progeny. Of the species which do change, only a few within the same country change at the same time; and all modifications are slowly effected. I have also shown that the intermediate varieties which probably at first existed in the intermediate zones, would be liable to be supplanted by the allied forms on either hand; for the latter, from existing in greater numbers, would generally be modified and improved at a quicker rate than the intermediate varieties, which existed in lesser numbers; so that the intermediate varieties would, in the long run, be supplanted and exterminated.

On this doctrine of the extermination of an infinitude of connecting links, between the living and extinct inhabitants of the world, and at each successive period between the extinct and still older species, why is not every geological formation charged with such links? Why does not every collection of fossil remains afford plain evidence of the gradation and mutation of the forms of life? Although geological research has undoubtedly revealed the former existence of many links, bringing numerous forms of life much closer together, it does not yield the infinitely many fine gradations between past and present species required on the theory; and this is the most obvious of the many objections which may be urged against it. Why, again, do whole groups of allied species appear, though this appearance is often false, to have come in suddenly on the successive geological stages? Although we now know that organic beings appeared on this globe, at a period incalculably remote, long before the lowest bed of the Cambrian system was deposited, why do we not find beneath this system great piles of strata stored with the remains of the progenitors of the Cambrian fossils? For on the theory, such strata must somewhere have been deposited at these ancient and utterly unknown epochs of the world's history.

I can answer these questions and objections only on the supposition that the geological record is far more imperfect than most geologists believe. The number of specimens in all our museums is absolutely as nothing compared with the countless generations of countless species which have certainly existed. The parent-form of any two or more species would not be in all its characters directly intermediate between its modified offspring, any more than the rock-pigeon is directly intermediate in crop and tail between its descendants, the pouter and fantail pigeons. We should not be able to recognise a species as the parent of another and modified species, if we were to examine the two ever so closely, unless we possessed most of the intermediate links; and owing to the imperfection of the geological record, we have no just right to expect to find so many links. If two or three, or even more linking forms were discovered, they would simply be ranked by many naturalists as so many new species, more especially if found in different geological sub-stages, let their differences be ever so slight. Numerous existing doubtful forms could be named which are probably varieties; but who will pretend that in future ages so many fossil links will be discovered, that naturalists will be able to decide whether or not these doubtful forms ought to be called varieties? Only a small portion of the world has been geologically explored. Only organic beings of certain classes can be preserved in a fossil condition, at least in any great number. Many species when once formed never undergo any further change but become extinct without leaving modified descendants; and the periods, during which species have undergone modification, though long as measured by years, have probably been short in comparison with the periods during which they retain the same form. It is the dominant and widely ranging species which vary most frequently and vary most, and varieties are often at first local—both causes rendering the discovery of intermediate links in any one formation less likely. Local varieties will not spread into other and distant regions until they are considerably modified and improved; and when they have spread, and are discovered in a geological formation, they appear as if suddenly created there, and will be simply classed as new species. Most formations have been intermittent in their accumulation; and their duration has probably been shorter than the average duration of specific forms. Successive formations are in most cases separated from each other by blank intervals of time of great length; for fossiliferous formations thick enough to resist future degradations can as a general rule be accumulated only where much sediment is deposited on the subsiding bed of the sea. During the alternate periods of elevation and of stationary level the record will generally be blank. During these latter periods there will probably be more variability in the forms of life; during periods of subsidence, more extinction.

With respect to the absence of strata rich in fossils beneath the Cambrian formation, I can recur only to the hypothesis given in the tenth chapter; namely, that though our continents and oceans have endured for an enormous period in nearly their present relative positions, we have no reason to assume that this has always been the case; consequently formations much older than any now known may lie buried beneath the great oceans. With respect to the lapse of time not having been sufficient since our planet was consolidated for the assumed amount of organic change, and this objection, as urged by Sir William Thompson, is probably one of the gravest as yet advanced, I can only say, firstly, that we do not know at what rate species change as measured by years, and secondly, that many philosophers are not as yet willing to admit that we know enough of the constitution of the universe and of the interior of our globe to speculate with safety on its past duration.

That the geological record is imperfect all will admit; but that it is imperfect to the degree required by our theory, few will be inclined to admit. If we look to long enough intervals of time, geology plainly declares that species have all changed; and they have changed in the manner required by the theory, for they have changed slowly and in a graduated

manner. We clearly see this in the fossil remains from consecutive formations invariably being much more closely related to each other, than are
the fossils from widely separated formations.

Such is the sum of the several chief objections and difficulties which
may be justly urged against the theory; and I have now briefly recapitulated the answers and explanations which, as far as I can see, may be giv-
en. I have felt these difficulties far too heavily during many years to
doubt their weight. But it deserves especial notice that the more important objections relate to questions on which we are confessedly ignorant;
nor do we know how ignorant we are. We do not know all the possible
transitional gradations between the simplest and the most perfect organs;
it cannot be pretended that we know all the varied means of Distribution
during the long lapse of years, or that we know how imperfect is the Geological Record. Serious as these several objections are, in my judgment
they are by no means sufficient to overthrow the theory of descent with
subsequent modification.

Now let us turn to the other side of the argument. Under domestication
we see much variability, caused, or at least excited, by changed conditions of life; but often in so obscure a manner, that we are tempted to
consider the variations as spontaneous. Variability is governed by many
complex laws,—by correlated growth, compensation, the increased use
and disuse of parts, and the definite action of the surrounding conditions.
There is much difficulty in ascertaining how largely our domestic productions have been modified; but we may safely infer that the amount has
been large, and that modifications can be inherited for long periods. As
long as the conditions of life remain the same, we have reason to believe
that a modification, which has already been inherited for many generations, may continue to be inherited for an almost infinite number of generations. On the other hand, we have evidence that variability when it has
once come into play, does not cease under domestication for a very long
period; nor do we know that it ever ceases, for new varieties are still occasionally produced by our oldest domesticated productions.

Variability is not actually caused by man; he only unintentionally exposes organic beings to new conditions of life, and then nature acts on the
organisation and causes it to vary. But man can and does select the variations given to him by nature, and thus accumulates them in any desired
manner. He thus adapts animals and plants for his own benefit or pleasure. He may do this methodically, or he may do it unconsciously by preserving the individuals most useful or pleasing to him without any intention of altering the breed. It is certain that he can largely influence the
character of a breed by selecting, in each successive generation, individual
differences so slight as to be inappreciable except by an educated eye.
This unconscious process of selection has been the great agency in the formation of the most distinct and useful domestic breeds. That many
breeds produced by man have to a large extent the character of natural

species, is shown by the inextricable doubts whether many of them are varieties or aboriginally distinct species.

There is no reason why the principles which have acted so efficiently under domestication should not have acted under nature. In the survival of favoured individuals and races, during the constantly-recurrent Struggle for Existence, we see a powerful and ever-acting form of Selection. The struggle for existence inevitably follows from the high geometrical ratio of increase which is common to all organic beings. This high rate of increase is proved by calculation,—by the rapid increase of many animals and plants during a succession of peculiar seasons, and when naturalised in new countries. More individuals are born than can possibly survive. A grain in the balance may determine which individuals shall live and which shall die,—which variety or species shall increase in number, and which shall decrease, or finally become extinct. As the individuals of the same species come in all respects into the closest competition with each other, the struggle will generally be most severe between them; it will be almost equally severe between the varieties of the same species, and next in severity between the species of the same genus. On the other hand the struggle will often be severe between beings remote in the scale of nature. The slightest advantage in certain individuals, at any age or during any season, over those with which they come into competition, or better adaptation in however slight a degree to the surrounding physical conditions, will, in the long run, turn the balance.

With animals having separated sexes, there will be in most cases a struggle between the males for the possession of the females. The most vigorous males, or those which have most successfully struggled with their conditions of life, will generally leave most progeny. But success will often depend on the males having special weapons, or means of defence, or charms; and a slight advantage will lead to victory.

As geology plainly proclaims that each land has undergone great physical changes, we might have expected to find that organic beings have varied under nature, in the same way as they have varied under domestication. And if there has been any variability under nature, it would be an unaccountable fact if natural selection had not come into play. It has often been asserted, but the assertion is incapable of proof, that the amount of variation under nature is a strictly limited quantity. Man, though acting on external characters alone and often capriciously, can produce within a short period a great result by adding up mere individual differences in his domestic productions; and every one admits that species present individual differences. But, besides such differences, all naturalists admit that natural varieties exist, which are considered sufficiently distinct to be worthy of record in systematic works. No one has drawn any clear distinction between individual differences and slight varieties; or between more plainly marked varieties and sub-species, and species. On separate continents, and on different parts of the same continent when divided by barriers of any kind, and on outlying islands, what a multitude of forms exist, which some experienced naturalists rank as varieties, others as geographical races or sub-species, and others as distinct, though closely allied species!

If then, animals and plants do vary, let it be ever so slightly or slowly, why should not variations or individual differences, which are in any way beneficial, be preserved and accumulated through natural selection, or the survival of the fittest? If man can by patience select variations useful to him, why, under changing and complex conditions of life, should not variations useful to nature's living products often arise, and be preserved or selected? What limit can be put to this power, acting during long ages and rigidly scrutinising the whole constitution, structure, and habits of each creature,—favouring the good and rejecting the bad? I can see no limit to this power, in slowly and beautifully adapting each form to the most complex relations of life. The theory of natural selection, even if we look no farther than this, seems to be in the highest degree probable. I have already recapitulated, as fairly as I could, the opposed difficulties and objections: now let us turn to the special facts and arguments in favour of the theory.

On the view that species are only strongly marked and permanent varieties, and that each species first existed as a variety, we can see why it is that no line of demarcation can be drawn between species, commonly supposed to have been produced by special acts of creation, and varieties which are acknowledged to have been produced by secondary laws. On this same view we can understand how it is that in a region where many species of a genus have been produced, and where they now flourish, these same species should present many varieties; for where the manufactory of species has been active, we might expect, as a general rule, to find it still in action; and this is the case if varieties be incipient species. Moreover, the species of the larger genera, which afford the greater number of varieties or incipient species, retain to a certain degree the character of varieties; for they differ from each other by a less amount of difference than do the species of smaller genera. The closely allied species also of the larger genera apparently have restricted ranges, and in their affinities they are clustered in little groups round other species—in both respects resembling varieties. These are strange relations on the view that each species was independently created, but are intelligible if each existed first as a variety.

As each species tends by its geometrical rate of reproduction to increase inordinately in number; and as the modified descendants of each species will be enabled to increase by as much as they become more diversified in habits and structure, so as to be able to seize on many and widely different places in the economy of nature, there will be a constant tendency in natural selection to preserve the most divergent offspring of any one species. Hence, during a long-continued course of modification, the slight differences characteristic of varieties of the same species, tend to be augmented into the greater differences characteristic of the species of the

same genus. New and improved varieties will inevitably supplant and exterminate the older, less improved, and intermediate varieties; and thus
species are rendered to a large extent defined and distinct objects. Dominant species belonging to the larger groups within each class tend to give
birth to new and dominant forms; so that each large group tends to become still larger, and at the same time more divergent in character. But as
all groups cannot thus go on increasing in size, for the world would not
hold them, the more dominant groups beat the less dominant. This tendency in the large groups to go on increasing in size and diverging in character, together with the inevitable contingency of much extinction, explains the arrangement of all the forms of life in groups subordinate to
groups, all within a few great classes, which has prevailed throughout all
time. This grand fact of the grouping of all organic beings under what is
called the Natural System, is utterly inexplicable on the theory of creation.

As natural selection acts solely by accumulating slight, successive, favourable variations, it can produce no great or sudden modifications; it
can act only by short and slow steps. Hence, the canon of "Natura non
facit saltum," which every fresh addition to our knowledge tends to confirm, is on this theory intelligible. We can see why throughout nature the
same general end is gained by an almost infinite diversity of means, for
every peculiarity when once acquired is long inherited, and structures already modified in many different ways have to be adapted for the same
general purpose. We can, in short, see why nature is prodigal in variety,
though niggard in innovation. But why this should be a law of nature if
each species has been independently created no man can explain.

Many other facts are, as it seems to me, explicable on this theory. How
strange it is that a bird, under the form of a woodpecker, should prey on
insects on the ground; that upland geese which rarely or never swim,
should possess webbed feet; that a thrush-like bird should dive and feed
on sub-aquatic insects; and that a petrel should have the habits and
structure fitting it for the life of an awk! and so in endless other cases.
But on the view of each species constantly trying to increase in number,
with natural selection always ready to adapt the slowly varying descendants of each to any unoccupied or ill-occupied place in nature, these facts
cease to be strange, or might even have been anticipated.

We can to a certain extent understand how it is that there is so much
beauty throughout nature; for this may be largely attributed to the agency of selection. That beauty, according to our sense of it, is not universal,
must be admitted by every one who will look at some venomous snakes,
at some fishes, and at certain hideous bats with a distorted resemblance
to the human face. Sexual selection has given the most brilliant colours,
elegant patterns, and other ornaments to the males, and sometimes to
both sexes of many birds, butterflies, and other animals. With birds it has
often rendered the voice of the male musical to the female, as well as to
our ears. Flowers and fruit have been rendered conspicuous by brilliant
colours in contrast with the green foliage, in order that the flowers may be

readily seen, visited and fertilised by insects, and the seeds disseminated by birds. How it comes that certain colours, sounds, and forms should give pleasure to man and the lower animals,—that is, how the sense of beauty in its simplest form was first acquired,—we do not know any more than how certain odours and flavours were first rendered agreeable.

As natural selection acts by competition, it adapts and improves the inhabitants of each country only in relation to their co-inhabitants; so that we need feel no surprise at the species of any one country, although on the ordinary view supposed to have been created and specially adapted for that country, being beaten and supplanted by the naturalised productions from another land. Nor ought we to marvel if all the contrivances in nature be not, as far as we can judge, absolutely perfect, as in the case even of the human eye; or if some of them be abhorrent to our ideas of fitness. We need not marvel at the sting of the bee, when used against an enemy, causing the bee's own death; at drones being produced in such great numbers for one single act, and being then slaughtered by their sterile sisters; at the astonishing waste of pollen by our fir-trees; at the instinctive hatred of the queen-bee for her own fertile daughters; at the ichneumonidæ feeding within the living bodies of caterpillars; or at other such cases. The wonder indeed is, on the theory of natural selection, that more cases of the want of absolute perfection have not been detected.

The complex and little known laws governing the production of varieties are the same, as far as we can judge, with the laws which have governed the production of distinct species. In both cases physical conditions seem to have produced some direct and definite effect, but how much we cannot say. Thus, when varieties enter any new station, they occasionally assume some of the characters proper to the species of that station. With both varieties and species, use and disuse seem to have produced a considerable effect; for it is impossible to resist this conclusion when we look, for instance, at the logger-headed duck, which has wings incapable of flight, in nearly the same condition as in the domestic duck; or when we look at the burrowing tucu-tucu, which is occasionally blind, and then at certain moles, which are habitually blind and have their eyes covered with skin; or when we look at the blind animals inhabiting the dark caves of America and Europe. With varieties and species, correlated variation seems to have played an important part, so that when one part has been modified other parts have been necessarily modified. With both varieties and species, reversions to long-lost characters occasionally occur. How inexplicable on the theory of creation is the occasional appearance of stripes on the shoulders and legs of the several species of the horse-genus and of their hybrids! How simply is this fact explained if we believe that these species are all descended from a striped progenitor, in the same manner as the several domestic breeds of the pigeon are descended from the blue and barred rock-pigeon!

On the ordinary view of each species having been independently created, why should specific characters, or those by which the species of the same genus differ from each other, be more variable than generic characters in which they all agree? Why, for instance, should the colour of a flower be more likely to vary in any one species of a genus, if the other species possess differently coloured flowers, than if all possessed the same coloured flowers? If species are only well-marked varieties, of which the characters have become in a high degree permanent, we can understand this fact; for they have already varied since they branched off from a common progenitor in certain characters, by which they have come to be specifically distinct from each other; therefore these same characters would be more likely again to vary than the generic characters which have been inherited without change for an immense period. It is inexplicable on the theory of creation why a part developed in a very unusual manner in one species alone of a genus, and therefore, as we may naturally infer, of great importance to that species, should be eminently liable to variation; but, on our view, this part has undergone, since the several species branched off from a common progenitor, an unusual amount of variability and modification, and therefore we might expect the part generally to be still variable. But a part may be developed in the most unusual manner, like the wing of a bat, and yet not be more variable than any other structure, if the part be common to many subordinate forms, that is, if it has been inherited for a very long period; for in this case, it will have been rendered constant by long-continued natural selection.

Glancing at instincts, marvellous as some are, they offer no greater difficulty than do corporeal structures on the theory of the natural selection of successive slight, but profitable modifications. We can thus understand why nature moves by graduated steps in endowing different animals of the same class with their several instincts. I have attempted to show how much light the principle of gradation throws on the admirable architectural powers of the hive-bee. Habit no doubt often comes into play in modifying instincts; but it certainly is not indispensable, as we see in the case of neuter insects, which leave no progeny to inherit the effects of long-continued habit. On the view of all the species of the same genus having descended from a common parent, and having inherited much in common, we can understand how it is that allied species, when placed under widely different conditions of life, yet follow nearly the same instincts; why the thrushes of tropical and temperate South America, for instance, line their nests with mud like our British species. On the view of instincts having been slowly acquired through natural selection, we need not marvel at some instincts being not perfect and liable to mistakes, and at many instincts causing other animals to suffer.

If species be only well-marked and permanent varieties, we can at once see why their crossed offspring should follow the same complex laws in their degrees and kinds of resemblance to their parents,—in being absorbed into each other by successive crosses, and in other such points,—as do the crossed offspring of acknowledged varieties. This similarity would be a strange fact, if species had been independently created and varieties had been produced through secondary laws.

If we admit that the geological record is imperfect to an extreme degree, then the facts, which the record does give, strongly support the theory of descent with modification. New species have come on the stage slowly and at successive intervals; and the amount of change, after equal intervals of time, is widely different in different groups. The extinction of species and of whole groups of species which has played so conspicuous a part in the history of the organic world, almost inevitably follows from the principle of natural selection; for old forms are supplanted by new and improved forms. Neither single species nor groups of species reappear when the chain of ordinary generation is once broken. The gradual diffusion of dominant forms, with the slow modification of their descendants, causes the forms of life, after long intervals of time, to appear as if they had changed simultaneously throughout the world. The fact of the fossil remains of each formation being in some degree intermediate in character between the fossils in the formations above and below, is simply explained by their intermediate position in the chain of descent. The grand fact that all extinct beings can be classed with all recent beings, naturally follows from the living and the extinct being the offspring of common parents. As species have generally diverged in character during their long course of descent and modification, we can understand why it is that the more ancient forms, or early progenitors of each group, so often occupy a position in some degree intermediate between existing groups. Recent forms are generally looked upon as being, on the whole, higher in the scale of organisation than ancient forms; and they must be higher, in so far as the later and more improved forms have conquered the older and less improved forms in the struggle for life; they have also generally had their organs more specialised for different functions. This fact is perfectly compatible with numerous beings still retaining simple and but little improved structures, fitted for simple conditions of life; it is likewise compatible with some forms having retrograded in organisation, by having become at each stage of descent better fitted for new and degraded habits of life. Lastly, the wonderful law of the long endurance of allied forms on the same continent,—of marsupials in Australia, of edentata in America, and other such cases,—is intelligible, for within the same country the existing and the extinct will be closely allied by descent.

Looking to geographical distribution, if we admit that there has been during the long course of ages much migration from one part of the world to another, owing to former climatal and geographical changes and to the many occasional and unknown means of dispersal, then we can understand, on the theory of descent with modification, most of the great leading facts in Distribution. We can see why there should be so striking a parallelism in the distribution of organic beings throughout space, and in their geological succession throughout time; for in both cases the beings have been connected by the bond of ordinary generation, and the means of modification have been the same. We see the full meaning of the wonderful fact, which has struck every traveller, namely, that on the same continent, under the most diverse conditions, under heat and cold, on mountain and lowland, on deserts and marshes, most of the inhabitants within each great class are plainly related; for they are the descendants of the same progenitors and early colonists. On this same principle of former migration, combined in most cases with modification, we can understand, by the aid of the Glacial period, the identity of some few plants, and the close alliance of many others, on the most distant mountains, and in the northern and southern temperate zones; and likewise the close alliance of some of the inhabitants of the sea in the northern and southern temperate latitudes, though separated by the whole intertropical ocean. Although two countries may present physical conditions as closely similar as the same species ever require, we need feel no surprise at their inhabitants being widely different, if they have been for a long period completely sundered from each other; for as the relation of organism to organism is the most important of all relations, and as the two countries will have received colonists at various periods and in different proportions, from some other country or from each other, the course of modification in the two areas will inevitably have been different.

On this view of migration, with subsequent modification, we see why oceanic islands are inhabited by only few species, but of these, why many are peculiar or endemic forms. We clearly see why species belonging to those groups of animals which cannot cross wide spaces of the ocean, as frogs and terrestrial mammals, do not inhabit oceanic islands; and why, on the other hand, new and peculiar species of bats, animals which can traverse the ocean, are found on islands far distant from any continent. Such cases as the presence of peculiar species of bats on oceanic islands and the absence of all other terrestrial mammals, are facts utterly inexplicable on the theory of independent acts of creation.

The existence of closely allied or representative species in any two areas, implies, on the theory of descent with modification, that the same parent-forms formerly inhabited both areas; and we almost invariably find that wherever many closely allied species inhabit two areas, some identical species are still common to both. Wherever many closely allied yet distinct species occur, doubtful forms and varieties belonging to the same groups likewise occur. It is a rule of high generality that the inhabitants of each area are related to the inhabitants of the nearest source whence immigrants might have been derived. We see this in the striking relation of nearly all plants and animals of the Galapagos archipelago, of Juan Fernandez, and of the other American islands, to the plants and animals of the neighbouring American mainland; and of those of the Cape de Verde archipelago, and of the other African islands to the African mainland. It must be admitted that these facts receive no explanation on the theory of creation.

The fact, as we have seen, that all past and present organic beings can be arranged within a few great classes, in groups subordinate to groups, and with the extinct groups often falling in between the recent groups, is intelligible on the theory of natural selection with its contingencies of extinction and divergence of character. On these same principles we see how it is, that the mutual affinities of the forms within each class are so com-

plex and circuitous. We see why certain characters are far more serviceable than others for classification;—why adaptive characters, though of
paramount importance to the beings, are of hardly any importance in
classification; why characters derived from rudimentary parts, though of
no service to the beings, are often of high classificatory value; and why
embryological characters are often the most valuable of all. The real affinities of all organic beings, in contradistinction to their adaptive resemblances, are due to inheritance or community of descent. The Natural
System is a genealogical arrangement, with the acquired grades of difference, marked by the terms, varieties, species, genera, families, &c.; and
we have to discover the lines of descent by the most permanent characters whatever they may be and of however slight vital importance.

The similar framework of bones in the hand of a man, wing of a bat, fin
of the porpoise, and leg of the horse,—the same number of vertebræ forming the neck of the giraffe and of the elephant,—and innumerable other
such facts, at once explain themselves on the theory of descent with slow
and slight successive modifications. The similarity of pattern in the wing
and in the leg of a bat, though used for such different purpose,—in the
jaws and legs of a crab,—in the petals, stamens, and pistils of a flower, is
likewise, to a large extent, intelligible on the view of the gradual modification of parts or organs, which were aboriginally alike in an early progenitor in each of these classes. On the principle of successive variations not
always supervening at an early age, and being inherited at a corresponding not early period of life, we clearly see why the embryos of mammals,
birds, reptiles, and fishes should be so closely similar, and so unlike the
adult forms. We may cease marvelling at the embryo of an air-breathing
mammal or bird having branchial slits and arteries running in loops, like
those of a fish which has to breathe the air dissolved in water by the aid
of well-developed branchiæ.

Disuse, aided sometimes by natural selection, will often have reduced
organs when rendered useless under changed habits or conditions of life;
and we can understand on this view the meaning of rudimentary organs.
But disuse and selection will generally act on each creature, when it has
come to maturity and has to play its full part in the struggle for existence,
and will thus have little power on an organ during early life; hence the
organ will not be reduced or rendered rudimentary at this early age. The
calf, for instance, has inherited teeth, which never cut through the gums
of the upper jaw, from an early progenitor having well-developed teeth;
and we may believe, that the teeth in the mature animal were formerly
reduced by disuse, owing to the tongue and palate, or lips, having become
excellently fitted through natural selection to browse without their aid;
whereas in the calf, the teeth have been left unaffected, and on the principle of inheritance at corresponding ages have been inherited from a remote period to the present day. On the view of each organism with all its
separate parts having been specially created, how utterly inexplicable is
it that organs bearing the plain stamp of inutility, such as the teeth in the

embryonic calf or the shrivelled wings under the soldered wing-covers of
many beetles, should so frequently occur. Nature may be said to have
taken pains to reveal her scheme of modification, by means of rudimentary organs, of embryological and homologous structures, but we are too
blind to understand her meaning.

I have now recapitulated the facts and considerations which have thoroughly convinced me that species have been modified, during a long
course of descent. This has been effected chiefly through the natural selection of numerous successive, slight, favourable variations; aided in an
important manner by the inherited effects of the use and disuse of parts;
and in an unimportant manner, that is in relation to adaptive structures,
whether past or present, by the direct action of external conditions, and
by variations which seem to us in our ignorance to arise spontaneously. It
appears that I formerly underrated the frequency and value of these latter forms of variation, as leading to permanent modifications of structure
independently of natural selection. But as my conclusions have lately
been much misrepresented, and it has been stated that I attribute the
modification of species exclusively to natural selection, I may be permitted to remark that in the first edition of this work, and subsequently, I
placed in a most conspicuous position—namely, at the close of the Introduction—the following words: "I am convinced that natural selection has
been the main but not the exclusive means of modification." This has
been of no avail. Great is the power of steady misrepresentation; but the
history of science shows that fortunately this power does not long endure.

It can hardly be supposed that a false theory would explain, in so satisfactory a manner as does the theory of natural selection, the several large
classes of facts above specified. It has recently been objected that this is
an unsafe method of arguing; but it is a method used in judging of the
common events of life, and has often been used by the greatest natural
philosophers. The undulatory theory of light has thus been arrived at;
and the belief in the revolution of the earth on its own axis was until lately supported by hardly any direct evidence. It is no valid objection that
science as yet throws no light on the far higher problem of the essence or
origin of life. Who can explain what is the essence of the attraction of
gravity? No one now objects to following out the results consequent on
this unknown element of attraction; notwithstanding that Leibnitz formerly accused Newton of introducing "occult qualities and miracles into
philosophy."

I see no good reason why the views given in this volume should shock
the religious feelings of any one. It is satisfactory, as showing how transient such impressions are, to remember that the greatest discovery ever
made by man, namely, the law of the attraction of gravity, was also attacked by Leibnitz, "as subversive of natural, and inferentially of revealed, religion." A celebrated author and divine has written to me that
"he has gradually learnt to see that it is just as noble a conception of the
Deity to believe that He created a few original forms capable of self-de-

velopment into other and needful forms, as to believe that He required a fresh act of creation to supply the voids caused by the action of His laws."

Why, it may be asked, until recently did nearly all the most eminent living naturalists and geologists disbelieve in the mutability of species? It cannot be asserted that organic beings in a state of nature are subject to no variation; it cannot be proved that the amount of variation in the course of long ages is a limited quality; no clear distinction has been, or can be, drawn between species and well-marked varieties. It cannot be maintained that species when intercrossed are invariably sterile, and varieties invariably fertile; or that sterility is a special endowment and sign of creation. The belief that species were immutable productions was almost unavoidable as long as the history of the world was thought to be of short duration; and now that we have acquired some idea of the lapse of time, we are too apt to assume, without proof, that the geological record is so perfect that it would have afforded us plain evidence of the mutation of species, if they had undergone mutation.

But the chief cause of our natural unwillingness to admit that one species has given birth to clear and distinct species, is that we are always slow in admitting great changes of which we do not see the steps. The difficulty is the same as that felt by so many geologists, when Lyell first insisted that long lines of inland cliffs had been formed, and great valleys excavated, by the agencies which we see still at work. The mind cannot possibly grasp the full meaning of the term of even a million years; it cannot add up and perceive the full effects of many slight variations, accumulated during an almost infinite number of generations.

Although I am fully convinced of the truth of the views given in this volume under the form of an abstract, I by no means expect to convince experienced naturalists whose minds are stocked with a multitude of facts all viewed, during a long course of years, from a point of view directly opposite to mine. It is so easy to hide our ignorance under such expressions as the "plan of creation," "unity of design," &c., and to think that we give an explanation when we only re-state a fact. Any one whose disposition leads him to attach more weight to unexplained difficulties than to the explanation of a certain number of facts will certainly reject the theory. A few naturalists, endowed with much flexibility of mind, and who have already begun to doubt the immutability of species, may be influenced by this volume; but I look with confidence to the future,—to young and rising naturalists, who will be able to view both sides of the question with impartiality. Whoever is led to believe that species are mutable will do good service by conscientiously expressing his conviction; for thus only can the load of prejudice by which this subject is overwhelmed be removed.

Several eminent naturalists have of late published their belief that a multitude of reputed species in each genus are not real species; but that other species are real, that is, have been independently created. This seems to me a strange conclusion to arrive at. They admit that a multitude of forms, which till lately they themselves thought were special creations, and which are still thus looked at by the majority of naturalists, and which consequently have all the external characteristic features of true species,—they admit that these have been produced by variation, but they refuse to extend the same view to other and slightly different forms. Nevertheless they do not pretend that they can define, or even conjecture, which are the created forms of life, and which are those produced by secondary laws. They admit variation as a *vera causa* in one case, they arbitrarily reject it in another, without assigning any distinction in the two cases. The day will come when this will be given as a curious illustration of the blindness of preconceived opinion. These authors seem no more startled at a miraculous act of creation than at an ordinary birth. But do they really believe that at innumerable periods in the earth's history certain elemental atoms have been commanded suddenly to flash into living tissues? Do they believe that at each supposed act of creation one individual or many were produced? Were all the infinitely numerous kinds of animals and plants created as eggs or seed, or as full grown? and in the case of mammals, were they created bearing the false marks of nourishment from the mother's womb? Undoubtedly some of these same questions cannot be answered by those who believe in the appearance or creation of only a few forms of life, or of some one form alone. It has been maintained by several authors that it is as easy to believe in the creation of a million beings as of one; but Maupertuis' philosophical axiom "of least action" leads the mind more willingly to admit the smaller number; and certainly we ought not to believe that innumerable beings within each great class have been created with plain, but deceptive, marks of descent from a single parent.

As a record of a former state of things, I have retained in the foregoing paragraphs, and elsewhere, several sentences which imply that naturalists believe in the separate creation of each species; and I have been much censured for having thus expressed myself. But undoubtedly this was the general belief when the first edition of the present work appeared. I formerly spoke to very many naturalists on the subject of evolution, and never once met with any sympathetic agreement. It is probable that some did then believe in evolution, but they were either silent, or expressed themselves so ambiguously that it was not easy to understand their meaning. Now things are wholly changed, and almost every naturalist admits the great principle of evolution. There are, however, some who still think that species have suddenly given birth, through quite unexplained means, to new and totally different forms: but, as I have attempted to show, weighty evidence can be opposed to the admission of great and abrupt modifications. Under a scientific point of view, and as leading to further investigation, but little advantage is gained by believing that new forms are suddenly developed in an inexplicable manner from old and widely different forms, over the old belief in the creation of species from the dust of the earth.

It may be asked how far I extend the doctrine of the modification of species. The question is difficult to answer, because the more distinct the forms are which we consider, by so much the arguments in favour of community of descent become fewer in number and less in force. But some arguments of the greatest weight extend very far. All the members of whole classes are connected together by a chain of affinities, and all can be classed on the same principle, in groups subordinate to groups. Fossil remains sometimes tend to fill up very wide intervals between existing orders.

Organs in a rudimentary condition plainly show that an early progenitor had the organ in a fully developed condition; and this in some cases implies an enormous amount of modification in the descendants. Throughout whole classes various structures are formed on the same pattern, and at a very early age the embryos closely resemble each other. Therefore I cannot doubt that the theory of descent with modification embraces all the members of the same great class or kingdom. I believe that animals are descended from at most only four or five progenitors, and plants from an equal or lesser number.

Analogy would lead me one step farther, namely, to the belief that all animals and plants are descended from some one prototype. But analogy may be a deceitful guide. Nevertheless all living things have much in common, in their chemical composition, their cellular structure, their laws of growth, and their liability to injurious influences. We see this even in so trifling a fact as that the same poison often similarly affects plants and animals; or that the poison secreted by the gall-fly produces monstrous growths on the wild rose or oak-tree. With all organic beings excepting perhaps some of the very lowest, sexual production seems to be essentially similar. With all, as far as is at present known the germinal vesicle is the same; so that all organisms start from a common origin. If we look even to the two main divisions—namely, to the animal and vegetable kingdoms—certain low forms are so far intermediate in character that naturalists have disputed to which kingdom they should be referred. As Professor Asa Gray has remarked, "the spores and other reproductive bodies of many of the lower algæ may claim to have first a characteristically animal, and then an unequivocally vegetable existence." Therefore, on the principle of natural selection with divergence of character, it does not seem incredible that, from such low and intermediate form, both animals and plants may have been developed; and, if we admit this, we must likewise admit that all the organic beings which have ever lived on this earth may be descended from some one primordial form. But this inference is chiefly grounded on analogy and it is immaterial whether or not it be accepted. No doubt it is possible, as Mr. G. H. Lewes has urged, that at the first commencement of life many different forms were evolved; but if so we may conclude that only a very few have left modified descendants. For, as I have recently remarked in regard to the members of each great kingdom, such as the Vertebrata Articulata &c., we have distinct evidence in their embryological homologous and rudimentary structures.

that within each kingdom all the members are descended from a single progenitor.

When the views advanced by me in this volume, and by Mr. Wallace, or when analogous views on the origin of species are generally admitted, we can dimly foresee that there will be a considerable revolution in natural history. Systematists will be able to pursue their labours as at present; but they will not be incessantly haunted by the shadowy doubt whether this or that form be a true species. This, I feel sure and I speak after experience, will be no slight relief. The endless disputes whether or not some fifty species of British brambles are good species will cease. Systematists will have only to decide (not that this will be easy) whether any form be sufficiently constant and distinct from other forms, to be capable of definition; and if definable, whether the differences be sufficiently important to deserve a specific name. This latter point will become a far more essential consideration than it is at present; for differences, however slight, between any two forms if not blended by intermediate gradations, are looked at by most naturalists as sufficient to raise both forms to the rank of species.

Hereafter we shall be compelled to acknowledge that the only distinction between species and well-marked varieties is, that the latter are known, or believed, to be connected at the present day by intermediate gradations, whereas species were formerly thus connected. Hence, without rejecting the consideration of the present existence of intermediate gradations between any two forms we shall be led to weigh more carefully and to value higher the actual amount of difference between them. It is quite possible that forms now generally acknowledged to be merely varieties may hereafter be thought worthy of specific names; and in this case scientific and common language will come into accordance. In short, we shall have to treat species in the same manner as those naturalists treat genera, who admit that genera are merely artificial combinations made for convenience. This may not be a cheering prospect; but we shall at least be free from the vain search for the undiscovered and undiscoverable essence of the term species.

The other and more general departments of natural history will rise greatly in interest. The terms used by naturalists, of affinity, relationship, community of type, paternity, morphology, adaptive characters, rudimentary and aborted organs, &c., will cease to be metaphorical, and will have a plain signification. When we no longer look at an organic being as a savage looks at a ship, as something wholly beyond his comprehension; when we regard every production of nature as one which has had a long history; when we contemplate every complex structure and instinct as the summing up of many contrivances, each useful to the possessor, in the same way as any great mechanical invention is the summing up of the labour, the experience, the reason, and even the blunders of numerous workmen; when we thus view each organic being, how far more interesting—I speak from experience—does the study of natural history become!

A grand and almost untrodden field of inquiry will be opened, on the causes and laws of variation, on correlation, on the effects of use and disuse, on the direct action of external conditions, and so forth. The study of domestic productions will rise immensely in value. A new variety raised by man will be a more important and interesting subject for study than one more species added to the infinitude of already recorded species. Our classifications will come to be, as far as they can be so made, genealogies; and will then truly give what may be called the plan of creation. The rules for classifying will no doubt become simpler when we have a definite object in view. We possess no pedigrees or armorial bearings; and we have to discover and trace the many diverging lines of descent in our natural genealogies, by characters of any kind which have long been inherited. Rudimentary organs will speak infallibly with respect to the nature of long-lost structures. Species and groups of species which are called aberrant, and which may fancifully be called living fossils, will aid us in forming a picture of the ancient forms of life. Embryology will often reveal to us the structure, in some degree obscured, of the prototype of each great class.

When we feel assured that all the individuals of the same species, and all the closely allied species of most genera, have within a not very remote period descended from one parent, and have migrated from some one birth-place; and when we better know the many means of migration, then, by the light which geology now throws, and will continue to throw, on former changes of climate and of the level of the land, we shall surely be enabled to trace in an admirable manner the former migrations of the inhabitants of the whole world. Even at present, by comparing the differences between the inhabitants of the sea on the opposite sides of a continent, and the nature of the various inhabitants on that continent, in relation to their apparent means of immigration, some light can be thrown on ancient geography.

The noble science of Geology loses glory from the extreme imperfection of the record. The crust of the earth with its imbedded remains must not be looked at as a well-filled museum, but as a poor collection made at hazard and at rare intervals. The accumulation of each great fossiliferous formation will be recognised as having depended on an unusual concurrence of favourable circumstances, and the blank intervals between the successive stages as having been of vast duration. But we shall be able to gauge with some security the duration of these intervals by a comparison of the preceding and succeeding organic forms. We must be cautious in attempting to correlate as strictly contemporaneous two formations, which do not include many identical species, by the general succession of the forms of life. As species are produced and exterminated by slowly acting and still existing causes, and not by miraculous acts of creation; and as the most important of all causes of organic change is one which is almost independent of altered and perhaps suddenly altered physical conditions, namely, the mutual relation of organism to organism,—the improvement of one organism entailing the improvement or the extermination of others; it follows, that the amount of organic change in the fossils of consecutive formations probably serves as a fair measure of the relative though not actual lapse of time. A number of species, however, keeping in a body might remain for a long period unchanged, whilst within the same period several of these species by migrating into new countries and coming into competition with foreign associates, might become modified; so that we must not overrate the accuracy of organic change as a measure of time.

In the future I see open fields for far more important researches. Psychology will be securely based on the foundation already well laid by Mr. Herbert Spencer, that of the necessary acquirement of each mental power and capacity by gradation. Much light will be thrown on the origin of man and his history.

Authors of the highest eminence seem to be fully satisfied with the view that each species has been independently created. To my mind it accords better with what we know of the laws impressed on matter by the Creator, that the production and extinction of the past and present inhabitants of the world should have been due to secondary causes, like those determining the birth and death of the individual. When I view all beings not as special creations, but as the lineal descendants of some few beings which lived long before the first bed of the Cambrian system was deposited, they seem to me to become ennobled. Judging from the past, we may safely infer that not one living species will transmit its unaltered likeness to a distant futurity. And of the species now living very few will transmit progeny of any kind to a far distant futurity; for the manner in which all organic beings are grouped, shows that the greater number of species in each genus, and all the species in many genera, have left no descendants, but have become utterly extinct. We can so far take a prophetic glance into futurity as to foretell that it will be the common and widely-spread species, belonging to the larger and dominant groups within each class, which will ultimately prevail and procreate new and dominant species. As all the living forms of life are the lineal descendants of those which lived long before the Cambrian epoch, we may feel certain that the ordinary succession by generation has never once been broken, and that no cataclysm has desolated the whole world. Hence we may look with some confidence to a secure future of great length. And as natural selection works solely by and for the good of each being, all corporeal and mental endowments will tend to progress towards perfection.

It is interesting to contemplate a tangled bank, clothed with many plants of many kinds, with birds singing on the bushes, with various insects flitting about, and with worms crawling through the damp earth, and to reflect that these elaborately constructed forms, so different from each other, and dependent upon each other in so complex a manner, have all been produced by laws acting around us. These laws, taken in the largest sense, being Growth with Reproduction; Inheritance which is almost implied by reproduction; Variability from the indirect and direct action of the conditions of life, and from use and disuse: a Ratio of Increase so high as to lead to a Struggle for Life, and as a consequence to Natural Selection, entailing Divergence of Character and the Extinction of less-improved forms. Thus, from the war of nature, from famine and death, the most exalted object which we are capable of conceiving, namely, the production of the higher animals, directly follows. There is grandeur in this view of life, with its several powers, having been originally breathed by the Creator into a few forms or into one; and that, whilst this planet has gone cycling on according to the fixed law of gravity, from so simple a beginning endless forms most beautiful and most wonderful have been, and are being evolved.

GLOSSARY

OF THE

PRINCIPAL SCIENTIFIC TERMS USED IN THE PRESENT VOLUME*

ABERRANT.—Forms or groups of animals or plants which deviate in important characters from their nearest allies, so as not to be easily included in the same group with them, are said to be aberrant.

ABERRATION (in Optics).—In the refraction of light by a convex lens the rays passing through different parts of the lens are brought to a focus at slightly different distances,—this is called *spherical aberration;* at the same time the coloured rays are separated by the prismatic action of the lens and likewise brought to a focus at different distances,—this is *chromatic aberration.*

ABNORMAL.—Contrary to the general rule.

ABORTED.—An organ is said to be aborted, when its development has been arrested at a very early stage.

ALBINISM.—Albinos are animals in which the usual colouring matters characteristic of the species have not been produced in the skin and its appendages. Albinism is the state of being an albino.

ALGÆ.—A class of plants including the ordinary sea-weeds and the filamentous fresh-water weeds.

ALTERNATION OF GENERATIONS.—This term is applied to a peculiar mode of reproduction which prevails among many of the lower animals, in which the egg produces a living form quite different from its parent, but from which the parent-form is reproduced by a process of budding, or by the division of the substance of the first product of the egg.

AMMONITES.—A group of fossil, spiral, chambered shells, allied to the existing pearly Nautilus, but having the partitions between the chambers waved in complicated patterns at their junction with the outer wall of the shell.

ANALOGY.—That resemblance of structures which depends upon similarity of function, as in the wings of insects and birds. Such structures are said to be *analogous,* and to be *analogues* of each other.

* I am indebted to the kindness of Mr. W. S. Dallas for this Glossary, which has been given because several readers have complained to me that some of the terms used were unintelligible to them. Mr. Dallas has endeavoured to give the explanations of the terms in as popular a form as possible.

ANIMALCULE.—A minute animal: generally applied to those visible only by the microscope.

ANNELIDS.—A class of worms in which the surface of the body exhibits a more or less distinct division into rings or segments, generally provided with appendages for locomotion and with gills. It includes the ordinary marine worms, the earthworms, and the leeches.

ANTENNÆ.—Jointed organs appended to the head in Insects, Crustacea and Centipedes, and not belonging to the mouth.

ANTHERS.—The summits of the stamens of flowers, in which the pollen or fertilising dust is produced.

APLACENTALIA, APLACENTATA or Aplacental Mammals. See *Mammalia*.

ARCHETYPAL.—Of or belonging to the Archetype, or ideal primitive form upon which all the beings of a group seem to be organised.

ARTICULATA.—A great division of the Animal Kingdom characterised generally by having the surface of the body divided into rings called segments, a greater or less number of which are furnished with jointed legs (such as Insects, Crustaceans and Centipedes).

ASYMMETRICAL.—Having the two sides unlike.

ATROPHIED.—Arrested in development at a very early stage.

BALANUS.—The genus including the common Acorn-shells which live in abundance on the rocks of the sea-coast.

BATRACHIANS.—A class of animals allied to the Reptiles, but undergoing a peculiar metamorphosis, in which the young animal is generally aquatic and breathes by gills. (*Examples,* Frogs, Toads, and Newts.)

BOULDERS.—Large transported blocks of stone generally imbedded in clays or gravels.

BRACHIOPODA.—A class of marine Mollusca, or soft-bodied animals, furnished with a bivalve shell, attached to submarine objects by a stalk which passes through an aperture in one of the valves, and furnished with fringed arms, by the action of which food is carried to the mouth.

BRANCHIÆ.—Gills or organs for respiration in water.

BRANCHIAL.—Pertaining to gills or branchiæ.

CAMBRIAN SYSTEM.—A Series of very ancient Palæozoic rocks, between the Laurentian and the Silurian. Until recently these were regarded as the oldest fossiliferous rocks.

CANIDÆ.—The Dog-family, including the Dog, Wolf, Fox, Jackal, &c.

CARAPACE.—The shell enveloping the anterior part of the body in Crustaceans generally; applied also to the hard shelly pieces of the Cirripedes.

CARBONIFEROUS.—This term is applied to the great formation which includes, among other rocks, the coal-measures. It belongs to the oldest, or Palæozoic, system of formations.

CAUDAL.—Of or belonging to the tail.

CEPHALOPODS.—The highest class of the Mollusca, or soft-bodied animals, characterised by having the mouth surrounded by a greater or less number of fleshy arms or tentacles, which, in most living species, are furnished with sucking-cups. (*Examples,* Cuttle-fish, Nautilus.)

CETACEA.—An order of Mammalia, including the Whales, Dolphins, &c., having the form of the body fish-like, the skin naked, and only the fore-limbs developed.

CHELONIA.—An order of Reptiles including the Turtles, Tortoises, &c.

CIRRIPEDES.—An order of Crustaceans including the Barnacles and Acorn-shells. Their young resemble those of many other Crustaceans in form; but when mature they are always attached to other objects, either directly or by means of a stalk, and their bodies are enclosed by a calcareous shell composed of several pieces, two of which can open to give issue to a bunch of curled, jointed tentacles, which represent the limbs.

COCCUS.—The genus of Insects including the Cochineal. In these the male is a minute, winged fly, and the female generally a motionless, berry-like mass.

COCOON.—A case usually of silky material, in which insects are frequently enveloped during the second or resting-stage (pupa) of their existence. The term "cocoon-stage" is here used as equivalent to "pupa-stage."

CŒLOSPERMOUS.—A term applied to those fruits of the Umbelliferæ which have the seed hollowed on the inner face.

COLEOPTERA.—Beetles, an order of Insects, having a biting mouth and the first pair of wings more or less horny, forming sheaths for the second pair, and usually meeting in a straight line down the middle of the back.

COLUMN.—A peculiar organ in the flowers of Orchids, in which the stamens, style and stigma (or the reproductive parts) are united.

COMPOSITÆ or COMPOSITOUS PLANTS.—Plants in which the inflorescence consists of numerous small flowers (florets) brought together into a dense head, the base of which is enclosed by a common envelope. (*Examples,* the Daisy, Dandelion, &c.)

CONFERVÆ.—The filamentous weeds of fresh water.

CONGLOMERATE.—A rock made up of fragments of rock or pebbles, cemented together by some other material.

COROLLA.—The second envelope of a flower usually composed of coloured, leaf-like organs (petals), which may be united by their edges either in the basal part or throughout.

CORRELATION.—The normal coincidence of one phenomenon, character, &c., with another.

CORYMB.—A bunch of flowers in which those springing from the lower part of the flower stalk are supported on long stalks so as to be nearly on a level with the upper ones.

COTYLEDONS.—The first or seed-leaves of plants.

CRUSTACEANS.—A class of articulated animals, having the skin of the body generally more or less hardened by the deposition of calcareous matter, breathing by means of gills. (*Examples,* Crab, Lobster, Shrimp, &c.)

CURCULIO.—The old generic term for the Beetles known as Weevils, characterised by their four-jointed feet, and by the head being produced into a sort of beak, upon the sides of which the antennæ are inserted.

CUTANEOUS.—Of or belonging to the skin.

DEGRADATION.—The wearing down of land by the action of the sea or of meteoric agencies.

DENUDATION.—The wearing away of the surface of the land by water.

DEVONIAN SYSTEM or formation.—A series of Palæozoic rocks, including the Old Red Sandstone.

DICOTYLEDONS or DICOTYLEDONOUS PLANTS.—A class of plants characterised by having two seed-leaves, by the formation of new wood between the bark and the old wood (exogenous growth) and by the reticulation of the veins of the leaves. The parts of the flowers are generally in multiples of five.

DIFFERENTIATION.—The separation or discrimination of parts or organs which in simpler forms of life are more or less united.

DIMORPHIC.—Having two distinct forms.—Dimorphism is the condition of the appearance of the same species under two dissimilar forms.

DIŒCIOUS.—Having the organs of the sexes upon distinct individuals.

DIORITE.—A peculiar form of Greenstone.

DORSAL.—Of or belonging to the back.

EDENTATA.—A peculiar order of Quadrupeds, characterised by the absence of at least the middle incisor (front) teeth in both jaws. (*Examples*, the Sloths and Armadillos.)

ELYTRA.—The hardened fore-wings of Beetles, serving as sheaths for the membranous hind-wings, which constitute the true organs of flight.

EMBRYO.—The young animal undergoing development within the egg or womb.

EMBRYOLOGY.—The study of the development of the embryo.

ENDEMIC.—Peculiar to a given locality.

ENTOMOSTRACA.—A division of the class Crustacea, having all the segments of the body usually distinct, gills attached to the feet or organs of the mouth, and the feet fringed with fine hairs. They are generally of small size.

EOCENE.—The earliest of the three divisions of the Tertiary epoch of geologists. Rocks of this age contain a small proportion of shells identical with species now living.

EPHEMEROUS INSECTS.—Insects allied to theMay-fly.

FAUNA.—The totality of the animals naturally inhabiting a certain country or region, or which have lived during a given geological period.

FELIDÆ.—The Cat-family.

FERAL.—Having become wild from a state of cultivation or domestication.

FLORA.—The totality of the plants growing naturally in a country, or during a given geological period.

FLORETS.—Flowers imperfectly developed in some respects, and collected into a dense spike or head, as in the Grasses, the Dandelion, &c.

FŒTAL.—Of or belonging to the fœtus, or embryo in course of development.

FORAMINIFERA.—A class of animals of very low organisation, and generally of small size, having a jelly-like body, from the surface of which delicate filaments can be given off and retracted for the prehension of external objects, and having a calcareous or sandy shell, usually divided into chambers, and perforated with small apertures.

FOSSILIFEROUS.—Containing fossils.

FOSSORIAL.—Having a faculty of digging. The Fossorial Hymenoptera are a group of Wasp-like Insects, which burrow in sandy soil to make nests for their young.

FRENUM (pl. FRENA).—A small band or fold of skin.

FUNGI (sing. FUNGUS).—A class of cellular plants, of which Mushrooms, Toadstools, and Moulds, are familiar examples.

FURCULA.—The forked bone formed by the union of the collar-bones in many birds, such as the common Fowl.

GALLINACEOUS BIRDS.—An order of Birds of which the common Fowl, Turkey, and Pheasant, are well-known examples.

GALLUS.—The genus of birds which includes the common Fowl.

GANGLION.—A swelling or knot from which nerves are given off as from a centre.

GANOID FISHES.—Fishes covered with peculiar enamelled bony scales. Most of them are extinct.

GERMINAL VESICLE.—A minute vesicle in the eggs of animals, from which development of the embryo proceeds.

GLACIAL PERIOD.—A period of great cold and of enormous extension of ice upon the surface of the earth. It is believed that glacial periods have occurred repeatedly during the geological history of the earth, but the term is generally applied to the close of the Tertiary epoch, when nearly the whole of Europe was subjected to an arctic climate.

GLAND.—An organ which secretes or separates some peculiar product from the blood or sap of animals or plants.

GLOTTIS.—The opening of the windpipe into the œsophagus or gullet.

GNEISS.—A rock approaching granite in composition, but more or less laminated, and really produced by the alteration of a sedimentary deposit after its consolidation.

GRALLATORES.—The so-called Wading-birds (Storks, Cranes, Snipes, &c.), which are generally furnished with long legs, bare of feathers above the heel, and have no membranes between the toes.

GRANITE.—A rock consisting essentially of crystals of felspar and mica in a mass of quartz.

HABITAT.—The locality in which a plant or animal naturally lives.

HEMIPTERA.—An order or sub-order of Insects, characterised by the possession of a jointed beak or rostrum, and by having the fore-wings horny in the basal portion and membranous at the extremity, where they cross each other. This group includes the various species of Bugs.

HERMAPHRODITE.—Possessing the organs of both sexes.

HOMOLOGY.—That relation between parts which results from their development from corresponding embryonic parts, either in different animals, as in the case of the arm of man, the foreleg of a quadruped, and the wing of a bird; or in the same individual, as in the case of the fore and hind legs in quadrupeds, and the segments or rings and their appendages of which the body of a worm, a centipede, &c., is composed. The latter is called *serial homology*. The parts which stand in such a relation to each other are said to be *homologous,* and one such part or organ is called the *homologue* of the other. In different plants the parts of the flower are homologous, and in general these parts are regarded as homologous with leaves.

HOMOPTERA.—An order or sub-order of Insects having (like the Hemiptera) a jointed beak, but in which the fore-wings are either wholly membranous or wholly leathery. The *Cicadæ,* Frog-hoppers, and *Aphides,* are well-known examples.

HYBRID.—The offspring of the union of two distinct species.

HYMENOPTERA.—An order of insects possessing biting jaws and usually four membranous wings in which there are a few veins. Bees and Wasps are familiar examples of this group.

HYPERTROPHIED.—Excessively developed.

ICHNEUMONIDÆ.—A family of Hymenopterous insects, the members of which lay their eggs in the bodies or eggs of other insects.

IMAGO.—The perfect (generally winged) reproductive state of an insect.

INDIGENS.—The aboriginal animal or vegetable inhabitants of a country or region.

INFLORESCENCE.—The mode of arrangement of the flowers of plants.

INFUSORIA.—A class of microscopic Animalcules, so called from their having originally been observed in infusions of vegetable matters. They consist of a gelatinous material enclosed in a delicate membrane, the whole or part of which is furnished with short vibrating hairs (called cilia), by means of which the animalcules swim through the water or convey the minute particles of their food to the orifice of the mouth.

INSECTIVOROUS.—Feeding on Insects.

INVERTEBRATA, or INVERTEBRATE ANIMALS.—Those animals which do not possess a backbone or spinal column.

LACUNÆ.—Spaces left among the tissues in some of the lower animals, and serving in place of vessels for the circulation of the fluids of the body.

LAMELLATED.—Furnished with lamellæ or little plates.

LARVA (pl. LARVÆ).—The first condition of an insect at its issuing from the egg, when it is usually in the form of a grub, caterpillar, or maggot.

LARYNX.—The upper part of the windpipe opening into the gullet.

LAURENTIAN.—A group of greatly altered and very ancient rocks, which is greatly developed along the course of the St. Laurence, whence the name. It is in these that the earliest known traces of organic bodies have been found.

LEGUMINOSÆ.—An order of plants represented by the common Peas and Beans, having an irregular flower in which one petal stands up like a wing, and the stamens and pistil are enclosed in a sheath formed by two other petals. The fruit is a pod (or legume).

LEMURIDÆ.—A group of four-handed animals, distinct from the Monkeys and approaching the Insectivorous Quadrupeds in some of their characters and habits. Its members have the nostrils curved or twisted, and a claw instead of a nail upon the first finger of the hind hands.

LEPIDOPTERA.—An order of Insects, characterised by the possession of a spiral proboscis, and of four large more or less scaly wings. It includes the well-known Butterflies and Moths.

LITTORAL.—Inhabiting the seashore.

LOESS.—A marly deposit of recent (Post-Tertiary) date, which occupies a great part of the valley of the Rhine.

MALACOSTRACA.—The higher division of the Crustacea, including the ordinary Crabs, Lobsters, Shrimps, &c., together with the Woodlice and Sand-hoppers.

MAMMALIA.—The highest class of animals, including the ordinary hairy quadrupeds, the Whales, and Man, and characterised by the production of living young which are nourished after birth by milk from the teats (*Mammæ, Mammary glands*) of the mother. A striking difference in embryonic development has led to the division of this class into two great groups; in one of these, when the embryo has attained a certain stage, a vascular connection, called the *placenta,* is formed between the embryo and the mother; in the other this is wanting, and the young are produced in a very incomplete state. The former, including the greater part of the class, are called *Placental mammals;* the latter, or *Aplacental mammals,* include the Marsupials and Monotremes (*Ornithorhynchus*).

MAMMIFEROUS.—Having mammæ or teats (see MAMMALIA).

MANDIBLES, in Insects.—The first or uppermost pair of jaws, which are generally solid, horny, biting organs. In Birds the term is applied to both jaws with their horny coverings. In Quadrupeds the mandible is properly the lower jaw.

MARSUPIALS.—An order of Mammalia in which the young are born in a very incomplete state of development, and carried by the mother, while sucking, in a ventral pouch (marsupium), such as the Kangaroos, Opossums, &c. (see MAMMALIA).

MAXILLÆ, in Insects.—The second or lower pair of jaws, which are composed of several joints and furnished with peculiar jointed appendages called palpi, or feelers.

MELANISM.—The opposite of albinism; an undue development of colouring material in the skin and its appendages.

METAMORPHIC ROCKS.—Sedimentary rocks which have undergone alteration, generally by the action of heat, subsequently to their deposition and consolidation.

MOLLUSCA.—One of the great divisions of the Animal Kingdom, including those animals which have a soft body, usually furnished with a shell, and in which the nervous ganglia, or centres, present no definite general arrangement. They are generally known under the denomination of "shell-fish;" the cuttle-fish, and the common snails, whelks, oysters, mussels, and cockles, may serve as examples of them.

MONOCOTYLEDONS, or MONOCOTYLEDONOUS PLANTS.—Plants in which the seed sends up only a single seed-leaf (or cotyledon); characterised by the absence of consecutive layers of wood in the stem (endogenous growth), by the veins of the leaves being generally straight, and by the parts of the flowers being generally in multiples of three. (*Examples,* Grasses, Lilies, Orchids, Palms, &c.)

MORAINES.—The accumulations of fragments of rock brought down by glaciers.

MORPHOLOGY.—The law of form or structure independent of function.

MYSIS-STAGE.—A stage in the development of certain Crustaceans (Prawns), in which they closely resemble the adults of a genus *(Mysis)* belonging to a slightly lower group.

NASCENT.—Commencing development.

NATATORY.—Adapted for the purpose of swimming.

NAUPLIUS-FORM.—The earliest stage in the development of many Crustacea, especially belonging to the lower groups. In this stage the animal has a short body, with indistinct indications of a division into segments, and three pairs of fringed limbs. This form of the common fresh-water *Cyclops* was described as a distinct genus under the name of *Nauplius*.

NEURATION.—The arrangement of the veins or nervures in the wings of Insects.

NEUTERS.—Imperfectly developed females of certain social insects (such as Ants and Bees), which perform all the labours of the community. Hence they are also called *workers*.

NICTITATING MEMBRANE.—A semi-transparent membrane, which can be drawn across the eye in Birds and Reptiles, either to moderate the effects of a strong light or to sweep particles of dust, &c., from the surface of the eye.

OCELLI.—The simple eyes or stemmata of Insects, usually situated on the crown of the head between the great compound eyes.

ŒSOPHAGUS.—The gullet.

OOLITIC.—A great series of secondary rocks, so called from the texture of some of its members, which appear to be made up of a mass of small *egg-like* calcareous bodies.

OPERCULUM.—A calcareous plate employed by many Mollusca to close the aperture of their shell. The *opercular valves* of Cirripedes are those which close the aperture of the shell.

ORBIT.—The bony cavity for the reception of the eye.

ORGANISM.—An organised being, whether plant or animal.

ORTHOSPERMOUS.—A term applied to those fruits of the Umbelliferæ which have the seed straight.

OSCULANT.—Forms or groups apparently intermediate between and connecting other groups are said to be osculant.

OVA.—Eggs.

OVARIUM or OVARY (in plants).—The lower part of the pistil or female organ of the flower, containing the ovules or incipient seeds; by growth after the other organs of the flower have fallen, it usually becomes converted into the fruit.

OVIGEROUS.—Egg-bearing.

OVULES (of plants).—The seeds in the earliest condition.

PACHYDERMS.—A group of Mammalia, so called from their thick skins, and including the Elephant, Rhinoceros, Hippopotamus, &c.

PALÆOZOIC.—The oldest system of fossiliferous rocks.

PALPI.—Jointed appendages to some of the organs of the mouth in Insects and Crustacea.

PAPILIONACEÆ.—An order of Plants (see LEGUMINOSÆ).—The flowers of these plants are called *papilionaceous,* or butterfly-like, from the fancied resemblance of the expanded superior petals to the wings of a butterfly.

PARASITE.—An animal or plant living upon or in, and at the expense of, another organism.

PARTHENOGENESIS.—The production of living organisms from unimpregnated eggs or seeds.

PEDUNCULATED.—Supported upon a stem or stalk. The pedunculated oak has its acorns borne upon a footstool.

PELORIA or PELORISM.—The appearance of regularity of structure in the flowers of plants which normally bear irregular flowers.

PELVIS.—The bony arch to which the hind limbs of vertebrate animals are articulated.

PETALS.—The leaves of the corolla, or second circle of organs in a flower. They are usually of delicate texture and brightly coloured.

PHYLLODINEOUS.—Having flattened, leaf-like twigs or leafstalks instead of true leaves.

PIGMENT.—The colouring material produced generally in the superficial parts of animals. The cells secreting it are called *pigment-cells.*

PINNATE.—Bearing leaflets on each side of a central stalk.

PISTILS.—The female organs of a flower, which occupy a position in the centre of the other floral organs. The pistil is generally divisible into the ovary or germen, the style and the stigma.

PLACENTALIA, PLACENTATA, or Placental Mammals.—See MAMMALIA.

PLANTIGRADES.—Quadrupeds which walk upon the whole sole of the foot, like the Bears.

PLASTIC.—Readily capable of change.

PLEISTOCENE PERIOD.—The latest portion of the Tertiary epoch.

PLUMULE (in plants).—The minute bud between the seed-leaves of newly-germinated plants.

PLUTONIC ROCKS.—Rocks supposed to have been produced by igneous action in the depths of the earth.

POLLEN.—The male element in flowering plants; usually a fine dust produced by the anthers, which, by contact with the stigma effects the fecundation of the seeds. This impregnation is brought about by means of tubes *(pollen-tubes)* which issue from the pollen-grains adhering to the stigma, and penetrate through the tissues until they reach the ovary.

POLYANDROUS (flowers).—Flowers having many stamens.

POLYGAMOUS PLANTS.—Plants in which some flowers are unisexual and others hermaphrodite. The unisexual (male and female) flowers, may be on the same or on different plants.

POLYMORPHIC.—Presenting many forms.

POLYZOARY.—The common structure formed by the cells of the Polyzoa, such as the well-known Sea-mats.

PREHENSILE.—Capable of grasping.

PREPOTENT.—Having a superiority of power.

PRIMARIES.—The feathers forming the tip of the wing of a bird, and inserted upon that part which represents the hand of man.

PROCESSES.—Projecting portions of bones, usually for the attachment of muscles, ligaments, &c.

PROPOLIS.—A resinous material collected by the Hive-Bees from the opening buds of various trees.

PROTEAN.—Exceedingly variable.

PROTOZOA.—The lowest great division of the Animal Kingdom. These animals are composed of a gelatinous material, and show scarcely any trace of distinct organs. The Infusoria, Foraminifera, and Sponges, with some other forms, belong to this division.

PUPA (pl. PUPÆ).—The second stage in the development of an Insect, from which it emerges in the perfect (winged) reproductive form. In most insects the *pupal stage* is passed in perfect repose. The *chrysalis* is the pupal state of butterflies.

RADICLE.—The minute root of an embryo plant.

RAMUS.—One half of the lower jaw in the Mammalia. The portion which rises to articulate with the skull is called the *ascending ramus*.

RANGE.—The extent of country over which a plant or animal is naturally spread. *Range in time* expresses the distribution of a species or group through the fossiliferous beds of the earth's crust.

RETINA.—The delicate inner coat of the eye, formed by nervous filaments spreading from the optic nerve, and serving for the perception of the impressions produced by light.

RETROGRESSION.—Backward development. When an animal, as it approaches maturity, becomes less perfectly organised than might be expected from its early stages and known relationships, it is said to undergo a *retrograde development* or *metamorphosis*.

RHIZOPODS.—A class of lowly organised animals (Protozoa), having a gelatinous body, the surface of which can be protruded in the form of root-like processes or filaments, which serve for locomotion and the prehension of food. The most important order is that of the Foraminifera.

RODENTS.—The gnawing Mammalia, such as the Rats, Rabbits, and Squirrels. They are especially characterised by the possession of a single pair of chisel-like cutting teeth in each jaw, between which and the grinding teeth there is a great gap.

RUBUS.—The Bramble Genus.

RUDIMENTARY.—Very imperfectly developed.

RUMINANTS.—The group of Quadrupeds which ruminate or chew the cud, such as oxen, sheep, and deer. They have divided hoofs, and are destitute of front teeth in the upper jaw.

SACRAL.—Belonging to the sacrum, or the bone composed usually of two or more united vertebræ to which the sides of the pelvis in vertebrate animals are attached.

SARCODE.—The gelatinous material of which the bodies of the lowest animals (Protozoa) are composed.

SCUTELLÆ.—The horny plates with which the feet of birds are generally more or less covered, especially in front.

SEDIMENTARY FORMATIONS.—Rocks deposited as sediments from water.

SEGMENTS.—The transverse rings of which the body of an articulate animal or Annelid is composed.

SEPALS.—The leaves or segments of the calyx, or outermost envelope of an ordinary flower. They are usually green, but sometimes brightly coloured.

SERRATURES.—Teeth like those of a saw.

SESSILE.—Not supported on a stem or footstalk.

SILURIAN SYSTEM.—A very ancient system of fossiliferous rocks belonging to the earlier part of the Palæozoic series.

SPECIALISATION.—The setting apart of a particular organ for the performance of a particular function.

SPINAL CORD.—The central portion of the nervous system in the Vertebrata, which descends from the brain through the arches of the vertebræ, and gives off nearly all the nerves to the various organs of the body.

STAMENS.—The male organs of flowering plants, standing in a circle within the petals. They usually consist of a filament and an anther, the anther being the essential part in which the pollen, or fecundating dust, is formed.

STERNUM.—The breast-bone.

STIGMA.—The apical portion of the pistil in flowering plants.

STIPULES.—Small leafy organs placed at the base of the footstalks of the leaves in many plants.

STYLE.—The middle portion of the perfect pistil, which rises like a column from the ovary and supports the stigma at its summit.

SUBCUTANEOUS.—Situated beneath the skin.

SUCTORIAL.—Adapted for sucking.

SUTURES (in the skull).—The lines of junction of the bones of which the skull is composed.

TARSUS (pl. TARSI).—The jointed feet of articulate animals, such as Insects.

TELEOSTEAN FISHES.—Fishes of the kind familiar to us in the present day, having the skeleton usually completely ossified and the scales horny.

TENTACULA or TENTACLES.—Delicate fleshy organs of prehension or touch possessed by many of the lower animals.

TERTIARY.—The latest geological epoch, immediately preceding the establishment of the present order of things.

TRACHEA.—The windpipe or passage for the admission of air to the lungs.

TRIDACTYLE.—Three-fingered, or composed of three movable parts attached to a common base.

TRILOBITES.—A peculiar group of extinct Crustaceans, somewhat resembling the Woodlice in external form, and, like some of them, capable of rolling themselves up into a ball. Their remains are found only in the Palæozoic rocks, and most abundantly in those of Silurian age.

TRIMORPHIC.—Presenting three distinct forms.

UMBELLIFERÆ.—An order of plants in which the flowers, which contain five stamens and a pistil with two styles, are supported upon footstalks which spring from the top of the flower stem and spread out like the wires of an umbrella, so as to bring all the flowers in the same head (*umbel*) nearly to the same level. (*Examples*, Parsley and Carrot).

UNGULATA.—Hoofed quadrupeds.

UNICELLULAR.—Consisting of a single cell.

VASCULAR.—Containing blood-vessels.

VERMIFORM.—Like a worm.

VERTEBRATA: or VERTEBRATE ANIMALS.—The highest division of the animal kingdom, so called from the presence in most cases of a backbone composed of numerous joints or *vertebræ*, which constitutes the centre of the skeleton and at the same time supports and protects the central parts of the nervous system.

WHORLS.—The circles or spiral lines in which the parts of plants are arranged upon the axis of growth.

WORKERS.—See neuters.

ZOËA-STAGE.—The earliest stage in the development of many of the higher Crustacea, so called from the name of *Zoëa* applied to these young animals when they were supposed to constitute a peculiar genus.

ZOÖIDS.—In many of the lower animals (such as the Corals, Medusæ, &c.) reproduction takes place in two ways, namely, by means of eggs and by a process of budding with or without separation from the parent of the product of the latter, which is often very different from that of the egg. The individuality of the species is represented by the whole of the form produced between two sexual reproductions; and these forms, which are apparently individual animals, have been called *zooids*.

THE DESCENT OF MAN

AND

SELECTION IN RELATION TO SEX

THE DESCENT OF MAN

AND

SELECTION IN RELATION TO SEX

INTRODUCTION

THE nature of the following work will be best understood by a brief account of how it came to be written. During many years I collected notes
on the origin or descent of man, without any intention of publishing on
the subject, but rather with the determination not to publish, as I
thought that I should thus only add to the prejudices against my views.
It seemed to me sufficient to indicate, in the first edition of my 'Origin of
Species,' that by this work "light would be thrown on the origin of man
and his history;'" and this implies that man must be included with other
organic beings in any general conclusion respecting his manner of appearance on this earth. Now the case wears a wholly different aspect. When a
naturalist like Carl Vogt ventures to say in his address as President of
the National Institution of Geneva (1869), "personne, en Europe au
moins, n'ose plus soutenir la création indépendante et de toutes pièces,
des espèces," it is manifest that at least a large number of naturalists
must admit that species are the modified descendants of other species;
and this especially holds good with the younger and rising naturalists.
The greater number accept the agency of natural selection; though some
urge, whether with justice the future must decide, that I have greatly
overrated its importance. Of the older and honoured chiefs in natural
science, many unfortunately are still opposed to evolution in every form.

In consequence of the views now adopted by most naturalists, and
which will ultimately, as in every other case, be followed by others who
are not scientific, I have been led to put together my notes, so as to see
how far the general conclusions arrived at in my former works were applicable to man. This seemed all the more desirable, as I had never deliberately applied these views to a species taken singly. When we confine
our attention to any one form, we are deprived of the weighty arguments
derived from the nature of the affinities which connect together whole
groups of organisms—their geographical distribution in past and present times, and their geological succession. The homological structure, embryological development, and rudimentary organs of a species remain to
be considered, whether it be man or any other animal, to which our attention may be directed; but these great classes of facts afford, as it appears

to me, ample and conclusive evidence in favour of the principle of gradual evolution. The strong support derived from the other arguments should, however, always be kept before the mind.

The sole object of this work is to consider, firstly, whether man, like every other species, is descended from some pre-existing form; secondly, the manner of his development; and thirdly, the value of the differences between the so-called races of man. As I shall confine myself to these points, it will not be necessary to describe in detail the differences between the several races—an enormous subject which has been fully discussed in many valuable works. The high antiquity of man has recently been demonstrated by the labours of a host of eminent men, beginning with M. Boucher de Perthes; and this is the indispensable basis for understanding his origin. I shall, therefore, take this conclusion for granted, and may refer my readers to the admirable treatises of Sir Charles Lyell, Sir John Lubbock, and others. Nor shall I have occasion to do more than to allude to the amount of difference between man and the anthropomorphous apes; for Prof. Huxley, in the opinion of most competent judges, has conclusively shewn that in every visible character man differs less from the higher apes, than these do from the lower members of the same order of Primates.

This work contains hardly any original facts in regard to man; but as the conclusions at which I arrived, after drawing up a rough draft, appeared to me interesting, I thought that they might interest others. It has often and confidently been asserted, that man's origin can never be known: but ignorance more frequently begets confidence than does knowledge: it is those who know little, and not those who know much, who so positively assert that this or that problem will never be solved by science. The conclusion that man is the co-descendant with other species of some ancient, lower, and extinct form, is not in any degree new. Lamarck long ago came to this conclusion, which has lately been maintained by several eminent naturalists and philosophers; for instance, by Wallace, Huxley, Lyell, Vogt, Lubbock, Büchner, Rolle, &c.,[1] and especially by Häckel. This last naturalist, besides his great work, 'Generelle Morphologie' (1866), has recently (1868, with a second edit. in 1870), published his 'Natürliche Schöpfungsgeschichte,' in which he fully discusses the genealogy of man. If this work had appeared before my essay had been written, I should probably never have completed it. Almost all the conclusions at which I have arrived I find confirmed by this naturalist,

[1] As the works of the first-named authors are so well known, I need not give the titles; but as those of the latter are less well known in England, I will give them:— 'Sechs Vorlesungen über die Darwin'sche Theorie:' zweite Auflage, 1868, von Dr. L. Büchner; translated into French under the title 'Conférences sur la Théorie Darwinienne,' 1869. 'Der Mensch, im Lichte der Darwin'schen Lehre,' 1865, von Dr. F. Rolle. I will not attempt to give references to all the authors who have taken the same side of the question. Thus G. Canestrini has published ('Annuario della Soc. d. Nat.,' Modena, 1867, p. 81) a very curious paper on rudimentary characters, as bearing on the origin of man. Another work has (1869) been published by Dr. Francesco Barrago, bearing in Italian the title of "Man, made in the image of God, was also made in the image of the ape."

whose knowledge on many points is much fuller than mine. Wherever I have added any fact or view from Prof. Häckel's writings, I give his authority in the text; other statements I leave as they originally stood in my manuscript, occasionally giving in the foot-notes references to his works, as a confirmation of the more doubtful or interesting points.

During many years it has seemed to me highly probable that sexual selection has played an important part in differentiating the races of man; but in my 'Origin of Species' (this edition, p. 68) I contented myself by merely alluding to this belief. When I came to apply this view to man, I found it indispensable to treat the whole subject in full detail.[2] Consequently the second part of the present work, treating of sexual selection, has extended to an inordinate length, compared with the first part; but this could not be avoided.

I had intended adding to the present volumes an essay on the expression of the various emotions by man and the lower animals. My attention was called to this subject many years ago by Sir Charles Bell's admirable work. This illustrious anatomist maintains that man is endowed with certain muscles solely for the sake of expressing his emotions. As this view is obviously opposed to the belief that man is descended from some other and lower form, it was necessary for me to consider it. I likewise wished to ascertain how far the emotions are expressed in the same manner by the different races of man. But owing to the length of the present work, I have thought it better to reserve my essay for separate publication.

[2] Prof. Häckel was the only author who, at the time when this work first appeared, had discussed the subject of sexual selection, and had seen its full importance, since the publication of the 'Origin'; and this he did in a very able manner in his various works.

PART I

THE DESCENT OR ORIGIN OF MAN

CHAPTER I

THE EVIDENCE OF THE DESCENT OF MAN FROM SOME LOWER FORM

Nature of the evidence bearing on the origin of man—Homologous structures in man and the lower animals—Miscellaneous points of correspondence—Development—Rudimentary structures, muscles, sense-organs, hair, bones, reproductive organs, &c.—The bearing of these three great classes of facts on the origin of man.

HE who wishes to decide whether man is the modified descendant of some pre-existing form, would probably first enquire whether man varies, however slightly, in bodily structure and in mental faculties; and if so, whether the variations are transmitted to his offspring in accordance with the laws which prevail with the lower animals. Again, are the variations the result, as far as our ignorance permits us to judge, of the same general causes, and are they governed by the same general laws, as in the case of other organisms; for instance, by correlation, the inherited effects of use and disuse, &c.? Is man subject to similar malconformations, the result of arrested development, of reduplication of parts, &c., and does he display in any of his anomalies reversion to some former and ancient type of structure? It might also naturally be enquired whether man, like so many other animals, has given rise to varieties and sub-races, differing but slightly from each other, or to races differing so much that they must be classed as doubtful species? How are such races distributed over the world; and how, when crossed, do they react on each other in the first and succeeding generations? And so with many other points.

The enquirer would next come to the important point, whether man tends to increase at so rapid a rate, as to lead to occasional severe struggles for existence; and consequently to beneficial variations, whether in body or mind, being preserved, and injurious ones eliminated. Do the races or species of men, whichever term may be applied, encroach on and replace one another, so that some finally become extinct? We shall see that all these questions, as indeed is obvious in respect to most of them, must be answered in the affirmative, in the same manner as with the lower animals. But the several considerations just referred to may be conveniently deferred for a time: and we will first see how far the bodily structure of man shows traces, more or less plain, of his descent from some lower form. In succeeding chapters the mental powers of man, in comparison with those of the lower animals, will be considered.

The Bodily Structure of Man.—It is notorious that man is constructed on the same general type or model as other mammals. All the bones in his skeleton can be compared with corresponding bones in a monkey, bat, or seal. So it is with his muscles, nerves, blood-vessels and internal viscera. The brain, the most important of all the organs, follows the same law, as shewn by Huxley and other anatomists. Bischoff,[1] who is a hostile witness, admits that every chief fissure and fold in the brain of man has its analogy in that of the orang; but he adds that at no period of development do their brains perfectly agree; nor could perfect agreement be expected, for otherwise their mental powers would have been the same. Vulpian[2] remarks: "Les différences réelles qui existent entre l'encéphale de l'homme et celui des singes supérieurs, sont bien minimes. Il ne faut pas se faire d'illusions à cet égard. L'homme est bien plus près des singes anthropomorphes par les caractères anatomiques de son cerveau que ceux-ci ne le sont non seulement des autres mammifères, mais même de certains quadrumanes, des guenons et des macaques." But it would be superfluous here to give further details on the correspondence between man and the higher mammals in the structure of the brain and all other parts of the body.

It may, however, be worth while to specify a few points, not directly or obviously connected with structure, by which this correspondence or relationship is well shewn.

Man is liable to receive from the lower animals, and to communicate to them, certain diseases, as hydrophobia, variola, the glanders, syphilis, cholera, herpes, &c.;[3] and this fact proves the close similarity [4] of their tissues and blood, both in minute structure and composition, far more plainly than does their comparison under the best microscope, or by the aid of the best chemical analysis. Monkeys are liable to many of the same non-contagious diseases as we are; thus Rengger,[5] who carefully observed for a long time the *Cebus Azaræ* in its native land, found it liable to catarrh, with the usual symptoms, and which, when often recurrent, led to consumption. These monkeys suffered also from apoplexy, inflammation of the bowels, and cataract in the eye. The younger ones when shedding their milk-teeth often died from fever. Medicines produced the same effect on them as on us. Many kinds of monkeys have a strong taste for tea, coffee, and spirituous liquors: they will also, as I have myself

---

[1] 'Grosshirnwindungen des Menschen,' 1868, s. 96. The conclusions of this author, as well as those of Gratiolet and Aeby, concerning the brain, will be discussed by Prof. Huxley in the Appendix alluded to in the Preface to this edition.

[2] 'Leç. sur la Phys.' 1866, p. 890, as quoted by M. Dally, 'L'Ordre des Primates et le Transformisme,' 1868, p. 29.

[3] Dr. W. Lauder Lindsay has treated this subject at some length in the 'Journal of Mental Science,' July 1871; and in the 'Edinburgh Veterinary Review,' July 1858.

[4] A Reviewer has criticised ('British Quarterly Review,' Oct. 1st, 1871, p. 472) what I have here said with much severity and contempt; but as I do not use the term identity, I cannot see that I am greatly in error. There appears to me a strong analogy between the same infection or contagion producing the same result, or one closely similar, in two distinct animals, and the testing of two distinct fluids by the same chemical reagent.

[5] 'Naturgeschichte der Säugethiere von Paraguay,' 1830, s. 50.

seen, smoke tobacco with pleasure.[6] Brehm asserts that the natives of north-eastern Africa catch the wild baboons by exposing vessels with strong beer, by which they are made drunk. He has seen some of these animals, which he kept in confinement, in this state; and he gives a laughable account of their behaviour and strange grimaces. On the following morning they were very cross and dismal; they held their aching heads with both hands, and wore a most pitiable expression: when beer or wine was offered them, they turned away with disgust, but relished the juice of lemons.[7] An American monkey, an Ateles, after getting drunk on brandy, would never touch it again, and thus was wiser than many men. These trifling facts prove how similar the nerves of taste must be in monkeys and man, and how similarly their whole nervous system is affected.

Man is infested with internal parasites, sometimes causing fatal effects; and is plagued by external parasites, all of which belong to the same genera or families as those infesting other mammals, and in the case of scabies to the same species.[8] Man is subject, like other mammals, birds, and even insects,[9] to that mysterious law, which causes certain normal processes, such as gestation, as well as the maturation and duration of various diseases, to follow lunar periods. His wounds are repaired by the same process of healing; and the stumps left after the amputation of his limbs, especially during an early embryonic period, occasionally possess some power of regeneration, as in the lowest animals.[10]

The whole process of that most important function, the reproduction of the species, is strikingly the same in all mammals, from the first act of courtship by the male,[11] to the birth and nurturing of the young. Monkeys are born in almost as helpless a condition as our own infants; and in certain genera the young differ fully as much in appearance from the

[6] The same tastes are common to some animals much lower in the scale. Mr. A. Nicols informs me that he kept in Queensland, in Australia, three individuals of the *Phaseolarctus cinereus;* and that, without having been taught in any way, they acquired a strong taste for rum, and for smoking tobacco.

[7] Brehm, 'Thierleben,' B. i. 1864, s. 75, 86. On the Ateles, s. 105. For other analogous statements, see s. 25, 107.

[8] Dr. W. Lauder Lindsay, 'Edinburgh Vet. Review,' July 1858, p. 13.

[9] With respect to insects see Dr. Laycock, "On a General Law of Vital Periodicity," 'British Association,' 1842. Dr. Macculloch, 'Silliman's North American Journal of Science,' vol. xvii. p. 305, has seen a dog suffering from tertian ague. Hereafter I shall return to this subject.

[10] I have given the evidence on this head in my 'Variation of Animals and Plants under Domestication,' vol. ii. p. 15, and more could be added.

[11] Mares e diversis generibus Quadrumanorum sine dubio dignoscunt feminas humanas a maribus. Primum, credo, odoratu, postea aspectu. Mr. Youatt, qui diu in Hortis Zoologicis (Bestiariis) medicus animalium erat, vir in rebus observandis cautus et sagax, hoc mihi certissime probavit, et curatores ejusdem loci et alii e ministris confirmaverunt. Sir Andrew Smith et Brehm notabant idem in Cynocephalo. Illustrissimus Cuvier etiam narrat multa de hâc re, quâ ut opinor, nihil turpius potest indicari inter omnia hominibus et Quadrumanis communia. Narrat enim Cynocephalum quendam in furorem incidere aspectu feminarum aliquarem, sed nequaquam accendi tanto furore ab omnibus. Semper eligebat juniores, et dignoscebat in turbâ, et advocabat voce gestûque.

adults, as do our children from their full-grown parents.[12] It has been urged by some writers, as an important distinction, that with man the young arrive at maturity at a much later age than with any other animal: but if we look to the races of mankind which inhabit tropical countries the difference is not great, for the orang is believed not to be adult till the age of from ten to fifteen years.[13] Man differs from woman in size, bodily strength, hairiness, &c., as well as in mind, in the same manner as do the two sexes of many mammals. So that the correspondence in general structure, in the minute structure of the tissues, in chemical composition and in constitution, between man and the higher animals, especially the anthropomorphous apes, is extremely close.

Embryonic Development.—Man is developed from an ovule, about the 125th of an inch in diameter, which differs in no respect from the ovules of other animals. The embryo itself at a very early period can hardly be distinguished from that of other members of the vertebrate kingdom. At this period the arteries run in arch-like branches, as if to carry the blood to branchiæ which are not present in the higher vertebrata, though the slits on the sides of the neck still remain (*f, g*, fig. 1), marking their former position. At a somewhat later period, when the extremities are developed, "the feet of lizards and mammals," as the illustrious Von Baer remarks, "the wings and feet of birds, no less than the hands and feet of man, all arise from the same fundamental form." It is, says Prof. Huxley,[14] "quite in the later stages of development that the young human being presents marked differences from the young ape, while the latter departs as much from the dog in its developments, as the man does. Startling as this last assertion may appear to be, it is demonstrably true."

As some of my readers may never have seen a drawing of an embryo, I have given one of man and another of a dog, at about the same early stage of development, carefully copied from two works of undoubted accuracy.[15]

After the foregoing statements made by such high authorities, it would be superfluous on my part to give a number of borrowed details, shewing that the embryo of man closely resembles that of other mammals. It may, however, be added, that the human embryo likewise resembles certain low forms when adult in various points of structure. For instance, the heart at first exists as a simple pulsating vessel; the excreta are voided

---

[12] This remark is made with respect to Cynocephalus and the anthropomorphous apes by Geoffroy Saint-Hilaire and F. Cuvier, 'Hist. Nat. des Mammifères,' tom. i. 1824.

[13] Huxley, 'Man's Place in Nature,' 1863, p. 34.

[14] 'Man's Place in Nature,' 1863, p. 67.

[15] The human embryo (upper fig.) is from Ecker, 'Icones Phys.,' 1851–1859, tab. xxx. fig. 2. This embryo was ten lines in length, so that the drawing is much magnified. The embryo of the dog is from Bischoff, 'Entwicklungsgeschichte des Hunde-Eies,' 1845, tab. xi. fig. 42 B. This drawing is five times magnified, the embryo being twenty-five days old. The internal viscera have been omitted, and the uterine appendages in both drawings removed. I was directed to these figures by Prof. Huxley, from whose work, 'Man's Place in Nature,' the idea of giving them was taken. Häckel has also given analogous drawings in his 'Schöpfungsgeschichte.'

through a cloacal passage; and the os coccyx projects like a true tail, "extending considerably beyond the rudimentary legs." [16] In the embryos of all air-breathing vertebrates, certain glands, called the corpora Wolffiana,

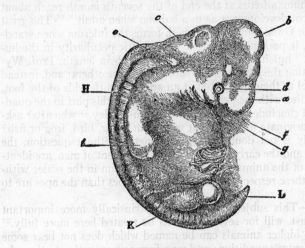

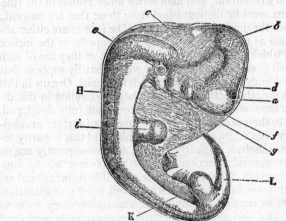

FIG. 1.—Upper figure human embryo, from Ecker. Lower figure that of a dog, from Bischoff.

a. Fore-brain, cerebral hemispheres, &c.
b. Mid-brain, corpora quadrigemina.
c. Hind-brain, cerebellum, medulla oblongata.
d. Eye. *e.* Ear. *f.* First visceral arch. *g.* Second visceral arch.
H. Vertebral columns and muscles in process of development.
i. Anterior ⎱
K. Posterior ⎰ extremities.
L. Tail or os coccyx.

[16] Prof. Wyman in 'Proc. of American Acad. of Sciences,' vol. iv. 1860, p. 17.

correspond with, and act like the kidneys of mature fishes.[17] Even at a later embryonic period, some striking resemblances between man and the lower animals may be observed. Bischoff says "that the convolutions of the brain in a human fœtus at the end of the seventh month reach about the same stage of development as in a baboon when adult." [18] The great toe, as Professor Owen remarks,[19] "which forms the fulcrum when standing or walking, is perhaps the most characteristic peculiarity in the human structure;" but in an embryo, about an inch in length, Prof. Wyman [20] found "that the great toe was shorter than the others; and, instead of being parallel to them, projected at an angle from the side of the foot, thus corresponding with the permanent condition of this part in the quadrumana." I will conclude with a quotation from Huxley,[21] who after asking, does man originate in a different way from a dog, bird, frog or fish? says, "the reply is not doubtful for a moment; without question, the mode of origin, and the early stages of the development of man, are identical with those of the animals immediately below him in the scale: without a doubt in these respects, he is far nearer to apes than the apes are to the dog."

Rudiments.—This subject, though not intrinsically more important than the two last, will for several reasons be treated here more fully.[22] Not one of the higher animals can be named which does not bear some part in a rudimentary condition; and man forms no exception to the rule. Rudimentary organs must be distinguished from those that are nascent; though in some cases the distinction is not easy. The former are either absolutely useless, such as the mammæ of male quadrupeds, or the incisor teeth of ruminants which never cut through the gums; or they are of such slight service to their present possessors, that we can hardly suppose that they were developed under the conditions which now exist. Organs in this latter state are not strictly rudimentary, but they are tending in this direction. Nascent organs, on the other hand, though not fully developed, are of high service to their possessors, and are capable of further development. Rudimentary organs are eminently variable; and this is partly intelligible, as they are useless, or nearly useless, and consequently are no longer subjected to natural selection. They often become wholly suppressed. When this occurs, they are nevertheless liable to occasional reappearance through reversion—a circumstance well worthy of attention.

The chief agents in causing organs to become rudimentary seem to have been disuse at that period of life when the organ is chiefly used (and

---

[17] Owen, 'Anatomy of Vertebrates,' vol. i. p. 533.
[18] 'Die Grosshirnwindungen des Menschen,' 1868, s. 95.
[19] 'Anatomy of Vertebrates,' vol. ii. p. 553.
[20] 'Proc. Soc. Nat. Hist.' Boston, 1863, vol. ix. p. 185.
[21] 'Man's Place in Nature,' p. 65.
[22] I had written a rough copy of this chapter before reading a valuable paper, "Caratteri rudimentali in ordine all' origine dell' uomo" ('Annuario della Soc. d. Nat.,' Modena, 1867, p. 81), by G. Canestrini, to which paper I am considerably indebted. Häckel has given admirable discussions on this whole subject, under the title of Dysteleology, in his 'Generelle Morphologie' and 'Schöpfungsgeschichte'

this is generally during maturity), and also inheritance at a correspond-ing period of life. The terms "disuse" does not relate merely to the less-ened action of muscles, but includes a diminished flow of blood to a part or organ, from being subjected to fewer alternations of pressure, or from becoming in any way less habitually active. Rudiments, however, may occur in one sex of those parts which are normally present in the other sex; and such rudiments, as we shall hereafter see, have often originated in a way distinct from those here referred to. In some cases, organs have been reduced by means of natural selection, from having become injur-ious to the species under changed habits of life. The process of reduction is probably often aided through the two principles of compensation and economy of growth; but the later stages of reduction, after disuse has done all that can fairly be attributed to it, and when the saving to be ef-fected by the economy of growth would be very small,[23] are difficult to understand. The final and complete suppression of a part, already useless and much reduced in size, in which case neither compensation nor econ-omy can come into play, is perhaps intelligible by the aid of the hypothe-sis of pangenesis. But as the whole subject of rudimentary organs has been discussed and illustrated in my former works,[24] I need here say no more on this head.

Rudiments of various muscles have been observed in many parts of the human body;[25] and not a few muscles, which are regularly present in some of the lower animals can occasionally be detected in man in a great-ly reduced condition. Every one must have noticed the power which many animals, especially horses, possess of moving or twitching their skin; and this is effected by the *panniculus carnosus*. Remnants of this muscle in an efficient state are found in various parts of our bodies; for instance, the muscle on the forehead, by which the eyebrows are raised. The *platysma myoides*, which is well developed on the neck, belongs to this system. Prof. Turner, of Edinburgh, has occasionally detected, as he informs me, muscular fasciculi in five different situations, namely in the axillæ, near the scapulæ, &c., all of which must be referred to the system of the *panniculus*. He has also shewn [26] that the *musculus sternalis* or *sternalis brutorum*, which is not an extension of the *rectus abdominalis*, but is closely allied to the *panniculus*, occurred in the proportion of about three per cent. in upward of 600 bodies: he adds, that this muscle affords "an excellent illustration of the statement that occasional and rudiment-ary structures are especially liable to variation in arrangement."

[23] Some good criticisms on this subject have been given by Messrs. Murie and Mi-vart, in 'Transact. Zoolog. Soc.' 1869, vol. vii. p. 92.

[24] 'Variation of Animals and Plants under Domestication,' vol. ii. pp. 317 and 397. See also 'Origin of Species,' this edit. p. 346.

[25] For instance, M. Richard ('Annales des Sciences Nat.,' 3d series, Zoolog. 1852, tom. xviii. p. 13) describes and figures rudiments of what he calls the "muscle pédieux de la main," which he says is sometimes "infiniment petit." Another muscle, called "le tibial postérieur," is generally quite absent in the hand, but appears from time to time in a more or less rudimentary condition.

[26] Prof. W. Turner, 'Proc. Royal Soc. Edinburgh,' 1866–67, p. 65.

Some few persons have the power of contracting the superficial muscles on their scalps; and these muscles are in a variable and partially rudimentary condition. M. A. de Candolle has communicated to me a curious instance of the long-continued persistence or inheritance of this power, as well as of its unusual development. He knows a family, in which one member, the present head of the family, could, when a youth, pitch several heavy books from his head by the movement of the scalp alone; and he won wagers by performing this feat. His father, uncle, grandfather, and his three children possess the same power to the same unusual degree. This family became divided eight generations ago into two branches; so that the head of the above-mentioned branch is cousin in the seventh degree to the head of the other branch. This distant cousin resides in another part of France; and on being asked whether he possessed the same faculty, immediately exhibited his power. This case offers a good illustration how persistent may be the transmission of an absolutely useless faculty, probably derived from our remote semi-human progenitors; since many monkeys have, and frequently use the power, of largely moving their scalps up and down.[27]

The extrinsic muscles which serve to move the external ear, and the intrinsic muscles which move the different parts, are in a rudimentary condition in man, and they all belong to the system of the *panniculus;* they are also variable in development, or at least in function. I have seen one man who could draw the whole ear forwards; other men can draw it upwards; another who could draw it backwards;[28] and from what one of these persons told me, it is probable that most of us, by often touching our ears, and thus directing our attention towards them, could recover some power of movement by repeated trials. The power of erecting and directing the shell of the ears to the various points of the compass, is no doubt of the highest service to many animals, as they thus perceive the direction of danger; but I have never heard, on sufficient evidence, of a man who possessed this power, the one which might be of use to him. The whole external shell may be considered a rudiment, together with the various folds and prominences (helix and anti-helix, tragus and anti-tragus, &c.) which in the lower animals strengthen and support the ear when erect, without adding much to its weight. Some authors, however, suppose that the cartilage of the shell serves to transmit vibrations to the acoustic nerve; but Mr. Toynbee,[29] after collecting all the known evidence on this head, concludes that the external shell is of no distinct use. The ears of the chimpanzee and orang are curiously like those of man, and the proper muscles are likewise but very slightly developed.[30] I am

[27] See my 'Expression of the Emotions in Man and Animals,' 1872, p. 144.

[28] Canestrini quotes Hyrtl. ('Annuario della Soc. dei Naturalisti,' Modena, 1897, p. 97) to the same effect.

[29] 'The Diseases of the Ear,' by J. Toynbee, F. R. S., 1860, p. 12. A distinguished physiologist, Prof. Preyer, informs me that he had lately been experimenting on the function of the shell of the ear, and has come to nearly the same conclusion as that given here.

[30] Prof. A. Macalister, 'Annals and Mag. of Nat. History,' vol. vii., 1871, p. 342.

also assured by the keepers in the Zoological Gardens that these animals never move or erect their ears; so that they are in an equally rudimentary condition with those of man, as far as function is concerned. Why these animals, as well as the progenitors of man, should have lost the power of erecting their ears, we can not say. It may be, though I am not satisfied with this view, that owing to their arboreal habits and great strength they were but little exposed to danger, and so during a lengthened period moved their ears but little, and thus gradually lost the power of moving them. This would be a parallel case with that of those large and heavy birds, which, from inhabiting oceanic islands, have not been exposed to the attacks of beasts of prey, and have consequently lost the power of using their wings for flight. The inability to move the ears in man and several apes is, however, partly compensated by the freedom with which they can move the head in a horizontal plane, so as to catch sounds from all directions. It has been asserted that the ear of man alone possesses a lobule; but "a rudiment of it is found in the gorilla;" [31] and, as I hear from Prof. Preyer, it is not rarely absent in the negro.

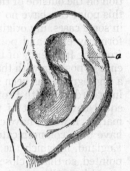

FIG. 2.—Human Ear, modelled and drawn by Mr. Woolner.

a. The projecting point.

The celebrated sculptor, Mr. Woolner, informs me of one little peculiarity in the external ear, which he has often observed both in men and women, and of which he perceived the full significance. His attention was first called to the subject whilst at work on his figure of Puck, to which he had given pointed ears. He was thus led to examine the ears of various monkeys, and subsequently more carefully those of man. The peculiarity consists in a little blunt point, projecting from the inwardly folded margin, or helix. When present, it is developed at birth, and according to Prof. Ludwig Meyer, more frequently in man than in woman. Mr. Woolner made an exact model of one such case, and sent me the accompanying drawing. (Fig. 2.) These points not only project inwards towards the centre of the ear, but often a little outwards from its plane, so as to be visible when the head is viewed from directly in front or behind. They are variable in size, and somewhat in position, standing either a little higher or lower; and they sometimes occur on one ear and not on the other. They are not confined to mankind, for I observed a case in one of the spider-monkeys (*Ateles beelzebuth*) in our Zoological Gardens; and Mr. E. Ray Lankester informs me of another case in a chimpanzee in the gardens at Hamburg. The helix obviously consists of the extreme margin of the ear folded inwards; and this folding appears to be in some manner connected with the whole external ear being permanently pressed backwards. In many monkeys, which do not stand high in the order, as

[31] Mr. St. George Mivart, 'Elementary Anatomy,' 1873, p. 396.

baboons and some species of macacus,[32] the upper portion of the ear is slightly pointed, and the margin is not at all folded inwards; but if the margin were to be thus folded, a slight point would necessarily project inwards towards the centre, and probably a little outwards from the plane of the ear; and this I believe to be their origin in many cases. On the other hand, Prof. L. Meyer, in an able paper recently published,[33] maintains that the whole case is one of mere variability; and that the projections are not real ones, but are due to the internal cartilage on each side of the points not having been fully developed. I am quite ready to admit that this is the correct explanation in many instances, as in those figured by Prof. Meyer, in which there are several minute points, or the whole margin is sinuous. I have myself seen, through the kindness of Dr. L. Down, the ear of a microcephalous idiot, on which there is a projection on the outside of the helix, and not on the inward folded edge, so that this point can have no relation to a former apex of the ear. Nevertheless in some cases, my original view, that the points are vestiges of the tips of formerly erect and pointed ears, still seems to me probable. I think so from the frequency of their occurrence, and from the general correspondence in position with that of the tip of a pointed ear. In one case, of which a photograph has been sent me, the projection is so large, that supposing, in accordance with Prof. Meyer's view, the ear to be made perfect by the equal development of the cartilage throughout the whole extent of the margin, it would have covered fully one-third of the whole ear. Two cases have been communicated to me, one in North America, and the other in England, in which the upper margin is not at all folded inwards, but is pointed, so that it closely resembles the pointed ear of an ordinary quadruped in outline. In one of these cases, which was that of a young child, the father compared the ear with the drawing which I have given [34] of the ear of a monkey, the *Cynopithecus niger,* and says that their outlines are closely similar. If, in these two cases, the margin had been folded inwards in the normal manner, an inward projection must have been formed. I may add that in two other cases the outline still remains somewhat pointed, although the margin of the upper part of the ear is normally folded inwards—in one of them, however, very narrowly. The following woodcut (No. 3) is an accurate copy of a photograph of the fœtus of an orang (kindly sent me by Dr. Nitsche), in which it may be seen how different the pointed outline of the ear is at this period from its adult condition, when it bears a close general resemblance to that of man. It is evident that the folding over of the tip of such an ear, unless it changed greatly during its further development, would give rise to a point projecting inwards. On the whole, it still seems to me probable that the points in question are in some cases, both in man and apes, vestiges of a former condition.

[32] See also some remarks, and the drawings of the ears of the Lemuroidea, in Messrs. Murie and Mivart's excellent paper in 'Transact. Zoolog. Soc.' vol. vii. 1869, pp. 6 and 90.

[33] Ueber das Darwin'sche Spitzohr, Archiv für Path. Anat. und Phys. 1871, p. 485.

[34] 'The Expression of the Emotions,' p. 136.

The nictitating membrane, or third eyelid, with its accessory muscles and other structures, is especially well developed in birds, and is of much functional importance to them, as it can be rapidly drawn across the whole eye-ball. It is found in some reptiles and amphibians, and in certain fishes, as in sharks. It is fairly well developed in the two lower divisions of the mammalian series, namely, in the monotremata and marsupials, and in some few of the higher mammals, as in the walrus. But in

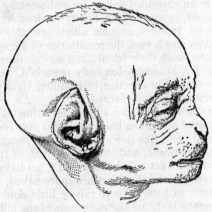

FIG. 3.—Fœtus of an Orang. Exact copy of a photograph, shewing the form of the ear at this early age.

man, the quadrumana, and most other mammals, it exists, as is admitted by all anatomists, as a mere rudiment, called the semilunar fold.[35]

The sense of smell is of the highest importance to the greater number of mammals—to some, as the ruminants, in warning them of danger; to others, as the carnivora, in finding their prey; to others, again, as the wild boar, for both purposes combined. But the sense of smell is of extremely slight service, if any, even to the dark coloured races of men, in whom it is much more highly developed than in the white and civilised races.[36] Nevertheless it does not warn them of danger, nor guide them to

[35] Müller's 'Elements of Physiology,' Eng. translat., 1842, vol. ii. p. 1117. Owen, 'Anatomy of Vertebrates,' vol. iii. p. 260; ibid. on the Walrus, 'Proc. Zoolog. Soc.' November 8th, 1854. See also R. Knox, 'Great Artists and Anatomists,' p. 106. This rudiment apparently is somewhat larger in Negroes and Australians than in Europeans, see Carl Vogt, 'Lectures on Man,' Eng. translat. p. 129.

[36] The account given by Humboldt of the power of smell possessed by the natives of South America is well known, and has been confirmed by others. M. Houzeau ('Études sur les Facultés Mentales,' &c., tom. i. 1872, p. 91) asserts that he repeatedly made experiments, and proved that Negroes and Indians could recognise persons in the dark by their odour. Dr. W. Ogle has made some curious observations on the connection between the power of smell and the colouring matter of the mucous membrane of the olfactory region as well as of the skin of the body. I have, therefore, spoken in the text of the dark-coloured races having a finer sense of smell than the white races. See his paper, 'Medico-Chirurgical Transactions,' London, vol. liii., 1870, p. 276.

their food; nor does it prevent the Esquimaux from sleeping in the most fetid atmosphere, nor many savages from eating half-putrid meat. In Europeans the power differs greatly in different individuals, as I am assured by an eminent naturalist who possesses this sense highly developed, and who has attended to the subject. Those who believe in the principle of gradual evolution, will not readily admit that the sense of smell in its present state was originally acquired by man, as he now exists. He inherits the power in an enfeebled and so far rudimentary condition, from some early progenitor, to whom it was highly serviceable, and by whom it was continually used. In those animals which have this sense highly developed, such as dogs and horses, the recollection of persons and of places is strongly associated with their odour; and we can thus perhaps understand how it is, as Dr. Maudsley has truly remarked,[37] that the sense of smell in man "is singularly effective in recalling vividly the ideas and images of forgotten scenes and places."

Man differs conspicuously from all the other Primates in being almost naked. But a few short straggling hairs are found over the greater part of the body in the man, and fine down on that of a woman. The different races differ much in hairiness; and in the individuals of the same race the hairs are highly variable, not only in abundance, but likewise in position: thus in some Europeans the shoulders are quite naked, whilst in others they bear thick tufts of hair.[38] There can be little doubt that the hairs thus scattered over the body are the rudiments of the uniform hairy coat of the lower animals. This view is rendered all the more probable, as it is known that fine, short, and pale-coloured hairs on the limbs and other parts of the body, occasionally become developed into "thickset, long, and rather coarse dark hairs," when abnormally nourished near old-standing inflamed surfaces.[39]

I am informed by Sir James Paget that often several members of a family have a few hairs in their eyebrows much longer than the others; so that even this slight peculiarity seems to be inherited. These hairs, too, seem to have their representatives; for in the chimpanzee, and in certain species of Macacus, there are scattered hairs of considerable length rising from the naked skin above the eyes, and corresponding to our eyebrows; similar long hairs project from the hairy covering of the superciliary ridges in some baboons.

The fine wool-like hair, or so-called lanugo, with which the human fœtus during the sixth month is thickly covered, offers a more curious case. It is first developed, during the fifth month, on the eyebrows and face, and especially round the mouth, where it is much longer than that on the head. A moustache of this kind was observed by Eschricht [40] on a

---

[37] 'The Physiology and Pathology of Mind,' 2nd edit. 1868, p. 134.

[38] Eschricht, Ueber die Richtung der Haare am menschlichen Körper, 'Müller's Archiv für Anat. und Phys.' 1837, s. 47. I shall often have to refer to this very curious paper.

[39] Paget, 'Lectures on Surgical Pathology,' 1853, vol. i. p. 71.

[40] Eschricht, ibid. s. 40, 47.

female fœtus; but this is not so surprising a circumstance as it may at first appear, for the two sexes generally resemble each other in all external characters during an early period of growth. The direction and arrangement of the hairs on all parts of the fœtal body are the same as in the adult, but are subject to much variability. The whole surface, including even the forehead and ears, is thus thickly clothed; but it is a significant fact that the palms of the hands and the soles of the feet are quite naked, like the inferior surfaces of all four extremities in most of the lower animals. As this can hardly be an accidental coincidence, the woolly covering of the fœtus probably represents the first permanent coat of hair in those mammals which are born hairy. Three or four cases have been recorded of persons born with their whole bodies and faces thickly covered with fine long hairs; and this strange condition is strongly inherited, and is correlated with an abnormal condition of the teeth.[41] Prof. Alex. Brandt informs me that he has compared the hair from the face of a man thus characterised, aged thirty-five, with the lanugo of a fœtus, and finds it quite similar in texture; therefore, as he remarks, the case may be attributed to an arrest of development in the hair, together with its continued growth. Many delicate children, as I have been assured by a surgeon to a hospital for children, have their backs covered by rather long silky hairs; and such cases probably come under the same head.

It appears as if the posterior molar or wisdom-teeth were tending to become rudimentary in the more civilised races of man. These teeth are rather smaller than the other molars, as is likewise the case with the corresponding teeth in the chimpanzee and orang; and they have only two separate fangs. They do not cut through the gums till about the seventeenth year, and I have been assured that they are much more liable to decay, and are earlier lost than the other teeth; but this is denied by some eminent dentists. They are also much more liable to vary, both in structure and in the period of their development, than the other teeth.[42] In the Melanian races, on the other hand, the wisdom-teeth are usually furnished with three separate fangs, and are generally sound; they also differ from the other molars in size, less than in the Caucasian races.[43] Prof. Schaaffhausen accounts for this difference between the races by "the posterior dental portion of the jaw being always shortened" in those that are civilised,[44] and this shortening may, I presume, be attributed to civilised men habitually feeding on soft, cooked food, and thus using their jaws less. I am informed by Mr. Brace that it is becoming quite a common practice in the United States to remove some of the molar teeth of chil-

---

[41] See my 'Variation of Animals and Plants under Domestication,' vol. ii. p. 327. Prof. Alex. Brandt has recently sent me an additional case of a father and son, born in Russia, with these peculiarities. I have received drawings of both from Paris

[42] Dr. Webb, 'Teeth in Man and the Anthropoid Apes,' as quoted by Dr. C. Carter Blake in 'Anthropological Review,' July 1867, p. 299

[43] Owen, 'Anatomy of Vertebrates,' vol. iii. pp. 320, 321. and 325.

[44] 'On the Primitive Form of the Skull,' Eng. translat. in 'Anthropological Review.' Oct. 1868, p. 426.

dren, as the jaw does not grow large enough for the perfect development of the normal number.[45]

With respect to the alimentary canal, I have met with an account of only a single rudiment, namely the vermiform appendage of the cæcum. The cæcum is a branch or diverticulum of the intestine, ending in a cul-de-sac, and is extremely long in many of the lower vegetable-feeding mammals. In the marsupial koala it is actually more than thrice as long as the whole body.[46] It is sometimes produced into a long gradually-tapering point, and is sometimes constricted in parts. It appears as if, in consequence of changed diet or habits, the cæcum had become much shortened in various animals, the vermiform appendage being left as a rudiment of the shortened part. That this appendage is a rudiment, we may infer from its small size, and from the evidence which Prof. Canestrini[47] has collected of its variability in man. It is occasionally quite absent, or again is largely developed. The passage is sometimes completely closed for half or two-thirds of its length, with the terminal part consisting of a flattened solid expansion. In the orang this appendage is long and convoluted: in man it arises from the end of the short cæcum, and is commonly from four to five inches in length, being only about the third of an inch in diameter. Not only is it useless, but it is sometimes the cause of death, of which fact I have lately heard two instances: this is due to small hard bodies, such as seeds, entering the passage, and causing inflammation.[48]

In some of the lower Quadrumana, in the Lemuridæ and Carnivora, as well as in many marsupials, there is a passage near the lower end of the humerus, called the supra-condyloid foramen, through which the great nerve of the fore limb and often the great artery pass. Now in the humerus of man, there is generally a trace of this passage, which is sometimes fairly well developed, being formed by a depending hook-like process of bone, completed by a band of ligament. Dr. Struthers,[49] who has closely attended to the subject, has now shewn that this peculiarity is sometimes inherited, as it has occurred in a father, and in no less than four out of his seven children. When present, the great nerve invariably passes through it; and this clearly indicates that it is the homologue and rudiment of the

---

[45] Prof. Montegazza writes to me from Florence, that he has lately been studying the last molar teeth in the different races of man, and has come to the same conclusion as that given in my text, viz., that in the higher or civilized races they are on the road towards atrophy or elimination.

[46] Owen, 'Anatomy of Vertebrates,' vol. iii. pp. 416, 434, 441.

[47] 'Annuario della Soc. d. Nat.' Modena, 1867, p. 94.

[48] M. C. Martins ("De l'Unité Organique," in 'Revue des Deux Mondes,' June 15, 1862, p. 16), and Häckel ('Generelle Morphologie,' B. ii. s. 278), have both remarked on the singular fact of this rudiment sometimes causing death.

[49] With respect to inheritance, see Dr. Struthers in the 'Lancet,' Feb. 15, 1873, and another important paper, ibid., Jan. 24, 1863, p. 83. Dr. Knox, as I am informed, was the first anatomist who drew attention to this peculiar structure in man; see his 'Great Artists and Anatomists,' p. 63. See also an important memoir on this process by Dr. Gruber, in the 'Bulletin de l'Acad. Imp. de St. Pétersbourg,' tom xii. 1867, p. 448.

supra-condyloid foramen of the lower animals. Prof. Turner estimates, as he informs me, that it occurs in about one per cent. of recent skeletons But if the occasional development of this structure in man is, as seems probable, due to reversion, it is a return to a very ancient state of things, because in the higher Quadrumana it is absent.

There is another foramen or perforation in the humerus, occasionally present in man, which may be called the inter-condyloid. This occurs, but not constantly, in various anthropoid and other apes,[50] and likewise in many of the lower animals. It is remarkable that this perforation seems to have been present in man much more frequently during ancient times than recently. Mr. Busk[51] has collected the following evidence on this head: Prof. Broca "noticed the perforation in four and a half per cent. of the arm-bones collected in the 'Cimetière du Sud,' at Paris; and in the Grotto of Orrony, the contents of which are referred to the Bronze period, as many as eight humeri out of thirty-two were perforated; but this extraordinary proportion, he thinks, might be due to the cavern having been a sort of 'family vault.' Again, M. Dupont found thirty per cent. of perforated bones in the caves of the Valley of the Lesse, belonging to the Reindeer period; whilst M. Leguay, in a sort of *dolmen* at Argenteuil, observed twenty-five per cent. to be perforated; and M. Pruner-Bey found twenty-six per cent. in the same condition in bones from Vauréal. Nor should it be left unnoticed that M. Pruner-Bey states that this condition is common in Guanche skeletons." It is an interesting fact that ancient races, in this and several other cases, more frequently present structures which resemble those of the lower animals than do the modern One chief cause seems to be that the ancient races stand somewhat nearer in the long line of descent to their remote animal-like progenitors.

In man, the os coccyx, together with certain other vertebræ hereafter to be described, though functionless as a tail, plainly represent this part in other vertebrate animals. At an early embryonic period it is free, and projects beyond the lower extremities; as may be seen in the drawing (Fig. 1.) of a human embryo. Even after birth it has been known, in certain rare and anomalous cases,[52] to form a small external rudiment of a tail. The os coccyx is short, usually including only four vertebræ, all anchylosed together: and these are in a rudimentary condition, for they consist, with the exception of the basal one, of the centrum alone.[53] They

[50] Mr. St. George Mivart, 'Transact. Phil. Soc.' 1867, p. 310.

[51] "On the Caves of Gibraltar," 'Transact. Internat. Congress of Prehist. Arch.' Third Session, 1869, p. 159. Prof. Wyman has lately shewn (Fourth Annual Report, Peabody Museum, 1871, p. 20), that this perforation is present in thirty-one per cent. of some human remains from ancient mounds in the Western United States, and in Florida. It frequently occurs in the negro.

[52] Quatrefages has lately collected the evidence on this subject. 'Revue des Cours Scientifiques,' 1867–1868, p. 625. In 1840 Fleischmann exhibited a human fœtus bearing a free tail, which, as is not always the case, included vertebral bodies; and this tail was critically examined by the many anatomists present at the meeting of naturalists at Erlangen (see Marshall in Niederländischen Archiv Für Zoologie, December 1871).

[53] Owen, 'On the Nature of Limbs,' 1849, p. 114.

are furnished with some small muscles; one of which, as I am informed by Prof. Turner, has been expressly described by Theile as a rudimentary repetition of the extensor of the tail, a muscle which is so largely developed in many mammals

The spinal cord in man extends only as far downwards as the last dorsal or first lumbar vertebra; but a thread-like structure (the *filum terminale*) runs down the axis of the sacral part of the spinal canal, and even along the back of the coccygeal bones. The upper part of this filament, as Prof. Turner informs me, is undoubtedly homologous with the spinal cord; but the lower part apparently consists merely of the *pia mater*, or vascular investing membrane. Even in this case the os coccyx may be said to possess a vestige of so important a structure as the spinal cord, though no longer enclosed within a bony canal. The following fact, for which I am also indebted to Prof. Turner, shews how closely the os coccyx corresponds with the true tail in the lower animals: Luschka has recently discovered at the extremity of the coccygeal bones a very peculiar convoluted body, which is continuous with the middle sacral artery; and this discovery led Krause and Meyer to examine the tail of a monkey (Macacus), and of a cat, in both of which they found a similarly convoluted body, though not at the extremity.

The reproductive system offers various rudimentary structures; but these differ in one important respect from the foregoing cases. Here we are not concerned with the vestige of a part which does not belong to the species in an efficient state, but with a part efficient in the one sex, and represented in the other by a mere rudiment. Nevertheless, the occurrence of such rudiments is as difficult to explain, on the belief of the separate creation of each species, as in the foregoing cases. Hereafter I shall have to recur to these rudiments, and shall shew that their presence generally depends merely on inheritance, that is, on parts acquired by one sex having been partially transmitted to the other. I will in this place only give some instances of such rudiments. It is well known that in the males of all mammals, including man, rudimentary mammæ exist. These in several instances have become well developed, and have yielded a copious supply of milk. Their essential identity in the two sexes is likewise shewn by their occasional sympathetic enlargement in both during an attack of the measles. The *vesicula prostatica*, which has been observed in many male mammals, is now universally acknowledged to be the homologue of the female uterus, together with the connected passage. It is impossible to read Leuckart's able description of this organ, and his reasoning, without admitting the justness of his conclusion. This is especially clear in the case of those mammals in which the true female uterus bifurcates, for in the males of these the vesicula likewise bifurcates.[54] Some other rudimentary structures belonging to the reproductive system might have been here adduced.[55]

[54] Leuckart, in Todd's 'Cyclop. of Anat.' 1849–52, vol. iv. p. 1415. In man this organ is only from three to six lines in length, but, like so many other rudimentary parts, it is variable in development as well as in other characters.

[55] See, on this subject, Owen, 'Anatomy of Vertebrates,' vol, iii. pp. 675, 676, 706.

The bearing of the three great classes of facts now given is unmistakable. But it would be superfluous fully to recapitulate the line of argument given in detail in my 'Origin of Species.' The homological construction of the whole frame in the members of the same class is intelligible, if we admit their descent from a common progenitor, together with their subsequent adaptation to diversified conditions. On any other view, the similarity of pattern between the hand of a man or monkey, the foot of a horse, the flipper of a seal, the wing of a bat, &c., is utterly inexplicable.[56] It is no scientific explanation to assert that they have all been formed on the same ideal plan. With respect to development, we can clearly understand, on the principle of variation supervening at a rather late embryonic period, and being inherited at a corresponding period, how it is that the embryos of wonderfully different forms should still retain, more or less perfectly, the structure of their common progenitor. No other explanation has ever been given of the marvellous fact that the embryos of a man, dog, seal, bat, reptile, &c., can at first hardly be distinguished from each other. In order to understand the existence of rudimentary organs, we have only to suppose that a former progenitor possessed the parts in question in a perfect state, and that under changed habits of life they became greatly reduced, either from simple disuse, or through the natural selection of those individuals which were least encumbered with a superfluous part, aided by the other means previously indicated.

Thus we can understand how it has come to pass that man and all other vertebrate animals have been constructed on the same general model, why they pass through the same early stages of development, and why they retain certain rudiments in common. Consequently we ought frankly to admit their community of descent; to take any other view, is to admit that our own structure, and that of all the animals around us, is a mere snare laid to entrap our judgment. This conclusion is greatly strengthened, if we look to the members of the whole animal series, and consider the evidence derived from their affinities or classification, their geographical distribution and geological succession. It is only our natu-

[56] Prof. Bianconi, in a recently published work, illustrated by admirable engravings ('La Théorie Darwinienne et la création dite indépendante,' 1874), endeavours to show that homological structures, in the above and other cases, can be fully explained on mechanical principles, in accordance with their uses. No one has shewn so well, how admirably such structures are adapted for their final purpose; and this adaptation can, as I believe, be explained through natural selection. In considering the wing of a bat, he brings forward (p. 218) what appears to me (to use Auguste Comte's words) a mere metaphysical principle, namely, the preservation "in its integrity of the mammalian nature of the animal." In only a few cases does he discuss rudiments, and then only those parts which are partially rudimentary, such as the little hoofs of the pig and ox, which do not touch the ground; these he shows clearly to be of service to the animal. It is unfortunate that he did not consider such cases as the minute teeth, which never cut through the jaw in the ox, or the mammæ of male quadrupeds, or the wings of certain beetles, existing under the soldered wing-covers, or the vestiges of the pistil and stamens in various flowers, and many other such cases. Although I greatly admire Prof. Bianconi's work, yet the belief now held by most naturalists seems to me left unshaken, that homological structures are inexplicable on the principle of mere adaptation.

ral prejudice, and that arrogance which made our forefathers declare that they were descended from demi-gods, which leads us to demur to this conclusion. But the time will before long come, when it will be thought wonderful that naturalists, who were well acquainted with the comparative structure and development of man, and other mammals, should have believed that each was the work of a separate act of creation.

CHAPTER II

ON THE MANNER OF DEVELOPMENT OF MAN FROM SOME LOWER FORM

Variability of body and mind in man—Inheritance—Causes of variability—Laws of variation the same in man as in the lower animals—Direct action of the conditions of life—Effects of the increased use and disuse of parts—Arrested development—Reversion—Correlated variation—Rate of increase—Checks to increase—Natural selection—Man the most dominant animal in the world—Importance of his corporeal structure—The causes which have led to his becoming erect—Consequent changes of structure—Decrease in size of the canine teeth—Increased size and altered shape of the skull—Nakedness—Absence of a tail—Defenceless condition of man.

It is manifest that man is now subject to much variability. No two individuals of the same race are quite alike. We may compare millions of faces, and each will be distinct. There is an equally great amount of diversity in the proportions and dimensions of the various parts of the body; the length of the legs being one of the most variable points.[1] Although in some quarters of the world an elongated skull, and in other quarters a short skull prevails, yet there is great diversity of shape even within the limits of the same race, as with the aborigines of America and South Australia—the latter a race "probably as pure and homogeneous in blood, customs, and language as any in existence"—and even with the inhabitants of so confined an area as the Sandwich Islands.[2] An eminent dentist assures me that there is nearly as much diversity in the teeth as in the features. The chief arteries so frequently run in abnormal courses, that it has been found useful for surgical purposes to calculate from 1040 corpses how often each course prevails.[3] The muscles are eminently variable: thus those of the foot were found by Prof. Turner[4] not to be strictly alike in any two out of fifty bodies; and in some the deviations were considerable. He adds, that the power of performing the appropriate movements must have been modified in accordance with the several deviations. Mr. J. Wood has recorded[5] the occurrence of 295 muscular vari-

---

[1] 'Investigations in Military and Anthropolog. Statistics of American Soldiers,' by B. A. Gould, 1869, p. 256.

[2] With respect to the "Cranial forms of the American aborigines," see Dr. Aitken Meigs in 'Proc. Acad. Nat. Sci.' Philadelphia, May, 1868. On the Australians, see Huxley, in Lyell's 'Antiquity of Man,' 1863, p. 87. On the Sandwich Islanders, Prof. J. Wyman, 'Observations on Crania,' Boston, 1868, p. 18.

[3] 'Anatomy of the Arteries,' by R. Quain. Preface, vol. i. 1844.

[4] 'Transact. Royal Soc. Edinburgh,' vol. xxiv. pp. 175, 189.

[5] 'Proc. Royal Soc.' 1867, p. 544; also 1868, pp. 483, 524. There is a previous paper, 1866, p. 229.

ations in thirty-six subjects, and in another set of the same number no less than 558 variations, those occurring on both sides of the body being only reckoned as one. In the last set, not one body out of the thirty-six was "found totally wanting in departures from the standard descriptions of the muscular system given in anatomical text books." A single body presented the extraordinary number of twenty-five distinct abnormalities. The same muscle sometimes varies in many ways: thus Prof. Macalister describes [6] no less than twenty distinct variations in the *palmaris accessorius.*

The famous old anatomist, Wolff,[7] insists that the internal viscera are more variable than the external parts: *Nulla particula est quæ non aliter et aliter in aliis se habeat hominibus.* He has even written a treatise on the choice of typical examples of the viscera for representation. A discussion on the beau-ideal of the liver, lungs, kidneys, &c., as of the human face divine, sounds strange in our ears.

The variability or diversity of the mental faculties in men of the same race, not to mention the greater differences between the men of distinct races, is so notorious that not a word need here be said. So it is with the lower animals. All who have had charge of menageries admit this fact, and we see it plainly in our dogs and other domestic animals. Brehm especially insists that each individual monkey of those which he kept tame in Africa had its own peculiar disposition and temper: he mentions one baboon remarkable for its high intelligence; and the keepers in the Zoological Gardens pointed out to me a monkey, belonging to the New World division, equally remarkable for intelligence. Rengger, also, insists on the diversity in the various mental characters of the monkeys of the same species which he kept in Paraguay; and this diversity, as he adds, is partly innate, and partly the result of the manner in which they have been treated or educated.[8]

I have elsewhere [9] so fully discussed the subject of Inheritance, that I need here add hardly anything. A greater number of facts have been collected with respect to the transmission of the most trifling, as well as of the most important characters in man, than in any of the lower animals; though the facts are copious enough with respect to the latter. So in regard to mental qualities, their transmission is manifest in our dogs, horses, and other domestic animals. Besides special tastes and habits, general intelligence, courage, bad and good temper, &c., are certainly transmitted. With man we see similar facts in almost every family; and we now know, through the admirable labours of Mr. Galton,[10] that genius which implies a wonderfully complex combination of high faculties, tends to be inherited; and, on the other hand, it is too certain that insanity and deteriorated mental powers likewise run in families.

[6] 'Proc. R. Irish Academy,' vol. x. 1868, p. 141.
[7] 'Act. Acad. St. Petersburg,' 1778, part ii. p. 217.
[8] Brehm, 'Thierleben,' B. i. s. 58, 87. Rengger, 'Säugethiere von Paraguay,' s. 57.
[9] 'Variation of Animals and Plants under Domestication,' vol. ii. chap. xii.
[10] 'Hereditary Genius: an Inquiry into its Laws and Consequences, 1869.

With respect to the causes of variability, we are in all cases very ignorant; but we can see that in man as in the lower animals, they stand in some relation to the conditions to which each species has been exposed, during several generations. Domesticated animals vary more than those in a state of nature; and this is apparently due to the diversified and changing nature of the conditions to which they have been subjected. In this respect the different races of man resemble domesticated animals, and so do the individuals of the same race, when inhabiting a very wide area, like that of America. We see the influence of diversified conditions in the more civilised nations; for the members belonging to different grades of rank, and following different occupations, present a greater range of character than do the members of barbarous nations. But the uniformity of savages has often been exaggerated, and in some cases can hardly be said to exist.[11] It is, nevertheless, an error to speak of man, even if we look only to the conditions to which he has been exposed, as "far more domesticated"[12] than any other animal. Some savage races, such as the Australians, are not exposed to more diversified conditions than are many species which have a wide range. In another and much more important respect, man differs widely from any strictly domesticated animal; for his breeding has never long been controlled, either by methodical or unconscious selection. No race or body of men has been so completely subjugated by other men, as that certain individuals should be preserved, and thus unconsciously selected, from somehow excelling in utility to their masters. Nor have certain male and female individuals been intentionally picked out and matched, except in the well-known case of the Prussian grenadiers; and in this case man obeyed, as might have been expected, the law of methodical selection; for it is asserted that many tall men were reared in the villages inhabited by the grenadiers and their tall wives. In Sparta, also, a form of selection was followed, for it was enacted that all children should be examined shortly after birth; the well-formed and vigorous being preserved, the others left to perish.[13]

[11] Mr. Bates remarks ('The Naturalist on the Amazons,' 1863, vol. ii. p. 159), with respect to the Indians of the same South American tribe, "no two of them were at all similar in the shape of the head; one man had an oval visage with fine features, and another was quite Mongolian in breadth and prominence of cheek, spread of nostrils, and obliquity of eyes."

[12] Blumenbach, 'Treatises on Anthropolog.' Eng. translat., 1865, p. 205.

[13] Mitford's 'History of Greece,' vol. i. p. 282. It appears also from a passage in Xenophon's 'Memorabilia,' B. ii. 4 (to which my attention has been called by the Rev. J. N. Hoare), that it was a well recognised principle with the Greeks, that men ought to select their wives with a view to the health and vigour of their children. The Grecian poet, Theognis, who lived 550 B. C., clearly saw how important selection, if carefully applied, would be for the improvement of mankind. He saw, likewise, that wealth often checks the proper action of sexual selection. He thus writes:

> "With kine and horses, Kurnus! we proceed
> By reasonable rules, and choose a breed
> For profit and increase, at any price:
> Of a sound stock, without defect or vice.

If we consider all the races of man as forming a single species, his range is enormous; but some separate races, as the Americans and Polynesians, have very wide ranges. It is a well-known law that widely-ranging species are much more variable than species with restricted ranges; and the variability of man may with more truth be compared with that of widely-ranging species, than with that of domesticated animals.

Not only does variability appear to be induced in man and the lower animals by the same general causes, but in both the same parts of the body are effected in a closely analogous manner. This has been proved in such full detail by Godron and Quatrefages, that I need here only refer to their works.[14] Monstrosities, which graduate into slight variations, are likewise so similar in man and the lower animals, that the same classification and the same terms can be used for both, as has been shewn by Isidore Geoffroy St.-Hilaire.[15] In my work on the variation of domestic animals, I have attempted to arrange in a rude fashion the laws of variation under the following heads:—The direct and definite action of changed conditions, as exhibited by all or nearly all the individuals of the same species, varying in the same manner under the same circumstances. The effects of the long-continued use or disuse of parts. The cohesion of homologous parts. The variability of multiple parts. Compensation of growth; but of this law I have found no good instance in the case of man. The effects of the mechanical pressure of one part on another; as of the pelvis on the cranium of the infant in the womb. Arrests of development, leading to the diminution or suppression of parts. The reappearance of long-lost characters through reversion. And lastly, correlated variation. All these so-called laws apply equally to man and the lower animals; and most of them even to plants. It would be superfluous here to discuss all of them;[16] but several are so important, that they must be treated at considerable length.

> But, in the daily matches that we make,
> The price is everything: for money's sake,
> Men marry: women are in marriage given
> The churl or ruffian, that in wealth has thriven,
> May match his offspring with the proudest race:
> Thus everything is mix'd, noble and base!
> If then in outward manner, form, and mind,
> You find us a degraded, motley kind,
> Wonder no more, my friend! the cause is plain,
> And to lament the consequence is vain."
> (The works of J. Hookham Frere, vol. ii. 1872, p. 334.)

[14] Godron, 'De l'Espèce,' 1859, tom. ii. livre 3. Quatrefages, 'Unité de l'Espèce Humaine,' 1861. Also Lectures on Anthropology, given in the 'Revue des Cours Scientifiques,' 1866-1868.

[15] 'Hist. Gén. et Part. des Anomalies de l'Organisation,' in three volumes, tom. i. 1832.

[16] I have fully discussed these laws in my 'Variation of Animals and Plants under Domestication,' vol. ii. chap. xxii. and xxiii. M. J. P. Durand has lately (1868) published a valuable essay 'De l'Influence des Milieux,' &c. He lays much stress, in the case of plants, on the nature of the soil.

The Direct and Definite Action of Changed Conditions.—This is a most perplexing subject. It cannot be denied that changed conditions produce some, and occasionally a considerable effect, on organisms of all kinds; and it seems at first probable that if sufficient time were allowed this would be the invariable result. But I have failed to obtain clear evidence in favour of this conclusion; and valid reasons may be urged on the other side, at least as far as the innumerable structures are concerned, which are adapted for special ends. There can, however, be no doubt that changed conditions induce an almost indefinite amount of fluctuating variability, by which the whole organisation is rendered in some degree plastic.

In the United States, above 1,000,000 soldiers, who served in the late war, were measured, and the States in which they were born and reared were recorded.[17] From this astonishing number of observations it is proved that local influences of some kind act directly on stature; and we further learn that "the State where the physical growth has in great measure taken place, and the State of birth, which indicates the ancestry, seem to exert a marked influence on the stature." For instance, it is established, "that residence in the Western States, during the years of growth, tends to produce increase of stature." On the other hand, it is certain that with sailors, their life delays growth, as shewn "by the great difference between the statures of soldiers and sailors at the ages of seventeen and eighteen years." Mr. B. A. Gould endeavoured to ascertain the nature of the influences which thus act on stature; but he arrived only at negative results, namely that they did not relate to climate, the elevation of the land, soil, nor even "in any controlling degree" to the abundance or the need of the comforts of life. This latter conclusion is directly opposed to that arrived at by Villermé, from the statistics of the height of the conscripts in different parts of France. When we compare the differences in stature between the Polynesian chiefs and the lower orders within the same islands, or between the inhabitants of the fertile volcanic and low barren coral islands of the same ocean,[18] or again between the Fuegians on the eastern and western shores of their country, where the means of subsistence are very different, it is scarcely possible to avoid the conclusion that better food and greater comfort do influence stature. But the preceding statements shew how difficult it is to arrive at any precise result. Dr. Beddoe has lately proved that, with the inhabitants of Britain, residence in towns and certain occupations have a deteriorating influence on height; and he infers that the result is to a certain extent inherited, as is likewise the case in the United States. Dr. Beddoe further believes that

---

[17] 'Investigations in Military and Anthrop. Statistics,' &c. 1869, by B. A. Gould, p. 93, 107, 126, 131, 134.

[18] For the Polynesians, see Prichard's 'Physical Hist. of Mankind,' vol. v. 1847, p. 145, 283. Also Godron, 'De l'Espèce,' tom. ii. p. 289. There is also a remarkable difference in appearance between the closely-allied Hindoos inhabiting the Upper Ganges and Bengal; see Elphinstone's 'History of India,' vol. i. p 324.

wherever a "race attains its maximum of physical development, it rises highest in energy and moral vigour." [19]

Whether external conditions produce any other direct effect on man is not known. It might have been expected that differences of climate would have had a marked influence, inasmuch as the lungs and kidneys are brought into activity under a low temperature, and the liver and skin under a high one.[20] It was formerly thought that the colour of the skin and the character of the hair were determined by light or heat; and although it can hardly be denied that some effect is thus produced, almost all observers now agree that the effect has been very small, even after exposure during many ages. But this subject will be more properly discussed when we treat of the different races of mankind. With our domestic animals there are grounds for believing that cold and damp directly affect the growth of the hair; but I have not met with any evidence on this head in the case of man.

Effects of the increased Use and Disuse of Parts.—It is well known that use strengthens the muscles in the individual, and complete disuse, or the destruction of the proper nerve, weakens them. When the eye is destroyed, the optic nerve often becomes atrophied. When an artery is tied, the lateral channels increase not only in diameter, but in the thickness and strength of their coats. When one kidney ceases to act from disease, the other increases in size, and does double work. Bones increase not only in thickness, but in length, from carrying a greater weight.[21] Different occupations, habitually followed, lead to changed proportions in various parts of the body. Thus it was ascertained by the United States Commission [22] that the legs of the sailors employed in the late war were longer by 0.217 of an inch than those of the soldiers, though the sailors were on an average shorter men; whilst their arms were shorter by 1.09 of an inch, and therefore, out of proportion, shorter in relation to their lesser height. This shortness of the arms is apparently due to their greater use, and is an unexpected result: but sailors chiefly use their arms in pulling, and not in supporting weights. With sailors, the girth of the neck and the depth of the instep are greater, whilst the circumference of the chest, waist, and hips is less, than in soldiers.

Whether the several foregoing modifications would become hereditary, if the same habits of life were followed during many generations, is not known, but it is probable. Rengger [23] attributes the thin legs and thick arms of the Payaguas Indians to successive generations having passed nearly their whole lives in canoes, with their lower extremities mo-

[19] 'Memoirs, Anthropolog. Soc.' vol. iii. 1867-69, pp. 561, 565, 567.

[20] Dr. Brakenridge, 'Theory of Diathesis,' 'Medical Times,' June 19 and July 17, 1869.

[21] I have given authorities for these several statements in my 'Variation of Animals under Domestication,' vol. ii. pp. 297-300. Dr. Jaeger, "Ueber das Längenwachsthum der Knochen," 'Jenaischen Zeitschrift,' B. v. Heft. i.

[22] 'Investigations,' &c. By B. A. Gould, 1869, p. 288.

[23] 'Säugethiere von Paraguay,' 1830, s. 4.

tionless. Other writers have come to a similar conclusion in analogous cases. According to Cranz,[24] who lived for a long time with the Esquimaux, "the natives believe that ingenuity and dexterity in seal-catching (their highest art and virtue) is hereditary; there is really something in it, for the son of a celebrated seal-catcher will distinguish himself, though he lost his father in childhood." But in this case it is mental aptitude, quite as much as bodily structure, which appears to be inherited. It is asserted that the hands of English labourers are at birth larger than those of the gentry.[25] From the correlation which exists, at least in some cases,[26] between the development of the extremities and of the jaws, it is possible that in those classes which do not labour much with their hands and feet, the jaws would be reduced in size from this cause. That they are generally smaller in refined and civilized men than in hard-working men or savages, is certain. But with savages, as Mr. Herbert Spencer[27] has remarked, the greater use of the jaws in chewing coarse, uncooked food, would act in a direct manner on the masticatory muscles, and on the bones to which they are attached. In infants, long before birth, the skin on the soles of the feet is thicker than on any other part of the body;[28] and it can hardly be doubted that this is due to the inherited effects of pressure during a long series of generations.

It is familiar to every one that watchmakers and engravers are liable to be short-sighted, whilst men living much out of doors, and especially savages, are generally long-sighted.[29] Short-sight and long-sight certainly tend to be inherited.[30] The inferiority of Europeans, in comparison with savages, in eyesight and in the other senses, is no doubt the accumulated and transmitted effect of lessened use during many generations; for Rengger[31] states that he has repeatedly observed Europeans, who had been brought up and spent their whole lives with the wild Indians, who nevertheless did not equal them in the sharpness of their senses. The same naturalist observes that the cavities in the skull for the reception of the several sense-organs are larger in the American aborigines than in Europeans; and this probably indicates a corresponding difference in the dimensions of the organs themselves. Blumenbach has also remarked

[24] 'History of Greenland,' Eng translat. 1767, vol. i. p. 230.
[25] 'Intermarriage.' By Alex. Walker, 1838, p. 377.
[26] 'The Variation of Animals under Domestication,' vol. i. p. 173.
[27] 'Principles of Biology,' vol. i. p. 455.
[28] Paget, 'Lectures on Surgical Pathology,' vol. ii. 1853, p. 209.
[29] It is a singular and unexpected fact that sailors are inferior to landsmen in their mean distance of distinct vision. Dr. B. A. Gould ('Sanitary Memoirs of the War of the Rebellion,' 1869, p. 530), has proved this to be the case; and he accounts for it by the ordinary range of vision in sailors being "restricted to the length of the vessel and the height of the masts."
[30] 'The Variation of Animals under Domestication,' vol. i. p. 8.
[31] 'Säugethiere von Paraguay,' s. 8, 10. I have had good opportunities for observing the extraordinary power of eyesight in the Fuegians. See also Lawrence ('Lectures on Physiology,' &c., 1822, p. 404) on this same subject. M. Giraud-Teulon has recently collected ('Revue des Cours Scientifiques,' 1870, p. 625) a large and valuable body of evidence proving that the cause of short-sight, *"C'est le travail assidu de près."*

on the large size of the nasal cavities in the skulls of the American aborigines, and connects this fact with their remarkably acute power of smell.
The Mongolians of the plains of Northern Asia, according to Pallas, have
wonderfully perfect senses; and Prichard believes that the great breadth
of their skulls across the zygomas follows from their highly-developed
sense-organs.[32]

The Quechua Indians inhabit the lofty plateaux of Peru; and Alcide
d'Orbigny states[33] that, from continually breathing a highly rarefied atmosphere, they have acquired chests and lungs of extraordinary dimensions. The cells, also, of the lungs are larger and more numerous than in
Europeans. These observations have been doubted, but Mr. D. Forbes
carefully measured many Aymaras, an allied race, living at the height of
between 10,000 and 15,000 feet; and he informs me[34] that they differ
conspicuously from the men of all other races seen by him in the circumference and length of their bodies. In his table of measurements, the stature of each man is taken at 1000, and the other measurements are reduced to this standard. It is here seen that the extended arms of the Aymaras are shorter than those of Europeans, and much shorter than those
of Negroes. The legs are likewise shorter; and they present this remarkable peculiarity, that in every Aymara measured, the femur is actually
shorter than the tibia. On an average, the length of the femur to that of
the tibia is as 211 to 252; whilst in two Europeans, measured at the same
time, the femora to the tibiæ were as 244 to 230; and in three Negroes
as 258 to 241. The humerus is likewise shorter relatively to the forearm.
This shortening of that part of the limb which is nearest to the body, appears to be, as suggested to me by Mr. Forbes, a case of compensation in
relation with the greatly increased length of the trunk. The Aymaras present some other singular points of structure, for instance, the very small
projection of the heel.

These men are so thoroughly acclimatised to their cold and lofty
abode, that when formerly carried down by the Spaniards to the low eastern plains, and when now tempted down by high wages to the gold-wash-
ings, they suffer a frightful rate of mortality. Nevertheless Mr. Forbes
found a few pure families which had survived during two generations:
and he observed that they still inherited their characteristic peculiarities.
But it was manifest, even without measurement, that these peculiarities
had all decreased; and on measurement, their bodies were found not to
be so much elongated as those of the men on the high plateau; whilst
their femora had become somewhat lengthened, as had their tibiæ, although in a less degree. The actual measurements may be seen by consulting Mr. Forbes's memoir. From these observations, there can, I think,
be no doubt that residence during many generations at a great elevation

[32] Prichard, 'Phys. Hist. of Mankind,' on the authority of Blumenbach, vol. i.
1851, p. 311; for the statement by Pallas, vol. iv. 1844, p. 407.
[33] Quoted by Prichard, 'Researches into the Phys. Hist. of Mankind,' vol. v. p. 463.
[34] Mr. Forbes' valuable paper is now published in the 'Journal of the Ethnological
Soc. of London,' new series. vol. ii. 1870, p. 193.

tends, both directly and indirectly, to induce inherited modifications in the proportions of the body.[35]

Although man may not have been much modified during the latter stages of his existence through the increased or decreased use of parts, the facts now given shew that his liability in this respect has not been lost; and we positively know that the same law holds good with the lower animals. Consequently we may infer that when at a remote epoch the progenitors of man were in a transitional state, and were changing from quadrupeds into bipeds, natural selection would probably have been greatly aided by the inherited effects of the increased or diminished use of the different parts of the body.

Arrests of Development.—There is a difference between arrested development and arrested growth, for parts in the former state continue to grow whilst still retaining their early condition. Various monstrosities come under this head; and some, as a cleft palate, are known to be occasionally inherited. It will suffice for our purpose to refer to the arrested brain-development of microcephalous idiots, as described in Vogt's memoir.[36] Their skulls are smaller, and the convolutions of the brain are less complex than in normal men. The frontal sinus, or the projection over the eye-brows, is largely developed, and the jaws are prognathous to an *"effrayant"* degree; so that these idiots somewhat resemble the lower types of mankind. Their intelligence, and most of their mental faculties, are extremely feeble. They cannot acquire the power of speech, and are wholly incapable of prolonged attention, but are much given to imitation. They are strong and remarkably active, continually gambolling and jumping about, and making grimaces. They often ascend stairs on all-fours; and are curiously fond of climbing up furniture or trees. We are thus reminded of the delight shewn by almost all boys in climbing trees; and this again reminds us how lambs and kids, originally alpine animals, delight to frisk on any hillock, however small. Idiots also resemble the lower animals in some other respects; thus several cases are recorded of their carefully smelling every mouthful of food before eating it. One idiot is described as often using his mouth in aid of his hands, whilst hunting for lice. They are often filthy in their habits, and have no sense of decency; and several cases have been published of their bodies being remarkably hairy.[37]

Reversion.—Many of the cases to be here given, might have been introduced under the last heading. When a structure is arrested in its de-

[35] Dr. Wilckens ('Landwirthschaft. Wochenblatt,' No. 10, 1869) has lately published an interesting Essay shewing how domestic animals, which live in mountainous regions, have their frames modified.

[36] 'Mémoire sur les Microcéphales,' 1867, pp. 50, 125, 169, 171, 184-198.

[37] Prof. Laycock sums up the character of brute-like idiots by calling them *theroid;* 'Journal of Mental Science,' July, 1863. Dr. Scott ('The Deaf and Dumb,' 2nd edit., 1870, p. 10) has often observed the imbeciles smelling their food. See, on this same subject, and on the hairiness of idiots, Dr. Maudsley, 'Body and Mind,' 1870, pp. 46-51. Pinel has also given a striking case of hairiness in an idiot.

velopment, but still continues growing, until it closely resembles a corresponding structure in some lower and adult member of the same group,
it may in one sense be considered as a case of reversion. The lower members in a group give us some idea how the common progenitor was probably constructed; and it is hardly credible that a complex part, arrested
at an early phase of embryonic development, should go on growing so as
ultimately to perform its proper function, unless it had acquired such
power during some earlier state of existence, when the present exceptional or arrested structure was normal. The simple brain of a microcephalous
idiot, in as far as it resembles that of an ape, may in this sense be said to
offer a case of reversion.[38] There are other cases which come more strictly

---

[38] In my 'Variation of Animals under Domestication' (vol. ii. p. 57), I attributed
the not very rare cases of supernumerary mammæ in women to reversion. I was led
to this as a probable conclusion, by the additional mammæ being generally placed
symmetrically on the breast; and more especially from one case, in which a single
efficient mamma occurred in the inguinal region of a woman, the daughter of another woman with supernumerary mammæ. But I now find (see, for instance, Prof.
Preyer, 'Der Kampf um das Dasein,' 1869, s. 45) that *mammæ erraticæ* occur in other situations, as on the back, in the armpit, and on the thigh; the mammæ in this
latter instance having given so much milk that the child was thus nourished. The
probability that the additional mammæ are due to reversion is thus much weakened;
nevertheless, it still seems to me probable, because two pairs are often found symmetrically on the breast; and of this I myself have received information in several
cases. It is well known that some Lemurs normally have two pairs of mammæ on
the breast. Five cases have been recorded of the presence of more than a pair of
mammæ (of course rudimentary) in the male sex of mankind; see 'Journal of Anat. and Physiology,' 1872, p. 56, for a case given by Dr. Handyside, in which two
brothers exhibited this peculiarity; see also a paper by Dr. Bartels, in 'Reichert's
and du Bois-Reymond's Archiv.,' 1872, p. 304. In one of the cases alluded to by Dr.
Bartels, a man bore five mammæ, one being medial and placed above the navel;
Meckel von Hemsbach thinks that this latter case is illustrated by a medial mamma
occurring in certain Cheiroptera. On the whole, we may well doubt if additional
mammæ would ever have been developed in both sexes of mankind, had not his early
progenitors been provided with more than a single pair.
    In the above work (vol. ii. p. 12), I also attributed, though with much hesitation,
the frequent cases of polydactylism in men and various animals to reversion. I was
partly led to this through Prof. Owen's statement, that some of the Ichthyopterygia
possess more than five digits, and therefore, as I supposed, had retained a primordial
condition; but Prof. Gegenbaur ('Jenaischen Zeitschrift,' B. v. Heft 3, s. 341), disputes Owen's conclusion. On the other hand, according to the opinion lately advanced
by Dr. Günther, on the paddle of Ceratodus, which is provided with articulated bony
rays on both sides of a central chain of bones, there seems no great difficulty in admitting that six or more digits on one side, or on both sides, might reappear through
reversion. I am informed by Dr. Zouteveen that there is a case on record of a man
having twenty-four fingers and twenty-four toes! I was chiefly led to the conclusion
that the presence of supernumerary digits might be due to reversion from the fact
that such digits, not only are strongly inherited, but, as I then believed, had the
power of regrowth after amputation, like the normal digits of the lower vertebrata.
But I have explained in the Second Edition of my Variation under Domestication
why I now place little reliance on the recorded cases of such regrowth. Nevertheless
it deserves notice, inasmuch as arrested development and reversion are intimately related processes; that various structures in an embryonic or arrested condition, such
as a cleft palate, bifid uterus, &c., are frequently accompanied by polydactylism.
This has been strongly insisted on by Meckel and Isidore Geoffroy St.-Hilaire. But
at present it is the safest course to give up altogether the idea that there is any rela-

under our present head of reversion. Certain structures, regularly occurring in the lower members of the group to which man belongs, occasionally make their appearance in him, though not found in the normal human embryo; or, if normally present in the human embryo, they become abnormally developed, although in a manner which is normal in the lower members of the group. These remarks will be rendered clearer by the following illustrations.

In various mammals the uterus graduates from a double organ with two distinct orifices and two passages, as in the marsupials, into a single organ, which is in no way double except from having a slight internal fold, as in the higher apes and man. The rodents exhibit a perfect series of gradations between these two extreme states. In all mammals the uterus is developed from two simple primitive tubes, the inferior portions of which form the cornua; and it is in the words of Dr. Farre, "by the coalescence of the two cornua at their lower extremities that the body of the uterus is formed in man; while in those animals in which no middle portion or body exists, the cornua remain ununited. As the development of the uterus proceeds, the two cornua become gradually shorter, until at length they are lost, or, as it were, absorbed into the body of the uterus." The angles of the uterus are still produced into cornua, even in animals as high up in the scale as the lower apes and lemurs.

Now in women, anomalous cases are not very infrequent, in which the mature uterus is furnished with cornua, or is partially divided into two organs; and such cases, according to Owen, repeat "the grade of concentrative development," attained by certain rodents. Here perhaps we have an instance of a simple arrest of embryonic development, with subsequent growth and perfect functional development; for either side of the partially double uterus is capable of performing the proper office of gestation. In other and rarer cases, two distinct uterine cavities are formed, each having its proper orifice and passage.[39] No such stage is passed through during the ordinary development of the embryo; and it is difficult to believe, though perhaps not impossible, that the two simple, minute, primitive tubes should know how (if such an expression may be used) to grow into two distinct uteri, each with a well-constructed orifice and passage, and each furnished with numerous muscles, nerves, glands and vessels, if they had not formerly passed through a similar course of development, as in the case of existing marsupials. No one will pretend that so perfect a structure as the abnormal double uterus in woman could be the result of mere chance. But the principle of reversion, by which a long-lost structure is called back into existence, might serve as the guide for its full development, even after the lapse of an enormous interval of time.

tion between the development of supernumerary digits and reversion to some lowly organized progenitor of man.

[39] See Dr. A. Farre's well-known article in the 'Cyclopædia of Anatomy and Physiology,' vol. v. 1859, p. 642. Owen, 'Anatomy of Vertebrates,' vol. iii., 1868, p. 687 Professor Turner in 'Edinburgh Medical Journal,' February 1865.

Professor Canestrini, after discussing the foregoing and various analogous cases, arrives at the same conclusion as that just given. He adduces another instance, in the case of the malar bone, [40] which, in some of the Quadrumana and other mammals, normally consists of two portions. This is its condition in the human fœtus when two months old; and through arrested development, it sometimes remains thus in man when adult, more especially in the lower prognathous races. Hence Canestrini concludes that some ancient progenitor of man must have had this bone normally divided into two portions, which afterwards became fused together. In man the frontal bone consists of a single piece, but in the embryo, and in children, and in almost all the lower mammals, it consists of two pieces separated by a distinct suture. This suture occasionally persists more or less distinctly in man after maturity; and more frequently in ancient than in recent crania, especially, as Canestrini has observed, in those exhumed from the Drift, and belonging to the brachycephalic type. Here again he comes to the same conclusion as in the analogous case of the malar bones. In this, and other instances presently to be given, the cause of ancient races approaching the lower animals in certain characters more frequently than do the modern races, appears to be, that the latter stand at a somewhat greater distance in the long line of descent from their early semi-human progenitors.

Various other anomalies in man, more or less analogous to the foregoing, have been advanced by different authors, as cases of reversion; but these seem not a little doubtful, for we have to descend extremely low in the mammalian series, before we find such structures normally present. [41]

In man, the canine teeth are perfectly efficient instruments for mastica-

---

[40] 'Annuario della Soc. dei Naturalisti in Modena,' 1867, p. 83. Prof. Canestrini gives extracts on this subject from various authorities. Laurillard remarks, that as he has found a complete similarity in the form, proportions, and connection of the two malar bones in several human subjects and in certain apes, he cannot consider this disposition of the parts as simply accidental. Another paper on this same anomaly has been published by Dr. Saviotti in the 'Gazzetta delle Cliniche,' Turin, 1871, where he says that traces of the division may be detected in about two per cent. of adult skulls; he also remarks that it more frequently occurs in prognathous skulls, not of the Aryan race, than in others. See also G. Delorenzi on the same subject; 'Tre nuovi casi d'anomalia dell' osso malare,' Torino, 1872. Also, E. Morselli, 'Sopra una rara anomalia dell' osso malare,' Modena, 1872. Still more recently Gruber has written a pamphlet on the division of this bone. I give these references because a reviewer, without any grounds or scruples, has thrown doubts on my statements.

[41] A whole series of cases is given by Isid. Geoffroy St.-Hilaire, 'Hist. des Anomalies,' tom. iii. p. 437. A reviewer ('Journal of Anat. and Physiology,' 1871, p. 366) blames me much for not having discussed the numerous cases, which have been recorded, of various parts arrested in their development. He says that, according to my theory, "every transient condition of an organ, during its development, is not only a means to an end, but once was an end in itself." This does not seem to me necessarily to hold good. Why should not variations occur during an early period of development, having no relation to reversion; yet such variations might be preserved and accumulated, if in any way serviceable, for instance, in shortening and simplifying the course of development? And again, why should not injurious abnormalities, such as atrophied or hypertrophied parts, which have no relation to a former state of existence, occur at an early period, as well as during maturity?

tion. But their true canine character, as Owen [42] remarks, "is indicated by the conical form of the crown, which terminates in an obtuse point, is convex outward and flat or sub-concave within, at the base of which surface there is a feeble prominence. The conical form is best expressed in the Melanian races, especially the Australian. The canine is more deeply implanted, and by a stronger fang than the incisors." Nevertheless, this tooth no longer serves man as a special weapon for tearing his enemies or prey; it may, therefore, as far as its proper function is concerned, be considered as rudimentary. In every large collection of human skulls some may be found, as Häckel [43] observes, with the canine teeth projecting considerably beyond the others in the same manner as in the anthropomorphous apes, but in a less degree. In these cases, open spaces between the teeth in the one jaw are left for the reception of the canines of the opposite jaw. An inter-space of this kind in a Kaffir skull, figured by Wagner, is surprisingly wide. [44] Considering how few are the ancient skulls which have been examined, compared to recent skulls, it is an interesting fact that in at least three cases the canines project largely; and in the Naulette jaw they are spoken of as enormous. [45]

Of the anthropomorphous apes the males alone have their canines fully developed; but in the female gorilla, and in a less degree in the female orang, these teeth project considerably beyond the others; therefore the fact, of which I have been assured, that women sometimes have considerably projecting canines, is no serious objection to the belief that their occasional great development in man is a case of reversion to an ape-like progenitor. He who rejects with scorn the belief that the shape of his own canines, and their occasional great development in other men, are due to our early forefathers having been provided with these formidable weapons, will probably reveal, by sneering, the line of his descent. For though he no longer intends, nor has the power, to use these teeth as weapons, he will unconsciously retract his "snarling muscles" (thus named by Sir C. Bell), [46] so as to expose them ready for action, like a dog prepared to fight.

Many muscles are occasionally developed in man, which are proper to the Quadrumana or other mammals. Professor Vlacovich [47] examined forty male subjects, and found a muscle, called by him the ischio-pubic, in nineteen of them; in three others there was a ligament which represented this muscle; and in the remaining eighteen no trace of it. In only two out of thirty female subjects was this muscle developed on both sides, but in three others the rudimentary ligament was present. This muscle, therefore, appears to be much more common in the male than in the female sex; and on the belief in the descent of man from some lower

[42] 'Anatomy of Vertebrates,' vol. iii. 1868, p. 323.

[43] 'Generelle Morphologie,' 1866, B. ii. s. clv.

[44] Carl Vogt's 'Lectures on Man,' Eng. translat. 1864, p. 151.

[45] C. Carter Blake, on a jaw from La Naulette, 'Anthropolog. Review,' 1867, p 295. Schaaffhausen, ibid. 1868, p. 426.

[46] 'The anatomy of Expression,' 1844, pp. 110, 131.

[47] Quoted by Prof. Canestrini in the 'Annuario,' &c., 1867, p. 90.

form, the fact is intelligible; for it has been detected in several of the lower animals, and in all of these it serves exclusively to aid the male in the act of reproduction.

Mr. J. Wood, in his valuable series of papers,[48] has minutely described a vast number of muscular variations in man, which resemble normal structures in the lower animals. The muscles which closely resemble those regularly present in our nearest allies, the Quadrumana, are too numerous to be here even specified. In a single male subject, having a strong bodily frame, and well-formed skull, no less than seven muscular variations were observed, all of which plainly represented muscles proper to various kinds of apes. This man, for instance, had on both sides of his neck a true and powerful *"levator claviculæ,"* such as is found in all kinds of apes, and which is said to occur in about one out of sixty human subjects.[49] Again, this man had "a special abductor of the metatarsal bone of the fifth digit, such as Professor Huxley and Mr. Flower have shewn to exist uniformly in the higher and lower apes." I will give only two additional cases; the *acromio-basilar* muscle is found in all mammals below man, and seems to be correlated with a quadrupedal gait,[50] and it occurs in about one out of sixty human subjects. In the lower extremities Mr. Bradley[51] found an *abductor ossis metatarsi quinti* in both feet of man; this muscle had not up to that time been recorded in mankind, but is always present in the anthropomorphous apes. The muscles of the hands and arms—parts which are so eminently characteristic of man—are extremely liable to vary, so as to resemble the corresponding muscles in the lower animals.[52] Such resemblances are either perfect or imperfect; yet in the latter case they are manifestly of a transitional nature. Certain variations are more common in man, and others in woman, without our being able to assign any reason. Mr. Wood, after describing numerous variations, makes the following pregnant remark: "Notable departures from the ordinary type of muscular structures run in grooves or directions, which must be taken to indicate some unknown factor, of much importance to a comprehensive knowledge of general and scientific anatomy."[53]

[48] These papers deserve careful study by any one who desires to learn how frequently our muscles vary, and in varying come to resemble those of the Quadrumana. The following references relate to the few points touched on in my text: 'Proc. Royal Soc.' vol. xiv. 1865, pp. 379-384; vol. xv. 1866, pp. 241, 242; vol. xv. 1867, p. 544; vol. xvi. 1868, p. 524. I may here add that Dr. Murie and Mr. St. George Mivart have shewn in their Memoir on the Lemuroidea ('Transact. Zoolog. Soc.' vol. vii. 1869, p. 96), how extraordinarily variable some of the muscles are in these animals, the lowest members of the Primates. Gradations, also, in the muscles leading to structures found in animals still lower in the scale, are numerous in the Lemuroidea.

[49] See also Prof. Macalister in 'Proc. R. Irish Academy,' vol. x. 1868, p. 124.

[50] Mr. Champneys in 'Journal of Anat. and Phys.' Nov., 1871, p. 178.

[51] 'Journal of Anat. and Phys.' May, 1872, p. 421.

[52] Prof. Macalister (ibid. p. 121) has tabulated his observations, and finds that muscular abnormalities are most frequent in the fore-arms, secondly, in the face, thirdly, in the foot, &c.

[53] The Rev. Dr. Haughton, after giving ('Proc. R. Irish Academy,' June 27, 1864, p. 715) a remarkable case of variation in the human *flexor pollicis longus*, adds, "This

That this unknown factor is reversion to a former state of existence may be admitted as in the highest degree probable.[54] It is quite incredible that a man should through mere accident abnormally resemble certain apes in no less than seven of his muscles, if there had been no genetic connection between them. On the other hand, if man is descended from some ape-like creature, no valid reason can be assigned why certain muscles should not suddenly reappear after an interval of many thousand generations, in the same manner as with horses, asses, and mules, dark-coloured stripes suddenly reappear on the legs, and shoulders, after an interval of hundreds, or more probably of thousands of generations.

These various cases of reversion are so closely related to those of rudimentary organs given in the first chapter, that many of them might have been indifferently introduced either there or here. Thus a human uterus furnished with cornua may be said to represent, in a rudimentary condition, the same organ in its normal state in certain mammals. Some parts which are rudimentary in man, as the os coccyx in both sexes, and the mammæ in the male sex, are always present; whilst others, such as the supracondyloid foramen, only occasionally appear, and therefore might have been introduced under the head of reversion. These several reversionary structures, as well as the strictly rudimentary ones, reveal the descent of man from some lower form in an unmistakable manner.

Correlated Variation.—In man, as in the lower animals, many structures are so intimately related, that when one part varies so does another, without our being able, in most cases, to assign any reason. We cannot say whether the one part governs the other, or whether both are governed by some earlier developed part. Various monstrosities, as I. Geoffroy repeatedly insists, are thus intimately connected. Homologous structures are particularly liable to change together, as we see on the opposite sides of the body, and in the upper and lower extremities. Meckel long ago remarked, that when the muscles of the arm depart from their proper type, they almost always imitate those of the leg; and so, conversely, with the

remarkable example shows that man may sometimes possess the arrangement of tendons of thumb and fingers characteristic of the macaque; but whether such a case should be regarded as a macaque passing upwards into a man, or a man passing downwards into a macaque, or as a congenital freak of nature, I cannot undertake to say." It is satisfactory to hear so capable an anatomist, and so embittered an opponent of evolutionism, admitting even the possibility of either of his first propositions. Prof. Macalister has also described ('Proc. R. Irish Acad.' vol. x. 1864, p. 138) variations in the *flexor pollicis longus,* remarkable from their relations to the same muscle in the Quadrumana.

[54] Since the first edition of this book appeared, Mr. Wood has published another memoir in the 'Phil. Transactions,' 1870, p. 83, on the varieties of the muscles of the human neck, shoulder, and chest. He here shows how extremely variable these muscles are, and how often and how closely the variations resemble the normal muscles of the lower animals. He sums up by remarking, "It will be enough for my purpose if I have succeeded in shewing the more important forms which, when occurring as varieties in the human subject, tend to exhibit in a sufficiently marked manner what may be considered as proofs and examples of the Darwinian principle of reversion, or law of inheritance, in this department of anatomical science."

muscles of the legs. The organs of sight and hearing, the teeth and hair, the colour of the skin and of the hair, colour and constitution, are more or less correlated.[55] Professor Schaaffhausen first drew attention to the relation apparently existing between a muscular frame and the strongly-pronounced supra-orbital ridges, which are so characteristic of the lower races of man.

Besides the variations which can be grouped with more or less probability under the foregoing heads, there is a large class of variations which may be provisionally called spontaneous, for to our ignorance they appear to arise without any exciting cause. It can, however, be shewn that such variations, whether consisting of slight individual differences, or of strongly-marked and abrupt deviations of structure, depend much more on the constitution of the organism than on the nature of the conditions to which it has been subjected.[56]

Rate of Increase.—Civilised populations have been known under favourable conditions, as in the United States, to double their numbers in twenty-five years; and, according to a calculation, by Euler, this might occur in a little over twelve years.[57] At the former rate, the present population of the United States (thirty millions), would in 657 years cover the whole terraqueous globe so thickly, that four men would have to stand on each square yard of surface. The primary or fundamental check to the continued increase of man is the difficulty of gaining subsistence, and of living in comfort. We may infer that this is the case from what we see, for instance, in the United States, where subsistence is easy, and there is plenty of room. If such means were suddenly doubled in Great Britain, our number would be quickly doubled. With civilised nations this primary check acts chiefly by restraining marriages. The greater death-rate of infants in the poorest classes is also very important; as well as the greater mortality, from various diseases, of the inhabitants of crowded and miserable houses, at all ages. The effects of severe epidemics and wars are soon counterbalanced, and more than counterbalanced, in nations placed under favourable conditions. Emigration also comes in aid as a temporary check, but, with the extremely poor classes, not to any great extent.

There is great reason to suspect, as Malthus has remarked, that the reproductive power is actually less in barbarous, than in civilised races. We know nothing positively on this head, for with savages no census has been taken; but from the concurrent testimony of missionaries, and of others who have long resided with such people, it appears that their families are usually small, and large ones rare. This may be partly accounted for, as

[55] The authorities for these several statements are given in my 'Variation of Animals under Domestication,' vol. ii. pp. 320-335.

[56] This whole subject has been discussed in chap. xxiii. vol. ii. of my 'Variation of Animals and Plants under Domestication.'

[57] See the ever memorable 'Essay on the Principle of Population,' by the Rev. T. Malthus, vol. i. 1826, pp. 6, 517.

it is believed, by the women suckling their infants during a long time; but it is highly probable that savages, who often suffer much hardships, and who do not obtain so much nutritious food as civilised men, would be actually less prolific. I have shewn in a former work,[58] that all our domesticated quadrupeds and birds, and all our cultivated plants, are more fertile than the corresponding species in a state of nature. It is no valid objection to this conclusion that animals suddenly supplied with an excess of food, or when grown very fat; and that most plants on sudden removal from very poor to very rich soil, are rendered more or less sterile. We might, therefore, expect that civilised men, who in one sense are highly domesticated, would be more prolific than wild men. It is also probable that the increased fertility of civilised nations would become, as with our domestic animals, an inherited character: it is at least known that with mankind a tendency to produce twins runs in families.[59]

Notwithstanding that savages appear to be less prolific than civilised people, they would no doubt rapidly increase if their numbers were not by some means rigidly kept down. The Santali, or hill-tribes of India, have recently afforded a good illustration of this fact; for, as shewn by Mr. Hunter,[60] they have increased at an extraordinary rate since vaccination has been introduced, other pestilences mitigated, and war sternly repressed. This increase, however, would not have been possible had not these rude people spread into the adjoining districts, and worked for hire. Savages almost always marry; yet there is some prudential restraint, for they do not commonly marry at the earliest possible age. The young men are often required to shew that they can support a wife; and they generally have first to earn the price with which to purchase her from her parents. With savages the difficulty of obtaining subsistence occasionally limits their number in a much more direct manner than with civilised people, for all tribes periodically suffer from severe famines. At such times savages are forced to devour much bad food, and their health can hardly fail to be injured. Many accounts have been published of their protruding stomachs and emaciated limbs after and during famines. They are then, also, compelled to wander much, and, as I was assured in Australia, their infants perish in large numbers. As famines are periodical, depending chiefly on extreme seasons, all tribes must fluctuate in number. They cannot steadily and regularly increase, as there is no artificial increase in the supply of food. Savages, when hard pressed, encroach on each other's territories, and war is the result; but they are indeed almost always at war with their neighbours. They are liable to many accidents on land and water in their search for food; and in some countries they suffer much from the larger beasts of prey. Even in India, districts have been depopulated by the ravages of tigers.

Malthus has discussed these several checks, but he does not lay stress enough on what is probably the most important of all, namely infanticide,

---

[58] 'Variation of Animals and Plants under Domestication,' vol. ii. pp. 111-113, 163.
[59] Mr. Sedgwick, 'British and Foreign Medico-Chirurg. Review,' July, 1863, p. 170.
[60] 'The Animals of Rural Bengal,' by W. W. Hunter, 1868, p. 259.

especially of female infants and the habit of procuring abortion. These practices now prevail in many quarters of the world; and infanticide seems formerly to have prevailed, as Mr. M'Lennan[61] has shewn on a still more extensive scale. These practices appear to have originated in savages recognising the difficulty, or rather the impossibility of supporting all the infants that are born. Licentiousness may also be added to the foregoing checks; but this does not follow from failing means of subsistence; though there is reason to believe that in some cases (as in Japan) it has been intentionally encouraged as a means of keeping down the population.

If we look back to an extremely remote epoch, before man had arrived at the dignity of manhood, he would have been guided more by instinct and less by reason than are the lowest savages at the present time. Our early semi-human progenitors would not have practised infanticide or polyandry; for the instincts of the lower animals are never so perverted[62] as to lead them regularly to destroy their own offspring, or to be quite devoid of jealousy. There would have been no prudential restraint from marriage, and the sexes would have freely united at an early age. Hence the progenitors of man would have tended to increase rapidly; but checks of some kind, either periodical or constant, must have kept down their numbers, even more severely than with existing savages. What the precise nature of these checks were, we cannot say, any more than with most other animals. We know that horses and cattle, which are not extremely prolific animals, when first turned loose in South America, increased at an enormous rate. The elephant, the slowest breeder of all known animals, would in a few thousand years stock the whole world. The increase of every species of monkey must be checked by some means; but not, as Brehm remarks, by the attacks of beasts of prey. No one will assume that the actual power of reproduction in the wild horses and cattle of America, was at first in any sensible degree increased; or that, as each district became fully stocked, this same power was diminished. No doubt in this case, and in all others, many checks concur, and different checks under different circumstances; periodical dearths, depending on unfavourable seasons, being probably the most important of all. So it will have been with the early progenitors of man.

Natural Selection.—We have now seen that man is variable in body and mind; and that the variations are induced, either directly or indirect-

[61] 'Primitive Marriage,' 1865.

[62] A writer in the 'Spectator' (March 12th, 1871, p. 320) comments as follows on this passage:—"Mr. Darwin finds himself compelled to reintroduce a new doctrine of the fall of man. He shews that the instincts of the higher animals are far nobler than the habits of savage races of men, and he finds himself, therefore, compelled to re-introduce,—in a form of the substantial orthodoxy of which he appears to be quite unconscious,—and to introduce as a scientific hypothesis the doctrine that man's gain of *knowledge* was the cause of a temporary but long-enduring moral deterioration as indicated by the many foul customs, especially as to marriage, of savage tribes. What does the Jewish tradition of the moral degeneration of man through his snatching at a knowledge forbidden him by his highest instinct assert beyond this?"

ly, by the same general causes, and obey the same general laws, as with the lower animals. Man has spread widely over the face of the earth, and must have been exposed, during his incessant migration,[63] to the most diversified conditions. The inhabitants of Tierra del Fuego, the Cape of Good Hope, and Tasmania in the one hemisphere, and of the Arctic regions in the other, must have passed through many climates, and changed their habits many times, before they reached their present homes.[64] The early progenitors of man must also have tended, like all other animals, to have increased beyond their means of subsistence; they must, therefore, occasionally have been exposed to a struggle for existence, and consequently to the rigid law of natural selection. Beneficial variations of all kinds will thus, either occasionally or habitually, have been preserved and injurious ones eliminated. I do not refer to strongly-marked deviations of structure, which occur only at long intervals of time, but to mere individual differences. We know, for instance, that the muscles of our hands and feet, which determine our powers of movement, are liable, like those of the lower animals,[65] to incessant variability. If then the progenitors of man inhabiting any district, especially one undergoing some change in its conditions, were divided into two equal bodies, the one half which included all the individuals best adapted by their powers of movement for gaining subsistence, or for defending themselves, would on an average survive in greater numbers, and procreate more offspring than the other and less well endowed half.

Man in the rudest state in which he now exists is the most dominant animal that has ever appeared on this earth. He has spread more widely than any other highly organised form: and all others have yielded before him. He manifestly owes this immense superiority to his intellectual faculties, to his social habits, which lead him to aid and defend his fellows, and to his corporeal structure. The supreme importance of these characters has been proved by the final arbitrament of the battle for life. Through his powers of intellect, articulate language has been evolved; and on this his wonderful advancement has mainly depended. As Mr. Chauncey Wright remarks: [66] "a psychological analysis of the faculty of language shews, that even the smallest proficiency in it might require more brain power than the greatest proficiency in any other direction." He has invented and is able to use various weapons, tools, traps, &c. with which he defends himself, kills or catches prey, and otherwise obtains food. He has made rafts or canoes for fishing or crossing over to neighbouring fertile islands. He has discovered the art of making fire, by which hard and stringy roots can be rendered digestible, and poisonous roots or

---

[63] See some good remarks to this effect by W. Stanley Jevons, "A Deduction from Darwin's Theory," 'Nature,' 1869, p. 231.

[64] Latham, 'Man and his Migrations,' 1851, p. 135.

[65] Messrs. Murie and Mivart in their 'Anatomy of the Lemuroidea' ('Transact. Zoolog. Soc.' vol. vii. 1869, pp. 96-98) say, "some muscles are so irregular in their distribution that they cannot be well classed in any of the above groups." These muscles differ even on the opposite sides of the same individual.

[66] Limits of Natural Selection, 'North American Review,' Oct. 1870, p. 295.

herbs innocuous. This discovery of fire, probably the greatest ever made by man, excepting language, dates from before the dawn of history. These several inventions, by which man in the rudest state has become so pre-eminent, are the direct results of the development of his powers of observation, memory, curiosity, imagination, and reason. I cannot, therefore, understand how it is that Mr. Wallace [67] maintains, that "natural selection could only have endowed the savage with a brain a little superior to that of an ape."

Although the intellectual powers and social habits of man are of paramount importance to him, we must not underrate the importance of his bodily structure, to which subject the remainder of this chapter will be devoted; the development of the intellectual and social or moral faculties being discussed in a later chapter.

Even to hammer with precision is no easy matter, as every one who has tried to learn carpentry will admit. To throw a stone with as true an aim as a Fuegian in defending himself, or in killing birds, requires the most consummate perfection in the correlated action of the muscles of the hand, arm, and shoulder, and, further, a fine sense of touch. In throwing a stone or spear, and in many other actions, a man must stand firmly on his feet; and this again demands the perfect co-adaptation of numerous muscles. To chip a flint into the rudest tool, or to form a barbed spear or hook from a bone, demands the use of a perfect hand; for, as a most capable judge, Mr. Schoolcraft,[68] remarks, the shaping fragments of stone into knives, lances, or arrow-heads, shews "extraordinary ability and long practice." This is to a great extent proved by the fact that primeval men practised a division of labour; each man did not manufacture his own flint tools or rude pottery, but certain individuals appear to have devoted themselves to such work, no doubt receiving in exchange the produce of the chase. Archæologists are convinced that an enormous interval of time elapsed before our ancestors thought of grinding chipped flints into smooth tools. One can hardly doubt, that a man-like animal who possessed a hand and arm sufficiently perfect to throw a stone with precision, or to form a flint into a rude tool, could, with sufficient practice, as far as mechanical skill alone is concerned, make almost anything which a civil-

---

[67] 'Quarterly Review,' April 1869, p. 392. This subject is more fully discussed in Mr. Wallace's 'Contributions to the Theory of Natural Selection,' 1870, in which all the essays referred to in this work are republished. The 'Essay on Man,' has been ably criticised by Prof. Claparède, one of the most distinguished zoologists in Europe, in an article published in the 'Bibliothèque Universelle,' June 1870. The remark quoted in my text will surprise every one who has read Mr. Wallace's celebrated paper on 'The origin of Human Races deduced from the Theory of Natural Selection,' originally published in the 'Anthropological Review,' May 1864, p. clviii. I cannot here resist quoting a most just remark by Sir J. Lubbock ('Prehistoric Times,' 1865, p. 479) in reference to this paper, namely, that Mr. Wallace, "with characteristic unselfishness, ascribes it (i. e. the idea of natural selection) unreservedly to Mr. Darwin, although, as is well known, he struck out the idea independently, and published it, though not with the same elaboration, at the same time."

[68] Quoted by Mr. Lawson Tait in his 'Law of Natural Selection,'—'Dublin Quarterly Journal of Medical Science,' Feb. 1869. Dr. Keller is likewise quoted to the same effect.

ised man can make. The structure of the hand in this respect may be compared with that of the vocal organs, which in the apes are used for uttering various signal-cries, or, as in one genus, musical cadences; but in man the closely similar vocal organs have become adapted through the inherited effects of use for the utterance of articulate language.

Turning now to the nearest allies of men, and therefore to the best representatives of our early progenitors, we find that the hands of the Quadrumana are constructed on the same general pattern as our own, but are far less perfectly adapted for diversified uses. Their hands do not serve for locomotion so well as the feet of a dog; as may be seen in such monkeys as the chimpanzee and orang, which walk on the outer margins of the palms, or on the knuckles.[69] Their hands, however, are admirably adapted for climbing trees. Monkeys seize thin branches or ropes, with the thumb on one side and the fingers and palm on the other, in the same manner as we do. They can thus also lift rather large objects, such as the neck of a bottle, to their mouths. Baboons turn over stones, and scratch up roots with their hands. They seize nuts, insects, or other small objects with the thumb in opposition to the fingers, and no doubt they thus extract eggs and young from the nests of birds. American monkeys beat the wild oranges on the branches until the rind is cracked, and then tear it off with the fingers of the two hands. In a wild state they break open hard fruits with stones. Other monkeys open mussel-shells with the two thumbs. With their fingers they pull out thorns and burs, and hunt for each other's parasites. They roll down stones, or throw them at their enemies: nevertheless, they are clumsy in these various actions, and, as I have myself seen, are quite unable to throw a stone with precision.

It seems to me far from true that because "objects are grasped clumsily" by monkeys, "a much less specialised organ of prehension" would have served them [70] equally well with their present hands. On the contrary, I see no reason to doubt that more perfectly constructed hands would have been an advantage to them, provided that they were not thus rendered less fitted for climbing trees. We may suspect that a hand as perfect as that of man would have been disadvantageous for climbing; for the most arboreal monkeys in the world, namely, Ateles in America Colobus in Africa, and Hylobates in Asia, are either thumbless, or their toes partially cohere, so that their limbs are converted into mere grasping hooks.[71]

As soon as some ancient member in the great series of the Primates came to be less arboreal, owing to a change in its manner of procuring subsistence, or to some change in the surrounding conditions, its habitual

[69] Owen, 'Anatomy of Vertebrates,' vol. iii. p. 71.

[70] 'Quarterly Review,' April 1869, p. 392.

[71] In *Hylobates syndactylus*, as the name expresses, two of the toes regularly cohere; and this, as Mr. Blyth informs me, is occasionally the case with the toes of *H. agilis, lar*, and *leuciscus*. Colobus is strictly arboreal and extraordinarily active (Brehm, 'Thierleben,' B. i. s. 50), but whether a better climber than the species of the allied genera, I do not know. It deserves notice that the feet of the sloths, the most arboreal animals in the world, are wonderfully hook-like.

manner of progression would have been modified: and thus it would have been rendered more strictly quadrupedal or bipedal. Baboons frequent hilly and rocky districts, and only from necessity climb high trees; [72] and they have acquired almost the gait of a dog. Man alone has become a biped; and we can, I think, partly see how he has come to assume his erect attitude, which forms one of his most conspicuous characters. Man could not have attained his present dominant position in the world without the use of his hands, which are so admirably adapted to act in obedience to his will. Sir C. Bell [73] insists that "the hand supplies all instruments, and by its correspondence with the intellect gives him universal dominion." But the hands and arms could hardly have become perfect enough to have manufactured weapons, or to have hurled stones and spears with a true aim, as long as they were habitually used for locomotion and for supporting the whole weight of the body, or, as before remarked, so long as they were especially fitted for climbing trees. Such rough treatment would also have blunted the sense of touch, on which their delicate use largely depends. From these causes alone it would have been an advantage to man to become a biped; but for many actions it is indispensable that the arms and whole upper part of the body should be free; and he must for this end stand firmly on his feet. To gain this great advantage, the feet have been rendered flat; and the great toe has been peculiarly modified, though this has entailed the almost complete loss of its power of prehension. It accords with the principle of the division of physiological labour, prevailing throughout the animal kingdom, that as the hands became perfected for prehension, the feet should have become perfected for support and locomotion. With some savages, however, the foot has not altogether lost its prehensile power, as shewn by their manner of climbing trees, and of using them in other ways.[74]

If it be an advantage to man to stand firmly on his feet and to have his hands and arms free, of which, from his pre-eminent success in the battle of life, there can be no doubt, then I can see no reason why it should not have been advantageous to the progenitors of man to have become more and more erect or bipedal. They would thus have been better able to defend themselves with stones or clubs, to attack their prey, or otherwise to obtain food. The best built individuals would in the long run have succeeded best, and have survived in larger numbers. If the gorilla and a few allied forms had become extinct, it might have been argued, with great force and apparent truth, that an animal could not have been gradually converted from a quadruped into a biped, as all the individuals in an intermediate condition would have been miserably ill-fitted for progression.

[72] Brehm, 'Thierleben,' B. i. s. 80.

[73] "The Hand," &c. 'Bridgewater Treatise,' 1833, p. 38.

[74] Häckel has an excellent discussion on the steps by which man became a biped: 'Natürliche Schöpfungsgeschichte,' 1868, s. 507. Dr. Büchner ('Conférences sur la Théorie Darwinienne,' 1869, p. 135) has given good cases of the use of the foot as a prehensile organ by man; and has also written on the manner of progression of the higher apes, to which I allude in the following paragraph: see also Owen ('Anatomy of Vertebrates,' vol. iii. p. 71) on this latter subject.

But we know (and this is well worthy of reflection) that the anthropomorphous apes are now actually in an intermediate condition; and no one doubts that they are on the whole well adapted for their conditions of life. Thus the gorilla runs with a sidelong shambling gait, but more commonly progresses by resting on its bent hands. The long-armed apes occasionally use their arms like crutches, swinging their bodies forward between them, and some kinds of Hylobates, without having been taught, can walk or run upright with tolerable quickness; yet they move awkwardly, and much less securely than man. We see, in short, in existing monkeys a manner of progression intermediate between that of a quadruped and a biped; but, as an unprejudiced judge [75] insists, the anthropomorphous apes approach in structure more nearly to the bipedal than to the quadrupedal type.

As the progenitors of man became more and more erect, with their hands and arms more and more modified for prehension and other purposes, with their feet and legs at the same time transformed for firm support and progression, endless other changes of structure would have become necessary. The pelvis would have to be broadened, the spine peculiarly curved, and the head fixed in an altered position, all which changes have been attained by man. Prof. Schaaffhausen [76] maintains that "the powerful mastoid processes of the human skull are the result of his erect position;" and these processes are absent in the orang, chimpanzee, &c., and are smaller in the gorilla than in man. Various other structures, which appear connected with man's erect position, might here have been added. It is very difficult to decide how far these correlated modifications are the result of natural selection, and how far of the inherited effects of the increased use of certain parts, or of the action of one part on another. No doubt these means of change often co-operate: thus when certain muscles, and the crests of bone to which they are attached, become enlarged by habitual use, this shews that certain actions are habitually performed and must be serviceable. Hence the individuals which performed them best, would tend to survive in greater numbers.

The free use of the arms and hands, partly the cause and partly the result of man's erect position, appears to have led in an indirect manner to other modifications of structure. The early male forefathers of man were, as previously stated, probably furnished with great canine teeth; but as they gradually acquired the habit of using stones, clubs, or other weapons, for fighting with their enemies or rivals, they would use their jaws and teeth less and less. In this case, the jaws, together with the teeth, would become reduced in size, as we may feel almost sure from innumerable analogous cases. In a future chapter we shall meet with a closely parallel case, in the reduction or complete disappearance of the canine teeth in male ruminants, apparently in relation with the development of their horns; and in horses, in relation to their habit of fighting with their incisor teeth and hoofs.

In the adult male anthropomorphous apes, as Rütimeyer,[77] and others, have insisted, it is the effect on the skull of the great development of the jaw-muscles that causes it to differ so greatly in many respects from that of man, and has given to these animals "a truly frightful physiognomy." Therefore, as the jaws and teeth in man's progenitors gradually become reduced in size, the adult skull would have come to resemble more and more that of existing man. As we shall hereafter see, a great reduction of the canine teeth in the males would almost certainly affect the teeth of the females through inheritance.

As the various mental faculties gradually developed themselves the brain would almost certainly become larger. No one, I presume, doubts that the large proportion which the size of man's brain bears to his body, compared to the same proportion in the gorilla or orang, is closely connected with his higher mental powers. We meet with closely analogous facts with insects, for in ants the cerebral ganglia are of extraordinary dimensions, and in all the Hymenoptera these ganglia are many times larger than in the less intelligent orders, such as beetles.[78] On the other hand, no one supposes that the intellect of any two animals or of any two men can be accurately gauged by the cubic contents of their skulls. It is certain that there may be extraordinary mental activity with an extremely small absolute mass of nervous matter: thus the wonderfully diversified instincts, mental powers, and affections of ants are notorious, yet their cerebral ganglia are not so large as the quarter of a small pin's head. Under this point of view, the brain of an ant is one of the most marvellous atoms of matter in the world, perhaps more so than the brain of a man.

The belief that there exists in man some close relation between the size of the brain and the development of the intellectual faculties is supported by the comparison of the skulls of savage and civilised races, of ancient and modern people, and by the analogy of the whole vertebrate series. Dr. J. Barnard Davis has proved,[79] by many careful measurements, that the mean internal capacity of the skull in Europeans is 92.3 cubic inches; in Americans 87.5; in Asiatics 87.1; and in Australians only 81.9 cubic inches. Professor Broca [80] found that the nineteenth century skulls from graves in Paris were larger than those from vaults of the twelfth century, in the proportion of 1484 to 1426; and that the increased size, as ascertained by measurements, was exclusively in the frontal part of the skull —the seat of the intellectual faculties. Prichard is persuaded that the

---

[77] 'Die Grenzen der Thierwelt, eine Betrachtung zu Darwin's Lehre,' 1868, s. 51.

[78] Dujardin, 'Annales des Sc. Nat.' 3rd series Zoolog. tom. xiv. 1850, p. 203. See also Mr. Lowne, 'Anatomy and Phys. of the *Musca vomitoria*,' 1870, p. 14. My son, Mr. F. Darwin, dissected for me the cerebral ganglia of the *Formica rufa*.

[79] 'Philosophical Transactions,' 1869, p. 513.

[80] 'Les Sélections,' M. P. Broca, 'Revue d'Anthropologies,' 1873; see also, as quoted in C. Vogt's 'Lectures on Man,' Eng. Translat. 1864, pp. 88, 90. Prichard, 'Phys. Hist. of Mankind,' vol. i. 1838, p. 305.

present inhabitants of Britain have "much more capacious braincases" than the ancient inhabitants. Nevertheless, it must be admitted that some skulls of very high antiquity, such as the famous one of Neanderthal, are well developed and capacious.[81] With respect to the lower animals, M. E. Lartet, [82] by comparing the crania of tertiary and recent mammals belonging to the same groups, has come to the remarkable conclusion that the brain is generally larger and the convolutions are more complex in the more recent forms. On the other hand, I have shewn[83] that the brains of domestic rabbits are considerably reduced in bulk, in comparison with those of the wild rabbit or hare; and this may be attributed to their having been closely confined during many generations, so that they have exerted their intellect, instincts, senses and voluntary movements but little.

The gradually increasing weight of the brain and skull in man must have influenced the development of the supporting spinal column, more especially whilst he was becoming erect. As this change of position was being brought about, the internal pressure of the brain will also have influenced the form of the skull; for many facts shew how easily the skull is thus effected. Ethnologists believe that it is modified by the kind of cradle in which infants sleep. Habitual spasms of the muscles, and a cicatrix from a severe burn, have permanently modified the facial bones. In young persons whose heads have become fixed either sideways or backwards, owing to disease, one of the two eyes has changed its position, and the shape of the skull has been altered apparently by the pressure of the brain in a new direction.[84] I have shewn that with long-eared rabbits even so trifling a cause as the lopping forward of one ear drags forward almost every bone of the skull on that side; so that the bones on the opposite side no longer strictly correspond. Lastly, if any animal were to increase or diminish much in general size, without any change in its mental powers, or if the mental powers were to be much increased or diminished, without any great change in the size of the body, the shape of the skull would almost certainly be altered. I infer this from my observations on domestic rabbits, some kinds of which have become very much larger than the wild animal, whilst others have retained nearly the same size, but in both cases the brain has been much reduced relatively to the size of the body. Now

[81] In the interesting article just referred to, Prof. Broca has well remarked, that in civilised nations, the average capacity of the skull must be lowered by the preservation of a considerable number of individuals, weak in mind and body, who would have been promptly eliminated in the savage state. On the other hand, with savages, the average includes only the more capable individuals, who have been able to survive under extremely hard conditions of life. Broca thus explains the otherwise inexplicable fact, that the mean capacity of the skull of the ancient Troglodytes of Lozère is greater than that of modern Frenchmen.

[82] 'Comptes-rendus des Sciences,' &c., June 1, 1868.

[83] 'The Variation of Animals and Plants under Domestication,' vol. i. pp. 124-129.

[84] Schaaffhausen gives from Blumenbach and Busch, the cases of the spasms and cicatrix, in 'Anthropolog. Review,' Oct. 1868, p. 420. Dr. Jarrold ('Anthropologia,' 1808, pp. 115, 116) adduces from Camper and from his own observations, cases of the modification of the skull from the head being fixed in an unnatural position. He believes that in certain trades, such as that of a shoemaker, where the head is habitually held forward, the forehead becomes more rounded and prominent.

I was at first much surprised on finding that in all these rabbits the skull
had become elongated or dolichocephalic; for instance, of two skulls of
nearly equal breadth, the one from a wild rabbit and the other from a
large domestic kind, the former was 3.15 and the latter 4.3 inches in
length.[85] One of the most marked distinctions in different races of men is
that the skull in some is elongated, and in others rounded; and here the
explanation suggested by the case of the rabbits may hold good; for
Welcker finds that short "men incline more to brachycephaly, and tall
men to dolichocephaly;" [86] and tall men may be compared with the larger and longer-bodied rabbits, all of which have elongated skulls, or are
dolichocephalic.

From these several facts we can understand, to a certain extent, the
means by which the great size and more or less rounded form of the skull
have been acquired by man; and these are characters eminently distinctive of him in comparison with the lower animals.

Another most conspicuous difference between man and the lower animals is the nakedness of his skin. Whales and porpoises (Cetacea), dugongs (Sirenia) and the hippopotamus are naked; and this may be advantageous to them for gliding through the water; nor would it be injurious to them from the loss of warmth, as the species, which inhabit the
colder regions, are protected by a thick layer of blubber, serving the same
purpose as the fur of seals and otters. Elephants and rhinoceroses are almost hairless; and as certain extinct species, which formerly lived under
an Arctic climate, were covered with long wool or hair, it would almost
appear as if the existing species of both genera had lost their hairy covering from exposure to heat. This appears the more probable, as the elephants in India which live on elevated and cool districts are more hairy [87]
than those on the lowlands. May we then infer that man became divested
of hair from having aboriginally inhabited some tropical land? That the
hair is chiefly retained in the male sex on the chest and face, and in both
sexes at the junction of all four limbs with the trunk, favours this inference—on the assumption that the hair was lost before man became erect;
for the parts which now retain most hair would then have been most protected from the heat of the sun. The crown of the head, however, offers a
curious exception, for at all times it must have been one of the most exposed parts, yet it is thickly clothed with hair. The fact, however, that
the other members of the order of Primates, to which man belongs, although inhabiting various hot regions, are well clothed with hair, generally thickest on the upper surface,[88] is opposed to the supposition that

---

[85] 'Variation of Animals,' &c., vol. i. p. 117, on the elongation of the skull; p. 119,
on the effect of the lopping of one ear.

[86] Quoted by Schaaffhausen, in 'Anthropolog. Review,' Oct. 1868, p. 419.

[87] Owen, 'Anatomy of Vertebrates,' vol. iii. p. 619.

[88] Isidore Geoffroy St.-Hilaire remarks ('Hist. Nat. Générale,' tom. ii. 1859, pp.
215-217) on the head of man being covered with long hair; also on the upper surfaces of monkeys and of other mammals being more thickly clothed than the lower
surfaces. This has likewise been observed by various authors. Prof. P. Gervais ('Hist.
Nat. des Mammifères,' tom. i. 1854, p. 28), however, states that in the Gorilla the

man became naked through the action of the sun. Mr. Belt believes [89] that within the tropics it is an advantage to man to be destitute of hair, as he is thus enabled to free himself of the multitude of ticks (acari) and other parasites, with which he is often infested, and which sometimes cause ulceration. But whether this evil is of sufficient magnitude to have led to the denudation of his body through natural selection, may be doubted, since none of the many quadrupeds inhabiting the tropics have, as far as I know, acquired any specialised means of relief. The view which seems to me the most probable is that man, or rather primarily woman, became divested of hair for ornamental purposes, as we shall see under Sexual Selection; and, according to this belief, it is not surprising that man should differ so greatly in hairiness from all other Primates, for characters, gained through sexual selection, often differ to an extraordinary degree in closely related forms.

According to a popular impression, the absence of a tail is eminently distinctive of man; but as those apes which come nearest to him are destitute of this organ, its disappearance does not relate exclusively to man. The tail often differs remarkably in length within the same genus: thus in some species of Macacus it is longer than the whole body, and is formed of twenty-four vertebræ; in others it consists of a scarcely visible stump, containing only three or four vertebræ. In some kinds of baboons there are twenty-five, whilst in the mandrill there are ten very small stunted caudal vertebræ, or, according to Cuvier,[90] sometimes only five. The tail, whether it be long or short, almost always tapers towards the end; and this, I presume, results from the atrophy of the terminal muscles, together with their arteries and nerves, through disuse, leading to the atrophy of the terminal bones. But no explanation can at present be given of the great diversity which often occurs in its length. Here, however, we are more specially concerned with the complete external disappearance of the tail. Professor Broca has recently shewn [91] that the tail in all quadrupeds consists of two portions, generally separated abruptly from each other; the basal portion consists of vertebræ, more or less perfectly channelled and furnished with apophyses like ordinary vertebræ; whereas those of the terminal portion are not channelled, are almost smooth, and scarcely resemble true vertebræ. A tail, though not externally visible, is really present in man and the anthropomorphous apes, and is constructed on exactly the same pattern in both. In the terminal portion the vertebræ, constituting the *os coccyx*, are quite rudimentary, being much reduced in size and number. In the basal portion, the vertebræ are likewise few, are unit-

hair is thinner on the back, where it is partly rubbed off, than on the lower surface.

[89] The 'Naturalist in Nicaragua,' 1874, p. 209. As some confirmation of Mr. Belt's view, I may quote the following passage from Sir W. Denison ('Varieties of Vice-Regal Life,' vol. i. 1870, p. 440): "It is said to be a practice with the Australians, when the vermin get troublesome, to singe themselves."

[90] Mr. St. George Mivart, 'Proc. Zoolog. Soc.' 1865, pp. 562, 583. Dr. J. E. Gray, 'Cat. Brit. Mus.: Skeletons.' Owen, 'Anatomy of Vertebrates,' vol. ii. p. 517. Isidore Geoffroy, 'Hist. Nat. Gén.' tom. ii. p. 244.

[91] 'Revue d'Anthropologie,' 1872; 'La Constitution des Vertèbres caudales.'

ed firmly together, and are arrested in development; but they have been rendered much broader and flatter than the corresponding vertebræ in the tails of other animals: they constitute what Broca calls the accessory sacral vertebræ. These are of functional importance by supporting certain internal parts and in other ways; and their modification is directly connected with the erect or semi-erect attitude of man and the anthropomorphous apes. This conclusion is the more trustworthy, as Broca formerly held a different view, which he has now abandoned. The modification, therefore, of the basal caudal vertebræ in man and the higher apes may have been effected, directly or indirectly, through natural selection.

But what are we to say about the rudimentary and variable vertebræ of the terminal portion of the tail, forming the *os coccyx?* A notion which has often been, and will no doubt again be ridiculed, namely, that friction has had something to do with the disappearance of the external portion of the tail, is not so ridiculous as it at first appears. Dr. Anderson [92] states that the extremely short tail of *Macacus brunneus* is formed of eleven vertebræ, including the imbedded basal ones. The extremity is tendinous and contains no vertebræ; this is succeeded by five rudimentary ones, so minute that together they are only one line and a half in length, and these are permanently bent to one side in the shape of a hook. The free part of the tail, only a little above an inch in length, includes only four more small vertebræ. This short tail is carried erect; but about a quarter of its total length is doubled on to itself to the left; and this terminal part, which includes the hook-like portion, serves "to fill up the interspace between the upper divergent portion of the callosities;" so that the animal sits on it, and thus renders it rough and callous. Dr. Anderson thus sums up his observations: "These facts seem to me to have only one explanation; this tail, from its short size, is in the monkey's way when it sits down, and frequently becomes placed under the animal while it is in this attitude; and from the circumstance that it does not extend beyond the extremity of the ischial tuberosities, it seems as if the tail originally had been bent round by the will of the animal, into the interspace between the callosities, to escape being pressed between them and the ground, and that in time the curvature became permanent, fitting in of itself when the organ happens to be sat upon." Under these circumstances it is not surprising that the surface of the tail should have been roughened and rendered callous, and Dr. Murie,[93] who carefully observed this species in the Zoological Gardens, as well as three other closely allied forms with slightly longer tails, says that when the animal sits down, the tail "is necessarily thrust to one side of the buttocks; and whether long or short its root is consequently liable to be rubbed or chafed." As we now have evidence that mutilations occasionally produce an inherited effect,[94] it is not very

---

[92] 'Proc. Zoolog. Soc.,' 1872, p. 210.

[93] 'Proc. Zoolog. Soc.,' 1872, p. 786.

[94] I allude to Dr. Brown-Séquard's observations on the transmitted effect of an operation causing epilepsy in guinea-pigs, and likewise more recently on the analogous effects of cutting the sympathetic nerve in the neck. I shall hereafter have occasion

improbable that in short-tailed monkeys, the projecting part of the tail, being functionally useless, should after many generations have become rudimentary and distorted, from being continually rubbed and chafed. We see the projecting part in this condition in the *Macacus brunneus*, and absolutely aborted in the *M. ecaudatus* and in several of the higher apes. Finally, then, as far as we can judge, the tail has disappeared in man and the anthropomorphous apes, owing to the terminal portion having been injured by friction during a long lapse of time; the basal and embedded portion having been reduced and modified, so as to become suitable to the erect or semi-erect position.

I have now endeavoured to shew that some of the most distinctive characters of man have in all probability been acquired, either directly, or more commonly indirectly, through natural selection. We should bear in mind that modifications in structure or constitution which do not serve to adapt an organism to its habits of life, to the food which it consumes, or passively to the surrounding conditions, cannot have been thus acquired. We must not, however, be too confident in deciding what modifications are of service to each being: we should remember how little we know about the use of many parts, or what changes in the blood or tissues may serve to fit an organism for a new climate or new kinds of food. Nor must we forget the principle of correlation, by which, as Isidore Geoffroy has shewn in the case of man, many strange deviations of structure are tied together. Independently of correlation, a change in one part often leads, through the increased or decreased use of other parts, to other changes of a quite unexpected nature. It is also well to reflect on such facts, as the wonderful growth of galls on plants caused by the poison of an insect, and on the remarkable changes of colour in the plumage of parrots when fed on certain fishes, or inoculated with the poison of toads;[95] for we can thus see that the fluids of the system, if altered for some special purpose, might induce other changes. We should especially bear in mind that modifications acquired and continually used during past ages for some useful purpose, would probably become firmly fixed, and might be long inherited.

Thus a large yet undefined extension may safely be given to the direct and indirect results of natural selection; but I now admit, after reading the essay by Nägeli on plants, and the remarks by various authors with respect to animals, more especially those recently made by Professor Broca, that in the earlier editions of my 'Origin of Species' I perhaps attributed too much to the action of natural selection or the survival of the fittest. I have altered the fifth edition of the 'Origin' so as to confine my remarks to adaptive changes of structure; but I am convinced, from the light gained during even the last few years, that very many structures

to refer to Mr. Salvin's interesting case of the apparently inherited effects of motmots biting off the barbs of their own tail-feathers. See also on the general subject 'Variation of Animals and Plants under Domestication,' vol. ii. pp. 22-24.

[95] 'The Variation of Animals and Plants under Domestication,' vol. ii. pp. 280, 282.

which now appear to us useless, will hereafter be proved to be useful, and will therefore come within the range of natural selection. Nevertheless, I did not formerly consider sufficiently the existence of structures, which, as far as we can at present judge, are neither beneficial nor injurious; and this I believe to be one of the greatest oversights as yet detected in my work. I may be permitted to say, as some excuse, that I had two distinct objects in view; firstly, to shew that species had not been separately created, and secondly, that natural selection had been the chief agent of change, though largely aided by the inherited effects of habit, and slightly by the direct action of the surrounding conditions. I was not, however, able to annul the influence of my former belief, then almost universal, that each species had been purposely created; and this led to my tacit assumption that every detail of structure, excepting rudiments, was of some special, though unrecognised, service. Any one with this assumption in his mind would naturally extend too far the action of natural selection, either during past or present times. Some of those who admit the principle of evolution, but reject natural selection, seem to forget, when criticising my book, that I had the above two objects in view; hence if I have erred in giving to natural selection great power, which I am very far from admitting, or in having exaggerated its power, which is in itself probable, I have at least, as I hope, done good service in aiding to overthrow the dogma of separate creations.

It is, as I can now see, probable that all organic beings, including man, possess peculiarities of structure, which neither are now, nor were formerly of any service to them, and which, therefore, are of no physiological importance. We know not what produces the numberless slight differences between the individuals of each species, for reversion only carries the problem a few steps backwards, but each peculiarity must have had its efficient cause. If these causes, whatever they may be, were to act more uniformly and energetically during a lengthened period (and against this no reason can be assigned), the result would probably be not a mere slight individual difference, but a well-marked and constant modification, though one of no physiological importance. Changed structures, which are in no way beneficial, cannot be kept uniform through natural selection, though the injurious will be thus eliminated. Uniformity of character would, however, naturally follow from the assumed uniformity of the exciting causes, and likewise from the free intercrossing of many individuals. During successive periods, the same organism might in this manner acquire successive modifications, which would be transmitted in a nearly uniform state as long as the exciting causes remained the same and there was free intercrossing. With respect to the exciting causes we can only say, as when speaking of so-called spontaneous variations, that they relate much more closely to the constitution of the varying organism, than to the nature of the conditions to which it has been subjected.

Conclusion.—In this chapter we have seen that as man at the present day is liable, like every other animal, to multiform individual differences or slight variations, so no doubt were the early progenitors of man; the variations being formerly induced by the same general causes, and governed by the same general and complex laws as at present. As all animals tend to multiply beyond their means of subsistence, so it must have been with the progenitors of man; and this would inevitably lead to a struggle for existence and to natural selection. The latter process would be greatly aided by the inherited effects of the increased use of parts, and these two processes would incessantly react on each other. It appears, also, as we shall hereafter see, that various unimportant characters have been acquired by man through sexual selection. An unexplained residuum of change must be left to the assumed uniform action of those unknown agencies, which occasionally induce strongly marked and abrupt deviations of structure in our domestic productions.

Judging from the habits of savages and of the greater number of the Quadrumana, primeval men, and even their ape-like progenitors, probably lived in society. With strictly social animals, natural selection sometimes acts on the individual, through the preservation of variations which are beneficial to the community. A community which includes a large number of well-endowed individuals increases in number, and is victorious over other less favoured ones; even although each separate member gains no advantage over the others of the same community. Associated insects have thus acquired many remarkable structures, which are of little or no service to the individual, such as the pollen-collecting apparatus, or the sting of the worker-bee, or the great jaws of soldier-ants. With the higher social animals, I am not aware that any structure has been modified solely for the good of the community, though some are of secondary service to it. For instance, the horns of ruminants and the great canine teeth of baboons appear to have been acquired by the males as weapons for sexual strife, but they are used in defence of the herd or troop. In regard to certain mental powers the case, as we shall see in the fifth chapter, is wholly different; for these faculties have been chiefly, or even exclusively, gained for the benefit of the community, and the individuals thereof have at the same time gained an advantage indirectly.

It has often been objected to such views as the foregoing, that man is one of the most helpless and defenceless creatures in the world; and that during his early and less well-developed condition, he would have been still more helpless. The Duke of Argyll, for instance, insists [96] that "the human frame has diverged from the structure of brutes, in the direction of greater physical helplessness and weakness. That is to say, it is a divergence which of all others it is most impossible to ascribe to mere natural selection." He adduces the naked and unprotected state of the body, the absence of great teeth or claws for defence, the small strength and speed of man, and his slight power of discovering food or of avoiding danger by smell. To these deficiencies there might be added one still more serious, namely, that he cannot climb quickly, and so escape from

[96] 'Primeval Man,' 1869, p. 66.

enemies. The loss of hair would not have been a great injury to the inhabitants of a warm country. For we know that the unclothed Fuegians can exist under a wretched climate. When we compare the defenceless state of man with that of apes, we must remember that the great canine teeth with which the latter are provided, are possessed in their full development by the males alone, and are chiefly used by them for fighting with their rivals; yet the females, which are not thus provided, manage to survive.

In regard to bodily size or strength, we do not know whether man is descended from some small species, like the chimpanzee, or from one as powerful as the gorilla; and, therefore, we cannot say whether man has become larger and stronger, or smaller and weaker, than his ancestors. We should, however, bear in mind that an animal possessing great size, strength, and ferocity, and which, like the gorilla, could defend itself from all enemies, would not perhaps have become social: and this would most effectually have checked the acquirement of the higher mental qualities, such as sympathy and the love of his fellows. Hence it might have been an immense advantage to man to have sprung from some comparatively weak creature.

The small strength and speed of man, his want of natural weapons, &c., are more than counterbalanced, firstly, by his intellectual powers, through which he has formed for himself weapons, tools, &c., though still remaining in a barbarous state, and, secondly, by his social qualities which lead him to give and receive aid from his fellow-men. No country in the world abounds in a greater degree with dangerous beasts than Southern Africa; no country presents more fearful physical hardships than the Arctic regions; yet one of the puniest of races, that of the Bushmen, maintains itself in Southern Africa, as do the dwarfed Esquimaux in the Arctic regions. The ancestors of man were, no doubt, inferior in intellect, and probably in social disposition, to the lowest existing savages; but it is quite conceivable that they might have existed, or even flourished, if they had advanced in intellect, whilst gradually losing their brute-like powers, such as that of climbing trees, &c. But these ancestors would not have been exposed to any special danger, even if far more helpless and defenceless than any existing savages, had they inhabited some warm continent or large island, such as Australia, New Guinea, or Borneo, which is now the home of the orang. And natural selection arising from the competition of tribe with tribe, in some such large area as one of these, together with the inherited effects of habit, would, under favourable conditions, have sufficed to raise man to his present high position in the organic scale.

CHAPTER III

COMPARISON OF THE MENTAL POWERS OF MAN AND THE LOWER ANIMALS

The difference in mental power between the highest ape and the lowest savage, immense—Certain instincts in common—The emotions—Curiosity—Imitation—Attention—Memory—Imagination—Reason—Progressive improvement—Tools and weapons used by animals—Abstraction, self-consciousness—Language—Sense of Beauty—Belief in God, spiritual agencies, superstitions.

WE have seen in the last two chapters that man bears in his bodily structure clear traces of his descent from some lower form; but it may be urged that, as man differs so greatly in his mental power from all other animals, there must be some error in this conclusion. No doubt the difference in this respect is enormous, even if we compare the mind of one of the lowest savages, who has no words to express any number higher than four, and who uses hardly any abstract terms for common objects or for the affections,[1] with that of the most highly organised ape. The difference would, no doubt, still remain immense, even if one of the higher apes had been improved or civilised as much as a dog has been in comparison with its parent-form, the wolf or jackal. The Fuegians rank amongst the lowest barbarians; but I was continually struck with surprise how closely the three natives on board H. M. S. "Beagle," who had lived some years in England, and could talk a little English, resembled us in disposition and in most of our mental faculties. If no organic being excepting man had possessed any mental power, or if his powers had been of a wholly different nature from those of the lower animals, then we should never have been able to convince ourselves that our high faculties had been gradually developed. But it can be shewn that there is no fundamental difference of this kind. We must also admit that there is a much wider interval in mental power between one of the lowest fishes, as a lamprey or lancelet, and one of the higher apes, than between an ape and man; yet this interval is filled up by numberless gradations.

Nor is the difference slight in moral disposition between a barbarian, such as the man described by the old navigator Byron, who dashed his child on the rocks for dropping a basket of sea-urchins, and a Howard or Clarkson; and in intellect, between a savage who uses hardly any abstract terms, and a Newton or Shakespeare. Differences of this kind between the highest men of the highest races and the lowest savages, are

---

[1] See the evidence on those points, as given by Lubbock, 'Prehistoric Times,' p. 354, &c.

connected by the finest gradations. Therefore it is possible that they might pass and be developed into each other.

My object in this chapter is to shew that there is no fundamental difference between man and the higher mammals in their mental faculties. Each division of the subject might have been extended into a separate essay, but must here be treated briefly. As no classification of the mental powers has been universally accepted, I shall arrange my remarks in the order most convenient for my purpose; and will select those facts which have struck me most, with the hope that they may produce some effect on the reader.

With respect to animals very low in the scale, I shall give some additional facts under Sexual Selection, shewing that their mental powers are much higher than might have been expected. The variability of the faculties in the individuals of the same species is an important point for us, and some few illustrations will here be given. But it would be superfluous to enter into many details on this head, for I have found on frequent enquiry, that it is the unanimous opinion of all those who have long attended to animals of many kinds, including birds, that the individuals differ greatly in every mental characteristic. In what manner the mental powers were first developed in the lowest organisms, is as hopeless an enquiry as how life itself first originated. These are problems for the distant future, if they are ever to be solved by man.

As man possesses the same senses as the lower animals, his fundamental intuitions must be the same. Man has also some few instincts in common, as that of self-preservation, sexual love, the love of the mother for her new-born offspring, the desire possessed by the latter to suck, and so forth. But man, perhaps, has somewhat fewer instincts than those possessed by the animals which come next to him in the series. The orang in the Eastern islands, and the chimpanzee in Africa, build platforms on which they sleep; and, as both species follow the same habit, it might be argued that this was due to instinct, but we cannot feel sure that it is not the result of both animals having similar wants, and possessing similar powers of reasoning. These apes, as we may assume, avoid the many poisonous fruits of the tropics, and man has no such knowledge: but as our domestic animals, when taken to foreign lands, and when first turned out in the spring, often eat poisonous herbs, which they afterwards avoid, we cannot feel sure that the apes do not learn from their own experience or from that of their parents what fruits to select. It is, however, certain, as we shall presently see, that apes have an instinctive dread of serpents, and probably of other dangerous animals.

The fewness and the comparative simplicity of the instincts in the higher animals are remarkable in contrast with those of the lower animals. Cuvier maintained that instinct and intelligence stand in an inverse ratio to each other; and some have thought that the intellectual faculties of the higher animals have been gradually developed from their instincts. But Pouchet, in an interesting essay,[2] has shewn that no such inverse

[2] 'L'Instinct chez les Insectes,' 'Revue des Deux Mondes,' Feb. 1870, p. 690.

ratio really exists. Those insects which possess the most wonderful instincts are certainly the most intelligent. In the vertebrate series, the least intelligent members, namely fishes and amphibians, do not possess complex instincts; and amongst mammals the animal most remarkable for its instincts, namely the beaver, is highly intelligent, as will be admitted by every one who has read Mr. Morgan's excellent work.[3]

Although the first dawnings of intelligence, according to Mr. Herbert Spencer,[4] have been developed through the multiplication and co-ordination of reflex actions, and although many of the simpler instincts graduate into reflex actions, and can hardly be distinguished from them, as in the case of young animals sucking, yet the more complex instincts seem to have originated independently of intelligence. I am, however, very far from wishing to deny that instinctive actions may lose their fixed and untaught character, and be replaced by others performed by the aid of the free will. On the other hand, some intelligent actions, after being performed during several generations, become converted into instincts and are inherited, as when birds on oceanic islands learn to avoid man. These actions may then be said to be degraded in character, for they are no longer performed through reason or from experience. But the greater number of the more complex instincts appear to have been gained in a wholly different manner, through the natural selection of variations of simpler instinctive actions. Such variations appear to arise from the same unknown causes acting on the cerebral organisation, which induce slight variations or individual differences in other parts of the body; and these variations, owing to our ignorance, are often said to arise spontaneously. We can, I think, come to no other conclusion with respect to the origin of the more complex instincts, when we reflect on the marvellous instincts of sterile worker-ants and bees, which leave no offspring to inherit the effects of experience and of modified habits.

Although, as we learn from the above-mentioned insects and the beaver, a high degree of intelligence is certainly compatible with complex instincts, and although actions, at first learnt voluntarily can soon through habit be performed with the quickness and certainty of a reflex action, yet it is not improbable that there is a certain amount of interference between the development of free intelligence and of instinct,—which latter implies some inherited modification of the brain. Little is known about the functions of the brain, but we can perceive that as the intellectual powers become highly developed, the various parts of the brain must be connected by very intricate channels of the freest intercommunication; and as a consequence each separate part would perhaps tend to be less well fitted to answer to particular sensations or associations in a definite and inherited—that is instinctive—manner. There seems even to exist some relation between a low degree of intelligence and a strong tendency to the formation of fixed, though not inherited habits; for as a sagacious physician remarked to me, persons who are slightly imbecile tend to act

---

[3] 'The American Beaver and His Works,' 1868.
[4] 'The Principles of Psychology,' 2nd edit. 1870, pp. 418-443.

in everything by routine or habit; and they are rendered much happier if this is encouraged.

I have thought this digression worth giving, because we may easily underrate the mental powers of the higher animals, and especially of man, when we compare their actions founded on the memory of past events, on foresight, reason, and imagination, with exactly similar actions instinctively performed by the lower animals; in this latter case the capacity of performing such actions has been gained, step by step, through the variability of the mental organs and natural selection, without any conscious intelligence on the part of the animal during each successive generation. No doubt, as Mr. Wallace has argued,[5] much of the intelligent work done by man is due to imitation and not to reason; but there is this great difference between his actions and many of those performed by the lower animals, namely, that man cannot, on his first trial, make, for instance, a stone hatchet or a canoe, through his power of imitation. He has to learn his work by practice; a beaver, on the other hand, can make its dam or canal, and a bird its nest, as well, or nearly as well, and a spider its wonderful web, quite as well,[6] the first time it tries as when old and experienced.

To return to our immediate subject: the lower animals, like man, manifestly feel pleasure and pain, happiness and misery. Happiness is never better exhibited than by young animals, such as puppies, kittens, lambs, &c., when playing together, like our own children. Even insects play together, as has been described by that excellent observer, P. Huber,[7] who saw ants chasing and pretending to bite each other, like so many puppies.

The fact that the lower animals are excited by the same emotions as ourselves is so well established, that it will not be necessary to weary the reader by many details. Terror acts in the same manner on them as on us, causing the muscles to tremble, the heart to palpitate, the sphincters to be relaxed, and the hair to stand on end. Suspicion, the offspring of fear, is eminently characteristic of most wild animals. It is, I think, impossible to read the account given by Sir E. Tennent, of the behaviour of the female elephants, used as decoys, without admitting that they intentionally practise deceit, and well know what they are about. Courage and timidity are extremely variable qualities in the individuals of the same species, as is plainly seen in our dogs. Some dogs and horses are ill-tempered, and easily turn sulky; others are good-tempered; and these qualities are certainly inherited. Every one knows how liable animals are to furious rage, and how plainly they shew it. Many, and probably true, anecdotes have been published on the long-delayed and artful revenge of various animals. The accurate Rengger, and Brehm[8] state that the American and

[5] 'Contributions to the Theory of Natural Selection,' 1870, p. 212.
[6] For the evidence on this head, see Mr. J. Traherne Moggridge's most interesting work, 'Harvesting Ants and Trap-door Spiders,' 1873, pp. 126, 128.
[7] 'Recherches sur les Mœurs des Fourmis,' 1810, p. 173.
[8] All the following statements, given on the authority of these two naturalists, are taken from Rengger's 'Naturgesch. der Säugethiere von Paraguay,' 1830, s. 41-57, and from Brehm's 'Thierleben', B. i. s. 10-87.

African monkeys which they kept tame, certainly revenged themselves. Sir Andrew Smith, a zoologist whose scrupulous accuracy was known to many persons, told me the following story of which he was himself an eye-witness; at the Cape of Good Hope an officer had often plagued a certain baboon, and the animal, seeing him approaching one Sunday for parade, poured water into a hole and hastily made some thick mud, which he skilfully dashed over the officer as he passed by, to the amusement of many bystanders. For long afterwards the baboon rejoiced and triumphed whenever he saw his victim.

The love of a dog for his master is notorious; as an old writer quaintly says,[9] "A dog is the only thing on this earth that luvs you more than he luvs himself."

In the agony of death a dog has been known to caress his master, and every one has heard of the dog suffering under vivisection, who licked the hand of the operator; this man, unless the operation was fully justified by an increase of our knowledge, or unless he had a heart of stone, must have felt remorse to the last hour of his life.

As Whewell[10] has well asked, "who that reads the touching instances of maternal affection, related so often of the women of all nations, and of the females of all animals, can doubt that the principle of action is the same in the two cases?" We see maternal affection exhibited in the most trifling details; thus Rengger observed an American monkey (a Cebus) carefully driving away the flies which plagued her infant; and Duvaucel saw a Hylobates washing the faces of her young ones in a stream. So intense is the grief of female monkeys for the loss of their young, that it invariably caused the death of certain kinds kept under confinement by Brehm in N. Africa. Orphan monkeys were always adopted and carefully guarded by the other monkeys, both males and females. One female baboon had so capacious a heart that she not only adopted young monkeys of other species, but stole young dogs and cats, which she continually carried about. Her kindness, however, did not go so far as to share her food with her adopted offspring, at which Brehm was surprised, as his monkeys always divided everything quite fairly with their own young ones. An adopted kitten scratched this affectionate baboon, who certainly had a fine intellect, for she was much astonished at being scratched, and immediately examined the kitten's feet, and without more ado bit off the claws.[11] In the Zoological Gardens, I heard from the keeper that an old baboon (*C. chacma*) had adopted a Rhesus monkey; but when a young drill and mandrill were placed in the cage, she seemed to perceive that these monkeys, though distinct species, were her nearer relatives, for she at once rejected the Rhesus and adopted both of them. The young

[9] Quoted by Dr. Lauder Lindsay, in his 'Physiology of Mind in the Lower Animals;' 'Journal of Mental Science,' April 1871, p. 38.

[10] 'Bridgewater Treatise,' p. 263.

[11] A critic, without any grounds ('Quarterly Review,' July, 1871, p. 72), disputes the possibility of this act as described by Brehm, for the sake of discrediting my work. Therefore I tried, and found that I could readily seize with my own teeth the sharp little claws of a kitten nearly five weeks old.

Rhesus, as I saw, was greatly discontented at being thus rejected, and it would, like a naughty child, annoy and attack the young drill and mandrill whenever it could do so with safety; this conduct exciting great indignation in the old baboon. Monkeys will also, according to Brehm, defend their master when attacked by any one, as well as dogs to whom they are attached, from the attacks of other dogs. But we here trench on the subjects of sympathy and fidelity, to which I shall recur. Some of Brehm's monkeys took much delight in teasing a certain old dog whom they disliked, as well as other animals, in various ingenious ways.

Most of the more complex emotions are common to the higher animals and ourselves. Every one has seen how jealous a dog is of his master's affection, if lavished on any other creature; and I have observed the same fact with monkeys. This shews that animals not only love, but have desire to be loved. Animals manifestly feel emulation. They love approbation or praise; and a dog carrying a basket for his master exhibits in a high degree self-complacency or pride. There can, I think, be no doubt that a dog feels shame, as distinct from fear, and something very like modesty when begging too often for food. A great dog scorns the snarling of a little dog, and this may be called magnanimity. Several observers have stated that monkeys certainly dislike being laughed at; and they sometimes invent imaginary offences. In the Zoological Gardens I saw a baboon who always got into a furious rage when his keeper took out a letter or book and read it aloud to him; and his rage was so violent that, as I witnessed on one occasion, he bit his own leg till the blood flowed. Dogs shew what may be fairly called a sense of humour, as distinct from mere play; if a bit of stick or other such object be thrown to one, he will often carry it away for a short distance; and then squatting down with it on the ground close before him, will wait until his master comes quite close to take it away. The dog will then seize it and rush away in triumph, repeating the same manœuvre, and evidently enjoying the practical joke.

We will now turn to the more intellectual emotions and faculties, which are very important, as forming the basis for the development of the higher mental powers. Animals manifestly enjoy excitement, and suffer from ennui, as may be seen with dogs, and, according to Rengger, with monkeys. All animals feel *Wonder,* and many exhibit *Curiosity.* They sometimes suffer from this latter quality, as when the hunter plays antics and thus attracts them; I have witnessed this with deer, and so it is with the wary chamois, and with some kinds of wild-ducks. Brehm gives a curious account of the instinctive dread, which his monkeys exhibited, for snakes; but their curiosity was so great that they could not desist from occasionally satiating their horror in a most human fashion, by lifting up the lid of the box in which the snakes were kept. I was so much surprised at this account, that I took a stuffed and coiled-up snake into the monkey-house at the Zoological Gardens, and the excitement thus caused was one of the most curious spectacles which I ever beheld. Three species of Cercopithecus were the most alarmed; they dashed about their cages, and uttered sharp signal cries of danger, which were understood by the other monkeys. A few young monkeys and one old Anubis baboon alone took no notice of the snake. I then placed the stuffed specimen on the ground in one of the larger compartments. After a time all the monkeys collected round it in a large circle, and staring intently, presented a most ludicrous appearance. They became extremely nervous; so that when a wooden ball, with which they were familiar as a plaything, was accident- ally moved in the straw, under which it was partly hidden, they all in- stantly started away. These monkeys behaved very differently when a dead fish, a mouse,[12] a living turtle, and other new objects were placed in their cages; for though at first frightened, they soon approached, handled and examined them. I then placed a live snake in a paper bag, with the mouth loosely closed, in one of the larger compartments. One of the mon- keys immediately approached, cautiously opened the bag a little, peeped in, and instantly dashed away. Then I witnessed what Brehm has de- scribed, for monkey after monkey, with head raised high and turned on one side, could not resist taking a momentary peep into the upright bag, at the dreadful object lying quietly at the bottom. It would almost appear as if monkeys had some notion of zoological affinities, for those kept by Brehm exhibited a strange, though mistaken, instinctive dread of inno- cent lizards and frogs. An orang, also, has been known to be much alarmed at the first sight of a turtle.[13]

The principle of *Imitation* is strong in man, and especially, as I have myself observed, with savages. In certain morbid states of the brain this tendency is exaggerated to an extraordinary degree: some hemiplegic pa- tients and others, at the commencement of inflammatory softening of the brain, unconsciously imitate every word which is uttered, whether in their own or in a foreign language, and every gesture or action which is performed near them.[14] Desor[15] has remarked that no animal voluntarily imitates an action performed by man, until in the ascending scale we come to monkeys, which are well known to be ridiculous mockers. Ani- mals, however, sometimes imitate each other's actions: thus two species of wolves, which had been reared by dogs, learned to bark, as does some- times the jackal,[16] but whether this can be called voluntary imitation is another question. Birds imitate the songs of their parents, and sometimes of other birds; and parrots are notorious imitators of any sound which they often hear. Dureau de la Malle gives an account[17] of a dog reared by a cat, who learnt to imitate the well-known action of a cat licking her paws, and thus washing her ears and face; this was also witnessed by the celebrated naturalist Audouin. I have received several confirmatory ac- counts; in one of these, a dog had not been suckled by a cat, but had been brought up with one, together with kittens, and had thus acquired the

---

[12] I have given a short account of their behaviour on this occasion in my 'Expres- sion of the Emotions,' p. 43.
[13] W. C. L. Martin, 'Nat. Hist. of Mammalia,' 1841, p. 405.
[14] Dr. Bateman 'On Aphasia,' 1870, p. 110.
[15] Quoted by Vogt, 'Mémoire sur les Microcéphales,' 1867, p. 168.
[16] 'The Variation of Animals and Plants under Domestication,' vol. i. p. 27.
[17] 'Annales des Sc. Nat.' (1st Series), tom. xxii. p. 397.

above habit, which he ever afterwards practised during his life of thirteen years. Dureau de la Malle's dog likewise learnt from the kittens to play with a ball by rolling it about with his fore paws, and springing on it. A correspondent assures me that a cat in his house used to put her paws into jugs of milk having too narrow a mouth for her head. A kitten of this cat soon learned the same trick, and practised it ever afterwards, whenever there was an opportunity.

The parents of many animals, trusting to the principle of imitation in their young, and more especially to their instinctive or inherited tendencies, may be said to educate them. We see this when a cat brings a live mouse to her kittens; and Dureau de la Malle has given a curious account (in the paper above quoted) of his observations on hawks which taught their young dexterity, as well as judgment of distances, by first dropping through the air dead mice and sparrows, which the young generally failed to catch, and then bringing them live birds and letting them loose.

Hardly any faculty is more important for the intellectual progress of man than *Attention*. Animals clearly manifest this power, as when a cat watches by a hole and prepares to spring on its prey. Wild animals sometimes become so absorbed when thus engaged, that they may be easily approached. Mr. Bartlett has given me a curious proof how variable this faculty is in monkeys. A man who trains monkeys to act in plays, used to purchase common kinds from the Zoological Society at the price of five pounds for each; but he offered to give double the price, if he might keep three or four of them for a few days, in order to select one. When asked how he could possibly learn so soon, whether a particular monkey would turn out a good actor, he answered that it all depended on their power of attention. If when he was talking and explaining anything to a monkey, its attention was easily distracted, as by a fly on the wall or other trifling object, the case was hopeless. If he tried by punishment to make an inattentive monkey act, it turned sulky. On the other hand, a monkey which carefully attended to him could always be trained.

It is almost superfluous to state that animals have excellent *Memories* for persons and places. A baboon at the Cape of Good Hope, as I have been informed by Sir Andrew Smith, recognised him with joy after an absence of nine months. I had a dog who was savage and averse to all strangers, and I purposely tried his memory after an absence of five years and two days. I went near the stable where he lived, and shouted to him in my old manner; he shewed no joy, but instantly followed me out walking, and obeyed me, exactly as if I had parted with him only half an hour before. A train of old associations, dormant during five years, had thus been instantaneously awakened in his mind. Even ants, as P. Huber[18] has clearly shewn, recognised their fellow-ants belonging to the same community after a separation of four months. Animals can certainly by some means judge of the intervals of time between recurrent events.

The *Imagination* is one of the highest prerogatives of man. By this fac-

18 'Les Mœurs des Fourmis,' 1810, p. 150.

ulty he unites former images and ideas, independently of the will, and thus creates brilliant and novel results. A poet, as Jean Paul Richter remarks,[19] "who must reflect whether he shall make a character say yes or no—to the devil with him; he is only a stupid corpse." Dreaming gives us the best notion of this power; as Jean Paul again says, "The dream is an involuntary art of poetry." The value of the products of our imagination depends of course on the number, accuracy, and clearness of our impressions, on our judgment and taste in selecting or rejecting the involuntary combinations, and to a certain extent on our power of voluntarily combining them. As dogs, cats, horses, and probably all the higher animals, even birds[20] have vivid dreams, and this is shewn by their movements and the sounds uttered, we must admit that they possess some power of imagination. There must be something special, which causes dogs to howl in the night, and especially during moonlight, in that remarkable and melancholy manner called baying. All dogs do not do so; and, according to Houzeau,[21] they do not then look at the moon, but at some fixed point near the horizon. Houzeau thinks that their imaginations are disturbed by the vague outlines of the surrounding objects, and conjure up before them fantastic images: if this be so, their feelings may almost be called superstitious.

Of all the faculties of the human mind, it will, I presume, be admitted that *Reason* stands at the summit. Only a few persons now dispute that animals possess some power of reasoning. Animals may constantly be seen to pause, deliberate, and resolve. It is a significant fact, that the more the habits of any particular animal are studied by a naturalist, the more he attributes to reason and the less to unlearnt instincts.[22] In future chapters we shall see that some animals extremely low in the scale apparently display a certain amount of reason. No doubt it is often difficult to distinguish between the power of reason and that of instinct. For instance, Dr. Hayes, in his work on 'The Open Polar Sea,' repeatedly remarks that his dogs, instead of continuing to draw the sledges in a compact body, diverged and separated when they came to thin ice, so that their weight might be more evenly distributed. This was often the first warning which the travellers received that the ice was becoming thin and dangerous. Now, did the dogs act thus from the experience of each individual, or from the example of the older and wiser dogs, or from an inherited habit, that is from instinct? This instinct, may possibly have arisen since the time, long ago, when dogs were first employed by the natives in drawing their sledges; or the Arctic wolves, the parent-stock of the Esquimaux dog, may have acquired an instinct impelling them not to attack their prey in a close pack, when on thin ice.

[19] Quoted in Dr. Maudsley's 'Physiology and Pathology of Mind,' 1868, pp. 19, 220.
[20] Dr. Jerdon, 'Birds of India,' vol. i. 1862, p. xxi. Houzeau says that his parokeets and canary-birds dreamt: 'Facultés Mentales,' tom. ii. p. 136.
[21] 'Facultés Mentales des Animaux,' 1872, tom. ii. p. 181.
[22] Mr. L. H. Morgan's work on 'The American Beaver,' 1868, offers a good illustration of this remark. I cannot help thinking, however, that he goes too far in underrating the power of instinct.

We can only judge by the circumstances under which actions are performed, whether they are due to instinct, or to reason, or to the mere association of ideas: this latter principle, however, is intimately connected with reason. A curious case has been given by Prof. Möbius,[23] of a pike, separated by a plate of glass from an adjoining aquarium stocked with fish, and who often dashed himself with such violence against the glass in trying to catch the other fishes, that he was sometimes completely stunned. The pike went on thus for three months, but at last learnt caution, and ceased to do so. The plate of glass was then removed, but the pike would not attack these particular fishes, though he would devour others which were afterwards introduced; so strongly was the idea of a violent shock associated in his feeble mind with the attempt on his former neighbours. If a savage, who had never seen a large plate-glass window, were to dash himself even once against it, he would for a long time afterwards associate a shock with a window-frame; but very differently from the pike, he would probably reflect on the nature of the impediment, and be cautious under analogous circumstances. Now with monkeys, as we shall presently see, a painful or merely a disagreeable impression, from an action once performed, is sometimes sufficient to prevent the animal from repeating it. If we attribute this difference between the monkey and the pike solely to the association of ideas being so much stronger and more persistent in the one than the other, though the pike often received much the more severe injury, can we maintain in the case of man that a similar difference implies the possession of a fundamentally different mind?

Houzeau relates[24] that, whilst crossing a wide and arid plain in Texas, his two dogs suffered greatly from thirst, and that between thirty and forty times they rushed down the hollows to search for water. These hollows were not valleys, and there were no trees in them, or any other difference in the vegetation, and as they were absolutely dry there could have been no smell of damp earth. The dogs behaved as if they knew that a dip in the ground offered them the best chance of finding water, and Houzeau has often witnessed the same behaviour in other animals.

I have seen, as I daresay have others, that when a small object is thrown on the ground beyond the reach of one of the elephants in the Zoological Gardens, he blows through his trunk on the ground beyond the object, so that the current reflected on all sides may drive the object within his reach. Again a well-known ethnologist, Mr. Westropp, informs me that he observed in Vienna a bear deliberately making with his paw a current in some water, which was close to the bars of his cage, so as to draw a piece of floating bread within his reach. These actions of the elephant and bear can hardly be attributed to instinct or inherited habit, as they would be of little use to an animal in a state of nature. Now, what is the difference between such actions, when performed by an uncultivated man, and by one of the higher animals?

The savage and the dog have often found water at a low level, and the

[23] 'Die Bewegungen der Thiere,' &c., 1873, p. 11.
[24] 'Facultés Mentales des Animaux,' 1872, tom. ii. p. 265.

coincidence under such circumstances has become associated in their minds. A cultivated man would perhaps make some general proposition on the subject; but from all that we know of savages it is extremely doubtful whether they would do so, and a dog certainly would not. But a savage, as well as a dog, would search in the same way, though frequently disappointed; and in both it seems to be equally an act of reason, whether or not any general proposition on the subject is consciously placed before the mind.[25] The same would apply to the elephant and the bear making currents in the air or water. The savage would certainly neither know nor care by what law the desired movements were effected; yet his act would be guided by a rude process of reasoning, as surely as would a philosopher in his longest chain of deductions. There would no doubt be this difference between him and one of the higher animals, that he would take notice of much slighter circumstances and conditions, and would observe any connection between them after much less experience; and this would be of paramount importance. I kept a daily record of the actions of one of my infants, and when he was about eleven months old, and before he could speak a single word, I was continually struck with the greater quickness, with which all sorts of objects and sounds were associated together in his mind, compared with that of the most intelligent dogs I ever knew. But the higher animals differ in exactly the same way in this power of association from those low in the scale, such as the pike, as well as in that of drawing inferences and of observation.

The promptings of reason, after very short experience, are well shewn by the following actions of American monkeys, which stand low in their order. Rengger, a most careful observer, states that when he first gave eggs to his monkeys in Paraguay, they smashed them, and thus lost much of their contents; afterwards they gently hit one end against some hard body, and picked off the bits of shell with their fingers. After cutting themselves only *once* with any sharp tool, they would not touch it again, or would handle it with the greatest caution. Lumps of sugar were often given them wrapped up in paper; and Rengger sometimes put a live wasp in the paper, so that in hastily unfolding it they got stung; after this had *once* happened, they always first held the packet to their ears to detect any movement within.[26]

The following cases relate to dogs. Mr. Colquhoun [27] winged two wild-ducks, which fell on the further side of a stream; his retriever tried to bring over both at once, but could not succeed; she then, though never before known to ruffle a feather, deliberately killed one, brought over the other, and returned for the dead bird. Col. Hutchinson relates

---

[25] Prof. Huxley has analysed with admirable clearness the mental steps by which a man, as well as a dog, arrives at a conclusion in a case analogous to that given in my text. See his article, 'Mr. Darwin's Critics,' in the 'Contemporary Review,' Nov. 1871, p. 462, and in his 'Critiques and Essays,' 1873, p. 279.

[26] Mr. Belt, in his most interesting work, 'The Naturalist in Nicaragua,' 1874 (p. 119), likewise describes various actions of a tamed Cebus, which, I think, clearly shew that this animal possessed some reasoning power.

[27] 'The Moor and the Loch,' p. 45. Col. Hutchinson on 'Dog Breaking,' 1850, p. 46.

that two partridges were shot at once, one being killed, the other wounded; the latter ran away, and was caught by the retriever, who on her return came across the dead bird; "she stopped, evidently greatly puzzled, and after one or two trials, finding she could not take it up without permitting the escape of the winged bird, she considered a moment, then deliberately murdered it by giving it a severe crunch, and afterwards brought away both together. This was the only known instance of her ever having wilfully injured any game." Here we have reason though not quite perfect, for the retriever might have brought the wounded bird first and then returned for the dead one, as in the case of the two wild-ducks. I give the above cases, as resting on the evidence of two independent witnesses, and because in both instances the retrievers, after deliberation, broke through a habit which is inherited by them (that of not killing the game retrieved), and because they shew how strong their reasoning faculty must have been to overcome a fixed habit.

I will conclude by quoting a remark by the illustrious Humboldt.[28] "The muleteers in S. America say, 'I will not give you the mule whose step is easiest, but *la mas racional*,—the one that reasons best;' " and as he adds, "this popular expression, dictated by long experience, combats the system of animated machines, better perhaps than all the arguments of speculative philosophy." Nevertheless some writers even yet deny that the higher animals possess a trace of reason; and they endeavor to explain away, by what appears to be mere verbiage,[29] all such facts as those above given.

It has, I think, now been shewn that man and the higher animals, especially the Primates, have some few instincts in common. All have the same senses, intuitions, and sensations,—similar passions, affections, and emotions, even the more complex ones, such as jealousy, suspicion, emulation, gratitude, and magnanimity; they practise deceit and are revengeful; they are sometimes susceptible to ridicule, and even have a sense of humour; they feel wonder and curiosity; they possess the same faculties of imitation, attention, deliberation, choice, memory, imagination, the association of ideas, and reason, though in very different degrees. The individuals of the same species graduate in intellect from absolute imbecility to high excellence. They are also liable to insanity, though far less often than in the case of man.[30] Nevertheless, many authors have insisted that man is divided by an insuperable barrier from all the lower animals

[28] 'Personal Narrative,' Eng. translat., vol. iii. p. 106.

[29] I am glad to find that so acute a reasoner as Mr. Leslie Stephen ('Darwinism and Divinity, Essays on Free-thinking,' 1873, p. 80), in speaking of the supposed impassable barrier between the minds of man and the lower animals, says, "The distinctions, indeed, which have been drawn, seem to us to rest upon no better foundation than a great many other metaphysical distinctions; that is, the assumption that because you can give two things different names, they must therefore have different natures. It is difficult to understand how anybody who has ever kept a dog, or seen an elephant, can have any doubt as to an animal's power of performing the essential processes of reasoning."

[30] See 'Madness in Animals,' by Dr. W. Lauder Lindsay, in 'Journal of Mental Science,' July 1871.

in his mental faculties. I formerly made a collection of above a score of such aphorisms, but they are almost worthless, as their wide difference and number prove the difficulty, if not the impossibility, of the attempt. It has been asserted that man alone is capable of progressive improvement; that he alone makes use of tools or fire, domesticates other animals, or possesses property; that no animal has the power of abstraction, or of forming general concepts, is self-conscious and comprehends itself; that no animal employs language; that man alone has a sense of beauty, is liable to caprice, has the feeling of gratitude, mystery, &c.; believes in God, or is endowed with a conscience. I will hazard a few remarks on the more important and interesting of these points.

Archbishop Sumner formerly maintained[31] that man alone is capable of progressive improvement. That he is capable of incomparably greater and more rapid improvement than is any other animal, admits of no dispute; and this is mainly due to his power of speaking and handing down his acquired knowledge. With animals, looking first to the individual, every one who has had any experience in setting traps, knows that young animals can be caught much more easily than old ones; and they can be much more easily approached by an enemy. Even with respect to old animals, it is impossible to catch many in the same place and in the same kind of trap, or to destroy them by the same kind of poison; yet it is improbable that all should have partaken of the poison, and impossible that all should have been caught in a trap. They must learn caution by seeing their brethren caught or poisoned. In North America, where the fur-bearing animals have long been pursued, they exhibit, according to the unanimous testimony of all observers, an almost incredible amount of sagacity, caution and cunning; but trapping has been there so long carried on, that inheritance may possibly have come into play. I have received several accounts that when telegraphs are first set up in any district, many birds kill themselves by flying against the wires, but that in the course of a very few years they learn to avoid this danger, by seeing, as it would appear, their comrades killed.[32]

If we look to successive generations, or to the race, there is no doubt that birds and other animals gradually both acquire and lose caution in relation to man or other enemies;[33] and this caution is certainly in chief part an inherited habit or instinct, but in part the result of individual experience. A good observer, Leroy,[34] states, that in districts where foxes are much hunted, the young, on first leaving their burrows, are incontestably much more wary than the old ones in districts where they are not much disturbed.

Our domestic dogs are descended from wolves and jackals,[35] and

[31] Quoted by Sir C. Lyell, 'Antiquity of Man,' p. 497.

[32] For additional evidence, with details, see M. Houzeau, 'Les Facultés Mentales,' tom. ii. 1872, p. 147.

[33] See, with respect to birds on oceanic islands, my 'Journal of Researches during the voyage of the "Beagle,"' 1845, p. 398. 'Origin of Species,' this ed. p. 305.

[34] 'Lettres Phil. sur l'Intelligence des Animaux,' nouvelle édit. 1802, p. 86.

[35] See the evidence on this head in chap. i. vol. i. 'On the Variation of Animals and Plants under Domestication.'

though they may not have gained in cunning, and may have lost in wariness and suspicion, yet they have progressed in certain moral qualities, such as in affection, trust-worthiness, temper, and probably in general intelligence. The common rat has conquered and beaten several other species throughout Europe, in parts of North America, New Zealand, and recently in Formosa, as well as on the mainland of China. Mr. Swinhoe,[36] who describes these two latter cases, attributes the victory of the common rat over the large *Mus coninga* to its superior cunning; and this latter quality may probably be attributed to the habitual exercise of all its faculties in avoiding extirpation by man, as well as to nearly all the less cunning or weak-minded rats having been continuously destroyed by him. It is, however, possible that the success of the common rat may be due to its having possessed greater cunning than its fellow-species, before it became associated with man. To maintain, independently of any direct evidence, that no animal during the course of ages has progressed in intellect or other mental faculties, is to beg the question of the evolution of species. We have seen that, according to Lartet, existing mammals belonging to several orders have larger brains than their ancient tertiary prototypes.

It has often been said that no animal uses any tool; but the chimpanzee in a state of nature cracks a native fruit, somewhat like a walnut, with a stone.[37] Rengger[38] easily taught an American monkey thus to break open hard palm-nuts; and afterwards of its own accord, it used stones to open other kinds of nuts, as well as boxes. It thus also removed the soft rind of fruit that had a disagreeable flavour. Another monkey was taught to open the lid of a large box with a stick, and afterwards it used the stick as a lever to move heavy bodies; and I have myself seen a young orang put a stick into a crevice, slip his hand to the other end, and use it in the proper manner as a lever. The tamed elephants in India are well known to break off branches of trees and use them to drive away the flies; and this same act has been observed in an elephant in a state of nature.[39] I have seen a young orang, when she thought she was going to be whipped, cover and protect herself with a blanket or straw. In these several cases stones and sticks were employed as implements; but they are likewise used as weapons. Brehm[40] states, on the authority of the well-known traveller Schimper, that in Abyssinia when the baboons belonging to one species (*C. gelada*) descend in troops from the mountains to plunder the fields, they sometimes encounter troops of another species (*C. hamadryas*), and then a fight ensues. The Geladas roll down great stones, which the Hamadryas try to avoid, and then both species, making a great uproar, rush furiously against each other. Brehm, when, accompanying the Duke of Coburg-Gotha, aided in an attack with firearms on a troop of baboons in the pass of Mensa in Abyssinia. The ba-

[36] 'Proc. Zoolog. Soc.' 1864, p. 186.
[37] Savage and Wyman in 'Boston Journal of Nat. Hist.' vol. iv. 1843–44, p. 383.
[38] 'Saugethiere von Paraguay,' 1830, s. 51–56.
[39] The 'Indian Field,' March 4, 1871.
[40] 'Thierleben,' B. i. s. 79, 82.

boons in return rolled so many stones down the mountain, some as large as a man's head, that the attackers had to beat a hasty retreat; and the pass was actually closed for a time against the caravan. It deserves notice that these baboons thus acted in concert. Mr. Wallace[41] on three occasions saw female orangs, accompanied by their young, "breaking off branches and the great spiny fruit of the Durian tree, with every appearance of rage; causing such a shower of missiles as effectually kept us from approaching too near the tree." As I have repeatedly seen, a chimpanzee will throw any object at hand at a person who offends him; and the before-mentioned baboon at the Cape of Good Hope prepared mud for the purpose.

In the Zoological Gardens, a monkey, which had weak teeth, used to break open nuts with a stone; and I was assured by the keepers that after using the stone, he hid it in the straw, and would not let any other monkey touch it. Here, then, we have the idea of property; but this idea is common to every dog with a bone, and to most or all birds with their nests.

The Duke of Argyll[42] remarks, that the fashioning of an implement for a special purpose is absolutely peculiar to man; and he considers that this forms an immeasurable gulf between him and the brutes. This is no doubt a very important distinction; but there appears to me much truth in Sir J. Lubbock's suggestion,[43] that when primeval man first used flint-stones for any purpose, he would have accidentally splintered them, and would then have used the sharp fragments. From this step it would be a small one to break the flints on purpose, and not a very wide step to fashion them rudely. This latter advance, however, may have taken long ages, if we may judge by the immense interval of time which elapsed before the men of the neolithic period took to grinding and polishing their stone tools. In breaking the flints, as Sir J. Lubbock likewise remarks, sparks would have been emitted, and in grinding them heat would have been evolved: thus the two usual methods of "obtaining fire may have originated." The nature of fire would have been known in the many volcanic regions where lava occasionally flows through forests. The anthropomorphous apes, guided probably by instinct, build for themselves temporary platforms; but as many instincts are largely controlled by reason, the simpler ones, such as this of building a platform, might readily pass into a voluntary and conscious act. The orang is known to cover itself at night with the leaves of the Pandanus; and Brehm states that one of his baboons used to protect itself from the heat of the sun by throwing a straw-mat over its head. In these several habits, we probably see the first steps towards some of the simpler arts, such as rude architecture and dress, as they arose amongst the early progenitors of man.

Abstraction, General Conceptions, Self-consciousness, Mental Individuality.—It would be very difficult for any one with even much more

[41] 'The Malay Archipelago,' vol. i. 1869, p. 87.
[42] 'Primeval Man,' 1869, pp. 145, 147.
[43] 'Prehistoric Times,' 1865, p. 473, &c.

knowledge than I possess, to determine how far animals exhibit any traces of these high mental powers. This difficulty arises from the impossibility of judging what passes through the mind of an animal; and again, the fact that writers differ to a great extent in the meaning which they attribute to the above terms, causes a further difficulty. If one may judge from various articles which have been published lately, the greatest stress seems to be laid on the supposed entire absence in animals of the power of abstraction, or of forming general concepts. But when a dog sees another dog at a distance, it is often clear that he perceives that it is a dog in the abstract; for when he gets nearer his whole manner suddenly changes, if the other dog be a friend. A recent writer remarks, that in all such cases it is a pure assumption to assert that the mental act is not essentially of the same nature in the animal as in man. If either refers what he perceives with his senses to a mental concept, then so do both.[44] When I say to my terrier, in an eager voice (and I have made the trial many times), "Hi, hi, where is it?" she at once takes it as a sign that something is to be hunted, and generally first looks quickly all around, and then rushes into the nearest thicket, to scent for any game, but finding nothing, she looks up into any neighbouring tree for a squirrel. Now do not these actions clearly shew that she had in her mind a general idea or concept that some animal is to be discovered and hunted?

It may be freely admitted that no animal is self-conscious, if by this term it is implied, that he reflects on such points, as whence he comes or whither he will go, or what is life and death, and so forth. But how can we feel sure that an old dog with an excellent memory and some power of imagination, as shewn by his dreams, never reflects on his past pleasures or pains in the chase? And this would be a form of self-consciousness. On the other hand, as Büchner [45] has remarked, how little can the hard-worked wife of a degraded Australian savage, who uses very few abstract words, and cannot count above four, exert her self-consciousness, or reflect on the nature of her own existence. It is generally admitted, that the higher animals possess memory, attention, association, and even some imagination and reason. If these powers, which differ much in different animals, are capable of improvement, there seems no great improbability in more complex faculties, such as the higher forms of abstraction, and self-consciousness, &c., having been evolved through the development and combination of the simpler ones. It has been urged against the views here maintained that it is impossible to say at what point in the ascending scale animals become capable of abstraction, &c.; but who can say at what age this occurs in our young children? We see at least that such powers are developed in children by imperceptible degrees.

That animals retain their mental individuality is unquestionable. When my voice awakened a train of old associations in the mind of the before-mentioned dog, he must have retained his mental individuality,

---

[44] Mr. Hookham, in a letter to Prof. Max Müller, in the 'Birmingham News,' May 1873.
[45] 'Conférences sur la Théorie Darwinienne,' French translat. 1869, p. 132.

although every atom of his brain had probably undergone change more than once during the interval of five years. This dog might have brought forward the argument lately advanced to crush all evolutionists, and said, "I abide amid all mental moods and all material changes. . . . The teaching that atoms leave their impressions as legacies to other atoms falling into the places they have vacated is contradictory of the utterance of consciousness, and is therefore false; but it is the teaching necessitated by evolutionism, consequently the hypothesis is a false one." [46]

Language.—This faculty has justly been considered as one of the chief distinctions between man and the lower animals. But man, as a highly competent judge, Archbishop Whately remarks, "is not the only animal that can make use of language to express what is passing in his mind, and can understand, more or less, what is so expressed by another." [47] In Paraguay the *Cebus azaræ* when excited utters at least six distinct sounds, which excite in other monkeys similar emotions.[48] The movements of the features and gestures of monkeys are understood by us, and they partly understand ours, as Rengger and others declare. It is a more remarkable fact that the dog, since being domesticated, has learnt to bark [49] in at least four or five distinct tones. Although barking is a new art, no doubt the wild parent-species of the dog expressed their feelings by cries of various kinds. With the domesticated dog we have the bark of eagerness, as in the chase; that of anger, as well as growling; the yelp or howl of despair, as when shut up; the baying at night; the bark of joy, as when starting on a walk with his master; and the very distinct one of demand or supplication, as when wishing for a door or window to be opened. According to Houzeau, who paid particular attention to the subject, the domestic fowl utters at least a dozen significant sounds.[50]

The habitual use of articulate language is, however, peculiar to man; but he uses, in common with the lower animals, inarticulate cries to express his meaning, aided by gestures and the movements of the muscles of the face.[51] This especially holds good with the more simple and vivid feelings, which are but little connected with our higher intelligence. Our cries of pain, fear, surprise, anger, together with their appropriate actions, and the murmur of a mother to her beloved child are more expressive than any words. That which distinguishes man from the lower animals is not the understanding of articulate sounds, for, as every one knows, dogs understand many words and sentences. In this respect they are at the same stage of development as infants, between the ages of ten and twelve months, who understand many words and short sentences, but cannot yet utter a single word. It is not the mere articulation which is our distinguishing character, for parrots and other birds possess this

[46] The Rev. Dr. J. M'Cann, 'Anti-Darwinism,' 1869, p. 13.
[47] Quoted in 'Anthropological Review,' 1864, p. 158.
[48] Rengger, ibid. s. 45.
[49] See my 'Variation of Animals and Plants under Domestication,' vol. i. p. 27.
[50] 'Facultés Mentales des Animaux,' tom. ii. 1872, p. 346–349.
[51] See a discussion on this subject in Mr. E. B. Tylor's very interesting work, 'Researches into the Early History of Mankind,' 1865, chaps. ii. to iv.

power. Nor is it the mere capacity of connecting definite sounds with definite ideas; for it is certain that some parrots, which have been taught to speak, connect unerringly words with things, and persons with events.[52] The lower animals differ from man solely in his almost infinitely larger power of associating together the most diversified sounds and ideas; and this obviously depends on the high development of his mental powers.

As Horne Tooke, one of the founders of the noble science of philology, observes, language is an art, like brewing or baking; but writing would have been a better simile. It certainly is not a true instinct, for every language has to be learnt. It differs, however, widely from all ordinary arts, for man has an instinctive tendency to speak, as we see in the babble of our young children; whilst no child has an instinctive tendency to brew, bake, or write. Moreover, no philologist now supposes that any language has been deliberately invented; it has been slowly and unconsciously developed by many steps.[53] The sounds uttered by birds offer in several respects the nearest analogy to language, for all the members of the same species utter the same instinctive cries expressive of their emotions; and all the kinds which sing, exert their power instinctively; but the actual song, and even the call-notes, are learnt from their parents or foster-parents. These sounds, as Daines Barrington[54] has proved, "are no more innate than language is in man." The first attempts to sing "may be compared to the imperfect endeavour in a child to babble." The young males continue practising, or as the bird-catchers say, "recording," for ten or eleven months. Their first essays show hardly a rudiment of the future song; but as they grow older we can perceive what they are aiming at; and at last they are said "to sing their song round." Nestlings which have learnt the song of a distinct species, as with the canary-birds educated in the Tyrol, teach and transmit their new song to their offspring. The slight natural differences of song in the same species inhabit-

---

[52] I have received several detailed accounts to this effect. Admiral Sir B. J. Sulivan, whom I know to be a careful observer, assures me that an African parrot, long kept in his father's house, invariably called certain persons of the household, as well as visitors, by their names. He said "good morning" to every one at breakfast, and "good night" to each as they left the room at night, and never reversed these salutations. To Sir B. J. Sulivan's father, he used to add to the "good morning" a short sentence, which was never once repeated after his father's death. He scolded violently a strange dog which came into the room through the open window; and he scolded another parrot (saying "you naughty polly") which had got out of its cage, and was eating apples on the kitchen table. See also, to the same effect, Houzeau on parrots, 'Facultés Mentales,' tom. ii. p. 309. Dr. A. Moschkau informs me that he knew a starling which never made a mistake in saying in German "good morning" to persons arriving, and "good bye, old fellow," to those departing. I could add several other such cases.

[53] See some good remarks on this head by Prof. Whitney, in his 'Oriental and Linguistic Studies,' 1873, p. 354. He observes that the desire of communication between man is the living force, which, in the development of language, "works both consciously and unconsciously; consciously as regards the immediate end to be attained; unconsciously as regards the further consequences of the act."

[54] Hon. Daines Barrington in 'Philosoph. Transactions,' 1773, p. 262. See also Dureau de la Malle, in 'Ann. des. Sc. Nat.' 3rd series, Zoolog. tom. x. p. 119.

ing different districts may be appositely compared, as Barrington remarks, "to provincial dialects;" and the songs of allied, though distinct species may be compared with the languages of distinct races of man. I have given the foregoing details to shew that an instinctive tendency to acquire an art is not peculiar to man.

With respect to the origin of articulate language, after having read on the one side the highly interesting works of Mr. Hensleigh Wedgwood, the Rev. F. Farrar, and Prof. Schleicher,[55] and the celebrated lectures of Prof. Max Müller on the other side, I cannot doubt that language owes its origin to the imitation and modification of various natural sounds, the voices of other animals, and man's own instinctive cries, aided by signs and gestures. When we treat of sexual selection we shall see that primeval man, or rather some early progenitor of man, probably first used his voice in producing true musical cadences, that is in singing, as do some of the gibbon-apes at the present day; and we may conclude from a widely-spread analogy, that this power would have been especially exerted during the courtship of the sexes,—would have expressed various emotions, such as love, jealousy, triumph,—and would have served as a challenge to rivals. It is, therefore, probable that the imitation of musical cries by articulate sounds may have given rise to words expressive of various complex emotions. The strong tendency in our nearest allies, the monkeys, in microcephalous idiots,[56] and in the barbarous races of mankind, to imitate whatever they hear deserves notice, as bearing on the subject of imitation. Since monkeys certainly understand much that is said to them by man, and when wild, utter signal-cries of danger to their fellows;[57] and since fowls give distinct warnings for danger on the ground, or in the sky from hawks (both, as well as a third cry, intelligible to dogs),[58] may not some unusually wise ape-like animal have imitated the growl of a beast of prey, and thus told his fellow-monkeys the nature of the expected danger? This would have been a first step in the formation of a language.

As the voice was used more and more, the vocal organs would have been strengthened and perfected through the principle of the inherited effects of use; and this would have reacted on the power of speech. But the relation between the continued use of language and the development of the brain, has no doubt been far more important. The mental powers in some early progenitor of man must have been more highly developed than in any existing ape, before even the most imperfect form of speech could have come into use; but we may confidently believe that the con-

---

[55] 'On the Origin of Language,' by H. Wedgwood, 1866. 'Chapters on Language,' by the Rev. F. W. Farrar, 1865. These works are most interesting. See also 'De la Phys. et de Parole,' par Albert Lemoine, 1865, p. 190. The work on this subject, by the late Prof. Aug. Schleicher, has been translated by Dr. Bikkers into English, under the title of 'Darwinism tested by the Science of Language,' 1869.

[56] Vogt, 'Mémoire sur les Microcéphales,' 1867, p. 169. With respect to savages, I have given some facts in my 'Journal of Researches,' &c., 1845, p. 206.

[57] See clear evidence on this head in the two works so often quoted, by Brehm and Rengger.

[58] Houzeau gives a very curious account of his observations on this subject in his 'Facultés Mentales des Animaux,' tom. ii. p. 348.

tinued use and advancement of this power would have reacted on the mind itself, by enabling and encouraging it to carry on long trains of thought. A complex train of thought can no more be carried on without the aid of words, whether spoken or silent, than a long calculation without the use of figures or algebra. It appears, also, that even an ordinary train of thought almost requires, or is greatly facilitated by some form of language, for the dumb, deaf, and blind girl, Laura Bridgman, was observed to use her fingers whilst dreaming.[59] Nevertheless, a long succession of vivid and connected ideas may pass through the mind without the aid of any form of language, as we may infer from the movements of dogs during their dreams. We have, also, seen that animals are able to reason to a certain extent, manifestly without the aid of language. The intimate connection between the brain, as it is now developed in us, and the faculty of speech, is well shewn by those curious cases of brain-disease in which speech is specially affected, as when the power to remember substantives is lost, whilst other words can be correctly used, or where substantives of a certain class, or all except the initial letters of substantives and proper names are forgotten.[60] There is no more improbability in the continued use of the mental and vocal organs leading to inherited changes in their structure and functions, than in the case of hand-writing, which depends partly on the form of the hand and partly on the disposition of the mind; and handwriting is certainly inherited.[61]

Several writers, more especially Prof. Max Müller,[62] have lately insisted that the use of language implies the power of forming general concepts; and that as no animals are supposed to possess this power, an impassable barrier is formed between them and man.[63] With respect to animals, I have already endeavoured to shew that they have this power, at least in a rude and incipient degree. As far as concerns infants of from ten to eleven months old, and deaf-mutes, it seems to me incredible, that they

[59] See remarks on this head by Dr. Maudsley, 'The Physiology and Pathology of Mind,' 2nd edit. 1868, p. 199.

[60] Many curious cases have been recorded. See, for instance, Dr. Bateman 'On Aphasia,' 1870, p. 27, 31, 53, 100, &c. Also, 'Inquiries Concerning the Intellectual Powers,' by Dr. Abercrombie, 1838, p. 150.

[61] 'The Variation of Animals and Plants under Domestication,' vol. ii. p. 6.

[62] Lectures on 'Mr. Darwin's Philosophy of Language,' 1873.

[63] The judgment of a distinguished philologist, such as Prof. Whitney, will have far more weight on this point than anything that I can say. He remarks ('Oriental and Linguistic Studies,' 1873, p. 297), in speaking of Bleek's views: "Because on the grand scale language is the necessary auxiliary of thought, indispensable to the development of the power of thinking, to the distinctness and variety and complexity of cognitions to the full mastery of consciousness; therefore he would fain make thought absolutely impossible without speech, identifying the faculty with its instrument. He might just as reasonably assert that the human hand cannnot act without a tool. With such a doctrine to start from, he cannot stop short of Müller's worst paradoxes, that an infant (in fans, not speaking) is not a human being, and that deaf-mutes do not become possessed of reason until they learn to twist their fingers into imitation of spoken words." Max Müller gives in italics ('Lectures on Mr. Darwin's Philosophy of Language,' 1873, third lecture) the following aphorism: "There is no thought without words, as little as there are words without thought." What a strange definition must here be given to the word thought!

should be able to connect certain sounds with certain general ideas as quickly as they do, unless such ideas were already formed in their minds. The same remark may be extended to the more intelligent animals; as Mr. Leslie Stephen observes,[64] "A dog frames a general concept of cats or sheep, and knows the corresponding words as well as a philosopher. And the capacity to understand is as good a proof of vocal intelligence, though in an inferior degree, as the capacity to speak."

Why the organs now used for speech should have been originally perfected for this purpose, rather than any other organs, it is not difficult to see. Ants have considerable powers of intercommunication by means of their antennæ, as shewn by Huber, who devotes a whole chapter to their language. We might have used our fingers as efficient instruments, for a person with practice can report to a deaf man every word of a speech rapidly delivered at a public meeting; but the loss of our hands, whilst thus employed, would have been a serious inconvenience. As all the higher mammals possess vocal organs, constructed on the same general plan as ours, and used as a means of communication, it was obviously probable that these same organs would be still further developed if the power of communication had to be improved; and this has been effected by the aid of adjoining and well adapted parts, namely the tongue and lips.[65] The fact of the higher apes not using their vocal organs for speech, no doubt depends on their intelligence not having been sufficiently advanced. The possession by them of organs, which with long-continued practice might have been used for speech, although not thus used, is paralleled by the case of many birds which possess organs fitted for singing, though they never sing. Thus, the nightingale and crow have vocal organs similarly constructed, these being used by the former for diversified song, and by the latter only for croaking.[66] If it be asked why apes have not had their intellects developed to the same degree as that of man, general causes only can be assigned in answer, and it is unreasonable to expect any thing more definite, considering our ignorance with respect to the successive stages of development through which each creature has passed.

The formation of different languages and of distinct species, and the proofs that both have been developed through a gradual process, are curiously parallel.[67] But we can trace the formation of many words further back than that of species, for we can perceive how they actually arose from the imitation of various sounds. We find in distinct languages strik-

[64] 'Essays on Free-thinking,' &c., 1873, p. 82.

[65] See some good remarks to this effect by Dr. Maudsley, 'The Physiology and Pathology of Mind,' 1868, p. 199.

[66] Macgillivray, 'Hist. of British Birds,' vol. ii. 1839, p. 29. An excellent observer, Mr. Blackwall, remarks that the magpie learns to pronounce single words, and even short sentences, more readily than almost any other British bird; yet, as he adds, after long and closely investigating its habits, he has never known it, in a state of nature, display any unusual capacity for imitation. 'Researches in Zoology,' 1834, p. 158.

[67] See the very interesting parallelism between the development of species and languages, given by Sir C. Lyell in 'The Geolog. Evidences of the Antiquity of Man,' 1863, chap. xxiii.

ing homologies due to community of descent, and analogies due to a similar process of formation. The manner in which certain letters or sounds change when others change is very like correlated growth. We have in both cases the reduplication of parts, the effects of long-continued use, and so forth. The frequent presence of rudiments, both in languages and in species, is still more remarkable. The letter *m* in the word *am*, means *I;* so that in the expression *I am*, a superfluous and useless rudiment has been retained. In the spelling also of words, letters often remain as the rudiments of ancient forms of pronunciation. Languages, like organic beings, can be classed in groups under groups; and they can be classed either naturally according to descent, or artificially by other characters. Dominant languages and dialects spread widely, and lead to the gradual extinction of other tongues. A language, like a species, when once extinct, never, as Sir C. Lyell remarks, reappears. The same language never has two birth-places. Distinct languages may be crossed or blended together.[68] We see variability in every tongue, and new words are continually cropping up; but as there is a limit to the powers of the memory, single words, like whole languages, gradually become extinct. As Max Müller[69] has well remarked:—"A struggle for life is constantly going on amongst the words and grammatical forms in each language. The better, the shorter, the easier forms are constantly gaining the upper hand, and they owe their success to their own inherent virtue." To these more important causes of the survival of certain words, mere novelty and fashion may be added; for there is in the mind of man a strong love for slight changes in all things. The survival or preservation of certain favoured words in the struggle for existence is natural selection.

The perfectly regular and wonderfully complex construction of the languages of many barbarous nations has often been advanced as a proof, either of the divine origin of these languages, or of the high art and former civilisation of their founders. Thus F. von Schlegel writes: "In those languages which appear to be at the lowest grade of intellectual culture, we frequently observe a very high and elaborate degree of art in their grammatical structure. This is especially the case with the Basque and the Lapponian, and many of the American languages."[70] But it is assuredly an error to speak of any language as an art, in the sense of its having been elaborately and methodically formed. Philologists now admit that conjugations, declensions, &c., originally existed as distinct words, since joined together; and as such words express the most obvious relations between objects and persons, it is not surprising that they should have been used by the men of most races during the earliest ages. With respect to perfection, the following illustration will best shew how easily we may err: a Crinoid sometimes consists of no less than 150,000 pieces of shell,[71] all arranged with perfect symmetry in radiating lines; but a

[68] See remarks to this effect by the Rev. F. W. Farrar, in an interesting article, entitled 'Philology and Darwinism,' in 'Nature,' March 24th, 1870, p. 528.

[69] 'Nature,' January 6th, 1870, p. 257.

[70] Quoted by C. S. Wake, 'Chapters on Man,' 1868, p. 101.

[71] Buckland, 'Bridgewater Treatise,' p. 411.

naturalist does not consider an animal of this kind as more perfect than a bilateral one with comparatively few parts, and with none of these parts alike, excepting on the opposite sides of the body. He justly considers the differentiation and specialisation of organs as the test of perfection. So with languages: the most symmetrical and complex ought not to be ranked above irregular, abbreviated, and bastardised languages, which have borrowed expressive words and useful forms of construction from various conquering, conquered, or immigrant races.

From these few and imperfect remarks I conclude that the extremely complex and regular construction of many barbarous languages, is no proof that they owe their origin to a special act of creation.[72] Nor, as we have seen, does the faculty of articulate speech in itself offer any insuperable objection to the belief that man has been developed from some lower form.

Sense of Beauty.—This sense has been declared to be peculiar to man. I refer here only to the pleasure given by certain colours, forms, and sounds, and which may fairly be called a sense of the beautiful; with cultivated men such sensations are, however, intimately associated with complex ideas and trains of thought. When we behold a male bird elaborately displaying his graceful plumes or splendid colours before the female, whilst other birds, not thus decorated, make no such display, it is impossible to doubt that she admires the beauty of her male partner. As women everywhere deck themselves with these plumes, the beauty of such ornaments cannot be disputed. As we shall see later, the nests of humming-birds, and the playing passages of bower-birds are tastefully ornamented with gaily-coloured objects; and this shews that they must receive some kind of pleasure from the sight of such things. With the great majority of animals, however, the taste for the beautiful is confined, as far as we can judge, to the attractions of the opposite sex. The sweet strains poured forth by many male birds during the season of love, are certainly admired by the females, of which fact evidence will hereafter be given. If female birds had been incapable of appreciating the beautiful colours, the ornaments, and voices of their male partners, all the labour and anxiety exhibited by the latter in displaying their charms before the females would have been thrown away; and this it is impossible to admit. Why certain bright colours should excite pleasure cannot, I presume, be explained, any more than why certain flavours and scents are agreeable; but habit has something to do with the result, for that which is at first unpleasant to our senses, ultimately becomes pleasant, and habits are inherited. With respect to sounds, Helmholtz has explained to a certain extent on physiological principles, why harmonies and certain cadences are agreeable. But besides this, sounds frequently recurring at irregular intervals are highly disagreeable, as every one will admit who has listened at night to the irregular flapping of a rope on board ship. The same principle seems to come into play with vision, as the eye prefers

[72] See some good remarks on the simplification of languages, by Sir. J. Lubbock, 'Origin of Civilisation,' 1870, p. 278.

symmetry or figures with some regular recurrence. Patterns of this kind
are employed by even the lowest savages as ornaments; and they have
been developed through sexual selection for the adornment of some male
animals. Whether we can or not give any reason for the pleasure thus derived from vision and hearing, yet man and many of the lower animals
are alike pleased by the same colours, graceful shading and forms, and
the same sounds.

The taste for the beautiful, at least as far as female beauty is concerned, is not of a special nature in the human mind; for it differs widely
in the different races of man, and is not quite the same even in the different nations of the same race. Judging from the hideous ornaments, and
the equally hideous music admired by most savages, it might be urged
that their æsthetic faculty was not so highly developed as in certain animals, for instance, as in birds. Obviously no animal would be capable of
admiring such scenes as the heavens at night, a beautiful landscape, or
refined music; but such high tastes are acquired through culture, and depend on complex associations; they are not enjoyed by barbarians or by
uneducated persons.

Many of the faculties, which have been of inestimable service to man
for his progressive advancement, such as the powers of the imagination,
wonder, curiosity, an undefined sense of beauty, a tendency to imitation,
and the love of excitement or novelty, could hardly fail to lead to capricious changes of customs and fashions. I have alluded to this point, because a recent writer[73] has oddly fixed on Caprice "as one of the most remarkable and typical differences between savages and brutes." But not
only can we partially understand how it is that man is from various conflicting influences rendered capricious, but that the lower animals are, as
we shall hereafter see, likewise capricious in their affections, aversions,
and sense of beauty. There is also reason to suspect that they love novelty, for its own sake.

Belief in God—Religion.—There is no evidence that man was aboriginally endowed with the ennobling belief in the existence of an Omnipo-
tent God. On the contrary there is ample evidence, derived not from
hasty travellers, but from men who have long resided with savages, that
numerous races have existed, and still exist, who have no idea of one or
more gods, and who have no words in their languages to express such an
idea.[74] The question is of course wholly distinct from that higher one,
whether there exists a Creator and Ruler of the universe; and this has
been answered in the affirmative by some of the highest intellects that
have ever existed.

If, however, we include under the term "religion" the belief in unseen
or spiritual agencies, the case is wholly different; for this belief seems to

---

[73] 'The Spectator,' Dec. 4th, 1869, p. 1430.

[74] See an excellent article on this subject by the Rev. F. W. Farrar, in the 'Anthropological Review,' Aug. 1864, p. ccxvii. For further facts see Sir J. Lubbock, 'Prehistoric Times,' 2nd edit. 1869, p. 564; and especially the chapters on Religion in his
'Origin of Civilisation,' 1870.

be universal with the less civilised races. Nor is it difficult to comprehend how it arose. As soon as the important faculties of the imagination, wonder, and curiosity, together with some power of reasoning, had become partially developed, man would naturally crave to understand what was passing around him, and would have vaguely speculated on his own existence. As Mr. M'Lennan[75] has remarked, "Some explanation of the phenomena of life, a man must feign for himself, and to judge from the universality of it, the simplest hypothesis, and the first to occur to men, seems to have been that natural phenomena are ascribable to the presence in animals, plants, and things, and in the forces of nature, of such spirits prompting to action as men are conscious they themselves possess." It is also probable, as Mr. Tylor has shewn, that dreams may have first given rise to the notion of spirits; for savages do not readily distinguish between subjective and objective impressions. When a savage dreams, the figures which appear before him are believed to have come from a distance, and to stand over him; or "the soul of the dreamer goes out on its travels, and comes home with a remembrance of what it has seen."[76] But until the faculties of imagination, curiosity, reason, &c., had been fairly well developed in the mind of man, his dreams would not have led him to believe in spirits, any more than in the case of a dog.

The tendency in savages to imagine that natural objects and agencies are animated by spiritual or living essences, is perhaps illustrated by a little fact which I once noticed: my dog, a full-grown and very sensible animal, was lying on the lawn during a hot and still day; but at a little distance a slight breeze occasionally moved an open parasol, which would have been wholly disregarded by the dog, had any one stood near it. As it was, every time that the parasol slightly moved, the dog growled fiercely and barked. He must, I think, have reasoned to himself in a rapid and unconscious manner, that movement without any apparent cause indicated the presence of some strange living agent, and that no stranger had a right to be on his territory.

The belief in spiritual agencies would easily pass into the belief in the existence of one or more gods. For savages would naturally attribute to spirits the same passions, the same love of vengeance or simplest form of

[75] 'The Worship of Animals and Plants,' in the 'Fortnightly Review,' Oct. 1, 1869, p. 422.

[76] Tylor, 'Early History of Mankind,' 1865, p. 6. See also the three striking chapters on the Development of Religion, in Lubbock's 'Origin of Civilisation,' 1870. In a like manner Mr. Herbert Spencer, in his ingenious essay in the 'Fortnightly Review' (May 1st, 1870, p. 535), accounts for the earliest forms of religious belief throughout the world, by man being led through dreams, shadows, and other causes, to look at himself as a double essence, corporeal and spiritual. As the spiritual being is supposed to exist after death and to be powerful, it is propitiated by various gifts and ceremonies, and its aid invoked. He then further shews that names or nicknames given from some animal or other object, to the early progenitors or founders of a tribe, are supposed after a long interval to represent the real progenitor of the tribe; and such animal or object is then naturally believed still to exist as a spirit, is held sacred, and worshipped as a god. Nevertheless I cannot but suspect that there is a still earlier and ruder stage, when anything which manifests power or movement is thought to be endowed with some form of life, and with mental faculties analogous to our own.

justice, and the same affections which they themselves feel. The Fuegians appear to be in this respect in an intermediate condition, for when the surgeon on board the "Beagle" shot some young ducklings as specimens, York Minster declared in the most solemn manner, "Oh, Mr. Bynoe, much rain, much snow, blow much;" and this was evidently a retributive punishment for wasting human food. So again he related how, when his brother killed a "wild man," storms long raged, much rain and snow fell. Yet we could never discover that the Fuegians believed in what we should call a God, or practised any religious rites; and Jemmy Button, with justifiable pride, stoutly maintained that there was no devil in his land. This latter assertion is the more remarkable, as with savages the belief in bad spirits is far more common than that in good ones.

The feeling of religious devotion is a highly complex one, consisting of love, complete submission to an exalted and mysterious superior, a strong sense of dependence,[77] fear, reverence, gratitude, hope for the future, and perhaps other elements. No being could experience so complex an emotion until advanced in his intellectual and moral faculties to at least a moderately high level. Nevertheless, we see some distant approach to this state of mind in the deep love of a dog for his master, associated with complete submission, some fear, and perhaps other feelings. The behaviour of a dog when returning to his master after an absence, and, as I may add, of a monkey to his beloved keeper, is widely different from that towards their fellows. In the latter case the transports of joy appear to be somewhat less, and the sense of equality is shewn in every action. Professor Braubach goes so far as to maintain that a dog looks on his master as on a god.[78]

The same high mental faculties which first led man to believe in unseen spiritual agencies, then in fetishism, polytheism, and ultimately in monotheism, would infallibly lead him, as long as his reasoning powers remained poorly developed, to various strange superstitions and customs. Many of these are terrible to think of—such as the sacrifice of human beings to a blood-loving god; the trial of innocent persons by the ordeal of poison or fire; witchcraft, &c.—yet it is well occasionally to reflect on these superstitions, for they shew us what an infinite debt of gratitude we owe to the improvement of our reason, to science, and to our accumulated knowledge. As Sir J. Lubbock[79] has well observed, "it is not too much to say that the horrible dread of unknown evil hangs like a thick cloud over savage life, and embitters every pleasure." These miserable and indirect consequences of our highest faculties may be compared with the incidental and occasional mistakes of the instincts of the lower animals.

[77] See an able article on the 'Physical Elements of Religion,' by Mr. L. Owen Pike, in 'Anthropolog. Review,' April, 1870, p. lxiii.

[78] 'Religion, Moral, &c., der Darwin'schen Art-Lehre,' 1869, s. 53. It is said (Dr. W. Lauder Lindsay, 'Journal of Mental Science,' 1871, p. 43), that Bacon long ago, and the poet Burns, held the same notion.

[79] 'Prehistoric Times,' 2nd edit. p. 571. In this work (p. 571) there will be found an excellent account of the many strange and capricious customs of savages.

CHAPTER IV

*The moral sense—Fundamental proposition—The qualities of social animals—Origin
of sociability—Struggle between opposed instincts—Man a social animal—The
more enduring social instincts conquer other less persistent instincts—The social
virtues alone regarded by savages—The self-regarding virtues acquired at a later
stage of development—The importance of the judgment of the members of the
same community on conduct—Transmission of moral tendencies—Summary*

I FULLY subscribe to the judgment of those writers[1] who maintain that of
all the differences between man and the lower animals, the moral sense
or conscience is by far the most important. This sense, as Mackintosh[2]
remarks, "has a rightful supremacy over every other principle of human
action;" it is summed up in that short but imperious word *ought,* so full
of high significance. It is the most noble of all the attributes of man, leading him without a moment's hesitation to risk his life for that of a fellow-
creature; or after due deliberation, impelled simply by the deep feeling of
right or duty, to sacrifice it in some great cause. Immanuel Kant ex-
claims, "Duty! Wondrous thought, that workest neither by fond insinu-
ation, flattery, nor by any threat, but merely by holding up thy naked
law in the soul, and so extorting for thyself always reverence, if not always obedience; before whom all appetites are dumb, however secretly
they rebel; whence thy original?"[3]

This great question has been discussed by many writers[4] of consummate ability; and my sole excuse for touching on it, is the impossibility
of here passing it over; and because, as far as I know, no one has approached it exclusively from the side of natural history. The investigation
possesses, also, some independent interest, as an attempt to see how far
the study of the lower animals throws light on one of the highest physical
faculties of man.

The following proposition seems to me in a high degree probable—
namely, that any animal whatever, endowed with well-marked social in-

[1] See, for instance, on this subject, Quatrefages, 'Unité de l'Espèce Humaine,' 1861,
p. 21, &c.

[2] 'Dissertation on Ethical Philosophy,' 1837, p. 231, &c.

[3] 'Metaphysics of Ethics,' translated by J. W. Semple, Edinb., 1836, p. 136.

[4] Mr. Bain gives a list ('Mental and Moral Science,' 1868, p. 543-725) of twenty-
six British authors who have written on this subject, and whose names are familiar
to every reader; to these, Mr. Bain's own name, and those of Mr. Lecky, Mr. Shad-
worth Hodgson, Sir J. Lubbock, and others, might be added.

stincts,[5] the parental and filial affections being here included, would inevitably acquire a moral sense or conscience, as soon as its intellectual powers had become as well, or nearly as well developed, as in man. For, *firstly*, the social instincts lead an animal to take pleasure in the society of its fellows, to feel a certain amount of sympathy with them, and to perform various services for them. The services may be of a definite and evidently instinctive nature; or there may be only a wish and readiness, as with most of the higher social animals, to aid their fellows in certain general ways. But these feelings and services are by no means extended to all the individuals of the same species, only to those of the same association. *Secondly*, as soon as the mental faculties had become highly developed, images of all past actions and motives would be incessantly passing through the brain of each individual: and that feeling of dissatisfaction, or even misery, which invariably results, as we shall hereafter see, from any unsatisfied instinct, would arise, as often as it was perceived that the enduring and always present social instinct had yielded to some other instinct, at the time stronger, but neither enduring in its nature, nor leaving behind it a very vivid impression. It is clear that many instinctive desires, such as that of hunger, are in their nature of short duration; and after being satisfied, are not readily or vividly recalled. *Thirdly*, after the power of language had been acquired, and the wishes of the community could be expressed, the common opinion how each member ought to act for the public good, would naturally become in a paramount degree the guide to action. But it should be borne in mind that however great weight we may attribute to public opinion, our regard for the approbation and disapprobation of our fellows depends on sympathy, which, as we shall see, forms an essential part of the social instinct, and is indeed its foundation-stone. *Lastly*, habit in the individual would ultimately play a very important part in guiding the conduct of each member; for the social instinct, together with sympathy, is, like any other instinct, greatly strengthened by habit, and so consequently would be obedience to the wishes and judgment of the community. These several subordinate propositions must now be discussed, and some of them at considerable length.

[5] Sir B. Brodie, after observing that man is a social animal ('Psychological Enquiries,' 1854, p. 192), asks the pregnant question, "ought not this to settle the disputed question as to the existence of a moral sense?" Similar ideas have probably occurred to many persons, as they did long ago to Marcus Aurelius. Mr. J. S. Mill speaks, in his celebrated work, 'Utilitarianism,' (1864, pp. 45, 46), of the social feelings as a "powerful natural sentiment," and as "the natural basis of sentiment for utilitarian morality." Again he says, "Like the other acquired capacities above referred to, the moral faculty, if not a part of our nature, is a natural out-growth from it; capable, like them, in a certain small degree of springing up spontaneously." But in opposition to all this, he also remarks, "if, as in my own belief, the moral feelings are not innate, but acquired, they are not for that reason less natural." It is with hesitation that I venture to differ at all from so profound a thinker, but it can hardly be disputed that the social feelings are instinctive or innate in the lower animals; and why should they not be so in man? Mr. Bain (see, for instance, 'The Emotions and the Will,' 1865, p. 481) and others believe that the moral sense is acquired by each individual during his lifetime. On the general theory of evolution this is at least extremely improbable. The ignoring of all transmitted mental qualities will, as it seems to me, be hereafter judged as a most serious blemish in the works of Mr. Mill.

It may be well first to premise that I do not wish to maintain that any strictly social animal, if its intellectual faculties were to become as active and as highly developed as in man, would acquire exactly the same moral sense as ours. In the same manner as various animals have some sense of beauty, though they admire widely different objects, so they might have a sense of right and wrong, though led by it to follow widely different lines of conduct. If, for instance, to take an extreme case, men were reared under precisely the same conditions as hive-bees, there can hardly be a doubt that our unmarried females would, like the worker-bees, think it a sacred duty to kill their brothers, and mothers would strive to kill their fertile daughters; and no one would think of interfering.[6] Nevertheless, the bee, or any other social animal, would gain in our supposed case, as it appears to me, some feeling of right or wrong, or a conscience. For each individual would have an inward sense of possessing certain stronger or more enduring instincts, and others less strong or enduring; so that there would often be a struggle as to which impulse should be followed; and satisfaction, dissatisfaction, or even misery would be felt, as past impressions were compared during their incessant passage through the mind. In this case an inward monitor would tell the animal that it would have been better to have followed the one impulse rather than the other. The one course ought to have been followed, and the other ought not; the one would have been right and the other wrong; but to these terms I shall recur.

Sociability.—Animals of many kinds are social; we find even distinct species living together; for example, some American monkeys; and united flocks of rooks, jackdaws, and starlings. Man shews the same feeling in his strong love for the dog, which the dog returns with interest. Every one must have noticed how miserable horses, dogs, sheep, &c., are when separated from their companions, and what strong mutual affection the two former kinds, at least, shew on their reunion. It is curious to speculate on the feelings of a dog, who will rest peacefully for hours in a room with his master or any of the family, without the least notice being taken of him; but if left for a short time by himself, barks or howls dismally. We will confine our attention to the higher social animals; and pass over insects, although some of these are social, and aid one another in many important

---

[6] Mr. H. Sidgwick remarks, in an able discussion on this subject (the 'Academy,' June 15th, 1872, p. 231), "a superior bee, we may feel sure, would aspire to a milder solution of the popular question." Judging, however, from the habits of many or most savages, man solves the problem by female infanticide, polyandry and promiscuous intercourse; therefore it may well be doubted whether it would be by a milder method. Miss Cobbe, in commenting ('Darwinism in Morals,' 'Theological Review,' April, 1872, p. 188-191) on the same illustration, says, the *principles* of social duty would be thus reversed; and by this, I presume, she means that the fulfilment of a social duty would tend to the injury of individuals; but she overlooks the fact, which she would doubtless admit, that the instincts of the bee have been acquired for the good of the community. She goes so far as to say that if the theory of ethics advocated in this chapter were ever generally accepted, "I cannot but believe that in the hour of their triumph would be sounded the knell of the virtue of mankind!" It is to be hoped that the belief in the permanence of virtue on this earth is not held by many persons on so weak a tenure.

ways. The most common mutual service in the higher animals is to warn one another of danger by means of the united senses of all. Every sportsman knows, as Dr. Jaeger remarks,[7] how difficult it is to approach animals in a herd or troop. Wild horses and cattle do not, I believe, make any danger-signal; but the attitude of any one of them who first discovers an enemy, warns the others. Rabbits stamp loudly on the ground with their hind-feet as a signal: sheep and chamois do the same with their forefeet, uttering likewise a whistle. Many birds, and some mammals, post sentinels, which in the case of seals are said[8] generally to be the females. The leader of a troop of monkeys acts as the sentinel, and utters cries expressive both of danger and of safety.[9] Social animals perform many little services for each other: horses nibble, and cows lick each other, on any spot which itches: monkeys search each other for external parasites; and Brehm states that after a troop of the *Cercopithecus griseoviridis* has rushed through a thorny brake, each monkey stretches itself on a branch, and another monkey sitting by, "conscientiously" examines its fur, and extracts every thorn or burr.

Animals also render more important services to one another: thus wolves and some other beasts of prey hunt in packs, and aid one another in attacking their victims. Pelicans fish in concert. The Hamadryas baboons turn over stones to find insects, &c.; and when they come to a large one, as many as can stand round, turn it over together and share the booty. Social animals mutually defend each other. Bull bisons in N. America, when there is danger, drive the cows and calves into the middle of the herd, whilst they defend the outside. I shall also in a future chapter give an account of two young wild bulls at Chillingham attacking an old one in concert, and of two stallions together trying to drive away a third stallion from a troop of mares. In Abyssinia, Brehm encountered a great troop of baboons who were crossing a valley: some had already ascended the opposite mountain, and some were still in the valley: the latter were attacked by the dogs, but the old males immediately hurried down from the rocks, and with mouths widely opened, roared so fearfully, that the dogs quickly drew back. They were again encouraged to the attack; but by this time all the baboons had reascended the heights, excepting a young one, about six months old, who, loudly calling for aid, climbed on a block of rock, and was surrounded. Now one of the largest males, a true hero, came down again from the mountain, slowly went to the young one, coaxed him, and triumphantly led him away—the dogs being too much astonished to make an attack. I cannot resist giving another scene which was witnessed by this same naturalist; an eagle seized a young Cercopithecus, which, by clinging to a branch, was not at once carried off; it

[7] 'Die Darwin'sche Theorie,' s. 101.
[8] Mr. R. Brown in 'Proc. Zoolog. Soc.' 1868, p. 409.
[9] Brehm, 'Thierleben,' B. i. 1864, s. 52, 79. For the case of the monkeys extracting thorns from each other, see s. 54. With respect to the Hamadryas turning over stones, the fact is given (s. 76) on the evidence of Alvarez, whose observations Brehm thinks quite trustworthy. For the cases of the old male baboons attacking the dogs, see s. 79; and with respect to the eagle, see s. 56.

cried loudly for assistance, upon which the other members of the troop, with much uproar, rushed to the rescue, surrounded the eagle, and pulled out so many feathers, that he no longer thought of his prey, but only how to escape. This eagle, as Brehm remarks, assuredly would never again attack a single monkey of a troop.[10]

It is certain that associated animals have a feeling of love for each other, which is not felt by non-social adult animals. How far in most cases they actually sympathise in the pains and pleasures of others, is more doubtful, especially with respect to pleasures. Mr. Buxton, however, who had excellent means of observation,[11] states that his macaws, which lived free in Norfolk, took "an extravagant interest" in a pair with a nest; and whenever the female left it, she was surrounded by a troop "screaming horrible acclamations in her honour." It is often difficult to judge whether animals have any feeling for the sufferings of others of their kind. Who can say what cows feel, when they surround and stare intently on a dying or dead companion; apparently, however, as Houzeau remarks, they feel no pity. That animals sometimes are far from feeling any sympathy is too certain; for they will expel a wounded animal from the herd, or gore or worry it to death. This is almost the blackest fact in natural history, unless, indeed, the explanation which has been suggested is true, that their instinct or reason leads them to expel an injured companion, lest beasts of prey, including man, should be tempted to follow the troop. In this case their conduct is not much worse than that of the North American Indians, who leave their feeble comrades to perish on the plains; or the Fijians, who, when their parents get old, or fall ill, bury them alive.[12]

Many animals, however, certainly sympathise with each other's distress or danger. This is the case even with birds. Captain Stansbury[13] found on a salt lake in Utah an old and completely blind pelican, which was very fat, and must have been well fed for a long time by his companions. Mr. Blyth, as he informs me, saw Indian crows feeding two or three of their companions which were blind; and I have heard of an analogous case with the domestic cock. We may, if we choose, call these actions instinctive; but such cases are much too rare for the development of any special instinct.[14] I have myself seen a dog, who never passed a cat who lay sick in a basket, and was a great friend of his, without giving her a few licks with his tongue, the surest sign of kind feeling in a dog.

---

[10] Mr. Belt gives the case of a spider-monkey (Ateles) in Nicaragua, which was heard screaming for nearly two hours in the forest, and was found with an eagle perched close by it. The bird apparently feared to attack as long as it remained face to face; and Mr. Belt believes, from what he has seen of the habits of these monkeys, that they protect themselves from eagles by keeping two or three together. 'The Naturalist in Nicaragua,' 1874, p. 118.

[11] 'Annals of Mag. of Nat. Hist.,' November, 1868, p. 382.

[12] Sir J. Lubbock, 'Prehistoric Times,' 2nd edit. p. 446.

[13] As quoted by Mr. L. H. Morgan, 'The American Beaver,' 1868, p. 272. Capt. Stansbury also gives an interesting account of the manner in which a very young pelican, carried away by a strong stream, was guided and encouraged in its attempts to reach the shore by half a dozen old birds.

[14] As Mr. Bain states, "effective aid to a sufferer springs from sympathy proper:" 'Mental and Moral Science,' 1868, p. 245.

It must be called sympathy that leads a courageous dog to fly at any one who strikes his master, as he certainly will. I saw a person pretending to beat a lady, who had a very timid little dog on her lap, and the trial had never been made before; the little creature instantly jumped away, but after the pretended beating was over, it was really pathetic to see how perseveringly he tried to lick his mistress's face, and comfort her. Brehm[15] states that when a baboon in confinement was pursued to be punished, the others tried to protect him. It must have been sympathy in the cases above given which led the baboons and Cercopitheci to defend their young comrades from the dogs and the eagle. I will give only one other instance of sympathetic and heroic conduct, in the case of a little American monkey. Several years ago a keeper at the Zoological Gardens showed me some deep and scarcely healed wounds on the nape of his own neck, inflicted on him, whilst kneeling on the floor, by a fierce baboon. The little American monkey, who was a warm friend of this keeper, lived in the same compartment, and was dreadfully afraid of the great baboon. Nevertheless, as soon as he saw his friend in peril, he rushed to the rescue, and by screams and bites so distracted the baboon that the man was able to escape, after, as the surgeon thought, running great risk of his life.

Besides love and sympathy, animals exhibit other qualities connected with the social instincts, which in us would be called moral; and I agree with Agassiz[16] that dogs possess something very like a conscience.

Dogs possess some power of self-command, and this does not appear to be wholly the result of fear. As Braubach[17] remarks, they will refrain from stealing food in the absence of their master. They have long been accepted as the very type of fidelity and obedience. But the elephant is likewise very faithful to his driver or keeper, and probably considers him as the leader of the herd. Dr. Hooker informs me that an elephant, which he was riding in India, became so deeply bogged that he remained stuck fast until the next day, when he was extricated by men with ropes. Under such circumstances elephants will seize with their trunks any object, dead or alive, to place under their knees, to prevent their sinking deeper in the mud; and the driver was dreadfully afraid lest the animal should have seized Dr. Hooker and crushed him to death. But the driver himself, as Dr. Hooker was assured, ran no risk. This forbearance under an emergency so dreadful for a heavy animal, is a wonderful proof of noble fidelity.[18]

All animals living in a body, which defend themselves or attack their enemies in concert, must indeed be in some degree faithful to one another; and those that follow a leader must be in some degree obedient. When the baboons in Abyssinia[19] plunder a garden, they silently follow their leader; and if an imprudent young animal makes a noise, he receives a slap from the others to teach him silence and obedience. Mr. Galton, who has had excellent opportunities for observing the half-wild cattle in S.

[15] 'Thierleben,' B. i. s. 85.
[16] 'De l'Espèce et de la Classe,' 1869, p. 97.
[17] 'Die Darwin'sche Art-Lehre,' 1869, s. 54.
[18] See also Hooker's 'Himalayan Journals,' vol. ii, 1854, p. 333.
[19] Brehm, 'Thierleben,' B. i. s. 76.

Africa, says,[20] that they cannot endure even a momentary separation
from the herd. They are essentially slavish, and accept the common determination, seeking no better lot than to be led by any one ox who has
enough self-reliance to accept the position. The men who break in these
animals for harness, watch assiduously for those who, by grazing apart,
shew a self-reliant disposition, and these they train as fore-oxen. Mr Galton adds that such animals are rare and valuable; and if many were born
they would soon be eliminated, as lions are always on the look-out for the
individuals which wander from the herd.

With respect to the impulse which leads certain animals to associate
together, and to aid one another in many ways, we may infer that in most
cases they are impelled by the same sense of satisfaction or pleasure
which they experience in performing other instinctive actions; or by the
same sense of dissatisfaction as when other instinctive actions are
checked. We see this in innumerable instances, and it is illustrated in a
striking manner by the acquired instincts of our domesticated animals;
thus a young shepherd-dog delights in driving and running round a flock
of sheep, but not in worrying them; a young fox-hound delights in hunting a fox, whilst some other kinds of dogs, as I have witnessed, utterly
disregard foxes. What a strong feeling of inward satisfaction must impel
a bird, so full of activity, to brood day after day over her eggs. Migratory
birds are quite miserable if stopped from migrating; perhaps they enjoy
starting on their long flight; but it is hard to believe that the poor pinioned goose, described by Audubon, which started on foot at the proper
time for its journey of probably more than a thousand miles, could have
felt any joy in doing so. Some instincts are determined solely by painful
feelings, as by fear, which leads to self-preservation, and is in some cases
directed towards special enemies. No one, I presume, can analyse the sensations of pleasure or pain. In many instances, however, it is probable
that instincts are persistently followed from the mere force of inheritance, without the stimulus of either pleasure or pain. A young pointer,
when it first scents game, apparently cannot help pointing. A squirrel in a
cage who pats the nuts which it cannot eat, as if to bury them in the
ground, can hardly be thought to act thus, either from pleasure or pain.
Hence the common assumption that men must be impelled to every action by experiencing some pleasure or pain may be erroneous. Although a
habit may be blindly and implicitly followed, independently of any pleasure or pain felt at the moment, yet if it be forcibly and abruptly checked,
a vague sense of dissatisfaction is generally experienced.

It has often been assumed that animals were in the first place rendered
social, and that they feel as a consequence uncomfortable when separated
from each other, and comfortable whilst together; but it is a more probable view that these sensations were first developed, in order that those
animals which would profit by living in society, should be induced to live
together, in the same manner as the sense of hunger and the pleasure of

[20] See his extremely interesting paper on 'Gregariousness in Cattle, and in Man,'
'Macmillan's Mag.' Feb. 1871, p. 353.

eating were, no doubt, first acquired in order to induce animals to eat. The feeling of pleasure from society is probably an extension of the parental or filial affections, since the social instinct seems to be developed by the young remaining for a long time with their parents; and this extension may be attributed in part to habit, but chiefly to natural selection. With those animals which were benefited by living in close association, the individuals which took the greatest pleasure in society would best escape various dangers, whilst those that cared least for their comrades, and lived solitary, would perish in greater numbers. With respect to the origin of the parental and filial affections, which apparently lie at the base of the social instincts, we know not the steps by which they have been gained; but we may infer that it has been to a large extent through natural selection. So it has almost certainly been with the unusual and opposite feeling of hatred between the nearest relations, as with the worker-bees which kill their brother drones, and with the queen-bees which kill their daughter-queens; the desire to destroy their nearest relations having been in this case of service to the community. Parental affection, or some feeling which replaces it, has been developed in certain animals extremely low in the scale, for example, in star-fishes and spiders. It is also occasionally present in a few members alone in a whole group of animals, as in the genus Forficula, or earwigs.

The all-important emotion of sympathy is distinct from that of love. A mother may passionately love her sleeping and passive infant, but she can hardly at such times be said to feel sympathy for it. The love of a man for his dog is distinct from sympathy, and so is that of a dog for his master. Adam Smith formerly argued, as has Mr. Bain recently, that the basis of sympathy lies in our strong retentiveness of former states of pain or pleasure. Hence, "the sight of another person enduring hunger, cold, fatigue, revives in us some recollection of these states, which are painful even in idea." We are thus impelled to relieve the sufferings of another, in order that our own painful feelings may be at the same time relieved. In like manner we are led to participate in the pleasures of others.[21] But I cannot see how this view explains the fact that sympathy is excited, in an immeasurably stronger degree, by a beloved, than by an indifferent person. The mere sight of suffering, independently of love, would suffice to call up in us vivid recollections and associations. The explanation may lie in the fact that, with all animals, sympathy is directed solely towards the members of the same community, and therefore towards known, and more or less beloved members, but not to all the individuals of the same

[21] See the first and striking chapter in Adam Smith's 'Theory of Moral Sentiments.' Also Mr. Bain's 'Mental and Moral Science,' 1868, p. 244, and 275-282. Mr. Bain states, that, "sympathy is, indirectly, a source of pleasure to the sympathiser;" and he accounts for this through reciprocity. He remarks that "the person benefited, or others in his stead, may make up, by sympathy and good offices returned, for all the sacrifice." But if, as appears to be the case, sympathy is strictly an instinct, its exercise would give direct pleasure, in the same manner as the exercise, as before remarked, of almost every other instinct.

species. This fact is not more surprising than that the fears of many animals should be directed against special enemies. Species which are not social, such as lions and tigers, no doubt feel sympathy for the suffering of their own young, but not for that of any other animal. With mankind, selfishness, experience, and imitation, probably add, as Mr. Bain has shown, to the power of sympathy; for we are led by the hope of receiving good in return to perform acts of sympathetic kindness to others; and sympathy is much strengthened by habit. In however complex a manner this feeling may have originated, as it is one of high importance to all those animals which aid and defend one another, it will have been increased through natural selection; for those communities, which included the greatest number of the most sympathetic members, would flourish best, and rear the greatest number of offspring.

It is, however, impossible to decide in many cases whether certain social instincts have been acquired through natural selection, or are the indirect result of other instincts and faculties, such as sympathy, reason, experience, and a tendency to imitation; or again, whether they are simply the result of long-continued habit. So remarkable an instinct as the placing sentinels to warn the community of danger, can hardly have been the indirect result of any of these faculties; it must, therefore, have been directly acquired. On the other hand, the habit followed by the males of some social animals of defending the community, and of attacking their enemies or their prey in concert, may perhaps have originated from mutual sympathy; but courage, and in most cases strength, must have been previously acquired, probably through natural selection.

Of the various instincts and habits, some are much stronger than others; that is, some either give more pleasure in their performance, and more distress in their prevention, than others; or, which is probably quite as important, they are, through inheritance, more persistently followed, without exciting any special feeling of pleasure or pain. We are ourselves conscious that some habits are much more difficult to cure or change than others. Hence a struggle may often be observed in animals between different instincts, or between an instinct and some habitual disposition; as when a dog rushes after a hare, is rebuked, pauses, hesitates, pursues again, or returns ashamed to his master; or as between the love of a female dog for her young puppies and for her master,—for she may be seen to slink away to them, as if half ashamed of not accompanying her master. But the most curious instance known to me of one instinct getting the better of another, is the migratory instinct conquering the maternal instinct. The former is wonderfully strong; a confined bird will at the proper season beat her breast against the wires of her cage, until it is bare and bloody. It causes young salmon to leap out of the fresh water, in which they could continue to exist, and thus unintentionally to commit suicide Every one knows how strong the maternal instinct is, leading even timid birds to face great danger, though with hesitation, and in opposition to the instinct of self-preservation. Nevertheless, the migratory instinct is so powerful, that late in the autumn swallows, house-martins, and swifts frequently desert their tender young, leaving them to perish miserably in their nests.[22]

We can perceive that an instinctive impulse, if it be in any way more beneficial to a species than some other or opposed instinct, would be rendered the more potent of the two through natural selection; for the individuals which had it most strongly developed would survive in larger numbers. Whether this is the case with the migratory in comparison with the maternal instinct, may be doubted. The great persistence, or steady action of the former at certain seasons of the year during the whole day, may give it for a time paramount force.

Man a social animal.—Every one will admit that man is a social being. We see this in his dislike of solitude, and in his wish for society beyond that of his own family. Solitary confinement is one of the severest punishments which can be inflicted. Some authors suppose that man primevally lived in single families; but at the present day, though single families, or only two or three together, roam the solitudes of some savage lands, they always, as far as I can discover, hold friendly relations with other families inhabiting the same district. Such families occasionally meet in council, and unite for their common defence. It is no argument against savage man being a social animal, that the tribes inhabiting adjacent districts are almost always at war with each other; for the social instincts never extend to all the individuals of the same species. Judging from the analogy of the majority of the Quadrumana, it is probable that the early ape-like progenitors of man were likewise social; but this is not of much importance for us. Although man, as he now exists, has few special instincts, having lost any which his early progenitors may have possessed, this is no reason why he should not have retained from an extremely remote period some degree of instinctive love and sympathy for his fellows. We are indeed all conscious that we do possess such sympathetic feelings;[23] but our consciousness does not tell us whether they are instinctive, having originated long ago in the same manner as with the lower animals, or whether they have been acquired by each of us during our early years. As man is a social animal, it is almost certain that he would inherit a tendency to be

[22] This fact, the Rev. L. Jenyns states (see his edition of 'White's Nat. Hist. of Selborne,' 1853, p. 204), was first recorded by the illustrious Jenner, in 'Phil. Transact.' 1824, and has since been confirmed by several observers, especially by Mr. Blackwall. This latter careful observer examined, late in the autumn, during two years, thirty-six nests; he found that twelve contained young dead birds, five contained eggs on the point of being hatched, and three, eggs not nearly hatched. Many birds, not yet old enough for a prolonged flight, are likewise deserted and left behind. See Blackwall, 'Researches in Zoology,' 1834, pp. 108, 118. For some additional evidence, although this is not wanted, see Leroy, 'Lettres Phil.' 1802, p. 217. For Swifts, Gould's 'Introduction to the Birds of Great Britain,' 1823, p. 5. Similar cases have been observed in Canada by Mr. Adams; 'Pop. Science Review,' July, 1873, p. 283.

[23] Hume remarks ('An Enquiry Concerning the Principles of Morals,' edit. of 1751, p. 132), "There seems a necessity for confessing that the happiness and misery of others are not spectacles altogether indifferent to us, but that the view of the former . . . communicates a secret joy; the appearance of the latter . . . throws a melancholy damp over the imagination."

faithful to his comrades, and obedient to the leader of his tribe; for these qualities are common to most social animals. He would consequently possess some capacity for self-command. He would from an inherited tendency be willing to defend, in concert with others, his fellow-men; and would be ready to aid them in any way, which did not too greatly interfere with his own welfare or his own strong desires.

The social animals which stand at the bottom of the scale are guided almost exclusively, and those which stand higher in the scale are largely guided, by special instincts in the aid which they give to the members of the same community; but they are likewise in part impelled by mutual love and sympathy, assisted apparently by some amount of reason. Although man, as just remarked, has no special instincts to tell him how to aid his fellow-men, he still has the impulse, and with his improved intellectual faculties would naturally be much guided in this respect by reason and experience. Instinctive sympathy would also cause him to value highly the approbation of his fellows; for, as Mr. Bain has clearly shewn,[24] the love of praise and the strong feeling of glory, and the still stronger horror of scorn and infamy, "are due to the workings of sympathy." Consequently man would be influenced in the highest degree by the wishes, approbation, and blame of his fellow-men, as expressed by their gestures and language. Thus the social instincts, which must have been acquired by man in a very rude state, and probably even by his early ape-like progenitors, still give the impulse to some of his best actions; but his actions are in a higher degree determined by the expressed wishes and judgment of his fellow-men, and unfortunately very often by his own strong selfish desires. But as love, sympathy and self-command become strengthened by habit, and as the power of reasoning becomes clearer, so that man can value justly the judgments of his fellows, he will feel himself impelled, apart from any transitory pleasure or pain, to certain lines of conduct. He might then declare—not that any barbarian or uncultivated man could thus think—I am the supreme judge of my own conduct, and in the words of Kant, I will not in my own person violate the dignity of humanity.

The more enduring Social Instincts conquer the less persistent Instincts.—We have not, however, as yet considered the main point, on which, from our present point of view, the whole question of the moral sense turns. Why should a man feel that he ought to obey one instinctive desire rather than another? Why is he bitterly regretful, if he has yielded to a strong sense of self-preservation, and has not risked his life to save that of a fellow-creature? or why does he regret having stolen food from hunger?

It is evident in the first place, that with mankind the instinctive impulses have different degrees of strength; a savage will risk his own life to save that of a member of the same community, but will be wholly indifferent about a stranger: a young and timid mother urged by the maternal instinct will, without a moment's hesitation, run the greatest danger for

[24] 'Mental and Moral Science,' 1868, p. 254.

her own infant, but not for a mere fellow-creature. Nevertheless many a civilized man, or even boy, who never before risked his life for another, but full of courage and sympathy, has disregarded the instinct of self-preservation, and plunged at once into a torrent to save a drowning man, though a stranger. In this case man is impelled by the same instinctive motive, which made the heroic little American monkey, formerly described, save his keeper, by attacking the great and dreaded baboon. Such actions as the above appear to be the simple result of the greater strength of the social or maternal instincts than that of any other instinct or motive; for they are performed too instantaneously for reflection, or for pleasure or pain to be felt at the time; though, if prevented by any cause, distress or even misery might be felt. In a timid man, on the other hand, the instinct of self-preservation might be so strong, that he would be unable to force himself to run any such risk, perhaps not even for his own child.

I am aware that some persons maintain that actions performed impulsively, as in the above cases, do not come under the dominion of the moral sense, and cannot be called moral. They confine this term to actions done deliberately, after a victory over opposing desires, or when prompted by some exalted motive. But it appears scarcely possible to draw any clear line of distinction of this kind.[25] As far as exalted motives are concerned, many instances have been recorded of savages, destitute of any feeling of general benevolence towards mankind, and not guided by any religious motive, who have deliberately sacrificed their lives as prisoners,[26] rather than betray their comrades; and surely their conduct ought to be considered as moral. As far as deliberation, and the victory over opposing motives are concerned, animals may be seen doubting between opposed instincts, in rescuing their offspring or comrades from danger; yet their actions, though done for the good of others, are not called moral. Moreover, anything performed very often by us, will at last be done without deliberation or hesitation, and can then hardly be distinguished from an instinct; yet surely no one will pretend that such an action ceases to be moral. On the contrary, we all feel that an act cannot be considered as perfect, or as performed in the most noble manner, unless it be done impulsively, without deliberation or effort, in the same manner as by a man in whom the requisite qualities are innate. He who is forced to overcome his fear or want of sympathy before he acts, deserves, however, in one way higher credit than the man whose innate disposition leads him to a good act without effort. As we cannot distinguish between motives, we rank all actions of a certain class as moral, if performed by a moral being. A moral being is one who is capable of comparing his past and future

[25] I refer here to the distinction between what has been called *material* and *formal* morality. I am glad to find that Professor Huxley ('Critiques and Addresses,' 1873, p. 287) takes the same view on this subject as I do. Mr. Leslie Stephen remarks ('Essays on Freethinking and Plain Speaking,' 1873, p. 83), "the metaphysical distinction between material and formal morality is as irrelevant as other such distinctions."
[26] I have given one such case, namely of three Patagonian Indians who preferred being shot, one after the other, to betraying the plans of their companions in war ('Journal of Researches,' 1845, p. 103).

actions or motives, and of approving or disapproving of them. We have no reason to suppose that any of the lower animals have this capacity; therefore, when a Newfoundland dog drags a child out of the water, or a monkey faces danger to rescue its comrade, or takes charge of an orphan monkey, we do not call its conduct moral. But in the case of man, who alone can with certainty be ranked as a moral being, actions of a certain class are called moral, whether performed deliberately, after a struggle with opposing motives, or impulsively through instinct, or from the effects of slowly-gained habit.

But to return to our more immediate subject. Although some instincts are more powerful than others, and thus lead to corresponding actions, yet it is untenable, that in man the social instincts (including the love of praise and fear of blame) possess greater strength, or have, through long habit, acquired greater strength than the instincts of self-preservation, hunger, lust, vengeance, &c. Why then does man regret, even though trying to banish such regret, that he has followed the one natural impulse rather than the other; and why does he further feel that he ought to regret his conduct? Man in this respect differs profoundly from the lower animals. Nevertheless we can, I think, see with some degree of clearness the reason of this difference.

Man, from the activity of his mental faculties, cannot avoid reflection: past impressions and images are incessantly and clearly passing through his mind. Now with those animals which live permanently in a body, the social instincts are ever present and persistent. Such animals are always ready to utter the danger-signal, to defend the community, and to give aid to their fellows in accordance with their habits; they feel at all times, without the stimulus of any special passion or desire, some degree of love and sympathy for them; they are unhappy if long separated from them, and always happy to be again in their company. So it is with ourselves. Even when we are quite alone, how often do we think with pleasure or pain of what others think of us,—of their imagined approbation or disapprobation; and this all follows from sympathy, a fundamental element of the social instincts. A man who possessed no trace of such instincts would be an unnatural monster. On the other hand, the desire to satisfy hunger, or any passion such as vengeance, is in its nature temporary, and can for a time be fully satisfied. Nor is it easy, perhaps hardly possible, to call up with complete vividness the feeling, for instance, of hunger; nor indeed, as has often been remarked, of any suffering. The instinct of self-preservation is not felt except in the presence of danger; and many a coward has thought himself brave until he has met his enemy face to face. The wish for another man's property is perhaps as persistent a desire as any that can be named; but even in this case the satisfaction of actual possession is generally a weaker feeling than the desire: many a thief, if not a habitual one, after success has wondered why he stole some article.[27]

[27] Enmity or hatred seems also to be a highly persistent feeling, perhaps more so than any other that can be named. Envy is defined as hatred of another for some excellence or success; and Bacon insists (Essay ix.), "Of all other affections envy is

A man cannot prevent past impressions often repassing through his mind; he will thus be driven to make a comparison between the impressions of past hunger, vengeance satisfied, or danger shunned at other men's cost, with the almost ever-present instinct of sympathy, and with his early knowledge of what others consider as praiseworthy or blameable. This knowledge cannot be banished from his mind, and from instinctive sympathy is esteemed of great moment. He will then feel as if he had been baulked in following a present instinct or habit, and this with all animals causes dissatisfaction, or even misery.

The above case of the swallow affords an illustration, though of a reversed nature, of a temporary though for the time strongly persistent instinct conquering another instinct, which is usually dominant over all others. At the proper season these birds seem all day long to be impressed with the desire to migrate; their habits change; they become restless, are noisy and congregate in flocks. Whilst the mother-bird is feeding, or brooding over her nestlings, the maternal instinct is probably stronger than the migratory; but the instinct which is the more persistent gains the victory, and at last, at a moment when her young ones are not in sight, she takes flight and deserts them. When arrived at the end of her long journey, and the migratory instinct has ceased to act, what an agony of remorse the bird would feel, if, from being endowed with great mental activity, she could not prevent the image constantly passing through her mind, of her young ones perishing in the bleak north from cold and hunger.

At the moment of action, man will no doubt be apt to follow the stronger impulse; and though this may occasionally prompt him to the noblest deeds, it will more commonly lead him to gratify his own desires at the expense of other men. But after their gratification when past and weaker impressions are judged by the ever-enduring social instinct, and by his deep regard for the good opinion of his fellows, retribution will surely come. He will then feel remorse, repentance, regret, or shame; this latter feeling, however, relates almost exclusively to the judgment of others. He will consequently resolve more or less firmly to act differently for the future; and this is conscience; for conscience looks backwards, and serves as a guide for the future.

---

the most importune and continual." Dogs are very apt to hate both strange men and strange dogs, especially if they live near at hand, but do not belong to the same family, tribe, or clan; this feeling would thus seem to be innate, and is certainly a most persistent one. It seems to be the complement and converse of the true social instinct. From what we hear of savages, it would appear that something of the same kind holds good with them. If this be so, it would be a small step in any one to transfer such feelings to any member of the same tribe if he had done him an injury and had become his enemy. Nor is it probable that the primitive conscience would reproach a man for injuring his enemy; rather it would reproach him, if he had not revenged himself. To do good in return for evil, to love your enemy, is a height of morality to which it may be doubted whether the social instincts would, by themselves, have ever led us. It is necessary that these instincts, together with sympathy, should have been highly cultivated and extended by the aid of reason, instruction, and the love or fear of God, before any such golden rule would ever be thought of and obeyed.

The nature and strength of the feelings which we call regret, shame, repentance or remorse, depend apparently not only on the strength of the violated instinct, but partly on the strength of the temptation, and often still more on the judgment of our fellows. How far each man values the appreciation of others, depends on the strength of his innate or acquired feeling of sympathy; and on his own capacity for reasoning out the remote consequences of his acts. Another element is most important, although not necessary, the reverence or fear of the Gods, or Spirits believed in by each man: and this applies especially in cases of remorse. Several critics have objected that though some slight regret or repentance may be explained by the view advocated in this chapter, it is impossible thus to account for the soul-shaking feeling of remorse. But I can see little force in this objection. My critics do not define what they mean by remorse, and I can find no definition implying more than an overwhelming sense of repentance. Remorse seems to bear the same relation to repentance, as rage does to anger, or agony to pain. It is far from strange that an instinct so strong and so generally admired, as maternal love, should, if disobeyed, lead to the deepest misery, as soon as the impression of the past cause of disobedience is weakened. Even when an action is opposed to no special instinct, merely to know that our friends and equals despise us for it is enough to cause great misery. Who can doubt that the refusal to fight a duel through fear has caused many men an agony of shame? Many a Hindoo, it is said, has been stirred to the bottom of his soul by having partaken of unclean food. Here is another case of what must, I think, be called remorse. Dr. Landor acted as a magistrate in West Australia, and relates,[28] that a native on his farm, after losing one of his wives from disease, came and said that "he was going to a distant tribe to spear a woman, to satisfy his sense of duty to his wife. I told him that if he did so, I would send him to prison for life. He remained about the farm for some months, but got exceedingly thin, and complained that he could not rest or eat, that his wife's spirit was haunting him, because he had not taken a life for hers. I was inexorable, and assured him that nothing should save him if he did." Nevertheless the man disappeared for more than a year, and then returned in high condition; and his other wife told Dr. Landor that her husband had taken the life of a woman belonging to a distant tribe; but it was impossible to obtain legal evidence of the act. The breach of a rule held sacred by the tribe, will thus, as it seems, give rise to the deepest feelings,—and this quite apart from the social instincts, excepting in so far as the rule is grounded on the judgment of the community. How so many strange superstitions have arisen throughout the world we know not; nor can we tell how some real and great crimes, such as incest, have come to be held in an abhorrence (which is not however quite universal) by the lowest savages. It is even doubtful whether in some tribes incest would be looked on with greater horror, than would the marriage of a man with a woman bearing the same name, though not a relation. "To violate this law is a crime which the Australians hold in

[28] 'Insanity in Relation to Law;' Ontario, United States, 1871, p. 1.

the greatest abhorrence, in this agreeing exactly with certain tribes of North America. When the question is put in either district, is it worse to kill a girl of a foreign tribe, or to marry a girl of one's own, an answer just opposite to ours would be given without hesitation."[29] We may, therefore, reject the belief, lately insisted on by some writers, that the abhorrence of incest is due to our possessing a special God-implanted conscience. On the whole it is intelligible, that a man urged by so powerful a sentiment as remorse, though arising as above explained, should be led to act in a manner, which he has been taught to believe serves as an expiation, such as delivering himself up to justice.

Man prompted by his conscience, will through long habit acquire such perfect self-command, that his desires and passions will at last yield instantly and without a struggle to his social sympathies and instincts, including his feeling for the judgment of his fellows. The still hungry, or the still revengeful man will not think of stealing food, or of wreaking his vengeance. It is possible, or as we shall hereafter see, even probable, that the habit of self-command may, like other habits, be inherited. Thus at last man comes to feel, through acquired and perhaps inherited habit, that it is best for him to obey his more persistent impulses. The imperious word *ought* seems merely to imply the consciousness of the existence of a rule of conduct, however it may have originated. Formerly it must have been often vehemently urged that an insulted gentleman *ought* to fight a duel. We even say that a pointer *ought* to point, and a retriever to retrieve game. If they fail to do so, they fail in their duty and act wrongly.

If any desire or instinct leading to an action opposed to the good of others still appears, when recalled to mind, as strong as, or stronger than, the social instinct, a man will feel no keen regret at having followed it; but he will be conscious that if his conduct were known to his fellows, it would meet with their disapprobation; and few are so destitute of sympathy as not to feel discomfort when this is realised. If he has no such sympathy, and if his desires leading to bad actions are at the time strong, and when recalled are not over-mastered by the persistent social instincts, and the judgment of others, then he is essentially a bad man;[30] and the sole restraining motive left is the fear of punishment, and the conviction that in the long run it would be best for his own selfish interests to regard the good of others rather than his own.

It is obvious that every one may with an easy conscience gratify his own desires, if they do not interfere with his social instincts, that is with the good of others; but in order to be quite free from self-reproach, or at least of anxiety, it is almost necessary for him to avoid the disapprobation, whether reasonable or not, of his fellow-men. Nor must he break through the fixed habits of his life, especially if these are supported by reason; for if he does, he will assuredly feel dissatisfaction. He must like-

---

[29] E. B. Tylor in 'Contemporary Review,' April, 1873, p. 707.

[30] Dr. Prosper Despine in his 'Psychologie Naturelle,' 1868 (tom. i. p. 243; tom. ii. p. 169) gives many curious cases of the worst criminals, who apparently have been entirely destitute of conscience.

wise avoid the reprobation of the one God or gods in whom, according to his knowledge or superstition, he may believe; but in this case the additional fear of divine punishment often supervenes.

The strictly Social Virtues at first alone regarded.—The above view of the origin and nature of the moral sense, which tells us what we ought to do, and of the conscience which reproves us if we disobey it, accords well with what we see of the early and undeveloped condition of this faculty in mankind. The virtues which must be practised, at least generally, by rude men, so that they may associate in a body, are those which are still recognised as the most important. But they are practised almost exclusively in relation to the men of the same tribe; and their opposites are not regarded as crimes in relation to the men of other tribes. No tribe could hold together if murder, robbery, treachery, &c., were common; consequently such crimes within the limits of the same tribe "are branded with everlasting infamy;" [31] but excite no such sentiment beyond these limits. A North-American Indian is well pleased with himself, and is honoured by others, when he scalps a man of another tribe; and a Dyak cuts off the head of an unoffending person, and dries it as a trophy. The murder of infants has prevailed on the largest scale throughout the world,[32] and has met with no reproach; but infanticide, especially of females, has been thought to be good for the tribe, or at least not injurious. Suicide during former times was not generally considered as a crime,[33] but rather, from the courage displayed, as an honourable act; and it is still practised by some semi-civilised and savage nations without reproach, for it does not obviously concern others of the tribe. It has been recorded that an Indian Thug conscientiously regretted that he had not robbed and strangled as many travellers as did his father before him. In a rude state of civilisation the robbery of strangers is, indeed, generally considered as honourable.

Slavery, although in some ways beneficial during ancient times,[34] is a great crime; yet it was not so regarded until quite recently, even by the most civilised nations. And this was especially the case, because the slaves belonged in general to a race different from that of their masters. As barbarians do not regard the opinion of their women, wives are commonly treated like slaves. Most savages are utterly indifferent to the suf-

[31] See an able article in the 'North British Review,' 1867, p. 395. See also Mr. W. Bagehot's articles on the Importance of Obedience and Coherence to Primitive Man, in the 'Fortnightly Review,' 1867, p. 529, and 1868, p. 457, &c.

[32] The fullest account which I have met with is by Dr. Gerland, in his 'Ueber dan Aussterben der Naturvölker,' 1868: but I shall have to recur to the subject of infanticide in a future chapter.

[33] See the very interesting discussion on Suicide in Lecky's 'History of European Morals,' vol. i, 1869, p. 223. With respect to savages, Mr. Winwood Reade informs me that the negroes of West Africa often commit suicide. It is well known how common it was amongst the miserable aborigines of South America after the Spanish conquest. For New Zealand, see the voyage of the "Novara," and for the Aleutian Islands, Müller, as quoted by Houzeau, 'Les Facultés Mentales,' &c., tom. ii. p. 136.

[34] See Mr. Bagehot, 'Physics and Politics,' 1872, p. 72.

ferings of strangers, or even delight in witnessing them. It is well known
that the women and children of the North American Indians aided in
torturing their enemies. Some savages take a horrid pleasure in cruelty
to animals,[35] and humanity is an unknown virtue. Nevertheless, besides
the family affections, kindness is common, especially during sickness, between the members of the same tribe, and is sometimes extended beyond
these limits. Mungo Park's touching account of the kindness of the negro
women of the interior to him is well known. Many instances could be
given of the noble fidelity of savages towards each other, but not to strangers; common experience justifies the maxim of the Spaniard, "Never,
never trust an Indian." There cannot be fidelity without truth; and this
fundamental virtue is not rare between the members of the same tribe:
thus Mungo Park heard the negro women teaching their young children
to love the truth. This, again, is one of the virtues which becomes so deeply rooted in the mind, that it is sometimes practised by savages, even at a
high cost, towards strangers; but to lie to your enemy has rarely been
thought a sin, as the history of modern diplomacy too plainly shews. As
soon as a tribe has a recognised leader, disobedience becomes a crime, and
even abject submission is looked at as a sacred virtue.

As during rude times no man can be useful or faithful to his tribe without courage, this quality has universally been placed in the highest rank;
and although in civilised countries a good yet timid man may be far more
useful to the community than a brave one, we cannot help instinctively
honouring the latter above a coward, however benevolent. Prudence, on
the other hand, which does not concern the welfare of others, though a
very useful virtue, has never been highly esteemed. As no man can practise the virtues necessary for the welfare of his tribe without self-sacrifice,
self-command, and the power of endurance, these qualities have been at
all times highly and most justly valued. The American savage voluntarily
submits to the most horrid tortures without a groan, to prove and
strengthen his fortitude and courage; and we cannot help admiring him,
or even an Indian Fakir, who, from a foolish religious motive, swings suspended by a hook buried in his flesh.

The other so-called self-regarding virtues, which do not obviously,
though they may really, affect the welfare of the tribe, have never been
esteemed by savages, though now highly appreciated by civilised nations.
The greatest intemperance is no reproach with savages. Utter licentiousness, and unnatural crimes, prevail to an astounding extent.[36] As soon,
however, as marriage, whether polygamous, or monogamous, becomes
common, jealousy will lead to the inculcation of female virtue; and this,
being honoured, will tend to spread to the unmarried females. How slowly it spreads to the male sex, we see at the present day. Chastity eminently requires self-command; therefore it has been honoured from a

---

[35] See, for instance, Mr. Hamilton's account of the Kaffirs, 'Anthropological Review,' 1870, p. xv.

[36] Mr. M'Lennan has given ('Primitive Marriage,' 1865, p. 176) a good collection
of facts on this head.

very early period in the moral history of civilised man. As a consequence of this, the senseless practice of celibacy has been ranked from a remote period as a virtue.[37] The hatred of indecency, which appears to us so natural as to be thought innate, and which is so valuable an aid to chastity, is a modern virtue, appertaining exclusively, as Sir G. Staunton remarks,[38] to civilised life. This is shewn by the ancient religious rites of various nations, by the drawings on the walls of Pompeii, and by the practices of many savages.

We have now seen that actions are regarded by savages, and were probably so regarded by primeval man, as good or bad, solely as they obviously affect the welfare of the tribe,—not that of the species, nor that of an individual member of the tribe. This conclusion agrees well with the belief that the so-called moral sense is aboriginally derived from the social instincts, for both relate at first exclusively to the community.

The chief causes of the low morality of savages, as judged by our standard, are, firstly, the confinement of sympathy to the same tribe. Secondly, powers of reasoning insufficient to recognise the bearing of many virtues, especially of the self-regarding virtues, on the general welfare of the tribe. Savages, for instance, fail to trace the multiplied evils consequent on a want of temperance, chastity, &c. And, thirdly, weak power of self-command; for this power has not been strengthened through long-continued, perhaps inherited, habit, instruction and religion.

I have entered into the above details on the immorality of savages,[39] because some authors have recently taken a high view of their moral nature, or have attributed most of their crimes to mistaken benevolence.[40] These authors appear to rest their conclusion on savages possessing those virtues which are serviceable, or even necessary, for the existence of the family and of the tribe,—qualities which they undoubtedly do possess. and often in a high degree.

Concluding Remarks.—It was assumed formerly by philosophers of the derivative [41] school of morals that the foundation of morality lay in a form of Selfishness; but more recently the "Greatest happiness principle" has been brought prominently forward. It is, however, more correct to speak of the latter principle as the standard, and not as the motive of conduct. Nevertheless, all the authors whose works I have consulted, with a few exceptions,[42] write as if there must be a distinct motive for every

[37] Lecky, 'History of European Morals,' vol. i. 1869, p. 109.

[38] 'Embassy to China,' vol. ii. p. 348.

[39] See on this subject copious evidence in Chap. vii. of Sir J. Lubbock, 'Origin of Civilisation,' 1870.

[40] For instance Lecky, 'Hist. European Morals,' vol. i. p. 124.

[41] This term is used in an able article in the 'Westminster Review,' Oct. 1869, p. 498. For the "Greatest happiness principle," see J. S. Mill, 'Utilitarianism,' p. 17.

[42] Mill recognises ('System of Logic,' vol. ii. p. 422) in the clearest manner, that actions may be performed through habit without the anticipation of pleasure. Mr. H. Sidgwick also, in his Essay on Pleasure and Desire ('The Contemporary Review,' April, 1872, p. 671), remarks: "To sum up, in contravention of the doctrine that our conscious active impulses are always directed towards the production of agreeable

action, and that this must be associated with some pleasure or displeasure. But man seems often to act impulsively, that is from instinct or long habit, without any consciousness of pleasure, in the same manner as does probably a bee or ant, when it blindly follows its instincts. Under circumstances of extreme peril, as during a fire, when a man endeavours to save a fellow-creature without a moment's hesitation, he can hardly feel pleasure; and still less has he time to reflect on the dissatisfaction which he might subsequently experience if he did not make the attempt. Should he afterwards reflect over his own conduct, he would feel that there lies within him an impulsive power widely different from a search after pleasure or happiness; and this seems to be the deeply planted social instinct.

In the case of the lower animals it seems much more appropriate to speak of their social instincts, as having been developed for the general good rather than for the general happiness of the species. The term, general good, may be defined as the rearing of the greatest number of individuals in full vigour and health, with all their faculties perfect, under the conditions to which they are subjected. As the social instincts both of man and the lower animals have no doubt been developed by nearly the same steps, it would be advisable, if found practicable, to use the same definition in both cases, and to take as the standard of morality, the general good or welfare of the community, rather than the general happiness; but this definition would perhaps require some limitation on account of political ethics.

When a man risks his life to save that of a fellow-creature, it seems also more correct to say that he acts for the general good, rather than for the general happiness of mankind. No doubt the welfare and the happiness of the individual usually coincide; and a contented, happy tribe will flourish better than one that is discontented and unhappy. We have seen that even at an early period in the history of man, the expressed wishes of the community will have naturally influenced to a large extent the conduct of each member; and as all wish for happiness, the "greatest happiness principle" will have become a most important secondary guide and object; the social instinct, however, together with sympathy (which leads to our regarding the approbation and disapprobation of others), having served as the primary impulse and guide. Thus the reproach is removed of laying the foundation of the noblest part of our nature in the base principle of selfishness; unless, indeed, the satisfaction which every animal feels, when it follows its proper instincts, and the dissatisfaction felt when prevented, be called selfish.

sensations in ourselves, I would maintain that we find everywhere in consciousness extra-regarding impulse, directed towards something that is not pleasure; that in many cases the impulse is so far incompatible with the self-regarding that the two do not easily co-exist in the same moment of consciousness." A dim feeling that our impulses do not by any means always arise from any contemporaneous or anticipated pleasure, has, I cannot but think, been one chief cause of the acceptance of the intuitive theory of morality, and of the rejection of the utilitarian or "Greatest happiness" theory. With respect to the latter theory the standard and the motive of conduct have no doubt often been confused, but they are really in some degree blended.

The wishes and opinions of the members of the same community, expressed at first orally, but later by writing also, either form the sole
guides of our conduct, or greatly reinforce the social instincts; such opinions, however, have sometimes a tendency directly opposed to these instincts. This latter fact is well exemplified by the *Law of Honour,* that is,
the law of the opinion of our equals, and not of all our countrymen. The
breach of this law, even when the breach is known to be strictly accordant with true morality, has caused many a man more agony than a real
crime. We recognise the same influence in the burning sense of shame
which most of us have felt, even after the interval of years, when calling
to mind some accidental breach of a trifling, though fixed, rule of eti-
quette. The judgment of the community will generally be guided by some
rude experience of what is best in the long run for all the members; but
this judgment will not rarely err from ignorance and weak powers of reasoning. Hence the strangest customs and superstitions, in complete opposition to the true welfare and happiness of mankind, have become all-
powerful throughout the world. We see this in the horror felt by a Hindoo
who breaks his caste, and in many other such cases. It would be difficult
to distinguish between the remorse felt by a Hindoo who has yielded to
the temptation of eating unclean food, from that felt after committing a
theft; but the former would probably be the more severe.

How so many absurd rules of conduct, as well as so many absurd
religious beliefs, have originated, we do not know; nor how it is that they
have become, in all quarters of the world, so deeply impressed on the
mind of men; but it is worthy of remark that a belief constantly inculcated during the early years of life, whilst the brain is impressible, appears to acquire almost the nature of an instinct; and the very essence of
an instinct is that it is followed independently of reason. Neither can we
say why certain admirable virtues, such as the love of truth, are much
more highly appreciated by some savage tribes than by others; [43] nor,
again, why similar differences prevail even amongst highly civilised nations. Knowing how firmly fixed many strange customs and superstitions
have become, we need feel no surprise that the self-regarding virtues,
supported as they are by reason, should now appear to us so natural as to
be thought innate, although they were not valued by man in his early
condition.

Notwithstanding many sources of doubt, man can generally and readily distinguish between the higher and lower moral rules. The higher are
founded on the social instincts, and relate to the welfare of others. They
are supported by the approbation of our fellow-men and by reason. The
lower rules, though some of them when implying self-sacrifice hardly deserve to be called lower, relate chiefly to self, and arise from public opinion, matured by experience and cultivation; for they are not practised by
rude tribes.

As man advances in civilisation, and small tribes are united into larger

[43] Good instances are given by Mr. Wallace in 'Scientific Opinion,' Sept. 15, 1869;
and more fully in his 'Contributions to the Theory of Natural Selection,' 1870, p. 353

communities, the simplest reason would tell each individual that he ought to extend his social instincts and sympathies to all the members of the same nation, though personally unknown to him. This point being once reached, there is only an artificial barrier to prevent his sympathies extending to the men of all nations and races. If, indeed, such men are separated from him by great differences in appearance or habits, experience unfortunately shews us how long it is, before we look at them as our fellow-creatures. Sympathy beyond the confines of man, that is, humanity to the lower animals, seems to be one of the latest moral acquisitions. It is apparently unfelt by savages, except towards their pets. How little the old Romans knew of it is shewn by their abhorrent gladiatorial exhibitions. The very idea of humanity, as far as I could observe, was new to most of the Gauchos of the Pampas. This virtue, one of the noblest with which man is endowed, seems to arise incidentally from our sympathies becoming more tender and more widely diffused, until they are extended to all sentient beings. As soon as this virtue is honoured and practised by some few men, it spreads through instruction and example to the young, and eventually becomes incorporated in public opinion.

The highest possible stage in moral culture is when we recognise that we ought to control our thoughts, and "not even in inmost thought to think again the sins that made the past so pleasant to us." [44] Whatever makes any bad action familiar to the mind, renders its performance by so much the easier. As Marcus Aurelius long ago said, "Such as are thy habitual thoughts, such also will be the character of thy mind; for the soul is dyed by the thoughts." [45]

Our great philosopher, Herbert Spencer, has recently explained his views on the moral sense. He says,[46] "I believe that the experiences of utility organised and consolidated through all past generations of the human race, have been producing corresponding modifications, which, by continued transmission and accumulation, have become in us certain faculties of moral intuition—certain emotions responding to right and wrong conduct, which have no apparent basis in the individual experiences of utility." There is not the least inherent improbability, as it seems to me, in virtuous tendencies being more or less strongly inherited; for, not to mention the various dispositions and habits transmitted by many of our domestic animals to their offspring, I have heard of authentic cases in which a desire to steal and a tendency to lie appeared to run in families of the upper ranks; and as stealing is a rare crime in the wealthy classes, we can hardly account by accidental coincidence for the tendency occurring in two or three members of the same family. If bad tendencies are transmitted, it is probable that good ones are likewise transmitted. That the state of the body by affecting the brain, has great influence on the moral tendencies is known to most of those who have suf-

---

[44] Tennyson, 'Idylls of the King,' p. 244.

[45] 'The Thoughts of the Emperor M. Aurelius Antoninus,' Eng. translat., 2nd edit., 1869, p. 112. Marcus Aurelius was born A. D. 121.

[46] Letter to Mr. Mill in Bain's 'Mental and Moral Science,' 1868, p. 722.

fered from chronic derangements of the digestion or liver. The same fact is likewise shewn by the "perversion or destruction of the moral sense being often one of the earliest symptoms of mental derangement;" [47] and insanity is notoriously often inherited. Except through the principle of the transmission of moral tendencies, we cannot understand the differences believed to exist in this respect between the various races of mankind.

Even the partial transmission of virtuous tendencies would be an immense assistance to the primary impulse derived directly and indirectly from the social instincts Admitting for a moment that virtuous tendencies are inherited, it appears probable, at least in such cases as chastity, temperance, humanity to animals, &c., that they become first impressed on the mental organization through habit, instruction and example, continued during several generations in the same family, and in a quite subordinate degree, or not at all, by the individuals possessing such virtues having succeeded best in the struggle for life. My chief source of doubt with respect to any such inheritance, is that senseless customs, superstitions, and tastes, such as the horror of a Hindoo for unclean food, ought on the same principle to be transmitted. I have not met with any evidence in support of the transmission of superstitious customs or senseless habits, although in itself it is perhaps not less probable than that animals should acquire inherited tastes for certain kinds of food or fear of certain foes.

Finally the social instincts, which no doubt were acquired by man as by the lower animals for the good of the community, will from the first have given to him some wish to aid his fellows, some feeling of sympathy, and have compelled him to regard their approbation and disapprobation. Such impulses will have served him at a very early period as a rude rule of right and wrong. But as man gradually advanced in intellectual power, and was enabled to trace the more remote consequences of his actions; as he acquired sufficient knowledge to reject baneful customs and superstitions; as he regarded more and more, not only the welfare, but the happiness of his fellow-men; as from habit, following on beneficial experience, instruction and example, his sympathies became more tender and widely diffused, extending to men of all races, to the imbecile, maimed, and other useless members of society, and finally to the lower animals,—so would the standard of his morality rise higher and higher. And it is admitted by moralists of the derivative school and by some intuitionists, that the standard of morality has risen since an early period in the history of man. [48]

As a struggle may sometimes be seen going on between the various instincts of the lower animals, it is not surprising that there should be a

[47] Maudsley, 'Body and Mind,' 1870, p. 60.
[48] A writer in the 'North British Review' (July, 1869. p. 531), well capable of forming a sound judgment, expresses himself strongly in favour of this conclusion. Mr. Lecky ('Hist. of Morals' vol. i. p. 143) seems to a certain extent to coincide therein.

struggle in man between his social instincts, with their derived virtues, and his lower, though momentarily stronger impulses or desires. This, as Mr. Galton [49] has remarked, is all the less surprising, as man has emerged from a state of barbarism within a comparatively recent period. After having yielded to some temptation we feel a sense of dissatisfaction, shame, repentance, or remorse, analogous to the feelings caused by other powerful instincts or desires, when left unsatisfied or baulked. We compare the weakened impression of a past temptation with the ever present social instincts, or with habits, gained in early youth and strengthened during our whole lives, until they have become almost as strong as instincts. If with the temptation still before us we do not yield, it is because either the social instinct or some custom is at the moment predominant, or because we have learnt that it will appear to us hereafter the stronger, when compared with the weakened impression of the temptation, and we realise that its violation would cause us suffering. Looking to future generations, there is no cause to fear that the social instincts will grow weaker, and we may expect that virtuous habits will grow stronger, becoming perhaps fixed by inheritance. In this case the struggle between our higher and lower impulses will be less severe, and virtue will be triumphant.

Summary of the last two Chapters.—There can be no doubt that the difference between the mind of the lowest man and that of the highest animal is immense. An anthropomorphous ape, if he could take a dispassionate view of his own case, would admit that though he could form an artful plan to plunder a garden—though he could use stones for fighting or for breaking open nuts, yet that the thought of fashioning a stone into a tool was quite beyond his scope. Still less, as he would admit, could he follow out a train of metaphysical reasoning, or solve a mathematical problem, or reflect on God, or admire a grand natural scene. Some apes, however, would probably declare that they could and did admire the beauty of the coloured skin and fur of their partners in marriage. They would admit, that though they could make other apes understand by cries some of their perceptions and simpler wants, the notion of expressing definite ideas by definite sounds had never crossed their minds. They might insist that they were ready to aid their fellow-apes of the same troop in many ways, to risk their lives for them, and to take charge of their orphans; but they would be forced to acknowledge that disinterested love for all living creatures, the most noble attribute of man, was quite beyond their comprehension.

Nevertheless the difference in mind between man and the higher animals, great as it is, certainly is one of degree and not of kind. We have seen that the senses and intuitions, the various emotions and faculties, such as love, memory, attention, curiosity, imitation, reason, &c., of

[49] See his remarkable work on 'Hereditary Genius,' 1869, p. 349. The Duke of Argyll ('Primeval Man,' 1869, p. 188) has some good remarks on the contest in man's nature between right and wrong.

which man boasts, may be found in an incipient, or even sometimes in a well-developed condition, in the lower animals. They are also capable of some inherited improvement, as we see in the domestic dog compared with the wolf or jackal. If it could be proved that certain high mental powers, such as the formation of general concepts, self-consciousness, &c., were absolutely peculiar to man, which seems extremely doubtful, it is not improbable that these qualities are merely the incidental results of other highly-advanced intellectual faculties; and these again mainly the result of the continued use of a perfect language. At what age does the new-born infant possess the power of abstraction, or become self-conscious, and reflect on its own existence? We cannot answer; nor can we answer in regard to the ascending organic scale. The half-art, half-instinct of language still bears the stamp of its gradual evolution. The ennobling belief in God is not universal with man; and the belief in spiritual agencies naturally follows from other mental powers. The moral sense perhaps affords the best and highest distinction between man and the lower animals; but I need say nothing on this head, as I have so lately endeavoured to shew that the social instincts,—the prime principle of man's moral constitution [50]—with the aid of active intellectual powers and the effects of habit, naturally lead to the golden rule, "As ye would that men should do to you, do ye to them likewise;" and this lies at the foundation of morality.

In the next chapter I shall make some few remarks on the probable steps and means by which the several mental and moral faculties of man have been gradually evolved. That such evolution is at least possible, ought not to be denied, for we daily see these faculties developing in every infant; and we may trace a perfect gradation from the mind of an utter idiot, lower than that of an animal low in the scale, to the mind of a Newton.

[50] 'The Thoughts of Marcus Aurelius,' &c., p. 139.

CHAPTER V

ON THE DEVELOPMENT OF THE INTELLECTUAL AND MORAL FACULTIES
DURING PRIMEVAL AND CIVILISED TIMES

Advancement of the intellectual powers through natural selection—Importance of imitation—Social and moral faculties—Their development within the limits of the same tribe—Natural selection as affecting civilised nations—Evidence that civilised nations were once barbarous.

THE subjects to be discussed in this chapter are of the highest interest, but are treated by me in an imperfect and fragmentary manner. Mr. Wallace, in an admirable paper before referred to,[1] argues that man, after he had partially acquired those intellectual and moral faculties which distinguish him from the lower animals, would have been but little liable to bodily modifications through natural selection or any other means. For man is enabled through his mental faculties "to keep with an unchanged body in harmony with the changing universe." He has great power of adapting his habits to new conditions of life. He invents weapons, tools, and various stratagems to procure food and to defend himself. When he migrates into a colder climate he uses clothes, builds sheds, and makes fires; and by the aid of fire cooks food otherwise indigestible. He aids his fellow-men in many ways, and anticipates future events. Even at a remote period he practised some division of labour.

The lower animals, on the other hand, must have their bodily structure modified in order to survive under greatly changed conditions. They must be rendered stronger, or acquire more effective teeth or claws, for defence against new enemies; or they must be reduced in size, so as to escape detection and danger. When they migrate into a colder climate, they must become clothed with thicker fur, or have their constitutions altered. If they fail to be thus modified, they will cease to exist.

The case, however, is widely different, as Mr. Wallace has with justice insisted, in relation to the intellectual and moral faculties of man. These faculties are variable; and we have every reason to believe that the variations tend to be inherited. Therefore, if they were formerly of high importance to primeval man and to his ape-like progenitors, they would have been perfected or advanced through natural selection. Of the high importance of the intellectual faculties there can be no doubt, for man mainly owes to them his predominant position in the world. We can see, that in the rudest state of society, the individuals who were the most

[1] 'Anthropological Review,' May, 1864, p. clviii.

sagacious, who invented and used the best weapons or traps, and who were best able to defend themselves, would rear the greatest number of offspring. The tribes, which included the largest number of men thus endowed, would increase in number and supplant other tribes. Numbers depend primarily on the means of subsistence, and this depends partly on the physical nature of the coutry, but in a much higher degree on the arts which are there practised. As a tribe increases and is victorious, it is often still further increased by the absorption of other tribes.[2] The stature and strength of the men of a tribe are likewise of some importance for its success, and these depend in part on the nature and amount of the food which can be obtained. In Europe the men of the Bronze period were supplanted by a race more powerful, and, judging from their sword-handles, with larger hands;[3] but their success was probably still more due to their superiority in the arts.

All that we know about savages, or may infer from their traditions and from old monuments, the history of which is quite forgotten by the present inhabitants, shew that from the remotest times successful tribes have supplanted other tribes. Relics of extinct or forgotten tribes have been discovered throughout the civilised regions of the earth, on the wild plains of America, and on the isolated islands in the Pacific Ocean. At the present day civilised nations are everywhere supplanting barbarous nations, excepting where the climate opposes a deadly barrier; and they succeed mainly, though not exclusively, through their arts, which are the products of the intellect. It is, therefore, highly probable that with mankind the intellectual faculties have been mainly and gradually perfected through natural selection; and this conclusion is sufficient for our purpose. Undoubtedly it would be interesting to trace the development of each separate faculty from the state in which it exists in the lower animals to that in which it exists in man; but neither my ability nor knowledge permits the attempt.

It deserves notice that, as soon as the progenitors of man became social (and this probably occurred at a very early period), the principle of imitation, and reason, and experience would have increased, and much modified the intellectual powers in a way, of which we see only traces in the lower animals. Apes are much given to imitation, as are the lowest savages; and the simple fact previously referred to, that after a time no animal can be caught in the same place by the same sort of trap, shews that animals learn by experience, and imitate the caution of others. Now, if some one man in a tribe, more sagacious than the others, invented a new snare or weapon, or other means of attack or defence, the plainest self-interest, without the assistance of much reasoning power, would prompt the other members to imitate him; and all would thus profit. The habitual practice of each new art must likewise in some slight degree strengthen the intellect. If the new invention were an important one, the tribe would

---

[2] After a time the members or tribes which are absorbed into another tribe assume, as Sir Henry Maine remarks ('Ancient Law,' 1861, p. 131), that they are the co-descendants of the same ancestors.

[3] Morlot, 'Soc. Vaud. Sc. Nat.' 1860, p. 294.

increase in number, spread, and supplant other tribes. In a tribe thus rendered more numerous there would always be a rather greater chance of the birth of other superior and inventive members. If such men left children to inherit their mental superiority, the chance of the birth of still more ingenious members would be somewhat better, and in a very small tribe decidedly better. Even if they left no children, the tribe would still include their blood-relations; and it has been ascertained by agriculturists[4] that by preserving and breeding from the family of an animal, which when slaughtered was found to be valuable, the desired character has been obtained.

Turning now to the social and moral faculties. In order that primeval men, or the ape-like progenitors of man, should become social, they must have acquired the same instinctive feelings, which impel other animals to live in a body; and they no doubt exhibited the same general disposition. They would have felt uneasy when separated from their comrades, for whom they would have felt some degree of love; they would have warned each other of danger, and have given mutual aid in attack or defence. All this implies some degree of sympathy, fidelity, and courage. Such social qualities, the paramount importance of which to the lower animals is disputed by no one, were no doubt acquired by the progenitors of man in a similar manner, namely, through natural selection, aided by inherited habit. When two tribes of primeval man, living in the same country, came into competition, if (other circumstances being equal) the one tribe included a great number of courageous, sympathetic and faithful members, who were always ready to warn each other of danger, to aid and defend each other, this tribe would succeed better and conquer the other. Let it be borne in mind how all-important in the never-ceasing wars of savages, fidelity and courage must be. The advantage which disciplined soldiers have over undisciplined hordes follows chiefly from the confidence which each man feels in his comrades. Obedience, as Mr. Bagehot has well shewn,[5] is of the highest value, for any form of government is better than none. Selfish and contentious people will not cohere, and without coherence nothing can be effected. A tribe rich in the above qualities would spread and be victorious over other tribes: but in the course of time it would, judging from all past history, be in its turn overcome by some other tribe still more highly endowed. Thus the social and moral qualities would tend slowly to advance and be diffused throughout the world.

But it may be asked, how within the limits of the same tribe did a large number of members first become endowed with these social and moral qualities, and how was the standard of excellence raised? It is extremely doubtful whether the offspring of the more sympathetic and benevolent

[4] I have given instances in my 'Variation of Animals under Domestication,' vol. ii. p. 196.
[5] See a remarkable series of articles on 'Physics and Politics,' in the 'Fortnightly Review,' Nov. 1867; April 1, 1868; July 1, 1869, since separately published.

parents, or of those who were the most faithful to their comrades, would be reared in greater numbers than the children of selfish and treacherous parents belonging to the same tribe. He who was ready to sacrifice his life, as many a savage has been, rather than betray his comrades, would often leave no offspring to inherit his noble nature. The bravest men, who were always willing to come to the front in war, and who freely risked their lives for others, would on an average perish in larger numbers than other men. Therefore it hardly seems probable, that the number of men gifted with such virtues, or that the standard of their excellence, could be increased through natural selection, that is, by the survival of the fittest; for we are not here speaking of one tribe being victorious over another.

Although the circumstances, leading to an increase in the number of those thus endowed within the same tribe, are too complex to be clearly followed out, we can trace some of the probable steps. In the first place, as the reasoning powers and foresight of the members became improved, each man would soon learn that if he aided his fellow-men, he would commonly receive aid in return. From this low motive he might acquire the habit of aiding his fellows; and the habit of performing benevolent actions certainly strengthens the feeling of sympathy which gives the first impulse to benevolent actions. Habits, moreover, followed during many generations probably tend to be inherited.

But another and much more powerful stimulus to the development of the social virtues, is afforded by the praise and the blame of our fellow-men. To the instinct of sympathy, as we have already seen, it is primarily due, that we habitually bestow both praises and blame on others, whilst we love the former and dread the latter when applied to ourselves; and this instinct no doubt was originally acquired, like all the other social instincts, through natural selection. At how early a period the progenitors of man in the course of their development, became capable of feeling and being impelled by, the praise or blame of their fellow-creatures, we cannot of course say. But it appears that even dogs appreciate encouragement, praise, and blame. The rudest savages feel the sentiment of glory, as they clearly show by preserving the trophies of their prowess, by their habit of excessive boasting, and even by the extreme care which they take of their personal appearance and decorations; for unless they regarded the opinion of their comrades, such habits would be senseless.

They certainly feel shame at the breach of some of their lesser rules, and apparently remorse, as shewn by the case of the Australian who grew thin and could not rest from having delayed to murder some other woman, so as to propitiate his dead wife's spirit. Though I have not met with any other recorded case, it is scarcely credible that a savage, who will sacrifice his life rather than betray his tribe, or one who will deliver himself up as a prisoner rather than break his parole,[6] would not feel remorse in his inmost soul, if he had failed in a duty, which he held sacred.

[6] Mr. Wallace gives cases in his 'Contributions to the Theory of Natural Selection,' 1870, p. 354.

We may therefore conclude that primeval man, at a very remote period, was influenced by the praise and blame of his fellows. It is obvious,
that the members of the same tribe would approve of conduct which appeared to them to be for the general good, and would reprobate that
which appeared evil. To do good unto others—to do unto others as ye
would they should do unto you—is the foundation-stone of morality. It
is, therefore, hardly possible to exaggerate the importance during rude
times of the love of praise and the dread of blame. A man who was not
impelled by any deep, instinctive feeling, to sacrifice his life for the good
of others, yet was roused to such actions by a sense of glory, would by
his example excite the same wish for glory in other men, and would
strengthen by exercise the noble feeling of admiration. He might thus do
far more good to his tribe than by begetting offspring with a tendency to
inherit his own high character.

With increased experience and reason, man perceives the more remote
consequences of his actions, and the self-regarding virtues, such as temperance, chastity, &c., which during early times are, as we have before
seen, utterly disregarded, come to be highly esteemed or even held sacred.
I need not, however, repeat what I have said on this head in the fourth
chapter. Ultimately our moral sense or conscience becomes a highly complex sentiment—originating in the social instincts, largely guided by the
approbation of our fellow-men, ruled by reason, self-interest, and in later
times by deep religious feelings, and confirmed by instruction and habit.

It must not be forgotten that although a high standard of morality
gives but a slight or no advantage to each individual man and his children over the other men of the same tribe, yet that an increase in the
number of well-endowed men and an advancement in the standard of
morality will certainly give an immense advantage to one tribe over another. A tribe including many members who, from possessing in a high
degree the spirit of patriotism, fidelity, obedience, courage, and sympathy, were always ready to aid one another, and to sacrifice themselves
for the common good, would be victorious over most other tribes; and
this would be natural selection. At all times throughout the world tribes
have supplanted other tribes; and as morality is one important element
in their success, the standard of morality and the number of well-endowed men will thus everywhere tend to rise and increase.

It is, however, very difficult to form any judgment why one particular
tribe and not another has been successful and has risen in the scale of
civilisation. Many savages are in the same condition as when first discovered several centuries ago. As Mr. Bagehot has remarked, we are apt
to look at the progress as normal in human society; but history refutes
this. The ancients did not even entertain the idea, nor do the Oriental
nations at the present day. According to another high authority, Sir
Henry Maine,[7] "the greatest part of mankind has never shewn a particle
of desire that its civil institutions should be improved." Progress seems to

---

[7] 'Ancient Law,' 1861, p. 22. For Mr. Bagehot's remarks, 'Fortnightly Review,'
April 1, 1868, p. 452.

depend on many concurrent favourable conditions, far too complex to be followed out. But it has often been remarked, that a cool climate, from leading to industry and to the various arts, has been highly favourable thereto. The Esquimaux, pressed by hard necessity, have succeeded in many ingenious inventions, but their climate has been too severe for continued progress. Nomadic habits, whether over wide plains, or through the dense forests of the tropics, or along the shores of the sea, have in every case been highly detrimental. Whilst observing the barbarous inhabitants of Tierra del Fuego, it struck me that the possession of some property, a fixed abode, and the union of many families under a chief, were the indispensable requisites for civilisation Such habits almost necessitate the cultivation of the ground; and the first steps in cultivation would probably result, as I have elsewhere shewn,[8] from some such accident as the seeds of a fruit-tree falling on a heap of refuse, and producing an unusually fine variety. The problem, however, of the first advance of savages towards civilisation is at present much too difficult to be solved.

Natural Selection as affecting Civilised Nations.—I have hitherto only considered the advancement of man from a semi-human condition to that of the modern savage. But some remarks on the action of natural selection on civilised nations may be worth adding. This subject has been ably discussed by Mr. W. R. Greg,[9] and previously by Mr. Wallace and Mr. Galton.[10] Most of my remarks are taken from these three authors. With savages, the weak in body or mind are soon eliminated; and those that survive commonly exhibit a vigorous state of health. We civilised men, on the other hand, do our utmost to check the process of elimination; we build asylums for the imbecile, the maimed, and the sick; we institute poor-laws; and our medical men exert their utmost skill to save the life of every one to the last moment. There is reason to believe that vaccination has preserved thousands, who from a weak constitution would formerly have succumbed to small-pox. Thus the weak members of civilised societies propagate their kind. No one who has attended to the breeding of domestic animals will doubt that this must be highly injurious to the race of man. It is surprising how soon a want of care, or care wrongly directed, leads to the degeneration of a domestic race; but excepting in the case of man himself, hardly any one is so ignorant as to allow his worst animals to breed.

The aid which we feel impelled to give to the helpless is mainly an in-

[8] 'The Variation of Animals and Plants under Domestication,' vol. i. p. 309.

[9] 'Fraser's Magazine,' Sept. 1868, p. 353. This article seems to have struck many persons, and has given rise to two remarkable essays and a rejoinder in the 'Spectator,' Oct. 3rd and 17th, 1868. It has also been discussed in the 'Q. Journal of Science,' 1869, p. 152, and by Mr. Lawson Tait in the 'Dublin Q. Journal of Medical Science,' Feb. 1869, and by Mr. E. Ray Lankester in his 'Comparative Longevity,' 1870, p. 128. Similar views appeared previously in the 'Australasian,' July 13, 1867. I have borrowed ideas from several of these writers.

[10] For Mr. Wallace, see 'Anthropolog. Review,' as before cited. Mr. Galton in 'Macmillan's Magazine,' Aug. 1865, p. 318; also his great work, 'Hereditary Genius,' 1870.

cidental result of the instinct of sympathy, which was originally acquired as part of the social instincts, but subsequently rendered, in the manner previously indicated, more tender and more widely diffused. Nor could we check our sympathy, even at the urging of hard reason, without deterioration in the noblest part of our nature. The surgeon may harden himself whilst performing an operation, for he knows that he is acting for the good of his patient; but if we were intentionally to neglect the weak and helpless, it could only be for a contingent benefit, with an overwhelming present evil. We must therefore bear the undoubtedly bad effects of the weak surviving and propagating their kind; but there appears to be at least one check in steady action, namely that the weaker and inferior members of society do not marry so freely as the sound; and this check might be indefinitely increased by the weak in body or mind refraining from marriage, though this is more to be hoped for than expected.

In every country in which a large standing army is kept up, the finest young men are taken by the conscription or are enlisted. They are thus exposed to early death during war, are often tempted into vice, and are prevented from marrying during the prime of life. On the other hand the shorter and feebler men, with poor constitutions, are left at home, and consequently have a much better chance of marrying and propagating their kind.[11]

Man accumulates property and bequeaths it to his children, so that the children of the rich have an advantage over the poor in the race for success, independently of bodily or mental superiority. On the other hand, the children of parents who are short-lived, and are therefore on an average deficient in health and vigour, come into their property sooner than other children, and will be likely to marry earlier, and leave a larger number of offspring to inherit their inferior constitutions. But the inheritance of property by itself is very far from an evil; for without the accumulation of capital the arts could not progress; and it is chiefly through their power that the civilised races have extended, and are now everywhere extending their range, so as to take the place of the lower races. Nor does the moderate accumulation of wealth interfere with the process of selection. When a poor man becomes moderately rich, his children enter trades or professions in which there is struggle enough, so that the able in body and mind succeed best. The presence of a body of well-instructed men, who have not to labour for their daily bread, is important to a degree which cannot be over-estimated; as all high intellectual work is carried on by them, and on such work, material progress of all kinds mainly depends, not to mention other and higher advantages. No doubt wealth when very great tends to convert men into useless drones, but their number is never large; and some degree of elimination here occurs, for we daily see rich men, who happen to be fools or profligate, squandering away their wealth.

Primogeniture with entailed estates is a more direct evil, though it may

---

[11] Prof. H. Fick ('Einfluss der Naturwissenschaft auf das Recht,' June, 1872) has some good remarks on this head, and on other such points.

formerly have been a great advantage by the creation of a dominant class, and any government is better than none. Most eldest sons, though they may be weak in body or mind, marry, whilst the younger sons, however superior in these respects, do not so generally marry. Nor can worthless eldest sons with entailed estates squander their wealth. But here, as elsewhere, the relations of civilised life are so complex that some compensatory checks intervene. The men who are rich through primogeniture are able to select generation after generation the more beautiful and charming women; and these must generally be healthy in body and active in mind. The evil consequences, such as they may be, of the continued preservation of the same line of descent, without any selection, are checked by men of rank always wishing to increase their wealth and power; and this they effect by marrying heiresses. But the daughters of parents who have produced single children, are themselves, as Mr. Galton[12] has shewn, apt to be sterile; and thus noble families are continually cut off in the direct line, and their wealth flows into some side channel; but unfortunately this channel is not determined by superiority of any kind.

Although civilisation thus checks in many ways the action of natural selection, it apparently favours the better development of the body, by means of good food and the freedom from occasional hardships. This may be inferred from civilised men having been found, wherever compared, to be physically stronger than savages.[13] They appear also to have equal powers of endurance, as has been proved in many adventurous expeditions. Even the great luxury of the rich can be but little detrimental; for the expectation of life of our aristocracy, at all ages and of both sexes, is very little inferior to that of healthy English lives in the lower classes.[14]

We will now look to the intellectual faculties. If in each grade of society the members were divided into two equal bodies, the one including the intellectually superior and the other the inferior, there can be little doubt that the former would succeed best in all occupations, and rear a greater number of children. Even in the lowest walks of life, skill and ability must be of some advantage; though in many occupations, owing to the great division of labour, a very small one. Hence in civilised nations there will be some tendency to an increase both in the number and in the standard of the intellectually able. But I do not wish to assert that this tendency may not be more than counterbalanced in other ways, as by the multiplication of the reckless and improvident; but even to such as these, ability must be some advantage.

It has often been objected to views like the foregoing, that the most eminent men who have ever lived have left no offspring to inherit their great intellect. Mr. Galton says,[15] "I regret I am unable to solve the simple question whether, and how far, men and women who are prodigies of genius are infertile. I have, however, shewn that men of eminence are by

---

[12] 'Hereditary Genius,' 1870, pp. 132-140.

[13] Quatrefages, 'Revue des Cours Scientifiques,' 1867-68, p. 659.

[14] See the fifth and sixth columns compiled from good authorities, in the table given in Mr. E. R. Lankester's 'Comparative Longevity,' 1870, p. 115.

[15] 'Hereditary Genius,' 1870, p. 330.

no means so." Great lawgivers, the founders of beneficent religions, great philosophers and discoverers in science, aid the progress of mankind in a far higher degree by their works than by leaving a numerous progeny. In the case of corporeal structures, it is the selection of the slightly better-endowed and the elimination of the slightly less well-endowed individuals, and not the preservation of strongly-marked and rare anomalies, that leads to the advancement of a species.[16] So it will be with the intellectual faculties, since the somewhat abler men in each grade of society succeed rather better than the less able, and consequently increase in number, if not otherwise prevented. When in any nation the standard of intellect and the number of intellectual men have increased, we may expect from the law of the deviation from an average, that prodigies of genius will, as shewn by Mr. Galton, appear somewhat more frequently than before.

In regard to the moral qualities, some elimination of the worst dispositions is always in progress even in the most civilised nations. Malefactors are executed, or imprisoned for long periods, so that they cannot freely transmit their bad qualities. Melancholic and insane persons are confined, or commit suicide. Violent and quarrelsome men often come to a bloody end. The restless who will not follow any steady occupation—and this relic of barbarism is a great check to civilisation[17]—emigrate to newly-settled countries, where they prove useful pioneers. Intemperance is so highly destructive, that the expectation of life of the intemperate, at the age of thirty for instance, is only 13.8 years; whilst for the rural labourers of England at the same age it is 40.59 years.[18] Profligate women bear few children, and profligate men rarely marry; both suffer from disease. In the breeding of domestic animals, the elimination of those individuals, though few in number, which are in any marked manner inferior, is by no means an unimportant element towards success. This especially holds good with injurious characters which tend to reappear through reversion, such as blackness in sheep; and with mankind some of the worst dispositions, which occasionally without any assignable cause make their appearance in families, may perhaps be reversions to a savage state, from which we are not removed by very many generations. This view seems indeed recognised in the common expression that such men are the black sheep of the family.

With civilised nations, as far as an advanced standard of morality, and an increased number of fairly good men are concerned, natural selection apparently effects but little; though the fundamental social instincts were originally thus gained. But I have already said enough, whilst treating of the lower races, on the causes which lead to the advance of morality, namely, the approbation of our fellow-men—the strengthening of our

[16] 'Origin of Species,' this edition, p. 78.
[17] 'Hereditary Genius,' 1870, p. 347.
[18] E. Ray Lankester, 'Comparative Longevity,' 1870, p. 115. The table of the intemperate is from Neison's 'Vital Statistics.' In regard to profligacy, see Dr. Farr, 'Influence of Marriage on Mortality,' 'Nat. Assoc. for the Promotion of Social Science,' 1858.

sympathies by habit—example and imitation—reason—experience, and even self-interest—instruction during youth, and religious feelings

A most important obstacle in civilised countries to an increase in the number of men of a superior class has been strongly insisted on by Mr. Greg and Mr. Galton,[19] namely, the fact that the very poor and reckless, who are often degraded by vice, almost invariably marry early, whilst the careful and frugal, who are generally otherwise virtuous, marry late in life, so that they may be able to support themselves and their children in comfort. Those who marry early produce within a given period not only a greater number of generations, but, as shewn by Dr. Duncan,[20] they produce many more children. The children, moreover, that are borne by mothers during the prime of life are heavier and larger, and therefore probably more vigorous, than those born at other periods. Thus the reckless, degraded, and often vicious members of society, tend to increase at a quicker rate than the provident and generally virtuous members. Or as Mr. Greg puts the case: "The careless, squalid, unaspiring Irishman multiplies like rabbits: the frugal, foreseeing, self-respecting, ambitious Scot, stern in his morality, spiritual in his faith, sagacious and disciplined in his intelligence, passes his best years in struggle and in celibacy, marries late, and leaves few behind him. Given a land originally peopled by a thousand Saxons and a thousand Celts—and in a dozen generations five-sixths of the population would be Celts, but five-sixths of the property, of the power, of the intellect, would belong to the one-sixth of Saxons that remained. In the eternal 'struggle for existence,' it would be the inferior and *less* favoured race that had prevailed—and prevailed by virtue not of its good qualities but of its faults."

There are, however, some checks to this downward tendency. We have seen that the intemperate suffer from a high rate of mortality, and the extremely profligate leave few offspring. The poorest classes crowd into towns, and it has been proved by Dr. Stark from the statistics of ten years in Scotland,[21] that at all ages the death-rate is higher in towns than in rural districts, "and during the first five years of life the town death-rate is almost exactly double that of the rural districts." As these returns include both the rich and the poor, no doubt more than twice the number of births would be requisite to keep up the number of the very poor inhabitants in the towns, relatively to those in the country. With women, marriage at too early an age is highly injurious; for it has been found in France that, "twice as many wives under twenty die in the year, as died out of the same number of the unmarried." The mortality, also, of hus-

[19] 'Fraser's Magazine,' Sept. 1868, p. 353. 'Macmillan's Magazine,' Aug. 1865, p. 318. The Rev. F. W. Farrar ('Fraser's Mag.,' Aug. 1870, p. 264) takes a different view.

[20] 'On the Laws of the Fertility of Women,' in 'Transact. Royal Soc.,' Edinburgh, vol. xxiv. p. 287; now published separately under the title of 'Fecundity, Fertility, and Sterility,' 1871. See, also, Mr. Galton, 'Hereditary Genius,' pp. 352-357, for observations to the above effect.

[21] 'Tenth Annual Report of Births, Deaths, &c., in Scotland,' 1867, p. xxix.

bands under twenty is "excessively high,"[22] but what the cause of this may be, seems doubtful. Lastly, if the men who prudently delay marrying until they can bring up their families in comfort, were to select, as they often do, women in the prime of life, the rate of increase in the better class would be only slightly lessened.

It was established from an enormous body of statistics, taken during 1853, that the unmarried men throughout France, between the ages of twenty and eighty, die in a much larger proportion than the married: for instance, out of every 1000 unmarried men, between the ages of twenty and thirty, 11.3 annually died, whilst of the married, only 6.5 died.[23] A similar law was proved to hold good, during the years 1863 and 1864, with the entire population above the age of twenty in Scotland: for instance, out of every 1000 unmarried men, between the ages of twenty and thirty, 14.97 annually died, whilst of the married only 7.24 died, that is less than half.[24] Dr. Stark remarks on this, "Bachelorhood is more destructive to life than the most unwholesome trades, or than residence in an unwholesome house or district where there has never been the most distant attempt at sanitary improvement." He considers that the lessened mortality is the direct result of "marriage, and the more regular domestic habits which attend that state." He admits, however, that the intemperate, profligate, and criminal classes, whose duration of life is low, do not commonly marry; and it must likewise be admitted that men with a weak constitution, ill health, or any great infirmity in body or mind, will often not wish to marry, or will be rejected. Dr. Stark seems to have come to the conclusion that marriage in itself is a main cause of prolonged life, from finding that aged married men still have a considerable advantage in this respect over the unmarried of the same advanced age; but every one must have known instances of men, who with weak health during youth did not marry, and yet have survived to old age, though remaining weak, and therefore always with a lessened chance of life or of marrying. There is another remarkable circumstance which seems to support Dr. Stark's conclusion, namely, that widows and widowers in France suffer in comparison with the married a very heavy rate of mortality; but Dr. Farr attributes this to the poverty and evil habits consequent on the disruption of the family, and to grief. On the whole we may conclude with Dr. Farr that the lesser mortality of married than of unmarried men, which seems to be a general law, "is mainly due to the constant elimination of imperfect types, and to the skilful selection of the finest individu-

---

[22] These quotations are taken from our highest authority on such questions, namely, Dr. Farr, in his paper 'On the Influence of Marriage on the Mortality of the French People,' read before the Nat. Assoc. for the Promotion of Social Science, 1858.

[23] Dr. Farr, ibid. The quotations given below are extracted from the same striking paper.

[24] I have taken the mean of the quinquennial means, given in 'The Tenth Annual Report of Births, Deaths, &c., in Scotland,' 1867. The quotation from Dr. Stark is copied from an article in the 'Daily News,' Oct. 17th, 1868, which Dr. Farr considers very carefully written.

als out of each successive generation;" the selection relating only to the marriage state, and acting on all corporeal, intellectual, and moral qualities.[25] We may, therefore, infer that sound and good men who out of prudence remain for a time unmarried, do not suffer a high rate of mortality.

If the various checks specified in the two last paragraphs, and perhaps others as yet unknown, do not prevent the reckless, the vicious and otherwise inferior members of society from increasing at a quicker rate than the better class of men, the nation will retrograde, as has too often occurred in the history of the world. We must remember that progress is no invariable rule. It is very difficult to say why one civilised nation rises, becomes more powerful, and spreads more widely, than another; or why the same nation progresses more quickly at one time than at another. We can only say that it depends on an increase in the actual number of the population, on the number of the men endowed with high intellectual and moral faculties, as well as on their standard of excellence. Corporeal structure appears to have little influence, except so far as vigour of body leads to vigour of mind.

It has been urged by several writers that as high intellectual powers are advantageous to a nation, the old Greeks, who stood some grades higher in intellect than any race that has ever existed,[26] ought, if the power of natural selection were real, to have risen still higher in the scale, increased in number, and stocked the whole of Europe. Here we have the tacit assumption, so often made with respect to corporeal structures, that there is some innate tendency towards continued development in mind and body. But development of all kinds depends on many concurrent favourable circumstances. Natural selection acts only tentatively. Individuals and races may have acquired certain indisputable advantages, and yet have perished from failing in other characters. The Greeks may have retrograded from a want of coherence between the many small states, from the small size of their whole country, from the practice of slavery, or from extreme sensuality; for they did not succumb until "they were enervated and corrupt to the very core."[27] The western nations of Europe, who now so immeasurably surpass their former savage progenitors, and stand at the summit of civilisation, owe little or none of their superiority to direct inheritance from the old Greeks, though they owe much to the written works of that wonderful people.

Who can positively say why the Spanish nation, so dominant at one time, has been distanced in the race. The awakening of the nations of Europe from the dark ages is a still more perplexing problem. At that early period, as Mr. Galton has remarked, almost all the men of a gentle nature, those given to meditation or culture of the mind, had no refuge

[25] Dr. Duncan remarks ('Fecundity, Fertility,' &c., 1871, p. 334) on this subject; "At every age the healthy and beautiful go over from the unmarried side to the married, leaving the unmarried columns crowded with the sickly and unfortunate."

[26] See the ingenious and original argument on this subject by Mr. Galton, 'Hereditary Genius,' pp. 340-342.

[27] Mr. Greg, 'Fraser's Magazine,' Sept. 1868, p. 357.

except in the bosom of a Church which demanded celibacy;[28] and this could hardly fail to have had a deteriorating influence on each successive generation. During this same period the Holy Inquisition selected with extreme care the freest and boldest men in order to burn or imprison them. In Spain alone some of the best men—those who doubted and questioned, and without doubting there can be no progress—were eliminated during three centuries at the rate of a thousand a year. The evil which the Catholic Church has thus effected is incalculable, though no doubt counterbalanced to a certain, perhaps to a large, extent in other ways; nevertheless, Europe has progressed at an unparalleled rate.

The remarkable success of the English as colonists, compared to other European nations, has been ascribed to their "daring and persistent energy;" a result which is well illustrated by comparing the progress of the Canadians of English and French extraction; but who can say how the English gained their energy? There is apparently much truth in the belief that the wonderful progress of the United States, as well as the character of the people, are the results of natural selection; for the more energetic, restless, and courageous men from all parts of Europe have emigrated during the last ten or twelve generations to that great country, and have there succeeded best.[29] Looking to the distant future, I do not think that the Rev. Mr. Zincke takes an exaggerated view when he says:[30] "All other series of events—as that which resulted in the culture of mind in Greece, and that which resulted in the empire of Rome—only appear to have purpose and value when viewed in connection with, or rather as subsidiary to . . . . the great stream of Anglo-Saxon emigration to the west." Obscure as is the problem of the advance of civilisation, we can at least see that a nation which produced during a lengthened period the greatest number of highly intellectual, energetic, brave, patriotic, and benevolent men, would generally prevail over less favoured nations.

Natural selection follows from the struggle for existence; and this from a rapid rate of increase. It is impossible not to regret bitterly, but whether wisely is another question, the rate at which man tends to increase; for this leads in barbarous tribes to infanticide and many other evils, and in civilised nations to abject poverty, celibacy, and to the late marriages of the prudent. But as man suffers from the same physical evils as the lower animals, he has no right to expect an immunity from the evils consequent on the struggle for existence. Had he not been subjected during primeval times to natural selection, assuredly he would never have attained to his present rank. Since we see in many parts of the world enormous areas of the most fertile land capable of supporting numerous happy homes, but

[28] 'Hereditary Genius,' 1870, pp. 357-359. The Rev. F. W. Farrar ('Fraser's Mag.,' Aug. 1870, p. 257) advances arguments on the other side. Sir C. Lyell had already ('Principles of Geology,' vol. ii. 1868, p. 489) in a striking passage called attention to the evil influence of the Holy Inquisition in having, through selection, lowered the general standard of intelligence in Europe.

[29] Mr. Galton, 'Macmillan's Magazine,' August, 1865, p. 325. See also, 'Nature,' 'On Darwinism and National Life,' Dec. 1869, p. 184.

[30] 'Last Winter in the United States,' 1868, p. 29.

peopled only by a few wandering savages, it might be argued that the struggle for existence had not been sufficiently severe to force man upwards to his highest standard. Judging from all that we know of man and the lower animals, there has always been sufficient variability in their intellectual and moral faculties, for a steady advance through natural selection. No doubt such advance demands many favourable concurrent circumstances; but it may well be doubted whether the most favourable would have sufficed, had not the rate of increase been rapid, and the consequent struggle for existence extremely severe. It even appears from what we see, for instance, in parts of S. America, that a people which may be called civilised, such as the Spanish settlers, is liable to become indolent and to retrograde, when the conditions of life are very easy. With highly civilised nations continued progress depends in a subordinate degree on natural selection; for such nations do not supplant and exterminate one another as do savage tribes. Nevertheless the more intelligent members within the same community will succeed better in the long run than the inferior, and leave a more numerous progeny, and this is a form of natural selection. The more efficient causes of progress seem to consist of a good education during youth whilst the brain is impressible, and of a high standard of excellence, inculcated by the ablest and best men, embodied in the laws, customs and traditions of the nation, and enforced by public opinion. It should, however, be borne in mind, that the enforcement of public opinion depends on our appreciation of the approbation and disapprobation of others; and this appreciation is founded on our sympathy, which it can hardly be doubted was originally developed through natural selection as one of the most important elements of the social instincts.[31]

On the evidence that all civilised nations were once barbarous.—The present subject has been treated in so full and admirable a manner by Sir J. Lubbock,[32] Mr. Tylor, Mr. M'Lennan, and others, that I need here give only the briefest summary of their results. The arguments recently advanced by the Duke of Argyll[33] and formerly by Archbishop Whately, in favour of the belief that man came into the world as a civilised being, and that all savages have since undergone degradation, seem to me weak in comparison with those advanced on the other side. Many nations, no doubt, have fallen away in civilisation, and some may have lapsed into utter barbarism, though on this latter head I have met with no evidence. The Fuegians were probably compelled by other conquering hordes to settle in their inhospitable country, and they may have become in consequence somewhat more degraded; but it would be difficult to prove that they have fallen much below the Botocudos, who inhabit the finest parts of Brazil.

[31] I am much indebted to Mr. John Morley for some good criticisms on this subject: see, also Broca, 'Les Sélections,' 'Revue d'Anthropologie,' 1872.
[32] 'On the Origin of Civilisation,' 'Proc. Ethnological Soc.,' Nov. 26, 1867.
[33] 'Primeval Man,' 1869.

The evidence that all civilised nations are the descendants of barbarians, consists, on the one side, of clear traces of their former low condition in still-existing customs, beliefs, language, &c.; and on the other side, of proofs that savages are independently able to raise themselves a few steps in the scale of civilisation, and have actually thus risen. The evidence on the first head is extremely curious, but cannot be here given: I refer to such cases as that of the art of enumeration, which, as Mr. Tylor clearly shews by reference to the words still used in some places, originated in counting the fingers, first of one hand and then of the other, and lastly of the toes. We have traces of this in our own decimal system, and in the Roman numerals, where, after the V., which is supposed to be an abbreviated picture of a human hand, we pass on to VI., &c., when the other hand no doubt was used. So again, "when we speak of three-score and ten, we are counting by the vigesimal system, each score thus ideally made, standing for 20—for 'one man' as a Mexican or Carib would put it."[34] According to a large and increasing school of philologists, every language bears the marks of its slow and gradual evolution. So it is with the art of writing, for letters are rudiments of pictorial representations. It is hardly possible to read Mr. M'Lennan's work [35] and not admit that almost all civilised nations still retain traces of such rude habits as the forcible capture of wives. What ancient nation, as the same author asks, can be named that was originally monogamous? The primitive idea of justice, as shewn by the law of battle and other customs of which vestiges still remain, was likewise most rude. Many existing superstitions are the remnants of former false religious beliefs. The highest form of religion—the grand idea of God hating sin and loving righteousness—was unknown during primeval times.

Turning to the other kind of evidence: Sir J. Lubbock has shewn that some savages have recently improved a little in some of their simpler arts. From the extremely curious account which he gives of the weapons, tools, and arts, in use amongst savages in various parts of the world, it cannot be doubted that these have nearly all been independent discoveries, excepting perhaps the art of making fire.[36] The Australian boomerang is a good instance of one such independent discovery. The Tahitians when first visited had advanced in many respects beyond the inhabitants of most of the other Polynesian islands. There are no just grounds for the belief that the high culture of the native Peruvians and Mexicans was de-

---

[34] 'Royal Institution of Great Britain,' March 15, 1867. Also, 'Researches into the Early History of Mankind,' 1865.

[35] 'Primitive Marriage,' 1865. See, likewise, an excellent article, evidently by the same author, in the 'North British Review,' July, 1869. Also, Mr. L. H. Morgan, 'A Conjectural Solution of the Origin of the Class, System of Relationship,' in 'Proc. American Acad. of Sciences,' vol. vii. Feb. 1868. Prof. Schaaffhausen ('Anthropolog. Review,' Oct. 1869, p. 373) remarks on "the vestiges of human sacrifices found both in Homer and the Old Testament."

[36] Sir J. Lubbock, 'Prehistoric Times,' 2nd edit. 1869, chap. xv. and xvi. et passim. See also the excellent 9th Chapter in Tylor's 'Early History of Mankind,' 2nd edit., 1870.

rived from abroad;[37] many native plants were there cultivated, and a few
native animals domesticated. We should bear in mind that, judging from
the small influence of most missionaries, a wandering crew from some
semi-civilised land, if washed to the shores of America, would not have
produced any marked effect on the natives, unless they had already become somewhat advanced. Looking to a very remote period in the history
of the world, we find, to use Sir J. Lubbock's well-known terms, a paleo-
lithic and neolithic period; and no one will pretend that the art of grinding rough flint tools was a borrowed one. In all parts of Europe, as far
east as Greece, in Palestine, India, Japan, New Zealand, and Africa, including Egypt, flint tools have been discovered in abundance; and of
their use the existing inhabitants retain no tradition. There is also indirect evidence of their former use by the Chinese and ancient Jews. Hence
there can hardly be a doubt that the inhabitants of these countries, which
include nearly the whole civilised world, were once in a barbarous condition. To believe that man was aboriginally civilised and then suffered utter degradation in so many regions, is to take a pitiably low view of human nature. It is apparently a truer and more cheerful view that progress
has been much more general than retrogression; that man has risen,
though by slow and interrupted steps, from a lowly condition to the highest standard as yet attained by him in knowledge, morals and religion.

[37] Dr. F. Müller has made some good remarks to this effect in the 'Reise der Novara: Anthropolog. Theil,' Abtheil. iii. 1868, s. 127.

CHAPTER VI

ON THE AFFINITIES AND GENEALOGY OF MAN

Position of man in the animal series—The natural system genealogical—Adaptive characters of slight value—Various small points of resemblance between man and the Quadrumana—Rank of man in the natural system—Birthplace and antiquity of man—Absence of fossil connecting links—Lower stages in the genealogy of man, as inferred, firstly from his affinities and secondly from his structure—Early androgynous condition of the Vertebrata—Conclusion.

EVEN if it be granted that the difference between man and his nearest allies is as great in corporeal structure as some naturalists maintain, and although we must grant that the difference between them is immense in mental power, yet the facts given in the earlier chapters appear to declare, in the plainest manner, that man is descended from some lower form, notwithstanding that connecting-links have not hitherto been discovered.

Man is liable to numerous, slight, and diversified variations, which are induced by the same general causes, are governed and transmitted in accordance with the same general laws, as in the lower animals. Man has multiplied so rapidly, that he has necessarily been exposed to struggle for existence, and consequently to natural selection. He has given rise to many races, some of which differ so much from each other, that they have often been ranked by naturalists as distinct species. His body is constructed on the same homological plan as that of other mammals. He passes through the same phases of embryological development. He retains many rudimentary and useless structures, which no doubt were once serviceable. Characters occasionally make their re-appearance in him, which we have reason to believe were possessed by his early progenitors. If the origin of man had been wholly different from that of all other animals, these various appearances would be mere empty deceptions; but such an admission is incredible. These appearances, on the other hand, are intelligible, at least to a large extent, if man is the co-descendant with other mammals of some unknown and lower form.

Some naturalists, from being deeply impressed with the mental and spiritual powers of man, have divided the whole organic world into three kingdoms, the Human, the Animal, and the Vegetable, thus giving to man a separate kingdom.[1] Spiritual powers cannot be compared or

[1] Isidore Geoffroy St.-Hilaire gives a detailed account of the position assigned to man by various naturalists in their classifications: 'Hist. Nat. Gén.' tom. ii. 1859, pp. 170-189.

classed by the naturalist: but he may endeavour to shew, as I have done, that the mental faculties of man and the lower animals do not differ in kind, although immensely in degree. A difference in degree, however great, does not justify us in placing man in a distinct kingdom, as will perhaps be best illustrated by comparing the mental powers of two insects, namely, a coccus or scale-insect and an ant, which undoubtedly belong to the same class. The difference is here greater than, though of a somewhat different kind from, that between man and the highest mammal. The female coccus, whilst young, attaches itself by its proboscis to a plant; sucks the sap, but never moves again; is fertilised and lays eggs; and this is its whole history. On the other hand, to describe the habits and mental powers of worker-ants, would require, as Pierre Huber has shewn, a large volume; I may, however, briefly specify a few points. Ants certainly communicate information to each other, and several unite for the same work, or for games of play. They recognise their fellow-ants after months of absence, and feel sympathy for each other. They build great edifices, keep them clean, close the doors in the evening, and post sentries. They make roads as well as tunnels under rivers, and temporary bridges over them, by clinging together. They collect food for the community, and when an object, too large for entrance, is brought to the nest, they enlarge the door, and afterwards build it up again. They store up seeds, of which they prevent the germination, and which, if damp, are brought up to the surface to dry. They keep aphides and other insects as milch-cows. They go out to battle in regular bands, and freely sacrifice their lives for the common weal. They emigrate according to a preconcerted plan. They capture slaves. They move the eggs of their aphides, as well as their own eggs and cocoons, into warm parts of the nest, in order that they may be quickly hatched; and endless similar facts could be given.[2] On the whole, the difference in mental power between an ant and a coccus is immense; yet no one has ever dreamed of placing these insects in distinct classes, much less in distinct kingdoms. No doubt the difference is bridged over by other insects; and this is not the case with man and the higher apes. But we have every reason to believe that the breaks in the series are simply the results of many forms having become extinct.

Professor Owen, relying chiefly on the structure of the brain, has divided the mammalian series into four sub-classes. One of these he devotes to man; in another he places both the Marsupials and the Monotremata; so that he makes man as distinct from all other mammals as are these two latter groups conjoined. This view has not been accepted, as far as I am aware, by any naturalist capable of forming an independent judgment; and therefore need not here be further considered.

We can understand why a classification founded on any single character or organ—even an organ so wonderfully complex and important as

---

[2] Some of the most interesting facts ever published on the habits of ants are given by Mr. Belt, in his 'Naturalist in Nicaragua,' 1874. See also Mr. Moggridge's admirable work, 'Harvesting Ants,' &c., 1873, also 'L'Instinct chez les Insectes,' by M George Pouchet, 'Revue des Deux Mondes,' Feb. 1870, p. 682.

the brain—or on the high development of the mental faculties, is almost sure to prove unsatisfactory. This principle has indeed been tried with hymenopterous insects; but when thus classed by their habits or instincts, the arrangement proved thoroughly artificial.[3] Classifications may, of course, be based on any character whatever, as on size, colour, or the element inhabited; but naturalists have long felt a profound conviction that there is a natural system. This system, it is now generally admitted, must be, as far as possible, genealogical in arrangement,—that is the co-descendants of the same form must be kept together in one group, apart from the co-descendants of any other form; but if the parent-forms are related, so will be their descendants, and the two groups together will form a larger group. The amount of difference between the several groups —that is the amount of modification which each has undergone—is expressed by such terms as genera, families, orders, and classes. As we have no record of the lines of descent, the pedigree can be discovered only by observing the degrees of resemblance between the beings which are to be classed. For this object numerous points of resemblance are of much more importance than the amount of similarity or dissimilarity in a few points. If two languages were found to resemble each other in a multitude of words and points of construction, they would be universally recognised as having sprung from a common source, notwithstanding that they differed greatly in some few words or points of construction. But with organic beings the points of resemblance must not consist of adaptations to similar habits of life: two animals may, for instance, have had their whole frames modified for living in the water, and yet they will not be brought any nearer to each other in the natural system. Hence we can see how it is that resemblances in several unimportant structures, in useless and rudimentary organs, or not now functionally active, or in an embryological condition, are by far the most serviceable for classification; for they can hardly be due to adaptations within a late period; and thus they reveal the old lines of descent or of true affinity.

We can further see why a great amount of modification in some one character ought not to lead us to separate widely any two organisms. A part which already differs much from the same part in other allied forms has already, according to the theory of evolution, varied much; consequently it would (as long as the organism remained exposed to the same exciting conditions) be liable to further variations of the same kind; and these, if beneficial, would be preserved, and thus be continually augmented. In many cases the continued development of a part, for instance, of the beak of a bird, or of the teeth of a mammal, would not aid the species in gaining its food, or for any other object; but with man we can see no definite limit to the continued development of the brain and mental faculties, as far as advantage is concerned. Therefore in determining the position of man in the natural or genealogical system, the extreme develop-

---

[3] Westwood, 'Modern Class of Insects,' vol. ii. 1840, p. 87.

ment of his brain ought not to outweigh a multitude of resemblances in other less important or quite unimportant points.

The greater number of naturalists who have taken into consideration the whole structure of man, including his mental faculties, have followed Blumenbach and Cuvier, and have placed man in a separate Order, under the title of the Bimana, and therefore on an equality with the orders of the Quadrumana, Carnivora, &c. Recently many of our best naturalists have recurred to the view first propounded by Linnæus, so remarkable for his sagacity, and have placed man in the same Order with the Quadrumana, under the title of the Primates. The justice of this conclusion will be admitted: for in the first place, we must bear in mind the comparative insignificance for classification of the great development of the brain in man, and that the strongly-marked differences between the skulls of man and the Quadrumana (lately insisted upon by Bischoff, Aeby, and others) apparently follow from their differently developed brains. In the second place, we must remember that nearly all the other and more important differences between man and the quadrumana are manifestly adaptive in their nature, and relate chiefly to the erect position of man; such as the structure of his hand, foot, and pelvis, the curvature of his spine, and the position of his head. The family of Seals offers a good illustration of the small importance of adaptive characters for classification. These animals differ from all other Carnivora in the form of their bodies and in the structure of their limbs, far more than does man from the higher apes; yet in most systems, from that of Cuvier to the most recent one by Mr. Flower,[4] seals are ranked as a mere family in the Order of the Carnivora. If man had not been his own classifier, he would never have thought of founding a separate order for his own reception.

It would be beyond my limits, and quite beyond my knowledge, even to name the innumerable points of structure in which man agrees with the other Primates. Our great anatomist and philosopher, Prof. Huxley, has fully discussed this subject,[5] and concludes that man in all parts of his organization differs less from the higher apes, than these do from the lower members of the same group. Consequently there "is no justification for placing man in a distinct order."

In an early part of this work I brought forward various facts, shewing how closely man agrees in constitution with the higher mammals; and this agreement must depend on our close similarity in minute structure and chemical composition. I gave, as instances, our liability to the same diseases, and to the attacks of allied parasites; our tastes in common for the same stimulants, and the similar effects produced by them, as well as by various drugs, and other such facts.

As small unimportant points of resemblance between man and the Quadrumana are not commonly noticed in systematic works, and as, when numerous, they clearly reveal our relationship, I will specify a few

[4] 'Proc. Zoolog. Soc.' 1863, p. 4.
[5] 'Evidence as to Man's Place in Nature,' 1863, p. 70, *et passim.*

such points. The relative position of our features is manifestly the same; and the various emotions are displayed by nearly similar movements of the muscles and skin, chiefly above the eyebrows and round the mouth. Some few expressions are, indeed, almost the same, as in the weeping of certain kinds of monkeys and in the laughing noise made by others, during which the corners of the mouth are drawn backwards, and the lower eyelids wrinkled. The external ears are curiously alike. In man the nose is much more prominent than in most monkeys; but we may trace the commencement of an aquiline curvature in the nose of the Hoolock Gibbon; and this in the *Semnopithecus nasica* is carried to a ridiculous extreme.

The faces of many monkeys are ornamented with beards, whiskers, or moustaches. The hair on the head grows to a great length in some species of Semnopithecus;[6] and in the Bonnet monkey (*Macacus radiatus*) it radiates from a point on the crown, with a parting down the middle. It is commonly said that the forehead gives to man his noble and intellectual appearance; but the thick hair on the head of the Bonnet monkey terminates downwards abruptly, and is succeeded by hair so short and fine that at a little distance the forehead, with the exception of the eyebrows, appears quite naked. It has been erroneously asserted that eyebrows are not present in any monkey. In the species just named the degree of nakedness of the forehead differs in different individuals; and Eschricht states[7] that in our children the limit between the hairy scalp and the naked forehead is sometimes not well defined; so that here we seem to have a trifling case of reversion to a progenitor, in whom the forehead had not as yet become quite naked.

It is well known that the hair on our arms tends to converge from above and below to a point at the elbow. This curious arrangement, so unlike that in most of the lower mammals, is common to the gorilla, chimpanzee, orang, some species of Hylobates, and even to some few American monkeys. But in *Hylobates agilis* the hair on the fore-arm is directed downwards or towards the wrist in the ordinary manner; and in *H. lar* it is nearly erect, with only a very slight forward inclination; so that in this latter species it is in a transitional state. It can hardly be doubted that with most mammals the thickness of the hair on the back and its direction, is adapted to throw off the rain; even the transverse hairs on the fore-legs of a dog may serve for this end when he is coiled up asleep. Mr. Wallace, who has carefully studied the habits of the orang, remarks that the convergence of the hair towards the elbow on the arms of the orang may be explained as serving to throw off the rain, for this animal during rainy weather sits with its arms bent, and with the hands clasped round a branch or over its head. According to Livingstone, the gorilla also "sits in pelting rain with his hands over his head."[8] If the

---

[6] Isid. Geoffroy, 'Hist. Nat. Gén.' tom. ii. 1859, p. 217.

[7] 'Ueber die Richtung der Haare,' &c., Müller's 'Archiv für Anat. und Phys.' 1837, s. 51.

[8] Quoted by Reade, 'The African Sketch Book,' vol. i., 1873, p. 152.

above explanation is correct, as seems probable, the direction of the hair on our own arms offers a curious record of our former state; for no one supposes that it is now of any use in throwing off the rain; nor, in our present erect condition, is it properly directed for this purpose.

It would, however, be rash to trust too much to the principle of adaptation in regard to the direction of the hair in man or his early progenitors; for it is impossible to study the figures given by Eschricht of the arrangement of the hair on the human fœtus (this being the same as in the adult) and not agree with this excellent observer that other and more complex causes have intervened. The points of convergence seem to stand in some relation to those points in the embryo which are last closed in during development. There appears, also, to exist some relation between the arrangement of the hair on the limbs, and the course of the medullary arteries.[9]

It must not be supposed that the resemblances between man and certain apes in the above and in many other points—such as in having a naked forehead, long tresses on the head, &c.—are all necessarily the result of unbroken inheritance from a common progenitor, or of subsequent reversion. Many of these resemblances are more probably due to analogous variation, which follows, as I have elsewhere attempted to shew,[10] from co-descended organisms having a similar constitution, and having been acted on by like causes inducing similar modifications. With respect to the similar direction of the hair on the fore-arms of man and certain monkeys, as this character is common to almost all the anthropomorphous apes, it may probably be attributed to inheritance; but this is not certain, as some very distinct American monkeys are thus characterised.

Although, as we have now seen, man has no just right to form a separate Order for his own reception, he may perhaps claim a distinct Sub-order or Family. Prof. Huxley, in his last work,[11] divides the Primates into three Sub-orders; namely, the Anthropidæ with man alone, the Simiadæ including monkeys of all kinds, and the Lemuridæ with the diversified genera of lemurs. As far as differences in certain important points of structure are concerned, man may no doubt rightly claim the rank of a Sub-order; and this rank is too low, if we look chiefly to his mental faculties. Nevertheless, from a genealogical point of view it appears that this rank is too high, and that man ought to form merely a Family, or possibly even only a Sub-family. If we imagine three lines of descent proceeding from a common stock, it is quite conceivable that two of them might after the lapse of ages be so slightly changed as still to remain as species of the same genus, whilst the third line might become so greatly

[9] On the hair in Hylobates, see 'Nat. Hist. of Mammals,' by C. L. Martin, 1841, p. 415. Also, Isid. Geoffroy on the American monkeys and other kinds, 'Hist. Nat. Gén.' vol. ii. 1859, p. 216, 243, Eschricht, ibid. s. 46, 55, 61. Owen, 'Anat. of Vertebrates,' vol. iii. p. 619. Wallace, 'Contributions to the Theory of Natural Selection,' 1870, p. 344.

[10] 'Origin of Species,' this edit., p. 117. 'The Variation of Animals and Plants under Domestication,' vol. ii. 1868, p. 348.

[11] 'An Introduction to the Classification of Animals,' 1869, p. 99.

modified as to deserve to rank as a distinct Sub-family, or even Order. But in this case it is almost certain that the third line would still retain through inheritance numerous small points of resemblance with the other two. Here, then, would occur the difficulty, at present insoluble, how much weight we ought to assign in our classifications to strongly-marked differences in some few points,—that is, to the amount of modification undergone; and how much to close resemblance in numerous unimportant points, as indicating the lines of descent or genealogy. To attach much weight to the few but strong differences is the most obvious and perhaps the safest course, though it appears more correct to pay great attention to the many small resemblances, as giving a truly natural classification.

In forming a judgment on this head with reference to man, we must glance at the classification of the Simiadæ. This family is divided by almost all naturalists into the Catarhine group, or Old World monkeys, all of which are characterised (as their name expresses) by the peculiar structure of their nostrils, and by having four premolars in each jaw; and into the Platyrhine group or New World monkeys (including two very distinct sub-groups), all of which are characterised by differently constructed nostrils, and by having six premolars in each jaw. Some other small differences might be mentioned. Now man unquestionably belongs in his dentition, in the structure of his nostrils, and some other respects, to the Catarhine or Old World division; nor does he resemble the Platyrhines more closely than the Catarhines in any characters, excepting in a few of not much importance and apparently of an adaptive nature. It is therefore against all probability that some New World species should have formerly varied and produced a man-like creature, with all the distinctive characters proper to the Old World division; losing at the same time all its own distinctive characters. There can, consequently, hardly be a doubt that man is an off-shoot from the Old World Simian stem; and that under a genealogical point of view he must be classed with the Catarhine division.[12]

The anthropomorphous apes, namely the gorilla, chimpanzee, orang, and hylobates, are by most naturalists separated from the other Old World monkeys, as a distinct sub-group. I am aware that Gratiolet, relying on the structure of the brain, does not admit the existence of this sub-group, and no doubt it is a broken one. Thus the orang, as Mr. St. G. Mivart remarks,[13] "is one of the most peculiar and aberrant forms to be found in the Order." The remaining non-anthropomorphous Old World monkeys, are again divided by some naturalists into two or three smaller sub-groups; the genus Semnopithecus, with its peculiar sacculated stom-

[12] This is nearly the same classification as that provisionally adopted by Mr. St. George Mivart ('Transact. Philosoph. Soc.' 1867, p. 300), who, after separating the Lemuridæ, divides the remainder of the Primates into the Hominidæ, the Simiadæ which answer to the Catarhines, the Cebidæ, and the Hapalidæ,—these two latter groups answering to the Platyrhines. Mr. Mivart still abides by the same view; see 'Nature,' 1871, p. 481.

[13] 'Transact. Zoolog. Soc.' vol. vi. 1867, p. 214.

ach, being the type of one such sub-group. But it appears from M. Gaudry's wonderful discoveries in Attica, that during the Miocene period a form existed there, which connected Semnopithecus and Macacus; and this probably illustrates the manner in which the other and higher groups were once blended together.

If the anthropomorphous apes be admitted to form a natural subgroup, then as man agrees with them, not only in all those characters which he possesses in common with the whole Catarhine group, but in other peculiar characters, such as the absence of a tail and of callosities, and in general appearance, we may infer that some ancient member of the anthropomorphous sub-group gave birth to man. It is not probable that, through the law of analogous variation, a member of one of the other lower sub-groups should have given rise to a man-like creature, resembling the higher anthropomorphous apes in so many respects. No doubt man, in comparison with most of his allies, has undergone an extraordinary amount of modification, chiefly in consequence of the great development of his brain and his erect position; nevertheless, we should bear in mind that he "is but one of several exceptional forms of Primates." [14]

Every naturalist, who believes in the principle of evolution, will grant that the two main divisions of the Simiadæ, namely the Catarhine and Platyrhine monkeys, with their sub-groups, have all proceeded from some one extremely ancient progenitor. The early descendants of this progenitor, before they had diverged to any considerable extent from each other, would still have formed a single natural group; but some of the species or incipient genera would have already begun to indicate by their diverging characters the future distinctive marks of the Catarhine and Platyrhine divisions. Hence the members of this supposed ancient group would not have been so uniform in their dentition, or in the structure of their nostrils, as are the existing Catarhine monkeys in one way and the Platyrhines in another way, but would have resembled in this respect the allied Lemuridæ, which differ greatly from each other in the form of their muzzles,[15] and to an extraordinary degree in their dentition.

The Catarhine and Platyrhine monkeys agree in a multitude of characters, as is shewn by their unquestionably belonging to one and the same Order. The many characters which they possess in common can hardly have been independently acquired by so many distinct species; so that these characters must have been inherited. But a naturalist would undoubtedly have ranked as an ape or a monkey, an ancient form which possessed many characters common to the Catarhine and Platyrhine monkeys, other characters in an intermediate condition, and some few, perhaps, distinct from those now found in either group. And as man from a genealogical point of view belongs to the Catarhine or Old World stock, we must conclude, however much the conclusion may revolt our pride,

[14] Mr. St. G. Mivart, 'Transact. Phil. Soc.' 1867, p. 410.
[15] Messrs. Murie and Mivart on the Lemuroidea, 'Transact. Zoolog. Soc.' vol. vii. 1869, p. 5.

that our early progenitors would have been properly thus designated.[16] But we must not fall into the error of supposing that the early progenitors of the whole Simian stock, including man, was identical with, or even closely resembled, any existing ape or monkey.

On the Birthplace and Antiquity of Man.—We are naturally led to enquire, where was the birthplace of man at that stage of descent when our progenitors diverged from the Catarhine stock? The fact that they belonged to this stock clearly shews that they inhabited the Old World; but not Australia nor any oceanic island, as we may infer from the laws of geographical distribution. In each great region of the world the living mammals are closely related to the extinct species of the same region. It is therefore probable that Africa was formerly inhabited by extinct apes closely allied to the gorilla and chimpanzee; and as these two species are now man's nearest allies, it is somewhat more probable that our early progenitors lived on the African continent than elsewhere. But it is useless to speculate on this subject; for two or three anthropomorphous apes, one the Dryopithecus [17] of Lartet, nearly as large as a man, and closely allied to Hylobates, existed in Europe during the Miocene age; and since so remote a period the earth has certainly undergone many great revolutions, and there has been ample time for migration on the largest scale.

At the period and place, whenever and wherever it was, when man first lost his hairy covering, he probably inhabited a hot country; a circumstance favourable for the frugiferous diet on which, judging from analogy, he subsisted. We are far from knowing how long ago it was when man first diverged from the Catarhine stock; but it may have occurred at an epoch as remote as the Eocene period; for that the higher apes had diverged from the lower apes as early as the Upper Miocene period is shewn by the existence of the Dryopithecus. We are also quite ignorant at how rapid a rate organisms, whether high or low in the scale, may be modified under favourable circumstances; we know, however, that some have retained the same form during an enormous lapse of time. From what we see going on under domestication, we learn that some of the co-descendants of the same species may be not at all, some a little, and some greatly changed, all within the same period. Thus it may have been with man, who has undergone a great amount of modification in certain characters in comparison with the higher apes.

The great break in the organic chain between man and his nearest allies, which cannot be bridged over by any extinct or living species, has often been advanced as a grave objection to the belief that man is descend-

---

[16] Häckel has come to this same conclusion. See 'Ueber die Entstehung des Menschengeschlechts,' in Virchow's 'Sammlung. gemein. wissen. Vortrage,' 1868, s. 61. Also his 'Natürliche Schöpfungsgeschichte,' 1868 in which he gives in detail his views on the genealogy of man.

[17] Dr. C. Forsyth Major, 'Sur les Singes Fossiles trouvés en Italie:' 'Soc. Ital. des Sc. Nat.' tom. xv. 1872.

ed from some lower form; but this objection will not appear of much weight to those who, from general reasons, believe in the general principle of evolution. Breaks often occur in all parts of the series, some being wide, sharp and defined, others less so in various degrees; as between the orang and its nearest allies—between the Tarsius and the other Lemuridæ—between the elephant, and in a more striking manner between the Ornithorhynchus or Echidna, and all other mammals. But these breaks depend merely on the number of related forms which have become extinct. At some future period, not very distant as measured by centuries, the civilised races of man will almost certainly exterminate, and replace, the savage races throughout the world. At the same time the anthropomorphous apes, as Professor Schaaffhausen has remarked,[18] will no doubt be exterminated. The break between man and his nearest allies will then be wider, for it will intervene between man in a more civilised state, as we may hope, even than the Caucasian, and some ape as low as a baboon, instead of as now between the negro or Australian and the gorilla.

With respect to the absence of fossil remains, serving to connect man with his ape-like progenitors, no one will lay much stress on this fact who reads Sir C. Lyell's discussion,[19] where he shews that in all the vertebrate classes the discovery of fossil remains has been a very slow and fortuitous process. Nor should it be forgotten that those regions which are the most likely to afford remains connecting man with some extinct ape-like creature, have not as yet been searched by geologists.

Lower Stages in the Genealogy of Man.—We have seen that man appears to have diverged from the Catarhine or Old World division of the Simiadæ, after these had diverged from the New World division. We will now endeavour to follow the remote traces of his genealogy, trusting principally to the mutual affinities between the various classes and orders, with some slight reference to the periods, as far as ascertained, of their successive appearance on the earth. The Lemuridæ stand below and near to the Simiadæ, and constitute a very distinct family of the Primates, or, according to Häckel and others, a distinct Order. This group is diversified and broken to an extraordinary degree, and includes many aberrant forms. It has, therefore, probably suffered much extinction. Most of the remnants survive on islands, such as Madagascar and the Malayan archipelago, where they have not been exposed to so severe a competition as they would have been on well-stocked continents. This group likewise presents many gradations, leading, as Huxley remarks,[20] "insensibly from the crown and summit of the animal creation down to creatures from which there is but a step, as it seems, to the lowest, smallest, and least intelligent of the placental mammalia." From these various considerations it is probable that the Simiadæ were originally developed from

[18] 'Anthropological Review,' April, 1867, p. 236.
[19] 'Elements of Geology,' 1865, pp. 583-585. 'Antiquity of Man,' 1863, p. 145.
[20] 'Man's Place in Nature,' p. 105.

the progenitors of the existing Lemuridæ; and these in their turn from forms standing very low in the mammalian series.

The Marsupials stand in many important characters below the placental mammals. They appeared at an earlier geological period, and their range was formerly much more extensive than at present. Hence the Placentata are generally supposed to have been derived from the Implacentata or Marsupials; not, however, from forms closely resembling the existing Marsupials, but from their early progenitors. The Monotremata are plainly allied to the Marsupials, forming a third and still lower division in the great mammalian series. They are represented at the present day solely by the Ornithorhynchus and Echidna; and these two forms may be safely considered as relics of a much larger group, representatives of which have been preserved in Australia through some favourable concurrence of circumstances. The Monotremata are eminently interesting, as leading in several important points of structure towards the class of reptiles.

In attempting to trace the genealogy of the Mammalia, and therefore of man, lower down in the series, we become involved in greater and greater obscurity; but as a most capable judge, Mr. Parker, has remarked, we have good reason to believe, that no true bird or reptile intervenes in the direct line of descent. He who wishes to see what ingenuity and knowledge can effect, may consult Prof. Häckel's works.[21] I will content myself with a few general remarks. Every evolutionist will admit that the five great vertebrate classes, namely, mammals, birds, reptiles, amphibians, and fishes, are descended from some one prototype; for they have much in common, especially during their embryonic state. As the class of fishes is the most lowly organised, and appeared before the others, we may conclude that all the members of the vertebrate kingdom are derived from some fishlike animal. The belief that animals so distinct as a monkey, an elephant, a humming-bird, a snake, a frog, and a fish, &c., could all have sprung from the same parents, will appear monstrous to those who have not attended to the recent progress of natural history. For this belief implies the former existence of links binding closely together all these forms, now so utterly unlike.

Nevertheless, it is certain that groups of animals have existed, or do now exist, which serve to connect several of the great vertebrate classes more or less closely. We have seen that the Ornithorhynchus graduates towards reptiles; and Prof. Huxley has discovered, and is confirmed by Mr. Cope and others, that the Dinosaurians are in many important characters intermediate between certain reptiles and certain birds—the birds referred to being the ostrich-tribe (itself a widely-diffused remnant of a

---

[21] Elaborate tables are given in his 'Generelle Morphologie' (B. ii. s. cliii. and s. 425); and with more especial reference to man in his 'Natürliche Schöpfungsgeschichte,' 1868. Prof. Huxley, in reviewing this latter work ('The Academy,' 1869, p. 42) says, that he considers the phylum or lines of descent of the Vertebrata to be admirably discussed by Häckel, although he differs on some points. He expresses, also, his high estimate of the general tenor and spirit of the whole work.

larger group) and the Archeopteryx, that strange Secondary bird, with a long lizard-like tail. Again, according to Prof. Owen,[22] the Ichthyosaurians—great sea-lizards furnished with paddles—present many affinities with fishes, or rather, according to Huxley, with amphibians; a class which, including in its highest division frogs and toads, is plainly allied to the Ganoid fishes. These latter fishes swarmed during the earlier geological periods, and were constructed on what is called a generalised type, that is, they presented diversified affinities with other groups of organisms. The Lepidosiren is also so closely allied to amphibians and fishes, that naturalists long disputed in which of these two classes to rank it; it, and also some few Ganoid fishes, have been preserved from utter extinction by inhabiting rivers, which are harbours of refuge, and are related to the great waters of the ocean in the same way that islands are to continents.

Lastly, one single member of the immense and diversified class of fishes, namely, the lancelet or amphioxus, is so different from all other fishes, that Häckel maintains that it ought to form a distinct class in the vertebrate kingdom. This fish is remarkable for its negative characters; it can hardly be said to possess a brain, vertebral column, or heart, &c.; so that it was classed by the older naturalists amongst the worms. Many years ago Prof. Goodsir perceived that the lancelet presented some affinities with the Ascidians, which are invertebrate, hermaphrodite, marine creatures permanently attached to a support. They hardly appear like animals, and consist of a simple, tough, leathery sack, with two small projecting orifices. They belong to the Mulluscoida of Huxley—a lower division of the great kingdom of the Mollusca; but they have recently been placed by some naturalists amongst the Vermes or worms. Their larvæ somewhat resemble tadpoles in shape,[23] and have the power of swimming freely about. Mr. Kovalevsky[24] has lately observed that the larvæ of Ascidians are related to the Vertebrata, in their manner of development, in the relative position of the nervous system, and in possessing a structure closely like the *chorda dorsalis* of vertebrate animals; and in this he has been since confirmed by Prof. Kupffer. M. Kovalevsky writes to me from Naples, that he has now carried these observations yet further, and should his results be well established, the whole will form a discovery of the very greatest value. Thus, if we may rely on embryology, ever the safest guide in classification, it seems that we have at last gained a clue to the source whence the Vertebrata were derived.[25] We should

---

[22] 'Palæontology,' 1860, p. 199.

[23] At the Falkland Islands I had the satisfaction of seeing, in April 1833, and therefore some years before any other naturalist, the locomotive larvæ of a compound Ascidian, closely allied to Synoicum, but apparently generically distinct from it. The tail was about five times as long as the oblong head, and terminated in a very fine filament. It was, as sketched by me under a simple microscope, plainly divided by transverse opaque partitions, which I presume represent the great cells figured by Kovalevsky. At an early stage of development the tail was closely coiled round the head of the larva.

[24] 'Mémoires de l'Acad. des Sciences de St. Pétersbourg,' tom. x. No. 15, 1866.

then be justified in believing that at an extremely remote period a group of animals existed, resembling in many respects the larvæ of our present Ascidians, which diverged into two great branches—the one retrograding in development and producing the present class of Ascidians, the other rising to the crown and summit of the animal kingdom by giving birth to the Vertebrata.

We have thus far endeavoured rudely to trace the genealogy of the Vertebrata by the aid of their mutual affinities. We will now look to man as he exists; and we shall, I think, be able partially to restore the structure of our early progenitors, during successive periods, but not in due order of time. This can be effected by means of the rudiments which man still retains, by the characters which occasionally make their appearance in him through reversion, and by the aid of the principles of morphology and embryology. The various facts, to which I shall here allude, have been given in the previous chapters.

The early progenitors of man must have been once covered with hair, both sexes having beards; their ears were probably pointed, and capable of movement; and their bodies were provided with a tail, having the proper muscles. Their limbs and bodies were also acted on by many muscles which now only occasionally reappear, but are normally present in the Quadrumana. At this or some earlier period, the great artery and nerve of the humerus ran through a supra-condyloid foramen. The intestine gave forth a much larger diverticulum or cæcum than that now existing. The foot was then prehensile, judging from the condition of the great toe in the fœtus; and our progenitors, no doubt, were arboreal in their habits, and frequented some warm, forest-clad land. The males had great canine teeth, which served them as formidable weapons. At a much earlier period the uterus was double; the excreta were voided through a cloaca; and the eye was protected by a third eyelid or nictitating membrane. At a still earlier period the progenitors of man must have been aquatic in their habits; for morphology plainly tells us that our lungs consist of a modified swim-bladder, which once served as a float. The clefts on the neck in the embryo of man show where the branchiæ once existed. In the lunar or weekly recurrent periods of some of our functions we apparently still retain traces of our primordial birthplace, a shore washed by the tides. At about this same early period the true kidneys were replaced by the corpora wolffiana. The heart existed as a simple pulsating vessel; and the chorda dorsalis took the place of a vertebral column. These early ancestors of man, thus seen in the dim recesses of time, must have been as

[25] But I am bound to add that some competent judges dispute this conclusion; for instance, M. Giard, in a series of papers in the 'Archives de Zoologie Expérimentale,' for 1872. Nevertheless, this naturalist remarks, p. 281, 'L'organisation de la larve ascidienne en dehors de toute hypothèse et de toute théorie, nous montre comment la nature peut produire la disposition fondamentale du type vertébré (l'existence d'une corde dorsale) chez un invertébré par la seule condition vitale de l'adaptation, et cette simple possibilité du passage supprime l'abime entre les deux sous-règnes, encore bien qu'en ignore par où le passage s'est fait en réalité.'

simply, or even still more simply organised than the lancelet or amphioxus.

There is one other point deserving a fuller notice. It has long been known that in the vertebrate kingdom one sex bears rudiments of various accessory parts, appertaining to the reproductive system, which properly belong to the opposite sex; and it has now been ascertained that at a very early embryonic period both sexes possess true male and female glands. Hence some remote progenitor of the whole vertebrate kingdom appears to have been hermaphrodite or androgynous.[26] But here we encounter a singular difficulty. In the mammalian class the males possess rudiments of a uterus with the adjacent passage, in their vesiculæ prostaticæ; they bear also rudiments of mammæ, and some male Marsupials have traces of a marsupial sack.[27] Other analogous facts could be added. Are we, then, to suppose that some extremely ancient mammal continued androgynous, after it had acquired the chief distinctions of its class, and therefore after it had diverged from the lower classes of the vertebrate kingdom? This seems very improbable, for we have to look to fishes, the lowest of all the classes, to find any still existent androgynous forms.[28] That various accessory parts, proper to each sex, are found in a rudimentary condition in the opposite sex, may be explained by such organs having been gradually acquired by the one sex, and then transmitted in a more or less imperfect state to the other. When we treat of sexual selection, we shall meet with innumerable instances of this form of transmission,—as in the case of the spurs, plumes, and brilliant colours, acquired for battle or ornament by male birds, and inherited by the females in an imperfect or rudimentary condition.

The possession by male mammals of functionally imperfect mammary organs is, in some respects, especially curious. The Monotremata have the proper milk-secreting glands with orifices, but no nipples; and as these animals stand at the very base of the mammalian series, it is probable that the progenitors of the class also had milk-secreting glands, but no nipples. This conclusion is supported by what is known of their man-

[26] This is the conclusion of Prof. Gegenbaur, one of the highest authorities in comparative anatomy: see 'Grundzüge der vergleich. Anat.' 1870, s. 876. The result has been arrived at chiefly from the study of the Amphibia; but it appears from the researches of Waldeyer (as quoted in 'Journal of Anat. and Phys.' 1869, p. 161), that the sexual organs of even "the higher vertebrata are, in their early condition, hermaphrodite." Similar views have long been held by some authors, though until recently without a firm basis.

[27] The male Thylacinus offers the best instance. Owen, 'Anatomy of Vertebrates,' vol. iii. p. 771.

[28] Hermaphroditism has been observed in several species of Serranus, as well as in some other fishes, where it is either normal and symmetrical, or abnormal and unilateral. Dr. Zouteveen has given me references on this subject, more especially to a paper by Prof. Halbertsma, in the 'Transact. of the Dutch Acad. of Sciences,' vol. xvi. Dr. Günther doubts the fact, but it has now been recorded by too many good observers to be any longer disputed. Dr. M. Lessona writes to me, that he has verified the observations made by Cavolini on Serranus. Prof. Ercolani has recently shewn ('Acad. delle Scienze,' Bologna, Dec. 28, 1871) that eels are androgynous.

ner of development; for Professor Turner informs me, on the authority of Kölliker and Langer, that in the embryo the mammary glands can be distinctly traced before the nipples are in the least visible; and the development of successive parts in the individual generally represents and accords with the development of successive beings in the same line of descent. The Marsupials differ from the Monotremata by possessing nipples; so that probably these organs were first acquired by the Marsupials, after they had diverged from, and risen above, the Monotremata, and were then transmitted to the placental mammals.[29] No one will suppose that the Marsupials still remained androgynous, after they had approximately acquired their present structure. How then are we to account for male mammals possessing mammæ? It is possible that they were first developed in the females and then transferred to the males, but from what follows this is hardly probable.

It may be suggested, as another view, that long after the progenitors of the whole mammalian class had ceased to be androgynous, both sexes yielded milk, and thus nourished their young; and in the case of the Marsupials, that both sexes carried their young in marsupial sacks. This will not appear altogether improbable, if we reflect that the males of existing syngnathous fishes receive the eggs of the females in their abdominal pouches, hatch them, and afterwards, as some believe, nourish the young; [30]—that certain other male fishes hatch the eggs within their mouths or branchial cavities;—that certain male toads take the chaplets of eggs from the females, and wind them round their own thighs, keeping them there until the tadpoles are born;—that certain male birds undertake the whole duty of incubation, and that male pigeons, as well as the females, feed their nestlings with a secretion from their crops. But the above suggestion first occurred to me from mammary glands of male mammals being so much more perfectly developed than the rudiments of the other accessory reproductive parts, which are found in the one sex though proper to the other. The mammary glands and nipples, as they exist in male mammals, can indeed hardly be called rudimentary; they are merely not fully developed, and not functionally active. They are sympathetically affected under the influence of certain diseases, like the same organs in the female. They often secrete a few drops of milk at birth and at puberty: this latter fact occurred in the curious case before referred to, where a young man possessed two pairs of mammæ. In man and some

[29] Prof. Gegenbaur has shewn ('Jenaische Zeitschrift,' Bd. vii. p. 212) that two distinct types of nipples prevail throughout the several mammalian orders, but that it is quite intelligible how both could have been derived from the nipples of the Marsupials, and the latter from those of the Monotremata. See, also, a memoir by Dr. Max Huss, on the mammary glands, ibid. B. viii. p. 176.

[30] Mr. Lockwood believes (as quoted in 'Quart. Journal of Science,' April, 1868, p. 269), from what he has observed of the development of Hippocampus, that the walls of the abdominal pouch of the male in some way afford nourishment. On male fishes hatching the ova in their mouths, see a very interesting paper by Prof. Wyman, in 'Proc. Boston Soc. of Nat. Hist.' Sept. 15, 1857; also Prof. Turner, in 'Journal of Anat. and Phys.' Nov. 1, 1866, p. 78. Dr. Günther has likewise described similar cases.

other male mammals these organs have been known occasionally to become so well developed during maturity as to yield a fair supply of milk. Now if we suppose that during a former prolonged period male mammals aided the females in nursing their offspring,[31] and that afterwards from some cause (as from the production of a smaller number of young) the males ceased to give this aid, disuse of the organs during maturity would lead to their becoming inactive; and from two well-known principles of inheritance, this state of inactivity would probably be transmitted to the males at the corresponding age of maturity. But at an earlier age these organs would be left unaffected, so that they would be almost equally well developed in the young of both sexes.

Conclusion.—Von Baer has defined advancement or progress in the organic scale better than any one else, as resting on the amount of differentiation and specialisation of the several parts of a being,—when arrived at maturity, as I should be inclined to add. Now as organisms have become slowly adapted to diversified lines of life by means of natural selection, their parts will have become more and more differentiated and specialised for various functions from the advantage gained by the division of physiological labour. The same part appears often to have been modified first for one purpose, and then long afterwards for some other and quite distinct purpose; and thus all the parts are rendered more and more complex. But each organism still retains the general type of structure of the progenitor from which it was aboriginally derived. In accordance with this view it seems, if we turn to geological evidence, that organisation on the whole has advanced throughout the world by slow and interrupted steps. In the great kingdom of the Vertebrata it has culminated in man. It must not, however, be supposed that groups of organic beings are always supplanted, and disappear as soon as they have given birth to other and more perfect groups. The latter, though victorious over their predecessors, may not have become better adapted for all places in the economy of nature. Some old forms appear to have survived from inhabiting protected sites, where they have not been exposed to very severe competition; and these often aid us in constructing our genealogies, by giving us a fair idea of former and lost populations. But we must not fall into the error of looking at the existing members of any lowly-organised group as perfect representatives of their ancient predecessors.

The most ancient progenitors in the kingdom of the Vertebrata, at which we are able to obtain an obscure glance, apparently consisted of a group of marine animals,[32] resembling the larvæ of existing Ascidians.

[31] Maddle. C. Royer has suggested a similar view in her 'Origine de l'Homme,' &c., 1870.

[32] The inhabitants of the seashore must be greatly affected by the tides; animals living either about the *mean* high-water mark, or about the *mean* low-water mark, pass through a complete cycle of tidal changes in a fortnight. Consequently, their food supply will undergo marked changes week by week. The vital functions of such animals, living under these conditions for many generations, can hardly fail to run their course in regular weekly periods. Now it is a mysterious fact that in the higher

These animals probably gave rise to a group of fishes, as lowly organised as the lancelet; and from these the Ganoids, and other fishes like the Lepidosiren, must have been developed. From such fish a very small advance would carry us on to the Amphibians. We have seen that birds and reptiles were once intimately connected together; and the Monotremata now connect mammals with reptiles in a slight degree. But no one can at present say by what line of descent the three higher and related classes, namely, mammals, birds, and reptiles, were derived from the two lower vertebrate classes, namely, amphibians and fishes. In the class of mammals the steps are not difficult to conceive which led from the ancient Monotremata to the ancient Marsupials; and from these to the early progenitors of the placental mammals. We may thus ascend to the Lemuridæ; and the interval is not very wide from these to the Simiadæ. The Simiadæ then branched off into two great stems, the New World and Old World monkeys; and from the latter, at a remote period, Man, the wonder and glory of the Universe, proceeded.

Thus we have given to man a pedigree of prodigious length, but not, it may be said, of noble quality. The world, it has often been remarked, appears as if it had long been preparing for the advent of man: and this, in one sense is strictly true, for he owes his birth to a long line of progenitors. If any single link in this chain had never existed, man would not have been exactly what he now is. Unless we wilfully close our eyes, we may, with our present knowledge, approximately recognise our parentage; nor need we feel ashamed of it. The most humble organism is something much higher than the inorganic dust under our feet; and no one with an unbiased mind can study any living creature, however humble, without being struck with enthusiasm at its marvellous structure and properties.

and now terrestrial Vertebrata, as well as in other classes, many normal and abnormal processes have one or more whole weeks as their periods; this would be rendered intelligible if the Vertebrata are descended from an animal allied to the existing tidal Ascidians. Many instances of such periodic processes might be given, as the gestation of mammals, the duration of fevers, &c. The hatching of eggs affords also a good example, for, according to Mr. Bartlett ('Land and Water,' Jan. 7, 1871), the eggs of the pigeon are hatched in two weeks; those of the fowl in three; those of the duck in four; those of the goose in five; and those of the ostrich in seven weeks. As far as we can judge, a recurrent period, if approximately of the right duration for any process or function, would not, when once gained, be liable to change; consequently it might be thus transmitted through almost any number of generations. But if the function changed, the period would have to change, and would be apt to change almost abruptly by a whole week. This conclusion, if sound, is highly remarkable; for the period of gestation in each mammal, and the hatching of each bird's eggs, and many other vital processes, thus betray to us the primordial birthplace of these animals.

CHAPTER VII

ON THE RACES OF MAN

The nature and value of specific characters—Application to the races of man—Arguments in favour of, and opposed to, ranking the so-called races of man as distinct species—Sub-species—Monogenists and polygenists—Convergence of character—Numerous points of resemblance in body and mind between the most distinct races of man—The state of man when he first spread over the earth—Each race not descended from a single pair—The extinction of races—The formation of races—The effects of crossing—Slight influence of the direct action of the conditions of life—Slight or no influence of natural selection—Sexual selection.

It is not my intention here to describe the several so-called races of men; but I am about to enquire what is the value of the differences between them under a classificatory point of view, and how they have originated. In determining whether two or more allied forms ought to be ranked as species or varieties, naturalists are practically guided by the following considerations; namely, the amount of difference between them, and whether such differences relate to few or many points of structure, and whether they are of physiological importance; but more especially whether they are constant. Constancy of character is what is chiefly valued and sought for by naturalists. Whenever it can be shewn, or rendered probable, that the forms in question have remained distinct for a long period, this becomes an argument of much weight in favour of treating them as species. Even a slight degree of sterility between any two forms when first crossed, or in their offspring, is generally considered as a decisive test of their specific distinctness; and their continued persistence without blending within the same area, is usually accepted as sufficient evidence, either of some degree of mutual sterility, or in the case of animals of some mutual repugnance to pairing.

Independently of fusion from intercrossing, the complete absence, in a well-investigated region, of varieties linking together any two closely-allied forms, is probably the most important of all the criterions of their specific distinctness; and this is a somewhat different consideration from mere constancy of character, for two forms may be highly variable and yet not yield intermediate varieties. Geographical distribution is often brought into play unconsciously and sometimes consciously; so that forms living in two widely separated areas, in which most of the other inhabitants are specifically distinct, are themselves usually looked at as distinct; but in truth this affords no aid in distinguishing geographical races from so-called good or true species.

Now let us apply these generally-admitted principles to the races of man, viewing him in the same spirit as a naturalist would any other animal. In regard to the amount of difference between the races, we must make some allowance for our nice powers of discrimination gained by the long habit of observing ourselves. In India, as Elphinstone remarks, although a newly-arrived European cannot at first distinguish the various native races, yet they soon appear to him extremely dissimilar; [1] and the Hindoo cannot at first perceive any difference between the several European nations. Even the most distinct races of man are much more like each other in form than would at first be supposed; certain negro tribes must be excepted, whilst others, as Dr. Rohlfs writes to me, and as I have myself seen, have Caucasian features. This general similarity is well shewn by the French photographs in the Collection Anthropologique du Muséum de Paris of the men belonging to various races, the greater number of which might pass for Europeans, as many persons to whom I have shewn them have remarked. Nevertheless, these men, if seen alive, would undoubtedly appear very distinct, so that we are clearly much influenced in our judgment by the mere colour of the skin and hair, by slight differences in the features, and by expression.

There is, however, no doubt that the various races, when carefully compared and measured, differ much from each other,—as in the texture of the hair, the relative proportions of all parts of the body,[2] the capacity of the lungs, the form and capacity of the skull, and even in the convolutions of the brain.[3] But it would be an endless task to specify the numerous points of difference. The races differ also in constitution, in acclimatisation and in liability to certain diseases. Their mental characteristics are likewise very distinct; chiefly as it would appear in their emotional, but partly in their intellectual faculties. Every one who has had the opportunity of comparison, must have been struck with the contrast between the taciturn, even morose, aborigines of S. America and the lighthearted, talkative negroes. There is a nearly similar contrast between the Malays and the Papuans,[4] who live under the same physical conditions, and are separated from each other only by a narrow space of sea.

We will first consider the arguments which may be advanced in favour of classing the races of man as distinct species, and then the arguments on the other side. If a naturalist, who had never before seen a Negro, Hottentot, Australian, or Mongolian, were to compare them, he would at once perceive that they differed in a multitude of characters,

---

[1] 'History of India,' 1841, vol. i. p. 323. Father Ripa makes exactly the same remark with respect to the Chinese.

[2] A vast number of measurements of Whites, Blacks, and Indians, are given in the 'Investigations in the Military and Anthropolog. Statistics of American Soldiers,' by B. A. Gould, 1869, pp. 298-358; 'On the capacity of the lungs,' p. 471. See also the numerous and valuable tables, by Dr. Weisbach, from the observations of Dr. Scherzer and Dr. Schwarz, in the 'Reise der Novara: Anthropolog. Theil,' 1867.

[3] See, for instance, Mr. Marshall's account of the brain of a Bushwoman, in 'Phil. Transact.' 1864, p. 519.

[4] Wallace, 'The Malay Archipelago,' vol. ii. 1869, p. 178.

some of slight and some of considerable importance. On enquiry he would find that they were adapted to live under widely different climates, and that they differed somewhat in bodily constitution and mental disposition. If he were then told that hundreds of similar specimens could be brought from the same countries, he would assuredly declare that they were as good species as many to which he had been in the habit of affixing specific names. This conclusion would be greatly strengthened as soon as he had ascertained that these forms had all retained the same character for many centuries; and that negroes, apparently identical with existing negroes, had lived at least 4000 years ago.[5] He would also hear, on the authority of an excellent observer, Dr. Lund,[6] that the human skulls found in the caves of Brazil, entombed with many extinct mammals, belonged to the same type as that now prevailing throughout the American Continent.

Our naturalist would then perhaps turn to geographical distribution, and he would probably declare that those forms must be distinct species, which differ not only in appearance, but are fitted for hot, as well as damp or dry countries, and for the Arctic regions. He might appeal to the fact that no species in the group next to man—namely, the Quadrumana, can resist a low temperature, or any considerable change of climate; and that the species which come nearest to man have never been reared to maturity, even under the temperate climate of Europe. He would be deeply impressed with the fact, first noticed by Agassiz,[7] that the different races of man are distributed over the world in the same zoological provinces, as those inhabited by undoubtedly distinct species and genera of mammals. This is manifestly the case with the Australian, Mongolian, and Negro races of man; in a less well-marked manner with the Hottentots; but plainly with the Papuans and Malays, who are separated, as Mr. Wallace has shewn, by nearly the same line which divides the great Malayan and Australian zoological provinces. The Aborigines of America range throughout the Continent; and this at first appears

[5] With respect to the figures in the famous Egyptian caves of Abou-Simbel, M. Pouchet says ('The Plurality of the Human Races,' Eng. translat., 1864, p. 50), that he was far from finding recognisable representations of the dozen or more nations which some authors believe that they can recognise. Even some of the most strongly-marked races cannot be identified with that degree of unanimity which might have been expected from what has been written on the subject. Thus Messrs. Nott and Gliddon ('Types of Mankind,' p. 148), state that Rameses II., or the Great, has features superbly European; whereas Knox, another firm believer in the specific distinctness of the races of man ('Races of Man,' 1850, p. 201), speaking of young Memnon (the same as Rameses II., as I am informed by Mr. Birch), insists in the strongest manner that he is identical in character with the Jews of Antwerp. Again, when I looked at the statue of Amunoph III., I agreed with two officers of the establishment, both competent judges, that he had a strongly-marked negro type of features; but Messrs. Nott and Gliddon (ibid. p. 146, fig. 53), describe him as a hybrid, but not of "negro intermixture."

[6] As quoted by Nott and Gliddon, 'Types of Mankind,' 1854, p. 439. They give also corroborative evidence; but C. Vogt thinks that the subject requires further investigation.

[7] 'Diversity of Origin of the Human Races,' in the 'Christian Examiner,' July, 1850.

opposed to the above rule, for most of the productions of the Southern and Northern halves differ widely: yet some few living forms, as the oppossum, range from the one into the other, as did formerly some of the gigantic Edentata. The Esquimaux, like other Arctic animals, extend round the whole polar regions. It should be observed that the amount of difference between the mammals of the several zoological provinces does not correspond with the degree of separation between the latter; so that it can hardly be considered as an anomaly that the Negro differs more, and the American much less from the other races of man, than do the mammals of the African and American continents from the mammals of the other provinces. Man, it may be added, does not appear to have aboriginally inhabited any oceanic island; and in this respect, he resembles the other members of his class.

In determining whether the supposed varieties of the same kind of domestic animal should be ranked as such, or as specifically distinct, that is, whether any of them are descended from distinct wild species, every naturalist would lay much stress on the fact of their external parasites being specifically distinct. All the more stress would be laid on this fact, as it would be an exceptional one; for I am informed by Mr. Denny that the most different kinds of dogs, fowls, and pigeons, in England, are infested by the same species of Pediculi or lice. Now Mr. A. Murray has carefully examined the Pediculi collected in different countries from the different races of man;[8] and he finds that they differ, not only in colour, but in the structure of their claws and limbs. In every case in which many specimens were obtained the differences were constant. The surgeon of a whaling ship in the Pacific assured me that when the Pediculi, with which some Sandwich Islanders on board swarmed, strayed on to the bodies of the English sailors, they died in the course of three or four days. These Pediculi were darker coloured, and appeared different from those proper to the natives of Chiloe in South America, of which he gave me specimens. These, again, appeared larger and much softer than European lice. Mr. Murray procured four kinds from Africa, namely, from the Negroes of the Eastern and Western coasts, from the Hottentots and Kaffirs; two kinds from the natives of Australia; two from North and two from South America. In these latter cases it may be presumed that the Pediculi came from natives inhabiting different districts. With insects slight structural differences, if constant, are generally esteemed of specific value: and the fact of the races of man being infested by parasites, which appear to be specifically distinct, might fairly be urged as an argument that the races themselves ought to be classed as distinct species.

Our supposed naturalist having proceeded thus far in his investigation, would next enquire whether the races of men, when crossed, were in any degree sterile. He might consult the work[9] of Professor Broca, a cautious and philosophical observer, and in this he would find good evidence that some races were quite fertile together, but evidence of an op-

<hr />

[8] 'Transact. R. Soc. of Edinburgh,' vol. xxii. 1861, p. 567.
[9] 'On the Phenomena of Hybridity in the Genus Homo,' Eng. translat. 1864.

posite nature in regard to other races. Thus it has been asserted that the native women of Australia and Tasmania rarely produce children to European men; the evidence, however, on this head has now been shewn to be almost valueless. The half-castes are killed by the pure blacks: and an account has lately been published of eleven half-caste youths murdered and burnt at the same time, whose remains were found by the police.[10] Again, it has often been said that when mulattoes intermarry, they produce few children; on the other hand, Dr. Bachman, of Charleston,[11] positively asserts that he has known mulatto families which have intermarried for several generations, and have continued on an average as fertile as either pure whites or pure blacks. Enquiries formerly made by Sir C. Lyell on this subject led him, as he informs me, to the same conclusion.[12] In the United States the census for the year 1854 included, according to Dr. Bachman, 405,751 mulattoes; and this number, considering all the circumstances of the case, seems small; but it may partly be accounted for by the degraded and anomalous position of the class, and by the profligacy of the women. A certain amount of absorption of mulattoes into negroes must always be in progress; and this would lead to an apparent diminution of the former. The inferior vitality of mulattoes is spoken of in a trustworthy work[13] as a well-known phenomenon; and this, although a different consideration from their lessened fertility, may perhaps be advanced as a proof of the specific distinctness of the parent races. No doubt both animal and vegetable hybrids, when produced from extremely distinct species, are liable to premature death; but the parents of mulattoes cannot be put under the category of extremely distinct species. The common Mule, so notorious for long life and vigour, and yet so sterile, shews how little necessary connection there is in hybrids between lessened fertility and vitality; other analogous cases could be cited.

Even if it should hereafter be proved that all the races of men were perfectly fertile together, he who was inclined from other reasons to rank them as distinct species, might with justice argue that fertility and ster-

[10] See the interesting letter by Mr. T. A. Murray, in the 'Anthropolog. Review,' April, 1868, p. liii. In this letter Count Strzelecki's statement that Australian women who have borne children to a white man, are afterwards sterile with their own race, is disproved. M. A. de Quatrefages has also collected ('Revue des Cours Scientifiques,' March, 1869, p. 239), much evidence that Australians and Europeans are not sterile when crossed.

[11] 'An Examination of Prof. Agassiz's Sketch of the Nat. Provinces of the Animal World,' Charleston, 1855, p. 44.

[12] Dr. Rohlfs writes to me that he found the mixed races in the Great Sahara, derived from Arabs, Berbers, and Negroes of three tribes, extraordinarily fertile. On the other hand, Mr. Winwood Reade informs me that the Negroes on the Gold Coast, though admiring white men and mulattoes, have a maxim that mulattoes should not intermarry, as the children are few and sickly. This belief, as Mr. Reade remarks, deserves attention, as white men have visited and resided on the Gold Coast for four hundred years, so that the natives have had ample time to gain knowledge through experience.

[13] 'Military and Anthropolog. Statistics of American Soldiers,' by B. A. Gould, 1869, p. 319.

ility are not safe criterions of specific distinctness. We know that these qualities are easily affected by changed conditions of life, or by close inter-breeding, and that they are governed by highly complex laws, for instance, that of the unequal fertility of converse crosses between the same two species. With forms which must be ranked as undoubted species, a perfect series exists from those which are absolutely sterile when crossed, to those which are almost or completely fertile. The degrees of sterility do not coincide strictly with the degrees of difference between the parents in external structures or habits of life. Man in many respects may be compared with those animals which have long been domesticated, and a large body of evidence can be advanced in favour of the Pallasian doctrine,[14] that domestication tends to eliminate the sterility which is so general a result of the crossing of species in a state of nature. From these several considerations, it may be justly urged that the perfect fertility of the intercrossed races of man, if established, would not absolutely preclude us from ranking them as distinct species.

Independently of fertility, the characters presented by the offspring from a cross have been thought to indicate whether or not the parent-forms ought to be ranked as species or varieties; but after carefully studying the evidence, I have come to the conclusion that no general rules of this kind can be trusted. The ordinary result of a cross is the production of a blended or intermediate form; but in certain cases some of the offspring take closely after one parent-form, and some after the other. This is especially apt to occur when the parents differ in characters which

---

[14] 'The Variation of Animals and Plants under Domestication,' vol. ii. p. 109. I may here remind the reader that the sterility of species when crossed is not a specially-acquired quality, but, like the incapacity of certain trees to be grafted together, is incidental on other acquired differences. The nature of these differences is unknown, but they relate more especially to the reproductive system, and much less so to external structure or to ordinary differences in constitution. One important element in the sterility of crossed species apparently lies in one or both having been long habituated to fixed conditions; for we know that changed conditions have a special influence on the reproductive system, and we have good reason to believe (as before remarked) that the fluctuating conditions of domestication tend to eliminate that sterility which is so general with species, in a natural state, when crossed. It has elsewhere been shewn by me (ibid. vol. ii. p. 185, and 'Origin of Species,' this edit. p. 219), that the sterility of crossed species has not been acquired through natural selection: we can see that when two forms have already been rendered very sterile, it is scarcely possible that their sterility should be augmented by the preservation or survival of the more and more sterile individuals; for, as the sterility increases, fewer and fewer offspring will be produced from which to breed, and at last only single individuals will be produced at the rarest intervals. But there is even a higher grade of sterility than this. Both Gärtner and Kölreuter have proved that in genera of plants, including many species, a series can be formed from species which, when crossed, yield fewer and fewer seeds, to species which never produce a single seed, but yet are affected by the pollen of the other species, as shewn by the swelling of the germen. It is here manifestly impossible to select the more sterile individuals, which have already ceased to yield seeds; so that the acme of sterility, when the germen alone is affected, cannot have been gained through selection. This acme, and no doubt the other grades of sterility, are the incidental results of certain unknown differences in the constitution of the reproductive system of the species which are crossed.

first appeared as sudden variations or monstrosities.[15] I refer to this point, because Dr. Rohlfs informs me that he has frequently seen in Africa the offspring of negroes crossed with members of other races, either completely black or completely white, or rarely piebald. On the other hand, it is notorious that in America mulattoes commonly present an intermediate appearance.

We have now seen that a naturalist might feel himself fully justified in ranking the races of man as distinct species; for he has found that they are distinguished by many differences in structure and constitution, some being of importance. These differences have, also, remained nearly constant for very long periods of time. Our naturalist will have been in some degree influenced by the enormous range of man, which is a great anomaly in the class of mammals, if mankind be viewed as a single species. He will have been struck with the distribution of the several so-called races, which accords with that of other undoubtedly distinct species of mammals. Finally, he might urge that the mutual fertility of all the races has not as yet been fully proved, and even if proved would not be an absolute proof of their specific identity.

On the other side of the question, if our supposed naturalist were to enquire whether the forms of man keep distinct like ordinary species, when mingled together in large numbers in the same country, he would immediately discover that this was by no means the case. In Brazil he would behold an immense mongrel population of Negroes and Portuguese; in Chiloe, and other parts of South America, he would behold the whole population consisting of Indians and Spaniards blended in various degrees.[16] In many parts of the same continent he would meet with the most complex crosses between Negroes, Indians, and Europeans; and judging from the vegetable kingdom, such triple crosses afford the severest test of the mutual fertility of the parent forms. In one island of the Pacific he would find a small population of mingled Polynesian and English blood; and in the Fiji Archipelago a population of Polynesian and Negritos crossed in all degrees. Many analogous cases could be added; for instance, in Africa. Hence the races of man are not sufficiently distinct to inhabit the same country without fusion; and the absence of fusion affords the usual and best test of specific distinctness.

Our naturalist would likewise be much disturbed as soon as he perceived that the distinctive characters of all the races were highly variable. This fact strikes every one on first beholding the negro slaves in Brazil, who have been imported from all parts of Africa. The same remark holds good with the Polynesians, and with many other races. It may be doubted whether any character can be named which is distinctive of a race and is constant. Savages, even within the limits of the same tribe, are not nearly so uniform in character, as has been often asserted. Hottentot women

---

[15] 'The Variation of Animals,' &c., vol. ii. p. 92.

[16] M. de Quatrefages has given ('Anthropolog. Review,' Jan. 1869, p. 22), an interesting account of the success and energy of the Paulistas in Brazil, who are a much crossed race of Portuguese and Indians, with a mixture of the blood of other races.

offer certain peculiarities, more strongly marked than those occurring in any other race, but these are known not to be of constant occurrence. In the several American tribes, colour and hairiness differ considerably; as does colour to a certain degree, and the shape of the features greatly, in the Negroes of Africa. The shape of the skull varies much in some races;[17] and so it is with every other character. Now all naturalists have learnt by dearly bought experience, how rash it is to attempt to define species by the aid of inconstant characters.

But the most weighty of all the arguments against treating the races of man as distinct species, is that they graduate into each other, independently in many cases, as far as we can judge, of their having intercrossed. Man has been studied more carefully than any other animal, and yet there is the greatest possible diversity amongst capable judges whether he should be classed as a single species or race, or as two (Virey), as three (Jacquinot), as four (Kant), five (Blumenbach), six (Buffon), seven (Hunter), eight (Agassiz), eleven (Pickering), fifteen (Bory St. Vincent), sixteen (Desmoulins), twenty-two (Morton), sixty (Crawfurd), or as sixty-three, according to Burke.[18] This diversity of judgment does not prove that the races ought not to be ranked as species, but it shews that they graduate into each other, and that it is hardly possible to discover clear distinctive characters between them.

Every naturalist who has had the misfortune to undertake the description of a group of highly varying organisms, has encountered cases (I speak after experience) precisely like that of man; and if of a cautious disposition, he will end by uniting all the forms which graduate into each other, under a single species; for he will say to himself that he has no right to give names to objects which he cannot define. Cases of this kind occur in the Order which include man, namely in certain genera of monkeys; whilst in other genera, as in Cercopithecus, most of the species can be determined with certainty. In the American genus Cebus, the various forms are ranked by some naturalists as species, by others as mere geographical races. Now if numerous specimens of Cebus were collected from all parts of South America, and those forms which at present appear to be specifically distinct, were found to graduate into each other by close steps, they would usually be ranked as mere varieties or races; and this course has been followed by most naturalists with respect to the races of man. Nevertheless, it must be confessed that there are forms, at least in the vegetable kingdom,[19] which we cannot avoid naming as spe-

---

[17] For instance, with the aborigines of America and Australia. Prof. Huxley says ('Transact. Internat. Congress of Prehist. Arch.' 1868, p. 105), that the skulls of many South Germans and Swiss are "as short and as broad as those of the Tartars," &c.

[18] See a good discussion on this subject in Waitz, 'Introduct. to Anthropology,' Eng. translat. 1863, pp. 198–208, 227. I have taken some of the above statements from H. Tuttle's 'Origin and Antiquity of Physical Man,' Boston, 1866, p. 35.

[19] Prof. Nägeli has carefully described several striking cases in his 'Botanische Mittheilungen,' B. ii. 1866, ss. 294–369. Prof. Asa Gray has made analogous remarks on some intermediate forms in the Compositæ of N. America.

cies, but which are connected together by numberless gradations, inde-
dependently of intercrossing.

Some naturalists have lately employed the term "sub-species" to designate forms which possess many of the characteristic of true species, but
which hardly deserve so high a rank. Now if we reflect on the weighty
arguments above given, for raising the races of man to the dignity of species, and the insuperable difficulties on the other side in defining them, it
seems that the term "sub-species" might here be used with propriety.
But from long habit the term "race" will perhaps always be employed.
The choice of terms is only so far important in that it is desirable to use,
as far as possible, the same terms for the same degrees of difference. Unfortunately this can rarely be done: for the larger genera generally include closely-allied forms, which can be distinguished only with much
difficulty, whilst the smaller genera within the same family include forms
that are perfectly distinct; yet all must be ranked equally as species. So
again, species within the same large genus by no means resemble each
other to the same degree: on the contrary, some of them can generally
be arranged in little groups round other species, like satellites round
planets.[20]

The question whether mankind consists of one or several species has
of late years been much discussed by anthropologists, who are divided
into the two schools of monogenists and polygenists. Those who do not
admit the principle of evolution, must look at species as separate creations, or as in some manner as distinct entities; and they must decide
what forms of man they will consider as species by the analogy of the
method commonly pursued in ranking other organic beings as species.
But it is a hopeless endeavour to decide this point, until some definition
of the term "species" is generally accepted; and the definition must not
include an indeterminate element such as an act of creation. We might as
well attempt without any definition to decide whether a certain number
of houses should be called a village, town, or city. We have a practical
illustration of the difficulty in the never-ending doubts whether many
closely-allied mammals, birds, insects, and plants, which represent each
other respectively in North America and Europe, should be ranked as
species or geographical races; and the like holds true of the productions
of many islands situated at some little distance from the nearest continent.

Those naturalists, on the other hand, who admit the principle of evolution, and this is now admitted by the majority of rising men, will feel no
doubt that all the races of man are descended from a single primitive
stock; whether or not they may think fit to designate the races as distinct
species, for the sake of expressing their amount of difference.[21] With our
domestic animals the question whether the various races have arisen
from one or more species is somewhat different. Although it may be admitted that all the races, as well as all the natural species within the same

[20] 'Origin of Species,' this edit. p. 47.
[21] See Prof. Huxley to this effect in the 'Fortnightly Review,' 1865, p. 275.

genus, have sprung from the same primitive stock, yet it is a fit subject for discussion, whether all the domestic races of the dog, for instance, have acquired their present amount of difference since some one species was first domesticated by man; or whether they owe some of their characters to inheritance from distinct species, which had already been differentiated in a state of nature. With man no such question can arise, for he cannot be said to have been domesticated at any particular period.

During an early stage in the divergence of the races of man from a common stock, the differences between the races and their number must have been small; consequently as far as their distinguishing characters are concerned, they then had less claim to rank as distinct species than the existing so-called races. Nevertheless, so arbitrary is the term of species, that such early races would perhaps have been ranked by some naturalists as distinct species, if their differences, although extremely slight, had been more constant than they are at present, and had not graduated into each other.

It is however possible, though far from probable, that the early progenitors of man might formerly have diverged much in character, until they became more unlike each other than any now existing races; but that subsequently, as suggested by Vogt,[22] they converge in character. When man selects the offspring of two distinct species for the same object, he sometimes induces a considerable amount of convergence, as far as general appearance is concerned. This is the case, as shown by Von Nathusius,[23] with the improved breeds of the pig, which are descended from two distinct species; and in a less marked manner with the improved breeds of cattle. A great anatomist, Gratiolet, maintains that the anthropomorphous apes do not form a natural sub-group; but that the orang is a highly developed gibbon or semnopithecus, the chimpanzee a highly developed macacus, and the gorilla a highly developed mandrill. If this conclusion, which rests almost exclusively on brain-characters, be admitted, we should have a case of convergence at least in external characters, for the anthropomorphous apes are certainly more like each other in many points, than they are to other apes. All analogical resemblances, as of a whale to a fish, may indeed be said to be cases of convergence; but this term has never been applied to superficial and adaptive resemblances. It would, however, be extremely rash to attribute to convergence close similarity of character in many points of structure amongst the modified descendants of widely distinct beings. The form of a crystal is determined solely by the molecular forces, and it is not surprising that dissimilar substances should sometimes assume the same form; but with organic beings we should bear in mind that the form of each depends on an infinity of complex relations, namely on variations, due to causes far too intricate to be followed,—on the nature of the variations preserved,

[22] 'Lectures on Man,' Eng. translat. 1864, p. 468.
[23] 'Die Racen des Schweines,' 1860, s. 46. 'Vorstudien für Geschichte, &c., Schweinescähdel,' 1864, s. 104. With respect to cattle, see M. de Quatrefages, 'Unité de l'Espèce Humaine,' 1861, p. 119.

these depending on the physical conditions, and still more on the surrounding organisms which compete with each,—and lastly, on inheritance (in itself a fluctuating element) from innumerable progenitors, all
of which have had their forms determined through equally complex relations. It appears incredible that the modified descendants of two organisms, if these differed from each other in a marked manner, should
ever afterwards converge so closely as to lead to a near approach to identity throughout their whole organisation. In the case of the convergent
races of pigs above referred to, evidence of their descent from two primitive stock is, according to Von Nathusius, still plainly retained, in certain bones of their skulls. If the races of man had descended, as is supposed by some naturalists, from two or more species, which differed from
each other as much, or nearly as much, as does the orang from the gorilla,
it can hardly be doubted that marked differences in the structure of certain bones would still be discoverable in man as he now exists.

Although the existing races of man differ in many respects, as in colour, hair, shape of skull, proportions of the body, &c., yet if their whole
structure be taken into consideration they are found to resemble each
other closely in a multitude of points. Many of these are of so unimportant or of so singular a nature, that it is extremely improbable that they
should have been independently acquired by aboriginally distinct species or races. The same remark holds good with equal or greater force
with respect to the numerous points of mental similarity between the
most distinct races of man. The American aborigines, Negroes and Europeans are as different from each other in mind as any three races that
can be named; yet I was incessantly struck, whilst living with the Feu-
gians on board the "Beagle," with the many little traits of character,
shewing how similar their minds were to ours; and so it was with a full-
blooded negro with whom I happened once to be intimate.

He who will read Mr. Tylor's and Sir J. Lubbock's interesting works[24]
can hardly fail to be deeply impressed with the close similarity between
the men of all races in tastes, dispositions and habits. This is shown by
the pleasure which they all take in dancing, rude music, acting, painting,
tattooing, and otherwise decorating themselves; in their mutual comprehension of gesture-language, by the same expression in their features, and
by the same inarticulate cries, when excited by the same emotions. This
similarity, or rather identity, is striking, when contrasted with the different expressions and cries made by distinct species of monkeys. There is
good evidence that the art of shooting with bows and arrows has not been
handed down from any common progenitor of mankind, yet as Westropp
and Nilsson have remarked,[25] the stone arrow-heads, brought from the

---

[24] Tylor's 'Early History of Mankind,' 1865: with respect to gesture-language, see
p. 54. Lubbock's 'Prehistoric Times,' 2nd edit. 1869.
[25] 'On Analogous Forms of Implements,' in 'Memoirs of Anthropolog. Soc.' by H.
M. Westropp. 'The Primitive Inhabitants of Scandinavia,' Eng. translat. edited by Sir
J. Lubbock, 1868, p. 104.

most distant parts of the world, and manufactured at the most remote periods, are almost identical; and this fact can only be accounted for by the various races having similar inventive or mental powers. The same observation has been made by archæologists[26] with respect to certain widely-prevalent ornaments, such as zig-zags, &c.; and with respect to various simple beliefs and customs, such as the burying of the dead under megalithic structures. I remember observing in South America,[27] that there, as in so many other parts of the world, men have generally chosen the summits of lofty hills, to throw up piles of stones, either as a record of some remarkable event, or for burying their dead.

Now when naturalists observe a close agreement in numerous small details of habits, tastes, and dispositions between two or more domestic races, or between nearly-allied natural forms, they use this fact as an argument that they are descended from a common progenitor who was thus endowed; and consequently that all should be classed under the same species. The same argument may be applied with much force to the races of man.

As it is improbable that the numerous and unimportant points of resemblance between the several races of man in bodily structure and mental faculties (I do not here refer to similar customs) should all have been independently acquired, they must have been inherited from progenitors who had these same characters. We thus gain some insight into the early state of man, before he had spread step by step over the face of the earth. The spreading of man to regions widely separated by the sea, no doubt, preceded any great amount of divergence of character in the several races; for otherwise we should sometimes meet with the same race in distinct continents; and this is never the case. Sir J. Lubbock, after comparing the arts now practised by savages in all parts of the world, specifies those which man could not have known, when he first wandered from his original birthplace; for if once learnt they would never have been forgotten.[28] He thus shews that "the spear, which is but a development of the knife-point, and the club, which is but a long hammer, are the only things left." He admits, however, that the art of making fire probably had been already discovered, for it is common to all the races now existing, and was known to the ancient cave-inhabitants of Europe. Perhaps the art of making rude canoes or rafts was likewise known; but as man existed at a remote epoch, when the land in many places stood at a very different level to what it does now, he would have been able, without the aid of canoes, to have spread widely. Sir J. Lubbock further remarks how improbable it is that our earliest ancestors could have "counted as high as ten, considering that so many races now in existence cannot get beyond four." Nevertheless, at this early period, the intellectual and social faculties of man

---

[26] Westropp, 'On Cromlechs,' &c., 'Journal of Ethnological Soc.' as given in 'Scientific Opinion,' June 2nd, 1869, p. 3.

[27] 'Journal of Researches: Voyage of the "Beagle,"' p. 46.

[28] 'Prehistoric Times,' 1869, page 574.

could hardly have been inferior in any extreme degree to those possessed at present by the lowest savages; otherwise primeval man could not have been so eminently successful in the struggle for life, as proved by his early and wide diffusion.

From the fundamental differences between certain languages, some philologists have inferred that when man first became widely diffused, he was not a speaking animal; but it may be suspected that languages, far less perfect than any now spoken, aided by gestures, might have been used, and yet have left no traces on subsequent and more highly-developed tongues. Without the use of some language, however imperfect, it appears doubtful whether man's intellect could have risen to the standard implied by his dominant position at an early period.

Whether primeval man, when he possessed but few arts, and those of the rudest kind, and when his power of language was extremely imperfect, would have deserved to be called man, must depend on the definition which we employ. In a series of forms graduating insensibly from some ape-like creature to man as he now exists, it would be impossible to fix on any definite point when the term "man" ought to be used. But this is a matter of very little importance. So again, it is almost a matter of indifference whether the so-called races of man are thus designated, or are ranked as species or sub-species; but the latter term appears the more appropriate. Finally, we may conclude that when the principle of evolution is generally accepted, as it surely will be before long, the dispute between the monogenists and the polygenists will die a silent and unobserved death.

One other question ought not to be passed over without notice, namely, whether, as is sometimes assumed, each sub-species or race of man has sprung from a single pair of progenitors. With our domestic animals a new race can readily be formed by carefully matching the varying offspring from a single pair, or even from a single individual possessing some new character; but most of our races have been formed, not intentionally from a selected pair, but unconsciously by the preservation of many individuals which have varied, however slightly, in some useful or desired manner. If in one country stronger and heavier horses, and in another country lighter and fleeter ones, were habitually preferred, we may feel sure that two distinct sub-breeds would be produced in the course of time, without any one pair having been separated and bred from, in either country. Many races have been thus formed, and their manner of formation is closely analogous to that of natural species. We know, also, that the horses taken to the Falkland Islands have, during successive generations, become smaller and weaker, whilst those which have run wild on the Pampas have acquired larger and coarser heads; and such changes are manifestly due, not to any one pair, but to all the individuals having been subjected to the same conditions, aided, perhaps, by the principle of reversion. The new sub-breeds in such cases are not descended from any

single pair, but from many individuals which have varied in different degrees, but in the same general manner; and we may conclude that the
races of man have been similarly produced, the modifications being either
the direct result of exposure to different conditions, or the indirect result
of some form of selection. But to this latter subject we shall presently
return.

On the Extinction of the Races of Man.—The partial or complete extinction of many races and sub-races of man is historically known. Humboldt saw in South America a parrot which was the sole living creature
that could speak a word of the language of a lost tribe. Ancient monuments and stone implements found in all parts of the world, about which
no tradition has been preserved by the present inhabitants, indicate much
extinction. Some small and broken tribes, remnants of former races, still
survive in isolated and generally mountainous districts. In Europe the
ancient races were all, according to Shaaffhausen,[29] "lower in the scale
than the rudest living savages;" they must therefore have differed, to a
certain extent, from any existing race. The remains described by Professor Broca from Les Eyzies, though they unfortunately appear to have belonged to a single family, indicate a race with a most singular combination of low or simious, and of high characteristics. This race is "entirely
different from any other, ancient or modern, that we have heard of." [30] It
differed, therefore, from the quaternary race of the caverns of Belgium.

Man can long resist conditions which appear extremely unfavourable
for his existence.[31] He has long lived in the extreme regions of the North,
with no wood for his canoes or implements, and with only blubber as fuel,
and melted snow as drink. In the southern extremity of America the Fuegians survive without the protection of clothes, or of any building worthy
to be called a hovel. In South Africa the aborigines wander over arid
plains, where dangerous beasts abound. Man can withstand the deadly
influence of the Terai at the foot of the Himalaya, and the pestilential
shores of tropical Africa.

Extinction follows chiefly from the competition of tribe with tribe, and
race with race. Various checks are always in action, serving to keep down
the numbers of each savage tribe,—such as periodical famines, nomadic
habits and the consequent deaths of infants, prolonged suckling, wars, accidents, sickness, licentiousness, the stealing of women, infanticide, and
especially lessened fertility. If any one of these checks increases in power,
even slightly, the tribe thus affected tends to decrease; and when of two
adjoining tribes one becomes less numerous and less powerful than the
other, the contest is soon settled by war, slaughter, cannibalism, slavery,

---

[29] Translation in 'Anthropological Review,' Oct. 1868, p. 431.
[30] 'Transact. Internat. Congress of Prehistoric Arch.' 1868, pp. 172–175. See also
Broca (translation) in 'Anthropological Review,' Oct., 1868, p. 410.
[31] Dr. Gerland, 'Ueber das Aussterben der Naturvölker,' 1868, s. 82.

and absorption. Even when a weaker tribe is not thus abruptly swept away, if it once begins to decrease, it generally goes on decreasing until it becomes extinct.[32]

When civilised nations come into contact with barbarians the struggle is short, except where a deadly climate gives its aid to the native race. Of the causes which lead to the victory of civilised nations, some are plain and simple, others complex and obscure. We can see that the cultivation of the land will be fatal in many ways to savages, for they cannot, or will not, change their habits. New diseases and vices have in some cases proved highly destructive; and it appears that a new disease often causes much death, until those who are most susceptible to its destructive influence are gradually weeded out;[33] and so it may be with the evil effects from spirituous liquors, as well as with the unconquerably strong taste for them shewn by so many savages. It further appears, mysterious as is the fact, that the first meeting of distinct and separated people generates disease.[34] Mr. Sproat, who in Vancouver Island closely attended to the subject of extinction, believed that changed habits of life, consequent on the advent of Europeans, induces much ill health. He lays, also, great stress on the apparently trifling cause that the natives become "bewildered and dull by the new life around them; they lose the motives for exertion, and get no new ones in their place."[35]

The grade of their civilisation seems to be a most important element in the success of competing nations. A few centuries ago Europe feared the inroads of Eastern barbarians; now any such fear would be ridiculous. It is a more curious fact, as Mr. Bagehot has remarked, that savages did not formerly waste away before the classical nations, as they now do before modern civilised nations; had they done so, the old moralists would have mused over the event; but there is no lament in any writer of that period over the perishing barbarians.[36] The most potent of all the causes of extinction, appears in many cases to be lessened fertility and ill-health, especially amongst the children, arising from changed conditions of life, notwithstanding that the new conditions may not be injurious in themselves. I am much indebted to Mr. H. H. Howorth for having called my attention to this subject, and for having given me information respecting it. I have collected the following cases.

When Tasmania was first colonised the natives were roughly estimated by some at 7000 and by others at 20,000. Their number was soon greatly reduced, chiefly by fighting with the English and with each other. After the famous hunt by all the colonists, when the remaining natives deliv-

---

[32] Gerland (ibid. s. 12) gives facts in support of this statement.

[33] See remarks to this effect in Sir H. Holland's 'Medical Notes and Reflections,' 1839, p. 390.

[34] I have collected ('Journal of Researches, Voyage of the "Beagle," ' p. 435) a good many cases bearing on this subject; see also Gerland, ibid. s. 8. Poeppig speaks of the "breath of civilisation as poisonous to savages."

[35] Sproat, 'Scenes and Studies of Savage Life,' 1868, p. 284.

[36] Bagehot, 'Physics and Politics,' 'Fortnightly Review,' April 1, 1868, p. 455.

ered themselves up to the government, they consisted only of 120 individuals,[37] who were in 1832 transported to Flinders Island. This island, situated between Tasmania and Australia, is forty miles long, and from twelve to eighteen miles broad: it seems healthy, and the natives were well treated. Nevertheless, they suffered greatly in health. In 1834 they consisted (Bonwick, p. 250) of forty-seven adult males, forty-eight adult females, and sixteen children, or in all of 111 souls. In 1835 only one hundred were left. As they continued rapidly to decrease, and as they themselves thought that they should not perish so quickly elsewhere, they were removed in 1847 to Oyster Cove in the southern part of Tasmania. They then consisted (Dec. 20th, 1847) of fourteen men, twenty-two women and ten children.[38] But the change of site did no good. Disease and death still pursued them, and in 1864 one man (who died in 1869), and three elderly women alone survived. The infertility of the women is even a more remarkable fact than the liability of all to ill-health and death. At the time when only nine women were left at Oyster Cove, they told Mr. Bonwick (p. 386), that only two had ever borne children: and these two had together produced only three children!

With respect to the cause of this extraordinary state of things, Dr. Story remarks that death followed the attempts to civilise the natives. "If left to themselves to roam as they were wont and undisturbed, they would have reared more children, and there would have been less mortality." Another careful observer of the natives, Mr. Davis, remarks, "The births have been few and the deaths numerous. This may have been in a great measure owing to their change of living and food; but more so to their banishment from the mainland of Van Diemen's Land, and consequent depression of spirits" (Bonwick, pp. 388, 390).

Similar facts have been observed in two widely different parts of Australia. The celebrated explorer, Mr. Gregory, told Mr. Bonwick, that in Queensland "the want of reproduction was being already felt with the blacks, even in the most recently settled parts, and that decay would set in." Of thirteen aborigines from Shark's Bay who visited Murchison River, twelve died of consumption within three months.[39]

The decrease of the Maories of New Zealand has been carefully investigated by Mr. Fenton, in an admirable Report, from which all the following statements, with one exception, are taken.[40] The decrease in number since 1830 is admitted by every one, including the natives themselves, and is still steadily progressing. Although it has hitherto been found impossible to take an actual census of the natives, their numbers were care-

[37] All the statements here given are taken from 'The last of the Tasmanians,' by J. Bonwick, 1870.

[38] This is the statement of the Governor of Tasmania, Sir W. Denison, 'Varieties of Vice-Regal Life,' 1870, vol. i. p. 67.

[39] For these cases, see Bonwick's 'Daily Life of the Tasmanians,' 1870, p. 90: and the 'Last of the Tasmanians,' 1870, p. 386.

[40] 'Observations on the Aboriginal Inhabitants of New Zealand,' published by the Government, 1859.

fully estimated by residents in many districts. The result seems trustworthy, and shows that during the fourteen years, previous to 1858, the decrease was 19.42 per cent. Some of the tribes, thus carefully examined, lived above a hundred miles apart, some on the coast, some inland; and their means of subsistence and habits differed to a certain extent (p. 28). The total number in 1858 was believed to be 53,700, and in 1872, after a second interval of fourteen years, another census was taken, and the number is given as only 36,359, shewing a decrease of 32.29 per cent![41] Mr. Fenton, after shewing in detail the insufficiency of the various causes, usually assigned in explanation of this extraordinary decrease, such as new diseases, the profligacy of the women, drunkenness, wars, &c., concludes on weighty grounds that it depends chiefly on the unproductiveness of the women, and on the extraordinary mortality of the young children (pp. 31, 34). In proof of this he shews (p. 33) that in 1844 there was one non-adult for every 2.57 adults; whereas in 1858 there was only one non-adult for every 3.27 adults. The mortality of the adults is also great. He adduces as a further cause of the decrease the inequality of the sexes; for fewer females are born than males. To this latter point, depending perhaps on a widely distinct cause, I shall return in a future chapter. Mr. Fenton contrasts with astonishment the decrease in New Zealand with the increase in Ireland; countries not very dissimilar in climate, and where the inhabitants now follow nearly similar habits. The Maories themselves (p. 35) "attribute their decadence, in some measure, to the introduction of new food and clothing, and the attendant change of habits;" and it will be seen, when we consider the influence of changed conditions on fertility, that they are probably right. The diminution began between the years 1830 and 1840; and Mr. Fenton shews (p. 40) that about 1830, the art of manufacturing putrid corn (maize), by long steeping in water, was discovered and largely practised; and this proves that a change of habits was beginning amongst the natives, even when New Zealand was only thinly inhabited by Europeans. When I visited the Bay of Islands in 1835, the dress and food of the inhabitants had already been much modified: they raised potatoes, maize, and other agricultural produce, and exchanged them for English manufactured goods and tobacco.

It is evident from many statements in the life of Bishop Patteson,[42] that the Melanesians of the New Hebrides and neighbouring archipelagoes, suffered to an extraordinary degree in health, and perished in large numbers, when they were removed to New Zealand, Norfolk Island, and other salubrious places, in order to be educated as missionaries.

The decrease of the native population of the Sandwich Islands is as notorious as that of New Zealand. It has been roughly estimated by those best capable of judging, that when Cook discovered the Islands in 1779, the population amounted to about 300,000. According to a loose census in

[41] 'New Zealand,' by Alex. Kennedy, 1873, p. 47.

[42] 'Life of J. C. Patteson,' by C. M. Younge, 1874; see more especially vol. i. p 530

1823, the numbers then were 142,050. In 1832, and at several subsequent periods, an accurate census was officially taken, but I have been able to obtain only the following returns:

YEAR.	NATIVE POPULATION. (Except during 1832 and 1836, when the few foreigners in the islands were included.)	Annual rate of decrease per cent., assuming it to have been uniform between the successive censuses; these censuses being taken at irregular intervals.
1832	130,313	
1836	108,579	4.46
1853	71,019	2.47
1860	67,084	0.81
1866	58,765	2.18
1872	51,531	2.17

We here see that in the interval of forty years, between 1832 and 1872, the population has decreased no less than sixty-eight per cent! This has been attributed by most writers to the profligacy of the women, to former bloody wars, and to the severe labour imposed on conquered tribes and to newly introduced diseases, which have been on several occasions extremely destructive. No doubt these and other such causes have been highly efficient, and may account for the extraordinary rate of decrease between the years 1832 and 1836; but the most potent of all the causes seems to be lessened fertility. According to Dr. Ruschenberger of the U. S. Navy, who visited these islands between 1835 and 1837, in one district of Hawaii, only twenty-five men out of 1134, and in another district only ten out of 637, had a family with as many as three children. Of eighty married women, only thirty-nine had ever borne children; and "the official report gives an average of half a child to each married couple in the whole island." This is almost exactly the same average as with the Tasmanians at Oyster Cove. Jarves, who published his History in 1843, says that "families who have three children are freed from all taxes; those having more, are rewarded by gifts of land and other encouragements." This unparalleled enactment by the government well shews how infertile the race had become. The Rev. A. Bishop stated in the Hawaiian 'Spectator' in 1839, that a large proportion of the children die at early ages, and Bishop Staley informs me that this is still the case, just as in New Zealand. This has been attributed to the neglect of the children by the women, but it is probably in large part due to innate weakness of constitution in the children, in relation to the lessened fertility of their parents. There is, moreover, a further resemblance to the case of New Zealand, in the fact that there is a large excess of male over female births: the census of 1872 gives 31,650 males to 25,247 females of all ages, that is 125.36 males for every 100 females; whereas in all civilised countries the females exceed the males. No doubt the profligacy of the women may in part account for their small fertility; but their changed habits of life is a much more probable cause, and which will at the same time account for the increased mortality, especially of the children. The islands were visited by Cook in 1779, by Vancouver in 1794, and often subsequently by whalers. In 1819 missionaries arrived, and found that idolatry had been already abolished and other changes effected by the king. After this period there was a rapid change in almost all the habits of life of the natives, and they soon became "the most civilised of the Pacific Islanders." One of my informants, Mr. Coan, who was born on the islands, remarks that the natives have undergone a greater change in their habits of life in the course of fifty years than Englishmen during a thousand years. From information received from Bishop Staley, it does not appear that the poorer classes have ever much changed their diet, although many new kinds of fruit have been introduced, and the sugar-cane is in universal use. Owing, however, to their passion for imitating Europeans, they altered their manner of dressing at an early period, and the use of alcoholic drinks became very general. Although these changes appear inconsiderable, I can well believe, from what is known with respect to animals, that they might suffice to lessen the fertility of the natives.[43]

Lastly, Mr. Macnamara states[44] that the low and degraded inhabitants of the Andaman Islands, on the eastern side of the Gulf of Bengal, are "eminently susceptible to any change of climate: in fact, take them away from their island homes, and they are almost certain to die, and that independently of diet or extraneous influences." He further states that the inhabitants of the Valley of Nepâl, which is extremely hot in summer, and also the various hill-tribes of India, suffer from dysentery and fever when on the plains; and they die if they attempt to pass the whole year there.

We thus see that many of the wilder races of man are apt to suffer much in health when subjected to changed conditions or habits of life, and not exclusively from being transported to a new climate. Mere alterations in habits, which do not appear injurious in themselves, seem to have this same effect; and in several cases the children are particularly

---

[43] The foregoing statements are taken chiefly from the following works: 'Jarves' History of the Hawaiian Islands,' 1843, p. 400–407. Cheever, 'Life in the Sandwich Islands,' 1851, p. 277. Ruschenberger is quoted by Bonwick, 'Last of the Tasmanians,' 1870, p. 378. Bishop is quoted by Sir E. Belcher, 'Voyage Round the World,' 1843, vol. i. p. 272. I owe the census of the several years to the kindness of Mr. Coan, at the request of Dr. Youmans of New York; and in most cases I have compared the Youmans figures with those given in several of the above-named works. I have omitted the census for 1850, as I have seen two widely different numbers given.

[44] 'The Indian Medical Gazette,' Nov. 1, 1871, p. 240.

liable to suffer. It has often been said, as Mr. Macnamara remarks, that man can resist with impunity the greatest diversities of climate and other changes; but this is true only of the civilised races. Man in his wild condition seems to be in this respect almost as susceptible as his nearest allies, the anthropoid apes, which have never yet survived long, when removed from their native country.

Lessened fertility from changed conditions, as in the case of the Tasmanians, Maories, Sandwich Islanders, and apparently the Australians, is still more interesting than their liability to ill-health and death; for even a slight degree of infertility, combined with those other causes which tend to check the increase of every population, would sooner or later lead to extinction. The diminution of fertility may be explained in some cases by the profligacy of the women (as until lately with the Tahitians), but Mr. Fenton has shewn that this explanation by no means suffices with the New Zealanders, nor does it with the Tasmanians.

In the paper above quoted, Mr. Macnamara gives reasons for believing that the inhabitants of districts subject to malaria are apt to be sterile; but this cannot apply in several of the above cases. Some writers have suggested that the aborigines of islands have suffered in fertility and health from long continued inter-breeding; but in the above cases infertility has coincided too closely with the arrival of Europeans for us to admit this explanation. Nor have we at present any reason to believe that man is highly sensitive to the evil effects of inter-breeding, especially in areas so large as New Zealand, and the Sandwich archipelago with its diversified stations. On the contrary, it is known that the present inhabitants of Norfolk Island are nearly all cousins or near relations, as are the Todas in India, and the inhabitants of some of the Western Islands of Scotland; and yet they seem not to have suffered in fertility.[45]

A much more probable view is suggested by the analogy of the lower animals. The reproductive system can be shewn to be susceptible to an extraordinary degree (though why we know not) to changed conditions of life; and this susceptibility leads both to beneficial and to evil results. A large collection of facts on this subject is given in chap. xviii. of vol. ii. of my 'Variation of Animals and Plants under Domestication,' I can here give only the briefest abstract; and every one interested in the subject may consult the above work. Very slight changes increase the health, vigour, and fertility of most or all organic beings, whilst other changes are known to render a large number of animals sterile. One of the most familiar cases, is that of tamed elephants not breeding in India; though they often breed in Ava, where the females are allowed to roam about the forests to some extent, and are thus placed under more natural conditions. The case of various American monkeys, both sexes of which have been kept for many years together in their own countries, and yet have

---

[45] On the close relationship of the Norfolk Islanders, see Sir W. Denison, 'Varieties of Vice-Regal Life,' vol. i., 1870, p. 410. For the Todas, see Col. Marshall's work, 1873, p. 110. For the Western Islands of Scotland, Dr. Mitchell, 'Edinburgh Medical Journal,' March to June, 1865.

very rarely or never bred, is a more apposite instance, because of their relationship to man. It is remarkable how slight a change in the conditions often induces sterility in a wild animal when captured; and this is the more strange as all our domesticated animals have become more fertile than they were in a state of nature; and some of them can resist the most unnatural conditions with undiminished fertility.[46] Certain groups of animals are much more liable than others to be affected by captivity; and generally all the species of the same group are affected in the same manner. But sometimes a single species in a group is rendered sterile, whilst the others are not so; on the other hand, a single species may retain its fertility whilst most of the others fail to breed. The males and females of some species when confined, or when allowed to live almost, but not quite free, in their native country, never unite; others thus circumstanced frequently unite but never produce offspring; others again produce some offspring, but fewer than in a state of nature; and as bearing on the above cases of man, it is important to remark that the young are apt to be weak and sickly, or malformed, and to perish at an early age.

Seeing how general is this law of the susceptibility of the reproductive system to changed conditions of life, and that it holds good with our nearest allies, the Quadrumana, I can hardly doubt that it applies to man in his primeval state. Hence if savages of any race are induced suddenly to change their habits of life, they become more or less sterile, and their young offspring suffer in health, in the same manner and from the same cause, as do the elephant and hunting-leopard in India, many monkeys in America, and a host of animals of all kinds, on removal from their natural conditions.

We can see why it is that aborigines, who have long inhabited islands, and who must have been long exposed to nearly uniform conditions, should be specially affected by any change in their habits, as seems to be the case. Civilised races can certainly resist changes of all kinds far better than savages; and in this respect they resemble domesticated animals, for though the latter sometimes suffer in health (for instance European dogs in India), yet they are rarely rendered sterile, though a few such instances have been recorded.[47] The immunity of civilised races and domesticated animals is probably due to their having been subjected to a greater extent, and therefore having grown somewhat more accustomed, to diversified or varying conditions, than the majority of wild animals; and to their having formerly immigrated or been carried from country to country, and to different families or sub-races having inter-crossed. It appears that a cross with civilised races at once gives to an aboriginal race an immunity from the evil consequences of changed conditions. Thus the crossed offspring from the Tahitians and English, when settled in Pitcairn Island, increased so rapidly that the Island was soon overstocked; and in June 1856 they were removed to Norfolk Island. They then consisted of 60 married persons and 134 children, making a total of 194.

---

[46] For the evidence on this head, see 'Variation of Animals,' &c., vol. ii. p. 111.

[47] 'Variation of Animals,' &c., vol. ii. p. 16.

Here they likewise increased so rapidly, that although sixteen of them returned to Pitcairn Island in 1859, they numbered in January 1868, 300 souls; the males and females being in exactly equal numbers. What a contrast does this case present with that of the Tasmanians; the Norfolk Islanders *increased* in only twelve and a half years from 194 to 300; whereas the Tasmanians *decreased* during fifteen years from 120 to 46, of which latter number only ten were children.[48]

So again in the interval between the census of 1866 and 1872 the natives of full blood in the Sandwich Islands decreased by 8081, whilst the half-castes, who are believed to be healthier, increased by 847; but I do not know whether the latter number includes the offspring from the half-castes, or only the half-castes of the first generation.

The cases which I have here given all relate to aborigines, who have been subjected to new conditions as the result of the immigration of civilised men. But sterility and ill-health would probably follow, if savages were compelled by any cause, such as the inroad of a conquering tribe, to desert their homes and to change their habits. It is an interesting circumstance that the chief check to wild animals becoming domesticated, which implies the power of their breeding freely when first captured, and one chief check to wild men, when brought into contact with civilisation, surviving to form a civilised race, is the same, namely, sterility from changed conditions of life.

Finally, although the gradual decrease and ultimate extinction of the races of man is a highly complex problem, depending on many causes which differ in different places and at different times; it is the same problem as that presented by the extinction of one of the higher animals—of the fossil horse, for instance, which disappeared from South America, soon afterwards to be replaced, within the same districts, by countless troups of the Spanish horse. The New Zealander seems conscious of this parallelism, for he compares his future fate with that of the native rat now almost exterminated by the European rat. Though the difficulty is great to our imagination, and really great, if we wish to ascertain the precise causes and their manner of action, it ought not to be so to our reason, as long as we keep steadily in mind that the increase of each species and each race is constantly checked in various ways; so that if any new check, even a slight one, be superadded, the race will surely decrease in number; and decreasing numbers will sooner or later lead to extinction; the end, in most cases, being promptly determined by the inroads of conquering tribes.

On the Formation of the Races of Man.—In some cases the crossing of distinct races has led to the formation of a new race. The singular fact that the Europeans and Hindoos, who belong to the same Aryan stock, and speak a language fundamentally the same, differ widely in appear-

---

[48] These details are taken from 'The Mutineers of the "Bounty," ' by Lady Belcher, 1870; and from 'Pitcairn Island,' ordered to be printed by the House of Commons, May 29th, 1863. The following statements about the Sandwich Islanders are from the 'Honolulu Gazette,' and from Mr. Coan.

ance, whilst Europeans differ but little from Jews, who belong to the Sem-
itic stock, and speak quite another language, has been accounted for by
Broca,[49] through certain Aryan branches having been largely crossed by
indigenous tribes during their wide diffusion. When two races in close
contact cross, the first result is a heterogeneous mixture: thus Mr. Hunter, in describing the Santali or hill-tribes of India, says that hundreds of
imperceptible gradations may be traced "from the black, squat tribes of
the mountains to the tall olive-coloured Brahman, with his intellectual
brow, calm eyes, and high but narrow head;" so that it is necessary in
courts of justice to ask the witnesses whether they are Santalis or Hindoos.[50] Whether a heterogeneous people, such as the inhabitants of some
of the Polynesian islands, formed by the crossing of two distinct races,
with few or no pure members left, would ever become homogeneous, is
not known from direct evidence. But as with our domesticated animals, a
cross-breed can certainly be fixed and made uniform by careful selection[51] in the course of a few generations, we may infer that the free intercrossing of a heterogeneous mixture during a long descent would supply
the place of selection, and overcome any tendency to reversion; so that
the crossed race would ultimately become homogeneous, though it might
not partake in an equal degree of the characters of the two parent-races.

Of all the differences between the races of man, the colour of the skin is
the most conspicuous and one of the best marked. It was formerly
thought that differences of this kind could be accounted for by long exposure to different climates; but Pallas first shewed that this is not ten-
able, and he has since been followed by almost all anthropologists.[52] This
view has been rejected chiefly because the distribution of the variously
coloured races, most of whom must have long inhabited their present
homes, does not coincide with corresponding differences of climate. Some
little weight may be given to such cases as that of the Dutch families,
who, as we hear on excellent authority,[53] have not undergone the least
change of colour after residing for three centuries in South Africa. An argument on the same side may likewise be drawn from the uniform appearance in various parts of the world of gipsies and Jews, though the
uniformity of the latter has been somewhat exaggerated.[54] A very damp
or a very dry atmosphere has been supposed to be more influential in
modifying the colour of the skin than mere heat; but as D'Orbigny in
South America, and Livingstone in Africa, arrived at diametrically oppo-

---

[49] 'On Anthropology,' translation 'Anthropolog. Review,' Jan. 1868, p. 38.

[50] 'The Annals of Rural Bengal,' 1868, p. 134.

[51] 'The Variation of Animals and Plants under Domestication,' vol. ii. p. 95.

[52] Pallas, 'Act. Acad. St. Petersburg,' 1780, part ii. p. 69. He was followed by Rudolphi, in his 'Beyträge zur Anthropologie,' 1812. An excellent summary of the evidence is given by Godron, 'De l'Espèce,' 1859, vol. ii. p. 246, &c.

[53] Sir Andrew Smith, as quoted by Knox, 'Races of Man,' 1850, p. 473.

[54] See De Quatrefages on this head, 'Revue des Cours Scientifiques,' Oct. 17, 1868,
p. 731.

site conclusions with respect to dampness and dryness, any conclusion on this head must be considered as very doubtful.[55]

Various facts, which I have given elsewhere, prove that the colour of the skin and hair is sometimes correlated in a surprising manner with a complete immunity from the action of certain vegetable poisons, and from the attacks of certain parasites. Hence it occurred to me, that negroes and other dark races might have acquired their dark tints by the darker individuals escaping from the deadly influence of the miasma of their native countries, during a long series of generations.

I afterwards found that this same idea had long ago occurred to Dr. Wells.[56] It has long been known that negroes, and even mulattoes, are almost completely exempt from the yellow-fever, so destructive in tropical America.[57] They likewise escape to a large extent the fatal intermittent fevers, that prevail along at least 2600 miles of the shores of Africa, and which annually cause one-fifth of the white settlers to die, and another fifth to return home invalided.[58] This immunity in the negro seems to be partly inherent, depending on some unknown peculiarity of constitution, and partly the result of acclimatisation. Pouchet[59] states that the negro regiments recruited near the Soudan, and borrowed from the Viceroy of Egypt for the Mexican war, escaped the yellow-fever almost equally with the negroes originally brought from various parts of Africa and accustomed to the climate of the West Indies. That acclimatisation plays a part, is shewn by the many cases in which negroes have become somewhat liable to tropical fevers, after having resided for some time in a colder climate.[60] The nature of the climate under which the white races have long resided, likewise has some influence on them; for during the fearful epidemic of yellow fever in Demerara during 1837, Dr. Blair found that the death-rate of the immigrants was proportional to the latitude of the country whence they had come. With the negro the immunity, as far as it is the result of acclimatisation, implies exposure during a prodigious length of time; for the aborigines of tropical America who have resided there from time immemorial, are not exempt from yellow fever; and the Rev. H. B. Tristram states, that there are districts in Northern Africa which the native inhabitants are compelled annually to leave, though the negroes can remain with safety.

---

[55] Livingstone's 'Travels and Researches in S. Africa,' 1857, pp. 338, 339. D'Orbigny, as quoted by Godron, 'De l'Espèce,' vol. ii. p. 266.

[56] See a paper read before the Royal Soc. in 1813, and published in his Essays in 1818. I have given an account of Dr. Wells' views in the Historical Sketch (p. xvi.) to my 'Origin of Species.' Various cases of colour correlated with constitutional peculiarities are given in my 'Variation of Animals under Domestication,' vol. ii. pp. 227, 335.

[57] See, for instance, Nott and Gliddon, 'Types of Mankind,' p. 68.

[58] Major Tulloch, in a paper read before the Statistical Society, April 20th, 1840, and given in the 'Athenæum,' 1840, p. 353.

[59] 'The Plurality of the Human Race' (translat.), 1864, p. 60.

[60] Quatrefages, 'Unité de l'Espèce Humaine,' 1861, p. 205. Waitz, 'Introduct. to Anthropology,' translat. vol. i. 1863, p. 124. Livingstone gives analogous cases in his 'Travels.'

That the immunity of the negro is in any degree correlated with the colour of his skin is a mere conjecture: it may be correlated with some difference in his blood, nervous system, or other tissues. Nevertheless, from the facts above alluded to, and from some connection apparently existing between complexion and a tendency to consumption, the conjecture seemed to me not improbable. Consequently I endeavoured, with but little success,[61] to ascertain how far it holds good. The late Dr. Daniell, who had long lived on the West Coast of Africa, told me that he did not believe in any such relation. He was himself unusually fair, and had withstood the climate in a wonderful manner. When he first arrived as a boy on the coast, an old and experienced negro chief predicted from his appearance that this would prove the case. Dr. Nicholson, of Antigua, after having attended to this subject, writes to me that dark-coloured Europeans escape the yellow fever more than those that are light-coloured. Mr. J. M. Harris altogether denies that Europeans with dark hair withstand a hot climate better than other men: on the contrary, experience has taught him in making a selection of men for service on the coast of Africa, to choose those with red hair.[62] As far, therefore, as these slight indications go, there seems no foundation for the hypothesis, that blackness has resulted from the darker and darker individuals having survived better during long exposure to fever-generating miasma.

[61] In the spring of 1862 I obtained permission from the Director-General of the Medical department of the Army, to transmit to the surgeons of the various regiments on foreign service a blank table, with the following appended remarks, but I have received no returns. "As several well-marked cases have been recorded with our domestic animals of a relation between the colour of the dermal appendages and the constitution; and it being notorious that there is some limited degree of relation between the colour of the races of man and the climate inhabited by them; the following investigation seems worth consideration. Namely, whether there is any relation in Europeans between the colour of their hair, and their liability to the diseases of tropical countries. If the surgeons of the several regiments, when stationed in unhealthy tropical districts, would be so good as first to count, as a standard of comparison, how many men, in the force whence the sick are drawn, have dark and light-coloured hair, and hair of intermediate or doubtful tints; and if a similar account were kept by the same medical gentleman, of all the men who suffered from malarious and yellow fevers, or from dysentery, it would soon be apparent, after some thousand cases had been tabulated, whether there exists any relation between the colour of the hair and constitutional liability to tropical diseases. Perhaps no such relation would be discovered, but the investigation is well worth making. In case any positive result were obtained, it might be of some practical use in selecting men for any particular service. Theoretically the result would be of high interest, as indicating one means by which a race of men inhabiting from a remote period an unhealthy tropical climate, might have become dark-coloured by the better preservation of dark-haired or dark-complexioned individuals during a long succession of generations."

[62] 'Anthropological Review,' Jan. 1866, p. xxi. Dr. Sharpe also says, with respect to India ('Man a Special Creation,' 1873, p. 118), "that it has been noticed by some medical officers that Europeans with light hair and florid complexions suffer less from diseases of tropical countries than persons with dark hair and sallow complexions; and, so far as I know, there appear to be good grounds for this remark." On the other hand, Mr. Heddle, of Sierra Leone, "who has had more clerks killed under him than any other man," by the climate of the West African Coast (W. Reade, 'African Sketch Book,' vol. ii. p. 522), holds a directly opposite view, as does Capt. Burton.

Dr. Sharpe remarks,[63] that a tropical sun, which burns and blisters a white skin, does not injure a black one at all; and, as he adds, this is not due to habit in the individual, for children only six or eight months old are often carried about naked, and are not affected. I have been assured by a medical man, that some years ago during each summer, but not during the winter, his hands became marked with light brown patches, like, although larger than freckles, and that these patches were never affected by sun-burning, whilst the white parts of his skin have on several occasions been much inflamed and blistered. With the lower animals there is, also, a constitutional difference in liability to the action of the sun between those parts of the skin clothed with white hair and other parts.[64] Whether the saving of the skin from being thus burnt is of sufficient importance to account for a dark tint having been gradually acquired by man through natural selection, I am unable to judge. If it be so, we should have to assume that the natives of tropical America have lived there for a much shorter time than the negroes in Africa, or the Papuans in the southern parts of the Malay archipelago, just as the lighter-coloured Hindoos have resided in India for a shorter time than the darker aborigines of the central and southern parts of the peninsula.

Although with our present knowledge we cannot account for the differences of colour in the races of man, through any advantage thus gained, or from the direct action of climate; yet we must not quite ignore the latter agency, for there is good reason to believe that some inherited effect is thus produced.[65]

We have seen in the second chapter that the conditions of life affect the development of the bodily frame in a direct manner, and that the effects are transmitted. Thus, as is generally admitted, the European settlers in the United States undergo a slight but extraordinary rapid change of appearance. Their bodies and limbs become elongated; and I hear from Col. Bernys that during the late war in the United States, good evidence was afforded of this fact by the ridiculous appearance presented by the German regiments, when dressed in ready-made clothes manufactured for the American market, and which were much too long for the men in every way. There is, also, a considerable body of evidence shewing that in the Southern States the house-slaves of the third generation present a markedly different appearance from the field-slaves.[66]

If, however, we look to the races of man as distributed over the world,

---

[63] 'Man a Special Creation,' 1873, p. 119.

[64] 'Variation of Animals and Plants under Domestication,' vol. ii. pp. 336, 337.

[65] See, for instance, Quatrefages ('Revue des Cours Scientifiques,' Oct. 10, 1868, p. 724) on the effects of residence in Abyssinia and Arabia, and other analogous cases. Dr. Rolle ('Der Mensch, seine Abstammung,' &c., 1865, s. 99) states, on the authority of Khanikof, that the greater number of German families settled in Georgia, have acquired in the course of two generations dark hair and eyes. Mr. D. Forbes informs me that the Quichuas in the Andes vary greatly in colour, according to the position of the valleys inhabited by them.

[66] Harlan, 'Medical Researches,' p. 532. Quatrefages ('Unité de l'Espèce Humaine,' 1861, p. 128) has collected much evidence on this head.

we must infer that their characteristic differences cannot be accounted for by the direct action of different conditions of life, even after exposure to them for an enormous period of time. The Esquimaux live exclusively on animal food; they are clothed in thick fur, and are exposed to intense cold and to prolonged darkness; yet they do not differ in any extreme degree from the inhabitants of Southern China, who live entirely on vegetable food, and are exposed almost naked to a hot, glaring climate. The unclothed Fuegians live on the marine productions of their inhospitable shores; the Botocudos of Brazil wander about the hot forests of the interior and live chiefly on vegetable productions; yet these tribes resemble each other so closely that the Fuegians on board the "Beagle" were mistaken by some Brazilians for Botocudos. The Botocudos again, as well as the other inhabitants of tropical America, are wholly different from the Negroes who inhabit the opposite shores of the Atlantic, are exposed to a nearly similar climate, and follow nearly the same habits of life.

Nor can the differences between the races of man be accounted for by the inherited effects of the increased or decreased use of parts, except to a quite insignificant degree. Men who habitually live in canoes, may have their legs somewhat stunted; those who inhabit lofty regions may have their chests enlarged; and those who constantly use certain sense-organs may have the cavities in which they are lodged somewhat increased in size, and their features consequently a little modified. With civilised nations, the reduced size of the jaws from lessened use—the habitual play of different muscles serving to express different emotions—and the increased size of the brain from greater intellectual activity, have together produced a considerable effect on their general appearance when compared with savages.[67] Increased bodily stature, without any corresponding increase in the size of the brain, may (judging from the previously adduced case of rabbits), have given to some races an elongated skull of the dolichocephalic type.

Lastly, the little-understood principle of correlated development has sometimes come into action, as in the case of great muscular development and strongly projecting supra-orbital ridges. The colour of the skin and hair are plainly correlated, as is the texture of the hair with its colour in the Mandans of North America.[68] The colour also of the skin, and the odour emitted by it, are likewise in some manner connected. With the breeds of sheep the number of hairs within a given space and the number of excretory pores are related.[69] If we may judge from the analogy of our domesticated animals, many modifications of structure in man probably come under this principle of correlated development.

[67] See Prof. Schauffhausen, translat. in 'Anthropological Review,' Oct. 1868. p. 429.
[68] Mr. Catlin states ('N. American Indians,' 3rd edit. 1842, vol. i. p. 49) that in the whole tribe of the Mandans, about one in ten or twelve of the members, of all ages and both sexes, have bright silvery grey hair, which is hereditary. Now this hair is as coarse and harsh as that of a horse's mane, whilst the hair of other colours is fine and soft.
[69] On the odour of the skin, Godron, 'Sur l'Espèce,' tom. ii. p. 217. On the pores of the skin, Dr. Wilckens, 'Die Aufgaben der Landwirth. Zootechnik,' 1869, s. 7.

We have now seen that the external characteristic differences between the races of man cannot be accounted for in a satisfactory manner by the direct action of the conditions of life, nor by the effects of the continued use of parts, nor through the principle of correlation. We are therefore led to enquire whether slight individual differences, to which man is eminently liable, may not have been preserved and augmented during a long series of generations through natural selection. But here we are at once met by the objection that beneficial variations alone can be thus preserved; and as far as we are enabled to judge, although always liable to err on this head, none of the differences between the races of man are of any direct or special service to him. The intellectual and moral or social faculties must of course be excepted from this remark. The great variability of all the external differences between the races of man, likewise indicates that they cannot be of much importance; for if important, they would long ago have been either fixed and preserved, or eliminated. In this respect man resembles those forms, called by naturalists protean or polymorphic, which have remained extremely variable, owing, as it seems, to such variations being of an indifferent nature, and to their having thus escaped the action of natural selection.

We have thus far been baffled in all our attempts to account for the differences between the races of man; but there remains one important agency, namely Sexual Selection, which appears to have acted powerfully on man, as on many other animals. I do not intend to assert that sexual selection will account for all the differences between the races. An unexplained residuum is left, about which we can only say, in our ignorance, that as individuals are continually born with, for instance, heads a little rounder or narrower, and with noses a little longer or shorter, such slight differences might become fixed and uniform, if the unknown agencies which induced them were to act in a more constant manner, aided by long-continued intercrossing. Such variations come under the provisional class, alluded to in our second chapter, which for want of a better term are often called spontaneous. Nor do I pretend that the effects of sexual selection can be indicated with scientific precision; but it can be shewn that it would be an inexplicable fact if man had not been modified by this agency, which appears to have acted powerfully on innumerable animals. It can further be shewn that the differences between the races of man, as in colour, hairiness, form of features, &c., are of a kind which might have been expected to come under the influence of sexual selection. But in order to treat this subject properly, I have found it necessary to pass the whole animal kingdom in review. I have therefore devoted to it the Second Part of this work. At the close I shall return to man, and, after attempting to shew how far he has been modified through sexual selection, will give a brief summary of the chapters in this First Part.

NOTE ON THE RESEMBLANCES AND DIFFERENCES IN THE STRUCTURE AND THE
DEVELOPMENT OF THE BRAIN IN MAN AND APES. BY PROFESSOR HUX-
LEY, F. R. S.

The controversy respecting the nature and the extent of the differences in
the structure of the brain in man and the apes, which arose some fifteen years
ago, has not yet come to an end, though the subject matter of the dispute is,
at present, totally different from what it was formerly. It was originally asserted and re-asserted, with singular pertinacity, that the brain of all the apes,
even the highest, differs from that of man, in the absence of such conspicuous
structures as the posterior lobes of the cerebral hemispheres, with the posterior cornu of the lateral ventricle and the *hippocampus minor,* contained in
those lobes, which are so obvious in man.

But the truth that the structures in question are as well developed in apes'
as in human brains, or even better; and that it is characteristic of all the *Primates* (if we exclude the Lemurs) to have these parts well developed, stands
at present on as secure a basis as any proposition in comparative anatomy.
Moreover, it is admitted by every one of the long series of anatomists who,
of late years, have paid special attention to the arrangement of the complicated sulci and gyri which appear upon the surface of the cerebral hemispheres
in man and the higher apes, that they are disposed after the very same pattern
in him, as in them. Every principal gyrus and sulcus of a chimpanzee's brain
is clearly represented in that of a man, so that the terminology which applies
to the one answers for the other. On this point there is no difference of opinion. Some years since, Professor Bischoff published a memoir [70] on the cerebral
convolutions of man and apes; and as the purpose of my learned colleague was
certainly not to diminish the value of the differences between apes and men in
this respect, I am glad to make a citation from him.

"That the apes, and especially the orang, chimpanzee and gorilla, come very
close to man in their organisation, much nearer than to any other animal, is a
well known fact, disputed by nobody. Looking at the matter from the point of
view of organisation alone, no one probably would ever have disputed the view
of Linnæus, that man should be placed, merely as a peculiar species, at the
head of the mammalia and of those apes. Both shew, in all their organs, so
close an affinity, that the most exact anatomical investigation is needed in order to demonstrate those differences which really exist. So it is with the brains.
The brains of man, the orang, the chimpanzee, the gorilla, in spite of all the
important differences which they present, come very close to one another" (l.
c. p. 101).

There remains, then, no dispute as to the resemblance in fundamental characters, between the ape's brain and man's: nor any as to the wonderfully close
similarity between the chimpanzee, orang and man, in even the details of the
arrangement of the gyri and sulci of the cerebral hemispheres. Nor, turning to
the differences between the brains of the highest apes and that of man, is
there any serious question as to the nature and extent of these differences.
It is admitted that the man's cerebral hemispheres are absolutely and relatively larger than those of the orang and chimpanzee; that his frontal lobes are
less excavated by the upward protrusion of the roof of the orbits; that his
gyri and sulci are, as a rule, less symmetrically disposed, and present a greater
number of secondary plications. And it is admitted that, as a rule, in man,

[70] 'Die Grosshirn-Windungen des Menschen;' 'Abhandlungen der K. Bayerischen
Akademie,' Bd. x., 1868.

the temporo-occipital or "external perpendicular" fissure, which is usually so strongly marked a feature of the ape's brain is but faintly marked. But it is also clear, that none of these differences constitutes a sharp demarcation between the man's and the ape's brain. In respect to the external perpendicular fissure of Gratiolet, in the human brain for instance, Professor Turner remarks: [71]

"In some brains it appears simply as an indentation of the margin of the hemisphere, but, in others, it extends for some distance more or less transversely outwards. I saw it in the right hemisphere of a female brain pass more than two inches outwards; and on another specimen, also the right hemisphere, it proceeded for four-tenths of an inch outwards, and then extended downwards, as far as the lower margin of the outer surface of the hemisphere. The imperfect definition of this fissure in the majority of human brains, as compared with its remarkable distinctness in the brain of most Quadrumana, is owing to the presence, in the former, of certain superficial, well marked, secondary convolutions which bridge it over and connect the parietal with the occipital lobe. The closer the first of these bridging gyri lies to the longitudinal fissure, the shorter is the external parieto-occipital fissure" (l. c. p. 12).

The obliteration of the external perpendicular fissure of Gratiolet, therefore, is not a constant character of the human brain. On the other hand, its full development is not a constant character of the higher ape's brain. For, in the chimpanzee, the more or less extensive obliteration of the external perpendicular sulcus by "bridging convolutions," on one side or the other, has been noted over and over again by Prof. Rolleston, Mr. Marshall, M. Broca and Professor Turner. At the conclusion of a special paper on this subject the latter writes: [72]

"The three specimens of the brain of a chimpanzee just described, prove that the generalisation which Gratiolet has attempted to draw of the complete absence of the first connecting convolution and the concealment of the second, as essentially characteristic features in the brain of this animal, is by no means universally applicable. In only one specimen did the brain, in these particulars, follow the law which Gratiolet has expressed. As regards the presence of the superior bridging convolution, I am inclined to think that it has existed in one hemisphere, at least, in a majority of the brains of this animal which have, up to this time, been figured or described. The superficial position of the second bridging convolution is evidently less frequent, and has as yet, I believe, only been seen in the brain (A) recorded in this communication. The asymmetrical arrangement in the convolutions of the two hemispheres, which previous observers have referred to in their descriptions, is also well illustrated in these specimens" (pp. 8, 9).

Even were the presence of the temporo-occipital, or external perpendicular, sulcus, a mark of distinction between the higher apes and man, the value of such a distinctive character would be rendered very doubtful by the structure of the brain in the Platyrhine apes. In fact, while the temporo-occipital is one of the most constant of sulci in the Catarhine, or Old World, apes, it is never very strongly developed in the New World apes; it is absent in the smaller Platyrhine; rudimentary in *Pithecia;* [73] and more or less obliterated by bridging convolutions in *Ateles.*

[71] 'Convolutions of the Human Cerebrum Topographically Considered,' 1866, p. 12.

[72] Notes more especially on the bridging convolutions in the Brain of the Chimpanzee, 'Proceedings of the Royal Society of Edinburgh,' 1865–6.

[73] Flower 'On the Anatomy of *Pithecia Monachus,*' 'Proceedings of the Zoological Society,' 1862.

A character which is thus variable within the limits of a single group can have no great taxonomic value.

It is further established, that the degree of asymmetry of the convolution of the two sides in the human brain is subject to much individual variation; and that, in those individuals of the Bushman race who have been examined, the gyri and sulci of the two hemispheres are considerably less complicated and more symmetrical than in the European brain, while, in some individuals of the chimpanzee, their complexity and asymmetry become notable. This is particularly the case in the brain of a young male chimpanzee figured by M. Broca. ('L'ordre des Primates,' p. 165, fig. 11.)

Again, as respects the question of absolute size, it is established that the difference between the largest and the smallest healthy human brain is greater than the difference between the smallest healthy human brain and the largest chimpanzee's or orang's brain.

Moreover, there is one circumstance in which the orang's and chimpanzee's brains resemble man's, but in which they differ from the lower apes, and that is the presence of two corpora candicantia—the *Cynomorpha* having but one.

In view of these facts I do not hesitate in this year 1874, to repeat and insist upon the proposition which I enunciated in 1863: [74]

"So far as cerebral structure goes, therefore, it is clear that man differs less from the chimpanzee or the orang, than these do even from the monkeys, and that the difference between the brain of the chimpanzee and of man is almost insignificant when compared with that between the chimpanzee brain and that of a Lemur."

In the paper to which I have referred, Professor Bischoff does not deny the second part of this statement, but he first makes the irrelevant remark that it is not wonderful if the brains of an orang and a Lemur are very different; and secondly, goes on to assert that, "If we successively compare the brain of a man with that of an orang; the brain of this with that of a chimpanzee; of this with that of a gorilla, and so on of a *Hylobates, Semnopithecus, Cynocephalus, Cercopithecus, Macacus, Cebus, Callithrix, Lemur, Stenops, Hapale,* we shall not meet with a greater, or even as great a break in the degree of development of the convolutions, as we find between the brain of a man and that of an orang or chimpanzee."

To which I reply, firstly, that whether this assertion be true or false, it has nothing whatever to do with the proposition enunciated in 'Man's Place in Nature,' which refers not to the development of the convolutions alone, but to the structure of the whole brain. If Professor Bischoff had taken the trouble to refer to p. 96 of the work he criticises, in fact, he would have found the following passage: "And it is a remarkable circumstance that though, so far as our present knowledge extends, there *is* one true structural break in the series of forms of Simian brains, this hiatus does not lie between man and the manlike apes, but between the lower and the lowest Simians, or in other words, between the Old and New World apes and monkeys and the Lemurs. Every Lemur which has yet been examined, in fact, has its cerebellum partially visible from above; and its posterior lobe, with the contained posterior cornu and hippocampus minor, more or less rudimentary. Every marmoset, American monkey, Old World monkey, baboon or manlike ape, on the contrary, has its cerebellum entirely hidden, posteriorly, by the cerebral lobes, and possesses a large posterior cornu with a well-developed hippocampus minor."

[74] 'Man's Place in Nature,' p. 102.

This statement was a strictly accurate account of what was known when it was made; and it does not appear to me to be more than apparently weakened by the subsequent discovery of the relatively small development of the posterior lobes in the Siamang and in the Howling monkey. Notwithstanding the exceptional brevity of the posterior lobes in these two species, no one will pretend that their brains, in the slightest degree, approach those of the Lemurs. And if, instead of putting *Hapale* out of its natural place, as Professor Bischoff most unaccountably does, we write the series of animals he has chosen to mention as follows: *Homo, Pithecus, Troglodytes, Hylobates, Semnopithecus, Cynocephalus, Cercopithecus, Macacus, Cebus, Callithrix, Hapale, Lemur, Stenops,* I venture to reaffirm that the great break in this series lies between *Hapale* and *Lemur,* and that this break is considerably greater than that between any other two terms of that series. Professor Bischoff ignores the fact that long before he wrote, Gratiolet had suggested the separation of the Lemurs from the other *Primates* on the very ground of the difference in their cerebral characters; and that Professor Flower had made the following observations in the course of his description of the brain of the Javan Loris: [75]

"And it is especially remarkable that, in the development of the posterior lobes, there is no approximation to the Lemurine, short hemisphered brain, in those monkeys which are commonly supposed to approach this family in other respects, viz., the lower members of the Platyrhine group."

So far as the structure of the adult brain is concerned, then, the very considerable additions to our knowledge, which have been made by the researches of so many investigators, during the past ten years, fully justify the statement which I made in 1863. But it has been said, that, admitting the similarity between the adult brains of man and apes, they are nevertheless, in reality, widely different, because they exhibit fundamental differences in the mode of their development. No one would be more ready than I to admit the force of this argument, if such fundamental differences of development really exist. But I deny that they do exist. On the contrary, there is a fundamental agreement in the development of the brain in men and apes.

Gratiolet originated the statement that there is a fundamental difference in the development of the brains of apes and that of man—consisting in this; that, in the apes, the sulci which first make their appearance are situated on the posterior region of the cerebral hemispheres, while, in the human fœtus, the sulci first become visible on the frontal lobes.[76]

This general statement is based upon two observations, the one of a Gibbon almost ready to be born, in which the posterior gyri were "well developed," while those of the frontal lobes were "hardly indicated" [77] (l. c. p. 39), and

---

[75] 'Transactions of the Zoological Society,' vol. v. 1862.

[76] "Chez tous les singes, les plis postérieurs se développent les premiers; les plis antérieurs se développent plus tard, aussi la vertèbre occipitale et la pariétale sont-elles relativement très-grandes chez le fœtus. L'Homme présente une exception remarquable quant à l'époque de l'apparition des plis frontaux, qui sont les premiers indiqués; mais le développement général du lobe frontal, envisagé seulement par rapport à son volume, suit les mêmes lois que dans les singes;" Gratiolet, 'Mémoire sur les plis cérébers,' de l'Homme et des Primateaux, p. 39, Tab. iv. fig. 3.

[77] Gratiolet's words are (l. c. p. 39): "Dans le fœtus dont il s'agit les plis cérébraux postérieurs sont bien développés, tandis que les plis du lobe frontal sont à peine indiqués." The figure, however (Pl. iv. fig. 3), shews the fissure of Rolando, and one of the frontal sulci, plainly enough. Nevertheless, M. Alix, in his 'Notice sur les travaux anthropologiques de Gratiolet' (Mém. de la Société d'Anthropologie de Paris,' 1868,

the other of a human fœtus at the 22nd or 23rd week of uterogestation, in which Gratiolet notes that the insula was uncovered, but that nevertheless "des incisures sèment de lobe antérieur, une scissure peu profonde indique la séparation du lobe occipital, trés-réduit, d'ailleurs dès cette époque. Le reste de la surface cérébrale est encore absolument lisse."

Three views of this brain are given in Plate II. figs. 1, 2, 3, of the work cited, shewing the upper, lateral and inferior views of the hemispheres, but not the inner view. It is worthy of note that the figure by no means bears out Gratiolet's description, inasmuch as the fissure (antero-temporal) on the posterior half of the face of the hemisphere is more marked than any of those vaguely indicated in the anterior half. If the figure is correct, it in no way justifies Gratiolet's conclusion: "Il y a donc entre ces cerveaux [those of a Callithrix and of a Gibbon] et celui du fœtus humain une différence fondamental. Chez celui-ci, longtemps avant que les plis temporaux apparissent, les plis frontaux *essayent* d'exister."

Since Gratiolet's time, however, the development of the gyri and sulci of the brain has been made the subject of renewed investigation by Schmidt, Bischoff, Pansch,[73] and more particularly by Ecker,[79] whose work is not only the latest, but by far the most complete, memoir on the subject.

The final results of their inquiries may be summed up as follows:—

1. In the human fœtus, the sylvian fissure is formed in the course of the third month of uterogestation. In this, and in the fourth month, the cerebral hemispheres are smooth and rounded (with the exception of the sylvian depression), and they project backwards far beyond the cerebellum.

2. The sulci, properly so called, begin to appear in the interval between the end of the fourth and the beginning of the sixth month of fœtal life, but Ecker is careful to point out that, not only the time, but the order, of their appearance is subject to considerable individual variation. In no case, however, are either the frontal or the temporal sulci the earliest.

The first which appears, in fact, lies on the inner face of the hemisphere (whence doubtless Gratiolet, who does not seem to have examined that face in his fœtus, overlooked it), and is either the internal perpendicular (occipito-parietal), or the calcarine sulcus, these two being close together and eventually running into one another. As a rule the occipito-parietal is the earlier of the two.

3. At the latter part of this period, another sulcus, the "posterio-parietal," or "Fissure of Rolando" is developed, and it is followed, in the course of the sixth month, by the other principal sulci of the frontal, parietal, temporal and occipital lobes. There is, however, no clear evidence that one of these constantly appears before the other; and it is remarkable that, in the brain at the period described and figured by Ecker (l. c. p. 212-13, Taf. II. figs. 1, 2, 3, 4),

page 32), writes thus: "Gratiolet a eu entre les mains le cerveau d'un fœtus de Gibbon, singe éminemment supérieur, et tellement rapproché de l'orang, que des naturalistes très-compétents l'ont rangé parmi les anthropoïdes. M. Huxley, par exemple, n'hésite pas sur ce point. Eh bien, c'est sur le cerveau d'un fœtus de Gibbon que Gratiolet a vu *les circonvolutions du lobe temporo-sphénoidal déjà développées lorsqu'il n'existent pas encore de plis sur le lobe frontal.* Il était donc bien autorisé à dise que, chez l'homme les circonvolutions apparaissent d'a en ω, tandis que chez les singes elles se développent d'ω en a."

[73] 'Ueber die typische Anordnung der Furchen und Windungen auf den Grosshirn-Hemisphären des Menschen und der Affen.' 'Archiv für Anthropologie,' iii., 1868.

[79] 'Zur Entwickelungs Geschichte der Furchen und Windungen der Grosshirn-Hemisphären im Fœtus des Menschen.' 'Archiv für Anthropologie,' iii., 1868.

the antero-temporal sulcus (*scissure parallèle*) so characteristic of the ape's brain, is as well, if not better developed than the fissure of Rolando, and is much more marked than the proper frontal sulci.

Taking the facts as they now stand, it appears to me that the order of the appearance of the sulci and gyri in the fœtal human brain is in perfect harmony with the general doctrine of evolution, and with the view that man has been evolved from some ape-like form; though there can be no doubt that that form was, in many respects, different from any member of the *Primates* now living.

Von Baer taught us, half a century ago, that, in the course of their development, allied animals put on at first, the characters of the greater groups to which they belong, and, by degrees, assume those which restrict them within the limits of their family, genus, and species; and he proved, at the same time, that no developmental stage of a higher animal is precisely similar to the adult condition of any lower animal. It is quite correct to say that a frog passes through the condition of a fish, inasmuch as at one period of its life the tadpole has all the characters of a fish, and if it went no further, would have to be grouped among fishes. But it is equally true that a tadpole is very different from any known fish.

In like manner, the brain of a human fœtus, at the fifth month, may correctly be said to be, not only the brain of an ape, but that of an Arctopithecine or marmoset-like ape; for its hemispheres, with their great posterior lobster, and with no sulci but the sylvian and the calcarine, present the characteristics found only in the group of the Arctopithecine *Primates*. But it is equally true, as Gratiolet remarks, that, in its widely open sylvian fissure, it differs from the brain of any actual marmoset. No doubt it would be much more similar to the brain of an advanced fœtus of a marmoset. But we know nothing whatever of the development of the brain in the marmosets. In the Platyrhini proper, the only observation with which I am acquainted is due to Pansch, who found in the brain of a fœtal *Cebus Apella,* in addition to the sylvian fissure and the deep calcarine fissure, only a very shallow antero-temporal fissure (*scissure parallète* of Gratiolet).

Now this fact, taken together with the circumstance that the antero-temporal sulcus is present in such Platyrhini as the Saimiri, which present mere traces of sulci on the anterior half of the exterior of the cerebral hemispheres, or none at all, undoubtedly, so far as it goes, affords fair evidence in favour of Gratiolet's hypothesis, that the posterior sulci appear before the anterior, in the brains of the *Platyrhini*. But, it by no means follows, that the rule which may hold good for the *Platyrhini* extends to the *Catarhini*. We have no information whatever respecting the development of the brain in the *Cynomorphia;* and, as regards the *Anthropomorpha,* nothing but the account of the brain of the Gibbon, near birth, already referred to. At the present moment there is not a shadow of evidence to show that the sulci of a chimpanzee's, or orang's, brain do not appear in the same order as a man's.

Gratiolet opens his preface with the aphorism: "Il est dangereux dans les sciences de conclure trop vite." I fear he must have forgotten this sound maxim by the time he had reached the discussion of the differences between men and apes, in the body of his work. No doubt, the excellent author of one of the most remarkable contributions to the just understanding of the mammalian brain which has ever been made, would have been the first to admit the insufficiency of his data had he lived to profit by the advance of inquiry. The misfortune is that his conclusions have been employed by persons incompetent to appreciate their foundation, as arguments in favour of obscur-antism.[80]

But it is important to remark that, whether Gratiolet was right or wrong in his hypothesis respecting the relative order of appearance of the temporal and frontal sulci, the fact remains; that, before either temporal or frontal sulci appear, the fœtal brain of man presents characters which are found only in the lowest group of the *Primates* (leaving out the Lemurs); and that this is exactly what we should expect to be the case, if man has resulted from the gradual modification of the same form as that from which the other *Primates* have sprung.

[80] For example, M. l'Abbé Lecomte in his terrible pamphlet 'Le Darwinisme et l'origine de l'Homme,' 1873.

PART II

SEXUAL SELECTION

CHAPTER VIII

PRINCIPLES OF SEXUAL SELECTION

Secondary sexual characters—Sexual selection—Manner of action—Excess of males—Polygamy—The male alone generally modified through sexual selection—Eagerness of the male—Variability of the male—Choice exerted by the female—Sexual compared with natural selection—Inheritance, at corresponding periods of life, at corresponding seasons of the year, and as limited by sex—Relations between the several forms of inheritance—Causes why one sex and the young are not modified through sexual selection—Supplement on the proportional numbers of the two sexes throughout the animal kingdom—The proportion of the sexes in relation to natural selection.

WITH animals which have their sexes separated, the males necessarily differ from the females in their organs of reproduction; and these are the primary sexual characters. But the sexes often differ in what Hunter has called secondary sexual characters, which are not directly connected with the act of reproduction; for instance, the male possesses certain organs of sense or locomotion, of which the female is quite destitute, or has them more highly-developed, in order that he may readily find or reach her; or again the male has special organs of prehension for holding her securely. These latter organs, of infinitely diversified kinds, graduate into those which are commonly ranked as primary, and in some cases can hardly be distinguished from them; we see instances of this in the complex appendages at the apex of the abdomen in male insects. Unless indeed we confine the term "primary" to the reproductive glands, it is scarcely possible to decide which ought to be called primary and which secondary.

The female often differs from the male in having organs for the nourishment or protection of her young, such as the mammary glands of mammals, and the abdominal sacks of the marsupials. In some few cases also the male possesses similar organs, which are wanting in the female, such as the receptacles for the ova in certain male fishes, and those temporarily developed in certain male frogs. The females of most bees are provided with a special apparatus for collecting and carrying pollen, and their ovipositor is modified into a sting for the defence of the larvæ and the community. Many similar cases could be given, but they do not here concern us. There are, however, other sexual differences quite unconnected with the primary reproductive organs, and it is with these that we are more especially concerned—such as the greater size, strength, and pugnacity of the male, his weapons of offence or means of defence against rivals, his gaudy colouring and various ornaments, his power of song, and other such characters.

567

Besides the primary and secondary sexual differences, such as the fore-going, the males and females of some animals differ in structures related to different habits of life, and not at all, or only indirectly, to the repro-ductive functions. Thus the females or certain flies (Culicidæ and Tab-anidæ) are blood-suckers, whilst the males, living on flowers, have mouths destitute of mandibles.[1] The males of certain moths and of some crustaceans (*e. g.* Tanais) have imperfect, closed mouths, and cannot feed. The complemental males of certain Cirripedes live like epiphytic plants either on the female or the hermaphrodite form, and are destitute of a mouth and of prehensile limbs. In these cases it is the male which has been modified, and has lost certain important organs, which the female possess. In other cases it is the female which has lost such parts; for in-stance, the female glow-worm is destitute of wings, as also are many fe-male moths, some of which never leave their cocoons. Many female para-sitic crustaceans have lost their natatory legs. In some weevil-beetles (Curculionidæ) there is a great difference between the male and female in the length of the rostrum or snout;[2] but the meaning of this and of many analogous differences, is not at all understood. Differences of struc-ture between the two sexes in relation to different habits of life are gener-ally confined to the lower animals; but with some few birds the beak of the male differs from that of the female. In the Huia of New Zealand the difference is wonderfully great, and we hear from Dr. Buller[3] that the male uses his strong beak in chiselling the larvæ of insects out of decayed wood, whilst the female probes the softer parts with her far longer, much curved and pliant beak: and thus they mutually aid each other. In most cases, differences of structure between the sexes are more or less directly connected with the propagation of the species: thus a female, which has to nourish a multitude of ova, requires more food than the male, and con-sequently requires special means for procuring it. A male animal, which lives for a very short time, might lose its organs for procuring food through disuse, without detriment; but he would retain his locomotive organs in a perfect state, so that he might reach the female. The female, on the other hand, might safely lose her organs for flying, swimming, or walking, if she gradually acquired habits which rendered such powers useless.

We are, however, here concerned only with sexual selection. This de-pends on the advantage which certain individuals have over others of the same sex and species solely in respect of reproduction. When, as in the cases above mentioned, the two sexes differ in structure in relation to different habits of life, they have no doubt been modified through natural selection, and by inheritance, limited to one and the same sex. So again the primary sexual organs, and those for nourishing or protecting the young, come under the same influence; for those individuals which gen-

[1] Westwood, 'Modern Class. of Insects,' vol. ii. 1840, p. 541. For the statement about Tanais, mentioned below, I am indebted to Fritz Müller.

[2] Kirby and Spence, 'Introduction to Entomology,' vol. iii. 1826, p. 309.

[3] 'Birds of New Zealand,' 1872, p. 66.

erated or nourished their offspring best, would leave, *cœteris paribus*, the greatest number to inherit their superiority; whilst those which generated or nourished their offspring badly, would leave but few to inherit their weaker powers. As the male has to find the female, he requires organs of sense and locomotion, but if these organs are necessary for the other purposes of life, as is generally the case, they will have been developed through natural selection. When the male has found the female, he sometimes absolutely requires prehensile organs to hold her; thus Dr. Wallace informs me that the males of certain moths cannot unite with the females if their tarsi or feet are broken. The males of many oceanic crustaceans, when adult, have their legs and antennæ modified in an extraordinary manner for the prehension of the female; hence we may suspect that it is because these animals are washed about by the waves of the open sea, that they require these organs in order to propagate their kind, and if so, their development has been the result of ordinary or natural selection. Some animals extremely low in the scale have been modified for this same purpose; thus the males of certain parasitic worms, when fully grown, have the lower surface of the terminal part of their bodies roughened like a rasp, and with this they coil round and permanently hold the females.[4]

When the two sexes follow exactly the same habits of life, and the male has the sensory or locomotive organs more highly developed than those of the female, it may be that the perfection of these is indispensable to the male for finding the female; but in the vast majority of cases, they serve only to give one male an advantage over another, for with sufficient time, the less well-endowed males would succeed in pairing with the females; and judging from the structure of the female, they would be in all other respects equally well adapted for their ordinary habits of life. Since in such cases the males have acquired their present structure, not from being better fitted to survive in the struggle for existence, but from having gained an advantage over other males, and from having transmitted this advantage to their male offspring alone, sexual selection must here have come into action. It was the importance of this distinction which led me to designate this form of selection as Sexual Selection. So again, if the chief service rendered to the male by his prehensile organs is to prevent the escape of the female before the arrival of other males, or when assaulted by them, these organs will have been perfected through sexual selection, that is by the advantage acquired by certain individuals over their rivals. But in most cases of this kind it is impossible to distinguish

---

[4] M. Perrier advances this case ('Revue Scientifique,' Feb. 1, 1873, p. 865) as one fatal to the belief in sexual selection, inasmuch as he supposes that I attribute all the differences between the sexes to sexual selection. This distinguished naturalist, therefore, like so many other Frenchmen, has not taken the trouble to understand even the first principles of sexual selection. An English naturalist insists that the claspers of certain male animals could not have been developed through the choice of the female! Had I not met with this remark, I should not have thought it possible for any one to have read this chapter and to have imagined that I maintain that the choice of the female had anything to do with the development of the prehensile organs in the male.

between the effects of natural and sexual selection. Whole chapters could be filled with details on the differences between the sexes in their sensory, locomotive, and prehensile organs. As, however, these structures are not more interesting than others adapted for the ordinary purposes of life I shall pass them over almost entirely, giving only a few instances under each class.

There are many other structures and instincts which must have been developed through sexual selection—such as the weapons of offence and the means of defence—of the males for fighting with and driving away their rivals—their courage and pugnacity—their various ornaments—their contrivances for producing vocal or instrumental music—and their glands for emitting odours, most of these latter structures serving only to allure or excite the female. It is clear that these characters are the result of sexual and not of ordinary selection, since unarmed, unornamented, or unattractive males would succeed equally well in the battle for life and in leaving a numerous progeny, but for the presence of better endowed males. We may infer that this would be the case, because the females, which are unarmed and unornamented, are able to survive and procreate their kind. Secondary sexual characters of the kind just referred to, will be fully discussed in the following chapters, as being in many respects interesting, but especially as depending on the will, choice, and rivalry of the individuals of either sex. When we behold two males fighting for the possession of the female, or several male birds displaying their gorgeous plumage, and performing strange antics before an assembled body of females, we cannot doubt that, though led by instinct, they know what they are about, and consciously exert their mental and bodily powers.

Just as man can improve the breeds of his game-cocks by the selection of those birds which are victorious in the cock-pit, so it appears that the strongest and most vigorous males, or those provided with the best weapons, have prevailed under nature, and have led to the improvement of the natural breed or species. A slight degree of variability leading to some advantage, however slight, in reiterated deadly contests would suffice for the work of sexual selection; and it is certain that secondary sexual characters are eminently variable. Just as man can give beauty, according to his standard of taste, to his male poultry, or more strictly can modify the beauty originally acquired by the parent species, can give to the Sebright bantam a new and elegant plumage, an erect and peculiar carriage—so it appears that female birds in a state of nature, have by a long selection of the more attractive males, added to their beauty or other attractive qualities. No doubt this implies powers of discrimination and taste on the part of the female which will at first appear extremely improbable; but by the facts to be adduced hereafter, I hope to be able to shew that the females actually have these powers. When, however, it is said that the lower animals have a sense of beauty, it must not be supposed that such sense is comparable with that of a cultivated man, with his multiform and complex associated ideas. A more just comparison would be between the taste for the beautiful in animals, and that in the lowest savages, who admire and deck themselves with any brilliant, glittering, or curious object.

From our ignorance on several points, the precise manner in which sexual selections acts is somewhat uncertain. Nevertheless if those naturalists who already believe in the mutability of species, will read the following chapters, they will, I think, agree with me, that sexual selection has played an important part in the history of the organic world. It is certain that amongst almost all animals there is a struggle between the males for the possession of the female. This fact is so notorious that it would be superfluous to give instances. Hence the females have the opportunity of selecting one out of several males, on the supposition that their mental capacity suffices for the exertion of a choice. In many cases special circumstances tend to make the struggle between the males particularly severe. Thus the males of our migratory birds generally arrive at their places of breeding before the females, so that many males are ready to contend for each female. I am informed by Mr. Jenner Weir, that the bird-catchers assert that this is invariably the case with the nightingale and blackcap, and with respect to the latter he can himself confirm the statement.

Mr. Swaysland of Brighton has been in the habit, during the last forty years, of catching our migratory birds on their first arrival, and he has never known the females of any species to arrive before their males. During one spring he shot thirty-nine males of Ray's wagtail (*Budytes Raii*) before he saw a single female. Mr. Gould has ascertained by the dissection of those snipes which arrive the first in this country, that the males come before the females. And the like holds good with most of the migratory birds of the United States.[5] The majority of the male salmon in our rivers, on coming up from the sea, are ready to breed before the females. So it appears to be with frogs and toads. Throughout the great class of insects the males almost always are the first to emerge from the pupal state, so that they generally abound for a time before any females can be seen.[6] The cause of this difference between the males and females in their periods of arrival and maturity is sufficiently obvious. Those males which annually first migrated into any country, or which in the spring were first ready to breed, or were the most eager, would leave the largest number of offspring; and these would tend to inherit similar instincts and constitutions. It must be borne in mind that it would have been impossible to change very materially the time of sexual maturity in the females, without at the same time interfering with the period of the production of the young—a period which must be determined by the seasons of the year.

[5] J. A. Allen, on the 'Mammals and Winter Birds of Florida,' Bull. Comp. Zoology, Harvard College, p. 268.

[6] Even with those plants in which the sexes are separate, the male flowers are generally mature before the female. As first shewn by C. K. Sprengel, many hermaphrodite plants are dichogamous; that is, their male and female organs are not ready at the same time, so that they cannot be self-fertilised. Now in such flowers, the pollen is in general matured before the stigma, though there are exceptional cases in which the female organs are before-hand.

On the whole there can be no doubt that with almost all animals, in which the sexes are separate, there is a constantly recurrent struggle between the males for the possession of the females.

Our difficulty in regard to sexual selection lies in understanding how it is that the males which conquer other males, or those which prove the most attractive to the females, leave a greater number of offspring to inherit their superiority than their beaten and less attractive rivals. Unless this result does follow, the characters which give to certain males an advantage over others, could not be perfected and augmented through sexual selection. When the sexes exist in exactly equal numbers, the worst-endowed males will (except where polygamy prevails), ultimately find females, and leave as many offspring, as well fitted for their general habits of life, as the best-endowed males. From various facts and considerations, I formerly inferred that with most animals, in which secondary sexual characters are well developed, the males considerably exceeded the females in number; but this is not by any means always true. If the males were to the females as two to one, or as three to two, or even in a somewhat lower ratio, the whole affair would be simple; for the better-armed or more attractive males would leave the largest number of offspring. But after investigating, as far as possible, the numerical proportion of the sexes, I do not believe that any great inequality in number commonly exists. In most cases sexual selection appears to have been effective in the following manner.

Let us take any species, a bird for instance, and divide the females inhabiting a district into two equal bodies, the one consisting of the more vigorous and better-nourished individuals, and the other of the less vigorous and healthy. The former, there can be little doubt, would be ready to breed in the spring before the others; and this is the opinion of Mr. Jenner Weir, who has carefully attended to the habits of birds during many years. There can also be no doubt that the most vigorous, best-nourished and earliest breeders would on an average succeed in rearing the largest number of fine offspring.[7] The males, as we have seen, are generally ready to breed before the females; the strongest, and with some species the best armed of the males, drive away the weaker; and the former would then unite with the more vigorous and better-nourished females, because they are the first to breed.[8] Such vigorous pairs would surely rear a larger number of offspring than the retarded females, which would be compelled to unite with the conquered and less powerful males, supposing the sexes to be numerically equal; and this is all that is wanted

[7] Here is excellent evidence on the character of the offspring from an experienced ornithologist. Mr. J. A. Allen, in speaking ('Mammals and Winter Birds of E. Florida,' p. 229) of the later broods, after the accidental destruction of the first, says, that these "are found to be smaller and paler-coloured than those hatched earlier in the season. In cases where several broods are reared each year, as a general rule the birds of the earlier broods seem in all respects the most perfect and vigorous."

[8] Hermann Müller has come to this same conclusion with respect to those female bees which are the first to emerge from the pupa each year. See his remarkable essay, 'Anwendung den Darwin'schen Lehre auf Bienen,' 'Verh. d. V. Jahrg,' xxix. p. 45.

to add, in the course of successive generations, to the size, strength and courage of the males, or to improve their weapons.

But in very many cases the males which conquer their rivals, do not obtain possession of the females, independently of the choice of the latter. The courtship of animals is by no means so simple and short an affair as might be thought. The females are most excited by, or prefer pairing with, the more ornamented males, or those which are the best songsters, or play the best antics; but it is obviously probable that they would at the same time prefer the more vigorous and lively males, and this has in some cases been confirmed by actual observation.[9] Thus the more vigorous females, which are the first to breed, will have the choice of many males; and though they may not always select the strongest or best armed, they will select those which are vigorous and well armed, and in other respects the most attractive. Both sexes, therefore, of such early pairs would as above explained, have an advantage over others in rearing offspring; and this apparently has sufficed during a long course of generations to add not only to the strength and fighting powers of the males, but likewise to their various ornaments or other attractions.

In the converse and much rarer case of the males selecting particular females, it is plain that those which were the most vigorous and had conquered others, would have the freest choice; and it is almost certain that they would select vigorous as well as attractive females. Such pairs would have an advantage in rearing offspring, more especially if the male had the power to defend the female during the pairing-season as occurs with some of the higher animals, or aided her in providing for the young. The same principles would apply if each sex preferred and selected certain individuals of the opposite sex; supposing that they selected not only the more attractive, but likewise the more vigorous individuals.

Numerical Proportion of the Two Sexes.—I have remarked that sexual selection would be a simple affair if the males were considerably more numerous than the females. Hence I was led to investigate, as far as I could, the proportions between the two sexes of as many animals as possible; but the materials are scanty. I will here give only a brief abstract of the results, retaining the details for a supplementary discussion, so as not to interfere with the course of my argument. Domesticated animals alone afford the means of ascertaining the proportional numbers at birth; but no records have been specially kept for this purpose. By indirect means, however, I have collected a considerable body of statistics, from which it appears that with most of our domestic animals the sexes are nearly equal at birth. Thus 25,560 births of race-horses have been recorded during twenty-one years, and the male births were to the female births as 99.7 to 100. In greyhounds the inequality is greater than with any other animal, for out of 6878 births during twelve years, the male

---

[9] With respect to poultry, I have received information, hereafter to be given, to this effect. Even with birds, such as pigeons, which pair for life, the female, as I hear from Mr. Jenner Weir, will desert her mate if he is injured or grows weak.

births were to the female as 110.1 to 100. It is, however, in some degree doubtful whether it is safe to infer that the proportion would be the same under natural conditions as under domestication; for slight and unknown differences in the conditions affect the proportion of the sexes. Thus with mankind, the male births in England are as 104.5, in Russia as 108.9, and with the Jews of Livonia as 120, to 100 female births. But I shall recur to this curious point of the excess of male births in the supplement to this chapter. At the Cape of Good Hope, however, male children of European extraction have been born during several years in the proportion of between 90 and 99 to 100 female children.

For our present purpose we are concerned with the proportions of the sexes, not only at birth, but also at maturity, and this adds another element of doubt; for it is a well-ascertained fact that with man the number of males dying before or during birth, and during the first two years of infancy, is considerably larger than that of females. So it almost certainly is with male lambs, and probably with some other animals. The males of some species kill one another by fighting; or they drive one another about until they become greatly emaciated. They must also be often exposed to various dangers, whilst wandering about in eager search for the females. In many kinds of fish the males are much smaller than the females, and they are believed often to be devoured by the latter, or by other fishes. The females of some birds appear to die earlier than the males; they are also liable to be destroyed on their nests, or whilst in charge of their young. With insects the female larvæ are often larger than those of the males, and would consequently be more likely to be devoured. In some cases the mature females are less active and less rapid in their movements than the males, and could not escape so well from danger. Hence, with animals in a state of nature, we must rely on mere estimation, in order to judge of the proportions of the sexes at maturity; and this is but little trustworthy, except when the inequality is strongly marked. Nevertheless, as far as a judgment can be formed, we may conclude from the facts given in the supplement, that the males of some few mammals, of many birds, of some fish and insects, are considerably more numerous than the females.

The proportion between the sexes fluctuates slightly during successive years: thus with race-horses, for every 100 mares born the stallions varied from 107.1 in one year to 92.6 in another year, and with greyhounds from 116.3 to 95.3. But had larger numbers been tabulated throughout an area more extensive than England, these fluctuations would probably have disappeared; and such as they are, would hardly suffice to lead to effective sexual selection in a state of nature. Nevertheless, in the cases of some few wild animals, as shewn in the supplement, the proportions seem to fluctuate either during different seasons or in different localities in a sufficient degree to lead to such selection. For it should be observed that any advantage, gained during certain years or in certain localities by those males which were able to conquer their rivals, or were the most attractive to the females, would probably be transmitted to the offspring, and would not subsequently be eliminated. During the succeeding seasons, when, from the equality of the sexes, every male was able to procure a female, the stronger or more attractive males previously produced would still have at least as good a chance of leaving offspring as the weaker or less attractive.

Polygamy.—The practice of polygamy leads to the same results as would follow from an actual inequality in the number of the sexes; for if each male secures two or more females, many males cannot pair; and the latter assuredly will be the weaker or less attractive individuals. Many mammals and some few birds are polygamous, but with animals belonging to the lower classes I have found no evidence of this habit. The intellectual powers of such animals are, perhaps, not sufficient to lead them to collect and guard a harem of females. That some relation exists between polygamy and the development of secondary sexual characters, appears nearly certain; and this supports the view that a numerical preponderance of males would be eminently favourable to the action of sexual selection. Nevertheless many animals, which are strictly monogamous, especially birds, display strongly-marked secondary sexual characters; whilst some few animals, which are polygamous, do not have such characters.

We will first briefly run through the mammals, and then turn to birds. The gorilla seems to be polygamous, and the male differs considerably from the female; so it is with some baboons, which live in herds containing twice as many adult females as males. In South America the *Mycetes caraya* present well-marked sexual differences, in colour, beard, and vocal organs; and the male generally lives with two or three wives: the male of the *Cebus capucinus* differs somewhat from the female, and appears to be polygamus.[10] Little is known on this head with respect to most other monkeys, but some species are strictly monogamous. The ruminants are eminently polygamous, and they present sexual differences more frequently than almost any other group of mammals; this holds good, especially in their weapons, but also in other characters. Most deer, cattle, and sheep are polygamous; as are most antelopes, though some are monogamous. Sir Andrew Smith, in speaking of the antelopes of South Africa, says that in herds of about a dozen there was rarely more than one mature male. The Asiatic *Antilope saiga* appears to be the most inordinate polygamist in the world; for Pallas[11] states that the male drives away all rivals, and collects a herd of about a hundred females and kids together; the female is hornless and has softer hair, but does not otherwise differ

---

[10] On the Gorilla, Savage and Wyman, 'Boston Journal of Nat. Hist.' vol. v. 1845–47, p. 423. On Cynocephalus, Brehm, 'Illust. Thierleben,' B. i. 1864, s. 77. On Mycetes, Rengger, 'Naturgesch.: Säugethiere von Paraguay,' 1830, ss. 14, 20. Cebus, Brehm, ibid. s. 108.

[11] Pallas, 'Spicilegia Zoolog., Fasc.' xii. 1777, p. 29. Sir Andrew Smith, 'Illustrations of the Zoology of S. Africa,' 1849, pl. 29, on the Kobus. Owen, in his 'Anatomy of Vertebrates' (vol. iii. 1868, p. 633) gives a table shewing incidentally which species of antelopes are gregarious.

much from the male. The wild horse of the Falkland Islands and of the Western States of N. America is polygamous, but, except in his greater size and in the proportions of his body, differs but little from the mare. The wild boar presents well-marked sexual characters, in his great tusks and some other points. In Europe and in India he leads a solitary life, except during the breeding-season; but as is believed by Sir W. Elliot, who has had many opportunities in India of observing this animal, he consorts at this season with several females. Whether this holds good in Europe is doubtful, but it is supported by some evidence. The adult male Indian elephant, like the boar, passes much of his time in solitude; but as Dr. Campbell states, when with others, "it is rare to find more than one male with a whole herd of females;" the larger males expelling or killing the smaller and weaker ones. The male differs from the female in his immense tusks, greater size, strength, and endurance; so great is the difference in these respects that the males when caught are valued at one-fifth more than the females.[12] The sexes of other pachydermatous animals differ very little or not at all, and, as far as known, they are not polygamists. Nor have I heard of any species in the Orders of Cheiroptera, Edentata, Insectivora and Rodents being polygamous, excepting that amongst the Rodents, the common rat, according to some rat-catchers, lives with several females. Nevertheless the two sexes of some sloths (Edentata) differ in the character and colour of certain patches of hair on their shoulders.[13] And many kinds of bats (Cheiroptera) present well-marked sexual differences, chiefly in the males possessing odoriferous glands and pouches, and by their being of a lighter colour.[14] In the great order of Rodents, as far as I can learn, the sexes rarely differ, and when they do so, it is but slightly in the tint of the fur.

As I hear from Sir Andrew Smith, the lion in South Africa sometimes lives with a single female, but generally with more, and, in one case, was found with as many as five females; so that he is polygamous. As far as I can discover, he is the only polygamist amongst all the terrestrial Carnivora, and he alone presents well-marked sexual characters. If, however, we turn to the marine Carnivora, as we shall hereafter see, the case is widely different; for many species of seals offer extraordinary sexual differences, and they are eminently polygamous. Thus, according to Péron, the male sea-elephant of the Southern Ocean always possesses several females, and the sea-lion of Forster is said to be surrounded by from twenty to thirty females. In the North, the male sea-bear of Steller is accompanied by even a greater number of females. It is an interesting fact, as Dr. Gill remarks,[15] that in the monogamous species, "or those living in small communities, there is little difference in size between the males and females; in the social species, or rather those of which the males have harems, the males are vastly larger than the females."

[12] Dr. Campbell, in 'Proc. Zoolog. Soc.' 1869, p. 138. See also an interesting paper, by Lieut. Johnstone, in 'Proc. Asiatic Soc. of Bengal,' May, 1868.
[13] Dr. Gray, in 'Annals and Mag. of Nat. Hist.' 1871, p. 302.
[14] See Dr. Dobson's excellent paper in 'Proc. Zoolog. Soc.' 1873, p. 241.
[15] The Eared Seals, 'American Naturalist,' vol. iv., Jan. 1871.

Amongst birds, many species, the sexes of which differ greatly from each other, are certainly monogamous. In Great Britain we see well-marked sexual differences, for instance, in the wild-duck which pairs with a single female, the common blackbird, and the bullfinch which is said to pair for life. I am informed by Mr. Wallace that the like is true of the Chatterers or Cotingidæ of South America, and of many other birds. In several groups I have not been able to discover whether the species are polygamous or monogamous. Lesson says that birds of paradise, so remarkable for their sexual differences, are polygamous, but Mr. Wallace doubts whether he had sufficient evidence. Mr. Salvin tells me he has been led to believe that humming-birds are polygamous. The male widow-bird, remarkable for his caudal plumes, certainly seems to be a polygamist.[16] I have been assured by Mr. Jenner Weir and by others, that it is somewhat common for three starlings to frequent the same nest; but whether this is a case of polygamy or polyandry has not been ascertained.

The Gallinaceæ exhibit almost as strongly marked sexual differences as birds of paradise or humming-birds, and many of the species are, as is well known, polygamous; others being strictly monogamous. What a contrast is presented between the sexes of the polygamous peacock or pheasant, and the monogamous guinea-fowl or partridge! Many similar cases could be given, as in the grouse tribe, in which the males of the polygamous capercailzie and black-cock differ greatly from the females; whilst the sexes of the monogamous red grouse and ptarmigan differ very little. In the Cursores, except amongst the bustards, few species offer strongly-marked sexual differences, and the great bustard (*Otis tarda*) is said to be polygamous. With the Grallatores, extremely few species differ sexually, but the ruff (*Machetes pugnax*) affords a marked exception, and this species is believed by Montagu to be a polygamist. Hence it appears that amongst birds there often exists a close relation between polygamy and the development of strongly-marked sexual differences. I asked Mr. Bartlett, of the Zoological Gardens, who has had very large experience with birds, whether the male tragopan (one of the Gallinaceæ) was polygamous, and I was struck by his answering, "I do not know, but should think so from his splendid colours."

It deserves notice that the instinct of pairing with a single female is easily lost under domestication. The wild-duck is strictly monogamous, the domestic-duck highly polygamous. The Rev. W. D. Fox informs me that out of some half-tamed wild-ducks, on a large pond in his neighborhood, so many mallards were shot by the game-keeper that only one was left for every seven or eight females; yet unusually large broods were reared. The guinea-fowl is strictly monogamous; but Mr. Fox finds that his birds succeed best when he keeps one cock to two or three hens. Canary-birds pair in a state of nature, but the breeders in England success-

---

[16] 'The Ibis,' vol. iii. 1861, p. 133, on the Progne Widow-bird. See also on the *Vidua axillaris,* ibid. vol. ii. 1860, p. 211. On the polygamy of the Capercailzie and Great Bustard, see L. Lloyd, 'Game Birds of Sweden,' 1867, p. 19, and 182. Montagu and Selby speak of the Black Grouse as polygamous and of the Red Grouse as monogamous.

fully put one male to four or five females. I have noticed these cases, as rendering it probable that wild monogamous species might readily become either temporarily or permanently polygamous.

Too little is known of the habits of reptiles and fishes to enable us to speak of their marriage arrangements. The stickle-back (Gasterosteus), however, is said to be a polygamist;[17] and the male during the breeding season differs conspicuously from the female.

To sum up on the means through which, as far as we can judge, sexual selection has led to the development of secondary sexual characters. It has been shewn that the largest number of vigorous offspring will be reared from the pairing of the strongest and best-armed males, victorious in contests over other males, with the most vigorous and best-nourished females, which are the first to breed in the spring. If such females select the more attractive, and at the same time vigorous males, they will rear a larger number of offspring than the retarded females, which must pair with the less vigorous and less attractive males. So it will be if the more vigorous males select the more attractive and at the same time healthy and vigorous females; and this will especially hold good if the male defends the female, and aids in providing food for the young. The advantage thus gained by the more vigorous pairs in rearing a larger number of offspring has apparently sufficed to render sexual selection efficient. But a large numerical preponderance of males over females will be still more efficient; whether the preponderance is only occasional and local, or permanent; whether it occurs at birth, or afterwards from the greater destruction of the females; or whether it indirectly follows from the practice of polygamy.

The Male generally more modified than the Female.—Throughout the animal kingdom, when the sexes differ in external appearance, it is, with rare exceptions, the male which has been the more modified; for, generally, the female retains a closer resemblance to the young of her own species, and to other adult members of the same group. The cause of this seems to lie in the males of almost all animals having stronger passions than the females. Hence it is the males that fight together and sedulously display their charms before the females; and the victors transmit their superiority to their male offspring. Why both sexes do not thus acquire the characters of their fathers, will be considered hereafter. That the males of all mammals eagerly pursue the females is notorious to every one. So it is with birds; but many cock birds do not so much pursue the hen, as display their plumage, perform strange antics, and pour forth their song in her presence. The male in the few fish observed seems much more eager than the female; and the same is true of alligators, and apparently of Batrachians. Throughout the enormous class of insects, as Kirby remarks,[18] "the law is, that the male shall seek the female." Two good authorities, Mr. Blackwell and Mr. C. Spence Bate, tell me that the

---

[17] Noel Humphreys, 'River Gardens,' 1857.
[18] Kirby and Spence, 'Introduction to Entomology,' vol. iii. 1826, p. 342.

males of spiders and crustaceans are more active and more erratic in their
habits than the females. When the organs of sense or locomotion are present in the one sex of insects and crustaceans and absent in the other, or
when, as is frequently the case, they are more highly developed in the one
than in the other, it is, as far as I can discover, almost invariably the male
which retains such organs, or has them most developed; and this shews
that the male is the more active member in the courtship of the sexes.[19]

The female, on the other hand, with the rarest exceptions, is less eager
than the male. As the illustrious Hunter[20] long ago observed, she generally "requires to be courted;" she is coy, and may often be seen endeavouring for a long time to escape from the male. Every observer of the
habits of animals will be able to call to mind instances of this kind. It is
shown by various facts, given hereafter, and by the results fairly attrib-
utable to sexual selection, that the female, though comparatively passive,
generally exerts some choice and accepts one male in preference to others.
Or she may accept, as appearances would sometimes lead us to believe,
not the male which is the most attractive to her, but the one which is the
least distasteful. The exertion of some choice on the part of the female
seems a law almost as general as the eagerness of the male.

We are naturally led to enquire why the male, in so many and such distinct classes, has become more eager than the female, so that he searches
for her, and plays the more active part in courtship. It would be no advantage and some loss of power if each sex searched for the other; but
why should the male almost always be the seeker? The ovules of plants
after fertilisation have to be nourished for a time; hence the pollen is necessarily brought to the female organs—being placed on the stigma, by
means of insects or the wind, or by the spontaneous movements of the
stamens; and in the Algæ, &c., by the locomotive power of the anthero-
zooids. With lowly-organised aquatic animals, permanently affixed to the
same spot and having their sexes separate, the male element is invariably
brought to the female; and of this we can see the reason, for even if the
ova were detached before fertilisation, and did not require subsequent
nourishment or protection, there would yet be greater difficulty in transporting them than the male element, because, being larger than the latter, they are produced in far smaller numbers. So that many of the lower
animals are, in this respect, analogous with plants.[21] The males of affixed
and aquatic animals having been led to emit their fertilising element in

---

[19] One parasitic Hymenopterous insect (Westwood, 'Modern Class. of Insects,' vol.
ii. p. 160) forms an exception to the rule, as the male has rudimentary wings, and
never quits the cell in which it is born, whilst the female has well-developed wings.
Audouin believes that the females of this species are impregnated by the males which
are born in the same cells with them; but it is much more probable that the females
visit other cells, so that close inter-breeding is thus avoided. We shall hereafter meet
in various classes, with a few exceptional cases, in which the female, instead of the
male, is the seeker and wooer.

[20] 'Essays and Observations,' edited by Owen, vol. i. 1861, p. 194.

[21] Prof. Sachs ('Lehrbuch der Botanik,' 1870, s. 633) in speaking of the male and
female reproductive cells, remarks, "verhält sich die eine bei der Vereinigung activ,
. . . die andere erscheint bei der Vereinigung passiv."

this way, it is natural that any of their descendants, which rose in the scale and became locomotive, should retain the same habit; and they would approach the female as closely as possible, in order not to risk the loss of the fertilising element in a long passage of it through the water. With some few of the lower animals, the females alone are fixed, and the males of these must be the seekers. But it is difficult to understand why the males of species, of which the progenitors were primordially free, should invariably have acquired the habit of approaching the females, instead of being approached by them. But in all cases, in order that the males should seek efficiently, it would be necessary that they should be endowed with strong passions; and the acquirement of such passions would naturally follow from the more eager leaving a larger number of offspring than the less eager.

The great eagerness of the males has thus indirectly led to their much more frequently developing secondary sexual characters than the females. But the development of such characters would be much aided, if the males were more liable to vary than the females—as I concluded they were—after a long study of domesticated animals. Von Nathusius, who has had very wide experience, is strongly of the same opinion.[22] Good evidence also in favour of this conclusion can be produced by a comparison of the two sexes in mankind. During the Novara Expedition[23] a vast number of measurements was made of various parts of the body in different races, and the men were found in almost every case to present a greater range of variation than the women; but I shall have to recur to this subject in a future chapter. Mr. J. Wood,[24] who has carefully attended to the variation of the muscles in man, puts in italics the conclusion that "the greatest number of abnormalities in each subject is found in the males." He had previously remarked that "altogether in 102 subjects, the varieties of redundancy were found to be half as many again as in females, contrasting widely with the greater frequency of deficiency in females before described." Professor Macalister likewise remarks[25] that variations in the muscles "are probably more common in males than females." Certain muscles which are not normally present in mankind are also more frequently developed in the male than in the female sex, although exceptions to this rule are said to occur. Dr. Burt Wilder[26] has tabulated the cases of 152 individuals with supernumerary digits, of which 86 were males, and 39, or less than half, females, the remaining 27 being of unknown sex. It should not, however, be overlooked that women would more frequently endeavour to conceal a deformity of this kind than men. Again, Dr. L. Meyer asserts that the ears of man are more va-

[22] 'Vortrage über Viehzucht," 1872, p. 63.
[23] 'Reise der Novara: Anthropolog. Theil,' 1867, ss. 216-269. The results were calculated by Dr. Weisbach from measurements made by Drs. K. Scherzer and Schwarz. On the greater variability of the males of domesticated animals, see my 'Variation of Animals and Plants under Domestication,' vol. ii. 1868, p. 75.
[24] 'Proceedings Royal Soc.' vol. xvi. July, 1868, pp. 519 and 524.
[25] 'Proc. Royal Irish Academy,' vol. x. 1868, p. 123.
[26] 'Mass. Med. Soc.' ii. No. 3, 1868, p. 9.

riable in form than those of a woman.[27] Lastly the temperature is more variable in man than in woman.[28]

The cause of the greater general variability in the male sex, than in the female is unknown, except in so far as secondary sexual characters are extraordinarily variable, and are usually confined to the males; and, as we shall presently see, this fact is, to a certain extent, intelligible. Through the action of sexual and natural selection male animals have been rendered in very many instances widely different from their females; but independently of selection the two sexes, from differing constitutionally, tend to vary in a somewhat different manner. The female has to expend much organic matter in the formation of her ova, whereas the male expends much force in fierce contests with his rivals, in wandering about in search of the female, in exerting his voice, pouring out odoriferous secretions, &c.: and this expenditure is generally concentrated within a short period. The great vigour of the male during the season of love seems often to intensify his colours, independently of any marked difference from the female.[29] In mankind, and even as low down in the organic scale as in the Lepidoptera, the temperature of the body is higher in the male than in the female, accompanied in the case of man by a slower pulse.[30] On the whole the expenditure of matter and force by the two sexes is probably nearly equal, though effected in very different ways and at different rates.

From the causes just specified the two sexes can hardly fail to differ somewhat in constitution, at least during the breeding season; and, although they may be subjected to exactly the same conditions, they will tend to vary in a different manner. If such variations are of no service to either sex, they will not be accumulated and increased by sexual or natural selection. Nevertheless, they may become permanent if the exciting cause acts permanently; and in accordance with a frequent form of inheritance they may be transmitted to that sex alone in which they first appeared. In this case the two sexes will come to present permanent, yet unimportant, differences of character. For instance, Mr. Allen shews that with a large number of birds inhabiting the northern and southern United States, the specimens from the south are darker-coloured than those from the north; and this seems to be the direct result of the difference in temperature, light, &c., between the two regions. Now, in some few cases, the two sexes of the same species appear to have been differently affected; in the *Agelœus phœniceus* the males have had their colours greatly intensi-

[27] 'Archiv für Path. Anat. und Phys.' 1871, p. 488.

[28] The conclusions recently arrived at by Dr. J. Stockton Hough, on the temperature of man, are given in the 'Pop. Sci. Review,' Jan. 1, 1874, p. 97.

[29] Prof. Mantegazza is inclined to believe ('Lettera a Carlo Darwin,' 'Archivio per l'Anthropologia,' 1871, p. 306) that the bright colours, common in so many male animals, are due to the presence and retention by them of the spermatic fluid; but this can hardly be the case; for many male birds, for instance young pheasants, become brightly coloured in the autumn of their first year.

[30] For mankind, see Dr. J. Stockton Hough, whose conclusions are given in the 'Pop. Science Review,' 1874, p. 97. See Girard's observations on the Lepidoptera, as given in the 'Zoological Record,' 1869, p. 347.

fied in the south; whereas with *Cardinalis virginianus* it is the females which have been thus affected; with *Quiscalus major* the females have been rendered extremely variable in tint, whilst the males remain nearly uniform.[31]

A few exceptional cases occur in various classes of animals, in which the females instead of the males have acquired well pronounced secondary sexual characters, such as brighter colours, greater size, strength, or pugnacity. With birds there has sometimes been a complete transposition of the ordinary characters proper to each sex; the females having become the more eager in courtship, the males remaining comparatively passive, but apparently selecting the more attractive females, as we may infer from the results. Certain hen birds have thus been rendered more highly coloured or otherwise ornamented, as well as more powerful and pugnacious than the cocks; these characters being transmitted to the female offspring alone.

It may be suggested that in some cases a double process of selection has been carried on; that the males have selected the more attractive females, and the latter the more attractive males. This process, however, though it might lead to the modification of both sexes, would not make the one sex different from the other, unless indeed their tastes for the beautiful differed; but this is a supposition too improbable to be worth considering in the case of any animal, excepting man. There are, however, many animals in which the sexes resemble each other, both being furnished with the same ornaments, which analogy would lead us to attribute to the agency of sexual selection. In such cases it may be suggested with more plausibility, that there has been a double or mutual process of sexual selection; the more vigorous and precocious females selecting the more attractive and vigorous males, the latter rejecting all except the more attractive females. But from what we know of the habits of animals, this view is hardly probable, for the male is generally eager to pair with any female. It is more probable that the ornaments common to both sexes were acquired by one sex, generally the male, and then transmitted to the offspring of both sexes. If, indeed, during a lengthened period the males of any species were greatly to exceed the females in number, and then during another lengthened period, but under different conditions, the reverse were to occur, a double, but not simultaneous, process of sexual selection might easily be carried on, by which the two sexes might be rendered widely different.

We shall hereafter see that many animals exist, of which neither sex is brilliantly coloured or provided with special ornaments, and yet the members of both sexes or of one alone have probably acquired simple colours, such as white or black, through sexual selection. The absence of bright tints or other ornaments may be the result of variations of the right kind never having occurred, or of the animals themselves having preferred plain black or white. Obscure tints have often been developed

[31] 'Mammals and Birds of E. Florida, pp. 234, 280, 295.

through natural selection for the sake of protection, and the acquirement through sexual selection of conspicuous colours, appears to have been sometimes checked from the danger thus incurred. But in other cases the males during long ages may have struggled together for the possession of the females, and yet no effect will have been produced, unless a larger number of offspring were left by the more successful males to inherit their superiority, than by the less successful: and this, as previously shewn, depends on many complex contingencies.

Sexual selection acts in a less rigorous manner than natural selection. The latter produces its effects by the life or death at all ages of the more or less successful individuals. Death, indeed, not rarely ensues from the conflicts of rival males. But generally the less successful male merely fails to obtain a female, or obtains a retarded and less vigorous female later in the season, or, if polygamous, obtains fewer females; so that they leave fewer, less vigorous, or no offspring. In regard to structures acquired through ordinary or natural selection, there is in most cases, as long as the conditions of life remain the same, a limit to the amount of advantageous modification in relation to certain special purposes; but in regard to structures adapted to make one male victorious over another, either in fighting or in charming the female, there is no definite limit to the amount of advantageous modification; so that as long as the proper variations arise the work of sexual selection will go on. This circumstance may partly account for the frequent and extraordinary amount of variability presented by secondary sexual characters. Nevertheless, natural selection will determine that such characters shall not be acquired by the victorious males, if they would be highly injurious, either by expending too much of their vital powers, or by exposing them to any great danger. The development, however, of certain structures—of the horns, for instance, in certain stags—has been carried to a wonderful extreme; and in some cases to an extreme which, as far as the general conditions of life are concerned, must be slightly injurious to the male. From this fact we learn that the advantages which favoured males derive from conquering other males in battle or courtship, and thus leaving a numerous progeny, are in the long run greater than those derived from rather more perfect adaptation to their conditions of life. We shall further see, and it could never have been anticipated, that the power to charm the female has sometimes been more important than the power to conquer other males in battle.

LAWS OF INHERITANCE

In order to understand how sexual selection has acted on many animals of many classes, and in the course of ages has produced a conspicuous result, it is necessary to bear in mind the laws of inheritance, as far as they are known. Two distinct elements are included under the term "inheritance"—the transmission, and the development of characters; but as these generally go together, the distinction is often overlooked. We see this distinction in those characters which are transmitted through the early years of life, but are developed only at maturity or during old age. We see the same distinction more clearly with secondary sexual characters, for these are transmitted through both sexes, though developed in one alone. That they are present in both sexes, is manifest when two species, having strongly-marked sexual characters, are crossed, for each transmits the characters proper to its own male and female sex to the hybrid offspring of either sex. The same fact is likewise manifest, when characters proper to the male are occasionally developed in the female when she grows old or becomes diseased, as, for instance, when the common hen assumes the flowing tail-feathers, hackles, comb, spurs, voice, and even pugnacity of the cock. Conversely, the same thing is evident, more or less plainly, with castrated males. Again, independently of old age or disease, characters are occasionally transferred from the male to the female, as when, in certain breeds of the fowl, spurs regularly appear in the young and healthy females. But in truth they are simply developed in the female; for in every breed each detail in the structure of the spur is transmitted through the female to her male offspring. Many cases will hereafter be given, where the female exhibits, more or less perfectly, characters proper to the male, in whom they must have been first developed, and then transferred to the female. The converse case of the first development of characters in the female and of transference to the male, is less frequent; it will therefore be well to give one striking instance. With bees the pollen-collecting apparatus is used by the female alone for gathering pollen for the larvæ, yet in most of the species it is partially developed in the males to whom it is quite useless, and it is perfectly developed in the males of Bombus or the humble-bee.[32] As not a single other Hymenopterous insect, not even the wasp, which is closely allied to the bee, is provided with a pollen-collecting apparatus, we have no grounds for supposing that male bees primordially collected pollen as well as the females; although we have some reason to suspect that male mammals primordially suckled their young as well as the females. Lastly, in all cases of reversion, characters are transmitted through two, three, or many more generations, and are then developed under certain unknown favourable conditions. This important distinction between transmission and development will be best kept in mind by the aid of the hypothesis of pangenesis. According to this hypothesis, every unit or cell of the body throws off gemmules or undeveloped atoms, which are transmitted to the offspring of both sexes, and are multiplied by self-division. They may remain undeveloped during the early years of life or during successive generations; and their development into units or cells, like those from which they were derived, depends on their affinity for, and union with other units or cells previously developed in the due order of growth.

Inheritance at corresponding Periods of Life.—This tendency is well established. A new character, appearing in a young animal, whether it

[32] H. Müller, 'Anwendung der Darwin'schen Lehre,' &c. Verh. d. n. V. Jahrg. xxix. p. 42.

lasts throughout life or is only transient, will, in general, reappear in the offspring at the same age and last for the same time. If, on the other hand, a new character appears at maturity, or even during old age, it tends to reappear in the offspring at the same advanced age. When deviations from this rule occur, the transmitted characters much oftener appear before, than after the corresponding age. As I have dwelt on this subject sufficiently in another work,[33] I will here merely give two or three instances, for the sake of recalling the subject to the reader's mind. In several breeds of the Fowl, the down-covered chickens, the young birds in their first true plumage, and the adults differ greatly from one another, as well as from their common parent-form, the *Gallus bankiva;* and these characters are faithfully transmitted by each breed to their offspring at the corresponding periods of life. For instance, the chickens of spangled Hamburgs, whilst covered with down, have a few dark spots on the head and rump, but are not striped longitudinally, as in many other breeds; in their first true plumage, "they are beautifully pencilled," that is each feather is transversely marked by numerous dark bars; but in their second plumage the feathers all become spangled or tipped with a dark round spot.[34] Hence in this breed variations have occurred at, and been transmitted to, three distinct periods of life. The Pigeon offers a more remarkable case, because the aboriginal parent species does not undergo any change of plumage with advancing age, excepting that at maturity the breast becomes more iridescent; yet there are breeds which do not acquire their characteristic colours until they have moulted two, three, or four times; and these modifications of plumage are regularly transmitted.

Inheritance at corresponding Seasons of the Year.—With animals in a state of nature, innumerable instances occur of characters appearing periodically at different seasons. We see this in the horns of the stag, and in the fur of arctic animals which becomes thick and white during the winter. Many birds acquire bright colours and other decorations during the breeding-season alone. Pallas states,[35] that in Siberia domestic cattle and horses become lighter-coloured during the winter; and I have myself observed, and heard of similar strongly marked changes of colour, that is, from brownish cream-colour or reddish-brown to a perfect white, in several ponies in England. Although I do not know that this tendency to change the colour of the coat during different seasons is transmitted, yet it probably is so, as all shades of colour are strongly inherited by the

[33] 'The Variation of Animals and Plants under Domestication,' vol. ii. 1868, p. 75. In the last chapter but one, the provisional hypothesis of pangenesis, above alluded to, is fully explained.

[34] These facts are given on the high authority of a great breeder, Mr. Teebay; see Tegetmeier's 'Poultry Book,' 1868, p. 158. On the characters of chickens of different breeds, and on the breeds of the pigeon, alluded to in the following paragraph, see 'Variation of Animals,' &c., vol. i. pp. 160, 249; vol. ii. p. 77.

[35] 'Novæ species Quadrupedum e Glirium ordine,' 1778, p. 7. On the transmission of colour by the horse, see 'Variation of Animals, &c., under Domestication,' vol. i. p. 51 Also vol. ii. p. 71, for a general discussion on 'Inheritance as limited by Sex.'

horse. Nor is this form of inheritance, as limited by the seasons, more remarkable than its limitation by age or sex.

Inheritance as Limited by Sex.—The equal transmission of characters to both sexes is the commonest form of inheritance, at least with those animals which do not present strongly-marked sexual differences, and indeed with many of these. But characters are somewhat commonly transferred exclusively to that sex, in which they first appear. Ample evidence on this head has been advanced in my work on 'Variation under Domestication,' but a few instances may here be given. There are breeds of the sheep and goat, in which the horns of the male differ greatly in shape from those of the female; and these differences, acquired under domestication, are regularly transmitted to the same sex. As a rule, it is the females alone in cats which are tortoise-shell, the corresponding colour in the males being rusty-red. With most breeds of the fowl, the characters proper to each sex are transmitted to the same sex alone. So general is this form of transmission that it is an anomaly when variations in certain breeds are transmitted equally to both sexes. There are also certain sub-breeds of the fowl in which the males can hardly be distinguished from one another, whilst the females differ considerably in colour. The sexes of the pigeon in the parent-species do not differ in any external character; nevertheless, in certain domesticated breeds the male is coloured differently from the female.[36] The wattle in the English Carrier pigeon, and the crop in the Pouter, are more highly developed in the male than in the female; and although these characters have been gained through long-continued selection by man, the slight differences between the sexes are wholly due to the form of inheritance which has prevailed; for they have arisen, not from, but rather in opposition to, the wish of the breeder.

Most of our domestic races have been formed by the accumulation of many slight variations; and as some of the successive steps have been transmitted to one sex alone, and some to both sexes, we find in the different breeds of the same species all gradations between great sexual dissimilarity and complete similarity. Instances have already been given with the breeds of the fowl and pigeon, and under nature analogous cases are common. With animals under domestication, but whether in nature I will not venture to say, one sex may lose characters proper to it, and may thus come somewhat to resemble the opposite sex; for instance, the males of some breeds of the fowl have lost their masculine tail-plumes and hackles. On the other hand, the differences between the sexes may be increased under domestication, as with merino sheep, in which the ewes have lost their horns. Again, characters proper to one sex may suddenly appear in the other sex; as in those sub-breeds of the fowl in which the hens acquire spurs whilst young; or, as in certain Polish sub-breeds, in which the females, as there is reason to believe, originally acquired a

---

[36] Dr. Chapuis, 'Le Pigeon Voyageur Belge,' 1865, p. 87. Boitard et Corbié, 'Les Pigeons de Volière,' &c. 1824, p. 173. See, also, on similar differences in certain breeds at Modena, 'Le variazioni dei Colombi domestici,' del Paolo Bonizzi, 1873.

crest, and subsequently transferred it to the males. All these cases are intelligible on the hypothesis of pangenesis; for they depend on the gemmules of certain parts, although present in both sexes, becoming, through the influence of domestication, either dormant or developed in either sex.

There is one difficult question which it will be convenient to defer to a future chapter; namely, whether a character at first developed in both sexes, could through selection be limited in its development to one sex alone. If, for instance, a breeder observed that some of his pigeons (of which the characters are usually transferred in an equal degree to both sexes) varied into pale blue, could he by long-continued selection make a breed, in which the males alone should be of this tint, whilst the females remained unchanged? I will here only say, that this, though perhaps not impossible, would be extremely difficult; for the natural result of breeding from the pale-blue males would be to change the whole stock of both sexes to this tint. If, however, variations of the desired tint appeared, which were from the first limited in their development to the male sex, there would not be the least difficulty in making a breed with the two sexes of a different colour, as indeed has been effected with a Belgian breed, in which the males alone are streaked with black. In a similar manner, if any variation appeared in a female pigeon, which was from the first sexually limited in its development to the females, it would be easy to make a breed with the females alone thus characterised; but if the variation was not thus originally limited, the process would be extremely difficult, perhaps impossible.[37]

On the Relation between the Period of Development of a Character and its Transmission to one Sex or to both Sexes.—Why certain characters should be inherited by both sexes, and other characters by one sex alone, namely by that sex in which the character first appeared, is in most cases quite unknown. We cannot even conjecture why with certain sub-breeds of the pigeon, black striæ, though transmitted through the female, should be developed in the male alone, whilst every other character is equally transferred to both sexes. Why, again, with cats, the tortoise-shell colour should, with rare exceptions, be developed in the female alone. The very same character, such as deficient or super-numerary digits, colour-blindness, &c., may with mankind be inherited by the males alone of one family, and in another family by the females alone, though in both cases transmitted through the opposite as well as through the same sex.[38]

[37] Since the publication of the first edition of this work, it has been highly satisfactory to me to find the following remarks (the 'Field,' Sept. 1872) from so experienced a breeder as Mr. Tegetmeier. After describing some curious cases in pigeons, of the transmission of colour by one sex alone, and the formation of a sub-breed with this character, he says: "It is a singular circumstance that Mr. Darwin should have suggested the possibility of modifying the sexual colours of birds by a course of artificial selection. When he did so, he was in ignorance of these facts that I have related; but it is remarkable how very closely he suggested the right method of procedure."

[38] References are given in my 'Variation of Animals under Domestication,' vol. ii. p.

Although we are thus ignorant, the two following rules seem often to hold good—that variations which first appear in either sex at a late period of life, tend to be developed in the same sex alone; whilst variations which first appear early in life in either sex tend to be developed in both sexes. I am, however, far from supposing that this is the sole determining cause. As I have not elsewhere discussed this subject, and it has an important bearing on sexual selection, I must here enter into lengthy and somewhat intricate details.

It is in itself probable that any character appearing at an early age would tend to be inherited equally by both sexes, for the sexes do not differ much in constitution before the power of reproduction is gained. On the other hand, after this power has been gained and the sexes have come to differ in constitution, the gemmules (if I may again use the language of pangenesis) which are cast off from each varying part in the one sex would be much more likely to possess the proper affinities for uniting with the tissues of the same sex, and thus becoming developed, than with those of the opposite sex.

I was first led to infer that a relation of this kind exists, from the fact that whenever and in whatever manner the adult male differs from the adult female, he differs in the same manner from the young of both sexes. The generality of this fact is quite remarkable: it holds good with almost all mammals, birds, amphibians, and fishes; also with many crustaceans, spiders, and some few insects, such as certain orthoptera and libellulæ. In all these cases the variations, through the accumulation of which the male acquired his proper masculine characters, must have occurred at a somewhat late period of life; otherwise the young males would have been similarly characterised; and conformably with our rule, the variations are transmitted to and developed in the adult males alone. When, on the other hand, the adult male closely resembles the young of both sexes (these, with rare exceptions, being alike), he generally resembles the adult female; and in most of these cases the variations through which the young and old acquired their present characters, probably occurred, according to our rule, during youth. But there is here room for doubt, for characters are sometimes transferred to the offspring at an earlier age than that at which they first appeared in the parents, so that the parents may have varied when adult, and have transferred their characters to their offspring whilst young. There are, moreover, many animals, in which the two sexes closely resemble each other, and yet both differ from their young; and here the characters of the adults must have been acquired late in life; nevertheless, these characters, in apparent contradiction to our rule, are transferred to both sexes. We must not, however, overlook the possibility or even probability of successive variations of the same nature occurring, under exposure to similar conditions, simultaneously in both sexes at a rather late period of life; and in this case the variations would be transferred to the offspring of both sexes at a corresponding late age; and there would then be no real contradiction to the rule that variations occurring late in life are transferred exclusively to the sex in which they first appeared. This latter rule seems to hold true more gen-erally than the second one, namely, that variations which occur in either sex early in life tend to be transferred to both sexes. As it was obviously impossible even to estimate in how large a number of cases throughout the animal kingdom these two propositions held good, it occurred to me to investigate some striking or crucial instances, and to rely on the result.

An excellent case for investigation is afforded by the Deer family. In all the species, but one, the horns are developed only in the males, though certainly transmitted through the females, and capable of abnormal de-velopment in them. In the reindeer, on the other hand, the female is pro-vided with horns; so that in this species, the horns ought, according to our rule, to appear early in life, long before the two sexes are mature and have come to differ much in constitution. In all the other species the horns ought to appear later in life, which would lead to their develop-ment in that sex alone, in which they first appeared in the progenitor of the whole Family. Now in seven species, belonging to distinct sections of the family and inhabiting different regions, in which the stags alone bear horns, I find that the horns first appear at periods, varying from nine months after birth in the roebuck to ten, twelve or even more months in the stags of the six other and larger species.[39] But with the reindeer the case is widely different; for, as I hear from Prof. Nilsson, who kindly made special enquiries for me in Lapland, the horns appear in the young animals within four or five weeks after birth, and at the same time in both sexes. So that here we have a structure, developed at a most unusu-ally early age in one species of the family, and likewise common to both sexes in this one species alone.

In several kinds of antelopes, only the males are provided with horns, whilst in the greater number both sexes bear horns. With respect to the period of development, Mr. Blyth informs me that there was at one time in the Zoological Gardens a young koodoo (*Ant. strepsiceros*), of which the males alone are horned, and also the young of a closely-allied species, the eland (*Ant. oreas*), in which both sexes are horned. Now it is in strict conformity with our rule, that in the young male koodoo, although ten months old, the horns were remarkably small, considering the size ulti-mately attained by them; whilst in the young male eland, although only three months old, the horns were already very much larger than in the koodoo. It is also a noticeable fact that in the prong-horned antelope,[40] only a few of the females, about one in five, have horns, and these are in a

[39] I am much obliged to Mr. Cupples for having made enquiries for me in regard to the Roebuck and Red Deer of Scotland from Mr. Robertson, the experienced head-forester to the Marquis of Breadalbane. In regard to Fallow-deer, I have to thank Mr. Eyton and others for information. For the *Cervus alces* of N. America, see 'Land and Water,' 1868, pp. 221 and 254; and for the *C. Virginianus* and *strongyloceros* of the same continent, see J. D. Caton, in 'Ottawa Acad. of Nat. Sc.' 1868, p. 13. For *Cervus Eldi* of Pegu, see Lieut. Beaven, 'Proc. Zoolog. Soc.' 1867, p. 762.

[40] *Antilocapra Americana*. I have to thank Dr. Canfield for information with respect to the horns of the female: see also his paper in 'Proc. Zoolog. Soc.' 1866, p. 109. Also Owen, 'Anatomy of Vertebrates,' vol. iii. p. 627.

rudimentary state, though sometimes above four inches long; so that as far as concerns the possession of horns by the males alone, this species is in an intermediate condition, and the horns do not appear until about five or six months after birth. Therefore in comparison with what little we know of the development of the horns in other antelopes, and from what we do know with respect to the horns of deer, cattle, &c., those of the prong-horned antelope appear at an intermediate period of life,—that is, not very early, as in cattle and sheep, nor very late, as in the larger deer and antelopes. The horns of sheep, goats, and cattle, which are well developed in both sexes, though not quite equal in size, can be felt, or even seen, at birth or soon afterwards.[41] Our rule, however, seems to fail in some breeds of sheep, for instance merinos, in which the rams alone are horned; for I cannot find on enquiry,[42] that the horns are developed later in life in this breed than in ordinary sheep in which both sexes are horned. But with domesticated sheep the presence or absence of horns is not a firmly fixed character; for a certain proportion of the merino ewes bear small horns, and some of the rams are hornless; and in most breeds hornless ewes are occasionally produced.

Dr. W. Marshall has lately made a special study of the protuberances so common on the heads of birds,[43] and he comes to the following conclusion:—that with those species in which they are confined to the males, they are developed late in life; whereas with those species in which they are common to the two sexes, they are developed at a very early period. This is certainly a striking confirmation of my two laws of inheritance.

In most of the species of the splendid family of the Pheasants, the males differ conspicuously from the females, and they acquire their ornaments at a rather late period of life. The eared pheasant (*Crossoptilon auritum*), however, offers a remarkable exception, for both sexes possess the fine caudal plumes, the large ear-tufts and the crimson velvet about the head; I find that all these characters appear very early in life in accordance with rule. The adult male can, however, be distinguished from the adult female by the presence of spurs; and conformably with our rule, these do not begin to be developed before the age of six months, as I am assured by Mr. Bartlett, and even at this age, the two sexes can hardly be distinguished.[44] The male and female Peacock differ conspicu-

---

[41] I have been assured that the horns of the sheep in North Wales can always be felt, and are sometimes even an inch in length, at birth. Youatt says ('Cattle,' 1834, p. 277), that the prominence of the frontal bone in cattle penetrates the cutis at birth, and that the horny matter is soon formed over it.

[42] I am greatly indebted to Prof. Victor Carus for having made enquiries for me, from the highest authorities, with respect to the merino sheep of Saxony. On the Guinea coast of Africa there is, however, a breed of sheep in which, as with merinos, the rams alone bear horns; and Mr. Winwood Reade informs me that in one case observed by him, a young ram, born on Feb. 10th, first shewed horns on March 6th, so that in this instance, in conformity with rule, the development of the horns occurred at a later period of life than in Welsh sheep, in which both sexes are horned.

[43] 'Ueber die knöchernen Schädelhöcker der Vögel' in the 'Niederlandischen Archiv für Zoologie,' Band I. Heft 2, 1872.

[44] In the common peacock (*Pavo cristatus*) the male alone possesses spurs, whilst

ously from each other in almost every part of their plumage, except in the elegant head-crest, which is common to both sexes; and this is developed very early in life, long before the other ornaments, which are confined to the male. The wild-duck offers an analogous case, for the beautiful green speculum on the wings is common to both sexes, though duller and somewhat smaller in the female, and it is developed early in life, whilst the curled tail-feathers and other ornaments of the male are developed later.[45] Between such extreme cases of close sexual resemblance and wide dissimilarity, as those of the Crossoptilon and peacock, many intermediate ones could be given, in which the characters follow our two rules in their order of development.

As most insects emerge from the pupal state in a mature condition, it is doubtful whether the period of development can determine the transference of their characters to one or to both sexes. But we do not know that the coloured scales, for instance, in two species of butterflies, in one of which the sexes differ in colour, whilst in the other they are alike, are developed at the same relative age in the cocoon. Nor do we know whether all the scales are simultaneously developed on the wings of the same species of butterfly, in which certain coloured marks are confined to one sex, whilst others are common to both sexes. A difference of this kind in the period of development is not so improbable as it may at first appear; for with the Orthoptera, which assume their adult state, not by a single metamorphosis, but by a succession of moults, the young males of some species at first resemble the females, and acquire their distinctive masculine characters only at a later moult. Strictly analogous cases occur at the successive moults of certain male crustaceans.

We have as yet considered the transference of characters, relatively to their period of development, only in species in a natural state; we will now turn to domesticated animals, and first touch on monstrosities and diseases. The presence of supernumerary digits, and the absence of certain phalanges, must be determined at an early embryonic period—the

---

both sexes of the Java Peacock (*P. muticus*) offer the unusual case of being furnished with spurs. Hence I fully expected that in the latter species they would have been developed earlier in life than in the common peacock; but M. Hegt of Amsterdam informs me, that with young birds of the previous year, of both species, compared on April 23rd, 1869, there was no difference in the development of the spurs. The spurs, however, were as yet represented merely by slight knobs or elevations. I presume that I should have been informed if any difference in the rate of development had been observed subsequently.

[45] In some other species of the Duck family the speculum differs in a greater degree in the two sexes; but I have not been able to discover whether its full development occurs later in life in the males of such species, than in the male of the common duck, as ought to be the case according to our rule. With the allied *Mergus cucullatus* we have, however, a case of this kind: the two sexes differ conspicuously in general plumage, and to a considerable degree in the speculum, which is pure white in the male and greyish-white in the female. Now the young males at first entirely resemble the females, and have a greyish-white speculum, which becomes pure white at an earlier age than that at which the adult male acquires his other and more strongly-marked sexual differences: see Audubon, 'Ornithological Biography,' vol. iii. 1835, pp. 249–250.

tendency to profuse bleeding is at least congenital, as is probably colour-blindness—yet these peculiarities, and other similar ones, are often limited in their transmission to one sex; so that the rule that characters, developed at an early period, tend to be transmitted to both sexes, here wholly fails. But this rule, as before remarked, does not appear to be nearly so general as the converse one, namely, that characters which appear late in life in one sex are transmitted exclusively to the same sex. From the fact of the above abnormal peculiarities becoming attached to one sex, long before the sexual functions are active, we may infer that there must be some difference between the sexes at an extremely early age. With respect to sexually-limited diseases, we know too little of the period at which they originate, to draw any safe conclusion. Gout, however, seems to fall under our rule, for it is generally caused by intemperance during manhood, and is transmitted from the father to his sons in a much more marked manner than to his daughters.

In the various domestic breeds of sheeps, goats, and cattle, the males differ from their respective females in the shape or development of their horns, forehead, mane, dewlap, tail, and hump on the shoulders; and these peculiarities, in accordance with our rule, are not fully developed until a rather late period of life. The sexes of dogs do not differ, except that in certain breeds, especially in the Scotch deerhound, the male is much larger and heavier than the female; and, as we shall see in a future chapter, the male goes on increasing in size to an unusually late period of life, which, according to rule, will account for his increased size being transmitted to his male offspring alone. On the other hand, the tortoise-shell colour, which is confined to female cats, is quite distinct at birth, and this case violates the rule. There is a breed of pigeons in which the males alone are streaked with black, and the streaks can be detected even in the nestlings; but they become more conspicuous at each successive moult, so that this case partly opposes and partly supports the rule. With the English Carrier and Pouter pigeons, the full development of the wattle and the crop occurs rather late in life, and conformably with the rule, these characters are transmitted in full perfection to the males alone. The following cases perhaps come within the class previously alluded to, in which both sexes have varied in the same manner at a rather late period of life, and have consequently transferred their new characters to both sexes at a corresponding late period; and if so, these cases are not opposed to our rule:—there exist sub-breeds of the pigeon, described by Neumeister,[46] in which both sexes change their colour during two or three moults (as is likewise the case with the Almond Tumbler), nevertheless, these changes, though occurring rather late in life, are common to both sexes. One variety of the Canary-bird, namely the London Prize, offers a nearly analogous case.

With the breeds of the Fowl the inheritance of various characters by one or both sexes, seem generally determined by the period at which such

---

[46] 'Das Ganze der Taubenzucht,' 1837, s. 21, 24. For the case of the streaked pigeons, see Dr. Chapuis, 'Le pigeon voyageur Belge,' 1855, p. 87.

characters are developed. Thus in all the many breeds in which the adult male differs greatly in colour from the female, as well as from the wild parent-species, he differs also from the young male, so that the newly-acquired characters must have appeared at a rather late period of life. On the other hand, in most of the breeds in which the two sexes resemble each other, the young are coloured in nearly the same manner as their parents, and this renders it probable that their colours first appeared early in life. We have instances of this fact in all black and white breeds, in which the young and old of both sexes are alike; nor can it be maintained that there is something peculiar in a black or white plumage, which leads to its transference to both sexes; for the males alone of many natural species are either black or white, the females being differently coloured. With the so-called Cuckoo sub-breeds of the fowl, in which the feathers are transversely pencilled with dark stripes, both sexes and the chickens are coloured in nearly the same manner. The laced plumage of the Sebright bantam is the same in both sexes, and in the young chickens the wing-feathers are distinctly, though imperfectly laced. Spangled Hamburgs, however, offer a partial exception; for the two sexes, though not quite alike, resemble each other more closely than do the sexes of the aboriginal parent-species; yet they acquire their characteristic plumage late in life, for the chickens are distinctly pencilled. With respect to other characters beside colour, in the wild-parent species and in most of the domestic breeds, the males alone possess a well-developed comb; but in the young of the Spanish fowl it is largely developed at a very early age, and, in accordance with this early development in the male, it is of unusual size in the adult female. In the Game breeds pugnacity is developed at a wonderfully early age, of which curious proofs could be given; and this character is transmitted to both sexes, so that the hens, from their extreme pugnacity, are now generally exhibited in separate pens. With the Polish breeds the bony protuberance of the skull which supports the crest is partially developed even before the chickens are hatched, and the crest itself soon begins to grow, though at first feebly;[47] and in this breed the adults of both sexes are characterised by a great bony protuberance and an immense crest.

Finally, from what we have now seen of the relation which exists in many natural species and domesticated races, between the period of the development of their characters and the manner of their transmission—for example, the striking fact of the early growth of the horns in the reindeer, in which both sexes bear horns, in comparison with their much later growth in the other species in which the male alone bears horns—we may conclude that one, though not the sole cause of characters being exclusively inherited by one sex, is their development at a late age. And sec-

[47] For full particulars and references on all these points respecting the several breeds of the Fowl, see 'Variation of Animals and Plants under Domestication,' vol. i. pp. 250, 256. In regard to the higher animals, the sexual differences which have arisen under domestication are described in the same work under the head of each species.

ondly, that one, though apparently a less efficient cause of characters being inherited by both sexes, is their development at an early age, whilst the sexes differ but little in constitution. It appears, however, that some difference must exist between the sexes even during a very early embryonic period, for characters developed at this age not rarely become attached to one sex.

Summary and concluding remarks.—From the foregoing discussion on the various laws of inheritance, we learn that the characters of the parents often, or even generally, tend to become developed in the offspring of the same sex, at the same age, and periodically at the same season of the year, in which they first appeared in the parents. But these rules, owing to unknown causes, are far from being fixed. Hence during the modification of a species, the successive changes may readily be transmitted in different ways; some to one sex, and some to both; some to the offspring at one age, and some to the offspring at all ages. Not only are the laws of inheritance extremely complex, but so are the causes which induce and govern variability. The variations thus induced are preserved and accumulated by sexual selection, which is in itself an extremely complex affair, depending, as it does, on the ardour in love, the courage, and the rivalry of the males, as well as on the powers of perception, the taste, and will of the female. Sexual selection will also be largely dominated by natural selection tending towards the general welfare of the species. Hence the manner in which the individuals of either or both sexes have been affected through sexual selection cannot fail to be complex in the highest degree.

When variations occur late in life in one sex, and are transmitted to the same sex at the same age, the other sex and the young are left unmodified. When they occur late in life, but are transmitted to both sexes at the same age, the young alone are left unmodified. Variations, however, may occur at any period of life in one sex or in both, and be transmitted to both sexes at all ages, and then all the individuals of the species are similarly modified. In the following chapters it will be seen that all these cases frequently occur in nature.

Sexual selection can never act on any animal before the age for reproduction arrives. From the great eagerness of the male it has generally acted on this sex and not on the females. The males have thus become provided with weapons for fighting with their rivals, with organs for discovering and securely holding the female, and for exciting or charming her. When the sexes differ in these respects, it is also, as we have seen, an extremely general law that the adult male differs more or less from the young male; and we may conclude from this fact that the successive variations, by which the adult male became modified, did not generally occur much before the age for reproduction. Whenever some or many of the variations occurred early in life, the young males would partake more or less of the characters of the adult males; and differences of this kind between the old and young males may be observed in many species of animals.

It is probable that young male animals have often tended to vary in a manner which would not only have been of no use to them at an early age, but would have been actually injurious—as by acquiring bright colours, which would render them conspicuous to their enemies, or by acquiring structures, such as great horns, which would expend much vital force in their development. Variations of this kind occurring in the young males would almost certainly be eliminated through natural selection. With the adult and experienced males, on the other hand, the advantages derived from the acquisition of such characters, would more than counterbalance some exposure to danger, and some loss of vital force.

As variations which give to the male a better chance of conquering other males, or of finding, securing, or charming the opposite sex, would, if they happened to arise in the female, be of no service to her, they would not be preserved in her through sexual selection. We have also good evidence with domesticated animals, that variations of all kinds are, if not carefully selected, soon lost through intercrossing and accidental deaths. Consequently in a state of nature, if variations of the above kind chanced to arise in the female line, and be transmitted exclusively in this line, they would be extremely liable to be lost. If, however, the females varied and transmitted their newly acquired characters to their offspring of both sexes, the characters which were advantageous to the males would be preserved by them through sexual selection, and the two sexes would in consequence be modified in the same manner, although such characters were of no use to the females: but I shall hereafter have to recur to these more intricate contingencies. Lastly, the females may acquire, and apparently have often acquired by transference, characters from the male sex.

As variations occurring later in life, and transmitted to one sex alone, have incessantly been taken advantage of and accumulated through sexual selection in relation to the reproduction of the species; therefore it appears, at first sight, an unaccountable fact that similar variations have not frequently been accumulated through natural selection, in relation to the ordinary habits of life. If this had occurred, the two sexes would often have been differently modified, for the sake, for instance, of capturing prey or of escaping from danger. Differences of this kind between the two sexes do occasionally occur, especially in the lower classes. But this implies that the two sexes follow different habits in their struggles for existence, which is a rare circumstance with the higher animals. The case, however, is widely different with the reproductive functions, in which respect the sexes necessarily differ. For variations in structure which are related to these functions, have often proved of value to one sex, and from having arisen at a late period of life, have been transmitted to one sex alone; and such variations, thus preserved and transmitted, have given rise to secondary sexual characters.

In the following chapters, I shall treat of the secondary sexual characters in animals of all classes, and shall endeavour in each case to apply the principles explained in the present chapter. The lowest classes will detain us for a very short time, but the higher animals, especially birds, must be treated at considerable length. It should be borne in mind that for reasons already assigned, I intend to give only a few illustrative instances of the innumerable structures by the aid of which the male finds the female, or, when found, holds her. On the other hand, all structures and instincts by the aid of which the male conquers other males, and by which he allures or excites the female, will be fully discussed, as these are in many ways the most interesting.

Supplement on the proportional numbers of the two sexes in animals belonging to various classes.

As no one, as far as I can discover, has paid attention to the relative numbers of the two sexes throughout the animal kingdom, I will here give such materials as I have been able to collect, although they are extremely imperfect. They consist in only a few instances of actual enumeration, and the numbers are not very large. As the proportions are known with certainty only in mankind, I will first give them as a standard of comparison.

Man.—In England during ten years (from 1857 to 1866) the average number of children born alive yearly was 707,120, in the proportion of 104.5 males to 100 females. But in 1857 the male births throughout England were as 105.2, and in 1865 as 104.0 to 100. Looking to separate districts, in Buckinghamshire (where about 5000 children are annually born) the *mean* proportion of male to female births, during the whole period of the above ten years, was as 102.8 to 100; whilst in N. Wales (where the average annual births are 12,873) it was as high as 106.2 to 100. Taking a still smaller district, viz., Rutlandshire (where the annual births average only 739), in 1864 the male births were as 114.6, and in 1862 as only 97.0 to 100; but even in this small district the average of the 7385 births during the whole ten years, was as 104.5 to 100: that is in the same ratio as throughout England.[48] The proportions are sometimes slightly disturbed by unknown causes; thus Prof. Faye states "that in some districts of Norway there has been during a decennial period a steady deficiency of boys, whilst in others the opposite condition has existed." In France during forty-four years the male to the female births have been as 106.2 to 100; but during this period it has occurred five times in one department, and six times in another, that the female births have exceeded the males. In Russia the average proportion is as high as 108.9, and in Philadelphia in the United States as 110.5 to 100.[49] The

---

[48] 'Twenty-ninth Annual Report of the Registrar-General for 1866.' In this report (p. xii.) a special decennial table is given.

[49] For Norway and Russia, see abstract of Prof. Faye's researches, in 'British and Foreign Medico-Chirurg. Review,' April, 1867, pp. 343, 345. For France, the 'Annuaire pour l'An 1867,' p. 213. For Philadelphia, Dr. Stockton Hough, 'Social Science

average for Europe, deduced by Bickes from about seventy million births, is 106 males to 100 females. On the other hand, with white children born at the Cape of Good Hope, the proportion of males is so low as to fluctuate during successive years between 90 and 99 males for every 100 females. It is a singular fact that with Jews the proportion of male births is decidedly larger than with Christians: thus in Prussia the proportion is as 113, in Breslau as 114, and in Livonia as 120 to 100; the Christian births in these countries being the same as usual, for instance, in Livonia as 104 to 100.[50]

Prof. Faye remarks that "a still greater preponderance of males would be met with, if death struck both sexes in equal proportion in the womb and during birth. But the fact is, that for every 100 still-born females, we have in several countries from 134.6 to 144.9 still-born males. During the first four or five years of life, also, more male children die than females, for example in England, during the first year, 126 boys die for every 100 girls—a proportion which in France is still more unfavourable."[51] Dr. Stockton-Hough accounts for these facts in part by the more frequent defective development of males than of females. We have before seen that the male sex is more variable in structure than the female; and variations in important organs would generally be injurious. But the size of the body, and especially of the head, being greater in male than female infants is another cause: for the males are thus more liable to be injured during parturition. Consequently the still-born males are more numerous; and, as a highly competent judge, Dr. Crichton Browne,[52] believes, male infants often suffer in health for some years after birth. Owing to this excess in the death-rate of male children, both at birth and for some time subsequently, and owing to the exposure of grown men to various dangers, and to their tendency to emigrate, the females in all old-settled countries, where statistical records have been kept,[53] are found to preponderate considerably over the males.

Assoc.' 1874. For the Cape of Good Hope, Quetelet as quoted by Dr. H. H. Zouteveen, in the Dutch Translation of this work (vol. i. p. 417), where much information is given on the proportion of the sexes.

[50] In regard to the Jews, see M. Thury, 'La Loi de Production des Sexes,' 1863, p. 25.

[51] 'British and Foreign Medico-Chirurg. Review,' April, 1867, p. 343. Dr. Stark also remarks ('Tenth Annual Reports of Births, Deaths, &c., in Scotland,' 1867, p. xxviii.) that "These examples may suffice to show that, at almost every stage of life, the males in Scotland have a greater liability to death and a higher death-rate than the females. The fact, however, of this peculiarity being most strongly developed at that infantile period of life when the dress, food, and general treatment of both sexes are alike, seems to prove that the higher male death-rate is an impressed, natural, and constitutional peculiarity due to sex alone."

[52] 'West Riding Lunatic Asylum Reports,' vol. i. 1871, p. 8. Sir J. Simpson has proved that the head of the male infant exceeds that of the female by 3-8ths of an inch in circumference, and by 1-8th in transverse diameter. Quetelet has shown that woman is born smaller than man; see Dr. Duncan, 'Fecundity, Fertility, Sterility,' 1871, p. 382.

[53] With the savage Guaranys of Paraguay, according to the accurate Azara ('Voyages dans l'Amérique merid.' tom. ii. 1809, p. 60, 179), the women are to the men in the proportion of 14 to 13.

It seems at first sight a mysterious fact that in different nations, under different conditions and climates, in Naples, Prussia, Westphalia, Holland, France, England and the United States, the excess of male over female births is less when they are illegitimate than when legitimate.[54] This has been explained by different writers in many different ways, as from the mothers being generally young, from the large proportion of first pregnancies, &c. But we have seen that male infants, from the large size of their heads, suffer more than female infants during parturition; and as the mothers of illegitimate children must be more liable than other women to undergo bad labours, from various causes, such as attempts at concealment by tight lacing, hard work, distress of mind, &c., their male infants would proportionably suffer. And this probably is the most efficient of all the causes of the proportion of males to females born alive being less amongst illegitimate children than amongst the legitimate. With most animals the greater size of the adult male than of the female, is due to the stronger males having conquered the weaker in their struggles for the possession of the females, and no doubt it is owing to this fact that the two sexes of at least some animals differ in size at birth. Thus we have the curious fact that we may attribute the more frequent deaths of male than female infants, especially amongst the illegitimate, at least in part to sexual selection.

It has often been supposed that the relative age of the two parents determine the sex of the offspring; and Prof. Leuckart[55] has advanced what he considers sufficient evidence, with respect to man and certain domesticated animals, that this is one important though not the sole factor in the result. So again the period of impregnation relatively to the state of the female has been thought by some to be the efficient cause; but recent observations discountenance this belief. According to Dr. Stockton-Hough,[56] the season of the year, the poverty or wealth of the parents, residence in the country or in cities, the crossing of foreign immigrants, &c., all influence the proportion of the sexes. With mankind, polygamy has also been supposed to lead to the birth of a greater proportion of female infants; but Dr. J. Campbell[57] carefully attended to this subject in the harems of Siam, and concludes that the proportion of male to female births is the same as from monogamous unions. Hardly any animal has been rendered so highly polygamous as the English race-horse, and we shall immediately see that his male and female offspring are almost exactly equal in number. I will now give the facts which I have collected with respect to the proportional numbers of the sexes of various animals; and will then briefly discuss how far selection has come into play in determining the result.

---

[54] Babbage, 'Edinburgh Journal of Science,' 1829, vol. i. p. 88; also p. 90, on still-born children. On illegitimate children in England, see 'Report of Registrar-General for 1866,' p. xv.

[55] Leuckart, in Wagner 'Handwörterbuch der Phys,' B. iv. 1853, s. 774.

[56] Social Science Assoc. of Philadelphia, 1874.

[57] 'Anthropological Review,' April, 1870, p. cviii.

Horses.—Mr. Tegetmeier has been so kind as to tabulate for me from the 'Racing Calendar' the births of race-horses during a period of twenty-one years, viz., from 1846 to 1867; 1849 being omitted, as no returns were that year published. The total births were 25,560,[58] consisting of 12,763 males and 12,797 females, or in the proportion of 99.7 males to 100 females. As these numbers are tolerably large, and as they are drawn from all parts of England, during several years, we may with much confidence conclude that with the domestic horse, or at least with the race-horse, the two sexes are produced in almost equal numbers. The fluctuations in the proportions during successive years are closely like those which occur with mankind, when a small and thinly-populated area is considered; thus in 1856 the male horses were as 107.1, and in 1867 as only 92.6 to 100 females. In the tabulated returns the proportions vary in cycles, for the males exceeded the females during six successive years; and the females exceeded the males during two periods each of four years; this, however, may be accidental; at least I can detect nothing of the kind with man in the decennial table in the Registrar's Report for 1866.

Dogs.—During a period of twelve years, from 1857 to 1868, the births of a large number of greyhounds, throughout England, were sent to the 'Field' newspaper; and I am again indebted to Mr. Tegetmeier for carefully tabulating the results. The recorded births were 6878, consisting of 3605 males and 3273 females, that is, in the proportion of 110.1 males to 100 females. The greatest fluctuations occurred in 1864, when the proportion was as 95.3 males, and in 1867, as 116.3 males to 100 females. The above average proportion of 110.1 to 100 is probably nearly correct in the case of the greyhound, but whether it would hold with other domesticated breeds is in some degree doubtful. Mr. Cupples has enquired from several great breeders of dogs, and finds that all without exception believe that females are produced in excess; but he suggests that this belief may have arisen from females being less valued, and from the consequent disappointment producing a stronger impression on the mind.

Sheep.—The sexes of sheep are not ascertained by agriculturists until several months after birth, at the period when the males are castrated; so that the following returns do not give the proportions at birth. Moreover, I find that several great breeders in Scotland, who annually raise some thousand sheep, are firmly convinced that a larger proportion of males than of females die during the first year or two. Therefore the proportion of males would be somewhat larger at birth than at the age of castration. This is a remarkable coincidence with what, as we have seen, occurs with mankind, and both cases probably depend on the same cause. I have received returns from four gentlemen in England who have bred Lowland sheep, chiefly Leicesters, during the last ten to sixteen years; they amount altogether to 8965 births, consisting of 4407 males and 4558 females; that is in the proportion of 96.7 males to 100 females. With respect to Cheviot and black-faced sheep bred in Scotland, I have received returns from six breeders, two of them on a large scale, chiefly for the years 1867-1869, but some of the returns extend back to 1862. The total number recorded amounts to 50,685, consisting of 25,071 males and 25,-

---

[58] During eleven years a record was kept of the number of mares which proved barren or prematurely slipped their foals; and it deserves notice, as shewing how infertile these highly-nurtured and rather closely-interbred animals have become, that not far from one-third of the mares failed to produce living foals. Thus during 1866, 809 male colts and 816 female colts were born, and 743 mares failed to produce offspring. During 1867, 836 males and 902 females were born, and 794 mares failed.

614 females, or in the proportion of 97.9 males to 100 females. If we take the English and Scotch returns together, the total number amounts to 59,650, consisting of 29,478 males and 30,172 females, or as 97.7 to 100. So that with sheep at the age of castration the females are certainly in excess of the males, but probably this would not hold good at birth.[59]

Of *Cattle* I have received returns from nine gentlemen of 982 births, too few to be trusted; these consisted of 477 bull-calves and 505 cow-calves; i.e., in the proportion of 94.4 males to 100 females. The Rev. W. D. Fox informs me that in 1867 out of 34 calves born on a farm in Derbyshire only one was a bull. Mr. Harrison Weir has enquired from several breeders of *Pigs,* and most of them estimate the male to the female births as about 7 to 6. This same gentleman has bred *Rabbits* for many years, and has noticed that a far greater number of bucks are produced than does. But estimations are of little value.

Of mammalia in a state of nature I have been able to learn very little. In regard to the common rat, I have received conflicting statements. Mr. R. Elliot, of Laighwood, informs me that a rat-catcher assured him that he had always found the males in great excess, even with the young in the nest. In consequence of this, Mr. Elliot himself subsequently examined some hundred old ones, and found the statement true. Mr. F. Buckland has bred a large number of white rats, and he also believes that the males greatly exceed the females. In regard to Moles, it is said that "the males are much more numerous than the females:"[60] and as the catching of these animals is a special occupation, the statement may perhaps be trusted. Sir A. Smith, in describing an antelope of S. Africa[61] (*Kobus ellipsiprymnus*), remarks, that in the herds of this and other species, the males are few in number compared with the females: the natives believe that they are born in this proportion; others believe that the younger males are expelled from the herds, and Sir A. Smith says, that though he has himself never seen herds consisting of young males alone, others affirm that this does occur. It appears probable that the young when expelled from the herd, would often fall a prey to the many beasts of prey of the country.

BIRDS

With respect to the *Fowl,* I have received only one account, namely, that out of 1001 chickens of a highly-bred stock of Cochins, reared during eight years by Mr. Stretch, 487 proved males and 514 females; i.e., as 94.7 to 100. In regard to domestic pigeons there is good evidence either that the males are produced in excess, or that they live longer; for these birds invariably pair, and single males, as Mr. Tegetmeier informs me, can always be purchased cheaper than females. Usually the two birds reared from the two eggs laid in the same nest are a male and a female; but Mr. Harrison Weir, who has been so large a breeder, says that he has often bred two cocks from the same nest, and seldom two hens; moreover, the hen is generally the weaker of the two, and more liable to perish.

[59] I am much indebted to Mr. Cupples for having procured for me the above returns from Scotland, as well as some of the following returns on cattle. Mr. R. Elliot, of Laighwood, first called my attention to the premature deaths of the males,—a statement subsequently confirmed by Mr. Aitchison and others. To this latter gentleman, and to Mr. Payan, I owe my thanks for large returns as to sheep.

[60] Bell, 'History of British Quadrupeds,' p. 100.

[61] 'Illustrations of the Zoology of S. Africa,' 1849, pl. 29.

With respect to birds in a state of nature, Mr. Gould and others [62] are convinced that the males are generally the more numerous; and as the young males of many species resemble the females, the latter would naturally appear to be the more numerous. Large numbers of pheasants are reared by Mr. Baker of Leadenhall from eggs laid by wild birds, and he informs Mr. Jenner Weir that four or five males to one female are generally produced. An experienced observer remarks,[63] that in Scandinavia the broods of the capercailzie and black-cock contain more males than females; and that with the Dal-ripa (a kind of ptarmigan) more males than females attend the *leks* or places of courtship; but this latter circumstance is accounted for by some observers by a greater number of hen birds being killed by vermin. From various facts given by White of Selborne,[64] it seems clear that the males of the partridge must be in considerable excess in the south of England; and I have been assured that this is the case in Scotland. Mr. Weir on enquiring from the dealers, who receive at certain seasons large numbers of ruffs (*Machetes pugnax*), was told that the males are much the more numerous. This same naturalist has also enquired for me from the birdcatchers, who annually catch an astonishing number of various small species alive for the London market, and he was unhesitatingly answered by an old and trustworthy man, that with the chaffinch the males are in large excess: he thought as high as 2 males to 1 female, or at least as high as 5 to 3.[65] The males of the blackbird, he likewise maintained, were by far the more numerous, whether caught by traps or by netting at night. These statements may apparently be trusted, because this same man said that the sexes are about equal with the lark, the twite (*Linaria montana*), and goldfinch. On the other hand, he is certain that with the common linnet, the females preponderate greatly, but unequally during different years; during some years he has found the females to the males as four to one. It should, however, be borne in mind, that the chief season for catching birds does not begin till September, so that with some species partial migrations may have begun, and the flocks at this period often consist of hens alone. Mr. Salvin paid particular attention to the sexes of the humming-birds in Central America, and is convinced that with most of the species the males are in excess; thus one year he procured 204 specimens belonging to ten species, and these consisted of 166 males and of only 38 females. With two other species the females were in excess: but the proportions apparently vary either during different seasons or in different localities; for on one occasion the males of *Campylopterus hemileucurus* were to the females as 5 to 2, and on another occasion [66] in exactly the reversed ratio. As bearing on this latter point, I may add, that Mr. Powys found in Corfu and Epirus the sexes of the Chaffinch keeping apart, and "the females by far the most numerous;" whilst in Palestine Mr. Tristram found "the male flocks appearing greatly to exceed the female in number." [67] So again with the *Quiscalus major*, Mr. G. Taylor [68]

[62] Brehm ('Illust. Thierleben,' B. iv. s. 990) comes to the same conclusion.

[63] On the authority of L. Lloyd, 'Game Birds of Sweden,' 1867, pp. 12, 132.

[64] 'Nat. Hist. of Selborne,' letter xxix. edit. of 1825, vol. i. p. 139.

[65] Mr. Jenner Weir received similar information, on making enquiries during the following year. To shew the number of living chaffinches caught, I may mention that in 1869 there was a match between two experts, and one man caught in a day 62, and another 40, male chaffinches. The greatest number ever caught by one man in a single day was 70.

[66] 'Ibis,' vol. ii. p. 260, as quoted in Gould's 'Trochilidæ,' 1861, p. 52. For the foregoing proportions, I am indebted to Mr. Salvin for a table of his results.

[67] 'Ibis,' 1860, p. 137; and 1867, p. 369.

[68] 'Ibis,' 1862, p. 187.

says, that in Florida there were "very few females in proportion to the males," whilst in Honduras the proportion was the other way, the species there having the character of a polygamist.

FISH

With Fish the proportional numbers of the sexes can be ascertained only by catching them in the adult or nearly adult state; and there are many difficulties in arriving at any just conclusion.[69] Infertile females might readily be mistaken for males, as Dr. Günther has remarked to me in regard to trout. With some species the males are believed to die soon after fertilising the ova. With many species the males are of much smaller size than the females, so that a large number of males would escape from the same net by which the females were caught. M. Carbonnier,[70] who has especially attended to the natural history of the pike (*Esox lucius*), states that many males, owing to their small size, are devoured by the larger females; and he believes that the males of almost all fish are exposed from this same cause to greater danger than the females. Nevertheless, in the few cases in which the proportional numbers have been actually observed, the males appear to be largely in excess. Thus Mr. R. Buist, the superintendent of the Stormontfield experiments, says that in 1865, out of 70 salmon first landed for the purpose of obtaining the ova, upwards of 60 were males. In 1867 he again "calls attention to the vast disproportion of the males to the females. We had at the outset at least ten males to one female." Afterwards females sufficient for obtaining ova were procured. He adds, "from the great proportion of the males, they are constantly fighting and tearing each other on the spawning-beds."[71] This disproportion, no doubt, can be accounted for in part, but whether wholly is doubtful, by the males ascending the rivers before the females. Mr. F. Buckland remarks in regard to trout, that "it is a curious fact that the males preponderate very largely in number over the females. It *invariably* happens that when the first rush of fish is made to the net, there will be at least seven or eight males to one female found captive. I cannot quite account for this; either the males are more numerous than the females, or the latter seek safety by concealment rather than flight." He then adds, that by carefully searching the banks sufficient females for obtaining ova can be found.[72] Mr. H. Lee informs me that out of 212 trout taken for this purpose in Lord Portsmouth's park, 150 were males and 62 females.

The males of the Cyprinidæ likewise seem to be in excess; but several members of this Family, viz., the carp, tench, bream and minnow, appear regularly to follow the practice, rare in the animal kingdom, of polyandry; for the female whilst spawning is always attended by two males, one on each side, and in the case of the bream by three or four males. This fact is so well known, that it is always recommended to stock a pond with two male tenches to one female, or at least with three males to two females. With the minnow, an excellent observer states, that on the spawning-beds the males are ten times as numerous as the females; when a female comes amongst the males,

[69] Leuckart quotes Bloch (Wagner, 'Handwörterbuch der Phys.,' B. iv. 1853, s. 175), that with fish there are twice as many males as females.
[70] Quoted in the 'Farmer,' March 18, 1869, p. 369.
[71] 'The Stormontfield Piscicultural Experiments,' 1866, p. 23. The 'Field' newspaper, June 29th, 1867.
[72] 'Land and Water,' 1868, p. 41.

"she is immediately pressed closely by a male on each side; and when they have been in that situation for a time, are superseded by other two males."[73]

INSECTS

In this great Class, the Lepidoptera almost alone affords means for judging of the proportional numbers of the sexes; for they have been collected with special care by many good observers, and have been largely bred from the egg or caterpillar state. I had hoped that some breeders of silk-moths might have kept an exact record, but after writing to France and Italy, and consulting various treatises, I cannot find that this has ever been done. The general opinion appears to be that the sexes are nearly equal, but in Italy, as I hear from Professor Canestrini, many breeders are convinced that the females are produced in excess. This same naturalist, however, informs me, that in the two yearly broods of the Ailanthus silk-moth (*Bombyx cynthia*), the males greatly preponderate in the first, whilst in the second the two sexes are nearly equal, or the females rather in excess.

In regard to Butterflies in a state of nature, several observers have been much struck by the apparently enormous preponderance of the males.[74] Thus Mr. Bates,[75] in speaking of several species, about a hundred in number, which inhabit the Upper Amazons, says that the males are much more numerous than the females, even in the proportion of a hundred to one. In North America, Edwards, who had great experience, estimates in the genus Papilio the males to the females as four to one; and Mr. Walsh, who informs me of this statement, says that with *P. turnus* this is certainly the case. In South Africa, Mr. R. Trimen found the males in excess in 19 species; [76] and in one of these, which swarms in open places, he estimated the number of males as fifty to one female. With another species, in which the males are numerous in certain localities, he collected only five females during seven years. In the island of Bourbon, M. Maillard states that the males of one species of Papilio are twenty times as numerous as the females.[77] Mr. Trimen informs me that as far as he has himself seen, or heard from others, it is rare for the females of any butterfly to exceed the males in number; but three South African species perhaps offer an exception. Mr. Wallace [78] states that the females of *Ornithoptera crœsus*, in the Malay archipelago, are more common and more easily caught than the males; but this is a rare butterfly. I may here add, that in Hyperythra, a genus of moths, Guenée says, that from four to five females are sent in collections from India for one male.

When this subject of the proportional numbers of the sexes of insects was brought before the Entomological Society,[79] it was generally admitted that the males of most Lepidoptera, in the adult or imago state, are caught in greater numbers than the females: but this fact was attributed by various observers

[73] Yarrell, 'Hist. British Fishes,' vol. i. 1826, p. 307; on the *Cyprinus carpio*, p. 331; on the *Tinca vulgaris*, p. 331; on the *Abramis brama*, p. 336. See, for the minnow (*Leuciscus phoxinus*), 'Loudon's Mag. of Nat. Hist.' vol. v. 1832, p. 682.

[74] Leuckart quotes Meinecke (Wagner, 'Handwörterbuch der Phys.' B. iv. 1853, s. 775) that the males of Butterflies are three or four times as numerous as the females.

[75] 'The Naturalist on the Amazons,' vol. ii. 1863, p. 228, 347.

[76] Four of these cases are given by Mr. Trimen in his 'Rhopalocera Africæ Australis.'

[77] Quoted by Trimen, 'Transect. Ent. Soc.' vol. v. part iv. 1866, p. 330.

[78] 'Transact. Linn. Soc.' vol. xxv. p. 37.

[79] 'Proc. Entomolog. Soc.' Feb. 17th, 1868.

to the more retiring habits of the females, and to the males emerging earlier from the cocoon. This latter circumstance is well known to occur with most Lepidoptera, as well as with other insects. So that, as M. Personnat remarks, the males of the domesticated *Bombyx Yamamai*, are useless at the beginning of the season, and the females at the end, from the want of mates.[80] I cannot, however, persuade myself that these causes suffice to explain the great excess of males, in the above cases of certain butterflies which are extremely common in their native countries. Mr. Stainton, who has paid very close attention during many years to the smaller moths, informs me that when he collected them in the imago state, he thought that the males were ten times as numerous as the females, but that since he has reared them on a large scale from the caterpillar state, he is convinced that the females are the more numerous. Several entomologists concur in this view. Mr. Doubleday, however, and some others, take an opposite view, and are convinced that they have reared from the eggs and caterpillars a larger proportion of males than of females.

Besides the more active habits of the males, their earlier emergence from the cocoon, and in some cases their frequenting more open stations, other causes may be assigned for an apparent or real difference in the proportional numbers of the sexes of Lepidoptera, when captured in the imago state, and when reared from the egg or caterpillar state. I hear from Professor Canestrini, that it is believed by many breeders in Italy, that the female caterpillar of the silk-moth suffers more from the recent disease than the male; and Dr. Staudinger informs me that in rearing Lepidoptera more females die in the cocoon than males. With many species the female caterpillar is larger than the male, and a collector would naturally choose the finest specimens, and thus unintentionally collect a larger number of females. Three collectors have told me that this was their practice; but Dr. Wallace is sure that most collectors take all the specimens which they can find of the rarer kinds, which alone are worth the trouble of rearing. Birds when surrounded by caterpillars would probably devour the largest; and Professor Canestrini informs me that in Italy some breeders believe, though on insufficient evidence, that in the first broods of the Ailanthus silkmoth, the wasps destroy a larger number of the female than of the male caterpillars. Dr. Wallace further remarks that female caterpillars, from being larger than the males, require more time for their development, and consume more food and moisture: and thus they would be exposed during a longer time to danger from ichneumons, birds, &c., and in times of scarcity would perish in greater numbers. Hence it appears quite possible that in a state of nature, fewer female Lepidoptera may reach maturity than males; and for our special object we are concerned with their relative numbers at maturity, when the sexes are ready to propagate their kind.

The manner in which the males of certain moths congregate in extraordinary numbers round a single female, apparently indicates a great excess of males, though this fact may perhaps be accounted for by the earlier emergence of the males from their cocoons. Mr. Stainton informs me that from twelve to twenty males, may often be seen congregated round a female *Elachista rufocinerea*. It is well known that if a virgin *Lasiocampa quercus* or *Saturnia carpini* be exposed in a cage, vast numbers of males collect round her, and if confined in a room will even come down the chimney to her. Mr Doubleday believes that he has seen from fifty to a hundred males of both

[80] Quoted by Dr. Wallace in 'Proc. Ent. Soc.' 3rd series, vol. v. 1867, p. 487.

these species attracted in the course of a single day by a female in confinement. In the Isle of Wight Mr. Trimen exposed a box in which a female of the Lasiocampa had been confined on the previous day, and five males soon endeavored to gain admittance. In Australia, Mr. Verreaux, having placed the female of a small Bombyx in a box in his pocket, was followed by a crowd of males, so that about 200 entered the house with him.[81]

Mr. Doubleday has called my attention to M. Staudinger's [82] list of Lepidoptera, which gives the prices of the males and females of 300 species or well-marked varieties of butterflies (Rhopalocera). The prices for both sexes of the very common species are of course the same; but in 114 of the rarer species they differ; the males being in all cases, excepting one, the cheaper. On an average of the prices of the 113 species, the price of the male to that of the female is as 100 to 149; and this apparently indicates that inversely the males exceed the females in the same proportion. About 2000 species or varieties of moths (Heterocera) are catalogued, those with wingless females being here excluded on account of the difference in habits between the two sexes: of these 2000 species, 141 differ in price according to sex, the males of 130 being cheaper, and those of only 11 being dearer than the females. The average price of the males of the 130 species, to that of the females, is as 100 to 143. With respect to the butterflies in this priced list, Mr. Doubleday thinks (and no man in England has had more experience), that there is nothing in the habits of the species which can account for the difference in the prices of the two sexes, and that it can be accounted for only by an excess in the number of the males. But I am bound to add that Dr. Staudinger informs me, that he is himself of a different opinion. He thinks that the less active habits of the females and the earlier emergence of the males will account for his collectors securing a larger number of males than of females, and consequently for the lower prices of the former. With respect to specimens reared from the caterpillar-state, Dr. Staudinger believes, as previously stated, that a greater number of females than of males die whilst confined in the cocoons. He adds that with certain species one sex seems to preponderate over the other during certain years.

Of direct observations on the sexes of Lepidoptera, reared either from eggs or caterpillars, I have received only the few following cases:—

So that in these eight lots of cocoons and eggs, males were produced in excess. Taken together the proportion of males is as 122.7 to 100 females. But the numbers are hardly large enough to be trustworthy.

On the whole, from these various sources of evidence, all pointing in the same direction, I infer that with most species of Lepidoptera, the mature males generally exceed the females in number, whatever the proportions may be at their first emergence from the egg.

With reference to the other Orders of insects, I have been able to collect very little reliable information. With the stag-beetle (*Lucanus cervus*) "the males appear to be much more numerous than the females;" but when, as Cornelius remarked during 1867, an unusual number of these beetles appeared in one part of Germany, the females appeared to exceed the males as six to one. With one of the Elateridæ, the males are said to be much more numerous than the females, and "two or three are often found united with one female;"[83]

[81] Blanchard, 'Métamorphoses, Mœurs des Insectes,' 1868, pp. 225–226.
[82] 'Lepidopteren-Doubletten Liste,' Berlin, No. x. 1866.
[83] Günther's 'Record of Zoological Literature,' 1867, p. 260. On the excess of female Lucanus, ibid. p. 250. On the males of Lucanus in England, Westwood, 'Modern Class of Insects,' vol. i. p. 187. On the Siagonium, ibid. p. 172.

	Males.	Females.
The Rev. J. Hellins [84] of Exeter reared, during 1868, imagos of 73 species, which consisted of	153	137
Mr. Albert Jones of Eltham reared, during 1868, imagos of 9 species, which consisted of	159	126
During 1869 he reared imagos from 4 species, consisting of	114	112
Mr. Buckler of Emsworth, Hants, during 1869, reared imagos from 74 species, consisting of	180	169
Dr. Wallace of Colchester reared from one brood of Bombyx cynthia	52	48
Dr. Wallace raised, from cocoons of Bombyx Pernyi sent from China, during 1869	224	123
Dr. Wallace raised, during 1868 and 1869, from two lots of cocoons of Bombyx yama-mai	52	46
Total	934	761

so that here polyandry seems to prevail." With Siagonium (Staphylinidæ), in which the males are furnished with horns, "the females are far more numerous than the opposite sex." Mr. Janson stated at the Entomological Society that the females of the bark-feeding *Tomicus villosus* are so common as to be a plague, whilst the males are so rare as to be hardly known.

It is hardly worth while saying anything about the proportion of the sexes in certain species and even groups of insects, for the males are unknown or very rare, and the females are parthenogenetic, that is, fertile without sexual union; examples of this are afforded by several of the Cynipidæ.[85] In all the gall-making Cynipidæ known to Mr. Walsh, the females are four or five times as numerous as the males; and so it is, as he informs me, with the gall-making Cecidomyiidæ (Diptera). With some common species of Saw-flies (Tenthredinæ) Mr. F. Smith has reared hundreds of specimens from larvæ of all sizes, but has never reared a single male; on the other hand, Curtis says,[86] that with certain species (Athalia), bred by him, the males were to the females as six to one; whilst exactly the reverse occurred with the mature insects of the same species caught in the fields. In the family of Bees, Hermann Müller,[87] collected a large number of specimens of many species, and reared others from the cocoons, and counted the sexes. He found that the males of some species greatly exceeded the females in number; in others the reverse occurred; and in others the two sexes were nearly equal. But as in most cases the males emerge from the cocoons before the females, they are at the commencement of the breeding season practically in excess. Müller also observed that the relative number of the two sexes in some species differed much in different localities. But as H. Müller has himself remarked to me, these re-

[84] This naturalist has been so kind as to send me some results from former years, in which the females seemed to preponderate; but so many of the figures were estimates, that I found it impossible to tabulate them.

[85] Walsh, in 'The American Entomologist,' vol. i. 1869, p. 103. F. Smith, 'Record of Zoological Lit.,' 1867, p. 328.

[86] 'Farm Insects,' pp. 45–46.

[87] 'Anwendung der Darwinschen Lehre Verh. d. n. V. Jahrg. xxiv.'

marks must be received with some caution, as one sex might more easily escape observation than the other. Thus his brother Fritz Müller has noticed in Brazil that the two sexes of the same species of bee sometimes frequent different kinds of flowers. With respect to the Orthoptera, I know hardly anything about the relative number of the sexes: Körte,[88] however, says that out of 500 locusts which he examined, the males were to the females as five to six. With the Neuroptera, Mr. Walsh states that in many, but by no means in all the species of the Odonatous group, there is a great overplus of males: in the genus Hetærina, also, the males are generally at least four times as numerous as the females. In certain species in the genus Gomphus the males are equally in excess, whilst in two other species, the females are twice or thrice as numerous as the males. In some European species of Psocus thousands of females may be collected without a single male, whilst with other species of the same genus both sexes are common.[89] In England, Mr. MacLachlan has captured hundreds of the female *Apatania muliebris*, but has never seen the male; and of *Boreus hyemalis* only four or five males have been seen here.[90] With most of these species (excepting the Tenthredinæ) there is at present no evidence that the females are subject to parthenogenesis; and thus we see how ignorant we are of the causes of the apparent discrepancy in the proportion of the two sexes.

In the other classes of the Articulata I have been able to collect still less information. With spiders, Mr. Blackwall, who has carefully attended to this class during many years, writes to me that the males from their more erratic habits are more commonly seen, and therefore appear more numerous. This is actually the case with a few species; but he mentions several species in six genera,[91] in which the females appear to be much more numerous than the males. The small size of the males in comparison with the females (a peculiarity which is sometimes carried to an extreme degree), and their widely different appearance, may account in some instances for their rarity in collections.[92]

Some of the lower Crustaceans are able to propagate their kind sexually, and this will account for the extreme rarity of the males; thus Von Siebold[93] carefully examined no less than 13,000 specimens of Apus from twenty-one localities, and amongst these he found only 319 males. With some other forms (as Tanais and Cypris), as Fritz Müller informs me, there is reason to believe that the males are much shorter-lived than the females; and this would explain their scarcity, supposing the two sexes to be at first equal in number. On the other hand, Müller has invariably taken far more males than females of the Diastylidæ and of Cypridina on the shores of Brazil: thus with a species in the latter genus, 63 specimens caught the same day included 57 males; but he suggests that this preponderance may be due to some unknown difference in the habits of the two sexes. With one of the higher Brazilian crabs, namely a Gelasimus, Fritz Müller found the males to be more numerous than the fe-

---

[88] 'Die Strich, Zug oder Wanderheuschrecke,' 1828, p. 20.

[89] 'Observations on N. American Neuroptera,' by H. Hagen and B. D. Walsh, 'Proc. Ent. Soc. Philadelphia,' Oct. 1863, pp. 168, 223, 239.

[90] 'Proc. Ent. Soc. London,' Feb. 17, 1868.

[91] Another great authority with respect to this class, Prof. Thorell of Upsala ('On European Spiders,' 1869–70, part i. p. 205), speaks as if female spiders were generally commoner than the males.

[92] See, on this subject, Mr. O. P. Cambridge, as quoted in 'Quarterly Journal of Science,' 1868, page 429.

[93] 'Beit. zur Parthenogenesis,' p. 174.

males. According to the large experience of Mr. C. Spence Bate, the reverse seems to be the case with six common British crabs, the names of which he has given me.

The proportion of the sexes in relation to natural selection.

There is reason to suspect that in some cases man has by selection indirectly influenced his own sex-producing powers. Certain women tend to produce during their whole lives more children of one sex than of the other: and the same holds good of many animals, for instance, cows and horses; thus Mr. Wright of Yeldersley House informs me that one of his Arab mares, though put seven times to different horses, produced seven fillies. Though I have very little evidence on this head, analogy would lead to the belief, that the tendency to produce either sex would be inherited like almost every other peculiarity, for instance, that of producing twins; and concerning the above tendency a good authority, Mr. J. Downing, has communicated to me facts which seem to prove that this does occur in certain families of short-horn cattle. Col. Marshall[94] has recently found on careful examination that the Todas, a hill-tribe of India, consist of 112 males and 84 females of all ages—that is in a ratio of 133.3 males to 100 females. The Todas, who are polyandrous in their marriages, during former times invariably practised female infanticide; but this practice has now been discontinued for a considerable period. Of the children born within late years, the males are more numerous than the females, in the proportion of 124 to 100. Colonel Marshall accounts for this fact in the following ingenious manner. "Let us for the purpose of illustration take three families as representing an average of the entire tribe; say that one mother gives birth to six daughters and no sons; a second mother has six sons only, whilst the third mother has three sons and three daughters. The first mother, following the tribal custom, destroys four daughters and preserves two. The second retains her six sons. The third kills two daughters and keeps one, as also her three sons. We have then from the three families, nine sons and three daughters, with which to continue the breed. But whilst the males belong to families in which the tendency to produce sons is great, the females are of those of a converse inclination. Thus the bias strengthens with each generation, until, as we find, families grow to have habitually more sons than daughters."

That this result would follow from the above form of infanticide seems almost certain; that is if we assume that a sex-producing tendency is inherited. But as the above numbers are so extremely scanty, I have searched for additional evidence, but cannot decide whether what I have found is trustworthy; nevertheless the facts are, perhaps, worth giving. The Maories of New Zealand have long practised infanticide; and Mr. Fenton[95] states that he "has met with instances of women who have destroyed four, six, and even seven children, mostly females. However, the

[94] 'The Todas,' 1873, pp. 100, 111, 194, 196.
[95] 'Aboriginal Inhabitants of New Zealand; Government Report,' 1859, p. 36.

universal testimony of those best qualified to judge, is conclusive that this custom has for many years been almost extinct. Probably the year 1835 may be named as the period of its ceasing to exist." Now amongst the New Zealanders, as with the Todas, male births are considerably in excess. Mr. Fenton remarks (p. 30), "One fact is certain, although the exact period of the commencement of this singular condition of the disproportion of the sexes cannot be demonstratively fixed, it is quite clear that this course of decrease was in full operation during the years 1830 to 1844, when the non-adult population of 1844 was being produced, and has continued with great energy up to the present time." The following statements are taken from Mr. Fenton (p. 26), but as the numbers are not large, and as the census was not accurate, uniform results cannot be expected. It should be borne in mind in this and the following cases, that the normal state of every population is an excess of women, at least in all civilised countries, chiefly owing to the greater mortality of the male sex during youth, and partly to accidents of all kinds later in life. In 1858, the native population of New Zealand was estimated as consisting of 31,667 males and 24,303 females of all ages, that is in the ratio of 130.3 males to 100 females. But during this same year, and in certain limited districts, the numbers were ascertained with much care, and the males of all ages were here 753 and the females 616; that is in the ratio of 122.2 males to 100 females. It is more important for us that during this same year of 1858, the *non-adult* males within the same district were found to be 178, and the *non-adult* females 142, that is in the ratio of 125.3 to 100. It may be added that in 1844, at which period female infanticide had only lately ceased, the *non-adult* males in one district were 281, and the *non-adult* females only 194, that is in the ratio of 144.8 males to 100 females.

In the Sandwich Islands, the males exceed the females in number. Infanticide was formerly practised there to a frightful extent, but was by no means confined to female infants, as is shown by Mr. Ellis,[96] and as I have been informed by Bishop Staley and the Rev. Mr. Coan. Nevertheless, another apparently trustworthy writer, Mr. Jarves,[97] whose observations apply to the whole archipelago, remarks:—"Numbers of women are to be found, who confess to the murder of from three to six or eight children," and he adds, "females from being considered less useful than males were more often destroyed." From what is known to occur in other parts of the world, this statement is probable; but must be received with much caution. The practice of infanticide ceased about the year 1819, when idolatry was abolished and missionaries settled in the Islands. A careful census in 1839 of the adult and taxable men and women in the island of Kauai and in one district of Oahu (Jarves, p. 404), gives 4723 males and 3776 females; that is in the ratio of 125.08 to 100. At the same time the number of males under fourteen years in Kauai and under eight-

---

[96] 'Narrative of a Tour through Hawaii,' 1826, p. 298.
[97] 'History of the Sandwich Islands,' 1843, p. 93.

een in Oahu was 1797, and of females of the same ages 1429; and here we have the ratio of 125.75 males to 100 females.

In a census of all the islands in 1850,[98] the males of all ages amount to 36,272, and the females to 33,128, or as 109.49 to 100. The males under seventeen years amounted to 10,773, and the females under the same age to 9593, or as 112.3 to 100. From the census of 1872, the proportion of males of all ages (including half-castes) to females, is as 125.36 to 100. It must be borne in mind that all these returns for the Sandwich Islands give the proportion of living males to living females, and not of the births; and judging from all civilised countries the proportion of males would have been considerably higher if the numbers had referred to births.[99]

From the several foregoing cases we have some reason to believe that infanticide practised in the manner above explained, tends to make a male-producing race; but I am far from supposing that this practice in the case of man, or some analogous process with other species, has been the sole determining cause of an excess of males. There may be some unknown law leading to this result in decreasing races, which have already become somewhat infertile. Besides the several causes previously alluded to, the greater facility of parturition amongst savages, and the less consequent injury to their male infants, would tend to increase the proportion of live-born males to females. There does not, however, seem to be any necessary connection between savage life and a marked excess of males; that is if we may judge by the character of the scanty offspring of the

[98] This is given in the Rev. H. T. Cheever's 'Life in the Sandwich Islands,' 1851, p. 277.

[99] Dr. Coulter, in describing ('Journal R. Geograph. Soc.,' vol. v. 1835, p. 67) the state of California about the year 1830, says that the natives, reclaimed by the Spanish missionaries, have nearly all perished, or are perishing, although well treated, not driven from their native land, and kept from the use of spirits. He attributes this, in great part, to the undoubted fact that the men greatly exceed the women in number; but he does not know whether this is due to a failure of female offspring, or to more females dying during early youth. The latter alternative, according to all analogy, is very improbable. He adds that "infanticide, properly so called, is not common, though very frequent recourse is had to abortion." If Dr. Coulter is correct about infanticide, this case cannot be advanced in support of Colonel Marshall's view. From the rapid decrease of the reclaimed natives, we may suspect that, as in the cases lately given, their fertility has been diminished from changed habits of life.

I had hoped to gain some light on this subject from the breeding of dogs; inasmuch as in most breeds, with the exception, perhaps, of greyhounds, many more female puppies are destroyed than males, just as with the Toda infants. Mr. Cupples assures me that this is usual with Scotch deerhounds. Unfortunately, I know nothing of the proportion of the sexes in any breed, excepting greyhounds, and there the male births are to the females as 110.1 to 100. Now from enquiries made from many breeders, it seems that the females are in some respects more esteemed, though otherwise troublesome; and it does not appear that the female puppies of the best-bred dogs are systematically destroyed more than the males, though this does sometimes take place to a limited extent. Therefore I am unable to decide whether we can, on the above principles, account for the preponderance of male births in greyhounds. On the other hand, we have seen that with horses, cattle, and sheep, which are too valuable for the young of either sex to be destroyed, if there is any difference, the females are slightly in excess.

lately existing Tasmanians and of the crossed offspring of the Tahitians now inhabiting Norfolk Island.

As the males and females of many animals differ somewhat in habits and are exposed in different degrees to danger, it is probable that in many cases, more of one sex than of the other are habitually destroyed. But as far as I can trace out the complication of causes, an indiscriminate though large destruction of either sex would not tend to modify the sex-producing power of the species. With strictly social animals, such as bees or ants, which produce a vast number of sterile and fertile females in comparison with the males, and to whom this preponderance is of paramount importance, we can see that those communities would flourish best which contained females having a strong inherited tendency to produce more and more females; and in such cases an unequal sex-producing tendency would be ultimately gained through natural selection. With animals living in herds or troops, in which the males come to the front and defend the herd, as with the bisons of North America and certain baboons, it is conceivable that a male-producing tendency might be gained by natural selection; for the individuals of the better defended herds would leave more numerous descendants. In the case of mankind the advantage arising from having a preponderance of men in the tribe is supposed to be one chief cause of the practice of female infanticide.

In no case, as far as we can see, would an inherited tendency to produce both sexes in equal numbers or to produce one sex in excess, be a direct advantage or disadvantage to certain individuals more than to others; for instance, an individual with a tendency to produce more males than females would not succeed better in the battle for life than an individual with an opposite tendency; and therefore a tendency of this kind could not be gained through natural selection. Nevertheless, there are certain animals (for instance, fishes and cirripedes) in which two or more males appear to be necessary for the fertilisation of the female; and the males accordingly largely preponderate, but it is by no means obvious how this male-producing tendency could have been acquired. I formerly thought that when a tendency to produce the two sexes in equal numbers was advantageous to the species, it would follow from natural selection, but I now see that the whole problem is so intricate that it is safer to leave its solution for the future.

CHAPTER IX

These characters absent in the lowest classes—Brilliant colours—Mollusca—Annelids —Crustacea, secondary sexual characters strongly developed; dimorphism; colour; characters not acquired before maturity—Spiders, sexual colours of; stridulation of the males—Myriapoda.

WITH animals belonging to the lower classes, the two sexes are not rarely united in the same individual, and therefore secondary sexual characters cannot be developed. In many cases where the sexes are separate, both are permanently attached to some support, and the one cannot search or struggle for the other. Moreover it is almost certain that these animals have too imperfect senses and much too low mental powers, to appreciate each other's beauty or other attractions, or to feel rivalry.

Hence in these classes or sub-kingdoms, such as the Protozoa, Cœlenterata, Echinodermata, Scolecida, secondary sexual characters, of the kind which we have to consider. do not occur: and this fact agrees with the belief that such characters in the higher classes have been acquired through sexual selection, which depends on the will, desire, and choice of either sex. Nevertheless some few apparent exceptions occur; thus, as I hear from Dr. Baird, the males of certain Entozoa, or internal parasitic worms, differ slightly in colour from the females; but we have no reason to suppose that such differences have been augmented through sexual selection. Contrivances by which the male holds the female, and which are indispensable for the propagation of the species, are independent of sexual selection, and have been acquired through ordinary selection.

Many of the lower animals, whether hermaphrodites or with separate sexes, are ornamented with the most brilliant tints, or are shaded and striped in an elegant manner; for instance, many corals and sea-anemones (Actiniæ), some jelly-fish (Medusæ, Porpita, &c.), some Planariæ, many star-fishes, Echini, Ascidians, &c.; but we may conclude from the reasons already indicated, namely, the union of the two sexes in some of these animals, the permanently affixed condition of others, and the low mental powers of all, that such colours do not serve as a sexual attraction, and have not been acquired through sexual selection. It should be borne in mind that in no case have we sufficient evidence that colours have been thus acquired, except where one sex is much more brilliantly

or conspicuously coloured than the other, and where there is no difference
in habits between the sexes sufficient to account for their different colours. But the evidence is rendered as complete as it can ever be, only
when the more ornamented individuals, almost always the males, voluntarily display their attractions before the other sex; for we cannot believe
that such display is useless, and if it be advantageous, sexual selection
will almost inevitably follow. We may, however, extend this conclusion
to both sexes, when coloured alike, if their colours are plainly analogous
to those of one sex alone in certain other species of the same group.

How, then, are we to account for the beautiful or even gorgeous colours
of many animals in the lowest classes? It appears doubtful whether such
colours often serve as a protection; but that we may easily err on this
head, will be admitted by every one who reads Mr. Wallace's excellent
essay on this subject. It would not, for instance, at first occur to any one
that the transparency of the Medusæ, or jelly-fish, is of the highest service to them as a protection; but when we are reminded by Häckel that
not only the medusæ, but many floating mollusca, crustaceans, and even
small oceanic fishes partake of this same glass-like appearance, often accompanied by prismatic colours, we can hardly doubt that they thus escape the notice of pelagis birds and other enemies. M. Giard is also convinced[1] that the bright tints of certain sponges and ascidians serve as a
protection. Conspicuous colours are likewise beneficial to many animals
as a warning to their would-be devourers that they are distasteful, or that
they possess some special means of defence; but this subject will be discussed more conveniently hereafter.

We can, in our ignorance of most of the lowest animals, only say that
their bright tints result either from the chemical nature or the minute
structure of their tissues, independently of any benefit thus derived.
Hardly any colour is finer than that of arterial blood; but there is no reason to suppose that the colour of the blood is in itself any advantage;
and though it adds to the beauty of the maiden's cheek, no one will pretend that it has been acquired for this purpose. So again with many animals, especially the lower ones, the bile is richly coloured; thus, as I am
informed by Mr. Hancock, the extreme beauty of the Eolidæ (naked sea-
slugs) is chiefly due to the biliary glands being seen through the translucent integuments—this beauty being probably of no service to these animals. The tints of the decaying leaves in an American forest are described
by every one as gorgeous; yet no one supposes that these tints are of the
least advantage to the trees. Bearing in mind how many substances closely analogous to natural organic compounds have been recently formed by
chemists, and which exhibit the most splendid colours, it would have been
a strange fact if substances similarly coloured had not often originated,
independently of any useful end thus gained, in the complex laboratory
of living organisms.

[1] 'Archives de Zoolog. Expér.,' Oct. 1872, p. 563.

The sub-kingdom of the Mollusca.—Throughout this great division of the animal kingdom, as far as I can discover, secondary sexual characters, such as we are here considering, never occur. Nor could they be expected in the three lowest classes, namely, in the Ascidians, Polyzoa, and Brachiopods (constituting the Molluscoida of some authors), for most of these animals are permanently affixed to a support or have their sexes united in the same individual. In the Lamellibranchiata, or bivalve shells, hermaphroditism is not rare. In the next higher classes of the Gasteropoda, or univalve shells, the sexes are either united or separate. But in the latter case the males never possess special organs for finding, securing, or charming the females, or for fighting with other males. As I am informed by Mr. Gwyn Jeffreys, the sole external difference between the sexes consists in the shell sometimes differing a little in form; for instance, the shell of the male periwinkle (*Littorina littorea*) is narrower and has a more elongated spire than that of the female. But differences of this nature, it may be presumed, are directly connected with the act of reproduction, or with the development of the ova.

The Gasteropoda, though capable of locomotion and furnished with imperfect eyes, do not appear to be endowed with sufficient mental powers for the members of the same sex to struggle together in rivalry, and thus to acquire secondary sexual characters. Nevertheless with the pulmoniferous gasteropods, or land-snails, the pairing is preceded by courtship; for these animals, though hermaphrodites, are compelled by their structure to pair together. Agassiz remarks,[2] "Quiconque a eu l'occasion d'observer les amours des limaçons, ne saurait mettre en doute la séduction déployée dans les mouvements et les allures qui préparent et accomplissent le double embrassement de ces hermaphrodites." These animals appear also susceptible of some degree of permanent attachment: an accurate observer, Mr. Lonsdale, informs me that he placed a pair of landsnails (*Helix pomatia*), one of which was weakly, into a small and ill-provided garden. After a short time the strong and healthy individual disappeared, and was traced by its track of slime over a wall into an adjoining well-stocked garden. Mr. Lonsdale concluded that it had deserted its sickly mate; but after an absence of twenty-four hours it returned, and apparently communicated the result of its successful exploration, for both then started along the same track and disappeared over the wall.

Even in the highest class of the Mollusca, the Cephalopoda or cuttlefishes, in which the sexes are separate, secondary sexual characters of the present kind do not, as far as I can discover, occur. This is a surprising circumstance, as these animals possess highly-developed sense-organs and have considerable mental powers, as will be admitted by every one who has watched their artful endeavours to escape from an enemy.[3] Certain Cephalopoda, however, are characterised by one extraordinary sexual character, namely that the male element collects within one of the arms

---

[2] 'De l'Espèce et de la Class.' &c., 1869, p. 106.

[3] See, for instance, the account which I have given in my 'Journal of Researches,' 1845, p. 7.

or tentacles, which is then cast off, and clinging by its sucking-discs to the female, lives for a time an independent life. So completely does the cast-off arm resemble a separate animal, that it was described by Cuvier as a parasitic worm under the name of Hectocotyle. But this marvellous structure may be classed as a primary rather than as a secondary sexual character.

Although with the Mollusca sexual selection does not seem to have come into play; yet many univalve and bivalve shells, such as volutes, cones, scallops, &c., are beautifully coloured and shaped. The colours do not appear in most cases to be of any use as a protection; they are probably the direct result, as in the lowest classes, of the nature of the tissues; the patterns and the sculpture of the shell depending on its manner of growth. The amount of light seems to be influential to a certain extent; for although, as repeatedly stated by Mr. Gwyn Jeffreys, the shells of some species living at a profound depth are brightly coloured, yet we generally see the lower surfaces, as well as the parts covered by the mantle, less highly-coloured than the upper and exposed surfaces.[4] In some cases, as with shells living amongst corals or brightly-tinted sea-weeds, the bright colours may serve as a protection.[5] But that many of the nudibranch mollusca, or sea-slugs, are as beautifully coloured as any shells, may be seen in Messrs. Alder and Hancock's magnificent work; and from information kindly given me by Mr. Hancock, it seems extremely doubtful whether these colours usually serve as a protection. With some species this may be the case, as with one kind which lives on the green leaves of algæ, and is itself bright-green. But many brightly-coloured, white, or otherwise conspicuous species, do not seek concealment; whilst again some equally conspicuous species, as well as other dull-coloured kinds, live under stones and in dark recesses. So that with these nudibranch molluscs, colour apparently does not stand in any close relation to the nature of the places which they inhabit.

These naked sea-slugs are hermaphrodites, yet they pair together, as do land-snails, many of which have extremely pretty shells. It is conceivable that two hermaphrodites, attracted by each other's greater beauty, might unite and leave offspring which would inherit their parents' greater beauty. But with such lowly-organised creatures this is extremely improbable. Nor is it at all obvious how the offspring from the more beautiful pairs of hermaphrodites would have any advantage over the offspring of the less beautiful, so as to increase in number, unless indeed vigour and beauty generally coincided. We have not here the case of a number of males becoming mature before the females, with the more beautiful males selected by the more vigorous females. If, indeed, brilliant colours were

[4] I have given ('Geolog. Observations on Volcanic Islands,' 1844, p. 53) a curious instance of the influence of light on the colours of a frondescent incrustation, deposited by the surf on the coast-rocks of Ascension, and formed by the solution of triturated sea-shells.

[5] Dr. Morse has lately discussed this subject in his paper on the Adaptive Coloration of Mollusca, 'Proc. Boston Soc. of Nat. Hist.' vol. xiv., April, 1871.

beneficial to a hermaphrodite animal in relation to its general habits of life, the more brightly-tinted individuals would succeed best and would increase in number; but this would be a case of natural and not of sexual selection.

Sub-kingdom of the Vermes; Class, *Annelida (or Sea-worms).*—In this class, although the sexes, when separate, sometimes differ from each other in characters of such importance that they have been placed under distinct genera or even families, yet the differences do not seem of the kind which can be safely attributed to sexual selection. These animals are often beautifully coloured, but as the sexes do not differ in this respect, we are but little concerned with them. Even the Nemertians, though so lowly organised, "vie in beauty and variety of colouring with any other group in the invertebrate series;" yet Dr. McIntosh[6] cannot discover that these colours are of any service. The sedentary annelids become duller-coloured, according to M. Quatrefages,[7] after the period of reproduction; and this I presume may be attributed to their less vigorous condition at that time. All these worm-like animals apparently stand too low in the scale for the individuals of either sex to exert any choice in selecting a partner, or for the individuals of the same sex to struggle together in rivalry.

Sub-kingdom of the Arthropoda; Class, *Crustacea.*—In this great class we first meet with undoubted secondary sexual characters, often developed in a remarkable manner. Unfortunately the habits of crustaceans are very imperfectly known, and we cannot explain the uses of many structures peculiar to one sex. With the lower parasitic species the males are of small size, and they alone are furnished with perfect swimming-legs, antennæ and sense-organs; the females being destitute of these organs, with their bodies often consisting of a mere distorted mass. But these extraordinary differences between the two sexes are no doubt related to their widely different habits of life, and consequently do not concern us. In various crustaceans, belonging to distinct families, the anterior antennæ are furnished with peculiar thread-like bodies, which are believed to act as smelling-organs, and these are much more numerous in the males than in the females. As the males, without any unusual development of their olfactory organs, would almost certainly be able sooner or later to find the females, the increased number of the smelling-threads has probably been acquired through sexual selection, by the better provided males having been the more successful in finding partners and in producing offspring. Fritz Müller has described a remarkable dimorphic species of Tanais, in which the male is represented by two distinct forms, which never graduate into each other. In the one form the male is furnished with more numerous smelling-threads, and in the other form with

---

[6] See his beautiful monograph on 'British Annelids,' part i. 1873, p. 3.

[7] See M. Perrier, 'l'Origine de l'Homme d'après Darwin,' 'Revue Scientifique,' Feb. 1873, p. 866.

more powerful and more elongated chelæ or pincers, which serve to hold the female. Fritz Müller suggests that these differences between the two male forms of the same species may have originated in certain individuals having varied in the number of the smelling-threads, whilst other individuals varied in the shape and size of their chelæ; so that of the former, those which were best able to find the female, and of the latter, those which were best able to hold her, have left the greatest number of progeny to inherit their respective advantages.[8]

In some of the lower crustaceans, the right anterior antenna of the male differs greatly in structure from the left, the latter resembling in its simple tapering joints the antennæ of the female. In the male the modified antenna is either swollen in the middle or angularly bent, or converted (fig. 4) into an elegant, and sometimes wonderfully complex, prehensile organ.[9] It serves, as I hear from Sir J. Lubbock, to hold the female, and for this same purpose one of the two posterior legs (b) on the same side of the body is converted into a forceps. In another family the inferior or posterior antennæ are "curiously zigzagged" in the males alone.

In the higher crustaceans the anterior legs are developed into chelæ or pincers; and these are generally larger in the male than in the female,— so much so that the market value of the male edible crab (*Cancer pagurus*), according to Mr. C. Spence Bate, is five times as great as that of the female. In many species the chelæ are of unequal size on the opposite side of the body, the right-hand one being, as I am informed by Mr. Bate, generally, though not invariably, the largest. This inequality is also often much greater in the male than in the female. The two chelæ of the male often differ in structure (figs. 5, 6, and 7), the smaller one resembling that of the female. What advantage is gained by their inequality in size on the opposite sides of the body, and by the inequality being much greater in the male than in the female; and why, when they are of equal size, both are often much larger in the male than in the female, is not known. As I hear from Mr. Bate, the chelæ are sometimes

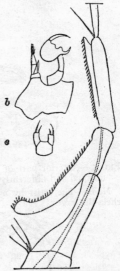

Fig. 4.—Labidocera Darwinii (from Lubbock).

a. Part of right anterior antenna of male, forming a prehensile organ.

b. Posterior pair of thoracic legs of male.

c. Ditto of female.

---

[8] 'Facts and Arguments for Darwin,' English translat. 1869, p. 20. See the previous discussion on the olfactory threads. Sars has described a somewhat analogous case (as quoted in 'Nature,' 1870, p. 455) in a Norwegian crustacean, the *Pontoporeia affinis*.

[9] See Sir J. Lubbock in 'Annals and Mag. of Nat. Hist.' vol. xi. 1853, pl. i. and x.; and vol. xii. (1853) pl. vii. See also Lubbock in 'Transact. Ent. Soc.' vol. iv. new series, 1856–1858, p. 8. With respect to the zigzagged antennæ mentioned below, see Fritz Müller, 'Facts and Arguments for Darwin,' 1869, p. 40, foot-note.

of such length and size that they cannot possibly be used for carrying food to the mouth. In the males of certain fresh-water prawns (Palæmon) the right leg is actually longer than the whole body.[10] The great size of the one leg with its chelæ may aid the male in fighting with his rivals; but this will not account for their inequality in the female on the opposite sides of the body. In Gelasimus, according to a statement quo-

FIG. 5.—Anterior part of body of Callianassa (from Milne-Edwards), showing the unequal and differently-constructed right and left-hand chelæ of the male.

N. B.—The artist by mistake has reversed the drawing and made the left-hand chela the largest.

FIG. 6.   FIG. 7.

FIG. 6.—Second leg of male Orchestia Tucuratinga (from Fritz Müller).
FIG. 7.—Ditto of female.

ted by Milne-Edwards,[11] the male and the female live in the same burrow, and this shews that they pair; the male closes the mouth of the burrow with one of its chelæ, which is enormously developed; so that here it indirectly serves as a means of defence. Their main use, however, is probably to seize and to secure the female, and this in some instances, as with Gammarus, is known to be the case. The male of the hermit or soldier crab (*Pagurus*) for weeks together, carries about the shell in-

[10] See a paper by Mr. C. Spence Bate, with figures, in 'Proc. Zoolog. Soc.,' 1868, p. 363; and on the nomenclature of the genus, ibid. p. 585. I am greatly indebted to Mr. Spence Bate for nearly all the above statements with respect to the chelæ of the higher crustaceans.

[11] 'Hist. Nat. des Crust.' tom. ii. 1837, p. 50.

habited by the female.[12] The sexes, however, of the common shore-crab
(*Carcinus mœnas*), as Mr. Bate informs me, unite directly after the female has moulted her hard shell, when she is so soft that she would be
injured if seized by the strong pincers of the male; but as she is caught
and carried about by the male before moulting, she could then be seized
with impunity.

Fritz Müller states that certain species of Melita are distinguished
from all other amphipods by the females having "the coxal lamellæ of the
penultimate pair of feet produced into hook-like processes, of which the
males lay hold with the hands of the first pair." The development of these
hook-like processes has probably followed from those females which were
the most securely held during the act of reproduction, having left the
largest number of offspring. Another Brazilian amphipod (*Orchestia
Darwinii,* fig. 8) presents a case of dimorphism, like that of Tanais; for
there are two male forms, which differ in the structure of their chelæ.[13]
As either chela would certainly suffice to hold the female,—for both are
now used for this purpose,—the two male forms probably originated by
some having varied in one manner and some in another; both forms having derived certain special, but nearly equal advantages, from their differently shaped organs.

It is not known that male crustaceans fight together for the possession
of the females, but it is probably the case; for with most animals when
the male is larger than the female, he seems to owe his greater size to his
ancestors having fought with other males during many generations. In
most of the orders, especially in the highest or the Brachyura, the male is
larger than the female; the parasitic genera, however, in which the sexes
follow different habits of life, and most of the Entomostraca must be excepted. The chelæ of many crustaceans are weapons well adapted for
fighting. Thus when a Devil-crab (*Portunus puber*) was seen by a son of
Mr. Bate fighting with a *Carcinus mœnas,* the latter was soon thrown on
its back, and had every limb torn from its body. When several males of a
Brazilian Gelasimus, a species furnished with immense pincers, were
placed together in a glass vessel by Fritz Müller, they mutilated and
killed one another. Mr. Bate put a large male *Carcinus mœnas* into a pan
of water, inhabited by a female which was paired with a smaller male;
but the latter was soon dispossessed. Mr. Bate adds, "if they fought, the
victory was a bloodless one, for I saw no wounds." This same naturalist
separated a male sand-skipper (so common on our sea-shores), *Gammarus marinus,* from its female, both of whom were imprisoned in the same
vessel with many individuals of the same species. The female, when thus
divorced, soon joined the others. After a time the male was put again into
the same vessel; and he then, after swimming about for a time, dashed into the crowd, and without any fighting at once took away his wife. This
fact shews that in the Amphipoda, an order low in the scale, the males
and females recognise each other, and are mutually attached.

[12] Mr. C. Spence Bate, 'Brit. Assoc., Fourth Report on the Fauna of S. Devon.'
[13] Fritz Müller, 'Facts and Arguments for Darwin,' 1869, pp. 25-28.

The mental powers of the Crustacea are probably higher than at first sight appears probable. Any one who tries to catch one of the shore-crabs, so common on tropical coasts, will perceive how wary and alert they are. There is a large crab (*Birgus latro*), found on coral islands, which makes a thick bed of the picked fibres of the cocoa-nut, at the bottom of a deep

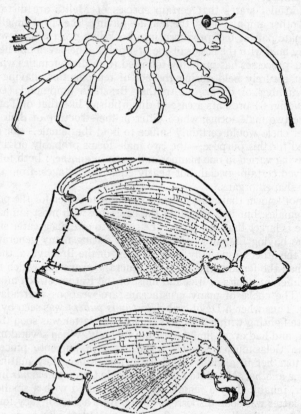

FIG. 8.—Orchestia Darwinii (from Fritz Müller), showing the differently-constructed chelæ of the two male forms.

burrow. It feeds on the fallen fruit of this tree by tearing off the husk, fibre by fibre; and it always begins at that end where the three eye-like depressions are situated. It then breaks through one of these eyes by hammering with its heavy front pincers, and turning round, extracts the albuminous core with its narrow posterior pincers. But these actions are probably instinctive, so that they would be performed as well by a young animal as by an old one. The following case, however, can hardly be so considered: a trustworthy naturalist, Mr. Gardner,[14] whilst watching a shore-crab (Gelasimus) making its burrow, threw some shells towards the hole. One rolled in, and three other shells remained within a few inches of the mouth. In about five minutes the crab brought out the shell which had fallen in, and carried it away to a distance of a foot; it then saw the three other shells lying near, and evidently thinking that they might likewise roll in, carried them to the spot where it had laid the first. It would, I think, be difficult to distinguish this act from one performed by man by the aid of reason.

Mr. Bate does not know of any well-marked case of difference of colour in the two sexes of our British crustaceans, in which respect the sexes of the higher animals so often differ. In some cases, however, the males and females differ slightly in tint, but Mr. Bate thinks not more than may be accounted for by their different habits of life, such as by the male wandering more about, and being thus more exposed to the light. Dr. Power tried to distinguish by colour the sexes of the several species which inhabit Mauritius, but failed, except with one species of Squilla, probably *S. stylifera,* the male of which is described as being "of a beautiful bluish-green," with some of the appendages cherry-red, whilst the female is clouded with brown and grey, "with the red about her much less vivid than in the male."[15] In this case, we may suspect the agency of sexual selection. From M. Bert's observations on Daphnia, when placed in a vessel illuminated by a prism, we have reason to believe that even the lowest crustaceans can distinguish colours. With Saphirina (an oceanic genus of Entomostraca), the males are furnished with minute shields or cell-like bodies, which exhibit beautiful changing colours; these are absent in the females, and in both sexes of one species.[16] It would, however, be extremely rash to conclude that these curious organs serve to attract the females. I am informed by Fritz Müller, that in the female of a Brazilian species of Gelasimus, the whole body is of a nearly uniform greyish-brown. In the male the posterior part of the cephalo-thorax is pure white, with the anterior part of a rich green, shading into dark brown; and it is remarkable that these colours are liable to change in the course of a few minutes—the white becoming dirty grey or even black, the green "losing much of its brilliancy." It deserves especial notice that the males do not acquire their bright colours until they become mature. They appear to be much more numerous than the females; they differ also in the larger size of their chelæ. In some species of the genus, probably in all, the sexes pair and inhabit the same burrow. They are also, as we have seen, highly intelligent animals. From these various considerations it seems probable that the male in this species has become gaily ornamented in order to attract or excite the female.

[14] 'Travels in the Interior of Brazil,' 1846, p. 111. I have given, in my 'Journal of Researches,' p. 463, an account of the habits of the Birgus.
[15] Mr. Ch. Fraser, in 'Proc. Zoolog. Soc.' 1869, p. 3. I am indebted to Mr. Bate for Dr. Power's statement.
[16] Claus, 'Die freilebenden Copepoden,' 1863, s. 35.

It has just been stated that the male Gelasimus does not acquire his conspicuous colours until mature and nearly ready to breed. This seems a general rule in the whole class in respect to the many remarkable structural differences between the sexes. We shall hereafter find the same law prevailing throughout the great sub-kingdom of the Vertebrata; and in all cases it is eminently distinctive of characters which have been acquired through sexual selection. Fritz Müller[17] gives some striking instances of this law; thus the male sand-hopper (Orchestia) does not, until nearly full grown, acquire his large claspers, which are very differently constructed from those of the female; whilst young, his claspers resemble those of the female.

Class, *Arachnida* (Spiders).—The sexes do not generally differ much in colour, but the males are often darker than the females, as may be seen in Mr. Blackwall's magnificent work.[18] In some species, however, the difference is conspicuous: thus the female of *Sparassus smaragdulus* is dullish green, whilst the adult male has the abdomen of a fine yellow, with three longitudinal stripes of rich red. In certain species of Thomisus the sexes closely resemble each other, in others they differ much; and analogous cases occur in many other genera. It is often difficult to say which of the two sexes departs most from the ordinary coloration of the genus to which the species belong; but Mr. Blackwall thinks that, as a general rule, it is the male; and Canestrini[19] remarks that in certain genera the males can be specifically distinguished with ease, but the females with great difficulty. I am informed by Mr. Blackwall that the sexes whilst young usually resemble each other; and both often undergo great changes in colour during their successive moults, before arriving at maturity. In other cases the male alone appears to change colour. Thus the male of the above bright-coloured Sparassus at first resembles the female, and acquires his peculiar tints only when nearly adult. Spiders are possessed of acute senses, and exhibit much intelligence; as is well known, the females often shew the strongest affection for their eggs, which they carry about enveloped in a silken web. The males search eagerly for the females, and have been seen by Canestrini and others to fight for possession of them. This same author says that the union of the two sexes has been observed in about twenty species; and he asserts positively that the female rejects some of the males who court her, threatens them with open mandibles, and at last after long hesitation accepts the chosen one. From these several considerations, we may admit with some confidence that the well-marked differences in colour between the sexes of certain species are the results of sexual selection; though we have not here the best kind of evidence,—the display by the male of his ornaments. From the extreme va-

---

[17] 'Facts and Arguments,' &c., p. 79.

[18] 'A History of the Spiders of Great Britain,' 1861-64. For the following facts, see pp. 77, 88, 102.

[19] This author has recently published a valuable essay on the 'Caratteri sessuali secondarii degli Arachnidi,' in the 'Atti della Soc. Veneto-Trentina di Sc. Nat. Padova,' vol. i. Fasc. 3, 1873.

riability of colour in the male of some species, for instance of *Theridion lineatum*, it would appear that these sexual characters of the males have not as yet become well fixed. Canestrini draws the same conclusion from the fact that the males of certain species present two forms, differing from each other in the size and length of their jaws; and this reminds us of the above cases of dimorphic crustaceans.

The male is generally much smaller than the female, sometimes to an extraordinary degree,[20] and he is forced to be extremely cautious in making his advances, as the female often carries her coyness to a dangerous pitch. De Greer saw a male that "in the midst of his preparatory caresses was seized by the object of his attentions, enveloped by her in a web and then devoured, a sight which, as he adds, filled him with horror and indignation."[21] The Rev. O. P. Cambridge[22] accounts in the following manner for the extreme smallness of the male in the genus Nephila. "M. Vinson gives a graphic account of the agile way in which the diminutive male escapes from the ferocity of the female, by gliding about and playing hide and seek over her body and along her gigantic limbs: in such a pursuit it is evident that the chances of escape would be in favour of the smallest males, whilst the larger ones would fall early victims; thus gradually a diminutive race of males would be selected, until at last they would dwindle to the smallest possible size compatible with the exercise of their generative functions,—in fact probably to the size we now see them, i. e., so small as to be a sort of parasite upon the female, and either beneath her notice, or too agile and too small for her to catch without great difficulty."

Westring has made the interesting discovery that the males of several species of Theridion[23] have the power of making a stridulating sound, whilst the females are mute. The apparatus consists of a serrated ridge at the base of the abdomen, against which the hard hinder part of the thorax is rubbed; and of this structure not a trace can be detected in the females. It deserves notice that several writers, including the well-known arachnologist Walckenaer, have declared that spiders are attracted by music.[24] From the analogy of the Orthoptera and Homoptera, to be described in the next chapter, we may feel almost sure that the stridulation serves, as Westring also believes, to call or to excite the female; and this

[20] Aug. Vinson ('Aranéides des Iles de la Réunion,' pl. vi. figs. 1 and 2) gives a good instance of the small size of the male in *Epeira nigra*. In this species, as I may add, the male is testaceous and the female black with legs banded with red. Other even more striking cases of inequality in size between the sexes have been recorded ('Quarterly Journal of Science,' 1868, July, p. 429); but I have not seen the original accounts.

[21] Kirby and Spence, 'Introduction to Entomology,' vol. i. 1818, p. 280.

[22] 'Proc. Zoolog. Soc.' 1871, p. 621.

[23] *Theridion* (*Asagena*, Sund.) *serratipes, 4-punctatum et guttatum;* see Westring, in Kroyer, 'Naturhist. Tidskrift,' vol. iv. 1842-1843, p. 349; and vol. ii. 1846-1849, p. 342. See, also, for other species, 'Araneæ Suecicæ,' p. 184.

[24] Dr. H. H. van Zouteveen, in his Dutch translation of this work (vol. i. p. 444) has collected several cases.

is the first case known to me in the ascending scale of the animal kingdom of sounds emitted for this purpose.[25]

Class, *Myriapoda*.—In neither of the two orders in this class, the millipedes and centipedes, can I find any well-marked instances of such sexual differences as more particularly concern us. In *Glomeris limbata*, however, and perhaps in some few other species, the males differ slightly in colour from the females; but this Glomeris is a highly variable species. In the males of the Diplopoda, the legs belonging either to one of the anterior or of the posterior segments of the body are modified into prehensile hooks which serve to secure the female. In some species of Iulus the tarsi of the male are furnished with membraneous suckers for the same purpose. As we shall see when we treat of Insects, it is a much more unusual circumstance, that it is the female in Lithobius, which is furnished with prehensile appendages at the extremity of her body for holding the male.[26]

[25] Hilgendorf, however, has lately called attention to an analogous structure in some of the higher crustaceans, which seems adapted to produce sound; see 'Zoological Record,' 1869, page 603.

[26] Walckenaer et P. Gervais, 'Hist. Nat. des Insectes: Apteres,' tom. iv. 1847, pp. 17, 19, 68

CHAPTER X

SECONDARY SEXUAL CHARACTERS OF INSECTS

Diversified structures possessed by the males for seizing the females—Differences between the sexes, of which the meaning is not understood—Difference in size between the sexes—Thysanura—Diptera—Hemiptera—Homoptera, musical powers possessed by the males alone—Orthoptera, musical instruments of the males, much diversified in structure; pugnacity; colours—Neuroptera, sexual differences in colour—Hymenoptera, pugnacity and colours—Coleoptera, colours; furnished with great horns, apparently as a . ornament; battles; stridulating organs generally common to both sexes.

IN the immense class of insects the sexes sometimes differ in their loco-motive-organs, and often in their sense-organs, as in the pectinated and beautifully plumose antennæ of the males of many species. In Chloëon, one of the Ephemeræ, the male has great pillared eyes, of which the female is entirely destitute.[1] The ocelli are absent in the females of certain insects, as in the Multillidæ; and here the females are likewise wingless. But we are chiefly concerned with structures by which one male is enabled to conquer another, either in battle or courtship, through his strength, pugnacity, ornaments, or music. The innumerable contrivances, therefore, by which the male is able to seize the female, may be briefly passed over. Besides the complex structures at the apex of the abdomen, which ought perhaps to be ranked as primary organs,[2] "it is astonishing," as Mr. B. D. Walsh[3] has remarked, "how many different organs are worked in by nature for the seemingly insignificant object of enabling the male to grasp the female firmly." The mandibles or jaws are sometimes used for this purpose; thus the male *Corydalis cornutus* (a neuropterous insect in some degree allied to the Dragon flies, &c.) has immense curved jaws, many

---

[1] Sir J. Lubbock, 'Transact. Linnean Soc.' vol. xxv. 1866, p. 484. With respect to the Mutillidæ see Westwood, 'Modern Class. of Insects,' vol. ii. p. 213.

[2] These organs in the male often differ in closely-allied species, and afford excellent specific characters. But their importance, from a functional point of view, as Mr. R. MacLachlan has remarked to me, has probably been overrated. It has been suggested, that slight differences in these organs would suffice to prevent the intercrossing of well-marked varieties or incipient species, and would thus aid in their development. That this can hardly be the case, we may infer from the many recorded cases (see, for instance, Bronn, 'Geschichte der Natur,' B. ii. 1843, s. 164; and Westwood, 'Transact. Ent. Soc.' vol. iii. 1842, p. 195) of distinct species having been observed in union. Mr. MacLachlan informs me (vide 'Stett. Ent. Zeitung,' 1867, s. 155) that when several species of Phryganidæ, which present strongly-pronounced differences of this kind, were confined together by Dr. Aug. Meyer, *they coupled,* and one pair produced fertile ova.

[3] 'The Practical Entomologist,' Philadelphia, vol. ii. May, 1867, p. 88.

times longer than those of the female; and they are smooth instead of being toothed, so that he is thus enabled to seize her without injury.[4] One
of the stag-beetles of North America (*Lucanus elaphus*) uses his jaws,
which are much larger than those of the female, for the same purpose, but
probably likewise for fighting. In one of the sand-wasps (*Ammophila*)
the jaws in the two sexes are closely alike, but are used for widely different
purposes: the males, as Professor Westwood observes, "are exceedingly
ardent, seizing their partners round the neck
with their sickle-shaped jaws;"[5] whilst the
females use these organs for burrowing in
sand-banks and making their nests.

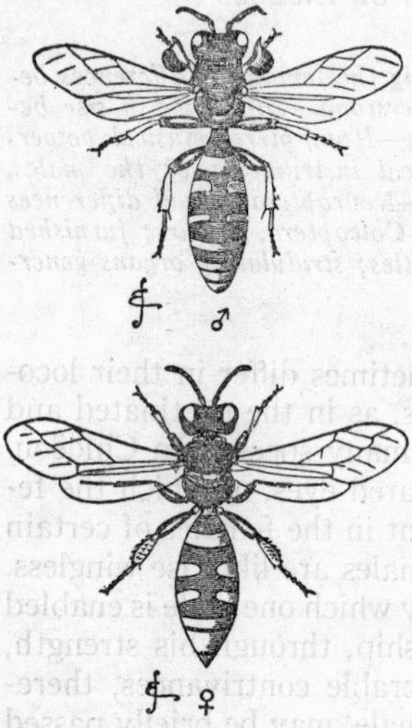

The tarsi of the front-legs are dilated in
many male beetles, or are furnished with
broad cushions of hairs; and in many genera
of water-beetles they are armed with a
round flat sucker, so that the male may adhere to the slippery body of the female. It is
a much more unusual circumstance that the
females of some water-beetles (Dytiscus)
have their elytra deeply grooved, and in
Acilius sulcatus thickly set with hairs, as an
aid to the male. The females of some other
water-beetles (Hydroporus) have their elytra punctured for the same purpose.[6] In the
male of *Crabro cribrarius* (fig. 9), it is the
tibia which is dilated into a broad horny
plate, with minute membraneous dots, giving to it a singular appearance like that of
a riddle.[7] In the male of Penthe (a genus
of beetles) a few of the middle joints of
the antennæ are dilated and furnished on the inferior surface with
cushions of hair, exactly like those on the tarsi of the Carabidæ, "and
obviously for the same end." In male dragon-flies, "the appendages at the
tip of the tail are modified in an almost infinite variety of curious patterns
to enable them to embrace the neck of the female." Lastly, in the males
of many insects, the legs are furnished with peculiar spines, knobs or

FIG. 9.—Crabro cribrarius.
Upper figure, male; lower
figure, female.

[4] Mr. Walsh, ibid. p. 107.

[5] 'Modern Classification of Insects,' vol. ii. 1840, pp. 205, 206. Mr. Walsh, who
called my attention to the double use of the jaws, says that he has repeatedly observed this fact.

[6] We have here a curious and inexplicable case of dimorphism, for some of the females of four European species of Dysticus, and of certain species of Hydroporus,
have their elytra smooth; and no intermediate gradations between the sulcated or
punctured, and the quite smooth elytra have been observed. See Dr. H. Schaum, as
quoted in the 'Zoologist,' vol. v.-vi. 1847-48, p. 1896. Also Kirby and Spence, 'Introduction to Entomology,' vol. iii. 1826, p. 305.

[7] Westwood, 'Modern Class.' vol. ii. p. 193. The following statement about Penthe,
and others in inverted commas, are taken from Mr. Walsh, 'Practical Entomologist,'
Philadelphia, vol. iii. p. 88.

spurs; or the whole leg is bowed or thickened, but this is by no means invariably a sexual character; or one pair, or all three pairs are elongated, sometimes to an extravagant length.[8]

The sexes of many species in all the orders present differences, of which the meaning is not understood. One curious case is that of a beetle (fig. 10), the male of which has left mandible much enlarged; so that the mouth is greatly distorted. In another Carabidous beetle, Eurygnathus,[9] we have the case, unique as far as known to Mr. Wollaston, of the head of the female being much broader and larger, though in a variable degree, than that of the male. Any number of such cases could be given. They abound in the Lepidoptera: one of the most extraordinary is that certain male butterflies have their fore-legs more or less atrophied, with the tibiæ and tarsi reduced to mere rudimentary knobs. The wings, also, in the two sexes often differ in neuration,[10] and sometimes considerably in outline, as in the *Aricoris epitus,* which was shewn to me in the British Museum by Mr. A. Butler. The males of certain South American butterflies have tufts of hair on the margins of the wings, and horny excrescences on the discs of the posterior pair.[11] In several British butterflies, as shewn by Mr. Wonfor, the males alone are in parts clothed with peculiar scales.

The use of the bright light of the female glow-worm has been subject to much discussion. The male is feebly luminous, as are the larvæ and even the eggs. It has been supposed by some authors that the light serves to frighten away enemies, and by others to guide the male to the female. At last, Mr. Belt [12] appears to have solved the difficulty: he finds that all the Lampyridæ which he has tried are highly distasteful to insectivorous mammals and birds. Hence it is in accordance with Mr. Bates' view, hereafter to be explained, that many insects mimic the Lampyridæ closely, in order to be mistaken for them, and thus to escape destruction. He further believes that the luminous species profit by being at once recognised as unpalatable. It is probable that the same explanation may be extended to the Elators, both sexes of which are highly luminous. It is not known why the

Fig. 10.—Taphroderes distortus (much enlarged). Upper figure, male; lower figure, female.

[8] Kirby and Spence, 'Introduct.' &c., vol. iii. pp. 332-336.
[9] 'Insecta Maderensia,' 1854, page 20.
[10] E. Doubleday, 'Annals and Mag. of Nat. Hist.' vol. i. 1848, p. 379. I may add that the wings in certain Hymenoptera (see Shuckard, 'Fossorial Hymenop.' 1837, pp. 39-43) differ in neuration according to sex.
[11] H. W. Bates, in 'Journal of Proc. Linn. Soc.' vol. vi. 1862, p. 74. Mr. Wonfor's observations are quoted in 'Popular Science Review,' 1868, p. 343.
[12] 'The Naturalist in Nicaragua,' 1874, pp. 316-320. On the phosphorescence of the eggs, see 'Annals and Mag. of Nat. Hist.' 1871, Nov., p. 372.

wings of the female glow-worm have not been developed; but in her present state she closely resembles a larva, and as larvæ are so largely preyed on by many animals, we can understand why she has been rendered so much more luminous and conspicuous than the male; and why the larvæ themselves are likewise luminous.

Difference in Size between the Sexes.—With insects of all kinds the males are commonly smaller than the females; and this difference can often be detected even in the larval state. So considerable is the difference between the male and female cocoons of the silk-moth (*Bombyx mori*), that in France they are separated by a particular mode of weighing.[13] In the lower classes of the animal kingdom, the greater size of the females seems generally to depend on their developing an enormous number of ova; and this may to a certain extent hold good with insects. But Dr. Wallace has suggested a much more probable explanation. He finds, after carefully attending to the development of the caterpillars of *Bombyx cynthia* and *yamamai,* and especially to that of some dwarfed caterpillars reared from a second brood on unnatural food, "that in proportion as the individual moth is finer, so is the time required for its metamorphosis longer; and for this reason the female, which is the larger and heavier insect, from having to carry her numerous eggs, will be preceded by the male, which is smaller and has less to mature."[14] Now as most insects are short-lived, and as they are exposed to many dangers, it would manifestly be advantageous to the female to be impregnated as soon as possible. This end would be gained by the males being first matured in large numbers ready for the advent of the females; and this again would naturally follow, as Mr. A. R. Wallace has remarked,[15] through natural selection; for the smaller males would be first matured, and thus would procreate a large number of offspring which would inherit the reduced size of their male parents, whilst the larger males from being matured later would leave fewer offspring.

There are, however, exceptions to the rule of male insects being smaller than the females: and some of these exceptions are intelligible. Size and strength would be an advantage to the males, which fight for the possession of the females; and in these cases, as with the stag-beetle (Lucanus), the males are larger than the females. There are, however, other beetles which are not known to fight together, of which the males exceed the females in size; and the meaning of this fact is not known; but in some of these cases, as with the huge Dynastes and Megasoma, we can at least see that there would be no necessity for the males to be smaller than the females, in order to be matured before them, for these beetles are not short-lived, and there would be ample time for the pairing of the sexes. So again, male dragon-flies (Libellulidæ) are sometimes sensibly larger, and never smaller, than the females;[16] and as Mr. MacLachlan believes, they do

---

[13] Robinet, 'Vers à Soie,' 1848, p. 207.

[14] 'Transact. Ent. Soc.' 3rd series, vol. v. p. 486.

[15] 'Journal of Proc. Ent. Soc.' Feb. 4th, 1867, p. lxxi.

[16] For this and other statements on the size of the sexes, see Kirby and Spence, ibid. vol. iii. p. 300; on the duration of life in insects, see p. 344.

not generally pair with the females until a week or fortnight has elapsed, and until they have assumed their proper masculine colours. But the most curious case, shewing on what complex and easily-overlooked relations, so trifling a character as difference in size between the sexes may depend, is that of the aculeate Hymenoptera; for Mr. F. Smith informs me that throughout nearly the whole of this large group, the males, in accordance with the general rule, are smaller than the females, and emerge about a week before them; but amongst the Bees, the males of *Apis mellifica, Anthidium manicatum,* and *Anthophora acervorum,* and amongst the Fosseres, the males of the *Methoca ichneumonides,* are larger than the females. The explanation of this anomaly is that a marriage flight is absolutely necessary with these species, and the male requires great strength and size in order to carry the female through the air. Increased size has here been acquired in opposition to the usual relation between size and the period of development, for the males, though larger, emerge before the smaller females.

We will now review the several Orders, selecting such facts as more particularly concern us. The Lepidoptera (Butterflies and Moths) will be retained for a separate chapter.

Order, *Thysanura.*—The members of this lowly organised order are wingless, dull-coloured, minute insects, with ugly, almost misshapen heads and bodies. Their sexes do not differ, but they are interesting as shewing us that the males pay sedulous court to the females even low down in the animal scale. Sir J. Lubbock[17] says: "It is very amusing to see these little creatures (*Smynthurus luteus*) coquetting together. The male, which is much smaller than the female, runs round her, and they butt one another, standing face to face and moving backward and forward like two playful lambs. Then the female pretends to run away and the male runs after her with a queer appearance of anger, gets in front and stands facing her again; then she turns coyly round, but he, quicker and more active, scuttles round too, and seems to whip her with his antennæ; then for a bit they stand face to face, play with their antennæ, and seem to be all in all to one another."

Order, *Diptera* (Flies).—The sexes differ little in colour. The greatest difference, known to Mr. F. Walker, is in the genus Bibio, in which the males are blackish or quite black, and the females obscure brownish-orange. The genus Elaphomyia, discovered by Mr. Wallace[18] in New Guinea, is highly remarkable, as the males are furnished with horns, of which the females are quite destitute. The horns spring from beneath the eyes, and curiously resemble those of a stag, being either branched or palmated. In one of the species, they equal the whole body in length. They might be thought to be adapted for fighting, but as in one species they are of a beautiful pink colour, edged with black, with a pale central stripe,

---

[17] 'Transact. Linnean Soc.' vol. xxvi. 1868, p. 296.
[18] 'The Malay Archipelago,' vol. ii., 1869, p. 313.

and as these insects have altogether a very elegant appearance, it is perhaps more probable that they serve as ornaments. That the males of some Diptera fight together is certain; Prof. Westwood[19] has several times seen this with the Tipulæ. The males of other Diptera apparently try to win the females by their music: H. Müller[20] watched for some time two males of an Eristalis courting a female; they hovered above her, and flew from side to side, making a high humming noise at the same time. Gnats and mosquitoes (Culicidæ) also seem to attract each other by humming; and Prof. Mayer has recently ascertained that the hairs on the antennæ of the male vibrate in unison with the notes of a tuning-fork, within the range of the sounds emitted by the female. The longer hairs vibrate sympathetically with the graver notes, and the shorter hairs with the higher ones. Landois also asserts that he has repeatedly drawn down a whole swarm of gnats by uttering a particular note. It may be added that the mental faculties of the Diptera are probably higher than in most other insects, in accordance with their highly-developed nervous system.[21]

Order, *Hemiptera* (Field-Bugs).—Mr. J. W. Douglas, who has particularly attended to the British species, has kindly given me an account of their sexual differences. The males of some species are furnished with wings, whilst the females are wingless; the sexes differ in the form of their bodies, elytra, antennæ and tarsi; but as the signification of these differences are unknown, they may be here passed over. The females are generally larger and more robust than the males. With British, and, as far as Mr. Douglas knows, with exotic species, the sexes do not commonly differ much in colour; but in about six British species the male is considerably darker than the female, and in about four other species the female is darker than the male. Both sexes of some species are beautifully coloured; and as these insects emit an extremely nauseous odour, their conspicuous colours may serve as a signal that they are unpalatable to insectivorous animals. In some few cases their colours appear to be directly protective: thus Prof. Hoffmann informs me that he could hardly distinguish a small pink and green species from the buds on the trunks of lime-trees, which this insect frequents.

Some species of Reduvidæ make a stridulating noise; and, in the case of *Pirates stridulus*, this is said[22] to be effected by the movement of the neck within the prothoracic cavity. According to Westring, *Reduvius personatus* also stridulates. But I have no reason to suppose that this is a sexual character, excepting that with non-social insects there seems to be no use for sound-producing organs, unless it be as a sexual call.

Order, *Homoptera*.—Every one who has wandered in a tropical forest must have been astonished at the din made by the male Cicadæ. The fe-

[19] 'Modern Classification of Insects,' vol. ii. 1840, p. 526.
[20] Anwendung, &c., 'Verh. d. n. V. Jahrg.' xxix. p. 80. Mayer, in 'American Naturalist,' 1874, p. 236.
[21] See Mr. B. T. Lowne's interesting work, 'On the Anatomy of the Blowfly, Musca vomitoria,' 1870, p. 14. He remarks (p. 33) that, "the captured flies utter a peculiar plaintive note, and that this sound causes other flies to disappear."
[22] Westwood, 'Modern Class. of Insects,' vol. ii. p. 473.

males are mute; as the Grecian poet Xenarchus says, "Happy the Cicadas live, since they all have voiceless wives." The noise thus made could be plainly heard on board the "Beagle," when anchored at a quarter of a mile from the shore of Brazil; and Captain Hancock says it can be heard at the distance of a mile. The Greeks formerly kept, and the Chinese now keep these insects in cages for the sake of their song, so that it must be pleasing to the ears of some men.[23] The Cicadidæ usually sing during the day, whilst the Fulgoridæ appear to be night-songsters. The sound, according to Landois,[24] is produced by the vibration of the lips of the spiracles, which are set into motion by a current of air emitted from the tracheæ; but this view has lately been disputed. Dr. Powell appears to have proved[25] that it is produced by the vibration of a membrane, set into action by a special muscle. In the living insect, whilst stridulating, this membrane can be seen to vibrate; and in the dead insect the proper sound is heard, if the muscle, when a little dried and hardened, is pulled with the point of a pin. In the female the whole complex musical apparatus is present, but is much less developed than in the male, and is never used for producing sound.

With respect to the object of the music, Dr. Hartman, in speaking of the *Cicada septemdecim* of the United States, says,[26] "the drums are now (June 6th and 7th, 1851) heard in all directions. This I believe to be the martial summons from the males. Standing in thick chestnut sprouts about as high as my head, where hundreds were around me, I observed the females coming around the drumming males." He adds, "this season (Aug. 1868) a dwarf pear tree in my garden produced about fifty larvæ of *Cic. pruinosa;* and I several times noticed the females to alight near a male while he was uttering his clanging notes." Fritz Müller writes to me from S. Brazil that he has often listened to a musical contest between two or three males of a species with a particularly loud voice, seated at a considerable distance from each other: as soon as one had finished his song, another immediately begun, and then another. As there is so much rivalry between the males, it is probable that the females not only find them by their sounds, but that, like female birds, they are excited or allured by the male with the most attractive voice.

I have not heard of any well-marked cases of ornamental differences between the sexes of the Homoptera. Mr. Douglas informs me that there are three British species, in which the male is black or marked with black bands, whilst the females are pale-coloured or obscure.

Order, *Orthoptera* (Crickets and Grasshoppers).—The males in the three saltatorial families in this Order are remarkable for their musical

[23] These particulars are taken from Westwood's 'Modern Classification of Insects,' vol. ii. 1840, page 422. See, also, on the Fulgoridæ Kirby and Spence, 'Introduct.' volume ii. page 401.

[24] 'Zeitschrift für wissenschaft Zoolog.' B. xvii. 1867, s. 152-158.

[25] 'Transact. New Zealand Institute,' vol. v. 1873, p. 286.

[26] I am indebted to Mr. Walsh for having sent me this extract from a 'Journal of the Doings of Cicada septemdecim' by Dr. Hartman.

powers, namely the Achetidæ or crickets, the Locustidæ for which there is
no equivalent English name, and the Acridiidæ or grasshoppers. The
stridulation produced by some of the Locustidæ is so loud that it can be
heard during the night at the distance of a mile;[27] and that made by certain species is not unmusical even to the human ear, so that the Indians
on the Amazons keep them in wicker cages. All observers agree that the
sounds serve either to call or excite the
mute females. With respect to the migratory locusts of Russia, Körte has given[28]
an interesting case of selection by the female of a male. The males of this species
(*Pachytylus migratorius*) whilst coupled
with the female stridulate from anger or
jealousy, if approached by other males.
The house-cricket when surprised at
night uses its voice to warn its fellows.[29]
In North America the Katydid (*Platyphyllum concavum*, one of the Locustidæ) is described[30] as mounting on the
upper branches of a tree, and in the evening beginning "his noisy babble, while
rival notes issue from the neighbouring
trees, and the graves resound with the
call of *Katy-did-she-did* the live-long
night." Mr. Bates, in speaking of the
European field-cricket (one of the Achetidæ), says "the male has been observed
to place himself in the evening at the
entrance of his burrow, and stridulate until a female approaches, when
the louder notes are succeeded by a more subdued tone, whilst the successful musician caresses with his antennæ the mate he has won."[31] Dr.
Scudder was able to excite one of these insects to answer him, by rubbing
on a file with a quill."[32] In both sexes a remarkable auditory apparatus
has been discovered by Von Siebold, situated in the front legs.[33]

In the three Families the sounds are differently produced. In the males
of the Achetidæ both wing-covers have the same apparatus; and this in
the field cricket (*Gryllus campestris*, fig. 11) consists, as described by

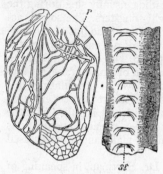

Fig. 11.—Gryllus c a m p e s t r i s
(from Landois).

Right-hand figure, under side of
part of a wing-nervure, much
magnified, showing the teeth
(st). Left-hand figure, upper
surface of wing-cover, with the
projecting, smooth nervure, *r*,
across which the teeth *(st)* are
scraped.

[27] L. Guilding, 'Transact. Linn. Soc.' vol. xv. p. 154.
[28] I state this on the authority of Köppen, 'Ueber die Heuschrecken in Südruss-
land,' 1866, p. 32, for I have in vain endeavoured to procure Körte's work.
[29] Gilbert White, 'Nat. Hist. of Selborne,' vol. ii. 1825, p. 262.
[30] Harris, 'Insects of New England,' 1842, p. 128.
[31] 'The Naturalist on the Amazons,' vol. i. 1863, p. 252. Mr. Bates gives a very interesting discussion on the gradations in the musical apparatus of the three families.
See also Westwood, 'Modern Class.' vol. ii. pp. 445 and 453.
[32] 'Proc. Boston Soc. of Nat. Hist.' vol. xi. April, 1868.
[33] 'Nouveau Manuel d'Anat. Comp.' (French translat.), tom. i, 1850, p. 567.

Landois,[34] of from 131 to 138 sharp, transverse ridges or teeth (*st*) on the under side of one of the nervures of the wing-cover. This toothed nervure is rapidly scraped across a projecting, smooth, hard nervure (*r*) on the upper surface of the opposite wing. First one wing is rubbed over the other, and then the movement is reversed. Both wings are raised a little at the same time, so as to increase the resonance. In some species the wing-covers of the males are furnished at the base with a talc-like plate.[35] I here give a drawing (fig. 12) of the teeth on the under side of the nervure of another species of Gryllus, viz., *G. domesticus*.

With respect to the formation of these teeth, Dr. Gruber has shewn[36] that they have been developed by the aid of selection, from the minute scales and hairs with which the wings and body are covered, and I came to the same conclusion with respect to those of the Coleoptera. But Dr. Gruber further shews that their development is in part directly due to the stimulus from the friction of one wing over the other.

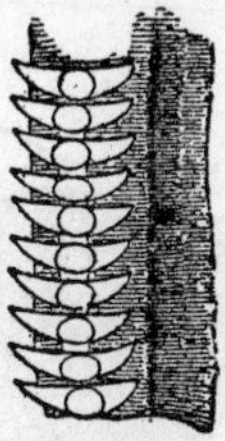

FIG. 12.—Teeth of Nervure of Gryllus domesticus (from Landois).

In the Locustidæ the opposite wing-covers differ from each other in structure (fig. 13), and the action cannot, as in the last family, be reversed. The left wing, which acts as the bow, lies over the right wing which serves as the fiddle. One of the nervures (*a*) on the under surface of the former is finely serrated, and is scraped across the prominent nervures on the upper surface of the opposite or right wing. In our British *Phasgonura viridissima* it appeared to me that the serrated nervure is rubbed against the rounded hind-corner of the opposite wing, the edge of which is thickened, coloured brown, and very sharp. In the right wing, but not in the left, there is a little plate, as transparent as talc, surrounded by nervures, and called the speculum. In *Ephippiger vitium*, a member of this same family, we have a curious subordinate modification; for the wing-covers are greatly reduced in size, but "the posterior part of the pro-thrax is elevated into a kind of dome over the wing-covers, and which has probably the effect of increasing the sound."[37]

We thus see that the musical apparatus is more differentiated or specialised in the Locustidæ (which include, I believe, the most powerful performers in the Order), than in the Achetidæ, in which both wing-covers have the same structure and the same function.[38] Landois, however, detected in one of the Locustidæ, namely in Decticus, a short and narrow row of small teeth, mere rudiments, on the inferior surface of the right wing-cover, which underlies the other and is never used as the bow. I observed the same rudimentary structure on the under side of the right

[34] 'Zeitschrift für wissenschaft. Zoolog.' B. xvii. 1867, s. 117.

[35] Westwood, 'Modern Class. of Insects,' vol. i. p. 440.

[36] 'Ueber der Tonapparat der Locustiden, ein Beitrag zum Darwinismus,' 'Zeitsch. für wissensch. Zoolog.' B. xxii. 1872, p. 100.

[37] Westwood, 'Modern Class. of Insects,' vol. i. p. 453.

[38] Landois, 'Zeitsch. f. wiss. Zoolog.' B. xvii. 1867, s. 121, 122.

wing-cover in *Phasgonura viridissima*. Hence we may infer with confidence that the Locustidæ are descended from a form, in which, as in the existing Achetidæ, both wing-covers had serrated nervures on the under surface, and could be indifferently used as the bow; but that in the Locustidæ the two wing-covers gradually became differentiated and perfected, on the principle of the division of labour, the one to act exclusively as the bow, and the other as the fiddle. Dr. Gruber takes the same view, and has shewn that rudimentary teeth are commonly found on the inferior surface of the right wing. By what steps the more simple apparatus in the

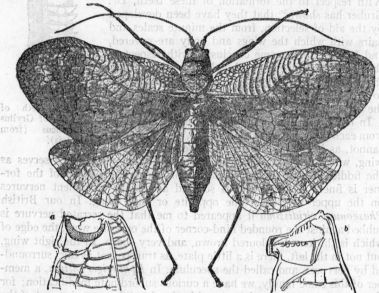

FIG. 13.—Chlorocœlus Tanana (from Bates). *a, b*, Lobes of opposite wing-covers.

Achetidæ originated, we do not know, but it is probable that the basal portions of the wing-covers originally overlapped each other as they do at present; and that the friction of the nervures produced a grating sound, as is now the case with the wing-covers of the females.[39] A grating sound thus occasionally and accidentally made by the males, if it served them ever so little as a love-call to the females, might readily have been intensified through sexual selection, by variations in the roughness of the nervures having been continually preserved.

In the last and third Family, namely the Acridiidæ or grasshoppers, the stridulation is produced in a very different manner, and according to Dr.

[39] Mr. Walsh also informs me that he has noticed that the female of the *Platyphyllum concavum*, "when captured makes a feeble grating noise by shuffling her wing-covers together."

Scudder, is not so shrill as in the preceding Families. The inner surface of the femur (fig. 14, r) is furnished with a longitudinal row of minute, elegant, lancet-shaped, elastic teeth, from 85 to 93 in number;[40] and these are scraped across the sharp, projecting nervures on the wing-covers, which are thus made to vibrate and resound. Harris[41] says that when one of the males begins to play, he first "bends the shank of the hind-leg

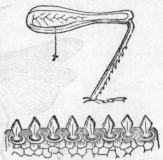

beneath the thigh, where it is lodged in a furrow designed to receive it, and then draws the leg briskly up and down. He does not play both fiddles together, but alternately, first upon one and then on the other." In many species, the base of the abdomen is hollowed out into a great cavity which is believed to act as a resounding board. In Pneumora (fig. 15), a S. African genus belonging to the same family, we meet with a new and remarkable modification; in the males a small notched ridge projects obliquely from each side of the abdomen, against which the hind femora are rubbed.[42] As the male is furnished with wings (the female being wingless), it is remarkable

FIG. 14.—Hind-leg of Stenobothrus pratorum: r, the stridulating ridge; lower figure, the teeth forming the ridge, much magnified (from Landois).

that the thighs are not rubbed in the usual manner against the wing-covers; but this may perhaps be accounted for by the unusually small size of the hind-legs. I have not been able to examine the inner surface of the thighs, which, judging from analogy, would be finely serrated. The species of Pneumora have been more profoundly modified for the sake of stridulation than any other orthopterous insect; for in the male the whole body has been converted into a musical instrument, being distended with air, like a great pellucid bladder, so as to increase the resonance. Mr. Trimen informs me that at the Cape of Good Hope these insects make a wonderful noise during the night.

In the three foregoing families, the females are almost always destitute of an efficient musical apparatus. But there are a few exceptions to this rule, for Dr. Gruber has shewn that both sexes of *Ephippiger vitium* are thus provided; though the organs differ in the male and female to a certain extent. Hence we cannot suppose that they have been transferred from the male to the female, as appears to have been the case with the secondary sexual characters of many other animals. They must have been independently developed in the two sexes, which no doubt mutually call to each other during the season of love. In most other Locustidæ (but not according to Landois in Decticus) the females have rudiments of the stridulatory organs proper to the male; from whom it is probable that

[40] Landois, ibid. s. 113.
[41] 'Insects of New England,' 1842, p. 133.
[42] Westwood, 'Modern Classification,' vol. i. p. 462.

these have been transferred. Landois also found such rudiments on the
under surface of the wing-covers of the female Achetidæ, and on the femora of the female Acridiidæ. In the Homoptera, also, the females have
the proper musical apparatus in a functionless state; and we shall hereafter meet in other divisions of the animal kingdom with many instances

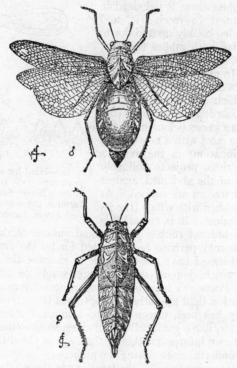

FIG. 15.—Pneumora (from specimens in the British Museum). Upper
figure, male; lower figure, female.

of structures proper to the male being present in a rudimentary condition
in the female.

Landois has observed another important fact, namely, that in the females of the Acridiidæ, the stridulating teeth on the femora remain
throughout life in the same condition in which they first appear during
the larval state in both sexes. In the males, on the other hand, they become further developed, and acquire their perfect structure at the last
moult, when the insect is mature and ready to breed.

From the facts now given, we see that the means by which the males
of the Orthoptera produce their sounds are extremely diversified, and are

altogether different from those employed by the Homoptera.[43] But throughout the animal kingdom we often find the same object gained by the most diversified means; this seems due to the whole organisation having undergone multifarious changes in the course of ages, and as part after part varied different variations were taken advantage of for the same general purpose. The diversity of means for producing sound in the three families of the Orthoptera and in the Homoptera, impresses the mind with the high importance of these structures to the males, for the sake of calling or alluring the females. We need feel no surprise at the amount of modification which the Orthoptera have undergone in this respect, as we now know, from Dr. Scudder's remarkable discovery,[44] that there has been more than ample time. This naturalist has lately found a fossil insect in the Devonian formation of New Brunswick, which is furnished with "the well-known tympanum or stridulating apparatus of the male Locustidæ." The insect, though in most respects related to the Neuroptera, appears, as is so often the case with very ancient forms, to connect the two related Orders of the Neuroptera and Orthoptera.

I have but little more to say on the Orthoptera. Some of the species are very pugnacious: when two male field-crickets (*Gryllus campestris*) are confined together, they fight till one kills the other; and the species of Mantis are described as manœuvring with their sword-like front-limbs, like hussars with their sabres. The Chinese keep these insects in little bamboo cages, and match them like game-cocks.[45] With respect to colour, some exotic locusts are beautifully ornamented; the posterior wings being marked with red, blue, and black; but as throughout the Order the sexes rarely differ much in colour, it is not probable that they owe their bright tints to sexual selection. Conspicuous colours may be of use to these insects, by giving notice that they are unpalatable. Thus it has been observed[46] that a bright-coloured Indian locust was invariably rejected when offered to birds and lizards. Some cases, however, are known of sexual differences in colour in this Order. The male of an American cricket[47] is described as being as white as ivory, whilst the female varies from almost white to greenish-yellow or dusky. Mr. Walsh informs me that the adult male of *Spectrum femoratum* (one of the Phasmidæ) "is of a shining brownish-yellow colour; the adult female being of a dull, opaque, cinereous brown; the young of both sexes being green." Lastly, I may mention that the male of one curious kind of cricket[48] is furnished with

[43] Landois has recently found in certain Orthoptera rudimentary structures closely similar to the sound-producing organs in the Homoptera; and this is a surprising fact. See 'Zeitschr. für wissensch Zoolog.' B. xxii. Heft 3, 1871. p. 348.

[44] 'Transact. Ent. Soc.' 3rd series, vol. ii. ('Journal of Proceedings,' p. 117).

[45] Westwood, 'Modern Class. of Insects,' vol. i. p. 427; for crickets, p. 445.

[46] Mr. Ch. Horne, in 'Proc. Ent. Soc.' May 3, 1869, p. xii.

[47] The *Œcanthus nivalis*. Harris, 'Insects of New England,' 1842, p. 124. The two sexes of *Œ. pellucidus* of Europe differ, as I hear from Victor Carus, in nearly the same manner.

[48] Platyblemnus: Westwood, 'Modern Class.' vol. i. p. 447.

"a long membranous appendage, which falls over the face like a veil;" but what its use may be, is not known.

Order, *Neuroptera.*—Little need here be said, except as to colour. In the Ephemeridæ the sexes often differ slightly in their obscure tints;[49] but it is not probable that the males are thus rendered attractive to the females. The Libellulidæ, or dragon-flies, are ornamented with splendid green, blue, yellow, and vermilion metallic tints; and the sexes often differ. Thus, as Prof. Westwood remarks,[50] the males of some of the Agrionidæ, "are of a rich blue with black wings, whilst the females are fine green with colourless wings." But in *Agrion Ramburii* these colours are exactly reversed in the two sexes.[51] In the extensive N. American genus of Hetærina, the males alone have a beautiful carmine spot at the base of each wing. In *Anax junius* the basal part of the abdomen in the male is a vivid ultramarine blue, and in the female grass-green. In the allied genus Gomphus, on the other hand, and in some other genera, the sexes differ but little in colour. In closely-allied forms throughout the animal kingdom, similar cases of the sexes differing greatly, or very little, or not at all, are of frequent occurrence. Although there is so wide a difference in colour between the sexes of many Libellulidæ, it is often difficult to say which is the more brilliant; and the ordinary coloration of the two sexes is reversed, as we have just seen, in one species of Agrion. It is not probable that their colours in any case have been gained as a protection. Mr. MacLachlan, who has closely attended to this family, writes to me that dragon-flies—the tyrants of the insect-world—are the least liable of any insect to be attacked by birds or other enemies, and he believes that their bright colours serve as a sexual attraction. Certain dragon-flies apparently are attracted by particular colours: Mr. Patterson observed[52] that the Agrionidæ, of which the males are blue, settled in numbers on the blue float of a fishing line; whilst two other species were attracted by shining white colours.

It is an interesting fact, first noticed by Schelver, that, in several genera belonging to two sub-families, the males on first emergence from the pupal state, are coloured exactly like the females; but that their bodies in a short time assume a conspicuous milky-blue tint, owing to the exudation of a kind of oil, soluble in ether and alcohol. Mr. MacLachlan believes that in the male of *Libellula depressa* this change of colour does not occur until nearly a fortnight after the metamorphosis, when the sexes are ready to pair.

Certain species of Neurothemis present, according to Brauer,[53] a cu-

[49] B. D. Walsh, the 'Pseudo-neuroptera of Illinois,' in 'Proc. Ent. Soc. of Philadelphia,' 1862, p. 361.

[50] 'Modern Class.' vol. ii. p. 37.

[51] Walsh, ibid. p. 381. I am indebted to this naturalist for the following facts on Hetærina, Anax, and Gomphus.

[52] 'Transact. Ent. Soc.' vol. i. 1836, p. lxxxi.

[53] See abstract in the 'Zoological Record' for 1867, p. 450.

rious case of dimorphism, some of the females having ordinary wings, whilst others have them "very richly netted, as in the males of the same species." Brauer "explains the phenomenon on Darwinian principles by the supposition that the close netting of the veins is a secondary sexual character in the males, which has been abruptly transferred to some of the females, instead of, as generally occurs, to all of them." Mr. Mac-Lachlan informs me of another instance of dimorphism in several species of Agrion, in which some individuals are of an orange colour, and these are invariably females. This is probably a case of reversion; for in the true Libellulæ, when the sexes differ in colour, the females are orange or yellow; so that supposing Agrion to be descended from some primordial form which resembled the typical Libellulæ in its sexual characters, it would not be surprising that a tendency to vary in this manner should occur in the females alone.

Although many dragon-flies are large, powerful, and fierce insects, the males have not been observed by Mr. MacLachlan to fight together, excepting, as he believes, in some of the smaller species of Agrion. In another group in this Order, namely, the Termites or white ants, both sexes at the time of swarming may be seen running about, "the male after the female, sometimes two chasing one female, and contending with great eagerness who shall win the prize."[54] The *Atropos pulsatorius* is said to make a noise with its jaws, which is answered by other individuals.[55]

Order, *Hymenoptera*.—That inimitable observer, M. Fabre,[56] in describing the habits of Cerceris, a wasp-like insect, remarks that "fights frequently ensue between the males for the possession of some particular female, who sits an apparently unconcerned beholder of the struggle for supremacy, and when the victory is decided, quietly flies away in company with the conqueror." Westwood[57] says that the males of one of the saw-flies (Tenthredinæ) "have been found fighting together, with their mandibles locked." As M. Fabre speaks of the males of Cerceris striving to obtain a particular female, it may be well to bear in mind that insects belonging to this Order have the power of recognising each other after long intervals of time, and are deeply attached. For instance, Pierre Huber, whose accuracy no one doubts, separated some ants, and when, after an interval of four months, they met others which had formerly belonged to the same community, they recognised and caressed one another with their antennæ. Had they been strangers they would have fought together. Again, when two communities engage in a battle, the ants on the same side sometimes attack each other in the general confusion, but they soon perceive their mistake, and the one ant soothes the other.[58]

In this Order slight differences in colour, according to sex, are com-

---

[54] Kirby and Spence, 'Introduct. to Entomology,' vol. ii. 1818, p. 35.

[55] Houzeau, 'Les Facultés Mentales,' &c. Tom. i. p. 104.

[56] See an interesting article, 'The Writings of Fabre,' in 'Nat. Hist. Review,' April 1862, p. 122.

[57] 'Journal of Proc. of Entomolog. Soc.' Sept. 7th, 1863, p. 169.

[58] P. Huber, 'Recherches sur les Mœurs des Fourmis,' 1810, pp. 150, 165.

mon, but conspicuous differences are rare except in the family of Bees; yet both sexes of certain groups are so brilliantly coloured—for instance in Chrysis, in which vermilion and metallic greens prevail—that we are tempted to attribute the result to sexual selection. In the Ichneumonidæ, according to Mr. Walsh,[59] the males are almost universally lighter-coloured than the females. On the other hand, in the Tenthredinidæ the males are generally darker than the females. In the Siricidæ the sexes frequently differ; thus the male of *Sirex juvencus* is banded with orange, whilst the female is dark purple; but it is difficult to say which sex is the more ornamented. In *Tremex columbœ* the female is much brighter coloured than the male. I am informed by Mr. F. Smith, that the male ants of several species are black, the females being testaceous.

In the family of Bees, especially in the solitary species, as I hear from the same entomologist, the sexes often differ in colour. The males are generally the brighter, and in Bombus as well as in Apathus, much more variable in colour than the females. In *Anthophora retusa* the male is of a rich fulvous-brown, whilst the female is quite black: so are the females of several species of Xylocopa, the males being bright yellow. On the other hand the females of some species, as of *Andræna fulva,* are much brighter coloured than the males. Such differences in colour can hardly be accounted for by the males being defenceless and thus requiring protection, whilst the females are well defended by their stings. H. Müller,[60] who has particularly attended to the habits of bees, attributes these differences in colour in chief part to sexual selection. That bees have a keen perception of colour is certain. He says that the males search eagerly and fight for the possession of the females; and he accounts through such contests for the mandibles of the males being in certain species larger than those of the females. In some cases the males are far more numerous than the females, either early in the season, or at all times and places, or locally; whereas the females in other cases are apparently in excess. In some species the more beautiful males appear to have been selected by the females; and in others the more beautiful females by the males. Consequently in certain genera (Müller, p. 42), the males of the several species differ much in appearance, whilst the females are almost indistinguishable; in other genera the reverse occurs. H. Müller believes (p. 82) that the colours gained by one sex through sexual selection have often been transferred in a variable degree to the other sex, just as the pollen-collecting apparatus of the female has often been transferred to the male, to whom it is absolutely useless.[61]

[59] 'Proc. Entomolog. Soc. of Philadelphia,' 1866, pp. 238, 239.
[60] 'Anwendung der Darwinschen Lehr auf Bienen.' Verh. d. n. Jahrg. xxix.
[61] M. Perrier in his article 'la Sélection sexuelle d'après Darwin' ('Revue Scientifique,' Feb. 1873, p. 868), without apparently having reflected much on the subject, objects that as the males of social bees are known to be produced from unfertilised ova, they could not transmit new characters to their male offspring. This is an extraordinary objection. A female bee fertilised by a male, which presented some character facilitating the union of the sexes, or rendering him more attractive to the female, would lay eggs which would produce only females; but these young females

Mutilla Europœa makes a stridulating noise; and according to Gou-
reau[62] both sexes have this power. He attributes the sound to the friction
of the third and preceding abdominal segments, and I find that these surfaces are marked with very fine concentric ridges; but so is the projecting thoracic collar into which the head articulates, and this collar, when
scratched with the point of a needle, emits the proper sound. It is rather
surprising that both sexes should have the power of stridulating, as the
male is winged and the female wingless. It is notorious that Bees express
certain emotions, as of anger, by the tone of their humming; and according to H. Müller (p. 80), the males of some species make a peculiar singing noise whilst pursuing the females.

Order, *Coleoptera* (Beetles).—Many beetles are coloured so as to resemble the surfaces which they habitually frequent, and they thus escape
detection by their enemies. Other species, for instance diamond-beetles,
are ornamented with splendid colours, which are often arranged in
stripes, spots, crosses, and other elegant patterns. Such colours can hardly
serve directly as a protection, except in the case of certain flower-feeding
species; but they may serve as a warning or means of recognition, on the
same principle as the phosphorescence of the glow-worm. As with beetles
the colours of the two sexes are generally alike, we have no evidence that
they have been gained through sexual selection; but this is at least possible, for they may have been developed in one sex and then transferred
to the other; and this view is even in some degree probable in those
groups which possess other well-marked secondary sexual characters.
Blind beetles, which cannot of course behold each other's beauty, never,
as I hear from Mr. Waterhouse, jun., exhibit bright colours, though they
often have polished coats; but the explanation of their obscurity may be
that they generally inhabit caves and other obscure stations.
Some Longicorns, especially certain Prionidæ, offer an exception to the
rule that the sexes of beetles do not differ in colour. Most of these insects
are large and splendidly coloured. The males in the genus Pyrodes,[63]

would next year produce males; and will it be pretended that such males would not
inherit the characters of their male grandfathers? To take a case with ordinary animals as nearly parallel as possible: if a female of any white quadruped or bird were
crossed by a male of a black breed, and the male and female offspring were paired
together, will it be pretended that the grandchildren would not inherit a tendency to
blackness from their male grandfather? The acquirement of new characters by the
sterile worker-bees is a much more difficult case, but I have endeavoured to show in
my 'Origin of Species,' how these sterile beings are subjected to the power of natural
selection.
[62] Quoted by Westwood, 'Modern Class. of Insects,' vol. ii. p. 214.
[63] *Pyrodes pulcherrimus,* in which the sexes differ conspicuously, has been described
by Mr. Bates in 'Transact. Ent. Soc.' 1869, p. 50. I will specify the few other cases
in which I have heard of a difference in colour between the sexes of beetles. Kirby
and Spence ('Introduct. to Entomology,' vol. iii. p. 301) mention a Cantharis, Me-
loe, Rhagium, and the *Leptura testacea;* the male of the latter being testaceous, with
a black thorax, and the female of a dull red all over. These two latter beetles belong
to the family of Longicorns. Messrs. R. Trimen and Waterhouse, jun., inform me of
two Lamellicorns, viz., a Peritrichia and Trichius, the male of the latter being more

which I saw in Mr. Bates's collection, are generally redder but rather duller than the females, the latter being coloured of a more or less splendid golden-green. On the other hand, in one species the male is golden-green, the female being richly tinted with red and purple. In the genus Esmeralda the sexes differ so greatly in colour that they have been ranked as distinct species; in one species both are of a beautiful shining green, but the male has a red thorax. On the whole, as far as I could judge, the females of those Prionidæ, in which the sexes differ, are coloured more

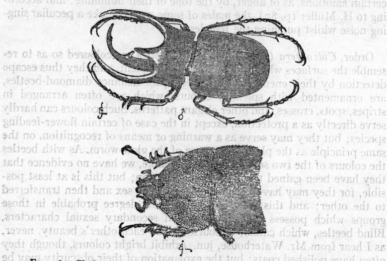

FIG. 16.—Chalcosoma atlas. Upper figure, male (reduced); lower figure, female (nat. size).

richly than the males, and this does not accord with the common rule in regard to colour, when acquired through sexual selection.

A most remarkable distinction between the sexes of many beetles is presented by the great horns which rise from the head, thorax, and clypeus of the males; and in some few cases from the under surface of the body. These horns, in the great family of the Lamellicorns, resemble those of various quadrupeds, such as stags, rhinoceroses, &c., and are wonderful both from their size and diversified shapes. Instead of describing them, I have given figures of the males and females of some of the more remarkable forms. (Figs. 16 to 20.) The females generally exhibit rudiments of the horns in the form of small knobs or ridges; but some are destitute of even the slightest rudiment. On the other hand, the horns are nearly as well developed in the female as in the male *Phanæus lancifer;*

obscurely coloured than the female. In *Tillus elongatus* the male is black, and the female always, as it is believed, of a dark blue colour, with a red thorax. The male, also, of *Orsodacna atra*, as I hear from Mr. Walsh, is black, the female (the so-called *O. ruficollis*) having a rufous thorax.

and only a little less well developed in the females of some other species of this genus and of Copris. I am informed by Mr. Bates that the horns do not differ in any manner corresponding with the more important char-

FIG. 17.—Copris isidis. (Left-hand figures, males.)

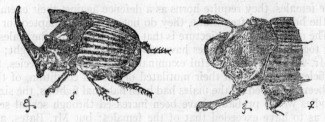

FIG. 18.—Phanæus faunus.

FIG. 19.—Dipelicus cantori.

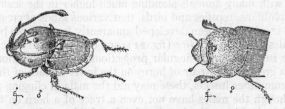

FIG. 20.—Onthophagus rangifer, enlarged.

acteristic differences between the several subdivisions of the family: thus within the same section of the genus Onthophagus, there are species which have a single horn, and others which have two.

In almost all cases, the horns are remarkable for their excessive variability; so that a graduated series can be formed, from the most highly developed males to others so degenerate that they can barely be distinguished from the females. Mr. Walsh[64] found that in *Phanœus carnifex* the horns were thrice as long in some males as in others. Mr. Bates, after examining above a hundred males of *Onthophagus rangifer* (fig. 20), thought that he had at last discovered a species in which the horns did not vary; but further research proved the contrary.

The extraordinary size of the horns, and their widely different structure in closely-allied forms, indicate that they have been formed for some purpose; but their excessive variability in the males of the same species leads to the inference that this purpose cannot be of a definite nature. The horns do not show marks of friction, as if used for any ordinary work. Some authors suppose[65] that as the males wander about much more than the females, they require horns as a defence against their enemies; but as the horns are often blunt, they do not seem well adapted for defence. The most obvious conjecture is that they are used by the males for fighting together; but the males have never been observed to fight; nor could Mr. Bates, after a careful examination of numerous species, find any sufficient evidence, in their mutilated or broken condition, of their having been thus used. If the males had been habitual fighters, the size of their bodies would probably have been increased through sexual selection, so as to have exceeded that of the females; but Mr. Bates, after comparing the two sexes in above a hundred species of the Copridæ, did not find any marked difference in this respect amongst well-developed individuals. In Lethrus, moreover, a beetle belonging to the same great division of the Lamellicorns, the males are known to fight, but are not provided with horns, though their mandibles are much larger than those of the female.

The conclusion that the horns have been acquired as ornaments is that which best agrees with the fact of their having been so immensely, yet not fixedly, developed,—as shewn by their extreme variability in the same species, and by their extreme diversity in closely-allied species. This view will at first appear extremely improbable; but we shall hereafter find with many animals standing much higher in the scale, namely fishes, amphibians, reptiles and birds, that various kinds of crests, knobs, horns and combs have been developed apparently for this sole purpose.

The males of *Onitis furcifer* (fig. 21), and of some other species of the genus, are furnished with singular projections on their anterior femora, and with a great fork or pair of horns on the lower surface of the thorax. Judging from other insects, these may aid the male in clinging to the female. Although the males have not even a trace of a horn on the upper surface of the body, yet the females plainly exhibit a rudiment of a single horn on the head (fig. 22, *a*), and of a crest (*b*) on the thorax. That the

---

[64] 'Proc. Entomolog. Soc. of Philadelphia,' 1864, p. 228.
[65] Kirby and Spence, 'Introduct. Entomolog.' vol. iii. p. 300.

slight thoracic crest in the female is a rudiment of a projection proper to the male, though entirely absent in the male of this particular species, is clear: for the female of *Bubas bison* (a genus which comes next to Onitis) has a similar slight crest on the thorax, and the male bears a great projection in the same situation. So, again, there can hardly be a doubt that the little point (*a*) on the head of the female *Onitis furcifer*, as well as on the head of the females of two or three allied species, is a rudimentary representative of the cephalic horn, which is common to the males of so many Lamellicorn beetles, as in Phanæus (fig. 18).

The old belief that rudiments have been created to complete the scheme of nature is here so far from holding good, that we have a com-

FIG. 21.—Onitis furci-   FIG. 22.—Left-hand figure, male of Onitis furcifer, male, viewed   fer, viewed laterally. Right-hand figure, fe-
from beneath.   male. *a*. Rudiment of cephalic horn. *b*. Trace
                           of thoracic horn or crest.

plete inversion of the ordinary state of things in the family. We may reasonably suspect that the males originally bore horns and transferred them to the females in a rudimentary condition, as in so many other Lamellicorns. Why the males subsequently lost their horns, we know not; but this may have been caused through the principle of compensation, owing to the development of the large horns and projections on the lower surface; and as these are confined to the males, the rudiments of the upper horns on the females would not have been thus obliterated.

The cases hitherto given refer to the Lamellicorns, but the males of some few other beetles, belonging to two widely distinct groups, namely, the Curculionidæ and Staphylinidæ, are furnished with horns—in the former on the lower surface of the body,[66] in the latter on the upper surface of the head and thorax. In the Staphylinidæ, the horns of the males are extraordinarily variable in the same species, just as we have seen with the Lamellicorns. In Siagonium we have a case of dimorphism, for the males can be divided into two sets, differing greatly in the size of their bodies and in the development of their horns, without intermediate gradations. In a species of Bledius (fig. 23), also belonging to the Staphylinidæ, Professor Westwood states that, "male specimens can be found in the same locality in which the central horn of the thorax is very large,

[66] Kirby and Spence, 'Introduct. Entomolog.' vol. iii. p. 329.

but the horns of the head quite rudimental; and others, in which the thoracic horn is much shorter, whilst the protuberances on the head are long."[67] Here we apparently have a case of compensation, which throws light on that just given, of the supposed loss of the upper horns by the males of *Onitis.*

Law of Battle.—Some male beetles, which seem ill-fitted for fighting, nevertheless engage in conflicts for the possession of the females. Mr. Wallace[68] saw two males of *Leptorhynchus angustatus,* a linear beetle with a much elongated rostrum, "fighting for a female, who stood close by busy at her boring. They pushed at each other with their rostra, and clawed and thumped, apparently in the greatest rage." The smaller male, however, "soon ran away, acknowledging himself vanquished." In some few cases male beetles are well adapted for fighting, by possessing great

Fig. 23.—Bledius taurus, magnified. Left-hand figure, male; right-hand figure, female.

toothed mandibles, much larger than those of the females. This is the case with the common stag-beetle (*Lucanus cervus*), the males of which emerge from the pupal state about a week before the other sex, so that several may often be seen pursuing the same female. At this season they engage in fierce conflicts. When Mr. A. H. Davis[69] enclosed two males with one female in a box, the larger male severely pinched the smaller one, until he resigned his pretensions. A friend informs me that when a boy he often put the males together to see them fight, and he noticed that they were much bolder and fiercer than the females, as with the higher animals. The males would seize hold of his finger, if held in front of them, but not so the females, although they have stronger jaws. The males of many of the Lucanidæ as well as of the above-mentioned Leptorhynchus, are larger and more powerful insects than the females. The two sexes of *Lethrus cephalotes* (one of the Lamellicorns) inhabit the same burrow; and the male has larger mandibles than the female. If, during the breeding season, a strange male attempts to enter the burrow, he is attacked; the female does not remain passive, but closes the mouth of the burrow, and encourages her mate by continually pushing him on from behind; and the battle lasts until the aggressor is killed or runs away.[70] The two sexes of another Lamellicorn beetle, the *Ateuchus cicatricosus,* live in

[67] 'Modern Classification of Insects,' vol. i. p. 172: Siagonium, p. 172. In the British Museum I noticed one male specimen of Siagonium in an intermediate condition, so that the dimorphism is not strict.

[68] 'The Malay Archipelago,' vol. ii. 1869, p. 276. Riley, Sixth 'Report on insects of Missouri,' 1874, p. 115.

[69] 'Entomological Magazine,' vol. i. 1833, p. 82. See also on the conflicts of this species, Kirby and Spence, ibid. vol. iii. p. 314; and Westwood, ibid. vol. i. p. 187.

[70] Quoted from Fischer, in 'Dict. Class. d'Hist. Nat.' tom. x. p. 324.

pairs, and seem much attached to each other; the male excites the females to roll the balls of dung in which the ova are deposited; and if she
is removed, he becomes much agitated. If the
male is removed the female ceases all work,
and as M. Brulerie[71] believes, would remain
on the same spot until she died.

The great mandibles of the male Lucanidæ
are extremely variable both in size and structure, and in this respect resemble the horns on
the head and thorax of many male Lamellicorns and Staphylinidæ. A perfect series can be
formed from the best-provided to the worst-
provided or degenerate males. Although the
mandibles of the common stag-beetle, and
probably of many other species, are used as efficient weapons for fighting, it is doubtful
whether their great size can thus be accounted
for. We have seen that they are used by the
Lucanus elaphus of N. America for seizing the
female. As they are so conspicuous and so elegantly branched, and as owing to their great
length they are not well adapted for pinching,
the suspicion has crossed my mind that they
may in addition serve as an ornament, like the
horns on the head and thorax of the various
species above described. The male *Chiasogna-*
thus Grantii of S. Chile—a splendid beetle belonging to the same family—has enormously
developed mandibles (fig. 24); he is bold and
pugnacious; when threatened he faces round,
opens his great jaws, and at the same time
stridulates loudly. But the mandibles were not
strong enough to pinch my finger so as to cause
actual pain.

Sexual selection, which implies the possession of considerable perceptive powers and of
strong passions, seems to have been more effective with the Lamellicorns than with any
other family of beetles. With some species the

FIG. 24.—Chiasognathus
Grantii, reduced. Upper
figure, male; lower figure,
female.

males are provided with weapons for fighting; some live in pairs and
show mutual affection; many have the power of stridulating when excited;
many are furnished with the most extraordinary horns, apparently for the
sake of ornament; and some, which are diurnal in their habits, are gorgeously coloured. Lastly, several of the largest beetles in the world belong
to this family, which was placed by Linnæus and Fabricius at the head of
the Order.[72]

[71] 'Ann. Soc. Entomolog. France,' 1866, as quoted in 'Journal of Travel,' by A.
Murray, 1868, p. 135.
[72] Westwood, 'Modern Class.' vol. i. p. 184.

Stridulating organs.—Beetles belonging to many and widely distinct
families possess these organs. The sound thus produced can sometimes be
heard at the distance of several feet or even yards,[73] but it is not comparable with that made by the Orthoptera. The rasp generally consists of a
narrow, slightly-raised surface, crossed by very fine, parallel ribs, sometimes so fine as to cause iridescent colours, and having a very elegant appearance under the microscope. In some cases, as with Typhœus, minute,
bristly or scale-like prominences, with which the whole surrounding surface is covered in approximately parallel lines, could be traced passing
into the ribs of the rasp. The transition takes place by their becoming
confluent and straight, and at the same time more prominent and smooth.

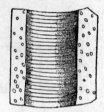 

Fig. 25.—Necrophorus (from Landois). *r.* The two rasps. Left-hand
figure, part of the rasp highly magnified.

A hard ridge on an adjoining part of the body serves as the scraper for
the rasp, but this scraper in some cases has been specially modified for
the purpose. It is rapidly moved across the rasp, or conversely the rasp
across the scraper.

These organs are situated in widely different positions. In the carrion-
beetles (Necrophorus) two parallel rasps (*r*, fig. 25) stand on the dorsal
surface of the fifth abdominal segment, each rasp [74] consisting of 126 to
140 fine ribs. These ribs are scraped against the posterior margins of the
elytra, a small portion of which projects beyond the general outline. In
many Crioceridæ, and in *Clythra 4-punctata* (one of the Chrysomelidæ),
and in some Tenebrionidæ, &c.,[75] the rasp is seated on the dorsal apex of
the abdomen, on the pygidium or pro-pygidium, and is scraped in the
same manner by the elytra. In Heterocerus, which belongs to another
family, the rasps are placed on the sides of the first abdominal segment,
and are scraped by ridges on the femora.[76] In certain Curculionidæ and

[73] Wollaston, 'On certain Musical Curculionidæ,' 'Annals and Mag. of Nat. Hist.'
vol. vi. 1860, p. 14.
[74] Landois, 'Zeitschrift für wiss. Zoolog.' B. xvii. 1867, s. 127.
[75] I am greatly indebted to Mr. G. B. Crotch for having sent me many prepared
specimens of various beetles belonging to these three families and to others, as well
as for valuable information. He believes that the power of stridulation in the Clythra has not been previously observed. I am also much indebted to Mr. E. W. Jan-
con, for information and specimens. I may add that my son, Mr. F. Darwin, finds
that *Dermestes murinus* stridulates, but he searched in vain for the apparatus. Sco-
lytus has lately been described by Dr. Chapman as a stridulator, in the 'Entomologist's Monthly Magazine,' vol. vi. p. 130.
[76] Schiödte, translated in 'Annals and Mag. of Nat. Hist.' vol. xx. 1867, p. 37.

Carabidæ,[77] the parts are completely reversed in position, for the rasps are seated on the inferior surface of the elytra, near their apices, or along their outer margins, and the edges of the abdominal segments serve as the scrapers. In *Pelobius Hermanni* (one of Dytiscidæ or water-beetles) a strong ridge runs parallel and near to the sutural margin of the elytra, and is crossed by ribs, coarse in the middle part, but becoming gradually finer at both ends, especially at the upper end; when this insect is held under water or in the air, a stridulating noise is produced by the extreme horny margin of the abdomen being scraped against the rasps. In a great number of long-horned beetles (Longicornia) the organs are situated quite otherwise, the rasp being on the meso-thorax, which is rubbed against the pro-thorax; Landois counted 238 very fine ribs on the rasp of *Cerambyx heros*.

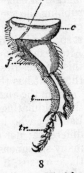

Many Lamellicorns have the power of stridulating, and the organs differ greatly in position. Some species stridulate very loudly, so that when Mr. F. Smith caught a *Trox sabulosus,* a gamekeeper, who stood by, thought he had caught a mouse; but I failed to discover the proper organs in this beetle. In Geotrupes and Typhœus, a narrow ridge runs obliquely across (*r,* fig. 26) the coxa of each hindleg (having in *G. stercorarius* 84 ribs), which is scraped by a specially projecting part of one of the abdominal segments. In the nearly allied *Copris lunaris,* an excessively narrow fine rasp runs along the sutural margin of the elytra, with another short rasp near the basal outer margin; but in some other Coprini the rasp is seated, according to Leconte,[78] on the dorsal surface of the abdomen. In Oryctes it is seated on the pro-pygidium; and, according to the same entomologist, in some other Dynastini, on the under surface of the elytra. Lastly, Westring states that in *Omaloplia brunnea* the rasp is placed on

FIG. 26.—Hind-leg of Geotrupes stercorarius (from Landois). *r.* Rasp. *c.* Coxa. *f.* Femur. *t.* Tibia. *tr.* Tarsi.

the pro-sternum, and the scraper on the meta-sternum, the parts thus occupying the under surface of the body, instead of the upper surface as in the Longicorns.

We thus see that in the different coleopterous families the stridulating organs are wonderfully diversified in position, but not much in structure. Within the same family some species are provided with these organs, and others are destitute of them. This diversity is intelligible, if we suppose that originally various beetles made a shuffling or hissing noise by the

[77] Westring has described (Kroyer, 'Naturhist. Tidskrift,' B. ii. 1848-49, p. 334) the stridulating organs in these two, as well as in other families. In the Carabidæ I have examined *Ealphrus uliginosus* and *Blethisa multipunctata,* sent to me by Mr. Crotch. In Blethisa the transverse ridges on the furrowed border of the abdominal segment do not, as far as I could judge, come into play in scraping the rasps on the elytra.

[78] I am indebted to Mr. Walsh, of Illinois, for having sent me extracts from Leconte's 'Introduction to Entomology,' pp. 101, 143.

rubbing together of any hard and rough parts of their bodies, which happened to be in contact; and that from the noise thus produced being in some way useful, the rough surfaces were gradually developed into regular stridulating organs. Some beetles as they move, now produce, either intentionally or unintentionally, a shuffling noise, without possessing any proper organs for the purpose. Mr. Wallace informs me that the *Euchirus longimanus* (a Lamellicorn, with the anterior legs wonderfully elongated in the male) "makes, whilst moving, a low hissing sound by the protrusion and contraction of the abdomen; and when seized it produces a grating sound by rubbing its hind-legs against the edges of the elytra." The hissing sound is clearly due to a narrow rasp running along the sutural margin of each elytron; and I could likewise make the grating sound by rubbing the shagreened surface of the femur against the granulated margin of the corresponding elytron; but I could not here detect any proper rasp; nor is it likely that I could have overlooked it in so large an insect. After examining Cychrus, and reading what Westring has written about this beetle, it seems very doubtful whether it possesses any true rasp, though it has the power of emitting a sound.

From the analogy of the Orthoptera and Homoptera, I expected to find the stridulating organs in the Coleoptera differing according to sex; but Landois, who has carefully examined several species, observed no such difference; nor did Westring; nor did Mr. G. R. Crotch in preparing the many specimens which he had the kindness to send me. Any difference in these organs, if slight, would, however, be difficult to detect, on account of their great variability. Thus, in the first pair of specimens of *Necrophorus humator* and of *Pelobius* which I examined, the rasp was considerably larger in the male than in the female; but not so with succeeding specimens. In *Geotrupes stercorarius* the rasp appeared to me thicker, opaquer, and more prominent in three males than in the same number of females; in order, therefore, to discover whether the sexes differed in their power of stridulating, my son, Mr. F. Darwin, collected fifty-seven living specimens, which he separated into two lots, according as they made a greater or less noise, when held in the same manner. He then examined all these specimens, and found that the males were very nearly in the same proportion to the females in both the lots. Mr. F. Smith has kept alive numerous specimens of *Monoynchus pseudacori* (Curculionidæ), and is convinced that both sexes stridulate, and apparently in an equal degree.

Nevertheless, the power of stridulating is certainly a sexual character in some few Coleoptera. Mr. Crotch discovered that the males alone of two species of Heliopathes (Tenebrionidæ) possess stridulating organs. I examined five males of *H. gibbus,* and in all these there was a well-developed rasp, partially divided into two, on the dorsal surface of the terminal abdominal segment; whilst in the same number of females there was not even a rudiment of the rasp, the membrane of this segment being transparent, and much thinner than in the male. In *H. cribratostriatus* the male has a similar rasp, excepting that it is not partially divided into two portions, and the female is completely destitute of this organ; the male in addition has on the apical margins of the elytra, on each side of the suture, three or four short longitudinal ridges, which are crossed by extremely fine ribs, parallel to and resembling those on the abdominal rasp; whether these ridges serve as an independent rasp, or as a scraper for the abdominal rasp, I could not decide: the female exhibits no trace of this latter structure.

Again, in three species of the Lamellicorn genus Oryctes, we have a nearly parallel case. In the females of *O. gryphus* and *nasicornis* the ribs on the rasp of the pro-pygidium are less continuous and less distinct than in the males; but the chief difference is that the whole upper surface of this segment, when held in the proper light, is seen to be clothed with hairs, which are absent or are represented by excessively fine down in the males. It should be noticed that in all Coleoptera the effective part of the rasp is destitute of hairs. In *O. senegalensis* the difference between the sexes is more strongly marked, and this is best seen when the proper abdominal segment is cleaned and viewed as a transparent object. In the female the whole surface is covered with little separate crests, bearing spines; whilst in the male these crests in proceeding towards the apex, become more and more confluent, regular, and naked; so that three-fourths of the segment is covered with extremely fine parallel ribs, which are quite absent in the female. In the females, however, of all three species of Oryctes, a slight grating or stridulating sound is produced, when the abdomen of a softened specimen is pushed backwards and forwards.

In the case of the Heliopathes and Oryctes there can hardly be a doubt that the males stridulate in order to call or to excite the females; but with most beetles the stridulation apparently serves both sexes as a mutual call. Beetles stridulate under various emotions, in the same manner as birds use their voices for many purposes besides singing to their mates. The great Chiasognathus stridulates in anger or defiance; many species do the same from distress or fear, if held so that they cannot escape; by striking the hollow stems of trees in the Canary Islands, Messrs. Wollaston and Crotch were able to discover the presence of beetles belonging to the genus Acalles by their stridulation. Lastly, the male Ateuchus stridulates to encourage the female in her work, and from distress when she is removed.[79] Some naturalists believe that beetles make this noise to frighten away their enemies; but I cannot think that a quadruped or bird, able to devour a large beetle, would be frightened by so slight a sound. The belief that the stridulation serves as a sexual call is supported by the fact that death-ticks (*Anobium tessellatum*) are well known to answer each other's ticking, and, as I have myself observed, a tapping noise artificially made. Mr. Doubleday also informs me that he has sometimes observed a female ticking,[80] and in an hour or two afterwards has

[79] M. P. de la Brulerie, as quoted in 'Journal of Travel,' A. Murray, vol. i. 1868, p. 135.
[80] According to Mr. Doubleday, "the noise is produced by the insect raising itself on its legs as high as it can, and then striking its thorax five or six times, in rapid

found her united with a male, and on one occasion surrounded by several males. Finally, it is probable that the two sexes of many kinds of beetles were at first enabled to find each other by the slight shuffling noise produced by the rubbing together of the adjoining hard parts of their bodies; and that as those males or females which made the greatest noise succeeded best in finding partners, rugosities on various parts of their bodies were gradually developed by means of sexual selection into true stridulating organs.

succession, against the substance upon which it is sitting." For references on this subject see Landois, 'Zeitschrift für wissen. Zoolog.' B. xvii. s. 181. Olivier says (as quoted by Kirby and Spence, 'Introduct.' vol. ii. p. 395) that the female of *Pimelia striata* produces a rather loud sound by striking her abdomen against any hard substance, "and that the male, obedient to this call, soon attends her, and they pair."

CHAPTER XI

INSECTS, *continued*—ORDER LEPIDOPTERA

BUTTERFLIES AND MOTHS

Courtship of butterflies—Battles—Ticking noise—Colours common to both sexes, or more brilliant in the males—Examples—Not due to the direct action of the conditions of life—Colours adapted for protection—Colours of moths—Display—Perceptive powers of the Lepidoptera—Variability—Causes of the difference in colour between the males and females—Mimicry, female butterflies more brilliantly coloured than the males—Bright colours of caterpillars—Summary and concluding remarks on the secondary sexual characters of insects—Birds and insects compared.

IN this great Order the most interesting points for us are the differences in colour between the sexes of the same species, and between the distinct species of the same genus. Nearly the whole of the following chapter will be devoted to this subject; but I will first make a few remarks on one or two other points. Several males may often be seen pursuing and crowding round the same female. Their courtship appears to be a prolonged affair, for I have frequently watched one or more males pirouetting round a female until I was tired, without seeing the end of the courtship. Mr. A. G. Butler also informs me that he has several times watched a male courting a female for a full quarter of an hour; but she pertinaciously refused him, and at last settled on the ground and closed her wings, so as to escape from his addresses.

Although butterflies are weak and fragile creatures, they are pugnacious, and an Emperor butterfly[1] has been captured with the tips of its wings broken from a conflict with another male. Mr. Collingwood, in speaking of the frequent battles between the butterflies of Borneo, says, "They whirl round each other with the greatest rapidity, and appear to be incited by the greatest ferocity."

The *Ageronia feronia* makes a noise like that produced by a toothed wheel passing under a spring catch, and which can be heard at the distance of several yards: I noticed this sound at Rio de Janeiro, only when two of these butterflies were chasing each other in an irregular course, so that it is probably made during the courtship of the sexes.[2]

[1] *Apatura Iris:* 'The Entomologist's Weekly Intelligence,' 1859, p. 139. For the Bornean Butterflies, see C. Collingwood, 'Rambles of a Naturalist,' 1868, p. 183.

[2] See my 'Journal of Researches,' 1845, p. 33. Mr. Doubleday has detected ('Proc Ent. Soc.' March 3rd, 1845, p. 123) a peculiar membranous sac at the base of the front wings, which is probably connected with the production of the sound. For the

Some moths also produce sounds; for instance, the males of *Theoco-phora fovea*. On two occasions Mr. F. Buchanan White[3] heard a sharp quick noise made by the male of *Hylophila prasinana*, and which he believes to be produced, as in Cicada, by an elastic membrane, furnished with a muscle. He quotes, also, Guenée, that Setina produces a sound like the ticking of a watch, apparently by the aid of "two large tympaniform vesicles, situated in the pectoral region;" and these "are much more developed in the male than in the female." Hence the sound-producing organs in the Lepidoptera appear to stand in some relation with the sexual functions. I have not alluded to the well-known noise made by the Death's Head Sphinx, for it is generally heard soon after the moth has emerged from its cocoon.

Giard has always observed that the musky odour, which is emitted by two species of Sphinx moths, is peculiar to the males;[4] and in the higher classes we shall meet with many instances of the males alone being odoriferous.

Every one must have admired the extreme beauty of many butterflies and of some moths; and it may be asked, are their colours and diversified patterns the result of the direct action of the physical conditions to which these insects have been exposed, without any benefit being thus derived? Or have successive variations been accumulated and determined as a protection, or for some unknown purpose, or that one sex may be attractive to the other? And, again, what is the meaning of the colours being widely different in the males and females of certain species, and alike in the two sexes of other species of the same genus? Before attempting to answer these questions a body of facts must be given.

With our beautiful English butterflies, the admiral, peacock, and painted lady (Vanessæ), as well as many others, the sexes are alike. This is also the case with the magnificent Heliconidæ, and most of the Danaidæ in the tropics. But in certain other tropical groups, and in some of our English butterflies, as the purple emperor, orange-tip, &c. (*Apatura Iris* and *Anthocharis cardamines*), the sexes differ either greatly or slightly in colour. No language suffices to describe the splendour of the males of some tropical species. Even within the same genus we often find species presenting extraordinary differences between the sexes, whilst others have their sexes closely alike. Thus in the South American genus Epicalia, Mr. Bates, to whom I am indebted for most of the following facts, and for looking over this whole discussion, informs me that he knows twelve species, the two sexes of which haunt the same stations (and this is not always the case with butterflies), and which, therefore, cannot have been differently affected by external conditions.[5] In nine of these twelve spe-

case of Thecophora, see 'Zoological Record,' 1869, p. 401. For Mr. Buchanan White's observations, 'The Scottish Naturalist,' July 1872, p. 214.

[3] 'The Scottish Naturalist,' July 1872, p. 213.

[4] 'Zoological Record,' 1869, p. 347.

[5] See also Mr. Bates's paper in 'Proc. Ent. Soc. of Philadelphia,' 1865, p. 206. Also Mr. Wallace on the same subject, in regard to Diadema, in 'Transact. Entomolog. Soc. of London,' 1869, p. 278.

cies the males rank amongst the most brilliant of all butterflies, and differ so greatly from the comparatively plain females that they were formerly placed in distinct genera. The females of these nine species resemble each other in their general type of coloration; and they likewise resemble both sexes of the species in several allied genera found in various parts of the world. Hence we may infer that these nine species, and probably all the others of the genus, are descended from an ancestral form which was coloured in nearly the same manner. In the tenth species the female still retains the same general colouring, but the male resembles her, so that he is coloured in a much less gaudy and contrasted manner than the males of the previous species. In the eleventh and twelfth species, the females depart from the usual type, for they are gaily decorated almost like the males, but in a somewhat less degree. Hence in these two latter species the bright colours of the males seem to have been transferred to the females; whilst in the tenth species the male has either retained or recovered the plain colours of the female, as well as of the parent-form of the genus. The sexes in these three cases have thus been rendered nearly alike, though in an opposite manner. In the allied genus Eubagis, both sexes of some of the species are plain-coloured and nearly alike; whilst with the greater number the males are decorated with beautiful metallic tints in a diversified manner, and differ much from their females. The females throughout the genus retain the same general style of colouring, so that they resemble one another much more closely than they resemble their own males.

In the genus Papilio, all the species of the Æneas group are remarkable for their conspicuous and strongly contrasted colours, and they illustrate the frequent tendency to gradation in the amount of difference between the sexes. In a few species, for instance in *P. ascanius,* the males and females are alike; in others the males are either a little brighter, or very much more superb than the females. The genus Junonia, allied to our Vanessæ, offers a nearly parallel case, for although the sexes of most of the species resemble each other, and are destitute of rich colours, yet in certain species, as in *J. œnone,* the male is rather more bright-coloured than the female, and in a few (for instance *J. andremiaja*) the male is so different from the female that he might be mistaken for an entirely distinct species.

Another striking case was pointed out to me in the British Museum by Mr. A. Butler, namely, one of the tropical American Theclæ, in which both sexes are nearly alike and wonderfully splendid; in another species the male is coloured in a similarly gorgeous manner, whilst the whole upper surface of the female is of a dull uniform brown. Our common little English blue butterflies of the genus Lycæna, illustrate the various differences in colour between the sexes, almost as well, though not in so striking a manner, as the above exotic genera. In *Lycœena agestis* both sexes have wings of a brown colour, bordered with small ocellated orange spots, and are thus alike. In *L. œgon* the wings of the males are of a fine blue, bordered with black, whilst those of the female are brown, with a similar border, closely resembling the wings of *L. agestis*. Lastly, in *L. arion* both sexes are of a blue colour and are very like, though in the female the edges of the wings are rather duskier, with the black spots plainer; and in a bright blue Indian species both sexes are still more alike.

I have given the foregoing details in order to show, in the first place, that when the sexes of butterflies differ, the male as a general rule is the more beautiful, and departs more from the usual type of colouring of the group to which the species belongs. Hence in most groups the females of the several species resemble each other much more closely than do the males. In some cases, however, to which I shall hereafter allude, the females are coloured more splendidly than the males. In the second place, these details have been given to bring clearly before the mind that within the same genus, the two sexes frequently present every gradation from no difference in colour, to so great a difference that it was long before the two were placed by entomologists in the same genus. In the third place, we have seen that when the sexes nearly resemble each other, this appears due either to the male having transferred his colours to the female, or to the male having retained, or perhaps recovered, the primordial colours of the group. It also deserves notice that in those groups in which the sexes differ, the females usually somewhat resemble the males, so that when the males are beautiful to an extraordinary degree, the females almost invariably exhibit some degree of beauty. From the many cases of gradation in the amount of difference between the sexes, and from the prevalence of the same general type of coloration throughout the whole of the same group, we may conclude that the causes have generally been the same which have determined the brilliant colouring of the males alone of some species, and of both sexes of other species.

As so many gorgeous butterflies inhabit the tropics, it has often been supposed that they owe their colours to the great heat and moisture of these zones; but Mr. Bates[6] has shown by the comparison of various closely-allied groups of insects from the temperate and tropical regions, that this view cannot be maintained; and the evidence becomes conclusive when brilliantly-coloured males and plain-coloured females of the same species inhabit the same district, feed on the same food, and follow exactly the same habits of life. Even when the sexes resemble each other, we can hardly believe that their brilliant and beautifully-arranged colours are the purposeless result of the nature of the tissues and of the action of the surrounding conditions.

With animals of all kinds, whenever colour has been modified for some special purpose, this has been, as far as we can judge, either for direct or indirect protection, or as an attraction between the sexes. With many species of butterflies the upper surfaces of the wings are obscure; and this in all probability leads to their escaping observation and danger. But butterflies would be particularly liable to be attacked by their enemies when at rest; and most kinds whilst resting raise their wings vertically

[6] 'The Naturalist on the Amazons,' vol. i. 1863, p. 19.

over their backs, so that the lower surface alone is exposed to view. Hence it is this side which is often coloured so as to imitate the objects on which these insects commonly rest. Dr. Rössler, I believe, first noticed the similarity of the closed wings of certain Vanessæ and other butterflies to the bark of trees. Many analogous and striking facts could be given. The most interesting one is that recorded by Mr. Wallace[7] of a common Indian and Sumatran butterfly (Kallima) which disappears like magic when it settles on a bush; for it hides its head and antennæ between its closed wings, which, in form, colour and veining, cannot be distinguished from a withered leaf with its footstalk. In some other cases the lower surfaces of the wings are brilliantly coloured, and yet are protective; thus in *Thecla rubi* the wings when closed are of an emerald green, and resemble the young leaves of the bramble, on which in spring this butterfly may often be seen seated. It is also remarkable that in very many species in which the sexes differ greatly in colour on their upper surface, the lower surface is closely similar or identical in both sexes, and serves as a protection.[8]

Although the obscure tints both of the upper and under sides of many butterflies no doubt serve to conceal them, yet we cannot extend this view to the brilliant and conspicuous colours on the upper surface of such species as our admiral and peacock Vanessæ, our white cabbage-butterflies (Pieris), or the great swallow-tail Papilio which haunts the open fens—for these butterflies are thus rendered visible to every living creature. In these species both sexes are alike; but in the common brimstone butterfly (*Gonepteryx rhamni*), the male is of an intense yellow, whilst the female is much paler; and in the orange-tip (*Anthocharis cardamines*) the males alone have their wings tipped with bright orange. Both the males and females in these cases are conspicuous, and it is not credible that their difference in colour should stand in any relation to ordinary protection. Prof. Weismann remarks,[9] that the female of one of the Lycænæ expands her brown wings when she settles on the ground, and is then almost invisible; the male, on the other hand, as if aware of the danger incurred from the bright blue of the upper surface of his wings, rests with them closed; and this shows that the blue colour cannot be in any way protective. Nevertheless, it is probable that conspicuous colours are indirectly beneficial to many species, as a warning that they are unpalatable. For in certain other cases, beauty has been gained through the imitation of other beautiful species, which inhabit the same district and enjoy an immunity from attack by being in some way offensive to their enemies; but then we have to account for the beauty of the imitated species.

As Mr. Walsh has remarked to me, the females of our orange-tip butterfly, above referred to, and of an American species (*Anth. genutia*)

---

[7] See the interesting article in the 'Westminster Review,' July, 1867, p. 10. A woodcut of the Kallima is given by Mr. Wallace in 'Hardwicke's Science Gossip,' September, 1867, p. 196.

[8] Mr. G. Fraser, in 'Nature,' April, 1871, p. 489.

[9] 'Einfluss der Isolirung au di. Artbildung,' 1872, p. 58.

probably show us the primordial colours of the parent-species of the genus; for both sexes of four or five widely-distributed species are coloured in nearly the same manner. As in several previous cases, we may here infer that it is the males of *Anth. cardamines* and *genutia* which have departed from the usual type of the genus. In the *Anth. sara* from California, the orange-tips to the wings have been partially developed in the female; but they are paler than in the male, and slightly different in some other respects. In an allied Indian form, the *Iphias glaucippe*, the orange-tips are fully developed in both sexes. In this Iphias, as pointed out to me by Mr. A. Butler, the under surface of the wings marvellously resembles a pale-coloured leaf; and in our English orange-tip, the under surface resembles the flower-head of the wild parsley, on which the butterfly often rests at night.[10] The same reason which compels us to believe that the lower surfaces have here been coloured for the sake of protection, leads us to deny that the wings have been tipped with bright orange for the same purpose, especially when this character is confined to the males.

Most Moths rest motionless during the whole or greater part of the day with their wings depressed; and the whole upper surface shaded and coloured in an admirable manner, as Mr. Wallace has remarked, for escaping detection. The front-wings of the Bombycidæ,[11] when at rest, generally overlap and conceal the hind-wings; so that the latter might be brightly coloured without much risk; and they are in fact often thus coloured. During flight, moths would often be able to escape from their enemies; nevertheless, as the hind-wings are then fully exposed to view, their bright colours must generally have been acquired at some little risk. But the following fact shews how cautious we ought to be in drawing conclusions on this head. The common Yellow Under-wings (Triphæna) often fly about during the day or early evening, and are then conspicuous from the colour of their hind-wings. It would naturally be thought that this would be a source of danger; but Mr. J. Jenner Weir believes that it actually serves them as a means of escape, for birds strike at these brightly coloured and fragile surfaces, instead of at the body. For instance, Mr. Weir turned into his aviary a vigorous specimen of *Triphœna pronuba*, which was instantly pursued by a robin; but the bird's attention being caught by the coloured wings, the moth was not captured until after about fifty attempts, and small portions of the wings were repeatedly broken off. He tried the same experiment, in the open air, with a swallow and *T. fimbria;* but the large size of this moth probably interfered with its capture.[12] We are thus reminded of a statement made by Mr. Wallace,[13] namely, that in the Brazilian forests and Malayan islands, many common and highly-decorated butterflies are weak flyers, though furnished with a broad expanse of wing; and they "are often captured with pierced and broken wings, as if they had been seized by birds, from which

[10] See the interesting observations by T. W. Wood, 'The Student,' Sept. 1868, p. 81.

[11] Mr. Wallace in 'Hardwicke's Science Gossip,' September, 1867, page 193.

[12] See also, on this subject, Mr. Weir's paper in 'Transact. Ent. Soc.' 1869, p. 23.

[13] 'Westminster Review,' July 1867, p. 16.

they had escaped: if the wings had been much smaller in proportion to the body, it seems probable that the insect would more frequently have been struck or pierced in a vital part, and thus the increased expanse of the wings may have been indirectly beneficial."

Display.—The bright colours of many butterflies and of some moths are specially arranged for display, so that they may be readily seen. During the night colours are not visible, and there can be no doubt that the nocturnal moths, taken as a body, are much less gaily decorated than butterflies, all of which are diurnal in their habits. But the moths of certain families, such as the Zygænidæ, several Sphingidæ, Uraniidæ, some Arctiidæ and Saturniidæ, fly about during the day or early evening, and many of these are extremely beautiful, being far brighter coloured than the strictly nocturnal kinds. A few exceptional cases, however, of bright-coloured nocturnal species have been recorded.[14]

There is evidence of another kind in regard to display. Butterflies, as before remarked, elevate their wings when at rest, but whilst basking in the sunshine often alternately raise and depress them, thus exposing both surfaces to full view; and although the lower surface is often coloured in an obscure manner as a protection, yet in many species it is as highly decorated as the upper surface, and sometimes in a very different manner. In some tropical species the lower surface is even more brilliantly coloured than the upper.[15] In the English fritillaries (*Argynnis*) the lower surface alone is ornamented with shining silver. Nevertheless, as a general rule, the upper surface, which is probably more fully exposed, is coloured more brightly and diversely than the lower. Hence the lower surface generally affords to entomologists the more useful character for detecting the affinities of the various species. Fritz Müller informs me that three species of Castnia are found near his house in S. Brazil: of two of them the hind-wings are obscure, and are always covered by the front-wings when these butterflies are at rest; but the third species has black hind-wings, beautifully spotted with red and white, and these are fully expanded and displayed whenever the butterfly rests. Other such cases could be added.

If we now turn to the enormous group of moths, which, as I hear from Mr. Stainton, do not habitually expose the under surface of their wings to full view, we find this side very rarely coloured with a brightness greater than, or even equal to, that of the upper side. Some exceptions to the rule, either real or apparent, must be noticed, as the case of Hypopyra.[16] Mr. Trimen informs me that in Guenée's great work, three moths are fig-

---

[14] For instance, Lithosia; but Prof. Westwood ('Modern Class. of Insects,' vol. ii. p. 390) seems surprised at this case. On the relative colours of diurnal and nocturnal Lepidoptera, see ibid. pp. 333 and 392; also Harris, 'Treatise on the Insects of New England,' 1842, p. 315.

[15] Such differences between the upper and lower surfaces of the wings of several species of Papilio may be seen in the beautiful plates to Mr. Wallace's 'Memoir on the Papilionidæ of the Malayan Region,' in 'Transactions Linn. Society,' vol. xxv. part i. 1865.

[16] See Mr. Wormald on this moth: 'Proc. Ent. Soc.' March 2nd, 1868.

ured, in which the under surface is much the more brilliant. For instance, in the Australian Gastrophora the upper surface of the fore-wing is pale greyish-ochreous, while the lower surface is magnificently ornamented by an ocellus of cobalt-blue, placed in the midst of a black mark, surrounded by orange-yellow, and this by bluish-white. But the habits of these three moths are unknown; so that no explanation can be given of their unusual style of colouring. Mr. Trimen also informs me that the lower surface of the wings in certain other Geometræ [17] and quadrifid Noctuæ are either more variegated or more brightly-coloured than the upper surface; but some of these species have the habit of "holding their wings quite erect over their backs, retaining them in this position for a considerable time," and thus exposing the under surface to view. Other species, when settled on the ground or herbage, now and then suddenly and slightly lift up their wings. Hence the lower surface of the wings being brighter than the upper surface in certain moths is not so anomalous as it at first appears. The Saturniidæ include some of the most beautiful of all moths, their wings being decorated, as in our British Emperor moth, with fine ocelli; and Mr. T. W. Wood [18] observes that they resemble butterflies in some of their movements; "for instance, in the gentle waving up and down of the wings as if for display, which is more characteristic of diurnal than of nocturnal Lepidoptera."

It is a singular fact that no British moths which are brilliantly coloured, and, as far as I can discover, hardly any foreign species, differ much in colour according to sex; though this is the case with many brilliant butterflies. The male, however, of one American moth, the *Saturnia Io,* is described as having its fore-wings deep yellow, curiously marked with purplish-red spots; whilst the wings of the female are purple-brown, marked with grey lines.[19] The British moths which differ sexually in colour are all brown, or of various dull yellow tints, or nearly white. In several species the males are much darker than the females,[20] and these belong to groups which generally fly about during the afternoon. On the other hand, in many genera, as Mr. Stainton informs me, the males have the hind-wings whiter than those of the female—of which fact *Agrotis exclamationis* offers a good instance. In the Ghost Moth (*Hepialus hu-*

[17] See also an account of the S. American genus Erateina (one of the Geomatræ) in 'Transact. Ent. Soc.' new series, vol. v. pl. xv. and xvi.

[18] 'Proc. Ent. Soc. of London,' July 6, 1868, p. xxvii.

[19] Harris, 'Treatise,' &c., edited by Flint, 1862, p. 395.

[20] For instance, I observe in my son's cabinet that the males are darker than the females in the *Lasiocampa quercus, Odonestis potatoria, Hypogymna dispar, Dasychira pudibunda,* and *Cycnia mendica.* In this latter species the difference in colour between the two sexes is strongly marked; and Mr. Wallace informs me that we here have, as he believes, an instance of protective mimicry confined to one sex, as will hereafter be more fully explained. The white female of the Cycnia resembles the very common *Spilosoma menthrasti,* both sexes of which are white; and Mr. Stainton observed that this latter moth was rejected with utter disgust by a whole brood of young turkeys, which were fond of eating other moths; so that if the Cycnia was commonly mistaken by British birds for the Spilosoma, it would escape being devoured, and its white deceptive colour would thus be highly beneficial.

muli) the difference is more strongly marked; the males being white, and the females yellow with darker markings.[21] It is probable that in these cases the males are thus rendered more conspicuous, and more easily seen by the females whilst flying about in the dusk.

From the several foregoing facts it is impossible to admit that the brilliant colours of butterflies, and of some few moths, have commonly been acquired for the sake of protection. We have seen that their colours and elegant patterns are arranged and exhibited as if for display. Hence I am led to believe that the females prefer or are most excited by the more brilliant males; for on any other supposition the males would, as far as we can see, be ornamented to no purpose. We know that ants and certain Lamellicorn beetles are capable of feeling an attachment for each other, and that ants recognise their fellows after an interval of several months. Hence there is no abstract improbability in the Lepidoptera, which probably stand nearly or quite as high in the scale as these insects, having sufficient mental capacity to admire bright colours. They certainly discover flowers by colour. The Humming-bird Sphinx may often be seen to swoop down from a distance on a bunch of flowers in the midst of green foliage; and I have been assured by two persons abroad, that these moths repeatedly visit flowers painted on the walls of a room, and vainly endeavour to insert their proboscis into them. Fritz Müller informs me that several kinds of butterflies in S. Brazil shew an unmistakable preference for certain colours over others: he observed that they very often visited the brilliant red flowers of five or six genera of plants, but never the white or yellow flowering species of the same and other genera, growing in the same garden; and I have received other accounts to the same effect. As I hear from Mr. Doubleday, the common white butterfly often flies down to a bit of paper on the ground, no doubt mistaking it for one of its own species. Mr. Collingwood [22] in speaking of the difficulty in collecting certain butterflies in the Malay Archipelago, states that "a dead specimen pinned upon a conspicuous twig will often arrest an insect of the same species in its headlong flight, and bring it down within easy reach of the net, especially if it be of the opposite sex."

The courtship of butterflies is, as before remarked, a prolonged affair. The males sometimes fight together in rivalry; and many may be seen pursuing or crowding round the same female. Unless, then, the females prefer one male to another, the pairing must be left to mere chance, and this does not appear probable. If, on the other hand, the females habitually, or even occasionally, prefer the more beautiful males, the colours of the latter will have been rendered brighter by degrees, and will have been transmitted to both sexes or to one sex, according to the law of inheri-

---

[21] It is remarkable, that in the Shetland Islands the male of this moth, instead of differing widely from the female, frequently resembles her closely in colour (see Mr. MacLachlan, 'Transact. Ent. Soc.' vol. ii. 1866, p. 459). Mr. G. Fraser suggests ('Nature,' April 1871, p. 489) that at the season of the year when the ghost-moth appears in these northern islands, the whiteness of the males would not be needed to render them visible to the females in the twilight night.

[22] 'Rambles of a Naturalist in the Chinese Seas,' 1868, p. 182.

tance which has prevailed. The process of sexual selection will have been much facilitated, if the conclusion can be trusted, arrived at from various kinds of evidence in the supplement to the ninth chapter; namely, that the males of many Lepidoptera, at least in the imago state, greatly exceed the females in number.

Some facts, however, are opposed to the belief that female butterflies prefer the more beautiful males; thus, as I have been assured by several collectors, fresh females may frequently be seen paired with battered, faded, or dingy males; but this is a circumstance which could hardly fail often to follow from the males emerging from their cocoons earlier than the females. With moths of the family of the Bombycidæ, the sexes pair immediately after assuming the imago state; for they cannot feed, owing to the rudimentary condition of their mouths. The females, as several entomologists have remarked to me, lie in an almost torpid state, and appear not to evince the least choice in regard to their partners. This is the case with the common silk-moth (*B. mori*), as I have been told by some continental and English breeders. Dr. Wallace, who has had great experience in breeding *Bombyx cynthia,* is convinced that the females evince no choice or preference. He has kept above 300 of these moths together, and has often found the most vigorous females mated with stunted males. The reverse appears to occur seldom; for, as he believes, the more vigorous males pass over the weakly females, and are attracted by those endowed with most vitality. Nevertheless, the Bombycidæ, though obscurely-coloured, are often beautiful to our eyes from their elegant and mottled shades.

I have as yet only referred to the species in which the males are brighter coloured than the females, and I have attributed their beauty to the females for many generations having chosen and paired with the more attractive males. But converse cases occur, though rarely, in which the females are more brilliant than the males; and here, as I believe, the males have selected the more beautiful females, and have thus slowly added to their beauty. We do not know why in various classes of animals the males of some few species have selected the more beautiful females instead of having gladly accepted any female, as seems to be the general rule in the animal kingdom; but if, contrary to what generally occurs with the Lepidoptera, the females were much more numerous than the males, the latter would be likely to pick out the more beautiful females. Mr. Butler shewed me several species of Callidryas in the British Museum, in some of which the females equalled, and in others greatly surpassed the males in beauty; for the females alone have the borders of their wings suffused with crimson and orange, and spotted with black. The plainer males of these species closely resemble each other, shewing that here the females have been modified; whereas in those cases, where the males are the more ornate, it is these which have been modified, the females remaining closely alike.

In England we have some analogous cases, though not so marked. The females alone of two species of Thecla have a bright-purple or orange patch on their fore-wings. In Hipparchia the sexes do not differ much; but it is the female of *H. janira* which has a conspicuous light-brown patch on her wings; and the females of some of the other species are brighter coloured than their males. Again, the females of *Colias edusa* and *hyale* have "orange or yellow spots on the black marginal border, represented in the males only by thin streaks;" and in Pieris it is the females which "are ornamented with black spots on the fore-wings, and these are only partially present in the males." Now the males of many butterflies are known to support the females during their marriage flight; but in the species just named it is the females which support the males; so that the part which the two sexes play is reversed, as is their relative beauty. Throughout the animal kingdom the males commonly take the more active share in wooing, and their beauty seems to have been increased by the females having accepted the more attractive individuals; but with these butterflies, the females take the more active part in the final marriage ceremony, so that we may suppose that they likewise do so in the wooing; and in this case we can understand how it is that they have been rendered the more beautiful. Mr. Meldola, from whom the foregoing statements have been taken, says in conclusion: "Though I am not convinced of the action of sexual selection in producing the colours of insects, it cannot be denied that these facts are strikingly corroborative of Mr. Darwin's views."[23]

As sexual selection primarily depends on variability, a few words must be added on this subject. In respect to colour there is no difficulty, for any number of highly variable Lepidoptera could be named. One good instance will suffice. Mr. Bates shewed me a whole series of specimens of *Papilio sesostris* and *P. chilrenœ;* in the latter the males varied much in the extent of the beautifully enamelled green patch on the fore-wings, and in the size of the white mark, and of the splendid crimson stripe on the hind-wings; so that there was a great contrast amongst the males between the most and the least gaudy. The male of *Papilio sesostris* is much less beautiful than of *P. childrenœ;* and it likewise varies a little in the size of the green patch on the fore-wings, and in the occasional appearance of the small crimson stripe on the hind-wings, borrowed, as it would seem, from its own female; for the females of this and of many other species in the Æneas group possess this crimson stripe. Hence between the brightest specimens of *P. sesostris* and the dullest of *P. childrenœ,* there was but a small interval; and it was evident that as far as mere variability is concerned, there would be no difficulty in permanently increasing the beauty of either species by means of selection. The variability is here almost confined to the male sex; but Mr. Wallace and Mr. Bates have shewn [24] that the females of some species are extremely variable, the

---

[23] 'Nature,' April 27th, 1871, p. 508. Mr. Meldola quotes Donzel, in 'Soc. Ent. de France,' 1837, p. 77, on the flight of butterflies whilst pairing. See also Mr. G. Fraser, in 'Nature,' April 20th, 1871, p. 489, on the sexual differences of several British butterflies.

[24] Wallace on the Papilionidæ of the Malayan Region, in 'Transact. Linn. Soc.'

males being nearly constant. In a future chapter I shall have occasion to shew that the beautiful eye-like spots, or ocelli, found on the wings of many Lepidoptera, are eminently variable. I may here add that these ocelli offer a difficulty on the theory of sexual selection; for though appearing to us so ornamental, they are never present in one sex and absent in the other, nor do they ever differ much in the two sexes.[25] This fact is at present inexplicable; but if it should hereafter be found that the formation of an ocellus is due to some change in the tissues of the wings, for instance, occurring at a very early period of development, we might expect, from what we know of the laws of inheritance, that it would be transmitted to both sexes, though arising and perfected in one sex alone.

On the whole, although many serious objections may be urged, it seems probable that most of the brilliantly-coloured species of Lepidoptera owe their colours to sexual selection, excepting in certain cases, presently to be mentioned, in which conspicuous colours have been gained through mimicry as a protection. From the ardour of the male throughout the animal kingdom, he is generally willing to accept any female; and it is the female which usually exerts a choice. Hence, if sexual selection has been efficient with the Lepidoptera, the male, when the sexes differ, ought to be the more brilliantly coloured, and this undoubtedly is the case. When both sexes are brilliantly coloured and resemble each other, the characters acquired by the males appear to have been transmitted to both. We are led to this conclusion by cases, even within the same genus, of gradation from an extraordinary amount of difference to identity in colour between the two sexes.

But it may be asked whether the difference in colour between the sexes may not be accounted for by other means besides sexual selection. Thus the males and females of the same species of butterfly are in several cases known [26] to inhabit different stations, the former commonly basking in the sunshine, the latter haunting gloomy forests. It is therefore possible that different conditions of life may have acted directly on the two sexes; but this is not probable [27] as in the adult state they are exposed to different conditions during a very short period; and the larvæ of both are exposed to the same conditions. Mr. Wallace believes that the difference between the sexes is due not so much to the males having been modified, as to the females having in all or almost all cases acquired dull colours for the sake of protection. It seems to me, on the contrary, far more probable that it is the males which have been chiefly modified through sexual selection, the females having been comparatively little changed. We can

vol. xxv. 1865, pp. 8, 36. A striking case of a rare variety, strictly intermediate between two other well-marked female varieties, is given by Mr. Wallace. See also Mr. Bates, in 'Proc. Entomolog. Soc.' Nov. 19th, 1866, p. xl.

[25] Mr. Bates was so kind as to lay this subject before the Entomological Society, and I have received answers to this effect from several entomologists.

[26] H. W. Bates, 'The Naturalist on the Amazons,' vol. ii. 1863, p. 228. A. R. Wallace, in 'Transact. Linn. Soc.' vol. xxv. 1865, p. 10.

[27] On this whole subject see 'The Variation of Animals and Plants under Domestication,' 1868, vol. ii. chap. xxiii.

thus understand how it is that the females of allied species generally resemble one another so much more closely than do the males. They thus
shew us approximately the primordial colouring of the parent-species of
the group to which they belong. They have, however, almost always been
somewhat modified by the transfer to them of some of the successive
variations, through the accumulation of which the males were rendered
beautiful. But I do not wish to deny that the females alone of some species may have been specially modified for protection. In most cases the
males and females of distinct species will have been exposed during their
prolonged larval state to different conditions, and may have been thus
affected; though with the males any slight change of colour thus caused
will generally have been masked by the brilliant tints gained through sexual selection. When we treat of Birds, I shall have to discuss the whole
question, as to how far the differences in colour between the sexes are due
to the males having been modified through sexual selection for ornamental purposes, or to the females having been modified through natural selection for the sake of protection, so that I will here say but little on the
subject.

In all the cases in which the more common form of equal inheritance
by both sexes has prevailed, the selection of bright-coloured males would
tend to make the females bright-coloured; and the selection of dull-coloured females would tend to make the males dull. If both processes were
carried on simultaneously, they would tend to counteract each other; and
the final result would depend on whether a greater number of females
from being well protected by obscure colours, or a greater number of
males by being brightly-coloured and thus finding partners, succeeded in
leaving more numerous offspring.

In order to account for the frequent transmission of characters to one
sex alone, Mr. Wallace expresses his belief that the more common form
of equal inheritance by both sexes can be changed through natural selection into inheritance by one sex alone, but in favour of this view I can discover no evidence. We know from what occurs under domestication that
new characters often appear, which from the first are transmitted to one
sex alone; and by the selection of such variations there would not be the
slightest difficulty in giving bright colours to the males alone, and at the
same time or subsequently, dull colours to the females alone. In this manner the females of some butterflies and moths have, it is probable, been
rendered inconspicuous for the sake of protection, and widely different
from their males.

I am, however, unwilling without distinct evidence to admit that two
complex processes of selection, each requiring the transference of new
characters to one sex alone, have been carried on with a multitude of species,—that the males have been rendered more brilliant by beating their
rivals, and the females more dull-coloured by having escaped from their
enemies. The male, for instance, of the common brimstone butterfly (Gonepteryx), is of a far more intense yellow than the female, though she is
equally conspicuous; and it does not seem probable that she specially ac-

quired her pale tints as a protection, though it is probable that the male acquired his bright colours as a sexual attraction. The female of *Anthocharis cardamines* does not possess the beautiful orange wing-tips of the male; consequently she closely resembles the white butterflies (Pieris) so common in our gardens; but we have no evidence that this resemblance is beneficial to her. As, on the other hand, she resembles both sexes of several other species of the genus inhabiting various quarters of the world, it is probable that she has simply retained to a large extent her primordial colours.

Finally, as we have seen, various considerations lead to the conclusion that with the greater number of brilliantly-coloured Lepidoptera it is the male which has been chiefly modified through sexual selection; the amount of difference between the sexes mostly depending on the form of inheritance which has prevailed. Inheritance is governed by so many unknown laws or conditions, that it seems to us to act in a capricious manner;[28] and we can thus, to a certain extent, understand how it is that with closely allied species the sexes either differ to an astonishing degree, or are identical in colour. As all the successive steps in the process of variation are necessarily transmitted through the female, a greater or less number of such steps might readily become developed in her; and thus we can understand the frequent gradations from an extreme difference to none at all between the sexes of allied species. These cases of gradation, it may be added, are much too common to favour the supposition that we here see females actually undergoing the process of transition and losing their brightness for the sake of protection; for we have every reason to conclude that at any one time the greater number of species are in a fixed condition.

Mimicry.—This principle was first made clear in an admirable paper by Mr. Bates,[29] who thus threw a flood of light on many obscure problems. It had previously been observed that certain butterflies in S. America belonging to quite distinct families, resembled the Heliconidæ so closely in every stripe and shade of colour, that they could not be distinguished save by an experienced entomologist. As the Heliconidæ are coloured in their usual manner, whilst the others depart from the usual colouring of the groups to which they belong, it is clear that the latter are the imitators, and the Heliconidæ the imitated. Mr. Bates further observed that the imitating species are comparatively rare, whilst the imitated abound, and that the two sets live mingled together. From the fact of the Heliconidæ being conspicuous and beautiful insects, yet so numerous in individuals and species, he concluded that they must be protected from the attacks of enemies by some secretion or odour; and this conclusion has now been amply confirmed,[30] especially by Mr. Belt. Hence Mr.

---

[28] 'The Variation of Animals and Plants under Domestication,' vol. ii. chap. xii. p. 17.

[29] 'Transact. Linn. Soc.' vol. xxiii. 1862, p. 495.

[30] 'Proc. Ent. Soc.' Dec. 3, 1866, p. xlv.

Bates inferred that the butterflies which imitate the protected species have acquired their present marvellously deceptive appearance through variation and natural selection, in order to be mistaken for the protected kinds, and thus to escape being devoured. No explanation is here attempted of the brilliant colours of the imitated, but only of the imitating butterflies. We must account for the colours of the former in the same general manner, as in the cases previously discussed in this chapter. Since the publication of Mr. Bates' paper, similar and equally striking facts have been observed by Mr. Wallace in the Malayan region, by Mr. Trimen in South Africa, and by Mr. Riley in the United States.[31]

As some writers have felt much difficulty in understanding how the first steps in the process of mimicry could have been effected through natural selection, it may be well to remark that the process probably commenced long ago between forms not widely dissimilar in colour. In this case even a slight variation would be beneficial, if it rendered the one species more like the other; and afterwards the imitated species might be modified to an extreme degree through sexual selection or other means, and if the changes were gradual, the imitators might easily be led along the same track, until they differed to an equally extreme degree from their original condition; and they would thus ultimately assume an appearance or colouring wholly unlike that of the other members of the group to which they belonged. It should also be remembered that many species of Lepidoptera are liable to considerable and abrupt variations in colour. A few instances have been given in this chapter; and many more may be found in the papers of Mr. Bates and Mr. Wallace.

With several species the sexes are alike, and imitate the two sexes of another species. But Mr. Trimen gives, in the paper already referred to, three cases in which the sexes of the imitated form differ from each other in colour, and the sexes of the imitating form differ in a like manner. Several cases have also been recorded where the females alone imitate brilliantly-coloured and protected species, the males retaining "the normal aspect of their immediate congeners." It is here obvious that the successive variations by which the female has been modified have been transmitted to her alone. It is, however, probable that some of the many successive variations would have been transmitted to, and developed in, the males had not such males been eliminated by being thus rendered less attractive to the females; so that only those variations were preserved which were from the first strictly limited in their transmission to the female sex. We have a partial illustration of these remarks in a statement by Mr. Belt;[32] that the males of some of the Leptalides, which imitate protected species, still retain in a concealed manner some of their original

---

[31] Wallace, 'Transact. Linn. Soc.' vol. xxv. 1865, p. i.; also, 'Transact. Ent. Soc.' vol. iv. (3rd series), 1867, p. 301. Trimen, 'Linn. Transact.' vol. xxvi. 1869, p. 497. Riley, 'Third Annual Report on the Noxious Insects of Missouri,' 1871, pp. 163-168. This latter essay is valuable, as Mr. Riley here discusses all the objections which have been raised against Mr. Bates's theory.

[32] 'The Naturalist in Nicaragua,' 1874, p. 385.

characters. Thus in the males "the upper half of the lower wing is of a pure white, whilst all the rest of the wings is barred and spotted with black, red and yellow, like the species they mimic. The females have not this white patch, and the males usually conceal it by covering it with the upper wing, so that I cannot imagine its being of any other use to them than as an attraction in courtship, when they exhibit it to the females, and thus gratify their deep-seated preference for the normal colour of the Order to which the Leptalides belong."

Bright Colours of Caterpillars.—Whilst reflecting on the beauty of many butterflies, it occurred to me that some caterpillars were splendidly coloured; and as sexual selection could not possibly have here acted, it appeared rash to attribute the beauty of the mature insect to this agency, unless the bright colours of their larvæ could be somehow explained. In the first place, it may be observed that the colours of caterpillars do not stand in any close correlation with those of the mature insect. Secondly, their bright colours do not serve in any ordinary manner as a protection. Mr. Bates informs me, as an instance of this, that the most conspicuous caterpillar which he ever beheld (that of a Sphinx) lived on the large green leaves of a tree on the open llanos of South America; it was about four inches in length, transversely banded with black and yellow, and with its head, legs, and tail of a bright red. Hence it caught the eye of any one who passed by, even at the distance of many yards, and no doubt that of every passing bird.

I then applied to Mr. Wallace, who has an innate genius for solving difficulties. After some consideration he replied: "Most caterpillars require protection, as may be inferred from some kinds being furnished with spines or irritating hairs, and from many being coloured green like the leaves on which they feed, or being curiously like the twigs of the trees on which they live." Another instance of protection, furnished me by Mr. J. Mansel Weale, may be added, namely, that there is a caterpillar of a moth which lives on the mimosas in South Africa, and fabricates for itself a case quite indistinguishable from the surrounding thorns. From such considerations Mr. Wallace thought it probable that conspicuously coloured caterpillars were protected by having a nauseous taste; but as their skin is extremely tender, and as their intestines readily protrude from a wound, a slight peck from the beak of a bird would be as fatal to them as if they had been devoured. Hence, as Mr. Wallace remarks, "distastefulness alone would be insufficient to protect a caterpillar unless some outward sign indicated to its would-be destroyer that its prey was a disgusting morsel." Under these circumstances it would be highly advantageous to a caterpillar to be instantaneously and certainly recognised as unpalatable by all birds and other animals. Thus the most gaudy colours would be serviceable, and might have been gained by variation and the survival of the most easily-recognised individuals.

This hypothesis appears at first sight very bold, but when it was brought before the Entomological Society [33] it was supported by various statements; and Mr. J. Jenner Weir, who keeps a large number of birds in an aviary, informs me that he has made many trials, and finds no exception to the rule, that all caterpillars of nocturnal and retiring habits with smooth skins, all of a green colour, and all which imitate twigs, are greedily devoured by his birds. The hairy and spinose kinds are invariably rejected, as were four conspicuously-coloured species. When the birds rejected a caterpillar, they plainly shewed, by shaking their heads, and cleansing their beaks, that they were disgusted by the taste. [34] Three conspicuous kinds of caterpillars and moths were also given to some lizards and frogs, by Mr. A. Butler, and were rejected, though other kinds were eagerly eaten. Thus the probability of Mr. Wallace's view is confirmed, namely, that certain caterpillars have been made conspicuous for their own good, so as to be easily recognised by their enemies, on nearly the same principle that poisons are sold in coloured bottles by druggists for the good of man. We cannot, however, at present thus explain the elegant diversity in the colours of many caterpillars; but any species which had at some former period acquired a dull, mottled, or striped appearance, either in imitation of surrounding objects, or from the direct action of climate, &c., almost certainly would not become uniform in colour, when its tints were rendered intense and bright; for in order to make a caterpillar merely conspicuous, there would be no selection in any definite direction.

Summary and Concluding Remarks on Insects.—Looking back to the several Orders, we see that the sexes often differ in various characters, the meaning of which is not in the least understood. The sexes, also, often differ in their organs of sense and means of locomotion, so that the males may quickly discover and reach the females. They differ still oftener in the males possessing diversified contrivances for retaining the females when found. We are, however, here concerned only in a secondary degree with sexual differences of these kinds.

In almost all the Orders, the males of some species, even of weak and delicate kinds, are known to be highly pugnacious; and some few are furnished with special weapons for fighting with their rivals. But the law of battle does not prevail nearly so widely with insects as with the higher animals. Hence it probably arises, that it is in only a few cases that the males have been rendered larger and stronger than the females. On the contrary, they are usually smaller, so that they may be developed within a shorter time, to be ready in large numbers for the emergence of the females.

[33] 'Proc. Entomolog. Soc.' Dec. 3rd, 1866, p. xlv., and March 4th, 1867, p. lxxx.

[34] See Mr. J. Jenner Weir's paper on Insects and Insectivorous Birds, in 'Transact. Ent. Soc.' 1869, p. 21; also Mr. Butler's paper, ibid. p. 27. Mr. Riley has given analogous facts in the 'Third Annual Report on the Noxious Insects of Missouri,' 1871, p. 148. Some opposed cases are, however, given by Dr. Wallace and M. H. d'Orville; see 'Zoological Record,' 1869, p. 349.

In two families of the Homoptera and in three of the Orthoptera, the males alone possess sound-producing organs in an efficient state. These are used incessantly during the breeding-season, not only for calling the females, but apparently for charming or exciting them in rivalry with other males. No one who admits the agency of selection of any kind, will, after reading the above discussion, dispute that these musical instruments have been acquired through sexual selection. In four other Orders the members of one sex, or more commonly of both sexes, are provided with organs for producing various sounds, which apparently serve merely as call-notes. When both sexes are thus provided, the individuals which were able to make the loudest or most continuous noise would gain partners before those which were less noisy, so that their organs have probably been gained through sexual selection. It is instructive to reflect on the wonderful diversity of the means for producing sound, possessed by the males alone, or by both sexes, in no less than six Orders. We thus learn how effectual sexual selection has been in leading to modifications which sometimes, as with the Homoptera, relate to important parts of the organisation.

From the reasons assigned in the last chapter, it is probable that the great horns possessed by the males of many Lamellicorn, and some other beetles, have been acquired as ornaments. From the small size of insects, we are apt to undervalue their appearance. If we could imagine a male Chalcosoma (fig. 16), with its polished bronzed coat of mail, and its vast complex horns, magnified to the size of a horse, or even of a dog, it would be one of the most imposing animals in the world.

The colouring of insects is a complex and obscure subject. When the male differs slightly from the female, and neither are brilliantly-coloured, it is probable that the sexes have varied in a slightly different manner, and that the variations have been transmitted by each sex to the same. without any benefit or evil thus accruing. When the male is brilliantly-coloured and differs conspicuously from the female, as with some dragon-flies and many butterflies, it is probable that he owes his colours to sexual selection; whilst the female has retained a primordial or very ancient type of colouring, slightly modified by the agencies before explained. But in some cases the female has apparently been made obscure by variations transmitted to her alone, as a means of direct protection; and it is almost certain that she has sometimes been made brilliant, so as to imitate other protected species inhabiting the same district. When the sexes resemble each other and both are obscurely coloured, there is no doubt that they have been in a multitude of cases so coloured for the sake of protection. So it is in some instances when both are brightly-coloured, for they thus imitate protected species, or resemble surrounding objects such as flowers; or they give notice to their enemies that they are unpalatable. In other cases in which the sexes resemble each other and are both brilliant, especially when the colours are arranged for display, we may conclude that they have been gained by the male sex as an attraction, and have been transferred to the female. We are more especially led to this conclusion whenever the same type of coloration prevails throughout a whole group, and we find that the males of some species differ widely in colour from the females, whilst others differ slightly or not at all with intermediate gradations connecting these extreme states.

In the same manner as bright colours have often been partially transferred from the males to the females, so it has been with the extraordinary horns of many Lamellicorn and some other beetles. So again, the sound-producing organs proper to the males of the Homoptera and Orthoptera have generally been transferred in a rudimentary, or even in a nearly perfect condition, to the females; yet not sufficiently perfect to be of any use. It is also an interesting fact, as bearing on sexual selection, that the stridulating organs of certain male Orthoptera are not fully developed until the last moult; and that the colours of certain male dragonflies are not fully developed until some little time after their emergence from the pupal state, and when they are ready to breed.

Sexual selection implies that the more attractive individuals are preferred by the opposite sex; and as with insects, when the sexes differ, it is the male which, with some rare exceptions, is the more ornamented, and departs more from the type to which the species belongs;—and as it is the male which searches eagerly for the female, we must suppose that the females habitually or occasionally prefer the more beautiful males, and that these have thus acquired their beauty. That the females in most or all the Orders would have the power of rejecting any particular male, is probable from the many singular contrivances possessed by the males, such as great jaws, adhesive cushions, spines, elongated legs, &c., for seizing the female; for these contrivances shew that there is some difficulty in the act, so that her concurrence would seem necessary. Judging from what we know of the perceptive powers and affections of various insects, there is no antecedent improbability in sexual selection having come largely into play; but we have as yet no direct evidence on this head, and some facts are opposed to the belief. Nevertheless, when we see many males pursuing the same female, we can hardly believe that the pairing is left to blind chance—that the female exerts no choice, and is not influenced by the gorgeous colours or other ornaments with which the male is decorated.

If we admit that the females of the Homoptera and Orthoptera appreciate the musical tones of their male partners, and that the various instruments have been perfected through sexual selection, there is little improbability in the females of other insects appreciating beauty in form or colour, and consequently in such characters having been thus gained by the males. But from the circumstance of colour being so variable, and from its having been so often modified for the sake of protection, it is difficult to decide in how large a proportion of cases sexual selection has played a part. This is more especially difficult in those Orders, such as Orthoptera, Hymenoptera, and Coleoptera, in which the two sexes rarely differ much in colour; for we are then left to mere analogy. With the Coleoptera, however, as before remarked, it is in the great Lamellicorn group, placed by some authors at the head of the Order, and in which we sometimes see a mutual attachment between the sexes, that we find the males of some species possessing weapons for sexual strife, others furnished with wonderful horns, many with stridulating organs, and others ornamented with splendid metallic tints. Hence it seems probable that all these characters have been gained through the same means, namely sexual selection. With butterflies we have the best evidence, as the males sometimes take pains to display their beautiful colours; and we cannot believe that they would act thus, unless the display was of use to them in their courtship.

When we treat of Birds, we shall see that they present in their secondary sexual characters the closest analogy with insects. Thus, many male birds are highly pugnacious, and some are furnished with special weapons for fighting with their rivals. They possess organs which are used during the breeding-season for producing vocal and instrumental music. They are frequently ornamented with combs, horns, wattles and plumes of the most diversified kinds, and are decorated with beautiful colours, all evidently for the sake of display. We shall find that, as with insects, both sexes in certain groups are equally beautiful, and are equally provided with ornaments which are usually confined to the male sex. In other groups both sexes are equally plain-coloured and unornamented. Lastly, in some few anomalous cases, the females are more beautiful than the males. We shall often find, in the same group of birds, every gradation from no difference between the sexes, to an extreme difference. We shall see that female birds, like female insects, often possess more or less plain traces or rudiments of characters which properly belong to the males and are of use only to them. The analogy, indeed, in all these respects between birds and insects is curiously close. Whatever explanation applies to the one class probably applies to the other; and this explanation, as we shall hereafter attempt to shew in further detail, is sexual selection.

CHAPTER XII

SECONDARY SEXUAL CHARACTERS OF FISHES,
AMPHIBIANS, AND REPTILES

FISHES: *Courtship and battles of the males—Larger size of the females—Males, bright colours and ornamental appendages; other strange characters—Colours and appendages acquired by the males during the breeding-season alone—Fishes with both sexes brilliantly coloured—Protective colours—The less conspicuous colours of the female cannot be accounted for on the principle of protection—Male fishes building nests, and taking charge of the ova and young.* AMPHIBIANS: *Differences in structure and colour between the sexes—Vocal organs.* REPTILES: *Chelonians—Crocodiles—Snakes, colours in some cases protective—Lizards, battles of—Ornamental appendages—Strange differences in structure between the sexes—Colours—Sexual differences almost as great as with birds.*

WE have now arrived at the great sub-kingdom of the Vertebrata, and will commence with the lowest class, that of Fishes. The males of Plagiostomous fishes (sharks, rays) and of Chimæroid fishes are provided with claspers which serve to retain the female, like the various structures possessed by many of the lower animals. Besides the claspers, the males of many rays have clusters of strong sharp spines on their heads, and several rows along "the upper outer surface of their pectoral fins." These are present in the males of some species, which have other parts of their bodies smooth. They are only temporarily developed during the breeding-season; and Dr. Günther suspects that they are brought into action as prehensile organs by the doubling inwards and downwards of the two sides of the body. It is a remarkable fact that the females and not the males of some species, as of *Raia clavata,* have their backs studded with large hook-formed spines.[1]

The males alone of the capelin (*Mallotus villosus,* one of Salmonidæ), are provided with a ridge of closely-set, brush-like scales, by the aid of which two males, one on each side, hold the female, whilst she runs with great swiftness on the sandy beach, and there deposits her spawn.[2] The widely distinct *Monacanthus scopas* presents a somewhat analogous structure. The male, as Dr. Günther informs me, has a cluster of stiff, straight spines, like those of a comb, on the sides of the tail; and these in a specimen six inches long were nearly one and a half inches in length; the female has in the same place a cluster of bristles, which may be compared with those of a tooth-brush. In another species, *M. peronii,* the

[1] Yarrell's 'Hist. of British Fishes,' vol. ii. 1836, pp. 417, 425, 436. Dr. Günther informs me that the spines in *R. clavata* are peculiar to the female.
[2] 'The Am. Nat.,' April, 1871, p. 119.

male has a brush like that possessed by the female of the last species, whilst the sides of the tail in the female are smooth. In some other species of the same genus the tail can be perceived to be a little roughened in the male and perfectly smooth in the female; and lastly in others, both sexes have smooth sides.

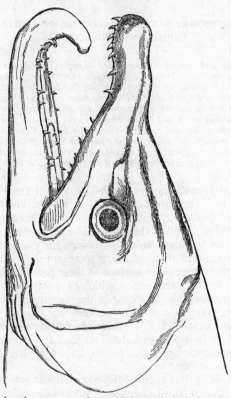

FIG. 27.—Head of male common salmon (*Salmo salar*) during the breeding-season.

[This drawing, as well as all the others in the present chapter, have been executed by the well-known artist, Mr. G. Ford, from specimens in the British Museum, under the kind superintendence of Dr. Günther.]

The males of many fish fight for the possession of the females. Thus the male stickleback (*Gasterosteus leiurus*) has been described as "mad with delight," when the female comes out of her hiding-place and surveys the nest which he has made for her. "He darts round her in every direction, then to his accumulated materials for the nest, then back again in an instant; and as she does not advance he endeavours to push her with his snout, and then tries to pull her by the tail and side-spine to the nest." [3] The males are said to be polygamists; [4] they are extraordinarily bold and pugnacious, whilst "the females are quite pacific." Their battles are at times desperate; "for these puny combatants fasten tight on each other for several seconds, tumbling over and over again until their strength appears completely exhausted." With the rough-tailed stickle-

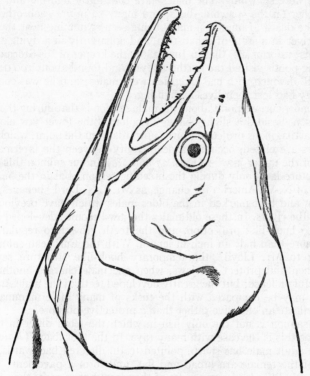

FIG. 28.—Head of female salmon.

back (*G. trachurus*) the males whilst fighting swim round and round each other, biting and endeavouring to pierce each other with their raised lateral spines. The same writer adds,[5] "the bite of these little furies is very severe. They also use their lateral spines with such fatal effect, that I have seen one during a battle absolutely rip his opponent quite open, so that he sank to the bottom and died." When a fish is conquered, "his gallant bearing forsakes him; his gay colours fade away; and he hides his disgrace among his peaceable companions, but is for some time the constant object of his conqueror's persecution."

[3] See Mr. R. Warington's interesting articles in 'Annals and Mag. of Nat. Hist.' October, 1852, and November, 1855.
[4] Noel Humphreys, 'River Gardens,' 1857.
[5] Loudon's 'Mag. of Nat. History,' vol. iii. 1830, p. 331.

The male salmon is as pugnacious as the little stickleback; and so is the male trout, as I hear from Dr. Günther. Mr. Shaw saw a violent contest between two male salmon which lasted the whole day; and Mr. R. Buist, Superintendent of Fisheries, informs me that he has often watched from the bridge at Perth the males driving away their rivals, whilst the females were spawning. The males "are constantly fighting and tearing each other on the spawning-beds, and many so injure each other as to cause the death of numbers, many being seen swimming near the banks of the river in a state of exhaustion, and apparently in a dying state." [6] Mr. Buist informs me, that in June 1868, the keeper of the Stormontfield breeding-ponds visited the northern Tyne and found about 300 dead salmon, all of which with one exception were males; and he was convinced that they had lost their lives by fighting.

The most curious point about the male salmon is that during the breeding-season, besides a slight change in colour, "the lower jaw elongates, and a cartilaginous projection turns upwards from the point, which, when the jaws are closed, occupies a deep cavity between the intermaxillary bones of the upper jaw." [7] (Figs. 27 and 28.) In our salmon this change of structure lasts only during the breeding-season; but in the *Salmo lycaodon* of N.-W. America the change, as Mr. J. K. Lord [8] believes, is permanent, and best marked in the older males which have previously ascended the rivers. In these old males the jaw becomes developed into an immense hook-like projection, and the teeth grow into regular fangs, often more than half an inch in length. With the European salmon, according to Mr. Lloyd, [9] the temporary hook-like structure serves to strengthen and protect the jaws, when one male charges another with wonderful violence; but the greatly developed teeth of the male American salmon may be compared with the tusks of many male mammals, and they indicate an offensive rather than a protective purpose.

The salmon is not the only fish in which the teeth differ in the two sexes; as this is the case with many rays. In the thornback (*Raia clavata*) the adult male has sharp, pointed teeth, directed backwards, whilst those of the female are broad and flat, and form a pavement; so that these teeth differ in the two sexes of the same species more than is usual in distinct genera of the same family. The teeth of the male become sharp only when he is adult: whilst young they are broad and flat like those of the female. As so frequently occurs with secondary sexual characters, both sexes of some species of rays (for instance *R. batis*), when adult, possess sharp pointed teeth; and here a character, proper to and primarily gained by the male, appears to have been transmitted to the offspring of both sexes. The teeth are likewise pointed in both sexes of *R. maculata*,

---

[6] 'The Field,' June 29th, 1867. For Mr. Shaw's statements, see 'Edinburgh Review,' 1843. Another experienced observer (Scrope's 'Days of Salmon Fishing,' p. 60) remarks that like the stag, the male would, if he could, keep all other males away.

[7] Yarrell, 'History of British Fishes,' vol. ii. 1836, p. 10.

[8] 'The Naturalist in Vancouver's Island,' vol. i. 1866, p. 54.

[9] 'Scandinavian Adventures,' vol. i. 1854, p. 100, 104.

but only when quite adult; the males acquiring them at an earlier age than the females. We shall hereafter meet with analogous cases in certain birds, in which the male acquires the plumage common to both sexes when adult, at a somewhat earlier age than does the female. With other species of rays the males even when old never possess sharp teeth, and consequently the adults of both sexes are provided with broad, flat teeth like those of the young, and like those of the mature females of the above-mentioned species.[10] As the rays are bold, strong and voracious fish, we may suspect that the males require their sharp teeth for fighting with their rivals; but as they possess many parts modified and adapted for the prehension of the female, it is possible that their teeth may be used for this purpose.

In regard to size, M. Carbonnier [11] maintains that the female of almost all fishes is larger than the male; and Dr. Günther does not know of a single instance in which the male is actually larger than the female. With some Cyprinodonts the male is not even half as large. As in many kinds of fishes the males habitually fight together, it is surprising that they have not generally become larger and stronger than the females through the effects of sexual selection. The males suffer from their small size, for according to M. Carbonnier, they are liable to be devoured by the females of their own species when carnivorous, and no doubt by other species. Increased size must be in some manner of more importance to the females, than strength and size are to the males for fighting with other males; and this perhaps is to allow of the production of a vast number of ova.

In many species the male alone is ornamented with bright colours; or these are much brighter in the male than the female. The male, also, is sometimes provided with appendages which appear to be of no more use to him for the ordinary purposes of life, than are the tail feathers to the peacock. I am indebted for most of the following facts to the kindness of Dr. Günther. There is reason to suspect that many tropical fishes differ sexually in colour and structure; and there are some striking cases with our British fishes. The male *Callionymus lyra* has been called the *gemmeous dragonet* "from its brilliant gem-like colours." When fresh caught from the sea the body is yellow of various shades, striped and spotted with vivid blue on the head; the dorsal fins are pale brown with dark longitudinal bands; the ventral, caudal, and anal fins being bluish-black. The female, or sordid dragonet, was considered by Linnæus, and by many subsequent naturalists, as a distinct species; it is of a dingy reddish-brown, with the dorsal fin brown and the other fins white. The sexes differ also in the proportional size of the head and mouth, and in the position of the eyes; [12] but the most striking difference is the extraordinary elonga-

[10] See Yarrell's account of the rays in his 'Hist. of British Fishes,' vol. ii. 1836, p. 416, with an excellent figure, and pp. 422, 432.

[11] As quoted in 'The Farmer,' 1868, p. 369.

[12] I have drawn up this description from Yarrell's 'British Fishes,' vol. i. 1836, pp. 261 and 266.

tion in the male (fig. 29) of the dorsal fin. Mr. W. Saville Kent remarks
that this "singular appendage appears from my observations of the species in confinement, to be subservient to the same end as the wattles,
crests, and other abnormal adjuncts of the male in gallinaceous birds, for
the purpose of fascinating their mates." [13] The young males resemble the
adult females in structure and colour. Throughout the genus Callionymus,[14] the male is generally much more brightly spotted than the female,

FIG. 29.—Callionymus lyra. Upper figure, male; lower figure, female.
N. B. The lower figure is more reduced than the upper.

and in several species, not only the dorsal, but the anal fin is much elongated in the males.

The male of the *Cottus scorpious,* or sea-serpent, is slenderer and
smaller than the female. There is also a great difference in colour between
them. It is difficult, as Mr. Lloyd [15] remarks, "for any one, who has not
seen this fish during the spawning-season, when its hues are brightest, to
conceive the admixture of brilliant colours with which it, in other respects
so ill-favoured, is at that time adorned." Both sexes of the *Labrus mixtus,* although very different in colour, are beautiful; the male being
orange with bright blue stripes, and the female bright red with some
black spots on the back.

In the very distinct family of the Cyprinodontidæ—inhabitants of the

[13] 'Nature,' July 1873, p. 264.

[14] 'Catalogue of Acanth. Fishes in the British Museum,' by Dr. Günther, 1861, pp.
138–151.

[15] 'Game Birds of Sweden,' &c., 1867, p. 466.

fresh waters of foreign lands—the sexes sometimes differ much in various characters. In the male of the *Mollienesia petenensis*,[16] the dorsal fin is greatly developed and is marked with a row of large, round, ocellated, bright-coloured spots; whilst the same fin in the female is smaller, of a different shape, and marked only with irregularly curved brown spots. In the male the basal margin of the anal fin is also a little produced and dark coloured. In the male of an allied form, the *Xiphophorus Hellerii* (fig.

FIG. 30.—Xiphophorus Hellerii. Upper figure, male; lower figure, female.

30), the inferior margin of the caudal fin is developed into a long filament, which, as I hear from Dr. Günther, is striped with bright colours. This filament does not contain any muscles, and apparently cannot be of any direct use to the fish. As in the case of the Callionymus, the males whilst young resemble the adult females in colour and structure. Sexual differences such as these may be strictly compared with those which are so frequent with gallinaceous birds.[17]

In a siluroid fish, inhabiting the fresh waters of South America, the *Plecostomus barbatus*[18] (fig. 31), the male has its mouth and inter-operculum fringed with a beard of stiff hairs, of which the female shows hardly a trace. These hairs are of the nature of scales. In another species of the same genus, soft flexible tentacles project from the front part of the head of the male, which are absent in the female. These tentacles are prolongations of the true skin, and therefore are not homologous with the

---

[16] With respect to this and the following species I am indebted to Dr. Günther for information: see also his paper on the 'Fishes of Central America,' in 'Transact. Zoolog. Soc.' vol. vi. 1868, p. 485.

[17] Dr. Günther makes this remark; 'Catalogue of Fishes in the British Museum,' vol iii. 1861, p. 141.

[18] See Dr. Günther on this genus, in 'Proc. of the Zoolog. Soc.' 1868, page 232.

stiff hairs of the former species; but it can hardly be doubted that both serve the same purpose. What this purpose may be, is difficult to conjecture; ornament does not here seem probable, but we can hardly suppose

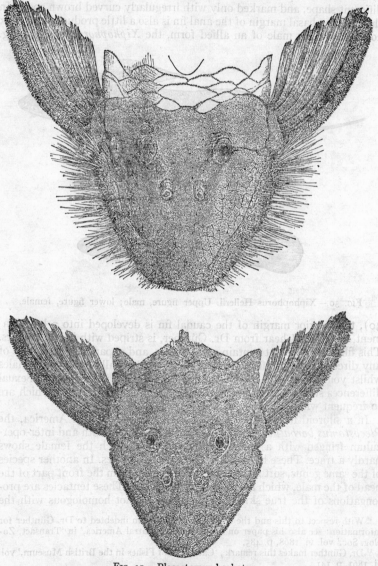

FIG. 31.—Plecostomus barbatus.
Upper figure, head of male; lower figure, female.

that stiff hairs and flexible filaments can be useful in any ordinary way to the males alone. In that strange monster, the *Chimæra monstrosa,* the male has a hook-shaped bone on the top of the head, directed forwards, with its end rounded and covered with sharp spines; in the female "this crown is altogether absent," but what its use may be to the male is utterly unknown.[19]

The structures as yet referred to are permanent in the male after he has arrived at maturity; but with some Blennies, and in another allied genus,[20] a crest is developed on the head of the male only during the breeding-season, and the body at the same time becomes more brightly-coloured. There can be little doubt that this crest serves as a temporary sexual ornament, for the female does not exhibit a trace of it. In other species of the same genus both sexes possess a crest, and in at least one species neither sex is thus provided. In many of the Chromidæ, for instance in Geophagus and especially in Cichla, the males, as I hear from Professor Agassiz,[21] have a conspicuous protuberance on the forehead, which is wholly wanting in the females and in the young males. Professor Agassiz adds, "I have often observed these fishes at the time of spawning when the protuberance is largest, and at other seasons when it is totally wanting, and the two sexes shew no difference whatever in the outline of the profile of the head. I never could ascertain that it subserves any special function, and the Indians on the Amazon know nothing about its use." These protuberances resemble, in their periodical appearance, the fleshy carbuncles on the heads of certain birds; but whether they serve as ornaments must remain at present doubtful.

I hear from Professor Agassiz and Dr. Günther, that the males of those fishes, which differ permanently in colour from the females, often become more brilliant during the breeding-season. This is likewise the case with a multitude of fishes, the sexes of which are identical in colour at all other seasons of the year. The tench, roach, and perch may be given as instances. The male salmon at this season is "marked on the cheeks with orange-coloured stripes, which give it the appearance of a Labrus, and the body partakes of a golden orange tinge. The females are dark in colour, and are commonly called black-fish." [22] An analogous and even greater change takes place with the *Salmo eriox* or bull trout; the males of the char (*S. umbla*) are likewise at this season rather brighter in colour than the females.[23] The colours of the pike (*Esox reticulatus*) of the United States, especially of the male, become, during the breeding-season, exceedingly intense, brilliant, and iridescent.[24] Another striking instance out of many is afforded by the male stickleback (*Gasterosteus*

---

[19] F. Buckland, in 'Land and Water,' July 1868, p. 377, with a figure. Many other cases could be added of structures peculiar to the male, of which the uses are not known.

[20] Dr. Günther, 'Catalogue of Fishes,' vol. iii. pp. 221 and 240.

[21] See also 'A Journey in Brazil,' by Prof. and Mrs. Agassiz, 1868, page 220.

[22] Yarrell, 'British Fishes,' vol. ii. 1836, pp. 10, 12, 35.

[23] W. Thompson, in 'Annals and Mag. of Nat. Hist.,' vol. vi. 1841, p. 440.

[24] 'The American Agriculturalist,' 1868, p. 100.

leiurus), which is described by Mr. Warington,[25] as being then "beautiful beyond description." The back and eyes of the female are simply brown and the belly white. The eyes of the male, on the other hand, are "of the most splendid green, having a metallic lustre like the green feathers of some humming-birds. The throat and belly are of a bright crimson, the back of an ashy-green, and the whole fish appears as though it were somewhat translucent and glowed with an internal incandescence." After the breeding season these colours all change, the throat and belly become of a paler red, the back more green, and the glowing tints subside.

With respect to the courtship of fishes, other cases have been observed since the first edition of this book appeared, besides that already given of the stickleback. Mr. W. S. Kent says that the male of the *Labrus mixtus,* which, as we have seen, differs in colour from the female, makes "a deep hollow in the sand of the tank, and then endeavours in the most persuasive manner to induce a female of the same species to share it with him, swimming backwards and forwards between her and the completed nest, and plainly exhibiting the greatest anxiety for her to follow." The males of *Cantharus lineatus* become, during the breeding-season, of deep leaden-black; they then retire from the shoal, and excavate a hollow as a nest. "Each male now mounts vigilant guard over his respective hollow, and vigorously attacks and drives away any other fish of the same sex. Towards his companions of the opposite sex his conduct is far different; many of the latter are now distended with spawn, and these he endeavours by all the means in his power to lure singly to his prepared hollow, and there to deposit the myriad ova with which they are laden, which he then protects and guards with the greatest care." [26]

A more striking case of courtship, as well as of display, by the males of a Chinese Macropus has been given by M. Carbonnier, who carefully observed these fishes under confinement.[27] The males are most beautifully coloured, more so than the females. During the breeding-season they contend for the possession of the females; and, in the act of courtship, expand their fins, which are spotted and ornamented with brightly coloured rays, in the same manner, according to M. Carbonnier, as the peacock. They then also bound about the females with much vivacity, and appear by "l'étalage de leurs vives couleurs chercher à attirer l'attention des femelles, lesquelles ne paraissaient indifférentes à ce manége, elles nageaient avec une molle lenteur vers les mâles et semblaient se complaire dans leur voisinage." After the male has won his bride, he makes a little disc of froth by blowing air and mucus out of his mouth. He then collects the fertilised ova, dropped by the female, in his mouth; and this caused M. Carbonnier much alarm, as he thought that they were going to be devoured. But the male soon deposits them in the disc of froth, afterwards guarding them, repairing the froth, and taking care of the young when hatched. I mention these particulars because, as we shall presently see,

[25] 'Annals and Mag. of Nat. Hist.' Oct. 1852.
[26] 'Nature,' May, 1873, p. 25.
[27] 'Bulletin de la Société d'Acclimation,' Paris, July, 1869, and Jan. 1870.

there are fishes, the males of which hatch their eggs in their mouths; and those who do not believe in the principle of gradual evolution might ask how could such a habit have originated; but the difficulty is much diminished when we know that there are fishes which thus collect and carry the eggs; for if delayed by any cause in depositing them, the habit of hatching them in their mouths might have been acquired.

To return to our more immediate subject. The case stands thus: female fishes, as far as I can learn, never willingly spawn except in the presence of the males; and the males never fertilise the ova except in the presence of the females. The males fight for the possession of the females. In many species, the males whilst young resemble the females in colour; but when adult become much more brilliant, and retain their colours throughout life. In other species the males become brighter than the females and otherwise more highly ornamented, only during the season of love. The males sedulously court the females, and in one case, as we have seen, take pains in displaying their beauty before them. Can it be believed that they would thus act to no purpose during their courtship? And this would be the case, unless the females exert some choice and select those males which please or excite them most. If the female exerts such choice, all the above facts on the ornamentation of the males become at once intelligible by the aid of sexual selection.

We have next to inquire whether this view of the bright colours of certain male fishes having been acquired through sexual selection can, through the law of the equal transmission of characters to both sexes, be extended to those groups in which the males and females are brilliant in the same, or nearly the same degree and manner. In such a genus as Labrus, which includes some of the most splendid fishes in the world—for instance, the Peacock Labrus (*L. pavo*), described,[28] with pardonable exaggeration, as formed of polished scales of gold, encrusting lapis-lazuli, rubies, sapphires, emeralds, and amethysts—we may, with much probability, accept this belief; for we have seen that the sexes in at least one species of the genus differ greatly in colour. With some fishes, as with many of the lowest animals, splendid colours may be the direct result of the nature of their tissues and of the surrounding conditions, without the aid of selection of any kind. The gold-fish (*Cyprinus auratus*), judging from the analogy of the golden variety of the common carp, is perhaps a case in point, as it may owe its splendid colours to a single abrupt variation, due to the conditions to which this fish has been subjected under confinement. It is, however, more probable that these colours have been intensified through artificial selection, as this species has been carefully bred in China from a remote period.[29] Under natural conditions it does

[28] Bory de Saint Vincent, in 'Dict. Class. d'Hist. Nat.' tom. ix. 1826, p. 151.

[29] Owing to some remarks on this subject, made in my work 'On the Variation of Animals under Domestication,' Mr. W. F. Mayers ('Chinese Notes and Queries,' Aug. 1868, p. 123) has searched the ancient Chinese encyclopedias. He finds that gold-fish were first reared in confinement during the Sung Dynasty, which commenced A. D. 960. In the year 1129 these fishes abounded. In another place it is said that since the year 1548 there has been "produced at Hangchow a variety called the fire-fish, from

not seem probable that beings so highly organised as fishes, and which live under such complex relations, should become brilliantly coloured without suffering some evil or receiving some benefit from so great a change, and consequently without the intervention of natural selection.

What, then, are we to conclude in regard to the many fishes, both sexes of which are splendidly coloured? Mr. Wallace [30] believes that the species which frequent reefs, where corals and other brightly-coloured organisms abound, are brightly coloured in order to escape detection by their enemies; but according to my recollection they were thus rendered highly conspicuous. In the fresh-waters of the tropics there are no brilliantly-coloured corals or other organisms for the fishes to resemble; yet many species in the Amazons are beautifully coloured, and many of the carnivorous Cyprinidæ in India are ornamented with "bright longitudinal lines of various tints." [31] Mr. M'Clelland, in describing these fishes, goes so far as to suppose that "the peculiar brilliancy of their colours" serves as "a better mark for king-fishers, terns, and other birds which are destined to keep the number of these fishes in check;" but at the present day few naturalists will admit that any animal has been made conspicuous as an aid to its own destruction. It is possible that certain fishes may have been rendered conspicuous in order to warn birds and beasts of prey that they were unpalatable, as explained when treating of caterpillars; but it is not, I believe, known that any fish, at least any fresh-water fish, is rejected from being distasteful to fish-devouring animals. On the whole, the most probable view in regard to the fishes, of which both sexes are brilliantly coloured, is that their colours were acquired by the males as a sexual ornament, and were transferred equally, or nearly so, to the other sex.

We have now to consider whether, when the male differs in a marked manner from the female in colour or in other ornaments, he alone has been modified, the variations being inherited by his male offspring alone; or whether the female has been specially modified and rendered inconspicuous for the sake of protection, such modifications being inherited only by the females. It is impossible to doubt that colour has been gained by many fishes as a protection: no one can examine the speckled upper surface of a flounder, and overlook its resemblance to the sandy bed of the sea on which it lives. Certain fishes, moreover, can through the action of the nervous system change their colours in adaptation to surrounding objects, and that within a short time. [32] One of the most striking instances ever recorded of an animal being protected by its colour (as far as it can be judged of in preserved specimens), as well as by its form, is that given by Dr. Günther [33] of a pipe-fish, which, with its reddish streaming fila-

its intensely red colour. It is universally admired, and there is not a household where it is not cultivated, *in rivalry as to its colour,* and as a source of profit."

[30] 'Westminster Rev.,' July 1867, p. 7.

[31] 'Indian Cyprinidæ,' by Mr. M'Clelland, 'Asiatic Researches,' vol. xix. part ii. 1839, p. 230.

[32] G. Pouchet, L'Institut. Nov. 1, 1871, p. 134.

[33] 'Proc. Zoolog. Soc.' 1865, p. 327, pl. xiv. and xv.

ments, is hardly distinguishable from the sea-weed to which it clings with its prehensile tail. But the question now under consideration is whether the females alone have been modified for this object. We can see that one sex will not be modified through natural selection for the sake of protection more than the other, supposing both to vary, unless one sex is exposed for a longer period to danger, or has less power of escaping from such danger than the other; and it does not appear that with fishes the sexes differ in these respects. As far as there is any difference, the males, from being generally smaller and from wandering more about, are exposed to greater danger than the females; and yet, when the sexes differ, the males are almost always the more conspicuously coloured. The ova are fertilised immediately after being deposited; and when this process lasts for several days, as in the case of the salmon,[34] the female, during the whole time, is attended by the male. After the ova are fertilised they are, in most cases, left unprotected by both parents, so that the males and females, as far as oviposition is concerned, are equally exposed to danger, and both are equally important for the production of fertile ova; consequently the more or less brightly-coloured individuals of either sex would be equally liable to be destroyed or preserved, and both would have an equal influence on the colours of their offspring.

Certain fishes belonging to several families, make nests, and some of them take care of their young when hatched. Both sexes of the bright-coloured *Crenilabrus massa* and *melops* work together in building their nests with sea-weed, shells, &c.[35] But the males of certain fishes do all the work, and afterward take exclusive charge of the young. This is the case with the dull-coloured gobies,[36] in which the sexes are not known to differ in colour, and likewise with the sticklebacks (Gasterosteus), in which the males become brilliantly coloured during the spawning season. The male of the smooth-tailed stickleback (*G. leiurus*) performs the duties of a nurse with exemplary care and vigilance during a long time, and is continually employed in gently leading back the young to the nest, when they stray too far. He courageously drives away all enemies including the females of his own species. It would indeed be no small relief to the male, if the female, after depositing her eggs, were immediately devoured by some enemy, for he is forced incessantly to drive her from the nest.[37]

The males of certain other fishes inhabiting South America and Ceylon, belonging to two distinct Orders, have the extraordinary habit of hatching within their mouths, or branchial cavities, the eggs laid by the females.[38] I am informed by Professor Agassiz that the males of the Am-

[34] Yarrell, 'Brit. Fishes,' vol. ii. p. 11.
[35] According to the observations of M. Gerbe; see Günther's 'Record of Zoolog. Literature,' 1865, p. 194.
[36] Cuvier, 'Règne Animal,' vol. ii. 1829, p. 242.
[37] See Mr. Warington's most interesting description of the habits of the *Gasterosteus leiurus* in 'Annals and Mag. of Nat. Hist.' November 1855.
[38] Prof. Wyman, in 'Proc. Boston Soc. of Nat. Hist.' Sept. 15, 1857. Also Prof Turner, in 'Journal of Anatomy and Phys.' Nov. 1, 1866, p. 78. Dr. Günther has likewise described other cases.

azonian species which follow this habit, "not only are generally brighter than the females, but the difference is greater at the spawning-season than at any other time." The species of Geophagus act in the same manner; and in this genus, a conspicuous protuberance becomes developed on the forehead of the males during the breeding-season. With the various species of Chromids, as Professor Agassiz likewise informs me, sexual differences in colour may be observed, "whether they lay their eggs in the water among aquatic plants, or deposit them in holes, leaving them to come out without further care, or build shallow nests in the river mud, over which they sit, as our Pomotis does. It ought also to be observed that these sitters are among the brightest species in their respective families; for instance, Hygrogonus is bright green, with large black ocelli, encircled with the most brilliant red." Whether with all the species of Chromids it is the male alone which sits on the eggs is not known. It is, however, manifest that the fact of the eggs being protected or unprotected by the parents, has had little or no influence on the differences in colour between the sexes. It is further manifest, in all the cases in which the males take exclusive charge of the nests and young, that the destruction of the brighter-coloured males would be far more influential on the character of the race, than the destruction of the brighter-coloured females; for the death of the male during the period of incubation or nursing would entail the death of the young, so that they could not inherit his peculiarities; yet, in many of these very cases the males are more conspicuously coloured than the females.

In most of the Lophobranchii (Pipe-fish, Hippocampi, &c.) the males have either marsupial sacks or hemispherical depressions on the abdomen, in which the ova laid by the female are hatched. The males also shew great attachment to their young.[39] The sexes do not commonly differ much in colour; but Dr. Günther believes that the male Hippocampi are rather brighter than the females. The genus Solenostoma, however, offers a curious exceptional case,[40] for the female is much more vividly-coloured and spotted than the male, and she alone has a marsupial sack and hatches the eggs; so that the female of Solenostoma differs from all the other Lophobranchii in this latter respect, and from almost all other fishes, in being more brightly-coloured than the male. It is improbable that this remarkable double inversion of character in the female should be an accidental coincidence. As the males of several fishes, which take exclusive charge of the eggs and young, are more brightly coloured than the females, and as here the female Solenostoma takes the same charge and is brighter than the male, it might be argued that the conspicuous colours of that sex which is the more important of the two for the welfare of the offspring, must be in some manner protective. But from the large number of fishes, of which the males are either permanently or

---

[39] Yarrell, 'Hist. of British Fishes,' vol. ii. 1836, pp. 329, 338.

[40] Dr. Günther, since publishing an account of this species in 'The Fishes of Zanzibar,' by Col. Playfair, 1866, p. 137, has re-examined the specimens, and has given me the above information.

periodically brighter than the females, but whose life is not at all more important for the welfare of the species than that of the female, this view can hardly be maintained. When we treat of birds we shall meet with analogous cases, where there has been a complete inversion of the usual attributes of the two sexes, and we shall then give what apears to be the probable explanation, namely, that the males have selected the more attractive females, instead of the latter having selected, in accordance with the usual rule throughout the animal kingdom, the more attractive males.

On the whole we may conclude, that with most fishes, in which the sexes differ in colour or in other ornamental characters, the males originally varied, with their variations transmitted to the same sex, and accumulated through sexual selection by attracting or exciting the females. In many cases, however, such characters have been transferred, either partially or completely, to the females. In other cases, again, both sexes have been coloured alike for the sake of protection; but in no instance does it appear that the female alone has had her colours or other characters specially modified for this latter purpose.

The last point which need be noticed is that fishes are known to make various noises, some of which are described as being musical. Dr. Dufossé, who has especially attended to this subject, says that the sounds are voluntarily produced in several ways by different fishes: by the friction of the pharyngeal bones—by the vibration of certain muscles attached to the swim-bladder, which serves as a resounding board—and by the vibration of the intrinsic muscles of the swim-bladder. By this latter means the Trigla produces pure and long-drawn sounds which range over nearly an octave. But the most interesting case for us is that of two species of Ophidium, in which the males alone are provided with a sound-producing apparatus, consisting of small movable bones, with proper muscles, in connection with the swim-bladder.[41] The drumming of the Umbrinas in the European seas is said to be audible from a depth of twenty fathoms; and the fishermen of Rochelle assert "that the males alone make the noise during the spawning-time; and that it is possible by imitating it, to take them without bait."[42] From this statement, and more especially from the case of Ophidium, it is almost certain that in this, the lowest class of the Vertebrata, as with so many insects and spiders, sound-producing instruments have, at least in some cases, been developed through sexual selection, as a means for bringing the sexes together.

AMPHIBIANS.

Urodela.—I will begin with the tailed amphibians. The sexes of salamanders or newts often differ much both in colour and structure. In some

---

[41] 'Comptes Rendus.' Tom. xlvi. 1858, p. 353. Tom. xlvii. 1858, p. 916. Tom. liv. 1862, p. 393. The noise made by the Umbrinas (*Sciæna aquila*), is said by some authors to be more like that of a flute or organ, than drumming: Dr. Zouteveen, in the Dutch translation of this work (vol. ii. p. 36), gives some further particulars on the sounds made by fishes.

[42] The Rev. C. Kingsley, in 'Nature,' May 1870, p. 40.

species prehensile claws are developed on the fore-legs of the males during the breeding-season: and at this season in the male *Triton palmipes* the hind-feet are provided with a swimming-web, which is almost completely absorbed during the winter; so that their feet then resemble those of the female.[43] This structure no doubt aids the male in his eager search and pursuit of the female. Whilst courting her he rapidly vibrates the end of his tail. With our common newts (*Triton punctatus* and *cristatus*) a deep, much indented crest is developed along the back and tail of the male during the breeding-season, which disappears during the winter. Mr. St. George Mivart informs me that it is not furnished with muscles,

FIG. 32.—Triton cristatus (half natural size, from Bell's 'British Reptiles').
Upper figure, male during the breeding season; lower figure, female.

and therefore cannot be used for locomotion. As during the season of courtship it becomes edged with bright colours, there can hardly be a doubt that it is a masculine ornament. In many species the body presents strongly contrasted, though lurid tints, and these become more vivid during the breeding-season. The male, for instance, of our common little newt (*Triton punctatus*) is "brownish-grey above, passing into yellow beneath, which in the spring becomes a rich bright orange, marked everywhere with round dark spots." The edge of the crest also is then tipped with bright red or violet. The female is usually of a yellowish-brown colour with scattered brown dots, and the lower surface is often quite plain.[44] The young are obscurely tinted. The ova are fertilised during the act of deposition, and are not subsequently tended by either parent. We may therefore conclude that the males have acquired their strongly-marked colours and ornamental appendages through sexual selection; these being transmitted either to the male offspring alone, or to both sexes.

Anura or *Batrachia*.—With many frogs and toads the colours evident-

[43] Bell, 'History of British Reptiles,' 2nd edit. 1849, pp. 156–159.
[44] Bell, 'History of British Reptiles,' 2nd edit. 1849, pp. 146, 151.

ly serve as a protection, such as the bright green tints of tree frogs and the obscure mottled shades of many terrestrial species. The most conspicuously-coloured toad which I ever saw, the *Phryniscus nigricans,*[45] had the whole upper surface of the body as black as ink, with the soles of the feet and parts of the abdomen spotted with the brightest vermilion. It crawled about the bare sandy or open grassy plains of La Plata under a scorching sun, and could not fail to catch the eye of every passing creature. These colours are probably beneficial by making this animal known to all birds of prey as a nauseous mouthful.

In Nicaragua there is a little frog "dressed in a bright livery of red and blue" which does not conceal itself like most other species, but hops about during the daytime, and Mr. Belt says [46] that as soon as he saw its happy sense of security, he felt sure that it was uneatable. After several trials he succeeded in tempting a young duck to snatch up a young one, but it was instantly rejected; and the duck "went about jerking its head, as if trying to throw off some unpleasant taste."

With respect to sexual differences of colour, Dr. Günther does not know of any striking instance either with frogs or toads; yet he can often distinguish the male from the female by the tints of the former being a little more intense. Nor does he know of any striking difference in external structure between the sexes, excepting the prominences which become developed during the breeding-season on the front legs of the male, by which he is enabled to hold the female.[47] It is surprising that these animals have not acquired more strongly-marked sexual characters; for though cold-blooded their passions are strong. Dr. Günther informs me that he has several times found an unfortunate female toad dead and smothered from having been so closely embraced by three or four males. Frogs have been observed by Professor Hoffman in Giessen fighting all day long during the breeding-season, and with so much violence that one had its body ripped open.

Frogs and toads offer one interesting sexual difference, namely, in the musical powers possessed by the males; but to speak of music, when applied to the discordant and overwhelming sounds emitted by male bull-frogs and some other species, seems, according to our taste, a singularly inappropriate expression. Nevertheless, certain frogs sing in a decidedly pleasing manner. Near Rio Janeiro I used often to sit in the evening to listen to a number of little Hylæ, perched on blades of grass close to the water, which sent forth sweet chirping notes in harmony. The various sounds are emitted chiefly by the males during the breeding-season, as in the case of the croaking of our common frog.[48] In accordance with this fact the vocal organs of the males are more highly-developed than those

---

[45] 'Zoology of the Voyage of the "Beagle," ' 1843. Bell. ibid. p. 49.

[46] 'The Naturalist in Nicaragua,' 1874, p. 321.

[47] The male alone of the *Bufo sikimmensis* (Dr. Anderson, 'Proc. Zoolog. Soc.' 1871, p. 204) has two plate-like callosities on the thorax and certain rugosities on the fingers, which perhaps subserve the same end as the above-mentioned prominences.

[48] Bell, 'Hist. Brit. Rep.' 1849, p. 93.

of the females. In some genera the males alone are provided with sacs which open into the larynx.[49] For instance, in the edible frog (*Rana esculenta*) "the sacs are peculiar to the males, and become, when filled with air in the act of croaking, large globular bladders, standing out one on each side of the head, near the corners of the mouth." The croak of the male is thus rendered exceedingly powerful; whilst that of the female is only a slight groaning noise.[50] In the several genera of the family the vocal organs differ considerably in structure, and their development in all cases may be attributed to sexual selection.

REPTILES.

Chelonia.—Tortoises and turtles do not offer well-marked sexual differences. In some species, the tail of the male is longer than that of the female. In some, the plastron or lower surface of the shell of the male is slightly concave in relation to the back of the female. The male of the mud-turtle of the United States (*Chrysemys picta*) has claws on its front feet twice as long as those of the female; and these are used when the sexes unite.[51] With the huge tortoise of the Galapagos Islands (*Testudo nigra*) the males are said to grow to a larger size than the females: during the pairing-season, and at no other time, the male utters a hoarse bellowing noise, which can be heard at the distance of more than a hundred yards; the female, on the other hand, never uses her voice.[52]

With the *Testudo elegans* of India, it is said "that the combats of the males may be heard at some distance, from the noise they produce in butting against each other." [53]

Crocodilia.—The sexes apparently do not differ in colour; nor do I know that the males fight together, though this is probable, for some kinds make a prodigious display before the females. Bartram [54] describes the male alligator as striving to win the female by splashing and roaring in the midst of a lagoon, "swollen to an extent ready to burst, with its head and tail lifted up, he springs or twirls round on the surface of the water, like an Indian chief rehearsing his feats of war." During the season of love, a musky odour is emitted by the submaxiliary glands of the crocodile, and pervades their haunts.[55]

Ophidia.—Dr. Günther informs me that the males are always smaller than the females, and generally have longer and slenderer tails; but he knows of no other difference in external structure. In regard to colour, he can almost always distinguish the male from the female, by his more strongly-pronounced tints; thus the black zigzag band on the back of the

[49] J. Bishop, in 'Todd's Cyclop. of Anat. and Phys.' vol. iv. p. 1503.
[50] Bell, ibid. pp. 112–114.
[51] Mr. C. J. Maynard, 'The American Naturalist,' Dec. 1869, p. 555.
[52] See my 'Journal of Researches during the Voyage of the "Beagle," ' 1845, p. 384.
[53] Dr. Günther, 'Reptiles of British India,' 1864, p. 7.
[54] 'Travels through Carolina,' &c., 1791, p. 128.
[55] Owen, 'Anatomy of Vertebrates,' vol. i. 1866, p. 615.

male English viper is more distinctly defined than in the female. The difference is much plainer in the rattle-snakes of N. America, the male of which, as the keeper in the Zoological Gardens shewed me, can at once be distinguished from the female by having more lurid yellow about its whole body. In S. Africa the *Bucephalus capensis* presents an analogous difference, for the female "is never so fully variegated with yellow on the sides as the male." [56] The male of the Indian *Dipsas cynodon,* on the other hand, is blackish-brown, with the belly partly black, whilst the female is reddish or yellowish-olive, with the belly either uniform yellowish or marbled with black. In the *Tragops dispur* of the same country the male is bright green, and the female bronze-coloured. [57] No doubt the colours of some snakes are protective, as shewn by the green tints of tree-snakes, and the various mottled shades of the species which live in sandy places; but it is doubtful whether the colours of many kinds, for instance of the common English snake and viper, serve to conceal them; and this is still more doubtful with the many foreign species which are coloured with extreme elegance. The colours of certain species are very different in the adult and young states. [58]

During the breeding-season the anal scent-glands of snakes are in active function; [59] and so it is with the same glands in lizards, and as we have seen with the submaxiliary glands of crocodiles. As the males of most animals search for the females, these odoriferous glands probably serve to excite or charm the female, rather than to guide her to the spot where the male may be found. Male snakes, though appearing so sluggish, are amorous; for many have been observed crowding round the same female, and even round her dead body. They are not known to fight together from rivalry. Their intellectual powers are higher than might have been anticipated. In the Zoological Gardens they soon learn not to strike at the iron bar with which their cages are cleaned; and Dr. Keen of Philadelphia informs me that some snakes which he kept learned after four or five times to avoid a noose, with which they were at first easily caught. An excellent observer in Ceylon, Mr. E. Layard, saw [60] a cobra thrust its head through a narrow hole and swallow a toad. "With this encumbrance he could not withdraw himself; finding this, he reluctantly disgorged the precious morsel, which began to move off; this was too much for snake philosophy to bear, and the toad was again seized, and again was the snake, after violent efforts to escape, compelled to part with its prey. This time, however, a lesson had been learnt, and the toad was seized by one leg, withdrawn, and then swallowed in triumph."

The keeper in the Zoological Gardens is positive that certain snakes, for instance Crotalus and Python, distinguish him from all other persons.

[56] Sir Andrew Smith, 'Zoolog. of S. Africa: Reptilia,' 1849, pl. x.
[57] Dr. A. Günther, 'Reptiles of British India,' Ray Soc. 1864, pages 304, 308.
[58] Dr. Stoliczka, 'Journal of Asiatic Soc. of Bengal,' vol. xxxix. 1870, pp. 205, 211.
[59] Owen, 'Anatomy of Vertebrates,' vol. i. 1866, p. 615.
[60] 'Rambles in Ceylon,' in 'Annals and Magazine of Natural History,' 2nd series, vol. ix. 1852, page 333.

Cobras kept together in the same cage apparently feel some attachment towards each other.[61]

It does not, however, follow because snakes have some reasoning power, strong passions and mutual affection, that they should likewise be endowed with sufficient taste to admire brilliant colours in their partners, so as to lead to the adornment of the species through sexual selection. Nevertheless, it is difficult to account in any other manner for the extreme beauty of certain species; for instance, of the coral-snakes of S. America, which are of a rich red with black and yellow transverse bands. I well remember how much surprise I felt at the beauty of the first coral-snake which I saw gliding across a path in Brazil. Snakes coloured in this peculiar manner, as Mr. Wallace states on the authority of Dr. Günther,[62] are found nowhere else in the world except in S. America, and here no less than four genera occur. One of these, Elaps, is venomous; a second and widely-distinct genus is doubtfully venomous, and the two others are quite harmless. The species belonging to these distinct genera inhabit the same districts, and are so like each other that no one "but a naturalist would distinguish the harmless from the poisonous kinds." Hence, as Mr. Wallace believes, the innocuous kinds have probably acquired their colours as a protection, on the principle of imitation; for they would naturally be thought dangerous by their enemies. The cause, however, of the bright colours of the venomous Elaps remains to be explained, and this may perhaps be sexual selection.

Snakes produce other sounds besides hissing. The deadly *Echis carinata* has on its sides some oblique rows of scales of a peculiar structure with serrated edges; and when this snake is excited these scales are rubbed against each other, which produces "a curious prolonged, almost hissing sound." [63] With respect to the rattling of the rattle-snake, we have at last some definite information: for Professor Aughey states,[64] that on two occasions, being himself unseen, he watched from a little distance a rattlesnake coiled up with head erect, which continued to rattle at short intervals for half an hour: and at last he saw another snake approach, and when they met they paired. Hence he is satisfied that one of the uses of the rattle is to bring the sexes together. Unfortunately he did not ascertain whether it was the male or the female which remained stationary and called for the other. But it by no means follows from the above fact that the rattle may not be of use to snakes in other ways, as a warning to animals which would otherwise attack them. Nor can I quite disbelieve the several accounts which have appeared of their thus paralysing their prey with fear. Some other snakes also make a distinct noise by rapidly vibrating their tails against the surrounding stalks of plants; and I have myself heard this in the case of a Trigonocephalus in S. America.

Lacertilia.—The males of some, probably of many kinds of lizards,

[61] Dr. Günther, 'Reptiles of British India,' 1864, p. 340.
[62] 'Westmin. Rev.,' July 1, 1867, p. 32.
[63] Dr. Anderson, 'Proc. Zoolog. Soc.' 1871, p. 196.
[64] 'The American Naturalist,' 1873, p. 85.

fight together from rivalry. Thus the arboreal *Anolis cristatellus* of S.
America is extremely pugnacious: "During the spring and early part of
the summer, two adult males rarely meet without a contest. On first seeing one another, they nod their heads up and down three or four times,
and at the same time expanding the frill or pouch beneath the throat;
their eyes glisten with rage, and after waving their tails from side to side
for a few seconds, as if to gather energy, they dart at each other furiously, rolling over and over, and holding firmly with their teeth. The conflict
generally ends in one of the combatants
losing his tail, which is often devoured by
the victor." The male of this species is
considerably larger than the female;[65] and
this, as far as Dr. Günther has been able
to ascertain, is the general rule with lizards of all kinds. The male alone of the
Cyrtodactylus rubidus of the Andaman
Islands possesses pre-anal pores; and these
pores, judging from analogy, probably
serve to emit an odour.[66]

Fig. 33.—Sitana minor. Male with
the gular pouch expanded
(from Günther's 'Reptiles of
India').

   The sexes often differ greatly in various
external characters. The male of the
above-mentioned Anolis is furnished with
a crest which runs along the back and
tail, and can be erected at pleasure; but of this crest the female does
not exhibit a trace. In the Indian *Cophotis ceylanica,* the female has
a dorsal crest, though much less developed than in the male; and
so it is, as Dr. Günther informs me, with the females of many Iguan-
as, Chameleons, and other lizards. In some species, however, the crest is
equally developed in both sexes, as in the *Iguana tuberculata.* In the genus Sitana, the males alone are furnished with a large throat-pouch (fig.
33), which can be folded up like a fan, and is coloured blue, black, and
red; but these splendid colours are exhibited only during the pairing-season. The female does not possess even a rudiment of this appendage. In
the *Anolis cristatellus,* according to Mr. Austen, the throat pouch, which
is bright red marbled with yellow, is present in the female, though in a
rudimental condition. Again, in certain other lizards, both sexes are equally well provided with throat pouches. Here we see with species belonging
to the same group, as in so many previous cases, the same character either
confined to the males, or more largely developed in them than in the females, or again equally developed in both sexes. The little lizards of the
genus Draco, which glide through the air on their rib-supported para-
chutes, and which in the beauty of their colours baffle description, are furnished with skinny appendages to the throat "like the wattles of gallinaceous birds." These become erected when the animal is excited. They oc-

---

[65] Mr. N. L. Austen kept these animals alive for a considerable time; see 'Land and
Water,' July 1867, p. 9.
[66] Stoliczka, 'Journal of the Asiatic Society of Bengal,' vol. xxxiv. 1870, p. 166.

cur in both sexes, but are best developed when the male arrives at maturity, at which age the middle appendage is sometimes twice as long as the
head. Most of the species likewise have a low crest running along the
neck; and this is much more developed in the full-grown males than in
the females or young males.[67]

A Chinese species is said to live in pairs during the spring; "and if one
is caught, the other falls from the tree to the ground, and allows itself to
be captured with impunity,"—I presume from despair.[68]

There are other and much more remarkable differences between the
sexes of certain lizards. The male of *Ceratophora aspera* bears on the extremity of his snout an appendage half as long as the head. It is cylindri-

FIG. 34.—Ceratophora Stoddartii. Upper figure, male;
lower figure, female.

cal, covered with scales, flexible, and apparently capable of erection: in the female it is
quite rudimental. In a second species of the
same genus a terminal scale forms a minute
horn on the summit of the flexible appendage; and in a third species (*C. Stoddartii*,
fig. 34) the whole appendage is converted into a horn, which is usually of a white colour,
but assumes a purplish tint when the animal
is excited. In the adult male of this latter
species the horn is half an inch in length, but
it is of quite minute size in the female and in
the young. These appendages, as Dr. Günther has remarked to me, may be compared
with the combs of gallinaceous birds, and
apparently serve as ornaments.

In the genus Chamæleon we come to the acme of difference between the
sexes. The upper part of the skull of the male *C. bifurcus* (fig. 35), an inhabitant of Madagascar, is produced into two great, solid, bony projections, covered with scales like the rest of the head; and of this wonderful
modification of structure the female exhibits only a rudiment. Again, in
Chamæleo Owenii (fig. 36), from the West Coast of Africa, the male
bears on his snout and forehead three curious horns, of which the female
has not a trace. These horns consist of an excrescence of bone covered
with a smooth sheath, forming part of the general integuments of the
body, so that they are identical in structure with those of a bull, goat, or
other sheath-horned ruminant. Although the three horns differ so much
in appearance from the two great prolongations of the skull in *C. bifurcus,* we can hardly doubt that they serve the same general purpose in the
economy of these two animals. The first conjecture, which will occur to
every one, is that they are used by the males for fighting together; and as

[67] All the foregoing statements and quotations, in regard to Cophotis, Sitana and
Draco, as well as the following facts in regard to Ceratophora and Chamæleon, are
from Dr. Günther himself, or from his magnificent work on the 'Reptiles of British
India,' Ray Soc. 1864, pp. 122, 130, 135.
[68] Mr. Swinhoe, 'Proc. Zoolog. Soc.' 1870, p. 240.

these animals are very quarrelsome,[69] this is probably a correct view. Mr. T. W. Wood also informs me that he once watched two individuals of *C. pumilus* fighting violently on the branch of a tree; they flung their heads about and tried to bite each other; they then rested for a time and afterwards continued their battle.

With many lizards the sexes differ slightly in colour, the tints and stripes of the males being brighter and more distinctly defined than in the females. This, for instance, is the case with the above Cophotis and with the *Acanthodactylus capensis* of S. Africa. In a Cordylus of the latter country, the male is either much redder or greener than the female. In the

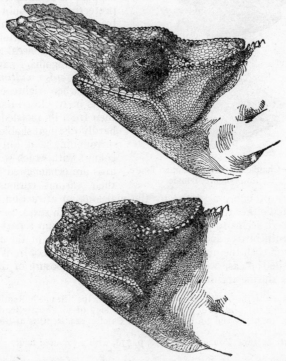

Fig. 35.—Chamæleo bifurcus. Upper figure male; lower figure, female.

Indian *Calotes nigrilabris* there is a still greater difference; the lips also of the male are black, whilst those of the female are green. In our common little viviparous lizard (*Zootoca vivipara*) "the under side of the body and base of the tail in the male are bright orange, spotted with black; in the female these parts are pale-greyish-green without spots." [70]

[69] Dr. Bucholz, 'Monatsbericht K. Preuss. Akad.' Jan. 1874, p. 78.
[70] Bell, 'History of British Reptiles,' 2nd edit. 1849, p. 40.

We have seen that the males alone of Sitana possess a throat-pouch; and this is splendidly tinted with blue, black, and red. In the *Proctotretus tenuis* of Chile the male alone is marked with spots of blue, green, and coppery-red.[71] In many cases the males retain the same colours throughout the year, but in others they become much brighter during the breeding-season; I may give as an additional instance the *Calotes maria*, which at this season has a bright red head, the rest of the body being green.[72]

FIG. 36.—Chamæleo Owenii. Upper figure, male; lower figure, female.

Both sexes of many species are beautifully coloured exactly alike; and there is no reason to suppose that such colours are protective. No doubt with the bright green kinds which live in the midst of vegetation, this colour serves to conceal them; and in N. Patagonia I saw a lizard (*Proctotretus multimaculatus*) which, when frightened, flattened its body, closed its eyes, and then from its mottled tints was hardly distinguishable from the surrounding sand. But the bright colours with which so many lizards are ornamented, as well as their various curious appendages, were probably acquired by the males as an attraction, and then transmitted either to their male offspring, or to both sexes. Sexual selection, indeed, seems to have played almost as important a part with reptiles as with birds; and the less conspicuous colours of the females in comparison with the males cannot be accounted for, as Mr. Wallace believes to be the case with birds, by the greater exposure of the females to danger during incubation.

[71] For Proctotretus see 'Zoology of the Voyage of the "Beagle": Reptiles,' by Mr. Bell, p. 8. For the Lizards of S. Africa, see 'Zoology of S. Africa: Reptiles,' by Sir Andrew Smith, pl. 25 and 39. For the Indian Calotes, see 'Reptiles of British India,' by Dr. Günther, p. 143.

[72] Günther in 'Proc. Zoolog. Soc.' 1870, p. 778, with a coloured figure.

CHAPTER XIII

SECONDARY SEXUAL CHARACTERS OF BIRDS

Sexual differences—Law of battle—Special weapons—Vocal organs—Instrumental music—Love-antics and dances—Decorations, permanent and seasonal—Double and single annual moults—Display of ornaments by the males.

SECONDARY sexual characters are more diversified and conspicuous in birds, though not perhaps entailing more important changes of structure, than in any other class of animals. I shall, therefore, treat the subject at considerable length. Male birds sometimes, though rarely, possess special weapons for fighting with each other. They charm the female by vocal or instrumental music of the most varied kinds. They are ornamented by all sorts of combs, wattles, protuberances, horns, air-distended sacks, top-knots, naked shafts, plumes and lengthened feathers gracefully springing from all parts of the body. The beak and naked skin about the head, and the feathers, are often gorgeously coloured. The males sometimes pay their court by dancing, or by fantastic antics performed either on the ground or in the air. In one instance, at least, the male emits a musky odour, which we may suppose serves to charm or excite the female; for that excellent observer, Mr. Ramsay,[1] says of the Australian musk-duck (*Biziura lobata*) that "the smell which the male emits during the summer months is confined to that sex, and in some individuals is retained throughout the year; I have never, even in the breeding-season, shot a female which had any smell of musk." So powerful is this odour during the pairing-season, that it can be detected long before the bird can be seen.[2] On the whole, birds appear to be the most æsthetic of all animals, excepting of course man, and they have nearly the same taste for the beautiful as we have. This is shown by our enjoyment of the singing of birds, and by our women, both civilised and savage, decking their heads with borrowed plumes, and using gems which are hardly more brilliantly coloured than the naked skin and wattles of certain birds. In man, how-ever, when cultivated, the sense of beauty is manifestly a far more complex feeling, and is associated with various intellectual ideas.

Before treating of the sexual characters with which we are here more particularly concerned, I may just allude to certain differences between the sexes which apparently depend on differences in their habits of life;

[1] 'Ibis,' vol. iii. (new series), 1867, p. 414.
[2] Gould, 'Handbook to the Birds of Australia,' 1865, vol. ii. p. 383.

for such cases, though common in the lower, are rare in the higher classes. Two humming-birds belonging to the genus Eustephanus, which inhabit the island of Juan Fernandez, were long thought to be specifically distinct, but are now known, as Mr. Gould informs me, to be the male and female of the same species, and they differ slightly in the form of the beak. In another genus of humming-birds (*Grypus*), the beak of the male is serrated along the margin and hooked at the extremity, thus differing much from that of the female. In the Neomorpha of New Zealand, there is, as we have seen, a still wider difference in the form of the beak in relation to the manner of feeding of the two sexes. Something of the same kind has been observed with the goldfinch (*Carduelis elegans*), for I am assured by Mr. J. Jenner Weir that the bird-catchers can distinguish the males by their slightly longer beaks. The flocks of males are often found feeding on the seeds of the teazle (Dipsacus), which they can reach with their elongated beaks, whilst the females more commonly feed on the seeds of the betony or Scrophularia. With a slight difference of this kind as a foundation, we can see how the beaks of the two sexes might be made to differ greatly through natural selection. In some of the above cases, however, it is possible that the beaks of the males may have been first modified in relation to their contests with other males; and that this afterwards led to slightly changed habits of life.

Law of Battle.—Almost all male birds are extremely pugnacious, using their beaks, wings, and legs for fighting together. We see this every spring with our robins and sparrows. The smallest of all birds, namely the humming-bird, is one of the most quarrelsome. Mr. Gosse [3] describes a battle in which a pair seized hold of each other's beaks, and whirled round and round, till they almost fell to the ground; and M. Montes de Oca, in speaking of another genus of humming-bird, says that two males rarely meet without a fierce aërial encounter: when kept in cages "their fighting has mostly ended in the splitting of the tongue of one of the two, which then surely dies from being unable to feed." [4] With Waders, the males of the common water-hen (*Gallinula chloropus*) "when pairing, fight violently for the females: they stand nearly upright in the water and strike with their feet." Two were seen to be thus engaged for half an hour, until one got hold of the head of the other, which would have been killed had not the observer interfered; the female all the time looking on as a quiet spectator.[5] Mr. Blyth informs me that the males of an allied bird (*Gallicrex cristatus*) are a third larger than the females, and are so pugnacious during the breeding-season that they are kept by the natives of Eastern Bengal for the sake of fighting. Various other birds are kept in India for the same purpose, for instance, the bulbuls (*Pycnonotus hæmorrhous*) which "fight with great spirit." [6]

[3] Quoted by Mr. Gould, 'Introduction to the Trochilidæ,' 1861, page 29.
[4] Gould, ibid, p. 52.
[5] W. Thompson, 'Nat. Hist. of Ireland: Birds,' vol. ii. 1850, p. 327.
[6] Jerdon, 'Birds of India,' 1863, vol. ii. p. 96.

The polygamous ruff (*Machetes pugnax*, fig. 37) is notorious for his extreme pugnacity; and in the spring, the males, which are considerably larger than the females, congregate day after day at a particular spot, where the females propose to lay their eggs. The fowlers discover these spots by the turf being trampled somewhat bare. Here they fight very much like game-cocks, seizing each other with their beaks and striking with their wings. The great ruff of feathers round the neck is then erected,

FIG. 37.—The Ruff or Machetes pugnax (from Brehm's 'Thierleben').

and according to Col. Montagu "sweeps the ground as a shield to defend the more tender parts;" and this is the only instance known to me in the case of birds of any structure serving as a shield. The ruff of feathers, however, from its varied and rich colours probably serves in chief part as an ornament. Like most pugnacious birds, they seem always ready to fight, and when closely confined, often kill each other; but Montagu observed that their pugnacity becomes greater during the spring, when the long feathers on their necks are fully developed; and at this period the least movement by any one bird provokes a general battle.[7] Of the pugnacity of web-footed birds, two instances will suffice: in Guiana "bloody fights occur during the breeding-season between the males of the wild musk-duck (*Cairina moschata*); and where these fights have occurred the river is covered for some distance with feathers."[8] Birds which seem ill-

[7] Macgillivray, 'Hist. Brit. Birds,' vol. iv. 1852, pp. 177–181.
[8] Sir R. Schomburgk, in 'Journal of R. Geograph. Soc.' vol. xiii. 1843, p. 31.

adapted for fighting engage in fierce conflicts; thus the stronger males of the pelican drive away the weaker ones, snapping with their huge beaks and giving heavy blows with their wings. Male snipe fight together, "tugging and pushing each other with their bills in the most curious manner imaginable." Some few birds are believed never to fight; this is the case, according to Audubon, with one of the woodpeckers of the United States (*Picu sauratus*), although "the hens are followed by even half a dozen of their gay suitors." [9]

The males of many birds are larger than the females, and this no doubt is the result of the advantage gained by the larger and stronger males over their rivals during many generations. The difference in size between the two sexes is carried to an extreme point in several Australian species; thus the male musk-duck (Biziura), and the male *Cincloramphus cruralis* (allied to our pipits) are by measurement actually twice as large as their respective females. [10] With many other birds the females are larger than the males; and, as formerly remarked, the explanation often given, namely, that the females have most of the work in feeding their young, will not suffice. In some few cases, as we shall hereafter see, the females apparently have acquired their greater size and strength for the sake of conquering other females and obtaining possession of the males.

The males of many gallinaceous birds, especially of the polygamous kinds, are furnished with special weapons for fighting with their rivals, namely spurs, which can be used with fearful effect. It has been recorded by a trustworthy writer [11] that in Derbyshire a kite struck at a game-hen accompanied by her chickens, when the cock rushed to the rescue, and drove his spur right through the eye and skull of the aggressor. The spur was with difficulty drawn from the skull, and as the kite, though dead, retained his grasp, the two birds were firmly locked together; but the cock when disentangled was very little injured. The invincible courage of the game-cock is notorious: a gentleman who long ago witnessed the brutal scene, told me that a bird had both its legs broken by some accident in the cockpit, and the owner laid a wager that if the legs could be spliced so that the bird could stand upright, he would continue fighting. This was effected on the spot, and the bird fought with undaunted courage until he received his death-stroke. In Ceylon a closely allied, wild species, the *Gallus Stanleyi*, is known to fight desperately "in defence of his seraglio," so that one of the combatants is frequently found dead. [12] An Indian partridge (*Ortygornis gularis*), the male of which is furnished with strong and sharp spurs, is so quarrelsome "that the scars of former fights disfigure the breast of almost every bird you kill." [13]

The males of almost all gallinaceous birds, even those which are not

---

[9] 'Ornithological Biography,' vol. i. p. 191. For pelicans and snipes, see vol. iii. pp. 138, 477.

[10] Gould, 'Handbook of Birds of Australia,' vol. i. page 395; vol. ii. page 383.

[11] Mr. Hewitt in the 'Poultry Book by Tegetmeier,' 1866, p. 137.

[12] Layard, 'Annals and Magazine of Natural History,' vol. xiv. 1854, p. 63.

[13] Jerdon, 'Birds of India,' vol. iii. p. 574.

furnished with spurs, engage during the breeding-season in fierce conflicts. The Capercailzie and Black-cock (*Tetrao urogallus* and *T. tetrix*),
which are both polygamists, have regular appointed places, where during
many weeks they congregate in numbers to fight together and to display
their charms before the females. Dr. W. Kovalevsky informs me that in
Russia he has seen the snow all bloody on the arenas where the capercailzie have fought; and the black-cocks "make the feathers fly in every direction," when several "engage in a battle royal." The elder Brehm gives
a curious account of the Balz, as the love-dances and love-songs of the
Black-cock are called in Germany. The bird utters almost continuously
the strangest noises: "he holds his tail up and spreads it out like a fan,
he lifts up his head and neck with all the feathers erect, and stretches his
wings from the body. Then he takes a few jumps in different directions
sometimes in a circle, and presses the under part of his beak so hard
against the ground that the chin feathers are rubbed off. During these
movements he beats his wings and turns round and round. The more ardent he grows the more lively he becomes, until at last the bird appears
like a frantic creature." At such times the black-cocks are so absorbed
that they become almost blind and deaf, but less so than the capercailzie:
hence bird after bird may be shot on the same spot, or even caught by the
hand. After performing these antics the males begin to fight: and the
same black-cock, in order to prove his strength over several antagonists,
will visit in the course of one morning several Balz-places, which remain
the same during successive years.[14]

The peacock with his long train appears more like a dandy than a
warrior, but he sometimes engages in fierce contests: the Rev. W. Darwin Fox informs me that at some little distance from Chester two peacocks became so excited whilst fighting, that they flew over the whole
city, still engaged, until they alighted on the top of St. John's tower.

The spur, in those gallinaceous birds which are thus provided, is generally single; but Polyplectron (see fig. 51, p. 729) has two or more on
each leg; and one of the Blood-pheasants (*Ithaginis cruentus*) has been
seen with five spurs. The spurs are generally confined to the male, being
represented by mere knobs or rudiments in the female; but the females of
the Java peacock (*Pavo muticus*) and, as I am informed by Mr. Blyth, of
the small fire-backed pheasant (*Euplocamus erythropthalmus*) possess
spurs. In Galloperdix it is usual for the males to have two spurs, and for
the females to have only one on each leg.[15] Hence spurs may be considered as a masculine structure, which has been occasionally more or less
transferred to the females. Like most other secondary sexual characters,
the spurs are highly variable, both in number and development, in the
same species.

Various birds have spurs on their wings. But the Egyptian goose
(*Chenalopex ægyptiacus*) has only "bare obtuse knobs," and these prob-

---

[14] Brehm, 'Ilust. Thierleben,' 1867, B. iv. s. 351. Some of the foregoing statements
are taken from L. Lloyd, 'Game Birds of Sweden,' &c., 1867, p. 79.

[15] Jerdon, 'Birds of India; on Ithaginis,' vol. iii. p. 523; on Galloperdix, p. 541.

ably shew us the first steps by which true spurs have been developed in other species. In the spur-winged goose, *Plectropterus gambensis,* the males have much larger spurs than the females; and they use them, as I

FIG. 38.—Palamedea cornuta (from Brehm), shewing the double wing-spurs, and the filament on the head.

am informed by Mr. Bartlett, in fighting together, so that, in this case, the wing-spurs serve as sexual weapons; but according to Livingstone, they are chiefly used in the defence of the young. The Palamedea (fig. 38) is armed with a pair of spurs on each wing; and these are such formidable weapons that a single blow has been known to drive a dog howling away. But it does not appear that the spurs in this case, or in that of some of the spur-winged rails, are larger in the male than in the female.[16] In certain plovers, however, the wing-spurs must be considered as a sexual character. Thus in the male of our common peewit (*Vanellus cristatus*) the tubercle on the shoulder of the wing becomes more prominent during the breeding-season, and the males fight together. In some species of Lobivanellus a similar tubercle becomes developed during the breeding-season "into a short horny spur." In the Australian *L. lobatus* both sexes have spurs, but these are much larger in the males than in the females. In an allied bird, the *Hoplopterus armatus*, the spurs do not increase in size during the breeding-season; but these birds have been seen in Egypt to fight together, in the same manner as our peewits, by turning suddenly in the air and striking sideways at each other, sometimes with fatal results. Thus also they drive away other enemies.[17]

The season of love is that of battle; but the males of some birds, as of the game-fowl and ruff, and even the young males of the wild turkey and grouse,[18] are ready to fight whenever they meet. The presence of the female is the *teterrima belli causa*. The Bengali baboos make the pretty little males of the amadavat (*Estrelda amandava*) fight together by placing three small cages in a row, with a female in the middle; after a little time the two males are turned loose, and immediately a desperate battle ensues.[19] When many males congregate at the same appointed spot and fight together, as in the case of grouse and various other birds, they are generally attended by the females,[20] which afterwards pair with the victorious combatants. But in some cases the pairing precedes instead of succeeding the combat: thus according to Audubon,[21] several males of the Virginian goat-sucker (*Caprimulgus virgianus*) "court, in a highly entertaining manner the female, and no sooner has she made her choice, than her approved gives chase to all intruders, and drives them beyond his dominions." Generally the males try to drive away or kill their rivals before they pair. It does not, however, appear that the females invariably

[16] For the Egyptian goose, see Macgillivray, 'British Birds,' vol. iv. p. 639. For Plectropterus, 'Livingstone's Travels,' p. 254. For Palamedea, Brehm's 'Thierleben,' B. iv. s. 740. See also on this bird Azara, 'Voyages dans l'Amérique mérid.' tom. iv. 1809, pp. 179, 253.

[17] See, on our peewit, Mr. R. Carr in 'Land and Water,' Aug. 8th, 1868, p. 46. In regard to Lobivanellus, see Jerdon's 'Birds of India,' vol. iii. p. 647, and Gould's 'Handbook of Birds of Australia,' vol. ii. p. 220. For the Holopterus, see Mr. Allen in the 'Ibis,' vol. v. 1863, p. 156.

[18] Audubon, 'Ornith. Biography,' vol. ii. p. 492; vol. i. pp. 4–13.

[19] Mr. Blyth, 'Land and Water,' 1867, p. 212.

[20] Richardson on *Tetrao umbellus* 'Fauna Bor. Amer.: Birds,' 1831, p. 343. L. Lloyd, 'Game Birds of Sweden,' 1867, pp. 22, 79, on the capercailzie and black-cock. Brehm, however, asserts ('Thierleben,' &c., B. iv. s. 352) that in Germany the grey-hens do not generally attend the Balzen of the black-cocks, but this is an exception to the common rule; possibly the hens may lie hidden in the surrounding bushes, as is known to be the case with the gray-hens in Scandinavia, and with other species in N. America.

[21] 'Ornith. Biography,' vol. ii. p. 275.

prefer the victorious males. I have indeed been assured by Dr. W. Kova-levsky that the female capercailzie sometimes steals away with a young male who has not dared to enter the arena with the older cocks, in the same manner as occasionally happens with the does of the red-deer in Scotland. When two males contend in presence of a single female, the victor, no doubt, commonly gains his desire; but some of these battles are caused by wandering males trying to distract the peace of an already mated pair.[22]

Even with the most pugnacious species it is probable that the pairing does not depend exclusively on the mere strength and courage of the male; for such males are generally decorated with various ornaments, which often become more brilliant during the breeding-season, and which are sedulously displayed before the females. The males also endeavour to charm or excite their mates by love-notes, songs, and antics; and the courtship is, in many instances, a prolonged affair. Hence it is not prob-able that the females are indifferent to the charms of the opposite sex, or that they are invariably compelled to yield to the victorious males. It is more probable that the females are excited, either before or after the con-flict, by certain males, and thus unconsciously prefer them. In the case of *Tetrao umbellus,* a good observer [23] goes so far as to believe that the bat-tles of the male "are all a sham, performed to show themselves to the greatest advantage before the admiring females who assemble around; for I have never been able to find a maimed hero, and seldom more than a broken feather." I shall have to recur to this subject, but I may here add that with the *Tetrao cupido* of the United States, about a score of males assemble at a particular spot, and, strutting about, make the whole air resound with their extraordinary noises. At the first answer from a fe-male the males begin to fight furiously, and the weaker give way; but then, according to Audubon, both the victors and vanquished search for the female, so that the females must either then exert a choice, or the bat-tle must be renewed. So, again, with one of the field-starlings of the Uni-ted States (*Sturnella ludoviciana*) the males engage in fierce conflicts, "but at the sight of a female they all fly after her as if mad." [24]

Vocal and instrumental music.—With birds the voice serves to express various emotions, such as distress, fear, anger, triumph, or mere happi-ness. It is apparently sometimes used to excite terror, as in the case of the hissing noise made by some nestling-birds. Audubon [25] relates that a night-heron (*Ardea nycticorax,* Linn.), which he kept tame, used to hide itself when a cat approached, and then "suddenly start up uttering one of the most frightful cries, apparently enjoying the cat's alarm and flight."

[22] Brehm, 'Thierleben,' &c., B. iv. 1867, p. 990. Audubon, 'Ornith. Biography,' vol. ii. p. 492.
[23] 'Land and Water,' July 25th, 1868, p. 14.
[24] Audubon's 'Ornitholog. Biography;' on *Tetrao cupido,* vol. ii. p. 492; on the Sturnus, vol. ii. p. 219.
[25] 'Ornithological Biograph.,' vol. v. p. 601.

The common domestic cock clucks to the hen, and the hen to her chickens, when a dainty morsel is found. The hen, when she has laid an egg, "repeats the same note very often, and concludes with the sixth above, which she holds for a longer time;" [26] and thus she expresses her joy. Some social birds apparently call to each other for aid; and as they flit from tree to tree, the flock is kept together by chirp answering chirp. During the nocturnal migrations of geese and other water-fowl, sonorous clangs from the van may be heard in the darkness overhead, answered by clangs in the rear. Certain cries serve as danger signals, which, as the sportsman knows to his cost, are understood by the same species and by others. The domestic cock crows, and the humming-bird chirps, in triumph over a defeated rival. The true song, however, of most birds and various strange cries are chiefly uttered during the breeding-season, and serve as a charm, or merely as a call-note, to the other sex.

Naturalists are much divided with respect to the object of the singing of birds. Few more careful observers ever lived than Montagu, and he maintained that the "males of song-birds and of many others do not in general search for the female, but, on the contrary, their business in the spring is to perch on some conspicuous spot, breathing out their full and amorous notes, which, by instinct, the female knows, and repairs to the spot to choose her mate." [27] Mr. Jenner Weir informs me that this is certainly the case with the nightingale. Bechstein, who kept birds during his whole life, asserts, "that the female canary always chooses the best singer, and that in a state of nature the female finch selects that male out of a hundred whose notes please her most." [28] There can be no doubt that birds closely attend to each other's song. Mr. Weir has told me of the case of a bullfinch which had been taught to pipe a German waltz, and who was so good a performer that he cost ten guineas; when this bird was first introduced into a room where other birds were kept and he began to sing, all the others, consisting of about twenty linnets and canaries, ranged themselves on the nearest side of their cages, and listened with the greatest interest to the new performer. Many naturalists believe that the singing of birds is almost exclusively "the effect of rivalry and emulation," and not for the sake of charming their mates. This was the opinion of Daines Barrington and White of Selborne, who both especially attended to this subject.[29] Barrington, however, admits that "superiority in song gives to birds an amazing ascendancy over others, as is well known to bird-catchers."

It is certain that there is an intense degree of rivalry between the males in their singing. Bird-fanciers match their birds to see which will sing longest; and I was told by Mr. Yarrell that a first-rate bird will some-

---

[26] The Hon. Daines Barrington, 'Philosoph. Transactions' 1773, page 252.

[27] 'Ornithological Dictionary,' 1833, p. 475.

[28] 'Naturgeschichte der Stubenvögel,' 1840, s. 4. Mr. Harrison Weir likewise writes to me:—"I am informed that the best singing males generally get a mate first, when they are bred in the same room."

[29] 'Philosophical Transactions,' 1773, p. 263. White's 'Natural History of Selborne,' 1825, vol. i. p. 246.

times sing till he drops down almost dead, or according to Bechstein,[30] quite dead from rupturing a vessel in the lungs. Whatever the cause may be, male birds, as I hear from Mr. Wier, often die suddenly during the season of song. That the habit of singing is sometimes quite independent of love is clear, for a sterile, hybrid canary-bird has been described [31] as singing whilst viewing itself in a mirror, and then dashing at its own image; it likewise attacked with fury a female canary, when put into the same cage. The jealousy excited by the act of singing is constantly taken advantage of by bird-catchers; a male in good song, is hidden and protected, whilst a stuffed bird, surrounded by limed twigs, is exposed to view. In this manner, as Mr. Weir informs me, a man has in the course of a single day caught fifty, and in one instance, seventy, male chaffinches. The power and inclination to sing differ so greatly with birds that although the price of an ordinary male chaffinch is only sixpence, Mr. Weir saw one bird for which the bird-catcher asked three pounds; the test of a really good singer being that it will continue to sing whilst the cage is swung round the owner's head.

That male birds should sing from emulation as well as for charming the female, is not at all incompatible; and it might have been expected that these two habits would have concurred, like those of display and pugnacity. Some authors, however, argue that the song of the male can not serve to charm the female, because the females of some few species, such as of the canary, robin, lark, and bullfinch, especially when in a state of widowhood, as Bechstein remarks, pour forth fairly melodious strains. In some of these cases the habit of singing may be in part attributed to the females having been highly fed and confined,[32] for this disturbs all the functions connected with the reproduction of the species. Many instances have already been given of the partial transference of secondary masculine characters to the female, so that it is not at all surprising that the females of some species should possess the power of song. It has also been argued, that the song of the male cannot serve as a charm, because the males of certain species, for instance of the robin, sing during the autumn.[33] But nothing is more common than for animals to take pleasure in practising whatever instinct they follow at other times for some real good. How often do we see birds which fly easily, gliding and sailing through the air obviously for pleasure? The cat plays with the captured mouse, and the cormorant with the captured fish. The weaver-bird (Ploceus), when confined in a cage, amuses itself by neatly weaving blades of grass between the wires of its cage. Birds which habitually fight during the breeding-season are generally ready to fight at all times; and the males of the capercailzie sometimes hold their *Balzen* or *leks* at the usual

---

[30] 'Naturgesch. der Stubenvögel,' 1840, s. 252.

[31] Mr. Bold, 'Zoologist,' 1843-44, p. 659.

[32] D. Barrington, 'Phil. Trans.' 1773, 262. Bechstein, 'Stubenvögel,' 1840, s. 4.

[33] This is likewise the case with the water-ouzel, see Mr. Hepburn in the 'Zoologist,' 1845-46, p. 1068.

place of assemblage during the autumn.[34] Hence it is not at all surprising that male birds should continue singing for their own amusement after the season for courtship is over.

As shewn in a previous chapter, singing is to a certain extent an art, and is much improved by practice. Birds can be taught various tunes, and even the unmelodious sparrow has learnt to sing like a linnet. They acquire the song of their foster parents,[35] and sometimes that of their neighbours.[36] All the common songsters belong to the Order of Insessores, and their vocal organs are much more complex than those of most other birds; yet it is a singular fact that some of the Insessores, such as ravens, crows, and magpies, possess the proper apparatus,[37] though they never sing, and do not naturally modulate their voices to any great extent. Hunter asserts [38] that with the true songsters the muscles of the larynx are stronger in the males than in the females; but with this slight exception there is no difference in the vocal organs of the two sexes, although the males of most species sing so much better and more continuously than the females.

It is remarkable that only small birds properly sing. The Australian genus Menura, however, must be excepted; for the *Menura Alberti,* which is about the size of a half-grown turkey, not only mocks other birds, but "its own whistle is exceedingly beautiful and varied." The males congregate and form *"corroborying* places," where they sing, raising and spreading their tails like peacocks, and drooping their wings.[39] It is also remarkable that birds which sing well are rarely decorated with brilliant colours or other ornaments. Of our British birds, excepting the bullfinch and goldfinch, the best songsters are plain-coloured. The kingfisher, bee-eater, roller, hoopoe, woodpeckers, &c., utter harsh cries; and the brilliant birds of the tropics are hardly ever songsters.[40] Hence bright colours and the power of song seem to replace each other. We can perceive that if the plumage did not vary in brightness, or if bright colours were dangerous to the species, other means would be employed to charm the females; and melody of voice offers one such means.

In some birds the vocal organs differ greatly in the two sexes. In the *Tetrao cupido* (fig. 39) the male has two bare, orange-coloured sacks, one on each side of the neck; and these are largely inflated when the male, during the breeding-season, makes his curious hollow sound, audible at a great distance. Audubon proved that the sound was intimately connected with this apparatus (which reminds us of the air-sacks on each

[34] L. Lloyd, 'Game Birds of Sweden,' 1867, p. 25.

[35] Barrington, ibid. p. 264, Bechstein, ibid. s. 5.

[36] Dureau de la Malle gives a curious instance ('Annales des Sc. Nat.' 3rd series, Zoolog. tom. x. p. 118) of some wild blackbirds in his garden in Paris, which naturally learnt a republican air from a caged bird.

[37] Bishop, in 'Todd's Cyclop. of Anatomy and Phys.' vol. iv. page 1496.

[38] As stated by Barrington in 'Philosophical Transactions,' 1773, page 262.

[39] Gould, 'Handbook to the Birds of Australia,' vol. i. 1865, pp. 308–310. See also Mr. T. W. Wood in the 'Student,' April 1870, p. 125.

[40] See remarks to this effect in Gould's 'Introduction to the Trochilidæ,' 1861, p. 22.

side of the mouth of certain male frogs), for he found that the sound was much diminished when one of the sacks of a tame bird was pricked, and when both were pricked it was altogether stopped. The female has "a

FIG. 39.—Tetrao cupido: male. (T. W. Wood.)

somewhat similar, though smaller naked space of skin on the neck; but this is not capable of inflation." [41] The male of another kind of grouse (*Tetrao urophasianus*), whilst courting the female, has his "bare yellow œsophagus inflated to a prodigious size, fully half as large as the body;" and he then utters various grating, deep, hollow tones. With his neck-feathers erect, his wings lowered, and buzzing on the ground, and his long pointed tail spread out like a fan, he displays a variety of grotesque attitudes. The œsophagus of the female is not in any way remarkable. [42]

It seems now well made out that the great throat pouch of the European male bustard (*Otis tarda*), and of at least four other species, does not, as was formerly supposed, serve to hold water, but is connected with the utterance during the breeding-season of a peculiar sound resembling "oak." [43] A crow-like bird inhabiting South America (*Cephalopterus or-*

[41] 'The Sportsman and Naturalist in Canada,' by Major W. Ross King, 1866, pp. 144–146. Mr. T. W. Wood gives in the 'Student' (April, 1870, p. 116) an excellent account of the attitude and habits of this bird during its courtship. He states that the ear-tufts or neck-plumes are erected, so that they meet over the crown of the head. See his drawing, fig. 39.

[42] Richardson, 'Fauna Bor. American: Birds,' 1831, p. 359. Audubon, ibid. vol. iv. p. 507.

[43] The following papers have been lately written on this subject: Prof. A. Newton, in the 'Ibis,' 1862, p. 107; Dr. Cullen, ibid. 1865, p. 145; Mr. Flower, in 'Proc. Zool.

natus, fig. 40) is called the umbrella-bird, from its immense top knot, formed of bare white quills surmounted by dark-blue plumes, which it can elevate into a great dome no less than five inches in diameter, covering the whole head. This bird has on its neck a long, thin, cylindrical fleshy appendage, which is thickly clothed with scale-like blue feathers. It probably serves in part as an ornament, but likewise as a resounding apparatus; for Mr. Bates found that it is connected "with an unusual development of the trachea and vocal organs." It is dilated when the bird utters its singularly deep, loud and long sustained fluty note. The head-crest and neck-appendage are rudimentary in the female.[44]

The vocal organs of various web-footed and wading birds are extraordinarily complex, and differ to a certain extent in the two sexes. In some cases the trachea is convoluted, like a French horn, and is deeply embedded in the sternum. In the wild swan (*Cygnus ferus*) it is more deeply embedded in the adult male than in the adult female or young male. In the male Merganser the enlarged portion of the trachea is furnished with an additional pair of muscles.[45] In one of the ducks, however, namely *Anas punctata,* the bony enlargement is only a little more developed in the male than in the female.[46] But the meaning of these differences in the trachea of the two sexes of the Anatidæ is not understood; for the male is not always the more vociferous; thus with the common duck, the male hisses, whilst the female utters a loud quack.[47] In both sexes of one of the cranes (*Grus virgo*) the trachea penetrates the sternum, but presents "certain sexual modifications." In the male of the black stork there is also a well-marked sexual difference in the length and curvature of the bronchi.[48] Highly important structures have, therefore, in these cases been modified according to sex.

It is often difficult to conjecture whether the many strange cries and notes uttered by male birds during the breeding-season serve as a charm or merely as a call to the female. The soft cooing of the turtle-dove and of many pigeons, it may be presumed, pleases the female. When the female of the wild turkey utters her call in the morning, the male answers by a note which differs from the gobling noise made, when with erected feath-

---

Soc.' 1865, p. 747; and Dr. Murie, in 'Proc. Zool. Soc.' 1868, p. 471. In this latter paper an excellent figure is given of the male Australian Bustard in full display with the sack distended. It is a singular fact that the sack is not developed in all the males of the same species.

[44] Bates, 'The Naturalist on the Amazons,' 1863, vol. ii. p. 284; Wallace, in 'Proc. Zool. Soc.' 1850, p. 206. A new species, with a still larger neck-appendage (*C. penduliger*), has lately been discovered, see 'Ibis,' vol. i. p. 457.

[45] Bishop, in Todd's 'Cyclop. of Anatomy and Phys.' vol. iv. page 1499.

[46] Prof. Newton, 'Proc. Zoolog. Soc.' 1871, p. 651.

[47] The spoonbill (Platalea) has its trachea convoluted into a figure of eight, and yet this bird (Jerdon 'Birds of India,' vol. iii. p. 763) is mute but Mr. Blyth informs me that the convolutions are not constantly present, so that perhaps they are now tending towards abortion.

[48] 'Elements of Comp. Anat.' by R. Wagner, Eng. translat. 1845, p. 111. With respect to the swan, as given above, Yarrell's 'History of British Birds,' second edition 1845, vol. iii. p. 193.

ers, rustling wings and distended wattles, he puffs and struts before her.[49] The *spel* of the black-cock certainly serves as a call to the female, for it has been known to bring four or five females from a distance to a male under confinement; but as the black-cock continues his *spel* for hours during successive days, and in the case of the capercailzie "with an agony of passion," we are led to suppose that the females which are present are thus charmed.[50] The voice of the common rook is known to alter during the breeding-season, and is therefore in some way sexual.[51] But what

FIG. 40.—The Umbrella-bird or Cephalopterus ornatus, male (from Brehm.)

shall we say about the harsh screams of, for instance, some kinds of macaws; have these birds as bad taste for musical sounds as they apparently have for colour, judging by the inharmonious contrast of their bright yellow and blue plumage? It is indeed possible that without any advantage being thus gained, the loud voices of many male birds may be the result of the inherited effects of the continued use of their vocal organs when excited by the strong passions of love, jealousy and rage; but to this point we shall recur when we treat of quadrupeds.

[49] C. L. Bonaparte, quoted in the 'Naturalist Library: Birds,' vol. xiv. p. 126.
[50] L. Lloyd, 'The Game Birds of Sweden,' &c., 1867, pp. 22, 81.
[51] Jenner, 'Phil. Trans.,' 1824, p. 20.

We have as yet spoken only of the voice, but the males of various birds practise, during their courtship, what may be called instrumental music. Peacocks and Birds of Paradise rattle their quills together. Turkey-cocks scrape their wings against the ground, and some kinds of grouse thus produce a buzzing sound. Another North American grouse, the *Tetrao umbellus*, when with his tail erect, his ruffs displayed, "he shows off his finery to the females, who lie hid in the neighbourhood," drums by rapidly striking his wings together above his back, according to Mr. R. Haymond, and not, as Audubon thought, by striking them against his sides. The sound thus produced is compared by some to distant thunder, and by others to the quick roll of a drum. The female never drums, "but flies directly to the place where the male is thus engaged." The male of the Kalij-pheasant, in the Himalayas, "often makes a singular drumming noise with his wings, not unlike the sound produced by shaking a stiff piece of cloth." On the west coast of Africa the little black-weavers (Ploceus?) congregate in a small party on the bushes round a small open space, and sing and glide through the air with quivering wings, "which make a rapid whirring sound like a child's rattle." One bird after another thus performs for hours together, but only during the courting-season. At this season, and at no other time, the males of certain night-jars (Caprimulgus) make a strange booming noise with their wings. The various species of wood-peckers strike a sonorous branch with their beaks, with so rapid a vibratory movement that "the head appears to be in two places at once." The sound thus produced is audible at a considerable distance but cannot be described; and I feel sure that its source would never be conjectured by any one hearing it for the first time. As this jarring sound is made chiefly during the breeding-season, it has been considered as a love-song; but it is perhaps more strictly a love-call. The female, when driven from her nest, has been observed thus to call her mate, who answered in the same manner and soon appeared. Lastly, the male Hoopoe (*Upupa epops*) combines vocal and instrumental music; for during the breeding-season this bird, as Mr. Swinhoe observed, first draws in air, and then taps the end of its beak perpendicularly down against a stone or the trunk of a tree, "when the breath being forced down the tubular bill produces the correct sound." If the beak is not thus struck against some object, the sound is quite different. Air is at the same time swallowed, and the œsophagus thus becomes much swollen; and this probably acts as a resonator, not only with the hoopoe, but with pigeons and other birds.[52]

[52] For the foregoing facts see, on Birds of Paradise, Brehm, 'Thierleben,' Band iii. s. 325. On Grouse, Richardson, 'Fauna Bor. Americ.: Birds,' pp. 343 and 359; Major W. Ross King, 'The Sportsman in Canada,' 1866, p. 156; Mr. Haymond, in Prof. Cox's 'Geol. Survey of Indiana,' p. 227; Audubon, 'American Ornitholog. Biograph.' vol. i. p. 216. On the Kalij-pheasant, Jerdon. 'Birds of India,' vol. iii. p. 533. On the Weavers, 'Livingstone's Expedition to the Zambesi,' 1865, p. 425. On Woodpeckers, Macgillivray, 'Hist. of British Birds,' vol. iii. 1840, pp. 84, 88, 89, and 95. On the Hoopoe, Mr. Swinhoe, in 'Proc. Zoolog. Soc.' June 23, 1863 and 1871, p. 348. On the Night-jar, Audubon, ibid. vol. ii. p. 255, and 'American Naturalist,' 1873, p. 672. The English Night-jar likewise makes in the spring a curious noise during its rapid flight.

In the foregoing cases sounds are made by the aid of structures already present and otherwise necessary; but in the following cases certain feathers have been specially modified for the express purpose of producing sounds. The drumming, bleating, neighing, or thundering noise (as expressed by different observers) made by the common snipe (*Scolopax gallinago*) must have surprised every one who has ever heard it. This bird, during the pairing-season, flies to "perhaps a thousand feet in height," and after zig-zagging about for a time descends to the earth in a curved line, with outspread tail and quivering pinions, and surprising velocity. The sound is emitted only during this rapid descent. No one was

FIG. 41.—Outer tail feather of Scolopax gallinago (from 'Proc. Zool. Soc.' 1858).

able to explain the cause until M. Meves observed that on each side of the tail the outer feathers are peculiarly formed (fig. 41), having a stiff sabre-shaped shaft with the oblique barbs of unusual length, the outer webs being strongly bound together. He found that by blowing on these feathers, or by fastening them to a long thin stick and waving them rapidly through the air, he could reproduce the drumming noise made by the living bird. Both sexes are furnished with these feathers, but they are generally larger in the male than in the female, and emit a deeper note.

FIG. 42.—Outer tail-feather of Scolopax frenata.

FIG. 43.—Outer tail-feather of Scolopax javensis.

In some species, as in *S. frenata* (fig. 42), four feathers, and in *S. javensis* (fig. 43), no less than eight on each side of the tail are greatly modified. Different tones are emitted by the feathers of the different species when waved through the air; and the *Scolopax Wilsonii* of the United States makes a switching noise whilst descending rapidly to the earth.[53]

In the male of the *Chamæpetes unicolor* (a large gallinaceous bird of America), the first primary wing-feather is arched towards the tip and is much more attenuated than in the female. In an allied bird, the *Penelope nigra,* Mr. Salvin observed a male, which, whilst it flew downwards "with outstretched wings, gave forth a kind of crashing rushing noise," like the falling of a tree.[54] The male alone of one of the Indian bustards (*Sypheotides auritus*) has its primary wing-feathers greatly acuminated; and the

[53] See M. Meves' interesting paper in 'Proc. Zool. Soc.' 1858, p. 199. For the habits of the snipe, Macgillivray, 'Hist. British Birds,' vol. iv. p. 371. For the American snipe, Capt. Blakiston, 'Ibis,' vol. v. 1863, p. 131.

[54] Mr. Salvin, in 'Proc. Zool. Soc.' 1867, p. 160. I am much indebted to this distinguished ornithologist for sketches of the feathers of the Chamæpetes, and for other information.

male of an allied species is known to make a humming noise whilst courting the female.[55] In a widely different group of birds, namely Humming-
birds, the males alone of certain kinds have either the shafts of their primary wing-feathers broadly dilated, or the webs abruptly excised towards
the extremity. The male, for instance, of *Selasphorus platycercus*, when
adult, has the first primary wing-feather (fig. 44), thus excised. Whilst
flying from flower to flower he makes "a
shrill, almost whistling noise;"[56] but it did
not appear to Mr. Salvin that the noise was
intentionally made.

Lastly, in several species of a sub-genus
of Pipra or Manakin, the males, as described by Mr. Sclater, have their *secondary*
wing-feathers modified in a still more remarkable manner. In the brilliantly-coloured
P. deliciosa the first three secondaries are
thick-stemmed and curved towards the
body; in the fourth and fifth (fig. 45, *a*)
the change is greater; and in the sixth and
seventh (*b, c*) the shaft "is thickened to an

Fig. 44.—Primary wing-
feather of a Humming-
bird, the *Selasphorus platycercus* (from a sketch by
Mr. Salvin). Upper figure,
that of male; lower figure,
corresponding feather of
female.

extraordinary degree, forming a solid horny lump." The barbs also are
greatly changed in shape, in comparison with the corresponding feathers
(*d, e, f*) in the female. Even the bones of the wing, which support these
singular feathers in the male, are said by Mr. Fraser to be much thickened. These little birds make an extraordinary noise, the first "sharp note
being not unlike the crack of a whip."[57]

The diversity of the sounds, both vocal and instrumental, made by the
males of many birds during the breeding-season, and the diversity of the
means for producing such sounds, are highly remarkable. We thus gain a
high idea of their importance for sexual purposes, and are reminded of
the conclusion arrived at as to insects. It is not difficult to imagine the
steps by which the notes of a bird, primarily used as a mere call or for
some other purpose, might have been improved into a melodious love
song. In the case of the modified feathers, by which the drumming, whistling, or roaring noises are produced, we know that some birds during their
courtship flutter, shake, or rattle their unmodified feathers together; and
if the females were led to select the best performers, the males which possessed the strongest or thickest, or most attenuated feathers, situated on
any part of the body, would be the most successful; and thus by slow degrees the feathers might be modified to almost any extent. The females,
of course, would not notice each slight successive alteration in shape, but
only the sounds thus produced. It is a curious fact that in the same class
of animals, sounds so different as the drumming of the snipe's tail, the

[55] Jerdon, 'Birds of India,' vol. iii. pp. 618, 621.
[56] Gould, 'Introduction to the Trochilidæ,' 1861, p. 49. Salvin, 'Proc. Zoolog. Soc.'
1867, p. 160.
[57] Sclater, in 'Proc. Zool. Soc.' 1860, p. 90, and in 'Ibis,' vol. iv. 1862, p. 175. Also
Salvin, in 'Ibis,' 1860, p. 37.

tapping of the woodpecker's beak, the harsh trumpet-like cry of certain water-fowl, the cooing of the turtle-dove, and the song of the nightingale, should all be pleasing to the females of the several species. But we must not judge of the tastes of distinct species by a uniform standard; nor must we judge by the standard of man's taste. Even with man, we should

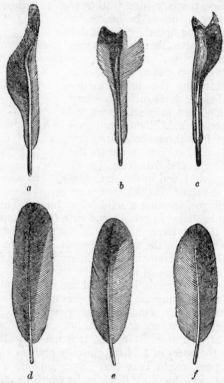

FIG. 45.—Secondary wing-feathers of *Pipra deliciosa* (from Mr. Sclater, in 'Proc. Zool. Soc.' 1860). The three upper feathers, *a, b, c,* from the male; the three lower corresponding feathers, *d, e, f,* from the female.

a and *d,* fifth secondary wing-feather of male and female, upper surface.
b and *e,* sixth secondary, upper surface.   *c* and *f,* seventh secondary, lower surface.

remember what discordant noises, the beating of tom-toms and the shrill notes of reeds, please the ears of savages. Sir S. Baker remarks,[58] that "as the stomach of the Arab prefers the raw meat and reeking liver taken hot from the animal, so does his ear prefer his equally coarse and discordant music to all other."

Love Antics and Dances.—The curious love gestures of some birds have already been incidentally noticed; so that little need here be added.

[58] 'The Nile Tributaries of Abyssinia,' 1867, p. 203.

In Northern America large numbers of a grouse, the *Tetrao phasianellus*, meet every morning during the breeding-season on a selected level spot, and here they run round and round in a circle of about fifteen or twenty feet in diameter, so that the ground is worn quite bare, like a fairy-ring. In these Partridge-dances, as they are called by the hunters, the birds assume the strangest attitudes, and run round, some to the left and some to the right. Audubon describes the males of a heron (*Ardea herodias*) as walking about on their long legs with great dignity before the females, bidding defiance to their rivals. With one of the disgusting carrion-vul-

FIG. 46.—Bower-bird, Chlamydera maculata, with bower (from Brehm).

tures (*Cathartes jota*) the same naturalist states that "the gesticulations and parade of the males at the beginning of the love-season are extremely ludicrous." Certain birds perform their love-antics on the wing, as we have seen with the black African weaver, instead of on the ground. During the spring our little white-throat (*Sylvia cinerea*) often rises a few feet or yards in the air above some bush, and "flutters with a fitful and fantastic motion, singing all the while, and then drops to its perch." The great English bustard throws himself into indescribably odd attitudes whilst courting the female, as has been figured by Wolf. An allied Indian bustard (*Otis bengalensis*) at such times "rises perpendicularly into the air with a hurried flapping of his wings, raising his crest and puffing out the feathers of his neck and breast, and then drops to the ground;" he repeats this manœuvre several times, at the same time humming in a peculiar tone. Such females as happen to be near "obey this saltatory summons," and when they approach he trails his wings and spreads his tail like a turkey-cock.[59]

But the most curious case is afforded by three allied genera of Australian birds, the famous Bower-birds,—no doubt the co-descendants of some ancient species which first acquired the strange instinct of constructing bowers for performing their love-antics. The bowers (fig. 46), which, as we shall hereafter see, are decorated with feathers, shells, bones, and leaves, are built on the ground for the sole purpose of courtship, for their nests are formed in trees. Both sexes assist in the erection of the bowers, but the male is the principal workman. So strong is this instinct that it is practised under confinement, and Mr. Strange has described[60] the habits of some Satin Bower-birds which he kept in an aviary in New South Wales. "At times the male will chase the female all over the aviary, then go to the bower, pick up a gay feather or a large leaf, utter a curious kind of note, set all his feathers erect, run round the bower and become so excited that his eyes appear ready to start from his head; he continues opening first one wing then the other, uttering a low, whistling note, and, like the domestic cock, seems to be picking up something from the ground, until at last the female goes gently towards him." Captain Stokes has described the habits and "play-houses" of another species, the Great Bower-bird, which was seen "amusing itself by flying backwards and forwards, taking a shell alternately from each side, and carrying it through the archway in its mouth." These curious creations, formed solely as halls of assemblage, where both sexes amuse themselves and pay their court, must cost the birds much labor. The bower, for instance, of the Fawn-breasted species, is nearly four feet in length, eighteen inches in height, and is raised on a thick platform of sticks.

Decoration.—I will first discuss the cases in which the males are ornamented either exclusively or in a much higher degree than the females, and in a succeeding chapter those in which both sexes are equally ornamented, and finally the rare cases in which the female is somewhat more brightly-coloured than the male. As with the artificial ornaments used by savage and civilised men, so with the natural ornaments of birds, the head is the chief seat of decoration.[61] The ornaments, as mentioned at the commencement of this chapter, are wonderfully diversified. The plumes on the front or back of the head consist of variously-shaped feathers, sometimes capable of erection or expansion, by which their beautiful colours are fully displayed. Elegant ear-tufts (see fig. 39, ante) are occa-

---

[59] For *Tetrao phasianellus,* see Richardson, 'Fauna, Bor. America,' p. 361, and for further particulars Capt. Blakiston, 'Ibis,' 1863, p. 125. For the Cathartes and Ardea, Audubon, 'Ornith. Biography,' vol. ii. p. 51, and vol. iii. p. 89. On the White-throat, Macgillivray, 'Hist. British Birds,' vol. ii. p. 354. On the Indian Bustard, Jerdon, 'Birds of India,' vol. iii. p. 618.

[60] Gould, 'Handbook to the Birds of Australia,' vol. i. pp. 444, 449, 455. The bower of the Satin Bower-bird may be seen in the Zoölogical Society's Gardens, Regent's Park.

[61] See remarks to this effect, on the 'Feeling of Beauty among Animals,' by Mr. J. Shaw, in the 'Athenæum,' Nov. 24th, 1866, p. 681.

sionally present. The head is sometimes covered with velvety down, as with the pheasant; or is naked and vividly coloured. The throat, also, is sometimes ornamented with a beard, wattles, or caruncles. Such appendages are generally brightly-coloured, and no doubt serve as ornaments, though not always ornamental in our eyes; for whilst the male is in the act of courting the female, they often swell and assume vivid tints, as in the male turkey. At such times the fleshy appendages about the head of the male Tragopan pheasant (*Ceriornis Temminckii*) swell into a large lappet on the throat and into two horns, one on each side of the splendid top-knot; and these are then coloured of the most intense blue which I have ever beheld.[62] The African hornbill (*Bucorax abyssinicus*) inflates the scarlet bladder-like wattle on its neck, and with its wings drooping and tail expanded "makes quite a grand appearance."[63] Even the iris of the eye is sometimes more brightly-coloured in the male than in the female; and this is frequently the case with the beak, for instance, in our common blackbird. In *Buceros corrugatus*, the whole beak and immense casque are coloured more conspicuously in the male than in the female; and "the oblique grooves upon the sides of the lower mandible are peculiar to the male sex."[64]

The head, again, often supports fleshy appendages, filaments, and solid protuberances. These, if not common to both sexes, are always confined to the males. The solid protuberances have been described in detail by Dr. W. Marshall,[65] who shews that they are formed either of cancellated bone coated with skin, or of dermal and other tissues. With mammals true horns are always supported on the frontal bones, but with birds various bones have been modified for this purpose; and in species of the same group the protuberances may have cores of bone, or be quite destitute of them, with intermediate gradations connecting these two extremes. Hence, as Dr. Marshall justly remarks, variations of the most different kinds have served for the development through sexual selection of these ornamental appendages. Elongated feathers or plumes spring from almost every part of the body. The feathers on the throat and breast are sometimes developed into beautiful ruffs and collars. The tail-feathers are frequently increased in length; as we see in the tail-coverts of the peacock, and in the tail itself of the Argus pheasant. With the peacock even the bones of the tail have been modified to support the heavy tail-coverts.[66] The body of the Argus is not larger than that of a fowl; yet the length from the end of the beak to the extremity of the tail is no less than five feet three inches,[67] and that of the beautifully ocellated secondary wing-feathers nearly three feet. In a small African night-jar (*Cosmetornis vex-*

[62] See Dr. Murie's account with coloured figures in 'Proc. Zoolog. Soc.' 1872, p. 730.
[63] Mr. Monteiro, 'Ibis,' vol. iv. 1862, p. 339.
[64] 'Land and Water,' 1868, p. 217.
[65] 'Ueber die Schädelhöcker,' &c., 'Niederländischen Archiv für Zoologie,' B. I. Heft 2, 1872.
[66] Dr. W. Marshall, 'Über den Vogelschwanz,' ibid. B. I. Heft 2, 1872.
[67] Jardine's 'Naturalist Library: Birds,' vol. xiv. p. 166.

illarius) one of the primary wing-feathers, during the breeding-season, attains a length of twenty-six inches, whilst the bird itself is only ten inches in length. In another closely-allied genus of night-jars, the shafts of the elongated wing-feathers are naked, except at the extremity, where

Fig. 47.—Paradisea Papuana (T. W. Wood).

there is a disc.[68] Again, in another genus of night-jars, the tail-feathers are even still more prodigiously developed. In general the feathers of the tail are more often elongated than those of the wings, as any great elonga-

[68] Sclater, in the 'Ibis,' vol. vi. 1864, p. 114; Livingstone, 'Expedition to the Zambesi,' 1865, p. 66.

tion of the latter impedes flight. We thus see that in closely-allied birds ornaments of the same kind have been gained by the males through the development of widely different feathers.

It is a curious fact that the feathers of species belonging to very distinct groups have been modified in almost exactly the same peculiar manner. Thus the wing-feathers in one of the above-mentioned night-jars are bare along the shaft, and terminate in a disc; or are, as they are sometimes called, spoon or racket-shaped. Feathers of this kind occur in the tail of a motmot (*Eumomota superciliaris*), of a king-fisher, finch, humming-bird, parrot, several Indian drongos (Dicrurus and Edolius, in one of which the disc stands vertically), and in the tail of certain birds of paradise. In these latter birds, similar feathers, beautifully ocellated, ornament the head, as is likewise the case with some gallinaceous birds. In an Indian bustard (*Sypheotides auritus*) the feathers forming the ear-tufts, which are about four inches in length, also terminate in discs.[69] It is a most singular fact that the motmots, as Mr. Salvin has clearly shown,[70] give to their tail feathers the racket-shape by biting off the barbs, and, further, that this continued mutilation has produced a certain amount of inherited effect.

Again, the barbs of the feathers in various widely-distinct birds are filamentous or plumose, as with some herons, ibises, birds of paradise, and Gallinaceæ. In other cases the barbs disappear, leaving the shafts bare from end to end; and these in the tail of the *Paradisea apoda* attain a length of thirty-four inches: [71] in *P. Papuana* (fig. 47) they are much shorter and thin. Smaller feathers when thus denuded appear like bristles, as on the breast of the turkey-cock. As any fleeting fashion in dress comes to be admired by man, so with birds a change of almost any kind in the structure or colouring of the feathers in the male appears to have been admired by the female. The fact of the feathers in widely distinct groups having been modified in an analogous manner no doubt depends primarily on all the feathers having nearly the same structure and manner of development, and consequently tending to vary in the same manner. We often see a tendency to analogous variability in the plumage of our domestic breeds belonging to distinct species. Thus top-knots have appeared in several species. In an extinct variety of the turkey, the top-knot consisted of bare quills surmounted with plumes of down, so that they somewhat resembled the racket-shaped feathers above described. In certain breeds of the pigeon and fowl the feathers are plumose, with some tendency in the shafts to be naked. In the Sebastopol goose the scapular feathers are greatly elongated, curled, or even spirally twisted, with the margins plumose.[72]

[69] Jerdon, 'Birds of India,' vol. iii. p. 620.

[70] 'Proc. Zoolog. Soc.' 1873, p. 429.

[71] Wallace, in 'An. and Mag. of Nat. Hist.,' vol. xx. 1857, p. 416, and in his 'Malay Archipelago,' vol. ii. 1869, p. 390.

[72] See my work on 'The Variation of Animals and Plants under Domestication,' vol. i. pp. 289, 293.

In regard to colour, hardly anything need here be said, for every one knows how splendid are the tints of many birds, and how harmoniously they are combined. The colours are often metallic and iridescent. Circular spots are sometimes surrounded by one or more differently shaded zones, and are thus converted into ocelli. Nor need much be said on the

FIG. 48.—Lophornis ornatus, male and female (from Brehm).

wonderful difference between the sexes of many birds. The common peacock offers a striking instance. Female birds of paradise are obscurely coloured and destitute of all ornaments, whilst the males are probably the most highly decorated of all birds, and in so many different ways that they must be seen to be appreciated. The elongated and golden-orange plumes which spring from beneath the wings of the *Paradisea apoda*, when vertically erected and made to vibrate, are described as forming a sort of halo, in the centre of which the head "looks like a little emerald sun with its rays formed by the two plumes." [73] In another most beauti-

Fig. 49.—Spathura underwoodi, male and female (from Brehm).

ful species the head is bald, "and of a rich cobalt blue, crossed by several lines of black velvety feathers." [74]

Male humming-birds (figs. 48 and 49) almost vie with birds of para-

[73] Quoted from M. de Lafresnaye in 'Annals and Mag. of Nat. Hist.' vol xiii. 1854, p. 157: see also Mr. Wallace's much fuller account in vol. xx. 1857, p. 412, and in his 'Malay Archipelago.'

[74] Wallace, 'The Malay Archipelago,' vol. ii. 1869, p. 405.

dise in their beauty, as every one will admit who has seen Mr. Gould's splendid volumes, or his rich collection. It is very remarkable in how many different ways these birds are ornamented. Almost every part of their plumage has been taken advantage of, and modified; and the modifications have been carried, as Mr. Gould shewed me, to a wonderful extreme in some species belonging to nearly every sub-group. Such cases are curiously like those which we see in our fancy breeds, reared by man for the sake of ornament; certain individuals originally varied in one character, and other individuals of the same species in other characters; and these have been seized on by man and much augmented—as shewn by the tail of the fantail-pigeon, the hood of the jacobin, the beak and wattle of the carrier, and so forth. The sole difference between these cases is that in the one, the result is due to man's selection, whilst in the other, as with humming-birds, birds of paradise, &c., it is due to the selection by the females of the more beautiful males.

I will mention only one other bird, remarkable from the extreme contrast in colour between the sexes, namely the famous bell-bird (*Chasmorhynchus niveus*) of S. America, the note of which can be distinguished at the distance of nearly three miles, and astonishes every one when first hearing it. The male is pure white, whilst the female is dusky-green; and white is a very rare colour in terrestrial species of moderate size and inoffensive habits. The male, also, as described by Waterton, has a spiral tube, nearly three inches in length, which rises from the base of the beak. It is jet-black, dotted over with minute downy feathers. This tube can be inflated with air, through a communication with the palate; and when not inflated hangs down on one side. The genus consists of four species, the males of which are very distinct, whilst the females, as described by Mr. Sclater in a very interesting paper, closely resemble each other, thus offering an excellent instance of the common rule that within the same group the males differ much more from each other than do the females. In a second species (*C. nudicollis*) the male is likewise snow-white, with the exception of a large space of naked skin on the throat and round the eyes, which during the breeding-season is of a fine green colour. In a third species (*C. tricarunculatus*) the head and neck alone of the male are white, the rest of the body being chestnut-brown, and the male of this species is provided with three filamentous projections half as long as the body—one rising from the base of the beak, and the two others from the corners of the mouth.[75]

The coloured plumage and certain other ornaments of the adult males are either retained for life, or are periodically renewed during the summer and breeding-season. At this same season the beak and naked skin about the head frequently change colour, as with some herons, ibises, gulls, one of the bell-birds just noticed, &c. In the white ibis, the cheeks, the inflatable skin of the throat, and the basal portion of the beak then

---

[75] Mr. Sclater, 'Intellectual Observer,' Jan. 1867. 'Waterton's Wanderings,' p. 118. See also Mr. Salvin's interesting paper, with a plate, in the 'Ibis,' 1865, p. 90.

become crimson.[76] In one of the rails, *Gallicrex cristatus,* a large red car-
uncle is developed during this period on the head of the male. So it is with
a thin horny crest on the beak of one of the pelicans, *P. erythrorhynchus;*
for, after the breeding-season, these horny crests are shed, like horns
from the heads of stags, and the shore of an island in a lake in Nevada
was found covered with these curious exuviæ.[77]

Changes of colour in the plumage according to the season depend, firstly on a double annual moult, secondly on an actual change of colour in
the feathers themselves, and thirdly on their dull-coloured margins being
periodically shed, or on these three processes more or less combined. The
shedding of the deciduary margins may be compared with the shedding
of their down by very young birds; for the down in most cases arises from
the summits of the first true feathers.[78]

With respect to the birds which annually undergo a double moult,
there are, firstly, some kinds, for instance snipes, swallow-plovers (Glareolæ), and curlews, in which the two sexes resemble each other, and do not
change colour at any season. I do not know whether the winter plumage
is thicker and warmer than the summer plumage, but warmth seems the
most probable end attained of a double moult, where there is no change
of colour. Secondly, there are birds, for instance, certain species of Totanus and other Grallatores, the sexes of which resemble each other, but
in which the summer and winter plumage differ slightly in colour. The
difference, however, in these cases is so small that it can hardly be an advantage to them; and it may, perhaps, be attributed to the direct action
of the different conditions to which the birds are exposed during the two
seasons. Thirdly, there are many other birds the sexes of which are alike,
but which are widely different in their summer and winter plumage.
Fourthly, there are birds the sexes of which differ from each other in colour; but the females, though moulting twice, retain the same colours
throughout the year, whilst the males undergo a change of colour, sometimes a great one, as with certain bustards. Fifthly and lastly, there are
birds the sexes of which differ from each other in both their summer and
winter plumage; but the male undergoes a greater amount of change at
each recurrent season than the female—of which the ruff (*Machetes pugnax*) offers a good instance.

With respect to the cause or purpose of the differences in colour between the summer and winter plumage, this may in some instances, as
with the ptarmigan,[79] serve during both seasons as a protection. When
the difference between the two plumages is slight it may perhaps be attributed, as already remarked, to the direct action of the conditions of life.

[76] 'Land and Water,' 1867, p. 394.

[77] Mr. D. G. Elliot, in 'Proc. Zool. Soc.' 1869, p. 589.

[78] Nitzsch's 'Pterylography,' edited by P. L. Sclater. Ray Soc. 1867, p. 14.

[79] The brown mottled summer plumage of the ptarmigan is of as much importance
to it, as a protection, as the white winter plumage; for in Scandinavia during the
spring, when the snow has disappeared, this bird is known to suffer greatly from
birds of prey, before it has acquired its summer dress: see Wilhelm von Wright, in
Lloyd, 'Game Birds of Sweden,' 1867, p. 125.

But with many birds there can hardly be a doubt that the summer plumage is ornamental, even when both sexes are alike. We may conclude that this is the case with many herons, egrets, &c., for they acquire their beautiful plumes only during the breeding-season. Moreover, such plumes, top-knots, &c., though possessed by both sexes, are occasionally a little more developed in the male than in the female; and they resemble the plumes and ornaments possessed by the males alone of other birds. It is also known that confinement, by affecting the reproductive system of male birds, frequently checks the development of their secondary sexual characters, but has no immediate influence on any other characters; and I am informed by Mr. Bartlett that eight or nine specimens of the Knot (*Tringa canutus*) retained their unadorned winter plumage in the Zoological Gardens throughout the year, from which fact we may infer that the summer plumage, though common to both sexes, partakes of the nature of the exclusively masculine plumage of many other birds.[80]

From the foregoing facts, more especially from neither sex of certain birds changing colour during either annual moult, or changing so slightly that the change can hardly be of any service to them, and from the females of other species moulting twice yet retaining the same colours throughout the year, we may conclude that the habit of annually moulting twice has not been acquired in order that the male should assume an ornamental character during the breeding-season; but that the double moult, having been originally acquired for some distinct purpose, has subsequently been taken advantage of in certain cases for gaining a nuptial plumage.

It appears at first sight a surprising circumstance that some closely-allied species should regularly undergo a double annual moult, and others only a single one. The ptarmigan, for instance, moults twice or even thrice in the year, and the blackcock only once: some of the splendidly coloured honey-suckers (Nectariniæ) of India and some sub-genera of obscurely coloured pipits (Anthus) have a double, whilst others have only a single annual moult.[81] But the gradations in the manner of moulting, which are known to occur with various birds, shew us how species, or whole groups, might have originally acquired their double annual moult, or having once gained the habit, have again lost it. With certain bustards and plovers the vernal moult is far from complete, some feathers being renewed, and some changed in colour. There is also reason to believe that with certain bustards and rail-like birds, which properly undergo a double moult, some of the older males retain their nuptial plumage throughout the year. A few highly modified feathers may merely be added dur-

[80] In regard to the previous statements on moulting, see, on snipes, &c., Macgillivray, 'Hist. Brit. Birds,' vol. iv. p. 371; on Glareolæ, curlews, and bustards, Jerdon, 'Birds of India,' vol. iii. pp. 615, 630, 683; on Totanus, ibid. p. 700; on the plumes of herons, ibid. p. 738, and Macgillivray, vol. iv. pp. 435 and 444, and Mr. Stafford Allen, in the 'Ibis,' vol. v. 1863, p. 33.

[81] On the moulting of the ptarmigan, see Gould's 'Birds of Great Britain.' On the honey-suckers, Jerdon, 'Birds of India,' vol. i. pp. 359, 365, 369. On the moulting of Anthus see Blyth, in 'Ibis,' 1867, p. 32.

ing the spring to the plumage, as occurs with the disc-formed tail-feathers of certain drongos (*Bhringa*) in India, and with the elongated feathers on the back, neck, and crest of certain herons. By such steps as these, the vernal moult might be rendered more and more complete, until a perfect double moult was acquired. Some of the birds of paradise retain their nuptial feathers throughout the year, and thus have only a single moult; others cast them directly after the breeding-season, and thus have a double moult; and others again cast them at this season during the first year, but not afterwards; so that these latter species are intermediate in their manner of moulting. There is also a great difference with many birds in the length of time during which the two annual plumages are retained; so that the one might come to be retained for the whole year, and the other completely lost. Thus in the spring *Machetes pugnax* retains his ruff for barely two months. In Natal the male widow-bird (*Chera progne*) acquires his fine plumage and long tail-feathers in December or January, and loses them in March; so that they are retained only for about three months. Most species, which undergo a double moult, keep their ornamental feathers for about six months. The male, however, of the wild *Gallus bankiva* retains his neck-hackles for nine or ten months; and when these are cast off, the underlying black feathers on the neck are fully exposed to view. But with the domesticated descendant of this species, the neck-hackles of the male are immediately replaced by new ones; so that we here see, as to part of the plumage, a double moult changed under domestication into a single moult.[82]

The common drake (*Anas boschas*), after the breeding-season, is well known to lose his male plumage for a period of three months, during which time he assumes that of the female. The male pin-tail duck (*Anas acuta*) loses his plumage for the shorter period of six weeks or two months; and Montague remarks that "this double moult within so short a time is a most extraordinary circumstance, that seems to bid defiance to all human reasoning." But the believer in the gradual modification of species will be far from feeling surprise at finding gradations of all kinds. If the male pin-tail were to acquire his new plumage within a still shorter period, the new male feathers would almost necessarily be mingled with the old, and both with some proper to the female; and this apparently is the case with the male of a not distantly-allied bird, namely the *Merganser serrator*, for the males are said to "undergo a change of plumage, which assimilates them in some measure to the female." By a little fur-

[82] For the foregoing statements in regard to partial moults, and on old males retaining their nuptial plumage, see Jerdon, on bustards and plovers, in 'Birds of India,' vol. iii. pp. 617, 637, 709, 711. Also Blyth in 'Land and Water,' 1867, p. 84. On the moulting of Paradisea, see an interesting article by Dr. W. Marshall, 'Archives Neerlandaises,' tom. vi. 1871. On the Vidua, 'Ibis,' vol. iii. 1861, p. 133. On the Drongoshrikes, Perdon, ibid. vol. i. p. 435. On the vernal moult of the *Herodias bubulcus*, Mr. S. S. Allen, in 'Ibis,' 1863, p. 33. On *Gallus bankiva*, Blyth, in 'Annals and Mag. of Nat. Hist.' vol. i. 1848, p. 455; see, also, on this subject, my 'Variation of Animals under Domestication,' vol. i. p. 236.

ther acceleration in the process, the double moult would be completely lost.[83]

Some male birds, as before stated, become more brightly coloured in the spring, not by a vernal moult, but either by an actual change of colour in the feathers, or by their obscurely-coloured deciduary margins being shed. Changes of colour thus caused may last for a longer or shorter time. In the *Pelecanus onocrotalus* a beautiful rosy tint, with lemon-coloured marks on the breast, overspreads the whole plumage in the spring; but these tints, as Mr. Sclater states, "do not last long, disappearing generally in about six weeks or two months after they have been attained." Certain finches shed the margins of their feathers in the spring, and then become brighter coloured, while other finches undergo no such change. Thus the *Fringilla tristis* of the United States (as well as many other American species) exhibits its bright colours only when the winter is past, whilst our goldfinch, which exactly represents this bird in habits, and our siskin, which represents it still more closely in structure, undergo no such annual change. But a difference of this kind in the plumage of allied species is not surprising, for with the common linnet, which belongs to the same family, the crimson forehead and breast are displayed only during the summer in England, whilst in Madeira these colours are retained throughout the year.[84]

Display by Male Birds of their Plumage.—Ornaments of all kinds, whether permanently or temporarily gained, are sedulously displayed by the males, and apparently serve to excite, attract, or fascinate the females. But the males will sometimes display their ornaments, when not in the presence of the females, as occasionally occurs with grouse at their balz-places, and as may be noticed with the peacock; this latter bird, however, evidently wishes for a spectator of some kind, and, as I have often seen, will show off his finery before poultry, or even pigs.[85] All naturalists who have closely attended to the habits of birds, whether in a state of nature or under confinement, are unanimously of opinion that the males take delight in displaying their beauty. Audubon frequently speaks of the male as endeavouring in various ways to charm the female. Mr. Gould, after describing some peculiarities in a male humming-bird, says he has no doubt that it has the power of displaying them to the greatest advantage before the female. Dr. Jerdon[86] insists that the beautiful plumage of the male serves "to fascinate and attract the female." Mr. Bartlett, at the Zoological Gardens, expressed himself to me in the strongest terms to the same effect.

[83] See Macgillivray, 'Hist. British Birds' (vol. v. pp. 34, 70, and 223), on the moulting of the Anatidæ, with quotations from Waterton and Montagu. Also Yarrell, 'Hist. of British Birds,' vol. iii. p. 243.

[84] On the pelican, see Sclater, in 'Proc. Zool. Soc.' 1868, p. 265. On the American finches, see Audubon, 'Ornith. Biography,' vol. i. pp. 174, 221, and Jerdon, 'Birds of India,' vol. ii. p. 383. On the *Fringilla cannabina* of Madeira, Mr. E. Vernon Harcourt, 'Ibis,' vol. v. 1863, p. 230.

[85] See also 'Ornamental Poultry,' by Rev. E. S. Dixon, 1848, p. 8.

[86] 'Birds of India,' introduct. vol. i. p. xxiv.; on the peacock, vol. iii. p. 507. See Gould's 'Introduction to the Trochilidæ,' 1861, pp. 15 and 111.

It must be a grand sight in the forests of India "to come suddenly on twenty or thirty pea-fowl, the males displaying their gorgeous trains, and strutting about in all the pomp of pride before the gratified females." The wild turkey-cock erects his glittering plumage, expands his finely-zoned tail and barred wing-feathers, and altogether, with his crimson and blue wattles, makes a superb, though, to our eye, grotesque appearance. Similar facts have already been given with respect to grouse of various kinds. Turning to another Order. The male *Rupicola crocea* (fig. 50) is one of

Fig. 50.—Rupicola crocea, male (T. W. Wood).

the most beautiful birds in the world, being of a splendid orange, with some of the feathers curiously truncated and plumose. The female is brownish-green, shaded with red, and has a much smaller crest. Sir R. Schomburgk has described their courtship; he found one of their meeting-places where ten males and two females were present. The space was from four to five feet in diameter, and appeared to have been cleared of every blade of grass and smoothed as if by human hands. A male "was capering, to the apparent delight of several others. Now spreading its wings, throwing up its head, or opening its tail like a fan; now strutting about with a hopping gait until tired, when it gabbled some kind of note, and was relieved by another. Thus three of them successively took the field, and then, with self-approbation, withdrew to rest." The Indians, in order to obtain their skins, wait at one of the meeting-places till the birds are eagerly engaged in dancing, and then are able to kill with their poisoned arrows four or five males, one after the other.[87] With birds of paradise a dozen or more full-plumaged males congregate in a tree to hold a dancing-party, as it is called by the natives: and here they fly about, raise their wings, elevate their exquisite plumes, and make them vibrate, and the whole tree seems, as Mr. Wallace remarks, to be filled with waving plumes. When thus engaged, they become so absorbed that a skilful archer may shoot nearly the whole party. These birds, when kept in confinement in the Malay Archipelago, are said to take much care in keeping their feathers clean; often spreading them out, examining them, and removing every speck of dirt. One observer, who kept several pairs alive, did not doubt that the display of the male was intended to please the female.[88]

The Gold and Amherst pheasants during their courtship not only expand and raise their splendid frills, but twist them, as I have myself seen, obliquely towards the female on whichever side she may be standing, obviously in order that a large surface may be displayed before her.[89] They likewise turn their beautiful tails and tail-coverts a little towards the same side. Mr. Bartlett has observed a male Polyplectron (fig. 51) in the act of courtship, and has shown me a specimen stuffed in the attitude then assumed. The tail and wing-feathers of this bird are ornamented with beautiful ocelli, like those on the peacock's train. Now when the peacock displays himself, he expands and erects his tail transversely to his body, for he stands in front of the female, and has to shew off, at the same time, his rich blue throat and breast. But the breast of the Polyplectron is obscurely coloured, and the ocelli are not confined to the tail-feathers. Consequently the Polyplectron does not stand in front of the female; but he erects and expands his tail-feathers a little obliquely, lowering the expanded wing on the same side, and raising that on the opposite side. In this attitude the ocelli over the whole body are exposed at the same time before the eyes of the admiring female in one grand bespangled expanse. To whichever side she may turn, the expanded wings and the obliquely-held tail are turned towards her. The male Tragopan pheasant acts in nearly the same manner, for he raises the feathers of the body, though not the wing itself, on the side which is opposite to the female, and which would otherwise be concealed, so that nearly all the beautifully spotted feathers are exhibited at the same time.

The Argus pheasant affords a much more remarkable case. The im-

---

[87] 'Journal of R. Geograph. Soc.' vol. x. 1840, p. 236.

[88] 'Annals and Mag. of Nat. Hist.' vol. xiii. 1854, p. 157; also Wallace, ibid. vol. xx. 1857, p. 412, and 'The Malay Archipelago,' vol. ii. 1869, p. 252. Also Dr. Bennett, as quoted by Brehm, 'Thierleben,' B. iii. s. 326.

[89] Mr. T. W. Wood has given ('The Student,' April, 1870, p. 115) a full account of this manner of display, by the Gold pheasant and by the Japanese pheasant, *Ph. versicolor;* and he calls it the lateral or one-sided display.

mensely developed secondary wing-feathers are confined to the male; and each is ornamented with a row of from twenty to twenty-three ocelli, above an inch in diameter. These feathers are also elegantly marked with

FIG. 51.—Polyplectron chinquis, male (T. W. Wood).

oblique stripes and rows of spots of a dark colour, like those on the skin of a tiger and leopard combined. These beautiful ornaments are hidden until the male shows himself off before the female. He then erects his tail, and expands his wing-feathers into a great, almost upright, circular fan or shield, which is carried in front of the body. The neck and head are held on one side, so that they are concealed by the fan; but the bird in order to see the female, before whom he is displaying himself, sometimes pushes his head between two of the long wing-feathers (as Mr. Bartlett has seen), and then presents a grotesque appearance. This must be a frequent habit with the bird in a state of nature, for Mr. Bartlett and his son

Fig. 52.—Side view of male Argus pheasant, whilst displaying before the female. Observed and sketched from nature by Mr. T. W. Wood.

on examining some perfect skins sent from the East, found a place between two of the feathers which was much frayed, as if the head had here frequently been pushed through. Mr. Wood thinks that the male can also peep at the female on one side, beyond the margin of the fan.

The ocelli on the wing-feathers are wonderful objects; for they are so

shaded that, as the Duke of Argyll remarks,[90] they stand out like balls lying loosely within sockets. When I looked at the specimen in the British
Museum, which is mounted with the wings expanded and trailing downwards, I was however greatly disappointed, for the ocelli appeared flat, or
even concave. But Mr. Gould soon made the case clear to me, for he held
the feathers erect, in the position in which they would naturally be displayed, and now from the light shining on them from above each ocellus
at once resembled the ornament called a ball and socket. These feathers
have been shown to several artists, and all have expressed their admiration at the perfect shading. It may well be asked, could such artistically •
shaded ornaments have been formed by means of sexual selection? But it
will be convenient to defer giving an answer to this question until we
treat in the next chapter of the principle of gradation.

The foregoing remarks relate to the secondary wing-feathers, but the
primary wing-feathers, which in most gallinaceous birds are uniformly
coloured, are in the Argus pheasant equally wonderful. They are of a soft
brown tint with numerous dark spots, each of which consists of two or
three black dots with a surrounding dark zone. But the chief ornament is
a space parallel to the dark-blue shaft, which in outline forms a perfect
second feather lying within the true feather. This inner part is coloured of
a lighter chestnut, and is thickly dotted with minute white points. I have
shewn this feather to several persons, and many have admired it even
more than the ball and socket feathers, and have declared that it was
more like a work of art than of nature. Now these feathers are quite hidden on all ordinary occasions, but are fully displayed, together with the
long secondary feathers, when they are all expanded together so as to
form the great fan or shield.

The case of the male Argus pheasant is eminently interesting, because
it affords good evidence that the most refined beauty may serve as a sexual charm, and for no other purpose. We must conclude that this is the
case, as the secondary and primary wing-feathers are not at all displayed,
and the ball and socket ornaments are not exhibited in full perfection until the male assumes the attitude of courtship. The Argus pheasant does
not possess brilliant colours, so that his success in love appears to depend
on the great size of his plumes, and on the elaboration of the most elegant
patterns. Many will declare that it is utterly incredible that a female bird
should be able to appreciate fine shading and exquisite patterns. It is undoubtedly a marvellous fact that she should possess this almost human
degree of taste. He who thinks that he can safely gauge the discrimination and taste of the lower animals may deny that the female Argus pheasant can appreciate such refined beauty; but he will then be compelled to
admit that the extraordinary attitudes assumed by the male during the
act of courtship, by which the wonderful beauty of his plumage is fully
displayed, are purposeless; and this is a conclusion which I for one will
never admit.

Although so many pheasants and allied gallinaceous birds carefully display their plumage before the females, it is remarkable, as Mr. Bartlett informs me, that this is not the case with the dull-coloured Eared and Cheer pheasants (*Crossoptilon auritum* and *Phasianus wallichii*); so that these birds seem conscious that they have little beauty to display. Mr. Bartlett has never seen the males of either of these species fighting together, though he has not had such good opportunities for observing the Cheer as the Eared pheasant. Mr. Jenner Weir, also, finds that all male birds with rich or strongly-characterised plumage are more quarrelsome than the dull-coloured species belonging to the same groups. The goldfinch, for instance, is far more pugnacious than the linnet, and the blackbird than the thrush. Those birds which undergo a seasonal change of plumage likewise become much more pugnacious at the period when they are most gaily ornamented. No doubt the males of some obscurely-coloured birds fight desperately together, but it appears that when sexual selection has been highly influential, and has given bright colours to the males of any species, it has also very often given a strong tendency to pugnacity. We shall meet with nearly analogous cases when we treat of mammals. On the other hand, with birds the power of song and brilliant colours have rarely been both acquired by the males of the same species; but in this case the advantage gained would have been the same, namely, success in charming the female. Nevertheless it must be owned that the males of several brilliantly coloured birds have had their feathers specially modified for the sake of producing instrumental music, though the beauty of this cannot be compared, at least according to our taste, with that of the vocal music of many songsters.

We will now turn to male birds which are not ornamented in any high degree, but which nevertheless display during their courtship whatever attractions they may possess. These cases are in some respects more curious than the foregoing, and have been but little noticed. I owe the following facts to Mr. Weir, who has long kept confined birds of many kinds, including all the British Fringillidæ and Emberizidæ. The facts have been selected from a large body of valuable notes kindly sent me by him. The bullfinch makes his advances in front of the female, and then puffs out his breast, so that many more of the crimson feathers are seen at once than otherwise would be the case. At the same time he twists and bows his black tail from side to side in a ludicrous manner. The male chaffinch also stands in front of the female, thus showing his red breast and "blue bell," as the fanciers call his head; the wings at the same time being slightly expanded, with the pure white bands on the shoulders thus rendered conspicuous. The common linnet distends his rosy breast, slightly expands his brown wings and tail, so as to make the best of them by exhibiting their white edgings. We must, however, be cautious in concluding that the wings are spread out solely for display, as some birds do so whose wings are not beautiful. This is the case with the domestic cock, but it is always the wing on the side opposite to the female which is expanded, and at the same time scraped on the ground. The male goldfinch behaves differently from all other finches: his wings are beautiful, the shoulders being black, with the dark-tipped wing-feathers spotted with white and edged with golden yellow. When he courts the female, he sways his body from side to side, and quickly turns his slightly expanded wings first to one side, then to the other, with a golden flashing effect. Mr. Weir informs me that no other British finch turns thus from side to side during his courtship, not even the closely-allied male siskin, for he would not thus add to his beauty.

Most of the British Buntings are plain coloured birds; but in the spring the feathers on the head of the male reed-bunting (*Emberiza schœniculus*) acquire a fine black colour by the abrasion of the dusky tips; and these are erected during the act of courtship. Mr. Weir has kept two species of Amadina from Australia: the *A. castanotis* is a very small and chastely coloured finch, with a dark tail, white rump, and jet-black upper tail-coverts, each of the latter being marked with three large conspicuous oval spots of white.[91] This species, when courting the female, slightly spreads out and vibrates these parti-coloured tail-coverts in a very peculiar manner. The male *Amadina Lathami* behaves very differently, exhibiting before the female his brilliantly spotted breast, scarlet rump, and scarlet upper tail-coverts. I may here add from Dr. Jerdon that the Indian bulbul (*Pycnonotus hœmorrhous*) has its under tail-coverts of a crimson colour, and these, it might be thought could never be well exhibited; but the bird "when excited often spreads them out laterally so that they can be seen even from above."[92] The crimson under tail-coverts of some other birds as with one of the woodpeckers, *Picus major,* can be seen without any such display. The common pigeon has iridescent feathers on the breast, and every one must have seen how the male inflates his breast whilst courting the female, thus showing them off to the best advantage. One of the beautiful bronze-winged pigeons of Australia (*Ocyphaps lophotes*) behaves, as described to me by Mr. Weir, very differently: the male, whilst standing before the female, lowers his head almost to the ground, spreads out and raises his tail, and half expands his wings. He then alternately and slowly raises and depresses his body, so that the iridescent metallic feathers are all seen at once, and glitter in the sun.

Sufficient facts have now been given to shew with what care male birds display their various charms, and this they do with the utmost skill. Whilst preening their feathers, they have frequent opportunities for admiring themselves, and of studying how best to exhibit their beauty. But as all the males of the same species display themselves in exactly the same manner, it appears that actions, at first perhaps intentional, have become instinctive. If so, we ought not to accuse birds of conscious vanity; yet when we see a peacock strutting about, with expanded and quivering tail-feathers, he seems the very emblem of pride and vanity.

[91] For the description of these birds, see Gould's 'Handbook to the Birds of Australia,' vol. i. 1865, p. 417.
[92] 'Birds of India,' vol. ii. p. 96.

The various ornaments possessed by the males are certainly of the highest importance to them, for in some cases they have been acquired at the expense of greatly impeded powers of flight or of running. The African night-jar (Cosmetornis), which during the pairing-season has one of its primary wing-feathers developed into a streamer of very great length, is thereby much retarded in its flight, although at other times remarkable for its swiftness. The "unwieldy size" of the secondary wing-feathers of the male Argus pheasant is said "almost entirely to deprive the bird of flight." The fine plumes of male birds of paradise trouble them during a high wind. The extremely long tail-feathers of the male widow-birds (Vidua) of Southern Africa render "their flight heavy;" but as soon as these are cast off they fly as well as the females. As birds always breed when food is abundant, the males probably do not suffer much inconvenience in searching for food from their impeded powers of movement; but there can hardly be a doubt that they must be much more liable to be struck down by birds of prey. Nor can we doubt that the long train of the peacock and the long tail and wing-feathers of the Argus pheasant must render them an easier prey to any prowling tiger-cat than would otherwise be the case. Even the bright colours of many male birds cannot fail to make them conspicuous to their enemies of all kinds. Hence, as Mr. Gould has remarked, it probably is that such birds are generally of a shy disposition, as if conscious that their beauty was a source of danger, and are much more difficult to discover or approach, than the sombre coloured and comparatively tame females or than the young and as yet unadorned males.[93]

It is a more curious fact that the males of some birds which are provided with special weapons for battle, and which in a state of nature are so pugnacious that they often kill each other, suffer from possessing certain ornaments. Cock-fighters trim the hackles and cut off the combs and gills of their cocks; and the birds are then said to be dubbed. An undubbed bird, as Mr. Tegetmeier insists, "is at a fearful disadvantage; the comb and gills offer an easy hold to his adversary's beak, and as a cock always strikes where he holds, when once he has seized his foe, he has him entirely in his power. Even supposing that the bird is not killed, the loss of blood suffered by an undubbed cock is much greater than that sustained by one that has been trimmed."[94] Young turkey-cocks in fighting always seize hold of each other's wattles; and I presume that the old birds fight in the same manner. It may perhaps be objected that the comb and wattles are not ornamental, and cannot be of service to the birds in this way; but even to our eyes, the beauty of the glossy black Spanish cock is much enhanced by his white face and crimson comb; and

[93] On the Cosmetornis, see Livingstone's 'Expedition to the Zambesi,' 1865, p. 66. On the Argus pheasant, Jardine's 'Nat. Hist. Lib.: Birds,' vol. xiv. p. 167. On Birds of Paradise, Lesson, quoted by Brehm, 'Thierleben,' B. iii. s. 325. On the widow-bird, Barrow's 'Travels in Africa,' vol. i. p. 243, and 'Ibis,' vol, iii, 1861, p. 133. Mr. Gould, on the shyness of male birds, 'Handbook to Birds of Australia,' vol. i. 1865, pp. 210, 457.

[94] Tegetmeier, 'The Poultry Book,' 1866, p. 139.

no one who has ever seen the splendid blue wattles of the male Tragopan pheasant distended in courtship can for a moment doubt that beauty is the object gained. From the foregoing facts we clearly see that the plumes and other ornaments of the males must be of the highest importance to them; and we further see that beauty is even sometimes more important than success in battle.

CHAPTER XIV

BIRDS—*continued*

*Choice exerted by the female—Length of courtship—Unpaired birds—Mental qual-
ities and taste for the beautiful—Preference or antipathy shewn by the female for
particular males—Variability of birds—Variations sometimes abrupt—Laws of
variation—Formation of ocelli—Gradations of character—Case of Peacock, Argus
pheasant, and Urosticte.*

WHEN the sexes differ in beauty or in the power of singing, or in producing what I have called instrumental music, it is almost invariably the
male who surpasses the female. These qualities, as we have just seen, are
evidently of high importance to the male. When they are gained for only
a part of the year it is always before the breeding-season. It is the male
alone who elaborately displays his varied attractions, and often performs
strange antics on the ground or in the air, in the presence of the female.
Each male drives away, or if he can, kills his rivals. Hence we may conclude that it is the object of the male to induce the female to pair with
him, and for this purpose he tries to excite or charm her in various ways;
and this is the opinion of all those who have carefully studied the habits
of living birds. But there remains a question which has an all-important
bearing on sexual selection, namely, does every male of the same species
excite and attract the female equally? Or does she exert a choice, and
prefer certain males? This latter question can be answered in the affirmative by much direct and indirect evidence. It is far more difficult to decide what qualities determine the choice of the females; but here again
we have some direct and indirect evidence that it is to a large extent the
external attractions of the male; though no doubt his vigour, courage,
and other mental qualities come into play. We will begin with the indirect evidence.

Length of Courtship.—The lengthened period during which both sexes
of certain birds meet day after day at an appointed place probably depends partly on the courtship being a prolonged affair, and partly on re-
iteration in the act of pairing. Thus in Germany and Scandinavia the bal-
zing or leks of the black-cocks last from the middle of March, all through
April into May. As many as forty or fifty, or even more birds congregate
at the leks; and the same place is often frequented during successive
years. The lek of the capercailzie lasts from the end of March to the middle or even end of May. In North America "the partridge dances" of the

Tetrao phasianellus "last for a month or more." Other kinds of grouse, both in North America and Eastern Siberia,[1] follow nearly the same habits. The fowlers discover the hillocks where the ruffs congregate by the grass being trampled bare, and this shews that the same spot is long frequented. The Indians of Guiana are well acquainted with the cleared arenas, where they expect to find the beautiful cocks of the Rock; and the natives of New Guinea know the trees where from ten to twenty male birds of paradise in full plumage congregate. In this latter case it is not expressly stated that the females meet on the same trees, but the hunters, if not specially asked, would probably not mention their presence, as their skins are valueless. Small parties of an African weaver (*Ploceus*) congregate, during the breeding-season, and perform for hours their graceful evolutions. Large numbers of the Solitary snipe (*Scolopax major*) assemble during dusk in a morass; and the same place is frequented for the same purpose during successive years; here they may be seen running about "like so many rats," puffing out their feathers, flapping their wings, and uttering the strangest cries.[2]

Some of the above birds,—the black-cock, capercailzie, pheasant-grouse, ruff, Solitary snipe, and perhaps others,—are, as is believed, polygamists. With such birds it might have been thought that the stronger males would simply have driven away the weaker, and then at once have taken possession of as many females as possible; but if it be indispensable for the male to excite or please the female, we can understand the length of the courtship and the congregation of so many individuals of both sexes at the same spot. Certain strictly monogamous species likewise hold nuptial assemblages; this seems to be the case in Scandinavia with one of the ptarmigans, and their leks last from the middle of March to the middle of May. In Australia the lyre-bird (*Menura superba*) forms "small round hillocks," and the *M. Alberti* scratches for itself shallow holes, or, as they are called by the natives, *corroborying places*, where it is believed both sexes assemble. The meetings of the *M. superba* are sometimes very large; and an account has lately been published [3] by a traveller, who heard in a valley beneath him, thickly covered with scrub, "a din which completely astonished" him; on crawling onwards he beheld, to his amazement, about one hundred and fifty of the magnificent lyre-cocks, "ranged in order of battle, and fighting with indescribable fury." The bowers of the Bower-birds are the resort of both sexes during the breeding-season; and "here the males meet and contend with each

[1] Nordman describes ('Bull. Soc. Imp. des Nat. Moscou,' 1861, tom. xxxiv. p. 264) the balzen of *Tetrao urogalloides* in Amur Land. He estimated the number of birds assembled at above a hundred, not counting the females, which lie hid in the surrounding bushes. The noises uttered differ from those of *T. urogallus*.

[2] With respect to the assemblages of the above-named grouse, see Brehm, 'Thierleben,' B. iv. s. 350; also L. Lloyd, 'Game Birds of Sweden,' 1867, pp. 19, 78. Richardson, 'Fauna Bor. Americana': Birds, p. 362. References in regard to the assemblages of other birds have already been given. On Paradisea, see Wallace, in 'Annals and Mag. of Nat. Hist.' vol. xx. 1857, p. 412. On the snipe, Lloyd, ibid. p. 221.

[3] Quoted by Mr. T. W. Wood in the 'Student,' April 1870, p. 125.

other for the favours of the female, and here the latter assemble and co-
quet with the males." With two of the genera, the same bower is resorted
to during many years.[4]

The common magpie (*Corvus pica*, Linn.), as I have been informed by
the Rev. W. Darwin Fox, used to assemble from all parts of Delamere
Forest, in order to celebrate the "great magpie marriage." Some years
ago these birds abounded in extraordinary numbers, so that a gamekeeper killed in one morning nineteen males, and another killed by a single
shot seven birds at roost together. They then had the habit of assembling
very early in the spring at particular spots, where they could be seen in
flocks, chattering, sometimes fighting, bustling and flying about the trees.
The whole affair was evidently considered by the birds as one of the highest importance. Shortly after the meeting they all separated, and were
then observed by Mr. Fox and others to be paired for the season. In any
district in which a species does not exist in large numbers, great assemblages cannot, of course, be held, and the same species may have different
habits in different countries. For instance, I have heard of only one instance, from Mr. Wedderburn, of a regular assemblage of black game in
Scotland, yet these assemblages are so well known in Germany and Scandinavia that they have received special names.

Unpaired Birds.—From the facts now given, we may conclude that the
courtship of birds belonging to widely different groups, is often a prolonged, delicate, and troublesome affair. There is even reason to suspect,
improbable as this will at first appear, that some males and females of
the same species, inhabiting the same district, do not always please each
other, and consequently do not pair. Many accounts have been published
of either the male or female of a pair having been shot, and quickly replaced by another. This has been observed more frequently with the magpie than with any other bird, owing perhaps to its conspicuous appearance and nest. The illustrious Jenner states that in Wiltshire one of a
pair was daily shot no less than seven times successively, "but all to no
purpose, for the remaining magpie soon found another mate"; and the
last pair reared their young. A new partner is generally found on the succeeding day; but Mr. Thompson gives the case of one being replaced on
the evening of the same day. Even after the eggs are hatched, if one of
the old birds is destroyed a mate will often be found; this occurred after
an interval of two days, in a case recently observed by one of Sir J. Lubbock's keepers.[5] The first and most obvious conjecture is that male magpies must be much more numerous than females; and that in the above
cases, as well as in many others which could be given, the males alone
had been killed. This apparently holds good in some instances, for the
gamekeepers in Delamere Forest assured Mr. Fox that the magpies and

---

[4] Gould, 'Handbook to the Birds of Australia,' vol. i. pp. 300, 308, 448, 451. On the
ptarmigan, above alluded to, see Lloyd, ibid, p. 129.

[5] On magpies, Jenner, in 'Phil. Transact.' 1824, p. 21. Macgillivray, 'Hist. British
Birds,' vol. i. p. 570. Thompson, in 'Annals and Magazine of Natural History' vol. viii.
1842, p. 494.

carrion-crows which they formerly killed in succession in large numbers near their nests, were all males; and they accounted for this fact by the males being easily killed whilst bringing food to the sitting females. Macgillivray, however, gives, on the authority of an excellent observer, an instance of three magpies successively killed on the same nest, which were all females; and another case of six magpies successively killed whilst sitting on the same eggs, which renders it probable that most of them were females; though, as I hear from Mr. Fox, the male will sit on the eggs when the female is killed.

Sir J. Lubbock's gamekeeper has repeatedly shot, but how often he could not say, one of a pair of jays (*Garrulus glandarius*), and has never failed shortly afterwards to find the survivor re-matched. Mr. Fox, Mr. F. Bond, and others have shot one of a pair of carrion-crows (*Corvus corone*), but the nest was soon again tenanted by a pair. These birds are rather common; but the peregrine-falcon (*Falco peregrinus*) is rare, yet Mr. Thompson states that in Ireland "if either an old male or female be killed in the breeding-season (not an uncommon circumstance), another mate is found within a very few days, so that the eyries, nothwithstanding such casualties, are sure to turn out their complement of young." Mr. Jenner Weir has known the same thing with the peregrine-falcons at Beachy Head. The same observer informs me that three kestrels (*Falco tinnunculus*), all males, were killed one after the other whilst attending the same nest; two of these were in mature plumage, but the third was in the plumage of the previous year. Even with the rare golden eagle (*Aquila chrysaëtos*), Mr. Birkbeck was assured by a trustworthy gamekeeper in Scotland, that if one is killed, another is soon found. So with the white owl (*Strix flammea*), "the survivor readily found a mate, and the mischief went on."

White of Selborne, who gives the case of the owl, adds that he knew a man, who from believing that partridges when paired were disturbed by the males fighting, used to shoot them; and though he had widowed the same female several times, she always soon found a fresh partner. This same naturalist ordered the sparrows, which deprived the house-martins of their nests, to be shot; but the one which was left, "be it cock or hen, presently procured a mate, and so for several times following." I could add analogous cases relating to the chaffinch, nightingale, and redstart. With respect to the latter bird (*Phœnicura ruticilla*), a writer expresses much surprise how the sitting female could so soon have given effectual notice that she was a widow, for the species was not common in the neighbourhood. Mr. Jenner Weir has mentioned to me a nearly similar case; at Blackheath he never sees or hears the note of the wild bullfinch, yet when one of his caged males has died, a wild one in the course of a few days has generally come and perched near the widowed female, whose call-note is not loud. I will give only one other fact, on the authority of this same observer; one of a pair of starlings (*Sturnus vulgaris*) was shot in the morning; by noon a new mate was found; this was again shot, but before night the pair was complete; so that the disconsolate widow or widower was thrice consoled during the same day. Mr. Engleheart also informs me that he used during several years to shoot one of a pair of starlings which built in a hole in a house at Blackheath; but the loss was always immediately repaired. During one season he kept an account, and found that he had shot thirty-five birds from the same nest; these consisted of both males and females, but in what proportion he could not say: nevertheless, after all this destruction, a brood was reared.[6]

These facts well deserve attention. How is it that there are birds enough ready to replace immediately a lost mate of either sex? Magpies, jays, carrion-crows, partridges, and some other birds, are always seen during the spring in pairs, and never by themselves; and these offer at first sight the most perplexing cases. But birds of the same sex, although of course not truly paired, sometimes live in pairs or in small parties, as is known to be the case with pigeons and partridges. Birds also sometimes live in triplets, as has been observed with starlings, carrion-crows, parrots, and partridges. With partridges two females have been known to live with one male, and two males with one female. In all such cases it is probable that the union would be easily broken; and one of the three would readily pair with a widow or widower. The males of certain birds may occasionally be heard pouring forth their love-song long after the proper time, shewing that they have either lost or never gained a mate. Death from accident or disease of one of a pair would leave the other free and single; and there is reason to believe that female birds during the breeding-season are especially liable to premature death. Again, birds which have had their nests destroyed, or barren pairs, or retarded individuals, would easily be induced to desert their mates, and would probably be glad to take what share they could of the pleasures and duties of rearing offspring although not their own.[7] Such contingencies as these probably explain most of the foregoing cases.[8] Nevertheless, it is a

[6] On the peregrine falcon, see Thompson, 'Nat. Hist. of Ireland: Birds,' vol. i. 1849, p. 39. On owls, sparrows, and partridges, see White, 'Nat. Hist. of Selborne,' edit. of 1825, vol. i. p. 139. On the Phœnicura, see Loudon's 'Mag. of Nat. Hist.' vol. vii. 1834, p. 245. Brehm ('Thierleben,' B. iv. s. 991) also alludes to cases of birds thrice mated during the same day.

[7] See White ('Nat. Hist. of Selborne,' 1825, vol. i. p. 140) on the existence, early in the season, of small coveys of male partridges, of which fact I have heard other instances. See Jenner, on the retarded state of the generative organs in certain birds, in 'Phil. Transact.' 1824. In regard to birds living in triplets. I owe to Mr. Jenner Weir the cases of the starlings and parrots, and to Mr. Fox, of partridges; on carrion-crows, see the 'Field,' 1868, p. 415. On various male birds singing after the proper period, see Rev. L. Jenyns, 'Observations in Natural History,' 1846, p. 87.

[8] The following case has been given ('The Times,' Aug. 6th, 1868) by the Rev. F. O. Morris, on the authority of the Hon. and Rev. O. W. Forester. "The gamekeeper here found a hawk's nest this year, with five young ones on it. He took four and killed them, but left one with its wings clipped as a decoy to destroy the old ones by. They were both shot next day, in the act of feeding the young one, and the keeper thought it was done with. The next day he came again and found two other charitable hawks, who had come with an adopted feeling to succour the orphan. These two he killed, and then left the nest. On returning afterwards he found two more charitable individuals on the same errand of mercy. One of these he killed; the other he also shot, but could not find. No more came on the like fruitless errand."

strange fact that within the same district, during the height of the breeding-season, there should be so many males and females always ready to
repair the loss of a mated bird. Why do not such spare birds immediately
pair together? Have we not some reason to suspect, and the suspicion has
occurred to Mr. Jenner Weir, that as the courtship of birds appears to be
in many cases prolonged and tedious, so it occasionally happens that certain males and females do not succeed, during the proper season, in exciting each other's love, and consequently do not pair? This suspicion
will appear somewhat less improbable after we have seen what strong antipathies and preferences female birds occasionally evince towards particular males.

Mental Qualities of Birds, and their Taste for the Beautiful.—Before
we further discuss the question whether the females select the more attractive males or accept the first whom they may encounter, it will be advisable briefly to consider the mental powers of birds. Their reason is
generally, and perhaps justly, ranked as low; yet some facts could be
given [9] leading to an opposite conclusion. Low powers of reasoning, however, are compatible, as we see with mankind, with strong affections,
acute perception, and a taste for the beautiful; and it is with these latter
qualities that we are here concerned. It has often been said that parrots
become so deeply attached to each other that when one dies the other
pines for a long time; but Mr. Jenner Weir thinks that with most birds
the strength of their affection has been much exaggerated. Nevertheless
when one of a pair in a state of nature has been shot, the survivor has
been heard for days afterwards uttering a plaintive call; and Mr. St.
John gives various facts proving the attachment of mated birds.[10] Mr.
Bennett relates [11] that in China after a drake of the beautiful mandarin
Teal had been stolen, the duck remained disconsolate, though sedulously
courted by another mandarin drake, who displayed before her all his
charms. After an interval of three weeks the stolen drake was recovered,
and instantly the pair recognised each other with extreme joy. On the
other hand, starlings, as we have seen, may be consoled thrice in the same
day for the loss of their mates. Pigeons have such excellent local memories, that they have been known to return to their former homes after an
interval of nine months, yet, as I hear from Mr. Harrison Weir, if a pair
which naturally would remain mated for life be separated for a few weeks
during the winter, and afterwards matched with other birds, the two,
when brought together again, rarely, if ever, recognise each other.

[9] I am indebted to Prof. Newton for the following passage from Mr. Adam's 'Travels of a Naturalist,' 1870, p. 278. Speaking of Japanese nut-hatches in confinement, he
says: "Instead of the more yielding fruit of the yew, which is the usual food of the
nut-hatch of Japan, at one time I substituted hard hazel-nuts. As the bird was unable to crack them, he placed them one by one in his water-glass, evidently with the
notion that they would in time become softer—an interesting proof of intelligence on
the part of these birds."

[10] 'A Tour in Sutherlandshire,' vol. i. 1849, p. 185. Dr. Buller says ('Birds of New
Zealand,' 1872, p. 56) that a male King Lory was killed; and the female "fretted and
moped, refused her food, and died of a broken heart."

[11] Wanderings in New South Wales,' vol. ii. 1834, p. 62.

Birds sometimes exhibit benevolent feelings; they will feed the deserted young ones even of distinct species, but this perhaps ought to be considered as a mistaken instinct. They will feed, as shewn in an earlier part
of this work, adult birds of their own species which have become blind.
Mr. Buxton gives a curious account of a parrot which took care of a frost-
bitten and crippled bird of a distinct species, cleansed her feathers, and
defended her from the attacks of the other parrots which roamed freely
about his garden. It is a still more curious fact that these birds apparently evince some sympathy for the pleasures of their fellows. When a
pair of cockatoos made a nest in an acacia tree, "it was ridiculous to see
the extravagant interest taken in the matter by the others of the same
species." These parrots, also, evinced unbounded curiosity, and clearly
had "the idea of property and possession." [12] They have good memories,
for in the Zoological Gardens they have plainly recognised their former
masters after an interval of some months.

Birds possess acute powers of observation. Every mated bird, of
course, recognises its fellow. Audubon states that a certain number of
mocking-thrushes (*Mimus polyglottus*) remain all the year round in
Louisiana, whilst others migrate to the Eastern States; these latter, on
their return, are instantly recognised, and always attacked, by their
southern brethren. Birds under confinement distinguish different persons,
as is proved by the strong and permanent antipathy or affection which
they shew, without any apparent cause, towards certain individuals. I
have heard of numerous instances with jays, partridges, canaries, and especially bullfinches. Mr. Hussey has described in how extraordinary a
manner a tamed partridge recognised everybody: and its likes and dislikes were very strong. This bird seemed "fond of gay colours, and no
new gown or cap could be put on without catching his attention." [13] Mr.
Hewitt has described the habits of some ducks (recently descended from
wild birds), which, at the approach of a strange dog or cat, would rush
headlong into the water, and exhaust themselves in their attempts to escape; but they knew Mr. Hewitt's own dogs and cats so well that they
would lie down and bask in the sun close to them. They always moved
away from a strange man, and so they would from the lady who attended
them if she made any great change in her dress. Audubon relates that he
reared and tamed a wild turkey which always ran away from any strange
dog; this bird escaped into the woods, and some days afterwards Audubon saw, as he thought, a wild turkey, and made his dog chase it; but, to
his astonishment, the bird did not run away, and the dog, when he came
up, did not attack the bird, for they mutually recognised each other as
old friends.[14]

[12] 'Acclimatization of Parrots,' by C. Buxton, M. P. 'Annals and Mag. of Nat. Hist,'
Nov. 1868, p. 381.
[13] 'The Zoologist,' 1847–'48, p. 1602.
[14] Hewitt on wild ducks, 'Journal of Horticulture,' Jan. 13, 1863, p. 39. Audubon
on the wild turkey, 'Ornith. Biography,' vol. i. p. 14. On the mocking-thrush, ibid. vol.
i p. 110.

Mr. Jenner Weir is convinced that birds pay particular attention to the colours of others birds, sometimes out of jealousy, and sometimes as a sign of kinship. Thus he turned a reed-bunting (*Emberiza schœniculus*), which had acquired its black head-dress, into his aviary, and the new-comer was not noticed by any bird, except by a bullfinch, which is like-wise black-headed. This bullfinch was a very quiet bird, and had never before quarrelled with any of its comrades, including another reed-bunt-ing, which had not as yet become black-headed: but the reed-bunting with a black head was so unmercifully treated that it had to be removed. *Spiza cyanea*, during the breeding-season, is of a bright blue colour; and though generally peaceable, it attacked *S. ciris*, which has only the head blue, and completely scalped the unfortunate bird. Mr. Weir was also ob-liged to turn out a robin, as it fiercely attacked all the birds in his aviary with any red in their plumage, but no other kinds; it actually killed a red-breasted crossbill, and nearly killed a goldfinch. On the other hand, he has observed that some birds, when first introduced, fly towards the species which resemble them most in colour, and settle by their sides.

As male birds display their fine plumage and other ornaments with so much care before the females, it is obviously probable that these appreci-ate the beauty of their suitors. It is, however, difficult to obtain direct evidence of their capacity to appreciate beauty. When birds gaze at themselves in a looking-glass (of which many instances have been re-corded) we cannot feel sure that it is not from jealousy of a supposed rival, though this is not the conclusion of some observers. In other cases it is difficult to distinguish between mere curiosity and admiration. It is perhaps the former feeling which, as stated by Lord Lilford,[15] attracts the ruff towards any bright object, so that, in the Ionian Islands, "it will dart down to a bright-coloured handkerchief, regardless of repeated shots." The common lark is drawn down from the sky, and is caught in large numbers, by a small mirror made to move and glitter in the sun. Is it admiration or curiosity which leads the magpie, raven, and some other birds to steal and secrete bright objects, such as silver articles or jewels?

Mr. Gould states that certain humming-birds decorate the outsides of their nests "with the utmost taste; they instinctively fasten thereon beautiful pieces of flat lichen, the larger pieces in the middle, and the smaller on the part attached to the branch. Now and then a pretty feath-er is intertwined or fastened to the outer sides, the stem being always so placed that the feather stands out beyond the surface." The best evidence, however, of a taste for the beautiful is afforded by the three genera of Australian bower-birds already mentioned. Their bowers (see fig. 46, p. 715), where the sexes congregate and play strange antics, are variously constructed, but what most concerns us is, that they are decorated by the several species in a different manner. The Satin bower-bird collects gaily-coloured articles, such as the blue tail-feathers of parrakeets, bleached bones and shells, which it sticks between the twigs or arranges at the en-

---

[15] The 'Ibis,' vol. ii. 1860, p. 344.

trance. Mr. Gould found in one bower a neatly-worked stone tomahawk and a slip of blue cotton, evidently procured from a native encampment. These objects are continually re-arranged, and carried about by the birds whilst at play. The bower of the Spotted bower-bird "is beautifully lined with tall grasses, so disposed that the heads nearly meet, and the decorations are very profuse." Round stones are used to keep the grass-stems in their proper places, and to make divergent paths leading to the bower. The stones and shells are often brought from a great distance. The Regent bird, as described by Mr. Ramsay, ornaments its short bower with bleached land-shells belonging to five or six species, and with "berries of various colours, blue, red, and black, which give it when fresh a very pretty appearance. Besides these there were several newly-picked leaves and young shoots of a pinkish colour, the whole shewing a decided taste for the beautiful." Well may Mr. Gould say that "these highly decorated halls of assembly must be regarded as the most wonderful instances of bird-architecture yet discovered;" and the taste, as we see, of the several species certainly differs.[16]

Preference for particular Males by the Females.—Having made these preliminary remarks on the discrimination and taste of birds, I will give all the facts known to me which bear on the preference shewn by the female for particular males. It is certain that distinct species of birds occasionally pair in a state of nature and produce hybrids. Many instances could be given: thus Macgillivray relates how a male blackbird and female thrush "fell in love with each other," and produced offspring.[17] Several years ago eighteen cases had been recorded of the occurrence in Great Britain of hybrids between the black grouse and pheasant; [18] but most of these cases may perhaps be accounted for by solitary birds not finding one of their own species to pair with. With other birds, as Mr. Jenner Weir has reason to believe, hybrids are sometimes the result of the casual intercourse of birds building in close proximity. But these remarks do not apply to the many recorded instances of tamed or domestic birds, belonging to distinct species, which have become absolutely fascinated with each other, although living with their own species. Thus Waterton [19] states that out of a flock of twenty-three Canada geese, a female paired with a solitary Bernicle gander, although so different in appearance and size; and they produced hybrid offspring. A male wigeon (*Mareca penelope*), living with females of the same species, has been known to pair with a pintail duck, *Querquedula acuta*. Lloyd describes the remarkable

[16] On the ornamented nests of humming-birds, Gould, 'Introduction to the Trochilidæ,' 1861, p. 19. On the bower-birds, Gould, 'Handbook to the Birds of Australia,' 1865, vol. i. pp. 444–461. Ramsay, in the 'Ibis,' 1867, p. 456.
[17] 'Hist of Brit. Birds,' vol. ii. p. 92.
[18] 'Zoologist,' 1853–1854, p. 3940.
[19] Waterton, 'Essays on Nat. His.' 2nd series, pp. 42 and 117. For the following statements see on the wigeon, Loudon's 'Mag. of Nat. Hist.' vol. ix. p. 616; L. Lloyd, 'Scandinavian Adventures,' vol. i. 1854, p. 452. Dixon, 'Ornamental and Domestic Poultry,' p. 137; Hewitt, in 'Journal of Horticulture,' Jan. 13, 1863, p. 40; Bechstein, 'Stubenvögel,' 1840, s. 230. Mr. J. Jenner Weir has lately given me an analogous case with ducks of two species.

attachment between a shield-drake (*Tadorna vulpanser*) and a common duck. Many additional instances could be given; and the Rev. E. S. Dixon remarks that "those who have kept many different species of geese together well know what unaccountable attachments they are frequently forming, and that they are quite as likely to pair and rear young with individuals of a race (species) apparently the most alien to themselves as with their own stock."

The Rev. W. D. Fox informs me that he possessed at the same time a pair of Chinese geese (*Anser cygnoides*), and a common gander with three geese. The two lots kept quite separate, until the Chinese gander seduced one of the common geese to live with him. Moreover, of the young birds hatched from the eggs of the common geese, only four were pure, the other eighteen proving hybrids; so that the Chinese gander seems to have had prepotent charms over the common gander. I will give only one other case; Mr. Hewitt states that a wild duck, reared in captivity "after breeding a couple of seasons with her own mallard, at once shook him off on my placing a male Pintail on the water. It was evidently a case of love at first sight, for she swam about the new-comer caressingly, though he appeared evidently alarmed and averse to her overtures of affection. From that hour she forgot her old partner. Winter passed by, and the next spring the Pintail seemed to have become a convert to her blandishments, for they nested and produced seven or eight young ones."

What the charm may have been in these several cases, beyond mere novelty, we cannot even conjecture. Colour, however, sometimes comes into play; for in order to raise hybrids from the siskin (*Fringilla spinus*) and the canary, it is much the best plan, according to Bechstein, to place birds of the same tint together. Mr. Jenner Weir turned a female canary into his aviary, where there were male linnets, goldfinches, siskins, greenfinches, chaffinches, and other birds, in order to see which she would choose; but there never was any doubt, and the greenfinch carried the day. They paired and produced hybrid offspring.

The fact of the female preferring to pair with one male rather than with another of the same species is not so likely to excite attention, as when this occurs, as we have just seen, between distinct species. The former cases can best be observed with domesticated or confined birds; but these are often pampered by high feeding, and sometimes have their instincts vitiated to an extreme degree. Of this latter fact I could give sufficient proofs with pigeons, and especially with fowls, but they cannot be here related. Vitiated instincts may also account for some of the hybrid unions above mentioned; but in many of these cases the birds were allowed to range freely over large ponds, and there is no reason to suppose that they were unnaturally stimulated by high feeding.

With respect to birds in a state of nature, the first and most obvious supposition which will occur to every one is that the female at the proper season accepts the first male whom she may encounter; but she has at least the opportunity for exerting a choice, as she is almost invariably pursued by many males. Audubon—and we must remember that he spent a long life in prowling about the forests of the United States and observing the birds—does not doubt that the female deliberately chooses her mate; thus, speaking of a woodpecker, he says the hen is followed by half-a-dozen gay suitors, who continue performing strange antics, "until a marked preference is shewn for one." The female of the red-winged starling (*Agelæus phœniceus*) is likewise pursued by several males, "until, becoming fatigued, she alights, receives their addresses, and soon makes a choice." He describes also how several male night-jars repeatedly plunge through the air with astonishing rapidity, suddenly turning, and thus making a singular noise; "but no sooner has the female made her choice than the other males are driven away." With one of the vultures (*Cathartes aura*) of the United States, parties of eight, ten, or more males and females assemble on fallen logs, "exhibiting the strongest desire to please mutually," and after many caresses, each male leads off his partner on the wing. Audubon likewise carefully observed the wild flocks of Canada geese (*Anser canadensis*), and gives a graphic description of their love-antics; he says that the birds which had been previously mated "renewed their courtship as early as the month of January, while the others would be contending or coquetting for hours every day, until all seemed satisfied with the choice they had made, after which, although they remained together, any person could easily perceive that they were careful to keep in pairs. I have observed also that the older the birds the shorter were the preliminaries of their courtship. The bachelors and old maids whether in regret, or not caring to be disturbed by the bustle, quietly moved aside and lay down at some distance from the rest." [20] Many similar statements with respect to other birds could be cited from this same observer.

Turning now to domesticated and confined birds, I will commence by giving what little I have learnt respecting the courtship of fowls. I have received long letters on this subject from Messrs. Hewitt and Tegetmeier, and almost an essay from the late Mr. Brent. It will be admitted by every one that these gentlemen, so well known from their published works, are careful and experienced observers. They do not believe that the females prefer certain males on account of the beauty of their plumage; but some allowance must be made for the artificial state under which these birds have long been kept. Mr. Tegetmeier is convinced that a gamecock, though disfigured by being dubbed and with his hackles trimmed, would be accepted as readily as a male retaining all his natural ornaments. Mr. Brent, however, admits that the beauty of the male probably aids in exciting the female; and her acquiescence is necessary. Mr. Hewitt is convinced that the union is by no means left to mere chance, for the female almost invariably prefers the most vigorous, defiant, and mettlesome male; hence it is almost useless, as he remarks, "to attempt true breeding if a game-cock in good health and condition runs the locality, for almost every hen on leaving the roosting-place will resort to the game-cock, even

[20] Audubon, 'Ornitholog. Biography,' vol. i. pp. 191, 349; vol. ii. pp. 42, 275; vol. iii. p. 2.

though that bird may not actually drive away the male of her own variety." Under ordinary circumstances the males and females of the fowl seem to come to a mutual understanding by means of certain gestures, described to me by Mr. Brent. But hens will often avoid the officious attentions of young males. Old hens, and hens of a pugnacious disposition, as the same writer informs me, dislike strange males, and will not yield until well beaten into compliance. Ferguson, however, describes how a quarrelsome hen was subdued by the gentle courtship of a Shanghai cock.[21]

There is reason to believe that pigeons of both sexes prefer pairing with birds of the same breed; and dovecot-pigeons dislike all the highly improved breeds.[22] Mr. Harrison Weir has lately heard from a trustworthy observer, who keeps blue pigeons, that these drive away all other coloured varieties, such as white, red, and yellow; and from another observer, that a female dun carrier could not, after repeated trials, be matched with a black male, but immediately paired with a dun. Again, Mr. Tegetmeier had a female blue turbit that obstinately refused to pair with two males of the same breed, which were successively shut up with her for weeks; but on being let out she would have immediately accepted the first blue dragon that offered. As she was a valuable bird, she was then shut up for many weeks with a silver (*i. e.*, very pale blue) male, and at last mated with him. Nevertheless, as a general rule, colour appears to have little influence on the pairing of pigeons. Mr. Tegetmeier, at my request, stained some of his birds with magenta, but they were not much noticed by the others.

Female pigeons occasionally feel a strong antipathy towards certain males, without any assignable cause. Thus MM. Boitard and Corbié, whose experience extended over forty-five years, state: "Quand une femelle éprouve de l'antipathie pour un mâle avec lequel on veut l'accoupler, malgré tous les feux de l'amour, malgré l'alpiste et le chènevis dont on la nourrit pour augmenter son ardeur, malgré un emprisonnement de six mois et même d'un an, elle refuse constamment ses caresses; les avances empressées, les agaceries, les tournoiemens, les tendres roucoulemens, rien ne peut lui plaire ni l'émouvoir; gonflée, boudeuse, blottie dans un coin de sa prison, elle n'en sort que pour boire et manger, ou pour repousser avec une espéce de rage des caresses devenues trop pressantes."[23] On the other hand, Mr. Harrison Weir has himself observed, and has heard from several breeders, that a female pigeon will occasionally take a strong fancy for a particular male, and will desert her own mate for him. Some females, according to another experienced observer, Riedel,[24] are of a profligate disposition, and prefer almost any stranger to their own

[21] 'Rare and Prize Poultry,' 1854, 27.

[22] 'Variation of Animals and Plants under Domestication,' vol. ii. p. 103.

[23] Boitard and Corbié, 'Les Pigeons, &c.,' 1824, p. 12. Prosper Lucas ('Traité de l'Héréd. Nat.' tom. ii. 1850, p. 296) has himself observed nearly similar facts with pigeons.

[24] 'Die Taubenzucht,' 1824, s. 86.

mate. Some amorous males, called by our English fanciers "gay birds," are so successful in their gallantries, that, as Mr. H. Weir informs me, they must be shut up on account of the mischief which they cause.

Wild turkeys in the United States, according to Audubon, "sometimes pay their addresses to the domesticated females, and are generally received by them with great pleasure." So that these females apparently prefer the wild to their own males.[25]

Here is a more curious case. Sir R. Heron during many years kept an account of the habits of the peafowl, which he bred in large numbers. He states that "the hens have frequently great preference to a particular peafowl. They were all so fond of on old pied cock, that one year, when he was confined, though still in view, they were constantly assembled close to the trellice-walls of his prison, and would not suffer a japanned peacock to touch them. On his being let out in the autumn, the oldest of the hens instantly courted him and was successful in her courtship. The next year he was shut up in a stable, and then the hens all courted his rival." [26] This rival was a japanned or black-winged peacock, to our eyes a more beautiful bird than the common kind.

Lichtenstein, who was a good observer and had excellent opportunities of observation at the Cape of Good Hope, assured Rudolphi that the female widow-bird (*Chera progne*) disowns the male when robbed of the long tail-feathers with which he is ornamented during the breeding-season. I presume that this observation must have been made on birds under confinement.[27] Here is an analogous case; Dr. Jaeger, [28] director of the Zoological Gardens of Vienna, states that a male silver-pheasant, who had been triumphant over all other males and was the accepted lover of the females, had his ornamental plumage spoiled. He was then immediately superseded by a rival, who got the upper hand and afterwards led the flock.

It is a remarkable fact, as shewing how important colour is in the courtship of birds, that Mr. Boardman, a well-known collector and observer of birds for many years in the Northern United States, has never in his large experience seen an albino paired with another bird; yet he has had opportunities of observing many albinos belonging to several species.[29] It can hardly be maintained that albinos in a state of nature are incapable of breeding, as they can be raised with the greatest facility under confinement. It appears, therefore, that we must attribute the fact that they do not pair to their rejection by their normally coloured comrades.

[25] 'Ornith. Biog.' vol. i. p. 13. See to the same effect, Dr. Bryant, in 'Allen's Mammals and Birds of Florida,' p. 344.
[26] 'Proc. Zool. Soc.' 1835, p. 54. The japanned peacock is considered by Mr. Sclater as a distinct species, and has been named *Pavo nigripennis;* but the evidence seems to me to shew that it is only a variety.
[27] Rudolphi, 'Beyträge zur Anthropologie,' 1812, s. 184.
[28] 'Die Darwin'sche Theorie, und ihre Stellung zu Moral und Religion,' 1869, s. 59.
[29] This statement is given by Mr. A. Leith Adams, in his 'Field and Forest Rambles,' 1873, p. 76, and accords with his own experience.

Female birds not only exert a choice, but in some few cases they court the male, or even fight together for his possession. Sir R. Heron states that with peafowl, the first advances are always made by the female; something of the same kind takes place, according to Audubon, with the older females of the wild turkey. With the capercailzie, the females flit round the male whilst he is parading at one of the places of assemblage, and solicit his attention.[30] We have seen that a tame wild-duck seduced an unwilling pintail drake after a long courtship. Mr. Bartlett believes that the Lophophorus, like many other gallinaceous birds, is naturally polygamous, but two females cannot be placed in the same cage with a male, as they fight so much together. The following instance of rivalry is more surprising as it relates to bullfinches, which usually pair for life. Mr. Jenner Weir introduced a dull-coloured and ugly female into his aviary, and she immediately attacked another mated female so unmercifully that the latter had to be separated. The new female did all the courtship, and was at last successful, for she paired with the male; but after a time she met with a just retribution, for, ceasing to be pugnacious, she was replaced by the old female, and the male then deserted his new and returned to his old love.

In all ordinary cases the male is so eager that he will accept any female, and does not, as far as we can judge, prefer one to the other; but, as we shall hereafter see, exceptions to this rule apparently occur in some few groups. With domesticated birds, I have heard of only one case of males shewing any preference for certain females, namely, that of the domestic cock, who, according to the high authority of Mr. Hewitt, prefers the younger to the older hens. On the other hand, in effecting hybrid unions between the male pheasant and common hens, Mr. Hewitt is convinced that the pheasant invariably prefers the older birds. He does not appear to be in the least influenced by their colour; but "is most capricious in his attachments:" [31] from some inexplicable cause he shews the most determined aversion to certain hens, which no care on the part of the breeder can overcome. Mr. Hewitt informs me that some hens are quite unattractive even to the males of their own species, so that they may be kept with several cocks during a whole season, and not one egg out of forty or fifty will prove fertile. On the other hand, with the Long-tailed duck (*Harelda glacialis*), "it has been remarked," says M. Ekström, "that certain females are much more courted than the rest. Frequently, indeed, one sees an individual surrounded by six or eight amorous males." Whether this statement is credible, I know not; but the native sportsmen shoot these females in order to stuff them as decoys.[32]

With respect to female birds feeling a preference for particular males, we must bear in mind that we can judge of choice being exerted only by

[30] In regard to peafowl, see Sir R. Heron, 'Proc. Zoolog. Soc.' 1835, p. 54, and the Rev. E. S. Dixon, 'Ornamental Poultry,' 1848, p. 8. For the turkey, Audubon, ibid. p. 4. For the capercailzie, Lloyd, 'Game Birds of Sweden,' 1867, p. 23.

[31] Mr. Hewitt, quoted in 'Tegetmeier's Poultry Book,' 1866, p. 165.

[32] Quoted in Lloyd's, 'Game Birds of Sweden,' p. 345.

analogy. If an inhabitant of another planet were to behold a number of young rustics at a fair courting a pretty girl, and quarrelling about her like birds at one of their places of assemblage, he would, by the eagerness of the wooers to please her and to display their finery, infer that she had the power of choice. Now with birds the evidence stands thus: they have acute powers of observation, and they seem to have some taste for the beautiful both in colour and sound. It is certain that the females occasionally exhibit, from unknown causes, the strongest antipathies and preferences for particular males. When the sexes differ in colour or in other ornaments the males with rare exceptions are the more decorated, either permanently or temporarily during the breeding-season. They sedulously display their various ornaments, exert their voices, and perform strange antics in the presence of the females. Even well-armed males, who, it might be thought, would altogether depend for success on the law of battle, are in most cases highly ornamented; and their ornaments have been acquired at the expense of some loss of power. In other cases ornaments have been acquired, at the cost of increased risk from birds and beasts of prey. With various species many individuals of both sexes congregate at the same spot, and their courtship is a prolonged affair. There is even reason to suspect that the males and females within the same district do not always succeed in pleasing each other and pairing.

What then are we to conclude from these facts and considerations? Does the male parade his charms with so much pomp and rivalry for no purpose? Are we not justified in believing that the female exerts a choice, and that she receives the addresses of the male who pleases her most? It is not probable that she consciously deliberates; but she is most excited or attracted by the most beautiful, or melodious, or gallant males. Nor need it be supposed that the female studies each stripe or spot of colour; that the peahen, for instance, admires each detail in the gorgeous train of the peacock—she is probably struck only by the general effect. Nevertheless, after hearing how carefully the male Argus pheasant displays his elegant primary wing-feathers, and erects his ocellated plumes in the right position for their full effect; or again, how the male goldfinch alternately displays his gold-bespangled wings, we ought not to feel too sure that the female does not attend to each detail of beauty. We can judge, as already remarked, of choice being exerted, only from analogy; and the mental powers of birds do not differ fundamentally from ours. From these various considerations we may conclude that the pairing of birds is not left to chance; but that those males, which are best able by their various charms to please or excite the female, are under ordinary circumstances accepted. If this be admitted, there is not much difficulty in understanding how male birds have gradually acquired their ornamental characters. All animals present individual differences, and as man can modify his domesticated birds by selecting the individuals which appear to him the most beautiful, so the habitual or even occasional preference by the female of the more attractive males would almost certainly lead to their modification; and such modifications might in the course of time be augmented to almost any extent, compatible with the existence of the species.

Variability of Birds, and especially of their Secondary Sexual Characters.—Variability and inheritance are the foundations for the work of selection. That domesticated birds have varied greatly, their variations being inherited, is certain. That birds in a state of nature have been modified into distinct races is now universally admitted.[33] Variations may be divided into two classes; those which appear to our ignorance to arise spontaneously, and those which are directly related to the surrounding conditions, so that all or nearly all the individuals of the same species are similarly modified. Cases of the latter kind have recently been observed with care by Mr. J. A. Allen,[34] who shews that in the United States many species of birds gradually become more strongly coloured in proceeding southward, and more lightly coloured in proceeding westward to the arid plains of the interior. Both sexes seem generally to be affected in a like manner, but sometimes one sex more than the other. This result is not incompatible with the belief that the colours of birds are mainly due to the accumulation of successive variations through sexual selection; for even after the sexes have been greatly differentiated, climate might produce an equal effect on both sexes, or a greater effect on one sex than on the other, owing to some constitutional difference.

Individual differences between the members of the same species are admitted by every one to occur under a state of nature. Sudden and strongly marked variations are rare; it is also doubtful whether if beneficial they would often be preserved through selection and transmitted to

[33] According to Dr. Blasius ('Ibis,' vol. ii. 1860, p. 297), there are 425 indubitable species of birds which breed in Europe, besides sixty forms, which are frequently regarded as distinct species. Of the latter, Blasius thinks that only ten are really doubtful, and that the other fifty ought to be united with their nearest allies; but this shews that there must be a considerable amount of variation with some of our European birds. It is also an unsettled point with naturalists, whether several North American birds ought to be ranked as specifically distinct from the corresponding European species. So again many North American forms which until lately were named as distinct species, are now considered to be local races.

[34] 'Mammals and Birds of East Florida,' also an 'Ornithological Reconnaissance of Kansas, &c.' Notwithstanding the influence of climate on the colours of birds, it is difficult to account for the dull or dark tints of almost all the species inhabiting certain countries, for instance, the Galapagos Islands under the equator, the wide temperate plains of Patagonia, and, as it appears, Egypt (see Mr. Hartshorne in the 'American Naturalist,' 1873, p. 747). These countries are open, and afford little shelter to birds; but it seems doubtful whether the absence of brightly coloured species can be explained on the principle of protection, for on the Pampas, which are equally open, though covered by green grass, and where the birds would be equally exposed to danger, many brilliant and conspicuously coloured species are common. I have sometimes speculated whether the prevailing dull tints of the scenery in the above-named countries may not have affected the appreciation of bright colours by the birds inhabiting them.

succeeding generations.[35] Nevertheless, it may be worth while to give the few cases which I have been able to collect, relating chiefly to colour,—simple albinism and melanism being excluded. Mr. Gould is well known to admit the existence of few varieties, for he esteems very slight differences as specific; yet he states [36] that near Bogota certain humming-birds belonging to the genus Cynanthus are divided into two or three races or varieties, which differ from each other in the colouring of the tail—"some having the whole of the feathers blue, while others have the eight central ones tipped with beautiful green." It does not appear that intermediate gradations have been observed in this or the following cases. In the males alone of one of the Australian parrakeets "the thighs in some are scarlet, in others grass-green." In another parrakeet of the same country "some individuals have the band across the wing-coverts bright-yellow, while in others the same part is tinged with red." [37] In the United States some few of the males of the Scarlet Tanager (*Tanagra rubra*) have "a beautiful transverse band of glowing red on the smaller wing-coverts;" [38] but this variation seems to be somewhat rare, so that its preservation through sexual selection would follow only under unusually favourable circumstances. In Bengal the Honey buzzard (*Pernis cristata*) has either a small rudimental crest on its head, or none at all: so slight a difference, however, would not have been worth notice, had not this same species possessed in Southern India "a well-marked occipital crest formed of several graduated feathers." [39]

The following case is in some respects more interesting. A pied variety of the raven, with the head, breast, abdomen, and parts of the wings and tail-feathers white, is confined to the Feroe Islands. It is not very rare there, for Graba saw during his visit from eight to ten living specimens. Although the characters of this variety are not quite constant, yet it has been named by several distinguished ornithologists as a distinct species. The fact of the pied birds being pursued and persecuted with much clamour by the other ravens of the island was the chief cause which led Brünnich to conclude that they were specifically distinct; but this is now

---

[35] I had always perceived ('Origin of Species') that rare and strongly-marked deviations of structure, deserving to be called monstrosities, could seldom be preserved through natural selection, and that the preservation of even highly-beneficial variations would depend to a certain extent on chance. I had also fully appreciated the importance of mere individual differences, and this led me to insist so strongly on the importance of that unconscious form of selection by man, which follows from the preservation of the most valued individuals of each breed, without any intention on his part to modify the characters of the breed. But until I read an able article in the 'North British Review' (March 1867, p. 289, *et seq.*), which has been of more use to me than any other Review, I did not see how great the chances were against the preservation of variations, whether slight or strongly pronounced, occurring only in single individuals.

[36] 'Introduction to the Trochlidæ,' p. 102.

[37] Gould, 'Handbook to Birds of Australia,' vol. ii. pp. 32 and 68.

[38] Audubon, 'Ornitholog. Biography,' 1838, vol. iv. p. 389.

[39] Jerdon, 'Birds of India,' vol. i. p. 108; and Mr. Blyth, in 'Land and Water,' 1868, p. 381.

known to be an error.[40] This case seems analogous to that lately given of albino birds not pairing from being rejected by their comrades.

In various parts of the northern seas a remarkable variety of the common Guillemot (*Uria troile*) is found; and in Feroe, one out of every five birds, according to Graba's estimation, presents this variation. It is characterised [41] by a pure white ring round the eye, with a curved narrow white line, an inch and a half in length, extending back from the ring. This conspicuous character has caused the bird to be ranked by several ornithologists as a distinct species under the name of *U. lacrymans,* but it is now known to be merely a variety. It often pairs with the common kind, yet intermediate gradations have never been seen; nor is this surprising, for variations which appear suddenly, are often, as I have elsewhere shewn,[42] transmitted either unaltered or not at all. We thus see that two distinct forms of the same species may co-exist in the same district, and we cannot doubt that if the one had possessed any advantage over the other, it would soon have been multiplied to the exclusion of the latter. If, for instance, the male pied ravens, instead of being persecuted by their comrades, had been highly attractive (like the above pied peacock) to the black female ravens their numbers would have rapidly increased. And this would have been a case of sexual selection.

With respect to the slight individual differences which are common, in a greater or less degree, to all the members of the same species, we have every reason to believe that they are by far the most important for the work of selection. Secondary sexual characters are eminently liable to vary, both with animals in a state of nature and under domestication.[43] There is also reason to believe, as we have seen in our eighth chapter, that variations are more apt to occur in the male than in the female sex. All these contingencies are highly favourable for sexual selection. Whether characters thus acquired are transmitted to one sex or to both sexes, depends, as we shall see in the following chapter, on the form of inheritance which prevails.

It is sometimes difficult to form an opinion whether certain slight differences between the sexes of birds are simply the result of variability with sexually-limited inheritance, without the aid of sexual selection, or whether they have been augmented through this latter process. I do not here refer to the many instances where the male displays splendid colours or other ornaments, of which the female partakes to a slight degree; for these are almost certainly due to characters primarily acquired by the male having been more or less transferred to the female. But what are we to conclude with respect to certain birds in which, for instance, the eyes

[40] Graba, 'Tagebuch Reise nach Färo,' 1830, s. 51–54. Macgillivray, 'Hist. British Birds,' vol. iii. p. 745. 'Ibis,' vol. v. 1863, p. 469.

[41] Graba, ibid. s. 54. Macgillivray, ibid. vol. v. p. 327.

[42] 'Variation of Animals and Plants under Domestication,' vol. ii. page 92.

[43] On these points see also 'Variation of Animals and Plants under Domestication,' vol. i. p. 253; vol. ii. pp. 73, 75.

differ slightly in colour in the two sexes? [44] In some cases the eyes differ conspicuously; thus with the storks of the genus *Xenorhynchus,* those of the male are blackish-hazel, whilst those of the females are gamboge-yellow; with many hornbills (Buceros), as I hear from Mr. Blyth,[45] the males have intense crimson eyes, and those of the females are white. In the *Buceros bicornis,* the hind margin of the casque and a stripe on the crest of the beak are black in the male, but not so in the female. Are we to suppose that these black marks and the crimson colour of the eyes have been preserved or augmented through sexual selection in the males? This is very doubtful; for Mr. Bartlett shewed me in the Zoological Gardens that the inside of the mouth of this Buceros is black in the male and flesh-coloured in the female; and their external appearance or beauty would not be thus affected. I observed in Chili [46] that the iris in the condor, when about a year old, is dark-brown, but changes at maturity into yellowish-brown in the male, and into bright red in the female. The male has also a small, longitudinal, leaden-coloured, fleshy crest or comb. The comb of many gallinaceous birds is highly ornamental, and assumes vivid colours during the act of courtship; but what are we to think of the dull-coloured comb of the condor, which does not appear to us in the least ornamental? The same question may be asked in regard to various other characters, such as the knob on the base of the beak of the Chinese goose (*Anser cygnoides*), which is much larger in the male than in the female. No certain answer can be given to these questions; but we ought to be cautious in assuming that knobs and various fleshy appendages cannot be attractive to the female, when we remember that with savage races of man various hideous deformities—deep scars on the face with the flesh raised into protuberances, the septum of the nose pierced by sticks or bones, holes in the ears and lips stretched widely open—are all admired as ornamental.

Whether or not unimportant differences between the sexes, such as those just specified, have been preserved through sxual selection, these differences, as well as all others, must primarily depend on the laws of variation. On the principle of correlated development, the plumage often varies on different parts of the body, or over the whole body, in the same manner. We see this well illustrated in certain breeds of the fowl. In all the breeds the feathers on the neck and loins of the males are elongated, and are called hackles; now when both sexes acquire a top-knot, which is a new character in the genus, the feathers on the head of the male become hackle-shaped, evidently on the principle of correlation; whilst those on the head of the female are of the ordinary shape. The colour also of the hackles forming the top-knot of the male, is often correlated with that of the hackles on the neck and loins, as may be seen by comparing these feathers in the Golden and Silver-spangled Polish, the Houdans,

---

[44] See, for instance, on the irides of a Podica and Gallicrex in 'Ibis,' vol. ii. 1860, p. 206; and vol. v. 1863, p. 426.

[45] See also Jerdon, 'Birds of India,' vol. i. pp. 243–245.

[46] 'Zoology of the Voyage of H. M. S. Beagle,' 1841, p. 6.

and Crève-cœur breeds. In some natural species we may observe exactly the same correlation in the colours of these same feathers, as in the males of the splendid Gold and Amherst pheasants.

The structure of each individual feather generally causes any change in its colouring to be symmetrical; we see this in the various laced, spangled, and pencilled breeds of the fowl; and on the principle of correlation the feathers over the whole body are often coloured in the same manner. We are thus enabled without much trouble to rear breeds with their plumage marked almost as symmetrically as in natural species. In laced and spangled fowls the coloured margins of the feathers are abruptly defined; but in a mongrel raised by me from a black Spanish cock glossed with green, and a white game-hen, all the feathers were greenish-black, excepting towards their extremities, which were yellowish-white; but between the white extremities and the black bases, there was on each feather a symmetrical, curved zone of dark-brown. In some instances the shaft of the feather determines the distribution of the tints; thus with the body-feathers of a mongrel from the same black Spanish cock and a silver-spangled Polish hen, the shaft, together with a narrow space on each side, was greenish-black, and this was surrounded by a regular zone of dark-brown, edged with brownish-white. In these cases we have feathers symmetrically shaded, like those which give so much elegance to the plumage of many natural species. I have also noticed a variety of the common pigeon with the wing-bars symmetrically zoned with three bright shades, instead of being simply black on a slaty-blue ground, as in the parent-species.

In many groups of birds the plumage is differently coloured in the several species, yet certain spots, marks, or stripes are retained by all. Analogous cases occur with the breeds of the pigeon, which usually retain the two wing-bars, though they may be coloured red, yellow, white, black, or blue, the rest of the plumage being of some wholly different tint. Here is a more curious case, in which certain marks are retained, though coloured in a manner almost exactly the opposite of what is natural; the aboriginal pigeon has a blue tail, with the terminal halves of the outer webs of the two outer tail feathers white; now there is a sub-variety having a white instead of a blue tail, with precisely that part black which is white in the parent-species.[47]

Formation and Variability of the Ocelli or eye-like Spots on the Plumage of Birds.—As no ornaments are more beautiful than the ocelli on the feathers of various birds, on the hairy coats of some mammals, on the scales of reptiles and fishes, on the skin of amphibians, on the wings of many Lepidoptera and other insects, they deserve to be especially noticed. An ocellus consists of a spot within a ring of another colour, like the pupil within the iris, but the central spot is often surrounded by additional concentric zones. The ocelli on the tail-coverts of the peacock offer a familiar example, as well as those on the wings of the peacock-butter-

---

[47] Bechstein, 'Naturgeschichte Deutschlands,' B. iv. 1795, s. 31, on a sub-variety of the Monck pigeon.

fly (Vanessa). Mr. Trimen has given me a description of a S. African moth (*Gynanisa isis*), allied to our Emperor moth, in which a magnificent ocellus occupies nearly the whole surface of each hinder wing; it consists of a black centre, including a semi-transparent crescent-shaped mark, surrounded by successive, ochre-yellow, black, ochre-yellow, pink, white, pink, brown, and whitish zones. Although we do not know the steps by which these wonderfully beautiful and complex ornaments have been developed, the process has probably been a simple one, at least with insects; for, as Mr. Trimen writes to me, "no characters of mere marking or coloration are so unstable in the Lepidoptera as the ocelli, both in number and size." Mr. Wallace, who first called my attention to this sub-

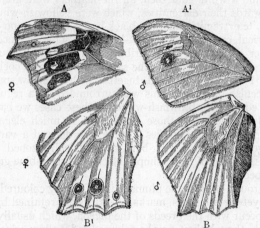

FIG. 53.—Cyllo leda, Linn., from a drawing by Mr. Trimen, shewing the extreme range of variation in the ocelli.

A. Specimen, from Mauritius, upper sur-   B. Specimen, from Java, upper surface
   face of fore-wing.   of hind-wing.
A¹. Specimen, from Natal, ditto.   B¹. Specimen, from Mauritius, ditto.

ject, shewed me a series of specimens of our common meadow-brown butterfly (*Hipparchia janira*) exhibiting numerous gradations from a simple minute black spot to an elegantly-shaded ocellus. In a S. African butterfly (*Cyllo leda*, Linn.), belonging to the same family, the ocelli are even still more variable. In some specimens (A, fig. 53) large spaces on the upper surface of the wings are coloured black, and include irregular white marks; and from this state a complete gradation can be traced into a tolerably perfect ocellus (A¹), and this results from the contraction of the irregular blotches of colour. In another series of specimens a gradation can be followed from excessively minute white dots, surrounded by a scarcely visible black line (B), into perfectly symmetrical and large ocelli (B¹).[48] In cases like these, the development of a perfect ocellus does not require a long course of variation and selection.

[48] This woodcut has been engraved from a beautiful drawing, most kindly made for

With birds and many other animals, it seems to follow from the comparison of allied species that circular spots are often generated by the breaking up and contraction of stripes. In the Tragopan pheasant faint white lines in the female represent the beautiful white spots in the male; [49] and something of the same kind may be observed in the two sexes of the Argus pheasant. However this may be, appearances strongly favour the belief that on the one hand, a dark spot is often formed by the colouring matter being drawn towards a central point from a surrounding zone, which latter is thus rendered lighter; and, on the other hand, that a white spot is often formed by the colour being driven away from a central point, so that it accumulates in a surrounding darker zone. In either case an ocellus is the result. The colouring matter seems to be a nearly constant quantity, but is redistributed, either centripetally or centrifugally. The feathers of the common guinea-fowl offer a good instance of white spots surrounded by darker zones; and wherever the white spots are large and stand near each other, the surrounding dark zones become confluent. In the same wing-feather of the Argus pheasant dark spots may be seen surrounded by a pale zone, and white spots by a dark zone. Thus the formation of an ocellus in its most elementary state appears to be a simple affair. By what further steps the more complex ocelli, which are surrounded by many successive zones of colour, have been generated, I will not pretend to say. But the zoned feathers of the mongrels from differently coloured fowls, and the extraordinary variability of the ocelli on many Lepidoptera, lead us to conclude that their formation is not a complex process, but depends on some slight and graduated change in the nature of the adjoining tissues.

Gradation of Secondary Sexual Characters.—Cases of gradation are important, as shewing us that highly complex ornaments may be acquired by small successive steps. In order to discover the actual steps by which the male of any existing bird has acquired his magnificent colours or other ornaments, we ought to behold the long line of his extinct progenitors; but this is obviously impossible. We may, however, generally gain a clue by comparing all the species of the same group, if it be a large one; for some of them will probably retain, at least partially, traces of their former characters. Instead of entering on tedious details respecting various groups, in which striking instances of gradation could be given, it seems the best plan to take one or two strongly marked cases, for instance that of the peacock, in order to see if light can be thrown on the steps by which this bird has become so splendidly decorated. The peacock is chiefly remarkable from the extraordinary length of his tail-coverts; the tail itself not being much elongated. The barbs along nearly the whole length of these feathers stand separate or are decomposed; but this is the case with the feathers of many species, and with some varieties of the domes-

me by Mr. Trimen; see also his description of the wonderful amount of variation in the coloration and shape of the wings of this butterfly, in his 'Rhopalocera Africæ Australis,' p. 186.

[49] Jerdon, 'Birds of India,' vol. iii. p. 517.

tic fowl and pigeon. The barbs coalesce towards the extremity of the shaft forming the oval disc or ocellus, which is certainly one of the most beautiful objects in the world. It consists of an iridescent, intensely blue, indented centre, surrounded by a rich green zone, this by a broad coppery-brown zone, and this by five other narrow zones of slightly different iridescent shades. A trifling character in the disc deserves notice; the barbs, for a space along one of the concentric zones are more or less destitute of their barbules, so that a part of the disc is surrounded by an almost transparent zone, which gives it a highly finished aspect. But I have elsewhere described [50] an exactly analogous variation in the hackles of a

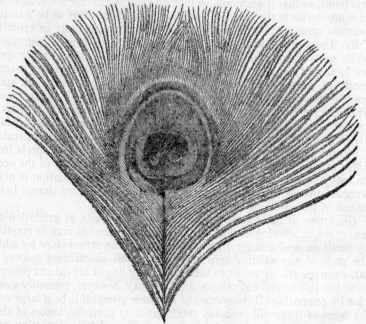

FIG. 54.—Feather of Peacock, about two-thirds of natural size, drawn by Mr. Ford. The transparent zone is represented by the outermost white zone, confined to the upper end of the disc.

sub-variety of the game-cock, in which the tips, having a metallic lustre, "are separated from the lower part of the feather by a symmetrically shaped transparent zone, composed of the naked portions of the barbs." The lower margin or base of the dark-blue centre of the ocellus is deeply indented on the line of the shaft. The surrounding zones likewise shew traces, as may be seen in the drawing (fig. 54), of indentations, or rather breaks. These indentations are common to the Indian and Javan peacocks (*Pavo cristatus* and *P. muticus*); and they seem to deserve particular at-

[50] "Variation of Animals and Plants under Domestication,' vol. i. p. 254.

tention, as probably connected with the development of the ocellus; but for a long time I could not conjecture their meaning.

If we admit the principle of gradual evolution, there must formerly have existed many species which presented every successive step between the wonderfully elongated tail-coverts of the peacock and the short tail-coverts of all ordinary birds; and again between the magnificent ocelli of the former, and the simpler ocelli or mere coloured spots on other birds; and so with all the other characters of the peacock. Let us look to the allied Gallinaceæ for any still-existing gradations. The species and sub-species of Polyplectron inhabit countries adjacent to the native land of the peacock; and they so far resemble this bird that they are sometimes called peacock-pheasants. I am also informed by Mr. Bartlett that they resemble the peacock in their voice and in some of their habits. During the spring the males, as previously described, strut about before the comparatively plain-coloured females, expanding and erecting their tail and wing-feathers, which are ornamented with numerous ocelli. I request the reader to turn back to the drawing (fig. 51, p. 729) of a Polyplectron. In *P. napoleonis* the ocelli are confined to the tail, and the back is of a rich metallic blue; in which respects this species approaches the Java Peacock. *P. hardwickii* possesses a peculiar top-knot, which is also somewhat like that of the Java peacock. In all species the ocelli on the wings and tail are either circular or oval, and consist of a beautiful, iridescent, greenish-blue or greenish-purple disc, with a black border. This border in *P. chinquis* shades into brown, edged with cream colour, so that the ocellus is here surrounded with variously shaded, though not bright, concentric zones. The unusual length of the tail-coverts is another

Fig. 55.—Part of a tail-covert of Polyplectron chinquis, with the two ocelli of nat. size.

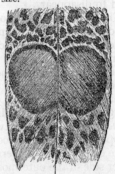

Fig. 56.—Part of a tail-covert of Polyplectron malaccense, with the two ocelli, partially confluent, of nat. size.

remarkable character in Polyplectron; for in some of the species they are half, and in others two-thirds as long as the true tail-feathers. The tail-coverts are ocellated as in the peacock. Thus the several species of Polyplectron manifestly make a graduated approach to the peacock in the length of their tail-coverts, in the zoning of the ocelli, and in some other characters.

Notwithstanding this approach, the first species of Polyplectron which I examined almost made me give up the search; for I found not only that the true tail-feathers, which in the peacock are quite plain, were ornamented with ocelli, but that the ocelli on all the feathers differed fundamentally from those of the peacock, in there being two on the same feather (fig. 55), one on each side of the shaft. Hence I concluded that the early progenitors of the peacock could not have resembled a Polyplectron. But on continuing my search, I observed that in some of the species the two ocelli stood very near each other; that in the tail-feathers of *P. hardwickii* they touched each other; and, finally, that on the tail-coverts of this same species as well as of *P. malaccense* (fig. 56) they were actually confluent. As the central part alone is confluent, an indentation is left at both the upper and lower ends; and the surrounding coloured zones are likewise indented. A single ocellus is thus formed on each tail-covert, though still plainly betraying its double origin. These confluent ocelli differ from the single ocelli of the peacock in having an indentation at both ends, instead of only at the lower or basal end. The explanation, however, of this difference is not difficult; in some species of Polyplectron the two oval ocelli on the same feather stand parallel to each other; in other species (as in *P. chinquis*) they converge towards one end; now the partial confluence of two convergent ocelli would manifestly leave a much deeper indentation at the divergent than at the convergent end. It is also manifest that if the convergence were strongly pronounced and the confluence complete, the indentation at the convergent end would tend to disappear.

The tail-feathers in both species of the peacock are entirely destitute of ocelli, and this apparently is related to their being covered up and concealed by the long tail-coverts. In this respect they differ remarkably from the tail-feathers of Polyplectron, which in most of the species are ornamented with larger ocelli than those on the tail-coverts. Hence I was led carefully to examine the tail-feathers of the several species, in order to discover whether their ocelli shewed any tendency to disappear; and to my great satisfaction, this appeared to be so. The central tail-feathers of *P. napoleonis* have the two ocelli on each side of the shaft perfectly developed; but the inner ocellus becomes less and less conspicuous on the more exterior tail-feathers, until a mere shadow or rudiment is left on the inner side of the outermost feather. Again, in *P. malaccense,* the ocelli on the tail-coverts are, as we have seen, confluent; and these feathers are of unusual length, being two-thirds of the length of the tail-feathers, so that in both these respects they approach the tail-coverts of the peacock. Now in *P. malaccense* the two central tail-feathers alone are ornamented, each with two brightly-coloured ocelli, the inner ocellus having completely disappeared from all the other tail-feathers. Consequently the tail-coverts and tail-feathers of this species of Polyplectron make a near approach in structure and ornamentation to the corresponding feathers of the peacock.

As far, then, as gradation throws light on the steps by which the magnificent train of the peacock has been acquired, hardly anything more is needed. If we picture to ourselves a progenitor of the peacock in an almost exactly intermediate condition between the existing peacock, with his enormously elongated tail-coverts, ornamented with single ocelli, and an ordinary gallinaceous bird with short tail-coverts, merely spotted with some colour, we shall see a bird allied to Polyplectron—that is, with tail-coverts, capable of erection and expansion, ornamented with two partially confluent ocelli, and long enough almost to conceal the tail-feathers, the latter having already partially lost their ocelli. The indentation of the central disc and of the surrounding zones of the ocellus, in both species of peacock, speaks plainly in favour of this view, and is otherwise inexplicable. The males of Polyplectron are no doubt beautiful birds, but their beauty, when viewed from a little distance, cannot be compared with that of the peacock. Many female progenitors of the peacock must, during a long line of descent, have appreciated this superiority; for they have unconsciously, by the continued preference for the most beautiful males, rendered the peacock the most splendid of living birds.

Argus pheasant.—Another excellent case for investigation is offered by the ocelli on the wing-feathers of the Argus pheasant, which are shaded in so wonderful a manner as to resemble balls lying loose within sockets, and consequently differ from ordinary ocelli. No one, I presume, will attribute the shading, which has excited the admiration of many experienced artists, to chance—to the fortuitous concourse of atoms of colouring matter. That these ornaments should have been formed through the selection of many successive variations, not one of which was originally intended to produce the ball-and-socket effect, seems as incredible as that one of Raphael's Madonnas should have been formed by the selection of chance daubs of paint made by a long succession of young artists, not one of whom intended at first to draw the human figure. In order to discover how the ocelli have been developed, we cannot look to a long line of progenitors, nor to many closely-allied forms, for such do not now exist. But fortunately the several feathers on the wing suffice to give us a clue to the problem, and they prove to demonstration that a gradation is at least possible from a mere spot to a finished ball-and-socket ocellus.

The wing-feathers, bearing the ocelli, are covered with dark stripes (fig. 57) or with rows of dark spots (fig. 59), each stripe or row of spots running obliquely down the outer side of the shaft to one of the ocelli. The spots are generally elongated in a line transverse to the row in which they stand. They often become confluent either in the line of the row— and then they form a longitudinal stripe—or transversely, that is, with the spots in the adjoining rows, and then they form transverse stripes. A spot sometimes breaks up into smaller spots, which still stand in their proper places.

It will be convenient first to describe a perfect ball-and-socket ocellus. This consists of an intensely black circular ring, surrounding a space shaded so as exactly to resemble a ball. The figure here given has been admirably drawn by Mr. Ford and well engraved, but a woodcut cannot exhibit the exquisite shading of the original. The ring is almost always slightly broken or interrupted (see fig. 57) at a point in the upper half, a little to the right of and above the white shade on the enclosed ball; it is also sometimes broken towards the base on the right hand. These little breaks have an important meaning. The ring is always much thickened, with the edges ill-defined towards the left-hand upper corner, the feather

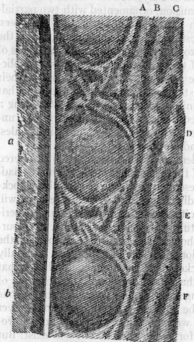

being held erect, in the position in which it is here drawn. Beneath this thickened part there is on the surface of the ball an oblique almost pure-white mark, which shades off downwards into a pale-leaden hue, and this into yellowish and brown tints, which insensibly become darker and darker towards the lower part of the ball. It is this shading which gives so admirably the effect of light shining on a convex surface. If one of the balls be examined, it will be seen that the lower part is of a brown tint and is indistinctly separated by a curved oblique line from the upper part which is yellower and more leaden; this curved oblique line runs at right angles to the longer axis of the white patch of light, and indeed of all the shading; but this difference in colour, which cannot of course be shewn in the woodcut, does not in the least interfere with the perfect shading of the ball. It should be particularly observed that each ocellus stands in obvious connection either with a dark stripe, or with a longitudinal row of dark spots, for both occur indifferently on the same feath-

FIG. 57.—Part of secondary wing-feather of Argus pheasant, shewing two perfect ocelli, *a* and *b*. A, B, C, D, &c., are dark stripes running obliquely down, each to an ocellus.

[Much of the web on both sides, especially to the left of the shaft, has been cut off.]

er. Thus in fig. 57 stripe A runs to ocellus *a;* B runs to ocellus *b;* stripe C is broken in the upper part, and runs down to the next succeeding ocellus, not represented in the woodcut; D to the next lower one, and so with the stripes E and F. Lastly, the several ocelli are separated from each other by a pale surface bearing irregular black marks.

I will next describe the other extreme of the series, namely, the first trace of an ocellus. The short secondary wing-feather (fig. 58), nearest to the body, is marked like the other feathers, with oblique, longitudinal, rather irregular, rows of very dark spots. The basal spot, or that nearest the shaft, in the five lower rows (excluding the lowest one) is a little larger than the other spots of the same row, and a little more elongated in a transverse direction. It differs also from the other spots by being bordered on its upper side with some dull fulvous shading. But this spot is not in any way more remarkable than those on the plumage of many birds, and might easily be overlooked. The next higher spot does not differ at all from the upper ones in the same row. The larger basal spots occupy exactly the same relative position on these feathers as do the perfect ocelli on the longer wing-feathers.

By looking to the next two or three succeeding wing-feathers, an absolutely insensible gradation can be traced from one of the last-described basal spots, together with the next higher one in the same row, to a curious ornament, which cannot be called an ocellus, and which I will name, from the want of a better term, an "elliptic ornament." These are shewn in the accompanying figure (fig. 59). We here see several oblique rows, A, B, C, D, &c. (see the lettered diagram on the right hand), of dark spots of the usual character. Each row of spots runs down to and is connected with one of the elliptic ornaments, in exactly the same manner as each stripe in fig. 57 runs down to, and is connected with, one of the ball-and-socket ocelli. Looking to any one row, for instance,

FIG. 58.—Basal part of the secondary wing-feather, nearest to the body.

B, in fig. 59, the lowest mark (*b*) is thicker and considerably longer than the upper spots, and has its left extremity pointed and curved upwards. This black mark is abruptly bordered on its upper side by a rather broad space of richly shaded tints, beginning with a narrow brown zone, which passes into orange, and this into a pale leaden tint, with the end towards the shaft much paler. These shaded tints together fill up the whole inner space of the elliptic ornament. The mark (*b*) corresponds in every respect with the basal shaded spot of the simple feather described in the last paragraph (fig. 58), but is more highly developed and more brightly coloured. Above and to the right of this spot (*b* fig. 59), with its bright shading, there is a long narrow, black mark (*c*), belonging to the same row, and which is arched a little downwards so as to face (*b*). This mark is sometimes broken into two portions. It is also narrowly edged on the lower side with a fulvous tint. To the left of and above *c*, in the same oblique direction, but always more or less distinct from it, there is another black mark (*d*). This mark is generally sub-triangular and irregular in shape, but in the one lettered in the diagram it is unusually narrow, elongated, and regular. It apparently consists of a lateral and broken prolongation of the mark (*c*), together with its confluence with a broken and prolonged part of the next spot above; but I do not feel sure of this. These three marks, *b*, *c*, and *d*, with the intervening bright shades, form together the so-called elliptic ornament. These ornaments placed parallel to the shaft, manifestly correspond in position with the ball-and-socket ocelli. Their extremely elegant appearance cannot be appreciated in the

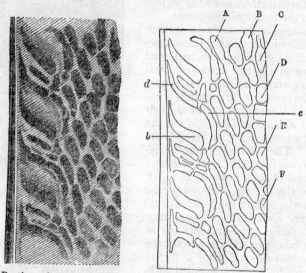

FIG. 59.—Portion of one of the secondary wing-feathers near to the body, shewing the so-called elliptic ornaments. The right-hand figure is given merely as a diagram for the sake of the letters of reference.

A, B, C, D, &c. Rows of spots running down to and forming the elliptic ornaments.
b. Lowest spot or mark in row B.

c. The next succeeding spot or mark in the same row.
d. Apparently a broken prolongation of the spot *c*. in the same row B.

drawing, as the orange and leaden tints, contrasting so well with the black marks, cannot be shewn.

Between one of the elliptic ornaments and a perfect ball-and-socket ocellus, the gradation is so perfect that it is scarcely possible to decide when the latter term ought to be used. The passage from the one into the other is effected by the elongation and greater curvature in opposite directions of the lower black mark (*b* fig. 59), and more especially of the upper one (*c*), together with the contraction of the elongated sub-triangular or narrow mark (*d*), so that at last these three marks become confluent, forming an irregular elliptic ring. This ring is gradually rendered more and more circular and regular, increasing at the same time in diameter. I have here given a drawing (fig. 60) of the natural size of an ocellus not as yet quite perfect. The lower part of the black ring is much more curved than is the lower mark in the elliptic ornament (*b* fig. 59). The upper part of the ring consists of two or three separate portions; and there is only a trace of the thickening of the portion which forms the black mark above the white shade. This white shade itself is not as yet much concentrated; and beneath it the surface is brighter coloured than in a perfect ball-and-socket ocellus. Even in the most perfect ocelli traces of the junction of three or four elongated black marks, by which the ring has been formed, may often be detected. The irregular sub-triangular or

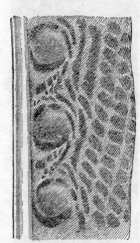

Fig. 60.—An ocellus in an intermediate condition between the elliptic ornament and the perfect ball-and-socket ocellus.

narrow mark (*d* fig. 59), manifestly forms, by its contraction and equalisation, the thickened portion of the ring above the white shade on a perfect ball-and-socket ocellus. The lower part of the ring is invariably a little thicker than the other parts (see fig. 57), and this follows from the lower black mark of the elliptic ornament (*b*. fig. 59) having originally been thicker than the upper mark (*c*). Every step can be followed in the process of confluence and modification; and the black ring which surrounds the ball of the ocellus is unquestionably formed by the un·ion and modification of the three black marks, *b, c, d*, of the elliptic ornament. The irregular zigzag black marks between the successive ocelli (see again fig. 57) are plainly due to the breaking up of the somewhat more regular but similar marks between the elliptic ornaments.

The successive steps in the shading of the ball-and-socket ocelli can be followed out with equal clearness. The brown, orange, and pale-leadened narrow zones, which border the lower black mark of the elliptic ornament, can be seen gradually to become more and more softened and shaded into each other, with the upper lighter part towards the left-hand corner rendered still lighter, so as to become almost white, and at the same time more contracted. But even in the most perfect ball-and-socket ocelli a slight difference in the tints, though not in the shading, between the upper and lower parts of the ball can be perceived, as before noticed; and the line of separation is oblique, in the same direction as the bright coloured shades of the elliptic ornaments. Thus almost every minute detail in the shape and colouring of the ball-and-socket ocelli can be shewn to follow from gradual changes in the elliptic ornaments; and the development of the latter can be traced by equally small steps from the union of two almost simple spots, the lower one (fig. 58) having some dull fulvous shading on its upper side.

The extremities of the longer secondary feathers which bear the perfect ball-and-socket ocelli, are peculiarly ornamented (fig. 61). The oblique longitudinal stripes suddenly cease upwards and become confused; and above this limit the whole upper end of the feather (*a*) is covered with white dots, surrounded by little black rings, standing on a dark ground. The oblique stripe belonging to the uppermost ocellus (*b*) is barely represented by a very short irregular black mark with the usual, curved, transverse base. As this stripe is thus abruptly cut off, we can perhaps understand from what has gone before, how it is that the upper thickened part of the ring is here absent; for, as before stated, this thickened part apparently stands in some relation with a broken prolongation from the next higher spot. From the absence of the upper and thickened part of the ring, the uppermost ocellus, though perfect in all other respects, appears as if its top had been obliquely sliced off. It would, I think, perplex any one, who believes that the plumage of the Argus pheasant was created as we now see it, to account for the imperfect condition of the uppermost ocellus. I should add that on the secondary wing-feather farthest from the body all the ocelli are smaller and less perfect than on the other feathers, and have the upper part of the ring deficient, as in the case just mentioned. The imperfection here seems to be connected with the fact that the spots on this feather shew less tendency than usual to become confluent into stripes; they are, on the contrary, often broken up into smaller spots, so that two or three rows run down to the same ocellus.

FIG. 61.—Portion near summit of one of the secondary wing-feathers, bearing perfect ball-and-socket ocelli.

a. Ornamented upper part.

b. Uppermost, imperfect ball-and-socket ocellus. (The shading above the white mark on the summit of the ocellus is here a little too dark.)

c. Perfect ocellus.

There still remains another very curious point, first observed by Mr. T. W. Wood,[51] which deserves attention. In a photograph, given me by Mr. Ward, of a specimen mounted as in the act of display, it may be seen that on the feathers which are held perpendicularly, the white marks on the ocelli, representing light reflected from a convex surface, are at the upper or further end, that is, are directed upwards; and the bird whilst displaying himself on the ground would naturally be illuminated from above. But here comes the curious point, the outer feathers are held almost hori-

[51] The 'Field,' May 28, 1870.

zontally, and their ocelli ought likewise to appear as if illuminated from above, and consequently the white marks ought to be placed on the upper sides of the ocelli; and, wonderful as is the fact, they are thus placed! Hence the ocelli on the several feathers, though occupying very different positions with respect to the light, all appear as if illuminated from above, just as an artist would have shaded them. Nevertheless they are not illuminated from strictly the same point as they ought to be; for the white marks on the ocelli of the feathers which are held almost horizontally, are placed rather too much towards the further end; that is they are not sufficiently lateral. We have, however, no right to expect absolute perfection in a part rendered ornamental through sexual selection, any more than we have in a part modified through natural selection for real use; for instance, in that wondrous organ the human eye. And we know what Helmholtz, the highest authority in Europe on the subject, has said about the human eye; that if an optician had sold him an instrument so carelessly made, he would have thought himself fully justified in returning it.[52]

We have now seen that a perfect series can be followed, from simple spots to the wonderful ball-and-socket ornaments. Mr. Gould, who kindly gave me some of these feathers, fully agrees with me in the completeness of the gradation. It is obvious that the stages in development exhibited by the feathers on the same bird do not at all necessarily shew us the steps passed through by the extinct progenitors of the species; but they probably give us the clue to the actual steps, and they at least prove to demonstration that a gradation is possible. Bearing in mind how carefully the male Argus pheasant displays his plumes before the female, as well as the many facts rendering it probable that female birds prefer the more attractive males, no one who admits the agency of sexual selection in any case will deny that a simple dark spot with some fulvous shading might be converted, through the approximation and modification of two adjoining spots, together with some slight increase of colour, into one of the so-called elliptic ornaments. These latter ornaments have been shewn to many persons, and all have admitted that they are beautiful, some thinking them even more so than the ball-and-socket ocelli. As the secondary plumes became lengthened through sexual selection, and as the elliptic ornaments increased in diameter, their colours apparently became less bright; and then the ornamentation of the plumes had to be gained by an improvement in the pattern and shading; and this process was carried on until the wonderful ball-and-socket ocelli were finally developed. Thus we can understand—and in no other way as it seems to me—the present condition and origin of the ornaments on the wing-feathers of the Argus pheasant.

From the light afforded by the principle of gradation—from what we know of the laws of variation—from the changes which have taken place

---

[52] 'Popular Lectures on Scientific Subjects,' Eng. trans. 1873, pp. 219, 227, 269, 390.

in many of our domesticated birds—and, lastly, from the character (as we shall hereafter see more clearly) of the immature plumage of young birds—we can sometimes indicate, with a certain amount of confidence, the probable steps by which the males have acquired their brilliant plumage and various ornaments; yet in many cases we are involved in complete darkness. Mr. Gould several years ago pointed out to me a humming-bird, the *Urosticte benjamini,* remarkable for the curious differences between the sexes. The male, besides a splendid gorget, has greenish-black tail-feathers, with the four *central* ones tipped with white; in the female, as with most of the allied species, the three *outer* tail-feathers on each side are tipped with white, so that the male has the four central, whilst the female has the six exterior feathers ornamented with white tips. What makes the case more curious is that, although the colouring of the tail differs remarkably in both sexes of many kinds of humming-birds, Mr. Gould does not know a single species, besides the Urosticte, in which the male has the four central feathers tipped with white.

The Duke of Argyll, in commenting on this case,[53] passes over sexual selection, and asks, "What explanation does the law of natural selection give of such specific varieties as these?" He answers "none whatever;" and I quite agree with him. But can this be so confidently said of sexual selection? Seeing in how many ways the tail-feathers of humming-birds differ, why should not the four central feathers have varied in this one species alone, so as to have acquired white tips? The variations may have been gradual, or somewhat abrupt as in the case recently given of the humming-birds near Bogota, in which certain individuals alone have the "central tail-feathers tipped with beautiful green." In the female of the Urosticte I noticed extremely minute or rudimental white tips to the two outer of the four central black tail-feathers; so that here we have an indication of change of some kind in the plumage of this species. If we grant the possibility of the central tail-feathers of the male varying in whiteness, there is nothing strange in such variations having been sexually selected. The white tips, together with the small white ear-tufts, certainly add, as the Duke of Argyll admits, to the beauty of the male; and whiteness is apparently appreciated by other birds, as may be inferred from such cases as the snow-white male of the Bell-bird. The statement made by Sir R. Heron should not be forgotten, namely, that his peahens, when debarred from access to the pied peacock, would not unite with any other male, and during that season produced no offspring. Nor is it strange that variations in the tail-feathers of the Urosticte should have been specially selected for the sake of ornament, for the next succeeding genus in the family takes its name of Metallura from the splendour of these feathers. We have, moreover, good evidence that humming-birds take especial pains in displaying their tail-feathers; Mr. Belt,[54] after describing the beauty of the *Florisuga mellivora,* says, "I have seen the female sitting on a branch, and two males displaying their charms in front

---

[53] 'The Reign of Law,' 1867, p. 247.
[54] 'The Naturalist in Nicaragua,' 1874, p. 112.

of her. One would shoot up like a rocket, then suddenly expanding the snow-white tail, like an inverted parachute, slowly descend in front of her, turning round gradually to shew off back and front. . . . The expanded white tail covered more space than all the rest of the bird, and was evidently the grand feature in the performance. Whilst one male was descending, the other would shoot up and come slowly down expanded. The entertainment would end in a fight between the two performers; but whether the most beautiful or the most pugnacious was the accepted suitor, I know not." Mr. Gould, after describing the peculiar plumage of the Urosticte, adds, "that ornament and variety is the sole object, I have myself but little doubt." [55] If this be admitted, we can perceive that the males which during former times were decked in the most elegant and novel manner would have gained an advantage, not in the ordinary struggle for life, but in rivalry with other males, and would have left a larger number of offspring to inherit their newly-acquired beauty.

[55] 'Introduction to the Trochilidæ,' 1861, p. 110.

CHAPTER XV

BIRDS—*continued*

Discussion as to why the males alone of some species, and both sexes of others, are brightly coloured—On sexually-limited inheritance, as applied to various structures and to brightly-coloured plumage—Nidification in relation to colour—Loss of nuptial plumage during the winter.

WE have in this chapter to consider why the females of many birds have not acquired the same ornaments as the male; and why, on the other hand, both sexes of many other birds are equally, or almost equally, ornamented? In the following chapter we shall consider the few cases in which the female is more conspicuously coloured than the male.

In my 'Origin of Species' [1] I briefly suggested that the long tail of the peacock would be inconvenient and the conspicuous black colour of the male capercailzie dangerous, to the female during the period of incubation: and consequently that the transmission of these characters from the male to the female offspring had been checked through natural selection. I still think that this may have occurred in some few instances: but after mature reflection on all the facts which I have been able to collect, I am now inclined to believe that when the sexes differ, the successive variations have generally been from the first limited in their transmission to the same sex in which they first arose. Since my remarks appeared, the subject of sexual coloration has been discussed in some very interesting papers by Mr. Wallace,[2] who believes that in almost all cases the successive variations tended at first to be transmitted equally to both sexes; but that the female was saved, through natural selection, from acquiring the conspicuous colours of the male, owing to the danger which she would thus have incurred during incubation.

This view necessitates a tedious discussion on a difficult point, namely, whether the transmission of a character, which is at first inherited by both sexes can be subsequently limited in its transmission to one sex alone by means of natural selection. We must bear in mind, as shewn in the preliminary chapter on sexual selection, that characters which are limited in their development to one sex are always latent in the other. An imaginary illustration will best aid us in seeing the difficulty of the case; we may suppose that a fancier wished to make a breed of pigeons, in which the males alone should be coloured of a pale blue, whilst the females retained their former slaty tint. As with pigeons characters of all

[1] Fourth edition, 1866, p. 241.
[2] 'Westminster Review,' July, 1867. 'Journal of Travel,' vol. i. 1868, p. 73.

kinds are usually transmitted to both sexes equally, the fancier would have to try to convert this latter form of inheritance into sexually-limited transmission. All that he could do would be to persevere in selecting every male pigeon which was in the least degree of a paler blue; and the natural result of this process, if steadily carried on for a long time, and if the pale variations were strongly inherited or often recurred, would be to make his whole stock of a lighter blue. But our fancier would be compelled to match, generation after generation, his pale blue males with slaty females, for he wishes to keep the latter of this colour. The result would generally be the production either of a mongrel piebald lot, or more probably the speedy and complete loss of the pale-blue tint; for the primordial slaty colour would be transmitted with prepotent force. Supposing, however, that some pale-blue males and slaty females were produced during each successive generation, and were always crossed together, then the slaty females would have, if I may use the expression, much blue blood in their veins, for their fathers, grandfathers, &c., will all have been blue birds. Under these circumstances it is conceivable (though I know of no distinct facts rendering it probable) that the slaty females might acquire so strong a latent tendency to pale-blueness, that they would not destroy this colour in their male offspring, their female offspring still inheriting the slaty tint. If so, the desired end of making a breed with the two sexes permanently different in colour might be gained.

The extreme importance, or rather necessity in the above case of the desired character, namely, pale-blueness, being present though in a latent state in the female, so that the male offspring should not be deteriorated, will be best appreciated as follows: the male of Sœmmerring's pheasant has a tail thirty-seven inches in length, whilst that of the female is only eight inches; the tail of the male common pheasant is about twenty inches, and that of the female twelve inches long. Now if the female Sœmmerring pheasant with her *short* tail were crossed with the male common pheasant, there can be no doubt that the male hybrid offspring would have a much *longer* tail than that of the pure offspring of the common pheasant. On the other hand, if the female common pheasant, with a tail much longer than that of the female Sœmmerring pheasant, were crossed with the male of the latter, the male hybrid offspring would have a much *shorter* tail than that of the pure offspring of Sœmmerring's pheasant.[3]

Our fancier, in order to make his new breed with the males of a pale-blue tint, and the females unchanged, would have to continue selecting the males during many generations; and each stage of paleness would have to be fixed in the males, and rendered latent in the females. The task would be an extremely difficult one, and has never been tried, but might possibly be successfully carried out. The chief obstacle would be the early and complete loss of the pale-blue tint, from the necessity of re-

[3] Temminck says that the tail of the female *Phasianus Sœmmerringii* is only six inches long, 'Planches coloriées,' vol. v. 1838, pp. 487 and 488: the measurements above given were made for me by Mr. Sclater. For the common pheasant, see Macgillivray, 'History of British Birds,' vol. i. pp. 118-121.

iterated crosses with the slaty female, the latter not having at first any *latent* tendency to produce pale-blue offspring.

On the other hand, if one or two males were to vary ever so slightly in paleness, and the variations were from the first limited in their transmission to the male sex, the task of making a new breed of the desired kind would be easy, for such males would simply have to be selected and matched with ordinary females. An analogous case has actually occurred, for there are breeds of the pigeon in Belgium [4] in which the males alone are marked with black striæ. So again Mr. Tegetmeier has recently shown [5] that dragons not rarely produce silver-coloured birds, which are almost always hens; and he himself has bred ten such females. It is on the other hand a very unusual event when a silver male is produced; so that nothing would be easier, if desired, than to make a breed of dragons with blue males and silver females. This tendency is indeed so strong that when Mr. Tegetmeier at last got a silver male and matched him with one of the silver females, he expected to get a breed with both sexes thus coloured; he was however disappointed, for the young male reverted to the blue colour of his grandfather, the young female alone being silver. No doubt with patience this tendency to reversion in the males, reared from an occasional silver male matched with a silver hen, might be eliminated, and then both sexes would be coloured alike; and this very process has been followed with success by Mr Esquilant in the case of silver turbits.

With fowls, variations of colour, limited in their transmission to the male sex, habitually occur. When this form of inheritance prevails, it might well happen that some of the successive variations would be transferred to the female, who would then slightly resemble the male, as actually occurs in some breeds. Or again, the greater number, but not all, of the successive steps might be transferred to both sexes, and the female would then closely resemble the male. There can hardly be a doubt that this is the cause of the male pouter pigeon having a somewhat larger crop, and of the male carrier pigeon having somewhat larger wattles, than their respective females; for fanciers have not selected one sex more than the other, and have had no wish that these characters should be more strongly displayed in the male than in the female, yet this is the case with both breeds.

The same process would have to be followed, and the same difficulties encountered, if it were desired to make a breed with the females alone of some new colour.

Lastly, our fancier might wish to make a breed with the two sexes differing from each other, and both from the parent species. Here the difficulty would be extreme, unless the successive variations were from the first sexually limited on both sides, and then there would be no difficulty. We see this with the fowl; thus the two sexes of the pencilled Hamburghs differ greatly from each other, and from the two sexes of the aboriginal *Gallus bankiva;* and both are now kept constant to their standard of ex-

[4] Dr. Chapius, 'Le Pigeon Voyageur Belge,' 1865, p. 87.
[5] The 'Field,' Sept. 1872.

cellence by continued selection, which would be impossible unless the distinctive characters of both were limited in their transmission.

The Spanish fowl offers a more curious case; the male has an immense comb, but some of the successive variations, by the accumulation of which it was acquired, appear to have been transferred to the female; for she has a comb many times larger than that of the females of the parent species. But the comb of the female differs in one respect from that of the male, for it is apt to lop over; and within a recent period it has been ordered by the fancy that this should always be the case, and success has quickly followed the order. Now the lopping of the comb must be sexually limited in its transmission, otherwise it would prevent the comb of the male from being perfectly upright, which would be abhorrent to every fancier. On the other hand, the uprightness of the comb in the male must likewise be a sexually-limited character, otherwise it would prevent the comb of the female from lopping over.

From the foregoing illustrations, we see that even with almost unlimited time at command, it would be an extremely difficult and complex, perhaps an impossible process, to change one form of transmission into the other through selection. Therefore, without distinct evidence in each case, I am unwilling to admit that this has been effected in natural species. On the other hand, by means of successive variations, which were from the first sexually limited in their transmission, there would not be the least difficulty in rendering a male bird widely different in colour or in any other character from the female; the latter being left unaltered, or slightly altered, or specially modified for the sake of protection.

As bright colours are of service to the males in their rivalry with other males, such colours would be selected whether or not they were transmitted exclusively to the same sex. Consequently the females might be expected often to partake of the brightness of the males to a greater or less degree; and this occurs with a host of species. If all the successive variations were transmitted equally to both sexes, the females would be indistinguishable from the males; and this likewise occurs with many birds. If, however, dull colours were of high importance for the safety of the female during incubation, as with many ground birds, the females which varied in brightness, or which received through inheritance from the males any marked accession of brightness, would sooner or later be destroyed. But the tendency in the males to continue for an indefinite period transmitting to their female offspring their own brightness, would have to be eliminated by a change in the form of inheritance; and this, as shewn by our previous illustration, would be extremely difficult. The more probable result of the long-continued destruction of the more brightly-coloured females, supposing the equal form of transmission to prevail, would be the lessening or annihilation of the bright colours of the males, owing to their continual crossing with the duller females. It would be tedious to follow out all the other possible results; but I may remind the reader that if sexually-limited variations in brightness occurred in the females, even if they were not in the least injurious to them and consequently were not eliminated, yet they would not be favoured or selected, for the male usually accepts any female, and does not select the more attractive individuals; consequently these variations would be liable to be lost, and would have little influence on the character of the race; and this will aid in accounting for the females being commonly duller-coloured than the males.

In the eighth chapter instances were given, to which many might here be added, of variations occurring at various ages, and inherited at the corresponding age. It was also shewn that variations which occur late in life are commonly transmitted to the same sex in which they first appear; whilst variations occurring early in life are apt to be transmitted to both sexes; not that all the cases of sexually-limited transmission can thus be accounted for. It was further shewn that if a male bird varied by becoming brighter whilst young, such variations would be of no service until the age for reproduction had arrived, and there was competition between rival males. But in the case of birds living on the ground and commonly in need of the protection of dull colors, bright tints would be far more dangerous to the young and inexperienced than to the adult males. Consequently the males which varied in brightness whilst young would suffer much destruction and be eliminated through natural selection; on the other hand, the males which varied in this manner when nearly mature, notwithstanding that they were exposed to some additional danger, might survive, and from being favoured through sexual selection, would procreate their kind. As a relation often exists between the period of variation and the form of transmission, if the bright-coloured young males were destroyed and the mature ones were successful in their courtship, the males alone would acquire brilliant colours and would transmit them exclusively to their male offspring. But I by no means wish to maintain that the influence of age on the form of transmission, is the sole cause of the great difference in brilliancy between the sexes of many birds.

When the sexes of birds differ in colour, it is interesting to determine whether the males alone have been modified by sexual selection, the females having been left unchanged, or only partially and indirectly thus changed; or whether the females have been specially modified through natural selection for the sake of protection. I will therefore discuss this question at some length, even more fully than its intrinsic importance deserves; for various curious collateral points may thus be conveniently considered.

Before we enter on the subject of colour, more especially in reference to Mr. Wallace's conclusions, it may be useful to discuss some other sexual differences under a similar point of view. A breed of fowls formerly existed in Germany [6] in which the hens were furnished with spurs; they were good layers, but they so greatly disturbed their nests with their spurs that they could not be allowed to sit on their own eggs. Hence at one time it appeared to me probable that with the females of the wild Gallinaceæ the development of spurs had been checked through natural

[6] Bechstein, 'Naturgesch. Deutschlands,' 1793, B. iii. s. 339.

selection, from the injury thus caused to their nests. This seemed all the more probable, as wing-spurs, which would not be injurious during incubation, are often as well-developed in the female as in the male; though in not a few cases they are rather larger in the male. When the male is furnished with leg-spurs the female almost always exhibits rudiments of them,—the rudiment sometimes consisting of a mere scale, as in Gallus. Hence it might be argued that the females had aboriginally been furnished with well-developed spurs, but that these had subsequently been lost through disuse or natural selection. But if this view be admitted, it would have to be extended to innumerable other cases; and it implies that the female progenitors of the existing spur-bearing species were once encumbered with an injurious appendage.

In some few genera and species, as in Galloperdix, Acomus, and the Javan peacock (*Pavo muticus*), the females, as well as the males, possess well-developed leg-spurs. Are we to infer from this fact that they construct a different sort of nest from that made by their nearest allies, and not liable to be injured by their spurs; so that the spurs have not been removed? Or are we to suppose that the females of these several species especially require spurs for their defence? It is a more probable conclusion that both the presence and absence of spurs in the females result from different laws of inheritance having prevailed, independently of natural selection. With the many females in which spurs appear as rudiments, we may conclude that some few of the successive variations, through which they were developed in the males, occurred very early in life, and were consequently transferred to the females. In the other and much rarer cases, in which the females possess fully developed spurs, we may conclude that all the successive variations were transferred to them; and that they gradually acquired and inherited the habit of not disturbing their nests.

The vocal organs and the feathers variously modified for producing sound, as well as the proper instincts for using them, often differ in the two sexes, but are sometimes the same in both. Can such differences be accounted for by the males having acquired these organs and instincts, whilst the females have been saved from inheriting them, on account of the danger to which they would have been exposed by attracting the attention of birds or beasts of prey? This does not seem to me probable, when we think of the multitude of birds which with impunity gladden the country with their voices during the spring.[7] It is a safer conclusion that, as vocal and instrumental organs are of special service only to the males during their courtship, these organs were developed through sexual selection and their constant use in that sex alone—the successive variations and the effects of use having been from the first more or less limited in transmission to the male offspring.

[7] Daines Barrington, however, thought it probable ('Phil. Transact.' 1773, p. 164) that few female birds sing, because the talent would have been dangerous to them during incubation. He adds, that a similar view may possibly account for the inferiority of the female to the male in plumage.

Many analogous cases could be adduced; those for instance of the plumes on the head being generally longer in the male than in the female, sometimes of equal length in both sexes, and occasionally absent in the female,—these several cases occurring in the same group of birds. It would be difficult to account for such a difference between the sexes by the female having been benefited by possessing a slightly shorter crest than the male, and its consequent diminution or complete suppression through natural selection. But I will take a more favourable case, namely the length of the tail. The long train of the peacock would have been not only inconvenient but dangerous to the peahen during the period of incubation and whilst accompanying her young. Hence there is not the least à priori improbability in the development of her tail having been checked through natural selection. But the females of various pheasants, which apparently are exposed on their open nests to as much danger as the peahen, have tails of considerable length. The females as well as the males of the *Menura superba* have long tails, and they build a domed nest, which is a great anomaly in so large a bird. Naturalists have wondered how the female Menura could manage her tail during incubation; but it is now known [8] that she "enters the nest head first, and then turns round with her tail sometimes over her back, but more often bent round by her side. Thus in time the tail becomes quite askew, and is a tolerable guide to the length of time the bird has been sitting." Both sexes of an Australian kingfisher (*Tanysiptera sylvia*) have the middle tail-feathers greatly lengthened, and the female makes her nest in a hole; and as I am informed by Mr. R. B. Sharpe these feathers become much crumpled during incubation.

In these two latter cases the great length of the tail-feathers must be in some degree inconvenient to the female; and as in both species the tail-feathers of the female are somewhat shorter than those of the male, it might be argued that their full development had been prevented through natural selection. But if the development of the tail of the peahen had been checked only when it became inconveniently or dangerously great, she would have retained a much longer tail than she actually possesses; for her tail is not nearly so long, relatively to the size of her body, as that of many female pheasants, nor longer than that of the female turkey. It must also be borne in mind that, in accordance with this view, as soon as the tail of the peahen became dangerously long, and its development was consequently checked, she would have continually reacted on her male progeny, and thus have prevented the peacock from acquiring his present magnificent train. We may therefore infer that the length of the tail in the peacock and its shortness in the peahen are the result of the requisite variations in the male having been from the first transmitted to the male offspring alone.

We are led to a nearly similar conclusion with respect to the length of the tail in the various species of pheasants. In the Eared pheasant (*Crossoptilon auritum*) the tail is of equal length in both sexes, namely, sixteen

[8] Mr. Ramsay, in 'Proc. Zoolog. Soc.' 1868, p. 50.

or seventeen inches; in the common pheasant it is about twenty inches long in the male and twelve in the female; in Sœmmerring's pheasant, thirty-seven inches in the male and only eight in the female; and lastly in Reeve's pheasant it is sometimes actually seventy-two inches long in the male and sixteen in the female. Thus in the several species, the tail of the female differs much in length, irrespectively of that of the male; and this can be accounted for, as it seems to me, with much more probability, by the laws of inheritance,—that is by the successive variations having been from the first more or less closely limited in their transmission to the male sex than by the agency of natural selection, resulting from the length of tail being more or less injurious to the females of these several allied species.

We may now consider Mr. Wallace's arguments in regard to the sexual coloration of birds. He believes that the bright tints originally acquired through sexual selection by the males would in all, or almost all cases, have been transmitted to the females, unless the transference had been checked through natural selection. I may here remind the reader that various facts opposed to this view have already been given under reptiles, amphibians, fishes and lepidoptera. Mr. Wallace rests his belief chiefly, but not exclusively, as we shall see in the next chapter, on the following statement,[9] that when both sexes are coloured in a very conspicuous manner, the nest is of such a nature as to conceal the sitting bird; but when there is a marked contrast of colour between the sexes, the male being gay and the female dull-coloured, the nest is open and exposes the sitting bird to view. This coincidence, as far as it goes, certainly seems to favour the belief that the females which sit on open nests have been specially modified for the sake of protection; but we shall presently see that there is another and more probable explanation, namely, that conspicuous females have acquired the instinct of building domed nests oftener than dull-coloured birds. Mr. Wallace admits that there are, as might have been expected, some exceptions to his two rules, but it is a question whether the exceptions are not so numerous as seriously to invalidate them.

There is in the first place much truth in the Duke of Argyll's remark[10] that a large domed nest is more conspicuous to an enemy, especially to all tree-haunting carnivorous animals, than a smaller open nest. Nor must we forget that with many birds which build open nests, the male sits on the eggs and aids the female in feeding the young: this is the case, for instance, with *Pyranga œstiva*,[11] one of the most splendid birds in the United States, the male being vermilion, and the female light brownish-green. Now if brilliant colours had been extremely dangerous to birds whilst sitting on their open nests, the males in these cases would have suffered greatly. It might, however, be of such paramount importance to the

[9] 'Journal of Travel,' edited by A. Murray, vol. i. 1868, p. 78.
[10] 'Journal of Travel,' edited by A. Murray, vol. i. 1868, p. 281.
[11] Audubon, 'Ornithological Biography,' vol. i. p. 233.

male to be brilliantly coloured, in order to beat his rivals, that this may have more than compensated some additional danger.

Mr. Wallace admits that with the King-crows (Dicrurus), Orioles, and Pittidæ, the females are conspicuously coloured, yet build open nests; but he urges that the birds of the first group are highly pugnacious and could defend themselves; that those of the second group take extreme care in concealing their open nests, but this does not invariably hold good; [12] and that with the birds of the third group the females are brightly coloured chiefly on the under surface. Besides these cases, pigeons which are sometimes brightly, and almost always conspicuously coloured, and which are notoriously liable to the attacks of birds of prey, offer a serious exception to the rule, for they almost always build open and exposed nests. In another large family, that of the humming-birds, all the species build open nests, yet with some of the most gorgeous species the sexes are alike; and in the majority, the females, though less brilliant than the males, are brightly coloured. Nor can it be maintained that all female humming-birds, which are brightly coloured, escape detection by their tints being green, for some display on their upper surfaces red, blue, and other colours.[13]

In regard to birds which build in holes or construct domed nests, other advantages, as Mr. Wallace remarks, besides concealment are gained, such as shelter from the rain, greater warmth, and in hot countries protection from the sun; [14] so that it is no valid objection to his view that many birds having both sexes obscurely coloured build concealed nests.[15] The female Horn-bill (*Buceros*), for instance, of India and Africa is protected during incubation with extraordinary care, for she plasters up with her own excrement the orifice of the hole in which she sits on her eggs, leaving only a small orifice through which the male feeds her; she is thus kept a close prisoner during the whole period of incubation; [16] yet female horn-bills are not more conspicuously coloured than many other birds of equal size which build open nests. It is a more serious objection to Mr. Wallace's view, as is admitted by him, that in some few groups the males are brilliantly coloured and the females obscure, and yet the latter hatch their eggs in domed nests. This is the case with the Grallinæ of Australia,

[12] Jerdon, 'Birds of India,' vol. ii. p. 108. Gould's 'Handbook of the Birds of Australia,' vol. i. p. 463.

[13] For instance, the female *Eupetomena macroura* has the head and tail dark blue with reddish loins; the female *Lampornis porphyrurus* is blackish-green on the upper surface, with the lores and sides of the throat crimson; the female *Eulampis jugularis* has the top of the head and back green, but the loins and the tail are crimson. Many other instances of highly conspicuous females could be given. See Mr. Gould's magnificent work on this family.

[14] Mr. Salvin noticed in Guatemala ('Ibis,' 1864, p. 375) that humming-birds were much more unwilling to leave their nests during very hot weather, when the sun was shining brightly, as if their eggs would be thus injured, than during cool, cloudy, or rainy weather.

[15] I may specify, as instances of dull-coloured birds building concealed nests, the species belonging to eight Australian genera described in Gould's 'Handbook of the Birds of Australia,' vol. i. pp. 340, 362, 365, 383, 387, 389, 391, 414.

[16] Mr. C. Horne, 'Proc. Zoolog. Soc.' 1869, p. 243.

the Superb Warblers (Maluridæ) of the same country, the Sun-birds (Nectariniæ), and with several of the Australian Honey-suckers or Meliphagidæ.[17]

If we look to the birds of England we shall see that there is no close and general relation between the colours of the female and the nature of the nest which is constructed. About forty of our British birds (excluding those of large size which could defend themselves) build in holes in banks, rocks, or trees, or construct domed nests. If we take the colours of the female goldfinch, bullfinch, or black-bird, as a standard of the degree of conspicuousness, which is not highly dangerous to the sitting female, then out of the above forty birds the females of only twelve can be considered as conspicuous to a dangerous degree, the remaining twenty-eight being inconspicuous.[18] Nor is there any close relation within the same genus between a well-pronounced difference in colour between the sexes, and the nature of the nest constructed. Thus the male house sparrow (*Passer domesticus*) differs much from the female, the male tree-sparrow (*P. montanus*) hardly at all, and yet both build well-concealed nests. The two sexes of the common fly-catcher (*Muscicapa grisola*) can hardly be distinguished, whilst the sexes of the pied fly-catcher (*M. luctuosa*) differ considerably, and both species build in holes or conceal their nests. The female blackbird (*Turdus merula*) differs much, the female ringouzel (*T. torquatus*) differs less, and the female common thrush (*T. musicus*) hardly at all from their respective males; yet all build open nests. On the other hand, the not very distantly-allied water-ouzel (*Cinclus aquaticus*) builds a domed nest, and the sexes differ about as much as in the ring-ouzel. The black and red grouse (*Tetrao tetrix* and *T. scoticus*) build open nests in equally well-concealed spots, but in the one species the sexes differ greatly, and in the other very little.

Notwithstanding the foregoing objections, I cannot doubt, after reading Mr. Wallace's excellent essay, that looking to the birds of the world, a large majority of the species in which the females are conspicuously coloured (and in this case the males with rare exceptions are equally conspicuous), build concealed nests for the sake of protection. Mr. Wallace enumerates [19] a long series of groups in which this rule holds good; but it will suffice here to give, as instances, the more familiar groups of king-

---

[17] On the nidification and colours of these latter species, see Gould's 'Handbook,' &c., vol. i. pp. 504, 527.

[18] I have consulted, on this subject, Macgillivray's 'British Birds,' and though doubts may be entertained in some cases in regard to the degree of concealment of the nest, and to the degree of conspicuousness of the female, yet the following birds, which all lay their eggs in holes or in domed nests, can hardly be considered, by the above standard, as conspicuous: Passer, 2 species; Sturnus, of which the female is considerably less brilliant than the male; Cinclus; Motallica boarula (?); Erithacus (?); Fruticola, 2 sp.; Saxicola; Ruticilla, 2 sp.; Sylvia, 3 sp.; Parus, 3 sp.; Mecistura Anorthura; Certhia; Sitta; Yunx; Muscicapa, 2 sp.; Hirundo, 3 sp.; and Cypselus. The females of the following 12 birds may be considered as conspicuous according to the same standard, viz., Pastor, Motacilla alba, Parus major and P. cærúleus, Upupa, Picus, 4 sp., Coracias, Alcedo, and Merops.

[19] 'Journal of Travel,' edited by A. Murray, vol. i. p. 78.

fishers, toucans, trogons, puff-birds (Capitonidæ), plantain-eaters (Musophagæ), woodpeckers, and parrots. Mr. Wallace believes that in these groups, as the males gradually acquired through sexual selection their brilliant colours, these were transferred to the females and were not eliminated by natural selection, owing to the protection which they already enjoyed from their manner of nidification. According to this view, their present manner of nesting was acquired before their present colours. But it seems to me much more probable that in most cases, as the females were gradually rendered more and more brilliant from partaking of the colours of the male, they were gradually led to change their instincts (supposing that they originally built open nests), and to seek protection by building domed or concealed nests. No one who studies, for instance, Audubon's account of the differences in the nests of the same species in the Northern and Southern United States,[20] will feel any great difficulty in admitting that birds, either by a change (in the strict sense of the word) of their habits, or through the natural selection of so-called spontaneous variations of instinct, might readily be led to modify their manner of nesting.

This way of viewing the relation, as far as it holds good, between the bright colours of female birds and their manner of nesting, receives some support from certain cases occurring in the Sahara Desert. Here, as in most other deserts, various birds, and many other animals, have had their colours adapted in a wonderful manner to the tints of the surrounding surface. Nevertheless there are, as I am informed by the Rev. Mr. Tristram, some curious exceptions to the rule; thus the male of the *Monticola cyanea* is conspicuous from his bright blue colour, and the female almost equally conspicuous from her mottled brown and white plumage; both sexes of two species of Dromolæa are of a lustrous black; so that these three species are far from receiving protection from their colours, yet they are able to survive, for they have acquired the habit of taking refuge from danger in holes or crevices in the rocks.

With respect to the above groups in which the females are conspicuously coloured and build concealed nests, it is not necessary to suppose that each separate species had its nidifying instinct specially modified; but only that the early progenitors of each group were gradually led to build domed or concealed nests, and afterwards transmitted this instinct, together with their bright colours, to their modified descendants. As far as it can be trusted, the conclusion is interesting, that sexual selection together with equal or nearly equal inheritance by both sexes, have indirectly determined the manner of nidification of whole groups of birds.

According to Mr. Wallace, even in the groups in which the females, from being protected in domed nests during incubation, have not had their bright colours eliminated through natural selection, the males often differ in a slight, and occasionally in a considerable degree from the fe-

[20] See many statements in the 'Ornithological Biography.' See also some curious observations on the nests of Italian birds by Eugenio Bettoni, in the 'Atti della Società Italiana,' vol. xi. 1869, p. 487.

males. This is a significant fact, for such differences in colour must be accounted for by some of the variations in the males having been from the first limited in transmission to the same sex; as it can hardly be maintained that these differences, especially when very slight, serve as a protection to the female. Thus all the species in the splendid group of the Trogons build in holes; and Mr. Gould gives figures [21] of both sexes of twenty-five species, in all of which, with one partial exception, the sexes differ sometimes slightly, sometimes conspicuously, in colour,—the males being always finer than the females, though the latter are likewise beautiful. All the species of kingfishers build in holes, and with most of the species the sexes are equally brilliant, and thus far Mr. Wallace's rule holds good; but in some of the Australian species the colours of the females are rather less vivid than those of the male; and in one splendidly-coloured species, the sexes differ so much that they were at first thought to be specifically distinct.[22] Mr. R. B. Sharpe, who has especially studied this group, has shewn me some American species (Ceryle) in which the breast of the male is belted with black. Again, in Carcineutes, the difference between the sexes is conspicuous: in the male the upper surface is dull-blue banded with black, the lower surface being partly fawn-coloured, and there is much red about the head; in the female the upper surface is reddish-brown banded with black, and the lower surface white with black markings. It is an interesting fact, as shewing how the same peculiar style of sexual colouring often characterises allied forms, that in three species of Dacelo the male differs from the female only in the tail being dull-blue banded with black, whilst that of the female is brown with blackish bars; so that here the tail differs in colour in the two sexes in exactly the same manner as the whole upper surface in the two sexes of Carcineutes.

With parrots, which likewise build in holes, we find analogous cases: in most of the species, both sexes are brilliantly coloured and indistinguishable, but in not a few species the males are coloured rather more vividly than the females, or even very differently from them. Thus, besides other strongly-marked differences, the whole under surface of the male King Lory (*Aprosmictus scapulatus*) is scarlet, whilst the throat and chest of the female is green tinged with red: in the *Euphema splendida* there is a similar difference, the face and wing coverts moreover of the female being of a paler blue than in the male.[23] In the family of the tits (*Parinæ*), which build concealed nests, the female of our common blue tomtit (*Parus cæruleus*), is "much less brightly coloured" than the male: and in the magnificent Sultan yellow tit of India the difference is greater.[24]

[21] See his 'Monograph of the Trogonidæ,' first edition.

[22] Namely Cyanalcyon. Gould's 'Handbook to the Birds of Australia,' vol. i. page 133; see, also, pages 130, 136.

[23] Every gradation of difference between the sexes may be followed in the parrots of Australia. See Gould's 'Handbook,' &c., vol. ii. pp. 14-102.

[24] Macgillivray's 'British Birds,' vol. ii. p. 433. Jerdon, 'Birds of India,' vol. ii. p 282.

Again, in the great group of the woodpeckers,[25] the sexes are generally nearly alike, but in the *Megapicus validus* all those parts of the head, neck, and breast, which are crimson in the male are pale brown in the female. As in several woodpeckers the head of the male is bright crimson, whilst that of the female is plain, it occurred to me that this colour might possibly make the female dangerously conspicuous, whenever she put her head out of the hole containing her nest, and consequently that this colour, in accordance with Mr. Wallace's belief, had been eliminated. This view is strengthened by what Malherbe states with respect to *Indopicus carlotta;* namely, that the young females, like the young males, have some crimson about their heads, but that this colour disappears in the adult female, whilst it is intensified in the adult male. Nevertheless the following considerations render this view extremely doubtful: the male takes a fair share in incubation,[26] and would be thus almost equally exposed to danger; both sexes of many species have their heads of an equally bright crimson; in other species the difference between the sexes in the amount of scarlet is so slight that it can hardly make any appreciable difference in the danger incurred; and lastly, the colouring of the head in the two sexes often differs slightly in other ways.

The cases, as yet given, of slight and graduated differences in colour between the males and females in the groups, in which as a general rule the sexes resemble each other, all relate to species which build domed or concealed nests. But similar gradations may likewise be observed in groups in which the sexes as a general rule resemble each other, but which build open nests.

. As I have before instanced the Australian parrots, so I may here instance, without giving any details, the Australian pigeons.[27] It deserves especial notice that in all these cases the slight differences in plumage between the sexes are of the same general nature as the occasionally greater differences. A good illustration of this fact has already been afforded by those kingfishers in which either the tail alone or the whole upper surface of the plumage differs in the same manner in the two sexes. Similar cases may be observed with parrots and pigeons. The differences in colour between the sexes of the same species are, also, of the same general nature as the differences in colour between the distinct species of the same group. For when in a group in which the sexes are usually alike, the male differs considerably from the female, he is not coloured in a quite new style. Hence we may infer that within the same group the special colours of both sexes when they are alike, and the colours of the male, when he differs slightly or even considerably from the female, have been in most cases determined by the same general cause; this being sexual selection.

It is not probable, as has already been remarked, that differences in colour between the sexes, when very slight, can be of service to the fe-

[25] All the following facts are taken from M. Malherbe's magnificent 'Monographie des Picidées,' 1861.

[26] Audubon's 'Ornithological Biography,' vol. ii. p. 75; see also the 'Ibis,' vol. i. p. 268.

[27] Gould's 'Handbook to the Birds of Australia,' vol. ii. pp. 109-149.

male as a protection. Assuming, however, that they are of service, they might be thought to be cases of transition; but we have no reason to believe that many species at any one time are undergoing change. Therefore we can hardly admit that the numerous females which differ very slightly in colour from their males are now all commencing to become obscure for the sake of protection. Even if we consider somewhat more marked sexual differences, is it probable, for instance, that the head of the female chaffinch,—the crimson on the breast of the female bullfinch,—the green of the female greenfinch,—the crest of the female golden-crested wren, have all been rendered less bright by the slow process of selection for the sake of protection? I cannot think so; and still less with the slight differences between the sexes of those birds which build concealed nests. On the other hand, the differences in colour between the sexes, whether great or small, may to a large extent be explained on the principle of the successive variations, acquired by the males through sexual selection, having been from the first more or less limited in their transmission to the females. That the degree of limitation should differ in different species of the same group will not surprise any one who has studied the laws of inheritance, for they are so complex that they appear to us in our ignorance to be capricious in their action.[28]

As far as I can discover there are few large groups of birds in which all the species have both sexes alike and brilliantly coloured, but I hear from Mr. Sclater, that this appears to be the case with the Musophagæ or plantain-eaters. Nor do I believe that any large group exists in which the sexes of all the species are widely dissimilar in colour: Mr. Wallace informs me that the chatterers of S. America (*Cotingidæ*) offer one of the best instances; but with some of the species, in which the male has a splendid red breast, the female exhibits some red on her breast; and the females of other species shew traces of the green and other colours of the males. Nevertheless we have a near approach to close sexual similarity or dissimilarity throughout several groups: and this, from what has just been said of the fluctuating nature of inheritance, is a somewhat surprising circumstance. But that the same laws should largely prevail with allied animals is not surprising. The domestic fowl has produced a great number of breeds and sub-breeds, and in these the sexes generally differ in plumage; so that it has been noticed as an unusual circumstance when in certain sub-breeds they resemble each other. On the other hand, the domestic pigeon has likewise produced a vast number of distinct breeds and sub-breeds, and in these, with rare exceptions, the two sexes are identically alike.

Therefore if other species of Gallus and Columba were domesticated and varied, it would not be rash to predict that similar rules of sexual similarity and dissimilarity, depending on the form of transmission, would hold good in both cases. In like manner the same form of transmission has generally prevailed under nature throughout the same

[28] See remarks to this effect in my work on 'Variation under Domestication,' vol ii. chap. xii.

groups, although marked exceptions to this rule occur. Thus within the same family or even genus, the sexes may be identically alike, or very different in colour. Instances have already been given in the same genus, as with sparrows, fly-catchers, thrushes and grouse. In the family of pheasants the sexes of almost all the species are wonderfully dissimilar, but are quite alike in the eared pheasant or *Crossoptilon auritum*. In two species of Chloephaga, a genus of geese, the male cannot be distinguished from the females, except by size; whilst in two others, the sexes are so unlike that they might easily be mistaken for distinct species.[29]

The laws of inheritance can alone account for the following cases, in which the female acquires, late in life, certain characters proper to the male, and ultimately comes to resemble him more or less completely. Here protection can hardly have come into play. Mr. Blyth informs me that the females of *Oriolus melanocephalus* and of some allied species, when sufficiently mature to breed, differ considerably in plumage from the adult males; but after the second or third moults they differ only in their beaks having a slight greenish tinge. In the dwarf bitterns (*Ardetta*), according to the same authority, "the male acquires his final livery at the first moult, the female not before the third or fourth moult; in the meanwhile she presents an intermediate garb, which is ultimately exchanged for the same livery as that of the male." So again the female *Falco peregrinus* acquires her blue plumage more slowly than the male. Mr. Swinhoe states that with one of the Drongo shrikes (*Dicrurus macrocercus*) the male, whilst almost a nestling, moults his soft brown plumage and becomes of a uniform glossy greenish-black; but the female retains for a long time the white striæ and spots on the axillary feathers; and does not completely assume the uniform black colour of the male for three years. The same excellent observer remarks that in the spring of the second year the female spoon-bill (Platalea) of China resembles the male of the first year, and that apparently it is not until the third spring that she acquires the same adult plumage as that possessed by the male at a much earlier age. The female *Bombycilla carolinensis* differs very little from the male, but the appendages, which like beads of red sealing-wax ornament the wing-feathers,[30] are not developed in her so early in life as in the male. In the male of an Indian parrakeet (*Palæornis javanicus*) the upper mandible is coral-red from his earliest youth, but in the female, as Mr. Blyth has observed with caged and wild birds, it is at first black and does not become red until the bird is at least a year old, at which age the sexes resemble each other in all respects. Both sexes of the wild turkey are ultimately furnished with a tuft of bristles on the breast, but in two-year-old birds the tuft is about four inches long in the male and hardly apparent in the female; when, however, the latter has reached her fourth year, it is from four to five inches in length.[31]

[29] The 'Ibis,' vol. vi. 1864, page 122.

[30] When the male courts the female, these ornaments are vibrated, and "are shewn off to great advantage," on the outstretched wings: A. Leith Adams, 'Field and Forest Rambles,' 1873, p. 153.

[31] On Ardetta, Translation of Cuvier's 'Règne Animal,' by Mr. Blyth, footnote, p.

These cases must not be confounded with those where diseased or old females abnormally assume masculine characters, nor with those where fertile females, whilst young, acquire the characters of the male, through variation or some unknown cause.[32] But all these cases have so much in common that they depend, according to the hypothesis of pangenesis, on gemmules derived from each part of the male being present, though latent, in the female; their development following on some slight change in the elective affinities of her constituent tissues.

A few words must be added on changes of plumage in relation to the season of the year. From reasons formerly assigned there can be little doubt that the elegant plumes, long pendant feathers, crests, &c., of egrets, herons, and many other birds, which are developed and retained only during the summer, serve for ornamental and nuptial purposes, though common to both sexes. The female is thus rendered more conspicuous during the period of incubation than during the winter; but such birds as herons and egrets would be able to defend themselves. As, however, plumes would probably be inconvenient and certainly of no use during the winter, it is possible that the habit of moulting twice in the year may have been gradually acquired through natural selection for the sake of casting off inconvenient ornaments during the winter. But this view cannot be extended to the many waders, whose summer and winter plumages differ very little in colour. With defenceless species, in which both sexes, or the males alone, become extremely conspicuous during the breeding season,—or when the males acquire at this season such long wing or tail-feathers as to impede their flight, as with Cosmetornis and Vidua,—it certainly at first appears highly probable that the second moult has been gained for the special purpose of throwing off these ornaments. We must, however, remember that many birds, such as some of the Birds of Paradise, the Argus pheasant and peacock, do not cast their plumes during the winter; and it can hardly be maintained that the constitution of these birds, at least of the Gallinaceæ, renders a double moult impossible, for the ptarmigan moults thrice in the year.[33] Hence it must be considered as doubtful whether the many species which moult their ornamental plumes or lose their bright colours during the winter, have acquired this habit on account of the inconvenience or danger which they would otherwise have suffered.

159. On the Peregrine Falcon, Mr. Blyth, in Charlesworth's 'Mag. of Nat. Hist.' vol. i. 1837, p. 304. On Dicrurus, 'Ibis,' 1863, p. 44. On the Platalea, 'Ibis,' vol. vi. 1864, p. 366. On the Bombycilla, Audubon's 'Ornitholog. Biography,' vol. i. p. 229. On the Palæornis, see, also, Jerdon, 'Birds of India,' vol. i. p. 263. On the wild turkey, Audubon, ibid. vol. i. p. 15; but I hear from Judge Caton that in Illinois the female very rarely acquires a tuft. Analogous cases with the females of Petrcocssyphus are given by Mr. R. Sharpe, 'Proc. Zoolog. Soc.' 1872, p. 496.

[32] Of these latter cases Mr. Blyth has recorded (Translation of Cuvier's 'Règne Animal,' p. 158) various instances with Lanius, Ruticilla, Linaria, and Anas. Audubon has also recorded a similar case ('Ornitholog. Biography,' vol. v. p. 519) with *Pyranga æstiva.*

[33] See Gould's 'Birds of Great Britain.'

I conclude, therefore, that the habit of moulting twice in the year was in most or all cases first acquired for some distinct purpose, perhaps for gaining a warmer winter covering; and that variations in the plumage occurring during the summer were accumulated through sexual selection, and transmitted to the offspring at the same season of the year; that such variations were inherited either by both sexes or by the males alone, according to the form of inheritance which prevailed. This appears more probable than that the species in all cases originally tended to retain their ornamental plumage during the winter, but were saved from this through natural selection, resulting from the inconvenience or danger thus caused.

I have endeavoured in this chapter to shew that the arguments are not trustworthy in favour of the view that weapons, bright colours, and various ornaments, are now confined to the males owing to the conversion, by natural selection, of the equal transmission of characters to both sexes, into transmission to the male sex alone. It is also doubtful whether the colours of many female birds are due to the preservation, for the sake of protection, of variations which were from the first limited in their transmission to the female sex. But it will be convenient to defer any further discussion on this subject until I treat, in the following chapter, of the differences in plumage between the young and old.

The immature plumage in relation to the character of the plumage in both sexes when adult—Six classes of cases—Sexual differences between the males of closely-allied or representative species—The female assuming the characters of the male —Plumage of the young in relation to the summer and winter plumage of the adults—On the increase of beauty in the birds of the world—Protective colouring —Conspicuously-coloured birds—Novelty appreciated—Summary of the four chapters on Birds.

WE must now consider the transmission of characters, as limited by age, in reference to sexual selection. The truth and importance of the principle of inheritance at corresponding ages need not here be discussed, as enough has already been said on the subject. Before giving the several rather complex rules or classes of cases, under which the differences in plumage between the young and the old, as far as known to me, may be included, it will be well to make a few preliminary remarks.

With animals of all kinds when the adults differ in colour from the young, and the colours of the latter are not, as far as we can see, of any special service, they may generally be attributed, like various embryological structures, to the retention of a former character. But this view can be maintained with confidence, only when the young of several species resemble each other closely, and likewise resemble other adult species belonging to the same group; for the latter are the living proofs that such a state of things was formerly possible. Young lions and pumas are marked with feeble stripes or rows of spots, and as many allied species both young and old are similarly marked, no believer in evolution will doubt that the progenitor of the lion and puma was a striped animal, and that the young have retained vestiges of the stripes, like the kittens of black cats, which are not in the least striped when grown up. Many species of deer, which when mature are not spotted, are whilst young covered with white spots, as are likewise some few species in the adult state. So again the young in the whole family of pigs (Suidæ), and in certain rather distantly allied animals, such as the tapir, are marked with dark longitudinal stripes; but here we have a character apparently derived from an extinct progenitor, and now preserved by the young alone. In all such cases the old have had their colours changed in the course of time, whilst the young have remained but little altered, and this has been effected through the principle of inheritance at corresponding ages.

This same principle applies to many birds belonging to various groups, in which the young closely resemble each other, and differ much from their respective adult parents. The young of almost all the Gallinaceæ, and of some distantly allied birds such as ostriches, are covered with longitudinally striped down; but this character points back to a state of things so remote that it hardly concerns us. Young cross-bills (Loxia) have at first straight beaks like those of other finches, and in their immature striated plumage they resemble the mature redpole and female siskin, as well as the young of the goldfinch, greenfinch, and some other allied species. The young of many kinds of buntings (Emberiza) resemble one another, and likewise the adult state of the common bunting, *E. miliaria*. In almost the whole large group of thrushes the young have their breasts spotted— a character which is retained throughout life by many species, but is quite lost by others, as by the *Turdus migratorius*. So again with many thrushes, the feathers on the back are mottled before they are moulted for the first time, and this character is retained for life by certain eastern species. The young of many species of shrikes (Lanius), of some woodpeckers, and of an Indian pigeon (*Chalcophaps indicus*), are transversely striped on the under surface; and certain allied species or whole genera are similarly marked when adult. In some closely-allied and resplendent Indian cuckoos (Chrysococcyx), the mature species differ considerably from one another in colour, but the young cannot be distinguished. The young of an Indian goose (*Sarkidiornis melanonotus*) closely resemble in plumage an allied genus, Dendrocygna, when mature.[1] Similar facts will hereafter be given in regard to certain herons. Young black-grouse (*Tetrao tetrix*) resemble the young as well as the old of certain other species, for instance the red-grouse or *T. scoticus*. Finally, as Mr. Blyth, who has attended closely to this subject, has well remarked, the natural affinities of many species are best exhibited in their immature plumage; and as the true affinities of all organic beings depend on their descent from a common progenitor, this remark strongly confirms the belief that the immature plumage approximately shews us the former or ancestral condition of the species.

Although many young birds, belonging to various families, thus give us a glimpse of the plumage of their remote progenitors, yet there are many other birds, both dull-coloured and bright-coloured, in which the young closely resemble their parents. In such cases the young of the different species cannot resemble each other more closely than do the parents; nor can they strikingly resemble allied forms when adult. They give us but little insight into the plumage of their progenitors, excepting in so far that, when the young and the old are coloured in the same general manner throughout a whole group of species, it is probable that their progenitors were similarly coloured.

---

[1] In regard to thrushes, shrikes, and woodpeckers, see Mr. Blyth, in Charlesworth's 'Mag. of Nat. Hist.' vol. i. 1837, p. 304; also footnote to his translation of Cuvier's 'Règne Animals,' p. 159. I give the case of Loxia on Mr. Blyth's information. On thrushes, see also Audubon, 'Ornith. Biog.' vol. ii. p. 195. On Chrysococcyx and Chalcophaps, Blyth, as quoted in Jerdon's 'Birds of India,' vol. iii. p. 485. On Sarkidiornis, Blyth, in 'Ibis,' 1867, p. 175.

We may now consider the classes of cases, under which the differences and resemblances between the plumage of the young and the old, in both sexes or in one sex alone, may be grouped. Rules of this kind were first enounced by Cuvier; but with the progress of knowledge they require some modification and amplification. This I have attempted to do, as far as the extreme complexity of the subject permits, from information derived from various sources; but a full essay on this subject by some competent ornithologist is much needed. In order to ascertain to what extent each rule prevails, I have tabulated the facts given in four great works, namely, by Macgillivray on the birds of Britain, Audubon on those of North America, Jerdon on those of India, and Gould on those of Australia. I may here premise, first, that the several cases or rules graduate into each other; and secondly, that when the young are said to resemble their parents, it is not meant that they are identically alike, for their colours are almost always less vivid, and the feathers are softer and often of a different shape.

RULES OR CLASSES OF CASES

I. When the adult male is more beautiful or conspicuous than the adult female, the young of both sexes in their first plumage closely resemble the adult female, as with the common fowl and peacock; or, as occasionally occurs, they resemble her much more closely than they do the adult male.

II. When the adult female is more conspicuous than the adult male, as sometimes though rarely occurs, the young of both sexes in their first plumage resemble the adult male.

III. When the adult male resembles the adult female, the young of both sexes have a peculiar first plumage of their own, as with the robin.

IV. When the adult male resembles the adult female, the young of both sexes in their first plumage resemble the adults, as with the kingfisher, many parrots, crows, hedge-warblers.

V. When the adults of both sexes have a distinct winter and summer plumage, whether or not the male differs from the female, the young resemble the adults of both sexes in their winter dress, or much more rarely in their summer dress, or they resemble the females alone. Or the young may have an intermediate character; or again they may differ greatly from the adults in both their seasonal plumages.

VI. In some few cases the young in their first plumage differ from each other according to sex; the young males resembling more or less closely the adult males, and the young females more or less closely the adult females.

CLASS I. In this class, the young of both sexes more or less closely resemble the adult female, whilst the adult male differs from the adult female, often in the most conspicuous manner. Innumerable instances in all Orders could be given; it will suffice to call to mind the common pheasant, duck, and house-sparrow. The cases under this class graduate into others. Thus the two sexes when adult may differ so slightly, and the young so slightly from the adults, that it is doubtful whether such cases ought to come under the present, or under the third or fourth classes. So again the young of the two sexes, instead of being quite alike, may differ in a slight degree from each other, as in our sixth class. These transitional cases, however, are few, or at least are not strongly pronounced, in comparison with those which come strictly under the present class.

The force of the present law is well shewn in those groups, in which, as a general rule, the two sexes and the young are all alike; for when in these groups the male does differ from the female, as with certain parrots, kingfishers, pigeons, &c., the young of both sexes resemble the adult female.[2] We see the same fact exhibited still more clearly in certain anomalous cases; thus the male of *Heliothrix auriculata* (one of the humming-birds) differs conspicuously from the female in having a splendid gorget and fine ear-tufts, but the female is remarkable from having a much longer tail than that of the male; now the young of both sexes resemble (with the exception of the breast being spotted with bronze) the adult female in all other respects, including the length of her tail, so that the tail of the male actually becomes shorter as he reaches maturity, which is a most unusual circumstance.[3] Again, the plumage of the male goosander (*Mergus merganser*) is more conspicuously coloured than that of the female, with the scapular and secondary wing-feathers much longer; but differently from what occurs, as far as I know, in any other bird, the crest of the adult male, though broader than that of the female, is considerably shorter, being only a little above an inch in length; the crest of the female being two and a half inches long. Now the young of both sexes entirely resemble the adult female, so that their crests are actually of greater length, though narrower, than in the adult male.[4]

When the young and the females closely resemble each other and both differ from the males, the most obvious conclusion is that the males alone have been modified. Even in the anomalous cases of the Heliothrix and Mergus, it is probable that originally both adult sexes were furnished— the one species with a much elongated tail, and the other with a much elongated crest—these characters having since been partially lost by the adult males from some unexplained cause, and transmitted in their diminished state to their male offspring alone, when arrived at the corresponding age of maturity. The belief that in the present class the male

[2] See, for instance, Mr. Gould's account ('Handbook to the Birds of Australia,' vol. i. p. 133) of Cyanalcyon (one of the Kingfishers), in which, however, the young male, though resembling the adult female, is less brilliantly coloured. In some species of Dacelo the males have blue tails, and the females brown ones; and Mr. R. B. Sharpe informs me that the tail of the young male of *D. gaudichaudi* is at first brown. Mr. Gould has described (ibid. vol. ii. pp. 14, 20, 37) the sexes and the young of certain black Cockatoos and of the King Lory, with the same rule prevails. Also Jerdon ('Birds of India,' vol. i. p. 260) on the *Palæornis rosa,* in which the young are more like the female than the male. See Audubon ('Ornith. Biograph.' vol. ii. p. 475) on the two sexes and the young of *Columba passerina.*

[3] I owe this information to Mr. Gould, who shewed me the specimens; see also his 'Introduction to the Trochilidæ,' 1861, p. 120 .

[4] Macgillivray, 'Hist. Brit. Birds,' vol. v. pp. 207-214.

alone has been modified, as far as the differences between the male and the female together with her young are concerned, is strongly supported by some remarkable facts recorded by Mr. Blyth,[5] with respect to closely-allied species which represent each other in distinct countries. For with several of these representative species the adult males have undergone a certain amount of change and can be distinguished; the females and the young from the distinct countries being indistinguishable, and therefore absolutely unchanged. This is the case with certain Indian chats (Thamnobia), with certain honey-suckers (Nectarinia), shrikes (Tephrodornis), certain kingfishers (Tanysiptera), Kalij pheasants (Gallophasis), and tree-partridges (Arboricola).

In some analogous cases, namely with birds having a different summer and winter plumage, but with the two sexes nearly alike, certain closely-allied species can easily be distinguished in their summer or nuptial plumage, yet are indistinguishable in their winter as well as in their immature plumage. This is the case with some of the closely-allied Indian wag-tails or Motacillæ. Mr. Swinhoe [6] informs me that three species of Ardeola, a genus of herons, which represent one another on separate continents, are "most strikingly different" when ornamented with their summer plumes, but are hardly, if at all, distinguishable during the winter. The young also of these three species in their immature plumage closely resemble the adults in their winter dress. This case is all the more interesting, because with two other species of Ardeola both sexes retain, during the winter and summer, nearly the same plumage as that possessed by the three first species during the winter and in their immature state; and this plumage, which is common to several distinct species at different ages and seasons, probably shews us how the progenitors of the genus were coloured. In all these cases, the nuptial plumage which we may assume was originally acquired by the adult males during the breeding-season, and transmitted to the adults of both sexes at the corresponding season, has been modified, whilst the winter and immature plumages have been left unchanged.

The question naturally arises, how is it that in these latter cases the winter plumage of both sexes, and in the former cases the plumage of the adult females, as well as the immature plumage of the young, have not been at all affected? The species which represent each other in distinct countries will almost always have been exposed to somewhat different conditions, but we can hardly attribute to this action the modification of the plumage in the males alone, seeing that the females and the young, though similarly exposed, have not been affected. Hardly any fact shews us more clearly how subordinate in importance is the direct action of the conditions of life, in comparison with the accumulation through se-

[5] See his admirable paper in the 'Journal of the Asiatic Soc. of Bengal,' vol. xix. 1850, p. 223; see also Jerdon, 'Birds of India,' vol. i. introduction, p. xxix. In regard to Tanysiptera, Prof. Schlegel told Mr. Blyth that he could distinguish several distinct races, solely by comparing the adult males.

[6] See also Mr. Swinhoe, in 'Ibis,' July 1863, p. 131; and a previous paper, with an extract from a note by Mr. Blyth, in 'Ibis,' January 1861, p. 25.

lection of indefinite variations, than the surprising difference between the sexes of many birds; for both will have consumed the same food, and have been exposed to the same climate. Nevertheless we are not precluded from believing that in the course of time new conditions may produce some direct effect either on both sexes, or from their constitutional differences chiefly on one sex. We see only that this is subordinate in importance to the accumulated results of selection. Judging, however, from a wide-spread analogy, when a species migrates into a new country (and this must precede the formation of representative species), the changed conditions to which they will almost always have been exposed will cause them to undergo a certain amount of fluctuating variability. In this case sexual selection, which depends on an element liable to change—the taste or admiration of the female—will have had new shades of colour or other differences to act on and accumulate; and as sexual selection is always at work, it would (from what we know of the results on domestic animals of man's unintentional selection), be surprising if animals inhabiting separate districts, which can never cross and thus blend their newly-acquired characters, were not, after a sufficient lapse of time, differently modified. These remarks likewise apply to the nuptial or summer plumage, whether confined to the males, or common to both sexes.

Although the females of the above closely-allied or representative species, together with their young, differ hardly at all from one another, so that the males alone can be distinguished, yet the females of most species within the same genus obviously differ from each other. The differences, however, are rarely as great as between the males. We see this clearly in the whole family of the Gallinaceæ: the females, for instance, of the common and Japan pheasant, and especially of the Gold and Amherst pheasant—of the silver pheasant and the wild fowl—resemble one another very closely in colour, whilst the males differ to an extraordinary degree. So it is with the females of most of the Cotingidæ, Fringillidæ, and many other families. There can indeed be no doubt that, as a general rule, the females have been less modified than the males. Some few birds, however, offer a singular and inexplicable exception; thus the females of *Paradisea apoda* and *P. papuana* differ from each other more than do their respective males; [7] the female of the latter species having the under surface pure white, whilst the female *P. apoda* is deep brown beneath. So, again, as I hear from Professor Newton, the males of two species of Oxynotus (shrikes), which represent each other in the islands of Mauritius and Bourbon,[8] differ but little in colour, whilst the females differ much. In the Bourbon species the female appears to have partially retained an immature condition of plumage, for at first sight she "might be taken for the young of the Mauritian species." These differences may be compared with those inexplicable ones, which occur independently of man's selec-

---

[7] Wallace, 'The Malay Archipelago,' vol. ii. 1869, p. 394.

[8] These species are described with coloured figures, by M. F. Pollen, in 'Ibis,' 1866, p. 275.

tion in certain sub-breeds of the game-fowl, in which the females are very different, whilst the males can hardly be distinguished.[9]

As I account so largely by sexual selection for the differences between the males of allied species, how can the differences between the females be accounted for in all ordinary cases? We need not here consider the species which belong to distinct genera; for with these, adaptation to different habits of life, and other agencies, will have come into play. In regard to the differences between the females within the same genus, it appears to me almost certain, after looking through various large groups, that the chief agent has been the greater or less transference to the female of the characters acquired by the males through sexual selection. In the several British finches, the two sexes differ either very slightly or considerably; and if we compare the females of the greenfinch, chaffinch, goldfinch, bullfinch, crossbill, sparrow, &c., we shall see that they differ from one another chiefly in the points in which they partially resemble their respective males; and the colours of the males may safely be attributed to sexual selection. With many gallinaceous species the sexes differ to an extreme degree, as with the peacock, pheasant, and fowl, whilst with other species there has been a partial or even complete transference of character from the male to the female. The females of the several species of Polyplectron exhibit in a dim condition, and chiefly on the tail, the splendid ocelli of their males. The female partridge differs from the male only in the red mark on her breast being smaller; and the female wild turkey only in her colours being much duller. In the guinea-fowl the two sexes are indistinguishable. There is no improbability in the plain, though peculiarly spotted plumage of this latter bird having been acquired through sexual selection by the males, and then transmitted to both sexes; for it is not essentially different from the much more beautifully spotted plumage, characteristic of the males alone of the Tragopan pheasants.

It should be observed that, in some instances, the transference of characters from the male to the female has been effected apparently at a remote period, the male having subsequently undergone great changes, without transferring to the female any of his later-gained characters. For instance, the female and the young of the black-grouse (*Tetrao tetrix*) resemble pretty closely both sexes and the young of the red-grouse (*T. scoticus*); and we may consequently infer that the black-grouse is descended from some ancient species, of which both sexes were coloured in nearly the same manner as the red-grouse. As both sexes of this latter species are more distinctly barred during the breeding season than at any other time, and as the male differs slightly from the female in his more strongly-pronounced red and brown tints,[10] we may conclude that his plumage has been influenced by sexual selection, at least to a certain extent. If so, we may further infer that the nearly similar plumage of the female black-grouse was similarly produced at some former period. But since this period the male black-grouse has acquired his fine black plum-

[9] 'Variation of Animals, &c.,' i. 251.
[10] Macgillivray, 'Hist. Brit. Birds,' vol. i. pp. 172-174.

age, with his forked and outwardly-curled tail-feathers; but of these characters there has hardly been any transference to the female, excepting that she shews in her tail a trace of the curved fork.

We may therefore conclude that the females of distinct though allied species have often had their plumage rendered more or less different by the transference in various degrees of characters acquired by the males through sexual selection, both during former and recent times. But it deserves especial attention that brilliant colours have been transferred much more rarely than other tints. For instance, the male of the red-throated blue-breast (*Cyanecula suecica*) has a rich blue breast, including a sub-triangular red mark; now marks of nearly the same shape have been transferred to the female, but the central space is fulvous instead of red, and is surrounded by mottled instead of blue feathers. The Gallina-ceæ offer many analogous cases; for none of the species, such as par-tridges, quails, guinea-fowls, &c., in which the colours of the plumage have been largely transferred from the male to the female, are brilliantly coloured. This is well exemplified with the pheasants, in which the male is generally so much more brilliant than the female; but with the Eared and Cheer pheasants (*Crossoptilon auritum* and *Phasianus wallichii*) the sexes closely resemble each other and their colours are dull. We may go so far as to believe that if any part of the plumage in the males of these two pheasants had been brilliantly coloured, it would not have been trans-ferred to the females. These facts strongly support Mr. Wallace's view that with birds which are exposed to much danger during incubation, the transference of bright colours from the male to the female has been checked through natural selection. We must not, however, forget that an-other explanation, before given, is possible; namely, that the males which varied and became bright, whilst they were young and inexperienced, would have been exposed to much danger, and would generally have been destroyed; the older and more cautious males, on the other hand, if they varied in a like manner, would not only have been able to survive, but would have been favoured in their rivalry with other males. Now varia-tions occurring late in life tend to be transmitted exclusively to the same sex, so that in this case extremely bright tints would not have been trans-mitted to the females. On the other hand, ornaments of a less conspicuous kind, such as those possessed by the Eared and Cheer pheasants, would not have been dangerous, and if they appeared during early youth, would generally have been transmitted to both sexes.

In addition to the effects of the partial transference of characters from the males to the females, some of the differences between the females of closely-allied species may be attributed to the direct or definite action of the conditions of life.[11] With the males, any such action would generally have been masked by the brilliant colours gained through sexual selec-tion; but not so with the females. Each of the endless diversities in plum-age which we see in our domesticated birds is, of course, the result of

---

[11] See, on this subject, chap. xxiii. in the 'Variation of Animals and Plants under Domestication.'

some definite cause; and under natural and more uniform conditions, some one tint, assuming that it was in no way injurious, would almost certainly sooner or later prevail. The free intercrossing of the many individuals belonging to the same species would ultimately tend to make any change of colour, thus induced, uniform in character.

No one doubts that both sexes of many birds have had their colours adapted for the sake of protection; and it is possible that the females alone of some species may have been modified for this end. Although it would be a difficult, perhaps an impossible process, as shewn in the last chapter, to convert one form of transmission into another through selection, there would not be the least difficulty in adapting the colours of the female, independently of those of the male, to surrounding objects, through the accumulation of variations which were from the first limited in their transmission to the female sex. If the variations were not thus limited, the bright tints of the male would be deteriorated or destroyed. Whether the females alone of many species have been thus specially modified, is at present very doubtful. I wish I could follow Mr. Wallace to the full extent; for the admission would remove some difficulties. Any variations which were of no service to the female as a protection would be at once obliterated, instead of being lost simply by not being selected, or from free intercrossing, or from being eliminated when transferred to the male and in any way injurious to him. Thus the plumage of the female would be kept constant in character. It would also be a relief if we could admit that the obscure tints of both sexes of many birds had been acquired and preserved for the sake of protection,—for example, of the hedge-warbler or kitty-wren (*Accentor modularis* and *Troglodytes vulgaris*), with respect to which we have no sufficient evidence of the action of sexual selection. We ought, however, to be cautious in concluding that colours which appear to us dull, are not attractive to the females of certain species; we should bear in mind such cases as that of the common house-sparrow, in which the male differs much from the female, but does not exhibit any bright tints. No one probably will dispute that many gallinaceous birds which live on the open ground, have acquired their present colours, at least in part, for the sake of protection. We know how well they are thus concealed; we know that ptarmigans, whilst changing from their winter to their summer plumage, both of which are protective, suffer greatly from birds of prey. But can we believe that the very slight differences in tints and markings between, for instance, the female blackgrouse and red-grouse serve as a protection? Are partridges, as they are now coloured, better protected than if they had resembled quails? Do the slight differences between the females of the common pheasant, the Japan and gold pheasants, serve as a protection, or might not their plumages have been interchanged with impunity? From what Mr. Wallace has observed of the habits of certain gallinaceous birds in the East, he thinks that such slight differences are beneficial. For myself, I will only say that I am not convinced.

Formerly when I was inclined to lay much stress on protection as accounting for the duller colours of female birds, it occurred to me that possibly both sexes and the young might aboriginally have been equally bright coloured; but that subsequently, the females from the danger incurred during incubation, and the young from being inexperienced, had been rendered dull as a protection. But this view is not supported by any evidence, and is not probable; for we thus in imagination expose during past times the females and the young to danger, from which it has subsequently been necessary to shield their modified descendants. We have, also, to reduce, through a gradual process of selection, the females and the young to almost exactly the same tints and markings, and to transmit them to the corresponding sex and period of life. On the supposition that the females and the young have partaken during each stage of the process of modification of a tendency to be as brightly coloured as the males, it is also a somewhat strange fact that the females have never been rendered dull-coloured without the young participating in the same change; for there are no instances, as far as I can discover, of species with the females dull and the young bright coloured. A partial exception, however, is offered by the young of certain woodpeckers, for they have "the whole upper part of the head tinged with red," which afterwards either decreases into a mere circular red line in the adults of both sexes, or quite disappears in the adult females.[12]

Finally, with respect to our present class of cases, the most probable view appears to be that successive variations in brightness or in other ornamental characters, occurring in the males at a rather late period of life have alone been preserved; and that most or all of these variations, owing to the late period of life at which they appeared, have been from the first transmitted only to the adult male offspring. Any variations in brightness occurring in the females or in the young, would have been of no service to them, and would not have been selected; and moreover, if dangerous, would have been eliminated. Thus the females and the young will either have been left unmodified, or (as is much more common) will have been partially modified by receiving through transference from the males some of his successive variations. Both sexes have perhaps been directly acted on by the conditions of life to which they have long been exposed: but the females from not being otherwise much modified, will best exhibit any such effects. These changes and all others will have been kept uniform by the free intercrossing of many individuals. In some cases, especially with ground birds, the females and the young may possibly have been modified, independently of the males, for the sake of protection, so as to have acquired the same dull-coloured plumage.

CLASS II.   *When the adult female is more conspicuous than the adult male, the young of both sexes in their first plumage resemble the adult male.*—This class is exactly the reverse of the last, for the females are here brighter coloured or more conspicuous than the males; and the young, as far as they are known, resemble the adult males instead of the adult females. But the difference between the sexes is never nearly so

---

[12] Audubon, 'Ornith. Biography,' vol. i. p. 193. Macgillivray, 'Hist. Brit. Birds,' vol. iii. p. 85. See also the case before given of *Indopicus carlotta*.

great as with many birds in the first class, and the cases are comparatively rare. Mr. Wallace, who first called attention to the singular relation
which exists between the less bright colours of the males and their performing the duties of incubation, lays great stress on this point,[13] as a
crucial test that obscure colours have been acquired for the sake of protection during the period of nesting. A different view seems to me more
probable. As the cases are curious and not numerous, I will briefly give all
that I have been able to find.

In one section of the genus Turnix, quail-like birds, the female is invariably larger than the male (being nearly twice as large in one of the
Australian species), and this is an unusual circumstance with the Gallinaceæ. In most of the species the female is more distinctly coloured and
brighter than the male,[14] but in some few species the sexes are alike. In
Turnix taigoor of India the male "wants the black on the throat and
neck, and the whole tone of the plumage is lighter and less pronounced
than that of the female." The female appears to be noisier, and is certainly much more pugnacious than the male; so that the females and not the
males are often kept by the natives for fighting, like game-cocks. As male
birds are exposed by the English bird-catchers for a decoy near a trap, in
order to catch other males by exciting their rivalry, so the females of this
Turnix are employed in India. When thus exposed the females soon begin
their "loud purring call, which can be heard a long way off, and any females within ear-shot run rapidly to the spot, and commence fighting
with the caged bird." In this way from twelve to twenty birds, all breeding females, may be caught in the course of a single day. The natives assert that the females after laying their eggs associate in flocks, and leave
the males to sit on them. There is no reason to doubt the truth of this assertion, which is supported by some observations made in China by Mr.
Swinhoe.[15] Mr. Blyth believes, that the young of both sexes resemble the
adult male.

The females of the three species of Painted Snipes (Rhynchæa, fig. 62)
"are not only larger but much more richly coloured than the males."[16]
With all other birds in which the trachea differs in structure in the two
sexes it is more developed and complex in the male than in the female;
but in the *Rhynchæa australis* it is simple in the male, whilst in the female it makes four distinct convolutions before entering the lungs.[17] The
female therefore of this species has acquired an eminently masculine
character. Mr. Blyth ascertained, by examining many specimens, that the
trachea is not convoluted in either sex of *R. bengalensis*, which species resembles *R. australis* so closely, that it can hardly be distinguished except

[13] 'Westminster Review,' July 1867, and A. Murray, 'Journal of Travel,' 1868, p. 83.
[14] For the Australian species, see Gould's 'Handbook,' &c., vol. ii. pp. 178, 180, 186,
and 188. In the British Museum specimens of the Australian Plain-wanderer (*Pedi-
onomus torquatus*) may be seen, shewing similar sexual differences.
[15] Jerdon, 'Birds of India,' vol. iii. p. 596. Mr. Swinhoe, in 'Ibis,' 1865, p. 542;
1866, pp. 131, 405.
[16] Jerdon, 'Birds of India,' vol. iii. p. 677.
[17] Gould's 'Handbook to the Birds of Australia,' vol. ii. p. 275.

by its shorter toes. This fact is another striking instance of the law that secondary sexual characters are often widely different in closely-allied forms, though it is a very rare circumstance when such differences relate to the female sex. The young of both sexes of *R. bengalensis* in their first plumage are said to resemble the mature male.[18] There is also reason to believe that the male undertakes the duty of incubation, for Mr. Swin-

FIG. 62.—Rhynchæa capensis (from Brehm).

hoe[19] found the females before the close of the summer associated in flocks, as occurs with the females of the Turnix.

The females of *Phalaropus fulicarius* and *P. hyperboreus* are larger, and in their summer plumage "more gaily attired than the males." But the difference in colour between the sexes is far from conspicuous. According to Professor Steenstrup, the male alone of *P. fulicarius* undertakes the duty of incubation; this is likewise shewn by the state of his breast-feathers during the breeding-season. The female of the dotterel plover (*Eudromias morinellus*) is larger than the male, and has the red and black tints on the lower surface, the white crescent on the breast, and

18 'The Indian Field,' Sept. 1858, p. 3.
19 'Ibis,' 1866, p. 298.

the stripes over the eyes, more strongly pronounced. The male also takes at least a share in hatching the eggs; but the female likewise attends to the young.[20] I have not been able to discover whether with these species the young resemble the adult males more closely than the adult females; for the comparison is somewhat difficult to make on account of the double moult.

Turning now to the Ostrich order: the male of the common cassowary (*Casuarius galeatus*) would be thought by any one to be the female, from his smaller size and from the appendages and naked skin about his head being much less brightly coloured; and I am informed by Mr. Bartlett that in the Zoological Gardens, it is certainly the male alone who sits on the eggs and takes care of the young.[21] The female is said by Mr. T. W. Wood [22] to exhibit during the breeding-season a most pugnacious disposition; and her wattles then become enlarged and more brilliantly coloured. So again the female of one of the emus (*Dromæus irroratus*) is considerably larger than the male, and she possesses a slight top-knot, but is otherwise indistinguishable in plumage. She appears, however, "to have greater power, when angry or otherwise excited, of erecting, like a turkey-cock, the feathers of her neck and breast. She is usually the more courageous and pugilistic. She makes a deep hollow guttural boom especially at night, sounding like a small gong. The male has a slenderer frame and is more docile, with no voice beyond a suppressed hiss when angry, or a croak." He not only performs the whole duty of incubation, but has to defend the young from their mother; "for as soon as she catches sight of her progeny she becomes violently agitated, and notwithstanding the resistance of the father appears to use her utmost endeavours to destroy them. For months afterwards it is unsafe to put the parents together, violent quarrels being the inevitable result, in which the female generally comes off conqueror."[23] So that with this emu we have a complete reversal not only of the parental and incubating instincts, but of the usual moral qualities of the two sexes; the females being savage, quarrelsome, and noisy, the males gentle and good. The case is very different with the African ostrich, for the male is somewhat larger than the female and has finer plumes with more strongly contrasted colours; nevertheless he undertakes the whole duty of incubation.[24]

[20] For these several statements, see Mr. Gould's 'Birds of Great Britain.' Prof. Newton informs me that he has long been convinced, from his own observations and from those of others, that the males of the above-named species take either the whole or a large share of the duties of incubation, and that they "shew much greater devotion towards their young, when in danger, than do the females." So it is, as he informs me, with *Limosa lapponica* and some few other Waders, in which the females are larger and have more strongly contrasted colours than the males.

[21] The natives of Ceram (Wallace, 'Malay Archipelago,' vol. ii. p. 150) assert that the male and female sit alternately on the eggs; but this assertion, as Mr. Bartlett thinks, may be accounted for by the female visiting the nest to lay her eggs.

[22] 'The Student,' April 1870, p. 124.

[23] See the excellent account of the habits of this bird under confinement, by Mr. A. W. Bennett, in 'Land and Water,' May 1868, p. 233.

[24] Mr. Sclater, on the incubation of the Struthiones, 'Proc. Zool. Soc.,' June 9, 1863. So it is with the *Rhea darwinii:* Captain Musters says ('At Home with the

I will specify the few other cases known to me, in which the female is more conspicuously coloured than the male, although nothing is known about the manner of incubation. With the carrion-hawk of the Falkland Islands (*Milvago leucurus*) I was much surprised to find by dissection that the individuals, which had all their tints strongly pronounced, with the cere and legs orange-coloured, were the adult females; whilst those with duller plumage and grey legs were the males or the young. In an Australian tree-creeper (*Climacteris erythrops*) the female differs from the male in "being adorned with beautiful, radiated, rufous markings on the throat, the male having this part quite plain." Lastly, in an Australian night-jar "the female always exceeds the male in size and in the brilliance of her tints; the males, on the other hand, have two white spots on the primaries more conspicuous than in the female." [25]

We thus see that the cases in which female birds are more conspicuously coloured than the males, with the young in their immature plumage resembling the adult males instead of the adult females, as in the previous class, are not numerous, though they are distributed in various Orders. The amount of difference, also, between the sexes is incomparably less than that which frequently occurs in the last class; so that the cause of the difference, whatever it may have been, has here acted on the females either less energetically or less persistently than on the males in the last class. Mr. Wallace believes that the males have had their colours rendered less conspicuous for the sake of protection during the period of incubation; but the difference between the sexes in hardly any of the foregoing cases appears sufficiently great for this view to be safely accepted. In some of the cases, the brighter tints of the female are almost confined to the lower surface, and the males, if thus coloured, would not have been exposed to danger whilst sitting on the eggs. It should also be borne in mind that the males are not only in a slight degree less conspicuously coloured than the females, but are smaller and weaker. They have, moreover, not only acquired the maternal instinct of incubation, but are less pugnacious and vociferous than the females, and in one instance have simpler vocal organs. Thus an almost complete transposition of the instincts, habits, disposition, colour, size, and of some points of structure, has been effected between the two sexes.

Patagonians,' 1871, p. 128), that the male is larger, stronger and swifter than the female, and of slightly darker colours; yet he takes sole charge of the eggs and of the young, just as does the male of the common species of Rhea.

[25] For the Milvago, see 'Zoology of the Voyage of the Beagle,' Birds, 1841, p. 16. For the Climacteris and Nightjar (Eurostopodus), see Gould's 'Handbook to the Birds of Australia,' vol. i. pp. 602 and 97. The new Zealand shieldrake (*Tadorna variegata*) offers a quite anomalous case; the head of the female is pue white, and her back is redder than that of the male; the head of the male is of a rich dark bronzed colour, and his back is clothed with finely pencilled slate-coloured feathers, so that altogether he may be considered as the more beautiful of the two. He is larger and more pugnacious than the female, and does not sit on the eggs. So that in all these respects this species comes under our first class of cases; but Mr. Sclater ('Proc. Zool. Soc.' 1866, p. 150) was much surprised to observe that the young of both sexes, when about three months old, resembled in their dark heads and necks the adult

Now if we might assume that the males in the present class have lost some of that ardour which is usual to their sex, so that they no longer search eagerly for the females; or, if we might assume that the females have become much more numerous than the males—and in the case of one Indian Turnix the females are said to be "much more commonly met with than the males" [26]—then it is not improbable that the females would have been led to court the males, instead of being courted by them. This indeed is the case to a certain extent with some birds, as we have seen with the peahen, wild turkey, and certain kinds of grouse. Taking as our guide the habits of most male birds, the greater size and strength as well as the extraordinary pugnacity of the females of the Turnix and emu, must mean that they endeavour to drive away rival females, in order to gain possession of the male; and on this view all the facts become clear; for the males would probably be most charmed or excited by the females which were the most attractive to them by their bright colours, other ornaments, or vocal powers. Sexual selection would then do its work, steadily adding to the attractions of the females; the males and the young being left not at all, or but little modified.

CLASS III. *When the adult male resembles the adult female, the young of both sexes have a peculiar first plumage of their own.*—In this class the sexes when adult resemble each other, and differ from the young. This occurs with many birds of many kinds. The male robin can hardly be distinguished from the female, but the young are widely different, with their mottled dusky-olive and brown plumage. The male and female of the splendid scarlet ibis are alike, whilst the young are brown; and the scarlet colour, though common to both sexes, is apparently a sexual character, for it is not well developed in either sex under confinement; and a loss of colour often occurs with brilliant males when they are confined. With many species of herons the young differ greatly from the adults; and the summer plumage of the latter, though common to both sexes, clearly has a nuptial character. Young swans are slate-coloured, whilst the mature birds are pure white; but it would be superfluous to give additional instances. These differences between the young and the old apparently depend, as in the last two classes, on the young having retained a former or ancient state of plumage, whilst the old of both sexes have acquired a new one. When the adults are bright coloured, we may conclude from the remarks just made in relation to the scarlet ibis and to many herons, and from the analogy of the species in the first class, that such colours have been acquired through sexual selection by the nearly mature males; but that, differently from what occurs in the first two classes, the transmission, though limited to the same age, has not been limited to the same sex. Consequently, the sexes when mature resemble each other and differ from the young.

males, instead of the adult females; so that it would appear in this case that the females have been modified, whilst the males and the young have retained a former state of plumage.

[26] Jerdon, 'Birds of India,' vol. iii. p. 598.

CLASS IV. *When the adult male resembles the adult female, the young of both sexes in their first plumage resemble the adults.*—In this class the young and the adults of both sexes, whether brilliantly or obscurely coloured, resemble each other. Such cases are, I think, more common than those in the last class. We have in England instances in the kingfisher, some woodpeckers, the jay, magpie, crow, and many small dull-coloured birds, such as the hedge-warbler or kitty-wren. But the similarity in plumage between the young and the old is never complete, and graduates away into dissimilarity. Thus the young of some members of the kingfisher family are not only less vividly coloured than the adults, but many of the feathers on the lower surface are edged with brown,[27]—a vestige probably of a former state of the plumage. Frequently in the same group of birds, even within the same genus, for instance in an Australian genus of parrakeets (Platycercus), the young of some species closely resemble, whilst the young of other species differ considerably, from their parents of both sexes, which are alike.[28] Both sexes and the young of the common jay are closely similar; but in the Canada jay (*Perisoreus canadensis*) the young differ so much from their parents that they were formerly described as distinct species.[29]

I may remark before proceeding that, under the present and next two classes of cases, the facts are so complex and the conclusions so doubtful, that any one who feels no especial interest in the subject had better pass them over.

The brilliant or conspicuous colours which characterise many birds in the present class, can rarely or never be of service to them as a protection; so that they have probably been gained by the males through sexual selection, and then transferred to the females and the young. It is, however, possible that the males may have selected the more attractive females; and if these transmitted their characters to their offspring of both sexes, the same results would follow as from the selection of the more attractive males by the females. But there is evidence that this contingency has rarely, if ever, occurred in any of those groups of birds in which the sexes are generally alike; for, if even a few of the successive variations had failed to be transmitted to both sexes, the females would have slightly exceeded the males in beauty. Exactly the reverse occurs under nature; for, in almost every group in which the sexes generally resemble each other, the males of some few species are in a slight degree more brightly coloured than the females. It is again possible that the females may have selected the more beautiful males, these males having reciprocally selected the more beautiful females; but it is doubtful whether this double process of selection would be likely to occur, owing to the greater eagerness of one sex than the other, and whether it would be more efficient than selection on one side alone. It is, therefore, the most probable view that sexual selection has acted, in the present class, as far as ornamental characters are concerned, in accordance with the general rule throughout the animal kingdom, that is, on the males; and that these have transmitted their grad-

[27] Jerdon, 'Birds of India,' vol. i. pp. 222, 228. Gould's 'Handbook to the Birds of Australia,' vol. i. pp. 124, 130.

[28] Gould, ibid. vol. ii. pp. 37, 46, 56.

[29] Audubon, 'Ornith. Biography,' vol. ii. p. 55.

ually-acquired colours, either equally or almost equally, to their offspring of both sexes.

Another point is more doubtful, namely, whether the successive variations first appeared in the males after they had become nearly mature, or whilst quite young. In either case sexual selection must have acted on the male when he had to compete with rivals for the possession of the female; and in both cases the characters thus acquired have been transmitted to both sexes and all ages. But these characters if acquired by the males when adult, may have been transmitted at first to the adults alone, and at some subsequent period transferred to the young. For it is known that, when the law of inheritance at corresponding ages fails, the offspring often inherit characters at an earlier age than that at which they first appeared in their parents.[30] Cases apparently of this kind have been observed with birds in a state of nature. For instance Mr. Blyth has seen specimens of *Lanius rufus* and of *Colymbus glacialis* which had assumed whilst young, in a quite anomalous manner, the adult plumage of their parents.[31] Again, the young of the common swan (*Cygnus olor*) do not cast off their dark feathers and become white until eighteen months or two years old; but Dr. F. Forel has described the case of three vigorous young birds, out of a brood of four, which were born pure white. These young birds were not albinos, as shewn by the color of their beaks and legs, which nearly resembled the same parts in the adults.[32]

It may be worth while to illustrate the above three modes by which, in the present class, the two sexes and the young may have come to resemble each other, by the curious case of the genus Passer.[33] In the house-sparrow (*P. domesticus*) the male differs much from the female and from the young. The young and the females are alike, and resemble to a large extent both sexes and the young of the sparrow of Palestine (*P. brachydactylus*), as well as of some allied species. We may therefore assume that the female and young of the house-sparrow approximately shew us the plumage of the progenitor of the genus. Now with the tree-sparrow (*P. montanus*) both sexes and the young closely resemble the male of the house-sparrow; so that they have all been modified in the same manner, and all depart from the typical colouring of their early progenitor. This may have been effected by a male ancestor of the tree-sparrow having varied, firstly, when nearly mature; or, secondly, whilst quite young, and by having in either case transmitted his modified plumage to the females and the young; or, thirdly, he may have varied when adult and transmitted his plumage to both adult sexes, and, owing to the failure of the law of inheritance at corresponding ages, at some subsequent period to his young.

It is impossible to decide which of these three modes has generally prevailed throughout the present class of cases. That the males varied whilst young, and transmitted their variations to their offspring of both sexes, is the most probable. I may here add that I have, with little success, endeavoured, by consulting various works, to decide how far the period of variation in birds has generally determined the transmission of characters to one sex or to both.

---

[30] 'Variation of Animals and Plants under Domestication,' vol. ii. p. 79.

[31] Charlesworth's 'Mag. of Nat. Hist.' vol. i. 1837, pp. 305, 306.

[32] 'Bulletin de la Soc. Vaudoise des Sc. Nat.' vol. x. 1869, p. 132. The young of the Polish swan, *Cygnus immutabilis* of Yarrell, are always white; but this species, as Mr. Sclater informs me, is believed to be nothing more than a variety of the domestic swan (*Cygnus olor*).

[33] I am indebted to Mr. Blyth for information in regard to this genus. The sparrow of Palestine belongs to the sub-genus Petronia.

The two rules, often referred to (namely, that variations occurring late in life are transmitted to one and the same sex, whilst those which occur early in life are transmitted to both sexes), apparently hold good in the first,[34] second, and fourth classes of cases; but they fail in the third, often in the fifth,[35] and in the sixth small class. They apply, however, as far as I can judge, to a considerable majority of the species; and we must not forget the striking generalisation by Dr. W. Marshall with respect to the protuberances on the heads of birds. Whether or not the two rules generally hold good, we may conclude from the facts given in the eighth chapter, that the period of variation is one important element in determining the form of transmission.

With birds it is difficult to decide by what standard we ought to judge of the earliness or lateness of the period of variation, whether by the age in reference to the duration of life, or to the power of reproduction, or to the number of moults through which the species passes. The moulting of birds, even within the same family, sometimes differs much without any assignable cause. Some birds moult so early, that nearly all the body feathers are cast off before the first wing-feathers are fully grown; and we cannot believe that this was the primordial state of things. When the period of moulting has been accelerated, the age at which the colours of the adult plumage are first developed will falsely appear to us to be earlier than it really is. This may be illustrated by the practice followed by some bird-fanciers, who pull out a few feathers from the breast of nestling bullfinches, and from the head or neck of young gold-pheasants, in order to ascertain their sex; for in the males, these feathers are immediately replaced by coloured ones.[36] The actual duration of life is known in but few birds, so that we can hardly judge by this standard. And, with reference to the period at which the power of reproduction is gained, it is a remarkable fact that various birds occasionally breed whilst retaining their immature plumage.[37]

The fact of birds breeding in their immature plumage seems opposed to the

---

[34] For instance, the males of *Tanagra œstiva* and *Fringilla cyanea* require three years, the male of *Fringilla ciris* four years, to complete their beautiful plumage. (See Audubon, 'Ornith. Biography,' vol. i. pp. 233, 280, 378.) The Harlequin duck takes three years (ibid. vol. iii. p. 614). The male of the Gold pheasant, as I hear from Mr. Jenner Weir, can be distinguished from the female when about three months old, but he does not acquire his full splendour until the end of the September in the following year.

[35] Thus the *Ibis tantalus* and *Grus americanus* take four years, the Flamingo several years, and the *Ardea ludovicana* two years, before they acquire their perfect plumage. See Audubon, ibid. vol. i. p. 221; vol. iii. pp. 133, 139, 211.

[36] Mr. Blyth, in Charlesworth's 'Mag. of Nat. Hist.' vol. i. 1837, p. 300. Mr. Bartlett has informed me in regard to gold-pheasants.

[37] I have noticed the following cases in Audubon's 'Ornith Biography.' The redstart of America (*Muscapica ruticilla,* vol. i. p. 203). The *Ibis tantalus* takes four years to come to full maturity, but sometimes breeds in the second year (vol. iii. p. 133). The *Grus americanus* takes the same time, but breeds before acquiring its full plumage (vol. iii. p. 211). The adults of *Ardea cœrulea* are blue, and the young white; and white, mottled, and mature blue birds may all be seen breeding together (vol. iv. p. 58): but Mr. Blyth informs me that certain herons apparently are dimorphic, for white and coloured individuals of the same age may be observed. The Harlequin duck (*Anas histrionica,* Linn.) takes three years to acquire its full plumage, though many birds breed in the second year (vol. iii. p. 614). The White-headed Eagle (*Falco leucocephalus,* vol. iii. p. 210) is likewise known to breed in its immature state. Some species of Oriolus (according to Mr. Blyth and Mr. Swinhoe, in 'Ibis,' July 1863, p. 68) likewise breed before they attain their full plumage.

belief that sexual selection has played as important a part, as I believe it has, in giving ornamental colours, plumes, &c., to the males, and, by means of equal transmission, to the females of many species. The objection would be a valid one, if the younger and less ornamental males were as successful in winning females and propagating their kind, as the older and more beautiful males. But we have no reason to suppose that this is the case. Audubon speaks of the breeding of the immature males of *Ibis tantalus* as a rare event, as does Mr. Swinhoe, in regard to the immature males of Oriolus.[38] If the young of any species in their immature plumage were more successful in winning partners than the adults, the adult plumage would probably soon be lost, as the males would prevail, which retained their immature dress for the longest period, and thus the character of the species would ultimately be modified.[39] If, on the other hand, the young never succeeded in obtaining a female, the habit of early reproduction would perhaps be sooner or later eliminated, from being superfluous and entailing waste of power.

The plumage of certain birds goes on increasing in beauty during many years after they are fully mature; this is the case with the train of the peacock, with some of the birds of paradise, and with the crest and plumes of certain herons, for instance, the *Ardea ludoviciana*.[40] But it is doubtful whether the continued development of such feathers is the result of the selection of successive beneficial variations (though this is the most probable view with birds of paradise) or merely of continuous growth. Most fishes continue increasing in size, as long as they are in good health and have plenty of food; and a somewhat similar law may prevail with the plumes of birds.

CLASS V. *When the adults of both sexes have a distinct winter and summer plumage, whether or not the male differs from the female, the young resemble the adults of both sexes in their winter dress, or much more rarely in their summer dress, or they resemble the females alone. Or the young may have an intermediate character; or, again, they may differ greatly from the adults in both their seasonal plumages.*—The cases in this class are singularly complex; nor is this surprising, as they depend on inheritance, limited in a greater or less degree in three different ways, namely, by sex, age, and the season of the year. In some cases the individuals of the same species pass through at least five distinct states of plumage. With the species, in which the male differs from the female during the summer season alone, or, which is rarer, during both seasons,[41] the young generally resemble the females,—as with the so-

---

[38] See the last foot-note.

[39] Other animals, belonging to quite distinct classes, are either habitually or occasionally capable of breeding before they have fully acquired their adult characters. This is the case with the young males of the salmon. Several amphibians have been known to breed whilst retaining their larval structure. Fritz Müller has shewn ('Facts and arguments for Darwin,' Eng. trans. 1869, p. 79) that the males of several amphipod crustaceans become sexually mature whilst young; and I infer that this is a case of premature breeding, because they have not as yet acquired their fully-developed claspers. All such facts are highly interesting, as bearing on one means by which species may undergo great modifications of character.

[40] Jerdon, 'Birds of India,' vol. iii. p. 507, on the peacock. Dr. Marshall thinks that the older and more brilliant males of birds of paradise, have an advantage over the younger males; see 'Archives Néerlandaises,' tom. vi. 1871.—On Ardea, Audubon, ibid. vol. iii. p. 139.

[41] For illustrative cases see vol. iv. of Macgillivray's 'Hist. Brit. Birds;' on Tringa, &c., pp. 229, 271; on the Machetes, p. 172; on the *Charadrius hiaticula*, p. 118; on the *Charadrius pluvialis*, p. 94.

called goldfinch of North America, and apparently with the splendid Maluri of Australia.[42] With these species, the sexes of which are alike during both the summer and winter, the young may resemble the adults, firstly, in their winter dress; secondly, and this is of much rarer occurrence, in their summer dress; thirdly, they may be intermediate between these two states; and, fourthly, they may differ greatly from the adults at all seasons. We have an instance of the first of these four cases in one of the egrets of India (*Buphus coromandus*), in which the young and the adults of both sexes are white during the winter, the adults becoming golden-buff during the summer. With the gaper (*Anastomus oscitans*) of India we have a similar case, but the colours are reversed: for the young and the adults of both sexes are grey and black during the winter, the adults becoming white during the summer.[43] As an instance of the second case, the young of the razor-bill (*Alca torda*, Linn.), in an early state of plumage, are coloured like the adults during the summer; and the young of the white-crowned sparrow of North America (*Fringilla leucophrys*), as soon as fledged, have elegant white stripes on their heads, which are lost by the young and the old during the winter.[44] With respect to the third case, namely, that of the young having an intermediate character between the summer and winter adult plumages, Yarrell[45] insists that this occurs with many waders. Lastly, in regard to the young differing greatly from both sexes in their adult summer and winter plumages, this occurs with some herons and egrets of North America and India,—the young alone being white.

I will make only a few remarks on these complicated cases. When the young resemble the females in their summer dress, or the adults of both sexes in their winter dress, the cases differ from those given under Classes I. and III. only in the characters originally acquired by the males during the breeding-season, having been limited in their transmission to the corresponding season. When the adults have a distinct summer and winter plumage, and the young differ from both, the case is more difficult to understand. We may admit as probable that the young have retained an ancient state of plumage; we can account by sexual selection for the summer or nuptial plumage of the adults, but how are we to account for their distinct winter plumage? If we could admit that this plumage serves in all cases as a protection, its acquirement would be a simple affair; but there seems no good reason for this admission. It may be suggested that the widely different conditions of life during the winter and summer have acted in a direct manner on the plumage; this may have had some effect, but I have not much confidence in so great a difference as we sometimes see between the two plumages, having been thus caused. A more probable explanation is, that an ancient style of plumage, partially modified through the transference of some characters from the summer plumage, has been retained by the adults during the winter. Finally, all the cases in our present class apparently depend on characters acquired by the adult males, having been variously limited in their transmission according to age,

[42] For the goldfinch of N. America, *Fringilla tristis*, Linn., see Audubon, 'Ornith. Biography,' vol. i. p. 172. For the Maluri, Gould's 'Handbook to the Birds of Australia,' vol. i. p. 318.

[43] I am indebted to Mr. Blyth for information as to the Buphus; see also Jerdon, 'Birds of India,' vol. iii. p. 749. On the Anastomus, see Blyth, in 'Ibis,' 1867, p. 173.

[44] On the Alca, see Macgillivray, 'Hist. Brit. Birds,' vol. v. p. 347. On the *Fringilla leucophrys*, Audubon, ibid. vol. ii. p. 89. I shall have hereafter to refer to the young of certain herons and egrets being white.

[45] 'History of British Birds,' vol. i. 1839, p. 159.

season, and sex; but it would not be worth while to attempt to follow out these complex relations.

CLASS VI. *The young in their first plumage differ from each other according to sex; the young males resembling more or less closely the adult males, and the young females more or less closely the adult females.*—The cases in the present class, though occurring in various groups, are not numerous; yet it seems the most natural thing that the young should at first somewhat resemble the adults of the same sex, and gradually become more and more like them. The adult male blackcap (*Sylvia atricapilla*) has a black head, that of the female being reddish-brown; and I am informed by Mr. Blyth, that the young of both sexes can be distinguished by this character even as nestlings. In the family of thrushes an unusual number of similar cases have been noticed; thus, the male blackbird (*Turdus merula*) can be distinguished in the nest from the female. The two sexes of the mocking bird (*Turdus polyglottus*, Linn.) differ very little from each other, yet the males can easily be distinguished at a very early age from the females by showing more pure white.[46] The males of a forest-thrush and of a rock-thrush (*Orocetes erythrogastra* and *Petrocincla cyanea*) have much of their plumage of a fine blue, whilst the females are brown; and the nestling males of both species have their main wing and tailfeathers edged with blue whilst those of the female are edged with brown.[47] In the young blackbird the wing-feathers assume their mature character and become black after the others; on the other hand, in the two species just named the wing-feathers become blue before the others. The most probable view with reference to the cases in the present class is that the males, differently from what occurs in Class I., have transmitted their colours to their male offspring at an earlier age than that at which they were first acquired; for, if the males had varied whilst quite young, their characters would probably have been transmitted to both sexes.[48]

In *Aïthurus polytmus*, a humming-bird, the male is splendidly coloured black and green, and two of the tail-feathers are immensely lengthened; the female has an ordinary tail and inconspicuous colours; now the young males, instead of resembling the adult female, in accordance with the common rule, begin from the first to assume the colours proper to their sex, and their tail-feathers soon become elongated. I owe this information to Mr. Gould, who has given me the following more striking and as yet unpublished case. Two humming-birds belonging to the genus Eustephanus, both beautifully coloured, inhabit the small island of Juan Fernandez, and have always been ranked as specifically distinct. But it has lately been ascertained that the one which is of a rich chestnut-brown colour with a golden-red head, is the male, whilst the other which is elegantly variegated with green and white with a metallic green head is the female. Now the young from the first somewhat re-

---

[46] Audubon, 'Ornith. Biography,' vol. i. p. 113.

[47] Mr. C. A. Wright, in 'Ibis,' vol. vi. 1864, p. 65. Jerdon, 'Birds of India,' vol. i. p. 515. See also on the blackbird, Blyth in Charlesworth's 'Mag. of Nat. History,' vol. i. 1837, p. 113.

[48] The following additional cases may be mentioned; the young males of *Tanagra rubra* can be distinguished from the young females (Audubon, 'Ornith. Biography,' vol. iv. p. 392), and so it is within the nestlings of a blue nuthatch, *Dendrophila frontalis* of India (Jerdon, 'Birds of India,' vol. i. p. 389). Mr. Blyth also informs me that the sexes of the stonechat, *Saxicola rubicola,* are distinguishable at a very early age. Mr. Slavin gives ('Proc. Zoolog. Soc.' 1870, p. 206) the case of a humming-bird, like the following one of Eustephanus.

semble the adults of the corresponding sex, the resemblance gradually becoming more and more complete.

In considering this last case, if as before we take the plumage of the young as our guide, it would appear that both sexes have been rendered beautiful independently; and not that one sex has partially transferred its beauty to the other. The male apparently has acquired his bright colours through sexual selection in the same manner as, for instance, the peacock or pheasant in our first class of cases; and the female in the same manner as the female Rhynchæa or Turnix in our second class of cases. But there is much difficulty in understanding how this could have been effected at the same time with the two sexes of the same species. Mr. Salvin states, as we have seen in the eighth chapter, that with certain humming birds the males greatly exceed the females in number, whilst with other species inhabiting the same country the females greatly exceed the males. If, then, we might assume that during some former lengthened period the males of the Juan Fernandez species had greatly exceeded the females in number, but that during another lengthened period the females had far exceeded the males, we could understand how the males at one time, and the females at another, might have been rendered beautiful by the selection of the brighter coloured individuals of either sex; both sexes transmitting their characters to their young at a rather earlier age than usual. Whether this is the true explanation I will not pretend to say; but the case is too remarkable to be passed over without notice.

We have now seen in all six classes, that an intimate relation exists between the plumage of the young and the adults, either of one sex or both. These relations are fairly well explained on the principle that one sex—this being in the great majority of cases the male—first acquired through variation and sexual selection bright colours or other ornaments, and transmitted them in various ways, in accordance with the recognised laws of inheritance. Why variations have occurred at different periods of life, even sometimes with species of the same group, we do not know, but with respect to the form of transmission, one important determining cause seems to be the age at which the variations first appear.

From the principle of inheritance at corresponding ages, and from any variations in colour which occurred in the males at an early age not being then selected—on the contrary being often eliminated as dangerous—whilst similar variations occurring at or near the period of reproduction have been preserved, it follows that the plumage of the young will often have been left unmodified, or but little modified. We thus get some insight into the colouring of the progenitors of our existing species. In a vast number of species in five out of our six classes of cases, the adults of one sex or of both are bright coloured, at least during the breeding-season, whilst the young are invariably less brightly coloured than the adults, or are quite dull coloured; for no instance is known, as far as I can discover, of the young of dull-coloured species displaying bright colours, or of the young of bright-coloured species being more brilliant than their parents. In the fourth class, however, in which the young and the old resemble each other, there are many species (though by no means all), of which the young are bright-coloured, and as these form old groups, we may infer that their early progenitors were likewise bright.

With this exception, if we look to the birds of the world, it appears that their beauty has been much increased since that period, of which their immature plumage gives us a partial record.

On the Colour of the Plumage in relation to Protection.—It will have been seen that I cannot follow Mr. Wallace in the belief that dull colours, when confined to the females, have been in most cases specially gained for the sake of protection. There can, however, be no doubt, as formerly remarked, that both sexes of many birds have had their colours modified, so as to escape the notice of their enemies; or in some instances, so as to approach their prey unobserved, just as owls have had their plumage rendered soft, that their flight may not be overheard. Mr. Wallace remarks [49] that "it is only in the tropics, among forests which never lose their foliage, that we find whole groups of birds, whose chief colour is green." It will be admitted by every one, who has ever tried, how difficult it is to distinguish parrots in a leaf-covered tree. Nevertheless, we must remember that many parrots are ornamented with crimson, blue, and orange tints, which can hardly be protective. Woodpeckers are eminently arboreal, but besides green species, there are many black, and black-and-white kinds—all the species being apparently exposed to nearly the same dangers. It is therefore probable that with tree-haunting birds, strongly-pronounced colours have been acquired through sexual selection, but that a green tint has been acquired oftener than any other, from the additional advantage of protection.

In regard to birds which live on the ground, every one admits that they are coloured so as to imitate the surrounding surface. How difficult it is to see a partridge, snipe, woodcock, certain plovers, larks, and night-jars when crouched on ground. Animals inhabiting deserts offer the most striking cases, for the bare surface affords no concealment, and nearly all the smaller quadrupeds, reptiles, and birds depend for safety on their colours. Mr. Tristram has remarked in regard to the inhabitants of the Sahara, that all are protected by their "isabelline or sand-colour." [50] Calling to my recollection the desert-birds of South America, as well as most of the ground-birds of Great Britain, it appeared to me that both sexes in such cases are generally coloured nearly alike. Accordingly, I applied to Mr. Tristram with respect to the birds of the Sahara, and he has kindly given me the following information. There are twenty-six species belonging to fifteen genera, which manifestly have their plumage coloured in a protective manner; and this colouring is all the more striking, as with most of these birds it differs from that of their congeners. Both sexes of thirteen out of the twenty-six species are coloured in the same manner; but these belong to genera in which this rule commonly prevails, so that they tell us nothing about the protective colours being the same in both sexes of desert-birds. Of the other thirteen species, three belong to genera in which the sexes usually differ from each other, yet here they have the

[49] 'Westminster Rev.' July, 1867, p. 5.
[50] 'Ibis,' 1859, vol. i. p. 429, *et seq.* Dr. Rohlfs, however, remarks to me in a letter that according to his experience of the Sahara, this statement is too strong.

sexes alike. In the remaining ten species, the male differs from the female; but the difference is confined chiefly to the under surface of the plumage, which is concealed when the bird crouches on the ground; the head and back being of the same sand-coloured hue in the two sexes. So that in these ten species the upper surfaces of both sexes have been acted on and rendered alike, through natural selection, for the sake of protection; whilst the lower surfaces of the males alone have been diversified, through sexual selection, for the sake of ornament. Here, as both sexes are equally well protected, we clearly see that the females have not been prevented by natural selection from inheriting the colours of their male parents; so that we must look to the law of sexually-limited transmission.

In all parts of the world both sexes of many soft-billed birds, especially those which frequent reeds or sedges, are obscurely coloured. No doubt if their colours had been brilliant, they would have been much more conspicuous to their enemies; but whether their dull tints have been specially gained for the sake of protection seems, as far as I can judge, rather doubtful. It is still more doubtful whether such dull tints can have been gained for the sake of ornament. We must, however, bear in mind that male birds, though dull-coloured, often differ much from their females (as with the common sparrow), and this leads to the belief that such colours have been gained through sexual selection, from being attractive. Many of the soft-billed birds are songsters; and a discussion in a former chapter should not be forgotten, in which it was shewn that the best songsters are rarely ornamented with bright tints. It would appear that female birds, as a general rule, have selected their mates either for their sweet voices or gay colours, but not for both charms combined. Some species, which are manifestly coloured for the sake of protection, such as the jack-snipe, woodcock, and night-jar, are likewise marked and shaded, according to our standard of taste, with extreme elegance. In such cases we may conclude that both natural and sexual selection have acted conjointly for protection and ornament. Whether any bird exists which does not possess some special attraction, by which to charm the opposite sex, may be doubted. When both sexes are so obscurely coloured that it would be rash to assume the agency of sexual selection, and when no direct evidence can be advanced shewing that such colours serve as a protection, it is best to own complete ignorance of the cause, or, which comes to nearly the same thing, to attribute the result to the direct action of the conditions of life.

Both sexes of many birds are conspicuously, though not brilliantly coloured, such as the numerous black, white, or piebald species; and these colours are probably the result of sexual selection. With the common blackbird, capercailzie, blackcock, black scoter-duck (Oidemia), and even with one of the birds of paradise (*Lophorina atra*), the males alone are black, whilst the females are brown or mottled; and there can hardly be a doubt that blackness in these cases has been a sexually selected character. Therefore it is in some degree probable that the complete or partial blackness of both sexes in such birds as crows, certain cockatoos, storks, and swans, and many marine birds, is likewise the result of sexual selection, accompanied by equal transmission to both sexes; for blackness can hardly serve in any case as a protection. With several birds, in which the male alone is black, and in others in which both sexes are black, the beak or skin about the head is brightly coloured, and the contrast thus afforded adds much to their beauty; we see this in the bright yellow beak of the male blackbird, in the crimson skin over the eyes of the blackcock and capercailzie, in the brightly and variously coloured beak of the scoter-drake (Oidemia), in the red beak of the chough (*Corvus graculus*, Linn.), of the black swan, and the black stork. This leads me to remark that it is not incredible that toucans may owe the enormous size of their beaks to sexual selection, for the sake of displaying the diversified and vivid stripes of colour, with which these organs are ornamented.[51] The naked skin, also, at the base of the beak and round the eyes is likewise often brilliantly coloured; and Mr. Gould, in speaking of one species,[52] says that the colours of the beak "are doubtless in the finest and most brilliant state during the time of pairing." There is no greater improbability that toucans should be encumbered with immense beaks, though rendered as light as possible by their cancellated structure, for the display of fine colours (an object falsely appearing to us unimportant), than that the male Argus pheasant and some other birds should be encumbered with plumes so long as to impede their flight.

In the same manner, as the males alone of various species are black, the females being dull-coloured; so in a few cases the males alone are either wholly or partially white, as with the several bell-birds of South America (Chasmorhynchus), the Antarctic goose (*Bernicla antarctica*), the silver-pheasant, &c., whilst the females are brown or obscurely mottled. Therefore, on the same principle as before, it is probable that both sexes of many birds, such as white cockatoos, several egrets with their beautiful plumes, certain ibises, gulls, terns, &c., have acquired their more or less completely white plumage through sexual selection. In some of these cases the plumage becomes white only at maturity. This is the case with certain gannets, tropic-birds, &c., and with the snow-goose (*Anser hyperboreus*). As the latter breeds on the "barren grounds," when not covered with snow, and as it migrates southward during the winter, there is no reason to suppose that its snow-white adult plumage serves as a protection. In the *Anastomus oscitans*, we have still better evidence

---

[51] No satisfactory explanation has ever been offered of the immense size, and still less of the bright colours, of the toucan's beak. Mr. Bates ('The Naturalist on the Amazons,' vol. ii. 1863, p. 341) states that they use their beaks for reaching fruit at the extreme tips of the branches; and likewise, as stated by other authors, for extracting eggs and young birds from the nests of other birds. But, as Mr. Bates admits, the beak "can scarcely be considered a very perfectly-formed instrument for the end to which it is applied." The great bulk of the beak, as shown by its breadth, depth, as well as length, is not intelligible on the view, that it serves merely as an organ of prehension. Mr. Belt believes ('The Naturalist in Nicaragua,' p. 197), that the principal use of the beak is as a defence against enemies, especially to the female whilst nesting in a hole in a tree.

[52] *Rhamphastos carinatus* Gould's 'Monograph of Ramphastidæ.'

that the white plumage is a nuptial character, for it is developed only during the summer; the young in their immature state, and the adults in their winter dress, being grey and black. With many kinds of gulls (Larus), the head and neck become pure white during the summer, being grey or mottled during the winter and in the young state. On the other hand, with the smaller gulls, or sea-mews (Gavia), and with some terns (Sterna), exactly the reverse occurs; for the heads of the young birds during the first year, and of the adults during the winter, are either pure white, or much paler coloured than during the breeding-season. These latter cases offer another instance of the capricious manner in which sexual selection appears often to have acted.[53]

That aquatic birds have acquired a white plumage so much oftener than terrestrial birds, probably depends on their large size and strong powers of flight, so that they can easily defend themselves or escape from birds of prey, to which moreover they are not much exposed. Consequently, sexual selection has not here been interfered with or guided for the sake of protection. No doubt with birds which roam over the open ocean, the males and females could find each other much more easily, when made conspicuous either by being perfectly white or intensely black; so that these colours may possibly serve the same end as the call-notes of many land-birds.[54] A white or black bird when it discovers and flies down to a carcase floating on the sea or cast up on the beach, will be seen from a great distance, and will guide other birds of the same and other species, to the prey; but as this would be a disadvantage to the first finders, the individuals which were the whitest or blackest would not thus procure more food than the less strongly coloured individuals. Hence conspicuous colours cannot have been gradually acquired for this purpose through natural selection.

As sexual selection depends on so fluctuating an element as taste, we can understand how it is that, within the same group of birds having nearly the same habits, there should exist white or nearly white, as well as black, or nearly black species,—for instance, both white and black cockatoos, storks, ibises, swans, terns, and petrels. Piebald birds likewise sometimes occur in the same groups together with black and white species; for instance, the black-necked swan, certain terns, and the common magpie. That a strong contrast in colour is agreeable to birds, we may conclude by looking through any large collection, for the sexes often differ from each other in the male having the pale parts of a purer white, and the variously coloured dark parts of still darker tints than the female.

[53] On Larus, Gavia, and Sterna, see Macgillivray, 'Hist. Brit. Birds,' vol. v. pp. 515, 584, 626. On the Anser hyperboreus, Audubon, 'Ornith. Biography,' vol. iv. p. 562. On the Anastomus, Mr. Blyth, in 'Ibis,' 1867, p. 173.

[54] It may be noticed that with vultures, which roam far and wide high in the air, like marine birds over the ocean, three or four species are almost wholly or largely white, and that many others are black. So that here again conspicuous colours may possibly aid the sexes in finding each other during the breeding-season.

It would even appear that mere novelty, or slight changes for the sake of change, have sometimes acted on female birds as a charm, like changes of fashion with us. Thus the males of some parrots can hardly be said to be more beautiful than the females, at least according to our taste, but they differ in such points, as in having a rose-coloured collar instead of "a bright emeraldine narrow green collar;" or in the male having a black collar instead of "a yellow demi-collar in front," with a pale roseate instead of a plum-blue head.[55] As so many male birds have elongated tail-feathers or elongated crests for their chief ornament, the shortened tail, formerly described in the male of a humming-bird, and the shortened crest of the male goosander, seem like one of the many changes of fashion which we admire in our own dresses.

Some members of the heron family offer a still more curious case of novelty in colouring having, as it appears, been appreciated for the sake of novelty. The young of the *Ardea asha* are white, the adults being dark slate-coloured; and not only the young, but the adults in their winter plumage, of the allied *Buphus coromandus* are white, this colour changing into a rich golden-buff during the breeding-season. It is incredible that the young of these two species, as well as of some other members of the same family,[56] should for any special purpose have been rendered pure white and thus made conspicuous to their enemies; or that the adults of one of these two species should have been specially rendered white during the winter in a country which is never covered with snow. On the other hand we have good reason to believe that whiteness has been gained by many birds as a sexual ornament. We may therefore conclude that some early progenitor of the *Ardea asha* and the Buphus acquired a white plumage for nuptial purposes, and transmitted this colour to their young; so that the young and the old became white like certain existing egrets; and that the whiteness was afterwards retained by the young, whilst it was exchanged by the adults for more strongly-pronounced tints. But if we could look still further back to the still earlier progenitors of these two species, we should probably see the adults dark-coloured. I infer that this would be the case, from the analogy of many other birds, which are dark whilst young, and when adult are white; and more especially from the case of the *Ardea gularis*, the colours of which are the reverse of those of *A. asha*, for the young are dark-coloured and the adults white, the young having retained a former state of plumage. It appears therefore that, during a long line of descent, the adult progenitors of the *Ardea asha*, the Buphus, and of some allies, have undergone the following changes of colour: first, a dark shade; secondly, pure white; and thirdly, owing to another change of fashion (if I may so express myself), their

---

[55] See Jerdon on the genus Palæornis, 'Birds of India,' vol. i. pp. 258-260.

[56] The young of *Ardea rufescens* and *A. cærulea* of the U. States are likewise white, the adults being coloured in accordance with their specific names. Audubon ('Ornith. Biography,' vol. iii. p. 416; vol. iv. p. 58) seems rather pleased at the thought that this remarkable change of plumage will greatly "disconcert the systematists."

present slaty, reddish, or golden-buff tints. These successive changes are intelligible only on the principle of novelty having been admired by birds for its own sake.

Several writers have objected to the whole theory of sexual selection, by assuming that with animals and savages the taste of the female for certain colours or other ornaments would not remain constant for many generations; that first one colour and then another would be admired, and consequently that no permanent effect could be produced. We may admit that taste is fluctuating, but it is not quite arbitrary. It depends much on habit, as we see in mankind; and we may infer that this would hold good with birds and other animals. Even in our own dress, the general character lasts long, and the changes are to a certain extent graduated. Abundant evidence will be given in two places in a future chapter, that savages of many races have admired for many generations the same cicatrices on the skin, the same hideously perforated lips, nostrils, or ears, distorted heads, &c.; and these deformities present some analogy to the natural ornaments of various animals. Nevertheless, with savages such fashions do not endure for ever, as we may infer from the differences in this respect between allied tribes on the same continent. So again the raisers of fancy animals certainly have admired for many generations and still admire the same breeds; they earnestly desire slight changes, which are considered as improvements, but any great or sudden change is looked at as the greatest blemish. With birds in a state of nature we have no reason to suppose that they would admire an entirely new style of coloration, even if great and sudden variations often occurred, which is far from being the case. We know that dovecot pigeons do not willingly associate with the variously coloured fancy breeds; that albino birds do not commonly get partners in marriage; and that the black ravens of the Feroe Islands chase away their piebald brethren. But this dislike of a sudden change would not preclude their appreciating slight changes, any more than it does in the case of man. Hence with respect to taste, which depends on many elements, but partly on habit and partly on a love of novelty, there seems no improbability in animals admiring for a very long period the same general style of ornamentation or other attractions, and yet appreciating slight changes in colours, form, or sound.

Summary of the Four Chapters on Birds.—Most male birds are highly pugnacious during the breeding-season, and some possess weapons adapted for fighting with their rivals. But the most pugnacious and the best armed males rarely or never depend for success solely on their power to drive away or kill their rivals, but have special means for charming the female. With some it is the power of song, or of giving forth strange cries, or instrumental music, and the males in consequence differ from the females in their vocal organs, or in the structure of certain feathers. From the curiously diversified means for producing various sounds, we gain a high idea of the importance of this means of courtship. Many birds endeavour to charm the females by love-dances or antics, performed on the ground or in the air, and sometimes at prepared places. But ornaments of many kinds, the most brilliant tints, combs and wattles, beautiful plumes, elongated feathers, top-knots, and so forth, are by far the commonest means. In some cases mere novelty appears to have acted as a charm. The ornaments of the males must be highly important to them, for they have been acquired in not a few cases at the cost of increased danger from enemies, and even at some loss of power in fighting with their rivals. The males of very many species do not assume their ornamental dress until they arrive at maturity, or they assume it only during the breeding-season, or the tints then become more vivid. Certain ornamental appendages become enlarged, turgid, and brightly coloured during the act of courtship. The males display their charms with elaborate care and to the best effect; and this is done in the presence of the females. The courtship is sometimes a prolonged affair, and many males and females congregate at an appointed place. To suppose that the females do not appreciate the beauty of the males, is to admit that their splendid decorations, all their pomp and display, are useless; and this is incredible. Birds have fine powers of discrimination, and in some few instances it can be shewn that they have a taste for the beautiful. The females, moreover, are known occasionally to exhibit a marked preference or antipathy for certain individual males.

If it be admitted that the females prefer, or are unconsciously excited by the more beautiful males, then the males would slowly but surely be rendered more and more attractive through sexual selection. That it is this sex which has been chiefly modified, we may infer from the fact that, in almost every genus where the sexes differ, the males differ much more from one another than do the females; this is well shewn in certain closely-allied representative species, in which the females can hardly be distinguished, whilst the males are quite distinct. Birds in a state of nature offer individual differences which would amply suffice for the work of sexual selection; but we have seen that they occasionally present more strongly marked variations which recur so frequently that they would immediately be fixed, if they served to allure the female. The laws of variation must determine the nature of the initial changes, and will have largely influenced the final result. The gradations, which may be observed between the males of allied species, indicate the nature of the steps through which they have passed. They explain also in the most interesting manner how certain characters have originated, such as the indented ocelli on the tail-feathers of the peacock, and the ball-and-socket ocelli on the wing-feathers of the Argus pheasant. It is evident that the brilliant colours, top-knots, fine plumes, &c., of many male birds cannot have been acquired as a protection; indeed, they sometimes lead to danger. That they are not due to the direct and definite action of the conditions of life, we may feel assured, because the females have been exposed to the same conditions, and yet often differ from the males to an extreme degree. Although it is probable that changed conditions acting during a lengthened period have in some cases produced a definite effect on both

sexes, or sometimes on one sex alone, the more important result will have
been an increased tendency to vary or to present more strongly-marked
individual differences; and such differences will have afforded an excellent ground-work for the action of sexual selection.

The laws of inheritance, irrespectively of selection, appear to have determined whether the characters acquired by the males for the sake of
ornament, for producing various sounds, and for fighting together, have
been transmitted to the males alone or to both sexes, either permanently,
or periodically during certain seasons of the year. Why various characters should have been transmitted sometimes in one way and sometimes
in another, is not in most cases known; but the period of variability
seems often to have been the determining cause. When the two sexes have
inherited all characters in common they necessarily resemble each other;
but as the successive variations may be differently transmitted, every
possible gradation may be found, even within the same genus, from the
closest similarity to the widest dissimilarity between the sexes. With
many closely-allied species, following nearly the same habits of life, the
males have come to differ from each other chiefly through the action of
sexual selection; whilst the females have come to differ chiefly from partaking more or less of the characters thus acquired by the males. The
effects, moreover, of the definite action of the conditions of life, will not
have been masked in the females, as in the males, by the accumulation
through sexual selection of strongly-pronounced colours and other ornaments. The individuals of both sexes, however affected, will have been
kept at each successive period nearly uniform by the free intercrossing
of many individuals.

With species, in which the sexes differ in colour, it is possible or probable that some of the successive variations often tended to be transmitted
equally to both sexes; but that when this occurred the females were prevented from acquiring the bright colours of the males, by the destruction
which they suffered during incubation. There is no evidence that it is possible by natural selection to convert one form of transmission into another. But there would not be the least difficulty in rendering a female
dull-coloured, the male being still kept bright-coloured, by the selection
of successive variations, which were from the first limited in their transmission to the same sex. Whether the females of many species have actually been thus modified, must at present remain doubtful. When, through
the law of the equal transmission of characters to both sexes, the females
were rendered as conspicuously coloured as the males, their instincts appear often to have been modified so that they were led to build domed
or concealed nests.

In one small and curious class of cases the characters and habits of the
two sexes have been completely transposed, for the females are larger,
stronger, more vociferous and brighter coloured than the males. They
have, also, become so quarrelsome that they often fight together for the
possession of the males, like the males of other pugnacious species for the
possession of the females. If, as seems probable, such females habitually

drive away their rivals, and by the display of their bright colours or other charms endeavour to attract the males, we can understand how it is that they have gradually been rendered, by sexual selection and sexually-limited transmission, more beautiful than the males—the latter being left unmodified or only slightly modified.

Whenever the law of inheritance at corresponding ages prevails but not that of sexually-limited transmission, then if the parents vary late in life —and we know that this constantly occurs with our poultry, and occasionally with other birds—the young will be left unaffected, whilst the adults of both sexes will be modified. If both these laws of inheritance prevail and either sex varies late in life, that sex alone will be modified, the other sex and the young being unaffected. When variations in brightness or in other conspicuous characters occur early in life, as no doubt often happens, they will not be acted on through sexual selection until the period of reproduction arrives; consequently if dangerous to the young, they will be eliminated through natural selection. Thus we can understand how it is that variations arising late in life have so often been preserved for the ornamentation of the males; the females and the young being left almost unaffected, and therefore like each other. With species having a distinct summer and winter plumage, the males of which either resemble or differ from the females during both seasons or during the summer alone, the degrees and kinds of resemblance between the young and the old are exceedingly complex; and this complexity apparently depends on characters, first acquired by the males, being transmitted in various ways and degrees, as limited by age, sex, and season.

As the young of so many species have been but little modified in colour and in other ornaments we are enabled to form some judgment with respect to the plumage of their early progenitors; and we may infer that the beauty of our existing species, if we look to the whole class, has been largely increased since that period, of which the immature plumage gives us an indirect record. Many birds, especially those which live much on the ground, have undoubtedly been obscurely coloured for the sake of protection. In some instances the upper exposed surface of the plumage has been thus coloured in both sexes, whilst the lower surface in the males alone has been variously ornamented through sexual selection. Finally, from the facts given in these four chapters, we may conclude that weapons for battle, organs for producing sound, ornaments of many kinds, bright and conspicuous colours, have generally been acquired by the males through variation and sexual selection, and have been transmitted in various ways according to the several laws of inheritance—the females and the young being left comparatively but little modified.[57]

---

[57] I am greatly indebted to the kindness of Mr. Sclater for having looked over these four chapters on birds, and the two following ones on mammals. In this way I have been saved from making mistakes about the names of the species, and from stating anything as a fact which is known to this distinguished naturalist to be erroneous. But of course he is not at all answerable for the accuracy of the statements quoted by me from various authorities.

CHAPTER XVII

SECONDARY SEXUAL CHARACTERS OF MAMMALS

The law of battle—Special weapons, confined to the males—Cause of absence of weapons in the female—Weapons common to both sexes, yet primarily acquired by the male—Other uses of such weapons—Their high importance—Greater size of the male—Means of defence—On the preference shown by either sex in the pairing of quadrupeds.

WITH mammals the male appears to win the female much more through the law of battle than through the display of his charms. The most timid animals, not provided with any special weapons for fighting, engage in desperate conflicts during the season of love. Two male hares have been seen to fight together until one was killed; male moles often fight, and sometimes with fatal results; male squirrels engage in frequent contests, "and often wound each other severely;" as do male beavers, so that "hardly a skin is without scars."[1] I observed the same fact with the hides of the guanacoes in Patagonia; and on one occasion several were so absorbed in fighting that they fearlessly rushed close by me. Livingstone speaks of the males of the many animals in Southern Africa as almost invariably shewing the scars received in former contests.

The law of battle prevails with aquatic as with terrestrial mammals. It is notorious how desperately male seals fight, both with their teeth and claws, during the breeding-season; and their hides are likewise often covered with scars. Male sperm-whales are very jealous at this season; and in their battles "they often lock their jaws together, and turn on their sides and twist about;" so that their lower jaws often become distorted.[2]

All male animals which are furnished with special weapons for fighting, are well known to engage in fierce battles. The courage and the desperate conflicts of stags have often been described; their skeletons have been found in various parts of the world, with the horns inextricably locked together, shewing how miserably the victor and vanquished had perished.[3]

[1] See Waterton's account of two hares fighting, 'Zoologist,' vol. i. 1843, p. 211. On moles, Bell, 'Hist. of British Quadrupeds,' 1st edit. p. 100. On squirrels, Audubon and Bachman, 'Viviparous Quadrupeds of N. America,' 1846, p. 269. On beavers, Mr. A. H. Green, in 'Journal of Lin. Soc. Zoolog.' vol. x. 1869, p. 362.

[2] On the battles of seals, see Capt. C. Abbott in 'Proc. Zool. Soc.' 1868, p. 191; Mr. R. Brown, ibid. 1868, p. 436; also L. Lloyd, 'Game Birds of Sweden,' 1867, p. 414; also Pennant. On the sperm-whale see Mr. J. H. Thompson, in 'Proc. Zool. Soc.' 1867, p. 246.

[3] See Scrope ('Art of Deer-stalking,' p. 17) on the locking of the horns with the *Cervus elaphus*. Richardson, in 'Fauna Bor. Americana,' 1829, p. 252, says that the

No animal in the world is so dangerous as an elephant in must. Lord Tankerville has given me a graphic description of the battles between the wild bulls in Chillingham Park, the descendants, degenerated in size but not in courage, of the gigantic *Bos primigenius*. In 1861 several contended for mastery; and it was observed that two of the younger bulls attacked in concert the old leader of the herd, overthrew and disabled him, so that he was believed by the keepers to be lying mortally wounded in a neighbouring wood. But a few days afterwards one the young bulls approached the wood alone; and then the "monarch of the chase," who had been lashing himself up for vengeance, came out and, in a short time, killed his antagonist. He then quietly joined the herd, and long held undisputed sway. Admiral Sir B. J. Sulivan informs me that, when he lived in the Falkland Islands, he imported a young English stallion, which frequented the hills near Port William with eight mares. On these hills there were two wild stallions, each with a small troop of mares; "and it is certain that these stallions would never have approached each other without fighting. Both had tried singly to fight the English horse and drive away his mares, but had failed. One day they came in *together* and attacked him. This was seen by the captain who had charge of the horses, and who, on riding to the spot, found one of the two stallions engaged with the English horse, whilst the other was driving away the mares, and had already separated four from the rest. The captain settled the matter by driving the whole party into a corral, for the wild stallions would not leave the mares."

Male animals which are provided with efficient cutting or tearing teeth for the ordinary purposes of life, such as the carnivora, insectivora, and rodents, are seldom furnished with weapons especially adapted for fighting with their rivals. The case is very different with the males of many other animals. We see this in the horns of stags and of certain kinds of antelopes in which the females are hornless. With many animals the canine teeth in the upper or lower jaw, or in both, are much larger in the males than in the females, or are absent in the latter, with the exception sometimes of a hidden rudiment. Certain antelopes, the musk-deer, camel, horse, boar, various apes, seals, and the walrus, offer instances. In the females of the walrus the tusks are sometimes quite absent.[4] In the male elephant of India and in the male dugong [5] the upper incisors form offensive weapons. In the male narwhal the left canine alone is developed into the well-known, spirally-twisted, so-called horn, which is sometimes from nine to ten feet in length. It is believed that the males use these horns for fighting together; for "an unbroken one can rarely be got, and occasion-

wapiti, moose, and reindeer have been found thus locked together. Sir A. Smith found at the Cape of Good Hope the skeletons of two gnus in the same condition.

[4] Mr. Lamont ('Seasons with the Sea-Horses,' 1861, p. 143) says that a good tusk of the male walrus weighs 4 pounds, and is longer than that of the female, which weighs about 3 pounds. The males are described as fighting ferociously. On the occasional absence of the tusks in the female, see Mr. R. Brown, 'Proc. Zool. Soc.' 1868, p. 429.

[5] Owen, 'Anatomy of Vertebrates,' vol. iii. p. 283.

ally one may be found with the point of another jammed into the broken place." [6] The tooth on the opposite side of the head in the male consists of a rudiment about ten inches in length, which is embedded in the jaw; but sometimes, though rarely, both are equally developed on the two sides. In the female both are always rudimentary. The male cachalot has a larger head than that of the female, and it no doubt aids him in his equatic battles. Lastly, the adult male ornithorhynchus is provided with a remarkable apparatus, namely a spur on the foreleg, closely resembling the poison-fang of a venomous snake; but according to Harting, the secretion from the gland is not poisonous; and on the leg of the female there is a hollow, apparently for the reception of the spur. [7]

When the males are provided with weapons which in the females are absent, there can be hardly a doubt that these serve for fighting with other males; and that they were acquired through sexual selection, and were transmitted to the male sex alone. It is not probable, at least in most cases, that the females have been prevented from acquiring such weapons, on account of their being useless, superfluous, or in some way injurious. On the contrary, as they are often used by the males for various purposes, more especially as a defence against their enemies, it is a surprising fact that they are so poorly developed, or quite absent, in the females of so many animals. With female deer the development during each recurrent season of great branching horns, and with female elephants the development of immense tusks, would be a great waste of vital power, supposing that they were of no use to the females. Consequently, they would have tended to be eliminated in the female through natural selection; that is, if the successive variations were limited in their transmission to the female sex, for otherwise the weapons of the males would have been injuriously affected, and this would have been a greater evil. On the whole, and from the consideration of the following facts, it seems probable that when the various weapons differ in the two sexes, this has generally depended on the kind of transmission which has prevailed.

As the reindeer is the one species in the whole family of Deer, in which the female is furnished with horns, though they are somewhat smaller, thinner, and less branched than in the male, it might naturally be thought that, at least in this case, they must be of some special service to her. The female retains her horns from the time when they are fully developed, namely, in September, throughout the winter until April or May, when she brings forth her young. Mr. Crotch made particular enquiries for me in Norway, and it appears that the females at this season conceal themselves for about a fortnight in order to bring forth their young, and then reappear, generally hornless. In Nova Scotia, however, as I hear from

[6] Mr. R. Brown, in 'Proc. Zool. Soc.' 1869, p. 553. See Prof. Turner, in 'Journal of Anat. and Phys.' 1872, p. 76, on the homological nature of these tusks. Also Mr. J. W. Clarke on two tusks being developed in the males, in 'Proc. Zoolog. Soc.' 1871, p. 42.
[7] Owen on the cachalot and Ornithorhynchus, ibid. vol. iii. pp. 638, 641. Harting is quoted by Dr. Zouteveen in the Dutch translat. of this work, vol. ii. p. 292.

Mr. H. Reeks, the female sometimes retains her horns longer. The male on the other hand casts his horns much earlier, towards the end of November. As both sexes have the same requirements and follow the same habits of life, and as the male is destitute of horns during the winter, it is improbable that they can be of any special service to the female during this season, which includes the larger part of the time during which she is horned. Nor is it probable that she can have inherited horns from some ancient progenitor of the family of deer, for, from the fact of the females of so many species in all quarters of the globe not having horns, we may conclude that this was the primordial character of the group.[8]

The horns of the reindeer are developed at a most unusually early age; but what the cause of this may be is not known. The effect has apparently been the transference of the horns to both sexes. We should bear in mind that horns are always transmitted through the female, and that she has a latent capacity for their development, as we see in old or diseased females.[9] Moreover the females of some other species of deer exhibit, either normally or occasionally, rudiments of horns; thus the female of *Cervulus moschatus* has "bristly tufts, ending in a knob, instead of a horn;" and "in most specimens of the female wapiti (*Cervus canadensis*) there is a sharp bony protuberance in the place of the horn." [10] From these several considerations we may conclude that the possession of fairly well-developed horns by the female reindeer, is due to the males having first acquired them as weapons for fighting with other males; and secondarily to their development from some unknown cause at an unusually early age in the males, and their consequent transference to both sexes.

Turning to the sheath-horned ruminants: with antelopes a graduated series can be formed, beginning with species, the females of which are completely destitute of horns—passing on to those which have horns so small as to be almost rudimentary (as with the *Antilocapra americana*, in which species they are present in only one out of four or five females [11]) —to those which have fairly developed horns, but manifestly smaller and thinner than in the male and sometimes of a different shape,[12]—and ending with those in which both sexes have horns of equal size. As with the

[8] On the structure and shedding of the horns of the reindeer, Hoffberg, 'Amœnitates Acad.' vol. iv. 1788, p. 149. See Richardson, 'Fauna Bor. Americana,' p. 241, in regard to the American variety or species: also Major W. Ross King, 'The Sportsman in Canada,' 1866, p. 80.

[9] Isidore Geoffroy St. Hilaire, 'Essais de Zoolog. Générale,' 1841, p. 513. Other masculine characters, besides the horns, are sometimes similarly transferred to the female; thus Mr. Boner, in speaking of an old female chamois ('Chamois Hunting in the Mountains of Bavaria,' 1860, 2nd edit. p. 363), says, "not only was the head very male-looking, but along the back there was a ridge of long hair, usually to be found only in bucks."

[10] On the Cervulus, Dr. Gray, 'Catalogue of Mammalia in the British Museum,' part iii. p. 220. On the *Cervus canadensis* or, wapiti, see Hon. J. D. Caton, 'Ottawa Acad. of Nat. Sciences,' May, 1868, p. 9.

[11] I am indebted to Dr. Canfield for this information, see also his paper in the 'Proc. Zoolog. Soc.' 1866, page 105.

[12] For instance the horns of the female *Ant. euchore* resemble those of a distinct species, viz. the *Ant. dorcas* var. *Corine,* see Desmarest, 'Mammalogie,' p. 455.

reindeer, so with antelopes, there exists, as previously shewn, a relation between the period of the development of the horns and their transmission to one or both sexes; it is therefore probable that their presence or absence in the females of some species, and their more or less perfect condition in the females of other species, depends, not on their being of any special use, but simply in inheritance. It accords with this view that even in the same restricted genus both sexes of some species, and the males alone of others, are thus provided. It is also a remarkable fact that, although the females of *Antilope bezoartica* are normally destitute of horns, Mr. Blyth has seen no less than three females thus furnished; and there was no reason to suppose that they were old or diseased.

In all the wild species of goats and sheep the horns are larger in the male than in the female, and are sometimes quite absent in the latter.[13] In several domestic breeds of these two animals, the males alone are furnished with horns; and in some breeds, for instance, in the sheep of North Wales, though both sexes are properly horned, the ewes are very liable to be hornless. I have been informed by a trustworthy witness, who purposely inspected a flock of these same sheep during the lambing season, that the horns at birth are generally more fully developed in the male than in the female. Mr. J. Peel crossed his Lonk sheep, both sexes of which always bear horns, with hornless Leicesters and hornless Shropshire Downs; and the result was that the male offspring had their horns considerably reduced, whilst the females were wholly destitute of them. These several facts indicate that, with sheep, the horns are a much less firmly fixed character in the females than in the males; and this leads us to look at the horns as properly of masculine origin.

With the adult musk-ox (*Ovibos moschatus*) the horns of the male are larger than those of the female, and in the latter the bases do not touch.[14] In regard to ordinary cattle Mr. Blyth remarks: "In most of the wild bovine animals the horns are both longer and thicker in the bull than in the cow, and in the cow-banteng (*Bos sondaicus*) the horns are remarkably small, and inclined much backwards. In the domestic races of cattle, both of the humped and humpless types, the horns are short and thick in the bull, longer and more slender in the cow and ox; and in the Indian buffalo, they are shorter and thicker in the bull, longer and more slender in the cow. In the wild gaour (*B. gaurus*) the horns are mostly both longer and thicker in the bull than in the cow." [15] Dr. Forsyth Major also informs me that a fossil skull, believed to be that of the female *Bos estruscus*, has been found in Val d'Arno, which is wholly without horns. In the *Rhinoceros simus*, as I may add, the horns of the female are generally longer but less powerful than in the male; and in some other species of rhinoceros they are said to be shorter in the female.[16] From these various

[13] Gray, 'Catalogue Mamm. Brit. Mus.' part iii. 1852, p. 160.
[14] Richardson, 'Fauna Bor. Americana,' p. 278.
[15] 'Land and Water,' 1867, p. 346.
[16] Sir Andrew Smith, 'Zoology of S. Africa,' pl. xix. Owen, 'Anatomy of Vertebrates,' vol. iii. p. 624.

facts we may infer as probable that horns of all kinds, even when they are equally developed in the two sexes, were primarily acquired by the male in order to conquer other males, and have been transferred more or less completely to the female.

The effects of castration deserve notice, as throwing light on this same point. Stags after the operation never renew their horns. The male reindeer, however, must be excepted, as after castration he does renew them. This fact, as well as the possession of horns by both sexes, seems at first to prove that the horns in this species do not constitute a sexual character;[17] but as they are developed at a very early age, before the sexes differ in constitution, it is not surprising that they should be unaffected by castration, even if they were aboriginally acquired by the male. With sheep both sexes properly bear horns; and I am informed that with Welch sheep the horns of the males are considerably reduced by castration; but the degree depends much on the age at which the operation is performed, as is likewise the case with other animals. Merino rams have large horns, whilst the ewes "generally speaking are without horns;" and in this breed castration seems to produce a somewhat greater effect, so that if performed at an early age the horns "remain almost undeveloped."[18] On the Guinea coast there is a breed in which the females never bear horns, and, as Mr. Winwood Reade informs me, the rams after castration are quite destitute of them. With cattle, the horns of the males are much altered by castration; for instead of being short and thick, they become longer than those of the cow, but otherwise resemble them. The *Antilope bezoartica* offers a somewhat analogous case: the males have long straight spiral horns, nearly parallel to each other, and directed backwards; the females occasionally bear horns, but these when present are of a very different shape, for they are not spiral, and spreading widely, bend round with the points forwards. Now it is a remarkable fact that, in the castrated male, as Mr. Blyth informs me, the horns are of the same peculiar shape as in the female, but longer and thicker. If we may judge from analogy, the female probably shews us, in these two cases of cattle and the antelope, the former condition of the horns in some early progenitor of each species. But why castration should lead to the reappearance of an early condition of the horns cannot be explained with any certainty. Nevertheless, it seems probable, that in nearly the same manner as the constitutional disturbance in the offspring, caused by a cross between two distinct species or races, often leads to the reappearance of long-lost characters;[19] so here, the disturbance in the constitu-

---

[17] This is the conclusion of Seidlitz, 'Die Darwinsche Theorie,' 1871, p. 47.

[18] I am much obliged to Prof. Victor Carus, for having made enquiries for me in Saxony on this subject. H. von Nathusius ('Viehzucht,' 1872, p. 64) says that the horns of sheep castrated at an early period, either altogether disappear or remain as mere rudiments; but I do not know whether he refers to merinos or to ordinary breeds.

[19] I have given various experiments and other evidence proving that this is the case, in my 'Variation of Animals and Plants under Domestication,' vol. ii., 1868, pp. 39-47.

tion of the individual, resulting from castration, produces the same effect.

The tusks of the elephant, in the different species or races, differ according to sex, nearly as do the horns of ruminants. In India and Malacca the males alone are provided with well-developed tusks. The elephant of Ceylon is considered by most naturalists as a distinct race, but by some as a distinct species, and here "not one in a hundred is found with tusks, the few that possess them being exclusively males." [20] The African elephant is undoubtedly distinct, and the female has large well-developed tusks, though not so large as those of the male.

These differences in the tusks of the several races and species of elephants—the great variability of the horns of deer, as notably in the wild reindeer—the occasional presence of horns in the female *Antilope bezoartica,* and their frequent absence in the female of *Antilocapra americana* —the presence of two tusks in some few male narwhals—the complete absence of tusks in some female walruses—are all instances of the extreme variability of secondary sexual characters, and of their liability to differ in closely-allied forms.

Although tusks and horns appear in all cases to have been primarily developed as sexual weapons, they often serve other purposes. The elephant uses his tusks in attacking the tiger; according to Bruce, he scores the trunks of trees until they can be thrown down easily, and he likewise thus extracts the farinaceous cores of palms; in Africa he often uses one tusk, always the same, to probe the ground and thus ascertain whether it will bear his weight. The common bull defends the herd with his horns; and the elk in Sweden has been known, according to Lloyd, to strike a wolf dead with a single blow of his great horns. Many similar facts could be given. One of the most curious secondary uses to which the horns of an animal may be occasionally put is that observed by Captain Hutton [21] with the wild goat (*Capra œgagrus*) of the Himalayas and, as it is also said with the ibex, namely that when the male accidentally falls from a height he bends inwards his head, and by alighting on his massive horns, breaks the shock. The female cannot thus use her horns, which are smaller, but from her more quiet disposition she does not need this strange kind of shield so much.

Each male animal uses his weapons in his own peculiar fashion. The common ram makes a charge and butts with such force with the bases of his horns, that I have seen a powerful man knocked over like a child. Goats and certain species of sheep, for instance the *Ovis cycloceros* of Afghanistan,[22] rear on their hind legs, and then not only butt, but "make a cut down and a jerk up, with the ribbed front of their scimitar-shaped horn, as with a sabre. When the *O. cycloceros* attacked a large domestic ram, who was a noted bruiser, he conquered him by the sheer novelty of

[20] Sir J. Emerson Tennent, 'Ceylon,' 1859, vol. ii. p. 274. For Malacca, 'Journal of Indian Archipelago,' vol. iv. p. 357.

[21] 'Calcutta Journal of Nat. Hist.' vol. ii. 1843, p. 526.

[22] Mr. Blyth, in 'Land and Water,' March, 1867, p. 134, on the authority of Capt. Hutton and others. For the wild Pembrokeshire goats, see the 'Field,' 1869, p. 150.

his mode of fighting, always closing at once with his adversary, and catching him across the face and nose with a sharp drawing jerk of the head, and then bounding out of the way before the blow could be returned." In Pembrokeshire a male goat, the master of a flock which during several generations had run wild, was known to have killed several males in single combat; this goat possessed enormous horns, measuring thirty-nine inches in a straight line from tip to tip. The common bull, as every one knows, gores and tosses his opponent; but the Italian buffalo is said never to use his horns, he gives a tremendous blow with his convex forehead, and then tramples on his fallen enemy with his knees—an instinct which the common bull does not possess.[23] Hence a dog who pins a buffalo by the nose is immediately crushed. We must, however, remember that the Italian buffalo has been long domesticated, and it is by no means certain that the wild parent-form had similar horns. Mr. Bartlett informs

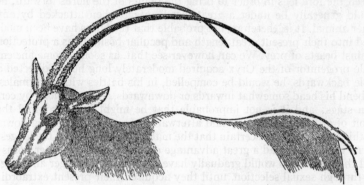

Fig. 63.—Oryx leucoryx, male (from the Knowsley Menagerie).

me that when a female Cape buffalo (*Bubalus caffer*) was turned into an enclosure with a bull of the same species, she attacked him, and he in return pushed her about with great violence. But it was manifest to Mr. Bartlett that, had not the bull shewn dignified forbearance, he could easily have killed her by a single lateral thrust with his immense horns. The giraffe uses his short, hair-covered horns, which are rather longer in the male than in the female, in a curious manner; for, with his long neck he swings his head to either side, almost upside down, with such force that I have seen a hard plank deeply indented by a single blow.

With antelopes it is sometimes difficult to imagine how they can possibly use their curiously-shaped horns; thus the springboc (*Ant. euchore*) has rather short upright horns, with the sharp points bent inwards almost at right angles, so as to face each other; Mr. Bartlett does not know how they are used, but suggests that they would inflict a fearful wound down each side of the face of an antagonist. The slightly-curved horns of

[23] M. E. M. Bailly, 'Sur l'usage des Cornes,' &c., 'Annal des Sc. Nat.' tom. ii. 1824, p. 369.

the *Oryx leucoryx* (fig. 63) are directed backwards, and are of such length that their points reach beyond the middle of the back, over which they extend in almost parallel lines. Thus they seem singularly ill-fitted for fighting; but Mr. Bartlett informs me that when two of these animals prepare for battle, they kneel down, with their heads between their fore-legs, and in this attitude the horns stand nearly parallel and close to the ground, with the points directed forwards and a little upwards. The combatants then gradually approach each other, and each endeavours to get the upturned points under the body of the other; if one succeeds in doing this, he suddenly springs up, throwing up his head at the same time, and can thus wound or perhaps even transfix his antagonist. Both animals always kneel down, so as to guard as far as possible against this manœuvre. It has been recorded that one of these antelopes has used his horn with effect even against a lion; yet from being forced to place his head between the fore legs in order to bring the points of the horns forward, he would generally be under a great disadvantage when attacked by any other animal. It is, therefore, not probable that the horns have been modified into their present great length and peculiar position, as a protection against beasts of prey. We can however see that, as soon as some ancient male progenitor of the Oryx acquired moderately long horns, directed a little backwards, he would be compelled, in his battles with rival males, to bend his head somewhat inwards or downwards, as is now done by certain stags; and it is not improbable that he might have acquired the habit of at first occasionally and afterwards of regularly kneeling down. In this case it is almost certain that the males which possessed the longest horns would have had a great advantage over others with shorter horns; and then the horns would gradually have been rendered longer and longer, through sexual selection, until they acquired their present extraordinary length and position.

With stags of many kinds the branches of the horns offer a curious case of difficulty; for certainly a single straight point would inflict a much more serious wound than several diverging ones. In Sir Philip Egerton's museum there is a horn of the red-deer (*Cervus elaphus*), thirty inches in length, with "not fewer than fifteen snags or branches;" and at Moritzburg there is still preserved a pair of antlers of a red-deer, shot in 1699 by Frederick I., one of which bears the astonishing number of thirty-three branches and the other twenty-seven, making altogether sixty branches. Richardson figures a pair of antlers of the wild reindeer with twenty-nine points.[24] From the manner in which the horns are branched, and more especially from deer being known occasionally to fight together by kicking with their fore feet,[25] M. Bailly actually comes to the conclusion that

[24] On the horns of red-deer, Owen, 'British Fossil Mammals,' 1846, p. 478; Richardson on the horns of the reindeer, 'Fauna Bor. Americana,' 1829, p. 240. I am indebted to Prof. Victor Carus, for the Moritzburg case.

[25] Hon. J. D. Caton ('Ottawa Acad. of Nat. Science,' May, 1868, p. 9) says that the American deer fight with their fore-feet, after "the question of superiority has been once settled and acknowledged in the herd." Bailly 'Sur l'usage des Cornes,' 'Annales des Sc. Nat.' tom. ii. 1824, p. 371.

their horns are more injurious than useful to them? But this author over-looks the pitched battles between rival males. As I felt much perplexed about the use or advantage of the branches, I applied to Mr. McNeill of Colonsay, who has long and carefully observed the habits of red-deer, and he informs me that he has never seen some of the branches brought into use, but that the brow antlers, from inclining downwards, are a great protection to the forehead, and their points are likewise used in attack. Sir Philip Egerton also informs me both as to red-deer and fallow-deer that, in fighting, they suddenly dash together, and getting their horns fixed against each other's bodies, a desperate struggle ensues. When one is at last forced to yield and turn round, the victor endeavours to plunge his brow antlers into his defeated foe. It thus appears that the upper branches are used chiefly or exclusively for pushing and fencing. Never-theless in some species the upper branches are used as weapons of off-ence; when a man was attacked by a wapiti deer (*Cervus canadensis*) in Judge Caton's park in Ottawa, and several men tried to rescue him, the stag "never raised his head from the ground; in fact he kept his face almost flat on the ground, with his nose nearly between his fore feet, ex-cept when he rolled his head to one side to take a new observation pre-paratory to a plunge." In this position the ends of the horns were direct-ed against his adversaries. "In rolling his head he necessarily raised it somewhat, because his antlers were so long that he could not roll his head without raising them on one side, while, on the other side they touched the ground." The stag by this procedure gradually drove the party of rescuers backwards to a distance of 150 or 200 feet; and the attacked man was killed.[26]

Although the horns of stags are efficient weapons, there can, I think, be no doubt that a single point would have been much more dangerous than a branched antler; and Judge Caton, who has had large experience with deer, fully concurs in this conclusion. Nor do the branching horns, though highly important as a means of defence against rival stags, appear perfectly well adapted for this purpose, as they are liable to become in-terlocked. The suspicion has therefore crossed my mind that they may serve in part as ornaments. That the branched antlers of stags as well as the elegant lyrated horns of certain antelopes, with their graceful double curvature (fig. 64), are ornamental in our eyes, no one will dispute. If, then, the horns, like the splendid accoutrements of the knights of old, add to the noble appearance of stags and antelopes, they may have been modified partly for this purpose, though mainly for actual service in bat-tle; but I have no evidence in favour of this belief.

An interesting case has lately been published, from which it appears that the horns of a deer in one district in the United States are now be-ing modified through sexual and natural selection. A writer in an excel-lent American Journal [27] says that he has hunted for the last twenty-one

---

[26] See a most interesting account in the Appendix to Hon. J. D. Caton's paper, as above quoted.

[27] 'The American Naturalist,' Dec. 1869, p. 552.

years in the Adirondacks, where the *Cervus virginianus* abounds. About fourteen years ago he first heard of *spike-horn bucks*. These became from year to year more common; about five years ago he shot one, and afterwards another, and now they are frequently killed. "The spike-horn differs greatly from the common antler of the *C. virginianus*. It consists of

FIG. 64.—Strepsiceros Kudu (from Sir Andrew Smith's 'Zoology of South Africa').

a single spike, more slender than the antler, and scarcely half so long, projecting forward from the brow, and terminating in a very sharp point. It gives a considerable advantage to its possessor over the common buck. Besides enabling him to run more swiftly through the thick woods and underbrush (every hunter knows that does and yearling bucks run much more rapidly than the large bucks when armed with their cumbrous antlers), the spike-horn is a more effective weapon than the common antler. With this advantage the spike-horn bucks are gaining upon the common bucks, and may, in time, entirely supersede them in the Adirondacks. Undoubtedly, the first spike-horn buck was merely an accidental freak of nature. But his spike-horns gave him an advantage, and enabled him to propagate his peculiarity. His descendants having a like advantage, have propagated the peculiarity in a constantly increasing ratio, till they are slowly crowding the antlered deer from the region they inhabit." A critic has well objected to this account by asking, why, if the simple horns are now so advantageous, were the branched antlers of the parent-form ever developed? To this I can only answer by remarking, that a new mode of attack with new weapons might be a great advantage, as shewn by the case of the *Ovis cycloceros*, who thus conquered a domestic ram famous for his fighting power. Though the branched antlers of a stag are well adapted for fighting with his rivals, and though it might be an advantage to the prong-horned variety slowly to acquire long and branched horns, if he had to fight only with others of the same kind, yet it by no means follows that branched horns would be the best fitted for conquering a foe differently armed. In the foregoing case of the *Oryx leucoryx*, it is almost certain that the victory would rest with an antelope having short horns, and who therefore did not need to kneel down, though an oryx might profit by having still longer horns, if he fought only with his proper rivals.

Male quadrupeds, which are furnished with tusks, use them in various ways, as in the case of horns. The boar strikes laterally and upwards; the musk-deer downwards with serious effect.[28] The walrus, though having so short a neck and so unwieldy a body, "can strike either upwards, or downwards, or sideways, with equal dexterity." [29] I was informed by the late Dr. Falconer, that the Indian elephant fights in a different manner according to the position and curvature of his tusks. When they are directed forwards and upwards he is able to fling a tiger to a great distance —it is said to even thirty feet; when they are short and turned downwards he endeavours suddenly to pin the tiger to the ground and, in consequence, is dangerous to the rider, who is liable to be jerked off the howdah.[30]

Very few male quadrupeds possess weapons of two distinct kinds specially adapted for fighting with rival males. The male muntjac-deer (Cervulus), however, offers an exception, as he is provided with horns and exserted canine teeth. But we may infer from what follows that one form of weapon has often been replaced in the course of ages by another. With ruminants the development of horns generally stands in an inverse relation with that of even moderately developed canine teeth. Thus camels, guanacoes, chevrotains, and musk-deer, are hornless, and they have efficient canines; these teeth being "always of smaller size in the females than in the males." The Camelidæ have, in addition to their true canines,

---

[28] Pallas, 'Spicilegia Zoologica,' fasc. xiii. 1779, p. 18.
[29] Lamont, 'Seasons with the Sea-Horses,' 1861, p. 141.
[30] See also Corse ('Philosoph. Transact.' 1799, p. 212) on the manner in which the short-tusked Mooknah variety attacks other elephants.

a pair of canine-shaped incisors in their upper jaws.[31] Male deer and antelopes, on the other hand, possess horns, and they rarely have canine teeth; and these, when present, are always of small size, so that it is doubtful whether they are of any service in their battles. In *Antilope montana* they exist only as rudiments in the young male, disappearing as he grows old; and they are absent in the female at all ages; but the females of certain other antelopes and of certain deer have been known occasionally to exhibit rudiments of these teeth.[32] Stallions have small canine teeth, which are either quite absent or rudimentary in the mare; but they do not appear to be used in fighting, for stallions bite with their incisors, and do not open their mouths wide like camels and guanacoes. Whenever the adult male possesses canines, now inefficient, whilst the female has either none or mere rudiments, we may conclude that the early male progenitor of the species was provided with efficient canines, which have been partially transferred to the females. The reduction of these teeth in the males seems to have followed from some change in their manner of fighting, often (but not in the horse) caused by the development of new weapons.

Tusks and horns are manifestly of high importance to their possessors, for their development consumes much organised matter. A single tusk of the Asiatic elephant—one of the extinct woolly species—and of the African elephant, have been known to weigh respectively 150, 160, and 180 pounds; and even greater weights have been given by some authors.[33] With deer, in which the horns are periodically renewed, the drain on the constitution must be greater; the horns, for instance, of the moose weigh from fifty to sixty pounds, and those of the extinct Irish elk from sixty to seventy pounds—the skull of the latter weighing on an average only five pounds and a quarter. Although the horns are not periodically renewed in sheep, yet their development, in the opinion of many agriculturists, entails a sensible loss to the breeder. Stags, moreover, in escaping from beasts of prey are loaded with an additional weight for the race, and are greatly retarded in passing through a woody country. The moose, for instance, with horns extending five and a half feet from tip to tip, although so skilful in their use that he will not touch or break a twig when walking quietly, cannot act so dexterously whilst rushing away from a pack of wolves. "During his progress he holds his nose up, so as to lay the horns horizontally back; and in this attitude cannot see the ground distinctly."[34] The tips of the horns of the great Irish elk were actually eight feet

---

[31] Owen, 'Anatomy of Vertebrates,' vol. iii. p. 349.

[32] See Rüppell (in 'Proc. Zoolog. Soc.' Jan. 12, 1836, p. 3) on the canines in deer and antelopes, with a note by Mr. Martin on a female American deer. See also Falconer ('Palæont. Memoirs and Notes,' vol. i. 1868, p. 576) on canines in an adult female deer. In old males of the musk-deer the canines (Pallas, 'Spic. Zoolog.' fasc. xiii. 1779, p. 18) sometimes grow to the length of three inches, whilst in old females a rudiment projects scarcely half an inch above the gums.

[33] Emerson Tennent, 'Ceylon,' 1859, vol. ii. p. 275; Owen, 'British Fossil Mammals,' 1846, p. 245.

[34] Richardson, 'Fauna Bor. Americana,' on the moose, *Alces palmata*, pp. 236, 237;

apart! Whilst the horns are covered with velvet, which lasts with red-deer for about twelve weeks, they are extremely sensitive to a blow; so that in Germany the stags at this time somewhat change their habits, and avoiding dense forests, frequent young woods and low thickets.[35] These facts remind us that male birds have acquired ornamental plumes at the cost of retarded flight, and other ornaments at the cost of some loss of power in their battles with rival males.

With mammals, when, as is often the case, the sexes differ in size, the males are almost always larger and stronger. I am informed by Mr. Gould that this holds good in a marked manner with the marsupials of Australia, the males of which appear to continue growing until an unusually late age. But the most extraordinary case is that of one of the seals (*Callorhinus ursinus*), a full-grown female weighing less than one-sixth of a full-grown male.[36] Dr. Gill remarks that it is with the polygamous seals, the males of which are well known to fight savagely together, that the sexes differ much in size; the monogamous species differing but little. Whales also afford evidence of the relation existing between the pugnacity of the males and their large size compared with that of the female; the males of the right-whales do not fight together, and they are not larger, but rather smaller, than their females; on the other hand, male sperm-whales fight much together, and their bodies are "often found scarred with the imprint of their rival's teeth," and they are double the size of the females. The greater strength of the male, as Hunter long ago remarked,[37] is invariably displayed in those parts of the body which are brought into action in fighting with rival males—for instance, in the massive neck of the bull. Male quadrupeds are also more courageous and pugnacious than the females. There can be little doubt that these characters have been gained, partly through sexual selection, owing to a long series of victories, by the stronger and more courageous males over the weaker, and partly through the inherited effects of use. It is probable that the successive variations in strength, size, and courage, whether due to mere variability or to the effects of use, by the accumulation of which male quadrupeds have acquired these characteristic qualities, occurred rather late in life, and were consequently to a large extent limited in their transmission to the same sex.

From these considerations I was anxious to obtain information as to the Scotch deer-hound, the sexes of which differ more in size than those of any other breed (though bloodhounds differ considerably), or than in any wild canine species known to me. Accordingly, I applied to Mr. Cup-

on the expanse of the horns, 'Land and Water,' 1869, p. 143. See also Owen, 'British Fossil Mammals,' on the Irish elk, pp. 447, 455.

[35] 'Forest Creatures,' by C. Boner, 1861, p. 60.

[36] See the very interesting paper by Mr. J. A. Allen in 'Bull. Mus. Comp. Zoolog. of Cambridge, United States,' vol. ii. No. 1, p. 82. The weights were ascertained by a careful observer, Capt. Bryant. Dr. Gill in 'The American Naturalist,' January 1871, Prof. Shaler on the relative size of the sexes of whales, 'American Naturalist,' January 1873.

[37] 'Animal Economy,' p. 45.

ples, well known for his success with this breed, who has with great kindness collected for me the following facts from various sources. Fine male dogs, measured at the shoulder, range from 28 inches, which is low, to 33 or even 34 inches in height; and in weight from 80 pounds, which is light, to 120 pounds, or even more. The females range in height from 23 to 27, or even to 28 inches; and in weight from 50 to 70, or even 80 pounds.[38] Mr. Cupples concludes that from 95 to 100 pounds for the male, and 70 for the female, would be a safe average; but there is reason to believe that formerly both sexes attained a greater weight. Mr. Cupples has weighed puppies when a fortnight old; in one litter the average weight of four males exceeded that of two females by six and a half ounces; in another litter the average weight of four males exceeded that of one female by less than one ounce; the same males when three weeks old, exceeded the female by seven and a half ounces, and at the age of six weeks by nearly fourteen ounces. Mr. Wright of Yeldersley House, in a letter to Mr. Cupples, says: "I have taken notes on the sizes and weights of puppies of many litters, and as far as my experience goes, dog-puppies as a rule differ very little from bitches till they arrive at about five or six months old; and then the dogs begin to increase, gaining upon the bitches both in weight and size. At birth, and for several weeks afterwards, a bitch-puppy will occasionally be larger than any of the dogs, but they are invariably beaten by them later." Mr. McNeill, of Colonsay, concludes that "the males do not attain their full growth till over two years old, though the females attain it sooner." According to Mr. Cupples' experience, male dogs go on growing in stature till they are from twelve to eighteen months old, and in weight till from eighteen to twenty-four months old; whilst the females cease increasing in stature at the age of from nine to fourteen or fifteen months, and in weight at the age of from twelve to fifteen months. From these various statements it is clear that the full difference in size between the male and female Scotch deer-hound is not acquired until rather late in life. The males almost exclusively are used for coursing, for, as Mr. McNeill informs me, the females have not sufficient strength and weight to pull down a full-grown deer. From the names used in old legends, it appears, as I hear from Mr. Cupples, that, at a very ancient period, the males were the most celebrated, the females being mentioned only as the mothers of famous dogs. Hence, during many generations, it is the male which has been chiefly tested for strength, size, speed, and courage, and the best will have been bred from. As, however, the males do not attain their full dimensions until rather late in life, they will have tended, in accordance with the law often indicated, to transmit their characters to their male offspring alone; and

[38] See also Richardson's 'Manual on the Dog,' p. 59. Much valuable information on the Scottish deer-hound is given by Mr. McNeill, who first called attention to the inequality in size between the sexes, in Scrope's 'Art of Deer-stalking.' I hope that Mr. Cupples will keep to his intention of publishing a full account and history of this famous breed.

thus the great inequality in size between the sexes of the Scotch deer-hound may probably be accounted for.

The males of some few quadrupeds possess organs or parts developed solely as a means of defence against the attacks of other males. Some kinds of deer use, as we have seen, the upper branches of their horns chiefly or exclusively for defending themselves; and the Oryx antelope, as I am informed by Mr. Bartlett, fences most skilfully with his long, gently curved horns; but these are likewise used as organs of offence. The same observer remarks that rhinoceroses in fighting, parry each other's sidelong blows with their horns, which clatter loudly together, as do the tusks of boars. Although wild boars fight desperately, they seldom, according to Brehm, receive fatal wounds, as the blows fall on each other's tusks, or on the layer of gristly skin covering the shoulder, called by the German hunters, the shield; and here we have a part specially modified for defence. With boars in the prime of life (see fig. 65) the tusks in the lower jaw are used for fighting, but they become in old age, as Brehm states, so much curved inwards and upwards over the snout that they can no longer be used in this way. They may, however, still serve, and even more effectively, as a means of defence. In compensation for the loss of the lower tusks as weapons of offence, those in the upper jaw, which always project a little laterally, increase in old age so much in length and curve so much upwards that they can be used for attack. Nevertheless, an old boar is not so dangerous to man as one at the age of six or seven years.[39]

FIG. 65.—Head of common wild boar, in prime of life (from Brehm).

In the full-grown male Babirusa pig of Celebes (fig. 66), the lower tusks are formidable weapons, like those of the European boar in the prime of life, whilst the upper tusks are so long and have their points so much curled inwards, sometimes even touching the forehead, that they are utterly useless as weapons of attack. They more nearly resemble horns than teeth, and are so manifestly useless as teeth that the animal was formerly supposed to rest his head by hooking them on to a branch! Their convex surfaces, however, if the head were held a little laterally, would serve as an excellent guard; and hence, perhaps, it is that in old animals they "are generally broken off, as if by fighting."[40] Here, then, we have the curious case of the upper tusks of the Babirusa regularly assuming during the prime of life a structure which apparently renders them fitted only for defence; whilst in the European boar the lower tusks

[39] Brehm, 'Thierleben,' ii. ss. 729-32.
[40] See Mr. Wallace's interesting account of this animal, 'The Malay Archipelago,' 1869, vol. i. p. 435.

assume in a less degree and only during old age nearly the same form, and then serve in like manner solely for defence.

In the wart-hog (*Phacochoerus œthiopicus*, fig. 67) the tusks in the upper jaw of the male curve upwards during the prime of life, and from being pointed serve as formidable weapons. The tusks in the lower jaw are sharper than those in the upper, but from their shortness it seems hardly possible that they can be used as weapons of attack. They must, however, greatly strengthen those in the upper jaw, from being ground so as to fit closely against their bases. Neither the upper nor the lower tusks

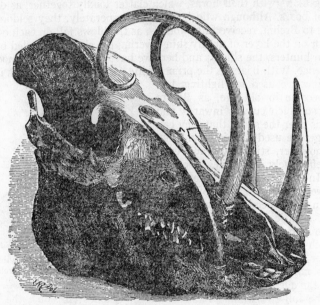

Fig. 66.—Skull of the Babirusa Pig (from Wallace's 'Malay Archipelago').

appear to have been specially modified to act as guards, though no doubt they are to a certain extent used for this purpose. But the wart-hog is not destitute of other special means of protection, for it has, on each side of the face, beneath the eyes, a rather stiff, yet flexible, cartilaginous, oblong pad (fig. 67), which projects two or three inches outwards; and it appeared to Mr. Bartlett and myself, when viewing the living animal, that these pads, when struck from beneath by the tusks of an opponent, would be turned upwards, and would thus admirably protect the somewhat prominent eyes. I may add, on the authority of Mr. Bartlett, that these boars when fighting stand directly face to face.

Lastly, the African river-hog (*Potomochoerus penicillatus*) has a hard cartilaginous knob on each side of the face beneath the eyes, which answers to the flexible pad of the wart-hog; it has also two bony prominences on the upper jaw above the nostrils. A boar of this species in the Zoological Gardens recently broke into the cage of the wart-hog. They fought all night long, and were found in the morning much exhausted, but not seriously wounded. It is a significant fact, as shewing the purposes of the above-described projections and excrescences, that these were covered with blood, and were scored and abraded in an extraordinary manner.

FIG. 67.—Head of female Æthiopian wart-hog, from 'Proc. Zool. Soc.' 1869, shewing the same characters as the male, though on a reduced scale.

N. B. When the engraving was first made, I was under the impression that it represented the male.

Although the males of so many members of the pig family are provided with weapons, and as we have just seen with means of defence, these weapons seem to have been acquired within a rather late geological period. Dr. Forsyth Major specifies [41] several miocene species, in none of which do the tusks appear to have been largely developed in the males; and Professor Rütimeyer was formerly struck with this same fact.

The mane of the lion forms a good defence against the attacks of rival lions, the one danger to which he is liable; for the males, as Sir A. Smith informs me, engage in terrible battles, and a young lion dares not approach an old one. In 1857 a tiger at Bromwich broke into the cage of a lion and a fearful scene ensued: "the lion's mane saved his neck and head from being much injured, but the tiger at last succeeded in ripping up his belly, and in a few minutes he was dead." [42] The broad ruff round the throat and chin of the Canadian lynx (*Felis canadensis*) is much longer in the male than in the female; but whether it serves as a defence I do not know. Male seals are well known to fight desperately together, and

---

[41] 'Atti della Soc. Italiana di Sc. Nat.' 1873, vol. xv. fasc. iv.
[42] 'The Times,' Nov. 10th, 1857. In regard to the Canada lynx, see Audubon and Bachman, 'Quadrupeds of North America,' 1846, p 139.

the males of certain kinds (*Otaria jubata*)[43] have great manes, whilst the females have small ones or none. The male baboon of the Cape of Good Hope (*Cynocephalus porcarius*) has a much longer mane and larger canine teeth than the female; and the mane probably serves as a protection, for, on asking the keepers in the Zoological Gardens, without giving them any clue to my object, whether any of the monkeys especially attacked each other by the nape of the neck, I was answered that this was not the case, except with the above baboon. In the Hamadryas baboon, Ehrenberg compares the mane of the adult male to that of a young lion, whilst in the young of both sexes and in the female the mane is almost absent.

It appeared to me probable that the immense woolly mane of the male American bison, which reaches almost to the ground, and is much more developed in the males than in the females, served as a protection to them in their terrible battles; but an experienced hunter told Judge Caton that he had never observed anything which favoured this belief. The stallion has a thicker and fuller mane than the mare; and I have made particular inquiries of two great trainers and breeders, who have had charge of many entire horses, and am assured that they "invariably endeavour to seize one another by the neck." It does not, however, follow from the foregoing statements, that when the hair on the neck serves as a defence, that it was originally developed for this purpose, though this is probable in some cases, as in that of the lion. I am informed by Mr. McNeill that the long hairs on the throat of the stag (*Cervus elaphus*) serve as a great protection to him when hunted, for the dogs generally endeavour to seize him by the throat; but it is not probable that these hairs were specially developed for this purpose; otherwise the young and the females would have been equally protected.

Choice in Pairing by either Sex of Quadrupeds.—Before describing in the next chapter, the differences between the sexes in voice, odours emitted, and ornaments, it will be convenient here to consider whether the sexes exert any choice in their unions. Does the female prefer any particular male, either before or after the males may have fought together for supremacy; or does the male, when not a polygamist, select any particular female? The general impression amongst breeders seems to be that the male accepts any female; and this owing to his eagerness, is, in most cases, probably the truth. Whether the female as a general rule indifferently accepts any male is much more doubtful. In the fourteenth chapter, on Birds, a considerable body of direct and indirect evidence was advanced, shewing that the female selects her partner; and it would be a strange anomaly if female quadrupeds, which stand higher in the scale and have higher mental powers, did not generally, or at least often, exert some choice. The female could in most cases escape, if wooed by a male that did not please or excite her; and when pursued by several

[43] Dr. Murie, on Otaria, 'Proc. Zoolog. Soc.' 1869, p. 109. Mr. J. A. Allen, in the paper above quoted (p. 75), doubts whether the hair, which is longer on the neck in the male than in the female, deserves to be called a mane.

males, as commonly occurs, she would often have the opportunity, whilst they were fighting together, of escaping with some one male, or at least of temporarily pairing with him. This latter contingency has often been observed in Scotland with female red-deer, as I am informed by Sir Philip Egerton and others.[44]

It is scarcely possible that much should be known about female quadrupeds in a state of nature making any choice in their marriage unions. The following curious details on the courtship of one of the eared seals (*Callorhinus ursinus*) are given [45] on the authority of Capt. Bryant, who had ample opportunities for observation. He says, "Many of the females on their arrival at the island where they breed appear desirous of returning to some particular male, and frequently climb the outlying rocks to overlook the rookeries, calling out and listening as if for a familiar voice. Then changing to another place they do the same again. . . . As soon as a female reaches the shore, the nearest male goes down to meet her, making meanwhile a noise like the clucking of a hen to her chickens. He bows to her and coaxes her until he gets between her and the water so that she cannot escape him. Then his manner changes, and with a harsh growl he drives her to a place in his harem. This continues until the lower row of harems is nearly full. Then the males higher up select the time when their more fortunate neighbours are off their guard to steal their wives. This they do by taking them in their mouths and lifting them over the heads of the other females, and carefully placing them in their own harem, carrying them as cats do their kittens. Those still higher up pursue the same method until the whole space is occupied. Frequently a struggle ensues between two males for the possession of the same female, and both seizing her at once pull her in two or terribly lacerate her with their teeth. When the space is all filled, the old male walks around complacently reviewing his family, scolding those who crowd or disturb the others, and fiercely driving off all intruders. This surveillance always keeps him actively occupied."

As so little is known about the courtship of animals in a state of nature, I have endeavoured to discover how far our domesticated quadrupeds evince any choice in their unions. Dogs offer the best opportunity for observation, as they are carefully attended to and well understood. Many breeders have expressed a strong opinion on this head. Thus, Mr. Mayhew remarks, "The females are able to bestow their affections; and tender recollections are as potent over them as they are known to be in other cases, where higher animals are concerned. Bitches are not always prudent in their loves, but are apt to fling themselves away on curs of low degree. If reared with a companion of vulgar appearance, there often springs up between the pair a devotion which no time can afterwards

[44] Mr. Boner, in his excellent description of the habits of the red-deer in Germany ('Forest Creatures,' 1861, p. 81) says, "while the stag is defending his rights against one intruder, another invades the sanctuary of his harem, and carries off trophy after trophy." Exactly the same thing occurs with seals, see Mr. J. A. Allen, ibid. p. 100.

[45] Mr. J. A. Allen in 'Bull. Mus. Comp. Zoolog. of Cambridge, United States,' vol. ii. No. 1, p. 99.

subdue. The passion, for such it really is, becomes of a more than romantic endurance." Mr. Mayhew, who attended chiefly to the smaller breeds, is convinced that the females are strongly attracted by males of a large size.[46] The well-known veterinary Blaine states[47] that his own female pug dog became so attached to a spaniel, and a female setter to a cur, that in neither case would they pair with a dog of their own breed until several weeks had elapsed. Two similar and trustworthy accounts have been given me in regard to a female retriever and a spaniel, both of which became enamoured with terrier-dogs.

Mr. Cupples informs me that he can personally vouch for the accuracy of the following more remarkable case, in which a valuable and wonderfully-intelligent female terrier loved a retriever belonging to a neighbour to such a degree, that she had often to be dragged away from him. After their permanent separation, although repeatedly showing milk in her teats, she would never acknowledge the courtship of any other dog, and to the regret of her owner never bore puppies. Mr. Cupples also states, that in 1868, a female deerhound in his kennel thrice produced puppies, and on each occasion shewed a marked preference for one of the largest and handsomest, but not the most eager, of four deerhounds living with her, all in the prime of life. Mr. Cupples has observed that the female generally favours a dog whom she has associated with and knows; her shyness and timidity at first incline her against a strange dog. The male, on the contrary, seems rather inclined towards strange females. It appears to be rare when the male refuses any particular female, but Mr. Wright, of Yeldersley House, a great breeder of dogs, informs me that he has known some instances; he cites the case of one of his own deerhounds, who would not take any notice of a particular female mastiff, so that another deerhound had to be employed. It would be superfluous to give, as I could, other instances, and I will only add that Mr. Barr, who has carefully bred many bloodhounds, states that in almost every instance particular individuals of opposite sexes shew a decided preference for each other. Finally, Mr. Cupples, after attending to this subject for another year, has written to me, "I have had full confirmation of my former statement, that dogs in breeding form decided preferences for each other, being often influenced by size, bright colour, and individual characters, as well as by the degree of their previous familiarity."

In regard to horses, Mr. Blenkiron, the greatest breeder of race-horses in the world, informs me that stallions are so frequently capricious in their choice, rejecting one mare and without any apparent cause taking to another, that various artifices have to be habitually used. The famous Monarque, for instance, would never consciously look at the dam of Gladiateur, and a trick had to be practised. We can partly see the reason why valuable race-horse stallions, which are in such demand as to be exhausted, should be so particular in their choice. Mr. Blenkiron has never

---

[46] 'Dogs: their Management,' by E. Mayhew, M.R.C.V.S., 2nd edit. 1864, pp. 187-192.

[47] Quoted by Alex. Walker 'On Intermarriage,' 1838, p. 276; see also p. 244.

known a mare reject a horse; but this has occurred in Mr. Wright's stable, so that the mare had to be cheated. Prosper Lucas [48] quotes various statements from French authorities, and remarks, "On voit des étalons qui s'éprennent d'une jument, et négligent toutes les autres." He gives, on the authority of Baëlen, similar facts in regard to bulls; and Mr. H. Reeks assures me that a famous short-horn bull belonging to his father "invariably refused to be matched with a black cow." Hoffberg, in describing the domesticated reindeer of Lapland says, "Fœminæ majores et fortiores mares præ cæteris admittunt, ad eos confugiunt, a junioribus agitatæ, qui hos in fugam conjiciunt." [49] A clergyman, who has bred many pigs, asserts that sows often reject one boar and immediately accept another.

From these facts there can be no doubt that, with most of our domesticated quadrupeds, strong individual antipathies and preferences are frequently exhibited, and much more commonly by the female than by the male. This being the case, it is improbable that the unions of quadrupeds in a state of nature should be left to mere chance. It is much more probable that the females are allured or excited by particular males, who possess certain characters in a higher degree than other males; but what these characters are, we can seldom or never discover with certainty.

[48] 'Traité de l'Héréd. Nat.' tom. ii. 1850, p. 296.
[49] 'Amœnitates Acad.' vol. iv. 1788, p. 160.

CHAPTER XVIII

SECONDARY SEXUAL CHARACTERS OF MAMMALS—*continued*

*Voice—Remarkable sexual peculiarities in seals—Odour—Development of the hair—
Colour of the hair and skin—Anomalous case of the female being more ornamented than the male—Colour and ornaments due to sexual selection—Colour
acquired for the sake of protection—Colour, though common to both sexes, often
due to sexual selection—On the disappearance of spots and stripes in adult quadrupeds—On the colours and ornaments of the Quadrumana—Summary.*

QUADRUPEDS use their voices for various purposes, as a signal of danger,
as a call from one member of a troop to another, or from the mother to
her lost offspring, or from the latter for protection to their mother; but
such uses need not here be considered. We are concerned only with the
difference between the voices of the sexes, for instance between that of
the lion and lioness, or of the bull and cow. Almost all male animals use
their voices much more during the rutting-season than at any other time;
and some, as the giraffe and porcupine,[1] are said to be completely mute
excepting at this season. As the throats (*i. e.* the larynx and thyroid
bodies [2]) of stags periodically become enlarged at the beginning of the
breeding-season, it might be thought that their powerful voices must be
somehow of high importance to them; but this is very doubtful. From
information given to me by two experienced observers, Mr. McNeill and
Sir P. Egerton, it seems that young stags under three years old do not
roar or bellow; and that the old ones begin bellowing at the commencement of the breeding-season, at first only occasionally and moderately,
whilst they restlessly wander about in search of the females. Their battles are prefaced by loud and prolonged bellowing, but during the actual
conflict they are silent. Animals of all kinds which habitually use their
voices utter various noises under any strong emotion, as when enraged
and preparing to fight; but this may merely be the result of nervous excitement, which leads to the spasmodic contraction of almost all the muscles of the body, as when a man grinds his teeth and clenches his fists
in rage or agony. No doubt stags challenge each other to mortal combat
by bellowing; but those with the more powerful voices, unless at the
same time the stronger, better-armed, and more courageous, would not
gain any advantage over their rivals.

It is possible that the roaring of the lion may be of some service to him
by striking terror into his adversary; for when enraged he likewise erects

[1] Owen, 'Anatomy of Vertebrates,' vol. iii. p. 585.
[2] Ibid. p. 595.

his mane and thus instinctively tries to make himself appear as terrible as possible. But it can hardly be supposed that the bellowing of the stag, even if it be of service to him in this way, can have been important enough to have led to the periodical enlargement of the throat. Some writers suggest that the bellowing serves as a call to the female; but the experienced observers above quoted inform me that female deer do not search for the male, though the males search eagerly for the females, as indeed might be expected from what we know of the habits of other male quadrupeds. The voice of the female, on the other hand, quickly brings to her one or more stags,[3] as is well known to the hunters who in wild countries imitate her cry. If we could believe that the male had the power to excite or allure the female by his voice, the periodical enlargement of his vocal organs would be intelligible on the principle of sexual selection, together with inheritance limited to the same sex and season; but we have no evidence in favour of this view. As the case stands, the loud voice of the stag during the breeding-season does not seem to be of any special service to him, either during his courtship or battles, or in any other way. But may we not believe that the frequent use of the voice, under the strong excitement of love, jealousy, and rage, continued during many generations, may at last have produced an inherited effect on the vocal organs of the stag, as well as of other male animals? This appears to me, in our present state of knowledge, the most probable view.

The voice of the adult male gorilla is tremendous, and he is furnished with a laryngeal sack, as is the adult male orang.[4] The gibbons rank among the noisiest of monkeys, and the Sumatra species (*Hylobates syndactylus*) is also furnished with an air sack; but Mr. Blyth, who has had opportunities for observation, does not believe that the male is noisier than the female. Hence, these latter monkeys probably use their voices as a mutual call; and this is certainly the case with some quadrupeds, for instance the beaver.[5] Another gibbon, the *H. agilis*, is remarkable, from having the power of giving a complete and correct octave of musical notes,[6] which we may reasonably suspect serves as a sexual charm; but I shall have to recur to this subject in the next chapter. The vocal organs of the American *Mycetes caraya* are one-third larger in the male than in the female, and are wonderfully powerful. These monkeys in warm weather make the forests resound at morning and evening with their overwhelming voices. The males begin the dreadful concert, and often continue it during many hours, the females sometimes joining in with their less powerful voices. An excellent observer, Rengger,[7] could not perceive that they were excited to begin by any special cause; he thinks that, like many birds, they delight in their own music, and try to excel each

---

[3] See, for instance, Major W. Ross King ('The Sportsman in Canada,' 1866, pp. 53, 131) on the habits of the moose and wild reindeer.

[4] Owen, 'Anatomy of Vertebrates,' vol. iii. p. 600.

[5] Mr. Green, in 'Journal of Linn. Society,' vol. x. Zoology, 1869, note 362.

[6] C. L. Martin, 'General Introduction to the Nat. Hist. of Mamm. Animals,' 1841, p. 431.

[7] 'Naturgeschichte der Säugethiere von Paraguay,' 1830, ss. 15, 21.

other. Whether most of the foregoing monkeys have acquired their powerful voices in order to beat their rivals and charm the females—or
whether the vocal organs have been strengthened and enlarged through
the inherited effects of long-continued use without any particular good
being thus gained—I will not pretend to say; but the former view, at
least in the case of the *Hylobates agilis,* seems the most probable.

I may here mention two very curious sexual peculiarities occurring in
seals, because they have been supposed by some writers to affect the
voice. The nose of the male sea-elephant (*Macrorhinus proboscideus*)
becomes greatly elongated during the breeding-season, and can then be
erected. In this state it is sometimes a foot in length. The female is not
thus provided at any period of life. The male makes a wild, hoarse, gurg-
ling noise, which is audible at a great distance and is believed to be
strengthened by the proboscis; the voice of the female being different.
Lesson compares the erection of the proboscis, with the swelling of the
wattles of male gallinaceous birds whilst courting the females. In another allied kind of seal, the bladder-nose (*Cystophora cristata*), the
head is covered by a great hood or bladder. This is supported by the septum of the nose, which is produced far backwards and rises into an internal crest seven inches in height. The hood is clothed with short hair,
and is muscular; it can be inflated until it more than equals the whole
head in size! The males when rutting, fight furiously on the ice, and their
roaring "is said to be sometimes so loud as to be heard four miles off."
When attacked they likewise roar or bellow; and whenever irritated the
bladder is inflated and quivers. Some naturalists believe that the voice is
thus strengthened, but various other uses have been assigned to this extraordinary structure. Mr. R. Brown thinks that it serves as a protection
against accidents of all kinds; but this is not probable, for, as I am assured by Mr. Lamont who killed 600 of these animals, the hood is rudimentary in the females, and it is not developed in the males during
youth.[8]

Odour.—With some animals, as with the notorious skunk of America,
the overwhelming odour which they emit appears to serve exclusively as
a defence. With shrew-mice (Sorex) both sexes possess abdominal scent-
glands, and there can be little doubt, from the rejection of their bodies by
birds and beasts of prey, that the odour is protective; nevertheless, the
glands become enlarged in the males during the breeding-season. In many
other quadrupeds the glands are of the same size in both sexes,[9] but their

[8] On the sea-elephant, see an article by Lesson, in 'Dict. Class. Hist. Nat.' tom.
xiii. p. 418. For the Cystophora, or Stemmatopus, see Dr. Dekay, 'Annals of Lyce-
um of Nat. Hist. New York,' vol. i. 1824, p. 94. Pennant has also collected information from the sealers on this animal. The fullest account is given by Mr. Brown, in
'Proc. Zoolog. Soc.' 1868, p. 435.

[9] As with the castoreum of the beaver, see Mr. L. H. Morgan's most interesting
work, 'The American Beaver,' 1868, p. 300. Pallas ('Spic. Zoolog.' fasc. viii. 1779, p.
23) has well discussed the odoriferous glands of mammals. Owen ('Anat. of Vertebrates,' vol. iii. p. 634) also gives an account of these glands, including those of the

uses are not known. In other species the glands are confined to the males, or are more developed than in the females; and they almost always become more active during the rutting-season. At this period the glands on the sides of the face of the male elephant enlarge, and emit a secretion having a strong musky odour. The males, and rarely the females, of many kinds of bats have glands and protrudable sacks situated in various parts; and it is believed that these are odoriferous.

The rank effluvium of the male goat is well known, and that of certain male deer is wonderfully strong and persistent. On the banks of the Plata I perceived the air tainted with the odour of the male *Cervus campestris,* at half a mile to leeward of a herd; and a silk handkerchief, in which I carried home a skin, though often used and washed, retained, when first unfolded, traces of the odour for one year and seven months. This animal does not emit its strong odour until more than a year old, and if castrated whilst young never emits it.[10] Besides the general odour, permeating the whole body of certain ruminants (for instance *Bos moschatus*) in the breeding-season, many deer, antelopes, sheep, and goats possess odoriferous glands in various situations, more especially on their faces. The so-called tear-sacks, or suborbital pits, come under this head. These glands secrete a semi-fluid fetid matter which is sometimes so copious as to stain the whole face, as I have myself seen in an antelope. They are "usually larger in the male than in the female, and their development is checked by castration."[11] According to Desmarest they are altogether absent in the female of *Antilope subgutturosa.* Hence, there can be no doubt that they stand in close relation with the reproductive functions. They are also sometimes present, and sometimes absent, in nearly allied forms. In the adult male musk-deer (*Moschus moschiferus*), a naked space round the tail is bedewed with an odoriferous fluid, whilst in the adult female, and in the male until two years old, this space is covered with hair and is not odoriferous. The proper musk-sack of this deer is from its position necessarily confined to the male, and forms an additional scent-organ. It is a singular fact that the matter secreted by this latter gland, does not, according to Pallas, change in consistence, or increase in quantity, during the rutting-season; nevertheless this naturalist admits that its presence is in some way connected with the act of reproduction. He gives, however, only a conjectural and unsatisfactory explanation of its use.[12]

In most cases, when only the male emits a strong odour during the breeding-season, it probably serves to excite or allure the female. We

elephant, and (p. 763) those of shrew-mice. On Bats, Mr. Dobson, 'Proc. Zool. Soc.' 1873, p. 241.
[10] Rengger, 'Naturgeschichte der Säugethiere von Paraguay,' 1830, s. 355. This observer also gives some curious particulars in regard to the odour.
[11] Owen, 'Anatomy of Vertebrates,' vol. iii. p. 632. See also Dr. Murie's observations on those glands in the 'Proc. Zoolog. Soc.' 1870, p. 340. Desmarest, On the *Antilope subgutturosa*, 'Mammalogie,' 1820, p. 455.
[12] Pallas 'Spicelegia Zoolog.' fasc. xiii. 1799, p. 24; Desmoulins, 'Dict. Class. d'Hist. Nat.' tom. iii. p. 586.

must not judge on this head by our own taste, for it is well known that rats are enticed by certain essential oils, and cats by valerian, substances far from agreeable to us; and that dogs, though they will not eat carrion, sniff and roll on it. From the reasons given when discussing the voice of the stag, we may reject the idea that the odour serves to bring the females from a distance to the males. Active and long-continued use cannot here have come into play, as in the case of the vocal organs. The odour emitted must be of considerable importance to the male, inasmuch as large and complex glands, furnished with muscles for everting the sack, and for closing or opening the orifice, have in some cases been developed. The development of these organs is intelligible through sexual selection, if the most odoriferous males are the most successful in winning the females, and in leaving offspring to inherit their gradually perfected glands and odours.

Development of the Hair.—We have seen that male quadrupeds often have the hair on their necks and shoulders much more developed than the females; and many additional instances could be given. This sometimes serves as a defence to the male during his battles; but whether the hair in most cases has been specially developed for this purpose, is very doubtful. We may feel almost certain that this is not the case, when only a thin and narrow crest runs along the back; for a crest of this kind would afford scarcely any protection, and the ridge of the back is not a place likely to be injured; nevertheless such crests are sometimes confined to the males, or are much more developed in them than in the females. Two antelopes, the *Tragelaphus scriptus* [13] (see fig. 70, p. 855) and *Portax picta* may be given as instances. When stags, and the males of the wild goat, are enraged or terrified, these crests stand erect; [14] but it cannot be supposed that they have been developed merely for the sake of exciting fear in their enemies. One of the above-named antelopes, the *Portax picta,* has a large well-defined brush of black hair on the throat, and this is much larger in the male than in the female. In the *Ammotragus tragelaphus* of North Africa, a member of the sheep-family, the fore-legs are almost concealed by an extraordinary growth of hair, which depends from the neck and upper halves of the legs; but Mr. Bartlett does not believe that this mantle is of the least use to the male, in whom it is much more developed than in the female.

Male quadrupeds of many kinds differ from the females in having more hair, or hair of a different character, on certain parts of their faces. Thus the bull alone has curled hair on the forehead. [15] In three closely-allied sub-genera of the goat family, only the males possess beards sometimes of large size; in two other sub-genera both sexes have a beard, but it disappears in some of the domestic breeds of the common goat; and

[13] Dr. Gray, 'Gleanings from the Menagerie at Knowsley,' pl. 28.
[14] Judge Caton on the Wapiti, 'Transact. Ottawa Acad. Nat. Sciences,' 1868, pp. 36, 40; Blyth, 'Land and Water,' on *Capra œgagrus,* 1867, p. 37.
[15] 'Hunter's Essays and Observations,' edited by Owen, 1861, vol. i. p. 236.

neither sex of the Hemitragus has a beard. In the ibex the beard is not developed during the summer, and it is so small at other times that it may be called rudimentary.[16] With some monkeys the beard is confined to the male, as in the orang; or is much larger in the male than in the female, as in the *Mycetes caraya* and *Pithecia satanas* (fig. 68). So it is with the whiskers of some species of Macacus,[17] and, as we have seen, with the manes of some species of baboons. But with most kinds of monkeys the various tufts of hair about the face and head are alike in both sexes.

The males of various members of the ox family (Bovidæ), and of cer-

FIG. 68.—Pithecia satanas, male (from Brehm).

tain antelopes, are furnished with a dewlap, or great fold of skin on the neck, which is much less developed in the female.

Now, what must we conclude with respect to such sexual differences as these? No one will pretend that the beards of certain male goats, or the dewlaps of the bull, or the crests of hair along the backs of certain male antelopes, are of any use to them in their ordinary habits. It is possible that the immense beard of the male Pithecia, and the large beard of the male orang, may protect their throats when fighting; for the keepers in the Zoological Gardens inform me that many monkeys attack each other by the throat; but it is not probable that the beard has been de-

[16] See Dr. Gray's 'Cat. of Mammalia in Brit. Museum,' part iii. 1852, p. 144.
[17] Rengger, 'Säugethiere,' &c. s. 14; Desmarest, 'Mammalogie,' p. 86.

veloped for a distinct purpose from that served by the whiskers, moustache, and other tufts of hair on the face; and no one will suppose that
these are useful as a protection. Must we attribute all these appendages
of hair or skin to mere purposeless variability in the male? It cannot be
denied that this is possible; for in many domesticated quadrupeds, certain characters, apparently not derived through reversion from any wild
parent form, are confined to the males, or are more developed in them
than in the females—for instance, the hump on the male zebu-cattle of
India, the tail of fat-tailed rams, the arched outline of the forehead in the
males of several breeds of sheep, and lastly, the mane, the long hairs on
the hind legs, and the dewlap of the male of the Berbura goat.[18] The
mane, which occurs only in the rams of an African breed of sheep, is a
true secondary sexual character, for, as I hear from Mr. Winwood Reade,
it is not developed if the animal be castrated. Although we ought to be
extremely cautious, as shewn in my work on 'Variation under Domestication,' in concluding that any character, even with animals kept by semi-
civilised people, has not been subjected to selection by man, and thus
augmented, yet in the cases just specified this is improbable; more especially as the characters are confined to the males, or are more strongly
developed in them than in the females. If it were positively known that
the above African ram is a descendant of the same primitive stock as the
other breeds of sheep, and if the Berbura male-goat with his mane, dewlap, &c., is descended from the same stock as other goats, then, assuming
that selection has not been applied to these characters, they must be due
to simple variability, together with sexually-limited inheritance.

Hence it appears reasonable to extend this same view to all analogous
cases with animals in a state of nature. Nevertheless I cannot persuade
myself that it generally holds good, as in the case of the extraordinary
development of hair on the throat and fore-legs of the male Ammotragus,
or in that of the immense beard of the male Pithecia. Such study as I
have been able to give to nature makes me believe that parts or organs
which are highly developed, were acquired at some period for a special
purpose. With those antelopes in which the adult male is more strongly-
coloured than the female, and with those monkeys in which the hair on
the face is elegantly arranged and coloured in a diversified manner, it
seems probable that the crests and tufts of hair were gained as ornaments; and this I know is the opinion of some naturalists. If this be correct, there can be little doubt that they were gained or at least modified
through sexual selection; but how far the same view may be extended to
other mammals is doubtful.

Colour of the Hair and of the Naked Skin.—I will first give briefly all
the cases known to me of male quadrupeds differing in colour from the females. With Marsupials, as I am informed by Mr. Gould, the sexes rarely

---

[18] See the chapters on these several animals in vol. i. of my 'Variation of Animals
under Domestication;' also vol. ii. p. 73; also chap xx. on the practice of selection by
semi-civilised people. For the Berbura goat, see Dr. Gray, 'Catalogue,' ibid. p. 157.

differ in this respect; but the great red kangaroo offers a striking exception, "delicate blue being the prevailing tint in those parts of the female which in the male are red." [19] In the *Didelphis opossum* of Cayenne the female is said to be a little more red than the male. Of the rodents, Dr. Gray remarks: "African squirrels, especially those found in the tropical regions, have the fur much brighter and more vivid at some seasons of the year than at others, and the fur of the male is generally brighter than that of the female." [20] Dr. Gray informs me that he specified the African squirrels, because, from their unusually bright colours, they best exhibit this difference. The female of the *Mus minutus* of Russia is of a paler and dirtier tint than the male. In a large number of bats the fur of the male is lighter than in the female.[21] Mr. Dobson also remarks, with respect to these animals: "Differences, depending partly or entirely on the possession by the male of fur of a much more brilliant hue, or distinguished by different markings or by the greater length of certain portions, are met only, to any appreciable extent, in the frugivorous bats in which the sense of sight is well developed." This last remark deserves attention, as bearing on the question whether bright colours are serviceable to male animals from being ornamental. In one genus of sloths, it is now established, as Dr. Gray states, "that the males are ornamented differently from the females—that is to say, that they have a patch of soft short hair between the shoulders, which is generally of a more or less orange colour, and in one species pure white. The females, on the contrary, are destitute of this mark."

The terrestrial Carnivora and Insectivora rarely exhibit sexual differences of any kind, including colour. The ocelot (*Felis pardalis*), however, is exceptional, for the colours of the female, compared with those of the male, are "moins apparentes, le fauve, étant plus terne, le blanc moins pur, les raies ayant moins de largeur et les taches moins de diamètre." [22] The sexes of the allied *Felis mitis* also differ, but in a less degree; the general hues of the female being rather paler than in the male, with the spots less black. The marine Carnivora or seals, on the other hand, sometimes differ considerably in colour, and they present, as we have already seen, other remarkable sexual differences. Thus the male of the *Otaria nigrescens* of the southern hemisphere is of a rich brown shade above; whilst the female, who acquires her adult tints earlier in life than the male, is dark-grey above, the young of both sexes being of a deep chocolate colour. The male of the northern *Phoca groenlandica* is tawny grey, with a curious saddle-shaped dark mark on the back; the female is much smaller, and has a very different appearance, being "dull white or yellowish

---

[19] *Osphranter rufus,* Gould, 'Mammals of Australia,' 1863, vol. ii. On the *Didelphis,* Desmarest, 'Mammalogie,' p. 256.

[20] 'Annals and Mag. of Nat. Hist.' Nov. 1867, p. 325. On the *Mus minutus,* Desmarest, 'Mammalogie,' p. 304.

[21] J. A. Allen, in 'Bulletin of Mus. Comp. Zoolog. of Cambridge, United States,' 1869, p. 207. Mr. Dobson on sexual characters in the Chiroptera, 'Proc. of the Zoolog. Society,' 1873, p. 241. Dr. Gray on Sloths, ibid. 1871, p. 436.

[22] Desmarest, 'Mammalogie,' 1820, p. 220. On *Felis mitis,* Rengger, ibid. s. 194.

straw-colour, with a tawny hue on the back;" the young at first are pure white, and can "hardly be distinguished among the icy hummocks and snow, their colour thus acting as a protection." [23]

With Ruminants sexual differences of colour occur more commonly than in any other order. A difference of this kind is general in the Strepsicerene antelopes; thus the male nilghau (*Portax picta*) is bluish-grey and much darker than the female, with the square white patch on the throat, the white marks on the fetlocks, and the black spots on the ears all much more distinct. We have seen that in this species the crests and tufts of hair are likewise more developed in the male than in the hornless female. I am informed by Mr. Blyth that the male, without shedding his hair, periodically becomes darker during the breeding-season. Young males cannot be distinguished from young females until about twelve months old; and if the male is emasculated before this period, he never, according to the same authority, changes colour. The importance of this latter fact, as evidence that the colouring of the Portax is of sexual origin, becomes obvious, when we hear [24] that neither the red summer coat nor the blue winter-coat of the Virginian deer is at all affected by emasculation. With most or all of the highly-ornamented species of Tragelaphus the males are darker than the hornless females, and their crests of hair are more fully developed. In the male of that magnificent antelope, the Derbyan eland, the body is redder, the whole neck much blacker, and the white band which separates these colours broader than in the female. In the Cape eland, also, the male is slightly darker than the female. [25]

In the Indian black-buck (*A. bezoartica*), which belongs to another tribe of antelopes, the male is very dark, almost black; whilst the hornless female is fawn-coloured. We meet in this species, as Mr. Blyth informs me, with an exactly similar series of facts, as in the *Portax picta,* namely, in the male periodically changing colour during the breeding-season, in the effects of emasculation on this change, and in the young of both sexes being indistinguishable from each other. In the *Antilope niger* the male is black, the female, as well as the young of both sexes, being brown; in *A. sing-sing* the male is much brighter coloured than the hornless female, and his chest and belly are blacker; in the male *A. caama*, the marks and lines which occur on various parts of the body are black, instead of brown as in the female; in the brindled gnu (*A. gorgon*) "the colours of the male are nearly the same as those of the female, only deeper and of a brighter hue." [26] Other analogous cases could be added.

[23] Dr. Murie on the Otaria, 'Proc. Zool. Soc.' 1869, p. 108. Mr. R. Brown on the *P. groenlandica,* ibid. 1868, p. 417. See also on the colours of seals, Desmarest, ibid. pp. 243, 249.

[24] Judge Caton, in 'Trans. Ottawa Acad. of Nat. Sciences,' 1868, p. 4.

[25] Dr. Gray, 'Cat. of Mamm. in Brit. Mus.' part iii. 1852, pp. 134–142; also Dr. Gray, 'Gleanings from the Menagerie of Knowsley,' in which there is a splendid drawing of the *Oreas derbianus:* see the text on Tragelaphus. For the Cape eland (*Oreas canna*), see Andrew Smith, 'Zoology of S. Africa,' pl. 41 and 42. There are also many of these Antelopes in the Zoological Gardens.

[26] On the *Ant. niger,* see 'Proc. Zool. Soc.' 1850, p. 133. With respect to an allied species, in which there is an equal sexual difference in colour, see Sir S. Baker, 'The

The Banteng bull (*Bos sondaicus*) of the Malayan Archipelago is almost black, with white legs and buttocks; the cow is of a bright dun, as are the young males until about the age of three years, when they rapidly change colour. The emasculated bull reverts to the colour of the female. The female Kemas goat is paler, and both it and the female *Capra œgagrus* are said to be more uniformly tinted than their males. Deer rarely present any sexual differences in colour. Judge Caton, however, informs me that in the males of the wapiti deer (*Cervus canadensis*) the neck, belly, and legs are much darker than in the female; but during the winter the darker tints gradually fade away and disappear. I may here mention that Judge Caton has in his park three races of the Virginian deer, which differs slightly in colour, but the differences are almost exclusively confined to the blue winter or breeding-coat; so that this case may be compared with those given in a previous chapter of closely-allied or representative species of birds, which differ from each other only in their breeding plumage.[27] The females of *Cervus paludosus* of S. America, as well as the young of both sexes, do not possess the black stripes on the nose and the blackish-brown line on the breast, which are characteristic of the adult males.[28] Lastly, as I am informed by Mr. Blyth, the mature male of the beautifully coloured and spotted axis deer is considerably darker than the female: and this hue the castrated male never acquires.

The last Order which we need consider is that of the Primates. The male of the *Lemur macaco* is generally coal-black, whilst the female is brown.[29] Of the Quadrumana of the New World, the females and young of *Mycetes caraya* are greyish-yellow and like each other; in the second year the young male becomes reddish-brown; in the third, black, excepting the stomach, which, however, becomes quite black in the fourth or fifth year. There is also a strongly-marked difference in colour between the sexes of *Mycetes seniculus* and *Cebus capucinus;* the young of the former, and I believe of the latter species, resembling the females. With *Pithecia leucocephala* the young likewise resemble the females, which are brownish-black above and light rusty-red beneath, the adult males being black. The ruff of hair round the face of *Ateles marginatus* is tinted yellow in the male and white in the female. Turning to the Old World, the males of *Hylobates hoolock* are always black, with the exception of a white band over the brows; the females vary from whity-brown to a dark tint mixed with black, but are never wholly black.[30] In the beautiful *Cer-*

Albert Nyanza,' 1866, vol. ii. p. 627. For the *A. sing-sing*, Gray, 'Cat. B. Mus.' p. 100 Desmarest, 'Mammalogie,' p. 468, on the *A. caama*. Andrew Smith, 'Zoology of S. Africa,' on the Gnu.

[27] 'Ottawa Academy of Sciences,' May 21, 1868, pp. 3, 5.

[28] S. Müller, on the Banteng, 'Zoog. Indischen Archipel.' 1839–1844, tab. 35; see also Raffles, as quoted by Mr. Blyth, in 'Land and Water,' 1867, p. 476. On Goats, Dr. Gray, 'Cat. Brit. Mus.' p. 146; Desmarest, 'Mammalogie,' p. 482. On the *Cervus paludosus*, Rengger, ibid. s. 345.

[29] Sclater, 'Proc. Zool. Soc.' 1866, p. i. The same fact has also been fully ascertained by MM. Pollen and van Dam. See, also, Dr. Gray in 'Annals and Mag. of Nat. Hist.' May 1871, p. 340.

[30] On Mycetes, Rengger, ibid. s. 14; and Brehm, 'Illustrirtes Thierleben,' B. i. s. 96,

copithecus diana, the head of the adult male is of an intense black, whilst that of the female is dark grey; in the former the fur between the thighs is of an elegant fawn colour, in the latter it is paler. In the beautiful and curious moustache monkey (*Cercopithecus cephus*) the only difference between the sexes is that the tail of the male is chestnut and that of the female grey; but Mr. Bartlett informs me that all the hues become more pronounced in the male when adult, whilst in the female they remain as they were during youth. According to the coloured figures given by Solomon Müller, the male of *Semnopithecus chrysomelas* is nearly black, the

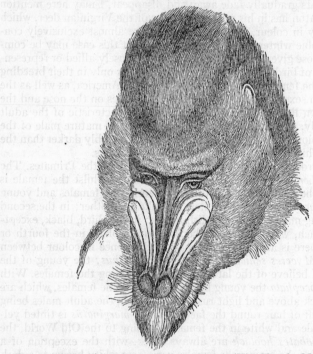

Fig. 69.—Head of male Mandrill (from Gervais, 'Hist. Nat. des Mammifères').

female being pale brown. In the *Cercopithecus cynosurus* and *griseoviridis* one part of the body, which is confined to the male sex, is of the most brilliant blue or green, and contrasts strikingly with the naked skin on the hinder part of the body, which is vivid red.

Lastly, in the baboon family, the adult male of *Cynocephalus hamadryas* differs from the female not only by his immense mane, but slightly in the colour of the hair and of the naked callosities. In the drill (*C. leucophæus*) the females and young are much paler-coloured, with less

107. On Ateles Desmarest, 'Mammalogie,' p. 75. On Hylobates, Blyth, 'Land and Water' 1867 p. 135. On the Semnopithecus S. Müller, 'Zoog. Indischen Archipel.' tab. x.

green, than the adult males. No other member in the whole class of mammals is coloured in so extraordinary a manner as the adult male mandrill (*C. mormon*). The face at this age becomes of a fine blue, with the ridge and tip of the nose of the most brilliant red. According to some authors, the face is also marked with whitish stripes, and is shaded in parts with black, but the colours appear to be variable. On the forehead there is a crest of hair, and on the chin a yellow beard. "Toutes les parties supérieures de leurs cuisses et le grand espace nu de leurs fesses sont également colorés du rouge le plus vif, avec un mélange de bleu qui ne manque réellement pas d'élégance." [31] When the animal is excited all the naked parts become much more vividly tinted. Several authors have used the strongest expressions in describing these resplendent colours, which they compare with those of the most brilliant birds. Another remarkable peculiarity is that when the great canine teeth are fully developed, immense protuberances of bone are formed on each cheek, which are deeply furrowed longitudinally, and the naked skin over them is brilliantly-coloured, as just described. (Fig. 69.) In the adult females and in the young of both sexes these protuberances are scarcely perceptible; and the naked parts are much less bright coloured, the face being almost black, tinged with blue. In the adult female, however, the nose at certain regular intervals of time becomes tinted with red.

In all the cases hitherto given the male is more strongly or brighter coloured than the female, and differs from the young of both sexes. But as with some few birds it is the female which is brighter coloured than the male, so with the Rhesus monkey (*Macacus rhesus*), the female has a large surface of naked skin round the tail, of a brilliant carmine red, which, as I was assured by the keepers in the Zoological Gardens, periodically becomes even yet more vivid, and her face also is pale red. On the other hand, in the adult male and in the young of both sexes (as I saw in the Gardens), neither the naked skin at the posterior end of the body, nor the face, shew a trace of red. It appears, however, from some published accounts, that the male does occasionally, or during certain seasons, exhibit some traces of the red. Although he is thus less ornamented than the female, yet in the larger size of his body, larger canine teeth, more developed whiskers, more prominent superciliary ridges, he follows the common rule of the male excelling the female.

I have now given all the cases known to me of a difference in colour between the sexes of mammals. Some of these may be the result of variations confined to one sex and transmitted to the same sex, without any good being gained, and therefore without the aid of selection. We have instances of this with our domesticated animals, as in the males of certain cats being rusty-red, whilst the females are tortoise-shell coloured. Analo-

---

[31] Gervais, 'Hist. Nat. des Mammifères,' 1854, p. 103. Figures are given of the skull of the male. Also Desmarest, 'Mammalogie,' p. 70. Geoffroy St.-Hilaire and F. Cuvier, 'Hist. Nat. des Mamm.' 1824, tom. i.

gous cases occur in nature: Mr. Bartlett has seen many black varieties of
the jaguar, leopard, vulpine phalanger, and wombat; and he is certain
that all, or nearly all these animals, were males. On the other hand, with
wolves, foxes, and apparently American squirrels, both sexes are occasionally born black. Hence it is quite possible that with some mammals a
difference in colour between the sexes, especially when this is congenital,
may simply be the result, without the aid of selection, of the occurrence
of one or more variations, which from the first were sexually limited in
their transmission. Nevertheless it is improbable that the diversified, vivid, and contrasted colours of certain quadrupeds, for instance, of the
above monkeys and antelopes, can thus be accounted for. We should bear
in mind that these colours do not appear in the male at birth, but only at
or near maturity; and that unlike ordinary variations, they are lost if the
male be emasculated. It is on the whole probable that the strongly-
marked colours and other ornamental characters of male quadrupeds are
beneficial to them in their rivalry with other males, and have consequently been acquired through sexual selection. This view is strengthened by
the differences in colour between the sexes occurring almost exclusively,
as may be collected from the previous details, in those groups and sub-
groups of mammals which present other and strongly-marked secondary
sexual characters; these being likewise due to sexual selection.

Quadrupeds manifestly take notice of colour. Sir S. Baker repeatedly
observed that the African elephant and rhinoceros attacked white or grey
horses with special fury. I have elsewhere shewn [32] that half-wild horses
apparently prefer to pair with those of the same colour, and that herds of
fallow-deer of different colours, though living together, have long kept
distinct. It is a more significant fact that a female zebra would not admit
the addresses of a male ass until he was painted so as to resemble a zebra,
and then, as John Hunter remarks, "she received him very readily. In
this curious fact, we have instinct excited by mere colour, which had so
strong an effect as to get the better of everything else. But the male did
not require this, the female being an animal somewhat similar to himself,
was sufficient to rouse him." [33]

In an earlier chapter we have seen that the mental powers of the higher
animals do not differ in kind, though greatly in degree, from the corresponding powers of man, especially of the lower and barbarous races;
and it would appear that even their taste for the beautiful is not widely
different from that of the Quadrumana. As the negro of Africa raises the
flesh on his face into parallel ridges "or cicatrices, high above the natural
surface, which unsightly deformities are considered great personal attractions;" [34]—as negroes and savages in many parts of the world paint their
faces with red, blue, white, or black bars,—so the male mandrill of Africa
appears to have acquired his deeply-furrowed and gaudily-coloured face

[32] 'The Variation of Animals and Plants under Domestication,' 1868, vol. ii. pp.
102, 103.
[33] 'Essays and Observations by J. Hunter,' edited by Owen, 1861, i. p. 194.
[34] Sir S. Baker, 'The Nile Tributaries of Abyssinia,' 1867.

from having been thus rendered attractive to the female. No doubt it is to us a most grotesque notion that the posterior end of the body should be coloured for the sake of ornament even more brilliantly than the face; but this is not more strange than that the tails of many birds should be especially decorated.

With mammals we do not at present possess any evidence that the males take pains to display their charms before the female; and the elaborate manner in which this is performed by male birds and other animals is the strongest argument in favour of the belief that the females admire, or are excited by, the ornaments and colours displayed before them. There is, however, a striking parallelism between mammals and birds in all their secondary sexual characters, namely in their weapons for fighting with rival males, in their ornamental appendages, and in their colours. In both classes, when the male differs from the female, the young of both sexes almost always resemble each other, and in a large majority of cases resemble the adult female. In both classes the male assumes the characters proper to his sex shortly before the age of reproduction; and if emasculated at an early period, loses them. In both classes the change of colour is sometimes seasonal, and the tints of the naked parts sometimes become more vivid during the act of courtship. In both classes the male is almost always more vividly or strongly coloured than the female, and is ornamented with larger crests of hair or feathers, or other such appendages. In a few exceptional cases the female in both classes is more highly ornamented than the male. With many mammals, and at least in the case of one bird, the male is more odoriferous than the female. In both classes the voice of the male is more powerful than that of the female. Considering this parallelism, there can be little doubt that the same cause, whatever it may be, has acted on mammals and birds; and the result, as far as ornamental characters are concerned, may be attributed, as it appears to me, to the long-continued preference of the individuals of one sex for certain individuals of the opposite sex, combined with their success in leaving a larger number of offspring to inherit their superior attractions.

Equal transmission of ornamental characters to both sexes.—With many birds, ornaments, which analogy leads us to believe were primarily acquired by the males, have been transmitted equally, or almost equally, to both sexes; and we may now enquire how far this view applies to mammals. With a considerable number of species, especially of the smaller kinds, both sexes have been coloured, independently of sexual selection, for the sake of protection; but not, as far as I can judge, in so many cases, nor in so striking a manner, as in most of the lower classes. Audubon remarks that he often mistook the musk-rat,[35] whilst sitting on the banks of a muddy stream, for a clod of earth, so complete was the resemblance. The hare on her form is a familiar instance of concealment through colour; yet this principle partly fails in a closely-allied species,

---

[35] *Fiber zibethicus,* Audubon and Bachman, 'The Quadrupeds of N. America,' 1846, p. 109.

the rabbit, for when running to its burrow, it is made conspicuous to the sportsman, and no doubt to all beasts of prey, by its upturned white tail. No one doubts that the quadrupeds inhabiting snow-clad regions have been rendered white to protect them from their enemies, or to favour their stealing on their prey. In regions where snow never lies for long, a white coat would be injurious; consequently, species of this colour are extremely rare in the hotter parts of the world. It deserves notice that many quadrupeds inhabiting moderately cold regions, although they do not assume a white winter dress, become paler during this season; and this apparently is the direct result of the conditions to which they have long been exposed. Pallas [36] states that in Siberia a change of this nature occurs with the wolf, two species of Mustela, the domestic horse, the *Equus hemionus,* the domestic cow, two species of antelopes, the musk-deer, the roe, elk, and reindeer. The roe, for instance, has a red summer and a greyish-white winter coat; and the latter may perhaps serve as a protection to the animal whilst wandering through the leafless thickets, sprinkled with snow and hoar-frost. If the above-named animals were gradually to extend their range into regions perpetually covered with snow, their pale winter-coats would probably be rendered through natural selection, whiter and whiter, until they became as white as snow.

Mr. Reeks has given me a curious instance of an animal profiting by being peculiarly coloured. He raised from fifty to sixty white and brown piebald rabbits in a large walled orchard; and he had at the same time some similarly coloured cats in his house. Such cats, as I have often noticed, are very conspicuous during day; but as they used to lie in watch during the dusk at the mouths of the burrows, the rabbits apparently did not distinguish them from their parti-coloured brethren. The result was that, within eighteen months, every one of these parti-coloured rabbits was destroyed; and there was evidence that this was effected by the cats. Colour seems to be advantageous to another animal, the skunk, in a manner of which we have had many instances in other classes. No animal will voluntarily attack one of these creatures on account of the dreadful odour which it emits when irritated; but during the dusk it would not easily be recognized and might be attacked by a beast of prey. Hence it is, as Mr. Belt believes,[37] that the skunk is provided with a great white bushy tail, which serves as a conspicuous warning.

Although we must admit that many quadrupeds have received their present tints either as a protection, or as an aid in procuring prey, yet with a host of species, the colours are far too conspicuous and too singularly arranged to allow us to suppose that they serve for these purposes. We may take as an illustration certain antelopes; when we see the square white patch on the throat, the white marks on the fetlocks, and the round black spots on the ears, all more distinct in the male of the *Portax picta,* than in the female;—when we see that the colours are more vivid, that

[36] 'Novæ species Quadrupedum e Glirium ordine,' 1778, page 7. What I have called the roe is the *Capreolus sibiricus subecaudatus* of Pallas.

[37] 'Naturalist in Nicaragua,' p. 249.

the narrow white lines on the flank and the broad white bar on the shoulder are more distinct in the male *Oreas derbyanus* than in the female;—when we see a similar difference between the sexes of the curiously-ornamented *Tragelaphus scriptus* (fig. 70),—we cannot believe that differences of this kind are of any service to either sex in their daily habits of life. It seems a much more probable conclusion that the various marks were first acquired by the males and their colours intensified through sexual selection, and then partially transferred to the females. If this view be

FIG. 70—Tragelaphus scriptus, male (from the Knowsley Menagerie).

admitted, there can be little doubt that the equally singular colours and marks of many other antelopes, though common to both sexes, have been gained and transmitted in a like manner. Both sexes, for instance, of the koodoo (*Strepsiceros kudu*) (fig. 64) have narrow white vertical lines on their hind flanks, and an elegant angular white mark on their foreheads. Both sexes in the genus Damalis are very oddly coloured; in *D. pygarga* the back and neck are purplish-red, shading on the flanks into black; and these colours are abruptly separated from the white belly and from a large white space on the buttocks; the head is still more oddly coloured, a large oblong white mask, narrowly-edged with black, covers the face up

to the eyes (fig. 71); there are three white stripes on the forehead, and
the ears are marked with white. The fawns of this species are of a uniform pale yellowish-brown. In *Damalis albifrons* the colouring of the head
differs from that in the last species in a single white stripe replacing the
three stripes, and in the ears being almost wholly white.[38] After having
studied to the best of my ability the sexual differences of animals belonging to all classes, I cannot avoid the conclusion that the curiously-ar-
ranged colours of many antelopes, though common to both sexes, are the
result of sexual selection primarily applied to the male.

The same conclusion may perhaps be extended to the tiger, one of the
most beautiful animals in the world, the sexes of which cannot be distin-

FIG. 71.—Damalis pygarga, male (from the Knowsley Menagerie).

guished by colour, even by the dealers in wild beasts. Mr. Wallace believes[39] that the striped coat of the tiger "so assimilates with the vertical
stems of the bamboo, as to assist greatly in concealing him from his approaching prey." But this view does not appear to me satisfactory. We
have some slight evidence that his beauty may be due to sexual selection,
for in two species of Felis the analogous marks and colours are rather
brighter in the male than in the female. The zebra is conspicuously
striped, and stripes cannot afford any protection in the open plains of

[38] See the fine plates in A. Smith's 'Zoology of S. Africa,' and Dr. Gray's 'Gleanings
from the Menagerie of Knowsley.'
[39] 'Westminster Review,' July 1, 1867, p. 5.

South Africa. Burchell [40] in describing a herd says, "their sleek ribs glistened in the sun, and the brightness and regularity of their striped coats presented a picture of extraordinary beauty, in which probably they are not surpassed by any other quadruped." But as throughout the whole group of the Equidæ the sexes are identical in colour, we have here no evidence of sexual selection. Nevertheless he who attributes the white and dark vertical stripes on the flanks of various antelopes to this process, will probably extend the same view to the Royal Tiger and beautiful Zebra.

We have seen in a former chapter that when young animals belonging to any class follow nearly the same habits of life as their parents, and yet are coloured in a different manner, it may be inferred that they have retained the colouring of some ancient and extinct progenitor. In the family of pigs, and in the tapirs, the young are marked with longitudinal stripes, and thus differ from all the existing adult species in these two groups. With many kinds of deer the young are marked with elegant white spots, of which their parents exhibit not a trace. A graduated series can be followed from the axis deer, both sexes of which at all ages and during all seasons are beautifully spotted (the male being rather more strongly coloured than the female), to species in which neither the old nor the young are spotted. I will specify some of the steps in this series. The Mantchurian deer (*Cervus mantchuricus*) is spotted during the whole year, but, as I have seen in the Zoological Gardens, the spots are much plainer during the summer, when the general colour of the coat is lighter, than during the winter, when the general colour is darker and the horns are fully developed. In the hog-deer (*Hyelaphus porcinus*) the spots are extremely conspicuous during the summer when the coat is reddish-brown, but quite disappear during the winter when the coat is brown.[41] In both these species the young are spotted. In the Virginian deer the young are likewise spotted, and about five per cent. of the adult animals living in Judge Caton's park, as I am informed by him, temporarily exhibit at the period when the red summer coat is being replaced by the bluish winter coat, a row of spots on each flank, which are always the same in number, though very variable in distinctness. From this condition there is but a very small step to the complete absence of spots in the adults at all seasons; and, lastly, to their absence at all ages and seasons, as occurs with certain species. From the existence of this perfect series, and more especially from the fawns of so many species being spotted, we may conclude that the now living members of the deer family are the descendants of some ancient species which, like the axis deer, was spotted at all ages and seasons. A still more ancient progenitor probably somewhat resembled the *Hyomoschus aquaticus*—for this animal is spotted, and the hornless

---

[40] 'Travels in South Africa,' 1824, vol. ii. p. 315.

[41] Dr. Gray, 'Gleanings from the Menagerie of Knowsley,' p. 64. Mr. Blyth, in speaking ('Land and Water,' 1869, p. 42) of the hog-deer of Ceylon, says it is more brightly spotted with white than the common hog-deer, at the season when it renews its horns.

males have large exserted canine teeth, of which some few true deer still retain rudiments. Hyomoschus, also, offers one of those interesting cases of a form linking together two groups, for it is intermediate in certain osteological characters between the pachyderms and ruminants, which were formerly thought to be quite distinct.[42]

A curious difficulty here arises. If we admit that coloured spots and stripes were first acquired as ornaments, how comes it that so many existing deer, the descendants of an aboriginally spotted animal, and all the species of pigs and tapirs, the descendants of an aboriginally striped animal, have lost in their adult state their former ornaments? I cannot satisfactorily answer this question. We may feel almost sure that the spots and stripes disappeared at or near maturity in the progenitors of our existing species, so that they were still retained by the young; and, owing to the law of inheritance at corresponding ages, were transmitted to the young of all succeeding generations. It may have been a great advantage to the lion and puma, from the open nature of their usual haunts, to have lost their stripes, and to have been thus rendered less conspicuous to their prey; and if the successive variations, by which this end was gained, occurred rather late in life, the young would have retained their stripes, as is now the case. As to deer, pigs, and tapirs, Fritz Müller has suggested to me that these animals, by the removal of their spots or stripes through natural selection, would have been less easily seen by their enemies; and that they would have especially required this protection, as soon as the carnivora increased in size and number during the tertiary periods. This may be the true explanation, but it is rather strange that the young should not have been thus protected, and still more so that the adults of some species should have retained their spots, either partially or completely, during part of the year. We know that, when the domestic ass varies and becomes reddish-brown, grey, or black, the stripes on the shoulders and even on the spine frequently disappear, though we cannot explain the cause. Very few horses, except dun-coloured kinds, have stripes on any part of their bodies, yet we have good reason to believe that the aboriginal horse was striped on the legs and spine, and probably on the shoulders.[43] Hence the disappearance of the spots and stripes in our adult existing deer, pigs, and tapirs, may be due to a change in the general colour of their coats; but whether this change was effected through sexual or natural selection, or was due to the direct action of the conditions of life, or to some other unknown cause, it is impossible to decide. An observation made by Mr. Sclater well illustrates our ignorance of the laws which regulate the appearance and disappearance of stripes; the species of Asinus which inhabit the Asiatic continent are destitute of stripes, not having even the cross shoulder-stripe, whilst those which inhabit Africa are conspicuously striped, with the partial exception of A.

[42] Falconer and Cautley, 'Proc. Geolog. Soc.' 1843; and Falconer's 'Pal. Memoirs,' vol. i. p. 196.
[43] 'The Variation of Animals and Plants under Domestication,' 1868, vol. i. pp. 61–64.

tæniopus, which has only the cross shoulder-stripe and generally some faint bars on the legs; and this species inhabits the almost intermediate region of Upper Egypt and Abyssinia.[44]

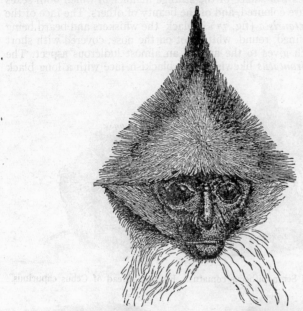

FIG. 72.—Head of Semnopithecus rubicundus. This and the following figures (from Prof. Gervais) are given to shew the odd arrangement and development of the hair on the head.

Quadrumana.—Before we conclude, it will be well to add a few remarks on the ornaments of monkeys. In most of the species the sexes resemble each other in colour, but in some, as we have seen, the males differ from the females, especially in the colour of the naked parts of the skin, in the development of the beard, whiskers, and mane. Many species are coloured either in so extraordinary or so beautiful a manner, and are furnished with such curious and elegant crests of hair, that we can hardly avoid looking at these characters as having been gained for the sake of ornament. The accompanying figures (figs. 72 to 76) serve to shew the arrangement of the hair on the face and head in several species. It is scarcely conceivable that these crests of hair, and the strongly contrasted colours of the fur and skin, can be the result of mere variability without the aid of selection; and it is inconceivable that they can be of use in any ordinary way to these animals. If so, they have probably been gained through sexual selection, though transmitted equally, or almost equally, to both sexes. With many of the Quadrumana, we have additional evi-

[44] 'Proc. Zool. Soc.' 1862, p. 164. See, also, Dr. Hartmann, 'Ann. d. Landw.' Dd. xliii. s. 222.

dence of the action of sexual selection in the greater size and strength of
the males, and in the greater development of their canine teeth, in comparison with the females.

A few instances will suffice of the strange manner in which both sexes
of some species are coloured, and of the beauty of others. The face of the
Cercopithecus petaurista (fig. 77) is black, the whiskers and beard being
white, with a defined, round, white spot on the nose, covered with short
white hair, which gives to the animal an almost ludicrous aspect. The
Semnopithecus frontatus likewise has a blackish face with a long black

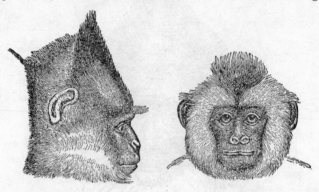

Fig. 73.—Head of Semnopithecus comatus.   Fig. 74.—Head of Cebus capucinus.

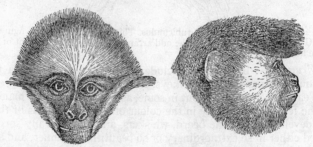

Fig. 75.—Head of Ateles marginatus.   Fig. 76.—Head of Cebus vellerosus.

beard, and a large naked spot on the forehead of a bluish-white colour.
The face of *Macacus lasiotus* is dirty flesh-coloured, with a defined red
spot on each cheek. The appearance of *Cercocebus æthiops* is grotesque,
with its black face, white whiskers and collar, chestnut head, and a large
naked white spot over each eyelid. In very many species, the beard, whiskers, and crests of hair round the face are of a different colour from the
rest of the head, and when different, are always of a lighter tint,[45] being

[45] I observed this fact in the Zoological Gardens; and many cases may be seen in
the coloured plates in Geoffroy St.-Hilaire and F. Cuvier, 'Histoire Nat. des Mammifères,' tom. i. 1824.

often pure white, sometimes bright yellow, or reddish. The whole face of the South American *Brachyurus calvus* is of a "glowing scarlet hue;" but this colour does not appear until the animal is nearly mature.[46] The nak-

FIG. 77. Cercopithecus petaurista (from Brehm).

ed skin of the face differs wonderfully in colour in the various species. It is often brown or flesh-colour, with parts perfectly white, and often as black as that of the most sooty negro. In the Brachyurus the scarlet tint is brighter than that of the most blushing Caucasian damsel. It is some-

[46] Bates, 'The Naturalist on the Amazons,' 1863, vol. ii. p. 310.

times more distinctly orange than in any Mongolian, and in several species it is blue, passing into violet or grey. In all the species known to Mr.
Bartlett, in which the adults of both sexes have strongly-coloured faces,
the colours are dull or absent during early youth. This likewise holds
good with the mandrill and Rhesus, in which the face and the posterior
parts of the body are brilliantly coloured in one sex alone. In these latter
cases we have reason to believe that the colours were acquired through
sexual selection; and we are naturally led to extend the same view to the
foregoing species, though both sexes when adult have their faces coloured
in the same manner.

Although many kinds of monkeys are far from beautiful according to
our taste, other species are universally admired for their elegant appearance and bright colours. The *Semnopithecus nemæus,* though peculiarly
coloured, is described as extremely pretty; the orange-tinted face is surrounded by long whiskers of glossy whiteness, with a line of chestnut-red
over the eyebrows; the fur on the back is of a delicate grey, with a square
patch on the loins, the tail and the fore-arms being of a pure white; a gorget of chestnut surmounts the chest; the thighs are black, with the legs
chestnut-red. I will mention only two other monkeys for their beauty;
and I have selected these as presenting slight sexual differences in colour,
which renders it in some degree probable that both sexes owe their elegant appearance to sexual selection. In the moustache-monkey (*Cercopithecus cephus*) the general colour of the fur is mottled-greenish with the
throat white; in the male the end of the tail is chestnut, but the face is
the most ornamented part, the skin being chiefly bluish-grey, shading
into a blackish tint beneath the eyes, with the upper lip of a delicate blue,
clothed on the lower edge with a thin black moustache; the whiskers are
orange-coloured, with the upper part black, forming a band which extends backwards to the ears, the latter being clothed with whitish hairs.
In the Zoological Society's Gardens I have often overheard visitors admiring the beauty of another monkey, deservedly called *Cercopithecus
diana* (fig. 78); the general colour of the fur is grey; the chest and inner
surface of the fore legs are white; a large triangular defined space on the
hinder part of the back is rich chestnut; in the male the inner sides of the
thighs and the abdomen are delicate fawn-coloured, and the top of the
head is black; the face and ears are intensely black, contrasting finely
with a white transverse crest over the eyebrows and a long white peaked
beard, of which the basal portion is black.[47]

In these and many other monkeys, the beauty and singular arrangement of their colours, and still more the diversified and elegant arrangement of the crests and tufts of hair on their heads, force the conviction on
my mind that these characters have been acquired through sexual selection exclusively as ornaments.

[47] I have seen most of the above monkeys in the Zoological Society's Gardens. The
description of the *Semnopithecus nemæus* is taken from Mr. W. C. Martin's 'Nat.
Hist. of Mammalia,' 1841, p. 460; see also pp. 475, 523.

Summary.—The law of battle for the possession of the female appears to prevail throughout the whole great class of mammals. Most naturalists will admit that the greater size, strength, courage, and pugnacity of the male, his special weapons of offence, as well as his special means of defence, have been acquired or modified through that form of selection which I have called sexual. This does not depend on any superiority in the general struggle for life, but on certain individuals of one sex, generally the male, being successful in conquering other males, and leaving a

FIG. 78.—Cercopithecus diana (from Brehm).

larger number of offspring to inherit their superiority than do the less successful males.

There is another and more peaceful kind of contest, in which the males endeavour to excite or allure the females by various charms. This is probably carried on in some cases by the powerful odours emitted by the males during the breeding-season; the odoriferous glands having been acquired through sexual selection. Whether the same view can be extended to the voice is doubtful, for the vocal organs of the males must have been strengthened by use during maturity, under the powerful excitements of love, jealousy or rage, and will consequently have been transmitted to the same sex. Various crests, tufts, and mantles of hair, which are either confined to the male, or are more developed in this sex than in the female, seem in most cases to be merely ornamental, though they sometimes serve as a defence against rival males. There is even reason to suspect that the branching horns of stags, and the elegant horns of certain antelopes, though properly serving as weapons of offence or defence, have been partly modified for ornament.

When the male differs in colour from the female, he generally exhibits darker and more strongly-contrasted tints. We do not in this class meet with the splendid red, blue, yellow, and green tints, so common with male birds and many other animals. The naked parts, however, of certain Quadrumana must be excepted; for such parts, often oddly situated, are brilliantly coloured in some species. The colours of the male in other cases may be due to simple variation, without the aid of selection. But when the colours are diversified and strongly pronounced, when they are not developed until near maturity, and when they are lost after emasculation, we can hardly avoid the conclusion that they have been acquired through sexual selection for the sake of ornament, and have been transmitted exclusively, or almost exclusively, to the same sex. When both sexes are coloured in the same manner, and the colours are conspicuous or curiously arranged, without being of the least apparent use as a protection, and especially when they are associated with various other ornamental appendages, we are led by analogy to the same conclusion, namely, that they have been acquired through sexual selection, although transmitted to both sexes. That conspicuous and diversified colours, whether confined to the males or common to both sexes, are as a general rule associated in the same groups and sub-groups with other secondary sexual characters serving for war or for ornament, will be found to hold good, if we look back to the various cases given in this and the last chapter.

The law of the equal transmission of characters to both sexes, as far as colour and other ornaments are concerned, has prevailed far more extensively with mammals than with birds; but weapons, such as horns and tusks, have often been transmitted either exclusively or much more perfectly to the males than to the females. This is surprising, for, as the males generally use their weapons for defence against enemies of all kinds, their weapons would have been of service to the females. As far as we can see, their absence in this sex can be accounted for only by the form of inheritance which has prevailed. Finally, with quadrupeds the contest between the individuals of the same sex, whether peaceful or bloody, has, with the rarest exceptions, been confined to the males; so that the latter have been modified through sexual selection, far more commonly than the females, either for fighting with each other or for alluring the opposite sex.

PART III
SEXUAL SELECTION IN RELATION TO MAN, AND CONCLUSION

CHAPTER XIX

SECONDARY SEXUAL CHARACTERS OF MAN

Differences between man and woman—Causes of such differences and of certain characters common to both sexes—Law of Battle—Difference in mental powers, and voice—On the influence of beauty in determining the marriages of mankind—Attention paid by savages to ornaments—Their ideas of beauty in woman—The tendency to exaggerate each natural peculiarity.

WITH mankind the differences between the sexes are greater than in most of the Quadrumana, but not so great as in some, for instance, the mandrill. Man on an average is considerably taller, heavier, and stronger than woman, with squarer shoulders and more plainly-pronounced muscles. Owing to the relation which exists between muscular development and the projection of the brows,[1] the superciliary ridge is generally more marked in man than in woman. His body, and especially his face, is more hairy, and his voice has a different and more powerful tone. In certain races the women are said to differ slightly in tint from the men. For instance, Schweinfurth, in speaking of a negress belonging to the Monbuttoos, who inhabit the interior of Africa a few degrees north of the Equator, says, "Like all her race, she had a skin several shades lighter than her husband's, being something of the colour of half-roasted coffee."[2] As the women labour in the fields and are quite unclothed, it is not likely that they differ in colour from the men owing to less exposure to the weather. European women are perhaps the brighter coloured of the two sexes, as may be seen when both have been equally exposed.

Man is more courageous, pugnacious and energetic than woman, and has a more inventive genius. His brain is absolutely larger, but whether or not proportionately to his larger body, has not, I believe, been fully ascertained. In woman the face is rounder; the jaws and the base of the skull smaller; the outlines of the body rounder, in parts more prominent; and her pelvis is broader than in man;[3] but this latter character may perhaps be considered rather as a primary than a secondary sexual character. She comes to maturity at an earlier age than man.

As with animals of all classes, so with man, the distinctive characters of the male sex are not fully developed until he is nearly mature; and if

---

[1] Schaaffhausen, translation in 'Anthropological Review,' Oct. 1868, pp. 419, 420, 427.

[2] 'The Heart of Africa,' English transl. 1873, vol. i. p. 544.

[3] Ecker, translation in 'Anthropological Review,' Oct. 1868, pp. 351–356. The comparison of the form of the skull in men and women has been followed out with much care by Welcker.

emasculated they never appear. The beard, for instance is a secondary sexual character, and male children are beardless, though at an early age they have abundant hair on the head. It is probably due to the rather late appearance in life of the successive variations whereby man has acquired his masculine characters, that they are transmitted to the male sex alone. Male and female children resemble each other closely, like the young of so many other animals in which the adult sexes differ widely; they likewise resemble the mature female much more closely than the mature male. The female, however, ultimately assumes certain distinctive characters, and in the formation of her skull, is said to be intermediate between the child and the man.[4] Again, as the young of closely allied though distinct species do not differ nearly so much from each other as do the adults, so it is with the children of the different races of man. Some have even maintained that race-differences cannot be detected in the infantile skull.[5] In regard to colour, the new-born negro child is reddish nut-brown, which soon becomes slaty-grey; the black colour being fully developed within a year in the Soudan, but not until three years in Egypt. The eyes of the negro are at first blue, and the hair chestnut-brown rather than black, being curled only at the ends. The children of the Australians immediately after birth are yellowish-brown, and become dark at a later age. Those of the Guaranys of Paraguay are whitish-yellow, but they acquire in the course of a few weeks the yellowish-brown tint of their parents. Similar observations have been made in other parts of America.[6]

I have specified the foregoing differences between the male and female sex in mankind, because they are curiously like those of the Quadrumana. With these animals the female is mature at an earlier age than the male; at least this is certainly the case in *Cebus azaræ*.[7] The males of most species are larger and stronger than the females, of which fact the gorilla affords a well-known instance. Even in so trifling a character as the greater prominence of the superciliary ridge, the males of certain monkeys differ from the females,[8] and agree in this respect with mankind. In the gorilla and certain other monkeys, the cranium of the adult male presents a strongly-marked sagittal crest, which is absent in the female; and Ecker found a trace of a similar difference between the two sexes in the Australians.[9] With monkeys when there is any difference in the voice, that of the

---

[4] Ecker and Welcker, ibid. pp. 352, 355; Vogt, 'Lectures on Man,' Eng. translat. p. 81.

[5] Schaaffhausen, 'Anthropolog. Review,' ibid. p. 429.

[6] Pruner-Bey, on negro infants as quoted by Vogt, 'Lectures on Man,' Eng. translat. 1864, p. 189: for further facts on negro infants, as quoted from Winterbottom and Camper, see Lawrence, 'Lectures on Physiology,' &c. 1822, p. 451. For the infants of the Guaranys, see Rengger, 'Säugethiere,' &c. s. 3. See also Godron, 'De l'Espèce,' tom. ii. 1859, p. 253. For the Australians, Waitz, 'Introduct. to Anthropology,' Eng. translat. 1863, p. 99.

[7] Rengger, 'Säugethiere,' &c. 1830, s. 49.

[8] As in *Macacus cynomolgus* (Desmarest, 'Mammalogie,' p. 65), and in *Hylobates agilis* (Geoffroy St.-Hilaire and F. Cuvier, 'Hist. Nat. des Mamm.' 1824, tom. i. p. 2).

[9] 'Anthropological Review,' Oct. 1868, p. 353.

male is the more powerful. We have seen that certain male monkeys have a well-developed beard, which is quite deficient, or much less developed in the female. No instance is known of the beard, whiskers, or moustache being larger in the female than in the male monkey. Even in the colour of the beard there is a curious parallelism between man and the Quadrumana, for with man when the beard differs in colour from the hair of the head, as is commonly the case, it is, I believe, almost always of a lighter tint, being often reddish. I have repeatedly observed this fact in England; but two gentlemen have lately written to me, saying that they form an exception to the rule. One of these gentlemen accounts for the fact by the wide difference in colour of the hair on the paternal and maternal sides of his family. Both had been long aware of this peculiarity (one of them having often been accused of dyeing his beard), and had been thus led to observe other men, and were convinced that the exceptions were very rare. Dr. Hooker attended to this little point for me in Russia, and found no exception to the rule. In Calcutta, Mr. J. Scott, of the Botanic Gardens, was so kind as to observe the many races of men to be seen there, as well as in some other parts of India, namely, two races of Sik-him, the Bhoteas, Hindoos, Burmese, and Chinese, most of which races have very little hair on the face; and he always found that when there was any difference in colour between the hair of the head and the beard, the latter was invariably lighter. Now with monkeys, as has already been stated, the beard frequently differs strikingly in colour from the hair of the head, and in such cases it is always of a lighter hue, being often pure white, sometimes yellow or reddish.[10]

In regard to the general hairiness of the body, the women in all races are less hairy than the men; and in some few Quadrumana the under side of the body of the female is less hairy than that of the male.[11] Lastly, male monkeys, like men, are bolder and fiercer than the females. They lead the troop, and when there is danger, come to the front. We thus see how close is the parallelism between the sexual differences of man and the Quadrumana. With some few species, however, as with certain baboons, the orang and the gorilla, there is a considerably greater difference between the sexes, as in the size of the canine teeth, in the development and colour of the hair, and especially in the colour of the naked parts of the skin, than in mankind.

All the secondary sexual characters of man are highly variable, even within the limits of the same race; and they differ much in the several

[10] Mr. Blyth informs me that he has only seen one instance of the beard, whiskers, &c., in a monkey becoming white with old age, as is so commonly the case with us. This, however, occurred in an aged *Macacus cynomolgus*, kept in confinement, whose moustaches were "remarkably long and human-like." Altogether this old monkey presented a ludicrous resemblance to one of the reigning monarchs of Europe, after whom he was universally nick-named. In certain races of man the hair on the head hardly ever becomes grey; thus Mr. D. Forbes has never, as he informs me, seen an instance with the Aymaras and Quichuas of S. America.

[11] This is the case with the females of several species of Hylobates, see Geoffroy St.-Hilaire and F. Cuvier, 'Hist. Nat. des Mamm.' tom. i. See, also, on *H. lar.* 'Penny Cyclopedia,' vol. ii. pp. 149, 150.

races. These two rules hold good generally throughout the animal kingdom. In the excellent observations made on board the *Novara*,[12] the male
Australians were found to exceed the females by only 65 millim. in height,
whilst with the Javans the average excess was 218 millim.; so that in this
latter race the difference in height between the sexes is more than thrice
as great as with the Australians. Numerous measurements were carefully
made of the stature, the circumference of the neck and chest, the length
of the back-bone and of the arms, in various races; and nearly all these
measurements shew that the males differ much more from one another
than do the females. This fact indicates that, as far as these characters
are concerned, it is the male which has been chiefly modified, since the
several races diverged from their common stock.

The development of the beard and the hairiness of the body differ remarkably in the men of distinct races, and even in different tribes or families of the same race. We Europeans see this amongst ourselves. In the
Island of St. Kilda, according to Martin,[13] the men do not acquire beards
until the age of thirty or upwards, and even then the beards are very thin.
On the Europæo-Asiatic continent, beards prevail until we pass beyond
India; though with the natives of Ceylon they are often absent, as was
noticed in ancient times by Diodorus.[14] Eastward of India beards disappear, as with the Siamese, Malays, Kalmucks, Chinese, and Japanese;
nevertheless, the Ainos,[15] who inhabit the northernmost islands of the Japan Archipelago, are the hairiest men in the world. With negroes the
beard is scanty or wanting, and they rarely have whiskers; in both sexes
the body is frequently almost destitute of fine down.[16] On the other hand,
the Papuans of the Malay Archipelago, who are nearly as black as negroes, possess well-developed beards.[17] In the Pacific Ocean the inhabitants of the Fiji Archipelago have large bushy beards, whilst those of the
not distant archipelagoes of Tonga and Samoa are beardless; but these
men belong to distinct races. In the Ellice group all the inhabitants belong to the same race; yet on one island alone, namely Nunemaya, "the
men have splendid beards;" whilst on the other islands "they have, as a
rule, a dozen straggling hairs for a beard."[18]

Throughout the great American continent the men may be said to be
beardless; but in almost all the tribes a few short hairs are apt to appear

---

[12] The results were deduced by Dr. Weisbach from the measurements made by Drs.
K. Scherzer and Schwarz, see 'Reise der Novara: Anthropolog. Theil,' 1867, ss. 216,
231, 234, 236, 239, 269.

[13] 'Voyage to St. Kilda' (3rd edit. 1753), p. 37.

[14] Sir J. E. Tennent, 'Ceylon,' vol. ii. 1859, p. 107.

[15] Quatrefages, 'Revue des Cours Scientifiques,' Aug. 29, 1868, p. 630; Vogt, 'Lectures on Man,' Eng. trans. p. 127.

[16] On the beards of negroes, Vogt, 'Lectures,' &c. p. 127; Waitz, 'Introduct. to Anthropology,' Engl. translat. 1863, vol. i. p. 96. It is remarkable that in the United
States ('Investigations in Military and Anthropological Statistics of American Soldiers,' 1869, p. 569) the pure negroes and their crossed offspring seem to have bodies
almost as hairy as Europeans.

[17] Wallace, 'The Malay Arch.' vol. ii. 1869, p. 178.

[18] Dr. J. Barnard Davis on Oceanic Races, in 'Anthropolog. Review,' April, 1870,
pp. 185, 191.

on the face, especially in old age. With the tribes of North America, Catlin estimates that eighteen out of twenty men are completely destitute by nature of a beard; but occasionally there may be seen a man, who has neglected to pluck out the hairs at puberty, with a soft beard an inch or two in length. The Guaranys of Paraguay differ from all the surrounding tribes in having a small beard, and even some hair on the body, but no whiskers.[19] I am informed by Mr. D. Forbes, who particularly attended to this point, that the Aymaras and Quichuas of the Cordillera are remarkably hairless, yet in old age a few straggling hairs occasionally appear on the chin. The men of these two tribes have very little hair on the various parts of the body where hair grows abundantly in Europeans, and the women have none on the corresponding parts. The hair on the head, however, attains an extraordinary length in both sexes, often reaching almost to the ground; and this is likewise the case with some of the N. American tribes. In the amount of hair, and in the general shape of the body, the sexes of the American aborigines do not differ so much from each other, as in most other races.[20] This fact is analogous with what occurs with some closely allied monkeys; thus the sexes of the chimpanzee are not as different as those of the orang or gorilla.[21]

In the previous chapters we have seen that with mammals, birds, fishes, insects, &c., many characters, which there is every reason to believe were primarily gained through sexual selection by one sex, have been transferred to the other. As this same form of transmission has apparently prevailed much with mankind, it will save useless repetition if we discuss the origin of characters peculiar to the male sex together with certain other characters common to both sexes.

Law of Battle.—With savages, for instance, the Australians, the women are the constant cause of war both between members of the same tribe and between distinct tribes. So no doubt it was in ancient times; "nam fuit ante Helenam mulier teterrima belli causa." With some of the North American Indians, the contest is reduced to a system. That excellent observer, Hearne,[22] says:—"It has ever been the custom among these people for the men to wrestle for any woman to whom they are attached; and, of course, the strongest party always carries off the prize. A weak man, unless he be a good hunter, and well-beloved, is seldom permitted to keep a wife that a stronger man thinks worth his notice. This custom prevails throughout all the tribes, and causes a great spirit of emulation among

[19] Catlin, 'North American Indians,' 3rd edit. 1842, vol. ii. p. 227. On the Guaranys, see Azara, 'Voyages dans l'Amérique Mérid.' tom. ii. 1809, p. 85; also Rengger, 'Säugethiere von Paraguay,' s. 3.

[20] Prof. and Mrs. Agassiz ('Journey in Brazil,' p. 530) remark that the sexes of the American Indians differ less than those of the negroes and of the higher races. See also Rengger, ibid. p. 3, on the Guaranys.

[21] Rütimeyer, 'Die Grenzen der Thierwelt; eine Betrachtung zu Darwin's Lehre,' 1868, s. 54.

[22] 'A Journey from Prince of Wales Fort,' 8vo edit. Dublin, 1796, p. 104. Sir. J. Lubbock ('Origin of Civilisation,' 1870, p. 69) gives other and similar cases in North America. For the Guanas of S. America see Azara, 'Voyages,' &c. tom. ii. p. 94.

their youth, who are upon all occasions, from their childhood, trying their strength and skill in wrestling." With the Guanas of South America, Azara states that the men rarely marry till twenty years old or more, as before that age they cannot conquer their rivals.

Other similar facts could be given; but even if we had no evidence on this head, we might feel almost sure, from the analogy of the higher Quadrumana,[23] that the law of battle had prevailed with man during the early stages of his development. The occasional appearance at the present day of canine teeth which project above the others, with traces of a diastema or open space for the reception of the opposite canines, is in all probability a case of reversion to a former state, when the progenitors of man were provided with these weapons, like so many existing male Quadrumana. It was remarked in a former chapter that as man gradually became erect, and continually used his hands and arms for fighting with sticks and stones, as well as for the other purposes of life, he would have used his jaws and teeth less and less. The jaws, together with their muscles, would then have been reduced through disuse, as would the teeth through the not well understood principles of correlation and economy of growth; for we everywhere see that parts, which are no longer of service, are reduced in size. By such steps the original inequality between the jaws and teeth in the two sexes of mankind would ultimately have been obliterated. The case is almost parallel with that of many male Ruminants, in which the canine teeth have been reduced to mere rudiments, or have disappeared, apparently in consequence of the development of horns. As the prodigious difference between the skulls of the two sexes in the orang and gorilla stands in close relation with the development of the immense canine teeth in the males, we may infer that the reduction of the jaws and teeth in the early male progenitors of man must have led to a most striking and favourable change in his appearance.

There can be little doubt that the greater size and strength of man, in comparison with woman, together with his broader shoulders, more developed muscles, rugged outline of body, his greater courage and pugnacity, are all due in chief part to inheritance from his half-human male ancestors. These characters would, however, have been preserved or even augmented during the long ages of man's savagery, by the success of the strongest and boldest men, both in the general struggle for life and in their contests for wives; a success which would have ensured their leaving a more numerous progeny than their less favoured brethren. It is not probable that the greater strength of man was primarily acquired through the inherited effects of his having worked harder than woman for his own subsistence and that of his family; for the women in all barbarous nations are compelled to work at least as hard as the men. With civilised people the arbitrament of battle for the possession of the women has long ceased; on the other hand, the men, as a general rule, have to work hard-

[23] On the fighting of the male gorillas, see Dr. Savage, in 'Boston Journal of Nat. Hist.' vol. v. 1847, p. 423. On *Presbytis entellus.* see the 'Indian Field,' 1859, p. 146.

er than the women for their joint subsistence, and thus their greater strength will have been kept up.

Difference in the Mental Powers of the two Sexes.—With respect to differences of this nature between man and woman, it is probable that sexual selection has played a highly important part. I am aware that some writers doubt whether there is any such inherent difference; but this is at least probable from the analogy of the lower animals which present other secondary sexual characters. No one disputes that the bull differs in disposition from the cow, the wild-boar from the sow, the stallion from the mare, and, as is well known to the keepers of menageries, the males of the larger apes from the females. Woman seems to differ from man in mental disposition, chiefly in her greater tenderness and less selfishness; and this holds good even with savages, as shewn by a well-known passage in Mungo Park's Travels, and by statements made by many other travellers. Woman, owing to her maternal instincts, displays these qualities towards her infants in an eminent degree; therefore it is likely that she would often extend them towards her fellow-creatures. Man is the rival of other men; he delights in competition, and this leads to ambition which passes too easily into selfishness. These latter qualities seem to be his natural and unfortunate birthright. It is generally admitted that with woman the powers of intuition, of rapid perception, and perhaps of imitation, are more strongly marked than in man; but some, at least, of these faculties are characteristic of the lower races, and therefore of a past and lower state of civilisation.

The chief distinction in the intellectual powers of the two sexes is shewn by man's attaining to a higher eminence, in whatever he takes up, than can woman—whether requiring deep thought, reason, or imagination, or merely the use of the senses and hands. If two lists were made of the most eminent men and women in poetry, painting, sculpture, music (inclusive both of composition and performance), history, science, and philosophy, with half-a-dozen names under each subject, the two lists would not bear comparison. We may also infer, from the law of the deviation from averages, so well illustrated by Mr. Galton, in his work on 'Hereditary Genius,' that if men are capable of a decided pre-eminence over women in many subjects, the average of mental power in man must be above that of woman.

Amongst the half-human progenitors of man, and amongst savages, there have been struggles between the males during many generations for the possession of the females. But mere bodily strength and size would do little for victory, unless associated with courage, perseverance, and determined energy. With social animals, the young males have to pass through many a contest before they win a female, and the older males have to retain their females by renewed battles. They have, also, in the case of mankind, to defend their females, as well as their young, from enemies of all kinds, and to hunt for their joint subsistence. But to avoid enemies or to attack them with success, to capture wild animals, and to fashion weapons, requires the aid of the higher mental faculties, namely, observation, reason, invention, or imagination. These various faculties will thus have been continually put to the test and selected during manhood; they will, moreover, have been strengthened by use during this same period of life. Consequently in accordance with the principle often alluded to, we might expect that they would at least tend to be transmitted chiefly to the male offspring at the corresponding period of manhood.

Now, when two men are put into competition, or a man with a woman, both possessed of every mental quality in equal perfection, save that one has higher energy, perseverance, and courage, the latter will generally become more eminent in every pursuit, and will gain the ascendancy.[24] He may be said to possess genius—for genius has been declared by a great authority to be patience; and patience, in this sense, means unflinching, undaunted perseverance. But this view of genius is perhaps deficient; for without the higher powers of the imagination and reason, no eminent success can be gained in many subjects. These latter faculties, as well as the former, will have been developed in man, partly through sexual selection, —that is, through the contest of rival males, and partly through natural selection,—that is, from success in the general struggle for life; and as in both cases the struggle will have been during maturity, the characters gained will have been transmitted more fully to the male than to the female offspring. It accords in a striking manner with this view of the modification and re-inforcement of many of our mental faculties by sexual selection, that, firstly, they notoriously undergo a considerable change at puberty,[25] and, secondly, that eunuchs remain throughout life inferior in these same qualities. Thus man has ultimately become superior to woman. It is, indeed, fortunate that the law of the equal transmission of characters to both sexes prevails with mammals; otherwise it is probable that man would have become as superior in mental endowment to woman, as the peacock is in ornamental plumage to the peahen.

It must be borne in mind that the tendency in characters acquired by either sex late in life, to be transmitted to the same sex at the same age, and of early acquired characters to be transmitted to both sexes, are rules which, though general, do not always hold. If they always held good, we might conclude (but I here exceed my proper bounds) that the inherited effects of the early education of boys and girls would be transmitted equally to both sexes; so that the present inequality in mental power between the sexes would not be effaced by a similar course of early training; nor can it have been caused by their dissimilar early training. In order that woman should reach the same standard as man, she ought, when nearly adult, to be trained to energy and perseverance, and to have her reason and imagination exercised to the highest point; and then she would probably transmit these qualities chiefly to her adult daughters.

[24] J. Stuart Mill remarks ('The Subjection of Women,' 1869, p. 122), "The things in which man most excels woman are those which require most plodding, and long hammering at single thoughts." What is this but energy and perseverance?

[25] Maudsley, 'Mind and Body,' p. 31.

All women, however, could not be thus raised, unless during many generations those who excelled in the above robust virtues were married, and produced offspring in larger numbers than other women. As before remarked of bodily strength, although men do not now fight for their wives, and this form of selection has passed away, yet during manhood, they generally undergo a severe struggle in order to maintain themselves and their families; and this will tend to keep up or even increase their mental powers, and, as a consequence, the present inequality between the sexes.[26]

Voice and Musical Powers.—In some species of Quadrumana there is a great difference between the adult sexes, in the power of their voices and in the development of the vocal organs; and man appears to have inherited this difference from his early progenitors. His vocal cords are about one-third longer than in woman, or than in boys; and emasculation produces the same effect on him as on the lower animals, for it "arrests that prominent growth of the thyroid, &c., which accompanies the elongation of the cords."[27] With respect to the cause of this difference between the sexes, I have nothing to add to the remarks in the last chapter on the probable effects of the long-continued use of the vocal organs by the male under the excitement of love, rage and jealousy. According to Sir Duncan Gibb,[28] the voice and the form of the larynx differ in the different races of mankind; but with the Tartars, Chinese, &c., the voice of the male is said not to differ so much from that of the female, as in most other races.

The capacity and love for singing or music, though not a sexual character in man, must not here be passed over. Although the sounds emitted by animals of all kinds serve many purposes, a strong case can be made out, that the vocal organs were primarily used and perfected in relation to the propagation of the species. Insects and some few spiders are the lowest animals which voluntarily produce any sound; and this is generally effected by the aid of beautifully constructed stridulating organs, which are often confined to the males. The sounds thus produced consist, I believe in all cases, of the same note, repeated rhythmically;[29] and this is sometimes pleasing even to the ears of man. The chief and, in some cases, exclusive purpose appears to be either to call or charm the opposite sex.

The sounds produced by fishes are said in some cases to be made only by the males during the breeding-season. All the air-breathing Vertebrata, necessarily possess an apparatus for inhaling and expelling air, with a pipe capable of being closed at one end. Hence when the primeval mem-

[26] An observation by Vogt bears on this subject: he says, "It is a remarkable circumstance, that the difference between the sexes, as regards the cranial cavity, increases with the development of the race, so that the male European excels much more the female, than the negro the negress. Welcker confirms this statement of Huschke from his measurements of negro and German skulls." But Vogt admits ('Lectures on Man,' Eng. translat. 1864, p. 81) that more observations are requisite on this point.
[27] Owen, 'Anatomy of Vertebrates,' vol. iii. p. 603.
[28] 'Journal of the Anthropolog. Soc.' April, 1869, p. lvii. and lxvi.
[29] Dr. Scudder, 'Notes on Stridulation,' in 'Proc. Boston Soc. of Nat. Hist.' vol. xi April, 1868.

bers of this class were strongly excited and their muscles violently contracted, purposeless sounds would almost certainly have been produced; and these, if they proved in any way serviceable, might readily have been modified or intensified by the preservation of properly adapted variations. The lowest Vertebrates which breathe air are Amphibians; and of these, frogs and toads possess vocal organs, which are incessantly used during the breeding-season, and which are often more highly developed in the male than in the female. The male alone of the tortoise utters a noise, and this only during the season of love. Male alligators roar or bellow during the same season. Every one knows how much birds use their vocal organs as a means of courtship; and some species likewise perform what may be called instrumental music.

In the class of Mammals, with which we are here more particularly concerned, the males of almost all the species use their voices during the breeding-season much more than at any other time; and some are absolutely mute excepting at this season. With other species both sexes, or only the females, use their voices as a love-call. Considering these facts, and that the vocal organs of some quadrupeds are much more largely developed in the male than in the female, either permanently or temporarily during the breeding-season; and considering that in most of the lower classes the sounds produced by the males, serve not only to call but to excite or allure the female, it is a surprising fact that we have not as yet any good evidence that these organs are used by male mammals to charm the females. The American *Mycetes caraya* perhaps forms an exception, as does the *Hylobates agilis*, an ape allied to man. This gibbon has an extremely loud but musical voice. Mr. Waterhouse states,[30] "It appeared to me that in ascending and descending the scale, the intervals were always exactly half-tones; and I am sure that the highest note was the exact octave to the lowest. The quality of the notes is very musical; and I do not doubt that a good violinist would be able to give a correct idea of the gibbon's composition, excepting as regards its loudness." Mr. Waterhouse then gives the notes. Professor Owen, who is a musician, confirms the foregoing statement, and remarks, though erroneously, that this gibbon "alone of brute mammals may be said to sing." It appears to be much excited after its performance. Unfortunately, its habits have never been closely observed in a state of nature; but from the analogy of other animals, it is probable that it uses its musical powers more especially during the season of courtship.

This gibbon is not the only species in the genus which sings, for my son, Francis Darwin, attentively listened in the Zoological Gardens to *H. leuciscus* whilst singing a cadence of three notes, in true musical intervals and with a clear musical tone. It is a more surprising fact that certain rodents utter musical sounds. Singing mice have often been mentioned and exhibited, but imposture has commonly been suspected. We have, however, at last a clear account by a well-known observer, the Rev. S. Lock-

[30] Given in W. C. L. Martin's 'General Introduction to Nat. Hist. of Mamm. Animals,' 1841, p. 432; Owen, 'Anatomy of Vertebrates,' vol. iii. p. 600.

wood,[31] of the musical powers of an American species, the *Hesperomys cognatus,* belonging to a genus distinct from that of the English mouse. This little animal was kept in confinement, and the performance was repeatedly heard. In one of the two chief songs, "the last bar would frequently be prolonged to two or three; and she would sometimes change from C sharp and D, to C natural and D, then warble on these two notes awhile, and wind up with a quick chirp on C sharp and D. The distinctness between the semitones was very marked, and easily appreciable to a good ear." Mr. Lockwood gives both songs in musical notation; and adds that though this little mouse "had no ear for time, yet she would keep to the key of B (two flats) and strictly in a major key." . . . "Her soft clear voice falls an octave with all the precision possible; then at the wind up, it rises again into a very quick trill on C sharp and D."

A critic has asked how the ears of man, and he ought to have added of other animals, could have been adapted by selection so as to distinguish musical notes. But this question shows some confusion on the subject; a noise is the sensation resulting from the co-existence of several aërial "simple vibrations" of various periods, each of which intermits so frequently that its separate existence cannot be perceived. It is only in the want of continuity of such vibrations, and in their want of harmony *inter se,* that a noise differs from a musical note. Thus an ear to be capable of discriminating noises—and the high importance of this power to all animals is admitted by every one—must be sensitive to musical notes. We have evidence of this capacity even low down in the animal scale: thus Crustaceans are provided with auditory hairs of different lengths, which have been seen to vibrate when the proper musical notes are struck.[32] As stated in a previous chapter, similar observations have been made on the hairs of the antennæ of gnats. It has been positively asserted by good observers that spiders are attracted by music. It is also well known that some dogs howl when hearing particular tones.[33] Seals apparently appreciate music, and their fondness for it "was well known to the ancients, and is often taken advantage of by the hunters at the present day."[34]

Therefore, as far as the mere perception of musical notes is concerned, there seems no special difficulty in the case of man or of any other animal. Helmholtz has explained on physiological principles why concords are agreeable, and discords disagreeable to the human ear; but we are little concerned with these, as music in harmony is a late invention. We are more concerned with melody, and here again, according to Helmholtz, it is intelligible why the notes of our musical scale are used. The ear analyses all sounds into their component "simple vibrations," although we are not conscious of this analysis. In a musical note the lowest in pitch of

[31] 'American Naturalist,' 1871, p. 761.

[32] Helmholtz, 'Théorie Phys. de la Musique,' 1868, p. 187.

[33] Several accounts have been published to this effect. Mr. Peach writes to me that an old dog of his howls when B flat is sounded on the flute, and to no other note. I may add another instance of a dog always whining, when one note on a concertina, which was out of tune, was played.

[34] Mr. R. Brown, in 'Proc. Zool. Soc.' 1868, p. 410.

these is generally predominant, and the others which are less marked are the octave, the twelfth, the second octave, &c., all harmonies of the fundamental predominant note; any two notes of our scale have many of these harmonic over-tones in common. It seems pretty clear then, that if an animal always wished to sing precisely the same song, he would guide himself by sounding those notes in succession, which possess many overtones in common—that is, he would choose for his song, notes which belong to our musical scale.

But if it be further asked why musical tones in a certain order and rhythm give man and other animals pleasure, we can no more give the reason than for the pleasantness of certain tastes and smells. That they do give pleasure of some kind to animals, we may infer from their being produced during the season of courtship by many insects, spiders, fishes, amphibians, and birds; for unless the females were able to appreciate such sounds and were excited or charmed by them, the persevering efforts of the males, and the complex structures often possessed by them alone, would be useless; and this it is impossible to believe.

Human song is generally admitted to be the basis or origin of instrumental music. As neither the enjoyment nor the capacity of producing musical notes are faculties of the least use to man in reference to his daily habits of life, they must be ranked amongst the most mysterious with which he is endowed. They are present, though in a very rude condition, in men of all races, even the most savage; but so different is the taste of the several races, that our music gives no pleasure to savages, and their music is to us in most cases hideous and unmeaning. Dr. Seemann, in some interesting remarks on this subject,[35] "doubt whether even amongst the nations of Western Europe, intimately connected as they are by close and frequent intercourse, the music of the one is interpreted in the same sense by the others. By travelling eastwards we find that there is certainly a different language of music. Songs of joy and dance-accompaniments are no longer, as with us, in the major keys, but always in the minor." Whether or not the half-human progenitors of man possessed, like the singing gibbons, the capacity of producing, and therefore no doubt of appreciating, musical notes, we know that man possessed these faculties at a very remote period. M. Lartet has described two flutes made out of the bones and horns of the reindeer, found in caves together with flint tools and the remains of extinct animals. The arts of singing and of dancing are also very ancient, and are now practised by all or nearly all the lowest races of man. Poetry, which may be considered as the offspring of song, is likewise so ancient, that many persons have felt astonished that it should have arisen during the earliest ages of which we have any record.

We see that the musical faculties, which are not wholly deficient in any race, are capable of prompt and high development, for Hottentots and Negroes have become excellent musicians, although in their native coun-

---

[35] 'Journal of Anthropolog. Soc.' Oct. 1870, p. clv. See also the several later chapters in Sir John Lubbock's 'Prehistoric Times,' second edition, 1869, which contain an admirable account of the habits of savages.

tries they rarely practise anything that we should consider music. Schweinfurth, however, was pleased with some of the simple melodies which he heard in the interior of Africa. But there is nothing anomalous in the musical faculties lying dormant in man: some species of birds which never naturally sing, can without much difficulty be taught to do so; thus a house-sparrow has learnt the song of a linnet. As these two species are closely allied, and belong to the order of Insessores, which includes nearly all the singing-birds in the world, it is possible that a progenitor of the sparrow may have been a songster. It is more remarkable that parrots, belonging to a group distinct from the Insessores, and having differently constructed vocal organs, can be taught not only to speak, but to pipe or whistle tunes invented by man, so that they must have some musical capacity. Nevertheless it would be very rash to assume that parrots are descended from some ancient form which was a songster. Many cases could be advanced of organs and instincts originally adapted for one purpose, having been utilised for some distinct purpose.[36] Hence the capacity for high musical development which the savage races of man possess, may be due either to the practice by our semi-human progenitors of some rude form of music, or simply to their having acquired the proper vocal organs for a different purpose. But in this latter case we must assume, as in the above instance of parrots, and as seems to occur with many animals, that they already possessed some sense of melody.

Music arouses in us various emotions, but not the more terrible ones of horror, fear, rage, &c. It awakens the gentler feelings of tenderness and love, which readily pass into devotion. In the Chinese annals it is said, "Music hath the power of making heaven descend upon earth." It likewise stirs up in us the sense of triumph and the glorious ardour for war. These powerful and mingled feelings may well give rise to the sense of sublimity. We can concentrate, as Dr. Seemann observes, greater intensity of feeling in a single musical note than in pages of writing. It is probable that nearly the same emotions, but much weaker and far less complex, are felt by birds when the male pours forth his full volume of song, in rivalry with other males, to captivate the female. Love is still the commonest theme of our songs. As Herbert Spencer remarks, "music arouses dormant sentiments of which we had not conceived the possibility, and do not know the meaning; or, as Richter says, tells us of things we have not seen and shall not see." Conversely, when vivid emotions are felt and expressed by the orator, or even in common speech, musical cadences and rhythm are instinctively used. The negro in Africa when excited often bursts forth in song; "another will reply in song, whilst the company, as

[36] Since this chapter was printed, I have seen a valuable article by Mr. Chauncey Wright ('North American Review,' Oct. 1870, page 293), who, in discussing the above subject, remarks, "There are many consequences of the ultimate laws or uniformities of nature, through which the acquisition of one useful power will bring with it many resulting advantages as well as limiting disadvantages, actual or possible, which the principle of utility may not have comprehended in its action." As I have attempted to shew in an early chapter of this work, this principle has an important bearing on the acquisition by man of some of his mental characteristics.

if touched by a musical wave, murmur a chorus in perfect unison." [37] Even monkeys express strong feelings in different tones—anger and impatience by low,—fear and pain by high notes.[38] The sensations and ideas thus excited in us by music, or expressed by the cadences of oratory, appear from their vagueness, yet depth, like mental reversions to the emotions and thoughts of a long-past age.

All these facts with respect to music and impassioned speech become intelligible to a certain extent, if we may assume that musical tones and rhythm were used by our half-human ancestors, during the season of courtship, when animals of all kinds are excited not only by love, but by the strong passions of jealousy, rivalry, and triumph. From the deeply-laid principle of inherited associations, musical tones in this case would be likely to call up vaguely and indefinitely the strong emotions of a long-past age. As we have every reason to suppose that articulate speech is one of the latest, as it certainly is the highest, of the arts acquired by man, and as the instinctive power of producing musical notes and rhythms is developed low down in the animal series, it would be altogether opposed to the principle of evolution, if we were to admit that man's musical capacity has been developed from the tones used in impassioned speech. We must suppose that the rhythms and cadences of oratory are derived from previously developed musical powers.[39] We can thus understand how it is that music, dancing, song, and poetry are such very ancient arts. We may go even further than this, and, as remarked in a former chapter, believe that musical sounds afforded one of the bases for the development of language.[40]

As the males of several quadrumanous animals have their vocal organs much more developed than in the females, and as a gibbon, one of the anthropomorphous apes, pours forth a whole octave of musical notes and may be said to sing, it appears probable that the progenitors of man, either the males or females or both sexes, before acquiring the power of ex-

---

[37] Winwood Reade, 'The Martyrdom of Man,' 1872, p. 441, and 'African Sketch Book,' 1873, vol. ii. p. 313.

[38] Rengger, 'Säugethiere von Paraguay,' s. 49.

[39] See the very interesting discussion on the 'Origin and Function of Music,' by Mr. Herbert Spencer, in his collected 'Essays,' 1858, p. 359. Mr. Spencer comes to an exactly opposite conclusion to that at which I have arrived. He concludes, as did Diderot formerly, that the cadences used in emotional speech afford the foundation from which music has been developed; whilst I conclude that musical notes and rhythm were first acquired by the male or female progenitors of mankind for the sake of charming the opposite sex. Thus musical tones became firmly associated with some of the strongest passions an animal is capable of feeling, and are consequently used instinctively, or through association when strong emotions are expressed in speech. Mr. Spencer does not offer any satisfactory explanation, nor can I, why high or deep notes should be expressive, both with man and the lower animals, of certain emotions. Mr. Spencer gives also an interesting discussion on the relations between poetry, recitative and song.

[40] I find in Lord Monboddo's 'Origin of Language,' vol. i. (1774), p. 469, that Dr. Blacklock likewise thought "that the first language among men was music, and that before our ideas were expressed by articulate sounds, they were communicated by tones varied according to different degrees of gravity and acuteness."

pressing their mutual love in articulate language, endeavoured to charm each other with musical notes and rhythm. So little is known about the use of the voice by the Quadrumana during the season of love, that we have no means of judging whether the habit of singing was first acquired by our male or female ancestors. Women are generally thought to possess sweeter voices than men, and as far as this serves as any guide, we may infer that they first acquired musical powers in order to attract the other sex.[41] But if so, this must have occurred long ago, before our ancestors had become sufficiently human to treat and value their women merely as useful slaves. The impassioned orator, bard, or musician, when with his varied tones and cadences he excites the strongest emotions in his hearers, little suspects that he uses the same means by which his half-human ancestors long ago aroused each other's ardent passions, during their courtship and rivalry.

The Influence of Beauty in determining the Marriages of Mankind.— In civilised life man is largely, but by no means exclusively, influenced in the choice of his wife by external appearance; but we are chiefly concerned with primeval times, and our only means of forming a judgment on this subject is to study the habits of existing semi-civilised and savage nations. If it can be shewn that the men of different races prefer women having various characteristics, or conversely with the women, we have then to enquire whether such choice, continued during many generations, would produce any sensible effect on the race, either on one sex or both according to the form of inheritance which has prevailed.

It will be well first to shew in some detail that savages pay the greatest attention to their personal appearance.[42] That they have a passion for ornament is notorious; and an English philosopher goes so far as to maintain, that clothes were first made for ornament and not for warmth. As Professor Waitz remarks, "however poor and miserable man is, he finds a pleasure in adorning himself." The extravagance of the naked Indians of South America in decorating themselves is shewn "by a man of large stature gaining with difficulty enough by the labour of a fortnight to procure in exchange the *chica* necessary to paint himself red."[43] The ancient barbarians of Europe during the Reindeer period brought to their caves any

[41] See an interesting discussion on this subject by Häckel, 'Generelle Morph.' B. ii. 1866, s. 246.

[42] A full and excellent account of the manner in which savages in all parts of the world ornament themselves, is given by the Italian traveller, Professor Mantegazza, 'Rio de la Plata, Viaggi e Studi,' 1867, pp. 525–545; all the following statements, when other references are not given, are taken from this work. See, also, Waitz, 'Introduction to Anthropolog.' Eng. translat. vol. i. 1863, p. 275, *et passim.* Lawrence also gives very full details in his 'Lectures on Physiology,' 1822. Since this chapter was written Sir J. Lubbock has published his 'Origin on Civilisation,' 1870, in which there is an interesting chapter on the present subject, and from which (pp. 42, 48) I have taken some facts about savages dyeing their teeth and hair, and piercing their teeth.

[43] Humboldt, 'Personal Narrative,' Eng. translat. vol. iv. p. 515; on the imagination shewn in painting the body, p. 522; on modifying the form of the calf of the leg, p. 466.

brilliant or singular objects which they happened to find. Savages at the present day everywhere deck themselves with plumes, necklaces, armlets, ear-rings, &c. They paint themselves in the most diversified manner. "If painted nations," as Humboldt observes, "had been examined with the same attention as clothed nations, it would have been perceived that the most fertile imagination and the most mutable caprice have created the fashions of painting, as well as those of garments."

In one part of Africa the eyelids are coloured black; in another the nails are coloured yellow or purple. In many places the hair is dyed of various tints. In different countries the teeth are stained black, red, blue, &c., and in the Malay Archipelago it is thought shameful to have white teeth "like those of a dog." Not one great country can be named, from the Polar regions in the north to New Zealand in the south, in which the aborigines do not tattoo themselves. This practice was followed by the Jews of old, and by the ancient Britons. In Africa some of the natives tattoo themselves, but it is a much more common practice to raise protuberances by rubbing salt into incisions made in various parts of the body; and these are considered by the inhabitants of Kordofan and Darfur "to be great personal attractions." In the Arab countries no beauty can be perfect until the cheeks "or temples have been gashed." [44] In South America, as Humboldt remarks, "a mother would be accused of culpable indifference towards her children, if she did not employ artificial means to shape the calf of the leg after the fashion of the country." In the Old and New Worlds the shape of the skull was formerly modified during infancy in the most extraordinary manner, as is still the case in many places, and such deformities are considered ornamental. For instance, the savages of Colombia [45] deem a much flattened head "an essential point of beauty."

The hair is treated with especial care in various countries; it is allowed to grow to full length, so as to reach to the ground, or is combed into "a compact frizzled mop, which is the Papuan's pride and glory." [46] In Northern Africa "a man requires a period of from eight to ten years to perfect his coiffure." With other nations the head is shaved, and in parts of South America and Africa even the eyebrows and eyelashes are eradicated. The natives of the Upper Nile knock out the four front teeth, saying that they do not wish to resemble brutes. Further south, the Bakotas knock out only the two upper incisors, which, as Livingstone [47] remarks, gives the face a hideous appearance, owing to the prominence of the lower jaw; but these people think the presence of the incisors most unsightly, and on beholding some Europeans, cried out, "Look at the great teeth!" The chief Sebituani tried in vain to alter this fashion. In various parts of Africa and in the Malay Archipelago the natives file the incisors

<hr />

[44] 'The Nile Tributaries,' 1867; 'The Albert N'yanza,' 1866, vol. i. p. 218.
[45] Quoted by Prichard, 'Phys. Hist. of Mankind,' 4th ed. vol. i. 1851, p. 321.
[46] On the Papuans, Wallace, 'The Malay Archipelago,' vol. ii. p. 445. On the coiffure of the Africans, Sir S. Baker, 'The Albert N'yanza,' vol. i. p. 210.
[47] 'Travels,' p. 533.

into points like those of a saw, or pierce them with holes, into which they insert studs.

As the face with us is chiefly admired for its beauty, so with savages it is the chief seat of mutilation. In all quarters of the world the septum, and more rarely the wings of the nose are pierced; rings, sticks, feathers, and other ornaments being inserted into the holes. The ears are everywhere pierced and similarly ornamented, and with the Botocudos and Lenguas of South America the hole is gradually so much enlarged that the lower edge touches the shoulder. In North and South America and in Africa either the upper or lower lip is pierced; and with the Botocudos the hole in the lower lip is so large that a disc of wood, four inches in diameter, is placed in it. Mantegazza gives a curious account of the shame felt by a South American native, and of the ridicule which he excited, when he sold his *tembeta*,—the large coloured piece of wood which is passed through the hole. In Central Africa the women perforate the lower lip and wear a crystal, which, from the movement of the tongue, has "a wriggling motion, indescribably ludicrous during conversation." The wife of the chief of Latooka told Sir S. Baker [48] that Lady Baker "would be much improved if she would extract her four front teeth from the lower jaw, and wear the long pointed polished crystal in her under lip." Further south with the Makalolo, the upper lip is perforated, and a large metal and bamboo ring, called a *pelelé*, is worn in the hole. "This caused the lip in one case to project two inches beyond the tip of the nose; and when the lady smiled, the contraction of the muscles elevated it over her eyes. 'Why do the women wear these things?' the venerable chief, Chinsurdi, was asked. Evidently surprised at such a stupid question, he replied, 'For beauty! They are the only beautiful things women have; men have beards, women have none. What kind of a person would she be without the pelelé? She would not be a woman at all with a mouth like a man, but no beard.' " [49]

Hardly any part of the body, which can be unnaturally modified, has escaped. The amount of suffering thus caused must have been extreme, for many of the operations require several years for their completion, so that the idea of their necessity must be imperative. The motives are various; the men paint their bodies to make themselves appear terrible in battle; certain mutilations are connected with religious rites, or they mark the age of puberty, or the rank of the man, or they serve to distinguish the tribes. Amongst savages the same fashions prevail for long perriods, [50] and thus mutilations, from whatever cause first made, soon come to be valued as distinctive marks. But self-adornment, vanity, and the admiration of others, seem to be the commonest motives. In regard to

[48] 'The Albert N'yanza,' 1866, vol. i. p. 217.

[49] Livingstone, 'British Association,' 1860; report given in the 'Athenæum,' July 7, 1860, p. 29.

[50] Sir S. Baker (ibid. vol. i. p. 210) speaking of the natives of Central Africa says, "every tribe has a distinct and unchanging fashion for dressing the hair." See Agassiz ('Journey in Brazil,' 1868, p. 318) on invariability of the tattooing of Amazonian Indians.

tattooing, I was told by the missionaries in New Zealand that when they tried to persuade some girls to give up the practice, they answered, "We must just have a few lines on our lips; else when we grow old we shall be so very ugly." With the men of New Zealand, a most capable judge [51] says, "to have fine tattooed faces was the great ambition of the young, both to render themselves attractive to the ladies, and conspicuous in war." A star tattooed on the forehead and a spot on the chin are thought by the women in one part of Africa to be irresistible attractions.[52] In most, but not all parts of the world, the men are more ornamented than the women, and often in a different manner; sometimes, though rarely, the women are hardly at all ornamented. As the women are made by savages to perform the greatest share of the work, and as they are not allowed to eat the best kinds of food, so it accords with the characteristic selfishness of man that they should not be allowed to obtain, or use the finest ornaments. Lastly, it is a remarkable fact, as proved by the foregoing quotations, that the same fashions in modifying the shape of the head, in ornamenting the hair, in painting, tattooing, in perforating the nose, lips, or ears, in removing or filing the teeth, &c., now prevail, and have long prevailed, in the most distant quarters of the world. It is extremely improbable that these practices, followed by so many distinct nations, should be due to tradition from any common source. They indicate the close similarity of the mind of man, to whatever race he may belong, just as do the almost universal habits of dancing, masquerading, and making rude pictures.

Having made these preliminary remarks on the admiration felt by savages for various ornaments, and for deformities most unsightly in our eyes, let us see how far the men are attracted by the appearance of their women, and what are their ideas of beauty. I have heard it maintained that savages are quite indifferent about the beauty of their women, valuing them solely as slaves; it may therefore be well to observe that this conclusion does not at all agree with the care which the women take in ornamenting themselves, or with their vanity. Burchell [53] gives an amusing account of a Bush-woman who used as much grease, red ochre, and shining powder "as would have ruined any but a very rich husband." She displayed also "much vanity and too evident a consciousness of her superiority." Mr. Winwood Reade informs me that the negroes of the West Coast often discuss the beauty of their women. Some competent observers have attributed the fearfully common practice of infanticide partly to the desire felt by the women to retain their good looks.[54] In several regions the women wear charms and use love-philters to gain the affections

[51] Rev. R. Taylor, 'New Zealand and its Inhabitants,' 1855, p. 152.
[52] Mantegazza, 'Viaggi e Studi,' p. 542.
[53] 'Travels in S. Africa,' 1824, vol. i. p. 414.
[54] See, for references, Gerland 'Ueber das Aussterben der Naturvölker,' 1868, ss. 51, 53, 55; also Azara, 'Voyages,' &c. tom. ii. p. 116.

of the men; and Mr. Brown enumerates four plants used for this purpose by the women of North-Western America.[55]

Hearne,[56] an excellent observer, who lived many years with the American Indians, says, in speaking of the women, "Ask a Northern Indian what is beauty, and he will answer, a broad flat face, small eyes, high cheek-bones, three or four broad black lines across each cheek, a low forehead, a large broad chin, a clumsy hook nose, a tawny hide, and breasts hanging down to the belt." Pallas, who visited the northern parts of the Chinese empire, says, "those women are preferred who have the Mandschú form; that is to say, a broad face, high cheek-bones, very broad noses, and enormous ears;"[57] and Vogt remarks that the obliquity of the eye, which is proper to the Chinese and Japanese, is exaggerated in their pictures for the purpose, as it "seems, of exhibiting its beauty, as contrasted with the eye of the red-haired barbarians." It is well known, as Huc repeatedly remarks, that the Chinese of the interior think Europeans hideous, with their white skins and prominent noses. The nose is far from being too prominent, according to our ideas, in the natives of Ceylon; yet "the Chinese in the seventh century, accustomed to the flat features of the Mongol races, were surprised at the prominent noses of the Cingalese; and Thsang described them as having 'the beak of a bird, with the body of a man.'"

Finlayson, after minutely describing the people of Cochin China, says that their rounded heads and faces are their chief characteristics; and, he adds, "the roundness of the whole countenance is more striking in the women, who are reckoned beautiful in proportion as they display this form of face." The Siamese have small noses with divergent nostrils, a wide mouth, rather thick lips, a remarkably large face, with very high and broad cheek-bones. It is, therefore, not wonderful that "beauty, according to our notion, is a stranger to them. Yet they consider their own females to be much more beautiful than those of Europe."[58]

It is well known that with many Hottentot women the posterior part of the body projects in a wonderful manner; they are steatopygous; and Sir Andrew Smith is certain that this peculiarity is greatly admired by the men.[59] He once saw a woman who was considered a beauty, and she was so immensely developed behind, that when seated on level ground she could not rise, and had to push herself along until she came to a slope. Some of the women in various negro tribes have the same peculiarity;

[55] On the vegetable productions used by the North-Western American Indians, in 'Pharmaceutical Journal,' vol. x.

[56] 'A Journey from Prince of Wales Fort,' 8vo. edit. 1796, p. 89.

[57] Quoted by Prichard, 'Phys. Hist. of Mankind,' 3rd edit. vol. iv. 1844, p. 519; Vogt, 'Lectures on Man,' Eng. translat. p. 129. On the opinion of the Chinese on the Cingalese, E. Tennent, 'Ceylon,' 1859, vol. ii. p. 107.

[58] Prichard, as taken from Crawfurd and Finlayson, 'Phys. Hist. of Mankind,' vol. iv. pp. 534, 535.

[59] Idem illustrissimus viator dixit mihi præcinctorium vel tabulam fœminæ, quod nobis teterrimum est, quondam permagno æstimari ab hominibus in hâc gente. Nunc res mutata est, et censent talem conformationem minime optandam esse.

and, according to Burton, the Somal men "are said to choose their wives by ranging them in a line, and by picking her out who projects farthest *a tergo*. Nothing can be more hateful to a negro than the opposite form." [60]

With respect to colour, the negroes rallied Mungo Park on the whiteness of his skin and the prominence of his nose, both of which they considered as "unsightly and unnatural conformations." He in return praised the glossy jet of their skins and the lovely depression of their noses; this they said was "honeymouth," nevertheless they gave him food. The African Moors, also, "knitted their brows and seemed to shudder" at the whiteness of his skin. On the eastern coast, the negro boys when they saw Burton, cried out, "Look at the white man; does he not look like a white ape?" On the western coast, as Mr. Winwood Reade informs me, the negroes admire a very black skin more than one of a lighter tint. But their horror of whiteness may be attributed, according to this same traveller, partly to the belief held by most negroes that demons and spirits are white, and partly to their thinking it a sign of ill-health.

The Banyai of the more southern part of the continent are negroes, but "a great many of them are of a light coffee-and-milk colour, and, indeed, this colour is considered handsome throughout the whole country;" so that here we have a different standard of taste. With the Kafirs, who differ much from negroes, "the skin, except among the tribes near Delagoa Bay, is not usually black, the prevailing colour being a mixture of black and red, the most common shade being chocolate. Dark complexions, as being most common, are naturally held in the highest esteem. To be told that he is light-coloured, or like a white man, would be deemed a very poor compliment by a Kafir. I have heard of one unfortunate man who was so very fair that no girl would marry him." One of the titles of the Zulu king is, "You who are black." [61] Mr. Galton, in speaking to me about the natives of S. Africa, remarked that their ideas of beauty seem very different from ours; for in one tribe two slim, slight, and pretty girls were not admired by the natives.

Turning to other quarters of the world; in Java, a yellow, not a white girl, is considered, according to Madame Pfeiffer, a beauty. A man of Cochin China "spoke with contempt of the wife of the English Ambassador, that she had white teeth like a dog, and a rosy colour like that of potato-flowers." We have seen that the Chinese dislike our white skin, and that the N. Americans admire "a tawny hide." In S. America, the Yuracaras, who inhabit the wooded, damp slopes of the eastern Cordillera, are remarkably pale-coloured, as their name in their own language expresses; nevertheless they consider European women as very inferior to their own. [62]

[60] 'The Anthropological Review,' November, 1864, p. 237. For additional references, see Waitz, 'Introduct. to Anthropology,' Eng. translat. 1863, vol. i. p. 105.

[61] Mungo Park's 'Travels in Africa,' 4to. 1816, pp. 53, 131. Burton's statement is quoted by Schaaffhausen, 'Archiv. für Anthropolog.' 1866, s. 163. On the Banyai, Livingstone, 'Travels,' p. 64. On the Kafirs, the Rev. J. Schooter, 'The Kafirs of Natal and the Zulu Country,' 1857, p. 1.

[62] For the Javans and Cochin-Chinese, see Waitz, 'Introduct. to Anthropology,'

In several of the tribes of North America the hair on the head grows to a wonderful length; and Catlin gives a curious proof how much this is esteemed, for the chief of the Crows was elected to this office from having the longest hair of any man in the tribe, namely ten feet and seven inches. The Aymaras and Quichuas of S. America, likewise have very long hair; and this, as Mr. D. Forbes informs me, is so much valued as a beauty, that cutting it off was the severest punishment which he could inflict on them. In both the Northern and Southern halves of the continent the natives sometimes increase the apparent length of their hair by weaving into it fibrous substances. Although the hair on the head is thus cherished, that on the face is considered by the North American Indians "as very vulgar," and every hair is carefully eradicated. This practice prevails throughout the American continent from Vancouver's Island in the north to Tierra del Fuego in the south. When York Minster, a Fuegian on board the 'Beagle,' was taken back to his country, the natives told him he ought to pull out the few short hairs on his face. They also threatened a young missionary, who was left for a time with them, to strip him naked, and pluck the hair from his face and body, yet he was far from being a hairy man. This fashion is carried so far that the Indians of Paraguay eradicate their eyebrows and eyelashes, saying that they do not wish to be like horses.[63]

It is remarkable that throughout the world the races which are almost completely destitute of a beard dislike hairs on the face and body, and take pains to eradicate them. The Kalmucks are beardless, and they are well known, like the Americans, to pluck out all straggling hairs; and so it is with the Polynesians, some of the Malays, and the Siamese. Mr. Veitch states that the Japanese ladies "all objected to our whiskers, considering them very ugly, and told us to cut them off, and be like Japanese men." The New Zealanders have short, curled beards; yet they formerly plucked out the hairs on the face. They had a saying that "there is no woman for a hairy man;" but it would appear that the fashion has changed in New Zealand, perhaps owing to the presence of Europeans, and I am assured that beards are now admired by the Maories.[64]

On the other hand, bearded races admire and greatly value their beards; among the Anglo-Saxons every part of the body had a recognised value; "the loss of the beard being estimated at twenty shillings, while the breaking of a thigh was fixed at only twelve."[65] In the East men

Eng. translat. vol. i. p. 305. On the Yuracaras, A. d'Orbigny, as quoted in Prichard, 'Phys. History of Mankind,' vol. v. 3rd edit. p. 476.

[63] 'North American Indians,' by G. Catlin, 3rd edit. 1842, vol. i. p. 49; vol. ii, p. 227. On the natives of Vancouver's Island, see Sproat, 'Scenes and Studies of Savage Life,' 1868, p. 25. On the Indians of Paraguay, Azara, 'Voyages,' tom. ii. p. 105.

[64] On the Siamese, Prichard, ibid. vol. iv. p. 533. On the Japanese, Veitch in 'Gardeners' Chronicle,' 1860, p. 1104. On the New Zealanders, Mantegazza, 'Viaggi e Studi,' 1867, p. 526. For the other nations mentioned, see references in Lawrence, 'Lectures on Physiology,' &c. 1822, p. 272.

[65] Lubbock, 'Origin of Civilisation,' 1870, p. 321.

swear solemnly by their beards. We have seen that Chinsurdi, the chief of the Makalolo in Africa, thought that beards were a great ornament. In the Pacific the Fijian's beard is "profuse and bushy, and is his greatest pride;" whilst the inhabitants of the adjacent archipelagoes of Tonga and Samoa are "beardless, and abhor a rough chin." In one island alone of the Ellice group "the men are heavily bearded, and not a little proud thereof." [66]

We thus see how widely the different races of man differ in their taste for the beautiful. In every nation sufficiently advanced to have made effigies of their gods or of their deified rulers, the sculptors no doubt have endeavoured to express their highest ideal of beauty and grandeur.[67] Under this point of view it is well to compare in our mind the Jupiter or Apollo of the Greeks with the Egyptian or Assyrian statues; and these with the hideous bas-reliefs on the ruined buildings of Central America.

I have met with very few statements opposed to this conclusion. Mr. Winwood Reade, however, who has had ample opportunities for observation, not only with the negroes of the West Coast of Africa, but with those of the interior who have never associated with Europeans, is convinced that their ideas of beauty are *on the whole* the same as ours; and Dr. Rohlfs writes to me to the same effect with respect to Bornu and the countries inhabited by the Pullo tribes. Mr. Reade found that he agreed with the negroes in their estimation of the beauty of the native girls; and that their appreciation of the beauty of European women corresponded with ours. They admire long hair, and use artificial means to make it appear abundant; they admire also a beard, though themselves very scantily provided. Mr. Reade feels doubtful what kind of nose is most appreciated; a girl has been heard to say, "I do not want to marry him, he has got no nose;" and this shows that a very flat nose is not admired. We should, however, bear in mind that the depressed, broad noses and projecting jaws of the negroes of the West Coast are exceptional types with the inhabitants of Africa. Notwithstanding the foregoing statements, Mr. Reade admits that negroes "do not like the colour of our skin; they look on blue eyes with aversion, and they think our noses too long and our lips too thin." He does not think it probable that negroes would ever prefer the most beautiful European woman, on the mere grounds of physical admiration, to a good-looking negress.[68]

[66] Dr. Barnard Davis quotes Mr. Prichard and others for these facts in regard to the Polynesians, in 'Anthropolog. Review,' April, 1870, pp. 185, 191.

[67] Ch. Comte has remarks to this effect in his 'Traité de Législation,' 3rd edit. 1837, p. 136.

[68] The 'African Sketch Book,' vol. ii. 1873, pp. 253, 394, 521. The Fuegians, as I have been informed by a missionary who long resided with them, consider European women as extremely beautiful; but from what we have seen of the judgment of the other aborigines of America, I cannot but think that this must be a mistake, unless indeed the statement refers to the few Fuegians who have lived for some time with Europeans, and who must consider us as superior beings. I should add that a most experienced observer, Capt. Burton, believes that a woman whom we consider beautiful is admired throughout the world. 'Anthropological Review,' March, 1864, p. 245.

The general truth of the principle, long ago insisted on by Humboldt,[69] that man admires and often tries to exaggerate whatever characters nature may have given him, is shown in many ways. The practice of beardless races extirpating every trace of a beard, and often all the hairs on the body affords one illustration. The skull has been greatly modified during ancient and modern times by many nations; and there can be little doubt that this has been practised, especially in N. and S. America, in order to exaggerate some natural and admired peculiarity. Many American Indians are known to admire a head so extremely flattened as to appear to us idiotic. The natives on the north-western coast compress the head into a pointed cone; and it is their constant practice to gather the hair into a knot on the top of the head, for the sake, as Dr. Wilson remarks, "of increasing the apparent elevation of the favourite conoid form." The inhabitants of Arakhan admire a broad, smooth forehead, and in order to produce it, they fasten a plate of lead on the heads of the new-born children. On the other hand, "a broad, well-rounded occiput is considered a great beauty" by the natives of the Fiji Islands.[70]

As with the skull, so with the nose; the ancient Huns during the age of Attila were accustomed to flatten the noses of their infants with bandages, "for the sake of exaggerating a natural conformation." With the Tahitians, to be called *long-nose* is considered as an insult, and they compress the noses and foreheads of their children for the sake of beauty. The same holds with the Malays of Sumatra, the Hottentots, certain Negroes, and the natives of Brazil.[71] The Chinese have by nature unusually small feet; [72] and it is well known that the women of the upper classes distort their feet to make them still smaller. Lastly, Humboldt thinks that the American Indians prefer colouring their bodies with red paint in order to exaggerate their natural tint; and until recently European women added to their naturally bright colours by rouge and white cosmetics; but it may be doubted whether barbarous nations have generally had any such intention in painting themselves.

In the fashions of our own dress we see exactly the same principle and the same desire to carry every point to an extreme; we exhibit, also, the same spirit of emulation. But the fashions of savages are far more permanent than ours; and whenever their bodies are artificially modified, this is necessarily the case. The Arab women of the Upper Nile occupy about three days in dressing their hair; they never imitate other tribes,

[69] 'Personal Narrative,' Eng. translat. vol. iv. p. 518, and elsewhere. Mantegazza, in his 'Viaggi e Studi,' strongly insists on this same principle.

[70] On the skulls of the American tribes, see Nott and Gliddon, 'Types of Mankind,' 1854, p. 440; Prichard, 'Phys. Hist. of Mankind,' vol. i. 3rd edit. p. 321; on the natives of Arakhan, ibid. vol. iv. p. 537. Wilson, 'Physical Ethnology,' Smithsonian Institution, 1863, p. 288; on the Fijians, p. 290. Sir J. Lubbock ('Prehistoric Times,' 2nd edit. 1869, p. 506) gives an excellent résumé on this subject.

[71] On the Huns, Godron, 'De l'Espèce,' tom. ii. 1859, p. 300. On the Tahitians, Waitz, 'Anthropolog.' Eng. translat. vol. i. p. 305. Marsden, quoted by Prichard, 'Phys. Hist. of Mankind,' 3rd edit. vol. v. p. 67. Lawrence, 'Lectures on Physiology,' p. 337.

[72] This fact was ascertained in the 'Reise der Novara: Anthropolog. Thiel,' Dr. Weisbach, 1867, s. 265.

"but simply vie with each other in the superlativeness of their own style."
Dr. Wilson, in speaking of the compressed skulls of various American
races, adds, "such usages are among the least eradicable, and long survive the shock of revolutions that change dynasties and efface more important national peculiarities." [73] The same principle comes into play in
the art of breeding; and we can thus understand, as I have elsewhere explained,[74] the wonderful development of the many races of animals and
plants, which have been kept merely for ornament. Fanciers always wish
each character to be somewhat increased; they do not admire a medium
standard; they certainly do not desire any great and abrupt change in the
character of their breeds; they admire solely what they are accustomed
to, but they ardently desire to see each characteristic feature a little more
developed.

The senses of man and of the lower animals seem to be so constituted
that brilliant colours and certain forms, as well as harmonious and rhyth-
mical sounds, give pleasure and are called beautiful; but why this should
be so we know not. It is certainly not true that there is in the mind of
man any universal standard of beauty with respect to the human body.
It is, however, possible that certain tastes may in the course of time become inherited, though there is no evidence in favour of this belief; and
if so, each race would possess its own innate ideal standard of beauty. It
has been argued [75] that ugliness consists in an approach to the structure
of the lower animals, and no doubt this is partly true with the more civilised nations, in which intellect is highly appreciated; but this explanation will hardly apply to all forms of ugliness. The men of each race prefer what they are accustomed to; they cannot endure any great change;
but they like variety, and admire each characteristic carried to a moderate extreme.[76] Men accustomed to a nearly oval face, to straight and regular features, and to bright colours, admire, as we Europeans know, these
points when strongly developed. On the other hand, men accustomed to a
broad face, with high cheek-bones, a depressed nose, and a black skin,
admire these peculiarities when strongly marked. No doubt characters of
all kinds may be too much developed for beauty. Hence a perfect beauty,
which implies many characters modified in a particular manner, will be in
every race a prodigy. As the great anatomist Bichat long ago said, if
every one were cast in the same mould, there would be no such thing as
beauty. If all our women were to become as beautiful as the Venus de'
Medici, we should for a time be charmed; but we should soon wish for
variety; and as soon as we had obtained variety, we should wish to see
certain characters a little exaggerated beyond the then existing common
standard.

[73] 'Smithsonian Institution,' 1863, p. 289. On the fashions of Arab women, Sir S.
Baker, 'The Nile Tributaries,' 1867, p. 121.

[74] 'The Variation of Animals and Plants under Domestication,' vol. i. p. 214; vol. ii.
p. 240.

[75] Schaaffhausen, 'Archiv. für Anthropôlogie,' 1866, s. 164.

[76] Mr. Bain has collected ('Mental and Moral Science,' 1868, pp. 304–314) about a
dozen more or less different theories of the idea of beauty; but none are quite the
same as that here given.

CHAPTER XX

SECONDARY SEXUAL CHARACTERS OF MAN—*continued*

On the effects of the continued selection of women according to a different standard of beauty in each race—On the causes which interfere with sexual selection in civilised and savage nations—Conditions favourable to sexual selection during primeval times—On the manner of action of sexual selection with mankind—On the women in savage tribes having some power to choose their husbands—Absence of hair on the body, and development of the beard—Colour of the skin—Summary.

WE have seen in the last chapter that with all barbarous races ornaments, dress, and external appearance are highly valued; and that the men judge of the beauty of their women by widely different standards. We must next inquire whether this preference and the consequent selection during many generations of those women, which appear to the men of each race the most attractive, has altered the character either of the females alone, or of both sexes. With mammals the general rule appears to be that characters of all kinds are inherited equally by the males and females; we might therefore expect that with mankind any characters gained by the females or by the males through sexual selection would commonly be transferred to the offspring of both sexes. If any change has thus been effected, it is almost certain that the different races would be differently modified, as each has its own standard of beauty.

With mankind, especially with savages, many causes interfere with the action of sexual selection as far as the bodily frame is concerned. Civilised men are largely attracted by the mental charms of women, by their wealth, and especially by their social position; for men rarely marry into a much lower rank. The men who succeed in obtaining the more beautiful women will not have a better chance of leaving a long line of descendants than other men with plainer wives, save the few who bequeath their fortunes according to primogeniture. With respect to the opposite form of selection, namely, of the more attractive men by the women, although in civilised nations women have free or almost free choice, which is not the case with barbarous races, yet their choice is largely influenced by the social position and wealth of the men; and the success of the latter in life depends much on their intellectual powers and energy, or on the fruits of these same powers in their forefathers. No excuse is needed for treating this subject in some detail; for, as the German philosopher Schopenhauer remarks, "the final aim of all love intrigues, be they comic or tragic, is really of more importance than all other ends in human life. What it all turns upon is nothing less than the composition of the next generation. . . . It is not the weal or woe of any one individual, but that of the human race to come, which is here at stake." [1]

There is, however, reason to believe that in certain civilised and semi-civilised nations sexual selection has effected something in modifying the bodily frame of some of the members. Many persons are convinced, as it appears to me with justice, that our aristocracy, including under this term all wealthy families in which primogeniture has long prevailed, from having chosen during many generations from all classes the more beautiful women as their wives, have become handsomer, according to the European standard, than the middle classes; yet the middle classes are placed under equally favourable conditions of life for the perfect development of the body. Cook remarks that the superiority in personal appearance "which is observable in the erees or nobles in all the other islands (of the Pacific) is found in the Sandwich Islands;" but this may be chiefly due to their better food and manner of life.

The old traveller Chardin, in describing the Persians, says their "blood is now highly refined by frequent intermixtures with the Georgians and Circassians, two nations which surpass all the world in personal beauty. There is hardly a man of rank in Persia who is not born of a Georgian or Circassian mother." He adds that they inherit their beauty, "not from their ancestors, for without the above mixture, the men of rank in Persia, who are descendants of the Tartars, would be extremely ugly." [2] Here is a more curious case; the priestesses who attended the temple of Venus Erycina at San-Giuliano in Sicily, were selected for their beauty out of the whole of Greece; they were not vestal virgins, and Quatrefages,[3] who states the foregoing fact, says that the women of San-Giuliano are now famous as the most beautiful in the island, and are sought by artists as models. But it is obvious that the evidence in all the above cases is doubtful.

The following case, though relating to savages, is well worth giving for its curiosity. Mr. Winwood Reade informs me that the Jollofs, a tribe of negroes on the west coast of Africa, "are remarkable for their uniformly fine appearance." A friend of his asked one of these men, "How is it that every one whom I meet is so fine looking, not only your men but your women?" The Jollof answered, "It is very easily explained: it has always been our custom to pick out our worst-looking slaves and to sell them." It need hardly be added that with all savages, female slaves serve as concubines. That this negro should have attributed, whether rightly or wrongly, the fine appearance of his tribe to the long-continued elimination of the ugly women is not so surprising as it may at first ap-

---

[1] 'Schopenhauer and Darwinism,' in 'Journal of Anthropology,' Jan. 1871, p. 323.
[2] These quotations are taken from Lawrence ('Lectures on Physiology,' &c. 1822, p. 393), who attributes the beauty of the upper classes in England to the men having long selected the more beautiful women.
[3] 'Anthropologie,' 'Revue des Cours Scientifiques,' Oct. 1868, p. 721.

pear; for I have elsewhere shewn [4] that negroes fully appreciate the importance of selection in the breeding of their domestic animals, and I could give from Mr. Reade additional evidence on this head.

The Causes which prevent or check the Action of Sexual Selection with Savages.—The chief causes are, first, so-called communal marriages or promiscuous intercourse; secondly, the consequences of female infanticide; thirdly, early betrothals; and lastly, the low estimation in which women are held, as mere slaves. These four points must be considered in some detail.

It is obvious that as long as the pairing of man, or of any other animal, is left to mere chance, with no choice exerted by either sex, there can be no sexual selection; and no effect will be produced on the offspring by certain individuals having had an advantage over others in their courtship. Now it is asserted that there exist at the present day tribes which practise what Sir J. Lubbock by courtesy calls communal marriages; that is, all the men and women in the tribe are husbands and wives to one another. The licentiousness of many savages is no doubt astonishing, but it seems to me that more evidence is requisite, before we fully admit that their intercourse is in any case promiscuous. Nevertheless all those who have most closely studied the subject,[5] and whose judgment is worth much more than mine, believe that communal marriage (this expression being variously guarded) was the original and universal form throughout the world, including therein the intermarriage of brothers and sisters. The late Sir A. Smith, who had travelled widely in S. Africa, and knew much about the habits of savages there and elsewhere, expressed to me the strongest opinion that no race exists in which woman is considered as the property of the community. I believe that his judgment was largely determined by what is implied by the term marriage. Throughout the following discussion I use the term in the same sense as when naturalists speak of animals as monogamous, meaning thereby that the male is accepted by or chooses a single female, and lives with her either during the breeding-season or for the whole year, keeping possession of her by the law of might; or, as when they speak of a polygamous species, meaning that the male lives with several females. This kind of marriage is all that concerns us here, as it suffices for the work of sexual selection. But I know that some of the writers above referred to imply by the term marriage a recognised right protected by the tribe.

[4] 'Variation of Animals and Plants under Domestication,' vol. i. p. 207.

[5] Sir J. Lubbock, 'The Origin of Civilisation,' 1870, chap. iii. especially pp. 60–67. Mr. M'Lennan, in his extremely valuable work on 'Primitive Marriage,' 1865, p. 163, speaks of the union of the sexes "in the earliest times as loose, transitory, and in some degree promiscuous." Mr. M'Lennan and Sir J. Lubbock have collected much evidence on the extreme licentiousness of savages at the present time. Mr. L. H. Morgan, in his interesting memoir of the classificatory system of relationship ('Proc. American Acad. of Sciences,' vol. vii. Feb. 1868, p. 475), concludes that polygamy and all forms of marriage during primeval times were essentially unknown. It appears also, from Sir J. Lubbock's work, that Bachofen likewise believes that communal intercourse originally prevailed.

The indirect evidence in favour of the belief of the former prevalence of communal marriages is strong, and rests chiefly on the terms of relationship which are employed between the members of the same tribe, implying a connection with the tribe, and not with either parent. But the subject is too large and complex for even an abstract to be here given, and I will confine myself to a few remarks. It is evident in the case of such marriages, or where the marriage tie is very loose, that the relationship of the child to its father cannot be known. But it seems almost incredible that the relationship of the child to its mother should ever be completely ignored, especially as the women in most savage tribes nurse their infants for a long time. Accordingly, in many cases the lines of descent are traced through the mother alone, to the exclusion of the father. But in other cases the terms employed express a connection with the tribe alone, to the exclusion even of the mother. It seems possible that the connection between the related members of the same barbarous tribe, exposed to all sorts of danger, might be so much more important, owing to the need of mutual protection and aid, than that between the mother and her child, as to lead to the sole use of terms expressive of the former relationships; but Mr. Morgan is convinced that this view is by no means sufficient.

The terms of relationship used in different parts of the world may be divided, according to the author just quoted, into two great classes, the classificatory and descriptive,—the latter being employed by us. It is the classificatory system which so strongly leads to the belief that communal and other extremely loose forms of marriage were originally universal. But as far as I can see, there is no necessity on this ground for believing in absolutely promiscuous intercourse; and I am glad to find that this is Sir J. Lubbock's view. Men and women, like many of the lower animals, might formerly have entered into strict though temporary unions for each birth, and in this case nearly as much confusion would have arisen in the terms of relationship as in the case of promiscuous intercourse. As far as sexual selection is concerned, all that is required is that choice should be exerted before the parents unite, and it signifies little whether the unions last for life or only for a season.

Besides the evidence derived from the terms of relationship, other lines of reasoning indicate the former wide prevalence of communal marriage. Sir J. Lubbock accounts for the strange and widely-extended habit of exogamy—that is, the men of one tribe taking wives from a distinct tribe, —by communism having been the original form of intercourse; so that a man never obtained a wife for himself unless he captured her from a neighbouring and hostile tribe, and then she would naturally have become his sole and valuable property. Thus the practice of capturing wives might have arisen; and from the honour so gained it might ultimately have become the universal habit. According to Sir J. Lubbock,[6] we can also thus understand "the necessity of expiation for marriage as

---

[6] 'Address to British Association On the Social and Religious Condition of the Lower Races of Man,' 1870, p. 20.

an infringement of tribal rites, since, according to old ideas, a man had no right to appropriate to himself that which belonged to the whole tribe." Sir J. Lubbock further gives a curious list of facts shewing that in old times high honour was bestowed on women who were utterly licentious; and this, as he explains, is intelligible, if we admit that promiscuous intercourse was the aboriginal, and therefore long revered custom of the tribe.[7]

Although the manner of development of the marriage-tie is an obscure subject, as we may infer from the divergent opinions on several points between the three authors who have studied it most closely, namely, Mr. Morgan, Mr. M'Lennan, and Sir J. Lubbock, yet from the foregoing and several other lines of evidence it seems probable[8] that the habit of marriage, in any strict sense of the word, has been gradually developed; and that almost promiscuous or very loose intercourse was once extremely common throughout the world. Nevertheless, from the strength of the feeling of jealousy all through the animal kingdom, as well as from the analogy of the lower animals, more particularly of those which come nearest to man, I cannot believe that absolutely promiscuous intercourse prevailed in times past, shortly before man attained to his present rank in the zoological scale. Man, as I have attempted to shew, is certainly descended from some ape-like creature. With the existing Quadrumana, as far as their habits are known, the males of some species are monogamous, but live during only a part of the year with the females: of this the orang seems to afford an instance. Several kinds, for example some of the Indian and American monkeys, are strictly monogamous, and associate all the year round with their wives. Others are polygamous, for example the gorilla and several American species, and each family lives separate. Even when this occurs, the families inhabiting the same district are probably somewhat social; the chimpanzee, for instance, is occasionally met with in large bands. Again, other species are polygamous, but several males, each with his own females, live associated in a body, as with several species of baboons[9]. We may indeed conclude from what we know of the jealousy of all male quadrupeds, armed, as many of them are, with special weapons for battling with their rivals, that promiscuous intercourse in a state of nature is extremely improbable. The pairing may not last for life, but only for each birth; yet if the males which are the strongest and best able to defend or otherwise assist their females and young, were to select the more attractive females, this would suffice for sexual selection.

[7] 'Origin of Civilisation,' 1870, p. 86. In the several works above quoted, there will be found copious evidence on relationship through the females alone, or with the tribe alone.

[8] Mr. C. Staniland Wake argues strongly ('Anthropologia,' March, 1874, p. 197) against the views held by these three writers on the former prevalence of almost promiscuous intercourse; and he thinks that the classificatory system of relationship can be otherwise explained.

[9] Brehm ('Illust. Thierleben,' B. i. p. 77) says Cynocephalus hamadryas lives in great troops containing twice as many adult females as adult males. See Rengger on American polygamous species, and Owen ('Anat. of Vertebrates,' vol. iii. p. 746) on American monogamous species. Other references might be added.

Therefore, looking far enough back in the stream of time, and judging from the social habits of man as he now exists, the most probable view is that he aboriginally lived in small communities, each with a single wife, or if powerful with several, whom he jealously guarded against all other men. Or he may not have been a social animal, and yet have lived with several wives, like the gorilla; for all the natives "agree that but one adult male is seen in a band; when the young male grows up, a contest takes place for mastery, and the strongest, by killing and driving out the others, establishes himself as the head of the community." [10] The younger males, being thus expelled and wandering about, would, when at last successful in finding a partner, prevent too close interbreeding within the limits of the same family.

Although savages are now extremely licentious, and although communal marriages may formerly have largely prevailed, yet many tribes practise some form of marriage, but of a far more lax nature than that of civilised nations. Polygamy, as just stated, is almost universally followed by the leading men in every tribe. Nevertheless there are tribes, standing almost at the bottom of the scale, which are strictly monogamous. This is the case with the Veddahs of Ceylon: they have a saying, according to Sir J. Lubbock,[11] "that death alone can separate husband and wife." An intelligent Kandyan chief, of course a polygamist, "was perfectly scandalised at the utter barbarism of living with only one wife, and never parting until separated by death." It was, he said, "just like the Wanderoo monkey." Whether savages who now enter into some form of marriage, either polygamous or monogamous, have retained this habit from primeval times, or whether they have returned to some form of marriage, after passing through a stage of promiscuous intercourse, I will not pretend to conjecture.

Infanticide.—This practice is now very common throughout the world, and there is reason to believe that it prevailed much more extensively during former times.[12] Barbarians find it difficult to support themselves and their children, and it is a simple plan to kill their infants. In South America some tribes, according to Azara, formerly destroyed so many infants of both sexes that they were on the point of extinction. In the Polynesian Islands women have been known to kill from four or five, to even ten of their children; and Ellis could not find a single woman who had not killed at least one. In a village on the eastern frontier of India Colonel MacCulloch found not a single female child. Wherever infanticide [13]

[10] Dr. Savage, in 'Boston Journal of Nat. Hist.' vol. v. 1845–47, p. 423.

[11] 'Prehistoric Times,' 1869, p. 424.

[12] Mr. M'Lennan, 'Primitive Marriage,' 1865. See especially on exogamy and infanticide, pp. 130, 138, 165.

[13] Dr. Gerland ('Ueber das Aussterben der Naturvölker,' 1868) has collected much information on infanticide, see especially ss. 27, 51, 54. Azara ('Voyages,' &c. tom. ii. pp. 94, 116) enters in detail on the motives. See also M'Lennan (ibid. p. 139) for cases in India. In the former reprints of the 2nd edition of this book an incorrect quotation from Sir G. Grey was unfortunately given in the above passage and has now been removed from the text.

prevails the struggle for existence will be in so far less severe, and all the members of the tribe will have an almost equally good chance of rearing their few surviving children. In most cases a larger number of female than of male infants are destroyed, for it is obvious that the latter are of more value to the tribe, as they will, when grown up, aid in defending it, and can support themselves. But the trouble experienced by the women in rearing children, their consequent loss of beauty, the higher estimation set on them when few, and their happier fate, are assigned by the women themselves, and by various observers, as additional motives for infanticide.

When, owing to female infanticide, the women of a tribe were few, the habit of capturing wives from neighbouring tribes would naturally arise. Sir J. Lubbock, however, as we have seen, attributes the practice in chief part to the former existence of communal marriage, and to the men having consequently captured women from other tribes to hold as their sole property. Additional causes might be assigned, such as the communities being very small, in which case, marriageable women would often be deficient. That the habit was most extensively practised during former times, even by the ancestors of civilised nations, is clearly shewn by the preservation of many curious customs and ceremonies, of which Mr. M'Lennan has given an interesting account. In our own marriages the "best man" seems originally to have been the chief abettor of the bridegroom in the act of capture. Now as long as men habitually procured their wives through violence and craft, they would have been glad to seize on any woman, and would not have selected the more attractive ones. But as soon as the practice of procuring wives from a distinct tribe was effected through barter, as now occurs in many places, the more attractive women would generally have been purchased. The incessant crossing, however, between tribe and tribe, which necessarily follows from any form of this habit, would tend to keep all the people inhabiting the same country nearly uniform in character; and this would interfere with the power of sexual selection in differentiating the tribes.

The scarcity of women, consequent on female infanticide, leads, also, to another practice, that of polyandry, still common in several parts of the world, and which formerly, as Mr. M'Lennan believes, prevailed almost universally: but this latter conclusion is doubted by Mr. Morgan and Sir J. Lubbock.[14] Whenever two or more men are compelled to marry one woman, it is certain that all the women of the tribe will get married, and there will be no selection by the men of the more attractive women. But under these circumstances the women no doubt will have the power of choice, and will prefer the more attractive men. Azara, for instance, describes how carefully a Guana woman bargains for all sorts of privileges, before accepting some one or more husbands; and the men in consequence take unusual care of their personal appearance. So amongst the Todas of India, who practise polyandry, the girls can accept or refuse

[14] 'Primitive Marriage,' p. 208; Sir J. Lubbock, 'Origin of Civilisation,' p. 100. See also Mr. Morgan, loc. cit., on the former prevalence of polyandry.

any man.[15] A very ugly man in these cases would perhaps altogether fail in getting a wife, or get one later in life; but the handsomer men, although more successful in obtaining wives, would not, as far as we can see, leave more offspring to inherit their beauty than the less handsome husbands of the same women.

Early Betrothals and Slavery of Women.—With many savages it is the custom to betroth the females whilst mere infants; and this would effectually prevent preference being exerted on either side according to personal appearance. But it would not prevent the more attractive women from being afterwards stolen or taken by force from their husbands by the more powerful men; and this often happens in Australia, America, and elsewhere. The same consequences with reference to sexual selection would to a certain extent follow, when women are valued almost solely as slaves or beasts of burden, as is the case with many savages. The men, however, at all times would prefer the handsomest slaves according to their standard of beauty.

We thus see that several customs prevail with savages which must greatly interfere with, or completely stop, the action of sexual selection. On the other hand, the conditions of life to which savages are exposed, and some of their habits, are favourable to natural selection; and this comes into play at the same time with sexual selection. Savages are known to suffer severely from recurrent famines; they do not increase their food by artificial means; they rarely refrain from marriage,[16] and generally marry whilst young. Consequently they must be subjected to occasional hard struggles for existence, and the favoured individuals will alone survive.

At a very early period, before man attained to his present rank in the scale, many of his conditions would be different from what now obtains amongst savages. Judging from the analogy of the lower animals, he would then either live with a single female, or be a polygamist. The most powerful and able males would succeed best in obtaining attractive females. They would also succeed best in the general struggle for life, and in defending their females, as well as their offspring, from enemies of all kinds. At this early period the ancestors of man would not be sufficiently advanced in intellect to look forward to distant contingencies; they would not foresee that the rearing of all their children, especially their female children, would make the struggle for life severer for the tribe. They would be governed more by their instincts and less by their reason than are savages at the present day. They would not at that period have partially lost one of the strongest of all instincts, common to all the lower animals, namely the love of their young offspring; and consequently they

---

[15] Azara, 'Voyages,' &c. tom. ii. pp. 92–95, Colonel Marshall 'Amongst tne Todas,' p. 212.

[16] Burchell says ('Travels in S. Africa,' vol. ii. 1824, p. 58), that among the wild nations of Southern Africa, neither men nor women ever pass their lives in a state of celibacy. Azara ('Voyages dans l'Amérique Merid.' tom. ii. 1809, p. 21) makes precisely the same remark in regard to the wild Indians of South America.

would not have practised female infanticide. Women would not have been thus rendered scarce, and polyandry would not have been practised; for hardly any other cause, except the scarcity of women seems sufficient to break down the natural and widely prevalent feeling of jealousy, and the desire of each male to possess a female for himself. Polyandry would be a natural stepping-stone to communal marriages or almost promiscuous intercourse; though the best authorities believe that this latter habit preceded polyandry. During primordial times there would be no early betrothals, for this implies foresight. Nor would women be valued merely as useful slaves or beasts of burden. Both sexes, if the females as well as the males were permitted to exert any choice, would choose their partners not for mental charms, or property, or social position, but almost solely from external appearance. All the adults would marry or pair, and all the offspring, as far as that was possible, would be reared; so that the struggle for existence would be periodically excessively severe. Thus during these times all the conditions for sexual selection would have been more favourable than at a later period, when man had advanced in his intellectual powers but had retrograded in his instincts. Therefore, whatever influence sexual selection may have had in producing the differences between the races of man, and between man and the higher Quadrumana, this influence would have been more powerful at a remote period than at the present day, though probably not yet wholly lost.

The Manner of Action of Sexual Selection with Mankind.—With primeval man under the favourable conditions just stated, and with those savages who at the present time enter into any marriage tie, sexual selection has probably acted in the following manner, subject to greater or less interference from female infanticide, early betrothals, &c. The strongest and most vigorous men—those who could best defend and hunt for their families, who were provided with the best weapons and possessed the most property, such as a large number of dogs or other animals,—would succeed in rearing a greater average number of offspring than the weaker and poorer members of the same tribes. There can, also, be no doubt that such men would generally be able to select the more attractive women. At present the chiefs of nearly every tribe throughout the world succeed in obtaining more than one wife. I hear from Mr. Mantell that, until recently, almost every girl in New Zealand who was pretty, or promised to be pretty, was *tapu* to some chief. With the Kafirs, as Mr. C. Hamilton states,[17] "the chiefs generally have the pick of the women for many miles round, and are most persevering in establishing or confirming their privilege." We have seen that each race has its own style of beauty, and we know that it is natural to man to admire each characteristic point in his domestic animals, dress, ornaments, and personal appearance, when carried a little beyond the average. If then the several foregoing propositions be admitted, and I cannot see that they are doubtful, it would be an inexplicable circumstance if the selection of the more

---

[17] 'Anthrop Rev.' Jan. 1870, p. xvi.

attractive women by the more powerful men of each tribe, who would rear on an average a greater number of children, did not after the lapse of many generations somewhat modify the character of the tribe.

When a foreign breed of our domestic animals is introduced into a new country, or when a native breed is long and carefully attended to, either for use or ornament, it is found after several generations to have undergone a greater or less amount of change whenever the means of comparison exist. This follows from unconscious selection during a long series of generations—that is, the preservation of the most approved individuals —without any wish or expectation of such a result on the part of the breeder. So again, if during many years two careful breeders rear animals of the same family, and do not compare them together or with a common standard, the animals are found to have become, to the surprise of their owners, slightly different.[18] Each breeder has impressed, as Von Nathusius well expresses it, the character of his own mind—his own taste and judgment—on his animals. What reason, then, can be assigned why similar results should not follow from the long-continued selection of the most admired women by those men of each tribe who were able to rear the greatest number of children? This would be unconscious selection, for an effect would be produced, independently of any wish or expectation on the part of the men who preferred certain women to others.

Let us suppose the members of a tribe, practising some form of marriage, to spread over an unoccupied continent, they would soon split up into distinct hordes, separated from each other by various barriers, and still more effectually by the incessant wars between all barbarous nations. The hordes would thus be exposed to slightly different conditions and habits of life, and would sooner or later come to differ in some small degree. As soon as this occurred, each isolated tribe would form for itself a slightly different standard of beauty; [19] and then unconscious selection would come into action through the more powerful and leading men preferring certain women to others. Thus the differences between the tribes, at first very slight, would gradually and inevitably be more or less increased.

With animals in a state of nature, many characters proper to the males, such as size, strength, special weapons, courage and pugnacity, have been acquired through the law of battle. The semi-human progenitors of man, like their allies the Quadrumana, will almost certainly have been thus modified; and, as savages still fight for the possession of their women, a similar process of selection has probably gone on in a greater or less degree to the present day. Other characters proper to the males of the lower animals, such as bright colours and various ornaments, have been acquir-

---

[18] 'The Variation of Animals and Plants under Domestication,' vol. ii. pp. 210–217.
[19] An ingenious writer argues, from a comparison of the pictures of Raphael, Rubens, and modern French artists, that the idea of beauty is not absolutely the same even throughout Europe: see the 'Lives of Haydn and Mozart,' by Bombet (otherwise M. Beyle), English translat. p. 278.

ed by the more attractive males having been preferred by the females. There are, however, exceptional cases in which the males are the selectors, instead of having been the selected. We recognise such cases by the females being more highly ornamented than the males,—their ornamental characters having been transmitted exclusively or chiefly to their female offspring. One such case has been described in the order to which man belongs, that of the Rhesus monkey.

Man is more powerful in body and mind than woman, and in the savage state he keeps her in a far more abject state of bondage than does the male of any other animal; therefore it is not surprising that he should have gained the power of selection. Women are everywhere conscious of the value of their own beauty; and when they have the means, they take more delight in decorating themselves with all sorts of ornaments than do men. They borrow the plumes of male birds, with which nature has decked this sex, in order to charm the females. As women have long been selected for beauty, it is not surprising that some of their successive variations should have been transmitted exclusively to the same sex; consequently that they should have transmitted beauty in a somewhat higher degree to their female than to their male offspring, and thus have become more beautiful, according to general opinion, than men. Women, however, certainly transmit most of their characters, including some beauty, to their offspring of both sexes; so that the continued preference by the men of each race for the more attractive women, according to their standard of taste, will have tended to modify in the same manner all the individuals of both sexes belonging to the race.

With respect to the other form of sexual selection (which with the lower animals is much the more common), namely, when the females are the selectors, and accept only those males which excite or charm them most, we have reason to believe that it formerly acted on our progenitors. Man in all probability owes his beard, and perhaps some other characters, to inheritance from an ancient progenitor who thus gained his ornaments. But this form of selection may have occasionally acted during later times; for in utterly barbarous tribes the women have more power in choosing, rejecting, and tempting their lovers, or of afterwards changing their husbands, than might have been expected. As this is a point of some importance, I will give in detail such evidence as I have been able to collect.

Hearne describes how a woman in one of the tribes of Arctic America repeatedly ran away from her husband and joined her lover; and with the Charruas of S. America, according to Azara, divorce is quite optional. Amongst the Abipones, a man on choosing a wife bargains with the parents about the price. But "it frequently happens that the girl rescinds what has been agreed upon between the parents and the bridegroom, obstinately rejecting the very mention of marriage." She often runs away, hides herself, and thus eludes the bridegroom. Captain Musters who lived with the Patagonians, says that their marriages are always settled by inclination; "if the parents make a match contrary to the daughter's will, she refuses and is never compelled to comply." In Tierra del Fuego a young man first obtains the consent of the parents by doing them some service, and then he attempts to carry off the girl; "but if she is unwilling, she hides herself in the woods until her admirer is heartily tired of looking for her, and gives up the pursuit; but this seldom happens." In the Fiji Islands the man seizes on the woman whom he wishes for his wife by actual or pretended force; but "on reaching the home of her abductor, should she not approve of the match, she runs to some one who can protect her; if, however, she is satisfied, the matter is settled forthwith." With the Kalmucks there is a regular race between the bride and bridegroom, the former having a fair start; and Clarke "was assured that no instance occurs of a girl being caught, unless she has a partiality to the pursuer." Amongst the wild tribes of the Malay Achipelago there is also a racing match; and it appears from M. Bourien's account, as Sir J. Lubbock remarks, that "the race, 'is not to the swift, nor the battle to the strong,' but to the young man who has the good fortune to please his intended bride." A similar custom, with the same result, prevails with the Koraks of North-Eastern Asia.

Turning to Africa: the Kafirs buy their wives, and girls are severely beaten by their fathers if they will not accept a chosen husband; but it is manifest from many facts given by the Rev. Mr. Shooter, that they have considerable power of choice. Thus very ugly, though rich men, have been known to fail in getting wives. The girls, before consenting to be betrothed, compel the men to shew themselves off first in front and then behind, and "exhibit their paces." They have been known to propose to a man, and they not rarely run away with a favoured lover. So again, Mr. Leslie, who was intimately acquainted with the Kafirs, says, "it is a mistake to imagine that a girl is sold by her father in the same manner, and with the same authority, with which he would dispose of a cow." Amongst the degraded Bushmen of S. Africa, "when a girl has grown up to womanhood without having been betrothed, which, however, does not often happen, her lover must gain her approbation, as well as that of the parents." [20] Mr. Winwood Reade made inquiries for me with respect to the negroes of Western Africa, and he informs me that "the women, at least among the more intelligent Pagan tribes, have no difficulty in getting the husbands whom they may desire, although it is considered unwomanly to ask a man to marry them. They are quite capable of falling in love, and of forming tender, passionate, and faithful attachments." Additional cases could be given.

[20] Azara 'Voyages,' &c. tom. ii. p. 23. Dobrizhoffer, 'An Account of the Abipones,' vol. ii. 1822, p. 207. Capt. Musters, in 'Proc. R. Geograph. Soc.,' vol. xv. p. 47. Williams on the Fiji Islanders, as quoted by Lubbock, 'Origin of Civilisation,' 1870, p. 79. On the Fuegians, King and Fitzroy, 'Voyages of the Adventure and Beagle,' vol. ii. 1839, p. 182. On the Kalmucks, quoted by M'Lennan, 'Primitive Marriage,' 1865, p. 32. On the Malays, Lubbock, ibid. p. 76. The Rev. J. Shooter, 'On the Kafirs of Natal,' 1857, pp. 52–60. Mr. D. Leslie, 'Kafir Character and Customs,' 1871, p. 4. On the Bush-men, Burchell, 'Travels in S. Africa,' ii. 1824, p. 59. On the Koraks by McKennan, as quoted by Mr. Wake, in 'Anthropologia,' Oct. 1873, p. 75.

We thus see that with savages the women are not in quite so abject a state in relation to marriage as has often been supposed. They can tempt the men whom they prefer, and can sometimes reject those whom they dislike, either before or after marriage. Preference on the part of the women, steadily acting in any one direction, would ultimately affect the character of the tribe; for the women would generally choose not merely the handsomest men, according to their standard of taste, but those who were at the same time best able to defend and support them. Such well-endowed pairs would commonly rear a larger number of offspring than the less favoured. The same result would obviously follow in a still more marked manner if there was selection on both sides; that is, if the more attractive, and at the same time more powerful men were to prefer, and were preferred by, the more attractive women. And this double form of selection seems actually to have occurred, especially during the earlier periods of our long history.

We will now examine a little more closely some of the characters which distinguished the several races of man from one another and from the lower animals, namely, the greater or less deficiency of hair on the body, and the colour of the skin. We need say nothing about the great diversity in the shape of the features and of the skull between the different races, as we have seen in the last chapter how different is the standard of beauty in these respects. These characters will therefore probably have been acted on through sexual selection; but we have no means of judging whether they have been acted on chiefly from the male or female side. The musical faculties of man have likewise been already discussed.

Absence of Hair on the Body, and its Development on the Face and Head.—From the presence of the woolly hair or lanugo on the human fœtus, and of rudimentary hairs scattered over the body during maturity, we may infer that man is descended from some animal which was born hairy and remained so during life. The loss of hair is an inconvenience and probably an injury to man, even in a hot climate, for he is thus exposed to the scorching of the sun, and to sudden chills, especially during wet weather. As Mr. Wallace remarks, the natives in all countries are glad to protect their naked backs and shoulders with some slight covering. No one supposes that the nakedness of the skin is any direct advantage to man; his body therefore cannot have been divested of hair through natural selection.[21] Nor, as shewn in a former chapter, have we any evidence that this can be due to the direct action of climate, or that it is the result of correlated development.

The absence of hair on the body is to a certain extent a secondary sex-

[21] 'Contributions to the Theory of Natural Selection,' 1870, p. 346. Mr. Wallace believes (p. 350) "that some intelligent power has guided or determined the development of man;" and he considers the hairless condition of the skin as coming under this head. The Rev. T. R. Stebbing, in commenting on this view ('Trans. of Devonshire Assoc. for Sci.,' 1870) remarks, that had Mr. Wallace "employed his usual ingenuity on the question of man's hairless skin, he might have seen the possibility of its selection through its superior beauty or the health attaching to superior cleanliness."

ual character; for in all parts of the world women are less hairy than men. Therefore we may reasonably suspect that this character has been gained through sexual selection. We know that the faces of several species of monkeys, and large surfaces at the posterior end of the body of other species, have been denuded of hair; and this we may safely attribute to sexual selection, for these surfaces are not only vividly coloured, but sometimes, as with the male mandrill and female rhesus, much more vividly in the one sex than in the other, especially during the breeding-season. I am informed by Mr. Bartlett that, as these animals gradually reach maturity, the naked surfaces grow larger compared with the size of their bodies. The hair, however, appears to have been removed, not for the sake of nudity, but that the colour of the skin may be more fully displayed. So again with many birds, it appears as if the head and neck had been divested of feathers through sexual selection, to exhibit the brightly-coloured skin.

As the body in woman is less hairy than in man, and as this character is common to all races, we may conclude that it was our female semi-human ancestors who were first divested of hair, and that this occurred at an extremely remote period before the several races had diverged from a common stock. Whilst our female ancestors were gradually acquiring this new character of nudity, they must have transmitted it almost equally to their offspring of both sexes whilst young; so that its transmission, as with the ornaments of many mammals and birds, has not been limited either by sex or age. There is nothing surprising in a partial loss of hair having been esteemed as an ornament by our ape-like progenitors, for we have seen that innumerable strange characters have been thus esteemed by animals of all kinds, and have consequently been gained through sexual selection. Nor is it surprising that a slightly injurious character should have been thus acquired; for we know that this is the case with the plumes of certain birds, and with the horns of certain stags.

The females of some of the anthropoid apes, as stated in a former chapter, are somewhat less hairy on the under surface than the males; and here we have what might have afforded a commencement for the process of denudation. With respect to the completion of the process through sexual selection, it is well to bear in mind the New Zealand proverb, "There is no woman for a hairy man." All who have seen photographs of the Siamese hairy family will admit how ludicrously hideous is the opposite extreme of excessive hairiness. And the king of Siam had to bribe a man to marry the first hairy woman in the family; and she transmitted this character to her young offspring of both sexes.[22]

Some races are much more hairy than others, especially the males; but it must not be assumed that the more hairy races, such as the European, have retained their primordial condition more completely than the naked races, such as the Kalmucks or Americans. It is more probable that the hairiness of the former is due to partial reversion; for characters which have been at some former period long inherited are always apt to return.

[22] 'The Variation of Animals and Plants under Domestication,' vol. ii. 1868, p. 237.

We have seen that idiots are often very hairy, and they are apt to revert in other characters to a lower animal type. It does not appear that a cold climate has been influential in leading to this kind of reversion; excepting perhaps with the negroes, who have been reared during several generations in the United States,[23] and possibly with the Ainos, who inhabit the northern islands of the Japan archipelago. But the laws of inheritance are so complex that we can seldom understand their action. If the greater hairiness of certain races be the result of reversion, unchecked by any form of selection, its extreme variability, even within the limits of the same race, ceases to be remarkable.[24]

With respect to the beard in man, if we turn to our best guide, the Quadrumana, we find beards equally developed in both sexes of many species, but in some, either confined to the males, or more developed in them than in the females. From this fact and from the curious arrangement, as well as the bright colours of the hair about the heads of many monkeys, it is highly probable, as before explained, that the males first acquired their beards through sexual selection as an ornament, transmitting them in most cases, equally or nearly so, to their offspring of both sexes. We know from Eschricht [25] that with mankind the female as well as the male fœtus is furnished with much hair on the face, especially round the mouth; and this indicates that we are descended from progenitors of whom both sexes were bearded. It appears therefore at first sight probable that man has retained his beard from a very early period, whilst woman lost her beard at the same time that her body became almost completely divested of hair. Even the colour of our beards seems to have been inherited from an ape-like progenitor; for when there is any difference in tint between the hair of the head and the beard, the latter is lighter coloured in all monkeys and in man. In those Quadrumana in which the male has a larger beard than that of the female, it is fully developed only at maturity, just as with mankind; and it is possible that only the later stages of development have been retained by man. In opposition to this

[23] 'Investigations into Military and Anthropological Statistics of American Soldiers,' by B. A. Gould, 1869; p. 568:—Observations were carefully made on the hairiness of 2129 black and coloured soldiers, whilst they were bathing; and by looking to the published table, "it is manifest at a glance that there is but little, if any, difference between the white and the black races in this respect." It is, however, certain that negroes in their native and much hotter land of Africa, have remarkably smooth bodies. It should be particularly observed, that both pure blacks and mulattoes were included in the above enumeration; and this is an unfortunate circumstance, as in accordance with a principle, the truth of which I have elsewhere proved, crossed races of man would be eminently liable to revert to the primordial hairy character of their early ape-like progenitors.

[24] Hardly any view advanced in this work has met with so much disfavour (see for instance, Spengel, 'Die Fortschritte des Darwinismus,' 1874, p. 80) as the above explanation of the loss of hair in mankind through sexual selection; but none of the opposed arguments seem to me of much weight, in comparison with the facts shewing that the nudity of the skin is to a certain extent a secondary sexual character in man and in some of the Quadrumana.

[25] 'Ueber die Richtung der Haare am Menschlichen Körper,' in Müller's 'Archiv für Anat. und Phys.' 1837, s. 40.

view of the retention of the beard from an early period is the fact of its great variability in different races, and even within the same race; for this indicates reversion,—long lost characters being very apt to vary on re-appearance.

Nor must we overlook the part which sexual selection may have played in later times; for we know that with savages the men of the beardless races take infinite pains in eradicating every hair from their faces as something odious, whilst the men of the bearded races feel the greatest pride in their beards. The women, no doubt, participate in these feelings, and if so sexual selection can hardly have failed to have effected something in the course of later times. It is also possible that the long-continued habit of eradicating the hair may have produced an inherited effect. Dr. Brown-Séquard has shewn that if certain animals are operated on in a particular manner, their offspring are affected. Further evidence could be given of the inheritance of the effects of mutilations; but a fact lately ascertained by Mr. Salvin [26] has a more direct bearing on the present question; for he has shewn that the motmots, which are known habitually to bite off the barbs of the two central tail-feathers, have the barbs of these feathers naturally somewhat reduced. [27] Nevertheless, with mankind the habit of eradicating the beard and the hairs on the body would probably not have arisen until these had already become by some means reduced.

It is difficult to form any judgment as to how the hair on the head became developed to its present great length in many races. Eschricht [28] states that in the human fœtus the hair on the face during the fifth month is longer than that on the head; and this indicates that our semi-human progenitors were not furnished with long tresses, which must therefore have been a late acquisition. This is likewise indicated by the extraordinary difference in the length of the hair in the different races; in the negro the hair forms a mere curly mat; with us it is of great length, and with the American natives it not rarely reaches to the ground. Some species of Semnopithecus have their heads covered with moderately long hair, and this probably serves as an ornament and was acquired through sexual selection. The same view may perhaps be extended to mankind, for we know that long tresses are now and were formerly much admired, as may be observed in the works of almost every poet; St. Paul says, "if a woman have long hair, it is a glory to her;" and we have seen that in North America a chief was elected solely from the length of his hair.

Colour of the Skin.—The best kind of evidence that in man the colour of the skin has been modified through sexual selection is scanty; for in most races the sexes do not differ in this respect, and only slightly, as we

---

[26] On the tail-feathers of Momotus, 'Proc. Zoolog. Soc.,' 1873, p. 429.

[27] Mr. Sproat has suggested ('Scenes and Studies of Savage Life,' 1868, p. 25) this same view. Some distinguished ethnologists, amongst others M. Gosse of Geneva, believe that artificial modifications of the skull tend to be inherited.

[28] 'Ueber die Richtung,' ibid. s. 40.

have seen, in others. We know, however, from the many facts already given that the colour of the skin is regarded by the men of all races as a highly important element in their beauty; so that it is a character which would be likely to have been modified through selection, as has occurred in innumerable instances with the lower animals. It seems at first sight a monstrous supposition that the jet-blackness of the negro should have been gained through sexual selection; but this view is supported by various analogies, and we know that negroes admire their own colour. With mammals, when the sexes differ in colour, the male is often black or much darker than the female; and it depends merely on the form of inheritance whether this or any other tint is transmitted to both sexes or to one alone. The resemblance to a negro in miniature of *Pithecia satanas* with his jet black skin, white rolling eyeballs, and hair parted on the top of the head, is almost ludicrous.

The colour of the face differs much more widely in the various kinds of monkeys than it does in the races of man; and we have some reason to believe that the red, blue, orange, almost white and black tints of their skin, even when common to both sexes, as well as the bright colours of their fur, and the ornamental tufts about the head, have all been acquired through sexual selection. As the order of development during growth, generally indicates the order in which the characters of a species have been developed and modified during previous generations; and as the newly-born infants of the various races of man do not differ nearly as much in colour as do the adults, although their bodies are as completely destitute of hair, we have some slight evidence that the tints of the different races were acquired at a period subsequent to the removal of the hair, which must have occurred at a very early period in the history of man.

Summary.—We may conclude that the greater size, strength, courage, pugnacity, and energy of man, in comparison with woman, were acquired during primeval times, and have subsequently been augmented, chiefly through the contests of rival males for the possession of the females. The greater intellectual vigour and power of invention in man is probably due to natural selection, combined with the inherited effects of habit, for the most able men will have succeeded best in defending and providing for themselves and for their wives and offspring. As far as the extreme intricacy of the subject permits us to judge, it appears that our male ape-like progenitors acquired their beards as an ornament to charm or excite the opposite sex, and transmitted them only to their male offspring. The females apparently first had their bodies denuded of hair, also as a sexual ornament; but they transmitted this character almost equally to both sexes. It is not improbable that the females were modified in other respects for the same purpose and by the same means; so that women have acquired sweeter voices and become more beautiful than men.

It deserves attention that with mankind the conditions were in many respects much more favourable for sexual selection during a very early period, when man had only just attained to the rank of manhood, than during later times. For he would then, as we may safely conclude, have been guided more by his instinctive passions, and less by foresight or reason. He would have jealously guarded his wife or wives. He would not have practised infanticide; nor valued his wives merely as useful slaves; nor have been betrothed to them during infancy. Hence we may infer that the races of men were differentiated, as far as sexual selection is concerned, in chief part at a very remote epoch; and this conclusion throws light on the remarkable fact that at the most ancient period, of which we have as yet any record, the races of man had already come to differ nearly or quite as much as they do at the present day.

The views here advanced, on the part which sexual selection has played in the history of man, want scientific precision. He who does not admit this agency in the case of the lower animals, will disregard all that I have written in the later chapters on man. We cannot positively say that this character, but not that, has been thus modified; it has however, been shewn that the races of man differ from each other and from their nearest allies, in certain characters which are of no service to them in their daily habits of life, and which it is extremely probable would have been modified through sexual selection. We have seen that with the lowest savages the people of each tribe admire their own characteristic qualities,—the shape of the head and face, the squareness of the cheek-bones, the prominence or depression of the nose, the colour of the skin, the length of the hair on the head, the absence of hair on the face and body, or the presence of a great beard, and so forth. Hence these and other such points could hardly fail to be slowly and gradually exaggerated, from the more powerful and able men in each tribe, who would succeed in rearing the largest number of offspring, having selected during many generations for their wives the most strongly characterised and therefore most attractive women. For my own part I conclude that of all the causes which have led to the differences in external appearance between the races of man, and to a certain extent between man and the lower animals, sexual selection has been the most efficient.

CHAPTER XXI

GENERAL SUMMARY AND CONCLUSION

Main conclusion that man is descended from some lower form—Manner of develop-
ment—Genealogy of man—Intellectual and moral faculties—Sexual Selection—
Concluding remarks.

A BRIEF summary will be sufficient to recall to the reader's mind the more
salient points in this work. Many of the views which have been advanced
are highly speculative, and some no doubt will prove erroneous; but I
have in every case given the reasons which have led me to one view rather than to another. It seemed worth while to try how far the principle of
evolution would throw light on some of the more complex problems in
the natural history of man. False facts are highly injurious to the progress of science, for they often endure long; but false views, if supported
by some evidence, do little harm, for every one takes a salutary pleasure
in proving their falseness: and when this is done, one path towards error
is closed and the road to truth is often at the same time opened.

The main conclusion here arrived at, and now held by many naturalists
who are well competent to form a sound judgment is that man is descended from some less highly organised form. The grounds upon which this
conclusion rests will never be shaken, for the close similarity between
man and the lower animals in embryonic development, as well as in innumerable points of structure and constitution, both of high and of the
most trifling importance,—the rudiments which he retains, and the abnormal reversions to which he is occasionally liable,—are facts which
cannot be disputed. They have long been known, but until recently they
told us nothing with respect to the origin of man. Now when viewed by
the light of our knowledge of the whole organic world, their meaning is
unmistakable. The great principle of evolution stands up clear and firm,
when these groups or facts are considered in connection with others, such
as the mutual affinities of the members of the same group, their geographical distribution in past and present times, and their geological succession. It is incredible that all these facts should speak falsely. He who is
not content to look, like a savage, at the phenomena of nature as discon-
nected, cannot any longer believe that man is the work of a separate act
of creation. He will be forced to admit that the close resemblance of the
embryo of man to that, for instance, of a dog—the construction of his
skull, limbs and whole frame on the same plan with that of other mammals, independently of the uses to which the parts may be put—the occasional re-appearance of various structures, for instance of several mus-

cles, which man does not normally possess, but which are common to the Quadrumana—and a crowd of analogous facts—all point in the plainest manner to the conclusion that man is the co-descendant with other mammals of a common progenitor.

We have seen that man incessantly presents individual differences in all parts of his body and in his mental faculties. These differences or variations seem to be induced by the same general causes, and to obey the same laws as with the lower animals. In both cases similar laws of inheritance prevail. Man tends to increase at a greater rate than his means of subsistence; consequently he is occasionally subjected to a severe struggle for existence, and natural selection will have effected whatever lies within its scope. A succession of strongly-marked variations of a similar nature is by no means requisite; slight fluctuating differences in the individual suffice for the work of natural selection; not that we have any reason to suppose that in the same species, all parts of the organisation tend to vary to the same degree. We may feel assured that the inherited effects of the long-continued use or disuse of parts will have done much in the same direction with natural selection. Modifications formerly of importance, though no longer of any special use, are long-inherited. When one part is modified, other parts change through the principle of correlation, of which we have instances in many curious cases of correlated monstrosities. Something may be attributed to the direct and definite action of the surrounding conditions of life, such as abundant food, heat or moisture; and lastly, many characters of slight physiological importance, some indeed of considerable importance, have been gained through sexual selection.

No doubt man, as well as every other animal, presents structures, which seem to our limited knowledge, not to be now of any service to him, nor to have been so formerly, either for the general conditions of life, or in the relations of one sex to the other. Such structures cannot be accounted for by any form of selection, or by the inherited effects of the use and disuse of parts. We know, however, that many strange and strongly-marked peculiarities of structure occasionally appear in our domesticated productions, and if their unknown causes were to act more uniformly, they would probably become common to all the individuals of the species. We may hope hereafter to understand something about the causes of such occasional modifications, especially through the study of monstrosities: hence the labours of experimentalists such as those of M. Camille Dareste, are full of promise for the future. In general we can only say that the cause of each slight variation and of each monstrosity lies much more in the constitution of the organism, than in the nature of the surrounding conditions; though new and changed conditions certainly play an important part in exciting organic changes of many kinds.

Through the means just specified, aided perhaps by others as yet undiscovered, man has been raised to his present state. But since he attained to the rank of manhood, he has diverged into distinct races, or as they may be more fitly called, sub-species. Some of these, such as the

Negro and European, are so distinct that, if specimens had been brought to a naturalist without any further information, they would undoubtedly have been considered by him as good and true species. Nevertheless all the races agree in so many unimportant details of structure and in so many mental peculiarities that these can be accounted for only by inheritance from a common progenitor; and a progenitor thus characterised would probably deserve to rank as man.

It must not be supposed that the divergence of each race from the other races, and of all from a common stock, can be traced back to any one pair of progenitors. On the contrary, at every stage in the process of modification, all the individuals which were in any way better fitted for their conditions of life, though in different degrees, would have survived in greater numbers than the less well-fitted. The process would have been like that followed by man, when he does not intentionally select particular individuals, but breeds from all the superior individuals, and neglects the inferior. He thus slowly but surely modifies his stock, and unconciously forms a new strain. So with respect to modifications acquired independently of selection, and due to variations arising from the nature of the organism and the action of the surrounding conditions, or from changed habits of life, no single pair will have been modified much more than the other pairs inhabiting the same country, for all will have been continually blended through free intercrossing.

By considering the embryological structure of man,—the homologies which he presents with the lower animals,—the rudiments which he retains,—and the reversions to which he is liable, we can partly recall in imagination the former condition of our early progenitors; and can approximately place them in their proper place in the zoological series. We thus learn that man is descended from a hairy, tailed quadruped, probably arboreal in its habits, and an inhabitant of the Old World. This creature, if its whole structure had been examined by a naturalist, would have been classed amongst the Quadrumana, as surely as the still more ancient progenitor of the Old and New World monkeys. The Quadrumana and all the higher mammals are probably derived from an ancient marsupial animal, and this through a long series of diversified forms, from some amphibian-like creature, and this again from some fish-like animal. In the dim obscurity of the past we can see that the early progenitor of all the Vertebrata must have been an aquatic animal provided with branchiæ, with the two sexes united in the same individual, and with the most important organs of the body (such as the brain and heart) imperfectly or not at all developed. This animal seems to have been more like the larvæ of the existing marine Ascidians than any other known form.

The high standard of our intellectual powers and moral disposition is the greatest difficulty which presents itself, after we have been driven to this conclusion on the origin of man. But every one who admits the principle of evolution, must see that the mental powers of the higher animals, which are the same in kind with those of man, though so different in degree, are capable of advancement. Thus the interval between the mental powers of one of the higher apes and of a fish, or between those of an ant and scale-insect, is immense; yet their development does not offer any special difficulty; for with our domesticated animals, the mental faculties are certainly variable, and the variations are inherited. No one doubts that they are of the utmost importance to animals in a state of nature. Therefore the conditions are favourable for their development through natural selection. The same conclusion may be extended to man; the intellect must have been all-important to him, even at a very remote period, as enabling him to invent and use language, to make weapons, tools, traps, &c., whereby with the aid of his social habits, he long ago became the most dominant of all living creatures.

A great stride in the development of the intellect will have followed, as soon as the half-art and half-instinct of language came into use; for the continued use of language will have reacted on the brain and produced an inherited effect; and this again will have reacted on the improvement of language. As Mr. Chauncey Wright [1] has well remarked, the largeness of the brain in man relatively to his body, compared with the lower animals, may be attributed in chief part to the early use of some simple form of language,—that wonderful engine which affixes signs to all sorts of objects and qualities, and excites trains of thought which would never arise from the mere impression of the senses, or if they did arise could not be followed out. The higher intellectual powers of man, such as those of ratiocination, abstraction, self-consciousness, &c., probably follow from the continued improvement and exercise of the other mental faculties.

The development of the moral qualities is a more interesting problem. The foundation lies in the social instincts, including under this term the family ties. These instincts are highly complex, and in the case of the lower animals give special tendencies towards certain definite actions; but the more important elements are love, and the distinct emotion of sympathy. Animals endowed with the social instincts take pleasure in one another's company, warn one another of danger, defend and aid one another in many ways. These instincts do not extend to all the individuals of the species, but only to those of the same community. As they are highly beneficial to the species, they have in all probability been acquired through natural selection.

A moral being is one who is capable of reflecting on his past actions and their motives—of approving of some and disapproving of others; and the fact that man is the one being who certainly deserves this designation. is the greatest of all distinctions between him and the lower animals. But in the fourth chapter I have endeavoured to shew that the moral sense follows, firstly, from the enduring and ever-present nature of the social instincts; secondly, from man's appreciation of the approbation and disapprobation of his fellows; and thirdly, from the high activ-

---

[1] 'On the Limits of Natural Selection,' in the 'North American Review,' Oct. 1870, p. 295.

ity of his mental faculties, with past impressions extremely vivid; and in these latter respects he differs from the lower animals. Owing to this condition of mind, man cannot avoid looking both backwards and forwards, and comparing past impressions. Hence after some temporary desire or passion has mastered his social instincts, he reflects and compares the now weakened impression of such past impulses with the ever-present social instincts; and he then feels that sense of dissatisfaction which all unsatisfied instincts leave behind them, he therefore resolves to act differently for the future,—and this is conscience. Any instinct, permanently stronger or more enduring than another, gives rise to a feeling which we express by saying that it ought to be obeyed. A pointer dog, if able to reflect on his past conduct, would say to himself, I ought (as indeed we say of him) to have pointed at that hare and not have yielded to the passing temptation of hunting it.

Social animals are impelled partly by a wish to aid the members of their community in a general manner, but more commonly to perform certain definite actions. Man is impelled by the same general wish to aid his fellows; but has few or no special instincts. He differs also from the lower animals in the power of expressing his desires by words, which thus become a guide to the aid required and bestowed. The motive to give aid is likewise much modified in man: it no longer consists solely of a blind instinctive impulse, but is much influenced by the praise or blame of his fellows. The appreciation and the bestowal of praise and blame both rest on sympathy; and this emotion, as we have seen, is one of the most important elements of the social instincts. Sympathy, though gained as an instinct, is also much strengthened by exercise or habit. As all men desire their own happiness, praise or blame is bestowed on actions and motives, according as they lead to this end; and as happiness is an essential part of the general good, the greatest-happiness principle indirectly serves as a nearly safe standard of right and wrong. As the reasoning powers advance and experience is gained, the remoter effects of certain lines of conduct on the character of the individual, and on the general good, are perceived; and then the self-regarding virtues come within the scope of public opinion, and receive praise, and their opposites blame. But with the less civilised nations reason often errs, and many bad customs and base superstitions come within the same scope, and are then esteemed as high virtues, and their breach as heavy crimes.

The moral faculties are generally and justly esteemed as of higher value than the intellectual powers. But we should bear in mind that the activity of the mind in vividly recalling past impressions is one of the fundamental though secondary bases of conscience. This affords the strongest argument for educating and stimulating in all possible ways the intellectual faculties of every human being. No doubt a man with a torpid mind, if his social affections and sympathies are well developed, will be led to good actions, and may have a fairly sensitive conscience. But whatever renders the imagination more vivid and strengthens the habit of recalling and comparing past impressions, will make the conscience more sensitive, and may even somewhat compensate for weak social affections and sympathies.

The moral nature of man has reached its present standard, partly through the advancement of his reasoning powers and consequently of a just public opinion, but especially from his sympathies having been rendered more tender and widely diffused through the effects of habit, example, instruction, and reflection. It is not improbable that after long practice virtuous tendencies may be inherited. With the more civilised races, the conviction of the existence of an all-seeing Deity has had a potent influence on the advance of morality. Ultimately man does not accept the praise or blame of his fellows as his sole guide, though few escape this influence, but his habitual convictions, controlled by reason, afford him the safest rule. His conscience then becomes the supreme judge and monitor. Nevertheless the first foundation or origin of the moral sense lies in the social instincts, including sympathy; and these instincts no doubt were primarily gained, as in the case of the lower animals, through natural selection.

The belief in God has often been advanced as not only the greatest, but the most complete of all the distinctions between man and the lower animals. It is however impossible, as we have seen, to maintain that this belief is innate or instinctive in man. On the other hand a belief in all-pervading spiritual agencies seems to be universal; and apparently follows from a considerable advance in man's reason, and from a still greater advance in his faculties of imagination, curiosity and wonder. I am aware that the assumed instinctive belief in God has been used by many persons as an argument for His existence. But this is a rash argument, as we should thus be compelled to believe in the existence of many cruel and malignant spirits, only a little more powerful than man; for the belief in them is far more general than in a beneficent Deity. The idea of a universal and beneficent Creator does not seem to arise in the mind of man, until he has been elevated by long-continued culture.

He who believes in the advancement of man from some low organised form, will naturally ask how does this bear on the belief in the immortality of the soul. The barbarous races of man, as Sir J. Lubbock has shewn, possess no clear belief of this kind; but arguments derived from the primeval beliefs of savages are, as we have just seen, of little or no avail. Few persons feel any anxiety from the impossibility of determining at what precise period in the development of the individual, from the first trace of a minute germinal vesicle, man becomes an immortal being; and there is no greater cause for anxiety because the period cannot possibly be determined in the gradually ascending organic scale.[2]

I am aware that the conclusions arrived at in this work will be denounced by some as highly irreligious; but he who denounces them is

[2] The Rev. J. A. Picton gives a discussion to this effect in his 'New Theories and the Old Faith,' 1870.

bound to shew why it is more irreligious to explain the origin of man as a distinct species by descent from some lower form, through the laws of variation and natural selection, than to explain the birth of the individual through the laws of ordinary reproduction. The birth both of the species and of the individual are equally parts of that grand sequence of events, which our minds refuse to accept as the result of blind chance. The understanding revolts at such a conclusion, whether or not we are able to believe that every slight variation of structure,—the union of each pair in marriage,—the dissemination of each seed,—and other such events, have all been ordained for some special purpose.

Sexual selection has been treated at great length in this work; for, as I have attempted to shew, it has played an important part in the history of the organic world. I am aware that much remains doubtful, but I have endeavoured to give a fair view of the whole case. In the lower divisions of the animal kingdom, sexual selection seems to have done nothing: such animals are often affixed for life to the same spot, or have the sexes combined in the same individual, or what is still more important, their perceptive and intellectual faculties are not sufficiently advanced to allow of the feelings of love and jealousy, or of the exertion of choice. When, however, we come to the Arthropoda and Vertebrata, even to the lowest classes in these two great Sub-Kingdoms, sexual selection has effected much.

In the several great classes of the animal kingdom,—in mammals, birds, reptiles, fishes, insects, and even crustaceans,—the differences between the sexes follow nearly the same rules. The males are almost always the wooers; and they alone are armed with special weapons for fighting with their rivals. They are generally stronger and larger than the females, and are endowed with the requisite qualities of courage and pugnacity. They are provided, either exclusively or in a much higher degree than the females, with organs for vocal or instrumental music, and with odoriferous glands. They are ornamental with infinitely diversified appendages, and with the most brilliant or conspicuous colours, often arranged in elegant patterns, whilst the females are unadorned. When the sexes differ in more important structures, it is the male which is provided with special sense-organs for discovering the female, with locomotive organs for reaching her, and often with prehensile organs for holding her. These various structures for charming or securing the female are often developed in the male during only part of the year, namely the breeding-season. They have in many cases been more or less transferred to the females; and in the latter case they often appear in her as mere rudiments. They are lost or never gained by the males after emasculation. Generally they are not developed in the male during early youth, but appear a short time before the age for reproduction. Hence in most cases the young of both sexes resemble each other; and the female somewhat resembles her young offspring throughout life. In almost every great class a few anomalous cases occur, where there has been an almost complete transposition of the characters proper to the two sexes; the females assuming characters which properly belong to the males. This surprising uniformity in the laws regulating the differences between the sexes in so many and such widely separated classes, is intelligible if we admit the action of one common cause, namely sexual selection.

Sexual selection depends on the success of certain individuals over others of the same sex, in relation to the propagation of the species; whilst natural selection depends on the success of both sexes, at all ages, in relation to the general conditions of life. The sexual struggle is of two kinds; in the one it is between individuals of the same sex, generally the males, in order to drive away or kill their rivals, the females remaining passive; whilst in the other, the struggle is likewise between the individuals of the same sex, in order to excite or charm those of the opposite sex, generally the females, which no longer remain passive, but select the more agreeable partners. This latter kind of selection is closely analogous to that which man unintentionally, yet effectually, brings to bear on his domesticated productions, when he preserves during a long period the most pleasing or useful individuals, without any wish to modify the breed.

The laws of inheritance determine whether characters gained through sexual selection by either sex shall be transmitted to the same sex, or to both; as well as the age at which they shall be developed. It appears that variations arising late in life are commonly transmitted to one and the same sex. Variability is the necessary basis for the action of selection, and is wholly independent of it. It follows from this, that variations of the same general nature have often been taken advantage of and accumulated through sexual selection in relation to the propagation of the species, as well as through natural selection in relation to the general purposes of life. Hence secondary sexual characters, when equally transmitted to both sexes can be distinguished from ordinary specific characters only by the light of analogy. The modifications acquired through sexual selection are often so strongly pronounced that the two sexes have frequently been ranked as distinct species, or even as distinct genera. Such strongly-marked differences must be in some manner highly important; and we know that they have been acquired in some instances at the cost not only of inconvenience, but of exposure to actual danger.

The belief in the power of sexual selection rests chiefly on the following considerations. Certain characters are confined to one sex; and this alone renders it probable that in most cases they are connected with the act of reproduction. In innumerable instances these characters are fully developed only at maturity, and often during only a part of the year, which is always the breeding-season. The males (passing over a few exceptional cases) are the more active in courtship; they are the better armed, and are rendered the more attractive in various ways. It is to be especially observed that the males display their attractions with elaborate care in the presence of the females; and that they rarely or never display them excepting during the season of love. It is incredible that all this should be purposeless. Lastly we have distinct evidence with some quadrupeds and birds, that the individuals of one sex are capable of feeling a strong antipathy or preference for certain individuals of the other sex.

Bearing in mind these facts, and the marked results of man's unconscious selection, when applied to domesticated animals and cultivated plants, it seems to me almost certain that if the individuals of one sex were during a long series of generations to prefer pairing with certain individuals of the other sex, characterised in some peculiar manner, the offspring would slowly but surely become modified in this same manner. I have not attempted to conceal that, excepting when the males are more numerous than the females, or when polygamy prevails, it is doubtful how the more attractive males succeed in leaving a large number of offspring to inherit their superiority in ornaments or other charms than the less attractive males; but I have shewn that this would probably follow from the females,—especially the more vigorous ones, which would be the first to breed,—preferring not only the more attractive but at the same time the more vigorous and victorious males.

Although we have some positive evidence that birds appreciate bright and beautiful objects, as with the bower-birds of Australia, and although they certainly appreciate the power of song, yet I fully admit that it is astonishing that the females of many birds and some mammals should be endowed with sufficient taste to appreciate ornaments, which we have reason to attribute to sexual selection; and this is even more astonishing in the case of reptiles, fish, and insects. But we really know little about the minds of the lower animals. It cannot be supposed, for instance, that male birds of paradise or peacocks should take such pains in erecting, spreading, and vibrating their beautiful plumes before the females for no purpose. We should remember the fact given on excellent authority in a former chapter, that several peahens, when debarred from an admired male, remained widows during a whole season rather than pair with another bird.

Nevertheless I know of no fact in natural history more wonderful than that of the female Argus pheasant should appreciate the exquisite shading of the ball-and-socket ornaments and the elegant patterns on the wing-feathers of the male. He who thinks that the male was created as he now exists must admit that the great plumes, which prevent the wings from being used for flight, and which are displayed during courtship and at no other time in a manner quite peculiar to this one species, were given to him as an ornament. If so, he must likewise admit that the female was created and endowed with the capacity of appreciating such ornaments. I differ only in the conviction that the male Argus pheasant acquired his beauty gradually, through the preference of the females during many generations for the more highly ornamented males; the æsthetic capacity of the females having been advanced through exercise or habit, just as our own taste is gradually improved. In the male through the fortunate chance of a few feathers, being left unchanged, we can distinctly trace how simple spots with a little fulvous shading on one side may have been developed by small steps into the wonderful ball-and-socket ornaments; and it is probable that they were actually thus developed.

Everyone who admits the principle of evolution, and yet feels great difficulty in admitting that female mammals, birds, reptiles, and fish, could have acquired the high taste implied by the beauty of the males, and which generally coincides with our own standard, should reflect that the nerve-cells of the brain in the highest as well as in the lowest members of the Vertebrate series, are derived from those of the common progenitor of this great Kingdom. For we can thus see how it has come to pass that certain mental faculties, in various and widely distinct groups of animals, have been developed in nearly the same manner and to nearly the same degree.

The reader who has taken the trouble to go through the several chapters devoted to sexual selection, will be able to judge how far the conclusions at which I have arrived are supported by sufficient evidence. If he accepts these conclusions he may, I think, safely extend them to mankind; but it would be superfluous here to repeat what I have so lately said on the manner in which sexual selection apparently has acted on man, both on the male and female side, causing the two sexes to differ in body and mind, and the several races to differ from each other in various characters, as well as from their ancient and lowly-organised progenitors.

He who admits the principle of sexual selection will be led to the remarkable conclusion that the nervous system not only regulates most of the existing functions of the body, but has indirectly influenced the progressive development of various bodily structures and of certain mental qualities. Courage, pugnacity, perseverance, strength and size of body, weapons of all kinds, musical organs, both vocal and instrumental, bright colours and ornamental appendages, have all been indirectly gained by the one sex or the other, through the exertion of choice, the influence of love and jealousy, and the appreciation of the beautiful in sound, colour or form; and these powers of the mind manifestly depend on the development of the brain.

Man scans with scrupulous care the character and pedigree of his horses, cattle, and dogs before he matches them; but when he comes to his own marriage he rarely, or never, takes any such care. He is impelled by nearly the same motives as the lower animals, when they are left to their own free choice, though he is in so far superior to them that he highly values mental charms and virtues. On the other hand he is strongly attracted by mere wealth or rank. Yet he might by selection do something not only for the bodily constitution and frame of his offspring, but for their intellectual and moral qualities. Both sexes ought to refrain from marriage if they are in any marked degree inferior in body or mind; but such hopes are Utopian and will never be even partially realised until the laws of inheritance are thoroughly known. Everyone does good service, who aids towards this end. When the principles of breeding and inheritance are better understood, we shall not hear ignorant members of our legislature rejecting with scorn a plan for ascertaining whether or not consanguineous marriages are injurious to man.

The advancement of the welfare of mankind is a most intricate problem: all ought to refrain from marriage who cannot avoid abject poverty for their children; for poverty is not only a great evil, but tends to its own increase by leading to recklessness in marriage. On the other hand, as Mr. Galton has remarked, if the prudent avoid marriage, whilst the reckless marry, the inferior members tend to supplant the better members of society. Man, like every other animal, has no doubt advanced to his present high condition through a struggle for existence consequent on his rapid multiplication; and if he is to advance still higher, it is to be feared that he must remain subject to a severe struggle. Otherwise he would sink into indolence, and the more gifted men would not be more successful in the battle of life than the less gifted. Hence our natural rate of increase, though leading to many and obvious evils, must not be greatly diminished by any means. There should be open competition for all men; and the most able should not be prevented by laws or customs from succeeding best and rearing the largest number of offspring. Important as the struggle for existence has been and even still is, yet as far as the highest part of man's nature is concerned there are other agencies more important. For the moral qualities are advanced, either directly or indirectly, much more through the effects of habit, the reasoning powers, instruction, religion, &c., than through natural selection; though to this latter agency may be safely attributed the social instincts, which afforded the basis for the development of the moral sense.

The main conclusion arrived at in this work, namely, that man is descended from some lowly organised form, will, I regret to think, be highly distasteful to many. But there can hardly be a doubt that we are descended from barbarians. The astonishment which I felt on first seeing a party of Fuegians on a wild and broken shore will never be forgotten by me, for the reflection at once rushed into my mind—such were our ancestors. These men were absolutely naked and bedaubed with paint, their long hair was tangled, their mouths frothed with excitement, and their expression was wild, startled, and distrustful. They possessed hardly any arts, and like wild animals lived on what they could catch; they had no government, and were merciless to every one not of their own small tribe. He who has seen a savage in his native land will not feel much shame, if forced to acknowledge that the blood of some more humble creature flows in his veins. For my own part I would as soon be descended from that heoric little monkey, who braved his dreaded enemy in order to save the life of his keeper, or from that old baboon, who descending from the mountains, carried away in triumph his young comrade from a crowd of astonished dogs—as from a savage who delights to torture his enemies, offers up bloody sacrifices, practises infanticide without remorse, treats his wives like slaves, knows no decency, and is haunted by the grossest superstitions.

Man may be excused for feeling some pride at having risen, though not through his own exertions, to the very summit of the organic scale; and the fact of his having thus risen, instead of having been aboriginally placed there, may give him hope for a still higher destiny in the distant future. But we are not here concerned with hopes or fears, only with the truth as far as our reason permits us to discover it; and I have given the evidence to the best of my ability. We must, however, acknowledge, as it seems to me, that man with all his noble qualities, with sympathy which feels for the most debased, with benevolence which extends not only to other men but to the humblest living creature, with his god-like intellect which has penetrated into the movements and constitution of the solar system—with all these exalted powers—Man still bears in his bodily frame the indelible stamp of his lowly origin.

SUPPLEMENTAL NOTE

ON

SEXUAL SELECTION IN RELATION TO MONKEYS

(*Reprinted from* NATURE, *November 2, 1876, page 18.*)

IN the discussion on Sexual Selection in my 'Descent of Man,' no case interested and perplexed me so much as the brightly-coloured hinder ends and adjoining parts of certain monkeys. As these parts are more brightly coloured in one sex than the other, and as they become more brilliant during the season of love, I concluded that the colours had been gained as a sexual attraction. I was well aware that I thus laid myself open to ridicule; though in fact it is not more surprising that a monkey should display his bright-red hinder end than that a peacock should display his magnificent tail. I had, however, at that time no evidence of monkeys exhibiting this part of their bodies during their courtship; and such display in the case of birds affords the best evidence that the ornaments of the males are of service to them by attracting or exciting the females. I have lately read an article by Joh. von Fischer, of Gotha, published in 'Der Zoologische Garten,' April 1876, on the expression of monkeys under various emotions, which is well worthy of study by any one interested in the subject, and which shews that the author is a careful and acute observer. In this article there is an account of the behaviour of a young male mandrill when he first beheld himself in a looking-glass, and it is added, that after a time he turned round and presented his red hinder end to the glass. Accordingly I wrote to Herr J. von Fischer to ask what he supposed was the meaning of this strange action, and he has sent me two long letters full of new and curious details, which will, I hope, be hereafter published. He says that he was himself at first perplexed by the above action, and was thus led carefully to observe several individuals of various other species of monkeys, which he has long kept in his house. He finds that not only the mandrill (*Cynocephalus mormon*) but the drill (*C. leucophœus*) and three other kinds of baboons (*C. hamadryas, sphinx,* and *babouin*), also *Cynopithecus niger,* and *Macacus rhesus* and *nemestrinus,* turn this part of their bodies, which in all these species is more or less brightly coloured, to him when they are pleased, and to other persons as a sort of greeting. He took pains to cure a *Macacus rhesus,* which he had kept for five years, of this indecorous habit, and at last succeeded. These monkeys are particularly apt to act in this manner, grinning at the same time, when first introduced to a new monkey, but often also to their old monkey friends; and after this mutual display they begin to play together. The young mandrill ceased spontaneously after a time to act in this manner towards his master, Von Fischer, but continued to do so towards persons who were strangers and to new monkeys. A young *Cynopithecus niger* never acted, excepting on one occasion, in this way towards his master, but frequently towards strangers, and continues to do so up to the present time. From these facts Von Fischer concludes that the monkeys which behaved in this manner before a looking-glass (viz., the mandrill, drill, *Cynopithecus niger, Macacus rhesus* and *nemestrinus*) acted as if their reflection were a new acquaintance. The mandrill and drill, which have their hinder ends especially ornamented, display it even whilst quite young, more frequently and more ostentatiously than do the other kinds. Next in order comes *Cynocephalus hamadryas,* whilst the other species act in this manner seldomer. The individuals, however, of the same species vary in this respect, and some which were very shy never displayed their hinder ends. It deserves especial attention that Von Fischer has never seen any species purposely exhibit the hinder part of its body, if not at all coloured. This remark applies to many individuals of *Macacus cynomolgus* and *Cercocebus radiatus* (which is closely allied to *M. rhesus*), to three species of Cercopithecus and several American monkeys. The habit of turning the hinder ends as a greeting to an old friend or new acquaintance, which seems to us so odd, is not really more so than the habits of many savages, for instance that of rubbing their bellies with their hands, or rubbing noses together. The habit with the mandrill and drill seems to be instinctive or inherited, as it was followed by very young animals; but it is modified or guided, like so many other instincts, by observation, for Von Fischer says that they take pains to make their display fully; and if made before two observers, they turn to him who seems to pay the most attention.

With respect to the origin of the habit, Von Fischer remarks that his monkeys like to have their naked hinder ends patted or stroked, and that they then grunt with pleasure. They often also turn this part of their bodies to other monkeys to have bits of dirt picked off, and so no doubt it would be with respect to thorns. But the habit with adult animals is connected to a certain extent with sexual feelings, for Von Fischer watched through a glass door a female *Cynopithecus niger,* and she during several days, "umdrehte und dem Männchen mit gurgelnden Tönen die stark geröthete Sitzfläche zeigte, was ich früher nie an diesem Thier bemerkt hatte. Beim Anblick dieses Gegenstandes erregte sich das Männchen sichtlich, denn es polterte heftig an den Stäben, ebenfalls gurgelnde Laute ausstossend." As all the monkeys which have the hinder parts of their bodies more or less brightly coloured live, according to Von Fischer, in open rocky places, he thinks that these colours serve to render one sex conspicuous at a distance to the other; but, as monkeys are such gregarious animals, I should have thought that there was no need for the sexes to recognise each other at a distance. It seems to me more probable that the bright colours, whether on the face or hinder end, or, as in the mandrill, on both, serve as a sexual ornament and attraction. Anyhow, as we now know that monkeys have the habit of turning their hinder ends towards other monkeys, it ceases to be at all surprising that it should have been this part of their bodies which has been more or less decorated. The fact that it is only the monkeys thus characterised which, as far as at present known, act in this manner as a greeting towards other monkeys renders it doubtful whether the habit was first acquired from some independent cause, and that afterwards the parts in question were coloured as a sexual ornament; or whether the colouring and the habit of turning round were first acquired through variation and sexual selection, and that afterwards the habit was retained as a sign of pleasure or as a greeting, through the principle of inherited association. This principle apparently comes into play on many occasions: thus it is generally admitted that the songs of birds serve mainly as an attraction during the season of love, and that the *leks,* or great congregations of the black-grouse, are connected with their courtship; but the habit of singing has been retained by some birds when they feel happy, for instance by the common robin, and the habit of congregating has been retained by the black-grouse during other seasons of the year.

I beg leave to refer to one other point in relation to sexual selection. It has been objected that this form of selection, as far as the ornaments of the males are concerned, implies that all females within the same district must possess and exercise exactly the same taste. It should, however, be observed, in the first place, that although the range of variation of a species may be very large, it is by no means indefinite. I have elsewhere given a good instance of this fact in the pigeon, of which there are at least a hundred varieties differing widely in their colours, and at least a score of varieties of the fowl differing in the same kind of way; but the range of colour in these two species is extremely distinct. Therefore the females of natural species cannot have an unlimited scope for their taste. In the second place, I presume that no supporter of the principle of sexual selection believes that the females select particular points of beauty in the males; they are merely excited or attracted in a greater degree by one male than by another, and this seems often to depend, especially with birds, on brilliant colouring. Even man, excepting perhaps an artist, does not analyse the slight differences in the features of the woman whom he may admire, on which her beauty depends. The male mandrill has not only the hinder end of his body, but his face gorgeously coloured and marked with oblique ridges, a yellow beard, and other ornaments. We may infer from what we see of the variation of animals under domestication, that the above several ornaments of the mandrill were gradually acquired by one individual varying a little in one way, and another individual in another way. The males which were the handsomest or the most attractive in any manner to the females would pair oftenest, and would leave rather more offspring than other males. The offspring of the former, although variously intercrossed, would either inherit the peculiarities of their fathers or transmit an increased tendency to vary in the same manner. Consequently the whole body of males inhabiting the same country would tend from the effects of constant intercrossing to become modified almost uniformly, but sometimes a little more in one character and sometimes in another, though at an extremely slow rate; all ultimately being thus rendered more attractive to the females. The process is like that which I have called unconscious selection by man, and of which I have given several instances. In one country the inhabitants value a fleet or light dog or horse, and in another country a heavier and more powerful one; in neither country is there any selection of individual animals with lighter or stronger bodies and limbs; nevertheless after a considerable lapse of time the individuals are found to have been modified in the desired manner almost uniformly, though differently in each country. In two absolutely distinct countries inhabited by the same species, the individuals of which can never during long ages have intermigrated and intercrossed, and where, moreover, the variations will probably not have been identically the same, sexual selection might cause the males to differ. Nor does the belief appear to me altogether fanciful that two sets of females, surrounded by a very different environment, would be apt to acquire somewhat different tastes with respect to form, sound, or colour. However this may be, I have given in my 'Descent of Man' instances of closely-allied birds inhabiting distinct countries, of which the young and the females cannot be distinguished, whilst the adult males differ considerably, and this may be attributed with much probability to the action of sexual selection.

INDEX TO THE ORIGIN OF SPECIES

INDEX

A.

T.

Tail of giraffe, 144.
—— of aquatic animals, 144.
——, prehensile, 170.
——, rudimentary, 349.
Tanais, dimorphic, 40.
Tarsi, deficient, 103.
Tausch, Dr., on umbelliferæ, 157.
Teeth and hair correlated, 109.
——, rudimentary, in embryonic, calf, 346, 366.
Tegetmeier, Mr., on cells of bees, 198, 201.
Temminck, on distribution aiding classification, 323.
Tendrils, their development, 176.
Thompson, Sir W., on the age of the habitable world, 252.
——, on the consolidation of the crust of the earth, 357.
Thouin, on grafts, 218.
Thrush, aquatic species of, 132.
——, mocking, of the Galapagos, 312.
——, young of, spotted, 339.
——, nest of, 208.
Thuret, M., on crossed fuci, 216.
Thwaites, Mr. on acclimatisation, 106.
Thylacinus, 327.
Tierra del Fuego, dogs of, 189.
——, plants of, 299.
Timber-drift, 286.
Time, lapse of, 236.
—— by itself not causing modification, 79.
Titmouse, 131.
Toads on islands, 307.
Tobacco, crossed varieties of, 228.
Tomes, Mr., on the distribution of bats, 308.
Transitions in varieties rare, 124.
Traquair, Dr., on flat-fish, 169.
Trautschold, on intermediate varieties, 243.
Trees on islands belong to peculiar orders, 307.
—— with separated sexes, 77.
Trifolium pratense, 59, 73.
—— incarnatum, 73.
Trigonia, 261.
Trilobites, 252.
——, sudden extinction of, 261.
Trimen, Mr., on imitating-insects, 330.
Trimorphism in plants, 40; 223.
Troglodytes, 208.
Tuco-tuco, blind, 104.
Tumbler pigeons, habits of, hereditary, 188.

——, young of, 342.
Turkey-cock, tuft of hair on breast, 70.
——, naked skin on head, 145.
——, young of, instinctively wild, 189.
Turnip and cabbage, analogous variations of, 117.
Type, unity of, 152.
Types, succession of, in same areas, 273.
Typotherium, 266.

U.

Udders enlarged by use, 18.
——, rudimentary, 346.
Ulex, young leaves of, 339.
Umbelliferæ, flowers and seeds of, 110.
——, outer and inner florets of, 157.
Unity of type, 152.
Uria lacrymans, 72.
Use, effects of, under domestication, 18.
——, effects of, in a state of nature, 102.
Utility, how far important in the construction of each part, 146.

V.

Valenciennes, on fresh-water fish, 302.
Variability of mongrels and hybrids, 229.
Variation under domestication, 15.
—— caused by reproductive system being affected by conditions of life, 16.
—— under nature, 38.
——, laws of, 101.
——, correlated, 18, 108, 146.
Variations appear at corresponding ages, 19, 67.
—— analogous in distinct species, 116.
Varieties, natural, 37.
——, struggle between, 60.
——, domestic, extinction of, 83.
——, transitional, rarity of, 124.
——, when crossed, fertile, 226.
Varieties, when crossed, sterile, 228.
——, classification of, 325.
Verbascum, sterility of, 212.
——, varieties of crossed, 228.
Verlot, M., on double stocks, 205.
Verneuil, M. de, on the succession of species, 263.
Vibracula of the Polyzoa, 174.
Viola, small imperfect flowers of, 157.
——, tricolor, 59.
Virchow, on the structure of the crystalline lens, 135.
Virginia, pigs of, 67.
Volcanic islands, denudation of, 237.
Vulture, naked skin on head, 145.

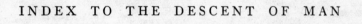

INDEX TO THE DESCENT OF MAN

INDEX

A.

Abbott, C., on the battles of seals, 818.

Abductor of the fifth metatarsal, presence of, in man, 426.

Abercrombie, Dr., on disease of the brain affecting speech, 464.

Abipones, marriage customs of the, 901.

Abortion, prevalence of the practice of, 430.

Abou-Simbel, caves of, 531.

Abramis brama, 603.

Abstraction, power of, in animals, 459.

Acalles, stridulation of, 651.

Acanthodactylus capensis, sexual differences of colour in, 695.

Accentor modularis, 795.

Acclimatisation, difference of, in different races of men, 530.

Achetidæ, stridulation of the, 632, 633, 634; rudimentary stridulating organs in female, 636.

Acilius sulcatus, elytra of the female, 626.

Acomus, development of spurs in the female of, 773.

Acridiidæ, stridulation of the, 634, 636; rudimentary stridulating organs in female, 636.

Acromio-basilar muscle, and quadrupetal gait, 426.

Acting, 539.

Actiniæ, bright colours of, 612.

Adams, Mr., migration of birds, 479; intelligence of nut-hatch, 741; on the *Bombycilla carolinensis*, 784.

Admiral butterfly, 657.

Adoption of the young of other animals by female monkeys, 449.

Advancement in the organic scale, Von Baer's definition of, 527.

Aeby, on the difference between the skulls of man and the quadrumana, 515.

Æsthetic faculty, not highly developed in savages, 468.

Affection, maternal, 449; manifestation of, by animals, 449; parental and filial, partly the result of natural selection, 478; mutual, of birds, 742; shewn by birds in confinement, for certain persons, 742.

Africa, probably the birthplace of man, 520; South, crossed population of, 535; South, retention of colour by the Dutch in, 551; South, proportion of the sexes in the butterflies of, 603; tattooing practised in, 881; Northern, coiffure of natives of, 882.

Agassiz, L., on conscience in dogs, 476; on the coincidence of the races of man with zoological provinces, 531; on the number of species of man, 536; on the courtship of the land-snails, 614; on the brightness of the colours of male fishes during the breeding season, 681; on the frontal protuberance of the males of *Geophagus* and *Cichla*, 681, 685; male fishes hatching ova in their mouths, 686; sexual differences in colour of chromids, 686; on the slight sexual differences of the South Americans, 871; on the tattooing of the Amazonian Indians, 884.

Age, in relation to the transmission of characters in birds, 787; variation in accordance with, in birds, 804.

Agelæus phœniceus, 581, 746.

Ageronia feronia, noise produced by, 653.

Agrion, dimorphism in, 638, 639.

Agrion Ramburii, sexes of, 638.

Agrionidæ, difference in the sexes of, 638.

Agrotis exclamationis, 660.

Ague, tertian, dog suffering from, 397.

Ainos, hairiness of the, 870.

Aitchison, Mr., on sheep, 600.

Aithurus polytmus, young of, 807.

Albino birds, 748.

Alca torda, young of, 806.

Alces palmata, 830.

Alder and Hancock, MM., on the nudibranch mollusca, 615.

Allen, J. A., vigour of birds earliest hatched, 571, 572; effect of difference of temperature, light, &c., on birds, 581; colours of birds, 751; on the relative size of the sexes of *Callorhinus ursinus*, 831; on the name of *Otaria jubata*, 836; on the pairing of seals, 836; on sexual differences in the colour of bats, 847.

—— S., on the habits of *Hoplopterus*, 703;

playing together, 448; memory in, 452; intercommunication of, by means of the antennæ, 465; habits of, 513; difference of the sexes in, 639; recognition of each other by, after separation, 639.

—— White, habits of, 638.

Anura, 688.

Apatania muliebris, male unknown, 607.

Apathus, difference of the sexes in, 640.

Apatura Iris, 653, 654.

Apes, difference of the young, from the adult, 398; semi-erect attitude of some, 434; mastoid processes of, 435; influences of the jaw-muscles on the physiognomy of, 436; female, destitute of large canines, 444; building platforms, 459; imitative faculties of, 497; anthropomorphous, 518; probable speedy extermination of the, 519; Gratiolet on the evolution of, 538; canine teeth of male, 820; females of some, less hairy beneath than the males, 904.

—— long-armed, their mode of progression, 435.

Aphasia, Dr. Bateman on, 464.

Apis mellifica, large male of, 629.

Apollo, Greek statues of, 888.

Apoplexy in *Cebus Azaræ,* 396.

Appendages, anal, of insects, 626.

Approbation, influence of the love of, 481, 486, 499.

Aprosmictus scapulatus, 781.

Apus, proportion of sexes, 607.

Aquatic birds, frequency of white plumage in, 812.

Aquila chrysaëtos, 739.

Arab women, elaborate and peculiar coiffure of, 889.

Arabs, fertility of crosses with other races, 533; gashing of cheeks and temples among the, 882.

Arakhan, artificial widening of the forehead by the natives of, 889.

Aboricola, young of, 791.

Archeopteryx, 523.

Arctiidæ, coloration of the, 659.

Ardea asha, rufescens, and *cærulea,* change of colour in, 813.

—— breeding in immature plumage, 805.

—— *gularis,* change of plumage in, 813.

—— *herodias,* love-gestures of the male, 715.

—— *ludoviciana,* age of mature plumage in, 805; continued growth of crest and plumes in the male of, 805.

—— *nycticorax,* cries of, 704.

Ardeola, young of, 791.

Ardetta, changes of plumage in, 784.

Argenteuil, 409.

Argus pheasant, 717, 734, 785; display of

plumage by the male, 728; ocellated spots of the, 757; gradation of characters in the, 761.

Argyll, Duke of, on the physical weakness of man, 443; the fashioning of implements peculiar to man, 459; on the contest in man between right and wrong, 494; on the primitive civilization of man, 509; on the plumage of the male Argus pheasant, 731; on *Urosticte Benjamini,* 768; on the nests of birds, 777.

Argynnis, colouring of the lower surface of, 659.

Aricoris epitus, sexual differences in the wings of, 627.

Aristocracy, increased beauty of the, 892.

Arms, proportions of, in soldiers and sailors, 418; direction of the hair on the, 516.

—— and hands, free use of, indirectly correlated with diminution of canines, 435.

Arrest of development, 421.

Arrow-heads, stone, general resemblance of, 539.

Arrows, use of, 539.

Arteries, variations in the course of the, 413.

Artery, effect of tying, upon the lateral channels, 418.

Arthropoda, 616.

Arts practised by savages, 541.

Ascension, coloured incrustation on the rocks of, 615.

Ascidia, affinity of the lancelet to, 523; tadpole-like larvæ of, 523.

Ascidians, 614; bright colours of some, 612.

Asinus, Asiatic and African species of, 858.

Asinus tæniopus, 858.

Ass, colour-variations of the, 858.

Ateles, effects of brandy on an, 397; absence of the thumb in, 433.

—— *beelzebuth,* ears of, 403.

—— *marginatus,* colour of the ruff of, 849; hair on the head of, 859.

Ateuchus cicatricosus, habits of, 646.

Ateuchus, stridulation of, 651.

Athalia, proportion of the sexes in, 606.

Atropus pulsatorius, 639.

Attention, manifestations of, in animals, 452.

Audouin, V., on a hymenopterous parasite with a sedentary male, 579.

Audubon, J. J., on the pinioned goose, 476; on the speculum of *Mergus cucullatus,* 591; on the pugnacity of male birds, 700, 703; on courtship of **Ca-**

824; curled frontal hair of the, 844.

Buller, Dr., on the Huia, 568; the attachment of birds, 741.

Bullfinch, sexual differences in the, 577; piping, 706; female, singing of the, 706; courtship of the, 732; widowed, finding a new mate, 740; attacking a reed-bunting, 743; nestling, sex ascertained by pulling out breast feathers, 804.

Bullfinches, distinguishing persons, 743; rivalry of female, 749.

Bulls, two young, attacking an old one, 474; wild, battles of, 819.

Bull-trout, male, colouring of, during the breeding season, 682.

Bunting, reed, head feathers of the male, 733; attacked by a bullfinch, 743.

Buntings, characters of young, 788.

Buphus coromandus, sexes and young of, 806; change of colour in, 813.

Burchell, Dr., on the zebra, 857; on the extravagance of a Bushwoman in adorning herself 884; celibacy unknown among the savages of South Africa, 898; on the marriage-customs of the Bushwomen, 902.

Burke, on the number of species of man, 536.

Burmese, colour of the beard in, 869.

Burton, Capt., on negro ideas of female beauty, 886; on a universal idea of beauty, 888.

Bushmen, 444; marriage among, 902.

Bushwoman, extravagant ornamentation of a, 884.

Bushwomen, marriage-customs of, 902.

Bustard, throat pouch of the male, 709; humming noise produced by a male, 712; Indian, ear-tufts of, 719.

Bustards, occurrence of sexual differences and of polygamy among the, 577; love-gestures of the male, 715; double moult in, 723, 724.

Butler, A. G., on sexual differences in the wings of *Aricoris epitus*, 627; courtship of butterflies, 653; on the colouring of the sexes in species of *Thecla*, 655; on the resemblance of *Iphias glaucippe* to a leaf, 658; on the rejection of certain moths and caterpillars by lizards and frogs, 669.

Butterfly, noise produced by a, 653; Emperor, 653, 654; meadow brown, instability of the ocellated spots of, 756.

Butterflies, proportion of the sexes in, 603; forelegs atrophied in some males, 627; sexual difference in the neuration of the wings of, 627; pugnacity of male, 653; protective resemblances of the lower surface of, 657; display of the

wings by, 659; white, alighting upon bits of paper, 661; attracted by a dead specimen of the same species, 661; courtship of, 661; male and female, inhabiting different stations, 664.

Buxton, C., observations on macaws, 475; on an instance of benevolence in a parrot, 742.

Buzzard, Indian honey-, variation the crest of, 752.

C.

Cabbage butterflies, 657.

Cachalot, large head of the male, 820.

Cadences, musical, perception of, by animals, 877.

Cæcum, 408; large, in the early progenitors of man, 524.

Cairina moschata, pugnacity of the male, 699.

Californian Indians, decrease of, 610.

Callianassa, chelæ of, figured, 618.

Callidryas, colours of sexes, 662.

Callionymus lyra, characters of the male, 677.

Callorhinus ursinus, relative size of the sexes of, 831; courtship of, 837.

Calotes maria, 696.

—— *nigrilabris*, sexual difference in the colour of, 695.

Cambridge, O. Pickard, on the sexes of spiders, 607; on the size of male *Nephila*, 623.

Camel, canine teeth of male, 819, 829.

Campbell, J., on the Indian elephant, 576; on the proportion of male and female births in the harems of Siam, 598.

Campylopterus hemileucurus, 601.

Canaries distinguishing persons, 742.

Canary, polygamy of the, 577; change of plumage in, after moulting, 592; female, selecting the best singing male, 705; sterile hybrid, singing of a, 706; female, singing of the, 706; selecting a greenfinch, 745; and siskin, pairing of, 745.

Cancer pagurus, 617.

Canestrini, G., on rudimentary characters and the origin of man, 390; on rudimentary characters, 400; on the movement of the ear in man, 402; on the variability of the vermiform appendage in man, 408; on the abnormal division of the malar bone in man, 424; on abnormal conditions of the human uterus, 423; on the persistence of the frontal suture in man, 424; on the proportion of the sexes in silk-moths, 603; second-

THE END.